Lecture Notes of the Institute for Computer Sciences, Social Informatics and Telecommunications Engineering 137

T0212704

More information about this series at http://www.springer.com/series/8197

Victor C.M. Leung · Min Chen
Jiafu Wan · Yin Zhang (Eds.)

Testbeds and Research Infrastructure: Development of Networks and Communities

9th International ICST Conference,
TridentCom 2014
Guangzhou, China, May 5–7, 2014
Revised Selected Papers

 Springer

Editors
Victor C.M. Leung
Electrical and Computer Engineering
The University of British Columbia
British Columbia
Canada

Jiafu Wan
School of Mechanical and Automotive
Engineering
South China University of Technology
Guangzhou
China

Min Chen
Huazhong University of Science and
Technology
Wuhan City
China

Yin Zhang
Huazhong University of Science and
Technology
Wuhan
China

ISSN 1867-8211   ISSN 1867-822X   (electronic)
Lecture Notes of the Institute for Computer Sciences, Social Informatics
and Telecommunications Engineering
ISBN 978-3-319-13325-6   ISBN 978-3-319-13326-3   (eBook)
DOI 10.1007/978-3-319-13326-3

Library of Congress Control Number: 2014956194

Springer Cham Heidelberg New York Dordrecht London
© Institute for Computer Sciences, Social Informatics and Telecommunications Engineering 2014

Printed on acid-free paper

Springer International Publishing AG Switzerland is part of Springer Science+Business Media
(www.springer.com)

Preface

It is a great pleasure to welcome you to the proceedings of the Ninth International Conference on Testbeds and Research Infrastructures for the Development of Networks and Communities (Tridentcom 2014). This year's conference continued its tradition of being the premier forum for presentation of results on cutting edge research in activities related to experimentation such as testing, verification, deployment, integration, management, and federation of such facilities as well as experimentation-oriented research based on implementation of novel schemes on research testbeds. The mission of the conference is to share novel basic research ideas as well as experimental applications in advanced networking area in addition to identifying new directions for future research and development.

In Tridentcom 2014, we received 149 paper submissions, and finally selected 49 regular papers. The acceptance rate was 32.89%.

Tridentcom 2014 gave researchers, vendors, providers, and users a unique opportunity to exchange ideas on past experience, requirements, needs, and visions for establishing the convergence of advanced networking and cloud computing. The conference consisted of six symposia that covered a broad range of research aspects. We hope that the conference proceedings will serve as a valuable reference to researchers and developers in the area.

We also hope that you find the papers in this volume interesting and thought-provoking. It will surely advance our understanding of advanced networking and doubtless open up new directions for research and development.

June 2014

Victor C.M. Leung
Min Chen
Jiafu Wan
Yin Zhang

Conference Organizing Committee

General Chair

Victor C.M. Leung   University of British Columbia, Canada

General Vice Chair

Min Chen   Huazhong University of Science and Technology,
China

TPC Chairs

Tarik Taleb   NEC Europe Ltd., Germany
Shiwen Mao   Auburn University, USA
Jiafu Wan   South China University of Technology, China

Workshop Chairs

Honggang Wang   University of Massachusetts Dartmouth, USA
Caifeng Zou   South China University of Technology, China

Local Arrangements Committee Chair

Jianqi Liu   Guangdong University of Technology, China
Yin Zhang   Huazhong University of Science and Technology,
China

International Advisory Committee

Han-Chieh Chao   National Ilan University, Taiwan
Xiaohu Ge   Huazhong University of Science and Technology,
China
Roy "Xiaorong" Lai   Confederal Network Inc., USA

Steering Committee Chair

Athanasios V. Vasilakos   University of Western Macedonia, Greece
Imrich Chlamtac   Create-Net, Italy

Publication Chair

Qiang Liu	Guangdong University of Technology, China
Chin-Feng Lai	National Ilan University, Taiwan

Tutorial Chair

Liang Zhou   Nanjing University of Posts and
Telecommunications, China

Publicity Chairs

Xiaofei Wang	Seoul National University, South Korea
Kai Lin	Dalian University of Technology, China

Web Chair

Yujun Ma   Huazhong University of Science and Technology,
China

Conference Secretary

Long Hu	Huazhong University of Science and Technology, China
Wei Cai	University of British Clombia, Canada

Conference Manager

Ruzanna Najaryan   EAI, Italy

Student Volunteers

Dan Guo	Huazhong University of Science and Technology, China
Zhuanli Cheng	Huazhong University of Science and Technology, China
Ran Li	Huazhong University of Science and Technology, China
Dung Ong Mau	Huazhong University of Science and Technology, China
Jialun Wang	Huazhong University of Science and Technology, China
Long Wang	Huazhong University of Science and Technology, China

Contents

Mobile Network, Wireless Network

Other Topics

Workshop on Mobile Cloud Computing (MCC 2014)

Testbed Virtualization

Software-Defined Infrastructure and the SAVI Testbed

Joon-Myung Kang[1]($\boxtimes$), Thomas Lin[2], Hadi Bannazadeh[2],
and Alberto Leon-Garcia[2]

[1] Network and Mobility Lab., HP Labs., Palo Alto, CA 94304, USA
joon-myung.kang@hp.com
[2] Department of Electrical and Computer Engineering,
University of Toronto, Toronto, ON M5S 3G4, Canada
t.lin@utoronto.ca, alberto.leongarcia@utoronto.ca,
hadi.bannazadeh@utoronto.ca

Abstract. In this paper we consider Software-Defined Infrastructure (SDI), a new concept for integrated control and management of converged heterogeneous resources. SDI enables programmability of infrastructure by enabling the support of cloud-based applications, customized network functions, and hybrid combinations of these. We motivate SDI in the context of a multi-tier cloud that includes massive-scale datacenters as well as a smart converged network edge. In SDI, a centralized SDI manager controls converged heterogeneous resources (i.e., computing, programmable hardware, and networking resources) using virtualization and a topology manager that provides the status of all resources and their connectivity. We discuss the design and implementation of SDI in the context of the Canadian SAVI testbed. We describe the current deployment of the SAVI testbed and applications that are currently supported in the testbed.

Keywords: Virtualization · Cloud computing · Software defined networking · Resource management

1 Introduction

The delivery of content and software applications is being revolutionized by application platforms that encompass massive datacenters, the Internet, and smart phones. Cloud computing, typically in very large remote datacenters, provide unprecedented flexibility and economies of scale in the support of applications. Software-defined networking (SDN) allows fine-grained control of application flows. Together cloud computing and SDN promise a future open marketplace where applications can be readily and rapidly programmed on a converged infrastructure. Major collaborative open source efforts are helping advance these two technologies, OpenStack [6] for cloud computing and OpenFlow [1] for SDN.

We view the cloud as being multi-tier in nature, with massive remote datacenters in one tier, and converged smart edge nodes closer to the users. Computing and networking resources in the smart edge are essential to support applications

© Institute for Computer Sciences, Social Informatics and Telecommunications Engineering 2014
V.C.M. Leung et al. (Eds.): TridentCom 2014, LNICST 137, pp. 3–13, 2014.
DOI: 10.1007/978-3-319-13326-3_1

with low-latency requirements, to execute security functions, and to promote efficient content distribution through local caching resources.

The location of the smart edge is roughly where telecom service providers are placed. Therefore it is natural that the design of the smart edge should consider the challenges of the service provider. The overarching challenge today is the need to invest huge capital expenditures to increase wireless capacity to accommodate higher traffic, while coping with slower revenue growth from competition and customer expectation for continual sustained improvement. We believe that virtualization can play a role in addressing these twin challenges.

The remote massive datacenter leverages virtualization of computing and networking resources to deliver flexibility and compelling economies of scale. In contrast, the smart edge is significantly smaller in scale and much more heterogeneous in its resources. The smart edge especially when defined to include wireless and wired access networks include nonconventional computing resources, namely FPGAs, network processors, ASICs for signal processing within purpose-built boxes. We believe that flexibility and economies of scale can be attained in the smart edge through the virtualization of computing, networking, and non-conventional computing resources and the introduction of control and management systems for converged resources.

Until recently, control and management approaches have focused on the separate management of different infrastructure resources. For example, cloud controllers such as OpenStack provide cloud resource provisioning, while network controllers such as an OpenFlow and other SDN controllers provide network control. In the smart edge, an integrated management and control system for converged network and generalized computing resources can be more effective in providing flexibility and performance in a cost-effective manner. Open interfaces for controlling and managing these shared heterogeneous resources can provide software programmability for dynamically deploying new functionality. In addition, advanced monitoring and measurement techniques and user access to infrastructure information can provide customized resource allocation or networking. Therefore, we need a "software-defined infrastrastructure (SDI) to satisfy their requirements beyond SDN and VMs.

In [2] we introduced the notion of SDI and in [3] we introduced the initial design of the control and management of the SAVI testbed. In this paper we first present the SDI architecture for designing a testbed for future applications and services, focusing specifically on the SDI manager and its associated topology manager. Next, we present the current design and implementation of the SAVI testbed and its control and management system for converged heterogeneous resources based on the SDI architecture. We describe the SAVI Testbed which has been deployed across much of Canada and used to demonstrate the management of physical and virtual resources. We also describe the hands-on workshop provided to SAVI researchers to promote the usage of the testbed. We describe a tutorial to introduce users to a configuration management service, as well as to the SDI manager to query and manage the physical and virtual network infrastructure in the SAVI testbed.

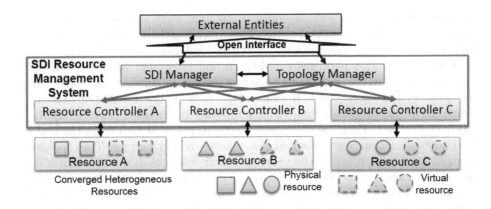

Fig. 1. A system architecture for SDI resource management

The paper is organized as follows. Section 2 describes a high-level system architecture of SDI using major components. Section 3 presents SAVI cluster configuration and heterogeneous resources and a design of SAVI testbed resource control and management system. The current SAVI testbed deployment and status are presented in Section 4. Finally, conclusion and future work are presented in Section 5.

2   Software-Defined Infrastructure

In this section, we define SDI and present an SDI resource management architecture for the converged heterogeneous resources. In SDI, "Software-Defined means providing open interfaces to: control and manage converged heterogeneous resources in different types of infrastructures for software programmability; and give an access to infrastructure resource information such as topology, usage data, etc. We design the SDI architecture to support those requirements.

Fig. 1 shows a high-level architecture of the SDI Resource Management System (RMS), in which an SDI manager can control and manage a resource of type A, B, and C using a corresponding resource controller A, B, or C, respectively. External entities obtain virtual resources in the converged heterogeneous resources via the SDI RMS through "Open Interfaces. The converged heterogeneous resources are composed of virtual resources and physical resources. Virtual resources include any resource virtualized on physical resources, such as virtual machines. Physical resources include any resource that can be abstracted or virtualized, such as computing servers, storage, network resources (routers or switches), and reconfigurable hardware resources.

The SDI RMS provides resource management functions for the converged heterogeneous resources to the external entities. These functions include provisioning, registry/configuration management, virtualization, allocation/scheduling, migration/scaling, monitoring/measurement, load balancing, energy management, fault management, performance management (delay, loss, etc.), and security management (authentication, policy, role, etc.). The external entities can be applications, users (service developers or providers), and high-level management systems.

The SDI manager performs coordinated and integrated resource management for converged heterogeneous resources through a resource controller and the topology manager. The SDI manager performs major integrated resource management functions based on resource topology information provided by the topology manager. Each resource controller is responsible for taking the high-level user descriptions and managing the resources of a given type. The topology manager maintains a list of the resources, their relationships, and monitoring and measurement data of each resource. Furthermore, the topology manager provides up-to-date resource information to the SDI manager for infrastructure-state-aware resource management. Examples of the integrated resource management functions that can be performed by the SDI manager include: fault tolerance, green networking (energy efficient and/or low-carbon emitting), path optimization, resource scheduling optimization, network-aware VM replacement, QoS support, real-time network monitoring, and flexible diagnostics.

3   SAVI Testbed Based on SDI Concept

The Smart Applications on Virtual Infrastructure (SAVI) project was established to investigate future application platforms designed for applications enablement [3]. We have developed a SAVI testbed system for controlling and managing converged virtual resources focused on computing and networking. In previous work [3], we extended Virtual Application on Network Infrastructure (VANI) [5] for supporting non-conventional computing resources. In this section we extend the previous SAVI testbed management system to one based on an SDI architecture that provides a uniform abstraction for heterogeneous resources. First, we present the SAVI cluster configuration and its heterogeneous resources. Second, we present a high-level design of our Control and Management system based on SDI. Third, we present an SDI manager which is a core component for integrated resource management. Finally, we present the topology manager which provides status of SAVI testbed nodes and resources.

3.1   SAVI Cluster

SAVI explores a multi-tier cloud that includes massive core datacenters, smart edge nodes, and access networks, wherein all resources are virtualized. SAVI has designed a node cluster that can provide virtualized and physical computing and networking resources, including heterogeneous resources. We anticipate that the Smart Edge will leverage these heterogeneous resources to provide greater service flexibility, improved resource utilization and cost efficiencies. A SAVI cluster provides heterogeneous resources interconnected by a 10GE OpenFlow fabric. SAVI has developed an approach to allow heterogeneous resources to be managed with OpenStack [6]. Currently, SAVI clusters include Intel Xeon servers, storage, OpenFlow switches, GPUs, NetFPGAs, Alteras DE5-Net and ATOM servers.

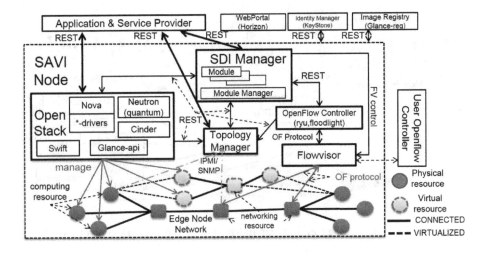

Fig. 2. Design of a control and management system for SAVI node [2]

3.2 High-Level Control and Management System Design

Fig. 2 shows the design of a control and management system for a SAVI node based on the SDI architecture to manage cloud and networking resources. A SAVI node controls and manages virtual resources using OpenStack and Open-Flow controller. In the Edge node (converged) network, a variety of heterogeneous computing and networking resources are available as shown in Fig. 2. The SDI manager controls and manages virtual computing resources by virtualizing physical computing resources using OpenStack. The OpenFlow controller is used for controlling networking resources. The OpenFlow controller receives all events from the OpenFlow switches and creates a flow table including actions. The SDI manager performs all management functions based on data provided by the OpenStack and the OpenFlow controller, and it determines appropriate actions for computing and networking resources using management modules inside.

The SDI manager has a module manager to manage specific functional modules such as a scheduling module, a networking control module, a fault-tolerant management module, or a green networking module. Details of each module are out of the scope of this paper. As in SDN, we have separated the data and control planes in the SAVI node. The OpenStack and OpenFlow controller are modules for communicating directly with computing and networking resources. The SDI manager in Fig. 2 is responsible for control and management tasks. The topology manager collects cloud computing resource information using OpenStack and networking resource information using OpenFlow. In addition, the topology manager can collect system information from the physical resources using IPMI and SNMP. Application and service providers can access not only control and management functions but also topology information through RESTful APIs which is a kind of open interfaces.

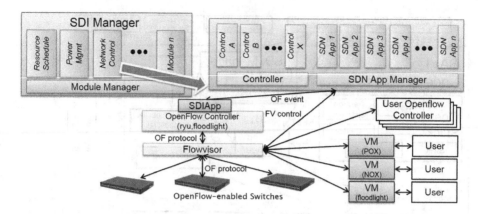

Fig. 3. SDI manager design and an expanded view of the network control module

In the SAVI testbed, we have used and extended the following projects from OpenStack: 1) Keystone for Identity management, 2) Nova for Compute and a cloud computing fabric controller, 3) Swift for Storage, a highly available, distributed, eventually consistent object/blob store, 4) Glance for Image management, 5) Neutron (formerly named Quantum) for network management, and 6) Cinder for volume management. Because the original OpenStack Nova does not support virtualization of unconventional resources such as FPGA, NetFPGA or GPU, we have extended Nova to support virtualization of such resources by adding new device drivers. These are depicted with *-drivers under Nova in Fig. 2.

We have used FlowVisor [8] as a controller that acts as a transparent proxy between OpenFlow switches and multiple OpenFlow controllers. FlowVisor creates rich slices of network resources and delegates control of each slice to a different controller, while enforcing isolation between the slices. Internally, we have used the Ryu OpenFlow controller [9] which serves as a network control proxy for the SDI networking control module. Through FlowVisor, any user can use his/her own OpenFlow controller, even though it is outside the SAVI testbed as shown in Fig. 3 [7].

3.3   SDI Manager

The SDI manager provides integrated resource management for converged heterogeneous resources by abstraction. As shown in Fig. 3, we have designed the SDI manager as a module platform where each module is pluggable and realizes a certain function of SDI control and management such as resource scheduling, power management, network control, and so on. The SDI manager includes not only predefined modules developed by us but also SDI services through open interfaces for end users such as resource allocation APIs. By providing SDI services, end users may easily implement their services/applications using available

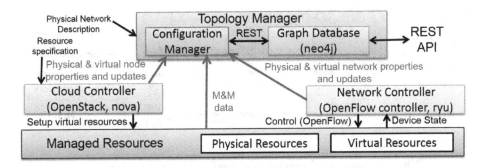

Fig. 4. Topology manager design

information from SAVI testbed and test them on the SAVI testbed. For instance, if an end user wants to allocate virtual machines based on CPU core temperature of physical servers, the SDI manager can provide an API to provide a list of available physical servers and measured properties including CPU core temperature. Based on the given information, the end user can develop his or her own resource allocation algorithm and apply it to SAVI TB through the resource allocation API given by the SDI manager.

For example, Fig. 3 shows a network control module which is a predefined module and enables SDN applications over the SDI manager. The module runs one or more network control applications (e.g., learning switch, topology discovery, FlowVisor control, etc.) using controllers A, B, ⋯ , and X which provides receiving and handling APIs. We have implemented an application (SDIApp in Fig. 3) running on the OpenFlow controller which forwards certain OpenFlow events to the network control module. In [7] we discussed the network control module, including how to control OpenFlow-enabled networks, manage virtual networks, and delegate control to user-defined OpenFlow controllers.

3.4 Topology Manager

Fig. 4 shows a high-level design for the topology manager where a configuration manager monitors the state and relationship between converged heterogeneous resources through a cloud controller and a network controller, and stores the monitored data to a graph database. In addition, the topology manager provides answers for the queries to the data from an SDI manager. The cloud controller and network controller each provide physical and virtual computing or networking resource properties, as well as associated monitoring and measurement data to the configuration manager.

The configuration manager builds a model by analyzing states and relationships of all monitored cloud and networking resources. We have used a graph for the model because all resources and their relationships can be represented by a set of vertices and edges with flexibility and simplicity. All physical and virtual resources are represented by a vertex and their relationship is represented

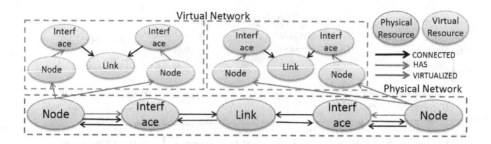

Fig. 5. Graph model example for cloud and networking resources

by an edge. For example, physical computing server, physical network interface, physical network link, virtual machine, virtual network interfaces, virtual network link, physical network switch, physical network port, virtual network switch, virtual network port, physical access point, and any other heterogeneous resources can be a vertex in a graph model. Each vertex has its own properties such as ID, name, and associated monitoring data. In addition, the graph model includes a set of subgraphs that represent a physical or a virtual network topology. Thus the configuration manager can store not only the state and relationship of converged heterogeneous resources, but also the physical and virtual network topology.

Fig. 5 shows a graph model example. In the SAVI TB, we have three types of network elements: Node, Interface, and Link. In the graph, a vertex represents one of the network elements with some dynamic properties. We also have three types of associations: CONNECTED, HAS, and VIRTUALIZED. In the graph, an edge represents the relationship. CONNECTED is used for one network element connected to another network element with a specified medium. HAS represents that a network element has another network element. VIRTUALIZED represents that a network element virtualizes another network element. In Fig. 5, physical resources are composed of a node, an interface and a link, and their relationships represent a physical network. Virtual resources can be virtualized on the physical resources and their relationships represent a virtual network.

We use a graph database for storing the graph model built by the configuration manager. The graph database is whiteboard friendly meaning that we can use the language of node, property, and relationship to describe our domain, so there is no need for a complicated object and relationship mapping tool to implement it in the database. We use the neo4j graph database, a popular open source graph database[10].

The topology manager provides topology information via REST APIs. It includes: 1) SAVI Node (physical server, switch, hardware sources, etc.), 2) Interface (network interface, switch port, etc.), 3) Link information, and 4) Topology.

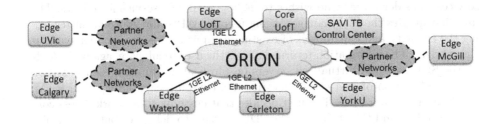

Fig. 6. Current deployment of SAVI testbed in Canadian universities

4   Current Deployment and Testing

Fig. 6 shows the current SAVI node and network topology deployed in seven Canadian universities. One core node and seven Edge nodes provide cloud computing and heterogeneous resources. Currently, the SAVI testbed has 550+ CPU cores, 10+ FPGA systems, 6+ GPU systems, 50+ TB storage, 10/1GE OpenFlow-enabled switches, and wireless access points. SAVI nodes in Ontario are connected by ORION (Ontario Research and Innovation Optical Network) with a 1GE L2 ethernet link, and elsewhere connectivity is through CANARIE (Canadian Research and Education Networks). The main SAVI testbed control center is located in the University of Toronto and provides resource management services for all infrastructures. Currently, we have a project to federate with GENI in the USA.

To provide an example of real operation in the SAVI testbed, we share our experience from a hands-on tutorial for 60+ researchers on July 2013. The tutorial introduced users to the topology management service and our SDI manager to query and manage the physical and virtual network infrastructure in SAVI testbed. The topology service provides the entire network topology to users through either RESTful APIs, a CLI client, or a Python library using a graph database. We showed how to use the service to get the topology from SAVI testbed and how to apply the information for VM resource scheduling. By default, each testbed tenant has a main network which is connected to a router to enable Internet access. However, users can define their own private networks isolated from the main network and the Internet. The tutorial showed how to create a private virtual network as well as a subnet for that network. Afterwards, users learned how to control the private network using their own SDN controller. In addition, SAVI researchers showed how to deploy and manage an application on the SAVI testbed using the Cross-Cloud Application Management Platform (XCAMP) [11]. Other applications and experiments running on the testbed involve big data analysis, multimedia services, resource scheduling, virtual data center embedding, and cloud deployment are running on the SAVI testbed.

Finally we describe a wireless use case for SDI. The SAVI testbed includes OpenFlow-enabled wireless access points with the added capability to virtualize WiFi. As an example of using SDI in the provisioning and control of end-to-end services, consider a user who wishes to deploy a wireless service for clients. The user first queries the SDI manager, using its open APIs, for information regarding the capacity and capabilities of existing computing resources on the various smart edges. The information returned allows the user to allocate, again via APIs on the SDI manager, virtualized servers on physical machines chosen based on some combination of user-chosen metrics (i.e. compute capabilities, free RAM, proximity to clients, etc.). The user decides that customized network access control is needed, and thus instructs the SDI manager to delegate control of a slice of the network to the user's own OpenFlow controller (which could be running in another VM on the smart edge). In order to connect clients, the user instructs the SDI manager to virtualize the wireless access points to enable a unique ESSID, seen by client devices as an independent WiFi network. Clients who connect via this ESSID will automatically be associated with the slice of network controlled by the user, and their traffic will be controlled accordingly based on the users OpenFlow controller. Other open APIs which enable monitoring and measurement allow the user to view the state and current utilization of their computing and network resources, in turn empowering the user to adjust the capacity and availability of their service as desired.

5   Concluding Remarks

In this paper we have presented an SDI architecture and resource management system for infrastructures consisting of converged heterogeneous virtualized resources. SDI promises to provide flexibility, performance, and cost effectiveness, especially in the smart edge of a multi-tiered cloud. As a practical operational example, we presented the design and implementation of the SAVI testbed based on the SDI concept. SAVI provides integrated resource management services through an SDI manager and topology manager. We also presented the current deployment and shared our experiences running applications on it.

Acknowledgments. The work is funded in part or completely by the SAVI project funded under the NSERC, Canada (NETGP394424-10) and by NRF, Korea (NRF-2013R1A6A3A03059975).

References

1. McKeown, N., Anderson, T., Balakrishnan, H., Parulkar, G., Peterson, L., Rexford, J., Shenker, S., Turner, J.: Openflow: enabling innovation in campus networks. SIGCOMM Comput. Commun. Rev. **38**(2), 69–74 (2008)
2. Kang, J.M., Bannazadeh, H., Leon-Garcia, A.: SAVI Testbed:Control and Management of Converged Virtual ICT Resources. In: 2013 IFIP IEEE Intl. Symposium on Integrated Network Management (IM 2013), Ghent, Belgium, pp. 664–667 (May 2014)
3. Kang, J.M., Bannazadeh, H., Rahimi, H., Lin, T., Faraji, M., Leon-Garcia, A.: Software-Defined Infrastructure and the Future Central Office. In: International Conference on Communications (ICC), Budapest, Hungary, pp. 225–229 (June 2013)

4. Lu, H., Shtern, M., Simmons, B., Smit, M., Litoiu, M.: Pattern-based Deployment Service for Next Generation Clouds. In: IEEE 9th World Congress on Services, Cloud Cup, Santa Clara, CA, pp. 464–471 (June 28, 2013)
5. Bannazadeh, H., Leon-Garcia, A., Redmond, K., Tam, G., Khan, A., Ma, M., Dani, S., Chow, P.: Virtualized Application Networking Infrastructure. In: Magedanz, T., Gavras, A., Thanh, N.H., Chase, J.S. (eds.) TridentCom 2010. LNICST, vol. 46, pp. 363–382. Springer, Heidelberg (2011)
6. Openstack. http://www.openstack.org
7. Lin, T., Kang, J.M., Bannazadeh, H., Leon-Garcia A.: Enabling SDN Applications on Software-Defined Infrastructure. In: IEEE IFIP Network Operations and Management Symposium (NOMS 2014), Krakow, Poland (accepted to appear, May 2014)
8. Sherwood, R., Gibby, G., Yapy, K.-K., Appenzellery, G., Casado, M., McKeown, N., Parulkary, G.: Flowvisor: A network virtualization layer, OpenFlow, Tech. Rep. OPENFLOW-TR-2009-1 (October 2009)
9. Tomonori, F.: Introduction to ryu sdn framework, Open Networking Summit (April 2013). http://osrg.github.io/ryu/slides/ONS2013-april-ryu-intro.pdf
10. Neo4j Graph Database. http://www.neo4j.org
11. Shtern, M., Simmons, B., Smit, M., Lu, H., Litoiu, M.: Introducing the Cross-Cloud Application Management Platform (XCAMP). Submitted to the 2014 International Conference on Software Engineering (2014)

A Networkless Data Exchange and Control Mechanism for Virtual Testbed Devices

Tim Gerhard$^{(\boxtimes)}$, Dennis Schwerdel, and Paul Müller

Integrated Communication Systems Lab, University of Kaiserslautern,
Kaiserslautern, Germany
{t_gerhard10,schwerdel,pmueller}@informatik.uni-kl.de

Abstract. Virtualization has become a key component of network test-beds. However, transmitting data or commands to the test nodes is still either a complicated task or makes use of the nodes' network interfaces, which may interfere with the experiment itself. This paper creates a model for the typical lifecycle of experiment nodes, and proposes a mechanism for networkless node control for virtual nodes in such a typical experiment lifecycle which has been implemented in an existing testbed environment.

Keywords: Testbed · Control Interface · Node Control

1 Introduction

Network research is becoming more important since the Internet and other computer networks have a growing influence on the world. For this area of research, network testbeds are a crucial tool for experimentation. These testbeds usually offer a number of devices distributed over the globe with certain connection configurations between them. The experimenters' influence on this setup and its variables depends mainly on the testbed's architecture.

An important aspect for the usage of a testbed is how the network devices can be controlled. For large experiments which have many network nodes it is not feasible to control every device by hand. Thus, the experimenter needs to have a controlling interface which can be automated, i.e. scripted. Many testbeds (such as PlanetLab [3] or EmuLab [2,7]) use the devices' networking capabilities to provide such an interface. Automation frontends for these testbeds like gush [1] also need a network connection to the devices.

However, in a networking testbed, a network interface (especially one connected to the Internet) may not be a good solution to the problem of controlling a device. There are several disadvantages when choosing this control method which have to be accounted for in the experiment design.

configuration. Depending on how node control is realized, there is either an additional network interface on every device or one of the interfaces which is being used in the experiment is also used for control. In the first case,

© Institute for Computer Sciences, Social Informatics and Telecommunications Engineering 2014
V.C.M. Leung et al. (Eds.): TridentCom 2014, LNICST 137, pp. 14–22, 2014.
DOI: 10.1007/978-3-319-13326-3_2

the experiment must be configured never to use the additional interface, even when routing over this interface would make more sense than routing over another one. In the second case, this interface is forced to support the traditional protocol stack including TCP/IP.

traffic. There may be uncontrolled traffic coming from the outside network to the experiment. This may affect measurements as this additional traffic uses bandwidth, may cause additional latency or interfere with the experiments in other ways.

connectivity. There may be experiments which may not be connected to the Internet for several reasons. For example, you cannot run a malware analysis while connected to the Internet without endangering the Internet (Such an experiment has been done on ToMaTo, using VNC as the node control method [5]).

Testbeds can provide a networkless control interface for these kinds of experiments, which will be shown in this paper. In Section 2, a model for automated node control will be developed. Section 3 describes how these operations can be realized in a host-guest system, section 4 introduces the actual implementation in the Topology Management Tool (ToMaTo [4,6]) and section 5 concludes this paper.

2 Requirements for Automated Control

After creating devices, the experimenter will usually install software on it (1), configure it (2), run the experiment (3) and then collect the resulting data (4). Step 1 consists of transmitting files to the device and then execute the installation routine. Step 2 also consists of running commands and maybe uploading some configuration files to the device. Step 3 can be initiated by a command, and step 4 is a file download from the device. Every additional interaction can also be possible through file transmission or sending commands.

For an automated control, one must be able to wait for a command to finish before continuing with the next step. Therefore, an automated control interface only needs these three operations: transmitting files between the controlling and the controlled device, executing commands or scripts on the controlled device and monitoring the progress of this execution.

Instead of allowing to directly execute a defined command, the controlled device can be configured to automatically execute a script identified by a certain file name after such a script has been uploaded. Uploads and downloads are done through archives, where the archive will be extracted to a certain directory after an upload, and the archive will be created from this directory again for download. For the purpose of describing, archive and directory can be viewed as equivalents.

A system which provides these three operations (upload and execute, query execution status, download) for its devices to its users without using the target device's network interfaces provides *Remote Execution and Transfer of Files for Vitual computers* (RexTFV).

3   Communication Between Host and Guest

This paper will focus on the interface between host and guest. It does not describe how the host is controlled by the user, but it is assumed that the additional commands can be integrated into the testbed's architecture.

Storage is a resource which is shared between host and guest. In general, the guest can access a part of the host's storage. This fact can be used to emulate a shared directory, which can then be used to provide the operations described in Section 2.

The *network-less Execution and Transfer Protocol* (nlXTP) uses such a shared directory to provide these operations between host and guest systems. The term *network-less* means that it does not make use of network interfaces.

RexTFV has been designed to work for virtual devices, but it can be used in any scenario where the controlling node can access the controlled node's storage.

3.1   Shared Directory

Virtualization systems can be categorized into container-based or full virtualization, which are completely different approaches to the problem of virtualizing computer systems. Thus, there are fundamental differences in the realization of the shared directory.

As will be shown in the next section, the shared directory has to provide the following:

- upload of an archive,
- download of an archive, and
- a frequent, scheduled reading of a certain file (the status file) by the host, written by the guest.

It is assumed that the user does not execute the upload and download operations while the guest is still working on the files, given the fact that the user knows when operations are running. Thus, only the scheduled reading of the status file has to cover possible inconsistency.

Container-Based Virtualization. Cantainer-based virtual machines (such as OpenVZ or VServer) aim at creating a different runtime environment, while host and guest system still share one kernel, including drivers. This means that the virtual machine is integrated into the host's scheduler and file system. In fact, the guest's root directory is simply a certain directory in the host's file system. Since nlXTP requires full control over the shared directory, this shared directory must be an otherwise unused subdirectory of the guest's file system.

Both host and guest can access the directory at any time, reading or writing. The only occurence of inconsistency may happen if the host reads a file which is at this point of time being written by the guest. To prevent this, the usual ways of preventing simultanous access to one file by multiple processes can be used. Alternatively, the file can be secured by a checksum.

Fig. 1. The virtual disk can be mounted in both systems simultaneously

Full Virtualization. In full virtualization systems (like KVM/QEMU or VirtualBox), such a shared file system can be realized by a virtual disk, which can
be accessed by both the host system and the guest system (see figure 1). This
disk needs to have a file system which is supported by both systems (in many
cases vFAT is suitable).

To avoid an inconsistent file system, host and guest must never write to this
disk at the same time, or before the cache of the other system has been written
back. Since it must be assumed that the disk is always mounted by the guest
system while it is turned on, the host system must only write on the disk while
the guest system is shut down. This means that archive uploads are unavailable
while the guest system is running.

Fig. 2. Access Sequence when the host performs an I/O operation on the shared
directory

However, the host system can still read the disk while the guest system is
turned on. To lower the probability of an inconsistent file system while reading, the host system only mounts the disk right before reading or writing, and
unmounts it right after the reading (see figure 2). Assuming a write-through
caching strategy by the guest, and given the assumption from above (the user
does not start a download while the the guest is still writing on the files), the
guest writing in the status file while the host is reading it remains the only
chance of inconsistency.

There may be three kinds of effects: (1) The file does not exist, (2) The
file does not fit into the boundaries described in the disk's file table or (3) the

file is being changed by the guest while the host is reading it (thus, the data is corrupted). To avoid all these errors, the guest secures the file content by a checksum. In case 1, the inconsistency can be detected directly (assuming that the file must exist; if it doesn't, the whole operation is pointless). In case 2, the checksum does not exist (or case 3 applies, depending on the implementation) and in case 3, the checksum validation will fail. If inconsistency is detected, the reading can be repeated after a short interval of time: just enough so the guest can finish the operation on the file.

3.2   Operations

NlXTP provides operations according to RexTFV in section 2. These are: upload & execute, query execution status and download. For the purpose of description, upload and execute can be seen as two different operations, where the execution automatically follows after an upload and is never called directly.

Upload. Depending on the realization of the shared directory, the upload may not be possible while the guest system is turned on. When the user uploads a file, the host deletes the current content of the shared directory, and then extracts the archive into this directory.

Execution. In order to provide the information for the status query, the script is not directly executed. Instead, a monitor program is called which then executes the script.

When uploading, there are three possible situations:

1. The guest system is turned off.
2. The guest system is turned on, and the host can invoke processes on the guest system.
3. The guest system is turned on, and the host cannot invoke processes on the guest system.

In case 1, the execution must be delayed until the guest system has been booted. On every guest system the monitor is executed at the boot process if the start script has been changed.

In case 2, the monitor is called by the host right after the archive has been extracted.

In case 3, the guest needs to run a daemon program which can react to changes in the shared directory. When a new start script appears, it executes the monitor. The same daemon may also handle case 1. In this case, the testbed must make sure that the daemon does not start the script before the archive has been completely extracted. One way of doing this is to not copy the start script into the shared directory before everything else is present.

Status Query. The status information consists of:

- Has the script finished? (*Done Flag*)
- Is the monitor still running? (*Running Info*)
- A custom string defined by the script (*Custom Status*)

This information is stored in a file called the status file, which is written by the monitor. The status file can be read by the host, which then provides the information to the testbed, which can make it accessible to the user.

The *Done Flag* will be set to true as soon as the monitor detects that the script process has terminated.

Since this termination cannot be detected if the monitor crashes or terminates before the script has been finished, the monitor repeatedly (i.e., every 2 minutes) writes the current timestamp into the *Running Info*. The host interprets this as a sequence number, and if it does not change for a certain amount of time, the monitor can be assumed to have stopped. Because the host only watches for changes, it is not necessary to synchronize the clocks. To hide complexity to the user, the host provides this information as a boolean value: The monitor is running or not.

The *Custom Status* can either be written by the start script, or the monitor provides a function which can be called by the script. This string may contain anything from a single value to an XML file. Since RexTFV provides an interface for the user (or any client program), this string can be used to send information from the virtual machine to the experimenter.

Additionally, the standard and error output of the script are being saved to the shared directory, where it can be downloaded as described in the next section.

Download. In order to download, the host packs the whole shared directory into an archive which can then be sent to the user.

This directory contains the start script's standard and error output, the status file, all the data which has been uploaded and not deleted, and all files which may have been generated in the shared directory by other programs and stored in this directory.

To avoid large downloads, the start script should delete unnecessary data like software packets after it has finished all other operations. In order to get all the necessary data, all programs should be configured to store their output data in this directory. If such a configuration is not possible, the start script must make sure to copy the data here after the experiment.

3.3   Architecture

RexTFV has been designed to not require any changes to the testbed's architecture, so that it can seemlessly integrated into an existing testbed by adding some function calls and adding these functions to the software controlling the hosts.

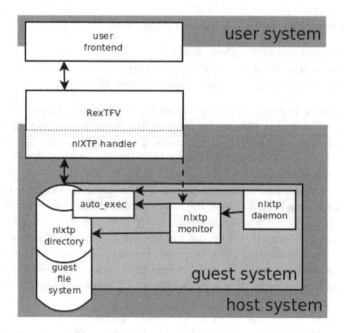

Fig. 3. Components of RexTFV using nlXTP and integration into the testbed

Figure 3 shows the distribution of components between guest, host and user system. Functions which are in the white area may be distributed as the testbed's architecture requires it. In general, the testbed must forward RexTFV function calls to the host system, and then use its nlXTP handler for communicating with the guest system, i.e. writing and reading from the shared directory, and eventually mounting and unmounting it. Since all function calls from the user to the nlXTP handler must run through the testbed, authentication and authorization for these operation can be checked by the testbed.

Function calls are always targeted at the host and never at the virtual devices. Thus, well-known technologies of network virtualization can be used to seperate this control-traffic from the traffic of the experiment in such a way that it becomes invisible for the experiment nodes. This way, this kind of control does not happen over the network from the point of view of the experiment nodes.

The operations from section 3.2 assume small programs on the guest system, the so-called "guest modules". These are the *nlXTP daemon*, which has to cover some cases for the auto-execution, and the *nlXTP monitor*, which has to execute the start script and write down the status information. In contrast to control over network, these requirements are low, because nlXTP does not require TCP/IP, SSH, user authentication or other complex programs on the devices, which are necessary for the core functionality.

If the guest modules are missing on a virtual machine, file transfers (the virtual floppy must be mounted manually), and the submission of status information (which must be written in the testbed-specific format in the status file)

are still possible in a manual way. This can also be used to install the guest modules manually on a newly created device. The only thing that would be impossible is the automatic execution of the start script.

4 Implementation

NlXTP has been implemented for the container-based OpenVZ and the full virtualization KVM. This proves that the concepts described in section 3 work. Since these concepts do not require or assume anything except the basic principles of container-based or full virtualization, they should work with other virtualization systems as well.

RexTFV has been implemented in ToMaTo using nlXTP. The functions can be found under the more user-friendly name *executable archives*.

5 Conclusion

RexTFV can be used to automate the lifecycle of devices in an experiment. When using nlXTP for host-to-guest and guest-to-host communication, it does not need any changes to the network configuration of a virtual machine, making it possible to run an experiment without ever connecting to the Internet, thus reducing noise from the outside which may affect the results. Furthermore, if an experimenter decides not to use RexTFV, its presence won't change the experiment's setup.

NlXTP makes use of the fact that the host and the guest system access the same physical storage to emulate a shared directory for network-less communication and is therefore only applicable in such a situation. It was specifically designed to avoid using an IP stack communication on experiment nodes.

Archives can not only be used for file transmission or single commands, but also for automating parts of or the whole experiment lifecycle on a testing node. In principle, the knowledge about which archives have been uploaded on which devices at what time in the experiment may, together with all testbed variables, determine the whole experiment. This can increase reproducibility and confirmability for the given experiment, if the archives are provided to the readers of a publication.

References

1. Albrecht, J., Huang, D.Y.: Managing Distributed Applications Using Gush. In: Magedanz, T., Gavras, A., Thanh, N.H., Chase, J.S. (eds.) TridentCom 2010. LNICST, vol. 46, pp. 401–411. Springer, Heidelberg (2011). http://link.springer.com/chapter/10.1007/978-3-642-17851-1_31
2. Bastin, N., Bavier, A., Blaine, J., Chen, J., Krishnan, N., Mambretti, J., McGeer, R., Ricci, R., Watts, N.: The instageni initiative: an architecture for distributed systems and advanced programmable networks. Computer Networks (2014). http://dl.acm.org/citation.cfm?id=2612045

3. Chun, B., Culler, D., Roscoe, T., Bavier, A., Peterson, L., Wawrzoniak, M., Bowman, M.: Planetlab: an overlay testbed for broad-coverage services. SIGCOMM Comput. Commun. Rev. 33(3), 3–12 (2003) ISSN 0146–4833. doi:10.1145/956993.956995. http://doi.acm.org/10.1145/956993.956995
4. Schwerdel, D., Hock, D., Günther, D., Reuther, B., Müller, P., Tran-Gia, P.: ToMaTo - A Network Experimentation Tool. In: Korakis, T., Li, H., Tran-Gia, P., Park, H.-S. (eds.) TridentCom 2011. LNICST, vol. 90, pp. 1–10. Springer, Heidelberg (2012). http://link.springer.com/chapter/10.1007/978-3-642-29273-6_1
5. Schwerdel, D., Reuther, B., Mueller, P.: Malware analysis in the tomato testbed (2011). http://dspace.icsy.de:12000/dspace/handle/123456789/350
6. Schwerdel, D., Reuther, B., Zinner, T., Mueller, P., Tran-Gia, P.: Future internet research and experimentation: The g-lab approach. Computer Networks 61(0), 102–117 (2014). ISSN 1389–1286. doi:http://dx.doi.org/10.1016/j.bjp.2013.12.023.. http://www.sciencedirect.com/science/article/pii/S1389128613004362 (Special issue on Future Internet) Testbeds - Part I
7. White, B., Lepreau, J., Stoller, L., Ricci, R., Guruprasad, S., Newbold, M., Hibler, M., Barb, C., Joglekar, A.: An integrated experimental environment for distributed systems and networks. pp. 255–270, Boston, MA (December 2002). http://dl.acm.org/citation.cfm?id=844152

The Tradeoff Between Single Aggregate and Multiple Aggregates in Designing GENI Experiments

Zongming Fei[1]([✉]), Ping Yi[1], and Jianjun Yang[2]

[1] Laboratory for Advanced Networking, Department of Computer Science,
University of Kentucky, Lexington, KY 40506, USA
`fei@netlab.uky.edu, yiping@netlab.uky.edu`
[2] Department of Computer Science, University of North Georgia,
Oakwood, GA 30566, USA
`jianjun.yang@ung.edu`

Abstract. The Global Environment for Network Innovations (GENI) provides a virtual laboratory for exploring future internets at scale. It consists of many geographically distributed aggregates for providing computing and networking resources for setting up network experiments. A key design question for GENI experimenters is where they should reserve the resources, and in particular whether they should reserve the resources from a single aggregate or from multiple aggregates. This not only depends on the nature of the experiment, but needs a better understanding of underlying GENI networks as well. This paper studies the performance of GENI networks, with a focus on the tradeoff between single aggregate and multiple aggregates in the design of GENI experiments from the performance perspective. The analysis of data collected will shed light on the decision process for designing GENI experiments.

Keywords: GENI · Network testbed · Network measurement · Experiment design

1 Introduction

The Global Environment for Network Innovations (GENI) is a project sponsored by National Science Foundation (NSF) with the aim to provide a collaborative environment to build a virtual laboratory for exploring future internets at scale [1,2]. It has attracted many universities and industrial partners to contribute their efforts towards developing a global federated network testbed for networking research and education. An experimenter can reserve both computing resources (such as PCs, virtual machines (VMs)), and networking resources (such as ION links, OpenFlow switches, VLANs, and GRE tunnels). GENI consists of many aggregates, each of which manages a set of resources [3]. Typically, a GENI aggregate is administrated and controlled by an institution which can impose its own policies about the allocation of the resources. As more GENI racks are

© Institute for Computer Sciences, Social Informatics and Telecommunications Engineering 2014
V.C.M. Leung et al. (Eds.): TridentCom 2014, LNICST 137, pp. 23–32, 2014.
DOI: 10.1007/978-3-319-13326-3_3

deployed on university campuses across the United States, GENI has grown to have tens of aggregates with resources available for network experiments [4].

One decision that needs to be made in designing a GENI experiment is whether to use resources from one aggregate or from multiple aggregates. It depends on the types of experiments to be performed. Some experiments such as multimedia applications may have a strict end-to-end delay requirement that cannot be satisfied by nodes distributed over a wide area. They may have to get resources from a single aggregate. On the other hand, there are experiments that need to test the behavior of protocols on how they react to the cross traffic from the real world. It may be preferable to have resources from multiple aggregates. There is also a question about which aggregates to choose to put the experimental nodes.

To make this decision, we need to have a good understanding of underlying networks. For example, what exactly can we get from links within an aggregate versus from multiple aggregates? How different are the bandwidths and latencies of links within an aggregate versus from multiple aggregates? What are their behaviors over a long period of time? We collect and analyze the measurement data and try to answer these questions. We expect that the analysis will provide helpful hints to the design of GENI experiments.

We understand that the distinction between single aggregate and multiple aggregates is not absolute. In a single aggregate experiment, the links generally have lower latencies and higher bandwidths. To make them suitable for an experiment that needs more realistic topology that has a wide variety of delays and bandwidths, we can add delay nodes in the middle of the topology to do traffic shaping, increasing the delay or reducing the bandwidth, or both. This added an element of simulations/emulations, instead of pure experimentations. The resulting topology will have some characteristics of multi-aggregate experiments. On the flip side of the coin are experiments using multiple aggregates. For large network experiments, the number of nodes usually exceeds the number of aggregates available. We have to allocate multiple nodes within an aggregate. Thus, even in a multi-aggregate experiment, we may still have links within an aggregate. In either case, we need to have an idea about delays and bandwidths of both single-aggregate links and cross-aggregate links.

In this paper, we present our study on performance of GENI networks, with a focus on the tradeoff between single aggregate and multiple aggregates in the design of GENI experiments from the performance perspective. We will analyze how the links behave differently over a period of time. The data collected will shed some light on the design process for choosing where the nodes in the experiment should be located.

The rest of the paper is structured as follows. Section 2 introduces related work and some background concepts. Section 3 describes the experiments we used to collect performance data. Section 4 presents the results about the latencies and bandwidths of the links within an aggregate and across aggregates. Section 5 concludes the paper.

2   Related Work

GENI has involved many universities and industry partners and grown significantly in recent years. It consists of multiple control frameworks [5,6] and has resources mainly on university campuses in the United States and several sites in other countries. It developed many tools supporting experimenters, such as Flack [7,8] of ProtoGENI [5].

Several early GENI projects investigated performance measurement [9–13] in the GENI environment. They have different focuses and generally emphasize on developing tools to enable users to collect performance data.

More recently, two major instrumentation and measurement efforts are under way in GENI. One is the Large-scale GENI Instrumentation and Measurement Infrastructure (GIMI) project [14], which makes use of OML library to instrument resources based on the ORBIT control framework. It can filter and process measurement flows, and consume measurement flows. The other is the GENI Measurement and Instrumentation Infrastructure (GEMINI) project [15]. It is based on earlier INSTOOLS system [9] and perfSONAR system [16]. It started with supporting ProtoGENI, but can now support nodes from other control frameworks as well. All these GENI measurement systems emphasize on building tools to support users to collect measurement data *after* their experiments have been set up. In contrast, this paper focuses on examining behaviors of different kinds of links in GENI networks and help users in the design process of their experiments.

3   Experiments for Data Collection

To measure the performance of links within an aggregate, we design a 11-node topology as shown in Fig. 1. In GENI, multiple virtual machines (VMs) can be allocated from a single raw physical machine/computer (PC). We want to measure both the links that connects two VMs from the same physical machine and the links that connects two VMs from two different physical machines. Theoretically, three VMs are enough because we can have two VMs from the same physical machine and the other one from a different physical machine. We can create both kinds of links with these three machines. However, if we create a topology with three VMs, most likely we will end up with three VMs from the same physical machine due to the allocation algorithm used in GENI aggregates. Even though we can bind a VM to a specific physical machine, the submission through the GENI Flack interface is not well supported. Our strategy is to specify a topology as shown in Fig. 1 with enough number of nodes so that they have to be allocated to different physical machines. We understand that we do not have to measure all the links. Rather we select four links as representatives.

We obtained the bandwidth and latency data for these four links using iperf [17] and ping over 10 days. One measurement (both bandwidth and latency) is taken for every hour, with 10 ECHO_REQUESTs for each ping.

To measure the performance of links from different aggregates, we select 10 aggregates and set up a mesh topology as shown in Fig. 2.

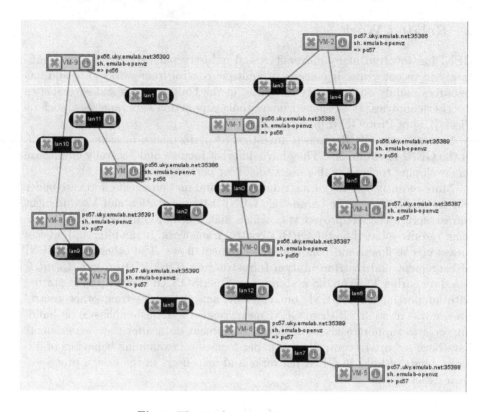

Fig. 1. The single-aggregate experiment

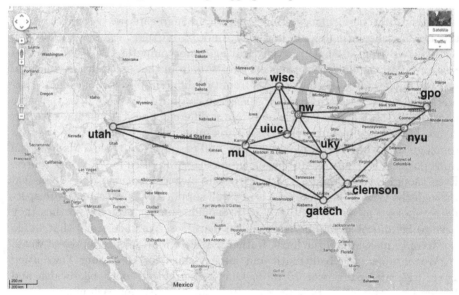

Fig. 2. The multi-aggregate experiment

4   Performance Results

We collected both latency and bandwidth information from these two experiments. Links in these two experiments can be divided into three categories:

Category 1 (**Same PC**): the links connecting two VMs that are allocated from the same physical machine;

Category 2 (**Same Aggregate**): the links connecting two VMs that are allocated from two different physical machines located in the same aggregate; and

Category 3 (**Different Aggregates**): the links connecting two VMs that are allocated from two different physical machines located in two different aggregates.

The first experiment covers the first two kinds of links, while the second experiment covers the third kind of links. We first calculate the averages of latencies and bandwidths over the 10 day period for each link. The results are summarized in Table 1.

The links in the Same PC category have similar performance. So we only choose two links (from VM-0 to VM-1, and from VM-6 to VM-7) as representatives. For the same reason, we only choose two links (from VM-0 to VM-6, and from VM-3 to VM-4) as representatives for the Same Aggregate category. However, the performance of the links from the Different Aggregates category varies a lot. So we include the results for all the links in the second experiment in the table.

As expected, the average latencies for the links in the Same PC category are the smallest, measured at 0.042ms and 0.045ms. The latencies for the links in the Same Aggregate category are about 2.5 times as large, but still in the range of one tenth of a second. They are both much smaller than the links connecting VMs from two different aggregates. The lowest latency we got is the link connecting VMs from the Northwestern aggregate and the UIUC aggregate, measured at 3ms, which are 30 times as large as that of the links from the Same Aggregate category. We see a wide variety of latencies measured for different cross-aggregate links, ranging from 3ms to 60ms. When designing a GENI experiment, we may take the difference in latencies into consideration for reserving GENI resources.

Table 1. Average latency and bandwidth

Category	link	Avg. Latency (ms)	Avg. Bandwidth (Mbits/second)
1. Same PC	VM-0 to VM-1	0.045	97.3
	VM-6 to VM-7	0.042	97.4
2. Same Aggregate	VM-0 to VM-6	0.115	474
	VM-3 to VM-4	0.116	469
3. Different Aggregates	21 links	from 3 to 60	from 34 to 94

While the average latencies give a general idea about the tradeoff between using nodes from a single aggregate versus from multiple aggregates, it is more interesting to observe how they change over time. Fig. 3(a) shows how the latency of the link from VM-0 to VM-1 in the first experiment change over the 10 day period. We can see that it always hovers around 0.045ms, with the highest at 0.084ms at one time and with the lowest at 0.034ms three times. It is relatively stable and close to its average value. Fig. 3(b) shows that the link from VM-6 to VM-7 displays the similar pattern.

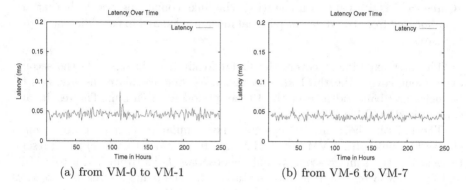

(a) from VM-0 to VM-1   (b) from VM-6 to VM-7

Fig. 3. Latency of the links connecting two VMs from the same PC

The latencies for the links connecting two VMs from two different PCs within an aggregate are larger than that of category 1 links as shown in Fig. 4. Also larger is the range these latencies change. However, we still see a very stable pattern in terms how they change over time.

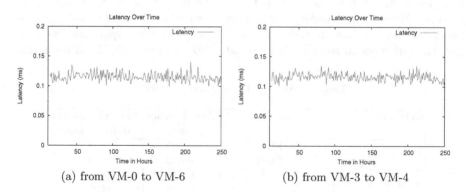

(a) from VM-0 to VM-6   (b) from VM-3 to VM-4

Fig. 4. Latency of the links connecting two VMs from two PCs within an aggregate

The latencies for category 3 links demonstrate a wider variety of patterns. For lack of space, we cannot present all of them in this paper. Instead, we choose two as representatives here to show how they can be quite different. Fig. 5(a) shows how the latency of the link from Kentucky to Missouri [1] change over time. The absolute range of the change is larger than those links from categories 1 and 2. However, the percentage of the change is not large. It is a totally different story for the link from Utah to Georgia Tech (Gatech) as shown in Fig. 5(b). Notice that the scales on y-axis in the figures are different. The range of the change in this case is almost 10 times as large as the average value. We can end up with a much more unpredictable behavior if we have VMs allocated from different aggregates.

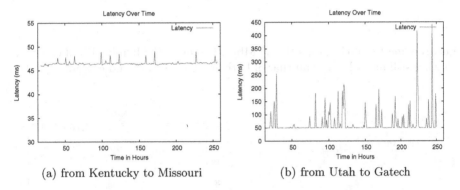

(a) from Kentucky to Missouri   (b) from Utah to Gatech

Fig. 5. Latency of the links connecting two VMs from two different aggregates

The latency of the links is only one factor to consider in designing GENI experiments. The other factor is the bandwidth of the links. From Table 1, we can see that category 1 links have a measured bandwidth of 97.3 Mbps. It can be higher because the two VMs these links attached to are located within the same physical machine. However, due to rate limit of the VMs, they are most likely capped at 100 Mbps. Fig. 6 shows how the bandwidth of these links change over time. Similar to the latency case, it stays close to the average level, appearing almost like a straight line.

Category 2 links achieve higher bandwidth, having average values at 474 Mbps and 469 Mbps. VMs in this case are connected with a gigabit switch. Because of the traffic from other experiments or load on the shared physical machines, the measured bandwidth is smaller than the maximal possible value. For the similar reason, we can see in Fig. 7 that it oscillates quite a lot over

---

[1] We use abbreviations here to indicate the VMs from a certain aggregate. "Kentucky" means the VM allocated from the University of Kentucky GENI aggregate. Similarly, "Missouri" means the VM allocated from the University of Missouri GENI aggregate. We use this convention for naming other VMs, too.

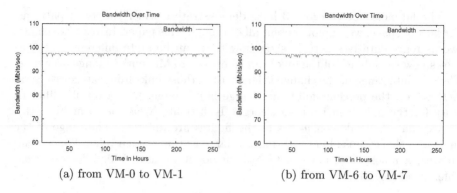

Fig. 6. Bandwidth of the links connecting two VMs from the same PC

time, ranging from 347 Mbps to 533 Mbps. However, the bandwidth of category 2 links is still much large than that of both category 1 links and category 3 links.

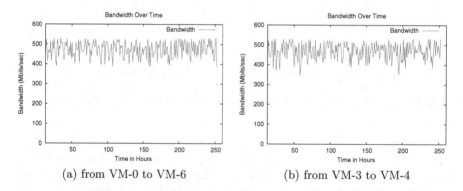

Fig. 7. Bandwidth of the links connecting two VMs from two PCs within an aggregate

We get a totally different picture for the links connecting two VMs from different aggregates. Depending on the links, we can get an average bandwidth as low as 34 Mbps and as high as 94 Mbps. They also change more wildly over time, as shown in Fig. 8. This is because these links are cross-Internet links that will compete with traffic from other applications. Their behaviors are much more unpredictable than those links within a single aggregate. For the same link from Utah to Gatech, we can get a bandwidth measure as low as 8.5 Mbps and as high as 90.5 Mbps. If we want to observe how a protocol performs and reacts to the real world traffic, this may be the link we should include in the experiment.

In summary, from the data we collected, we can see significant differences between single-aggregate links and cross-aggregate links in terms of latency and

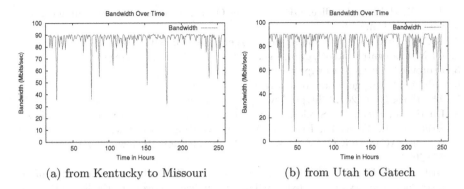

(a) from Kentucky to Missouri   (b) from Utah to Gatech

Fig. 8. Bandwidth of the links connecting two VMs from two different aggregates

bandwidth. Not only the average values are significantly different, but their behaviors over time can be quite different as well. When designing a GENI experiment, we can make use of performance data to decide where the nodes in the experiment should be located to meet the requirement.

5   Conclusion

Understanding the GENI networks is an important step in making a good design for GENI experiments. We focus on the performance aspect of the GENI networks by collecting latency and bandwidth data from two experiments. The results from this paper are only a snapshot of the GENI networks over a short period of time. However, the observed behaviors and the collected performance data of the links from different categories provide helpful information for GENI experimenters. As more researchers and educators use the GENI network testbed, there is a growing need to better understand all aspects of GENI.

Acknowledgments. We would like to thank Dr. Jim Griffioen for his comments on our earlier work on this topic. We also want to thank Mr. Hussamuddin Nasir and other members of the GEMINI project team for their help during the design and implementation of this project.

This material is based upon work supported in part by the National Science Foundation under Grant No. CNS-0834243 and CNS-1346688 Subcontracts 1925 and 1928. Any opinions, findings, and conclusions or recommendations expressed in this material are those of the authors and do not necessarily reflect the views of BBN Technologies Corp, the GENI Project Office, or the National Science Foundation.

References

1. The GENI Project Office, GENI System Overview. http://www.geni.net/docs/ GENISysOvrvw092908.pdf

2. The GENI Project Office, GENI System Overview. http://groups.geni.net/geni/wiki/GENIConcepts
3. GENI glossary. http://groups.geni.net/geni/wiki/GENIGlossary
4. GENI aggregates. http://groups.geni.net/geni/wiki/GeniAggregate
5. ProtoGENI. http://www.protogeni.net
6. ORCA. https://geni-orca.renci.org/trac/
7. The Flack GUI (2012). http://www.protogeni.net
8. Duerig, J., Ricci, R., Stoller, L., Strum, M., Wong, G., Carpenter, C., Fei, Z., Griffioen, J., Nasir, H., Reed, J., Wu, X.: Getting started with GENI: A user tutorial. ACM SIGCOMM Computer Communication Review (CCR) **42**(1), 72–77 (2012)
9. Griffioen, J., Fei, Z., Nasir, H., Wu, X., Reed, J., Carpenter, C.: The design of an instrumentation system for federated and virtualized network testbeds. In: Proc. of the First IEEE Workshop on Algoirthms and Operating Procedures of Federated Virtualized Networks (FEDNET), Maui, Hawaii (April 2012)
10. GIMS: High-speed packet capture for GENI (2011). http://gims.wail.wisc.edu/docs/Tutorial.html
11. Leveraging and abstracting measurements with perfSONAR(LAMP) (2011). http://groups.geni.net/geni/wiki/LAMP
12. Calyam, P., Schopis, P.: OnTimeMeasure: Centralized and distributed measurement orchestration software (2012). http://groups.geni.net/geni/wiki/OnTimeMeasure
13. Fahmy, S., Sharma, P.: Scalable, extensible, and safe monitoring of GENI clusters (2010). http://groups.geni.net/geni/attachment/wiki/ScalableMonitoring/design.pdf
14. GIMI: Large-scale GENI instrumentation and measurement infrastructure. http://groups.geni.net/geni/wiki/GIMI
15. GEMINI: A GENI measurement and instrumentation infrastructure. http://groups.geni.net/geni/wiki/GEMINI
16. PerfSONAR. http://www.perfsonar.net/
17. iperf - TCP and UDP bandwidth performance measurement tool. http://code.google.com/p/iperf/

Reproducible Software Appliances
for Experimentation

Cristian Ruiz[1]([✉]), Olivier Richard[1], and Joseph Emeras[2]

[1] INRIA Grenoble, Grenoble, France
{cristian.ruiz,olivier.richard}@imag.fr
[2] INRIA Nancy, Nancy, France
joseph.emeras@imag.fr

Abstract. Experiment reproducibility is a milestone of the scientific method. Reproducibility of experiments in computer science would bring several advantages such as code re-usability and technology transfer. The reproducibility problem in computer science has been solved partially, addressing particular class of applications or single machine setups. In this paper we present our approach oriented to setup complex environments for experimentation, environments that require a lot of configuration and the installation of several software packages. The main objective of our approach is to enable the exact and independent reconstruction of a given software environment and the reuse of code. We present a simple and small software appliance generator that helps an experimenter to construct a specific software stack that can be deployed on different available testbeds.

Keywords: Reproducible Research · Testbed · Virtual Appliances · Cloud Computing · Experiment Methodology

1 Introduction

In order to strengthen the results of a research it is important to carry out the experimental part under real environments. In some cases, these real environments consist in a complex software stack that normally comprises a configured operating system, kernel modules, run-time libraries, databases, special file systems, etc. The process of building those environments has two shortcomings: (a) It is a very time consuming task for the experimenter that depends on his/her expertise. (b) It is widely acknowledged that most of the time, it is hardly reproducible. A good practice at experimenting is to assure the reproducibility. For computational experiments this is a goal difficult to achieve and even a mere replication of the experiment is a challenge [8]. This is due to the numerous details that have to be taken into account. The process of repeating an experiment was carefully studied in [7] and among the many conclusions drawn, the difficulty of repeating published results was highly relevant.

© Institute for Computer Sciences, Social Informatics and Telecommunications Engineering 2014
V.C.M. Leung et al. (Eds.): TridentCom 2014, LNICST 137, pp. 33–42, 2014.
DOI: 10.1007/978-3-319-13326-3_4

With the advent of testbeds such as Grid'5000 [5] and FutureGrid [15], cloud-based testbeds like BonFIRE[1], the ubiquity of Cloud computing infrastructures and the virtualization technology that is accessible to almost anyone that has a computer with modest requirements. Now it is possible to deploy virtual machines or operating system images, which makes interesting the approach of software appliances for experimentation. In [12] the author gives 13 ways that replicability is enhanced by using virtual appliances and virtual machine snapshots. Another close approach is shown in [9] where snapshots of computer systems are stored and shared in the cloud making computational analysis more reproducible. A system to create executable papers is shown in [2], which relies on the use of virtual machines and aims at improving the interactions between authors, reviewers and readers with reproducilibity purposes.

Those approaches offer several advantages such as simplicity, portability, isolation and more importantly an exact replication of the environment but they incurred in high overheads in building, storing and transferring the final files obtained. Additionally, it is not clear the composition of the software stack and how it was configured. We lose the steps that let to their creation.

In this paper, we present our approach to reproduce a software environment for experimentation. The approach is based on a software appliance generator called Kameleon. We present the implementation of a persistent cache mechanism that stores every piece of data (e.g., software packages, configuration files, scripts, etc.) used to construct the software appliance. It presents a lightweight approach which enables the construction and exact post reconstruction of a given software appliance from text descriptions. Kameleon persistent cache mechanism presents three main advantages: (1) it can be used as a format to distribute and store individual and related software appliances (virtual cluster) incurring in less storage requirements; (2) *provenance of data*, anyone can look at the steps that led to the creation of a given experimental environment; (3) it helps to overcome widespread problems occasioned by small changes in binary versions, unavailability of software packages, changes in web addresses, etc.

This paper is structured as follows: In Section 2, some approaches to reproduce a given environment for experimentation are discussed. Then, our approach to set up the environment required for experimentation is described in Section 3. In Section 4, we show some experimental results and validation of our approach. Finally the conclusions are presented in Section 5.

2   Related Works

Experimenters have different options to make the environment for experimentation more reproducible. They can capture the environment where the experiment was run or they can use a more reproducible approach to set up the experiment from the beginning.

---

[1] http://www.bonfire-project.eu

2.1   Tools for Capturing the Environment of Experimentation

CDE [11] and ReproZip [6] are based on the capture of what it is necessary to run the experiment. They capture automatically software dependencies through the interception of Linux system calls. A package is created with all these dependencies enabling it to be run on different Linux distributions and versions. ReproZip unlike CDE allows the user to have more control over the final package created. Both tools provide the capacity of repeating a given experiment. However, they are aimed at single machine setups, they do not consider distributed environments and different environments that could interact between them.

2.2   Methods for Setting Up the Environment of Experimentation

Manual. The experimenter deploys a *golden image* that will be provisioned manually. The image modifications have to be saved some way (e.g snapshots) and several versions of the environment can be created with testing purposes. Possibly, the experimenter has to deal with the contextualization of the images or it could be done using the underlying testbed infrastructure. In terms of reproducibility, the experimenter end up with a set of pre-configured software appliances that can be deployed later on the platform by him/her or another experimenter. This approach is relevant due to its simplicity and has been used and mentioned in [9] and [2]. Despite its simplicity, the storing of software appliances or snapshots incurs in high storage costs.

Script Automation. It is as well based on the deployment of golden images, however, the provisioning part is automated using scripts. The experimenter possibly has no need to save the image, because it can be reconstructed from the golden image at each deployment. Many experimenters opt for this approach because it gives a certain degree of reproduciblity and automation and it is simple compared to using configuration management tools. This was used in [1] for deploying and scheduling thousands of virtual machines on Grid'5000 testbed. Script automation incurs in less overhead when the environment has to be transmitted, for post execution. Nevertheless, it is still dependent on the images provided by the underlying platform.

Configuration Management Tools. Unlike the previous approaches, the golden images are provisioned this time with the help of configuration management tools (e.g., *Chef*[2] or *Puppet*[3]) which gives to the experimenter a high degree of automation and reproducibility. However, the process of porting the non-existing software towards those tools is complex and some administration expertise is needed. In [14] it is shown the viability of reproducible eScience on the cloud through the use of configuration management tools. A similar approach is shown in [3].

---

[2] http://www.opscode.com/chef/
[3] https://puppetlabs.com/

Software Appliances. Experimenters can opt for software appliances that have to be contextualized at deployment time. In [13] the viability of this approach was shown. Those images can be either built or downloaded from existing testbed infrastructures (e.g Grid'5000, FutureGrid) or sites as TURNKEY [4] or Cloud market[5] oriented to Amazon EC2 images. Those images are independent from the ones provided by the platform and experimenters have access to more operating system flavors. The process of image building relies on widely available tools that will be analyzed in the next subsection.

2.3 Software Appliances Builders

We use the term software appliance, which is defined as a pre-built software that is combined with just enough operating system *(jeOS)* and can run on bare metal (real hardware) or inside a hypervisor. A virtual appliance is a type of software appliance, which is packed in a format that targets a specific platform (normally virtualization platform). A software appliance encompasses three layers:

- **Operating System**: In the broadest sense includes the most popular operating systems (e.g GNU/Linux, Windows, FreeBSD). This element of the appliance can also contain modifications and special configurations, for instance a modified kernel.
- **Platform Software**: This encompasses compiled languages such as C, C++ and interpreted languages such as Python and Ruby. Additionally, applications or middle-ware (e.g., MPI, MySQL, Hadoop, Apache, etc). All Those software components are already configured.
- **Application Software**: New software or modifications to be tested and studied.

Vagrant[6] and Veewee[7] are complementary tools to create and configure lightweight, reproducible, and portable development environments. Veewee automatically builds virtual machine images of different Linux distributions. Those images can be exported as so called *Boxes* that are run on top of the most popular virtualization technologies (e.g., VirtualBox, VMware, etc.). Vagrant provision these *Boxes* using industry-standard configuration management tools such as shell scripts, Chef or Puppet that will automatically install and configure software. The idea of Vagrant is the creation of disposable and consistent environments that can be re-built from scratch. BoxGrinder [8] creates appliances from simple plain text descriptions for various platforms. Unlike previous tools, it uses the host system to perform the image creation which results in a faster process. Those tools are widely used in Cloud infrastructures for generating customized virtual appliances. In theory any experimenter could reconstruct the

---

[4] http://www.turnkeylinux.org
[5] http://thecloudmarket.com/
[6] http://www.vagrantup.com/
[7] https://github.com/jedi4ever/veewee
[8] http://boxgrinder.org/

virtual appliances using the same tool and the same specifications provided by other experimenter. However, the main hurdle is the dependency on external repositories, for instance, 30% of Veewee definitions files point to repositories that not longer exist or some packages are missing for a complete installation.

3 Reproducible Software Appliances

We extended our previous work Kameleon [10] which is a very simple software appliance generator that enables the construction and exact post reconstruction of a given software appliance from text descriptions. It is targeted to make easier the reconstruction of custom software stacks in HPC, Grid, or Cloud-like environments. Kameleon takes care of the following steps in the process of software appliance generation:

- **Operating system**: Construction of the respective *O.S* file system layout, which encompasses the necessary binaries, libraries, configuration files in order to run. This depends on the distribution chosen for the software appliance.
- **Provision**: Installation of different software packages required for the appliance. This can be done through the package manager of the distribution chosen, from source tarballs, or using configuration management tools.
- **User's code**: This step will add user's modifications or applications that the user wants to experiment with.
- **Save output**: Save the generated image into a particular format: Virtual machine format, LiveCD, raw disk image, etc.

Kameleon approach is based on two contexts, namely *execution context* which is where Kameleon engine is executed (e.g., user's machine) and *construction context* in charge of generating the file system layout of the appliance. Kameleon can use different operating system-level virtualization techniques such as: *chroot* (the less isolated but the lightness one) or *Linux Containers* as well as full virtualization (*e.g., VirtualBox, kvm*) and real machine (the most isolated but the heaviest one). Each context has its own advantages and disadvantages. As exposed before, using the user's machine to build the appliance could result in a faster build process. Kameleon enables to take advantage of the most convenient approach given the user's requirements. The process of construction or reconstruction has to take care of some possible issues caused by, for example, isolation and portability. Special needs can be specified in Kameleon metadata.

Our previous work was extended mainly in two points: (1) Requirements for a reproducible software appliance were identified, (2) The implementation of a persistent cache mechanisim. Both points will be described next.

3.1 Requirements for a Reproducible Reconstruction

The approach for software appliance construction and reconstruction is based on four requirements:

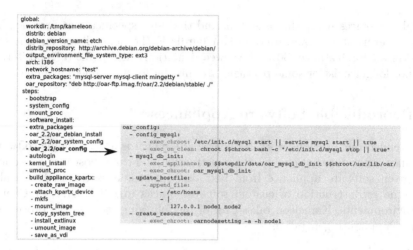

```
global:
    workdir: /tmp/kameleon
    distrib: debian
    debian_version_name: etch
    distrib_repository: http://archive.debian.org/debian-archive/debian/
    output_environment_file_system_type: ext3
    arch: i386
    network_hostname: "test"
    extra_packages: "mysql-server mysql-client mingetty "
    oar_repository: "deb http://oar-ftp.imag.fr/oar/2.2/debian/stable/ ./"
steps:
    - bootstrap
    - system_config
    - mount_proc
    - software_install:
    - extra_packages              oar_config:
    - oar_2.2/oar_debian_install    - config_mysql:
    - oar_2.2/oar_system_config       - exec_chroot: /etc/init.d/mysql start || service mysql start || true
    - oar_2.2/oar_config              - exec_on_clean: chroot $$chroot bash -c "/etc/init.d/mysql stop || true"
    - autologin                   - mysql_db_init:
    - kernel_install                - exec_appliance: cp $$stepdir/data/oar_mysql_db_init $$chroot/usr/lib/oar/
    - umount_proc                   - exec_chroot: oar_mysql_db_init
    - build_appliance_kpartx:     - update_hostfile:
       - create_raw_image           - append_file:
       - attach_kpartx_device         - /etc/hosts
       - mkfs                         - |
       - mount_image                      127.0.0.1 node1 node2
       - copy_system_tree         - create_resources:
       - install_extlinux           - exec_chroot: oarnodesetting -a -h node1
       - umount_image
       - save_as_vdi
```

Fig. 1. Recipe and step example

1. A recipe (Fig. 1) that describes how the software appliance is going to be built. This recipe is a higher level description easy to understand and contains some necessary meta-data in form of global variables and steps. For more details [10]
2. The *DATA* which is used as input of all the procedures described in the recipe. It encompasses software packages, tarballs, configuration files, control version repositores, scripts and every input data that make up a software appliance. Whenever used the term *DATA* in this paper, it will refer to this.
3. Kameleon engine consist in 700 lines of ruby code which parses the recipe and carry out the building. This part includes as well the persistent cache mechanism that will be described later on. This is the user interface to Kameleon.
4. Metadata that describes the compatibility and requirements between *execution context* and *construction context*.

Therefore, the problem of guaranteeing the exact reconstruction of software appliances is reduced to keeping the parts of Kameleon unchanged: (1) the recipe, (2) DATA (3) Kameleon engine. Two different experimenters having those three exact elements and fulfilling the requirements of context interactions (4) will generate the same software appliance. Kameleon can generate in an automatic and transparent way a cache file that will contain the exact *DATA* used during the process of construction along with the recipe, steps and metadata, all bundled together enabling the easy distribution. The low size of Kameleon engine and Polipo (less than 1MB) makes feasible the distribution of the exact versions used to create the environment, avoiding the incompatibility between versions. The whole process is depicted in Fig. 2. More information can be found in [10] or in Kameleon web site[9].

---

[9] kameleon.imag.fr

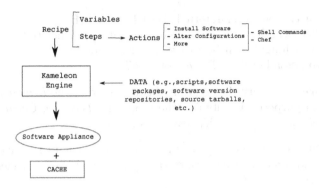

Fig. 2. Software appliance creation with Kameleon

3.2 Persistent Cache Mechanism

Our approach to achieve replicability is to use a persistent cache to capture all the *DATA* used during the construction. As we cannot guarantee that a particular download link will exist forever or always point to the same software with the same version. A persistent cache mechanism brings the two followings advantages: (a) Data can always be retrieved and (b) The software versions will be exactly the same.

Design. The caching mechanism has to be transparent and lightweight for the user in the two phases of the Kameleon approach: the construction of the software appliance, and its respective ulterior reconstruction. As most of *DATA* comes from the network (e.g., operating system, software packages), the obvious approach was to integrate a caching proxy for web. Such a caching proxy will capture transparently every piece of data downloaded using the network. However, there are still some parts of the *DATA* missing, because some files - that make the software appliance unique - are provided by the user from its local machine or even worse some packages cannot be cached. That is the reason why we opted for an approach consisting in two parts:

– A caching web proxy, that caches packages coming from the network. This relies on Polipo[10] which is a very small, portable and lightweight caching web proxy. We chose Polipo because it can run with almost zero configuration.
– Ad hoc procedures that cache what could not be cached using the caching web proxy (e.g., version control repositores, https traffic) and all data from the local machine. These Ad hoc procedures are based on simple actions depending on the data to cache. Modifications on the fly of the steps involved on those Ah doc procedures are necessary.

In order to make more clear the composition and limitations of the persistent cache, we define four properties of *DATA*:

---

[10] http://www.pps.jussieu.fr/~jch/software/polipo/

- Location: it can be either Internal (I) or External (E).
- Cacheability: whether it is possible to cache it (C) or not ($\bar{C}$).
- Method of caching: it can be Proxy (P) or Ad hoc (A).
- Scope: two possible values *Private* or *Public*.

The scope makes necessary the creation of two types of cache *Private* and *Public* for distribution purposes. Combining the properties *Location, Cacheability* and *Method of caching* we can identify five types of data:

- E,C,P: data which comes from an external location (e.g., local network, internet) and can be cached with the proxy (e.g., Software packages, tarballs, input data).
- E,C,A: same external location, however, it cannot be cached with the proxy (e.g., version control repositories, https traffic).
- E,$\bar{C}$: this data comes from an external location but can not be cached due to some restrictions (e.g., proprietary licenses) or due to its size it can not be stored (e.g., big databases).
- I,C,A: data that comes from the local machine and it is cached by some ad hoc procedures.
- I,$\bar{C}$: it comes form local machine but can not be cached.

4   Experimental Results and Validation

In order to show that our approach is very portable between versions of Linux distributions. We carried out successfully construction and reconstruction of different appliances as shown in Table 1 that consist in different flavors of GNU/Linux (Debian, Ubuntu) and middleware: OAR [4] a very lightweight batch scheduler, Hadoop[11] and TAU[12]. It was possible to reproduce old environments of test back to 2009. A design goal was to achieve a self contained cache. Hence, we tested the portability of the persistent cache mechanism. The aforementioned software appliances where reconstructed using their respective persistent cache files, the Kameleon engine and the Polipo binary which made only 984 K Bytes. This was tested in the following Linux distributions: Fedora 15, OpenSUSE 11.04, Ubuntu 10.4 and CentOS 6.0.

Table 1. Software appliances generated

Name	General Appliances Main software stack	Size [MB]	OAR Appliances			
			OAR Version	date of release	GNU/Linux version	Size [MB]
Hadoop	Java 1.6 Hadoop 1.03 Ubuntu 10.04 LTS	229	2.2.17	27 Nov 2009	Debian etch	112
			2.3.5	30 Nov 2009	Debian etch	113
	PAPI 5.1.0		2.4.7	11 Jan 2011	Debian Lenny	137
HPC Profiling	TAU 2.22 OpenMPI 1.6.4	226	2.5.0	5 Dec 2011	Debian Squeeze	140
	Debian Wheezy		2.5.2	23 May 2012	Debian Squeeze	140

---

[11] http://hadoop.apache.org/

[12] http://www.cs.uoregon.edu/research/tau/home.php

4.1   Building Old Environments

The persistent cache mechanism enable the building of environments generated at any point of time. It does so by using the same versions that are compatible with the scripts used at the moment of the first generation of the software appliance. Not using the same exact versions can sometimes generate unexpected errors that are time consuming and researchers do not want to deal with.

We faced those problems when building software appliances based on *Archlinux* distribution and on the OAR batch scheduler. Their current versions posed several incompatibility problems with the scripts used for generating the software appliances a year ago. The persistent cache mechanism enabled the reconstruction of these software appliances. All the examples presented in this paper can be reproduced accesing the Kameleon site[13].

5   Conclusions and Future Works

Experiment reproduciblity is a big challenge nowadays in computer science, a lot of tools have been proposed to address this problem, however there are still some environments and experiments that are difficult to tackle. Commonly, experimenters lack of expertise to setup complex environments necessary to reproduce a given experiment or to reuse the results obtained by someone else. We presented in this paper, a very lightweight approach that leverage existing software and allows an experimenter to reconstruct independently the same software environment used by another experimenter. Its design offers a low storage requirement and a total control on the environment creation which in turn allows the experimenter to understand the software environment and introduce modifications into the process. Furthermore, several methods to carry out the setup of the environment for experimentation were described and we show the advantages of our approach Kameleon. As a future work we plan to carry out more complex experiments with our approach and measure the gains in terms of reproducilibity and complexity as well as to study the contextualization of environments (e.g., post installation process) in different platforms.

Acknowledgments. Experiments presented in this paper were carried out using the Grid'5000 experimental testbed, being developed under the INRIA ALADDIN development action with support from CNRS, RENATER and several Universities as well as other funding bodies (see https://www.grid5000.fr).

References

1. Balouek, D., Lèbre, A., Quesnel, F.: Flauncher and DVMS - Deploying and Scheduling Thousands of Virtual Machines on Hundreds of Nodes Distributed Geographically. In: IEEE International Scalable Computing Challenge (SCALE 2013), held in conjunction with CCGrid 2013, Delft, Pays-Bas (2013)

---

[13] http://kameleon.imag.fr/

2. Brammer, G.R., Crosby, R.W., Matthews, S., Williams, T.L.: Paper mch: Creating dynamic reproducible science. Procedia CS **4**, 658–667 (2011)
3. Bresnahan, J., Freeman, T., LaBissoniere, D., Keahey, K.: Managing appliance launches in infrastructure clouds. In: Proceedings of the 2011 TeraGrid Conference: Extreme Digital Discovery, TG 2011, pp. 12:1–12:7. ACM, New York (2011)
4. Capit, N., Da Costa, G., Georgiou, Y., Huard, G., Martin, C., Mounie, G., Neyron, P., Richard, O.: A batch scheduler with high level components. In: Proceedings of the Fifth IEEE International Symposium on Cluster Computing and the Grid (CCGrid 2005), vol. 2, pp. 776–783. IEEE Computer Society, Washington, DC (2005)
5. Cappello, F., Desprez, F., Dayde, M., Jeannot, E., Jégou, Y., Lanteri, S., Melab, N., Namyst, R., Primet, P., Richard, O., Caron, E., Leduc, J., Mornet, G.: Grid'5000: a large scale, reconfigurable, controlable and monitorable Grid platform. In: 6th IEEE/ACM International Workshop on Grid Computing (Grid) (November 2005)
6. Chirigati, F., Shasha, D., Freire, J.: Reprozip: using provenance to support computational reproducibility. In: Proceedings of the 5th USENIX conference on Theory and Practice of Provenance, TaPP 2013, p. 1. USENIX Association, Berkeley (2013)
7. Clark, B., Deshane, T., Dow, E., Evanchik, S., Finlayson, M., Herne, J., Matthews, J.N.: Xen and the art of repeated research. In: Proceedings of the Annual Conference on USENIX Annual Technical Conference, ATEC 2004, p. 47. USENIX Association, Berkeley (2004)
8. Davison, A.P.: Automated capture of experiment context for easier reproducibility in computational research. Computing in Science Engineering **14**(4), 48–56 (2012)
9. Dudley, J.T., Butte, A.J.: In silico research in the era of cloud computing. Nature Biotechnology **28**(11), 1181–1185 (2010)
10. Emeras, J., Bzeznik, B., Richard, O., Georgiou, Y., Ruiz, C.: Reconstructing the software environment of an experiment with kameleon. In: Proceedings of the 5th ACM COMPUTE Conference: Intelligent and Scalable System Technologies, COMPUTE 2012, pp. 16:1–16:8. ACM, New York (2012)
11. Guo, P.J.: Cde: run any linux application on-demand without installation. In: Proceedings of the 25th international conference on Large Installation System Administration, LISA 2011, p. 2. USENIX Association, Berkeley (2011)
12. Howe, B.: Virtual appliances, cloud computing, and reproducible research. Computing in Science and Engg. **14**(4), 36–41 (2012)
13. Keahey, K., Freeman, T.: Contextualization: Providing one-click virtual clusters. In: Proceedings of the 2008 Fourth IEEE International Conference on eScience, ESCIENCE 2008, pp. 301–308. IEEE Computer Society, Washington, DC (2008)
14. Klinginsmith, J., Mahoui, M., Wu, Y.M.: Towards reproducible escience in the cloud. In: 2011 IEEE Third International Conference on Cloud Computing Technology and Science (CloudCom), pp. 582–586 (2011)
15. von Laszewski, G., Fox, G.C., Wang, F., Younge, A.J., Kulshrestha, A., Pike, G.G., Smith, W., Vockler, J., Figueiredo, R.J., Fortes, J., Keahey, K.: Design of the futuregrid experiment management framework. In: Gateway Computing Environments Workshop (GCE), pp. 1–10 (2010)

Heuristic Algorithm for Virtual Network Mapping Problem

Huynh Thi Thanh Binh[✉], Bach Hoang Vinh, Nguyen Hong Nhat,
and Le Hoang Linh

School of Information and Communication Technology,
Hanoi University of Science and Technology, Hanoi, Vietnam
binh.huynhthithanh@hust.edu.vn

Abstract. Nowadays, resource allocation for virtual networks (VNs) is brought as an imperative problem. For the characteristics of virtual networks, multiple virtual networks with different topo can co-exist on a shared infrastructure. A difficult point of problem is how to use the resource effectively and to satisfy the requirement of virtual network request. This problem is NP-hard. In this paper, we introduce a heuristic algorithm to solve this problem. To simulate a virtual network mapping problem in real world, we using two input data: an infrastructure network which is modeled by a connected graph and a set of virtual network request graphs with each graph contains their constraints, time and duration. The main purposes are to maximize the revenue and to minimize the cost when allocate the virtual networks to a substrate network. The experimental results are reported to show the efficiency of propose algorithm comparing to the Enhanced Greedy Node Mapping (EGNM) algorithm.

Keywords: Substrate network · Virtual network · Resource allocation · Heuristic algorithm

1 Introduction

In recent years, the network resources are being depleted. IPv4 has reached the limit, while people are still indifferent to IPv6. The physical resources are increasing improve, but have not been use effectively, leading to waste of resources. So, the necessary matter now is to use it in a suitable and efficient way. A given solution is Network virtualization. That means we can create multiple Virtual networks (VNs) which has different topologies, protocols and services. But all of them can run on and share resource of the same infrastructure, network virtualization promises better flexibility, security, manageability and decreased power consumption for the Internet [1]. This paper considers two processes of solving. The first is construction problem by giving the inputs, outputs and objective of the work. Second is our proposed algorithm that we use to improve the solutions.

However, the difficulty of this problem is how to optimal the allocation from virtual network to physical network and take full advantage of physical resource. Hence, several algorithms have been proposed to seek for a near optimal solution while reducing the complexity of the problem [2].i.e. in [3], Son H.Ngo et al. have introduce an improved heuristics for online node and link mapping which is improvement of

© Institute for Computer Sciences, Social Informatics and Telecommunications Engineering 2014
V.C.M. Leung et al. (Eds.): TridentCom 2014, LNICST 137, pp. 43–53, 2014.
DOI: 10.1007/978-3-319-13326-3_5

Yu'algorithm [4] by adding three more steps: sorting virtual nodes, using adaptive function and pre-checking invalid substrate links. With the best of our knowledge, almost mappings nowadays just start handling when the new requests come. Thus, we introduce a new way to approach the problem, which will use a new algorithm to pre-compute to speed up the processing. In this work, we give some criteria to evaluate and the objectives of problem, as well as an algorithm to generate the requirement of VNs. In that algorithm, we propose some improvements: sorting nodes by their degree and their available resource and compute before the time requests come. This resulted in two goals: maximize the revenue (B) and minimize the Cost (C). To simplified the goal, we decided to use the ratio of revenue to cost (B/C) as the only objective function and try to maximize this ratio. Experiment on 50-node topology of the substrate network and a set of virtual network requests, expected positive results and better than EGNM algorithms and Yu's Baseline virtual network embedding algorithm.

The rest of this paper is organized as follows. It starts with the introduction of problem formulation and related works. We describe about virtual network mapping problem at Section 2 and review some existing algorithms, on Section 3. Our new proposed algorithm is showed in section 4. Section 5 gives the experiments, computational and comparative results. The paper concludes with discussions and future works in section 6.

2   Problem Formulation

In this section, we give some overviews about virtual network embedding problem as well as an algorithm to solve it. We will define general substrate network, virtual network and set the main point to this problem which derived mainly from Son H.Ngo [2, 3] and Yu [4].

Input: A substrate network and a set of virtual network request:

Substrate Network
We define the substrate network as a graph $S = (N, L)$; where N is the set of substrate nodes and L is the set of substrate links of the network. Each node $n \in N$ has an associated free CPU resource - cs and each link $l \in L$ has an available bandwidth capacity - bs. Denoted by $N = \{n(cs)\}$ and $L = \{l(bs)\}$.
From that, we can define the available resource of each substrate node by:

$$AR(n) = cs \times \sum_{l \in L(n)} bs \qquad (1)$$

Where:- L(n) is the set of neighbor links of node n.
        - cs is the available resource of node n.
        - bs is bandwidth capacity of link l.

Virtual Network
The virtual network requests are modeled as $r = (V, E, t, d) \in R$, which is the set of requests. Where V, E are the set of vertices and edges of request, t is time when the request comes, and d is the duration of the request in turn.

Each vertex $v \in V$ has a CPU capacity requirement - cr and each edge $e \in E$ has a bandwidth capacity requirement - br. Denoted by $V = \{v(cr)\}$ and $E = \{e(br)\}$.

Each virtual node of virtual network has its required resource define as:

$$RR(v) = cr \times \sum_{e \in E(v)} br(e) \tag{2}$$

Where:- E(v) is the set of neighbor edges of vertex n.

- cr(v) is the required resource of vertex n.

- br(e) is required bandwidth of edge e.

Constrains

- Satisfying the most of virtual network requests not using the most resource.
- Each VN request is served with highest benefit.

Output

A set of graphs s' = $\{s_1, s_2...s_n\}$ where graph si is a result of mapping from virtual network r to physical network S.

Objectives

In this work, we are giving two main objectives: accept as many requests as possible (the acceptance ratio) and serve the VNs request with highest benefit brought while using the resource of physical network in optimal way. To do that, two quantities are given, that is revenue (B) and cost (C). And the objectives of this problem are maximizing revenue and minimizing the cost. However, it is difficult to satisfy both of them. So we decide to use the ratio of B to C to evaluate the final result.

The revenue here is determined by the total bandwidth of virtual link acceptance. The cost is evaluated by the number of substrate links of a path and the bandwidth was used in that path. In here, CPU resource is not the determining factor, and does not affect to the result of problem. Therefore, we decided to use only bandwidth to calculate the cost value.

- Maximize the Revenue calculate on set of request R:

$$B_{sum}(R) = \sum_{r_j \in R_A} B(r_j) = \sum_{r_j \in R_A} \sum_{e \in E(r_j)} br_e \tag{3}$$

Where: R_A is the set of requests that has accepted.

$E(r_j)$ is the set of request in R_A.

- Minimize the Cost calculate on output s':

$$C_{sum}(s') = \sum_{s_j \in s'} C(s_j) = \sum_{s_j \in s'} \sum_{p \in P(s_j)} length(p) \times bw_p \tag{4}$$

Where length(p) equal the number of link on that path.

Simplified, the goal is maximize this equation:

$$O = \frac{B_{sum}}{C_{sum}(s')} = \frac{\displaystyle\sum_{r_j \in R_A} \sum_{e \in E(r_j)} br_e}{\displaystyle\sum_{s_j \in s'} \sum_{p \in P(s_j)} length(p) \times bw_p} \tag{5}$$

3   Related Works

The problem can be divided into two main stages: node mapping and link mapping [1, 3, 4].

In [5], Adil et al. has given three main constraints associated with Virtual Network Embedding (VNE) problem. That is Node constraint, Link constrains and Admission control. Each kind of these maintain many types of constraint that must be satisfied. E.g. for node constraints, there are capacity and location. For link constraint, there are bandwidth and link propagation delay. And admission control is an important constraint that need to be implemented for two reasons: It ensure that demands of newly arrived VNs can be fulfilled by the substrate; resource allocation made to already mapped VNs is not violated.

In [4], Yu et al. use two algorithms for two stages which are Greedy Node Mapping (GNM) and Link Mapping with k-shortest path Algorithm.

GNM process all request arriving within a time-window as well as in the request queue, in decreasing order base on their revenue. For each request, they map its virtual nodes to substrate nodes which has maximum available resource. The pros of this method is to minimize the use of substrate resources at bottleneck nodes, which helps in satisfying the requirements of future VN requests which demand fewer resources [5].

And for link mapping, the selected nodes are connected following k-shortest paths algorithm to form a completed virtual network. A found path is accepted if it has enough bandwidth.

In [2], Son H.Ngo was improved the GNM algorithm of Yu, also the link mapping method. Using Enhance Greedy Node Mapping (EGNM), he lower the cost of problem for large scale application. They not only sort the requests base on their revenue but also sort the virtual nodes according to their require resource before mapping them to substrate node. By this way, virtual nodes with more required resource will be mapped to substrate nodes which have more available resource. They also re-calculate the available resource (AR) by adding a threshold T that is define as the ratio of CPU Load to Link Load on substrate network. Since then, the AR value of a node is depend on T.

At second stage, the Link mapping with Pre-checking using Dijkstra's algorithm was used. To satisfy the bandwidth constraint, they propose a pre-checking scheme that verifies the status of resource usage in the substrate network before the link mapping. The substrate links that do not have more or equal available bandwidth than requests will be removed from the graph. Then, the Dijkstra's algorithm will only search on the remaining links. This process helps to improve the acceptance ratio by assuring that once we find out a path, it will satisfy the bandwidth constraints [3].

In [6], Lischka et al. has combined two stages into only one stage. Then, with each incoming request, they used a backtrack algorithm to find a subgraph on substrate network that has the same form with virtual network. But a link on virtual network can be mapped with ε links on physical network. The disadvantage of this algorithm is that it waste more time to perform backtrack. Therefore it is not suited with the requests which have deadline to map.

Finally, the experiment's results in [3] show that, testing on the substrate node's size of 30 nodes and 50 nodes, the EGNM with pre-checked given the acceptance ratio and cumulative revenue better than GNM with k-shortest paths. But its revenue/cost ratio (B/C) is not good enough. Because the link mapping with Pre-checked has increased the cost by increasing the length of paths that satisfied the bandwidth constraints. Hence, decrease the B/C ratio.

According to this disadvantage, we propose a new method of node mapping and hoping it to simultaneously increase the revenue and decrease the cost while giving good acceptance ratio.

4   Proposed Algorithm

In this paper, we introduce a new way to approach the problem. Almost mappings nowadays just start handling when the new requests come. Thus, we propose a new algorithm to compute before meet a request to speed up the processing that is Path-Checking Adjacency Node Mapping (PCANM).

Some difficulties are the differences of the virtual networks' requirement and model. So, mapping them to the substrate network is also totally different. To simplified, we group the substrate node to the set with the same degree and add it into substrate list. This will help to predict the ability to provide resource of each node. Then, when the requests come, algorithm just has to search in this list instead of search in whole substrate network.

The arrangement, firstly, based on the degree of node, the nodes with the same degree will be sorted by their available resource. The virtual node, in another way, is only sorted by their required resource. The list is built before the arrival time of requests, auto update when a new request comes or another leaves.

Here are some briefly describe about PCANM. The ideal of this algorithm is simulating part of link mapping process while performing node mapping. Firstly, when the new requests come, we sort the virtual nodes in the order of descending of their required resource, and add it into list of virtual nodes. Then, take the one with largest required resource. For each virtual node was taken, we group the substrate node by their degree then compare the virtual node's degree with degrees of substrate nodes and the algorithm start processing from the group that has nearest greater than or equal with the virtual node's degree. In each group, the substrate nodes are sorted by their available resource in descending order. The final step before mapping is check whether the substrate node is satisfied the requirement of the virtual node or not and whether the substrate node (from the first one to the last one) is linked with other mapped substrate nodes or not and does any neighbors of this substrate node can be mapped with any neighbors of the virtual node or not.

Figure 1 describes the algorithm in general way. With two inputs: the virtual network r and substrate network S. At step 1, the algorithm finds and takes the virtual node which has highest required resource in r (the one has weight of 20). Then, we classify the substrate nodes into groups depends on their degree (step 2). At step 3, from the group which has the same degree with or nearest higher than the virtual node's degree, take the node with highest available resource (the one has weight of 35) to see if it can be mapped by the virtual node or not. The node that satisfied is the node has CPU resource greater than virtual node's CPU resource and has total bandwidth greater than virtual node's total bandwidth. If not, move to next substrate node in the group.

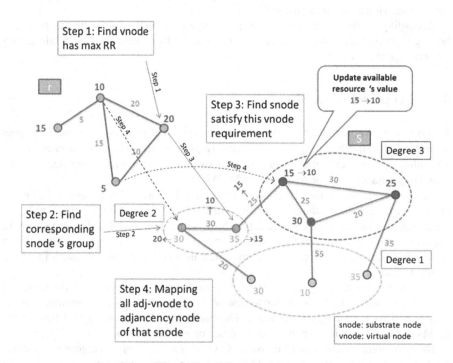

Fig. 1. Visualizing algorithm

Step 3.1 is a significant improvement in this algorithm, with the virtual node and substrate node that is recently mapped, we check their neighbor nodes to see if which node can be mapped to which. For next virtual nodes, we add one more step before map it to the substrate node, which is called connection testing step. In this step, the substrate node about to be mapped will be checked if it has the link to other mapped node. If not, the process then stops and continues with another node.

Following is PCANM's pseudo-code. In this pseudo-code, vNode stands for virtual node and sNode stands for substrate node.

Algorithm: PCANM $(S = (N, L), r = (V, E, t, d))$

```
Input:      Graph of substrate network S=(N,L); and virtual
            network request r=(V,E,t,d)
Output:     Set of results of mapping s'=(s₁',s₂',…sₙ')
begin
  1. Sort vNode according to their Required Resource
  2.   for each vNode do
  3.      if vNode was not mapped yet
  4.      failed = true
  5.      Sort substrate node according to their degree
          and Available Resource
  6.      for each sNode do
  7.         if can map vNode to sNode
  8.         Mark vNode is now being mapped to sNode
  9.         if sNode have links to other mapped sNode
 10.            failed = false
 11.            Map neighbor nodes of vNode to neighbor nodes
                of sNode.
 12                break
 13.            end if
 14.         end if
 15.      end for
 16.      if failed
 17.         NodeMappingFailed()
 18.      end if
 19.   end if
 20. end for
end
```

5   Experimental Results

5.1   Problem Instances

The Datasets
Substrate network:
Size of substrate network is the number of its nodes. We create three different topologies with the large number of node to experiment, which is 50-node topology, 100-node topology, and 200-node topology. Each pair of substrate nodes is connected with probability 0.2.

CPU resources of nodes follow distribution from 1 to 50.

Bandwidth resources of nodes follow distribution from 10 to 60.

Virtual network:

Size of VN is between 3 and 6 nodes. Each pair of virtual nodes is connected with probability 0.2

CPU and Bandwidth resources of nodes follow distribution from 1 to 25.

The appearance ratio of virtual network request is 40%.

5.2   Experiment Setup

We implemented two algorithms EGNM and PCANM in Java using Eclipse IDE. Each algorithm is simulated twenty times with three different topologies of substrate network: 50-node, 100-node and 200-node topology. Then we take the average of twenty times as the final result to compare. The network is generated randomly by a program written in Java.

5.3   Computational Results

We evaluate the performance of these algorithms based on 3 criteria: revenue/cost ratio, acceptance ratio, and revenue. The compared data is obtained during the implementation process. The formulas to calculate revenue value and revenue to cost ratio was given in (3) (4) (5). Acceptance ratio is defined as the proportion of arriving virtual network requests that are accepted.

Fig 2 and 3 show that the approximate results between two algorithms, but the B/C ratio of proposed algorithm is much better than the old algorithm.

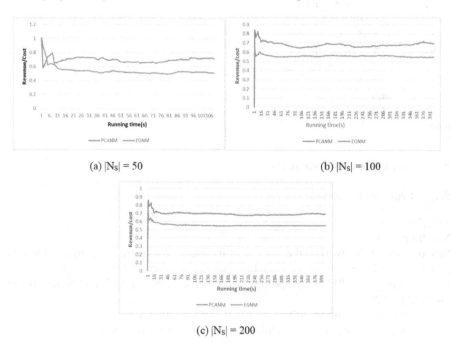

(a) $|N_S| = 50$ (b) $|N_S| = 100$

(c) $|N_S| = 200$

Fig. 2. Revenue/Cost (B/C) ratio compare between PCANM and EGNM based on the average data of twenty times running program

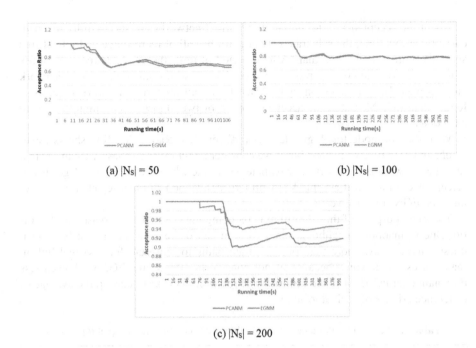

(a) |N$_S$| = 50   (b) |N$_S$| = 100

(c) |N$_S$| = 200

Fig. 3. Acceptance ratio compare between PCANM and EGNM based on the average data of twenty times running program

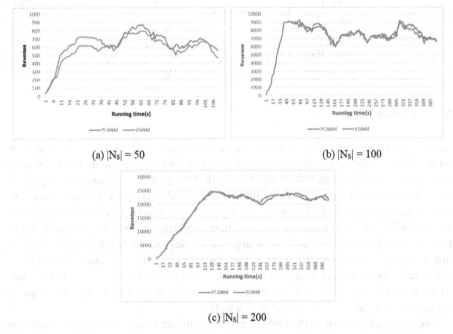

(a) |N$_S$| = 50   (b) |N$_S$| = 100

(c) |N$_S$| = 200

Fig. 4. Revenue compare between PCANM and EGNM based on the average data of twenty times running program

About the acceptance ratio, initial all of virtual networks are successfully mapped, cause by at this time, the substrate network still has all of its resource and lots of free space for virtual network to map. After a period of time, the available resource of SN is narrow down, the coming request can be denied, so not all of the virtual network are accepted. But the duration of PCANM to accept all virtual network requests is longer than EGNM. Later, the acceptance ratio of two algorithms asymptotic near to each other.

With the 200-node topologies test. For Acceptance Ratio, PCANM shows lower results in lately time of the test but if we consider about revenue chart, we can see that revenue of two algorithms is approximate each other, hence also PCANM got lower Acceptance Ratio but it accepts VN with larger revenue from that rejects lower revenue VN. EGNM is vice versa.

The main purpose of this algorithm is reducing the cost, since increase the B/C ratio. Due to mapping neighbors, this algorithm can decrease a lot of cost because it doesn't have to use more than one substrate paths to represent for a virtual link in many cases. Meanwhile, because of not considering this issue, EGNM showed less dominant than PCANM in the utilization of resources. Table 1 sums up the average of difference criteria of each algorithm.

Table 1. Average of criteria between two algorithms compare in different topologies

		EGNM	PCANM
Acceptance ratio	$|N_S| = 50$	0.75	0.77
	$|N_S| = 100$	0.81	0.81
	$|N_S| = 200$	0.96	0.94
Revenue/Cost	$|N_S| = 50$	0.54	0.69
	$|N_S| = 100$	0.55	0.68
	$|N_S| = 200$	0.55	0.69

6   Conclusion

In this paper, we proposed a totally new node mapping algorithm with 3 enhancements: sorting substrate nodes base on their degree and their available resource, mapping vertex's neighbor and checking path while taking node mapping. The algorithm maps the vertices of virtual network to the nodes of substrate network that is sorted by their degree and available resource. During the node mapping process, we examine the possibility of finding path of pairs of nodes, which improve the quality of node. Furthermore, by select the node with appropriate degree, we bring the possibility to map the neighbors of virtual nodes to the neighbors of substrate nodes. This significantly reduces the cost by mapping a link on virtual network to only one path on substrate network. Especially the list of physical nodes is created before the requests come, so it can reduces the amount of calculation.

The proposed approach (PCANM) has been compared with existing node mapping algorithms EGNM, which will be computing in time the request come. The evaluation results show that our presented algorithm gives higher performance in many important aspects. In term of revenue, PCANM is higher than EGNM about 10% in small topology (50 nodes) and 18% higher with the larger topology (200 nodes). The most significant improvement is revenue to cost ratio that is 28% better than EGNM's result and almost no change with the different data sets.

In the future work, we will try many different approaches and experiment with larger datasets in order to find the optimal solution for the problem.

References

1. Raihan Rahman, M., Aib, I., Boutaba, R.: Survivable Virtual Network Embedding. In: 9th International IFIP TC 6 Networking Conference Networking 2010, pp. 40–52 (2010)
2. Tran, H.V., Ngo, S.H.: An enhanced greedy node mapping algorithm for resource allocation in network virtualization, Journal of Science and Technology, 72–77 (2012)
3. Tran, H.V., Ngo, S.H.: Improved Heuristics for Online Node and Link Mapping Problem in Network Virtualization. In: The 13th International Conference on Computational Science and Applications (ICCSA 2013), pp.154–165 (June 2013)
4. Yu, M., Yi, Y., Rexford, J., Chiang, M.: Rethinking virtual network embedding: substrate support for path splitting and migration. SIGCOMM Comput. Commun. Rev. 38(2), pp. 17–29 (2008)
5. Razzaq, A., Hidell, M., Sjodin, P.: Virtual Network Embedding: A Hybrid Vertex Mapping Solution for Dynamic Resource Allocation. Journal of Electrical and Computer Engineering, 1–17 (2012)
6. Lischka, J., Karl, H.: A virtual network mapping algorithm based on subgraph isomorphism detection. In: The 1st ACM Workshop on Virtualized, Infrastructure Systems and Architectures, VISA 2009, p 81–88 (2009)
7. Chowdhury, N., Rahman, M.R., Boutaba, R.: Virtual network embedding with coordinated node and link mapping. In: IEEE INFOCOM 2009, pp. 783–791 (April 2009)

Virtualized Reconfigurable Hardware Resources in the SAVI Testbed

Stuart Byma[✉], Hadi Bannazadeh, Alberto Leon-Garcia, J. Gregory Steffan, and Paul Chow

University of Toronto, Toronto, Ontario, Canada
{bymastua,steffan,pc}@eecg.toronto.edu,
{hadi.bannazadeh,alberto.leongarcia}@utoronto.ca

Abstract. Reconfigurable hardware can allow acceleration of compute intensive tasks, provide line-rate packet processing capabilities, and in short, expand the range of experiments and applications that can be run on a testbed. Few large-scale networking testbeds have made any concerted effort towards the inclusion of virtualized reconfigurable devices, such as FPGAs, into their systems as allocatable resources. This changes with the SAVI testbed. In this paper, we present the current state of heterogeneous, reconfigurable hardware resources in the SAVI testbed, as well as how they are virtualized and facilitated to end-users through the Control and Management system. In addition, we present several use cases that show how beneficial these resources can be, including an in-network multicore multithreaded network processor programmable in C, and network-connected custom hardware modules.

Keywords: Testbeds · Reconfigurable hardware · Virtualization

1 Introduction

There are now quite a number of large-scale research testbeds in use or being developed [1]. Many of these have architectures that virtualize resources in some fashion, allowing researchers and users to have their own private subset of testbed resources. Often absent from these resources however, are reconfigurable devices, such as *Field Programmable Gate Arrays (FPGAs)*. It is highly desirable to incorporate these devices into testbeds, as there are many compute-intensive and high-speed processing tasks that they excel at. Many testbeds are focused on Future Internet or other networking themes where FPGAs can be very useful – they are capable of line-rate packet processing, being used in commercial equipment like routers and switches all the time, and their programmability allows the researcher to tailor their design to whatever paradigm or protocol necessary for their experiment.

In this paper, we introduce the different types of virtualized reconfigurable resources in the testbed of the *Smart Applications on Virtual Infrastructure (SAVI)* network [2,3]. The purpose of the SAVI network is to investigate future application platforms that rely on virtualized, flexible infrastructure. This infrastructure

© Institute for Computer Sciences, Social Informatics and Telecommunications Engineering 2014
V.C.M. Leung et al. (Eds.): TridentCom 2014, LNICST 137, pp. 54–64, 2014.
DOI: 10.1007/978-3-319-13326-3_6

is able to deploy large-scale, distributed systems that utilize the resources (wireless and wired networks, computing, devices) to deliver applications.

The SAVI testbed is a realization of this infrastructure, and is meant to be a testing ground for SAVI research in application platforms and Future Internet. The SAVI testbed implements a controlled and managed multi-tier cloud, consisting of Core and Smart Edge nodes connected by virtual networks over a large geographic region in Canada.

We describe in this paper how the heterogeneous resources in the Smart Edge nodes are enabled, and then present the different types of reconfigurable hardware resources in the SAVI testbed, and how each is controlled and managed. We present several use cases for these resources, showing how they allow researchers to run experiments and applications that were previously impossible, and how virtualized reconfigurable resources can easily outperform applications run in software on Virtual Machines (VMs).

We organize this paper as follows. Section 2 explores related and prior work in the research testbed field, dealing specifically with reconfigurable resources. In Section 3, we describe the SAVI testbed, it's architecture and capabilities, and examine it's software-defined infrastructure manager called *Janus*, describing how the system uses modifications to OpenStack to enable heterogeneous, non-Virtual Machine resources. Section 4 describes the different virtualized reconfigurable hardware resources in the testbed and how they are enabled and managed. In Section 5 we examine some use cases for these resources in the SAVI testbed, in particular network-connected custom hardware accelerators, and FPGA-based network processors. Section 6 looks at future work we hope to accomplish, and Section 7 concludes the paper.

2 Related Work

There has not been a significant amount of work on including reconfigurable hardware and FPGAs into research testbeds. The NetFPGA [4] has seen some use within GENI [5,6] and Internet2 [7,8], however it is unclear as to whether these are allocatable to end users as resources that are fully programmable and managed on the same level as VMs. The precursor to the SAVI testbed, *Virtualized Application Networking Infrastructure (VANI)* [9], integrated bare-metal servers with FPGA cards as resources, and the SAVI testbed builds on what began with VANI.

As far as we are aware, the SAVI testbed represents the first major push towards inclusion of reconfigurable hardware as resources on par with VMs, managed under the same system.

3 SAVI Testbed Control and Management

The SAVI testbed consists of several main components: Core data center nodes with traditional cloud computing resources (VMs, storage, network), Smart Edge nodes that complement traditional cloud resources with heterogeneous resources (bare-metal servers, FPGAs, GPUs), Access Nodes that provide wireless connectivity, the SAVI testbed network that interconnects all components, and a Control Center to orchestrate applications and experiments.

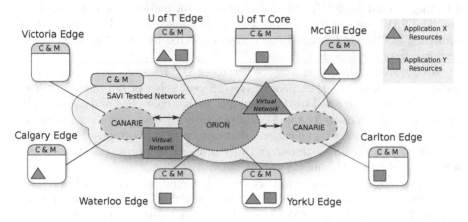

Fig. 1. The SAVI testbed. The ORION [10] and CANARIE [11] networks connect all components over a large geographic area of Canada. Experiments and applications can leverage virtualized resources from anywhere in the testbed.

Figure 1 shows the current state of the SAVI testbed. The components of the testbed are architected into a Control and Management (C & M) plane, and an Applications and Experiments plane. Our discussion will mostly be limited to the C & M plane, as we wish to describe how resources are controlled and managed in the system. We will also mainly limit our discussion to the Smart Edge node, as this is the component that contains the heterogeneous resources. A detailed overview of the entire SAVI testbed system is available in [2].

Figure 2 shows a diagram of the SAVI testbed Smart Edge. Resources in the system are virtualized using OpenStack [12], an open source cloud computing framework. OpenStack management forms the Smart Edge C & M plane in conjunction with the Software-Defined Infrastructure manager, called *Janus*. *Janus* offloads certain tasks from OpenStack, such as network control and resource scheduling, and also performs configuration management and orchestration of the testbed's OpenFlow-based *Software-Defined Network* (SDN). *Janus* uses *FlowVisor* (FV) to virtualize the network into slices, and users can run their own OpenFlow controller to manage their own private network slice. C & M services are all reachable through RESTful [13] APIs. OpenStack *Keystone* and *Glance* provide authentication and a global image registry respectively.

Of particular interest to this paper in Figure 2 is the *Nova* component of OpenStack, which is the part that allocates resources. The standard *Nova* only supports processor virtualization, where Virtual Machines (VMs) are booted on top of hypervisors that abstract away the physical hardware. The vision of the Smart Edge however, incorporates heterogeneous resources in addition to VMs. Thus *Nova* in the SAVI testbed is extended to enable it to manage these new resources.

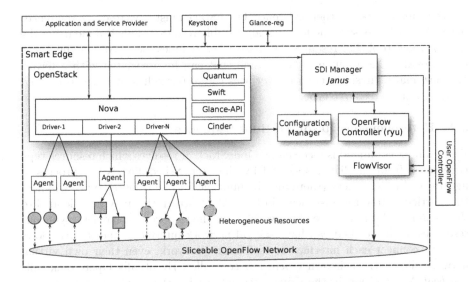

Fig. 2. The SAVI testbed Smart Edge node

3.1 Enabling Heterogeneous Resources

For OpenStack to manage different types of resources, they must all *appear* homogeneous in nature. To accomplish this, we use a *Driver-Agent* system. A driver for any resource implements required OpenStack management API methods, such as *boot, reboot, start, stop* and *release*. The driver then communicates these OpenStack management commands to an Agent, which carries them out directly on the resource, via a hypervisor or otherwise. In this fashion, OpenStack can manage all resources through the same interface. Figure 3 shows a diagram of the Driver-Agent system.

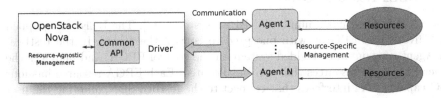

Fig. 3. The *Driver-Agent* abstraction used in the SAVI testbed OpenStack system

If a user desires to allocate a resource, they need to be able to specify what resource type they want – we extend the OpenStack notion of resource *flavor* to enable this. Usually, resource flavor refers to the number of virtual processors and amount of RAM to allocate to a VM. Here we extend *flavor* to also include resource *type*. The SAVI testbed currently has several of these additional resource types including GPUs, bare-metal servers, and reconfigurable hardware.

To be made aware of their existence, OpenStack must have resource references placed in its database – one for each allocatable resource. This is done using the *nova-manage* tool. The resource database entry includes the address of the Agent that provides the resource, a type name that can be associated with a flavor, and how many physical network interfaces the resource has. A flavor is created for each unique resource type.

3.2   Heterogeneous Resource Boot Sequence

When a boot command is received by OpenStack, it resolves which resource type is required from the flavor specified by the user. Scheduling is the process of figuring out which Agent (there may be multiple for one resource type) will host this particular resource instance – in the SAVI testbed, this may be offloaded to *Janus*. *Janus* also takes care of networking for the resource – some heterogeneous resources in the testbed can have several network interfaces, and *Janus* allows users to connect each interface to a different network, even their own virtual network slice with their own OpenFlow controller. Eventually OpenStack calls the *boot* API method in the driver associated with the required resource type and passes several parameters: the address of the Agent, the user-specified image, and the network information generated by *Janus* that belongs to the resource. The Agent takes the required steps to boot the resource and set up network connectivity, whatever they may be for the particular type, and acknowledges the driver request. A reference for the resource is then returned to the user.

4   Reconfigurable Devices as Resources

In the SAVI testbed, we use the *Driver-Agent* method to enable FPGA-based reconfigurable hardware resources as well. The following subsections describe the different FPGA resources available in the SAVI testbed.

4.1   BEE2 Board FPGAs

The SAVI testbed has a number of BEE2 systems [14]. The BEE2 is equipped with five Xilinx FPGAs, with one used to control the others. In the testbed, an Agent runs on an embedded system on the control FPGA, and manages the other FPGAs as resources that can be allocated. Each FPGA resource has four 10G-capable CX4 interfaces that connect to the testbed SDN, allowing the user to send and receive data from their hardware on the FPGA.

Since the user simply gets the entire device as a resource, they are responsible for designing and compiling their hardware using vendor tools, ensuring that their hardware ports match the correct pin locations on the BEE2, and ensuring that the hardware will function correctly. Once they generate a bitstream file for programming the FPGA, it is uploaded through the OpenStack *Glance* API as an image.

Note that we are again extending the definition of a concept in OpenStack. Normally, an "image" refers only to an Operating System (OS) image, however *Glance* allows any file type to be uploaded as an image. Therefore, for a BEE2 FPGA resource, the image will be a bitstream generated by the FPGA tools. For the BEE2 resource, the Agent will receive this image from the OpenStack controller via the driver, and simply configures it onto an unused FPGA. OpenStack sees the FPGA as any other resource thanks to the *Driver-Agent* abstraction, and the user can now make use of custom hardware acceleration in the SAVI testbed.

4.2 PCIe-Based FPGA Cards

To increase the range of different FPGA applications available to researchers, it is useful to have FPGAs closely coupled to processors so that the reconfigurable hardware can accelerate compute-intensive portions of software. The SAVI testbed provides several PCI-Express-based FPGA boards connected to physical servers: The NetFPGA, the NetFPGA10G [4] and the DE5Net [15]. The boards have varying FPGA device sizes and on-board memory, but have in common four network interfaces that are connected to the testbed SDN. The NetFPGA has four 1G Ethernet ports, while the NetFPGA10G and DE5Net have four 10G Ethernet ports. A researcher can now design custom hardware that can accelerate software tasks, provide line-rate packet processing, or a combination of both.

In addition to these boards, the testbed also contains MiniBEE [16] resources. The MiniBEE contains a conventional processor and an on-board FPGA connected through PCIe. It also has 10G network interfaces, a large amount of memory and an expansion port for additional FPGA peripherals.

Since the PCIe boards are required to be mounted inside physical servers, the SAVI testbed provides the server itself with the FPGA card attached as a resource. In the case of the MiniBEE, the entire system is also offered as a resource.

4.3 Fully Virtualized Hardware

With the BEE2 and PCIe-based SAVI testbed resources, the FPGAs are not as fully virtualized as they could be – OpenStack manages the resource, but a user still gets the entire physical device. This may not be quite as scalable or flexible as a fully virtualized approach, and also may not make full use of large FPGA's reconfigurable fabric. Therefore, we wish to virtualize FPGAs to a greater extent, in order to more closely match conventional cloud computing models. We have developed in the SAVI testbed a system that uses FPGA *partial reconfiguration* (PR), a technique to reconfigure only a portion of an FPGA at a time, to split the device into several virtual pieces [17]. Another custom driver and Agent allows OpenStack to manage each of these PR regions as a resource. We call these regions *Virtualized FPGA Resources*. Some hardware on the FPGA that is not partially reconfigured (called the *static logic*) forms an embedded system that interacts with the Agent, facilitating safe partial reconfiguration and setting up VFR networking. Buffering and arbitration in the static logic results in a three-cycle latency penalty for packet data streams into the VFRs, however throughput is only affected by a one-cycle stall per packet.

Figure 4 shows a diagram of this system. The system is implemented on one or several of the NetFPGA10G resources, showing how one resource in SAVI

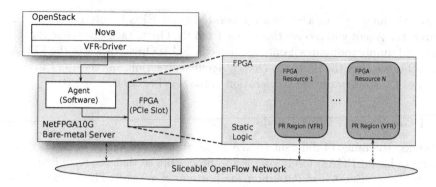

Fig. 4. Virtualized FPGA Resources in the SAVI testbed

can be used to provide additional, new resource types. Each VFR is connected through an arbiter in the static logic to the board's 10Gb Ethernet ports, and thus the testbed SDN. Researchers can make use of template Verilog HDL files and a script-based compile system to generate custom hardware that matches the interfaces to the VFRs and generate images of this hardware that can be uploaded via *Glance* and booted through OpenStack. The VFRs can be booted very quickly relative to VMs, taking around 2.6 seconds on average to get to a state where they are fully configured and able to process data. Because of this, VFR-based systems can scale extremely rapidly.

The system also significantly simplifies hardware design for the user. All chip level I/O, Ethernet interfacing and memory interfacing is done in the static logic of the system. The static logic therefore removes several complex, difficult integration tasks for users, and leaves them with a few standard, well-defined interfaces with which to build their system. This also makes it much easier to use tools like High-Level Synthesis instead of HDL design entry. Design and test time is greatly reduced, and researchers can set up prototypes and experiments much more quickly.

5   Use Cases

Researchers using the SAVI testbed now have access to FPGA-based hardware acceleration, either in-network, CPU-coupled over PCIe, or a combination of both. In this section we describe two use cases for the FPGA resources in the testbed.

5.1   A Multicore, Multithreaded Network Processor

NetThreads10G [18] is a port and expansion of the original NetThreads system by Martin Labrecque et al. [19]. Designed for the NetFPGA10G, it is a soft multicore, multithreaded network processor. Figure 5 shows a diagram of the system. Each of the four cores implements a modified MIPS instruction set, has a private instruction cache, and executes four-way multithreading. The four cores share access to a data cache, and a 20 packet capacity buffer, which is filled with incoming packets by hardware connected to the NetFPGA10G's 10Gb Ethernet stream interfaces. A set of 16 hardware locks enables safe sharing of data between threads, and the NetFPGA10G on-board RLDRAM provides 64MB of system memory.

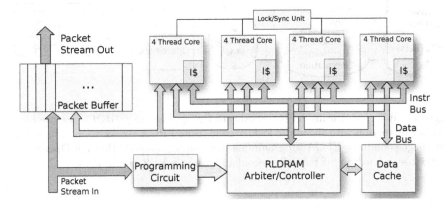

Fig. 5. The NetThreads architecture

The NetThreads framework also includes a MIPS gcc cross-compiler, and library providing rudimentary functions to read and write the packet buffer, allocate memory, and get and set the hardware locks for parallel programming. The NetThreads10G hardware contains a dedicated programming circuit that operates over Ethernet, meaning the system is programmable from anywhere in the testbed network.

The SAVI testbed researcher now has access to a gigabit-line-rate network processor that they can program easily in C – no hardware design necessary. Using the system is simple – since the hardware is already synthesized, placed, and routed, a user need only use the OpenStack API to allocate a NetFPGA10G resource and then program the NetThreads bitstream onto the device. A programmer application takes the output files of the cross-compiler and sends them over the network to the NetThreads system, whose programming circuit loads the software into memory and starts the processor system that can run many applications at line-rate.

5.2   A VFR-Based Load Balancer

Load balancing is an important part of large-scale cloud applications. In this section we demonstrate how an arbitrary protocol load balancer [17] can be implemented using the SAVI testbed's *Virtualized FPGA Resources*.

The load balancer is designed using a template Verilog file whose ports match those defined by the VFR system static logic. The hardware is designed to match a hypothetical protocol running on top of UDP, and distribute incoming packets to a number of servers. Servers send update packets to the load balancer, which tracks available server addresses in a memory. The balancer cycles through this memory as packets arrive, sending them to servers in a round-robin fashion. Figure 6 shows the VFR system compile and boot sequence.

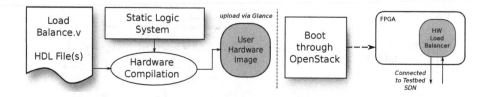

Fig. 6. Compiling and using VFRs. Hardware Design Language (HDL) files are compiled in conjunction with the static logic system using FPGA vendor tools. The generated image containing FPGA programming files can be "booted" through OpenStack, and the user's hardware is partially reconfigured into a VFR on the fly.

We compare the hardware load balancer to a software implementation run on a VM in the SAVI testbed. A client VM sends packets to the load balancer to be distributed amongst servers, and the servers send a direct response back to the client after receiving a packet from the load balancer. The round trip time is measured at the client and averaged over 10000 packets. Other VMs are used to inject additional traffic so that we can measure the approximate throughput capability of the software and hardware load balancers. A VM load balancer can only handle up to around 25MB/s before dropping packets and performing unpredictably. The VFR load balancer could handle over 100MB/s, even with the presence of the static logic virtualization layer, and did not drop a single packet. Figure 7 shows latency versus additional injection rate for software and hardware load balancers. Since each point is an average of 10000 packets, we show standard deviation as well.

This example shows how users of the SAVI testbed can offload network-based processing to VFRs and get a substantial performance gain through the simplified hardware design flow provided by the virtualization system.

6   Future Work

There is a significant amount of future work to be done with the reconfigurable resources in the SAVI testbed. We plan to continue adding to the number of physical FPGA resources in the system, and expand these resources to all Smart Edge nodes in the testbed.

We will also continue exploring the concept of *Virtualized FPGA Resources*, to see how closely they can be fit within the cloud computing model. This involves

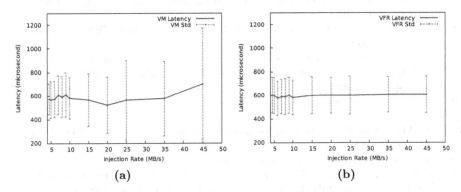

Fig. 7. (a) Latency through VM Load Balancer. (b) Latency through VFR hardware load balancer.

making them capable of more VM-like tasks, such as migration among physical machines. We also plan to investigate methods of chaining VFRs and other resources over the network at the system level – creating heterogeneous processing chains for arbitrary tasks.

7   Conclusion

We have presented the different types of reconfigurable resources in the SAVI testbed, and how they are enabled by the testbed's *Driver-Agent* abstraction for heterogeneous resources. Researchers using the SAVI testbed can use familiar management commands to access network-coupled and CPU-coupled FPGAs as cloud resources, and make use of either predefined or custom-designed hardware. These reconfigurable hardware resources will enable a new range of applications and experiments that were previously unavailable in the SAVI testbed, and the networking testbed community at large.

References

1. Pan, J., Paul, S., Jain, R.: A Survey of the Research on Future Internet Architectures. Communications Magazine, IEEE **49**(7), 26–36 (2011)
2. Joon-Myung K., Bannazadeh, H., Rahimi, H., Lin, T., Faraji, M., Leon-Garcia, A.: Software-Defined Infrastructure and the Future Central Office. In: IEEE International Conference on Communications Workshops (ICC), pp. 225–229 (2013)
3. Smit, M., Ng, J., Litoiu, M., Iszali, G., Leon-Garcia, A.: Smart Applications on Virtual Infrastructure. In: Proceedings of the 2011 Conference of the Center for Advanced Studies on Collaborative Research, CASCON 2011, pp. 381–381, Riverton (2011)
4. NetFPGA. NetFPGA 10G (2014). http://netfpga.org/
5. GENI. Global Environment for Networking Innovations (GENI) Project (2014). http://geni.net/

6. Emulab. ProtoGENI Nodes (2014). https://wiki.emulab.net/wiki/pgeniNodes
7. Internet2 (2014). http://www.internet2.edu/
8. Lockwood, J.: NetFPGA Update at GEC4. Presented at NSF GENI Engineering Conference (2009)
9. Redmond, K., Bannazadeh, H., Chow, P., Leon-Garcia, A.: Development of a Virtualized Application Networking Infrastructure Node. In: IEEE GLOBECOM Workshops, pp. 1–6 (2009)
10. ORION. Ontario Research and Innovation Optical Network (2014). http://www.orion.on.ca/
11. CANARIE. Canada's Advanced Research and Innovation Network (2014). http://www.canarie.ca/
12. OpenStack (2013). http://www.openstack.org/
13. Fielding, R.T.: REST: Architectural Styles and the Design of Network-Based Software Architectures. PhD thesis, University of California, Irvine (2000)
14. Chang, C., Wawrzynek, J., Brodersen, R.W.: BEE2: A High-End Reconfigurable Computing System. Design Test of Computers, IEEE **22**(2), 114–125 (2005)
15. Terasic Technologies Inc. DE5Net (2013). http://de5-net.terasic.com/
16. BEECube Inc. miniBEE - Research in a Box (2014). http://www.beecube.com/products/miniBEE.asp
17. Byma, S., Steffan, J.G., Bannazadeh, H., Leon-Garcia, A., Chow, P.: FPGAs in the Cloud: Booting Virtualized Hardware Accelerators with OpenStack. In: 22nd Internation Symposium on Field-Programmable Custom Computing Machines (FCCM). IEEE (2014)
18. Byma, S., Steffan, J.G., Chow, P.: NetThreads-10G: Software Packet Processing on NetFPGA-10G in a Virtualized Networking Environment Demonstration Abstract. In: 23rd International Conference on Field Programmable Logic and Applications (FPL). IEEE (2013)
19. Labrecque, M., Steffan, J.G., Salmon, G., Ghobadi, M., Ganjali, Y.: NetThreads: Programming NetFPGA with Threaded Software. In: NetFPGA Developers Workshop, vol. 9 (2009)

Network Measurement Virtual Observatory: An Integrated Database Environment for Internet Research and Experimentation

Tamás Sebők, Zsófia Kallus, Sándor Laki, Péter Mátray, József Stéger$^{(\boxtimes)}$, János Szüle, László Dobos, István Csabai, and Gábor Vattay

Department of Physics of Complex Systems, Eötvös Loránd University,
Budapest, Hungary
{sebok,kallus,laki,matray,steger,szule,dobos,
csabai,vattay}@complex.elte.hu

Abstract. To understand the long-term dynamics of networks engineers and network scientists collect tremendous amount of data and distribute them across many different data warehouses. In EU FP7 OpenLab project we developed the nmVO, which helps handling distinct data sources together in a common way efficiently. It also supports data collecting systems with a permanent data storage, such as SONoMA, and provides a public front-end to run measurements and access data, called GrayWulf. Furthermore, the on-line analysis of data, yielding the behavior and the structure of the Internet is convenient by using server side scientific functionalities.

Keywords: Database federation · Network measurement data · Virtual observatory

1 Introduction

The data tsunami of the last decade forced scientists to find new ways of dealing with data. It turned out early that the same data management problems and solutions can be shared among very distant fields of science disciplines. *Virtual Observatories* (VO) appeared originally for astronomical data [1] and later in other fields of science [2] to make the multi-terabyte science archives manageable and, most importantly, to make them accessible for researchers. As large archives of data became available on the Internet an obvious step forward was to try and federate these distant databases and provide a unified, searchable view of them to extract aggregated information. VOs provided a simple way to share data among members of research groups world-wide. Processing the unprecedented amounts of data required new techniques and relational database management systems have become an every day tool of astronomers, geophysicists, network scientists, biologists, etc. Soon data analysis kits also became part of VOs driven by the realization that in many cases the computation is much easier taken to the data than the data be downloaded to operate on. While certain computations can be

© Institute for Computer Sciences, Social Informatics and Telecommunications Engineering 2014
V.C.M. Leung et al. (Eds.): TridentCom 2014, LNICST 137, pp. 65–74, 2014.
DOI: 10.1007/978-3-319-13326-3_7

formulated in SQL, the lingua franca of VOs, other problems require extensions, preferably accessible from the same SQL interfaces. Recently, network research has been facing with very similar issues.

In this paper, we present the Network Measurement Virtual Observatory[1] (nmVO) designed to facilitate Internet related network sciences. Since it's first variant [3], which was developed mostly on the basis of existing VO technologies, it has gone through radical changes, becoming an integrated database environment covering various new functionalities from permanent object storage and data access capabilities to the federation of heterogeneous remote SQL-based data sources. In OneLab [4] project[2], nmVO has become the primary data federation tool, through which all kind of network measurement data collected by different research groups and stored in heterogeneous databases like PostgreSQL, MySQL or SQLServer can be accessed, analyzed and visualized with ease.

The rest of the paper is organized as follows. In Section 1.1 we give a brief introduction to the field of Internet network research. Section 1.2 presents SONoMA, the web-service-based abstraction layer developed to help execute experiments with a heterogeneous measurement infrastructure. The concept of nmVO is explained in Section 2.

1.1 Internet Measurements and Data Archives

Since the 1960's, Internet has gone through an enormous evolution, becoming one of the most complex artificial systems in the world. Besides the growth in its size, the high number of users and various applications generate huge amount of network traffic to be handled everyday. As a consequence, traffic control, forecasting, performance analysis and monitoring are becoming fundamental issues for network operators and interesting targets for researchers as well.

Similarly to other scientific areas, different network research groups make significant efforts to examine one or another aspects of this global system, using high variety of measurement tools and analysis methodologies. However, in order to reveal real dependences between various mechanisms and to obtain a global view on how the system works the data of different aspects need to be handled together. For example, queuing delay tomography [5] or loss inference methods require both topology and one-way delay or packet loss measurements. Inspired by this idea, the nmVO was established based on existing VO solutions [3] in 2007.

Since then, only few other efforts can be found in the literature that aim at helping the network research community with shared data. Many research groups publish their measurement results in raw files with various formats. Furthermore, there are only few attempts towards the standardization of network measurement data formats. For this, some papers propose JSON and XML [6,7] since they are flexible and descriptive enough, while others prefer ontology-driven semantic representations [8,9]. Recognizing this need, CAIDA[3] has created an Internet

---

[1] http://nm.vo.elte.hu

[2] http://www.onelab.eu

[3] The Cooperative Association for Internet Data Analysis - http://www.caida.org

measurement data meta catalog, called DatCat[4], which is basically a searchable registry of dataset descriptions. It helps to find, annotate, cite and publish data contributed by others. DatCat also contains detailed descriptions of data sets including their location, reproducibility, formatting, etc. In some cases, the raw files are also available at DatCat servers, while at other cases only a link points to the real location. The key difference between DatCat and VO concepts is that VOs aim at offering a unified SQL-based interface to query and fetch data, while DatCat does not deal with this issue at all.

1.2   The Service Oriented Network Measurement Architecture

Distributed network measurements are essential means to characterize the structure, the dynamics and the operational state of the Internet. Although in the last decades several measurement and monitoring systems have been created, the easy access of these infrastructures and the orchestration of complex measurements were not solved. In 2010, we laid down the basis of a network measurement framework, called SONoMA [10], serving originally the natural needs of the network measurement community. The SONoMA provides easy-to-use web services, see Fig. 1, to carry out large-scale network measurements from heterogeneous networking elements including PlanetLab[5] nodes, BlackFin-based APE boxes and Etoms[6]. This approach has opened the door to perform atomic and complex network measurements in real time, furthermore, it automatically stores the measurement results in nmVO.

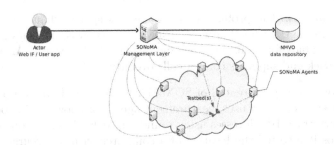

Fig. 1. The schematics of main SONoMA components and their control interactions

Recently, numerous new features have been added to SONoMA, especially focusing on making it more flexible, easier to extend and to support infrastructure monitoring. To this end the following enhancements have been applied:

---

[4] http://www.datcat.org
[5] http://www.planet-lab.org
[6] http://www.etomic.org

1. *Flexible tool extension:* The new measurement agents decouple the control and the implementation of tools. Now standard tools are also supported via drivers speaking different protocols (like SOAP, REST, SSH). E.g., measuring available bandwidth via `iperf`, getting *RTT* using `fping` or reading cpu load and memory usage from `/proc` are made easy.

2. *Harmonization of network tools and network measurements:* Various testbeds and devices could provide the same metric by different tools or their outputs may differ. In the new framework the operator defines a mapping for each tool, indicating metric types and units properly. Two configuration schema have been investigated and tested: a semantic approach and a close-code implementation.

3. *Periodic measurements:* In the former model of operation, measurements were carried out on demand, whereas now the definition of periodic and continuous measurements are also possible. In this way, the platform can be instrumented to provide their users with accurate and up-to-date information on the available resources.

4. *Permanent storage of data:* One of the key advantage of the SONoMA system is that all the measurement data are automatically stored in a permanent repository, in nmVO, enabling researchers to query and analyze their data back in time via a SQL-based querying interface. To avoid data losses, the new SONoMA variant does it more efficiently in a two-stage fashion. Collected data is first stored in a temporal SQLite repository files, serving as a fast first stage database. The records from this database are then transferred to the permanent database of nmVO. The new schema is made extensible, the back-end schema also flexible, supporting the extension with new metrics and tools.

5. *IPv6 readyness:* The problem of IPv4 address space exhaustion, made us investigate the IPv6 capability of SONoMA. The new configuration mapping schema enables for inclusion tools operating in IPv6 world. Also the web service back end supports control calls over IPv6.

To demonstrate the potential of SONoMA we built and operate *Spotter*[7], a geolocation service, which uses measurement agents of known GPS coordinates to localize arbitrary IP addresses using round trip delay information. With this service it possible to tell the location of a computer with an accuracy of a few ten kilometers.

2   Network Measurement Virtual Observatory

Historical experimental data are essential to understand the long-term dynamics and structure of the Internet. There have been numerous projects by large collaborations and small research groups to measure and analyze a wide range of network parameters. The collected data are amassed in archives dispersed around the world in incompatible data formats, often not even accessible on-line. One of

---

[7] http://spotter.etomic.org

the main goal of nmVO is to federate and/or co-locate these datasets and build an on-line data warehouse for network scientists and other experimenters. This data warehouse, however, is much more dynamic than most science archives. Network experiments consists of large series of micro-measurements (thousands or millions of pings and traceroutes), even conducting the experiments requires a large amount of initial data. Raw numbers from micro-measurements are ingested into the central nmVO archive before analysis. This not only allows data analysis programs to leverage the functionalities provided by the database server, but also to re-analyze the data later, either to verify earlier results, or to apply more sophisticated algorithms and validate new models.

2.1   The nmVO Infrastructure

In the early stages, nmVO benefited a lot from open software developed for existing VO solutions in different fields of science. The SQL query batch framework and user interface of the database system, called CasJobs, was originally borrowed from SkyServer [11], a database containing astronomical data. However, during its operation nmVO's weaknesses and shortcomings were recognized inspiring us to rethink the whole architecture from scratch. During this process, the usage requirements were also identified and taken into account, leading to a more flexible and complex integrated database solution for accessing, federating, analyzing and visualizing data related to Internet research and experimentation. Our aim was to create an integrated database solution whose benefits can be exploited by both testbed users, network scientists, tool and infrastructure providers, as well.

Figure 2 depicts the logical configuration of nmVO. One can observe that the heart of this system consists of three main components: A cluster of local database servers storing measurement data, an object store component and a data federation, analysis and visualization tool called GrayWulf that has fully replaced the CasJobs-based solution detailed in [3]. One can also observe that nmVO can provide and access to other remote data sources and tools. The integration of remote databases require only a few configuration steps that can be done through a web interface easily. After that the remotely stored data can be accessed through GrayWulf's web interface. The figure also shows the system provides each user with a small database (MyDB) where the results of user queries can be stored for further analysis or visualization. To demonstrate how external tools can be integrated into the system, we extended the local nmVO database with the capability to call SONoMA[8] [10] if the requested data is not available in the local database. Specific stored procedures have been implemented, calling the web-service methods of SONoMA to carry out ping, traceroute and other measurements. Thus, besides accessing existing data stored in the local repository, nmVO can automatically collect data from network measurement tools in a transparent way, by submitting an ordinary SQL-query.

---

[8] http://sonoma.etomic.org

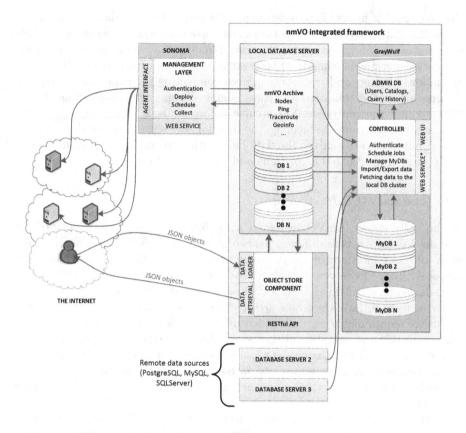

Fig. 2. The complex architecture of the nmVO environment

Finally, the object store component offers a RESTful interface to submit any kind of JSON objects for storing permanently in the local database of nmVO. Currently, Packet Tracking [12] and periodic `iperf` measurements are stored like this, but other types can easily be covered.

2.2 The Local nmVO Database

We have designed and built a multi-terabyte relational database to store archival and recent network measurement data including raw measurements and results from data analysis. The nmVO database [3] is organized into *Collections*. Collections group together measurements, sub-measurements and analyzed results belonging to the same experiment. A single experiment usually consists of thousands of micro-measurements. For example, in case of a geolocation experiment, in which we want to determine the most likely geographic coordinates of a given host, the network topology around the host has to be mapped with traceroute

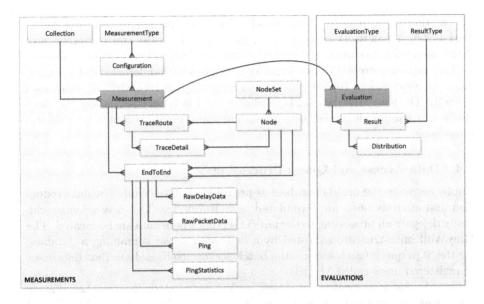

Fig. 3. A high-level view of the nmVO database schema. Measurements are organized into collections. Both raw measurements (Ping table) and results of analysis (PingStatistics table) are stored.

measurements, then delay roundtrip times along various routes have to be measured. Collection may contain multiple evaluations of the same raw data, usually based on different models, methods or initial parameters.

The two basic types of measurements the nmVO database stores are end-to-end measurements consisting of ping delay times and traceroutes consisting of router chains. For ping delays, raw measurements and aggregated delay times with statistics are stored.

The nmVO database is tightly integrated with a series of easy-to-use on-line network data analysis tools, many of them accessible directly from the database using SQL, or through intuitive web-based user interfaces. Figure 3 shows a high-level overview of the nmVO database schema.

Using SQL queries answering topology related questions is vastly simplified compared to any file-based approach. For example, one can easily determine the number of discovered paths between two given nodes, or the nature of route changes in a given network segment and time interval.

2.3   Federating Network Measurement Archives

Network experiments have been conducted by various groups around the world for years. Long-term dynamical analysis of the Internet is impossible without these data. The main issue of federation of data is their format. Historically, network scientists collected raw data in huge file, often storing redundant information using lengthy data models. To build the foundation of a federated system for network measurement, we designed a clear and comprehensive database schema to store raw data from a variety of typical network experiments.

Our system currently covers different databases with different database management systems, like Tophat which uses PostgreSQL or ETOMICDB which uses MySQL. The federated data set is reachable via a web interface, where the users easily can handle all of the joined databases and create complex queries and cross-joins.

2.4   Data Access and Query Processing

Public access to the nmVO database is provided via GrayWulf. The data reduction and analysis tasks are formulated as SQL queries. This way scientist can easily delegate all processing to the nmVO servers where data are co-located. The GrayWulf infrastructure is hosted by a dedicated server containing a database for the SQL query batch service, the batch service itself, and sandbox databases of registered users called MyDBs.

Besides local, co-located databases, nmVO can also connect to other, remote databases. Query results from remote databases get stored in the MyDB and can be joined with data from the local data sets. Users can also upload their own data to MyDB, and download data in various data formats.

An example query shows how to join tables from databases (nmVO: and TOPHAT:) with distinct locations. So location information is fetched from the local nmVO whereas path length is retrieved from the remote data source.

```
SELECT t.agent_id as src, t.destination_id as dst, t.hop as ip,
       t.hopcnt as hopcnt, r.lat as lat, r.lng as lon
FROM TOPHAT:traceroute_hops t
INNER JOIN nmVO:geo.routercity r ON t.hop = r.ip_string
WHERE t.first between '2012-06-07_0:0' and '2012-06-08_0:0'
```

2.5   Data Visualization

The best way to understand our data is the visualization. We built in a gnuplot based visualization tool, so the user can plot directly from database. It uses the servers resources, the plot displayed in the web interface either in HTML 5 canvas or one of many commonly used graphic format, such as postscript, PNG or JPEG. The visualization tool has 2 basic functions, plotting curves and histograms. Figure 4 shows a simple histogram made by the visualization tool.

2.6   Interactive Experiments

Since in nmVO databases are closely bound with the measurement infrastructure (SONoMA, Spotter) there is not anything to prevent us from initiating measurements directly from the database server, using SQL! Being able to conduct experiments straight from SQL scripts has a great potential. For example, missing data can be gathered on fly. To demonstrate how to integrate web services with databases, we wrapped the SONoMA ping web service interface into a SQL user-defined function.

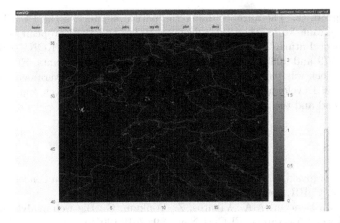

Fig. 4. Histogram of geographical coordinates made by the gnuplot based built in visualization tool

3 Summary

We have presented a brief introduction to the world of network measurements. To get a better understanding of the data network scientists use, first we introduced the methods and the basic infrastructure network measurements are done with. SONoMA, our open measurement management service was explained to show how time and effort can be reduced with a Virtual Observatory infrastructure to carry out otherwise complicated complex experiments. SONoMA, while remains easy to use, contains all the tools and has access to all the important testbeds that network scientists need. Building application on the basis of SONoMA is simple thanks to its web service interfaces. SONoMA is deeply integrated with the nmVO database to automatically store and publish measurement data.

We have introduced the concept of nmVO, a Virtual Observatory for Internet measurement data and demonstrated how technology developed for other fields of science can be reused to build scientific data repositories with minimal effort. The most important feature of nmVO is, however, that the database is tightly integrated with the measurement infrastructure. Tools work from data stored in the database and save results there. The nmVO database can be used as a cache to look up whether certain measurements have been done earlier, and reuse them if possible, saving on network traffic and measurement time. Archived measurements also allow for time-domain investigation of the network.

Another interesting feature of nmVO is that certain measurement tools are readily available from the SQL interface: experiments can be executed on the fly by calling stored procedures. This makes nmVO more like a real observatory than a virtual one.

Acknowledgments. The authors thank the partial support of the EU FP7 Open-Lab project (Grant No.287581), the European Union and the European Social Fund through project FuturICT.hu (grant no.: TAMOP-4.2.2.C-11/1/KONV-2012-0013), the OTKA 7779 and 103244, and the NAP 2005/KCKHA005 grants. EITKIC_12-1-2012-0001 project was partially supported by the Hungarian Government, managed by the National Development Agency, and financed by the Research and Technology Innovation Fund and the MAKOG Foundation.

References

1. George Djorgovski, S., Williams, R.: Virtual observatory: From concept to implementation. CoRR, abs/astro-ph/0504006 (2005)
2. Spaniol, M., Benczúr, A.A., Viharos, Z., Weikum, G.: Big web analytics: Toward a virtual web observatory. ERCIM News **89**, 2012 (2012)
3. Mátray, P., Csabai, I., Hága, P., Stéger, J., Dobos, L., Vattay, G.: Building a prototype for network measurement virtual observatory. In: MineNet, pp. 23–28. ACM (2007)
4. On federations..., (2009)
5. Rizzo, T., Steger, J., Péter, P., Csabai, I., Vattay, G.: High quality queueing information from accelerated active network tomography. In: TRIDENTCOM (2008)
6. Marcelo, B., et al.: Standardizing large-scale measurement platforms. ACM SIG-COMM Computer Communication Review **43**(1), 58–63 (2013)
7. Dhawan, M., et al.: Fathom: a browser-based network measurement platform. In: Proceedings of the 2012 ACM Conference on Internet Measurement Conference, ACM (2012)
8. van der Ham, J., Stéger, J., Laki, S., Kryftis, Y., Maglaris, V., de Laat, C.: The novi information models. Future Generation Computer Systems (2013)
9. Mátray, P., Csabai, I., Hága, P., Stéger, J., Vattay, G.: A semantic extension of the network measurement virtual observatory. Advances in Databases and Information Systems (2009)
10. Hullár, B., Laki, S., Stéger, J., Csabai, I., Vattay, G.: SONoMA: A service oriented network measurement architecture. In: Korakis, T., Li, H., Tran-Gia, P., Park, H.-S. (eds.) TridentCom 2011. LNICST, vol. 90, pp. 27–42. Springer, Heidelberg (2012)
11. Szalay, A.S., Gray, J., Thakar, A.R., Kunszt, P.Z., Malik, T., Raddick, J., Stoughton, C., vandenBerg, J.: The SDSS skyserver: Public access to the sloan digital sky server data (2002)
12. Santos, T., Henke, C., Schmoll, C., Zseby, T.: Multi-hop packet tracking for experimental facilities. SIGCOMM Comput. Commun. Rev. **40**(4), 447–448 (2010)

Internet of Things,
Vehicular Networks

A Reputation-Based Adaptive Trust Management System for Vehicular Clouds

Eun-Ju Lee and Ihn-Han Bae[(✉)]

School of IT Eng., Catholic University of Daegu, Gyeongsan, Korea
{eunjulee,ihbae}@cu.ac.kr

Abstract. Advances in vehicular networks, embedded devices and cloud computing will enable the formation of vehicular clouds of computing, communication, sensing, power and physical resources. Owing to the dynamic nature of the vehicular cloud, continuous monitoring on trust attributes in necessary to enforce service-level agreement, This paper proposes RA-VTrust, Reputation-based Adaptive Vehicular Trust model for efficiently evaluating the competence of a vehicular cloud service based on its multiple trust attributes. In RA-VTrust, an adaptive trust and a reputation managements based on variable precision rough sets are suggested to trust data mining and reputation knowledge discovery. The adaptive trust management provides cloud consumers with the most suitable trust for vehicular services because it is performed by considering vehicular service level agreement (VSLA) documents and reputation services. The performance of RA-VTrust is evaluated through a simulation.

Keywords: Cloud Computing · Reputation · Rough Sets · Service Level Agreement · Trust · Vehicular Cloud

1   Introduction

The vehicle of 2020 will be a core element of a Smarter Planet. The vehicle of the future will be a communications wonder and as yet another node on the Internet cloud, it will connect with other vehicles, the transportation infrastructure, homes, businesses and other sources. This connection will happen through a convergence of different electronic technologies and telematics that range from infotainment, speech recognition and linguistics, to thermal, power train and safety systems. Innovation will emerge mostly from software, electrical systems, sensors and driver-assistance services that will improve safety and the overall driving experience. At the same time, a new level of owner/vehicle personalization and customization will be delivered by leveraging a mobility framework over the cloud [1].

The trust mechanism provides a good way for improving the system security. It is a new and emerging security mode to provide security states, access control, reliability and polices for decision making by identifying and distributing the malicious entities based on converting and extracting the detected results from security mechanisms in different systems and collecting feedback assessments continually. Before interaction occurs between cloud providers and consumers, trust in the vehicular cloud relationship is very important to minimize the security risk and malicious attacks. Accordingly, we propose an RA-VTrust model for efficiently evaluating the competence of a vehicular cloud

© Institute for Computer Sciences, Social Informatics and Telecommunications Engineering 2014
V.C.M. Leung et al. (Eds.): TridentCom 2014, LNICST 137, pp. 77–86, 2014.
DOI: 10.1007/978-3-319-13326-3_8

service based on its multiple trust attributes. The RA-VTrust is designed on the VSLA model which supports the effective execution of automotive services in vehicular clouds, and evaluates the trustworthiness of the services of vehicular clouds through the collection of monitored evidence and the trust mining from the evidence using rough sets on the base of trust information system.

The rest of this paper is organized as follows. Section 2 surveys related work. Section 3 proposes VSLA model. Section 4 designs RA-VTrust system for vehicular clouds. Performance of RA-VTrust is described in Section 5. Section 6 concludes this paper.

2   Related Works

2.1   Vehicular Cloud

Cloud computing combines these two drivers: both usage and costs change based on user needs. Because of the flexible nature of cloud computing, it can meet user needs from an availability and performance perspective and still keep operating costs low because expenses are based on services that are actually used, as opposed to a capital investment that is based on projections of potential needs [1].

With the advent of smart phone in recent years, more and more intelligent vehicle services with cloud computing technique support can be easily implemented. This trend will become more obvious in the future as various types of sensors are embedded into the smart phone such as audio, video, accelerometer, GPS and biomedical sensors. Taking smart phone as an interface between human and internet as well as network, more and more customized services can be implemented in the future for vehicle users [2].

Advances in vehicular networks, embedded devices and cloud computing will enable the formation of vehicular clouds (VCs) of computing, communication, sensing, power and physical resources. There are two types of VCs. In the first type called Infrastructure-based VC, drivers will be able to access services by network communications involving the roadside infrastructure. In the second type called Autonomous VC (AVC), vehicles can be organized on-the-fly to form VC in support of emergences and other ad hoc events [3].

2.2   Cloud Service Level Agreement (CSLA)

As consumers move towards adopting such as a service-oriented architecture (SOA), the quality and reliability of the services become important aspects. However the demands of the service consumers vary significantly. It is not possible to fulfill all consumer expectations from the service provider perspective and hence a balance needs to be made via negotiation process. At the end of the negotiation process, provider and consumer commit to an agreement. In SOA terms, this agreement is referred to as a service level agreement (SLA). This SLA serves as the foundation for the expected level of service between the consumer and the provider. The QoS attributes that are generally part of SLA (such as response time and throughput) however change constantly and to enforce the agreement, these parameters need to be closely monitored [4].

Fig. 1. Vehicular cloud services

Vehicular cloud services (VCSs) that are illustrated Fig. 1 include many IT infrastructures, mobile devices, cloud services, traffic infrastructure, home network, and vehicles [5]. They interact with one another in vehicle-centric manner everywhere at anytime. The key challenges of the VCSs are discussed.

- Guarantee of Real-time Performance
  The vehicular service needs to assure the strict time constrains. If the specified timing is not met, controllability may be diminished or the system failure to work in the worst case. Accordingly, the guarantee of real-time performance in VCSs becomes a challenge.

- Assurance of Safety, Reliability and Security
  The automotive software must be safety-critical. Therefore safety and reliability are the critical requirements in the development of the vehicular software systems. Even if the information devices outside of vehicle are failed, the automotive ECU needs some mechanism to tolerate the impact of the failure.

2.3   Trust Models

Trust models have been proven useful for decision making in numerous service environments. The concepts have also been adapted in grid computing, cloud computing environments, and web services. In recent years, many scholars have made a lot of research on trust model for cloud computing. Alhamad *et al.* [6] developed a model for each of the dimensions for IaaS using fuzzy-set theory. Li, X. and Du, J. [7] represented Cloud-Trust, an adaptive trust management model for efficiently evaluating the competence of a cloud service based on its multiple trust attributes. Noor *et al.* [8] proposed a framework to improve ways on trust management in cloud environments. This framework helps distinguish between credible trust feedbacks and malicious trust feedbacks through a credibility model.

Also, a lot of trust and reputation management approaches for VANETs have been presented. Abumansoor *et al.* [9] proposed a trust evaluation model based on location information and verification in a NLOS (None Line Of Sight) condition. The model provides a trust attribute for applications and services to evaluate their own trust levels. Ding *et al.* [10] proposed an event-based reputation model to filter bogus warning messages, where a dynamic role-dependent reputation evaluation mechanism is presented to determine whether an incoming traffic message is significant and trustworthy to the driver. Yang, N. [11] proposed a trust and reputation management framework for VANETs. In the framework, a similarity mining technique is used for identifying similar message and similar vehicles, and a reputation evaluation algorithm is proposed for evaluating a new vehicle's reputation based on the similarity theory.

3   Vehicular Service Level Agreement (VSLA) Model

We present our VSLA architecture in Fig. 2. The VSLA supports the effective execution of automotive services in vehicular clouds that is inherently dynamic and the resource usage changes dynamically.

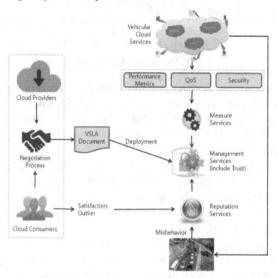

Fig. 2. VSLA architecture

In VSLA structure, we have assumed that the cloud provider and the cloud consumer already participated in the negotiation process and have an agreed set of service parameters. Once the VSLA document is established, it needs to be deployed. The term VSLA deployment is defined as the process of validating and distributing the VSLA, in part or full, to involved parties.

- Vehicular Cloud Services: While vehicular clouds have several services for vehicles and traffics, we consider only two types of vehicular services which are included in SaaS: driver assistance services and safety message dissemination services. Based on intelligent sensor technology, driver assistance services constantly monitor the vehicle surroundings as well as the driving behavior to detect potentially dangerous situations at an early stage. In critical driving situations, these systems warn and actively support the driver and, if necessary, intervene automatically in an effort to avoid a collision or to mitigate the consequences of the accident. Safety and comfort messages are the main types of messages transmitted in VANET. With the safety messages, the drivers can be made aware of the occurrence of accidents even in low visibility situations.

- Measurement Services: These services are responsible for measuring the runtime parameters of cloud provider resources. These services identify the following service parameters to enforce VSLA through vehicular cloud monitoring.

- Reputation Services: These services involve efficient storage of identities and past experiences concerning those identities. Positive or negative experiences may be stored, based on satisfactory completion of transactions, fulfillment of expectations, or some other form of verifiable fiduciary action. In the reputation service of our model, satisfaction and outlier are provided for the reputation of vehicular cloud applications. Also, misbehavior is provided for the reputation of vehicles.

4   RA-VTrust System

A vehicular cloud with the function of trust management is implemented by three layers: trust management layer, VSLA management layer and resource management layer (Fig. 3). The trust management layer is used to evaluate the trustworthiness of service provider through the collection of monitored evidence and the trust mining from the evidence using rough sets on the base of trust information system. The VSLA management layer is used to negotiate an agreement between two parties, where one is the user and another is the service provider. The resource management layer is charged by the service provider, and it provides a set of virtual machines that are configured according to user request and user reputation.

Specifically, each layer consists of several modules and databases. Theses modules and databases are listed as follows:

- Adaptive trust mechanism: This mechanism is the core of trust evaluation. Based on the following information bases, each user maintains a ATM to guide itself in evaluating cloud services through its direct interactions with these services.
  - User reputation information system: This information contains the vehicle reputation that is constructed from valid actions of moving nodes in VANETs and the user reputation that is based on outlier in voting of the satisfaction for vehicular services.
  - Evidence base: The measured and assessed information through service monitoring module is stored in evidence base.
  - Trust information system: The trust information system contains data on the objects of interested characterized in terms of some trust attributes.
- Service monitoring mechanism: This mechanism is needed to continuously measure and assess infrastructure or application behavior in terms of performance, reliability, power usage, ability to meet VSLAs, security, etc [14].
- VSLA manager: The service provider registers its services on VSLA management system. The service user negotiates with service provider about the VSLA details; they finally make an VSLA contract.
- Log information: This mechanism is managed by the cloud manager. Cloud manager sort high-performance cloud services for providing highly trusted resources when there are user requests.

Trust decision task for vehicular services is a multi-attribute decision-making problems based on monitored evidences by the service monitoring agent. Monitored trust evidence acts as initial input data. Each input data is m-dimensional vector, and it consists of m input evidences. We construct the trust information system (Table 1) for a vehicular service use it to initiate trusted knowledge discovery. The trust information system contains data on the objects of interested characterized in terms of some trust attributes and trust value according to the attribute data.

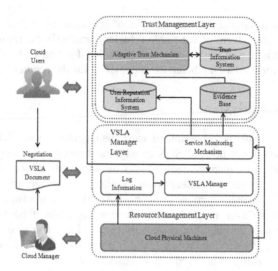

Fig. 3. RA-VTrust architecture

Table 1. The structure of trust information system

U	Th	Av	RT	Se	Sc	Trust
x_1	H	VH	VH	VH	H	VG
x_2	H	H	H	H	H	G
x_3	H	H	H	M	M	E
x_4	M	M	M	M	M	P
x_5	L	L	M	M	L	VP
x_6	M	H	H	H	M	E
x_7	H	H	VH	H	M	G
x_8	H	H	VH	VH	VH	VG
x_9	M	VH	H	VH	M	G
x_{10}	H	M	M	H	M	P
x_{11}	H	M	H	H	M	E
x_{12}	M	M	H	H	M	E

The trust information system consists of condition and decision attributes. The information system is denoted by S=(U, C, D), where U is a non-empty finite set of objects called universe of discourse, C and D represent conditional attributes and decision attributes of trust measurement, respectively. The information system uses five fuzzy sets for the input value of condition attributes and five fuzzy sets for the output value of decision attribute. In Table 1, C={Th, Av, RT, Se, Sc} denote the condition attribute, and D={Trust} denotes the decision attribute.

To enforce VSLA for a service, the RA-VTrust mechanism evaluates appropriate trusts in consideration of specified trust of VSLA, trust information system, the measured information of evidence base and user reputation. The relative classification error between the trust information system and the VSLA is computed by equation (1).

$$e(X,Y) = \sum_{i=1}^{n} \left[\left(\mu(x_i) - \mu(y_i) \right) \times w_i \right] \tag{1}$$

In equation (1), X and Y are the conditional attribute vectors of trust information system and VSLA, respectively. $\mu(x_i)$ and $\mu(y_i)$ represent the defuzzified values for the i-th elements of the conditional attributes of trust information system and VSLA, respectively. Also, n is the number of conditional attributes, and w_i is the relative weight of i-th conditional attribute. Therefore, the similarity between the trust information system and the VSLA is as follows:

$$s(X,Y)=1-e(X,Y) \tag{2}$$

We classify user reputation information into five fuzzy sets: VH, H, M, L, VL. Table 2 shows the allowable values of error, β, in the relative classification of user reputation information in case the trust degree of VSLA is E (excellent).

Table 2. Allowable classification error values for fuzzy reputation sets

Fuzzy reputation set	Allowable classification error value (β)
VH	[0.2, 0.3)
H	[0.1, 0.2)
M	[0.0. 0.1)
L	[-0.1, 0.0)
VL	Service suspension

Adaptive trust mechanism selects feasible trust objects from the trust information system through use of the specified trust of VSLA and the allowable classification error that depends on user reputation information. Then, it also selects the best trust that has the minimum classification error as the most suitable VSLA. The adaptive trust mechanism submits the best trust to VSLA manager. The VSLA manager submits the best trust to management services. The management services schedule and allocate the resources according to the best trust VSLA. The service monitoring mechanism is needed to continuously measure and assess infrastructure or application behavior regarding the execution of the service, and also forwards the values of trust attributes to evidence base. If these values of trust attributes of evidence base are different from the values of best trust attributes, the adaptive trust mechanism stores these values of trust attributes of evidence base in the trust information system.

To illustrate our idea, an example is used. Assume that the VSLA of the user who requests a vehicular service is (M, M, H, H, M, E), $w_i=(0.15, 0.2, 0.25, 0.25, 0.15)$, $\mu(VH)=1.0$, $\mu(H)=0.8$, $\mu(M)=0.6$, $\mu(L)=0.4$ and $\mu(VL)=0.2$. Firstly, if the user reputation is H, the feasible trust objects are computed as follows:

$$e(x_2,VSLA) = 0.2\times(0.15+0.2+0.15) = 0.1,$$

$$e(x_7,VSLA) = 0.2\times(0.15+0.2+0.25) = 0.12,$$

$$e(x_9,VSLA) = 0.2\times(0.4+0.25) = 0.13.$$

Accordingly, $x_2=(H, H, H, H, H, G)$ is selected as the best trust for the requested vehicular service.

Secondly, if the user reputation is L, the feasible trust objects are computed as follows:

$$e(x_4,VSLA) = 0.2\times(-0.25-0.25) = -0.1.$$

Accordingly, $x_4=(M, M, M, M, M, P)$ is selected as the best trust for the requested vehicular service. Therefore, the adaptive trust mechanism sends the best trust to VSLA manager and management services.

5   Performance Evaluation

The performance of proposed scheme is evaluated with the variation of reputation and trust values. The performance of RA-VTrust is compared with that of Alhamad [6]. Reputation and trust values are computed as follows:

- Reputation value variation
  The reputation value of each vehicle or its driver can be calculated by equation (3).

$$\text{Rep}_i^{(n)} = \begin{cases} \alpha \, \text{Rep}_i^{(n-1)} + (1-\alpha)r_i^{(n)}, & n > 1 \\ 0.5, & n = 1 \end{cases} \tag{3}$$

Where $0 \leq \alpha \leq 1$ and $r_i^{(n)}$ is the reputation value for the user i after confirming the n-th event message.

$$r_i^{(n)} = \begin{cases} 0.9, & \textit{if the } n-th \textit{ event message is rational behavor} \\ 0.7, & \textit{if the } n-th \textit{ satisfaction message is normal} \\ 0.3, & \textit{if the } n-th \textit{ satisfaction message is outlier} \\ 0.1, & \textit{if the } n-th \textit{ event message is misbehavior} \end{cases}$$

- Trust value variation
  The trust value for each vehicular service can be calculated by equation (4).

$$Trust_{val} = \sum_{i=1}^{n} w_i \mu(x_i), \tag{4}$$

where $0 \leq w_i \leq 1$ and the summation of w_i is 1. .

We evaluate the performance of RA-Trust in the MATLAB [12] by applying the parameters and values of Table 3.

Table 3. Simulation parameters

Parameter	Value
Number of service requests	50
Number of vehicles	10
Probability that abnormal event is occurred	0.1~0.7
μ(VH, H, M, L, VL)	1.0, 0.8, 0.6, 0.4, 0.2
w_i	(0.15, 0.2, 0.25, 0.25, 0.15)
Interval-valued for reputation fuzzy sets, {VH, H, M, L, VL}	{[1.0, 0.8], (0.8, 0.6], (0.6, 0.4], (0.4, 0.2], (0.2, 0.0]}
Interval-valued for trust fuzzy sets, {VG, G, E, P, VP}	{[1.0, 0.9], (0.9, 0.8], (0.8, 0.7], (0.7, 0.6], (0.6, 0.0]}
Initial value of reputation	0.5
Initial trust of VSLA	E

Fig. 4 and Fig. 5 show the evaluation results for reputation. Fig. 4 shows average reputation value according to the probability that abnormal event is occurred, where the larger abnormal probability, the smaller average reputation value. But, Alhamad model has a fixed reputation value even if abnormal events are occurred. Also, Fig. 5 shows the number of occurrences for reputation fuzzy sets according to the abnormal probability. The smaller abnormal probability has, the more high reputations (VH and H) are occurred, while the larger abnormal probability has, the more low reputations (L and VL) as compared with other abnormal probabilities are occurred. Additionally, we know that 8 service requests are suspended in case that abnormal probability is 0.7, but 2 service request is suspended in case that abnormal probability is 0.3 from Fig. 5.

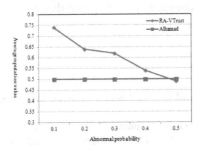

Fig. 4. Average reputation value with abnormal probability

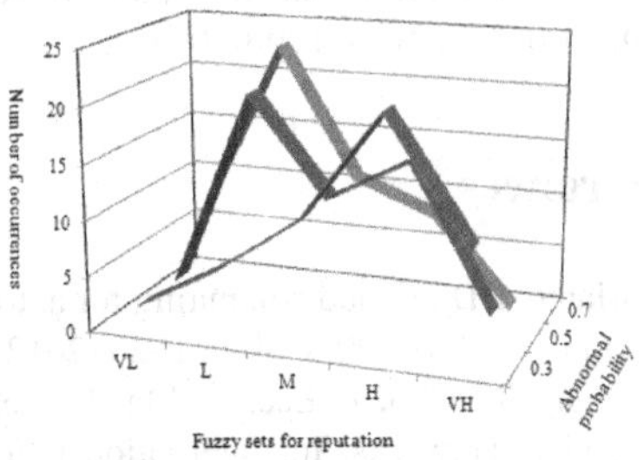

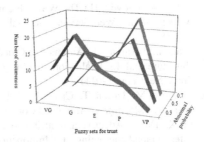

Fig. 5. The frequency of reputation fuzzy sets with abnormal probability

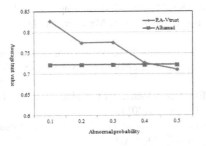

Fig. 6. Average trust value with abnormal probability

Fig. 7. The frequency of trust fuzzy sets with abnormal probability

Fig. 6 and Fig. 7 show the evaluation results for trust. Fig. 6 shows average trust value according to the probability that abnormal event is occurred. Similarly to reputation values, the larger abnormal probability, the smaller average trust value. But, Alhamad model has a fixed trust value even if abnormal events are occurred. Also, Fig. 7 shows the number of occurrences for trust fuzzy sets according to the abnormal probability. The smaller abnormal probability has, the more good trusts (VG and G) are occurred, while the larger abnormal probability has, the more poor trusts (P) are occurred. From the results of our simulation, we hereby confirm that our RA-VTrust is efficient adaptive trust management model for vehicular clouds regarding VSLA and reputation.

6   Conclusion

To development of efficient trust management model for the services of vehicular clouds, we propose firstly the VSLA which supports the effective execution of automotive services in vehicular clouds, and design next the RA-VTrust which evaluates the trustworthiness of service provider through the collection of monitored evidence and the trust mining from the evidence using trust information system. The performance of RA-VTrust is evaluated through a simulation. As a result, our RA-VTrust has proven to handle adaptively trust management for vehicular clouds regarding VSLA and reputation.

Our future work includes RA-VTrust extension which not only considers user and service reputations, but also has the service recommendation function that takes account of user service reputation.

References

1. Marco, J.D.: Cloud computing for automotive. IBM Global Business Services, IBM Cooperation, GIW03003USEN, 1–20 (2012)
2. Wang, T., Cho, J., Lee, S., Ma, T.: Real time services for future cloud computing enabled vehicle networks. In: International Conference on Wireless Communications and Signal Processing, pp. 1–5. IEEE Press, New York (2011)
3. Olariu, S., Eltoweissy, M., Younis, M.: Towards autonomous vehicular clouds. ICST Transactions on Mobile Communications and Applications. 11, 7–9 (2011)
4. Keller, A., Ludwig, H.: The WSLA Framework: Specifying and Monitoring Service Level Agreements for Web Services. Journal of Network and Systems Management. 11, 57–81 (2003)
5. Iwai, A., Aoyama, M.: Automotive Cloud Service Systems Based on Service-Oriented Architecture and Its Evaluation. In: Int. Conf. on Cloud Computing, pp. 638–645. IEEE Press, New York (2011)
6. Alhamad, M., Dillon, T., Cjanh, E.: A Trust-Evaluation Metric for Cloud applications. Int. Journal of Machine Learning and Computing. 1, 416–421(2011)
7. Li, X., Du, J.: Adaptive and attribute-based trust model for service-level agreement guarantee in cloud computing. IET Information Security 7, 39–50 (2012)
8. Noor, Talal H., Sheng, Quan Z.: Credibility-Based Trust Management for Services in Cloud Environments. In: Kappel, Gerti, Maamar, Zakaria, Motahari-Nezhad, Hamid R. (eds.) Service Oriented Computing. LNCS, vol. 7084, pp. 328–343. Springer, Heidelberg (2011)
9. Abumansoor, O., Boukerche, A.: Towards a Secure Trust Model for Vehicular Ad Hoc Networks Services. In: Global Telecommunications Conference, pp. 1–5. IEEE Press, New York (2011)
10. Ding, Q., Li, X., Zhou, X.: Reputation-based Trust Model in Vehicular Ad Hoc Networks. In: International Conference on Wireless Communications and Signal Processing, pp. 1–6. IEEE Press, New York (2010)
11. Yang, N.: A Similarity based Trust and Reputation Management Framework for VANETs. Int. Journal of Future Generation Communication and Networking. 6, 25–34(2013)
12. Kay M. G.: Basic Concepts in Matlab
    http://www.ise.ncsu.edu/kay/Basic_Concepts_in_Matlab.pdf

IPv6-Based Test Beds Integration Across Europe and China

Sébastien Ziegler[1(✉)], Michael Hazan[1], Huang Xiaohong[2], and Latif Ladid[3]

[1] Mandat International, 3 ch Champ-Baron, 1209 Geneva, Switzerland
{sziegler,mhazan}@mandint.org
[2] Beijing University of Post and Telecommunication, Beijing, China
huangxh@bupt.edu.cn
[3] University of Luxembourg, Kirchberg, Luxembourg
Latif.ladid@uni.lu

Abstract. The present article exposes a new approach in multiple test beds integration by using the IPv6 properties. It demonstrates the potential of such approach combined with 6LoWPAN and RESTful protocols, such as CoAP. It presents the results of an initial pilot between Mandat International (MI) and Beijing University of Post and Telecommunication (BUPT). Both partners have interconnected their respective test beds, respectively located in Geneva and Beijing. The article presents applied the conceptual model and its implementation. The article provides an overview of IPv6 impact and relevance for the Internet of Things, as well as future envisaged developments.

Keywords: Test bed · IPv6 · CoAP · 6LoWPAN · Internet of Things · IoT6 · ECIAO · Europe · China

1 Introduction

Over the last decades, the Internet has had a profound effect on the way we live and conduct business. The original ARPANET was conceived as a simple and reliable network of interconnected servers but the standardization of TCP/IP between 1974 and 1982 [1] has unexpectedly paved the way to the largest single market of human history. Since then, the Web has emerged and encompassed a huge numbers of connected applications and services. As more and more systems and actors were connected to the Web, the emergence of digital and social platforms was still a rather natural development, using the very same Internet architecture.

We are now facing a disruptive changes impacting the structure and scope of the Internet itself with the extension of the Internet to the Internet of Things and the transition towards the Internet Protocol version 6 (IPv6).

This paper explores the potential of these disruptions and demonstrates how IPv6 can ease the integration of distributed test beds located in different parts of the world to support experiments on the Internet of Things. We start by briefly introducing this evolution. We then present briefly the two research projects that have paved the way to this article: IoT6 [2] and ECIAO [3]. The rest of this paper then goes on to present

© Institute for Computer Sciences, Social Informatics and Telecommunications Engineering 2014
V.C.M. Leung et al. (Eds.): TridentCom 2014, LNICST 137, pp. 87–96, 2014.
DOI: 10.1007/978-3-319-13326-3_9

a model of IPv6 and CoAP based integration of test beds. We illustrates the relevance and consistency of our approach through the concrete fulfillment of a pilot for an integrated test bed involving sensors distributed between Geneva in Europe and Beijing in China.

2   IoT and IPv6 Convergence

For years, there was an implicit expectation that the growth of the Internet would be limited in a way which correlates to the World population. This expectation was continually strained as the number of websites and users connected to the Internet continued to grow and is not valid anymore, as we have entered a new era: the era of the Internet of Things. We are moving beyond a point of no return, with more devices connected to the Internet than human beings. While varying – attempts to estimate the number of connected devices in 2020 place the number as high as 50 Billion [4]. Each day our devices are becoming smaller, more pervasive and more mobile. The Internet is already used as a vehicle for many M2M connections, as it is used for Voice over IP and EPC tags management. We are increasingly seeing the Internet as a broad platform for the connectivity of many kinds of entities. We are rapidly moving towards a network in which machine-to-machine and machine-to-human communications will become more numerous than human initiated activities.

Since 1982, the Internet has benefited from the stable and well-designed Internet Protocol version 4 (IPv4). Unfortunately, however, IPv4 only has a capacity of about 4 billion theoretical public addresses (and fewer in practice). This corresponds to less than one public IP address per living adult on Earth – a number that was believed to be sufficient to address current and future needs at the time of its creation. Progressively, however, the growing allocation of public Internet addresses started to cause concerns, leading to restricted public allocation policies and the introduction of Network Address Translation (NAT) mechanisms to provide end-users with private (and sometimes volatile) addresses. Most users effectively became "Internet homeless", unaware that they were sharing potentially volatile public Internet addresses with others.

This continuous growth of the Internet convinced the IETF to deliver a new protocol with a larger addressing scheme, standardized in 1998 as the Internet Protocol version 6 (IPv6). [5] IPv6 is based on an addressing scheme of 2^{128} bits, split in two parts: 2^{64} bits for the network address and 2^{64} bits for the host ID. IPv6 is now globally deployed and a growing number of Internet Service Providers (ISP) are offering IPv6 connectivity.

The extended scheme offered by IPv6 enables an almost unlimited number of addresses, overcoming the scarcity issues of IPv4 and creating the necessary infrastructure for the exploding needs of the Internet of Things. The addressing scheme now available provides the possibility to allocate unique public Internet addresses to as many devices as needed, making each and every smart object Internet accessible through a unique, public and permanent address.

IPv6 is emerging as the natural answer to the emerging Internet of Things requirements. It provides a highly scalable addressing scheme [14, 15] as well as many useful features, such as stateless configuration mechanisms [6], as well as a native integration to the future Internet.

In parallel to IPv6, several IPv6-related standards have emerged, including among others: 6LoWPAN [7] providing a lighter version of IPv6 for constrained nodes and networks; CoAP [8] providing a light substitute to HTTP, RPL [9] providing a routing protocol for lossy networks; Mobility enablers, such as NEMO [10]; and new emerging standards such as 6TISCH [11].

3   Participating Projects

3.1   IoT6

In 2011, the IoT6 European research project [2] was initiated and designed by the coordinator of the UDG project[12]. It was started to further research the potential of IPv6 for heterogeneous integration and gathered together several academic and industrial research partners, including Mandat International and the University of Luxembourg. The objectives of IoT6 were to:

- Research the potential of IPv6 and related standards to support the future Internet of Things and to overcome its current fragmentation and lack of interoperability;
- To develop a highly scalable IPv6-based Service-Oriented Architecture to achieve interoperability, mobility, cloud computing integration and intelligence distribution among heterogeneous smart things components, applications and services; and
- To explore innovative forms of interactions with multi-protocol integration, mobile and cellular networks, cloud computing services (SaaS)[16], RFID [17] and Smart Things Information Service, information and intelligence distribution.

In other words, IoT6 explores the potential of IPv6 for horizontal integration (across various domains of the IoT) and vertical integration between the IoT and the Cloud. The main outcomes of the IoT6 project are recommendations on IPv6 features that can accelerate the Internet of Things coupled with an open and well-defined IPv6-based Service-Oriented Architecture that facilitates its exploitation.

3.2   ECIAO

The EU-China-FIRE Project is a 2 years (Aug. 2013 – Aug. 2015) EU-funded project, facilitating coordination and support to EU-China cooperation on Future Internet Experimental Research (FIRE) [18] and IPv6. China is a very large country pursuing its ICT[19] infrastructure development which could lead to pioneer the implementation of Future Internet advanced technologies as well as being a force to promote large scale IPv6 deployment more critically than EU due to lack of IPv4 resources. Since Europe is investing substantially in Future Internet Research and Experiment (FIRE) and could benefit from exchange and experience from large scale deployment requirements in China, the EU-China FIRE project is exploring mutual benefit cooperation activities. In addition to an interactive web portal, two large conferences and workshops will be organised and many public reports will help to increase awareness of benefits of cooperation between EU and China in the area of Future Internet research and experiments.

The EU-China FIRE project aims in particular to explore EU-China mutual benefit cooperation activities in:

- Strengthening EU-China joint research efforts on the Future Internet by developing interoperable solutions and common standards. Federation of test beds will be explored and interoperability initiatives will be undertaken.
- Reinforcing academic and industrial cooperation on Future Internet experimental research, through a better networking between European and Chinese actors. The EU-China FIRE web portal, linked also to leading social networks and with dedicated helpdesk services, will offer an efficient exchange platform stimulating cooperation between EU and China researchers. A minimum of five common research areas will be identified and documented.
- Exchanging good practices for IPv6 deployment and support the creation of interconnected IPv6 pilot(s) between Europe and China.

4   Initial Test Beds Overview

4.1   Mandat International Test Bed

Mandat International has built up a distributed test bed gathering heterogeneous sensors and actuators in two main locations:

- A smart office test bed in Geneva with end-users. This environment enables experimentations in real conditions, addressing the multidimensional nature of the Internet of Things.
- A university lab in Geneva with more technically focused experimentations.

The test bed has been used in several European research projects, addressing research topics such as energy efficiency, safety, smart buildings, WSN deployments and comfort. It intends to gather all kinds of devices, reflecting the inherent heterogeneity of the Internet of things. The deployed sensors and actuators are heterogeneous and can be split in three main categories:

- IP/6LoWPAN and CoAP based devices;
- IP but non-CoAP based devices;
- Non-IP devices.

The non-IP sensors and actuators are integrated to the IPv6 environment through the UDG technology [12] enabling multiprotocol interoperability and legacy protocol integration into IPv6.

The described pilot was focused on a subset of CoAP and 6LoWPAN sensors, accessible through global public IPv6 addresses.

4.2   BUPT Test Bed

BUPT has built up one 6lowpan based monitoring system, which is already deployed in the BUPT campus. Moreover, CoAP based platform is developing to support IoT application development and resource management.

As illustrated in Figure 1, the system is composed of three main parts: wireless sensor network (WSN) management system, WSN gateway (router) and wireless sensor nodes. The system can be used for collecting information, sending the alarm information and sharing data to the 3rd party. Figure 2 shows the software stack of the sensor network.

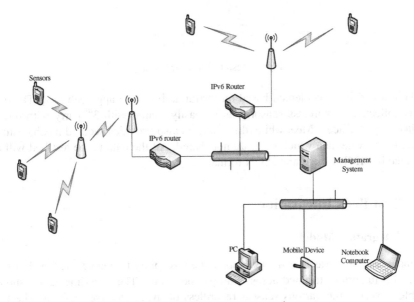

Fig. 1. WSN management system network structure

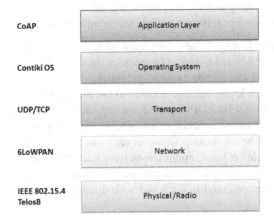

Fig. 2. Software stack

Since BUPT IoT platform is a dual-way system both for collecting measurement data and sending control commands, it is possible to do both remote and wireless monitoring and control in real time. Figure 3 shows a screen shot of the result of real-time measurement inside the campus.

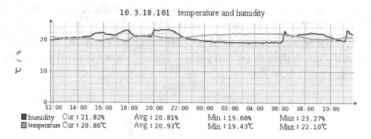

Fig. 3. Result of measurement

The test bed is implemented based on restful architecture approach [20]. The data that is collected by wireless sensors can be easily shared with 3rd party with restful architecture interface. Meanwhile, this platform also provides secured mechanism to protect the private data which users do not shared. All the data in the test bed will be presented by XML format and JSON format.

5   Test Beds Integration

5.1   Integration Model

The main objective was to test and validate the possibility to enable a test bed of sensors and actuators distributed across Europe and China. The experimentation should be able to access the various sensors regardless of their effective location. The first step of the joint pilot intends to demonstrate direct end-to-end access to distributed sensors located in Beijing and Geneva through IPv6.

The integration concept relies on a triple levels integration effort:

- At the sensor level, we have adopted a common interface and environment, by using 6LowPAN and CoAP. This enables the sensors to provide a RESTful interface, with a large scale capacity potential.
- At the network level, we have decided to use direct and secured IPv6 connection between both test beds. IPv6 provides a flexible and highly scalable network environment. A major concern was to enable a transparent interconnection from the sensor to the application wherever each one was located.
- At the application level, applications have been developed to interact with the CoAP enabled sensors. In order to demonstrate the integration, two websites are being implemented in each site with direct on-line access to sensors from both sides.

Figure 4 illustrates the integration model applied to both test beds.

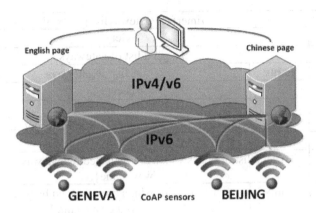

Fig. 4. Mutliple test bed integration model

5.2   REST Full Architecture Approach

RESTful architecture [20] approach is designed for Web applications, whose purpose is to reduce the complexity of the development and improve the scalability of the system. The RESTful architecture interfaces are designed according to the following principles:

1.   All the things on the Internet can be abstracted as resources.
2.   Each resource is corresponding to a unique resource identifier.
3.   Resources can be operated through generic connector interface.
4.   Various operations for resource will not change resource identifier.
5.   All operations are stateless.

The test bed of BUPT has implemented restful architecture approach. The data which is collected by wireless sensors can be accessed by restful architecture interface. However, the private data which users do not want to make public will be protected by the WSN management system. Data in the test bed is abstracted as resources which users can call through IPv6/IPv4. No matter what kind of system environment or the development environment that users use, they can easily access to these resources. Data in the test bed will be presented with XML format and JSON format.

According to data of the test bed, resources can be divided into 4 different types:

1.   A list of gateways.
2.   Lists of sensors which are managed by gateways.
3.   Real time data which is collected by sensors.
4.   History data of sensors which is stored in the database of WSN management system.

According to the types of resources, the interfaces are designed into 4 types. The following chart shows restful interfaces which are used to share with the 3rd party:

URL	/interface/gatewaylist.json(xml)	
Method	Get	
Function	To get a list of gateways.	
Output	Entity	A list of gateways.
Status	Success	
	Failure	
URL	/interface/{gateway name}/sensorlist.json(xml)	
Method	Get	
Function	To get a list of nodes which are managed by gateway named {gateway name}.	
Output	Entity	A list of nodes which are managed by gateway named {gateway name}
Status	Success	
	Failure	
URL	/interface/{sensor name}/realtime.json(xml)	
Method	Get	
Function	To get real time data which is collected by node named {sensor name}.	
Output	Entity	Real time data which is collected by node named {sensor name}
Status	Success	
	Failure	
URL	/interface/{sensor name}/{from time}/{to time}/history.json(xml)	
Method	Get	
Function	To get history data of the node named {sensor name} between {from time} and {to time}.	
Output	Entity	History data of the node named {sensor name} between {from time} and {to time}
Status	Success	
	Failure	

Form 1. The RESTful Interfaces of the Test beds

5.3   Initial Tests and Validation

A first step has been to deploy a joint IPv6 network between Beijing and Geneva. The IPv6 network has been tested and validated and can now provide direct and transparent interconnections. The connections can use SSL[21] and can be tunneled and secured with IPSec [22] if needed.

A first set of sensors have been connected on each site. They are remotely accessible and enable distant interactions from each site. On Geneva site for instance, wireless senor motes, including temperature and humidity sensor, as well as some actuators, including a heating valve and a light switch, are permanently deployed and accessible to the Chinese partners through their IPv6 address and CoAP interface.

6   Conclusions and Future Work

A first set of sensors and actuators have been successfully integrated into a common network enabling European and Chinese researchers to use them. They are remotely accessible and are paving the way to larger scale integration efforts. This initial pilot demonstrates the potential of IPv6 and CoAP for such integrations.

The current effort is oriented in three main directions:

- The extension of the test bed with additional sensors and actuators;
- The integration of other academic and industrial partners in view of addressing scalability requirements;
- The development of two web applications: one in China and one in Europe, providing and demonstrating simultaneous access to sensors deployed in both locations (Geneva and Beijing).

The authors will welcome and duly consider proposals from interested third parties to join the initial platform.

References

1. The Internet Protocol was initiated in 1974 with RFC 675 TCP/IP Specification of Internet Transmission Control Program. Its standardization was completed by the IETF in 1982 (1982)
2. IoT6, FP7 European Research Project. www.iot6.eu
3. ICIAO, FP7 European Research Project. http://www.euchina-fire.eu
4. Ericson white paper 284 23-3149 Uen, More than 50 billion connected devices (February 2011). http://www.ericsson.com/res/docs/whitepapers/wp-50-billions.pdf
5. Deering, S., Hinden, R.: IETF, IPv6 specifications defined in RFC 2460 Internet Protocol, Version 6 (IPv6) Specification (December 1998)
6. Thomson, S., Narten, T., Jinmei, T.: IETF, RFC 4862, IPv6 Stateless Address Autoconfiguration (September 2007)
7. IETF, RFC 4919, IPv6 over Low-Power Wireless Personal Area Networks (6LoWPANs): Overview, Assumptions, Problem Statement, and Goals (August 2007)
8. Shelby, Z., Hatke, K., Bormann, C.: Constrained Application Protocol (CoAP), Internet Draft, draft-ietf-core-coap-18 (December 2013)
9. IETF, RFC 6553, The Routing Protocol for Low-Power and Lossy Networks (RPL) (March 2012)
10. IETF, RFC 4919, IPv6 over Low-Power Wireless Personal Area Networks (6LoWPANs): Overview, Assumptions, Problem Statement, and Goals (August 2007)
11. IETF, RFC 3963, Network Mobility (NEMO) Basic Support Protocol (January 2005)
12. Universal Device Gateway was developed as a CTI project in Switzerland in (2006). wwww.devicegateway.com
13. IETF working group. http://datatracker.ietf.org/wg/6tisch/
14. Ziegler, S., Crettaz, C., Thomas, I.: IPv6 as a global addressing scheme and integrator for the Internet of Things and the Cloud IEEE PITSAC (accepted paper at)
15. Ziegler, S., Crettaz, C.: IoT6 usecase scenario & requirements," http://www.iot6.eu/images/stories/deliverables/IoT6_D1.1_v1.0.pdf

16. Buxmann, P., Hess, T., Lehmann, S.: Software as a Service. Wirtschaftsinformatik **50**(6), 500–503 (2008)
17. Brady M.J., Duan, D.W., Kodukula, V.S.R.: Radio frequency identification system: U.S. Patent 6,100,804[P]. (August 8, 2000)
18. Gavras, A., Karila, A., Fdida, S., et al.: Future internet research and experimentation: the FIRE initiative. ACM SIGCOMM Computer Communication Review **37**(3), 89–92 (2007)
19. McCormick, R., Scrimshaw, P.: Information and communications technology, knowledge and pedagogy. Education, Communication & Information **1**(1), 37–57 (2001)
20. Dinh, N.T., Kim, Y.: RESTful Architecture of Wireless Sensor Network for Building Management System. KSII Transactions on Internet & Information Systems 6(1) (2012)
21. Chou, W.: Inside SSL: the secure sockets layer protocol. IT professional **4**(4), 47–52 (2002)
22. Baldi, M.: Internet Protocol Security (2001)
23. Yang Tianle - IPv6 Mobile Deployment BP at China Mobile. IPv6 Project Manager in http://www.chinamobileltd.com/en/global/home.php China Mobile: http://www.euchina-fire.eu/wp-content/uploads/2013/10/ChinaMobileIPv6Progress_Tianle_web.pdf
24. U Jie - IPv6 deployment best practices by China Telecom. Senior Network Engineer, http://en.chinatelecom.com.cn/ China Telecom and Project Manager, China Next Generation Internet (http://www.cernet2.edu.cn/en/bg.htm CNGI): http://www.ipv6forum.com/dl/presentations/v6CT.pdf
25. Axel Clauberg - IPv6 Fixed Deployment Best Practices in Germany and Croatia: http://www.ipv6observatory.eu/wp-content/uploads/2012/11/01-06-Axel-Clauber1.pdf

Benchmarking Low-Resource Device Test-Beds for Real-Time Acoustic Data

Congduc Pham[1,2]($\boxtimes$) and Philippe Cousin[2]

[1] LIUPPA Laboratory, University of Pau, Pau, France
congduc.pham@univ-pau.fr
[2] Easy Global Market, Madrid, Spain
philippe.cousin@eglobalmark.com

Abstract. The EAR-IT project relies on 2 test-beds to demonstrate the use of acoustic data in smart environments: the smart city SmartSantander test-bed and the smart building HobNet test-beds. In this paper, we take a benchmarking approach to qualify the various EAR-IT test-bed based on WSN and IoT nodes with IEEE 802.15.4 radio technology. We will highlight the main performance bottlenecks when it comes to support transmission of acoustic data. We will also consider audio quality and energy aspects as part of our benchmark methodology in order to provide both performance and usability indicators. Experimentations of multi-hop acoustic data transmissions on the SmartSantander test-bed will be presented and we will demonstrate that streaming acoustic data can be realized in a multi-hop manner on low-resource device infrastructures.

Keywords: Benchmark · Internet of Thing · Acoustic · Smart Cities

1 Introduction

There is a growing interest in multimedia contents for surveillance applications in order to collect richer informations from the physical environment. Capturing, processing and transmitting multimedia information with small and low-resource device infrastructures such as Wireless Sensor Networks (WSN) or so-called Internet-of-Things (IoT) is quite challenging but the outcome is worth the effort and the range of surveillance applications that can be addressed will significantly increase. The EAR-IT project (www.ear-it.eu) is one of these original projects which focuses on large-scale "real-life" experimentations of intelligent acoustics for supporting high societal value applications and delivering new innovative range of services and applications mainly targeting to smart-buildings and smart-cities. One scenario that can be demonstrated is an on-demand acoustic data streaming feature for surveillance systems and management of emergencies. Other applications such as traffic density monitoring or ambulance tracking are also envisioned and are also requiring timely multi-hop communications between low-resource nodes. The EAR-IT project relies on 2 test-beds to demonstrate the use of acoustic data in smart environments: the smart city SmartSantander test-bed and the smart building HobNet test-bed.

© Institute for Computer Sciences, Social Informatics and Telecommunications Engineering 2014
V.C.M. Leung et al. (Eds.): TridentCom 2014, LNICST 137, pp. 97–106, 2014.
DOI: 10.1007/978-3-319-13326-3_10

There have been studies on multimedia sensors but few of them really consider timing on realistic hardware constraints for sending/receiving flows of packets [1–7]. In this paper, we take a benchmarking approach to qualify the various test-beds based on WSN and IoT nodes with IEEE 802.15.4 radio technology. We will highlight the main performance bottlenecks when it comes to support acoustic data. We will also consider audio quality and energy aspects as part of our benchmark methodology in order to provide both performance and usability indicators. The paper is then organized as follows: Section 2 reviews the EAR-IT test-beds and especially the various sensor node hardware. We will also present some audio sampling and transmission constraints. Section 3 will present our benchmark approach and experimental results showing the main performance bottlenecks. Section 4 will present the audio hardware we developed for the IoT nodes. In Section 5 we will present experimentations of multi-hop acoustic data transmissions on the SmartSantander test-bed and an analysis of the audio quality and energy consumption of the deployed system. Conclusions will be given in Section 6.

2   The EAR-IT Test-Beds

The EAR-IT test-beds consist in (i) the SmartSantander test-bed and (ii) the HobNet test-bed. The SmartSantander test-bed is a FIRE test-bed with 3 locations. One main location being the Santander city in north of Spain with more than 5000 nodes deployed across the city. This is the site we will use when referring to the SmartSantander test-bed. The HobNet test-bed is located at MANDAT Intl which is part of the University of Geneva and it is an in-door test-bed. Many information can be found on corresponding project web site (www.smartsantander.eu and www.hobnet-project.eu) but we will present in the following paragraphs some key information that briefly present the main characteristics of the deployed nodes.

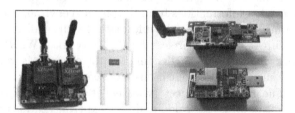

Fig. 1. Left: Santander's IoT node (left) and gateway (right). Right: HobNet's CM5000 & CM3000 AdvanticSys TelosB

2.1   The SmartSantander Test-Bed Hardware

IoT Nodes and Gateways. IoT nodes in the Santander test-bed are WaspMote sensor boards and gateways are Meshlium gateways, both from the Libelium company (www.libelium.com). Most of IoT nodes are also repeaters for multi-hops communication to the gateway. Figure 1(left) shows on the left part the WaspMote sensor node serving as IoT node and on the right part the gateway. The WaspMote is built around an Atmel ATmega1281 micro-controller running at 8MHz. There are 2 UARTs in the WaspMote that serve various purposes, one being to connect the micro-controller to the radio modules.

Radio Module. IoT nodes have one XBee 802.15.4 module and one XBee DigiMesh module. Differences between the 802.15.4 and the DigiMesh version are that Digimesh implements a proprietary routing protocols along with more advanced coordination/node discovery functions. In this paper, we only consider acoustic data transmission/relaying using the 802.15.4 radio module as the DigiMesh interface is reserved for management and service traffic. XBee 802.15.4 offers the basic 802.15.4 [8] PHY and MAC layer service set in non-beacon mode. Santander's nodes have the "pro" version set at 10mW transmit power with an advertised transmission range in line-of-sight environment of 750m. Details on the XBee/XBee-PRO 802.15.4 modules can be found from Digi's web site (www. digi.com).

2.2   The HobNet Test-Bed Hardware

HobNet is also a FIRE test-bed that focuses on Smart Buildings. Although the HobNet test-bed has several sites, within the EAR-IT project only the UNIGE test-bed at the University of Geneva with TelosB-based motes is concerned.

IoT Nodes. Sensor nodes in the HobNet test-bed consist in AdvanticSys TelosB motes, mainly CM5000 and CM3000, see figure 1(right), that are themselves based on the TelosB architecture. These motes are built around an TI MSP430 microcontroller with an embedded Texas Instrument CC2420 802.15.4 compatible radio module. Documentation on the AdvanticSys motes can be found on AdvanticSys web site (www.advanticsys.com). AdvanticSys motes run under the TinyOS system (www.tinyos.net). The last version of TinyOS is 2.1.2 and our tests use this version.

Radio Module. The CC2420 is less versatile than the XBee module but on the other hand more control on low-level operations can be achieved. The important difference compared to the previous Libelium WaspMote is that the radio module is connected to the microcontroller through an SPI bus instead of a serial UART line which normally would allow for much faster data transfer rates. The CC2420 radio specification and documentation are described in [9].

The default TinyOS configuration use a MAC protocol that is compatible with the 802.15.4 MAC (Low Power Listening features are disabled). The default TinyOS configuration also uses ActiveMessage (AM) paradigm to communicate. As we are using heterogeneous platforms we will rather the TKN154 IEEE 802.15.4 compliant API. We verified the performances of TKN154 against the TinyOS default MAC and found them greater.

2.3   Audio Sampling and Transmission Constraints

4KHz or 8KHz periodic 8-bit audio sampling implies to handle 1 byte of raw audio data once every 250us or 125us respectively. Then, when a sufficient number of samples have been buffered, these audio data must be encoded and transmitted while still maintaining the sampling process. For instance, if we take the maximum IEEE 802.15.4 payload size, i.e. 100 bytes, the audio sample time is 25ms and 12.5ms for 4KHz and 8KHz sampling respectively. Most of IoT nodes are based on low speed microcontroller (Atmel ATmega1281 at 8MHz for the Libelium WaspMote and TI MSP430 at 16MHz for the AdvanticSys) making simultaneous raw audio sampling and transmission (even without encoding) nearly impossible when using only the mote microcontroller.

3   Benchmarking IoT Nodes

The benchmark phase is intended to determine (i) the network performance indicators in terms of sending latency, relay latency, relay jitter and packet loss rates, (ii) audio quality indicators depending on the packet loss rates and (iii) energy consumption indicators. Regarding the network indicators we measured on real sensor hardware and communication API the time spent in a generic send() function, noted t_{send}, and the minimum time between 2 packet generation, noted t_{pkt}. t_{pkt} will typically take into account various counter updates and data manipulation so depending on the amount of processing required to get and prepare the data, t_{pkt} can be quite greater than t_{send}. With t_{send}, we can easily derive the maximum sending throughput that can be achieved if packets could be sent back-to-back, and with t_{pkt} we can have a more realistic sending throughput. In order to measure these 2 values, we developed a traffic generator with advanced timing functionalities. Packets are sent back-to-back with a minimum of data manipulation needed to maintain some statistics (counters) and to fill-in data into packets, which is the case in a real application. On the WaspMote, we increased the default serial baud rate between the microcontroller and the radio module from 38400 to 125000. The Libelium API has also been optimized to finally cut down the sending overheads by almost 3! Figure 2 shows t_{send} and t_{pkt} as the payload is varied.

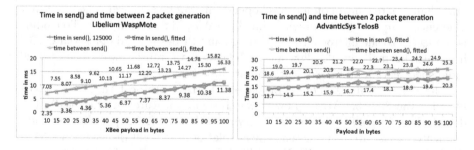

Fig. 2. Sending performances: WaspMote (left) and TelosB (right)

At the sending side, transmission of raw audio at 8KHz is clearly not possible as the time to send 100-byte packets is well above the available time window. 4KHz audio is possible on the WaspMote but not really feasible on the TelosB because the sampling process does interrupt the sending process which is already very close to the maximum time window allowed, i.e. 25ms.

In the next set of benchmark, we use a traffic generator to send packets to a receiver where we measured (i) the time needed by the mote to read the received data into user memory or application level, noted t_{read}, and (ii) the total time needed to relay a packet. Relay jitter is found to be quite small and easily handled with traditional playout buffer mechanisms.

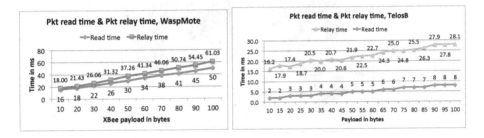

Fig. 3. Read and relaying performances: WaspMote (left) and TelosB (right)

On the WaspMote, we found that t_{read} is quite independent from the microcontroller to radio module communication baud rate because the main source of delays come from memory copies. We can see that when it comes to multi-hop transmissions, 4KHz raw audio is not feasible neither on WaspMote nor TelosB because the time window of 25ms for a 100-byte packets is not sufficient. We will describe in section 5 the audio quality and the energy benchmarking process.

4   Audio Hardware

To leverage the performance issues identified during the benchmark step, one common approach is to dedicate one of the 2 tasks to another microcontroller: (1) use another microcontroller to perform all the transmission operations (memory copies, frame formatting, ...) or (2) use another microcontroller to perform the sampling operations (generates interruptions, reads analog input, performs A/D conversion and possibly encodes the raw audio data). With the hardware platforms used in the EAR-IT project we can investigate these 2 solutions:

1. Libelium WaspMote uses an XBee radio module which has an embedded internal microcontroller that is capable of handling all the sending operations when running in so-called transparent mode (serial line replacement mode);
2. Develop a daughter audio board for the AdvanticSys TelosB mote that will perform the periodic sampling, encode the raw audio data with a given audio codec and fill in a buffer that will be periodically read by the host microcontroller, i.e. the TelosB MSP430.

Solution 1 on Libelium WaspMote. Solution 1 has been experimented and we successfully sampled at 8KHz to generate a 64000bps raw audio stream which is handled transparently by an XBee module running in transparent mode. Transmission is done very simply by writing the sample value in a register. However, we are still limited to 1-hop transmission because the transparent mode does not allow for dynamic destination address configuration making multi-hop transmissions difficult to configure. Moreover, as previously seen, the packet read overhead is very large on the WaspMote. The advantage is however to be able to increase the sampling rate from 4KHz to 8KHz when sending at 1-hop.

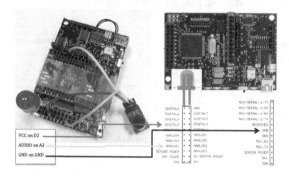

Fig. 4. Audio hardware on Libelium WaspMote

Solution 2 on AdvanticSys TelosB. The developed audio board will have its own microcontroller to handle the sampling operations and encode in real-time the raw audio data into Speex codec (www.speex.org). 8KHz sampling and 16-bits samples will be used to produce an optimized 8kbps encoded Speex audio stream (Speex encoding library is provided by Microchip). This audio board is designed and developed through a collaboration with IRISA/CAIRN research team and Feichter Electronics company (www.feichter-electronics.com). Here is a schematic of the audio board design:

Fig. 5. Left: Audio board schematic. Right: TelosB with the audio board

The audio board has a built-in omnidirectional MEMs microphone (ADMP404 from Analog Devices) but an external microphone can also be connected. The microphone signal output is amplified, digitized and filtered with the WM8940 audio codec. The audio board is built around a 16-bit Microchip dsPIC33EP512 microcontroller clocked at 47.5 MHz that offers enough processing power to encode the audio data in real-time. From the system perspective, the audio board sends the audio encoded data stream to the host microcontroller through an UART component. The host mote will periodically read the encoded data to periodically get fixed size encoded data packets that will be transmitted wirelessly through the communication stack. The speex codec at 8kbps works with 20ms audio frames: every 20ms 160 samples of 8-bit raw audio data is sent to the speex encoder to produce a 20-byte audio packet that will be sent to the host microcontroller through an UART line. These 20 bytes will be read by the host microcontroller and 4 framing bytes are added to the audio data. The first two framing bytes will be used by the receiver to recognize an audio packet. Then sequence number can be used to detect packet losses. The last framing size stores the audio payload size (in our case it is always 20 bytes). Framing bytes are optional but highly recommended. If framing bytes are not used, only a Start Of Frame byte is inserted to allow the speex audio decoder at the receiver end to detect truncated packets.

5   Experimentations

The WaspMote mote as an audio source using solution 1 is a straightforward solution therefore the experimentations described here use the AdvanticSys TelosB mote with the developed audio board but relay nodes consist in both Libelium WaspMote and AdvanticSys motes: some TelosB motes can be used on the Santander test-bed using WaspMote as relay nodes. The receiver consists in an AdvanticSys TelosB mote connected to a Linux computer to serve as a radio gateway.

The audio source can be controlled wirelessly with 3 commands: "D" command defines the next hop address, "C" command controls the audio board power (off/on) and "A" command defines the audio frame aggregation level which will be described later on. The relay nodes can also be controlled wirelessly and they mainly accept the "D" command to define the next hop address. The receiver will get audio packets from the AdvanticSys radio gateway, check for the framing bytes and feed the speex audio decoder with the encoded audio data. The audio decoder will produce a raw audio stream that can be played in real-time with play or stored in a file by using standard Unix redirection command. A play-out buffer threshold can be specified for play to compensate for variable packet jitter at the cost of higher play-out latencies.

We selected a location in Santander near the marina, see figure 6(left), to install the audio source and the relay nodes on the same street lamps than the one deployed by the Santander test-bed, see figure 6(right). We didn't perform tests on the HobNet test-bed yet, but we use both HobNet (AdvanticSys TelosB) and Santander (Libelium WaspMote) hardware as relay nodes. We placed our nodes on the street lamps indicated in figure 6(left), at locations 11, 392, 395 and the top-right gateway. The audio node is on location 11, the receiver is at the top-right gateway location and the 2 relay nodes are at location 392 and 395. With 2 relay nodes, the number of hops is 3. Most of IoT nodes deployed in Santander can reach their associated gateway in a maximum of 3 hops. The

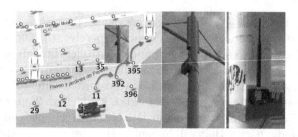

Fig. 6. Test of acoustic data streaming: topology

original IoT nodes of the Santander test-bed are placed on street lamp as shown in figure 6(left). We strapped our nodes as depicted by figure 6(right).

5.1 Multi-Hop Issues

We can see in figure 3 that on average an AdvanticSys TelosB relay node needs about 19ms to relay a 25-byte packet. However, sometimes relaying can take more than 20ms. As the audio source sends a 24-byte packet once every 20ms, it may happen that some packets are dropped at the relay node. We observed packet loss rates between 10% and 15% at the receiver. Figure 3 also shows that a WaspMote needs on average 24ms to relay a 25-byte packet. We also observed packet loss rates between 20% and 30% at the receiver.

In order to reduce the packet drop rate, we can aggregate 2 audio frames (noted A2) into 1 radio packet at the source therefore providing a 40ms time window for the relaying nodes. In this case, the radio packet payload is 48 bytes. The average relaying time is about 22ms for the TelosB and 37ms on the Wasp-Mote as shown in figure 3. While A2 is sufficient on the TelosB to provide a packet loss rate close to 0, the WaspMote still suffers from packet loss rates between 10% and 15% at the receiver because some relaying time are greater than 40ms. On the WaspMote, we can aggregate 3 audio frames (A3) to provide a 60ms time window which is enough to relay a 72-byte packet that needs about 48ms to be relayed. Doing so succeeded in having packet loss rate close to 0.

5.2 Audio Quality Benchmarking

In order to measure the receiving audio quality, we use the ITU-T P.862 PESQ software suite for narrowband audio to get an audio quality indicator (MOS-LQO) between the original audio data and the received audio data. Figure 7 shows for various packet loss rates the MOS-LQO indicator value when there is no audio aggregation, i.e. 1 audio frame in 1 radio packet. The first vertical bar (at 4.308) is the MOS-LQO value when comparing the speex encoded audio data to the uncompressed audio format[1]. It is usually admitted that a MOS-LQO of at

---

[1] Reader can listen at the various audio files at web.univ-pau.fr/~cpham/ SmartSantanderSample/speex

least 2.6 is of reasonably good quality. When there is a packet loss, it is possible
to detect it by the gap in the sequence number and use the appropriate speex
decoder mode. The red bars indicates the MOS-LQO values when packet losses
are detected. Without the packet loss detection feature, missing packets are
simply ignored and the speex decoder will simple decode the flow of available
received packets. We can see that it is always better to detect packet losses.
In figure 7 we can see that an AdvanticSys relay node without audio packet
aggregation (between 10% and 15% packet loss rate) still has an acceptable
MOS-LQO value. Using A2 aggregation makes the packet loss rate to be below
5% and therefore provides a good audio quality as indicated in figure 7(right).
When using Libelium WaspMote as relay nodes, A3 aggregation with packet
losses detection gives a MOS-LQO indicator of 3.4 and 2.9 for 5% and 10%
packet loss rates respectively.

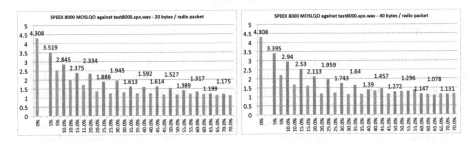

Fig. 7. MOS-LQO: A1(left) and A2(right) aggregation when pkt loss rate is varied

5.3   Energy Consumption Benchmarking

We also investigated the energy consumption of the audio source TelosB node
with the developed audio board. Figure 8(left) plots the measured energy consumption every 20ms. The first part of the figure shows the idle period where
the audio board is powered off and the radio module is on. Then, starting at
time 43s, the audio board is powered on to capture and encode in real-time during about 20s. The audio packets are sent wirelessly. Figure 8(right) shows the
cumulated energy consumption.

During idle period, the consumed energy is about 0.068J/s (68mW). During
audio capture with the radio sending, the consumed energy is about 0.33J/s

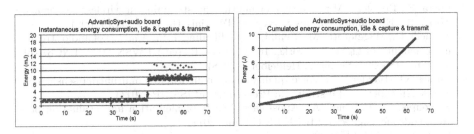

Fig. 8. Instantaneous (left) and Cumulated (right) energy consumption

(330mW). With 2 AA batteries providing about 18700J, we could continuously capture and transmit during more than 15 hours (2700000 audio frames)! With the WaspMote (although not shown due to space limitation), the 8KHz sampling and transmission process consumed about 0.610J/s (610mw) giving a continuous capture during more than 8 hours.

For relay, the WaspMote relay consumed about 0.236J/s (236mW) in listening mode and 0.238J for relaying a 72-byte radio packet in A3 mode, 3 audio frames (60B) + 3*4 framing bytes (12B). Again, with 2 AA batteries, in the best case the relay node can relay about 78606 radio packets before energy is down, i.e. 1h20m of audio. Data transmission in relaying has to use the API mode therefore the energy consumption is higher than in the case of transparent mode. However, given the results of our benchmarking process, we believe that periodic audio streaming scenarios are very possible in the context of a smart cities where most of sensor nodes can usually be recharged at night.

6   Conclusions

We took a benchmarking approach to study how acoustic data can be handled on low-resource device test-beds, highlighting communication overheads and bottlenecks that dramatically limit the relaying operations. We developed an audio board to sample and encode in real-time acoustic data and presented experimentations on the Santander EAR-IT test-bed for real-time acoustic data streaming. With appropriate audio aggregation to fit into relaying capabilities we demonstrated that streaming acoustic data is feasible on Smart Cities infrastructures with reasonably high audio quality and node lifetime.

Acknowledgments. This work is supported by the EU FP7 EAR-IT project, http://www.ear-it.eu

References

1. Rahimi, M., et al.: Cyclops: In situ image sensing and interpretation in wireless sensor networks. In: ACM SenSys (2005)
2. Mangharam, R., Rowe, A., Rajkumar, R., Suzuki, R.: Voice over sensor networks. In: 27th IEEE International of Real-Time Systems Symposium (2006)
3. Luo, L., et al.: Enviromic: Towards cooperative storage and retrieval in audio sensor networks. In: IEEE ICDCS (2007)
4. Misra, S., Reisslein, M.: A survey of multimedia streaming in wireless sensor networks. IEEE Communications Surveys & Tutorials 10, 1174–1179 (2008)
5. Brunelli, D., Maggiorotti, M., Benini, L., Bellifemine, F.L.: Analysis of audio streaming capability of zigbee networks. In: Verdone, R. (ed.) EWSN 2008. LNCS, vol. 4913, pp. 189–204. Springer, Heidelberg (2008)
6. Turkes, O., Baydere, S.: Voice quality analysis in wireless multimedia sensor networks: An experimental study. In: Proceedings of ISSNIP (2011)
7. Touloupis, E., Meliones, A., Apostolacos, S.: Implementation and evaluation of a voice codec for zigbee. In: IEEE ISCC (June 2011)
8. IEEE, Ieee std 802.15.4-2006. (2006)
9. Texas Instrument (accessed 4/12/2013). http://www.ti.com/lit/gpn/cc2420

UAVNet Simulation in UAVSim:
A Performance Evaluation and Enhancement

Ahmad Javaid[1], Weiqing Sun[2(✉)], and Mansoor Alam[1]

[1] Department of EECS, The University of Toledo, Ohio, USA
{ahmad.javaid,mansoor.alam2}@utoledo.edu
[2] Department of ET, The University of Toledo, Ohio, USA
weiqing.sun@utoledo.edu

Abstract. Several works have been done to design a simulation testbed for un-manned aerial vehicles (UAVs) in order to simulate the UAV Network (UAVNet) in a cost-effective manner. Our previously developed UAVSim is one of those attempts and has the capability of simulating large UAV networks as well while giving detailed results in terms of mobility modeling, traffic measurements, attack analysis, etc. The usefulness of such a simulation testbed cannot be guaranteed unless it is hardware independent. Therefore, we present a performance evaluation of such a recently developed software simulation testbed, UAVSim, using traditional and generic hardware available in any regu-lar computer laboratory, in order to show its usefulness in an academic research setup. We show performances for two different environments for two separate machines. Results show that the simulation time is quite predictable and rea-sonable for a particular network size.

Keywords: Testbed Performance · Simulation Testbed · UAVNet Security

1 Introduction

The domain of UAVs has broadened due to its application in every field. Initially, the primary focus of development was Military in nature but real world civil applications are on a rapid increase. With industries like pizza delivery [1] and local package de-livery [2] systems trying to use UAVs for their businesses, there are much more ap-plications to come. Nonetheless, the importance of their use in the military domain has only increased in the recent past and the inclusion of civil UAVs in the national airspace is being delayed due to several issues including security [3].

As several UAV use related issues are being addressed, the need of a secure and safe UAV system can't be ignored for neither military nor civil applications. Due to this reason, several researchers have developed different kinds of simulation testbeds in order to validate proper functioning of these systems and verify their characteristics before deployment. Software simulation testbeds developed using Matlab/Simulink [4], FlightGear [5], JSBSim/FlightGear [6] and Matlab/FlightGear [7] are some of the examples. All these simulation testbeds are focused on testing a single UAV model instead of modeling its behavior in the real world scenario. Some other simulation

© Institute for Computer Sciences, Social Informatics and Telecommunications Engineering 2014
V.C.M. Leung et al. (Eds.): TridentCom 2014, LNICST 137, pp. 107–115, 2014.
DOI: 10.1007/978-3-319-13326-3_11

testbeds using hardware along with software have also been developed where the hardware might be actual UAVs [8], [9], robots [10], [11], or just laptops [12], [13]. The only true software simulation testbed developed so far, called SPEEDES (Synchronous Parallel Environment for Emulation and Discrete Event Simulation) [14], simulates a swarm of UAVs on a high performance parallel computer so that it can match the actual speed and communication rate of the real UAVNet. Keeping all these important works focused on development of a simulation testbed for UAVs, we developed UAVSim.

The rest of the paper is organized to provide more details about UAVSim in Section 2 covering its design and features. Section 3 describes all the performance analysis done and related results and inferences. Section 4 concludes the paper and discusses possible future enhancements to the work.

2   UAVSim – Design and Features

As discussed in the previous Section, the focus of developing a simulation testbed has been simulating the behavior of a single UAV to check its working and proper functioning. Due to the use of a large number of UAVs nowadays, it is very much needed to judge the performance of these UAVs in a swarm of aircrafts when the authorities are talking about integrating UAVs in the National Airspace. Keeping all these requirements in mind, we initially worked on the UAV component level modeling, individual simulation, attack classification and attack modeling [15] and later developed a software simulation testbed called UAVSim for simulations of all sizes of UAV networks [16].

UAVSim is developed using the open source network simulator OMNeT++ and one of its independently developed open source modules called INET. The network design and higher level code is coded in NED, a language specifically designed for OMNeT++ while the lower level functioning is coded using C++ [17]. Although it has an in-built GUI and result analysis module, we developed most of the modules as per our requirement to make it more user-friendly.

One of the most important feature and primary focus of UAVSim is the security simulation of UAVNet. Several attacks have been implemented in the attack library of the testbed. Further, basic and advanced models of UAV have also been designed as well as the facility of using external models is provided. These external models are usually XML based and developed by other researchers. As mentioned earlier, the interactive GUI of UAVSim lets user vary various parameters while advanced users can directly manipulate the configuration files. Most performance tests were performed for security simulations and are reported in Section 3. Apart from supporting mobile wireless communication and UAV component level modeling capability, UAVSim also supports detailed network analysis at lower levels of the protocol stack. Further, attacks targeting different layers can also be designed, launched and tested in UAVSim. One of the most important features of UAVSim from user perspective is its user-friendly design and its ability to work on generic computing environment. Fig. 1 summarizes the important features and modules of UAVSim.

2.1 User-Friendly GUI Simulation

The simulation testbed supports both command line and graphical user interface. We have developed a custom GUI for UAVSim which lets basic users select possible options for some parameters. Users do not get a lot of independence in the basic GUI. While, the advanced users can edit all other parameters as well using the configuration file in the simulation project. The advanced user GUI is still under development and is expected to be finished soon. Although the GUI might cost some resource, it definitely can be counted as one of the performance parameters as the testbed has been designed to be used for all levels of users, basic, intermediate or advanced.

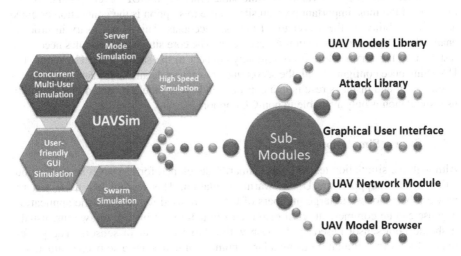

Fig. 1. UAVSim Design and Features. It shows the various modules [16] (*on the right*) which constitute UAVSim, as well as various simulation options.

2.2 Server Mode Simulation

In order to enhance the performance, a high performance computer can also be utilized in our simulation testbed. The connection details to a server or high performance computer can be set using the GUI by the administrator or the person setting up the testbed for the initial use. It should be noted that the core testbed simulation files should be installed on the server prior to this setup and *ssh* should be enabled on the high performance computer to enable seamless communication and execution.

2.3 High Speed (No-GUI) Simulation

While the testbed has a well-designed GUI, the aim of providing a non-GUI option was to enhance the performance. There is an option of express command mode execution as well, which prints the minimum required simulation statistics in order to let the user know that the simulation is running and the computer is not frozen. Using this option, the simulation can be run at the maximum speed and thus gives the best performance. This mode was primarily designed for Server mode simulation because the communication with the server might slow down execution. Nevertheless, this mode can be used on the desktop mode as well as the server mode.

2.4   Concurrent Multi-User Simulation

The testbed also provides a multi-user option which allows multiple users to concurrently run their simulations through their individual machines. This option utilizes the Server Mode of the testbed. As mentioned before, if the testbed needs to be used for the high speed simulation or, by several users at the same time, a non-GUI server option is available. One of the most important prerequisites to use this option is the connection oriented access availability on the server to all the user accounts. This is necessary in order to enable the independent simulation for each user. The core simulation modules need to be installed on the server while users remotely connect to the server using UAVSim. The UAVSim, once configured with the server and connection details, automatically connects to the server and displays results in a console window. It should be noted that the multi-user simulation is only available in non-GUI option.

2.5   Swarm Simulation

Although the simulation testbed was primarily developed for UAVNet security simulation, it also supports the UAV swarm simulation. This feature lets users test the network behavior when large numbers of UAVs are used for any specific application. The use can be commercial, civil or military in nature but in case of swarms, usually it should be a sensor based application with a large number of sensors. The performance for swarm simulation using a large number of nodes has also been evaluated.

3   Performance Results and Analysis

In order to demonstrate the usefulness of the simulation testbed, it is necessary to evaluate its performance using the already available computing infrastructure. Usually, in an academic or research setup, it is difficult to purchase new equipment as soon as it is needed. Therefore, enabling the use of a testbed to allow users to simulate the behavior of such a complicated network in the most cost-effective manner is of utmost importance. It should be noted that all simulations were 300 seconds in length. Other parameters are being varied in different performance tests.

3.1   Number of Wireless Nodes

We first evaluated the system performance with variable number of wireless nodes in the simulation scenario. Two cases were evaluated. Case I being variation of number of attack nodes while Case II involves use of just regular UAV nodes in order to show that UAVSim can be used for simulating UAV swarms as well as UAVNet security.

It is clear from Fig. 2 and 3 that the performance varies linearly (1:1) with the increasing number of malicious nodes. Since malicious nodes are responsible for most of the traffic in the network, the time varies linearly with respect to their number.

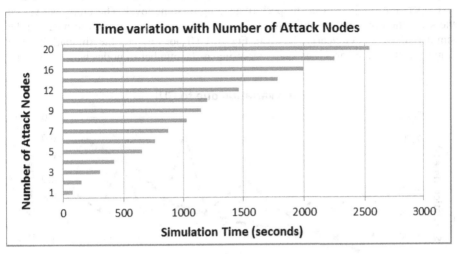

Fig. 2. Simulation time variation with varying number of Attack Nodes

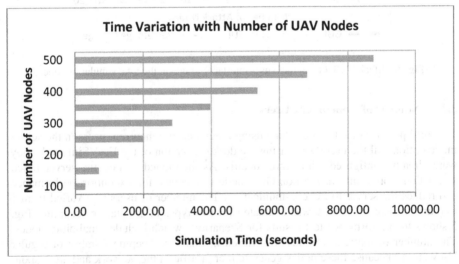

Fig. 3. Simulation time variation with varying number of regular UAV Nodes

Further, if we wish to perform simple UAV simulations using a large number of UAV nodes in absence of malicious nodes, the performance is again linearly dependent on the number of UAV nodes but the variation is about 1:100. This means that the addition of one malicious node would increase the simulation time about the same as adding 100 UAV nodes.

3.2   User Interface

The second performance metric was the user interface. It is clear that having a GUI displaying the network animation and various network statistics during a CPU intensive operation might impact the performance up to some level. Therefore, we varied the simulation parameter similar to the last performance test and tried to measure the simulation speed. As clearly shown in Fig. 4, GUI does impact the simulation up to some extent but the variations keep increasing as the number of nodes was increased.

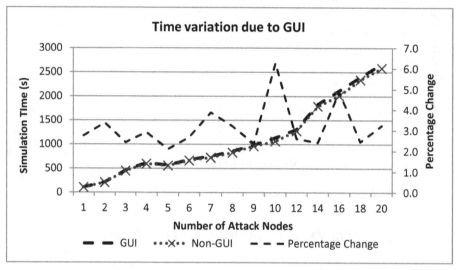

Fig. 4. Effect of GUI (graphical user interface) usage on the total simulation time

3.3   Number of Concurrent Users

The third performance test was done using a number of concurrent users in the server mode option. All the users were using the desktop version of the UAVSim while they were already configured with server details. As mentioned earlier, the server based simulation works only in the non-GUI mode to enhance the execution performance and reduce the server to PC communication. The number of users was varied from 1 to 6 and the execution time was evaluated for two types of simulation scenarios. Fig. 5 shows the performance test results for Scenario I, which included malicious nodes. The number of malicious nodes was varied in this case keeping number of regular UAVs as 10 because these nodes generate more traffic in the network and are responsible for increasing the execution time. On the contrary, Scenario II does not use malicious nodes and uses only regular UAV nodes and the results are shown in Fig. 6. Please note that the two separate vertical axes show the variation of simulation time for two different numbers of nodes in each case. The error bars show the maximum and minimum time while the points depict the average time.

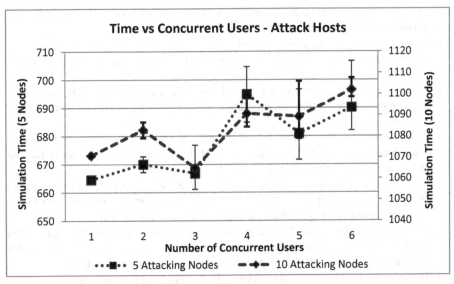

Fig. 5. Impact of number of concurrent users for 5 and 10 attack nodes

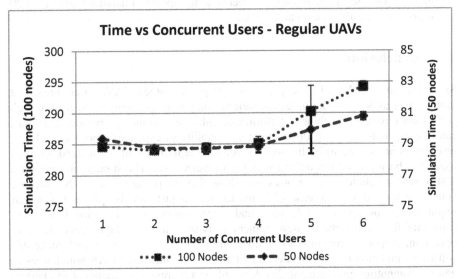

Fig. 6. Impact of number of concurrent users for 50 and 100 regular UAV hosts

3.4   Analysis

Various performance tests performed on UAVSim give us valuable insights in terms of the usability of the testbed. Although some simulation times are quite high in case of swarm simulations of a large number of nodes, for the primary purpose of security simulations, the performance is reasonable. Some important points which can be noted from the analysis are as follows –

- Simulation time varies almost linearly with the number of nodes in case of security simulations while in case of swarm simulations, the simulation time varies exponentially.
- Performing a simulation using the GUI has little impact on the performance. It can be easily inferred that the simulation being processor-intensive, is not affected by the use of graphics.
- Performance analysis for multiple users using the testbed in server mode reveals that the performance does get affected with increasing number of users but the overall percentage variation is less than 5% in all cases.
- Surprisingly, in some cases, the average simulation time is reduced when the number of concurrent users increases. But the variation in minimum and maximum shows that total system performance is not affected that much.
- The attack simulation for 20 attack nodes took less than an hour. Practically, this number would be much less, for example, we need 4 attack nodes for a GPS spoofing attack [18] and thus, the simulation capability is quite extensive.
- The increase in time due to the increase in the number of concurrent users can be easily predicted using the obtained simulation results. Since the variation is not exponential, the simulation testbed seems quite capable of handling more than 20 users concurrently on a regular server.

4   Conclusion

Simulation time analysis for the previously proposed testbed UAVSim are presented in this paper to demonstrate its use in generic computing environment instead of high performance parallel machines. Performance enhancement using advanced machines can't be ignored. However, due to the unavailability of expensive hardware, a lot of researchers are forced to be limited. Therefore, the usability of the testbed for such usage has been proved through various performance tests. The simulation time for a 300-second simulation for various cases show that the performance of the software simulation testbed is quite reasonable and lets user adjust various options as per their requirements. Interactive GUI, additional result analysis module, model browsing capability from other model development software, enhanced high speed mode of operation, support of concurrent users, etc. are some of the features which make this software simulation testbed an ideal simulation environment for UAV simulations in generic computing environment. Work is still in progress for enhancing the performance and adding various other features to make it more user-friendly.

References

1. Aamoth, D.: Delivering Domino's Pizza by Unmanned Helicopter: What Could Possibly Go Wrong? Time Magazine (June 2013).
   http://techland.time.com//06/03/delivering-dominos-pizza-by-unmanned-helicopter-what-could-possibly-go-wrong/#ixzz2rXl0mhfo (last accessed January 2014)

2. Chang, A.: With Prime Air, Amazon plans to deliver purchases via drones. LA Times (December 2013). http://articles.latimes.com/2013/dec/02/business/la-fi-tn-amazon-prime-air-20131202 (last accessed January 2014)
3. Integration of Civil Unmanned Aircraft Systems (UAS) in the National Airspace System (NAS) Roadmap, 1st edn., (2013). http://www.faa.gov/about/initiatives/uas/media/uas_roadmap_2013.pdf (Published November 2013)
4. Lu, P., Geng, Q.: Real-time simulation system for UAV based on Matlab/Simulink. In: 2011 IEEE 2nd International Conference on Computing, Control and Industrial Engineering (CCIE), vol. 1, pp. 399–404 (2011)
5. Zhang, J., Geng, Q, Fei, Q.: UAV flight control system modeling and simulation based on flightGear. In: International Conference on Automatic Control and Artificial Intelligence (ACAI 2012), pp. 2231–2234 (2012)
6. Kim, A., Wampler, B., Goppert, J., Hwang, I.: Cyber Attack Vulnerabilities Analysis for Unmanned Aerial Vehicles. In: Proceedings of Infotech @ Aerospace 2012 Conference, California (2012)
7. Qiang, Y., Bin, X., Yao, Z., Yanping, Y., Haotao, L., Wei, Z.: Visual simulation system for quadrotor unmanned aerial vehicles, 2011 30th Chinese Control Conference (CCC), pp. 454–459 (2011)
8. Brown, T.X., Doshi, S.K., Jadhav, S., Himmelstein, J.: Test Bed for a Wireless Network on Small UAVs. In: Proc. AIAA 3rd Unmanned Unlimited Technical Conference, Chicago, IL (2004)
9. Pereira, E., Sengupta, R., Hedrick, K.: The C3UV Testbed for Collaborative Control and Information Acquisition Using UAVs. In: 2013 American Control Conference, Washington DC, USA (2013)
10. Wu, J., Wang, W., Zhang, J., Wang, B.: Research of a kind of new UAV training simulator based on equipment simulation. In: International Conference on Electronic and Mechanical Engineering and Information Technology (EMEIT), vol. 9, pp. 4812–4815 (2011)
11. Yang, J., Li, H.: UAV Hardware-in-loop Simulation System Based on Right-angle Robot. In: 2012 4th International Conference on Intelligent Human-Machine Systems and Cybernetics (IHMSC), vol. 1, pp. 58–61 (2012)
12. Corner, J.J., Lamont, G.B.: Parallel simulation of UAV swarm scenarios. In: Proceedings of the 2004 Winter Simulation Conference, pp 355–363 (2004)
13. Hamilton, S., Hamilton, Jr., J.A.D., Schmoyer, Col. T.: Validating a network simulation testbed for army UAVs, In: Proceedings of the 2007 Winter Simulation Conference, WSC 2007, Washington (2007)
14. Chaumette, S., Laplace, R., Mazely, C., Miraulty, R.: SCUAL, Swarm of Communicating UAVs at LaBRI: an open UAVNet testbed. In: 2011 14th International Symposium on Wireless Personal Multimedia Communications (WPMC), France (2011)
15. Javaid, A., Sun, W., Devabhaktuni, V.K., Alam, M.: Cyber Security Threat Analysis and Modeling of an Unmanned Aerial Vehicle System. In: Proceeding of Conference on Homeland Security Technologies 2012, Boston (2012)
16. Javaid, A., Sun, W., Alam, M., UAVSim: A Simulation Testbed for Unmanned Aerial Vehicle Network Cyber Security Analysis. In: Proceeding of International Workshop on Wireless Networking and Control for Unmanned Autonomous Vehicles, Wi-UAV, Atlanta, GA (2013)
17. Varga, A.: The OMNeT++ discrete event simulation system. In: Proc. of the European Simulation Multiconference, Prague, Czech Republic (2001)
18. Tippenhauer, N.O., Pöpper, C., Rasmussen, K.B., Capkun, S.: On the requirements for successful GPS spoofing attacks. In: Proc. of the 18th ACM conference on Computer and communications security (2011)

Vehicular Inter-Networking via Named Data – An OPNET Simulation Study

Dung Ong Mau[1], Yin Zhang[1], Tarik Taleb[2], and Min Chen[1(✉)]

[1] School of Computer Science and Technology,
Huazhong University of Science and Technology,
1037 Luoyu Road, Wuhan 430074, China
omdung@gmail.com, {yin.zhang.cn,minchen}@ieee.org
[2] NEC Laboratories Europe, NEC Europe Ltd., Kurfrsten-Anlage 36,
69115 Heidelberg, Germany
talebtarik@ieee.org

Abstract. Named Data Networking (NDN) is proposed for effective content distribution when a large number of end-users demand for popular content at the same time. In this paper, NDN is implemented in Vehicular Ad-hoc NETwork (VANET) to meet its particular requirements, such that all of vehicles refer to the real time traffic status for safe driving. We propose Vehicular Named Data Networking according to three different vehicle communication mechanisms, which are vehicle-to-infrastructure (V2I), a hybrid of vehicle to road side unit (V2R) and vehicle to vehicle (V2V). Furthermore, this paper illustrates the experimental results conducted by OPNET Modeler, and proves that the solution with NDN enhances the Quality of Service (QoS) of VANET significantly.

Keywords: VANET · LTE · NDN · QoS

1 Introduction

Vehicular Ad-hoc NETwork (VANET) is the technique that uses moving vehicles as wireless nodes in a mobile network. And each wireless node takes a role as an end-user and wireless router to create a wide range communication. Motivated by the increasing demand for efficient and reliable information dissemination and retrieval, the Named Data Networking (NDN) architecture presents a simple and effective communication model [1]. In NDN, an interest packet (IntPk) and a data packet (DataPk) are two packet types mainly used to identify a content, which is typical hierarchical and human readable. NDN node maintains three data structures: Forwarding Information Base (FIB), Pending Interest Table (PIT) and Content Store (CS). Once NDN node receives a IntPk, it will lookup for a content in the CS. If the appropriate content is found, the DataPk will be send for a request, otherwise the IntPk will be checked in the PIT. The PIT takes a role to keep track on unsatisfied IntPks. After the PIT creates a new entry for unsatisfied IntPk, which is forwarded to upstream toward to a

© Institute for Computer Sciences, Social Informatics and Telecommunications Engineering 2014
V.C.M. Leung et al. (Eds.): TridentCom 2014, LNICST 137, pp. 116–125, 2014.
DOI: 10.1007/978-3-319-13326-3_12

potential content source based on the FIB's information. A returned DataPk will be sent to downstream and stored on the CS buffer. To maximize the probability of sharing and minimize upstream bandwidth demand, the CS should keep all arrived DataPks as long as possible. When the CS is about to get full or receive a new content, it will store the new one according to the replacement policy to leave space for the new content. Least Recently Used (LRU) and Least Frequently Used (LFU) are two dedicated replacement policies in original NDN. In [2], Giulio et al. propose V-NDN, applying the NDN to networking vehicles on the run. However, the design just illustrates NDNs promising potential to providing a unifying architecture, but does not provide more details about its feasibility, performance and practicability.

In this paper, we propose our solution, *Vehicular Named Data Networking*, by inheriting the basic principle of the NDN. However, extending the NDN model to the VANET is not straightforward application due to a lot of challenges in the vehicle environment such as the limited and intermittent connectivity, and the node mobility. The contribution of the paper as follows. We first introduce some meeting challenges in different types of vehicle communication mechanism. Then we discuss and evaluate the benefits brought by the NDN. The two schemes LRU and LFU are successfully constructed in the NDN node. Motivation from the NDN model simulation, the Vehicular Named Data Networking performance is taken into account by clearly comparison the VANET under two scenarios: with typical clients-server connection and with NDN connection.

The remainder of this paper is organized as follows. Section 2 provides the VANET background, and reactive routing applied for the NDN. Section 3 illustrates simulation and evaluation results for basic NDN model. Then, Section 4 portrays envisioned Vehicular Named Data Networking architecture of the simulation setup and discusses simulation results. Finally, Section 5 concludes this paper.

2   Background

2.1   VANET: An Overview

In vehicle-to-infrastructure (V2I) network, assistance transmission networks are required, such as 2.5G, 3G, 4G, to centrally manage all the vehicles communication [3]. With handover technique between radio cells, vehicles always keep pace with a server supplied VANET applications. For instance, a serving distance of mobile base stations operated at $900MHz$ carrier frequency is typically from $2km$ in microcell up to $35km$ in macrocell. Therefore, vehicles are least to handover between base stations. For this reason, proactive routing is utilized in V2I network. In this paper, we propose to use the latest cellular network: Long Term Evolution (LTE) [4] for V2I scheme.

Fig. 1(a) shows an example of V2I communication in LTE network. *Road-Side Units (RSUs)* are cameras to capture the road traffic status. An end point connection to RSUs can be LTE, Wireless Fidelity (WiFi) or wide area network (WAN). Vehicle subscribers request and receive an updated road traffic status

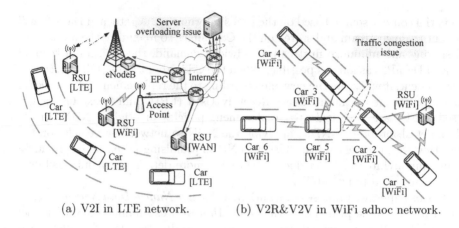

(a) V2I in LTE network.   (b) V2R&V2V in WiFi adhoc network.

Fig. 1. Two aspects of vehicle communication

from the server through LTE. Because of a large number of RSUs and vehicle subscribers, the server is easy to meet an overloading issue. Moreover, the current mobile networks are centralized management, e.g. in Long Term Evolution (LTE) network, all of Internet mobile traffic are come in and come out via the Evolved Packet Core (EPC) entity, leading to high requirement for a backbone mobile traffic. Especially in traffic jams, a group of nearby vehicles often requires the same information from the server (e.g. traffic status), which poses high redundancy contents in the backbone transmission.

In a hybrid network, vehicle-to-RSU (V2R) and vehicle-to-vehicle (V2V), multi-hop networking and a short range communication are critical. Typically, dedicated short range communication (DSRC) and wireless access in vehicular environments (WAVE) are utilized to directly exchange data between adjacent vehicles. However, with advances in smart-phone and tablet, the huge number of VANET applications are designed and installed on smart-phone by using available WiFi module on the mobile devices. The infrastructure-less network based on vehicles has greater challenges than fixed wireless networks caused by various speeds, traffic patterns, and driving environments. Therefore, reactive routing should be used in V2R&V2V scheme. Fig. 1(b) shows an example of V2R&V2V communication in WiFi ad-hoc network. At the wireless router node (e.g. Car_2) and RSU, they meet a traffic congestion issue when a huge number of vehicle subscribers are nearby RSU and request content at the same time. In this scheme, WiFi route may be the bottleneck of data transmission because all of wireless nodes share the bandwidth for the communication.

Due to the existing issues in VANET, both of V2I and V2R&V2V are proposed to implement with Named Data Networking (NDN) for better network performance (e.g. network traffic offloading, reducing traffic congestion and lower round trip time) than the typical clients-server connection [5].

2.2 Reactive Routing in NDN

In reactive routing, both a request node and an intermediate nodes do not have a routing table which is known as the FIB entity in NDN mechanism. For a wireless ad-hoc network to setup a reverse path from the server to an end-user, flooding is a fundamental mechanism to implement the multi-hop broadcasting the IntPk in order to build up the reverse path. However, broadcasting scheme causes several issues as follows; i.e., *i)* a burst transmission is generated by broadcasting all of received IntPks. Flooding in many cases, especially in a dense network, introduces significant communication overhead due to redundant re-broadcasting. *ii)* A loop network in routing is occurred when more than two intermediate nodes are within a radio range communication. And *iii)* a data burst of responding traffic is generated because there may exist many reverse paths from the server to the client. To alleviate the well-known broadcast storm problem, all broadcasting methods in VANET utilize position information to identify the next relay node. However, in the real-life scenario, a vehicle does not have knowledge about position information of both neighboring vehicles and RSUs. In order to restrict the number of nodes relaying the broadcasting data without addition requirement information, we suggest to minimize a hop count between the RSU and the target vehicle. The minimum hop count is taken place at intermediate nodes by checking the hop count value embedded in arrived IntPks before broadcasting. Typically, the first arrived packet in a bunch of new IntPk always has a minimum hop count and will be broadcasted. Then, all the same IntPk arrived later should be deleted. Fig. 2 shows the main operations for NDN vehicles.

3 Basic NDN Network Architecture

To evaluate the performance of NDN mechanism, we implemented NDN and conducted simulations using the OPNET Modeler 16.0 [6][7]. There are many simulators for VANET but none of them can provide a complete solution for simulating VANETs [8][9]. Among a number of simulation tools such as Vanet-MobiSim, SUMO, NS2, QualNet, etc., we would like to use OPNET because it supports for a realistic mobile network environment (e.g. 2.5G/3G/4G). In the simulation, NDN is overlayed over the IP layer. Indeed, we integrated the NDN processing modules into all network elements, such as mobile stations (MSs), Evolved Node B (eNodeB), routers, PCs, servers and IP Cloud.

3.1 Network Architecture

With every intention to consider a typical Internet network topology, we assumes the network topology as same as shown in Fig. 3 and we apply our new caching policies in both WAN and LTE network. The simulation LTE network includes three cells with 2000 meters of diameter for the radio coverage in each cell. Each cell has 1 eNodeB, 1 NDN processor node and 25 LTE MSs. And all the MSs

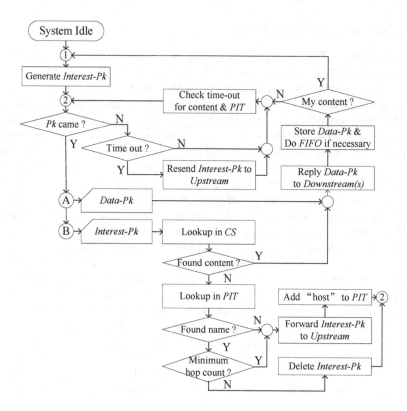

Fig. 2. NDN vehicle flow chart

request video content from the same server following a power function distribution. For example, a *Pareto* distribution: 20 MSs (80% traffic) request popular video contents while the other 5 MSs (20% traffic) request unpopular video items. There are two scenarios in the simulation,they are LRU and LFU, respectively. Hitting rate, coverage time to final state and a percentage of traffic offloading are important metrics to be verified in the simulation results. There are the same configuration and scenarios in WAN network. The simulation parameters we selected to reflect real-world implementations of in-network caching refers to the related work [10][11]. The simulations were run multiple times and the presented results are an average of these runs.

3.2   Performance Evaluation for Basic NDN Model

We first evaluate the performance of different content caching/replacement policies for different cache sizes. Let a relative cache size denote for the percentage of a cache size over a catalog size. In Fig. 4(a), the relative cache size in NDN node is increased by 0.06%, 0.1%, 0.16% and 0.2%. It should be noted that in the simulation, the catalog size(500000 files) is much greater than the cache size

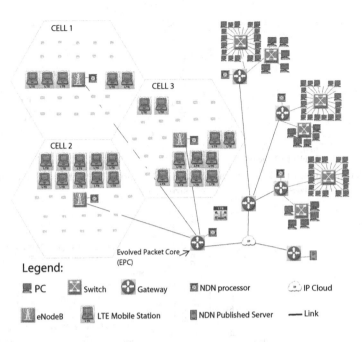

Fig. 3. Envisioned NDN network architecture

(equal or less than 1000 files). Therefore, the relative cache size is equal to or less than 0.2%.

In Fig. 4(a), the simulation results show that high hitting rates can be achieved with high cache sizes for all the simulated policies. In this figure, it is obvious that the increment of the hitting rate is not linear to the cache volume. Moreover, it also indicates that when the relative size is equal to 0.16%, the cache can handle most requests for popular contents. However, increasing to 0.2% the performance degrades, because of the tradeoff between cache volume (cost) and performance. Hence, there is consequently need to retrieve a suitable cache size.

In Fig. 4(b), it illustrates the LRU and LFU performance comparison when the relative cache size is set to 0.16%. The figure shows that LRU is just slightly higher than LFU. In Fig. 4(c), it illustrates the further comparison LRU and LFU for different relative cache sizes. Fig. 4(d) shows amount of traffic responding by the server under LRU and LFU schemes and relative cache size 0.1%. With higher hitting rate, lower requested traffic is fetched to the server, then higher percentage of traffic offloading is achieved. Because LRU and LFU have quite similar hitting rate, their capable of traffic offloading are similar too.

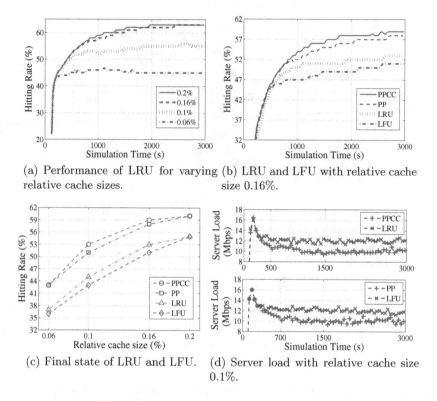

(a) Performance of LRU for varying relative cache sizes.

(b) LRU and LFU with relative cache size 0.16%.

(c) Final state of LRU and LFU.

(d) Server load with relative cache size 0.1%.

Fig. 4. LRU and LFU performance comparison

4   Simulation and Results

4.1   Network Simulation

Motivation from the NDN model simulation, we enhance Vehicular Named Data Networking simulation with two scenarios: V2I network and V2R&V2V network. V2I network simulation is illustrated in Fig. 5(a). There are three cells in LTE network, and each cell includes an eNodeB connected with NDN node. The eNodeB provides a radio communication within 2000 meters range while NDN node is added component to implement NDN protocol. Two RSUs that are implemented in each LTE cell, generate content with $64Kbps$ rate and transmit content to a server over LTE network. Data from different RSUs are distinguished by RSU identification (RSU_ID) and current geometric location. The server stores all received data from RSUs, and send the corresponding content to vehicles and NDN nodes. There are ten vehicles equipped with LTE mobile station. While vehicles are moving with $20km/h$ speed, they continuously send IntPks attached with their current geometric location (e.g. five seconds every IntPk), which is used to determine an appropriate content on the server/NDN node.

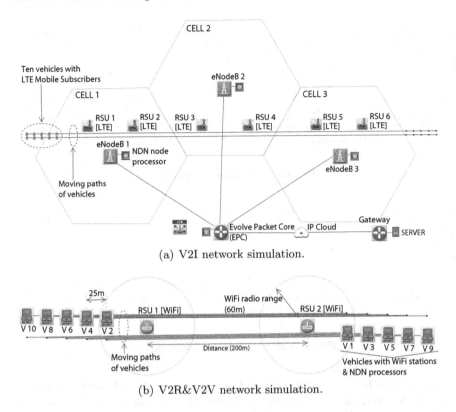

(a) V2I network simulation.

(b) V2R&V2V network simulation.

Fig. 5. VANDNET simulation

Fig. 5(b) demonstrates V2R&V2V network. There are two RSUs placed 200 meters apart. Ten vehicles divided into two groups moved slowly on two direction with $5km/h$ speed. Both RSUs and vehicles are equipped with WiFi card operated under IEEE802.11g standard and within 60 meters radio range. When the two flows of vehicles meet together, a traffic explosion caused by IntPks and DataPks happens. This scenario is useful to compare network performance between with and without NDN application. It should be noted that the typical speed of vehicles is about $40 - 80km/h$. However, we would like to determine the responding of the Vehicular Named Data Networking model in some of the worst situations, i.e., *i)* a group of vehicles move very slowly at handover areas in LTE/WiFi, and *ii)* a long time of the traffic explosion caused by IntPks and DataPks.

4.2   Simulation Results

Fig. 6(a) shows the vehicles would receive similar data results with or without NDN, but the data sent by the server is different. Without caching, all requests are fetched to the server which poses high redundancy content replied by the

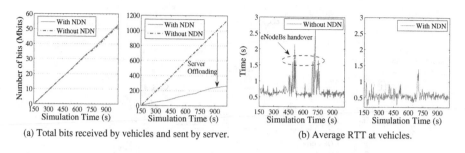

(a) Total bits received by vehicles and sent by server.   (b) Average RTT at vehicles.

Fig. 6. V2I simulation results

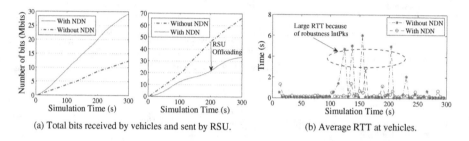

(a) Total bits received by vehicles and sent by RSU.   (b) Average RTT at vehicles.

Fig. 7. V2R&V2V simulation results

server. With caching, eNodeBs use available content to directly reply for IntPks from vehicles, and make the request bit rate received by the server to be reduced significantly. Fig. 6(b) shows the different results of round trip time (RTT) at vehicles with or without NDN schemes. A trajectory of ten vehicles are setup to move together and handover between eNodeBs around the 450th and the 750th second. At the roaming moment, vehicles are failed to received content, then they resent IntPks again to the server/NDN node. In the scheme with NDN, eNodeBs only need one content from server to reply all vehicles, while in the scheme without NDN, the server needs to send the same multiple copy of content to all vehicles.

Fig. 7(a) shows the different results between total bits sent by the RSUs and total bits received by the vehicle, which are caused by the following three reasons; i.e., *i)* with NDN mechanism, a minimum of IntPk is forwarded to the RSU, then a minimum of DataPk is sent out by RSU while with a typical clients-server connection, the RSU needs to reply all IntPks from vehicles. *ii)* With NDN mechanism, the IntPk can be intermediately satisfied by multiple one hop neighbor vehicles, while without NDN, the IntPk is only replied by the server. And *iii)* regarding to the bottleneck of WiFi link, all stations share the same physical channel. So that, the RSU and intermediate wireless nodes follows a *first in first serve* (FIFS) policy to serve for all stations. Fig. 7(b) presents an average RTT at vehicles. From the 100th to the 200th second, the traffic explosion is happened, and with NDN mechanism assistant, the RTT stability at vehicles is better than clients-server mechanism.

5   Conclusion

In this paper, we introduced the NDN with two original replacement policies that assist to off-load the traffic of the IP backbone as well as the server. Furthermore, we implement the Vehicular Named Data Networking model with two novel networks: V2I and V2R&V2V, respectively. The performance of the NDN model and the Vehicular Named Data Networking model were evaluated using computer simulations. With the obtained results, it is proved that NDN mechanism can improve the performance of the network significantly. In the future work, the Vehicular Named Data Networking model should be evaluated under various scenarios with a huge number of vehicles, mobility patterns and the prototype.

References

1. Jacobson, V., Smetters, D., Thornton, J., Plass, M., Briggs, N., Braynard, R.: Networking named content. Communication of the ACM **55**(1), 117–124 (2012)
2. Grassi, G., Pesavento, D., Wang, L., et al.: ACM HotMobile 2013 poster: vehicular inter-networking via named data. ACM SIGMOBILE Mobile Computing and Communications Review **17**(3), 23–24 (2013)
3. Yu, Y., Punihaole, T., Gerla, M., Sanadidi, M.Y.: Content Routing In the Vehicle Cloud. Military Communication **2012**, 1–6 (2012)
4. Zheng, K., Liu, F., Xiang, W., Xin, X.: Dynamic downlink aggregation carrier scheduling scheme for wireless networks. IET Communications **8**(1), 114–123 (2014)
5. TalebiFard, P., Leung, V.C.M.: A Content-Centric Perspective to Crowd-sensing in Vehicular Networking. In: Journal of Systems Architecture, 59(10) (2013).
6. OPNET Modeler. Available: www.opnet.com.
7. Chen, M.: OPNET Network Simulation, Press of Tsinghua University, ISBN 7-302-08232-4 (2004)
8. Martinez, F.J., Toh, C.K., Cano, J., Calafate, C.T., Manzoni, P.: A survey and comparative study of simulators for vehicular ad hoc networks (VANETs). Wireless Communications and Mobile Computing **11**(7), 813–828 (2011)
9. NS-3 based Named Data Networking (NDN) simulator. Available: http://ndnsim. net/index.html
10. Li, J., Wu, H., Liu, B., Lu, J., Wang, Y., Wang, X., Zhang, Y., Dong, L.: Popularity-driven Coordinated Caching in Named Data Networking. In: ACM/IEEE symposium on Architectures for networking and communications systems (ANCS), pp. 15–26 (Oct. 2012)
11. Rossi, D., Rossini, G.: Caching performance of content centric networks under multi-path routing (and more). Telecom ParisTech, Technical report, Paris, France (2011)

AnaVANET: An Experiment and Visualization Tool for Vehicular Networks

Manabu Tsukada[1]([✉]), José Santa[2,3], Satoshi Matsuura[4],
Thierry Ernst[5], and Kazutoshi Fujikawa[4]

[1] INRIA Paris - Rocquencourt, Le Chesnay, France
manabu.tsukada@inria.fr, tsukada@hongo.wide.ad.jp
[2] University Centre of Defence at the Spanish Air Force Academy, San Javier, Spain
[3] University of Murcia, Murcia, Spain
jose.santa@cud.upct.es, josesanta@um.es
[4] Nara Institute of Science and Technology, Nara, Japan
matsuura@is.naist.jp, fujikawa@itc.naist.jp
[5] CAOR Lab, Mines ParisTech, Paris, France
thierry.ernst@mines-paristech.fr

Abstract. The experimental evaluation of wireless and mobile networks is a challenge that rarely substitutes simulation in research works. This statement is even more evident in vehicular communications, due to the equipment and effort needed to obtain significant and realistic results. In this paper, key issues in vehicular experimental evaluation are analyzed by an evaluation tool called AnaVANET, especially designed for assessing the performance of vehicular networks. This software processes the output of well-known testing tools such as *ping* or *iperf*, together with navigation information, to generate geo-aware performance figures of merit both in numeric and graphical forms. Its main analysis capabilities are used to validate the good performance in terms of delay, packet delivery ratio and throughput of NEMO, when using a road-side segment based on IPv6 GeoNetworking.

Keywords: Vehicular Ad-hoc Networks · Experimental Evaluation · Wireless Multihop Communication · Network Mobility · Visualization Tool

1 Introduction

Vehicular networks are essential for Intelligent Transportation Systems (ITS) to optimize the road traffic and achieve safe, efficient and comfortable human mobility. Essentially, there are two main communication paradigms in vehicular communications, vehicle to vehicle (V2V) and vehicle to infrastructure (V2I), depending on whether the communication is performed directly between vehicles or using nodes locally or remotely installed on the road infrastructure.

When the V2V paradigm is considered, the research field is commonly called Vehicular Ad-hoc Networks, or VANET. Although there are a lot of works related

© Institute for Computer Sciences, Social Informatics and Telecommunications Engineering 2014
V.C.M. Leung et al. (Eds.): TridentCom 2014, LNICST 137, pp. 126–135, 2014.
DOI: 10.1007/978-3-319-13326-3_13

to VANET applications and basic research at physical, MAC and network layers, there is a significant lack of real evaluation analysis in this field, due to cost and effort implications. A number of experimentation works and supporting tools should be improved in the short term, in order to give real evidences to car manufacturers and road operators of the benefits of vehicular communications.

Conventional network measurement tools (e.g. *iperf*, *ping* or *traceroute*) assume fixed networks and assess network performances in a end-to-end basis. However, under dynamic network conditions such as in the vehicular networks case, it is difficult to measure detailed status of networks by using solely these tools, because vehicles are always changing their location and the performance of wireless channels fluctuates. In order to solve these issues, we have developed a packet analysis and visualization tool called AnaVANET [1], which considers the peculiarities of the vehicular environment for providing an exhaustive evaluation software for outdoor scenarios. Both V2V and V2I networks can be efficiently analyzed, thanks to the integrated features for collecting results, post-processing data, generate graphical figures of merit and, finally, publish the results in a dedicated web site (if desired).

The rest of the paper is organized as follows. Section 2 introduces the readers about the network layer protocols in vehicular networks experimentation. Then, the issues and requirements for evaluating vehicular networks are listed in Section 3. The evaluation methodology desired in this frame is described in Section 4 and, as a result of our analysis, the design and implementation of the AnaVANET evaluation tool is detailed in Section 5, together with a reference evaluation of a network testbed using the tool in Section 6. Finally, Section 7 concludes the paper summarizing the main results and addressing future works.

2   Network Protocols in Vehicular Networks

Network protocols in vehicular networks can be classified in infrastructure-less scenarios, i.e. V2V, and infrastructure-based scenarios, i.e. V2I, as showed in Fig. 1.

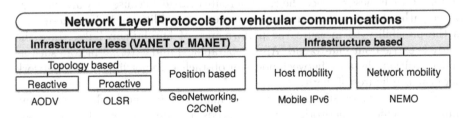

Fig. 1. Network Protocols in vehicular networks

The infrastructure-less scenario is well-known by the research area of VANET or Mobile Ad-hoc Networks (MANET). These approaches are designed to enable

---

[1] http://anavanet.net/

wireless communications in dynamic topologies without any infrastructure. Routing protocols here are further classified as *topology-based* and *position-based* routing protocols. Topology-based protocols were divided into two main branches by the IETF MANET working group: *reactive*, where nodes periodically exchange messages to create routes (*e.g.* AODV [1]), and *proactive*, in which control messages are exchanged on demand when it is necessary to reach a particular node (*e.g.* OLSR [2]).

Unlike topology based routing, position based routing does not need to maintain part of the network structure in order to forward packets towards the destination node. When routing packets based on position, nodes forward the packets with the aim of reaching the nodes within a geographical location. Thus, position based routing can eliminate the problem that appears in topology based protocols when routes become quickly unavailable in high mobility scenarios. In Greedy Perimeter Stateless Routing (GPSR) [3], for instance, the intermediate nodes make a decision based on the destination position and neighbor positions. The Car-to-Car Communication Consortium (C2CC) also specified the C2CNet protocol, which was later enhanced by the GeoNet project to support IPv6. Within the ITS standardization domain, GeoNetworking [4] is being completed by ETSI at the moment, integrating several geo-aware strategies to better route packets in vehicular networks.

On the other side, infrastructure-based protocols have been focused on the global connectivity of nodes to the Internet. Mobile IPv6 [5] solved the mobility problem for mobile hosts and, later, Network Mobility Basic support (NEMO) [6] provided a solution for the mobility of a whole network (e.g. a vehicle or bus), which has been recommended by the ISO TC204 WG16 to achieve Internet mobility for vehicles.

3   Issues and Requirements for VANET Evaluation

Using multi-hop and dynamic routing strategies presents a challenge in the evaluation of vehicular networks. Common end-to-end evaluation tools such as *ping6* and *iperf* are useless to track the effect of route change, because they are unaware of the path taken during a communication test. An additional lack of these tools is the possibility to measure the performance of hop-by-hop links, since the study is carried out end-to-end. Also, geographical and external factors such as nodes position, distance between nodes or obstacles are not linked with network performance figures of merit.

With the aim of summarizing these main requirements when evaluating multi-hop vehicular networks, the next needs are found essential by the software tools used in experimental campaigns for evaluating both V2V and V2I:

Path detection. The topology of a vehicular network with dynamic routing changes frequently as vehicles move, and the communication path is changed accordingly. Thus, the tool should take note of the communication path used in every moment.

Communication performance in links. Once the communication path is tracked, the tool should measure the performance in a link-by-link as well as end-to-end basis.

Geographical awareness. The network performance in a link depends on various geographical factors, such as the distance between the nodes, the movement speed and direction, and the existence of obstacles in the communication link. Thus, the evaluation tool should take the above geographical factors into account.

Intuitive visualization. Performance figures of merit and environmental information should be shown together in a synchronized way, and the spatio-temporal data series should be available in post process to play them at different speeds, stop when desired, or replayed freely as he or she wants.

Independence from network protocols. Given the various network layer protocols in vehicular communications, the evaluation tool should be independent from the one chosen.

Independent from devices. Since the configuration of vehicle and infrastructure devices may differ, the evaluation tool should not rely on any specific device functionality.

Adaptation to various scenarios. The software evaluation tool should accommodate to all possible communication scenarios (moving or static, urban or highway, etc.).

Easiness for data collection. Since a lot of experiments could be needed in a extensive campaign, the easiness of gathering data and deploying software modules in devices is essential.

As it is later described, the evaluation tool presented in this work (Ana-VANET) copes with the previous requirements.

4 Evaluation Methodology

The evaluation goals are to analyze which *testing conditions* affect which *data flows or network protocols*. For achieving this end it is necessary to design a proper evaluation methodology. Within it we should consider the tendency of results by repeating tests with the same settings or varying parameters under study, such as the network protocol, the mobility of nodes or the data volume. The overall analysis should be supported by a proper evaluation tool, such as the later presented **AnaVANET**. This section details both the testing conditions and the possible routing protocols to consider, as it is summarized in Fig. 2, by introducing the concept and presenting our real use case for testing the performance of NEMO over IPv6 GeoNetworking.

4.1 Testing Conditions

Testbed Platform. The testbed used for the evaluation of a network architecture should be carefully chosen to implement most relevant nodes in real software

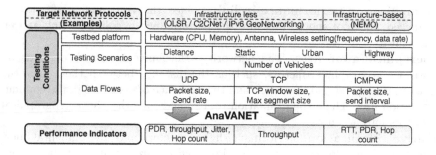

Fig. 2. Evaluation Methodology

and hardware. In vehicular communications, this is extremely important, since a good deployment could be needed in case of testing V2V multi-hop networks.

In our particular case, the testbed comprises a set of four vehicles and two roadside stations, as illustrated in Fig. 3. Each vehicle is equipped with a mobile router (MR), with at least two interfaces: an Ethernet link to connect mobile network nodes (MNNs) within the in-vehicle network, and a wireless adapter in ad-hoc mode used for both V2V and V2I communications. On the roadside, access routers (ARs) are prepared to be fixed on the top of a building or any other elevated point near the road. Each one provides two interfaces: an Ethernet link for a wired Internet access, and a wireless adapter in ad-hoc mode to connect with vehicles in the surroundings. At a backend point in the Internet, a home agent (HA) is installed to support Internet mobility of MRs by using NEMO.

Among the various testbed conditions, the hardware specification (CPU, memory, etc), antenna and wireless settings are important factors for the evaluation, since they will highly affect the results. In our case, MRs are Alix3d3 embedded boxes provided with a Linux 2.6.29.6 kernel. Each MR has a mini-pci wireless card Atheros AR5414 802.11 a/b/g Rev 0, and an antenna 2.4GHz 9dBi indoor OMNI RP-SMA6 is used. The frequency used has been 2.422Ghz and the data rate has been fixed to 6 Mbits/s.

Testing Scenarios. Fixing the evaluation scenarios beforehand is essential in the planning of a testing campaign. In general, the main factors that determine the possible scenarios are:

Mobility. Static scenarios can be chosen to test the network operation in a controlled way, but also dynamic ones can be used in a realistic evaluation. A dynamic scenario is considered in our case.

Location. The place in which the tests are carried out impacts on the network performance, due to signal propagation blockage issues above all. In our case a semi-urban scenario is used within the INRIA-Rocquencourt installations.

Number of vehicles. The number of hops between the source and the destination vehicles affect the communication delay and the higher probability of packet looses, due to route changes or MAC transmission issues. Up to four vehicles are considered in our case.

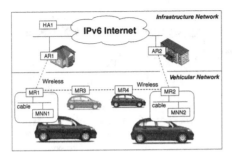

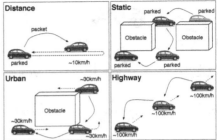

Fig. 3. Network Configuration   **Fig. 4.** Movement Scenarios

As summarized in Fig. 4, testing scenarios have been divided into urban and highway; mobility has been set to static, urban-like speed, and high speed.

4.2 Data Flows and Performance Indicators

A number or protocols and data flows can be set for evaluations, however, only the most representative and more used in the literature should be considered to study concrete performance indicators. For instance, in our case UDP, TCP and ICMPv6 are used to measure the network performance between two communication end-nodes (MNN to MNN) mounted within two vehicles:

UDP is a connection-less unidirectional transmission flow. The traffic is generated by *iperf* in our case. It is considered that with UDP the performance indicators under consideration can be the packet delivery ratio (PDR), throughput and jitter.

TCP is a connection-oriented bidirectional transmission flow. This traffic is also generated by *iperf* in our case. The performance indicator under consideration here has been the maximum throughput.

ICMPv6 is a bi-directional transmission flow. The traffic is generated by *ping6* in our case. The performance indicator under consideration can be the road trip delay time (RTT) and PDR.

5 System Design and Implementation of AnaVANET

AnaVANET (initially standing for Analyzer of VANET) is an evaluation tool implemented in Java to assess the performance of vehicular networks. It takes as input the logs generated by the *iperf*, *tcpdump* and/or *ping6*, together with navigation information in NMEA format, to compute the next performance metrics: network throughput, delay, jitter, hop count and list of intermediate nodes in the communication path, PDR end-to-end and hop-by-hop, speed, and instantaneous position.

AnaVANET is put in the context of the evaluation scenario described in the previous section in Fig. 5 , showing also the main inputs and outputs of the tool.

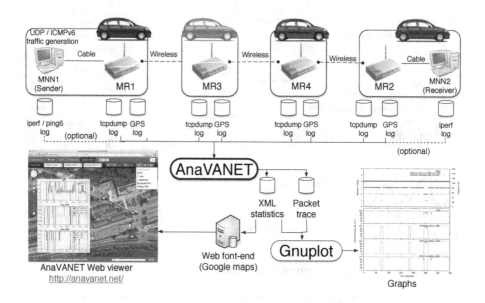

Fig. 5. Overview of AnaVANET

The sender MNN (left most vehicle) is in charge of generating data traffic, and both the sender and the receiver (right most vehicle) MNNs record a high level log, according to the application used to generate network traffic (*iperf* and *ping6* for the moment). All MRs record information about forwarded data packets by means of the *tcpdump* tool, and log the vehicle position continuously. All this data is post-processed by the AnaVANET core software and then analyzed. The tool traces all the data packets transmitted from the sender node to detect packet losses and calculate statistics for each link and end-to-end, and then merge all these per-hop information with transport level statistics of the traffic generator. As a result, AnaVANET outputs an XML file with statistics on a one-second basis, and a packet trace file with the path followed by each data packet.

Once generated, performance metrics can be graphically showed through plots generated by *gnuplot* and a website where all tests are available. The screenshot of the website is shown in left bottom of Fig. 5. Accessing the website one can replay the tests on a map to see momentary figures of merit.

On the map, the position and movement of the vehicle are depicted with the speed of each vehicle and the distance between them. The transferred data size, bandwidth, packet loss rate, RTT and jitter, for each link and end-to-end are displayed. The network performance is visualized by the width of links and the colors used to draw them.

6   Evaluation of NEMO over IPv6 GeoNetworking

Early versions of AnaVANET were designed for evaluating infrastructure less network protocols, as used in our previous works for analyzing OLSR in vehicular environments [7] and later tests of IPv6 over C2CNet [8] in the FP7 GeoNet project.

The current version of AnaVANET can also analyze infrastructure-based network protocols such as NEMO. In this section, we report a summary of the results collected in the evaluation of NEMO over IPv6 GeoNetworking when a vehicle connects with a node located in the Internet using two roadside units as access routers. The *umip.org*[2] implementation of NEMO is used and the *cargeo6.org*[3] software is used for IPv6 GeoNetworking. ICMPv6 and UDP evaluations in handover scenarios were performed at INRIA Paris-Rocquencourt campus with the two ARs previously presented in the testbed description. The speed of the vehicle was limited to less than 15 km/h, like in a low mobility urban scenario. The reader can directly click in Fig. 6 - Fig. 9 to see the correspondent result in the AnaVANET web viewer, to further perceive the details of the gathered results.

ICMPv6 echo requests (64 bytes) are sent from the MNN to a common computer located in the wired network twice in a second, which replies with ICMPv6 echo replies. The results collected in the ICMPv6 tests are plotted in Fig. 6. The lower part shows the itinerary of the vehicle and the locations of AR1 and AR2 on the map, whereas the upper part shows the RTT, the packet loss and the result of the mobility signaling. The X-axis and the Y-axis of the upper part are the latitude and the longitude of the vehicle, corresponding to the road stretch indicated in the lower part of the figure. When either the request or the reply is lost, the RTT is marked with a zero value and, at the same time, a packet loss is indicated. A binding registration success is plotted when the NEMO binding update (BU) and the corresponding binding acknowledgment (BA) are successfully processed. On the contrary, if either of them is lost, a binding registration fail is plotted at the position.

Fig. 7 shows the same results of the test, but referred to the test time. The upper graph shows the RTT and the distance to the two ARs; the middle one shows the PDR obtained with the two ARs; and, finally, the lower plot shows the status of the NEMO signaling. A NEMO success means that the binding registration has been successfully performed, and a fail indicates that either the BU or the BA has been lost.

The results collected in the UDP tests are plotted in Fig. 8. UDP packets are sent from the MNN to the wired node at a rate of 1 Mbps and a length of 1250 bytes. The lower part of the figure shows the itinerary of the vehicle, and the upper part corresponds to the PDR obtained with the ARs and the binding registration results, as in the previous case. The road stretch is the same one used above, but the vehicle moves on the contrary direction in this case.

In the time-mapped results showed in Fig. 9, the upper graph shows the UDP throughput from the MNN to the wired node, the middle part shows the PDR to the two ARs, and the lower plots the status of the NEMO signaling. Success of NEMO status means that the binding registration is successfully performed and Fail means that either the BU or the BA is lost.

---

[2] http://umip.org
[3] http://www.cargeo6.org

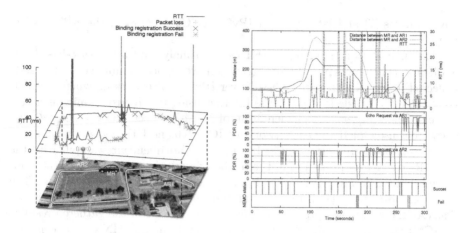

Fig. 6. Map-based RTT, Packet Losses and Mobility Signaling of ICMP evaluation in a handover scenario

Fig. 7. RTT, Packet Loss and Mobility Signaling of ICMP evaluation in a handover scenario

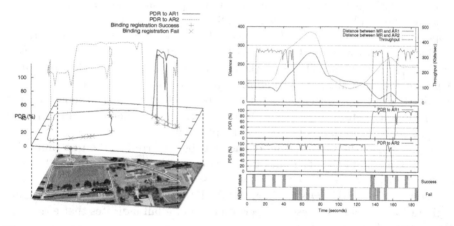

Fig. 8. Map-based PDR of UDP evaluation using NEMO over IPv6 GeoNetworking

Fig. 9. PDR of UDP evaluation using NEMO over IPv6 GeoNetworking

7 Conclusions and Future Work

The paper has presented the peculiarities of evaluating vehicular networks experimentally, through presenting the most used protocols and detailing the needs of the software tools to be used for this task. After that, the importance of the testing methodology is described, and a reference design of a vehicular network evaluation is used to exemplify it. The testbed design and implementation, testing scenarios, routing protocols and data flows, are found essential to be fixed beforehand to avoid improvisation during the testing campaign. The Ana-VANET platform is then presented as an efficient evaluation software to process the data gathered by common testing tools, and then generate lots of performance indicators of the trials. The capabilities of AnaVANET are exploited in a novel evaluation of NEMO over IPv6 GeoNetworking, using the tool to gather RTT, PDR and channel throughput information. The results reveal that mobile IPv6 connectivity can be maintained in a V2I case using GeoNetworking over WiFi to pass NEMO IPv6 traffic between vehicles and infrastructure.

Our future work includes, first, a link layer extension of the system to analyze the channel quality (RSSI), load ratio and coverage map. Second, it is considered the support for multicast data flows, since it is essential for the dissemination of events in vehicular networks. Third, we plan to evaluate a real application developed for cooperative ITS.

Acknowledgments. This work has been sponsored by the European 7th FP, through the ITSSv6 (contract 270519), FOTsis (contract 270447) and GEN6 (contract 297239) projects, and the Spanish Ministry of Science and Innovation, through the Walkie-Talkie project (TIN2011-27543-C03).

References

1. Perkins, C., Belding-Royer, E., Das, S.: Ad hoc On-Demand Distance Vector (AODV) Routing. RFC 3561 (Experimental) (July 2003)
2. Clausen, T., Jacquet, P.: Optimized Link State Routing Protocol (OLSR). RFC 3626 (Experimental) (October 2003)
3. Karp, B., Kung, H.T.: Gpsr: Greedy perimeter stateless routing for wireless networks. In: 6th Annual International Conference on Mobile Computing and Networking, MobiCom 2000, Boston, Massachusetts, USA, August 6-11, pp. 243–254. ACM / IEEE (August 2000)
4. Intelligent Transport Systems (ITS); Vehicular Communications; Part 4: Geographical Addressing and Forwarding for Point-to-Point and Point-to-Multipoint Communications; Sub-part 1: Media-Independent Functionality, ETSI TS 102 636-4-1 V1.1.1 (June 2011)
5. Perkins, C., Johnson, D., Arkko, J.: Mobility Support in IPv6. RFC 6275 (Proposed Standard) (July 2011)
6. Devarapalli, V., Wakikawa, R., Petrescu, A., Thubert, P.: Network Mobility (NEMO) Basic Support Protocol. RFC 3963 (Proposed Standard) (January 2005)
7. Santa, J., Tsukada, M., Ernst, T., Mehani, O., Gómez-Skarmeta, F.: Assessment of vanet multi-hop routing over an experimental platform. Int. J. Internet Protocol Technology 4 (2009)
8. Tsukada, M., Jemaa, I.B., Menouar, H., Zhang, W., Goleva, M., Ernst, T.: Experimental evaluation for IPv6 over VANET geographic routing. In: IWCMC 2010: Proceedings of the 6th International Wireless Communications and Mobile Computing Conference, pp. 736–741. ACM (2010)

A Smart Home Network Simulation Testbed for Cybersecurity Experimentation

Jizhou Tong[1], Weiqing Sun[2(✉)], and Lingfeng Wang[1]

[1] Department of EECS, The University of Toledo, Ohio, USA
{jizhou.tong,lingfeng.wang}@utoledo.edu
[2] Department of ET, The University of Toledo, Ohio, USA
weiqing.sun@utoledo.edu

Abstract. With the rapid development of smart home, it becomes essential to study techniques to safeguard the home area network (HAN) against various security attacks. In this paper, a smart home network simulation testbed has been developed for security research in this area. It is designed to feature high fidelity, cost-effectiveness and user-friendliness. The testbed enables users to specify the HAN network topology, communication protocols and appliances, as well as develop security mechanisms such as information flow tracking. For the evaluation purpose, two security mechanisms were implemented on the testbed and their effectiveness against attacks is studied using the developed testbed.

Keywords: Smart Home Network Simulation Testbed · Home Area Network · Smart Home Security · Cyber Security

1 Introduction

With the development of the Smart Grid and sophisticated network technologies, it is possible that intelligent information services can be enabled in a household environment. Smart home provides high-quality services to the users by deploying smart devices in the home area network (HAN), through which the Smart Grid connects with the consumers. ZigBee is the most popular network protocol used in the HAN thus far, which is a specification for a suite of high level communication protocols used to create personal area networks built from small, low power digital radios [1], [2].

However, the problem of cyber security becomes more and more important as the home becomes smarter, because malicious attacks may bring a significant impact to the HAN environment. For instance, attackers may obtain the control authority of the smart home through a well-designed attack. Under this condition, he or she can control all the appliances in the home, which may cause more serious consequences such as changing the room temperature or increasing the electricity consumption. Although the ZigBee protocol provides some security mechanisms, it is not sufficient to meet the security requirements of the smart home network. And advanced network security mechanisms should be deployed in the smart home network. In order to evaluate these

© Institute for Computer Sciences, Social Informatics and Telecommunications Engineering 2014
V.C.M. Leung et al. (Eds.): TridentCom 2014, LNICST 137, pp. 136–145, 2014.
DOI: 10.1007/978-3-319-13326-3_14

security mechanisms effectively, a smart home network testbed needs to be created which can support the experimentation of HAN security mechanisms. However, it will be costly to build and maintain a real smart home environment; therefore, we aim at building a cost-effective simulation testbed in this study.

In this paper, a smart home network testbed simulation environment is created. Two security mechanisms are implemented in this testbed to show that it can support the research on the HAN security mechanisms.

2 Possible Attacks in the Smart Home Communication Environment

In the smart home communication network, four types of attacks may occur, including radio jamming attack, device impersonation attack, replay attack and non-repudiation attack.

2.1 Radio Jamming Attack

Radio jamming is the process of transmission of radio signals that disrupt communication by decreasing the signal to noise ratio. A radio jamming attack can cut off the communication or result in a very high latency between the sender and the receiver. During the data packet transmission, the packet will be damaged in a jammed communication medium before it is received. A jamming attack can be launched by transmitting a constant stream of data in the same channel. In a smart home communication environment, this type of attack can delay the communication between the smart meter and home appliances for a long period of time.

2.2 Device Impersonation Attack

In an HAN environment, some advanced malicious devices can bypass the authentication mechanism and obtain the right of communicating. Then, they may disguise as any device in the HAN, which can lead to malicious data being logged into the HAN communication environment. If the malicious devices disguise itself as the smart meter, it will get the control rights of the HAN and can send the malicious control commands to all the home appliances, which may lead to undesired consequences. For instance, some appliances can be shut down unusually or the load of some appliances can be set too high. Additionally, if the malicious devices disguise as the home appliance, it may send the malicious data to the smart meter, which may cause abnormal operations such as losing control to the home appliances, no response to some requests from the home appliances or the smart meter turned off abnormally.

2.3 Replay Attack

A replay attack is the network attack in which the same valid message is resent or delayed maliciously or fraudulently. This type of attack is usually launched by the third parties. In the HAN communication environment, the attacker can intercept the authentication information of home appliances with the smart meter through a network monitoring tool. And then, the attacker can resend it to the smart meter. As a result, the attacker may invade the HAN successfully, which may cause the smart meter to overload. If the attacker launches the replay attack by controlling a home appliance, it may lead to the damage of the appliance by untimely activation.

2.4   Non-Repudiation Attack

Non-repudiation means that when a user uses or accepts one service, he or she cannot claim that the service is not used by him or her. In a smart grid communication environment, non-repudiation attack occurs when a customer denies using any service from the utility. In an HAN, the smart meter is controlled by the utility. The utility provides some necessary services to the HAN smart meter such as electricity real-time prices. The customer can deny the service of electricity real-time price in a smart meter by launching a non-repudiation attack, which may lead to economic losses for the utility companies.

3   Related Work

Previous research on the smart home simulator has been focused primarily on saving energy [3], [4]. A research to improve energy efficiency for smart building is presented in [5]. Some of them focus on the real home automation applications based on the sensors [6] and the method to create a test-bed for smart home [7], [8]. Some of the research work focuses on the smart home control systems [9], [10]. The machine to machine (M2M) network technology and its application in some areas such as healthcare and energy management are presented in [11] whose contribution is not only on the security issues of M2M network, but also on the quality of service and energy efficiency. Relatively little work has been done on how to create a smart home simulation platform for studying various security mechanisms in the HAN. Most of the current simulators for network simulation cannot meet the requirements for simulating a smart home environment with communication security mechanisms.

In [12], the authors carried out a research on several reality models to build a simulation platform for analyzing the network performances of the HAN. But, it primarily focuses on the network simulation of the HAN, and the security for the HAN is not considered in the study.

In [13], the authors present a multi-purpose scenario-based simulator for smart home. This simulator provides the ability to design the house plan and different virtual sensors and appliances. As a whole, this simulator can be good at simulating sensors and the appliances in the smart home. But the communication security is not considered in this smart home simulator.

In [14], the author presents a smart home simulation tool for energy consumption and production. This tool can give a graphical modeling platform of a smart home energy consumption based on the weather and energy price data input by the users. This simulation tool is good at simulating the energy consumption of a smart home. Nonetheless, as most of the smart home simulators, the network security mechanism in the smart home is not considered in the simulator.

4 Requirements of the Smart Home Network Simulation Testbed

Some key components are essential for building a smart home network simulation testbed for cybersecurity research. As shown in Fig. 1, there are four key components in a smart home environment, including the network module, control center module, home appliance module and security module. The control information is shown by green arrows and the status information is shown by yellow arrows. Control center can receive status information from home appliances and send proper control information to the appliances through the smart home network. The security module can secure the data transmission. The key design requirements and characteristics of the four modules are described later.

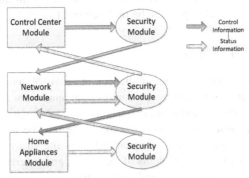

Fig. 1. Key Modules in Smart Home Network

4.1 Smart Home Network Module

The type of a smart home network can be wired or wireless. Wired communication is the fastest and most secure mode of the communication. But the cost for cabling and change in the existing structure of smart home needs to be considered. The wireless communication has an advantage over the wired communication since the wireless network is easy to install and configure in an HAN environment. The existing structure needs fewer modifications when the wireless communication is installed.

Various wireless technologies can be used for implementing a smart home network module such as Bluetooth, Wi-Fi (IEEE 802.11) and ZigBee (IEEE 802.15.4). From the comparison of these technologies, ZigBee is considered to be most suitable for the communication in the HAN of the smart grid. Because the master-slave architecture of Bluetooth has a limitation that only seven slaves can be added in a piconet, which is a constraint to the smart home network structure. The radio launched by Wi-Fi consumes a large amount of power. If Wi-Fi is used in the smart home network structure, batteries replacement in battery-operated home appliances may be required frequently. Compared with other wireless technologies, ZigBee provides a sufficient data rate for smart home network communication. Its radio consumes less power than other wireless technologies. In the simulation testbed, ZigBee protocol will be provided, and other communication technologies will be incorporated to fulfill the requirements of different users.

4.2   Control Center Module

The smart meter is the control center of an HAN environment, which is different from the traditional meter. The traditional meter in a house only collects the data of energy consumption of the home. There is no communication functionality in a traditional meter. For a smart meter, it can not only collect the energy consumption data of the whole house, but also indicate the energy consumption data of every home appliance. There are also some important network functions in the smart meter such as sending control commands to the home appliances, receiving the service information from the utility, collecting the feedback information from the home appliances in order to monitor their status, and providing the real-time electricity price to the customer. The communication between smart meter and home appliances is the single-hop communication. Because the smart meter needs to communicate with and control all the home appliances, the network type must be multi-channel.

4.3   Home Appliance Module

The biggest difference between home appliances in an HAN and traditional ones is that in an HAN they are controlled by the control commands sent from the smart meter through the home network environment. The traditional home appliances are controlled by using their switches. In a smart home, there may be no control switch on every home appliance. Instead, they are controlled by the smart meter through the HAN. Therefore, the network components of the sender and receiver need to be added to every home appliance in order to send their status to the smart meter and receive the control commands from the smart meter respectively. The type of the communication between every home appliance and the smart meter is single channel. The real-time status of the home appliances needs to be monitored by the smart meter. Some special home appliances like air-conditioners and heaters have multi-level power modes and can work under different modes. For these appliances, the smart meter can send different control commands to change their working modes.

4.4   Security Module

Network communication security is important to the smart home. In the testbed, a security module is designed so that users can develop their own security policies by using this module. The security module can have multiple security mechanisms, such as the information security checking mechanism and security label mechanism. These mechanisms can make the information flow secure during their transmission among the control center module, network module and home appliance module. The security module is embedded in all the other three modules. For instance, the control information will be checked by the security mechanisms of the security module before they are sent to the home appliance module through the network module. It will be sent after making sure that the data packet is legitimate.

5   Design and Implementation of the Smart Home Network Simulation Testbed

Based on the requirements of the simulation testbed, our simulator should be able to simulate the smart meter, various smart appliances and the HAN. Matlab/SimuLink provides a comprehensive tool to achieve the desired objective. It is able to simulate the power flow and communication flow in the smart home environment. For the communication network, TrueTime toolbox was used to facilitate the simulation of network protocols in a HAN. TrueTime is an add-on in Matlab/SimuLink, useful for real-time modeling of SimuLink models [15]. This toolbox facilitates co-simulation of controller task execution in real-time kernels network and transmission. It is developed in C++ language. One of its useful features lies in the network simulation including Ethernet, CAN, WLAN and ZigBee. Nonetheless, the TrueTime toolbox does not provide any security mechanism when a network control system is created. In order to facilitate the HAN security study, additional security models should be added on top of TrueTime toolbox. Based on TrueTime, smart home networks with user-specified configurations can be simulated.

5.1   The Structure of a Typical Smart Home Network

As seen from Fig. 2, there are ten appliances in the smart home. The smart meter is the smart control device, and other nine home appliances are controlled by the smart meter. The control commands are sent by the smart meter through the ZigBee network to the home appliances. After the control commands are received by the appliances, every appliance will give its energy usage information as a feedback to the smart meter through the ZigBee network so as to provide its current status.

Every appliance under control has three components: controller, actuator and sensor. These three components are logically independent with their appliance. They are embedded into each appliance. For every appliance, the control command is received by its controller. Then, the controller sends the control command to the actuator. After the actuator executes the command and changes the appliance status, the sensor sends the current status of the appliance back to the smart meter. The whole loop control process is shown in Fig. 3.

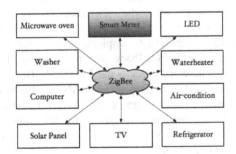

Fig. 2. Structure of a Typical Smart Home Network

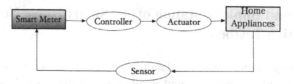

Fig. 3. The Process of Closed Loop Control

5.2   Smart Home Network Simulation Testbed Implementation

The testbed structure is shown in Fig. 4. Every block is a subsystem. The control center subsystem block simulates the functions of the smart meter which is the control center in the smart home. The ZigBee subsystem block is the TrueTime kernel network block which can simulate the wireless networks including 802.11 b/g (WLAN) and 802.15.4 (ZigBee).

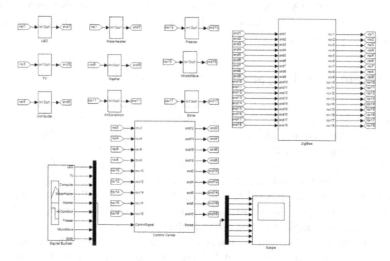

Fig. 4. Structure of the Smart Home Network Simulation Testbed

There are mainly two parts in the meter subsystem: one component sends control signals to the home appliances, while the other receives the energy usage feedback information from the home appliances. Meter subsystem uses nine TrueTime send blocks and TrueTime receive blocks to implement the function of sending control signals and receiving energy usage feedback information, respectively.

The TrueTime wireless network block is used in the ZigBee network subsystem. It provides two types of networks: ZigBee and WLAN. In this work, the ZigBee network is selected. Because the control signals sent to the nine home appliances and the energy usage feedback information received from the home appliances must go through the ZigBee network subsystem, the send port has 18 inputs and the receive port also has 18 outputs in this block.

For the home appliances subsystem, there are four types of blocks in the subsystem, which are TrueTime send block, TrueTime receive block, switch block and constant block. The TrueTime send block sends the energy usage feedback information to the meter subsystem through ZigBee network subsystem. The TrueTime receive block receives the control signal sent by the meter subsystem. The constant block with a value 0 represents the power off status of the home appliance. Another constant block with a different value for different home appliances subsystem represents the power of the home appliance. The switch block is connected with other three types of blocks. The control signal received by the TrueTime receive block can change the status of home appliance through controlling the switch block. Fig. 5 shows a LED subsystem. The power of the LED is 0.015 KW.

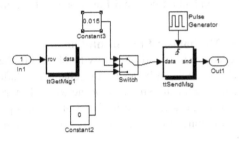

Fig. 5. LED Subsystem

5.3   Security Mechanism Implementation

Security mechanisms can be developed by the users based on the simulation testbed. Essentially, hook functions have been inserted into the network communication protocols. And users can develop code for those hook functions to implement their desired security mechanisms. The current testbed provides two such security mechanisms, which are information security checking mechanism and security label mechanism.

5.3.1   Information Security Checking Mechanism Implementation

Information security checking mechanism is designed to implement information flow control. In the smart home, the control information only can flow from the smart meter to the home appliances, and the feedback information can only flow from the home appliances to the smart meter.

The data type, source address and destination address will be checked before a message is sent or received in order to implement the information flow control presented above.

For example, the smart meter needs to send a control command to an appliance. For the sender, the data packet will be sent under the condition that the data type is control information, the destination address is a legal device and the source address is the control center. For the receiver, the data packet will be received under the condition that the data type is control information, the source address is the control center and the value of the destination address is correct.

From the process of the information security checking mechanism of the sender and receiver, the source address can be seen as sender ID; and the destination address can be seen as receiver ID. In order to implement the security checking mechanism, the legality of the sender and receiver ID must be checked in both of ttsend and ttreceive S-Function blocks in the smart meter block and home appliance blocks of the smart home network simulator. The sender ID, receiver ID and the number of nodes in the current network can be obtained by using pointers in the ttsend and ttreceive S-Function. If the values of the sender ID and receiver ID are less than the value of 0 or greater than the value of the number of nodes in the current network, they can be seen as illegal. And the ttsend and ttreceive S-Function will be terminated.

5.3.2   Security Label Mechanism Implementation

The security label mechanism is to add a security label field to the data packet before it is sent. The value of this label can be a string of characters defined by users, which make the data packet unique in the smart home network. Before the data packet is received, the receiver must check the security label of the data packet in order to ensure that the data packet belongs to the current network environment and the value of security label is correct.

A constant block called SecurityLabel has been added into the send block, which can be used to implement the security label mechanism. Under this condition, all the data packets sent by the send block of the smart home network will have a unique security label. For the receiver in this testbed, a security label checking function needs to be added into the ttreceive S-Function. For the process of the checking security label function, the value of the SecurityLabel is obtained through a pointer, and then the value is checked before the data packet is received. If the value of SecurityLabel field is equal to the specified value, the data packet will be received. If not, the data packet will be dropped.

6   Conclusions and Future Work

This paper presents a smart home network control system simulation testbed for studying HAN security mechanisms based on TrueTime toolbox. Two security mechanisms are provided in this simulator, which are information security checking mechanism and security label mechanism. The process of implementing the two security mechanisms demonstrated that this smart home network simulator can support the HAN security mechanisms effectively.

For the future work, more characteristics of the real home appliances will be implemented in the home appliances module. For example, some home appliances, including air-conditioners and heaters, have multiple energy consumption levels. In addition, a GUI will be designed to enhance the usability of the testbed. More security mechanisms will be implemented in this smart home network testbed, which can provide users more choices to conduct the research on the smart home network security.

References

1. Farahani, S.: ZigBee Wireless Networks and Transceivers. Newnes. pp. 1–3 (2008)
2. Guo, W., Healy, W.M., Zhou, M.: Interference Impacts on ZigBee-based Wireless Mesh Networks for Building Automation and Control. In: 2011 IEEE International Conference on Systems, Man, and Cybernetics, pp. 3452–3457 (2011)
3. Fensel, A., Tomic, S., Kumar, V., Stefanovic, M., Aleshin, S.V., Novikov, D.O.: SESAME-S: Semantic Smart Home System for Energy Efficiency. Informatik-Spektrum **36**(1), 46–57 (2012)
4. Jin, C.: A Smart Home Networking Simulation for Energy Saving. Carleton University (2011)
5. Louis, J.N.: Smart Buildings to Improve Energy Efficiency in the Residential Sector. University of Oulu (2012)
6. Gill, K., Yang, S.H., Yao, F., Lu, X.: A Zigbee-based Home Automation System. IEEE Trans. Consum. Electron **55**(2), 422–430 (2009)
7. Mekikis, P.V., Athanasiou, G., Fischione, C.: A Wireless Sensor Network Testbed for Event Detection in Smart Homes. In: 2013 IEEE International Conference on Distributed Computing in Sensor Systems, pp. 321–322 (2013)
8. Molitor, C., Benigni, A., Helmedag, A., Chen, K., Cali, D., Jahangiri, P., Muller, D., Monti, A.: Multiphysics Test Bed for Renewable Energy Systems in Smart Homes. IEEE Trans. Ind. Electron **60**(3), 1235–1248 (2013)
9. Perumal, T., Ramli, A., Leong, C.: Interoperability Framework for Smart Home Systems. IEEE Trans. Consum. Electron **57**(4), 1607–1611 (2011)
10. Suh, C., Ko, Y.B.: Design and Implementation of Intelligent Home Control Systems based on Active Sensor Networks. IEEE Trans. Consum. Electron **54**(3), 1177–1184 (2008)
11. Chen, M., Wan, J., Gonzalez, S., Liao, X., Leung, V.: A Survey of Recent Developments in Home M2M Networks. IEEE Communications Surveys and Tutorials (2013). doi:10.1109/SURV.2013.110113.00249
12. Liang, Y., Liu, P., Liu, J.: A Realities Model Simulation Platform of Wireless Home Area Network in Smart Grid. In: 2011 Asia-Pacific Power and Energy Engineering Conference, pp. 1–4 (2011)
13. Jahromi, Z.F., Rajabzadeh, A.: A Multi-Purpose Scenario-based Simulator for Smart House Environments. In: (IJCSIS) International Journal of Computer Science and Information Security, vol. 9, no. 1, pp. 13–18 (2011)
14. Krzyska, C.: Smart House Simulation Tool, Master thesis, Informatics and Mathematical Modelling, Technical University of Denmark, DTU (2006)
15. Cervin, A., Henriksson, D., Ohlin, M.: TRUETIME 2.0 beta - reference manual. Lund University (2010)

Connectivity Emulation Testbed
for IoT Devices and Networks

Nadir Javed$^{(\boxtimes)}$ and Bilhanan Silverajan

Tampere University of Technology, Tampere, Finland
{nadir.javed,bilhanan.silverajan}@tut.fi

Abstract. This paper describes our ongoing effort in creating a distributed highly scalable and resilient platform that can model network interactions among a very large number of devices, in terms of their wireless and wired network characteristics as well as multiradio hardware capabilities. Such an emulation platform was realized as a service overlay network atop the PlanetLab distributed testbed. Our initial results suggest that the approach undertaken is highly feasible to model both device heterogeneity ranging from simple sensors to more powerful devices, as well as wireless network characteristics to customize link reliability, channel throughput as well as bandwidth availability.

Keywords: IoT · PlanetLab · Testbed · Connectivity

1 Introduction

The Internet of Things (IoT) is expected to be constituted of billions of interconnected nodes and an equally significant number of networks [1]. These nodes comprise powerful devices as well as complexity and resource limited nodes such as sensors and actuators. In addition to high-speed fixed and wireless networks, the IoT is expected to comprise lossy, unreliable and limited bandwidth networks too. Such a diversity of connected nodes and networks inevitably impacts the types of service interactions as well as network communications, in both client-server, as well as peer-to-peer configurations. Nodes such as smart phones possess hardware allowing multiple radio technologies to co-exist, enabling multi-radio communication with other nodes using links of varying bandwidth and latency. Gateway nodes also allow packets from one kind of radio technology and access network to traverse another. Wireless sensor nodes introduce multi-hop relays into the network. Obviously this implies that measuring traffic flows among disparate types of networks, and traffic characteristics of pairwise node-based interactions are not trivial. The management of these networks and nodes, as well as lookups and discovery, are challenging problems to solve, considering the deployment scale.

In this paper, a scalable device and network emulation testbed for IoT is described, that allows such investigations to occur, from the device to the network, to subsequently execute services and monitor application level behavior.

© Institute for Computer Sciences, Social Informatics and Telecommunications Engineering 2014
V.C.M. Leung et al. (Eds.): TridentCom 2014, LNICST 137, pp. 146–155, 2014.
DOI: 10.1007/978-3-319-13326-3_15

This testbed, based on device-level interface characteristics and network conditions, resulted in a prototype architecture deployed atop PlanetLab [2]. PlanetLab guarantees neither constant network connectivity nor machine uptimes. Our prototype leverages both the availability of multiple hosts on demand, as well as link unreliability as positive aspects: Instantiation of emulated nodes does not impact overall system resources, while the intrinsic unreliability of host uptimes as well as connectivity can be typical of resource constrained nodes, which either go into sleep state or turn off their uplinks in an effort to conserve energy. The main objectives of our work are:

Network heterogeneity. Nodes in our testbed should feature emulation of several types of network interfaces and properties. Network connections feature diverse link characteristics, as well as link quality, packet loss and latency.

Flexibility. The testbed should serve as a foundation for wide research in deploying new types of services and applications, as well as the introduction of new application-level protocols. Such services, applications and protocols can be connection-oriented, connectionless, client-server or peer-to-peer based.

Scalability. The testbed should offer the ability to emulate and instantiate devices in the order of thousands to tens of thousands. Instantiation and management of instantiated emulated nodes should be accomplished using intuitive mechanisms that do not impact the execution nor the performance of the physical hosts atop which the emulated nodes run.

Remote Node Management. The testbed should allow remote configuration and management with a web-based front-end. Managing large numbers of nodes should be performed by allowing nodes to be tagged, for easy retrieval afterwards.

The rest of this paper is structured as follows: Section 2 presents related work. Sections 3 and 4 discuss the architecture, design as well as the implementation of important components in our testbed. Testing and verification is discussed in Section 5 while Section 6 concludes the paper.

2   Related Work

In published literature, a number of projects undertake active testbed research and deployment.

The MagNets project [3] aimed at deploying a next-generation wireless access network testbed infrastructure in the city of Berlin, where heterogeneous devices possessed by university students are allowed free access to an operator supported network. The Pan-European Laboratory (PanLab) concept [4] introduces a resource federation framework allowing multi-domain testbeds that provide heterogeneous crosslayer infrastructures for broad testing and experimentation. The SmartSantander [5] project aims to create a city-wide test facility for the experimentation of architectures, key enabling technologies, services and applications for the Internet of Things. It is conceived to provide a platform for large scale experimentation under real-life conditions. A unified testbed platform was developed to emulate LTE over Wired Ethernet, that can be used to examine the key aspects of an LTE system in realtime, including real time uplink and downlink scheduling, QoS parameters, and Android end-user applications [6]. The Distributed Network Emulator (DNEmu) [7] investigates how realistic network experiment can be performed involving globally distributed physical nodes under heterogeneous environments where a requirement of experimentation control between the real world network and emulated/simulated networks is introduced.

3 Design

We envision an emulation testbed with various device instances as shown in Figure 1a. The PlanetLab network is abstracted as a cloud, while squares represent PlanetLab nodes atop which various internetworked device instances and their available communication links are modeled. The network capabilities of such device instances are modeled focusing on the link reliability, bandwidth limitation and possible time delay.

As Figure 1.b shows, the testbed architecture comprises a central management server controlling and managing available PlanetLab hosts, setting up device instances on these hosts and emulating their network interfaces. An interface to the PlanetLab Central (PLC) server is used to fetch detailed node information such as node locations, addresses and uptime status. PLC provides an RPC-based API for this purpose [8].

A database is needed to maintain and record the state of the testbed. It used by the management server for storing and retrieving data essential for setting up a runtime environment, such as information for configuration of device instances as well as network links and characteristics. Such information is also retrieved by the webserver to be presented to the user for management and use of the emulated devices.

User-defined tags are supported by the platform to identify PlanetLab nodes and device instances, either individually or as groups. Tags associated with nodes and device instances are stored in the database as well.

This server also provides a web-based user-interface through which the platform can be deployed and managed. Figure 2 depicts browser windows, showing

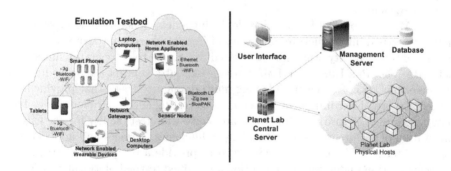

Fig. 1. a) Concept of device emulation on PlanetLab hosts b) Architecture and major components in the emulation platform

details of emulated devices such as the interfaces available for an emulated device instance, user-defined descriptions, device tags, number of instances and IDs.

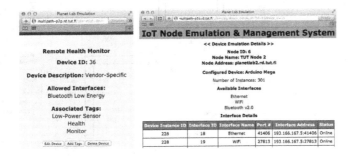

Fig. 2. Browser views of emulated devices

In this example, the user has defined device instances to emulate a remote health monitoring sensor and an Arduino device capable of communication over Bluetooth, Ethernet and WiFi based interfaces. The device ID is automatically generated and supplied by the system. The server also supplies other views aggregating all devices defined by a user, as well as physical PlanetLab nodes to be added into an existing testbed. The addition of various types of tags to be associated with PlanetLab nodes and devices to be emulated can be performed via this interface as well.

4   Implementation

Figure 3 presents a detailed view on how the emulation testbed has been implemented. The management server forms the core of the system which controls all the other components involved. The main system processes have been developed using PHP since the system uses a web based interface for user interaction. The user interface was implemented with a combination of HTML and JavaScript. To use the PLC API for fetching node information, a Python script was implemented. The database engine is based on MySQL. The server and the database use AJAX-based communication.

In order for the management server to set up the emulation testbed, it needs to be able to connect to the PlanetLab nodes defined by the user, and configure device instances. Therefore in addition to these components, SSH-based client functionality was also provided to the management server, with which it forms secure connections to PlanetLab nodes through which the required configuration commands are transmitted and the results are obtained. The SSH communication is established using public and private keys instead of passwords. The public key is uploaded to the PlanetLab Central server from where it gets propagated to all the hosts that are being used. The private key is stored on the management server and is used for authentication with the remote node.

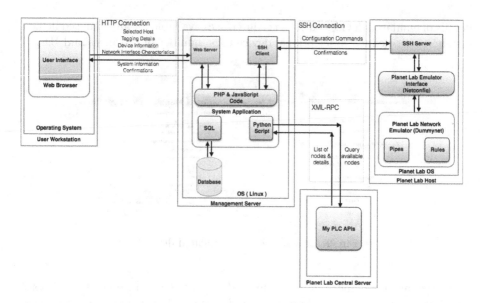

Fig. 3. Testbed implementation and existing connection types between them

PlanetLab provides a command-line tool for node-based bandwidth management. The tool is based on Dummynet, a powerful and flexible tool for testing network protocols and topologies [9]. Each physical machine runs a customized version of Dummynet that cannot be modified or replaced by end-users. Instead, a userspace command called *netconfig* is provided at each node for controlling bandwidth, network latency and packet loss ratio for incoming or outgoing connections, based on one or more known ports or addresses. In our testbed, we utilize *netconfig* to emulate both uplink and downlink of different network interfaces which are distinguished by using different port numbers. All incoming and outgoing traffic is monitored, and once a packet is detected having the same source or destination port number, rules are applied that have been specified for the traffic on that port number. For example, a sample *netconfig* configuration command invoked by an end-user for network emulation on a PlanetLab node could be:

```
host~> netconfig config SERVICE 6361 IN bw 2Mbit/s delay 2ms plr 0.2 OUT bw 1MBit/s delay 1ms plr 0.1
```

This configures the emulated link to intercept all the traffic flowing on port number 6361 and will force the incoming packets to a bandwidth of 2Mbit/s, cause a delay of 2 milliseconds and drop 20 % of the packets since the packet loss ratio is set to 0.2. Similarly all the outgoing packets will be forced to a bandwidth of 1Mbit/s, a delay of 1 millisecond and 10% packets will be dropped.

In order to start emulating the devices, the user first needs to add some nodes to the testbed, define the required network interfaces and their characteristics, define new devices in the system and associate the existing network interfaces to the device. After the required details are present, the user selects the nodes on which the devices are to be emulated. The system application at this point queries the database for node details and the list of available devices that can be emulated on the selected nodes. This information is then presented to the user who selects the device type and the number of instances that needs to be initialized on each node. The first part of the process is represented in Figure 4 as a message sequence chart showing the communication exchange between the different entities involved.

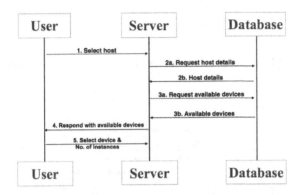

Fig. 4. First part of the message sequence for device emulation process

Once the server receives the user's choice of device and the number of instances that needs to be emulated, it queries the database for device details. The system application then queries the database for details of each associated interface. For each interface, a random port number is generated that is not being already used on the selected host for some other emulated link. Based on this port number and the interface details, a configuration command is generated by the system for execution on the node to emulate the requested network interface. This is the second part of the process and details can be seen in Figure 5.

After the configuration command is ready for all the required network interfaces of the device that is to be emulated, the system establishes an SSH connection with the selected PlanetLab node. Once the connection is established it executes in a loop all the configuration commands for each interface for each of the device instance that needs to be emulated. The system receives the result for each command that is executed and updates the records in database accordingly. Upon completion, the user is notified of the configuration results and is presented with the essential information required to utilize the newly instantiated device. This final part is represented in Figure 6.

After *netconfig* is executed on the PlanetLab node it creates the appropriate queues for handling the traffic, known as pipes, and also creates certain rules, which are then used for governing the flow of traffic through these pipes.

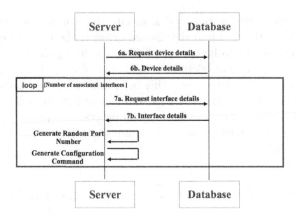

Fig. 5. Second part of the message sequence for device emulation process

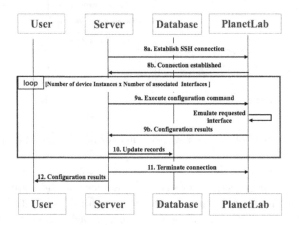

Fig. 6. Final part of the message sequence for device emulation process

Dummynet as an emulator makes use of these queues for enforcing the custom bandwidth, delays and packet drops. Every emulated network link has one or more pipes associated with it, and once the network packet matches the specified rule, it is put inside this pipe and the outward or inward flow is then controlled so that it conforms to the requested bandwidth. Similarly there could be some time constraints applied to the traffic flowing through the pipe for the latency effect and some packets could be randomly dropped from the queue depending on the packet loss ratio the user has configured.

5   Testing and Verification

The design and implementation of the emulation testbed were tested under live conditions on the PlanetLab environment. Unit testing was performed on the management server as well as the database, before widespread device instantiation was tested over approximately 50 Planetlab nodes, although it is relatively trivial to increase the number of testbed nodes to several hundreds or thousands. On each node, we successfully tested instantiation of at least 300 emulated devices as depicted in the earlier Fig. 2.

In order to verify that our testbed is configuring network interfaces properly, we tested the configured links across different emulated devices using a network measurement utility called *Iperf* [10]. *Iperf* works as a service in our device instances, supporting both client and server mode. It allowed us to create TCP and UDP streams between two hosts and provided throughput measurements for the underlying network.

To provide a simple example for this paper, we defined a test device in the testbed having a network interface with an uplink and downlink bandwidth of 5 Mbit/s and we deployed this device on a PlanetLab host. *Iperf* was then installed on this host and the bandwidth was measured for the traffic flowing on the port on which the interface has been configured.

Figure 7 shows the bandwidth measurement for the incoming traffic and Figure 8 shows the measurement for outgoing traffic. As it can be seen from these figures, the bandwidth observed on the configured interface conforms to the bandwidth that was configured.

```
[dcetut_Multipath_P2P@planetlab2 ~]$ iperf -s -p 5345
------------------------------------------------------------
Server listening on TCP port 5345
TCP window size: 85.3 KByte (default)
------------------------------------------------------------
[  4] local 193.166.167.5 port 5345 connected with 193.166.167.4 port 40390
[ ID] Interval       Transfer     Bandwidth
[  4]  0.0-10.6 sec  6.12 MBytes  4.83 Mbits/sec
```

Fig. 7. Incoming traffic bitrate verification

```
[dcetut_Multipath_P2P@planetlab2 ~]$ iperf -c planetlab1.rd.tut.fi -p 5345
------------------------------------------------------------
Client connecting to planetlab1.rd.tut.fi, TCP port 5345
TCP window size: 16.0 KByte (default)
------------------------------------------------------------
[  3] local 193.166.167.5 port 53143 connected with 193.166.167.4 port 5345
[ ID] Interval       Transfer     Bandwidth
[  3]  0.0-10.3 sec  6.12 MBytes  5.00 Mbits/sec
```

Fig. 8. Outgoing traffic bitrate verification

In order to verify that latency and packet loss factors are also functional on the interface, it was modified first to have a delay of 50ms along with the bandwidth of 5Mbit/s. The results obtained are shown in Figure 9, clearly showing a drop in the bandwidth due to the time delay on the interface.

Secondly the same interface was configured now to have a packet loss ratio of 0.1 i.e. 10 % of the packets on the interface would be dropped randomly. The results from this configuration are presented in Figure 10, also showing a drop in the observed bandwidth.

```
[dcetut_Multipath_P2P@planetlab2 ~]$ iperf -s -p 5345
------------------------------------------------------------
Server listening on TCP port 5345
TCP window size: 85.3 KByte (default)
------------------------------------------------------------
[  4] local 193.166.167.5 port 5345 connected with 193.166.167.4 port 43349
[ ID] Interval       Transfer     Bandwidth
[  4]  0.0-10.6 sec  5.62 MBytes  4.45 Mbits/sec
```

Fig. 9. Time delay affecting bandwidth

```
[dcetut_Multipath_P2P@planetlab2 ~]$ iperf -s -p 5345
------------------------------------------------------------
Server listening on TCP port 5345
TCP window size: 85.3 KByte (default)
------------------------------------------------------------
[  4] local 193.166.167.5 port 5345 connected with 193.166.167.4 port 58947
[ ID] Interval       Transfer     Bandwidth
[  4]  0.0-10.9 sec  1.62 MBytes  1.25 Mbits/sec
```

Fig. 10. Packet loss ratio

6   Conclusions and Future Work

The main outcome of this work has been the development of a distributed platform that allows us to emulate multiple devices on PlanetLab nodes that possess multiple links of varying characteristics to simulate fixed, wireless and virtual interfaces found in mobile devices and resource challenged nodes. While we achieved the target set out in our prototype testbed, we expect greater usefulness can be achieved by modeling other characteristics. These include various processor architectures, execution speeds as well as storage requirements. This remains a challenge as physical PlanetLab machines are highly homogeneous in terms of hardware as well as operating systems, typically running on x86-based workstations. However we remain optimistic that in future, research projects would arise to take on such a challenge for emulating the hardware characteristics of devices. This would undoubtedly affect startup and configuration times as well, as a PlanetLab node would have no idea of the type of device it is supposed to instantiate until the command is issued by the management server. In such a scenario, it can be envisioned that an additional component would be necessary in order to transfer binary device images to end-hosts for successful emulation.

The current architecture is aimed towards providing a single realm of control, i.e. the management of the emulated devices is centralized towards a single server while information about running nodes and their interfaces is stored in a single database. This is highly suitable for scenarios whereby management is controlled by a single organization. Such scenarios include a smart grid operator, nation-wide traffic management systems as well as smart city based management solutions. Commands for emulation are issued over the SSH protocol as blocking operations. As future work, we intend to investigate protocol driven approaches towards the instantiation and subsequent management of the emulated nodes. This would imply adding a management interface to each instantiated node over which well defined request and response messages would be sent to set or retrieve various types of information regarding the emulated nodes. Access control as well as transport layer security need to be well considered using this strategy.

While bandwidth and link characteristics were successfully controlled over TCP-based connection-oriented interactions, an operating system software bug on physical PlanetLab machines unfortunately prevented us from achieving similar results with UDP-based datagrams. At the time of writing, we are still in the process of troubleshooting the issue together with the PlanetLab administration. However, our results suggest that the approach undertaken is highly feasible to model both device heterogeneity ranging from simple sensors to more powerful devices, as well as wireless network characteristics to customize link reliability, channel throughput as well as bandwidth availability.

References

1. Ericsson, More than 50 Billion Connected Devices, White Paper (2011). http://www.ericsson.com/res/docs/whitepapers/wp50billions.pdf
2. PlanetLab International Testbed. http://www.planet-lab.org
3. Karrer, R.P., et al.: Magnets-experiences from deploying a joint research-operational next-generation wireless access network testbed. In: Testbeds and Research Infrastructure for the Development of Networks and Communities, TridentCom 2007, IEEE (2007)
4. Sebastian, W., et al.: Pan-European testbed and experimental facility federation-architecture refinement and implementation. International Journal of Communication Networks and Distributed Systems 5(1/2), 67–87 (2010)
5. Luis, S., et al.: SmartSantander: The meeting point between Future Internet research and experimentation and the smart cities. In: Future Network and Mobile Summit (FutureNetw), IEEE (2011)
6. Chertov, R., Kim, J., Chen, J.: LTE Emulation over Wired Ethernet. In: Korakis, T., Zink, M., Ott, M. (eds.) TridentCom 2012. LNICST, vol. 44, pp. 18–32. Springer, Heidelberg (2012)
7. Tazaki, H., Asaeda, H.: DNEmu: Design and Implementation of Distributed Network Emulation for Smooth Experimentation Control. In: Korakis, T., Zink, M., Ott, M. (eds.) TridentCom 2012. LNICST, vol. 44, pp. 162–177. Springer, Heidelberg (2012)
8. PlanetLab, PlanetLab Central API Documentation. https://www.planet-lab.eu/db/doc/PLCAPI.php
9. Carbone, M., Rizzo, L.: Dummynet Revisited. ACM SIGCOMM Computer Communication Review 40(2), 12–20 (2010)
10. Iperf project. http://iperf.sourceforge.net/

SDN, NDN

A Leading Routing Mechanism
for Neighbor Content Store

Du Chuan-zhen$^{(\boxtimes)}$, Zhang Yan, and Lan Ju-long

National Digital Switching System Engineering Technological R&D Center,
Zhengzhou 450002, China
duchzhen@126.com

Abstract. It is very easy for the nodes in Named Data Networking to ignore the neighbor nodes. To solve this issue, this paper proposes a leading routing mechanism for neighbor content store. Firstly, through building the interest clusters, the nodes are partitioned to different reigns to announce the information of content store. Secondly, the packets and the fast routing tables are designed. Finally, the best path is chosen to send the interest packets. The theoretical analysis and the simulation results show that this mechanism adequately uses the neighbor content and effectively decreases the average network delay. The server load is reduced by 30%.

Keywords: NDN · Content routing · Interest cluster · Neighbor content store

1 Introduction

With the rapid development of Internet technology and applications, and the rapid growth of Internet users, the way of the address of traditional IP network representing both the node location information and the identity information confuses the boundaries of the location and identification?, the limitations in the support of content distribution business become increasingly apparent. To solve this problem, in recent years, an innovative proposal of separating the hosts and contents in the network layer causes widespread concern. Content-centric networks become an important model and a developing trend of the future network.

NDN (Named Data Networking) proposes a new network architecture---- Named Data Network, using hierarchical data name instead of the IP address for data transfer, so that the data itself becomes a core element of the Internet architecture[1-2]. The architecture adopts the way of "Interest packets" to complete the multipoint access and distribution of contents in the form of announcement; "Data packets" along the reverse path of the interest packets passing the content to the requester achieve a balanced flow based on jump, try to reside the higher heat service content in the form of caching on the path to the node, and arrive at requesters in the shortest transmission path as much as possible.

Named Data Network directly based on the name of the routing and forwarding method can effectively solve the problems of exhaustion, mobility and extensibility in the IP network address space. NDN network router is responsible for name prefix announcement, spread by routing protocol in a network, and each router receiving the notice sets

© Institute for Computer Sciences, Social Informatics and Telecommunications Engineering 2014
V.C.M. Leung et al. (Eds.): TridentCom 2014, LNICST 137, pp. 159–173, 2014.
DOI: 10.1007/978-3-319-13326-3_16

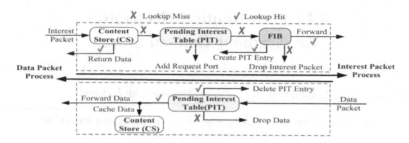

Fig. 1. NDN model of the network routing and forwarding

up its own FIB (Forwarding Information Base). When there are multiple Interest package requesting for the same data at the same time, the router will only forward the package firstly received and store these requests in the PIT (the Pending Interest Table).When the packets are sendedback, the router will find matching entries in the PIT, and forward packets to the interface according to the items shown in the list of interfaces. After that, the router will remove the corresponding PIT entries, and cache in the CS (Content Store).The CS is the router's buffer memory, using a buffer replacement strategy.

Named Data Network adopts the content-based routing method: node interest packets are directly forwarded to the source content server, and detect whether the nodes along the requesting path cache the requested content in the process of forwarding to achieve the goal of the shortest time of return data. Although compared with IP network, content-based routing method of the named data network improves the efficiency of the return packets, but such path-caching way cannot make full use of the neighboring cache which is not in the path. As shown in figure 2, the routing nodes around users store the corresponding data, but cannot make full use of them, which leads to the long path in the access of data.

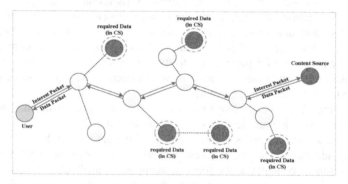

Fig. 2. The content retrieval process diagram in Named Data Network

As for the routing nodes' cache utilization problems in Named Data Network, related research has made certain progress and results. Shanbhag S 's team put forward a kind of SoCCeR service routing method, which turns the content routing problem into the service selection problem, and achieves to make full use of the nodes along the cache, while it still doesn't consider the cache content in neighboring nodes [5]. Literature [3] compares two different routing methods, and puts forward a hybrid routing method, namely establishing the routing to source server content and detecting the content copies of the node cache, but its starting point is to reduce the number of route entries and network costs. Literature [6] applys the routing based on potential energy to network content and designs the CATT routing cache perception target identification method. CATT method, however, before the request through the potential energy routing adopts the method of randomly forwarding. As a result, routing performance depends on the random initial value, and may lead to a longer path delay. Literature [7] proposes to establish the neighbor cache table's NCE routing strategy by detecting the neighbor nodes' cache content, so as to make full use of the neighbor node resources. But considering the large number of the contents in NDN, the detection method has difficulties in implementation, which would lead to the increase of the average response time of the contents' request. Literature [8] has carried on the qualitative analysis for the necessity and feasibility of the announcement of node copies. Although proposing to aggregate routing tables with the bloom filter, it still lacks the quantitative analysis and the concrete implementation for the routing mechanism. In addition, the above studies do not consider the update of node cache content according to the dynamic update of the heat and the differences between different content caches.

With the reference of the idea to create shortcut links in unstructured P2P networks in literature [9] and [10], this paper proposes a cache-oriented neighborhood for fast content routing (FCR), solving the problem of the construction of the neighboring routing cache in the Named Data Network. The structure of this paper is as follows: In Section 2 we mainly discuss the definition of FCR and explain the related concepts. In Section 3 we make a systematic analysis for the cost of cache notice between the content nodes and determine the notice way between adjacent nodes cache. In Section 4 we discuss the FCR mechanism based on nodes' interest clusters in detail. In Section 5 we provide some simulation experiments based on this mechanism and previous methods, compare the experiment results, and validate the feasibility and effectiveness of the mechanism.

2   Fast Content Routing

Content source server path is the shortest path for the user S to send interest packets to the source server D, during the process, the along nodes' set is $S = \{N_a, N_b, \ldots, N_m\}$, the response hop is H1.

2.1   Fast Content Path

Define the shortest path between the user node S and the required content of recent neighboring cache node N ($N \notin S$) as the FCP (Fast Content Path) for user S. During the process, the forwarding nodes are $S_{FCP} = \{N_A, N_B, \ldots, N_M\}$, the response hop is H2.

Among them, the routing node N as closest cache node for user S must make $H_2 \leq H_1$. Otherwise, the fact that content source is the latest cache is inconsistent with definitions. If user S has FCP (Fast Content Path), then $S_{FCP} \cap S \neq \varnothing$.

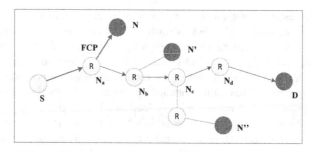

Fig. 3. Fast Content Path of the request nodes

Proof: Using the reduction to absurdity. Assume $S_{FCP} \cap S = \varnothing$, the routing node in the access network is N0.As the content source path must exist in the network, now we have $N_0 \in S$ and $N_0 \notin S_{FCP}$ .And then the access point N0 for S disconnects with routing node N, resulting the non-exist of FCP, which has a contradiction with the above known. Thus, the hypothesis doesn't succeed.

According to the principle that FCP at least has an intersection point with the server path. In search of the construction of FCP, only by $S = \{N_a, N_b, \ldots, N_m\}$ to achieve the stored content in other neighbor node N with its corresponding content C, and compute the corresponding routing.

2.2   The Cache Notification and Cost Analysis

The distribution of cache around nodes can mainly be obtained from two ways, namely detection and active notification. Although the detection can locate the specific content accurately, its two-way generating traffic makes the network costs too expensive, which leads the difficulty of mass deployment. Compared with detection, active notification method is one-way traffic. With the notice in a reasonable control range, the mass distribution of its own cache items can make the network costs to a minimum.

As assumption, the network topology is represented as $G = \{V, E\}$, V is the set of nodes, E is the collection of links. The number of nodes in the network is |V|. The size of notice packet is B, the average link rate is m. The cache of nodes always updates according to the heat of the content in NDN, the interval is T. In the network G, change at least |V| times and require N ($N \geq \log_m^{|V|}$, N is an integer) notices, only by this can send the updates of content cache to the whole nodes in the network. The cost of traffic is:

$$C = (m + m^2 + \ldots + m^N) \cdot B \cdot |V|$$
$$> m^N \cdot B \cdot |V|$$
$$\geq |V|^2 \cdot B$$

As the update time of the cache of the content node is just a few seconds, the cost of a time unit is $C/T \geq |V|^2 \cdot B/T$.

In order to reduce the cost of notice for the cached content, the proposed principle of the heuristic fast content routing announcement mechanism in this paper mainly contains two aspects:

A.   Set reasonable notice scale for neighboring cache content |V|

The Internet has the feature of the small world, which visit in close distance has the similarity to the cache of content [11]. Due to the same cluster nodes probably interested in the same class content, we propose to build the interest cluster based on interest correlation standard. Therefore, the notice of nodes cache is tedious and unnecessary in the network, which raises the utilization ratio of announcement content by narrowing the notice in the interest cluster. Based on this deduction, this paper proposes a heuristic fast content routing announcement mechanism to overcome the huge traffic cost brought by the flooding notice method.

B.   Choose the higher heat content to prolong the interval of notice time T

The routing lookup in NDN network starts with the frequently updates of the node contents' cache, which is dynamic and volatile. The frequently change of the cache items in the nodes has no significance for FCR. However, it may be cause the routing oscillation. Therefore, this paper proposes to notice only the higher heat node cache, which the steady part of the node resides data. Due of the frequently changing of the cache information not noticing outwards, it not only prolongs the advertisement interval, but also ensures the stability of the network node cache contents.

C.   Design the unique notification message structure in order to reduce the size of the notification message B

3   Leading Fast Content Routing Mechanism

The proposed heuristic neighboring cache notification mechanism based on node cache heat and the similarity of demand will be divided into certain interest network node clusters. Cluster nodes only notice the higher heat content cache in the internal, and those do not belong to the same cluster don't notice the cache. The construction of fast content routing can be roughly divided into three steps: cluster building, caching notices and fast route setup. After the completion of the fast routing tables, if received content request, the node would perform corresponding forwarding operations according to the sequential look-up of content store tables, pending interest tables, fast routing tables and forwarding information base.

3.1   The Construction of the Interest Node Cluster

In NDN, given the content request nodes as i and j, the interest content set is $C_{\text{interest}}(i)$, $C_{\text{interest}}(j)$. Their common interest set is $P_C = C_{\text{interest}}(i) \bigcap C_{\text{interest}}(j)$.

If node I requests certain content Mc times in the latest interval T, the IRC(Interest Relevancy Coefficient) is defined as:

$$\theta(i,j) = \frac{\sum\limits_{C \in P_C} [M_{C,i}^2 + M_{C,j}^2 - M_{C,j}M_{C,i}]}{T(\sum M_{C,i}M_{C,j} + d)} \quad (d \text{ is positive number})$$

Mc,i and Mc,j respectively represent the request number in the last interval T of node i and j .The closer Mc,i and Mc,j, the more important influence on $\theta(i,j)$ .This shows that node i and node j have a larger IRC. Oppositely, the IRC is smaller. Since Mc,i and Mc,j may be 0,so the positive number d $\neq$ 0.

3.2   The Selection of Core Nodes

The construction of an interest node cluster is not disorderly. Selecting the highest IRC Node (Leader Node) to build the interest cluster can increase the interests. Define the relevancy radio of node i, $\eta_i = \sum\limits_{j \in Neighbor(i)} \theta(i,j)$, η_i is the standard of the Leader Node, which is the sum of IRC of the neighbor nodes. The higher relevancy the leader nodes have, the larger interest the cluster will get.

Among interest clusters, the relevancy η_i is the priority for selecting nodes. The interest nodes notice the neighbor nodes. In order to reduce the traffic redundancy in the selection of leader nodes, the larger η_i the node have, the shorter time they will wait. When the nodes receive the larger priority notice, they would not notice their own η_i, yet only notice the larger priority node messages.

3.3   Define the Scope of the Interest Cluster

In order to reflect the advantage of a neighboring node to improve the efficiency of the fast route, the scope of request nodes of the cluster in named data network should not be too big ($H_2 \leq H_1$).Literature [7] has carried on the detailed research on the content network range announcement, pointing out that the average delay of network cluster at the scope of 2 just decrease by 3% than the scope of 1. As for the cache capable content network, most content requests can be satisfied within the scope of 1~2 (i.e. 3 jump range). Taking into account the superposition of two-way transmission delay, we will limit the scope of this paper notices set to 6-hop, namely Scope = 6, based on the literature [7]. The scope of the notice will be discussed through simulation experiments in later chapters.

3.4   Interest Cluster Construction Algorithm

According to that the interest correlation cluster building should consider caching content and its heat, the interest cluster can only notice some steady state cached data. The build process is as follows:

Table 1. Nodes Interest Cluster Construction Algorithm

Step1:	node N_i calculate η_i according to the current contents of the cache table and heat, and create announce packet P_i for N_i.
Step2:	After the waiting time T, the packet P_i is advertised to neighboring nodes, set the scope Scope and notice Hop values need to be forwarded to all interfaces.
Step3:	Within the time T, compare the received packets with information and notice the packet with a larger priority value out.
Step4:	In a cluster, the nodes with the best value of η_i will be set to the leader, it sends a confirmation message within a cluster, complete the Cluster.
Step5:	When all the contents of the cache node reaches a certain level or after a time interval T, re-content announcements.

4   Leading Neighboring Cache Notices

4.1   The Design of Notice Message

In order to achieve the neighboring cache of contents notice, the design of heuristic cache notification message in network is as follows:

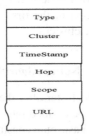

Fig. 4. Message format of heuristic neighboring cache notices

In the chart, Type format represents the type of message, the Cluster format records the number of the present cluster. TimeStamp format is used to record the sending time of messages, which can distinguish the latest version of notice message. Hop format is used to record the hops between the notice node and the present node, which can be used to represent the routing costs of notice to calculate the fast routing.

URL and Scope respectively are the name of required notice content (the naming mechanism in the NDN is in the form of a URL) and notice scope (hops). Hop would add one and the scope minus one when notice one hop with the end of 0 of the Scope. The neighbor nodes determine to continue notice according that whether the scope is 0. If scope is 0, the notice would stop.

4.2   The Choose of Notice Content

In order to avoid the notice message explosion caused by the frequent replacement of notification messages in the node cache, the notice content only choose the relatively stable (i.e. high heat value) content. Firstly the node cache sort the content by adopted caching strategies, select the top x % of the high heat copies to notice. If LRU strategy is used in such nodes, then they will notice the newly pumped cache queue x % to neighbor nodes, which is as follows:

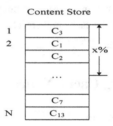

Fig. 5. The list of the heat nodes cache

Excessively frequent update may cause the miss of routing content items, any item of the current notice copy deleted by a node will trigger a new cache announcement, and the node will sent the information of the first node of x % cache in the current time sequence to all nodes within the cluster.

4.3   Leading Neighboring Cache Notice Algorithm

The node will be in separate to each cluster after the construction of the node cluster. The construction of fast routing can be divided into two stages: heuristic cache notice building and content delivery stage. Fast route construction mainly notices the content and builds the FCT (Fast Content Table). First of all, the cache nodes in the cluster make initialization before the announcement: node i sets the cluster number of itself, the content timestamp TSnew and the scope of its own announcement, and then forwards to all interfaces according to the first x %   cache content items based on the heat contents. Set the result of neighboring node j before receiving announcement: <NameC, Face, TSold, Hopold>. The timestamp TSold = 0 when there is no record for content C. It will implement such algorithm when node j receive the announcement of node i.

Table 2. Heuristic Neighboring Cache Notice Algorithm

Step1:	Nodes i and nodes j to determine whether the same cluster; If yes, proceed to step 2, otherwise discard the notice packet and jump to step 5.
Step2:	Determine if the contents of the current received notification packets are up to date. If $TS_{new} < TS_{old}$, the notification message is stale information and discards the packet, step 5; otherwise, proceed to Step 3.
Step3:	if $TS_{new} \geq TS_{old}$, the content of the notice is the latest entries; Receive notification packets and calculate the value of the received message Hop as routing consideration: $Hop_{new} \leftarrow Hop_0 + Hop(i, j)$ .if $Hop_{new} \geq Hop_{old}$, description routing costs are too high, dropped packets, perform step 5; otherwise, proceed to Step 4;
Step4:	Query convenient routing table FCT, update the URL corresponding entries,Fill Hop_{new} in the forwarding table routing consideration domain, and then decide whether to forward the contents of this notice forwarded to the next node depending on the size Scope value;
Step5:	The end of the notice

After the completion of the fast routing tables, nodes compare the current routing cost and server path cost in the FIB after receiving the interest request. If fast routing cost is smaller, then process the items in the fast routing table and create one item of FIB. Namely, nodes perform corresponding forwarding operations according to the sequential look-up of the content store table, FCT and FIB.

The forwarding process of the interest packets are as follows:

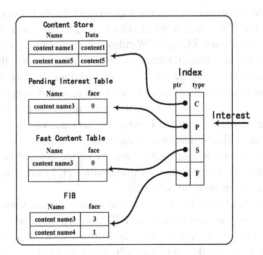

Fig. 6. The interest packets forwarding process in node

4.4   Fast Content Routing Algorithm

Node j would record contents name, arriving interfaces, and the price of this cache content after receiving the notification about the content C of its neighbor node i. Then it would implement the fast content routing algorithm.

Table 3. Fast Content Routing Algorithm

Step1:	Contrast Hop of this convenient route and the costof the forwarding information table to the content source server, if convenient route Hop is small, easy to create the entry in the routing table; otherwise delete the contents of the route entry corresponding convenient route.
Step2:	When there are several convenient route to the same content when forwarding interface Select the minimum cost of the interface as the next hop.

The format of FCT (Fast Content Table) built by the above algorithm is as follows:

Content Name	Face	Hop
/example.com/a	1	1
/example.com/b	2	3
/example.com/c	3	2

5   The Simulation Experiment and Result Analysis

These parts simulate an operation process topology in NDN network and its related performance using the C+ + and Matlab. The experimental environment is 4 GHZ Intel core 2 double processor PC with Windows 7 operating system. Firstly, build routing nodes based on the characteristics of named data network, then use the GT - ITM topology generation tool to generate a plane random network topology with 30 routing nodes, where the probability of any two routing nodes directly connected path is 0.3. Next, randomly select a node from the edge nodes as the server node of the network node of the whole content publishing and service, whose capacity is enough to store all the content objects. The rest of the nodes as ordinary routing nodes is directly connected with users, whose cache capacity of the content is B (assuming the same content object size, B represents the node number). In order to facilitate analysis, delay between adjacent nodes is set to 10ms.

For the convenience of measurement, set the content in the source server content object number N = 2000, assuming that the URL routing items are equal [13], which is set to 128 KB. Object content popularity follows Zipf-Mandelbrot distribution [3,4], namely the content popularity of the Kth object is: $P_k = H-1(\sigma, q, N)/(q+k)\sigma$. σ is the shape parameter, q is the mobility parameter, $\sigma=0.4$, $q=10$. $H(\sigma, q, N)$ is normalized correlation coefficient. Content routing nodes directly connect with the user host, who send interest packets (data request packets) to the associated content of the nodes. In the simulation of users' sending packets, we use the Poisson arrival features to satisfy the process [20] ($\lambda=4$) to arrive at each router node randomly. The simulation topology is shown as follows. The circle point represents router, the line represents link, the bandwidth is 100Mbps.

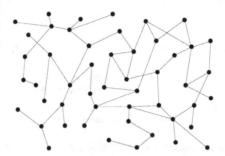

Fig. 7. The simulation topology

In order to effectively evaluate the experiment effect, this section simulates for the fast routing mechanism, and compares several previous methods of simulation at the same time. First one is the basic Content Routing mechanism of NDN network, regardless of the adjacent nodes cache, which directly forwards the request packet to the content source server [6], notes for SCR (Simple Content Routing). Next, it is the NCE strategy proposed by literature [7].The proposition of Literature [14] is the notice cached copy routing which is noted for ACC. When neighboring cache node content is missing in these three methods, it would directly forward the request packets to the content source. Finally, this section shows the simulation of the proposed heuristic fast content mechanism based on the interest nodes and FCR.

In order to validate the performance of the heuristic neighboring fast content mechanism, we choose the average delay of user requests and the content source server load as the standard to make comparison. The source server load is defined as the request packet number received during the simulation process.

5.1   Best Interest Cluster Scope

Figure 8 shows the influence on average delay and notice cost of different range announcement in the cluster building. According to the above simulation of the percentage of content announcement, take notice content to 60%. As the cluster radius increased, fast routing delay decreases. Heuristic notification message number also increases along with the cluster scope. From the figure, there happens the delay rotary phenomenon, which mainly caused by the large announcement scope, resulting that gradually close to the content source routing path length leads to the path delay picking up when the scope of interest cluster is more than 6 hops. Considering the impact on the performance and cost, the best range of cluster is 5.

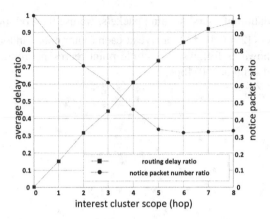

Fig. 8. The influence on time delay and the notification message number of interest cluster scope

5.2   The Proportion of Content Caching Announcement

Set the cache capacity B = 60, the total number of requests Nq = 2000.Set the proportion of content caching announcement x % as variables on the shortcut route delay performance simulation, the result is shown in figure 9. Gradually with the increase of circular ratio, time delay performance improves, but after the proportion is more than 80%, the average delay increased because the dynamic contents of the cache are part of the content of the frequent replacement notice to go out, causing the node forwarding the request to the removed content. As a result, it causes the missing of cache and increases the delay to get content from other nodes. In addition, with the expanding of notice range, this phenomenon of the increasing delay is more obvious.

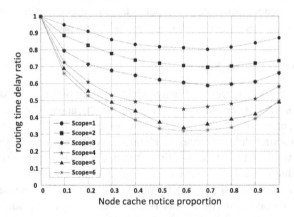

Fig. 9. The impact of the announcement ratio of cache content on performance

5.3   The Average Time Delay of the User Requests

The simulation process produced 2000 content requests. Define the single request delay as delay for a node from the content request to receive the requested data, then the simulation results of the average delay of the request contents is as shown in figure 10.

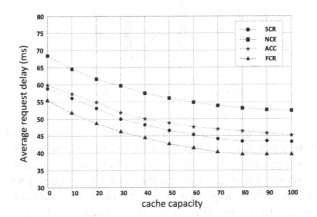

Fig. 10. The average time delay of the user requests

Seen from figure 10, the basic content routing in NDN has the largest time delay regardless of the copy in node. The methods of NCE and ACC both establish a copy of the neighbor node routing table, but they don't consider the differences in the heat of the neighbor node and the hit probability. The missing content situation is serious, which need to get from other resources, causing the increasing request delay. By contrast, the fast routing considers the update and delete of the cache node content. Once the cache content of announcement is replaced, then nodes update notification, and improve the hit probability of the request, which contributes to the minimum average request time delay.

5.4   Content Source Server Load

B= 60 cache capacity, content requests Nq = 2000. With the number of receiving interest in content server as norm, the performance of the server load simulation results as shown in figure 11. White represents the total number of request packets in the network, black for the number of received request packets for server.

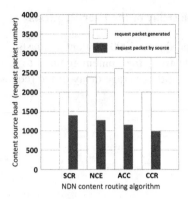

Fig. 11. Content source server load

From figure 11, the original NDN network routing way only routes the request to the determined server in the case that the total number of content requests is 2000, and thus it will not generate additional request packet. Lack of content, the ACE and NCE both have reroute request, which generate additional request packets. FCR will update notification timely to neighboring interest nodes within a cluster, so there is no reroute phenomenon. On the number of the received request packet for server, SCR is the most, because it only uses part of the forward path cache while the ACE, NCE and fast routing use the contents of the cache node resources, which effectively reduces the load of content server. Relative to the SCR, fast routing reduces about 30% on the server load.

6   Conclusion

The routing method improves the efficiency of the return packets through directly facing to the source server in the named data network, but cannot make full use of the neighboring cache content along the path. To solve this problem, this paper proposes the heuristic FCR (fast content routing) mechanism based on neighboring cache in interest clusters. Based on the small world feature of the Internet, we design heuristic announcement mechanism of cache contents in view of the different similarity between neighboring nodes in small community, and finally design the unique notification message structure and the reasonable notification scope to achieve fast content routing mechanism. Theoretical analysis and experimental results show that the method effectively reduces the average delay of the user request and the load of the source content server. Due to the frequently update of the content node, such fast content routing mechanism would lead to the expansion of the node routing table items. So how to aggregate and compress routing table items in the forward information base is the key point of further research and exploration.

This work was supported in part by a grant from the National Basic Research Program if China (973 Program) (No. 2012CB315902), the National Natural Science Foundation of China (No.61102074, 61170215, 61379120), Zhejiang Leading Team of Science and Technology Innovation (No. 2011R50010-03, 2011R50010-12, 2011R50010-19).

References

1. Carofiglio, G., Gallo, M., Muscariello, L.: Bandwidth and Storage Sharing Performance in Information Centric Networking[C]. In: Proceedings of ACM SIGCOMM ICN Workshop, 26–31(2011)
2. Tsilopoulos, C., Xylomenos, G.: Supporting Diverse Traffic Types in Information Centric Networks . In: Proceedings of ACM SIGCOMM ICN Workshop, 13–18(2011)
3. Chiocchetti, Raffaele, Rossi, Dario, Carofiglio, Giovanna, et al.: Exploit the Known or Explore the Unknown? Hamlet-Like Doubts in ICN[C]. Proceedings of ACM SIGCOMM ICN Workshop, Helsinki, Finland (2012)
4. Zhang Li-xia, Jacobson V, Tsudik Gene, et al. Named Data Networking (NDN) Project [R/OL]. http://named-data.org (2013)
5. Shanbhag, S., Schwan, N., Rimac, I., et al.: SoCCeR: services over content-centric routing. ACM SIGCOMM Workshop on Information-Centric Networking, Toronto, Canada (2011)
6. Eum, S., Nakauchi, K., Murata, M., et al.: CATT: Potential Based Routing with Content Caching for ICN. ACM SIGCOMM Workshop on Information-Centric Networking, Helsinki, Finland (2012)
7. Ye, R.: M. Xu, Neighbor Cache Explore Routing Strategy in NDN, Journal of Frontiers of Computer. Science and Technology 6, 593–601 (2012)
8. Wang, Y., Lee, K.: Advertising cached contents in the control plane: Necessity and feasibility. In IEEE INFOCOM, NOMEN Workshop (2012)
9. Sripanidkulchai, K, Maggs, B, Zhang, H.: Efficient Content Location Using Interest-Based Locality in Peer-to-Peer Systems. In: Proceedings of IEEE INFOCOM (2003)
10. Pireddo, L., Nascimento, M.A.: Taxonomy-Based Routing Indices for Peer-to-Peer Networks. In: Proceedings of the Workshop on Peer-to-Peer Information Retrieval, 27th International Annual ACM SIGIR Conference (2004)
11. Mcpherson, M., Lovin, L., Cook, J.: Birds of a feather: Homophily in social networks. In Annual Review of Sociology (2001)
12. Zhang, Y., Zhao, J., Cao, G., et al.: On Interest Locality in Content-Based Routing for Large-scale MANETs(2009)
13. Masinter, L., Berners-Lee, T., Fielding, R.T.: Uniform resource identifier (URI): Generic syntax (2005)
14. Wang, Y, Lee, K., Venkataraman, B., et al. Advertising cached contents in the control plane: Necessity and feasibility[C]//Computer Communications Workshops (INFOCOM WKSHPS), 2012 IEEE Conference on.(2012)

An OpenFlow Testbed for the Evaluation of Vertical Handover Decision Algorithms in Heterogeneous Wireless Networks

Ryan Izard[✉], Adam Hodges, Jianwei Liu, Jim Martin,
Kuang-Ching Wang, and Ke Xu

Clemson University, Clemson, SC 29634, USA
{rizard,hodges8,jianwel,jmarty,kwang,kxu}@clemson.edu

Abstract. This paper details a framework that leverages Software Defined Networking (SDN) features to provide a testbed for evaluating handovers for IPv4 heterogeneous wireless networks. The framework is intended to be an extension to the Global Environment for Network Innovations (GENI) testbed, but the essence of the framework can be applied on any OpenFlow (OF) enabled network. Our goal is to enable researchers to evaluate vertical handover decision algorithms using GENI resources, open source software, and low cost commodity hardware. The framework eliminates the triangle routing problem experienced by other previous IPv4-compatible IP mobility solutions. This paper provides an overview of the testbed framework, implementation details for our installation using GENI WiMAX resources, and a discussion of future work.

Keywords: Heterogeneous Wireless Networks · OpenFlow · IP Mobility · Testbeds · Vertical Handovers

1 Introduction

Wireless networks and mobile devices have evolved to the point where access to multiple radio access technologies (RATs) are commonplace. The combination of these RATs form a heterogeneous wireless network. It is in the best interest of both users and network operators that the network resources be distributed fairly and efficiently amongst all users within a heterogeneous wireless network [3]. Vertical handovers, or handovers between different RATs, cause interruptions in connectivity for mobile users during the process of obtaining a different IP address. This results in the temporary loss of IP connectivity. Another issue presented by a vertical handover is that typical network applications are not designed to support the use of multiple network interfaces.

Mobile IPv4 (RFC 5944) [7] provides a mechanism by which a mobile device can retain the use of an IP address even after it has associated with a foreign network. Upon migration, the mobile device reports its new IP address to the home network, and a tunnel is formed between the mobile device and a home

© Institute for Computer Sciences, Social Informatics and Telecommunications Engineering 2014
V.C.M. Leung et al. (Eds.): TridentCom 2014, LNICST 137, pp. 174–183, 2014.
DOI: 10.1007/978-3-319-13326-3_17

agent at the mobile device's home network. Egress traffic from the mobile device is routed normally, while ingress traffic is routed back to the home network and through the tunnel to the mobile device as illustrated in Fig. 1. The use of a tunnel creates what is known as the Mobile IP triangle routing problem, which adds delay and consumes extra network resources. The introduction of IPv6 features to Mobile IP (MIPv6) [8] running on an IPv6 network can alleviate the triangle through the use of what is known as route optimization. A limitation of these MIPv6 schemes is that they require custom software on the client to enable mobility.

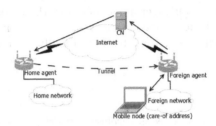

Fig. 1. Mobile IPv4 routing triangle problem

Many handover decision algorithms have been developed to alleviate the resource allocation problem presented by heterogeneous wireless networks. Most of these algorithms require the ability to make a handover decision based on the current conditions of all RATs. 802.21 [10] is a framework that was developed to support media independent handovers. The goal of this framework is to provide a standardized interface for every RAT that handover decision algorithms can utilize to create a global view of the available network states. An algorithm can build this global state by using 802.21 to query information, handle events, and issue commands. These algorithms can then use the global network state to intelligently trigger a handover. Testing vertical handover decision algorithms is nontrivial due to the cost and complexity of heterogeneous wireless network deployments and usually relies on network simulations [13]. We present a testbed design for evaluating these handover decision algorithms using real world wireless network resources.

The Global Environment for Network Innovations (GENI) [1] is a NSF sponsored effort to create a large scale testbed for network experimentation. One feature of GENI is its use of OpenFlow (OF) [2], a specification implemented by switches or routers that allows the forwarding plane to be modified by a controller in software. Recently, GENI has made strides towards enabling experimentation over wireless resources. It is a priority for GENI to provide mobile hosts with seamless vertical handovers using IPv4-compatible methods within GENI's heterogeneous wireless networks. This feature is desirable to researchers testing network applications as well as vertical handover decision algorithms.

Our contribution to this effort is the design of an OF-based, IPv4-compatible vertical handover testbed for use with GENI wireless networks. In the spirit of

GENI, researchers will be able to reserve and utilize the resources in our implementation of this testbed. However, due to the nature of wireless research, we anticipate that other researchers may need an implementation of the testbed on their own campus. Therefore, the majority of this paper describes the details of how we applied, designed, and implemented the framework to provide a versatile testbed. An understanding of the challenges and issues we encountered and resolved will provide insight and guidance to other researchers who plan on implementing this testbed on their campus.

The remainder of the paper is organized as follows. In Section 2, we discuss and contrast our solution to similar testbed efforts. Section 3 outlines the goals, requirements, limitations, and user model of our testbed. Section 4 describes the system design and implementation details. Section 5 contains a discussion of our future work to be completed on our testbed. Finally, we conclude the paper in Section 6.

2   Related Work

In an effort to bring heterogeneous wireless network testbed resources to GENI researchers, GENI has partnered with Open-Access Research Testbed for Next-Generation Wireless Networks (ORBIT) [9]. GENI WiMAX resources have been established at a number of universities across the US and are available for researchers to use. These resources are linked via a L2 tunnel to the GENI testbed. A subset of these campuses have received ORBIT nodes that can be accessed by experimenters through the ORBIT Management Framework (OMF). Clemson is one of the GENI WiMAX campuses with ORBIT nodes. These nodes are ideal for serving as mobile hosts within a vertical handover-enabled heterogeneous wireless network testbed.

The WiRover [5] project at Wisconsin-Madison is a system that utilizes multiple radios to increase the bandwidth and continuity of wireless network access for buses. WiRover uses pre-collected signal data along bus routes to allow their system to proactively make an intelligent handover decision. Although the WiRover project itself is not a testbed, the researchers' previous efforts in [6] include using the vehicular network as a testbed for a 3G-WiFi heterogeneous wireless network.

There are several existing heterogeneous wireless network testbeds that provide vertical handover capabilities. For example, [4] uses MIPv4 to achieve IP mobility, enabling the researchers to evaluate novel handover decision algorithms. Other testbeds, such as [11], do not have the requirement of IPv4 compatibility and can make use of MIPv6 and its route optimization features.

The proposal in [12] conceptualizes the client component of our testbed that we have detailed in section 4.1 of this paper. In this proposal, the researchers describe how such a client could participate in a Handover as a Service (HaaS) scheme. With HaaS, a central database makes the handover decision for a mobile host based on the mobile host's current location and historical network information for that location. We hope that our vertical handover decision testbed will eventually facilitate the implementation of the system discussed by the researchers in this proposal.

3   System Framework

The system framework utilizes OF to achieve IP mobility and application-transparent handovers. It is designed to be easily deployed to universities that have OF-enabled campuses or that can provide a subnet or VLAN for handover experimentation. The framework was developed and implemented at Clemson as a part of the GENI WiMAX project. Fig. 2 provides a general overview of how our testbed is constructed and how it integrates with the large-scale GENI testbed. At the architectural level, the framework allows OF-enabled mobile devices to roam across any OF-enabled wireless network. It requires a root OF switch as the testbed ingress/egress, as well as OF switches at each edge network. The challenge in building a testbed based on the framework is the required integration with existing network infrastructure at the campus. The testbed allows a mobile device to roam from wireless Network X (as illustrated in Fig. 2) to Network Y, preserving end-to-end socket connections that the device has with other hosts located either on the campus network or in the Internet. With these minimal assumptions, the testbed can be as simple or as complicated as desired. The design of our testbed can be divided into two major components: the network-level and the client-level.

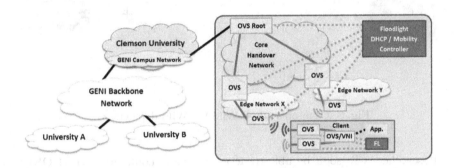

Fig. 2. Clemson testbed components and integration with GENI

The network-level component is required to manage and maintain client IP addresses, as well as the routing of client packets within the the testbed network. Both of these tasks are performed with a Floodlight (FL) OF controller, which maintains a global IP address pool and handles migration events within the testbed. To maintain the global IP address pool, a custom DHCP server module is integrated into FL. The FL controller is designed to be extensible to support other use cases; for example, in a HaaS framework, the FL controller could also make the handover decisions for the mobile devices in the network [12]. A key component of the network-level is an OF-enabled switch or Open vSwitch (OVS) located at the root, such that all IP mobility-enabled networks on the edge are descendants of this root. As descendants of the root switch, other OF switches or OVSs are deployed on the network-level in order to both route client packets and detect migration events. From a network operations point of view, benefits of this tree-like design include (1) a single point of integration with the campus infrastructure and (2) the requirement of no specialized hardware in the case where OVS is used in favor over physical OF switches.

The client-level component of the testbed exists entirely on-board the client and is responsible for both switching the active physical interface and maintaining all client sockets during such a handover event. To maintain active sockets, a default virtual network interface (VNI) is installed on the client. All applications send and receive packets through this VNI, and by nature of a virtual interface, it is not impacted by physical interface states. The client is also equipped with OVSs and its own FL OF controller. This controller is responsible for routing packets from the VNI's OVS, through the client-level OVS network, and then to the physical interface of choice as determined by a handover decision.

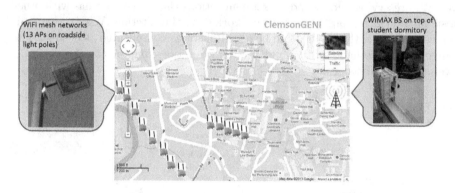

Fig. 3. Clemson's GENI WiMAX/WiFi deployment

Researchers will soon be able to access specially configured GENI ORBIT nodes, both stationary and vehicular, through the ORBIT Management Framework (OMF) [9]. These nodes will be pre-configured to enable researchers to test their applications and handover decision algorithms in the seamless handover environment we have designed. Each ORBIT mobile node will be within overlapping coverage of both WiFi and WiMAX networks. Fig. 3 depicts the wireless coverage areas available to GENI researchers on the Clemson main campus.

4   Testbed Implementation

On the network-level of the testbed, all WiFi APs are configured with Debian Linux 5.1.10, and all WiMAX gateways are configured with Debian Linux 6.0.7. On the client-level, testbed components have been verified on both Debian and Ubuntu Linux. All Linux distributions are using kernel 2.6.32. The FL OF controllers used on both the client and the network levels are sourced from FL 0.90. Each controller has been extended with custom modules to enable the vertical handover solution. Also common to both the network and the client are several OVS 1.9.0 virtual network bridges (OVSBs). A high-level diagram of the network-level is shown in Fig. 4.

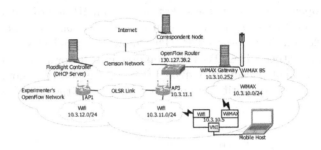

Fig. 4. Clemson testbed network configuration

4.1 Network Component

Within our testbed, the network component has the responsibility of maintaining the IP address pool for every mobility-enabled network. The network-level FL controller acts as a DHCP server, using DHCP requests as a trigger for migration. In the event of a migration, this Floodlight controller is also responsible for efficiently and quickly updating the client's location and thus the flow of its application packets.

The detection of a client connection and migration within the testbed is achieved through the use of OVSBs and OF flows (flows). These flows detect, encapsulate, and redirect client DHCP packets (on UDP destination port 67) to the network-level FL controller. This controller contains an integrated DHCP server module which, unlike traditional DHCP servers, associates an IP address lease with multiple MAC addresses. Each of these MAC addresses corresponds to a participating network interface (NIC) on the client. When processing a DHCP packet, the controller cross-references the MAC address of the DHCP packet with all available MAC address lists. Upon a successful match within a MAC address list, the controller assigns the client who initiated the request the corresponding IP. Then, upon a mobile host's initial connection or migration to a foreign network, flows are inserted in OVSBs starting at the testbed root and along every hop to the client's current location. These flows direct packets to and from the mobile client within the testbed. When a client migrates away from this network, any existing flows associated with the client are removed and replaced with flows along the path from the root to the newly-migrated foreign network. The use of a root switch and tree hierarchy allows the network-level controller to avoid undesirable triangle-routing in the event of a migration.

The mobility testbed includes many OVSBs within the network. As discussed previously, the network-level OVSBs connect to the network-level FL controller / DHCP server. These OVSBs are used in the detection of client migrations and the routing of client packets into and out of the testbed. Specifically, the OVSBs on the testbed edge detect client migration by intercepting DHCP request packets, while the OVSBs in the core direct the flow of client packets from the testbed root to the client on the testbed edge.

Each network-level node with OVSBs also uses OVS patch ports (OVSPPs). To ensure proper routing of packets destined for an IP not routable by a foreign network, OVSPPs are used to connect the external and internal facing OVSBs installed on the gateways/APs. This allows independent subnets to operate within the testbed. The OVSPPs, combined with flows that utilize these OVSPPs, force client packets to bypass Linux routing on each hop, thus supporting cross-subnet compatibility upon migration from the home network.

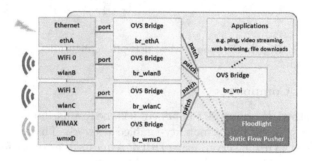

Fig. 5. Client Open vSwitch interface configuration

4.2   Client Component

Any mobile device should be able to connect to a network in our testbed and maintain an IP through a vertical or horizontal handover. However, if the handover is to be truly seamless to an application, there needs to be a persistent VNI for the application to use. The VNI abstracts the handover from the application and provides the application with an interface that is persistent for the duration the client is active. In addition to the VNI, the client should also be able to switch between interfaces in a manner that is simple and straightforward to the experimenter utilizing the testbed.

Similar to the network-level design, OVSBs are also utilized in the client to achieve a seamless handover. These client-level OVSBs are used in conjunction with a client-level FL OF controller and are installed for each mobility NIC on the client, as shown in Fig. 5. The local FL controller inserts flows in each OVSB via the integrated Static Flow Pusher. These flows route application packets from the client VNI to the NIC of choice. When a decision is made to switch NICs, the client will issue a DHCP request egress the new interface, which will then trigger the aforementioned events in the network-level. As a result, these OVSBs with FL-inserted flows allow the client to seamlessly switch from one network to another. All client-level tasks are encapsulated in shell scripts to provide testbed experimenters with a simple and single command to execute a handover.

Each client-level OVSB also contain OVSPPs. To ensure proper routing of packets from the VNI to the NIC of choice, OVSPPs are used to connect the VNI OVSB with the OVSB of each participating NIC installed on the client. (as seen in Fig. 5). The OVSPPs, combined with flows that utilize these OVSPPs, serve to link the VNI to each NIC's OVSB. These flows define the route (and thus the NIC) used by application packets.

The use of a VNI introduces a problem when associating with networks and routing packets to the client from the network-level. The MAC address of the VNI must be the same as that of the NIC, otherwise WiFi APs and other access mediums will not accept packets from or know how to route packets back to the client's VNI at the link layer. It is not reasonable to require the modification or "spoofing" of each NIC's MAC address to that of the VNI. The client-level solution to this problem is to perform MAC-rewrite within the client OVSBs. When an application generates packets, they are routed out of the client via flows on each OVSB. These flows contain actions to rewrite the source MAC address of all egress packets from that of the VNI to that of the NIC. The flows also contain actions to rewrite the destination MAC address of all ingress packets from that of the NIC to that of the VNI. This rewrite process allows the client to send and receive packets from its VNI with any associated network on the link layer. Due to a limitation of OF, ARP packets cannot be rewritten with flows; they must be processed instead by a controller. Thus, the client-level FL controller contains a custom module to rewrite all ARP packet MAC addresses within the controller itself. Although out-of-band processing of packets is inefficient as compared to in-band, ARP packets are not frequent, so an occasional rewrite within the controller is a compromise made in our client-level implementation.

4.3   Client-Network Signaling

The sequence of events that takes place when a client migrates to a foreign network is shown in Fig 6. To summarize the interaction between the two components, the events are as follows:

1. Client establishes L2 connection with the network and issues DHCP discover
2. Floodlight intercepts packet, allocates IP and responds with an offer
3. Client responds to offer by sending DHCP request
4. Floodlight intercepts request, triggers migration event and DHCP acks
5. Client receives DHCP ack, establishing L3 connectivity. Meanwhile, the network-level FL controller inserts flows at the root and gateway OVSBs and removes any existing flows belonging to the client.

After this process completes, the client will have established full network connectivity on a foreign network through the root node.

5   Future Work

We plan on integrating our vertical handover solution more tightly with GENI wireless efforts. This includes helping other campuses install our testing framework as well as using OMF to manage our mobile nodes. The GENI wireless

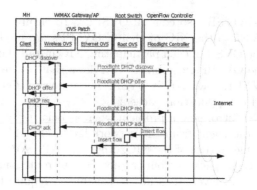

Fig. 6. Client Migration Sequence Diagram

community has taken steps towards using Android handheld devices as their test devices for mobility scenarios. To accommodate this, we will be investigating installing Open vSwitch on GENI Android devices and deploying our client component as an Android application. This will enable researchers to test their handover decision algorithms on Android mobile devices in a real-world heterogeneous wireless network.

6   Conclusion

This paper details a framework that leverages SDN features to provide a testbed for evaluating handovers for IPv4 heterogeneous wireless networks. Based on the framework, we have designed and implemented a testbed that we (as well as other researchers) can use to explore ideas related to vertical handovers. The testbed was implemented as a part of the GENI project which identified the need for an easily deployable method of achieving seamless vertical handovers in an IPv4 OF-enabled heterogeneous wireless environment. The testbed design presented in this paper meets these requirements and, as a proof-of-concept, has been implemented across wireless resources at the Clemson campus. The result is an IP mobility solution that is achieved solely through the use of OF features.

References

1. GENI (January 2014). http://www.geni.net/
2. OpenFlow (January 2014). https://www.opennetworking.org/
3. Amin, R.: Towards Viable Large Scale Heterogeneous Wireless Networks. Ph.D. thesis, Clemson University (2013)
4. Angoma, B., Erradi, M., Benkaouz, Y., Berqia, A., Akalay, M.C.: A vertical handoff implementation in a real testbed. Mobile Computing 1(1) (2012)
5. Hare, J., Hartung, L., Banerjee, S.: Beyond deployments and testbeds: Experiences with public usage on vehicular wifi hotspots. In: Proceedings of the 10th International Conference on Mobile Systems, Applications, and Services. MobiSys 2012, pp. 393–406 .ACM, New York, (2012). http://doi.acm.org/10.1145/2307636.2307673

6. Ormont, J., Walker, J., Banerjee, S., Sridharan, A., Seshadri, M., Machiraju, S.: A city-wide vehicular infrastructure for wide-area wireless experimentation. In: Proceedings of the Third ACM International Workshop on Wireless Network Testbeds, Experimental Evaluation and Characterization. WiNTECH 2008, pp. 3–10. ACM, New York (2008). http://doi.acm.org/10.1145/1410077.1410080
7. Perkins, C.: IP Mobility Support for IPv4, Revised. RFC 5944 (Proposed Standard) (Nov 2010). http://www.ietf.org/rfc/rfc5944.txt
8. Perkins, C., Johnson, D., Arkko, J.: Mobility Support in IPv6. RFC 6275 (Proposed Standard) (July 2011). http://www.ietf.org/rfc/rfc6275.txt
9. Rutgers, C., Princeton, Lucent Bell Labs, I.R., Thomson: Orbit lab (January 2014). http://www.orbit-lab.org/
10. Taniuchi, K., Ohba, Y., Fajardo, V., Das, S., Tauil, M., Cheng, Y.-H., Dutta, A., Baker, D., Yajnik, M., Famolari, D.: Ieee 802.21: Media independent handover: Features, applicability, and realization. Comm. Mag. **47**(1), 112–120 (2009). http://dx.doi.org/10.1109/MCOM.2009.4752687
11. Uddin, M.M., Pathan, A.S., Haseeb, S., Ahmed, M.: A test-bed analysis for seamless mipv6 handover in heterogeneous environment. In: 2011 IEEE 15th International Symposium on. Consumer Electronics (ISCE), pp. 89–94. IEEE (2011)
12. Xu, K., Izard, R., Yang, F., Wang, K.C., Martin, J.: Cloud-based handoff as a service for heterogeneous vehicular networks with openflow. In: Research and Educational Experiment Workshop (GREE), 2013 Second GENI pp. 45–49 (2013)
13. Yan, X., ekerciolu, Y.A., Narayanan, S.: A survey of vertical handover decision algorithms in fourth generation heterogeneous wireless networks. Computer Networks 54(11), 1848–1863 (2010). http://www.sciencedirect.com/science/article/pii/S1389128610000502

Utilizing OpenFlow, SDN and NFV in GPRS Core Network

Martin Nagy[✉] and Ivan Kotuliak

Faculty of Informatics and Information Technologies,
Slovak University of Technology in Bratislava, Ilkovičova 2, 84216, Bratislava, Slovakia
martinko.nagy@gmail.com, ivan.kotuliak@stuba.sk

Abstract. Since GPRS introduction, mobile networks had gone a long way, however GPRS with its EDGE enhancement is still widely used, but the architecture proves to be outdated, complex and often hard to integrate with other technologies. With the introduction of new networking approaches such as SDN and NFV, many problems regarding GPRS emerge. In this paper we present a new architecture for delivery of GPRS service which uses modern approaches such as SDN and NFV. This architecture simplifies the whole network by moving mobile network intelligence to the SDN controller, while removing old, complex nodes such as SGSN and GGSN and mobile protocols such as GTP. This brings the network flexibility, programmability, service elasticity and vendor independency. No changes on the radio access network or the mobile terminal are required to deploy our simplified GPRS architecture, so backward compatibility and interoperability is ensured. Proposed architecture was implemented and tested with real radio access network and mobile terminal.

Keywords: 3GPP networks · GPRS · SDN · Software Defined Networking · NFV · Network Functions Virtualization · OpenFlow · Signaling and user data separation · Wireless networks · Cellular networks · PCU-ng · PCUng · ePCU · vGSN · GRE

1   Introduction

Enormous traffic growth in today's networks causes problems to both network operators and network equipment vendors. Operators are unable to cope with the increasing network complexity and expenses which growing network brings. Vendors on the other hand are forced to bring new more powerful products to the market to satisfy the operator's needs.

The traffic growth however does not correspond to the revenue growth, but as mentioned before, operators are forced to invest in the transport infrastructure which decreases the revenue even more. Therefore the infrastructure becomes very complex mix of different transport and access technologies, often managed by various Observation, Administration and Management (OAM) systems.

Emerging approaches as Software Defined Networking (SDN) [1] and Network Function Virtualization (NFV) [2] seem as a solution, because they try to address many problems of the current networking industry.

© Institute for Computer Sciences, Social Informatics and Telecommunications Engineering 2014
V.C.M. Leung et al. (Eds.): TridentCom 2014, LNICST 137, pp. 184–193, 2014.
DOI: 10.1007/978-3-319-13326-3_18

Network appliances are expensive due to overall complexity, high performance and resiliency. Other problems include the vendor specific technologies and interfaces by which operators lock themselves to a single vendor, even they would wanted to choose every single networking element from a different network vendor.

Next problem is the time to market and flexibility of today's networks. Due to vendor specific technologies, proprietary or non-existent Application Programming Interfaces (APIs), introduction of new services has to be tightly consulted and cooperated with vendors, which increases the overall cost and time to market.

SDN and NFV promise to bring vendor independency, real-time analytics, more agile and flexible network management and quicker time to market. Mobile network equipment vendors have already released their first vision of SDN deployment in mobile networks, however they focus on the latest network technologies such as UMTS and LTE. There may be two reasons for this research aim. First is the better architectural fit of SDN and NFV to UMTS and LTE, because UMTS and LTE have split user-plane and control-plane transport over the network. Therefore it is more easy to use SDN in these networks, as SDN also builds on user and control plane separation. Second reason comes from the market. GPRS is an old technology and operators probably will not make serious investments to the GPRS based infrastructure in the future, therefore it does not make economic sense to invest into research of something, that might not generate enough revenue.

We, on the other hand, consider the SDN and NFV based GPRS network as interesting problem, as the 2G is still the most used mobile network due to its age, good coverage and penetration.

2   GPRS Network Basics

General Packet Radio Service (GPRS) is a technology which extends the standard Global System for Mobile Communication (GSM) network, so it can support packet switched data transport. It uses the same Radio Access Network (RAN) as the GSM does. RAN consists of Base Transceiver Station (BTS) and Base Station Controller (BSC). BTS is basically an antenna with modulation/demodulation and error correction circuitry. BSC controls a set of BTS and implements most of the logic of RAN. The GPRS capable BSC differs from GSM only BSC by an extra module called the Packet Control Unit (PCU). PCU splits incoming data from BTS into two types - packet switched traffic and circuit switched data/voice traffic.

Although RANs in GSM and GPRS network are fairly similar, the core network is totally different. GPRS adds totally new packet switched core network. It consists of Serving GPRS Support Node (SGSN) and Gateway GPRS Support Node (GGSN). SGSN connects to the BSC/PCU by an interface or more precisely reference point called Gb. SGSN may be connected to multiple BSCs via Gb interface. SGSN is responsible for mobility and session management, ciphering, authentication and packet routing from given BSC to correct GGSN and the other way (from GGSN to correct BSC).

SGSN may be connected to more GGSNs. GGSN is basically an IP based router which connects to SGSN by Gn reference point from one side and to external packet switched networks (Internet, intranet, VPN, etc.) from the other side (Gi reference point). Gn reference point is based on GPRS tunneling protocol (GTP). GTP suite can be further divided into GPRS Tunneling Protocol – user plane (GTP-u) and GPRS Tunneling Protocol – control plane (GTP-c). GTP-u is used for user data transfer from SGSN to GGSN, where the GTP-u header is removed and a plain IP packet is sent towards for example Internet over Gi interface. GTP-c is used for signaling between SGSN and GGSN (e.g. PDP context creation, deletion and modification) and SGSN-SGSN signaling during inter SGSN procedures (e.g. inter SGSN routing area update) when mobile station moves from domain served by one SGSN to domain served by another SGSN. Both SGSN and GGSN have connections to SGSNs and GGSNs in other countries and networks, for roaming purposes. This reference point is named Gp.

Additionally to network nodes mentioned above, there are other support nodes in the GPRS network such as Home Location Registry (HLR), Visitor Location Registry (VLR), Mobile Switching Center (MSC) and Equipment Identity Registry (EIR). All subscription data of the user is stored in HLR. Network elements such as SGSN or MSC communicate with HLR to acquire user profile data (e.g. subscribed services, authentication info). VLR is usually collocated with MSC and stores the information of all users served by MSC. MSC is basically a call router in circuit switched part of the network. EIR is used for whitelisting or blacklisting of certain terminals, for example the stolen ones.

Two concepts, that are unique to 3GPP mobile networks is Packet Data Protocol Context (PDP context) and the Access Point Name (APN). PDP context is a logical connection between SGSN and GGSN through which user data is transferred. This connection is established during procedure called PDP context activation, by which the mobile station acquires an IP address (among other connection parameters).

APN is a simple string, which identifies the external network to which the mobile station wants to connect. It has to noted, that APN specifies at the same time the GGSN and the service which mobile station wants to use. One example of common APN is "internet".

The typical scenario for GPRS mobile network consists of few procedures. First the mobile station has to connect to the network. This procedure is called the attach procedure. During this procedure the mobile network verifies the identity of the mobile station and assigns it a temporary identity for security purposes – Packet Temporary Mobile Station Identity (P-TMSI). Now the mobile station can send and receive SMS messages and calls. To send and receive packet switched data, it has to activate a PDP context. During this procedure, the mobile station specifies the service, to which it wants to connect (e.g. internet), QoS and other parameters. Network deduces the IP address of GGSN which provides requested service by a DNS resolution of APN and assigns an IP address to the mobile station. From this moment, the mobile station is able to communicate with external networks. All the user data traverses BTS, BSC/PCU, SGSN, GGSN and then finally leaves the mobile network. It has to be noted that in GPRS architecture, the signaling information (between BSC/PCU and SGSN) and user plane information are transported together over GPRS-Network Service (GPRS-NS) layer.

Later an enhancement of GPRS architecture came, called Enhanced Data rates for GPRS Evolution (EDGE), which brought higher order modulation and new coding schemes on the radio interface towards the mobile terminal. Changes required for EDGE deployment were mainly made in the radio access network.

Next generations of mobile networks such as Universal Mobile Telecommunications System (UMTS) and Long Term Evolution (LTE) will not be explained in this paper (Fig. 1.), detailed network architecture, principles and protocols can be found in 3GPP standards [3] [4] [5].

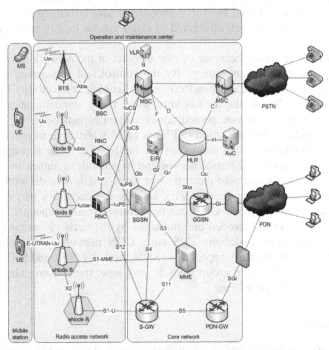

Fig. 1. GSM/GPRS/UMTS/LTE network with both packet switched and circuit switched parts of the network

2.1   Software Defined Network and Network Function Virtualization

Computer networks, even if highly distributed, combined both data and control plane from the start. Introduction of new services and features was slow and vendor dependent.

In general the term Software Defined Networking (SDN) stands for more programmable way of controlling the network behavior. It also includes forwarding (user plane) and control plane decoupling, so the control plane (network intelligence) is logically centralized in one single place [6].

SDN architecture can be generalized to three basic components: forwarder, controller, network/business applications.

In addition to mentioned three entities, reference points (interfaces) can be defined: northbound interface, southbound interface, westbound interface, eastbound interface.

SDN controller logically centralizes the network's intelligence and controls the forwarding plane by southbound interface. Moreover forwarding plane can be queried for statistical information or notifications can be received through this interface. The northbound interface of SDN controller is used for communication with various external networks and business applications which can query controller for information, for example network performance, topology, or request from controller some kind of action such as policing. Eastbound and westbound interfaces are used mainly in inter-controller communication, for example when each controller is located in different domain and they want to cooperate for example in path computation. It is worth noting, that all interfaces should be well standardized and information exchanged over these interfaces should be well abstracted to avoid vendor lock-in and emphasize fast adoption [7] [8].

All in all SDN promises decrease of overall costs of the network devices, increase of flexibility and easier management. By the control and forwarding plane decoupling, each plane can evolve independently while keeping compatibility through well-defined network APIs. As the area is very wide, many standardization bodies and vendors came up with their own, sometimes even open approaches.

Network Functions Virtualization (NFV) is ETSI's initiative to move specialized network functions from special and expensive hardware to general purpose x86/x64 computing architecture. It addresses networking in general, so numerous different use cases are proposed, for example there are use cases which consider virtualization of the Customer Premises Equipment (CPE), so only the necessary part of it is really present at the customer's place. CPEs can be therefore smaller, cheaper, more energy efficient and also more controlled and managed by the network operator. Other use cases include virtual base stations, IMS core, CDN networks and mobile network core. NFV is a complementary approach to SDN. Actually NFV and SND can benefit from each other. As the workgroup itself is very new, there is no exhaustive information available at the time being.

2.2   OpenFlow

As we built our new architecture on OpenFlow protocol, it is appropriate to introduce the OpenFlow protocol. It is the currently most popular SDN approach widely accepted in the academic community and the vendor community. OpenFlow splits the network into control plane and forwarding plane. Forwarding plane implemented by OpenFlow switches is managed by OpenFlow controller which is logically centralized.

OpenFlow switch behaves according to flow table, which consist of match criteria, actions and counters ordered in flow entries. Match criteria is a set of different protocol header fields and packets are compared against this criteria. Supported match criteria, actions and counters vary based on the OpenFlow version the switch and controller are compliant to. If the packet (flow) is matched, statistics are updated and corresponding action is executed. If packet does not match any entry in the flow table, forwarder can either drop the packet or send packet to the controller for further processing. OpenFlow protocol is used to add, delete and modify the flow table inside the OpenFlow Switch. A different protocol, OF-Config based on NetConf/Yang, was added to query OpenFlow switch capabilities and change parameters of the device. The most widespread version is 1.0 released in December 2009. Next versions of the switch specification and protocol added support for multiple flow tables, group flow table to manage multiple flows, IPv6 support, MPLS matching, meter support for QoS and support for multiple controllers. Due to its simplicity, OpenFlow was quickly adopted by the academic community and the commercial community. At the time being first commercial products are being introduced. Moreover many open source OpenFlow solutions exist [6].

3 Related Work

Mobile network operators and vendors are also trying to adopt the SDN philosophy to their use cases and benefit from the control and user plane decoupling, network programmability, scalability and reduction of expenses. However since the SDN approach is relatively new, no commercial deployment of SDN based mobile network was done yet.

For example Alcatel-Lucent/Bell-Labs proposed a concept of vertical forwarding. Vertical forwarding described by their approach basically means tunneling of data through the network [9]. Alcatel-Lucent sees the main disadvantage of carrier network in numerous of gateway nodes (mobility, security, etc.). These gateway nodes have often vendor specific interface and use specific signalization protocols as they execute specific functionality. As they pose a single point of failure, they must be extremely resilient which increases the cost of the equipment. To deal with these drawbacks, control plane and forwarding plane split is proposed in this approach. Intelligence and control of all gateways should be logically moved to the controller and forwarding plane should be realized on simple hardware. By using single controller of all gateways, network can react on failure of the network appliance and reroute traffic to the healthy nodes, without using special inter-gateway communication protocols.

Moreover control and data plane can evolve separately, upgrades and new protocols can be introduced separately for each element, where the change on one element will not affect the other.

Ericsson on the other hand proposed a GPRS Tunneling Protocol (GTP) extension for the OpenFlow protocol for Evolved Packet Core (EPC) [10]. This approach has been experimentally tested, however on UMTS architecture, where instead of MME, S-GW and P-GW a combination of SGSN and GGSN was used. It is worth noting that Ericsson has also patented this approach both in LTE/EPC [11] and in UMTS [12]. Authors of the paper argue, that EPC (and other 3GPP based mobile architectures) relies on two forms of routing, which are not coordinated, but on the other hand rely on each other. The first layer is the IP routing and second is GTP routing based on Tunnel Endpoint Identifiers (TEID) in GTP header. Coordination can be achieved, when the IP routing logic will be collocated with the GTP routing logic (MME, P-GW, S-GW, etc.).

Huawei with its MobileFlow architecture is defining an area of Software Defined Mobile Networks (SDMN) [13]. Architecture consists of MobileFlow Controller (MFC) and MobileFlow Forwarding Engines (MFFE). MFFE are somehow similar to OpenFlow forwarders, but little more feature rich (but still simpler than traditional network nodes). MFFEs are capable of for example GTP encapsulation, charging and policing. They implement the MobileFlow protocol on the Smf reference point. The control plane is similarly to OpenFlow centralized around MobileFlow Controller. MobileFlow uses MobileFlow protocol as a southbound protocol to communicate with MFFE. Controller is capable of communication with similar controllers via east-west interface, northbound interface is used to communicate with network applications. These applications can include EPC entities functionality (e.g. MME) or novel network applications. MobileFlow preserves the interoperability with existing UEs, therefore the changes in core network are transparent. Huawei successfully proved and tested their novel architecture by implementing UMTS and LTE network with real eNodeB and other simulated nodes.

All in all, it is evident that network vendors consider SDN as viable approach. However the market seems to be very conservative and the real commercial solutions are probably just yet to come.

4   Novel SDN and NFV Enabled GPRS Architecture

In traditional GPRS architecture, signaling and user plane data is transported together (between BSC/PCU and SGSN). For efficient use of SDN and NFV in the GPRS network, we have to separate these two types of information. This is desirably done as close to the radio access network as possible.

In our new GPRS architecture, we deploy a GPRS aware OpenFlow switch, which separates signaling and user plane data so streams of signaling only and user plane only messages are available. We call this new network element PCU for next generation networks (PCU-ng). The GPRS signaling is routed to the integrated GPRS control element called vGSN and the stream of user plane data is encapsulated into Generic Routing Encapsulation (GRE) protocol and routed to desired point (e.g. Internet).

vGSN combines functionalities of SGSN and GGSN from the classic GPRS architecture, mainly mobility management and security functions. For session management functions we use OpenFlow based SDN controller. SDN controller and vGSN communicate in order to setup, modify or teardown the sessions (PDP contexts) of the mobile stations. The advantage of splitting mobility and session management to two separated nodes is that architecture remains highly extensible for adding new mobility management nodes for future access technologies to the network with no or minimal impact on existing ones.

The session management in our architecture differs from the GPRS session management. We have substituted the GTP-u protocol, which is used only in mobile networks for something more common – GRE protocol (Generic Routing Encapsulation). Also tunnel management procedures have changed. Since we don't have a standalone SGSN and GGSN, there is no need for GTP-c signaling. The transport core network can easily be implemented by cheap OpenFlow GRE enabled switches. GRE tunnels are being created, modified or teardown by the SDN controller according to requests from vGSN. This is also an advantage since in classic GPRS architecture, a PDP context could be terminated only on GGSN. As our architecture does not have any GGSN node, we can terminate GRE tunnels anywhere we want, which enables further traffic flow optimization (e.g. offload Internet traffic from the network as soon as possible).

After the PDP context activation request from the mobile station, the vGSN informs the controller of the desired GRE tunnel/PDP context parameters. These include mainly the endpoint of the GRE tunnel deduced from the APN, the beginning of the tunnel given by source PCU-ng and QoS. SDN controller installs this GRE tunnel according to resources in the network and the user plane data can flow to and from the desired destination from this moment.

It has to be noted that the signaling messages towards mobile station remain the same, so no changes in protocol stack in BSC or mobile station is required.

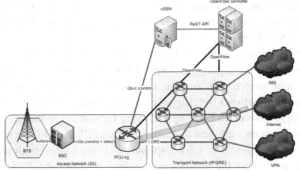

Fig. 2. New SDN/NFV based GPRS architecture

The PCU-ng operates as follows. It considers Service Access Point Identifiers (SAPI) 3, 5, 9, 11 in the GPRS-Logical Link Control (GPRS-LLC) layer header as the user data and the others as signaling. It has to be noted that signaling also includes GPRS transported SMS messages and Tunelling of Messages envelopes (TOM), but this can be handled as signaling in the vGSN. To match the LLC-SAPI field, OpenFlow protocol had to be extended to match all underlying protocols and fields. First the standard IP and UDP protocols are matched. Certain UDP port number tuples are considered as a transport for GPRS – Network Service layer (GPRS-NS), this is of course configurable. Inside GPRS-NS the Packed Data Unit (PDU) type field is matched. This field can either be GPRS-NS keepalive (NS_ALIVE/NS_ALIVE_ACK), which is forwarded to vGSN or other (NS_UNIDATA) which requires further processing. At GPRS-NS layer PCU-ng also processes the BSSGP Virtual Connection ID (BVCI) which identifies a virtual connection between BSC/PCU and SGSN. If the packet is NS_UNIDATA type, PCU-ng proceeds to further processing of Base Stations Subsystem GPRS Protocol (BSSGP) layer. First important field is the BSSGP PDU type, which can be again a BSSGP level signaling (e.g. FLOW-CONTROL-BVC, FLOW-CONTROL-BVC-ACK), or other types of messages (DL-UNIDATA, UL-UNIDATA). If other types of messages are matched, PCU-ng advances to analyzing the other fields such as Temporary Logical Level Identity (TLLI), which identifies the Mobile station. Last layer which is analyzed is the GPRS-Logical Link Layer (GPRS-LLC). Here only the Service Access Point Identifier is analyzed. Based on the value of this field, the PCU-ng decides whether the packet is a user plane message (SAPI=3, 5, 9, 11) or other (signaling, SMS, TOM).

5   Experimental Setup and Results

We implemented our solution from freely available open-source components. Our radio access network consists of open source hardware-based BTS. It provides one quad band GSM/GPRS TRX with an IP/Ethernet connection to the core network (Gb over IP). Base station is EDGE capable, however support in the PCU was not implemented yet. This missing support affects only the radio access network part and it is not important for our test setup. An open-source GPRS PCU (osmo-pcu [14]) resides on this hardware and connects to GPRS enabled OpenFlow forwarder – PCU-ng. This element implements custom GPRS OpenFlow actions (push/pop of BSSGP, GPRS-LLC and SNDC protocol headers) and custom GPRS match criteria (matching of selected information elements in GPRS related protocol headers) as enablers for the user and control plane separation. Our GPRS access controller module – vGSN is also based on open-source components, mainly osmo-sgsn [15] and open-ggsn [16]. vGSN combines the network intelligence of both nodes, while the data-path (user-plane processing) is moved to PCU-ng and other forwarders in the network.

OpenFlow components are based on ofsoftswitch (CPqD) [17] forwarder and RYU controller [18], both OpenFlow 1.3 compliant [19]. We cloned both project repositories and we are modifying the sources with a final goal to get GPRS support merged into project mainlines.

At the time being we are able to split the signaling and user plane data by PCU-ng and forward them to required locations. User plane data is moreover encapsulated into GRE as mentioned before. Extensive GRE tunnel management is in the development phase. Regarding the mobility management, as our current setup routes mobility and authentication messages towards circuit switched part of core network, we are not dealing with them right now on vGSN. However after the tunnel management work is done, the setup will be change to reflect the real topology and scenarios including mobility management with multiple BTS/BSC.

6   Conclusion

All in all we have significantly simplified the GPRS architecture from the point of overall infrastructure, by replacing complicated SGSN and GGSN nodes by extensible vGSN and SDN controller nodes, which can run on general x86/x64 architecture (NFV). In the legacy architecture, each PDP context had to be terminated only on GGSN node. In our architecture, PDP context can lead to any of the OpenFlow forwarders, which will strip off the GRE header and send user data to the external network. This enables offloading heavy traffic destined for the Internet from the core network as soon as possible. Next we have substituted the GTP protocol, which is only used in mobile networks for something very common and simple – GRE protocol (Generic Routing Encapsulation). The architecture is an enabler for seamless mobility as it has a single session manager (SDN controller) which will bring a single, not changing IP address for mobile devices changing their access networks. Moreover the architecture enables extensibility for future access networks.

Acknowledgments. This project was partially supported by Slovak National research grant 1/0676/12 and by the Tatra banka foundation under the contract No. 2012et011. We also want to thank all members of our research team, namely Ján Skalný, Tibor Hirjak, Martin Kalčok, Matúš Križan and Peter Balga.

References

1. Sezer, S., et al.: Are we ready for SDN? Implementation challenges for software-defined networks, Communications Magazine, **51**(7), pp.36–43, IEEE (July 2013)
2. ETSI: Network Functions Virtualization (2014). http://www.etsi.org/technologies-clusters/technologies/nfv
3. 3GPP: TS 23.060 rel. 10.12.0 – General Packet Radio Service (GPRS); Service description; Stage 2 (2013)
4. 3GPP: TS 23.401 rel. 10.11.0 – General Packet Radio Service (GPRS) enhancements for Evolved Universal Terrestrial Radio Access Network (E-UTRAN) access (2014)
5. 3GPP: TS 23.002 rel. 10.5.0 – Network architecture (2012)
6. Open Networking Foundation: Software-Defined Networking: The New Norm for Networks, ONF White Paper (2013). https://www.opennetworking.org/images/stories/downloads/sdn-resources/white-papers/wp-sdn-newnorm.pdf
7. Myung-ki, S., Ki-hyuk, N., Hyoung-jun, K.: Software-defined networking (SDN): A reference architecture and open APIs. In: ICT Convergence (ICTC), pp.360–361 (2012)
8. Myung-ki, S., Ki-hyuk, N.: Formal Specification Framework for Software-Defined Networks (2013). http://tools.ietf.org/html/draft-shin-sdn-formal-specification-03
9. Hampel, G., Steiner, M., Tian, B.: Applying Software-Defined Networking to the telecom domain. In: Computer Communications Workshops, pp.133–138 (2013)
10. Kempf, J., Johansson, B., Pettersson, S., Luning, H., Nilsson, T.: Moving the mobile evolved packet core to the cloud. In: WiMob (2012)
11. Johansson, B., et. al.: Implementing epc in a cloud computer with openflow data plane (2011). http://www.google.com/patents/WO2012160465A1
12. Johansson, B., et. al.: Implementing a 3G packet core in a cloud computer with OpenFlow data and control planes (2012). http://www.google.com/patents/US20130054761
13. Pentikousis, K., Yan, W., Weihua, H.: Mobileflow: Toward software-defined mobile networks. Communications Magazine, IEEE **51**(7), 44–53 (2013)
14. osmo-pcu (2014). http://openbsc.osmocom.org/trac/wiki/osmo-pcu
15. osmo-sgsn (2014). http://openbsc.osmocom.org/trac/wiki/osmo-sgsn
16. open-ggsn (2014). http://sourceforge.net/projects/ggsn/
17. ofsoftswitch (CPqD) (2014). https://github.com/CPqD/ofsoftswitch13
18. Nippon Telegraph and Telephone Corporation: Ryu SDN Framework (2014). http://osrg.github.io/ryu/
19. Open Networking Foundation: OpenFlow Switch Specification 1.3.0 (2012). https://www.opennetworking.org/images/stories/downloads/sdn-resources/onf-specifications/openflow/openflow-spec-v1.3.0.pdf

Investigating the Performance of Link Aggregation on OpenFlow Switches

Toan Nguyen-Duc[1]([⊠]), Hoang Tran-Viet[1], Kien Nguyen[1,2],
Quang Tran Minh[2], Son Hong Ngo[1], and Shigeki Yamada[2]

[1] Hanoi University of Science and Technology,
1 Dai-Co-Viet Street, Hanoi, Vietnam
{toan.nguyenduc1,hoang.tranviet}@hust.edu.vn,
sonnh@soict.hust.edu.vn
[2] National Institute of Informatics, 2-1-2 Hitotsubashi, Chiyoda-ku,
Tokyo 101-8430, Japan
{kienng,quangtran,shigeki}@nii.ac.jp

Abstract. In this paper, we extensively explore the operation of Link Aggregation (LA) on OpenFlow switches in comparison to the LA in conventional switches. The comparison of two LA implementations has been conducted in a real testbed under the UDP and TCP traffic loads. The testbed includes Pica8 P-3925 switches, which support two modes: an OpenFlow switch (i.e., using Open vSwitch) and a conventional switch (i.e., using the operating system called XorPlus). The evaluation results show that two LA implementations achieve similar performance in improving throughput. However, the XorPlus implementation provides a better resilience than the other. Specifically, the LA implementation on XorPlus spends less than 1.49538 seconds to switch the TCP traffic on the faulty link to the other links of a Link Aggregation Group (LAG) while the switchover time is four times longer on the Open vSwitch. In the case of UDP traffic, the maximum switchover time on the Open vSwitch is twice the one on XorPlus.

Keywords: Link aggregation · Resilient · Aggregation bandwidth · Openflow switch · Evaluation

1 Introduction

Link Aggregation refers to the capability of combining multiple physical cables into a logical link. The standardized link aggregation appears in IEEE 802.1AX [1], and is widely used for connecting pairs of networking devices. The link aggregation is prevalent because it provides a cost-effective way to improve bandwidth by simply adding new links alongside the existing ones instead of replacing the existing equipment with a higher-capacity link. For example, a 40Gbps aggregated bandwidth link is formed by aggregating four cables with capacity 10Gbps

© Institute for Computer Sciences, Social Informatics and Telecommunications Engineering 2014
V.C.M. Leung et al. (Eds.): TridentCom 2014, LNICST 137, pp. 194–202, 2014.
DOI: 10.1007/978-3-319-13326-3_19

each. Moreover, the link aggregation is also necessary since it increases the network resilience. When a physical cable of the logical link fails, the logical one continues to carry traffic over the remaining cables. Therefore, many network vendors have introduced LA supported in their hardware and software products. However, each vendor has its own commercial solutions which are closed to networking researchers. The same problem occurs in both the traditional manufacturers as well as the ones in the fast growing OpenFlow community.

The OpenFlow technology has been emerging with the concept of software defined networking, which provides innovation and flexibility in network operations and managements [2]. One of key features of the technology is the OpenFlow switch, whose specification is frequently updated by Open Networking Foundation. The switch is an extension of Ethernet switch, which also uses one or several internal forwarding tables. However, the switch has an extra interface, which is used to receive the control instructions from outside. The decoupling design of OpenFlow switch not only increases advanced functionalities but also reduces the cost and complexity of networking hardware. The OpenFlow switch was first deployed in an academic campus network [3], and the OpenFlow features have been supported by many networking vendors. More importantly, the OpenFlow has been successfully deployed in several production networks, such as Google WAN globally interconnecting datacenters [4]. However, several basic but important technologies such as Link Aggregation are recently added to the specification of OpenFlow Switch (version 1.1). Hence, it is necessary to extensively evaluate the technologies' performance in order to support the increasing deployments of OpenFlow.

There exist several related works on evaluations of OpenFlow switches [5, 6]. However, the works mainly focused on evaluating several basic networking parameters on data or control planes such as the throughput and latency. Besides that, there is also an investigation on the performance of specific OpenFlow hardware [7] targeting the scalability of OpenFlow switches. Different to other works, we investigate the operation of LA in OpenFlow switches, and compare its performance with the LA in conventional switches. The comparison of two LA implementations is conducted in a real testbed using Pica8 P-3295 switches [8] with UDP and TCP traffic. The switch supports two modes: an OpenFlow switch and a conventional switch. The mode OpenFlow switch is an open source Open vSwitch with the latest stable version 1.10.0 [9,10]. The mode conventional switch uses Pica8 operating system called Xorplus version 2.0.4. Our aim is to debug the traffic behaviours on the logical links of LA as well as investigate the benefits of LA on the network (e.g., increasing throughput, resilience, etc.). In term of network resilience, we measure the switchover time which is the duration of switching the traffic on the faulty link over the other links in a LAG.

The remainder of paper is organized as follows. In Section 2 we describe the theoretical background of our evaluation including basics of link aggregation, OpenFlow switch, and port mirroring. In Section 3, we present the LA evaluations and results. Finally, we conclude our work in section 4.

2   Theoretical Background

2.1   Link Aggregation

The first standard of Link Aggregation (LA) was introduced in the IEEE 802.3ad [11] in 2000. In 2008, LA was removed from the IEEE 802.3 and added to the IEEE Std 802.1AX-2008. LA is commonly used to connect pairs of networking devices (i.e., switches, routers, etc.), aiming to provide greater bandwidth at the network core. For example, LA which is made up of four links with capacity 10 Gbps each, can carry 40 Gbps. However, the traffic must be a mixture of connections since LA needs to keep the order of the packets. Moreover, LA potentially achieves resilience against link breakage since the failure only affects the carrying traffic that is automatically switched to the others if the connectivity still exists.

LA uses LAG to control static local information and the LA-related information must be configured (e.g., ports on networking devices). Each port has a Port ID and an operational key when it is belong to a LAG. The Port ID is combined with the system ID and the operational key to construct a LAG ID. On the transmitter, LA uses an Aggregator to distribute frame transmissions from a client to the appropriate ports in a LAG. On the receiver, the Aggregator collects received frames from the ports and pass them to the client transparently as shown in Fig. 1. Therefore, the receivers see all links in a LAG as a single logical link. The Aggregator also decides if a new link can join a LAG by comparing its operational Key to the operational Key of the port to which the link connect. Once the local device and its peer agree on the LAG, frames are distributed and collected on the aggregated link. LA uses Link Aggregation Control Protocol (LACP) for dynamic information exchanged between two LA-supported devices. The devices commonly referred to respectively as the "ACTOR" and the "PARTNER". One simple illustration of the communication is shown in

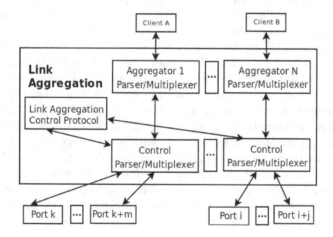

Fig. 1. Link Aggregation 802.1AX block diagram

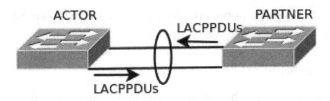

Fig. 2. Dynamic Link Aggregation

Fig. 2. Typically, LACP performs a number of tasks to support the communication between the devices. First, after a LAG is created on both devices, when cables are plugged in to the ports in a LAG, the ACTOR exchanges messages, such as protocol data units (PDUs) with the PARTNER. The messages allow LACP to determine whether or not both peers have the same system ID or have the same speed. If they do, the Collecting and Distributing flags in LACP PDUs are set, the aggregated link is capable of transmitting and receiving traffic. In the second step, LACP monitors the status of individual links to ensure their membership between ACTOR and PARTNER is still valid. In order to perform the monitoring, a periodic timer on the ACTOR will trigger transmission of PDUs to the PARTNER and vice versa. In a failure scenario, three LACPPDUs are exchanged without dependence on timer value. Consequently, the configuration resolves quickly to a stable configuration. In the third and last step, LACP controls the addition of links to the existing LAG as well as removes down links from the group.

2.2 OpenFlow Switch

An OpenFlow network consists mainly of OpenFlow switch(es) and OpenFlow controller(s). Essentially, the control of a switch, such as packet routing, is moved to the OpenFlow controller so that the controller administrator has full control over the switch. The controller interacts with the switch by using OpenFlow protocol. The function of the protocol is to install, modify or remove entries on a flow table of the switch. Each entry contains a flow description and a list of actions associated with that flow. When a packet reaches an OpenFlow switch, the switch extracts the packet header (e.g., MAC addresses, IP addresses, and TCP/UDP ports) and compares this information to the flow description of the flow table entries. If a matching entry is found, an action is applied to the packet. For example, the packet may be dropped or forwarded to one or more OpenFlow switch ports. If a matching is not found, the switch will ask the controller for the action that should be applied to all packets from the same flow. The decision is then sent to the switch and saved as an entry in the switch's flow table. The next incoming packets that belong to the same flow are then forwarded through the switch without referring to the controller. The earlier versions of OpenFlow Switch Specifications did not provide LA because their forwarding model simply supported drop, forwarding, and flood packets. Fortunately, since the version 1.1 of OpenFlow Switch specification, the concept of virtual port has been added to reuse the existing physical ports interface for additional functions like tunneling, and specially link aggregation, etc.

2.3 Port Mirroring

It is not easy to capture the traffic behaviors on individual links in a LAG because all the links are treated as a single one. We find that in order to obtain the behaviors, the technique named port mirroring [12] is extremely useful. The port mirroring is a fundamental option on packet switches and it is configurable remotely. The purpose of technique is to copy all incoming/outgoing packets on a switch port called mirrored port to another port called mirroring port. By doing so, we can monitor the traffic on the mirrored port by placing a packet capturing tool on the mirroring port. Moreover, the technique is also benefit for the evaluation of system resilience as later mention in Sections 3.

3 Evaluation

The testbed in our evaluation consists of two switches and three hosts as illustrated in Fig. 3. As mentioned earlier, the switches run either Open vSwitch or XorPlus. The switches are wired using two cables with capability 1Gbps each, which are formed a LAG. The steps of creating the LAG on the two OpenFlow swiches are implemented mostly following the two manuals of Pica switches [13,14]. In order to effectively collect the results, three Linux hosts, which are equipped with Intel Core I5, 4GB RAM, and Ubuntu 12.04 LTS 64 bit, are used as a traffic generator, receiver, and monitor. On the right side of topology (Fig. 3), the hosts H2 and H3 are attached to the switch SW2, through GE cables. On the left side, the host H1 has four 1Gbps networking cards shown as eth0, eth1, eth2, eth3, respectively. The eth2's duty is to receive the traffic from H2 and H3. The eth0 and eth1 are used to monitor the traffic on each member of the LAG by using Port Mirroring. In the evaluation, we generate the traffic from H2 and H3 to H1 using Iperf [15]. We capture the receiving traffic on the observed hosts using the tool named Bwm-ng [16].

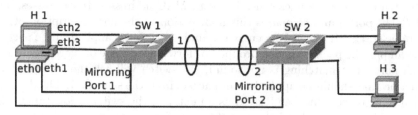

Fig. 3. Evaluation Testbed

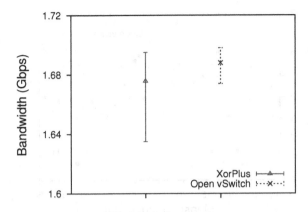

Fig. 4. TCP-related aggregation bandwidth measurement

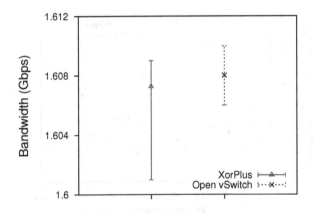

Fig. 5. UDP-related aggregation bandwidth measurement

3.1 Evaluating the Aggregation Bandwidth

The measurement procedure with TCP traffic is as follows. Initially, an Iperf server is started on H1 listening for incoming requests. Then, an Iperf client is enabled on H2, that attempts to establish communication with the Iperf server. After 5 seconds, another Iperf client, which share the same destination with the one on H2, is triggered on the host H3. The Iperf clients will be stopped after 90 seconds. We run the procedure 50 times on the two types of switches and the results for Open vSwitch and Xorplus are shown in Fig. 4. Figure 4 shows that the maximum TCP bandwidth of the LAG is about 1700 Mbps on Open vSwitch. This is only marginally higher than the maximum bandwidth of the LAG on XorPLus. We have also repeated the same procedure for the UDP traffic. The UDP bandwidth results are shown in Fig. 5. Similar to TCP traffic,

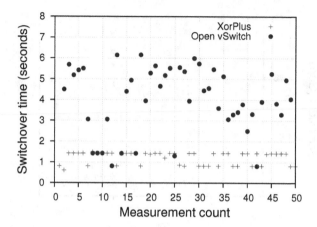

Fig. 6. TCP-related switchover time measurement results

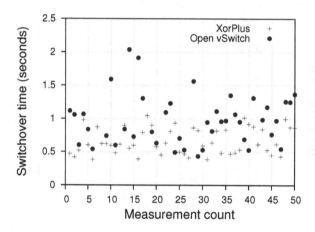

Fig. 7. UDP-related switchover time measurement results

the maximum UDP bandwidth of the LAG is 1600 Mbps and it is slightly higher bandwidth comparing to the other.

3.2 Evaluating the System Resilience

In order to evaluate how LA improves the system resilience, we observe the network performance when link failures occur. The focusing parameter is the switchover time, which is defined as the duration of switching the traffic from a faulty link to another aliveness link. Specifically, the switchover time t is the difference between the timestamp t1 carried by the last packet on the faulty link and the timestamp t2 on the first packet that goes over the alive one. The shorter switchover time, the fewer packet loss, and hence the shorter one leads to a better system resilience. In this evaluation, we use the same scenario as in Figure 3. The host H1 has three 1Gbps NICs called eth0, eth1 and eth2. The NICs are used to capture traffic on a computer aiming to avoid the problem of clock synchronization on different machines. As shown in the figure, Port 1 of SW1 connected to the first link of the LAG and Port 2 of SW 2 connected to the second one. SW1 was configured to copy the traffic on port 1 to another port. This port was then connected to H1's eth1. Similarity, the traffic on port 2 of SW2 was mirrored to another port which was connected to H1's eth0. As a result, H1 can monitor the network traffic on each link of the LAG. Tcpdump[17] was used to capture the details of packets being received over H1's eth0 and eth1.

In this evaluation, we also use both UDP and TCP traffic on the two types of switches. Each experiment has been repeated 50 times with random link failures, and the values of switchover time are presented in Fig. 6 and Fig. 7. Figure 6 shows that in the cases of TCP traffic the maximum switchover time on Open vSwitch is 6.15464 seconds, which is nearly four times longer than the one on Xorplus. However, the minimum switchover time on two types of switches is almost similar (0.815891 seconds compare to 0.607892 seconds). Figure 7 shows the UDP traffic switchover time on the switches. We can see the Open vSwitch spends maximum of 2.036 seconds to switch UDP traffic, which is twice longer than that time on Xorplus. Hence we confirms that LA enhances the system resilience since it can automatically switch the traffic. Besides that, the evaluation results also show that among two switches the conventional switch has a better resilience performance in term of switchover time.

4   Conclusion

We have evaluated the LA performance on OpenFlow switches and compared it against the one on conventional switches. The evaluation results confirm that the LA can spread the traffic load to all links in a LAG. Consequently, the aggregation bandwidth is increased linearly with the number of the aggregated links. Comparing the LA performance on the two types of switches, we found that the LA on OpenFlow switch provides a slightly lower throughput than the other. We also observed that LA enhances the system resilience since the capability of automatic switching the traffic on the faulty link to the aliveness links lets the LA keeps the logical link alive. Moreover, the LA implementation on XorPlus spends maximum of 1.49538 second to switch a TCP flow in the failure scenario. This period is four times faster than the one on OpenFlow switch. In the case of UDP traffic, it takes less than 2.036s for the LA implementation on the OpenFlow switch, but still twice longer than the LA on the conventional switches. We conclude that LA on Open vSwitch can be an alternative to the one on the conventional switch in improving throughput. However, the switches need to be furthermore optimized to achieve the equivalent performance in increasing system resilience.

In the future, we plan to extend the investigation on a LAG made up of more links. Moreover, we also plan to investigate the paths form by several

LAGs through multiple switches (i.e., multi-hop). Besides that, we are going to study the behavior and performance of LA under more complicated scenarios such as high throughput, or delay sensitive environments. Finally, we will explore the Fast Failover function of OpenFlow and compare the values of switchover time achieved by the Fast Failover and the one by LA.

References

1. IEEE Std 802.1AX-2008 (2008). http://standards.ieee.org/findstds/standard/802.1AX-2008.html
2. Lara, A., Kolasani, A., Ramamurthy, B.: Network innovation using openflow: A survey. IEEE Trans. Communications Surveys Tutorials **16**(1), 493–512 (2014)
3. McKeown, N., Anderson, T., Balakrishnan, H., Parulkar, G., Peterson, L., Rexford, J., Shenker, S., Turner, J.: Openflow: enabling innovation in campus networks. SIGCOMM Comput. Commun. Rev. 38(2) (2008)
4. Jain, S., Kumar, A., Mandal, S., Ong, J., Poutievski, L., Singh, A., Venkata, S., Wanderer, J., Zhou, J., Zhu, M., Zolla, J., Hölzle, U., Stuart, S., Vahdat, A.: B4: experience with a globally-deployed software defined wan. In: Proc. ACM SIG-COMM 2013, pp. 3–14 (2013)
5. Mateo, M.P.: OpenFlow Switching Performance. Master's thesis, Politecnico di Torino (July 2009). http://www.openflow.org/downloads/technicalreports/MS_Thesis_Polito_2009_Manuel_Palacin_OpenFlow.pdf
6. Bianco, A., Birke, R., Giraudo, L., Palacin, M.: Openflow switching: Data plane performance. In: Proc. IEEE International Conference on Communications (ICC), pp. 1–5 (2010)
7. PPELMAN, M.A.: Performance Analysis of OpenFlow Hardware. Master's thesis, University of Amsterdam (December 2012). http://www.delaat.net/rp/2011-2012/p18/report.pdf
8. Pica8   P-3295   Switch   specification.   http://www.pica8.org/document/pica8-datasheet-48x1gbe-p3290-p3295.pdf
9. Open vSwitch. http://openvswitch.org/
10. Pfaff, B., Pettit, J., Koponen, T., Amidon, K., Casado, M., Shenker, S.: Extending networking into the virtualization layer. In: Proc. of Workshop on Hot Topics in Networks (HotNets-VIII) (2009)
11. IEEE 802.3ad Link Aggregation Task Force (2000). http://www.ieee802.org/3/ad/
12. Zhang, J., Moore, A.: Traffic trace artifacts due to monitoring via port mirroring. In: Proc. IEEE End-to-End Monitoring Techniques and Services 2007, pp. 1–8 (2007)
13. PicOS 2.0.1 L2/L3 Configuration Guide. http://www.pica8.org/document/picos-2.0.1-12-13-configuration-guide.pdf
14. PicOS 2.0.1 OVS Configuration Guide. http://www.pica8.org/document/picos-2.0.1-ovs-configuration-guide.pdf
15. Iperf. http://iperf.sourceforge.net/
16. Bwm-ng. http://sourceforge.net/projects/bwmng/
17. Tcpump. http://www.tcpdump.org/

Large Scale Testbed Federation

SPICE Testbed: A DTN Testbed for Satellite and Space Communications

Ioannis Komnios[✉], Ioannis Alexiadis, Nikolaos Bezirgiannidis,
Sotiris Diamantopoulos, Sotirios-Angelos Lenas,
Giorgos Papastergiou, and Vassilis Tsaoussidis

Space Internetworking Center, Office 1, Building A, Panepistimioupoli Kimmeria,
Department of Electrical and Computer Engineering, Democritus University of Thrace,
67100 Xanthi, Greece
{ikomnios,ialex,nbezirgi,sdiaman,slenas,
gpapaste,vtsaousi}@ee.duth.gr

Abstract. This paper presents SPICE testbed, a state-of-the-art Delay Tolerant Networking testbed for satellite and space communications deployed at the Space Internetworking Center, Greece. The core of the testbed relies on the Bundle Protocol and its architecture has been designed to support multiple DTN implementations and a variety of underlying and overlying protocols. SPICE testbed is equipped with specialised hardware components for the accurate emulation of space links and ground stations, such as Portable Satellite Simulator (PSS) and CORTEX CRT system, as well as protocols and mechanisms specifically designed for space DTNs. Performance and functionality evaluations on SPICE testbed show that it is an ideal platform to evaluate new mechanisms in a variety of space communication scenarios.

Keywords: Delay Tolerant Networking · DTN Testbed · Bundle Protocol · ION · DTPC · BSS · BDTE · Space Communications · Interplanetary Internet

1   Introduction

Delay Tolerant Networking (DTN) [1] has emerged as a promising solution to the upcoming explosion in the volume of data produced by space assets and delivered to Earth. Since 2007, the Consultative Committee for Space Data Systems (CCSDS) [2] has formed a work group for the standardisation of space delay-tolerant protocols. SPICE researchers have been actively involved in the standardisation procedures and have developed a prototype DTN testbed for space communications under a contract of the European Space Agency (ESA) [3-5].

Due to the nature of space communications and the restricted amount of space assets, the design of a space-oriented DTN testbed does not necessarily need hundreds of nodes, but requires accurate emulation of space components and links that support diverse protocol stacks, depending on the nature of each asset. It is crucial to offer to researchers a realistic testing environment in order to evaluate, benchmark and optimise new protocols. In this context, SPICE testbed has received funding from EC's

© Institute for Computer Sciences, Social Informatics and Telecommunications Engineering 2014
V.C.M. Leung et al. (Eds.): TridentCom 2014, LNICST 137, pp. 205–215, 2014.
DOI: 10.1007/978-3-319-13326-3_20

FP7 SPICE project [6] in order to be enhanced with more nodes and specialised components that accurately emulate the functionality of typical ground stations, space links and satellites. Our aim is to build an experimental research environment for developing and evaluating a variety of new architectures and protocols for space communications. In particular, SPICE testbed presents the following key features:

i) *Realistic emulation of space communications.* Unlike the majority of existing DTN testbeds, which focus on terrestrial delay-tolerant communications, SPICE testbed provides a realistic experimental environment for satellite and space communications, including real and flight-ready components. Indeed, specialised hardware and software components have been incorporated into the testbed, enabling the testing, evaluation and validation of implemented mechanisms and protocols. Furthermore, a link with a geostationary satellite, namely HellasSat 2, is utilised on demand, to provide real satellite link characteristics for experimental purposes.

ii) *Compliance with typical equipment of major space agencies.* SPICE testbed incorporates typical components used by space agencies for the evaluation of protocols prior to mission launch. In particular, the Portable Satellite Simulator (PSS) [7] was built in compliance with ESA's requirements, while CORTEX CRT [8] is used by all major space agencies in their ground station facilities to support their missions. Finally, Satellite Tool Kit (STK) [9] is employed by mission designers as a tool to calculate not only exact satellite trajectories and contact durations, but also detailed communication characteristics, and perform link-budget analysis.

iii) *Interface provision for multiple underlying protocols.* SPICE testbed not only supports a variety of convergence layers for underlying protocols that comply with CCSDS standards and major space agencies, but also facilitates the development of novel routing, transport, and management schemes. Taking advantage of this functionality, SPICE researchers are able to validate such schemes against standardised protocols and perform interoperability testing.

iv) *Scalability.* SPICE testbed includes numerous nodes for the evaluation of complex communication scenarios that involve several space assets and can be further enhanced with virtual nodes installed on a high-performance server. Therefore, complex scenarios involving constellations of satellites (e.g., cubesats) and several end-users can be realistically modeled. It should also be mentioned that this scalability comes without adding any complexity, since the testbed is easily configured and controlled through dedicated workstations.

The remainder of the paper is structured as follows: Section 2 details the architecture of SPICE testbed and its major components. In Section 3 we refer to protocols and mechanisms that have been developed and evaluated in the testbed, along with sample results, while in Section 4 we present related work. The paper is concluded in Section 5.

2   SPICE Testbed Architecture and Components

2.1   SPICE Testbed Architecture

Notionally, the testbed comprises two distinct parts, namely the data plane and the control plane, and its architecture is depicted in Fig. 1. Data is transferred between nodes to emulate communication among space and ground assets through the data plane, while configuration scripts, control messages, and reports related to the emulation are managed through the control plane. Each plane is described in detail below.

Control plane - The control plane is responsible for (a) configuring and controlling the testbed nodes in real time based on user input, (b) monitoring the correct node operation, (c) collecting any associated performance statistics, and (d) delivering the experimental results to the researchers. These operations are coordinated by a main controller accessible via the internal network or the Internet. A hardware firewall restricts remote access, allowing only encrypted VPN connections. Researchers configure the experiments to be conducted through a user interface (UI), available at the main controller. Link characteristics and emulation parameters are either imported directly by the users or provided by the STK workstation after conducting the relevant simulations. Upon the completion of an experiment, results are collected and stored in the main controller.

Data plane – SPICE testbed supports the emulation of a wide variety of space and satellite communication scenarios, including present and future missions. These scenarios may involve (a) a number of landed assets, such as landers and rovers, that generate scientific data and can possibly form a planetary network, (b) a set of space assets near Earth or in deep Space (e.g. LEO/MEO/GEO satellites, spacecraft, planetary relay satellites etc.) that can produce and/or relay data, (c) terrestrial facilities such as typical ground stations (GS), mission operation centers (MOC) and end-users. Researchers are able to emulate all these types of space communications taking advantage of the diverse protocol stack configurations supported by SPICE testbed (Fig. 2).

In particular, an implementation of Proximity-1 [10] is employed as a CCSDS data link protocol to interconnect planetary nodes with relay satellites. Within space DTN network each space asset is emulated by a distinct DTN node. Depending on the objective of the emulation, researchers may use one of the three available CCSDS data link protocol implementations to interconnect space and ground station DTN networks:

Type I: Software-based emulation of the basic functionality of TM/TC/AOS protocols [11-13]. Space assets and ground stations are emulated using only ION-DTN implementation [14].

Type II: Software-based emulation of the full functionality of TM/TC/AOS protocols including Space Link Extension (SLE). Space assets are emulated using ION-DTN, as well as SIMSAT Software. Ground stations do not support DTN and receive AOS/TM/TC packets using SIMSAT.

Type III: Hardware-based emulation of the full functionality of TM/TC protocols. Space assets are emulated utilizing ION-DTN and the combination of SIMSAT and PSS. In this case, ground stations do not support DTN and only receive TM/TC frames using CORTEX CRT system.

Communication between a ground station (GS) and a mission operations center (MOC) can be either DTN-based (Type I) or SLE-based (Type II and Type III). Space data are then transferred to the end-users using ION-DTN. HellasSat 2 satellite may also be employed to provide real satellite link characteristics between DTN nodes.

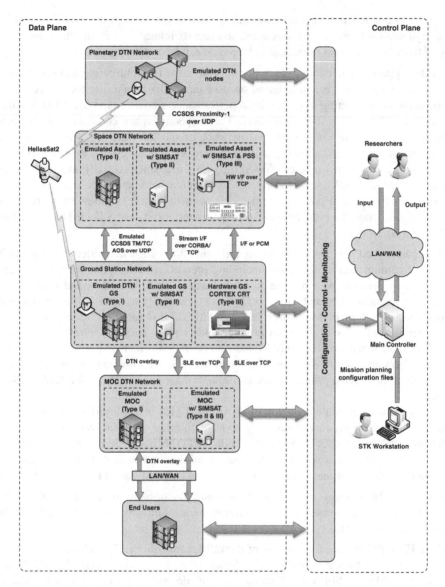

Fig. 1. SPICE Testbed Architecture

2.2   Hardware Components

DTN Nodes - The DTN nodes are fifteen rack-mounted servers used as distinct emulation nodes in experiments with network protocols of the DTN architecture. Each node is equipped with a quad-core Intel Xeon CPU operating at 2.4GHz with 4GB of RAM and 1TB of storage, running a Linux distribution. Private IP addresses are assigned to these servers so that they can communicate directly with each other locally. Additionally, they are divided into three groups of five, with a public

IP address used by each group for inbound/outbound Internet traffic. Inbound traffic is strictly limited to a few ports needed for remote access and the DTN frameworks. Users have the ability to gain access by means of an IPSec VPN, which is configured on a hardware firewall. Each server constitutes a standalone DTN node implementing the full DTN stack. In certain scenarios, where more DTN nodes are needed, the testbed core can be extended by employing a number of virtual machines. For this purpose a high-performance computer is used, featuring two hexa-core Intel Xeon CPUs, 24GB of RAM and 12TB of redundant storage. The high-performance computer runs a bare-metal hypervisor, VMware vSphere, which sets up the virtualization layer. This makes for a scalable testbed core capable of accommodating more than 35 nodes, enough to emulate most space missions.

Portable Satellite Simulator (PSS) - Portable Satellite Simulator Mark III (PSS) [7] is a generic PC based system capable of injecting telemetry into the downlink chain of a ground station and receiving telecommands from the uplink chain, complying with CCSDS recommendations and European Cooperation for Space Standardisation (ECSS) and ESA standards. PSS offers several monitoring and control interfaces and a maintenance interface, which allows controlling and monitoring the PSS locally at the ground station or remotely from the control center. PSS is deployed in the testbed as a state-of-the-art hardware satellite model, incorporating the link layer protocol stack of a real satellite.

CORTEX Command Ranging and Telemetry System (CORTEX CRT) - CORTEX CRT [8] is a state-of-the-art Telemetry and Telecommand base-band COTS. CORTEX CRT system allows a continuous improvement of the signal processing and supports future standards through telemetry processing, CCSDS telecommanding processing, ranging measurements etc. In essence, CORTEX CRT is able to decode and process telemetry data received from a satellite through an antenna and encode telecommand data transmitted to a satellite. CORTEX CRT has field-proven compatibility with most of satellites, high level of reliability with no preventive maintenance, and has been extensively used by many space agencies, including NASA, ESA and JAXA. Within SPICE testbed, CORTEX CRT emulates the functionality of a real ground station collecting and transmitting data from/to satellites.

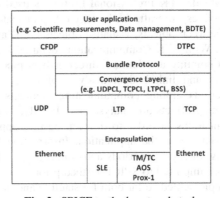

Fig. 2. SPICE testbed protocol stack

HellasSat 2 - A satellite link over HellasSat 2 has been set up at the premises of SPICE for the evaluation of Bundle Protocol (BP) [15] over a real satellite link, subject to errors and disruptions due to weather conditions.

2.3   Software Components

DTN Implementations - Interplanetary Overlay Network (ION) [14] is an implementation of the DTN architecture developed by Jet Propulsion Laboratory (JPL) and released as open source software. It includes implementations of the DTN Bundle Protocol, the Licklider Transmission Protocol (LTP) [16], Bundle Security Protocol (BSP) [17], and two CCSDS application protocols that have been adapted to run over the BP/LTP stack: class-1 (unacknowledged) CCSDS File Delivery Protocol (CFDP) [18] and Asynchronous Message Service (AMS) [19]. ION is the key DTN implementation of SPICE testbed, since it has been specifically designed for delay-tolerant space communications. Several protocols that have been developed by researchers of the Space Internetworking Center have been already incorporated in the latest ION release, and other are planned to be released in the following versions. **DTN2** [20], which is the reference implementation of the DTN architecture, and **IBR-DTN** [21], an implementation of the Bundle Protocol designed for embedded systems and smartphones are also included in the SPICE Testbed, mainly for interoperability testing purposes.

CCSDS File Delivery Protocol (CFDP) [18] - The ESA CFDP ground segment implementation provides a full implementation of the CCSDS File Delivery Protocol. ESA's CFDP provides a Java library and a daemon implementation for reliable and unreliable file transfer in space and on the ground. This implementation will be used by the European Space Agency on ground for upcoming space missions.

SIMSAT - SIMSAT [22] is a general-purpose real-time simulation infrastructure developed for ESA. SIMSAT supports standard simulation services such as cyclic and event-based real-time scheduling of models, logging of simulation events etc. The SIMSAT User Interface is used to coordinate experiments that utilise the Portable Satellite Simulator.

Satellite Tool Kit (STK) - STK [9] is an off-the-shelf mission modeling and analysis software for space, defense and intelligence systems and is used as an external component to the DTN testbed. STK Professional Edition is used to create and manage high-level objects (satellites, aircraft, facilities, etc.), propagate and orient vehicles, analyse relationships between objects, visualise objects in 2D and 3D and animate in real or simulated time. With STK Communications detailed transmitter and receiver elements with antenna pointing are defined, direct or bent pipe communication links over time are analysed and link budget analysis of each communication link is performed, contact periods among communicating elements are calculated, accidental/intentional jamming effects are analysed etc. Finally, Integration Module integrates with other applications in order to develop custom applications to automate repetitive tasks from outside of the application. Information like bandwidth, error rates, propagation delay, disruption periods and connectivity schedule constitute network parameters that are imported to SPICE testbed prior to each experiment. Several scenarios have been implemented so far both for satellite and deep-space communication experiments.

Netem - The netem tool [23], which is included in recent Linux kernel versions (2.6+), is used to alter networking properties and emulate variable delay, loss, duplication and re-ordering.

3   Protocols Designed and Evaluated

SPICE testbed is an ideal platform to evaluate different DTN implementations, protocols, applications and services. Its architecture and components have already contributed to the design, implementation, and optimization of novel algorithms and protocols, with respect to the challenging conditions of satellite and space communications [24-29]. Moreover, SPICE testbed has been used as the key testing platform in several European and ESA funded projects including FP7 SPICE, FP7 Space Data Routers [30], ESA's Extending Internet Into Space, ESA's BitTorrent study and more. In the following subsections, we briefly present sample works, along with experimental results obtained with SPICE testbed.

3.1   Delay-Tolerant Payload Conditioning

Delay-Tolerant Payload Conditioning (DTPC) protocol [31] is an end-to-end transport protocol that was designed in collaboration with NASA's Jet Propulsion Laboratory and is used on top of the Delay-Tolerant Networking (DTN) architecture, offering services such as controlled aggregation of application data units (ADUs) into DTPC *data items* with application-specific elision, end-to-end reliability, in-order delivery and duplicate suppression. A thorough evaluation procedure was developed to assure the correct functionality of the services offered by the DTPC protocol using up to 4 DTN nodes of SPICE testbed, as well as Netem to emulate various link properties (i.e. propagation delay, data rate and error rate). DTPC protocol was implemented into the ION-DTN software platform, along with two test applications for sending and receiving data, respectively. The evaluation scenarios are space-oriented in that propagation delays are in the order of seconds and contact times are scheduled. Therefore, LTP protocol was used as a convergence layer protocol in all bundle nodes. The time-sequence graph depicted in Fig. 3 tracks the delivery of ADUs at the receiver and shows that DTPC successfully retransmits items that were lost or considered lost due to loss of ACKs. In the latter case, the duplicate items are recognized as such and are discarded. DTPC protocol has been included in the official ION-DTN distribution since version 3.2.0.

3.2   Bundle Streaming Service

Bundle Streaming Service (BSS) [32] is a framework that supports the delivery of streaming media in DTN bundles. It exploits the characteristics of such networks to allow for reliable delay-tolerant streaming while improving the reception and storage of data streams. BSS is a joint work between Space Internetworking Center and Jet Propulsion Laboratory, NASA. It is incorporated into ION-DTN, along with two test applications for sending and receiving data, respectively, using the BSS framework. The extensive evaluation process of BSS mechanism was solely based on SPICE DTN testbed. In particular, several Space network configurations were emulated under different sets of network protocol stacks under variable propagation delays, high error rates, both symmetric and asymmetric network topologies in terms of communication link properties, as well as different number of communicating nodes and bundle sizes. The acquired results, presented in Fig. 4, show that BSS framework clearly outperforms ION's default forwarding mechanism (ipnfw) over the entire set of experiments.

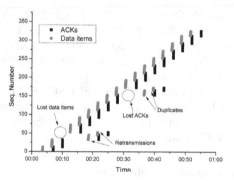

Fig. 3. DTPC - Evaluation of end-to-end reliability

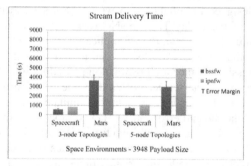

Fig. 4. Comparison between BSS and IPN forwarder based on stream delivery time of a representative sample of cases from Space scenarios

3.3 Delivery Time Estimation for Space Bundles

Bundle Delivery Time Estimation (BDTE) tool [33] is an application designed to work in an administrative framework and provide accurate predictions for end-to-end data delivery delays. It exploits a novel algorithmic method, based on the Contact Graph Routing algorithm [34], which predicts bundle route and calculates plausible arrival times along with the corresponding probabilities, based on measurements taken in network nodes and disseminated using DTN management protocol. The application development, as well as the design and implementation of the experimental database for supporting the application were developed in SPICE testbed and were included into the ION-DTN platform, with a plan to be released under the open source license. Fig. 5 depicts a sample BDTE application output, with the possible end-to-end arrival times of a bundle and the cumulative probability distribution.

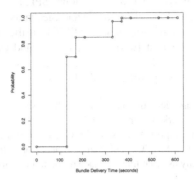

Fig. 5. BDTE output: Bundle delivery times and corresponding probabilities

4   Related Work

Given the specialised nature of space DTN communications, only a few testbeds have been developed on the field. The TATPA testbed [35] was one of the first proposals to integrate DTN in a satellite emulator. The authors of [36] have built a basic DTN testbed based on a space link simulator (SLS) and performed relay operations. This testbed consists of three nodes only and, thus, can only emulate small-scale scenarios. Similarly, Muri and McNair [37] have emulated a single optical flight terminal that relays data between two ground stations, focusing however on providing a high-capacity optical channel. As an extended approach, DTNbone [38] has been initiated as an interoperability-testing platform and consists of a collection of nodes worldwide running DTN bundle agents and applications. Given its distributed nature, each node of DTNBone is managed by the owner organisation and does not facilitate extensive testing. One of the most extended testbeds, namely the DTN Engineering Network (DEN) [39], has been developed by NASA and comprises physical and virtual machines and flight-like hardware located at different NASA centers and supporting universities. The DEN is configured with reference implementations of advanced communication protocols, including the Bundle Protocol and Licklider Transmission Protocol, and has been used by NASA to validate both software implementations and decentralized operational concepts. SPICE testbed constitutes a European alternative to DEN that provides an extended DTN experimental platform. In contrast to the closed DEN, SPICE testbed is widely available to the research community for validation and evaluation of existing protocols, as well as deployment and experimentation of newly developed mechanisms in a reliable, efficient DTN testbed.

5   Conclusions

Building a DTN testbed for satellite and space communications is a challenging task. Careful design is required to identify and fulfill the distinct requirements of present and future space missions. In this paper, we have presented a state-of-the-art DTN testbed that is scalable and includes several DTN nodes and specialised components that accurately emulate the whole protocol stack of satellite and space communications, as well as the operation of typical ground stations. SPICE testbed has leveraged the development and evaluation of novel protocols and mechanisms for space DTN. Promising results so far showcase the competence of SPICE testbed as an experimental platform with potential to be the first European validation and evaluation tool for future space internetworking protocols. Our aim is to encourage researchers to develop and test new space DTN concepts utilising SPICE testbed.

Acknowledgments. The research leading to these results has received funding from the European Community's Seventh Framework Programme ([FP7/2007-2013, FP7-REGPOT-2010-1, SP4 Capacities, Coordination and Support Actions) under Grant Agreement n° 264226 (Project title: Space Internetworking Center - SPICE). This paper reflects only the authors' views and the Community is not liable for any use that may be made of the information contained therein.

References

1. Fall, K.: A Delay-Tolerant Networking Architecture for Challenged Internets. In SIGCOMM, pp. 27–34 (2003)
2. The Consultative Committee for Space Data Systems (CCSDS). http://public.ccsds.org/default.aspx
3. Koutsogiannis, E., Diamantopoulos, S., Papastergiou, G., Komnios, I., Aggelis, A., Peccia, N.: Experiences from Architecting a DTN Testbed. Journal of Internet Engineering 3(1), 219–229 (2010). Kleidarithmos Press
4. Samaras, C., Komnios, I., Diamantopoulos, S., Koutsogiannis, E., Tsaoussidis, V., Papastergiou, G., Peccia, N.: Extending Internet into Space – ESA DTN Testbed Implementation and Evaluation. In: Granelli, F., Skianis, C., Chatzimisios, P., Xiao, Y., Redana, S. (eds.) MOBILIGHT 2009. LNICST, vol. 13, pp. 397–404. Springer, Heidelberg (2009)
5. Koutsogiannis, E., Diamantopoulos, S., Tsaoussidis, V.: A DTN Testbed Architecture. Workshop on the Emergence of Delay-/Disruption-Tolerant Networks (E-DTN), St. Petersburg, Russia, October (2009)
6. EC's FP7 Space Internetworking Center (SPICE) project. http://www.spice-center.org
7. Portable Satellite Simulator (PSS). http://www.spacelinkngt.com/PSSIMBU.html
8. CORTEX CRT system. http://www.zds-fr.com/en/products/10/satellite-ttc.html
9. Satellite Tool Kit (STK). http://www.agi.com/products/
10. Proximity-1 Space Link Protocol, CCSDS 211.0-R-3.1 (2002)
11. CCSDS Telemetry (TM) Space Data Link protocol Recommendation for Space Data Systems Standards. CCSDS 132.0-B (2003)
12. CCSDS Telecommand (TC) Space Data Link protocol Recommendation for Space Data Systems Standards. CCSDS 232.0-B-2 (2010)
13. AOS Space Data Link Protocol, CCSDS 732.0-B-1, Blue Book, Issue 1 (2003)
14. Interplanetary Overlay Network (ION-DTN), Jet Propulsion Laboratory Ohio University. http://sourceforge.net/projects/ion-dtn/
15. Scott, K., Burleigh, S.: Bundle Protocol Specification. IETF RFC 5050 (2007)
16. Ramadas, M., Burleigh, S., Farrell, S.: Licklider Transmission Protocol. IETF RFC 5326
17. Symington, S., Farrell, S., Weiss, H., Lovell, P.: Bundle Security Protocol Spec. RFC 6257
18. CCSDS File Delivery Protocol (CFDP) Recommendation for Space Data System Standards, CCSDS 727.0FBF4 (2007)
19. Asynchronous Message Service (AMS). http://trs-new.jpl.nasa.gov/dspace/bitstream/2014/37837/1/05-0923.pdf

20. DTN2 Delay Tolerant Networking Reference Implementation.
    `http://sourceforge.net/project/showfiles.php?group_id=101657`
21. Doering, M., Lahde, S., Morgenroth, J., Wolf, L.: IBR-DTN: an efficient implementation for embedded systems. In ACM CHANTS 2008. pp. 117–120. New York, ACM, NY (2008)
22. SIMSAT simulator. http://`www.terma.com/space/ground-segment/satellite-simulators/`
23. Network Emulator. `http://www.linuxfoundation.org/collaborate/workgroups/networking/netem`
24. Komnios, I., Diamantopoulos, S., Tsaoussidis, V.: Evaluation of Dynamic DTN Routing Protocols in Space Environment, 5th International Workshop on Satellite and Space Communications (IWSSC 2009). Sienna-Tuscany, Italy, September (2009)
25. Koutsogiannis, E., Papastergiou, G., Tsaoussidis, V.: Evaluation of CCSD File Delivery Protocol over Delay Tolerant Networks, 5th International Workshop on Satellite and Space Communications (IWSSC 2009). Sienna-Tuscany, Italy, September (2009)
26. Bezirgiannidis, N., Tsaoussidis, V.: Packet size and DTN transport service: Evaluation on a DTN Testbed. In: International Congress on Ultra Modern Telecommunications and Control Systems 2010, Moscow October (2010)
27. Papastergiou, G., Bezirgiannidis, N., Tsaoussidis, V.: On the Performance of Erasure Coding over Space DTNs. In: 10th International Conference on Wired/Wireless Internet Communications (WWIC 2012), Santorini, Greece, (June 2012)
28. Lenas, S.-A., Burleigh, S.C., Tsaoussidis, V.: Reliable Data Streaming over Delay Tolerant Networks. In: Koucheryavy, Y., Mamatas, L., Matta, I., Tsaoussidis, V. (eds.) WWIC 2012. LNCS, vol. 7277, pp. 358–365. Springer, Heidelberg (2012)
29. Clarke, N.L., Katos, V., Menesidou, S.-A., Ghita, B., Furnell, S.: A Novel Security Architecture for a Space-Data DTN. In: Koucheryavy, Y., Mamatas, L., Matta, I., Tsaoussidis, V. (eds.) WWIC 2012. LNCS, vol. 7277, pp. 342–349. Springer, Heidelberg (2012)
30. FP7 Space-Data Routers for Exploiting Space Data project.
    `http://www.spacedatarouters.eu`
31. Papastergiou, G., Alexiadis, I., Burleigh, S., Tsaoussidis, V.: Delay Tolerant Payload Conditioning protocol. J. Computer Networks. In press (2013)
32. Lenas, S.A., Burleigh, S., Tsaoussidis, V.: Bundle Streaming Service: Design, Implementation and Performance Evaluation. Transactions on Emerging Telecommunications Technologies. In press
33. Bezirgiannidis, N., Burleigh, S., Tsaoussidis, V.: Delivery Time Estimation for Space Bundles. Aerospace and Electronic Systems, IEEE Transactions 49(3), 1897–1910 (2013)
34. Burleigh, S.: Dynamic Routing for Delay-Tolerant Networking in Space. In SpaceOps2008, Heidelberg, Germany (May 2008)
35. Caini, C., Firincielli, R., Lacamera, D., Tamagnini, S., Tiraferri, D.: The TATPA Testbed, a Testbed for Advanced Transport Protocols and Architecture performance evaluation on wireless channels. In: Procedings TridentCom, pp. 1–7, Orlando, Florida (2007)
36. Sun, X., Yu, Q., Wang, R., Zhang, Q., Wei, Z., Hu, J., Vasilakos, A.: Performance of DTN protocols in space communications. Wireless Networks, pp. 1–19 (2013)
37. Muri, P., McNair, J.: A performance comparison of DTN protocols for high delay optical channels, pp. 183–188. In WCNCW, IEEE (2013)
38. Delay-Tolerant Network Research Group, DtnBone.
    `http://www.dtnrg.org/wiki/DtnBone`
39. Birrane, E., Collins, K., Scott, K.: The Delay Tolerant Networking Engineering Network – Constructing a Cross-Agency Supported Internetworking Testbed. In: SpaceOps 2012, Stockholm, Sweden (June 2012)

Empirical Analysis of IPv6 Transition Technologies Using the IPv6 Network Evaluation Testbed

Marius Georgescu$^{(\boxtimes)}$, Hiroaki Hazeyama, Youki Kadobayashi,
and Suguru Yamaguchi

Nara Institute of Science and Technology, Nara, Japan
{liviumarius-g,hiroa-ha,suguru}@is.naist.jp, youki-k@is.aist.nara.ac.jp
http://ipv6net.ro/

Abstract. IPv6 is yet to become more than a worthy successor of IPv4, which remains, for now, the dominant Internet Protocol. Behind this fact is the complicated transition period through which the Internet will have to go, until IPv6 will completely replace IPv4. This transition has presented the Internet Community with numerous challenges. One of these challenges is to decide which transition technology is more feasible for a particular network scenario. As an answer, this article is proposing the IPv6 Network Evaluation Testbed (IPv6NET), a research project whose ultimate goal is to obtain feasibility data in order to formulate a coherent, scenario-based IPv6 transition strategy. The paper presents the overview of IPv6NET, the testing methodology and empirical results for a specific network scenario. The scenario was introduced by the IETF and it was dedicated to an Enterprise Network which is using IPv6 as backbone technology. The Enterprise needs to convey communication tjo IPv4 capable nodes through the IPv6-only infrastructure. A suitable IPv6 transition implementation, covering multiple transition technologies, was tested in relation with this scenario. The presented empirical feasibility data includes network performance data such as: latency, throughput, packet loss, CPU load, and operational capability data, such as: configuration, troubleshooting and applications capability.

Keywords: IPv6 transition · IETF IPv6 scenario · 464 scenario · Enterprise Networks · IPv6NET · Asamap · MAPe, MAPt · DSLite · 464XLAT

1 Introduction

The Internet community found in IPv6 an answer for the continual expansion of the Internet, threatened by the limitations of IPv4. IPv6 uses an 128 bit address, extending the address space to $2^{128} \approx 3.4 \cdot 10^{38}$ unique IP addresses, enough for many years to come. However the light aura of IPv6 has dimmed since 1998, mainly because it is not able to communicate directly with its predecessor, IPv4. This introduced the Internet Community with a great challenge, usually called

© Institute for Computer Sciences, Social Informatics and Telecommunications Engineering 2014
V.C.M. Leung et al. (Eds.): TridentCom 2014, LNICST 137, pp. 216–228, 2014.
DOI: 10.1007/978-3-319-13326-3_21

the transition to IPv6. The transition is represented by the stages the Internet will have to withstand until IPv6 will completely replace IPv4.

Given the complexity of the current IPv4-dominated Internet, the Transition to IPv6 will be a long and complex process. So far, only a small number of production networks are IPv6 capable. The APNIC Labs IPv6 deployment report shows that only about 1.7 % of the users worldwide are currently using IPv6. IPv6 transition scenarios have been researched within the IETF by the v6ops and Softwire Working Groups. The scenarios were dedicated to four main types of networks: ISP Networks, Enterprise Networks, 3GPP Networks and Unmanaged Networks. The IETF ngtrans Working Group has made many efforts to propose and analyze viable transition mechanisms. Many transition mechanisms have been proposed and implemented. All have advantages and disadvantages considering a certain transition scenario, but no transition mechanism can be considered most feasible for all the scenarios. This opens many research opportunities. One of them is a scenario-based analysis of IPv6 transition implementations, and represents the ultimate goal of our research.

In this paper, we are proposing the IPv6 Network Evaluation Testbed (IPv6NET), which is dedicated to measuring the feasibility of transition mechanisms in a series of scenario-based network tests. As a study case, the article is focusing on one of the scenarios introduced by the IETF for Enteprise Networks in [4], targeting enterprises using an IPv6-only network infrastructure but with IPv4-capable nodes, which need to communicate over the IPv6 infrastructure.

The paper is organized as follows: section 2 presents related literature, section 3 introduces the IPv6NET concept and the testing methodology, in section 4 the empirical results are introduced and the feasibility of the tested implementation is analyzed in relation with the specific scenario, section 5 discusses our approach and lastly section 6 states the conclusions and future work.

2   Related Work

There are a variety of articles dedicated to IPv6 transition experimental environments in current literature. They can be generally classified into closed environments and open environments. The closed environments are usually small scale, local environments, which are isolated from production networks or the Internet. In [12], the performance of Linux operating systems is evaluated in relation to an IPv4-v6 Configured Tunnel and a 6to4 Tunnel. Four workstations were employed to build the testbed. In [14], differences in bandwidth requirements for common network applications like: remote login, web browsing, voice communication, database transaction, and video streaming are analyzed over 3 types of networks: IPv4-only, IPv6-only and a 6to4 tunneling mechanism. The environment was built using the OPNET simulator. Also based on the OPNET simulator was the testbed presented in [7], which analyzed the performance of transition mechanisms over a MPLS backbone. A common trait of the above mentioned closed environments, is the thorough performance analysis, which resulted in quantifiable data like: CPU and memory utilization, throughput, end-to-end delay, jitter and execution time.

However, before transition mechanisms are applied in a large scale environment, a systematic and quantitative performance analysis should be performed. This gets us to the second group of experimental environments, namely, open environments. They can be defined as experimental networks connected to a large scale production network or the Internet. [2] describes the lessons learned from deploying IPv6 in Google's heterogeneous corporate network. The report presents numerous operational troubles like: the lack of dual-stack support of the customer-premises equipments (CPE), or the immature IPv6 support of operating systems and applications. One of their conclusions was that the IPv6 transition can affect every operational aspect in a production environment, hence interoperability considerations have to be made. In [1], experiences with IPv6-only Networks are presented. NAT64 and DNS64 technologies are tested in two open environments: an office and a home environment. Common applications like: web browsing, streaming, instant messaging, VoIP, online gaming, file storage and home control were tested. Application issues in relation to the NAT64/DNS64 technology are identified, for example: Skype's limitation to connect to IPv6 destinations, or the lack of network operational diagnostics for certain standalone games. Experiences with IPv6-only Networks from previous WIDE Camp events in [9] present many meaningful interoperability data such as IPv6 capability of OSes, applications and network devices. Many operational issues have been identified. Some examples are: long fall-back routine, low DHCPv6 capability of certain OSes, lack of IPv6 support in some network devices, DNS64 overload, inappropriate AAAA replies or inappropriate selection of DNS resolvers. Considering these examples we can conclude that open environment testing has the potential of exposing interoperability issues, which can otherwise get overlooked.

Combing the advantages of the two testing methods can lead to a complete feasibility analysis. Hence the IPv6NET project is considering both methods for testing.

3   Testing Methodology on IPv6NET

The IPv6 Network Evaluation Testbed (IPv6NET) is dedicated to quantifying the feasibility of IPv6 transition implementations in relation to a specific network scenarios. IPv6NET has two main components: the testing component and the infrastructure component. The testing component has the following building blocks: a specific network scenario, an associated network template and a test methodology. The infrastructure component is represented by the implementations under test and the network test environment. As mentioned, we are considering building both closed and open environments.

The scenario targeted in this article was introduced by the IETF in [4] as Scenario 3. It is dedicated to an enterprise which decided to use IPv6 as the main protocol for network communications. Some applications and nodes, which are IPv4-capable would need to communicate over the IPv6 infrastructure. In order to achieve this, the Enterprise would need to apply an IPv6 transition technology, which would allow both protocols to coexist in the same environment. For simplicity, the technologies suitable for this specific scenario could be referred to as 464 technologies.

3.1 IPv6NET Feasibility Indicators and Metrics

This subsection presents some clarifications regarding the semantics used for the methodology associated with IPv6NET throughout this paper. For the empirical feasibility analysis presented in this article, we are using the term *feasibility indicator* as a generic classifier for performance metrics. For closed environment testing, the proposed feasibility indicator was *network performance*. Network performance indicates the technical feasibility of each technology in relation with existing computer network standards. To quantify network performance, we have used well established metrics, such as : *round-trip-delay, jitter, throughput, packet loss* and *CPU load*. For open-environment testing, we have proposed as feasibility indicator *operational capability*, which is showing how a certain technology fits in with the existing environment or how it manages to solve problems. To our best knowledge, there are no associated metrics for operational feasibility of network devices in current literature. Consequently we have introduced the following three metrics:

- *configuration capability*: measures how capable a network implementations is in terms of contextual configuration or reconfiguration
- *troubleshooting capability*: measures how capable a network implementation is at isolating and identifying faults
- *applications capability*: measures how capable a device is at ensuring compatibility with common user-side protocols

Details about the measurement process for these three metrics, as well as other methodology and infrastructure details, are presented in the following subsections.

3.2 Closed Environment

Infrastructure. The basic, small scale template for 464 technologies is composed of a set of network routers, a Customer Edge (CE) router which would encapsulate/translate the IPv4 packets in IPv6 packets, and a Provider Edge (PE) router, which would handle the decapsulation/translation from IPv6 back to IPv4. The IPv4-only backbone would be used for forwarding the IPv4 traffic. The IPv6 traffic would be directly forwarded by the IPv6 backbone. The closed experiment's design, presented in fig. 1a, follows the basic network template, including one Customer Edge (CE) machine and one Provider Edge (PE) machine.

Multiple technologies can be considered suitable for the 464 scenario: MAPe [15], MAPt [10], DSLite [6], 464XLAT [11]. Some implementations supporting these technologies have been proposed. One of those is the asamap vyatta distribution, which covers 4 of those technologies: MAPe, MAPt, DSLite and 464XLAT. Both 464 PE and 464CE machines have used as Operating System the asamap vyatta distribution.

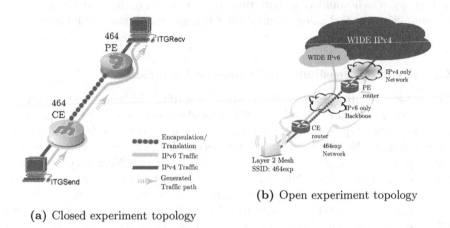

(b) Open experiment topology

(a) Closed experiment topology

Fig. 1. Experimental setup

The closed experiment has used as underlaying infrastructure the StarBED, a large scale general purpose network testbed, administered by the National Institute of Information and Communications Technology (NICT) of Japan. Four computers were used for this experiment: two for the devices under test (DUT), 464 PE and 464 CE, and two for the testing platform. The testing platform computers have used Ubuntu 12.04.3 server as base operating system. One of the computers preformed the ITGSend function, generating the traffic, while the other ran the ITGRecv function, receiving the generated traffic.

Methodology. The experimental workload was represented by the amount of traffic inserted into the experimental network. We have considered the combinations of frame size and frame rates displayed in Table 1. These have been recommended in RFC5180, IPv6 Benchmarking Methodology for Network Interconnect Devices, [13] as maximum frame rates × frame sizes for 10 Mbps Ethernet. 10 Mbps rates represent the first experimental baseline. For future tests we intend to expand to 100 Mbps as well as 1000Mbps. The traffic was generated using the Distributed Internet Traffic Generator (D-ITG) [3].

As other important parameters affecting the network performance we have considered: the IP version, IPv4 and IPv6, the upper layers protocols, UDP and TCP, the IPv6 transition technology and the IPv6 transition implementation. A full factorial design was employed, hence $12 \times 2 \times 2 \times 4 \times 1 = 192$ experiments were conducted. As recommended by RFC2544 [5], the duration of each experiment was 60 seconds after the first timestamp is sent. Each test was repeated 20 times and the reported value is the average of the recorded values.

3.3 Open Environment

Infrastructure. The open experiment topology, presented in fig. 1b also follows the basic, small scale 464 network template. The major difference is that

Table 1. *Framesize × Framerate*

No	Frame size	Frame rate	No	Frame size	Frame rate
1	64	14880	7	1518	812
2	128	8445	8	1522	810
3	256	4528	9	2048	604
4	512	2349	10	4096	303
5	1024	1197	11	8192	152
6	1280	961	12	9216	135

the testing platform was replaced by open up-link and down-link connections. The open environment was part of a bigger experimental network, which supplied Internet access to participants at the WIDE Camp 1309, a networking event, held between September 10 and September 13 2013, at Shinsu-Matsushiro Royal Hotel, Nagano, Japan. The 464 network consisted of two virtual machines, the Customer Edge machine (CE) and the Provider Edge machine (PE). The two machines have ran on a virtual environment constructed using a Dell PowerEdge R805 server and the Citrix Barebone XenServer 6.0 as hypervisor. The base implementation for all four tested transition technologies, MAPe, MAPt, DSLite, 464XLAT has been the asamap vyatta distribution. The technologies have been tested sequentially during the four days of the event. On the up-link, the IPv4 and IPv6 traffic was routed by a dual-stack core router. WIDE Camp participants were able to connect to the environments trough a single SSID, *464exp*, handled by the Layer 2 Cisco WiFi Mesh.

Methodology. For operational capability we have used as metrics: *configuration capability, troubleshooting capability* and *applications capability*. As measurement method for configuration capability, we have considered a number of configuration tasks, which have been inspired by the abstracted guidelines presented in [8]. The tasks can be organized in three generic groups, *initial setup,reconfiguration* and *confirmation*. For an easier referencing we have associated each task with a task code in accordance with the respective group association.

1. IinitialSetup1: Configure an encapsulation/translation virtual interface using a command line interface or a graphical user interface
2. IinitialSetup2: Save the current temporary configuration commands in a file which can be loaded at start-up
3. IinitialSetup3: Self configuration according to contextual configuration details
4. InitialSetup4: Display warnings in the case of misconfiguration and reject the mis-configured command
5. InitialSetup5: Display warnings in the case of missing command and reject saving the temporary configuration
6. InitialSetup6: Display contextual configuration commands help
7. Reconfiguration1: Convert current configuration settings to configuration commands

8. Reconfiguration2: Back-up and restore the current configuration
9. Confirmation1: Show the current configuration
10. Confirmation2: Show abstracted details for the 464 virtual interface

The configuration capability was measured as a ratio between the number of successfully completed configuration tasks and the total number of tasks. Similarly, for troubleshooting capability we have proposed a number of troubleshooting tasks. The tasks follow the fault isolation, fault determination and root cause analysis (RCA) guidelines presented in [8]. Consequently the tasks can be organized into the three generic categories: *fault isolation, fault determination* and root cause analysis RCA. For easy referencing, these tasks as well were associated with group codes:

1. FaultIsolation1: Capture and analyze IPv4 and IPv6 packets
2. FaultIsolation2: Send and receive contextual ICMP messages
3. FaultDetermination1: Identify a mis-configured contextual route
4. FaultDetermination2: Identify a mis-configured contextual line in the virtual 464 interface configuration
5. FaultDetermination3: Perform self-check troubleshooting sequence
6. RCA1: Log warning and error messages
7. RCA2: Display log
8. RCA3: Display in the user console the critical messages with contextual details
9. RCA4: Log statistical network interface information
10. RCA5: Display detailed statistical network interface information

The troubleshooting capability was also measured as a ratio of successful tasks over total number of troubleshooting tasks. To measure applications capability, we have tested a non-exhaustive list of common user applications in relation with the 464 transition technologies. The measurement result is presented as a ratio between the number of successfully tested application and the total number of applications.

4   Empirical Results

4.1   Closed Experiment Results

The network performance of the devices under test (DUTs) was compared with a Direct Connection setup in which the two test platform servers were connected directly. The results have been graphed as a function of frame size and the error bars present the margin of error for the mean, calculated at a 99% level of confidence. The latency results, composed of end-to-end delay 2 and jitter 3 show a slightly better performance for 464XLAT, by comparison with the rest of the technologies. Also, in average, translation-based technologies (MAPt, 464XLAT) had a better performance than encapsulation-based technologies (MAPe, DSLite).

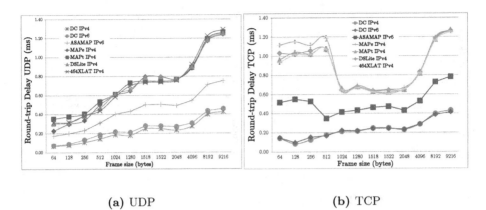

(a) UDP   (b) TCP

Fig. 2. Delay results

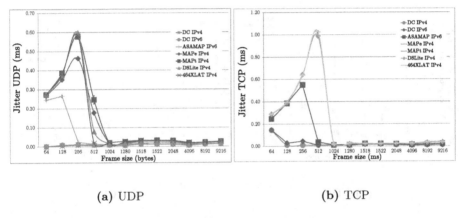

(a) UDP   (b) TCP

Fig. 3. Jitter results

The average throughput results, presented in fig. 4, show a similar performance for the four technologies. The overall average shows a small lead for DSLite and encapsulation-based technologies.

The loss rates, with the exception of some outliers for translation-based technologies over UDP (MAPt and 464XLAT), are very close to 0. For the outliers, the maximum loss-rate is approximately 0.003 %, considered negligible in most cases.

The average CPU load for the provider edge (PE) router, presented in fig. 5, shows a higher average CPU load for translation-based technologies(464XLAT and MAPt). By contrast, the average CPU load of the customer edge (CE) router, shown in fig. 6, is higher for the encapsulation-based technologies. As an overall MAPe seems to have the smallest impact on CPU load. Also notable is that encapsulation-based technologies outperformed the translation-based ones from this standpoint.

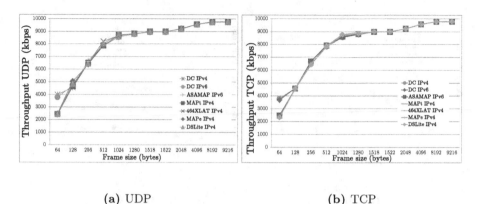

(a) UDP   (b) TCP

Fig. 4. Throughput results

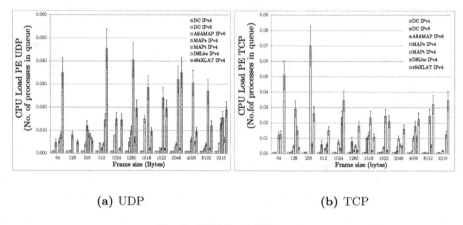

(a) UDP   (b) TCP

Fig. 5. CPU Load PE results

Considering the overall average of these measurements, the best performance was achieved by MAPe followed closely by DSLite, MAPt and 464XLAT. Also notable was the the IPv6-only connection outperformed all of the 464 technologies.

4.2 Open Experiment Results

During the four days of the WIDE Camp 1309 event, we had the chance to test the operational capability of the asamap implementation. The results for configuration and troubleshooting capability have been summarized in table 2.

Regarding the configuration capability, most of the tasks have been completed successfully. However, a self-configuration setup sequence is not yet available for the asamap implementation. Given the complexity of the transition technologies, a guided self-configuring setup would be a beneficial feature. For the troubleshooting capability as well, most of the tasks have been completed successfully. Two of the troubleshooting tasks couldn't be completed: FaultDe-termination3: Displaying critical messages with associated details and RCA3:

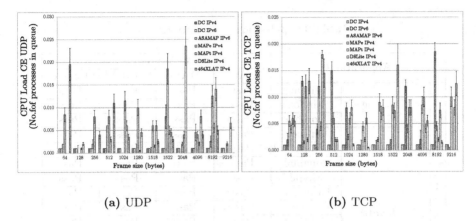

(a) UDP   (b) TCP

Fig. 6. CPU Load CE results

Table 2. Operation capability results

Operational Capability		Asamap			
		MAPe	MAPt	464XLAT	DSLite
Configuration Capability	IinitialSetup1	Pass	Pass	Pass	Pass
	IinitialSetup2	Pass	Pass	Pass	Pass
	IinitialSetup3	Fail	Fail	Fail	Fail
	IinitialSetup4	Pass	Pass	Pass	Pass
	IinitialSetup5	Pass	Pass	Pass	Pass
	InitialSetup6	Pass	Pass	Pass	Pass
	Reconfiguration1	Pass	Pass	Pass	Pass
	Reconfiguration2	Pass	Pass	Pass	Pass
	Confirmation1	Pass	Pass	Pass	Pass
	Confirmation2	Pass	Pass	Pass	Pass
Configuration capability result		9/10 = 0.9	9/10 = 0.9	9/10 = 0.9	9/10 = 0.9
Troubleshooting Capability	FaultIsolation1	Pass	Pass	Pass	Pass
	FaultIsolation2	Pass	Pass	Pass	Pass
	FaultDetermination1	Pass	Pass	Pass	Pass
	FaultDetermination2	Pass	Pass	Pass	Pass
	FaultDetermination3	Fail	Fail	Fail	Fail
	RCA1	Pass	Pass	Pass	Pass
	RCA2	Pass	Pass	Pass	Pass
	RCA3	Fail	Fail	Fail	Fail
	RCA4	Pass	Pass	Pass	Pass
	RCA5	Pass	Pass	Pass	Pass
Troubleshooting capability result		8/10 = 0.8	8/10 = 0.8	8/10 = 0.8	8/10 = 0.8

self-check sequence. Regarding the first one, some critical messages are displayed in the user console. However these are hard to interpret and understand. We believe this feature needs improvement. As for the second one, a self-check

Table 3. Applications capability results

Applications			Asamap			
			MAPe	MAPt	464XLAT	DSLite
Win 7 / Win 8 / Ubuntu 12.04 / Android 2.3	Browsing	Chrome	Pass	Pass	Pass	Pass
		Firefox	Pass	Pass	Pass	Pass
		Dolphin	Pass	Pass	Pass	Pass
	E-mail	Outlook	Pass	Pass	Pass	Pass
		Thunderbird	Pass	Pass	Pass	Pass
		Aquamail	Pass	Pass	Pass	Pass
	IM&VoIP	Skype	Pass	Pass	Pass	Pass
		Facebook	Pass	Pass	Pass	Pass
		Google+	Pass	Pass	Pass	Pass
		VoIP Buster	Pass	Pass	Pass	Pass
		Viber	Pass	Pass	Pass	Pass
		DigiOriunde	Pass	Pass	Pass	Pass
	VPN	OpenVPN	Pass	Pass	Pass	Pass
		Spotflux	Pass	Pass	Pass	Pass
	Cloud	Dropbox	Pass	Pass	Pass	Pass
		GDrive	Pass	Pass	Pass	Pass
	FTP	Filezilla	Pass	Pass	Pass	Pass
	Troubleshooting	puTTY	Pass	Pass	Pass	Pass
		WinSCP	Pass	Pass	Pass	Pass
		ConnectBot	Pass	Pass	Pass	Pass
Applications capability result			20/20 = 1	20/20 = 1	20/20 = 1	20/20 = 1

sequence is not available yet. This would represent a substantial improvement of the troubleshooting capability.

As for applications capability, inspired by [1], during the WIDE Camp event we have tested a non-exhaustive list of common applications. The full list of applications and the results are presented in table 3. To summarize we didn't encounter any applications troubles for any of the four technologies.

5   Discussion

IPv6 transition scenarios and IPv6 transition technologies have already been introduced for some time to the Internet Community. However the worldwide deployment rate of IPv6 is still very low. Given the complexity and the diversity of transition technologies, one of the biggest challenges is understanding which technology to use in a certain network scenario.

This article is proposing an answer to that challenge in the form of a network evaluation testbed, called IPv6NET. The contribution of this paper is represented by the detailed testing methodology associated with IPv6NET and the empirical feasibility results, which to our best knowledge represent a first in current literature.

Analyzing the empirical results, we found that one transition technology is *more feasible* than the rest, namely *MAPe*. We have also identified possible performance trends in IPv6 transition technologies benchmarking, for example encapsulation-based technologies seem to have better throughput performance and translation-based technologies better latency performance. A limitation of this method is represented by the lack of control data, since there is no similar alternative system to act as comparison base for the empirical results. We are planning to solve this by comparing the current open source based measurement system with existing commercial network benchmarking tools.

The empirical results can serve as a direct guideline to network operators faced with a similar transition scenario. One limitation of this approach is represented by the diversity and complexity of existing production networks by comparison with the presented scenario. However, by using the detailed methodology, any interested party could potentially implement it, and obtain customized feasibility data. The methodology can also serve as guideline for other researchers interested in joining this effort. Coping with a large number of technologies and their future developments may very well be solved by research collaboration. It can transform this project in an exhaustive IPv6 transition resource.

6   Conclusion

In this article we have introduced IPv6NET, a project aiming to empirically analyze the feasibility of IPv6 transition technologies in relation with specific network scenarios. From the methodology standpoint IPv6NET combines two types of testing environments, closed environments for thorough network performance data, and open environments for operational data. The network performance results, obtained in the close experiment, indicate MAPe as most feasible transition technology for the 464 scenario. However the other three technologies, DSLite, MAPt and 464XLAT follow it closely. As performance general guidelines, for latency, the translation-based technologies (464XLAT, MAPt) had a better performance. For throughput and CPU load the results were in favor of encapsulation-based technologies (MAPe, DSLite). Also a notable thing was that the IPv6-only connection outperformed all the 464 transition technologies.

In terms of applications capability we did not experience any application troubles. The operational capability results indicate that asamap had a good performance as well. Considering the overall operational results, we can safely conclude that the asamap vyatta distribution is a feasible implementation for the 464 network scenario.

For future work, we consider as first step increasing the scale of the network template. Regarding the open environment methodology, we are considering adding security as a feasibility indicator and proposing an associated metric. Another future step is proposing an unique general feasibility indicator (GFI), associated to each transition technology, which would help better centralize and compare the the results.

Acknowledgments. The authors would like to thank Mr. Masakazu Asama for providing the vyatta asamap distribution, upon which the experimental networks were implemented.

References

1. Arkko, J., Keranen, A.: Experiences from an IPv6-Only Network. RFC 6586 (Informational) (April 2012)
2. Babiker, H., Nikolova, I., Chittimaneni, K.K.: Deploying ipv6 in the google enterprise network lessons learned. In: Proceedings of the 25th International Conference on Large Installation System Administration, LISA 2011, p. 10. USENIX Association, Berkeley (2011)
3. Botta, A., Dainotti, A., Pescapè, A.: A tool for the generation of realistic network workload for emerging networking scenarios. Computer Networks **56**(15), 3531–3547 (2012)
4. Bound, J.: IPv6 Enterprise Network Scenarios. RFC 4057 (Informational) (June 2005)
5. Bradner, S. McQuaid, J.: Benchmarking methodology for network interconnect devices (1999)
6. Durand, A., Droms, R., Woodyatt, J., Lee, Y.: Dual-Stack Lite Broadband Deployments Following IPv4 Exhaustion. RFC 6333 (Proposed Standard) (August 2011)
7. Grayeli, P., Sarkani, S., Mazzuchi, T.: Performance analysis of ipv6 transition mechanisms over mpls. International Journal of Communication Networks and Information Security 4(2) (2012)
8. Harrington, D.: Guidelines for Considering Operations and Management of New Protocols and Protocol Extensions. RFC 5706 (Informational) (November 2009)
9. Hazeyama, H., Hiromi, R., Ishihara, T., Nakamura, O.: Experiences from IPv6-Only Networks with Transition Technologies in the WIDE Camp Spring 2012. draft-hazeyama-widecamp-ipv6-only-experience-01.txt (March 2012)
10. Hazeyama, H., Hiromi, R., Ishihara, T., Nakamura, O.: Experiences from IPv6-Only Networks with Transition Technologies in the WIDE Camp Spring 2012. draft-hazeyama-widecamp-ipv6-only-experience-01.txt (March 2012)
11. Mawatari, M., Kawashima, M., Byrne, C.: 464XLAT: Combination of Stateful and Stateless Translation. RFC 6877 (April 2013)
12. Narayan, S., Shang, P., Fan, N.: Network performance evaluation of internet protocols ipv4 and ipv6 on operating systems. In: Proceedings of the Sixth International Conference on Wireless and Optical Communications Networks, WOCN 2009, pp. 242–246. IEEE Press, Piscataway (2009)
13. Popoviciu, C., Hamza, A., Van de Velde, G., Dugatkin, D.: Ipv6 benchmarking methodology for network interconnect devices (2008)
14. Sasanus, S., Kaemarungsi, K.: Differences in bandwidth requirements of various applications due to ipv6 migration. In: Proceedings of the International Conference on Information Network 2012, ICOIN 2012, pp. 462–467. IEEE Computer Society, Washington, DC (2012)
15. Troan, O., Dec, W., Li, X., Bao, C., Matsushima, S., Murakami, T., Taylor, T.: Mapping of Address and Port with Encapsulation (MAP). draft-ietf-softwire-map-08 (August 2013)

NESSEE: An In-House Test Platform for Large Scale Tests of Multimedia Applications Including Network Behavior

Robert Lübke[✉], Daniel Schuster, and Alexander Schill

Computer Networks Group, Technische Universität Dresden, Dresden, Germany
{robert.luebke,daniel.schuster,alexander.schill}@tu-dresden.de

Abstract. This paper presents the test platform NESSEE that can be used for reproducing network behavior in large-scale experiments with distributed systems. The main target group of our platform consists of companies that require an easy-to-use in-house emulation environment for testing their developed applications. In our scenario we use NESSEE to test the video conferencing software of our industry partner Citrix. We illustrate this with examples from scalability, functional and network testing. The evaluation of the concepts shows its applicability in other scenarios as well.

Keywords: NESSEE · Emulation platform · Network characteristics · Application behavior · Testing

1 Introduction

During the development of an application, there should be a testing phase in which the application is executed under different real-world conditions. Various inputs are passed to the program to examine if it can meet its requirements and to find faulty behavior. In current software engineering models, this testing phase already starts in an early stage of the implementation using prototypes and is repeated regularly. This requires much coordination efforts, especially when testing large distributed systems. Therefore, there is the need of tool support and automation to facilitate this recurring process.

Every application communicating over a network must also be tested under various network conditions, especially if the overall system is distributed over several nodes. To do this you have to find a suitable environment to perform those tests in. Companies usually use the targeted *production environment* of the application for this. The results have great practical relevance, but often this approach is not feasible because of security reasons and confidentiality of the software. An alternative is a *dedicated test environment* with characteristics similar to the target environment. But rebuilding a global-scale infrastructure for large-scale experiments is time-consuming and expensive. *Simulation* is a synthetic approach, where the application itself and all necessary conditions, for

© Institute for Computer Sciences, Social Informatics and Telecommunications Engineering 2014
V.C.M. Leung et al. (Eds.): TridentCom 2014, LNICST 137, pp. 229–238, 2014.
DOI: 10.1007/978-3-319-13326-3_22

example the network behavior, are transformed into a model that is used for calculations. Due to model complexity it is only applicable in small scenarios. Furthermore, the abstraction of the original application under test may lead to less accurate tests and experiments. In the research community there are *federated test platforms* in which emulation can be used to reproduce network behavior. Emulation is a combined approach using the original application and calculating only some of the real-world conditions with a model. Unfortunately, these federated systems are missing means for automated testing and are not suitable for most companies.

We therefore developed own concepts for an in-house emulation platform for large-scale tests with distributed systems and implemented these in a testbed called NESSEE (Network Endpoint Server Scenario Emulation Environment). In conclusion, our main contributions are:

- combination of a large-scale testbed with the fine-grained emulation of multiple network characteristics
- emulation of application behavior
- means to continuously integrate into the application developer's work flow
- a generic specification of test cases using a scripting approach

The remainder of this paper is structured as follows. At first, we discuss the problems of performing large-scale tests with real-time multimedia applications and derive certain requirements. We then highlight similar approaches and discuss their shortcomings. Then we present the main concepts of our own approach, the NESSEE platform, and illustrate some of the experiments it allows to perform. After the evaluation of our concepts, we finally conclude the paper.

2   Problem Discussion and Requirements

In our use case we require a test platform for performing various experiments and different kinds of tests with the video conferencing solution of our industry partner Citrix. Especially those real-time multimedia applications which are offered as software as a service have to reach a certain quality level to meet the users' expectations. This requires an extensive testing phase including the reproduction of occurring real-world effects that could influence the application.

One major aspect that must not be concealed is the network with all its characteristics and technology-specific effects, including basic network parameters like bandwidth limitation, packet delay and loss as well as advanced network parameters and effects like packet reordering, duplication, jitter, connection hand overs and disconnects. In the real world, the systems running the application are connected with each other via multiple hops and the network behavior depends on concurrent traffic. Therefore, emulation of network topologies of any complexity and background traffic are required. All mentioned parameters and effects should be re-configurable during run time of the experiment to increase the flexibility. The dynamic reconfiguration should be based on time and user interaction.

The coordination effort for the testers should be as small as possible, especially the creation of test cases should be facilitated. Furthermore, the aim is to run automated tests, which require the emulation of the application behavior. When performing scalability tests, thousands of software under test (SUT) instances need to run on the test systems and they must be started and controlled in an automated way. To achieve this, the SUT must provide some kind of control interface that can be used by the emulation platform. The necessary adaptions of the SUT for this interface should be as slight as possible to emulate the real application behavior as precise as possible. Another way to reduce user efforts is to support current best practices of software engineering like continuous integration and test-driven development. The emulation platform should be able to seamlessly integrate into the application developer's work flow.

To be able to share test resources among users we require a multitenancy approach, allowing multiple users to run experiments concurrently. Of course, the emulation platform is supposed to handle multiple large experiments at once. This especially requires a good scalability of the overall system.

3   Related Work

In the last decade much research work has been done in the area of large testbeds for realistic measurements and experiments. FIRE [1] and GENI [3] are initiatives supporting the development of those testbeds. Some existing and well-established testbeds, each designed with different goals, are presented in the following.

OneLab [2] and PlanetLab [6] are very large and well-known testbeds supporting the development of new network services. PlanetLab provides more than thousand nodes all over the world that can be used for experiments. However, the number of users is also quite big which makes it difficult to reserve enough resources for own experiments. G-Lab [10] is an experimentation platform for future Internet studies and development with the main focus on routing, mobility and security. The G-Lab testing facilities are located in several German universities and consist of wired and wireless hardware with over 170 nodes. The Topology Management Tool [9] allows the user to create virtual network topologies using the G-Lab experimental facility. Emulab [11] is a network testbed offering various different experimental environments, for example emulation, simulation as well as live experimentation in the Internet. Resources like hosts, routers and networks are virtualized and the experimenter just specifies the desired topology and characteristics. The experiment itself is then launched on selected suitable machines and switches. Emulab is open source software and was used to build many independent testbeds all over the globe. ProtoGENI [8] extends Emulab and follows the approach of bridging different physical sites into one testbed. ORBIT [7] focuses on wireless network experiments. The experimental facilities consist of about 400 wireless nodes and support both, network emulation and field-trial capabilities. FEDERICA [4] is a European testbed very similar to GENI, using the concepts of sliced infrastructure for processing and networking.

Despite efforts of the providers the presented federated research testbeds do not completely fit the needs of companies, which prefer in-house solutions because of legal and security reasons. Some testbeds have complex registration procedures and unflexible membership dues for companies. Furthermore, all mentioned testbeds focus on research instead of software testing. They provide the means for manually performing non-recurring experiments. If the results of the experiment are successfully obtained, it usually gets archived. Software testing on the other hand requires recurring and reproducible test runs as well as means for automation. Beside the detailed reproduction of network conditions, automated software testing also requires the emulation of application behavior during the experiment. We therefore developed an own test platform that is chiefly based on well-established concepts of existing network testbeds, but that is also able to meet the requirements of testing software, especially multimedia applications.

4   Concepts of the NESSEE Test Platform

This section covers the main concepts of our own test platform called NESSEE. Its general architecture is illustrated in Figure 1. Client/server-based distributed systems and especially multimedia applications are the main focus of the platform. Therefore the environment consists of **Test Systems** for emulating the client- and server-side **Software Under Test** (SUT) behavior. As discussed previously companies usually prefer in-house solutions. Therefore the test systems are either physical or virtual machines inside the company network. If security is not that relevant, the test systems could of course be located at cloud computing providers. NESSEE integrates with Amazon EC2 allowing to start up and shut down virtual test systems dynamically. To achieve the large number of applications for scalability tests, multiple SUT instances must be executed on a test system. A performance metric is used to determine how many instances can be handled. Each test system further runs the **TestNodeModule** (TNM), which starts and controls the SUT instances via **Inter Process Communication** (IPC). Depending on the used operating system the supported IPC mechanisms are *COM* (Windows), *Unix command-line access*, *SSH* and a *custom IPC mechanism* using message passing. The SUT developer just has to implement one of these mechanisms to make the SUT controllable via NESSEE. As this usually requires only slight adaptations, it enables NESSEE to emulate the real application as accurately as possible without abstracting from the original SUT.

The central **NESSEE Server** coordinates all components involved, including the test systems running the TNM. It further collects log files from the SUT and NESSEE components and stores them in the central log repository for later inspection by the tester. A multi-tenant web front end can be used to control and configure the NESSEE Server. Additionally, one can use a Web service API to interact with NESSEE. This is especially useful for build and continuous integration software that automatically trigger NESSEE tests. Using this approach, NESSEE seamlessly integrates into the development process of the SUT.

The actual test cases are described in a dedicated format using the generic XML-based **Test Description Language** (TDL). It consists of modules describing the network conditions, the application behavior and the composition of the

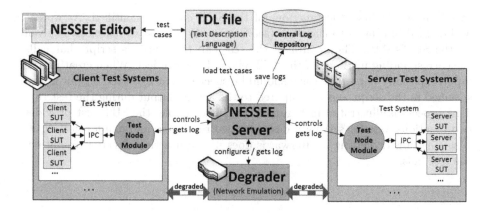

Fig. 1. General architecture of the NESSEE platform

test case. Additionally, the testers can use *JavaScript* to specify the application behavior within scripts. During the test, these scripts are executed by script engines inside the NESSEE Server and the TNM. The scripting approach provides the tester with all means of a programming language and therefore allows a flexible specification of the application behavior. The **NESSEE Editor** is a graphical environment for authoring TDL modules as well as scripts and thus reduces the efforts of test case creation.

The **Degrader** component is responsible for the emulation of the desired network behavior. It acts as a router for all test systems and artificially deteriorates the characteristics of all incoming traffic based on source IP address and port. Before a test run is started, the Degrader is configured by the NESSEE Server according to the network description of the test case. Among others, the Degrader emulates complex topologies, bandwidth limitations, packet delay, jitter, loss, reordering and duplication as well as connection handovers and disconnects. Detailed information about NESSEE's network emulation is given in [5].

5   Types of Experiments

This section discusses common types of experiments that are necessary when testing multimedia applications. We further illustrate and give concrete examples of how these experiments can be performed with the help of our previously discussed concepts.

5.1   Functional Testing

Functional testing is essential not only in the multimedia scenario, but for all kinds of software. The functions of the software are tested by providing input and comparing the output with the expectations that come from the software specification. At first, the functions of the SUT must be identified. As we use well-defined interfaces to the SUT (see Section 4) this list of functions is given by the SUT's API. The creator of the test can then write a script that calls the corresponding methods of the SUT via its helper object. When creating the input, especially borderline cases should be checked. The expected output is also specified in the script and is compared to the actual output during the test run. This process is illustrated in Figure 2. In this example, the SUT just provides two functions, one for setting a desired video resolution and one for getting it. If setting fails or getting it afterwards does not return the expected resolution, the test fails.

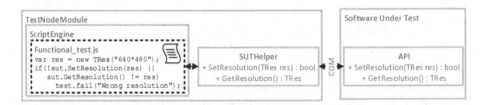

Fig. 2. Example of a functional test in the NESSEE platform

5.2   Scalability Testing

Scalability testing is a type of non-functional testing and its aim is to test whether or not a system behaves as expected when it is changed in size in order to meet a growing need. In multimedia applications, scalability plays an important role for server-side components, that serve a certain number of clients. The objective is to find out the maximum number of clients and to examine the behavior under heavy load.

With the presented concepts, NESSEE is able to handle those scalability tests with minimal coordination effort for the testers. Such large-scale tests are described in TDL like any other test and behavior of the applications can be scripted. The emulation platform automatically chooses suitable test systems, deploys and starts the SUT and the tester can concentrate on the test itself even if many test systems and SUT instances are involved in the test.

In our use case, we examine the scalability limitations of the video conferencing server components running experiments with up to 6,000 client SUT instances. Figure 3 is a screen shot of the web front end, giving an overview about involved SUT instances running on the test systems.

5.3   Network Testing

The aim of network testing is to examine the behavior of the software under various network conditions. Basically, every application communicating over a

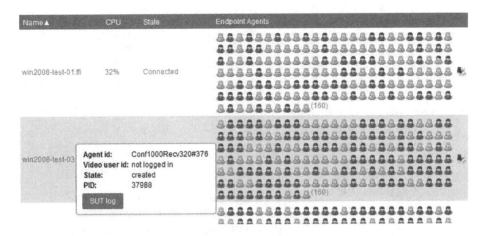

Fig. 3. In large-scale tests the web front end visualizes the states of the SUT instances with different icons and provides detailed information via tool tips

network should undergo those tests, but it is essential for real-time multimedia applications, because the quality and the user experience directly relate to the network conditions. As discussed in Section 4, the NESSEE emulation platform supports the fine-grained configuration of a variety of network parameters. But this configuration is not static as network testing requires the network conditions to change. Therefore, the testers have the possibility to reconfigure the characteristics manually using the web front end, but also automatically using the test scripts. Figure 4 illustrates this with an example of a network test. Changing the network characteristics is usually combined with one of the previously mentioned test types, functional or scalability testing.

6 Evaluation

NESSEE fulfills the analyzed functional requirements of a platform for automated tests of multimedia applications. In the evaluation of our concepts the non-functional requirement of scalability should be examined.

The **scalability and accuracy of the network emulation** components was already shown in previous work [5]. We evaluated the deviations of configured and actually measured values for various network characteristics in large and complex scenarios and produced the following results:

- data rate: ±3.50%
- packet delay: ±0.20%
- packet loss: ±0.10%
- packet reordering: ±0.13%
- packet duplication: ±0.00%

All parameters are emulated accurately, except for the data rate, which still needs improvement. We also observed effects like bandwidth sharing and the variation of delay (jitter).

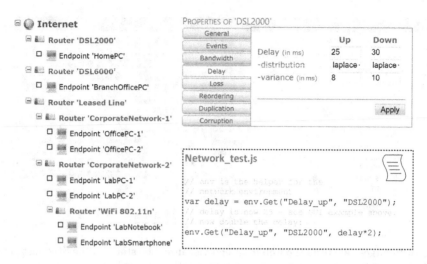

Fig. 4. For network tests the characteristics can be changed manually via the web front end and automatically via the test scripts

The **scalability of the script engine approach** was evaluated in multiple scenarios. We compared the NESSEE Script Engine with other similar engines regarding the performance of long-running functions, big data handling and multiple calls of smaller functions. Our engine did not always achieve best results, but it is sufficient for the usage inside the emulation environment. One quite important aspect is calling native code from JavaScript as illustrated in Figure 2 with the *sut* helper object that is resolved to the native class *SUTHelper*. This feature is used frequently by test scripts during the test run and therefore requires good performance. To evaluate this, we measured the execution time for a varying number of calls and compared it with other commonly used script engines. The results in Figure 5 show the very good performance of our script engine in comparison with other implementations.

We further investigated on the **scalability of the IPC approach** used to start and control the SUT. Regarding this, it is necessary to know how many SUT instances can be run on one machine at the same time. In our evaluation we used the COM interface that the video conferencing client provides and measured the starting time of a varying number of instances. The results of two different test machines are shown in Figure 6. Obviously, the results depend on the hardware performance. They show that it is possible to start over 500 instances of the SUT at the same time, although the start up phase was up to two minutes. Nonetheless, this amount of time is acceptable in such large-scale scenarios.

Beside these components, the **overall scalability** of the whole emulation platform was already shown in Section 5.2 with the illustration of the large-scale tests we performed with NESSEE.

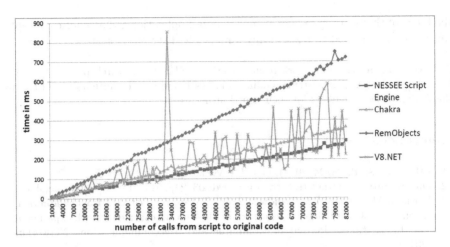

Fig. 5. Time for making calls from script to original code using different script engines

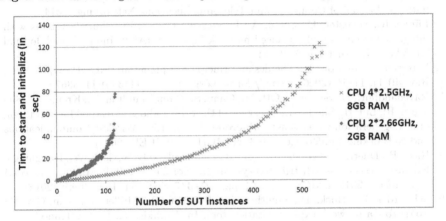

Fig. 6. Time to start a given number of SUT instances for two test systems

7   Conclusion

This paper presented concepts of a platform for various kinds of tests with multimedia applications. Most of the concepts originate from existing testbeds for network research and were adapted to the use case of automated software testing. Especially the in-house approach makes the platform attractive for companies. We implemented and evaluated our concepts in the NESSEE platform. Our main contribution is the combination of accurately emulating various network characteristics as well as application behavior inside a large-scale test platform. Furthermore, we provide means to continuously integrate testbed experiments in the software development workflow. Finally, we created a generic specification of test cases using a description language and a scripting approach. Although the focus of this work is testing of multimedia applications, the generic concepts can easily be adapted to tests of any large-scale distributed system.

Acknowledgments. This work results from the NESSEE research project that has been financed by Citrix Systems, Online Services Division. The authors would like to thank the project members for their contributing work.

References

1. FIRE (accessed: 03/24/2014). http://www.ict-fire.eu
2. Onelab. future internet testbeds (accessed: 03/24/2014). http://www.onelab.eu
3. Berman, M., Chase, J.S., Landweber, L., Nakao, A., Ott, M., Raychaudhuri, D., Ricci, R., Seskar, I.: Geni: A federated testbed for innovative network experiments. The International Journal of Computer and Telecommunications Networking, (2014)
4. Campanella, M., Farina, F.: The federica infrastructure and experience. The International Journal of Computer and Telecommunications Networking (2014)
5. Lübke, R., Schuster, D., Schill, A.: Large-scale tests of distributed systems with integrated emulation of advanced network behavior. IADIS International Journal on WWW/Internet **10**(2) (2012)
6. Peterson, L., Roscoe, T.: The design principles of planetlab. SIGOPS Oper. Syst. Rev. **40**(1), 11–16 (2006). http://doi.acm.org/10.1145/1113361.1113367
7. Raychaudhuri, D., Seskar, I., Ott, M., Ganu, S., Ramachandran, K., Kremo, H., Siracusa, R., Liu, H., Singh, M.: Overview of the orbit radio grid testbed for evaluation of next-generation wireless network protocols. In: IEEE Wireless Communications and Networking Conference, vol. 3, pp. 1664–1669. IEEE (2005)
8. Ricci, R., Duerig, J., Stoller, L., Wong, G., Chikkulapelly, S., Seok, W.: Designing a federated testbed as a distributed system. In: Korakis, T., Zink, M., Ott, M. (eds.) TridentCom 2012. LNICST, vol. 44, pp. 321–337. Springer, Heidelberg (2012)
9. Schwerdel, D., Hock, D., Günther, D., Reuther, B., Müller, P., Tran-Gia, P.: ToMaTo - a network experimentation tool. In: Korakis, T., Li, H., Tran-Gia, P., Park, H.-S. (eds.) TridentCom 2011. LNICST, vol. 90, pp. 1–10. Springer, Heidelberg (2012)
10. Schwerdel, D., Reuther, B., Zinner, T., Müller, P., Tran-Gia, P.: Future internet research and experimentation: The g-lab approach. The International Journal of Computer and Telecommunications Networking (2014)
11. White, B., Lepreau, J., Stoller, L., Ricci, R., Guruprasad, S., Newbold, M., Hibler, M., Barb, C., Joglekar, A.: An integrated experimental environment for distributed systems and networks. SIGOPS Oper. Syst. Rev. **36**(SI), 255–270 (2002). http://doi.acm.org/10.1145/844128.844152

Resources Description, Selection, Reservation and Verification on a Large-Scale Testbed

David Margery[1], Emile Morel[1], Lucas Nussbaum[2(✉)],
Olivier Richard[3], and Cyril Rohr[1]

[1] Inria, Nancy, France
{David.Margery,Emile.Morel,Cyril.Rohr}@inria.fr
[2] LORIA, CNRS, Inria, Université de Lorraine, Nancy, France
lucas.nussbaum@inria.fr
[3] LIG, CNRS, Inria, Université de Grenoble, Nancy, France
Olivier.Richard@inria.fr

Abstract. The management of resources on testbeds, including their description, reservation and verification, is a challenging issue, especially on of large scale testbeds such as those used for research on High Performance Computing or Clouds. In this paper, we present the solution designed for the Grid'5000 testbed in order to: (1) provide users with an in-depth and machine-parsable description of the testbed's resources; (2) enable multi-criteria selection and reservation of resources using a HPC resource manager; (3) ensure that the description of the resources remains accurate.

Keywords: Testbed · Resources · Discovery · Description · Reservation · Verification

1 Introduction

All scientific domains relying on experimental methodology require testbeds: particle colliders, synchrotrons, telescopes, greenhouses and experimental farms, etc. Computer science is not different, and the availability of testbeds is a requirement for solid science in fields such as distributed systems and networking.

When working on distributed systems such as Cloud computing infrastructures, high performance computing (HPC), peer-to-peer systems, or grid infrastructures, the scalability of solutions is often of central importance. To evaluate it, researchers rely on large-scale testbeds, much larger than what one laboratory or organization can usually fund and host, and often composed of a large number of resources scattered over various geographical locations.

Such testbeds and their resources raise a number of challenges, from both a testbed operator's and a user's point of view. Specifically, testbed operators need to keep track of all available resources, expose information about them to users, and make sure that they are still functioning adequately. Conversely, users need to be able to explore the resources and reserve them according to

© Institute for Computer Sciences, Social Informatics and Telecommunications Engineering 2014
V.C.M. Leung et al. (Eds.): TridentCom 2014, LNICST 137, pp. 239–247, 2014.
DOI: 10.1007/978-3-319-13326-3_23

their experimental needs. Those operations have a critical role in the quality of research performed on such testbeds, both by ensuring that the initial experimental results are not tainted by malfunctioning or misdocumented resources, and by enabling the experimenter to describe the experimental environment in a way suitable for reproducible research.

This paper describes the framework designed in the context of the Grid'5000 testbed [5,7], a large scale testbed focusing on Cloud, HPC, P2P and Grid computing, to address the challenges of resources description, selection, reservation and verification. The remainder of this paper is organized as follows. Section 2 describes the Grid'5000 testbed in order to provide the context of this work. Section 3 describes our multi-tier framework for resources management. Related work is discussed in Section 4. Finally, we conclude that paper in Section 5.

2   Context: The Grid'5000 Testbed

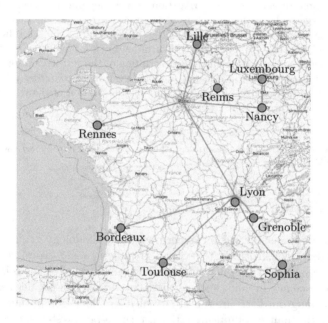

Fig. 1. Map of the Grid'5000 testbed

Started in 2003 and opened to the general public in 2004, the Grid'5000 project aims at providing a testbed for research on parallel and distributed systems, enabling researchers to validate their theoretical results and their software developments. It has been used for a large number of experiments, ranging from small scale to very large scale, and on a variety of topics: low level network protocols, virtualization environments, applications, etc. Grid'5000 has had between

500 and 600 active users per year since 2009, and at least 328 publications have been using Grid'5000.

As of 2014, Grid'5000 is composed of 11 sites (Figure 1), 26 clusters, 1260 nodes, and 8000 CPU cores. One particular focus of the testbed is the level of reconfiguration available to users: they can deploy their own software stacks (operating system, applications) on the bare metal using Kadeploy [10], with no particular constraint. They can also reconfigure the network to isolate their experiments on the ethernet level (VLAN), in order to protect it from external perturbations, or to protect the testbed from intrusive protocols involved in the experiment. Thanks to those reconfiguration capabilities, Grid'5000 enables users to work on Cloud or Grid middlewares (OpenStack, OpenNebula, Nimbus, gLite) for the duration of an experiment.

3   Resources Management in Grid'5000

Figure 2 provides a general overview of our framework designed in the context of the Grid'5000 project to manage resources. This framework is composed of three components:

- The *Reference API* (Section 3.1) contains the description of all resources, as a set of JSON documents.
- The *OAR resource manager* (Section 3.2) enables users to select and reserve resources.
- The *g5k-checks* tool (Section 3.3) is in charge of the verification of resources.

3.1   Resources Description with the Reference API

All resources descriptions are centralized in a NoSQL database, as a set of JSON documents that can be retrieved through a RESTful API. Those documents

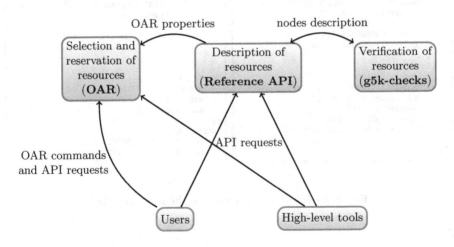

Fig. 2. General structure of resource management framework

```
"supported_job_types" : {              "network_adapters" : [
  "deploy" : true,                       {
  "besteffort" : true,                     "ip" : "172.16.68.1",
  "virtual" : "ivt"                        "rate" : 10000000000,
},                                         "mountable" : true,
"chassis" : {                              "interface" : "Ethernet",
  "serial" : "27Q7NZ1",                    "mounted" : true,
  "manufacturer" : "Dell Inc.",            "mac" : "b8:ca:3a:69:12:68",
  "name" : "PowerEdge R720"                "enabled" : true,
},                                         "version" : "82599EB",
"bios" : {                                 "device" : "eth0",
  "version" : 2,                           "ip6" : "fe80::baca:3aff:fe69:1268",
  "release_date" : "08/29/2013",           "network_address" : "graphite-1",
  "vendor" : "Dell Inc."                   "switch_port" : "F1",
},                                         "switch" : "gw-nancy",
"architecture" : {                         "management" : false,
  "platform_type" : "x86_64",              "driver" : "ixgbe",
  "smp_size" : 2,                          "vendor" : "intel"
  "smt_size" : 16                        },
},                                       {
"processor" : {                            "version" : "IDRAC7",
  "instruction_set" : "x86-64",            "ip" : "172.17.68.1",
  "cache_l1i" : 32768,                     "device" : "bmc",
  "version" : "E5-2650",                   "network_address" : "graphite-1-bmc",
  "cache_l2" : 262144,                     "switch_port" : "1/0/41",
  "model" : "Intel Xeon",                  "rate" : 100000000,
  "cache_l1d" : 32768,                     "switch" : "sgraphene3-ipmi",
  "cache_l3" : 20971520,                   "mountable" : false,
  "vendor" : "Intel",                      "interface" : "Ethernet",
  "clock_speed" : 2000000000              "mounted" : false,
},                                         "mac" : "f0:1f:af:e1:9a:0c",
"main_memory" : {                          "management" : true,
  "ram_size" : 270991937536,               "vendor" : "DELL",
},                                         "enabled" : true
"storage_devices" : [                    }
  {                                     ],
    "rev" : "DL10",                     "sensors" : {
    "model" : "INTEL SSDSC2BB30",         "power" : { "via" : { "pdu" : {
    "interface" : "SATA II",                 "uid" : "graphene-pdu9",
    "device" : "sda",                        "port" : 24
    "size" : 300069052416,                 },
    "driver" : "megaraid_sas"              "api" : { "metric" : "pdu" }
  },                                       },
  {                                      },
    "rev" : "DL10",                     "mic" : {
    "model" : "INTEL SSDSC2BB30",         "mic_model" : "7120P",
    "interface" : "SATA II",              "mic" : true,
    "device" : "sdb",                     "mic_count" : 1
    "size" : 300069052416,              },
    "driver" : "megaraid_sas"           "performance" : {
  }                                        "core_flops" : 13170000000,
],                                         "node_flops" : 187900000000
                                         }
```

Fig. 3. Description of one node in the Reference API

provide an in-depth description of most of the testbed's resources: nodes of course (Figure 3), but also network equipment (switches, routers) and other equipment such as power distribution units (PDU), with information such as the vendor, product name and reference, how the equipment is connected, and instructions on how to access remote control and measurement capabilities through SNMP.

This API is used by a number of tools, to generate documentation (list of all available resources), maps (e.g. network topology), and to enable remote control of resources. For example, the KaVLAN tool in charge of network isolation using VLAN reconfiguration on switches, relies on the mapping between nodes and network switches provided by the Reference API.

Most of the data in the Reference API is collected automatically by *g5k-checks*, which will be described in Section 3.3. A few data fields, whose value cannot be automatically discovered, require manual intervention from the testbed operator.

The data stored in the reference API is archived in a Git repository, which makes it possible to follow the testbed's evolutions over time, or retrieve the state of the testbed at a given date, which is useful in order to explain specific experimental results.

3.2   Resources Selection and Reservation with OAR

As the Grid'5000 infrastructure was originally designed by the HPC community, it felt natural at the time to use a HPC batch scheduler as the building block for resource reservation. The OAR resource manager [1,6] provides two main useful features in the context of a testbed.

Resources Properties. Most HPC resource managers such as Slurm [13] limit the structuring of resources in *partitions* of nodes considered identical. On the

---

Reserving two nodes for two hours. Nodes must have a GPU and power monitoring:

```
oarsub -p "wattmeter='YES' and gpu='YES'" -l nodes=2,walltime=2 -I
```

Reserving one node on cluster a, and two nodes with a 10 Gbps network adapter on cluster b:

```
oarsub -I -l "{cluster='a'}/nodes=1+{cluster='b' and eth10g='YES'}/nodes=2,walltime=2"
```

Advance reservation of 10 nodes on the same switch with support for Intel VT (virtualization):

```
oarsub -l "{virtual='ivt'}/switch=1/nodes=10,walltime=2" -r '2014-11-08 09:00:00'
```

Fig. 4. Example uses of OAR properties to request resources matching requirements

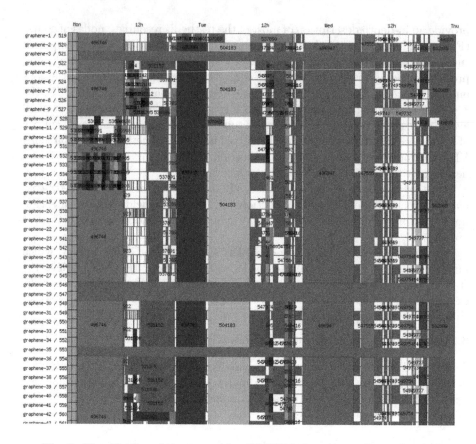

Fig. 5. Visualization of the usage of a Grid'5000 site using a Gantt diagram

other hand, with OAR, each node can be associated with a number of properties, that can later be used to request resources fulfilling specific needs, as shown in Figure 4. This enables users to request resources matching specific properties, rather than rely on explicit naming of requested resources: the burden of filtering resources for specific user requirements is transferred from the user to the resource manager.

On Grid'5000, OAR properties are generated automatically using data from the *Reference API*, and cover most of the data available in it. Also, resources are not limited to nodes. On Grid'5000, we also use OAR to reserve storage space and network subnets (for experiments requiring additional network addresses for virtual machines).

Advance Reservations of Resources. Most HPC resource managers focus on *batch* tasks, where the resource manager tries to start tasks as early as possible given available resources, but does not provide an opportunity for the user to specify when the resources should be allocated. This is a reasonable strategy for a HPC cluster, as the tasks do not require any user intervention. However, in the context of a testbed, most experiments require human intervention, as experiments that can run automatically without problems are quite rare.

OAR provides a *batch* scheduling mode, but also provides the possibility to request *advance reservation* of resources: at the time of the resource request, users can specify when they would like the resources to be allocated, and for which duration. On Grid'5000, this is coupled with a policy of only allowing large reservations of resources during nights and week-ends: during week days, this favors shared use of the testbed by many users so that they can prepare their experiments, and then run the actual experiments during nights and week-ends. OAR also provides a visualization of the planned reservations as a Gantt diagram (Figure 5).

3.3 Resources Verification with *g5k-checks*

A key challenge when maintaining a description of a testbed is to ensure that it is accurate. Inaccuracies could mislead researchers into making false assumptions, with dramatic consequences: incorrect results, publications that need to be retracted, etc. Unfortunately, hardware failures that have an impact on experiments are not uncommon: malfunctioning hard disk drives or broken RAM memory banks that result in less memory being available occur on a weekly, if not daily basis on Grid'5000.

On Grid'5000, we designed a tool called *g5k-checks*. *g5k-checks* is run when a node boots, and at regular intervals when no jobs are scheduled on a node. It is in charge of verifying that the node matches its description in the Reference API, by: (1) retrieving the current description of the node; (2) using several tools to acquire information on the node; (3) comparing the acquired information with the one from the Reference API, and marking the node as unavailable if the information does not match.

For most of its work, *g5k-checks* uses Ohai [2], a Ruby library to detect various attributes on a node. Additionally, it also relies on tools such as `ethtool` to gather the configuration of network interfaces.

g5k-checks has two additional modes of operation. First, it can be run directly by users during jobs where they pushed their own software environment to the nodes, which is useful in order to record the execution environment of a job. Second, testbed operators can use it to collect the information needed to fill the Reference API. This procedure is also a good opportunities to detect outliers among nodes, which are not uncommon when one installs a large new cluster.

3.4 Interfaces with External Tools

During the design of this framework, a lot of focus has been put in enabling external contributors to develop their own tools. Both the Reference API and OAR provide APIs that can be used to automate complex tasks. For example, one limitation of the Grid'5000 testbed is its distributed nature: each site has its own instance of the resource manager, which can make it hard to reserve a large number of resources on several sites at once. So one Grid'5000 user developed a tool, called Funk, that uses the Reference and OAR API to find resources matching a specification, and analyze the planning of reservations in order to find a matching time slot.

4   Related Work

Despite a large number of testbeds, both for Internet of Things and WSN [9] and for HPC and Cloud [8], our work is the only one presented as an integrated solution for the management of resources – most of the testbeds seem to only address a subset of the facets addressed in that paper.

Resource description and selection has been the focus on the more attention. Several solutions have been designed over the years, such as PlanetLab's SWORD [11], GENI's RSpec [3] or SensorML [4].

Most testbeds, especially in the WSN context, do not provide a way to reserve resources in advance. A notable exception is SensLab [12], which also uses OAR, and was actually inspired by our work on Grid'5000 (as both testbeds are mainly located in France).

Finally, while many tools can be used to explore the content of a resource (lshw, hwinfo) or to benchmark it, we are not aware of any other general attempt of comparing the results of such tools with a reference in order to detect malfunctioning hardware in the context of a testbed.

5   Conclusions and Future Work

In this paper, we presented an integrated, and fully-functional solution for the management of resources designed in the context of the Grid'5000 testbed. This solution provides users with an in-depth and machine-parsable (JSON) description of the testbed's resources. It enables multi-criteria selection and reservation of resources by using the OAR HPC job scheduler. Finally, it ensures that the description of resources remains accurate, by comparing it on a regular basis with information retrieving by a tool executed on each resource.

The main area of future improvement of this work is the verification of resources. Most of the tests currently implemented confirm the presence and the vendor & product information of a given piece of hardware, but do not verify its performance. It would be extremely useful to extend g5k-checks with some performance testing, especially for pieces of hardware that tend to fail frequently, such as hard disk drives. However, this needs to be balanced with the load imposed on the testbed by such testing – one need to use or design testing tools that are sufficiently efficient to provide an accurate performance measurement after a very short test.

References

1. OAR - a versatile resource and task manager for hpc clusters and other computing infrastructures. http://oar.imag.fr/
2. Ohai. http://docs.opscode.com/ohai.html
3. Rspec. http://www.protogeni.net/wiki/RSpec
4. Aloisio, G., Conte, D., Elefante, C., Epicoco, I., Marra, G.P., Mastrantonio, G., Quarta, G.: Sensorml for grid sensor networks. In: GCA, pp. 147–152 (2006)
5. Balouek, D., et al.: Adding virtualization capabilities to the grid'5000 testbed. In: Ivanov, I.I., van Sinderen, M., Leymann, F., Shan, T. (eds.) CLOSER 2012. CCIS, vol. 367, pp. 3–20. Springer, Heidelberg (2013). http://dx.doi.org/10.1007/978-3-319-04519-1_1
6. Capit, N., Da Costa, G., Georgiou, Y., Huard, G., Martin, C., Mounie, G., Neyron, P., Richard, O.: A batch scheduler with high level components. In: International Symposium on Cluster Computing and the Grid (CCGrid 2005), vol. 2, pp. 776–783 (May 2005)
7. Cappello, F., Desprez, F., Dayde, M., Jeannot, E., Jégou, Y., Lanteri, S., Melab, N., Namyst, R., Primet, P., Richard, O., Caron, E., Leduc, J., Mornet, G.: Grid'5000: A large scale, reconfigurable, controlable and monitorable Grid platform. In: 6th IEEE/ACM International Workshop on Grid Computing (Grid), pp. 99–106 (November 2005), http://hal.inria.fr/inria-00000284/en/
8. Desprez, F., Fox, G., Jeannot, E., Keahey, K., Kozuch, M., Margery, D., Neyron, P., Nussbaum, L., Pérez, C., Richard, O., Smith, W., Von Laszewski, G., Vöckler, J.: Supporting Experimental Computer Science. Rapport de recherche Argonne National Laboratory Technical Memo 326 (March 2012). http://hal.inria.fr/hal-00720815
9. Gluhak, A., Krco, S., Nati, M., Pfisterer, D., Mitton, N., Razafindralambo, T.: A survey on facilities for experimental internet of things research. IEEE Communications Magazine 49(11), 58–67 (2011)
10. Jeanvoine, E., Sarzyniec, L., Nussbaum, L.: Kadeploy3: Efficient and Scalable Operating System Provisioning. USENIX; login 38(1), 38–44 (2013)
11. Oppenheimer, D., Albrecht, J., Patterson, D., Vahdat, A.: Distributed resource discovery on planetlab with SWORD. In: Proceedings of the ACM/USENIX Workshop on Real, Large Distributed Systems (WORLDS) (2004)
12. Burin des Roziers, C., Chelius, G., Ducrocq, T., Fleury, E., Fraboulet, A., Gallais, A., Mitton, N., Noël, T., Vandaele, J.: Using SensLAB as a first class scientific tool for large scale wireless sensor network experiments. In: Domingo-Pascual, J., Manzoni, P., Palazzo, S., Pont, A., Scoglio, C. (eds.) NETWORKING 2011, Part I. LNCS, vol. 6640, pp. 147–159. Springer, Heidelberg (2011)
13. Yoo, A.B., Jette, M.A., Grondona, M.: SLURM: Simple linux utility for resource management. In: Feitelson, D.G., Rudolph, L., Schwiegelshohn, U. (eds.) JSSPP 2003. LNCS, vol. 2862, pp. 44–60. Springer, Heidelberg (2003)

Mobile Network, Wireless Network

Energy-Efficient Subcarrier Allocation for Downlink OFDMA Wireless Network

Changxiao Qiu, Fan Wu, Yu Ye, and Supeng Leng[✉]

School of Communication and Information Engineering,
University of Electronic Science and Technology of China,
Chengdu 610054, China
spleng@uestc.edu.cn

Abstract. For the downlink of OFDMA network without Quality of Service (QoS) provision, it has been proved that the network energy efficiency (EE) achieved by best Channel Quality Indicator (CQI) subcarrier allocation scheme is in close proximity to the optimal EE. However, for the downlink of OFDMA network with the provision of QoS, the existing algorithms directly assigning subcarriers have the problem of high complexity. This paper proposed a new subcarrier allocation algorithm by readjusting the subcarrier allocation obtained via the allocation principle of best CQI. The proposed algorithm attempts to maximize the EE of network, and at the meanwhile reduce computational complexity. Simulation experiments indicate that the proposed algorithm significantly reduces computational complexity and achieves nearly the same EE as the optimal solution.

Keywords: OFDMA · QoS · Subcarrier allocation · Energy efficiency · Computational complexity

1 Introduction

With the explosive growth of high-data-rate wireless services, energy consumption has drawn more and more attention. It has been reported in [1] that for many mobile operators, the radio access part takes up more than 70% of the total energy consumption. For both the user equipment (UE) side and base station side, energy-efficient design is increasingly important and becomes an inevitable trend.

Orthogonal frequency division multiple access (OFDMA) has been widely used for the next generation wireless communication system due to its performance of anti-inter- symbol interference. Hence, resource allocation in OFDMA network recently has focused on maximizing energy efficiency [2-16] rather than maximizing throughput [17-20]. In [3], the tradeoff between EE and SE (spectrum efficiency) with certain rate constraints has been addressed. In the energy-efficient resource allocation, circuit power is also accounted in addition to the transmitted power. Circuit power is assumed to be static in [3-10], while in [11-12] circuit power includes static power and dynamic power decided by data rate. A water-filling based subcarrier allocation

© Institute for Computer Sciences, Social Informatics and Telecommunications Engineering 2014
V.C.M. Leung et al. (Eds.): TridentCom 2014, LNICST 137, pp. 251–260, 2014.
DOI: 10.1007/978-3-319-13326-3_24

algorithm in a single cellular downlink OFDMA is proposed in [4]. In [5], energy efficient resource allocation in uplink and downlink OFDMA wireless network has been addressed with the consideration of network QoS. The proposed suboptimal subcarrier allocation algorithm which is named MDSA (Maximizing-EE-lower-bound-based Downlink Subcarrier Allocation) achieves the network EE closed to the optimal solution, while the calculation of each user's circuit power factor greatly increases the computational complexity. The uplink energy-efficient transmission is studied in single-cell OFDMA systems in [6-7]. In [8], the convex optimization theory is utilized to obtain the optimal joint subcarrier and power allocation, but it's too complex to achieve the resolutions of transcendental equations. The fading channels are assumed to be flat in [9], however the fading channels across all subcarriers are frequency selective in reality world. In [9-10], the proposed iteration algorithms both use time-sharing technique to achieve high EE performance, but the complexity depends on the number of iterations. The work in [13-16] investigates multi-cell resource allocation in interference-limited scenarios to improve network energy efficiency. Base station closed strategies are studied in [13-14] while game theory based resource allocation algorithms are proposed in [15-16]. All these related work directly allocate the subcarriers by specific techniques, while the computational complexity of proposed algorithms doesn't seem satisfactory.

In this paper, we address the energy-efficient resource allocation in downlink OFDMA wireless network with QoS in frequency selective fading channels. We model the problem of energy-efficient resource allocation as the optimization problem of maximizing EE under certain constraints. To reduce computational complexity, the optimization problem is decomposed into two subproblems-subcarrier allocation and power allocation. In subcarrier allocation, we propose BCSA (Best Channel quality Subcarrier Adjustment) algorithm which readjusts the subcarrier allocation obtained via the allocation principle of best channel quality. Based on the subcarrier allocation obtained in BCSA, we will use BPA (Bisection-based Power Adaptation) algorithm proposed in [5] to finish power allocation. Compared with MDSA, BCSA significantly reduces computational time and achieves comparable network EE. This will be demonstrated in simulation results.

The rest of the paper is organized as follows. Section 2 describes the system model and formulates the energy- efficient resource allocation problem. Section 3 tackles subcarrier and power allocation problems and proposes BCSA algorithm. This is followed by the performance comparison in section 4, and the paper is concluded in section 5.

2   System Model

A typical downlink OFDMA wireless network with a single base station transmitting towards K users is shown in figure 1. As described in [2], the EE is defined as transmitted bits per consumed joule and can be expressed as: EE = total data rate/total consumed power.

According to [5], assume that the channel state information (CSI) of K users across N subcarriers is known to the scheduler of the base station and each subcarrier is only assigned to one user during one scheduling period. The energy-efficient resource allocation problem for the OFDMA downlink transmission can be formulated as

$$\hat{\eta}_{EE} = \max_{p \in \rho, p \in p} \frac{\sum_{k \in \mathcal{K}} \sum_{n \in \mathcal{N}} \rho_{k,n} W \log_2 \left(1 + p_{k,n} \gamma_{k,n}\right)}{\zeta P + P_c} \tag{1a}$$

subject to

$$\sum_{k \in \mathcal{K}} \sum_{n \in \mathcal{N}} p_{k,n} = P \tag{1b}$$

$$\sum_{k \in \mathcal{K}} \rho_{k,n} = 1, \forall n \in \mathcal{N} \tag{1c}$$

$$\sum_{n \in \mathcal{N}} \rho_{k,n} r_{k,n} \ge R_{k,min}, \forall k \in \mathcal{K} \tag{1d}$$

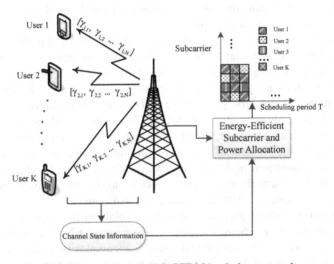

Fig. 1. A typical downlink OFDMA wireless network

Where $\hat{\eta}_{EE}$ is the optimal downlink network energy efficiency, the bandwidth of sub-carrier is W, P_c is circuit power of the base station, P is the total transmission power, and ζ is the reciprocal of drain efficiency of power amplifier. $\gamma_{k,n}$ is channel-gain-to-noise ratio (CNR) of the kth UE on the nth subcarrier. The CSI of the network can be expressed as $CNR = \left[\gamma_{k,n}\right]_{K \times N}$. $\mathcal{K} = \{1, 2, 3, ...K\}$ and $\mathcal{N} = \{1, 2, 3, ...N\}$ denote the sets of K subcarriers and N UEs, respectively. $\rho_{k,n} \in \{0,1\}$ indicates whether the nth subcarrier is assigned to the kth UE. The subcarrier allocation matrix ρ and power allocation matrix P can be expressed as

$$\rho \in \vec{\rho} = \left\{ \left[\rho_{k,n}\right]_{K \times N} \middle| \begin{array}{l} \rho_{k,n} \in \{0,1\}, \forall k \in \mathcal{K}, \forall n \in \mathcal{N} \\ \displaystyle\sum_{k \in \mathcal{K}} \rho_{k,n} \leq 1, \forall n \in \mathcal{N} \end{array} \right\} \tag{2}$$

$$p \in \vec{p} = \left\{ \left[p_{k,n}\right]_{K \times N} \middle| \begin{array}{l} p_{k,n} \geq 0, \ \forall k \in \mathcal{K}, \ \forall n \in \mathcal{N} \\ \displaystyle\sum_{k \in \mathcal{K}} \sum_{\forall n \in \mathcal{N}} p_{k,n} = P \end{array} \right\} \tag{3}$$

Besides, to guarantee QoS for each UE, the scheduler provides minimum rate $R_{k,min}$ for every user.

3   Energy-Efficient Resource Allocation

The resource allocation Problem (1) is generally NP hard for the optimal solution. To reduce the computational complexity, we decompose the problem into two subproblems. We first determine the subcarrier allocation and derive the power allocation by BPA algorithm based on water filling.

As to subcarrier allocation, a straightforward approach is to assign the subcarrier to the user which has the best channel quality. This allocation strategy is easy to implement and sometimes can lead satisfactory results, however it's not fair to the users whose channel quality are generally poor across all subcarriers. To balance high EE and computational complexity, [5] proposes MDSA which maximizes the minimum single-user EE. Numerical results show that the EE obtained by MDSA is close to that of the optimal solution. However, in MDSA, every user's circuit power factor needs to be solved, while the problem of solving circuit power factors is a multivariable and multi-constrained nonlinear optimization problem. The procedure increases the computational complexity and the circuit power factors need to be resolved once channel states change, which makes MDSA impractical in reality world.

For the network without guarantee of QoS, simulations have shown that the best CQI subcarrier allocation scheme can achieve the network EE which is very close to the optimal solution and the scheme takes very low complexity. In the situation with QoS, a promising solution is to readjust the subcarrier allocation obtained by best CQI, which can approach the optimal EE with low computational complexity. Based on this, we propose the BCSA algorithm which mainly readjusts the subcarriers between the highest EE UE and the lowest EE UE to achieve higher network EE. The EE of single UE is defined as

$$\eta_{EE,k} = \frac{R_k}{\zeta \sum_{n=1}^{N} p_{k,n} + \dfrac{\sum_{n=1}^{N} \rho_{k,n}}{N} P_c} \tag{4}$$

Where R_k is the total data rate for user k across the allocated subcarriers. The algorithm in detail is sketched in table 1. It starts by normalizing the CNR and determining the number of subcarriers allocated to each UE, which is shown from line 1 to line 2. The original subcarrier allocation is determined by choosing the best quality channel, which is described from line 3 to line 10. We readjust the subcarrier allocation between the highest EE UE and the lowest EE UE to improve the total network EE, which is illustrated from line 11 to line 13.

Table 1. Best channel state subcarrier adjustment (bcsa) algorithm

---

Algorithm   BCSA

Input: $\rho = \left[\rho_{k,n}\right]_{K \times N} \leftarrow 0_{K \times N}$, $\mathrm{CNR} = \left[\gamma_{k,n}\right]_{K \times N}$, P_c , ζ

$\{R_{k,min} \mid \forall k \in \mathcal{K}\}$, $M < N$

Output: $\rho = \left[\rho_{k,n}\right]_{K \times N}$

---

1. To calculate average channel gain for each user and normalize the $\gamma_{k,n}$

$$\overline{\gamma}_k \leftarrow \sum\nolimits_{n=1}^{N} \gamma_{k,n} / N ; \; \gamma_{k,n}^* \leftarrow \gamma_{k,n} / \overline{\gamma}_k ;$$

2. To determine the number of subcarriers assigned to each user

$$N_k \leftarrow \left[\left(R_{k,min} / \sum\nolimits_{k=1}^{K} R_{k,min}\right) * N\right];$$

3. **While** $\mathcal{N} \neq \varnothing$

4. $\quad\quad k^*, n^* \leftarrow \underset{\forall k \in \mathcal{K}, \forall n \in \mathcal{N}}{\mathrm{argmax}} \left(\gamma_{k,n}^*\right);$

5. $\quad\quad$ **If** $\sum\nolimits_{n=1}^{N} \rho_{k^*,n} < N_{k^*}$ **&&** $\sum\nolimits_{k=1}^{K} \rho_{k,n^*} = 0$

6. $\quad\quad\quad \rho_{k^*,n^*} \leftarrow 1; \; \gamma_{k^*,n^*}^* \leftarrow 0; \; \mathcal{N} \setminus \{n^*\};$

7. $\quad\quad$ **Else**

8. $\quad\quad\quad \gamma_{k^*,n^*}^* = 0;$

9. $\quad\quad$ **End**

10. **End**

11. Using single-user water filling [5] to obtain power allocation $P_{k,n}$ and data rate R_k for user k. According to (1a) and (4) to get the network EE η_{EE} , and the EE for user k $\eta_{EE,k}$.

12. Flag $\leftarrow 0; \mathcal{N} \leftarrow \{1,2,3,...N\};$

13. **Repeat**

$\quad\quad k_1 \leftarrow \underset{\forall k \in \mathcal{K}}{\arg\max}(\eta_{EE,k}); \quad k_2 \leftarrow \underset{\forall k \in \mathcal{K}}{\arg\min}(\eta_{EE,k});$

$\quad\quad [\alpha_n]_{1*N} \leftarrow [\mathrm{Inf}]_{1*N}; \;$ For the nth subcarrier assigned to user k_1 ,

$\quad\quad \alpha_n \leftarrow \gamma_{k_1,n} / \gamma_{k_2,n} ;$

$\quad\quad$ **If** Flag $\neq 0$

$\quad\quad\quad$ Flag $\leftarrow 0; \alpha_{Flag} \leftarrow \mathrm{Inf} ;$

$\quad\quad$ **End**

$\quad\quad n^* \leftarrow \underset{\forall n \in \mathcal{N}}{\arg\min}(\alpha_n); \; \rho_{k_1,n^*} \leftarrow 0; \; \rho_{k_2,n^*} \leftarrow 1;$

Table 1. (*continued*)

Using single-user water filling to obtain power allocation $p^*_{k_1,n}$, $p^*_{k_2,n}$

and data rate $R^*_{k_1}$, $R^*_{k_2}$ for user k_1 and k_2, respectively.   Ac-

cording to (1a) and (4) to get new EE, η^*_{EE,k_1}, η^*_{EE,k_2} and η^*_{EE}.

If $\eta^*_{EE} > \eta_{EE}$

$\quad \eta_{EE,k_1} \leftarrow \eta^*_{EE,k_1}$; $\eta_{EE,k_2} \leftarrow \eta^*_{EE,k_2}$; $\eta_{EE} \leftarrow \eta^*_{EE}$;

$\quad p_{k_1,n} \leftarrow p^*_{k_1,n}$; $p_{k_2,n} \leftarrow p^*_{k_2,n}$; $R_{k_1} \leftarrow R^*_{k_1}$; $R_{k_2} \leftarrow R^*_{k_2}$;

Else

$\quad \rho_{k_1,n^*} \leftarrow 1$; $\rho_{k_2,n^*} \leftarrow 0$; Flag $\leftarrow n^*$;

End

$\quad M \leftarrow M-1$;

Until $M = 0$;

Compared with MDSA algorithm, we don't calculate the power factor α_k [5] for each UE in BCSA algorithm. The complexity of the MDSA algorithm is roughly $\mathcal{O}(N_{OL}K/\delta^2 + N_{OL}N)$ times of water-filling, while $\mathcal{O}(N_{OL}K/\delta^2)$ is for the calculation of α_k and $\mathcal{O}(N_{OL}N)$ is for the subcarrier allocation. The complexity of BCSA algorithm is roughly $\mathcal{O}(N_{OL}M)$ where M is less than N and determined as a quarter of N in the following simulation. Obviously the complexity of BCSA is greatly less than that of MDSA.

After the subcarrier allocation is determined, we tackle the power allocation. As proved about problem (1) in [5], when $\boldsymbol{\rho}$ is fixed, η_{EE} is continuously differentiable and strictly quasiconcave in P, and can be easily obtained by the proposed algorithm which is named bisection-based power adaptation (BPA). Finally, the resource allocation is finished.

4   Performance Comparing

In this section, we use MATLAB to present simulation results to verify the benefit of BCSA compared with MDSA. We also simulate the PFB (Proportional Fairness Scheduling) algorithm which similarly determines the number of subcarriers allocated to each user and assigns every subcarrier to the user of best channel quality. In our simulation, the bandwidth of each subcarrier is 15kHz and the circuit power is 10W. For the downlink transmission, there are four UEs each with the same minimum rate requirement of 100 kbps. We assume that the drain efficiency of power amplifier is 38%.

The model of the wireless channel includes the distance dependent path loss, shadowing fading and small scale fading. The simulation parameters in detail are listed in Table 2.

Table 2. Simulation Parameter

Parameter	Setting
Number of users	4
Circuit power	10W
Number of subcarriers	<72
Bandwidth of subcarrier	15kHz
Shadowing standard deviation	7dB
Small scale fading distribution	Rayleigh distribution
Thermal noise spectral density	-174 dB/Hz
Minimum rate requirement	100kbps
Drain efficiency of power	0.38

To verify when ρ is fixed, η_{EE} is strictly quasiconcave in P, We determine ρ by allocating the subcarrier to the user whose channel quality is the best. Figure 2 shows the relationship between η_{EE} and total consumed power P with different circuit power. From it, we can see that η_{EE} is strictly quasiconcave in P even the circuit power is different and the network EE increases as the circuit power decreases.

Similarly, Figure 3 shows the relationship between η_{EE} and total consumed power P with different number of total subcarriers. It shows that η_{EE} is strictly quasiconcave in P even the number of subcarriers is different and the network EE increases as the number of total subcarriers increases.

Figure 4 compares the EE of algorithm MDSA, PFB and BCSA. From it, we can see that the EE of BCSA is higher than that of PFB, which is obvious as PFB is just similar with part of BCSA without the procedure of readjusting the subcarrier allocation. The EE of BCSA is a little lower than that of MDSA, sometimes even higher when the number of subcarriers is small.

Figure 5 plots the throughput corresponding to the EE in figure 4. We can find that the throughput of BCSA and MDSA are higher than that of PFB, while the throughput of BCSA is nearly close to that of MDSA. When the number of subcarriers is not large, the throughput of BCSA is higher than that of MDSA.

Like figure 5, Figure 6 plots the transmitted power corresponding to the EE in figure 4. It indicates that PFB consumes more power than MDSA and BCSA, while MDSA consumes less power than BCSA.

Figure 7 compares the CPU running time of the three algorithms. Compared with the left graph in the figure, in the right graph the CPU running time of MDSA doesn't include the time to calculate each user's circuit power factor. We can see that MDSA takes greatly more time than the other two algorithms so that it's impractical to implement in reality world. MDSA consumes the most time in the three algorithms even the time used to calculate factors is removed. It is easy to understand that PFB is less than BCSA as PFB is similar with part of BCSA. Compared with MDSA, BCSA consumes greatly less CPU running time.

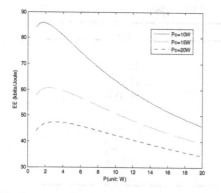

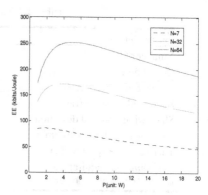

Fig. 2. Energy Efficiency-total translated Power relationship with Pc=10W, Pc=15W, Pc=20W, respectively. The number of subcarriers is 7.

Fig. 3. Energy Efficiency-total translated Power relationship with N=7, N=32, N=64, respectively. The circuit power is 10W.

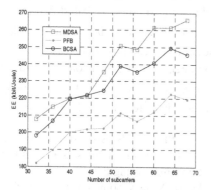

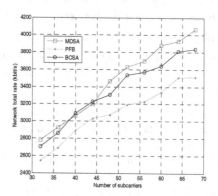

Fig. 4. Comparing of the EE for three algorithms as the number of subcarriers changes

Fig. 5. Comparing of the network total rate for three algorithms as the number of subcarriers changes

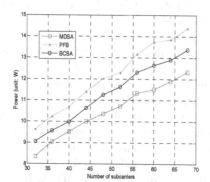

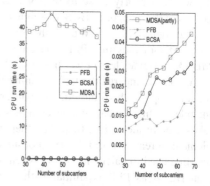

Fig. 6. Comparing of the transmitted power for three algorithms as the number of subcarriers changes

Fig. 7. Comparing of the CPU running time for three algorithms. The CPU is Intel(R) Core(TM)2 Duo CPU E7500 @2.94G.

5   Conclusion

This paper studies the energy-efficient resource allocation in downlink OFDMA wireless network. Although the subcarrier allocation MDSA algorithm achieves the close performance to the optimal EE of the network, but it takes impractical computational time to operate. To reduce the computational complexity, we propose the subcarrier allocation algorithm BCSA, which readjusts the subcarrier allocation in terms of the best channel quality. Simulation results show that the proposed algorithm with low complexity can achieve significant improvement on CPU execution time as well as the comparable EE of network with respect to the MDSA scheme.

Acknowledgment. This work is supported by the National S&T Major Project of China under Grant No.2013ZX03001-023, the 863 Project of China under Grant No. 2012AA011402, and the Program for New Century Excellent Talents in University (NCET-10-0294), China.

References

1. Edler, T., Lundberg, S.: Energy efficiency enhancements in radio access networks. In: Erricsson Rev. (2004)
2. Miao, G., Himayat, N., Li, G.Y., Swami, A.: Cross-layer optimization for energy-efficient wireless communications: a survey. Wiley. J Wireless Commun. Mobile Comput. 9(4), 529–542 (2009)
3. Xiong, C., Li, G.Y., Zhang, S., Chen, Y., Xu, S.: Energy- and spectral efficiency tradeoff in downlink OFDMA networks. IEEE Trans. Wireless Commun 10(1), 3874–3886 (2011)
4. Zheng, Z., Dan, L., Gong, S., Li, S.: Energy-Efficient Resource Allocation for Downlink OFDMA Systems. In: IEEE International Conference on Communications Workshops (ICC), Budapest, Hungary (2013)
5. Xiong, C., Li, G.Y., Zhang, S., Chen, Y., Xu, S.: Energy-Efficient Resource Allocation in OFDMA Networks. In: Proc. IEEE Global Communications Conference, Houston, Texas, USA (2012)
6. Miao, G.W., Himayat, N., Li, G.Y., Bormann, D.: Energy-efficient design in wireless OFDMA. In: IEEE International Conference on Communications, pp. 3307–3312 (2008)
7. Miao, G.W., Himayat, N., Li, G.Y., Talwar, S.: Low-complexity energy-efficient OFDMA. In: IEEE International Conference on Communications(ICC) (2009)
8. Zarakovitis, C., Ni, Q.: Energy efficient designs for communication systems: resolutions on inverse resource allocation principles. In: Communications Letters, pp. 1–4. IEEE (2013)
9. Akbari, A., Hoshyar, R., Tafazolli, R.: Energy-efficient resource allocation in wireless OFDMA systems. In: Proc. of IEEE 21st International Symposium on Personal Indoor and Mobile Radio Communications (PIMRC 2010), Istanbul Turkey, pp. 1731–1735 (2010)
10. Ng, D.W.K.: Lo, Schober, R.: Energy-Efficient Resource Allocation in OFDMA Systems with Hybrid Energy Harvesting Base Station. Wireless Communications 12(7), 1 (2013)
11. Isheden, C., Fettweis, G.P.: Energy-Efficient Multi-Carrier Link Adaptation with Sum Rate-Dependent Circuit Power. In: Proc. IEEE Global Telecommun. Conf. (2010)
12. Chatzipapas, A., Alouf, S., Mancuso, V.: On the minimization of power consumption in base stations using on/off power amplifiers. In: Online Conference on Green Communications (GreenCom), pp. 18–23. IEEE (2011)

13. Chen, H., Jiang, Y., Xu, J., Hu, H.: Energy-Efficient Coordinated Scheduling Mechanism for Cellular Communication Systems with Multiple Component Carriers. IEEE Journal on Selected Areas in Communications **31**(5), 959–968 (2013)
14. Su, L., Yang, C., Xu, Z.: Molisch, A.F.: Energy-efficient downlink transmission with base station closing in small cell networks. In: 2013 IEEE International Conference on Acoustics, Speech and Signal Processing (ICASSP), pp. 4784–4788 (2013)
15. Turyagyenda, C., O'Farrell, T., Guo, W.: Energy efficient coordinated radio resource management: a two player sequential game modelling for the long-term evolution downlink. Communications, IET **6**(14), 2239–2249 (2012)
16. Dabing, L., Lu, Z., Zheng, W.: Xiangming.: Energy efficient cross-layer resource allocation scheme based on potential games in LTE-A. In: 15th International Symposium on Wireless Personal Multimedia Communications (WPMC), pp. 623–627 (2012)
17. Huang, Y., Yang, L., Bengtsson, M., Ottersten, B.: Exploiting long-term channel correlation in limited feedback SDMA through channel phase codebook. IEEE Transactions on Signal Processing **59**(3), 1217–1228 (2011)
18. Huang, Y., Yang, L., Zhu, W.P.: A limited feedback SDMA with dynamic multiplexing order. Circuits, Systems and Signal Processing, Springer **29**(2), 247–262 (2010)
19. Fan, J., Li, Q.Y., Peng, G.Y.: Bingguang.: Adaptive Block-Level Resource Allocation in OFDMA Networks. IEEE Transactions on Wireless Communications **10**(11), 3966–3972 (2011)
20. Liao, H.-S., Chen, P.-Y., Chen, W.-T.: An Efficient Downlink Radio Resource Allocation with Carrier Aggregation in LTE-Advanced Networks. IEEE Transactions on Mobile Computing **PP**(99), 1 (2014)

SIMON: Seamless servIce MigratiON in Mobile Network

Dung Ong Mau, Jialun Wang, Long Wang, Long Hu,
Yujun Ma, and Yin Zhang[✉]

School of Computer Science and Technology, Huazhong University of Science
and Technology, 1037 Luoyu Road, Wuhan 430074, China
{omdung,jialun.cs,longwang.epic,longhu.cs,yujun.hust}@gmail.com,
yin.zhang.cn@ieee.org

Abstract. In the era of cloud and mobile social computing, a plethora
of mobile applications demand mobile stations (MSs) seamlessly interact
with the cloud anyplace in a real-time fashion. The mobility characteristic may cause a service on MS to be migrated between different Data
Centers (DC); otherwise, a packet delay is increased due to the fact
that a considerable geographical distance between MS and serving DC.
With a current networking architecture, IP address of either MS or virtual machine (VM) is changed because of the VM migration, and an IP
session between two peers is released and the service is disrupted as a
result. In this paper, we leverage the emerging Content Centric Networking (CCN) as a straightforward solution to these issues. Based on unique
content name identification, instead of IP address, service migration can
be continuous. Furthermore, a seamless service migration framework is
proposed to conduct the user's service request to the optimal DC, which
satisfies user requirements, minimizes the network usage and ensures
application Quality of Experience (QoE).

Keywords: Data Center · Cloud Computing · Virtual Machine Migration · Content Centric Networking

1 Introduction

Virtualization technology provides a better way to utilize computation resources,
improve scalability, reliability and availability while decrease operation costs.
With a huge number of advantages, virtualization technology is gaining more
and more interest in high-performance computing.

A hardware virtualization technique allows multiple operating systems as
known as virtual machines (VM) to run on a single cluster of physical hardware. The visualization hides underlying computing system and presents an
abstract computing platform by using a hypervisor (or virtual machine manager) [1]. In data center (DC), the number of physical machines can be reduced
by using virtualization that consolidates virtual appliances into shared servers,
which help to improve the efficiency of Information Technology (IT) systems.

© Institute for Computer Sciences, Social Informatics and Telecommunications Engineering 2014
V.C.M. Leung et al. (Eds.): TridentCom 2014, LNICST 137, pp. 261–270, 2014.
DOI: 10.1007/978-3-319-13326-3_25

Virtual appliances are virtual machine images containing everything needed to run a particular task (operating system, databases, configuration, software, etc.) that can be used as a *"black box"*. Obviously, it allows multiple virtual machines to be run on a single physical machine in order to provide more capability and increase the utilization level of the hardware.

Virtual machine (VM) migration is another important technique that always accompanies with the virtualization technology. Migration of VMs is a useful capability of virtualizing clusters and data centers. VM migration supports for the VM to be moved between physical machines (e.g. between two servers in the same DC) as known as live VM migration technique. Hence, the flexible management of available physical resources by making load balance and maintaining the infrastructure are easy to be done by VM migration and do not affect to available applications located on. VM migration is expected to be fast and VM service degradation is also expected to be low or even non-interruption during migration. In some previous works, the envision of VM migration occurs within internal DC and the VM needs to reserve the IP address [2,3]. However, it is a great challenge to migrate a VM to a different DC, as routine network operations would not allow non-continuous IP assignment.

It should be noted that VM migrates between different DCs only when all DCs are running the same hypervisor platform. Normally, cloud provider distributes many DCs in the large scale due to the growing business or other feasible condition when all DCs are handled by the same cloud provider [4]. In this paper, leveraging the emerging Content Centric Networking (CCN) strategy, we propose a novel method to support the VM migration without any service interruption. Specifically, communication with VM is identified via the name of the service running on it instead of IP address. The routing is found by the service name. In this way, services and VMs are decouple from their locations. Under framework proposed, our research focuses on designing a VM migration protocol between DCs and optimizing the Quality of Experiment (QoE). Furthermore, communications are expected to provide ubiquitous connectivity and continuously between machines and humans with Seamless servIce MigratiON (SIMON), instead of human intervention [5].

The remainder of this paper is organized as follows. In Section 2, we give the motivation and problem statement. Section 3 introduces the proposed seamless service migration framework. Section 4 portrays the envisioned network architecture of the simulation setup and introduces and discusses simulation results. Finally, Section 5 concludes this paper.

2   Motivation and Problem Statement

Cloud computing has been greatly developed in the IT market in recent years. With the multiple advantages and features, cloud computing supports a wide range of services, and the cloud provider upgrades its network by expanding a number of DCs. Thus, DCs are distributed over a wide area network (WAN) to cope with the growing number of business and users.

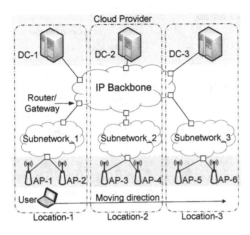

Fig. 1. Distributed Data Center

Fig. 1 presents three separate DCs under the same cloud provider that are geographically distributed and interconnected by the IP backbone network. In general, users in the location-1 access to the service running on DC-1. However, when a user moves to the location-2, it is likely that the user accesses to the subnetwork-2 but still uses the service on DC-1 in location-1 which is far from the user. The longer distance between the user and the appropriate VM, the more communication resources consume. Furthermore, it results in high packet latency and poor Quality of Experience (QoE). This intuitively results in an inefficient connectivity service caused by the absence of an optimal end-to-end connectivity. Therefore, there are following challenges.

- What is the suitable time to request for the optimal VM? Which entity can take a role to find out the optimal VM? And how to find out the optimal VM?
- Suppose that the user had enough information about the optimal VM, then VM is need to migrate. With the current network operation based on IP address, the IP address changing on VM will cause the IP session between user and VM being released.

This paper proposes a solution that address all these issues, defining a seamless service framework that interworks between a distributed DCs. Hereunder, the key feature of the proposed solution is to replace IP address connection by service/data identification in the context of Content Centric Networking (CCN).

3   Seamless Service Migration Framework

In this section, we consider a network topology showed in Fig.1 and we add a new component named *Controller* as illustrated in Fig.2. The controller can be an independent entity, or a software embedded into DCs [6, 7].

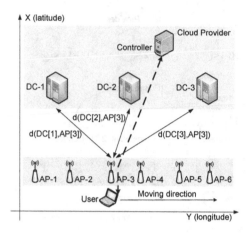

Fig. 2. Controller entity

In this paper, we focus on how to minimize a geographically distance between a mobile station (MS) and the optimal DC. Let $d(DC[i]AP[j])$ denote the distance between DC i and Access Point (AP) j, the controller can select the optimal DC k for AP j based on Equation (1) and (2).

$$d(DC[i]AP[j]) = \sqrt{(X_{DC[i]} - X_{AP[j]})^2 + (Y_{DC[i]} - Y_{AP[j]})^2} \qquad (1)$$

$$k_j = argmin\{d(DC[i]AP[j]), \forall i = 1, ..., N\} \qquad (2)$$

Functions of the controller include:

- Collecting and updating position, eg. latitude and longitude, of all DCs within a cloud provider.
- Pointing out the optimal VM to the MS based on the minimum distance location between the MS and the DC.
- Decision and management for VM migration between DCs.

By leveraging the concept of CCN [8], we replace IP address by content name identification. A specific application designed for CCN strategy is installed on MS, AP and DC. CCN is not only a theoretical strategy but also a capable of the real-life implementation. Indeed, many projects and prototypes have been implemented with CCN successfully [9–12]. CCN decouples location from identity and communication, and enables continuous communication in dynamic network environment. In CCN, the MS can switch to other network and continue to reserve former session or service regardless IP address. The service is identified by a location-independent unique name instead of the network address. Therefore, the MS can access the service without awareness about the allocation and migration of VMs.

Fig.3 shows the flow of messages and procedures carried out to establish a service session migrated to a different DC. In the initial state, DCs update their

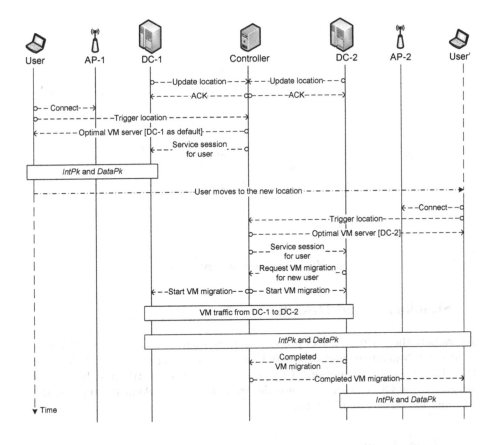

Fig. 3. Flowchart for the procedure of service migration

positions to the controller, which is confirmed by an acknowledgment (ACK) packet. A MS stays within the coverage of a radio station of AP-1. After connected successfully, the MS sends a trigger location packet to the controller. Based on the current location of the MS and a table of DCs' location, the controller selects the appropriate DC (as known as DC-1 in this example) and establishes a service session between MS and DC-1. As a default, we suppose that the service application for the MS is available on the DC-1.

In the second state, during the mobility of the MS, the MS becomes aware of either non-available AP or new AP service set identification (SSID). When connecting to a different AP, the MS will send a trigger location packet to the controller. Once the controller finds that the service is not available at DC-2, the service should be migrated from DC-1 to the optimal DC-2. Then a service session will be established between the MS and DC-2. In spite of a change in the IP address of both the MS and DC server, the service session continues without being torn down as all request and content are identified by the unique name.

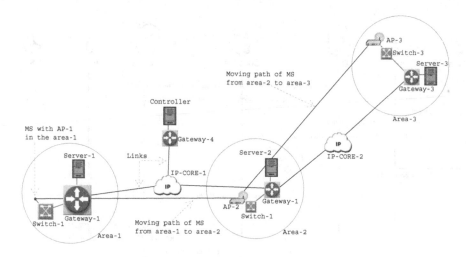

Fig. 4. Network simulation

4   Simulation and Results

To evaluate the performance of proposed service migration framework, we implemented CCN strategy and conducted simulations using the OPNET Modeler 16.0 [13,14]. In the simulations, CCN is overlayed over the IP layer. Indeed, we integrated the CCN processing modules into all network elements, such as MS, AP, routers, servers and IP Cloud.

4.1   Network Simulation

Fig.4 is a network simulation to demonstrate a procedure of the service migration in DC. There are three separate areas connected to IP core, which makes some delay for each packet passed through, e.g. constant distribution 0.01s. Each area includes one AP and one server. It should be noted that the server presents one or more VM servers.

In order to clarify the procedure of service migration in this scenario, there is only one MS moving from area-1 to area-2 and area-3. The trajectory of this MS is presented in Table 1. And Table 2 shows all the simulation parameters.

4.2   Simulation Results

Fig. 5 illustrates the status connectivity of the MS to APs and the time stamp tracking for using optimal server. Because of the mobility of the MS, it connects to APs with the SSID 1; 2; 3 respectively, while the SSID −1 indicates that non-AP is available. In the dashed line, the value one indicates that MS currently uses the optimal server and the value zero indicates that the MS is waiting for VM migration while it continues using non-optimal server.

Table 1. Trajectory of the MS

(X;Y) (m)	Distance (m)	Traverse time (s)	Ground speed (km/h)	Wait time (s)	Accom. time (s)
(0;0)	n/a	n/a	n/a	1800	1800
(6200;64)	6200	558	40	1800	4158
(10291;4774)	6239	561	40	1800	6519

Table 2. Simulation parameters

Element	Attribute	Value
WAN	Link between Gateway	OC-24 data rate
	Link for Switch,AP and server	1000 BaseX
	IP core latency	Constant 10ms
	Wireless interface	IEEE802.11g
CCN	CCN directory	$ccn://epic\_lab/myVM\_i$
	IntPk interval	50ms
	IntPk size	32B
	DataPk size	1500B
VM	VM size	1GB
	VM transfer rate	$12.10^6 bps$

Fig. 6(a) presents for the Round Trip Time (RTT) and data bit rate received by the MS. In Fig. 6(a), when the MS uses the optimal server, the RTT reaches a minimum delay because of the shortest distance between the MS and optimal server. However, as waiting for VM migration, the MS must continue using non-optimal server. As shown in Fig. 4 about network simulation, when the MS is not in the same area with its serving server, the IntPk and DataPk go through IP Core and got some delay. Therefore, Fig. 6(a) clearly shows that RTT in-case-of non-optimal server is greater than RTT in-case-of optimal server about $0.02s$.

Fig. 6(a) also illustrates the seamless VM migration in the context of CCN. Typically, the IP-connection will be dropped down when either source's or destination's IP are changed. Leverage from the concept of CCN, the data conversation is based on unique name of content and CCN supports well for the mobility of both producers and consumers.

Fig. 6(b) illustrates a traffic transmission between DCs caused by VM migration. In this simulation, we support that the size of a VM is 1GB and be transferred with a constant rate $(12.10^6 bps)$. Hence, it takes about $716s$ to complete transfer the VM. It also means that the MS keeps an former conversation with the un-optimal server within the first $716s$ until moving on the optimal server during the service migration.

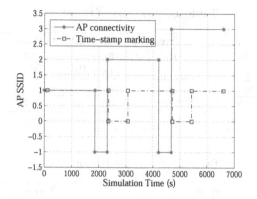

Fig. 5. AP connectivity and the time stamp tracking for using optimal server

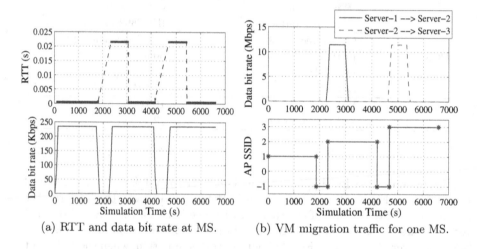

(a) RTT and data bit rate at MS.   (b) VM migration traffic for one MS.

Fig. 6. Simulation results for one MS

4.3   Evaluation

In order to evaluate the performance of our proposed framework, we expand the simulation by increasing the number of MSs up to 10. Moreover, we make a comparison between two mechanisms: with and without VM migration. Each MS occupies a separate VM in the server and distinguished by the name of content, (e.g. $ccn : //epic\_lab/myVM\_[i]$), where i refers to the identification of MS. The increasing number of MSs will affect most of simulation results, e.g. RTT and total VM migration traffic.

Fig. 7(a) shows a big gap of RTT between these two mechanisms. Obviously, without service migration, the RTT will increase as along as the MS is moving. In the contrary, with service migration, the MS does not only get the data latency delay because of a long communication, but also gets extra data latency because of the data burst caused by transferring VM traffic between servers.

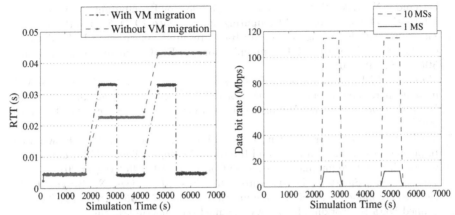

(a) The gap of RTT at MS between with/without VM migration.

(b) Total VM migration sent and received traffic for 1MS and 10MSs, respectively.

Fig. 7. Simulation results for 10 MSs in two scenarios

Finally, Fig. 7(b) illustrates the VM traffic rate sent and received by servers. In this scenario, all MSs have different services and each MS occupies one VM in the server. Moreover, all MSs have the same trajectory, so their service migration consume the same time.

5 Conclusion

In this paper, we investigate the challenges of seamless VM migration for DC. Then we introduce the framework supports continuity and QoE of mobile client with seamless service migration. It is considered that CCN strategy can be overlayed on any kind of network transmission (e.g. Internet layer is the most popular). Hence, the framework is thus highly feasible, practical, and standards-compliant without any major complexity being added to the current network architecture.

References

1. Zaw, E.P., Thein, N.L.: Improved Live VM Migration using LRU and Splay Tree Algorithm. International Journal of Computer Science and Telecommunications **3**(3), 1–7 (2012)
2. Anala, M.R., Kashyap, M., Shobha, G.: Application performance analysis during live migration of virtual machines. In: 2013 IEEE 3rd International Advance Computing Conference (IACC), pp. 366–372 (February 2013)
3. Li, K.K., Zheng, H., Wu, J.: Migration-based virtual machine placement in cloud systems. In: 2013 IEEE 2nd International Cloud Networking (CloudNet), pp. 83–90 (November 2013)

4. Fernando, N., Loke, S.W., Rahayu, W.: Mobile cloud computing: A survey. The International Journal of Grid Computing and eScience **29**(1), 84–106 (2013)
5. Zheng, K., Hu, F., Wang, W., et al.: Radio resource allocation in LTE-advanced cellular networks with M2M communications. IEEE Communications Magazine **50**(7), 184–192 (2012)
6. Mann, V., Vishnoi, A., Kannan, K., Kalyanaraman, S.: CrossRoads: Seamless VM mobility across data centers through software defined networking. In: 2012 IEEE Network Operations and Management Symposium (NOMS), pp. 88–96 (April 2012)
7. Taleb, T., Hasselmeyer, P., Mir, F.G.: Follow-Me Cloud: An OpenFlow-Based Implementation. In: 2013 IEEE and Internet of Things (iThings/CPSCom) Green Computing and Communications (GreenCom), pp. 240–245 (August 2013)
8. Jacobson, V., Smetters, D., Thornton, J., Plass, M., Briggs, N., Braynard, R.: Networking named content. Communication of the ACM **55**(1), 117–124 (2012)
9. Named Data Networking. http://www.named-data.net/index.html
10. NS-3 based Named Data Networking (NDN) simulator. http://ndnsim.net/index.html
11. Scalable and Adaptive Internet Solutions (SAIL) project. http://www.sail-project.eu/
12. Publish-Subscribe Internet Technology (PURSUIT) project. http://www.fp7-pursuit.eu/PursuitWeb/
13. OPNET Modeler. www.opnet.com
14. Chen, M.: OPNET Network Simulation. Press of Tsinghua University (2004) ISBN 7-302-08232-4

Multi-source Mobile Video Streaming: Load Balancing, Fault Tolerance, and Offloading with Prefetching

Dimitris Dimopoulos, Christos Boursinos, and Vasilios A. Siris[✉]

Mobile Multimedia Laboratory, Department of Informatics, Athens University of Economics and Business, Athens, Greece
vsiris@aueb.gr

Abstract. We present the design and experiments from a testbed implementation of multi-source mobile video streaming that combines three mechanisms: 1) load balancing among different paths from multiple sources, 2) resilience to link and server failures, and 3) enhanced offloading by exploiting mobility and throughput prediction to prefetch video data in caches located at hotspots that the mobile will encounter. Our testbed consists of an Android mobile video streaming client that can utilize both cellular and Wi-Fi interfaces and request different parts of a video from different servers, a server that accepts client requests for parts of a video, and a cache server that accepts client requests to proactively fetch parts of a video so that they are immediately available when the mobile client enters the cache server's hotspot.

1 Introduction

A major trend in mobile networks over the last few years is the exponential increase of powerful mobile devices, such as smartphones and tablets, with multiple heterogeneous wireless interfaces that include 3G/4G/LTE and Wi-Fi. The proliferation of such devices has resulted in a skyrocketing growth of mobile traffic, which in 2013 grew 81%, becoming nearly 18-times the global Internet traffic in 2000, and is expected to grow 10-fold from 2013 until 2018[1]. Moreover, mobile video traffic was 53% of the total traffic by the end of 2013 and is expected to be over two-thirds of the world's mobile data traffic by 2018. The increase of video traffic will further intensify the strain on cellular networks, hence reliable and efficient support for video traffic in future networks will be paramount.

Efficient support for video streaming in future mobile environments, in terms of both network resource utilization and energy consumption, will require

This research has been co-financed by the European Union (European Social Fund-ESF) and Greek national funds through the Operational Program "Education and Lifelong Learning" of the National Strategic Reference Framework (NSRF)-Research Funding Program: Aristeia II/I-CAN.

[1] Cisco Visual Networking Index: Global Mobile Data Traffic Forecast Update, 2013-2018, Feb. 5, 2014

© Institute for Computer Sciences, Social Informatics and Telecommunications Engineering 2014
V.C.M. Leung et al. (Eds.): TridentCom 2014, LNICST 137, pp. 271–281, 2014.
DOI: 10.1007/978-3-319-13326-3_26

integration of heterogeneous wireless technologies with complementary characteristics; this includes cellular networks with wide-area coverage and Wi-Fi hotspots with high throughput and energy efficient data transfer. Indeed, the industry has already verified the significance of mobile data offloading to exploit fixed broadband and Wi-Fi technology: globally, 33% of total mobile data traffic was offloaded onto Wi-Fi networks or femtocells in 2012[1].

The contribution of this paper is to present the design and experiments from the testbed implementation of a system for multi-source mobile video streaming that combines functions for load balancing and fault tolerance, in addition to implementing an innovative procedure for enhanced mobile data offloading that utilizes mobility and throughput prediction to prefetch video data in local caches at hotspots that a mobile will encounter. Indeed, prior work has verified that mobility and throughput prediction is possible; this paper is not concerned with developing a system for such prediction, but rather focuses on an actual implementation of mechanisms that exploit such prediction. The work in this paper is different from our previous work in [11,13] that considers mobile data offloading for delay tolerant traffic, which requires transferring a file within a time threshold, and delay sensitive traffic, which requires minimizing the file transfer time; unlike these traffic types, video streaming requires a continuous transfer of video data to avoid impact on a user's QoE (Quality of Experience), thus necessitates a totally different prefetching procedure and evaluation. Also, unlike [12] which contains trace-driven simulation, here we focus on the design and experiments from an actual implementation of enhanced offloading using prefetching, which is combined with mechanisms for load balancing and fault tolerance.

The rest of the paper is structured as follows: In Section 2 we present related work. In Section 3 we present the design of the multi-source mobile video streaming system and in Section 4 we present the mechanisms for load balancing, fault tolerance, and enhanced offloading using prefetching. In Section 5 we present experiments that illustrate the behavior of the system and the gains in terms of increased mobile data offloading and improved QoE.

2   Related Work

Prior work has demonstrated bandwidth predictability for both cellular networks [16] and Wi-Fi [7]. Bandwidth prediction for improving video streaming is investigated in [4,17], and for client-side pre-buffering to improve video streaming in [10]. The work in [4,10,17] focuses on cellular networks, whereas we consider integrated cellular and Wi-Fi networks. Moreover, our goal is not to develop a new system for mobility and bandwidth prediction, but to exploit such prediction to prefetch data in order to improve mobile video streaming.

Multi-source video streaming for improving robustness in mobile ad hoc networks is investigated in [9], which focuses on video and channel coding. The work in [2] investigates joint routing and rate allocation for multi-source video streaming in wireless mesh networks. Load balancing over multiple radio interfaces is investigated in [3], which focuses on client-side scheduling. [14] investigates load

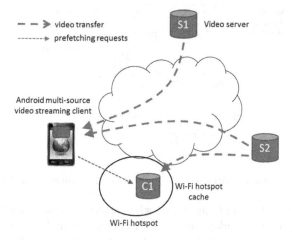

Fig. 1. The system architecture consists of an Android multi-source mobile video streaming client, video servers, and local hotspot caches for prefetching video data

balancing by probabilistically splitting a video flow across multiple radio interfaces based on video transmission patterns. The adaptation of P2P techniques for multi-source video streaming to Android clients is investigated in [8].

The feasibility of using prediction for prefetching is investigated in [1], which however does not propose or evaluate specific prefetching algorithms. Prefetching for improving video file delivery in cellular femtocell networks is investigated in [5], and to reduce the peak load of mobile networks by offloading traffic to Wi-Fi hotspots in [6]. Our work differs from the above work on multi-source streaming and prefetching in that it presents an actual testbed implementation of multi-source mobile video streaming that combines mechanisms for load balancing, fault tolerance, and an innovative procedure for prefetching video data in Wi-Fi hotspots that the mobile will encounter in order to improve video streaming.

3 System Design

The system consists of i) an Android client running in a mobile device that can playback a video while streaming different parts of the video from multiple servers, ii) video servers that accept requests for parts (chunks) of a video, and iii) caches located in Wi-Fi hotspots that accept requests from mobile clients to prefetch chunks of a video from a remote server, Figure 1. Next we describe in more detail each of these three entities.

The multi-source mobile video streaming client contains all the intelligence for downloading parts of a video file from multiple servers. In particular, the video streaming client implements the following three procedures:

- load balancing: the client measures the throughput that it receives data from different video servers, and adjusts the number of video chunks that it requests from each server based on the measured throughput.

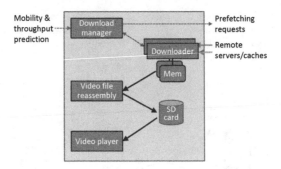

Fig. 2. Android multi-source mobile video streaming client design

- fault tolerance: the client can detect when a server or the path from a server is down, and request video chunks from another available server.
- enhanced offloading with prefetching: the client exploits mobility and throughput prediction to send to local caches in hotspots that it will encounter requests to prefetch parts of the video, so that they are immediately available when the mobile device connects to these hotspots.

The high-level design of the multi-source video client is shown in Figure 2. The download manager obtains mobility and throughput prediction information, based on which it instructs a local cache in the Wi-Fi hotspot that the mobile will encounter to prefetch video data. The video is segmented into multiple chunks that are contained in separate files. Each chunk is transferred to the mobile client through a separate TCP connection; this is performed by the downloader modules, Figure 2, where each downloader is responsible for transferring video data from a particular server. Such an approach for TCP-based video streaming, by breaking the video into multiple chunks, is used in the MPEG-DASH standard. However, we did not use the MPEG-DASH video standard because at the time of our implementation there was no stable MPEG-DASH video player for Android. Nevertheless, the design of the multi-source mobile video streaming client and the procedures implementing the aforementioned functionality are independent of the details of the protocol used for transferring video chunks.

To download video from multiple servers, the mobile client needs to know the IP addresses of these video servers, which can be included in the mobility prediction information or in metadata files such as MPEG-DASH's Media Presentation Description (MPD). Alternatively, knowledge of the video servers' IP addresses is not necessary in Information-Centric Network (ICN) architectures, where users request content based on the name for the content [15].

Unlike the multi-source mobile video streaming client which implements load balancing, fault tolerance, and prefetching, the video server simply accepts requests for video chunks, which are stored locally in separate files. Cache servers located in Wi-Fi hotspots are involved in video transfer only when prefetching is used. The advantages of prefetching are that transferring video data from a local hotspot cache can fully utilize the Wi-Fi throughput, which is typically higher than the backhaul throughput that connects the hotspot to the Internet. If the video is not prefetched, then the amount of video data transferred through the Wi-Fi hotspot is constrained by the available backhaul throughput.

4 Mechanisms

In this section we describe in more detail the three mechanisms implemented in the multi-source mobile video streaming client.

4.1 Load Balancing

This mechanism balances the load among the available servers, based on the throughput from each server. Specifically, the transfer of a video file occurs in rounds. In each round a specific number of video chunks C are transferred, which depends on the video playout rate R_{playout} and the chunk size S. In particular, the number of chunks C should satisfy $C \cdot S \geq R_{\mathrm{playout}} \cdot T$, where T is the time for transferring C chunks, and depends on the number of servers and the throughput from each server. Let r_i be the throughput from video server i measured in one round. If N is the number of servers, then the number of chunks c_i transferred from server i in the next round is given by

$$c_i = \frac{r_i}{\sum_{j=1}^{N} r_j} C \text{ for } i = 1, ..., N-1 \quad \text{and} \quad c_N = C - \sum_{i=1}^{N-1} c_i.$$

The throughput from each video server is measured by the downloaders, whereas the calculation of the number of video chunks that are requested from each server is performed in the download manager, Figure 2.

4.2 Fault Tolerance

The fault tolerance mechanism detects when a video server or a path from a server is down, in which case it downloads video chunks from an alternative server. Detection of a server or path fault is performed by the downloaders based on both a timeout (set to 50 milliseconds) for creating a new TCP connection and a broken TCP connection. Moreover, to handle the case of transient failures, the client periodically requests video data from a server that was previously down, allowing it to detect when the server becomes operational again.

4.3 Enhanced Offloading with Prefetching

Mobility prediction provides knowledge of how many Wi-Fi hotspots a mobile will encounter, when they will be encountered, and for how long the node will be in each hotspot's range. In addition to this mobility information, we assume that information on the estimated throughput in the Wi-Fi hotspots and the cellular network is also available; for the former, the information includes both the throughput for transferring data from a remote location, e.g., through an ADSL backhaul, and the throughput for transferring data from a local cache.

The procedure to exploit mobility and throughput prediction for prefetching is shown in Algorithm 1, which is implemented in the download manager of the multi-source mobile video streaming client. The algorithm extends the one investigated using trace-driven simulation in [12], by exploiting knowledge of the video buffer playout rate to reduce the throughput which it downloads video data over the mobile network. The procedure defines the mobile's actions when it exits a Wi-Fi hotspot, hence has only mobile access (Line 9), and when it enters a Wi-Fi hotspot (Line 14). Mobility and throughput prediction allows the mobile to determine when it will encounter the next Wi-Fi hotspot that has higher throughput than the cellular network's throughput. From the time to reach the next hotspot and the average video buffer playout rate, the mobile can estimate the position that the video stream is expected to reach (CurrentPosition + Offset) when it arrives at the next Wi-Fi hotspot (Line 10). It then sends a request to the cache in the next hotspot it will encounter to start caching video data from that position (Line 11). The video buffer playout rate is also used to estimate the throughput at which it should download video data while in the mobile network (Line 12).

Algorithm 1. Using mobility and throughput prediction to prefetch video data

---

1: **Variables:**
2: R_{playout}: average video buffer playout rate
3: $T_{\text{next Wi-Fi}}$: average time until node enters range of next Wi-Fi
4: *CurrentPosition*: current position of video stream
5: *Offset*: estimated offset of video stream when node enters next Wi-Fi hotspot
6: B: amount of video data in buffer
7: *RateMobile*: rate at which video is downloaded from mobile network
8: **Algorithm:**
9: **if** node exits Wi-Fi hotspot **then**
10:     *Offset* $\leftarrow R_{\text{playout}} \cdot T_{\text{next Wi-Fi}}$
11:     Start caching video stream in next Wi-Fi starting from *CurrentPosition + Offset*
12:     *RateMobile* $\leftarrow R_{\text{playout}} - \frac{B}{T_{\text{next WiFi}}}$
13:     Download video data from mobile network with rate *RateMobile*
14: **else if** node enters Wi-Fi hotspot **then**
15:     Transfer video data that has not been received up to *Offset* from original location
16:     Transfer video data from local cache
17:     Use remaining time in Wi-Fi hotspot to transfer video data from original location
18: **end if**

When the node enters a Wi-Fi hotspot, it might be missing some portion of the video stream up to the offset from which data was cached in the hotspot; this can occur if, due to time variations, the node reaches the Wi-Fi hotspot earlier than the time it had initially estimated. In this case, the missing data needs to be transferred from the video's original remote location (Line 15), through the hotspot's backhaul link. Also, the amount of data cached in the Wi-Fi hotspot can be smaller than the amount the node could download within the time it is in the hotspot's range. In this case, the node uses its remaining time in the Wi-Fi hotspot to transfer data, as above, from the video's original location (Line 17).

5   Experiments

In this section we present experimental results that illustrate the load balancing and resilience mechanisms and the performance gains of enhanced offloading with prefetching, in terms of a higher percentage of offloaded traffic and improved Quality of Experience (QoE), expressed through the reduced number of video pauses (or stalls). Our goal also includes demonstrating the flexibility provided by combining an actual multi-source mobile video streaming implementation with mobility emulation, in terms of time-varying connectivity type (mobile or Wi-Fi) and throughput, to execute experiments with different throughput values and different hotspot configurations.

5.1   Experiment Setup

In the beginning of each experiment the mobile client obtains a description of the experiment scenario in an XML (Extended Markup Language) file. The file specifies the mobile's connectivity, e.g. Wi-Fi or cellular, for different segments and the IP addresses of the video servers and caches (in the case of prefetching); the connectivity segments are specified by their starting time. Essentially, the scenario description file allows us to emulate the device's mobility, in terms of different connectivity scenarios, in addition to different maximum download rates for the mobile, Wi-Fi, and ADSL backhaul link; the latter is performed using the wondershaper network traffic shaping tool. The above mobility (in terms of time-varying connectivity type) and throughput emulation provides the necessary flexibility to perform experiments with a range of parameters and assess the performance of the system in scenarios with a different number, location, and throughput of Wi-Fi hotspots. Finally, our testbed implementation can support scenarios where both the mobile and WiFi interface are used simultaneously; this is achieved with the tethering feature of Android devices, which allows both the mobile and Wi-Fi interface to be simultaneously active.

The video used in the experiments was a 596 second clip from Big Buck Bunny, encoded at 1280x720 and with an average rate of approximately 1.65 Mbps. The video was segmented into 1229 chunks, each with size approximately 97 KBytes. In the experiments the multi-source mobile video streaming client was running on a Galaxy S2 smartphone with Android 4.0.4. The video and cache servers were running on two virtual machines with Ubuntu 13.10, executed in a workstation with VirtualBox 4.3.6.

5.2   Results

Load Balancing: Figure 3(a) shows the download throughput when video is streamed from two servers. Initially, the maximum throughput from each server is 1 and 3 Mbps. At approximately 40 seconds the maximum downlink rate from each server becomes 2 Mbps, and the achieved download throughput from both servers approaches this value. Of course, throughout the experiment the video is played back without any pauses (stalls).

Fault Tolerance: Figure 3(b) shows the download throughput from two servers. Initially, the load is balanced among the two servers. At approximately 40 seconds the second server falls and the download throughput from the first server increases. Later, at time 65 seconds the second server becomes available again and the load is again equally distributed between the two servers.

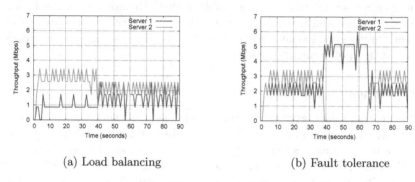

(a) Load balancing   (b) Fault tolerance

Fig. 3. Load balancing and fault tolerance

Enhanced Offloading with Prefetching: The next set of experiments show the performance gains that can be achieved with prefetching, in terms of the increased percentage of offloaded traffic and the improved video QoE through the reduction of the number of frame pauses (stalls). By default each experiment involves a total of 6 Wi-Fi hotspots, which the mobile encounters at time 0, 100, 200, 300, 400, and 500 seconds. The mobile is able to download video data in each hotspot for a duration of 20 seconds; note that prefetching cannot be performed in the first hotspot, since the experiments begin when the mobile is already in the first hotspot. We also assume that there is some randomness in the time a hotspot is encountered and in the maximum download throughput in each segment. The default variability of the time and throughput is 2% and 5%, respectively, while we also present results for different variabilities. A 5% variability for throughput 1 Mbps means that the actual throughput is randomly selected from the interval [950, 1050] Mbps, hence there is a mismatch between predicted and actual throughput. The graphs in this section show the average of five runs and the corresponding 95% confidence interval.

Percentage of offloaded traffic: Figure 4(a) shows the percentage of video traffic offloaded to Wi-Fi for three schemes: 1) no prefetching (i.e., when the mobile enters a hotspot the video is downloaded from a remote server using the maximum ADSL bauckhaul throughput), 2) prefetching and downloading of video data over the mobile network at the maximum rate, and 3) prefetching and downloading video data over the mobile network at a smaller rate, Algorithm 1. Observe that the percentage of offloaded traffic with prefetching increases when the Wi-Fi throughput increases, verifying that prefetching can utilize the higher

Wi-Fi throughput; on the other hand, without prefetching the percentage of offloading is independent of the Wi-Fi throughput, since the ADSL backhaul is the bottleneck. Also, a higher percentage of offloading is achieved with pre-fetching and reduction of the mobile throughput. Note that maximum offloading percentage is approximately 85%, since the video data transferred in the second mobile segment, which is approximately 15%, cannot be offloaded.

Figure 4(b) shows the percentage of offloading for a different number of hotspots: 4 hotspots located at times 0, 100, 300, and 500 seconds, and 3 hotspots located at times 0, 100, and 300 seconds. More hotspots allow a higher per-centage of offloading. Also, note that the two prefetching schemes achieve the same offloading for 3 hotspots; this occurs because when the number of hotspots is small, prefetching fully utilizes the available Wi-Fi throughput, hence Algo-rithm 1 uses the maximum mobile throughput. In general, the offloading gains depend on the location and duration of connectivity in hotspots. Moreover, higher values of the time variation (up to 10%) and throughput variation (up to 20%) yielded similar offloading results and are not included due to space constraints.

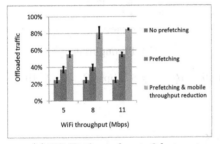
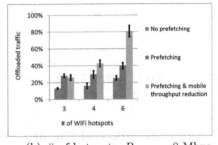

(a) Wi-Fi throughput, 6 hotspots   (b) # of hotspots, $R_{\text{Wi-Fi}} = 8$ Mbps

Fig. 4. Mobile video data offloading. $R_{\text{mobile}} = 2$ Mbps, $R_{\text{adsl}} = 3$ Mbps.

Improved video QoE: Next we investigate the improved QoE that can be achieved with prefetching, in terms of fewer video frame pauses. Figure 5 shows that the gains in terms of fewer pauses is higher when the mobile throughput is smaller; this is expected since more frame pauses occur when the mobile throughput is smaller, which is when the higher throughput of Wi-Fi can be utilized with prefetching to download more video data and avoid frame pauses; on the other hand, when prefetching is not used, while in a hotspot the video downloading rate is constrained by the ADSL throughput. Note that in the scenarios of this subsection traffic is downloaded over the mobile network using the maximum throughput, hence we do not differentiate between the two prefetching schemes considered in the previous subsection.

Influence of time and throughput variability: Figures 6(a) and 6(b) show the QoE for different time and throughput variabilities, respectively; these figures show that the variance of the measured pauses increases with higher variability, but prefetching still achieves fewer frame pauses.

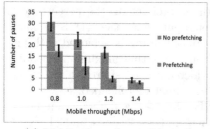

(a) Mobile throughput, 6 hotspots

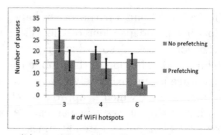

(b) # of hotspots, $R_{\mathrm{mobile}} = 1.2$ Mbps

Fig. 5. Mobile data QoE. $R_{\mathrm{Wi\text{-}Fi}} = 8$ Mbps, $R_{\mathrm{adsl}} = 3$ Mbps.

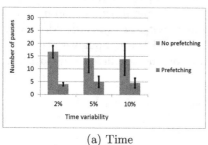

(a) Time

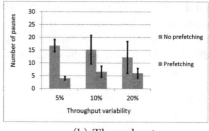

(b) Throughput

Fig. 6. Influence of time and throughput variability. $R_{\mathrm{Wi\text{-}Fi}} = 8$ Mbps, $R_{\mathrm{adsl}} = 3$ Mbps, $R_{\mathrm{mobile}} = 1.2$ Mbps.

6   Conclusions and Future Work

We have presented a testbed implementation of multi-source mobile video streaming for integrated cellular and Wi-Fi networks that combines mechanisms for load balancing, fault tolerance, and enhanced offloading with prefetching video data in local hotspot caches. Experimental results illustrate the functionality and performance of the above mechanisms in addition to the ability of the testbed framework to execute scenarios with different connectivity types, throughput values, and hotspot configurations. Future work includes extending the implementation to investigate QoE-aware adaptation of Scalable Video Coding (SVC) streaming.

References

1. Deshpande, P., Kashyap, A., Sung, C., Das, S.: Predictive Methods for Improved Vehicular WiFi Access. In: Proc. of ACM MobiSys (2009)
2. Ding, Y., Yang, Y., Xiao, L.: Multi-Path Routing and Rate Allocation for Multi-Source Video On-Demand Streaming in Wireless Mesh Networks. In: Proc. of IEEE INFOCOM (2011)

3. Evensen, K., Kaspar, D., Griwodz, C., Halvorsen, P., Hansen, A.F., Engelstad, P.: Improving the Performance of Quality-Adaptive Video Streaming over Multiple Heterogeneous Access Networks. In: Proc. of ACM, Multimedia Systems (2011)

4. Evensen, K., Petlund, A., Riiser, H., Vigmostad, P., Kaspar, D., Griwodz, C., Halvorsen, P.: Mobile Video Streaming Using Location-Based Network Prediction and Transparent Handover. In: Proc. of ACM NOSDAV (2011)

5. Golrezaei, N., Shanmugam, K., Dimakis, A.G., Molisch, A.F., Caire, G.: Femto-Caching: Wireless Video Content Delivery through Distributed Caching Helpers. In: Proc. of IEEE Infocom (2012)

6. Malandrino, F., Kurant, M., Markopoulou, A., Westphal, C., Kozat, U.C.: Proactive Seeding for Information Cascades in Cellular Networks. In: Proc. of IEEE Infocom (2012)

7. Nicholson, A.J., Noble, B.D.: BreadCrumbs: Forecasting Mobile Connectivity. In: Proc. of ACM Mobicom (2008)

8. Krieger, U.R., Eittenberger, P.M., Herbst, M.: RapidStream: P2P Streaming on Android. In: Proc. of 19th IEEE Intl Packet Video Workshop (2012)

9. Schierl, T., Ganger, K., Hellge, C., Wiedand, T., Stockhammer, T.: Svc-based miltisource streaming for robust video transmission in mobile ad hoc networks. IEEE Wireless Communications, 96–103 (October 2006)

10. Singh, V., Ott, J., Curcio, I.: Predictive Buffering for Streaming Video in 3G Networks. In: Proc. of IEEE WoWMoM (2012)

11. Siris, V.A., Anagnostopoulou, M.: Performance and Energy Efficiency of Mobile Data Offloading with Mobility Prediction and Prefetching. In: Proc. of IEEE Workshop on Convergence among Heterogeneous Wireless Systems in Future Internet (CONWIRE), co-located with IEEE WoWMoM (2013)

12. Siris, V.A., Anagnostopoulou, M., Dimopoulos, D.: Improving Mobile Video Streaming with Mobility Prediction and Prefetching in Integrated Cellular-WiFi Networks. In: 10th Int'l Conference on Mobile and Ubiquitous Systems: Computing, Networking and Services (Mobiquitous) (2013)

13. Siris, V.A., Kalyvas, D.: Enhancing Mobile Data Offloading with Mobility Prediction and Prefetching. In: Proc. of ACM MOBICOM MobiArch Workshop (2012)

14. Song, W., Zhuang, W.: Performance analysis of probabilistic multipath transmission of video streaming traffic over multi-radio wireless devices. IEEE Transactions on Wireless Communications 11(4), 1554–1564 (2012)

15. Xylomenos, G., Vasilakos, X., Tsilopoulos, C., Siris, V.A., Polyzos, G.C.: Caching and Mobility Support in a Publish-Subscribe Internet Architecture. IEEE Comm. Mag. 50(7), 128–136 (2012)

16. Yao, J., Kahnere, S.S., Hassan, M.: An Empirical Study of Bandwidth Predictability in Mobile Computing. In: Proc. of ACM WinTech (2008)

17. Yao, J., Kahnere, S.S., Hassan, M.: Quality Improvement of Mobile Video Using Geo-intelligent Rate Adaptation. In: Proc. of IEEE WCNC (2010)

Android-Based Testbed and Demonstration Environment for Cross-Layer Optimized Flow Mobility

Norbert Varga[1(✉)], László Bokor[1], and András Takács[2]

[1] Department of Networked Systems and Services,
Budapest University of Technology and Economics, Magyar Tudósok krt. 2,
H-1117 Budapest, Hungary
varga.norbert89@gmail.com, bokorl@hit.bme.hu
[2] Hungarian Academy of Sciences, Computer and Automation Research Institute,
Kende u. 13-17, H-1111 Budapest, Hungary
andras.takacs@sztaki.hu

Abstract. Nowadays, the spreading and development of multi-access mobile devices together with the proliferation of different radio access technologies make possible to users to actively benefit from the advances of heterogeneous and overlapping wireless networks. This fact and the varying characteristics of mobile applications in means of the required network resources and Quality of Service parameters invoke elaboration of effective flow-based mobility handling algorithms and their cross-layer optimization. Aiming to help research and development in the above topic, we propose an advanced, Android-based testbed and demonstration environment incorporating a cross-layer optimization platform and a flow-aware, client-based mobility management scheme. The testbed relies on MIP6D-NG, which is a client-based, multi-access Mobile IPv6 implementation with different extensions (e.g., Multiple Care-of Addresses registration, Flow Bindings etc.) and an advanced cross-layer communication API. We also introduce an adaptive flow handover system for multi-access environments based on cross-layer information transfer between the applications and the MIP6D-NG core, all implemented and evaluated in the proposed testbed.

Keywords: Android · Cross-layer-optimization · Mobile IPv6 · Flow Bindings · Vertical handover · Heterogeneous network · Mobility management · Testbed

1 Introduction

Recent Android devices are usually provided with multiple network interfaces, thus making able users to reach Internet resources using Wi-Fi or 3G/4G networks. The increasing number of heterogeneous and overlapping radio accesses [1] demand to design and implement algorithms which are able to exploit the available network resources. This motivated us to design and evaluate an extensive, modular, Android-based testbed environment with an advanced flow-aware mobility management framework working in different layers of the TCP/IP stack, a technique for cross-layer information transfer, and an adaptive decision algorithm operating as the engine of this fine-grained mobility management solution. With this system it became possible

© Institute for Computer Sciences, Social Informatics and Telecommunications Engineering 2014
V.C.M. Leung et al. (Eds.): TridentCom 2014, LNICST 137, pp. 282–292, 2014.
DOI: 10.1007/978-3-319-13326-3_27

to dynamically bind flows of any Android application to the available access networks and likewise to control the mobility management in the flow level. The decision core of the architecture manages the control of the flows of Android applications by determining the most appropriate interface (i.e., access network) for them. This decision algorithm is an exchangeable module in the testbed and able to optimize the binding of flows and to control the relevant mobility management tasks according to any aspect of the dynamically changing network environment. All the above features of the environment are using a real-time network measurement module continuously providing up-to-date information to the decision engine from the physical, MAC, IP, or even above layers. Based on the current/past network characteristics and the different optimization criteria selected by the mobile user, the decision engine will perform evaluation and in case of need, will send commands to the mobility execution module implemented by MIP6D-NG [2]. We used this testbed to evaluate the performance of different algorithm variants of adaptive cross-layer decision running on Android Smartphones.

The remainder of the paper is organized as follows. In Section 2, we introduce the related work on the existing solutions for cross-layer optimized flow mobility. Both theoretical and practical (i.e., implementation based) researches are depicted here. Section 3 introduces the architecture of our highly customized Android environment. Section 4 in turn details our overall testbed system setup. Section 5 presents our results. In Section 6 we conclude the paper and describe our future work.

2   Background and Related Work

Rapid evolution of wireless networking has provided wide-scale of different wireless access technologies like Bluetooth, ZigBee, 802.11a/b/g/n/p, 3G UMTS, LTE, LTE-A, WiMAX, etc. The complementary characteristic of the above architectures motivates network operators to integrate them in a supplementary and overlapping manner.

Benefits of such multi-access environments can only be exploited if mobility between the different networks is efficiently handled. The Mobile IPv6 [3] protocol family solves the session continuity for mobile nodes on the move. Two MIPv6 implementations are publicly available nowadays. Both the UMIP and the MIP6D-NG are Linux-based open source implementations of MIPv6 and its core extensions (NEMO [4], MCoA [5]). While UMIP [6] is the more mature and widespread solution, MIP6D-NG is a novel, emerging, more extendable implementation comprising some advanced and innovative functions which are not available in UMIP. From this set of pioneering features Flow Bindings [7] and a cross-layer communication API makes MIP6D-NG a promising client based cross-layer optimization supporting multi-access mobility management solution, and that was our motivation to apply it in our testbed architecture. However, further optimization can be achieved by assigning application flows to the appropriate interfaces using intelligent decisions and adaptivity based on the available network resources. Vertical handover and network flow mobility algorithms are the basics of an optimal and cross-layer driven mobility management method for future heterogeneous mobile networks.

2.1   Vertical Handover and Decision Algorithms

The literature on vertical handover (VHO) solutions is extensive. Many papers introduce special handover schemes, network topologies and architectures with decision
engines for VHO management (e.g. [8]). One of the most crucial elements of our
testbed is the decision engine, thus we start the introduction of the related work on the
most important VHO decision techniques and approaches.

We categorize the decision mechanisms based on the input parameters they rely
on. A summary about the used parameters for VHO decision can be found in [9],
where authors rate VHO algorithms into four categories: RSSI-, bandwidth-, cost-
based and combined solutions. In [9], Xiaohuan et al. also present a novel algorithm
but it does not rely on other inputs than RSSI. Majority of the existing algorithms use
only signal strength as input parameter (e.g., [10]), and authors usually evaluate their
solutions based on simulations or analytical calculations. However the RSSI based
techniques are the most widespread in the literature, the efficiency of this type of
VHO algorithms can be very low, if the parameters of other layers in the TCP/IP
stack (e.g., packet loss rate in L3) are not appropriate. Aiming to increase the efficiency of the applied decision scheme we have to use more input parameters, not only
signal strength. Authors of [11] and [12] follow this path and also rely on other input
parameter types (e.g., monetary cost, bandwidth, and user preferences) beside the
RSSI to design more a sophisticated handoff solution. Majority of the existing decision schemes are not capable to support decisions for flow level mobility management, meaning that during the handover all the flows are moved to another interface,
hence eliminating the possibility to differentiate between applications neither in the
VHO decision nor in the execution phase. For more fine-grained mobility management it is indispensable to define network flows and manipulate them separately
during handover events. The concept of network flows allows us to assign flows to
applications and link them to different interfaces. We can describe a flow with a 5-
tuple: source address and port, destination address and port, protocol type. We focus
on the literature of flow mobility in the following section.

2.2   Flow Mobility

Most of the papers in the subject discuss the definition and management of different
flows in protocol level [13]. In our testbed the advanced toolset of MIPD6-NG solves
all the protocol level questions of flow mobility management by relying on the Flow
Binding and MCoA RFCs, so we do not detail this in this paper. Instead, we focus on
the flow-aware VHO schemes and existing flow mobility implementations.

In [14], Haw et al. examine a multi-criteria VHO decision mechanism to manage
the network flows efficiently. In their flow mobility scenario two flows were defined
(FTP and VoIP), however the flow mobility was managed by the operator side and in
the context of the mostly theoretical content centric networking (CCN). Contrarily we
designed and implemented an IPv6 client-based mobility management which provides
more freedom to the end users and relies on the practical IPv6 networking schemes. In
[15] also a multi-criteria decision engine is presented. The introduced algorithm supports handover decisions based on network cost, signal strength, packet loss and predefined weight of the flows. This paper introduces theoretical results and doesn't
contain evaluation based on real implementations.

The articles above present only recommendations and/or simulation models for flow mobility management. The first publicly available Flow Bindings implementation was designed for Linux distributions by the authors of [16], however their implementation supported only NEMO environments, regular mobile nodes were not able to register or update network flows. Francois Hoguet et al. [17] showed a Linux based flow mobility environment and the possibilities of porting it to Android Smartphones. They used the UMIP's MIPv6 implementation and a proprietary flow binding solution. The authors measured the performance differences between a laptop and an Android Smartphone. This is a real implementation for Android devices, but does provide neither efficient flow mobility management nor complex decision engine. [18] and [19] also introduces a Linux based scheme, but this solution covers only a special NEMO use-case, always moves every flow (its predictive mobility management scheme prohibits separation of individual flows) and does not rely on the Flow Bindings RFCs. Ricardo Silva et al. [20] examine the mobility management on Android systems. They created a custom Android ROM to use the 3G and Wi-Fi interfaces simultaneously. IEEE 802.21 Media Independent Handover framework [21] is applied to support IPv6 based mobility. From this article also the flow mobility and the flow based decision mechanism are missing compared to our architecture.

3   Customized Android Architecture

In our proposed testbed environment the Mobile Node (MN) entity is realized by an Android Smartphone. The overall customized Android Smartphone architecture will be introduced in this section using a bottom-up approach (Fig. 1).

The mobile device must be able to run the MIP6D-NG daemon. MIP6D-NG requires special kernel therefore we modified the kernel part (added Mobile IPv6 support, MIP6D-NG compatibility, modified header files, external modules). To execute these modifications a custom ROM is required. The daemon runs on the native layer of the architecture. The porting MIP6D-NG to Android systems was a non-trivial task, because it required libraries and header files that do not exist on Android OS or if exists, differ from their original GNU Linux implementations. Therefore we created a cross-compiler toolchain which contains the ARM compatible versions of all the necessary components. We extended the NDK stand-alone toolchain[1] with our own libraries and header files. Other important daemons are located in this layer, such as Pingm6, Socat, and Lighttpd. Pingm6 is a modified Linux ping6 command which allows testing the flow mobility features. We used Socat for the UDP file transfer. Lighttpd is an open-source web server optimized for speed-critical environments. We used this for TCP video streaming purposes.

For multi-access communications, the MN needs the ability to communicate via two (3G and Wi-Fi) network interfaces (with IPv6 support) simultaneously. Despite the fact that recent Android devices usually possess multiple radio interfaces, even the newest Android OS versions (Android 4.4) do not allow the simultaneous usage of them. In fact, the built-in mechanisms for network interface management in Android phones are very simple: if a 3G interface is active and Wi-Fi is available, the 3G will

---

[1] Android NDK toolchain: http://developer.android.com/tools/sdk/ndk/index.html

shut down, while if only a 3G network is available, then the Wi-Fi interface will be in down state. Android OS designers are currently pushing a solution which saves battery power so only one interface can be active at the same time. To change the mechanism described above it was necessary to modify the source code of the `Service` `module` of the Android OS managing network connections. The `Service` `module` contains the `ConnectivityService.java` where the `handleMessage()` method of `NetworkStateTrackerHandler` class is responsible for the state management of network interfaces: a switch-case statement contains the implementation of each scenario. We implemented a new statement as an extension: if the 3G interface is active and Wi-Fi is available, then 3G should remain active, therefore real multi-access became usable. It meant that the Android OS itself also required modifications.

Another issue to be solved was that the 3G interface doesn't support native IPv6 on most Android devices. In order to solve this problem and also to provide portability of the testbed (i.e., testing and demonstration possibilities over any legacy IPv4 3G network) we were implementing an OpenVPN connection with a bridged interface on the Android Smartphone. Our custom ROM therefore contains the OpenVPN binary and the required `busybox` commands (e.g., `ifconfig`, `route`, etc.). In order to be able to create the bridge interface we needed the following kernel modules loaded: `bridge.ko`, `llc.ko`, `psnap.ko`, `p8022.ko`, `stp.ko`. To configure the environment variables of openvpn, the Smartphone runs the `OpenVPN-Settings` application. The OpenVPN server is located on a router, which provides an appropriate IPv6 prefix for the Android Smartphone 3G connection through the OpenVPN tunnel.

In order to perform the required modifications inside the source code of the Android OS and the kernel, a build environment was created which was able to make a custom ROM image with our MIP6D-NG ready kernel source code and with our modified Android OS code. We used CyanogenMod[2] Android sources and Andromadus[3] kernel tree distribution as a base code platform for our extensions. The result is a custom ROM with Android 4.1.2 and Kernel 3.0.57 with the appropriate patches and settings (MIP6D-NG requires kernel 3.x version, some kernel patches and special configuration). In the Java layer we designed and implemented a modular Android application comprising three main parts. The so called Radio Access Network Discovery Module (RANDM) is designed to measure the different parameters from multiple layers of the available networks (e.g., signal strength, delay, and packet loss). For signal strength measurements we used the `TelephonyManager` API. The packet loss and delay are calculated from the output of `Pingm6`. To run `Pingm6` (which is not a so called system binary) from Java layer we had to use an external library, the RootCommands[4]. RANDM forwards the measurement results to the Handover Decision and Execution Module (HDEM). HDEM is able to direct the Android OS to connect an available WiFi network using the `WifiConfiguration` and `WifiManager` APIs. The Handover Execution module (HEM) communicates with the native MIP6D-NG daemon, creates and sends flow register and flow update messages induced by the advanced decision algorithm. For the cross-layer information exchange a socket based communication scheme was designed and developed. The Handover Decision module (HDM) decides about the necessity of the

---

[2] CyanogenMod github: `https://github.com/CyanogenMod`

[3] Andromadus github: `https://github.com/Andromadus`

[4] RootCommands external library: `https://github.com/dschuermann/root-commands`

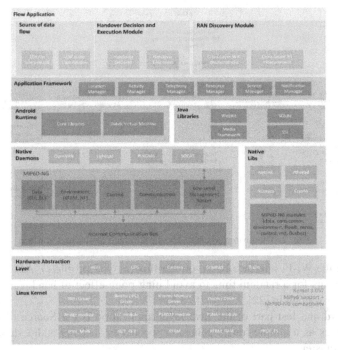

Fig. 1. Highly customized Android architecture

handoff based on the decision algorithm introduced in the next section. HDM directs the HEM to send flow register or update command to MIP6D-NG. The HDM is a modular, exchangeable part of the architecture, thus we can alternate the used decision algorithm very easily.

Currently we have three different decision mechanism implemented in our testbed: Static Flow Assignment (SFA), a purely Signal Strength based [9] (RSSI) and our custom cross-layer optimized algorithm. The SFA is able to register flows using MIP6D-NG, but cannot move them between the available interfaces. The RSSI algorithm reassigns the flows on the basis of the signal strength measurements of the available networks. Contrarily, our scheme relies on cross-layer information. The most important input parameters of our decision algorithm are the actual measurement data, the static information obtained during the network measurements in the currently used networks, and a knowledge database containing the information of all the previously visited networks. The first step of the algorithm is the registration of data flows to the default 3G interface using cross-layer communication between the application and the network layers. After this step starts the phase of passive measurements of Wi-Fi networks. If there are no available networks, the algorithm holds the flows on the 3G interface and waits for the appearance of new Wi-Fi access points. Otherwise starts the cross-layer measurements, in which it measures the signal strength from link-layer, and packet loss, RTT and jitter from network layer. If the parameters of the current measured network are not suitable for the QoS profile, the scheme starts to measure the next available network. If the measured QoS values are appropriate, the MN connects to this Wi-Fi network and moves the corresponding

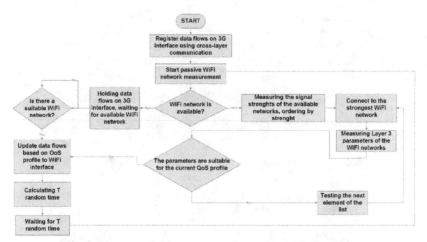

Fig. 2. The proposed cross-layer optimized decision algorithm

flow(s) to the Wi-Fi interface based on the flow(s) QoS profile(s). After that, the application waits for a random time to avoid ping-pong effect of handovers similarly to the solution applied in [22].

The third and last part of the Java layer application is the Source of Data Flows which serves as a simple traffic generator: produces an UPD audio stream and/or a TCP file transfer.

4   Overall Testbed Architecture

Fig. 3 presents the overall architecture of our testbed environment designed and implemented for real-life evaluation of advanced cross-layer optimized, flow level mobility management protocols and algorithms. The Home Agent is realized by a Dell Inspiron 7720 notebook running a MIP6D-NG daemon configured for Home Agent functionality. This entity requires special kernel configuration, which means the need of a MIP6D-NG compatible kernel.

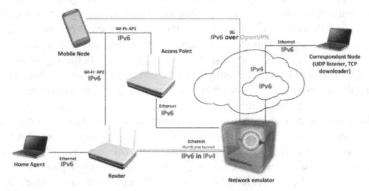

Fig. 3. The overall testbed architecture

A HTC Desire S Smartphone plays the role of the MN. In our testbed the core router is an ASUS WL500 with DD-WRTv24 OS (CrushedHat distribution). Two OpenVPN daemons are running on this router. On one hand an OpenVPN Server provides an appropriate IPv6 address for the 3G connection of Android Smartphone using RADVD[5]. On the other hand an OpenVPN client operates as an IPv6 over IPv4 or IPv6 over IPv6 tunnel, interconnecting the testbed with our IPv6 domain, independently of the router's actual IP access. It means that the overall architecture could be portable and in the worst case only recovers legacy IPv4 connection for the core router. Wanulator[6] network emulator nodes are also applied in the environment. This entity is a Linux distribution which allows us to manipulate the QoS parameters (e.g. delay, packet loss, jitter etc.) of the link to which it is connected (i.e., the wireless connections in the depicted setup). Using Wanulator we are able to evaluate different decision algorithms in any set of network QoS parameters.

5   Results

In order to present the feasibility of our testbed and to evaluate the proposed flow mobility decision algorithm, we implemented three measurement scenarios. In the first test case the significance of the lack of flow level mobility management is presented by the static flow assignment scheme that involves the following:

- the Smartphone connects to the Internet using only the 3G interface
- the Flow Application registers two different type of flows (e.g., TCP and UDP) to the MIP6D-NG, both statically assigned to the only available 3G interface
- a new Wi-Fi AP appears and the application connects to this new AP
- newly started flows, that favor Wi-Fi by their QoS profile can be registered to this newly available Wi-Fi, but ongoing sessions cannot be moved to use the novel access networks: they remain on the 3G connection

Relying on SFA we could communicate simultaneously with two different types of network, but because of the lack of fine-grained mobility, the data flows remain on the interface they were statically assigned to. Using such a static flow assignment algorithm we cannot exploit optimally the available network resources. On the contrary, our algorithm is able to handle the registered flows separately (e.g., we move only the TCP flow to the Wi-Fi (which has higher bandwidth value) and hold on the 3G interface the VoIP flow (which is reactive to the frequent handoffs). By running TCP and UDP tests we measured the amount of the transmitted data (audio and video files) of SFA and our proposal during transmissions of 90 seconds. Fig. 4 left part shows clearly that an algorithm which is able to dynamically move flows between interfaces (i.e., access networks) can transfer much more data. In case of the evaluated schemes in our scenario the average gain was 100.8%. Majority of handover decision algorithms in the literature are (purely) signal-strength based. The efficiency of this type of vertical handovers can be very low if the chosen network shows degraded QoS parameters in network layer of the TCP/IP stack (e.g., packet loss or high jitter occurs). In   order   to   highlight   this,   our   second   measurement   scenario

---

[5] Router Advertisement daemon: http://www.litech.org/radvd/
[6] Wanulator Network Simulator: http://wanulator.de/

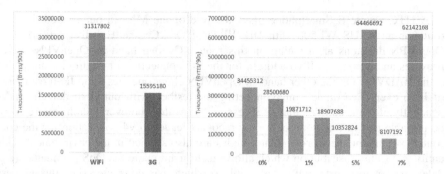

Fig. 4. Comparison between SFA (blue) and our algorithm (green) [left], comparison between RSSI (orange) and our algorithm (green) [right]

manipulates the network level parameters (e.g., packet loss) using the Wanulator box. This scenario from the RSSI algorithm's point of view:

- 3G network is available and the application connects to the 3G network
- the application registers two different types of flow to the 3G interface
- a new Wi-Fi network with good signal strength but high packet loss appears
- the application connects to this Wi-Fi network
- flows favoring Wi-Fi by their QoS profile will be moved to Wi-Fi

In this case the RSSI algorithm moves the data flows to the Wi-Fi interface, but because of the degraded network layer parameters it has much lower efficiency. On the contrary, our algorithm measures the packet loss and holds the flows on 3G interface until it finds an appropriate Wi-Fi network. Fig. 4 right part compares the two schemes: the amount of transmitted data over the TCP flow as a function of the packet loss is depicted. In the two cases (packet loss = 0% and 1%) the performance of RSSI algorithm is better, because our algorithm keeps the data of flows on 3G interface during the measurement session, while RSSI starts to use the Wi-Fi (which has a bigger bandwidth in the first and second test case) earlier. The measurement phase of our algorithm takes 20 seconds, but this will be enhanced in the future. The cumulative average gain of the cross-layer scheme in this scenario was 139%.

6   Conclusions

In this paper we aimed to present a highly customized Android-based testbed and demonstration environment involving a cross-layer optimization platform and a flow-aware, client-based mobility management scheme based on MIP6D-NG. We confirmed the applicability of our testbed by evaluating our flow mobility management proposal with the help of real-life measurements. We performed a comparison between our algorithm and two other scheme implemented from the literature (SFA, RSSI). As a part of our future activities in the designed testbed we are planning to refine our algorithm (e.g., decreasing the measurement period) and combining our client-based approach with network-based mobility management techniques.

Acknowledgement. The research leading to these results has received funding from the European Union's Seventh Framework Programme ([FP7/2007-2013]) under grant agreement n° 288502 (CONCERTO project). The authors are grateful to the many individuals whose work made this research possible.

References

1. Cisco Visual Networking Index, Global Mobile Data Traffic Forecast Update, 2013–2018 (February 05, 2014)
2. Takács, A., Bokor, L.: A Distributed Dynamic Mobility Architecture with Integral Cross-Layered and Context-Aware Interface for Reliable Provision of High Bitrate mHealth Services. In: Godara, B., Nikita, K.S. (eds.) MobiHealth. LNICST, vol. 61, pp. 369–379. Springer, Heidelberg (2013)
3. Johnson, D., Perkins, C., Arkko, J.: Mobility Support in IPv6. IETF (2004)
4. Devarapalli, V., Wakikawa, R., Petrescu, A., Thubert, P.: Network Mobility (NEMO) Basic Support Protocol. IETF (2005)
5. Wakikawa, R., Devarapalli, V., Tsirtsis, G., Ernst, T., Nagami, K.: Multiple Care-of Addresses Registration. IETF (2009)
6. UMIP, Mobile IPv6 and NEMO for Linux (2013)
7. Tsirtsis, G., Soliman, H., Montavont, N., Giaretta, G., Kuladinithi, K.: Flow Bindings in Mobile IPv6 and Network Mobility (NEMO) Basic Support. IETF (2011)
8. Salsano, S., Veltri, L., Polidoro, A., Ordine, A.: Architecture and testbed implementation of vertical handovers based on SIP session border controllers. Wirel. Pers. Commun. **43**(3), 1019–1034 (2007)
9. Yan, X., Şekercioğlu, Y.A., Narayanan, S.: A survey of vertical handover decision algorithms in Fourth Generation heterogeneous wireless networks. Comput. Netw. **54**(11), 1848–1863 (2010)
10. Mahardhika, G., Ismail, M., Mat, K.: Multi-criteria vertical handover decision in heterogeneous network. In: 2012 IEEE Symposium on ISWTA (2012)
11. Kim, J., Morioka, Y., Hagiwara, J.: An optimized seamless IP flow mobility management architecture for traffic offloading. In: NOMS (2012)
12. He, D., Chi, C., Chan, S., Chen, C., Bu, J., Yin, M.: A Simple and Robust Vertical Handoff Algorithm for Heterogeneous Wireless Mobile Networks. Wirel. Pers. Commun. **59**(2), 361–373 (2011)
13. De La Oliva, A., Bernardos, C.J., Calderon, M., Melia, T., Zuniga, J.C.: IP flow mobility: smart traffic offload for future wireless networks. IEEE Commun. Mag. (2011)
14. Haw, R., Hong, C.S.: A seamless content delivery scheme for flow mobility in Content Centric Network. In: 2012 14th Asia-Pacific Network Operations and Management Symposium (APNOMS), pp. 1–5 (2012)
15. Wang, Q., Atkinson, R., Dunlop, J.: Design and evaluation of flow handoff signalling for multihomed mobile nodes in wireless overlay networks. Comput. Netw. **52**(8), 1647–1674 (2008)
16. Ropitault, T., Montavont, N.: Implementation of Flow Binding Mechanism. In: Pervasive Computing and Communications, PerCom 2008 (2008)
17. Hoguet, F.: Network mobility for multi-homed Android mobile devices. Nicta, Eveleigh, Sydney, NSW, Australia, France (2012)

18. Kovacs, J., Bokor, L., Jeney, G.: Performance evaluation of GNSS aided predictive multihomed NEMO configurations. In: 2011 11th International Conference on ITS Telecommunications (ITST), pp. 293–298 (2011)
19. Jeney, G., Bokor, L., Mihaly, Z.: GPS aided predictive handover management for multihomed NEMO configurations. In: 2009 9th International Conference on Intelligent Transport Systems Telecommunications (ITST), pp. 69–73 (2009)
20. Silva, R., Carvalho, P., Sousa, P., Neves, P.: Enabling Heterogeneous Mobility in Android Devices. Mob. Netw. Appl. **16**(4), 518–528 (2011)
21. IEEE, IEEE Standard for Local and metropolitan area networks- Part 21: Media Independent Handover. IEEE (January 2009)
22. Inzerilli, T., Vegni, A.M., Neri, A., Cusani, R.: A Location-Based Vertical Handover Algorithm for Limitation of the Ping-Pong Effect. In: WIMOB 2008 (2008)

Bandwidth Efficient Adaptive Live Streaming with Cooperative Devices in Mobile Cloud Computing

Xiaoyi Zhang, Geng Xi, Kaiming Qu, and Lin Zhang$^{(\boxtimes)}$

School of Information and Communication Engineering,
Beijing University of Posts and Telecommunications, Beijing, China
Zhangxy_bupt@126.com, as_to@msn.cn, qukm90@gmail.com,
zhanglin@bupt.edu.cn

Abstract. Recent developments have heightened the optimization of Dynamic Adaptive Streaming over HTTP (DASH) services in mobile network condition (e.g. LTE/WIFI networks). The aim of this paper is to discuss how Mobile Cloud Computing (MCC) can assist DASH in a special scenario that a set of neighboring mobile devices take interests in watching the identical video stream. A mechanism is proposed to provide higher resolution live streaming with less expense (both in bandwidth and dollar-cost per device) by the cooperation among devices. The cloud-based live stream server will transcode the original stream segment according to the estimation of the devices' group bandwidth, every device then share received fragments (part of the segment) with each other through the free device-to-device interface, and finally gets the whole segment. An emulation testbed is realized with Android Smartphone implementation according to the proposed improvement to DASH. Experiments results demonstrate its performance with today's commercial players on the Quality of Experience (QoE), Peak Signal to Noise Ratio (PSNR) and network utilization across a range of scenarios.

Keywords: Dynamic Adaptive Streaming · Mobile Cloud Computing · Cooperative · Smartphone

1   Introduction

Recent technological advances are bringing Over-The-Top (OTT)-based video streaming services over mobile networks closer to reality. In mobile network, the available bandwidth differs among each device and changes over time. Compared with the wired Internet, it is even more important and difficult for the Dynamic Adaptive Streaming over HTTP (DASH) [1]service to select the proper video rate. The design of robust adaptive HTTP streaming algorithms is critical not only for the performance of video applications, but also the performance of the mobile network as a whole.

Today's most commercial DASH services are built on standard HTTP servers, the rate selection is solely realized by the client device[2]. However, in consideration of storage costs, it is very difficult to the server to provide numerous options of media

© Institute for Computer Sciences, Social Informatics and Telecommunications Engineering 2014
V.C.M. Leung et al. (Eds.): TridentCom 2014, LNICST 137, pp. 293–303, 2014.
DOI: 10.1007/978-3-319-13326-3_28

streaming quality, and if the client device bandwidth condition changes drastically, the appropriate media quality cannot be instantly switched, which degrades user experience. Mobile Cloud Computing (MCC) is an emerging technology to improve the quality of mobile services. MCC can improve the performance of mobile applications by offloading data processing from mobile devices to servers. With the help of MCC, the network condition of the whole mobile and server environment can be taken into consideration to determine the real-time transcoding procedure [3].

In this paper, we consider a scenario that a set of neighboring mobile devices take interests in watching the identical video stream. This scenario will occur when a group of users want to watch a live show or soccer game on their own mobile devices. The best stream coding rate may not be reached *if* the device asks for the stream separately. Worse still, when the mobile devices are within the same cover range of the base station, the network resource will be more scarce. However, if these users are willing to cooperate as a group, the mobile connections can be combined together to apply a better streaming rate and then extended by wireless Device to Device (D2D) links established through WiFi-Direct or Bluetooth [4].

Considering the above scenario, a cloud assisted real-time transcoding mechanism is proposed in this paper, which contains a bandwidth recorder, a media transcoder, a group-based resource manager and a HTTP live streaming server. This paper focus on our improvement to DASH and experiments on the emulated testbed with Android smartphones, aiming at providing better Quality of Experience (QoE) for mobile users.

The structure of the rest of the paper is as follows. Section 2 presents related work. Section 3 gives the scheme and the algorithm in details for each module in the system. Section 4 presents an emulation testbed and gives our analysis to the result. Finally, conclusions are drawn in Section 5.

2   Related Work

It is clear that the coding rate selection is determined by devices in most of the commercial DASH services. However, it is difficult to measure the accurate bandwidth of device-side above HTTP layer [2]. The natural variability of video content is taken into consideration to reduce the quality fluctuation rather than measured network bandwidth in [14], which do not consider the cooperation of mobile devices. The trade-offs problem is studied by [9] between the two QoE metrics—probability of interruption in media playback, and the initial waiting time before starting the playback.

A file downloading system within the adjacent cooperated mobile devices is proposed by [5], however the purpose of this paper is not aiming at streaming video. Furthermore, the paper [6] has considered the similar scenario, but the energy consumption is the main concern in this paper instead of QoE. Moreover, the device cooperation mechanism is quite simple that the captain device downloads the whole media content from cloud and sends it to its members by broadcasting. So the devices could not take advantage of cooperation which may lead to better video quality and less traffic cost. The system in [4] and [7] have nearly the same cooperation with this paper, but it does not consider DASH and cannot provide adaptive streaming to improve video quality.

A DASH based standard is presented in [10] considered the interoperability needs due to devices and servers that come from various vendors. Traditional methods demand multiple versions of the same video content with different bit rates stored on the server which may incur tremendous storage overhead, so cloud-assisted adaptive video streaming is proposed by [3] and [11]. A cloud based transcoder is proposed and implemented by [12] with an intermediate cloud platform to provide the format resolution considered the gap between Internet videos and mobile devices. In [13], a control-theoretic approach to select an appropriate bitrate is proposed with multiple content distribution servers but the author do not take advantage of the server cluster's computing capability and increase the burden of the client. However, these approaches on cloud do not consider the cooperation of mobile devices.

3   Proposed Scheme

In this paper, a prototype of the system in both the server side and the device side is implemented. In the remaining of this section, we give a basic overview of the modules in the functional entity and their interaction with each other. The following symbols are used in this section.

- ✓ N The number of devices.

- ✓ S_n^m The fragment of segment n sent to the device m, while S_n means the whole segment.

- ✓ L_n The length of the segment n.

- ✓ d_n^m The start position of the segment n sent to the device m.

- ✓ O_n^m The offset of the segment n sent to the device m.

- ✓ v_n^m The bandwidth of device m at the transmission of segment n.

- ✓ T_n^m The tuple (S_n^m, d_n^m, O_n^m) of segment n that device m share with others.

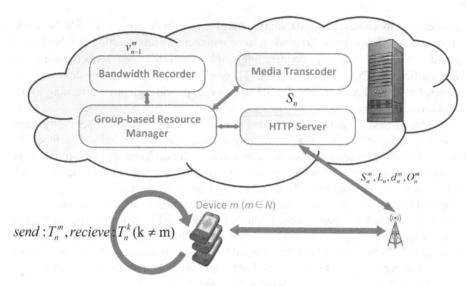

Fig. 1. System architecture

3.1 System Architecture

The system includes a cloud server and several cooperated mobile devices as shown in Figure 1. Before the startup, the devices should have been connected to each other with WiFi-Direct and connected to the server via Internet. And one device of the group should act as the **Captain Device** in charge of coordinating the other devices during the devices-setup period.

3.2 Modules on the Cloud Server

The **Group-based Resource Manager** controls the system on server side. When the **Captain Device** requests the playlist with the group number N, the **Group-based Resource Manager** creates a random certification key which is used to recognize the client devices as a group. It also takes the bandwidth information v_{n-1}^m from the **Bandwidth Recorder** and lets the **Media Transcoder** produce the video segment S_n in appropriate bit-rate. When connection starts, the length of package and the timestamp will be recorded in the **Bandwidth Recorder** and further provided to the **Group-based Resource Manager**. When predicting the network speed according to the group bandwidth, the highest possible value should using a safety margin as $(1-\alpha)v_{n-1}$ where α is usually in the range [0, 0.05].

The **Media Transcoder** produces the requested video segment with proper bit-rate to fit the network condition of the group of devices. When the devices want to get a video segment, the **Group-based Resource Manager** provides the original video segment and the target group bandwidth to **Media Transcoder**. The **Media Transcoder** outputs the appropriate video segment that can fulfill the group bandwidth capability.

The **HTTP Server** handles the HTTP request from the devices. When a captain device requests the play list, the **HTTP Server** notifies the **Group-based Resource Manager** to create a certification key, and sends the requested m3u8 list along with the key back to the device. When a video segment requests during the playing, the HTTP Server forwards the request to the **Group-based Resource Manager** to deal with.

3.3   Modules on Devices

The device side contains three modules which are **Device Resource Manager (DRM$_m$)**, **Device Downloader(DD$_m$)** and **Device Broadcaster(DB$_m$)**. The **DRM$_m$** takes charge of managing the whole operations on the devices such as segment caching, scheduling with other modules and interaction with Graphical User Interface (GUI). There is a list of segments in the server to be downloaded by each device. The **DD$_m$** cares about the fragment download from the server. If the **DD$_m$** receives the failure message from **DRM$_m$** which is broadcasted from other devices with the failure tuple T_n^m, all the devices try to request the server for failure fragment. Only one device can receive acknowledgement from the cloud and start to initiate the **DD$_m$** to download this failure tuple, where the decision mechanism is based on the wireless channel bandwidth and the download speed of each device. The **DB$_m$** is the coordinator that make all the devices available to connect with each other. The **DB$_m$** can deal with the broadcast message from other devices as well as sending the broadcast message to other devices. Finally when all the fragment of one segment are all received, then the **DRM$_m$** is responsible for assembling all the fragment to one whole segment and dispatch it to the video player.

3.4   Algorithm Procedure

Figure 2 shows the general sequence of flow for the device-setup period. During this period, the **Captain Device** requests the live video streaming playlist with the group number N from the server, and the server returns the list along with a random key which could be the certification of the group member. The **Captain Device** then broadcast the playlist and the key to other devices to start the playing.

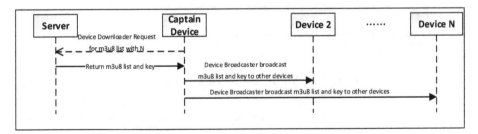

Fig. 2. Flow chart for the device-setup period

After receiving the play list, devices request the live video segments described in the list, as shown in Figure 3. At the first time the **HTTP Server** will simply divide the segment into equal fragments and send them to devices separately. For example, if the number of devices is N. The fragment size of each devices will be $S_1^m = \dfrac{1}{N} S_1$, where m indicates the mth device, and 1 indicates the first segment. When sending the fragments to devices, the server also provide the segment length L_1, start position d_1^m and offset O_1^m to the mth device so that the devices can record the fragment into appropriate position based on these information. When the **DD$_m$** receives the fragment, the **DB$_m$** directly broadcasts the fragment to other devices of the group through D2D interface. When all the fragments are collected, the **DRM$_m$** will assemble them into one whole segment and send it to the real-time video player. When the **DD$_m$** sends the request the server for the second segment with the key, the server will predict the network bandwidth of the group, according to the download speed of previous segment. Then the server transcodes the origin video into proper bit-rate to fit the network condition of the whole group, and separates it into fragments with different sizes according to the network ability of each device and send the $S_2^m = \left(v_1^m \middle/ \sum\limits_{k=1}^{N} v_1^k \right) S_2$ segment to the mth device, where v_1^m indicates the bandwidth of the mth device in the wireless channel at the first transmission. The server also provide the segment length L_2, start position d_2^m and offset O_2^m.

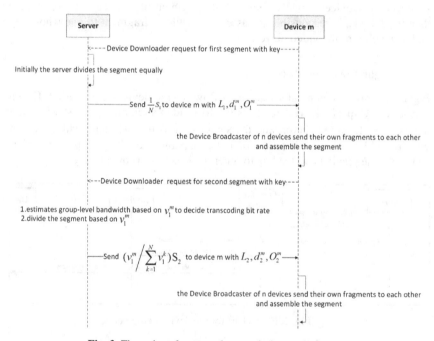

Fig. 3. Flow chart for normal transmission period

4   Testbed Emulation and Performance Analysis

We present an emulated testbed to testify the performance of the designed system, in order to show the advantage in QoE and network utilization. Finally, a PSNR measurement is used to evaluate the quality of the video segment.

4.1   Emulation Environment

Due to the complex smartphone system of the experiment environment and the control over the process, some conditions are set differently from the modules which will not affect the result. We use WiFi as HTTP downloading interface to simulate the 3G/4G connection in real system. Because it is more accurate to control network bandwidth as we want for the emulation in WiFi network than in 3G/4G, in order to repeat the scenarios in emulation. While WiFi module on mobile device is occupied by HTTP downloading, the Bluetooth on the device is used to exchange data between devices in the group. The details of transcoder in cloud are not closely related to the whole system, so we prepared up to 29 fixed streaming rate levels transcoded from an original 5000kbps video stream, in order to simulate the real-time transcoding approximately. The video stream lasts for 200 seconds which is divided into 20 trunk segments. While the minimum and maximum are 200kbps and 3000kbps with a step of 100kbps. And the small deviation towards the real appropriate transcoding will not affect our performance analysis and conclusions.

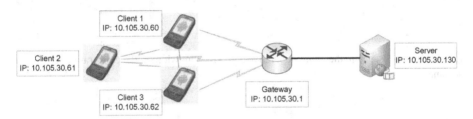

Fig. 4. Emulation environment architecture

The emulation environment network topology consists of three Android smartphones and a Linux server. Android devices in the system include client 1 as Samsung GT-I9070, client 2 as Samsung GT-I9100 and client 3 as Google Nexus S. The server has an 8 cores Intel Xeon E5-1620 CPU and 16GB RAM, and uses CentOS as its operating system.

4.2   Validation of Scheme on the Cloud Transcoder

This section shows the benefit of more effective network bandwidth utilization by the Media Transcoder. Traditional DASH server usually provides several fixed level of video stream as smooth, standard definition (SD) and high definition (HD) to face the network vibration. While in the transcoder scheme, definition level is more adaptive. Figure 5 (a) shows that using the transcoder scheme, the devices can get a video stream with a proper bit-rate closer to the limitation. The normal device get the DASH video with three fixed level which are 1000kbps, 1700kbps and 2500kbps in this case while the sim-transcoder device use our approach. The comparison indicates the video quality and network utilization with cloud transcoding is obviously improved. The bandwidth limit is emulated with network vibration by the Linux kernel Traffic Control (TC) module.

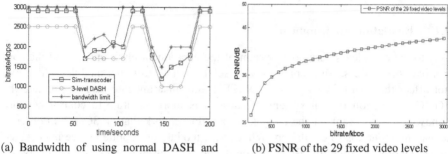

(a) Bandwidth of using normal DASH and Sim-transcoder

(b) PSNR of the 29 fixed video levels

Fig. 5. Performance of the Cloud Transcoder Scheme

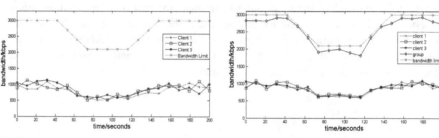

(a) Bandwidth usage in the non-cooperative scheme

(b) Bandwidth in the cooperative scheme

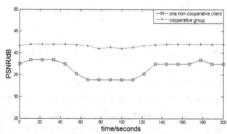

(c) PSNR comparison in the cooperative scheme and the non-cooperative scheme

Fig. 6. Bandwidth and PSNR Comparison in the cooperative scheme and the non-cooperative scheme

This paper uses the PSNR to measure the video streaming quality by calculating the image pixel difference between the original one and the received one. The computing formula of PSNR is well-known as $PSNR = 10 \times \log_{10} \left(\dfrac{\left(2^n - 1\right)^2}{MSE} \right)$ where MSE stands for the Mean Square Error between the original image and the compared one and n represents the number of bits occupied by each sampling point. The higher PSNR means the less distortion. For a video stream consists of N frames, the PSNR of the video is presented as the average value of the N frames' PSNR. In our case, a Linux open source tool called VQMT is used to calculate the value. Figure 5 (b) shows the PSNR of the 29 fixed video levels compared with the original 5000kbps one.

4.3   Performance of D2D Cooperation

This section describes the emulation result of the cooperative scheme and the non-cooperative scheme. In the non-cooperative scheme, three adjacent devices are watching the same live streaming video and competing for the network bandwidth in the range of same access point. Figure 6 (a) shows that devices in the non-cooperative scheme could own approximately one third of network bandwidth as competitors. As a result every device can only consume the video quality with rate lower than one third of the network bandwidth.

In the cooperation scheme, the requested bandwidth of the three devices is calculated as a group watching a streaming video synchronously. As shown in Figure 6 (b), although each device can only obtain part of the network bandwidth, the acquired video quality achieve better performance and more smooth facing to the network vibration. What's more, the network bandwidth is under higher resource utilization. Figure 6 (c) shows the PSNR between the non-cooperative and cooperative devices as mentioned in Figure 6 (a) and (b). It is observed that the PSNR is increased on average, which present that the media quality viewed by the user is on average better than the original mechanism.

As more component established on the device, more resource of computation and memory storage is cost. Figure 7 shows the CPU utilization and the memory usage of the each device in the cooperative scheme and the non-cooperative scheme. The CPU utilization of one device in the cooperative scheme is average 10 percent higher than those in the non-cooperative scheme, mainly because of the broadcasting mechanism. The same 10 percent higher usage also happens in the memory of the device.

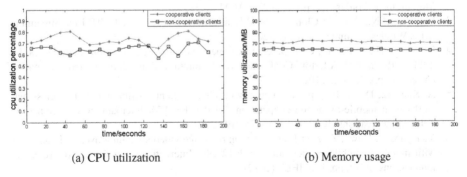

(a) CPU utilization   (b) Memory usage

Fig. 7. Resource usage of cooperative and non-cooperative

5   Conclusions and Future Work

In this paper, we have proposed an optimization solution for high resolution streaming video over HTTP in mobile network. We considered the scenario that a set of neighboring mobile devices take interests in watching the identical video stream. We have taken a pragmatic stance to work within the network constraints (w.r.t. resource sharing and adaptation) that have spurred the growth of video traffic by the help of mobile cloud computing. We proposed a framework to improve the quality of video services with the MCC and D2D technology. This article designs a cloud-assisted real-time transcoding mechanism based on DASH protocol, implements the bandwidth recorder, a media transcoder, a group-based resource manager and a HTTP live streaming server, and provides the optimum media quality. The experiments on our emulated network with Android smartphones show that this framework provides higher resolution live streaming with less expense, better QoE and more effective network utilization. According to the experimental results of the implemented testbed, the bandwidth utilization rate can be higher than 80 percent when the bandwidth is in steady state, even if the bandwidth is unstable, the bandwidth utilization rate is maintained at 60 percent - 80 percent. The PSNR analysis also shows that the video stream quality increased even with the network vibration due to the mechanism.

Fairness, efficiency, and stability are three potentially conflicting goals that a robust adaptive bit-rate selection algorithm must strive to achieve the Quality of Experience. In the future, we will try to present a principled understanding of bit-rate adaptation of DASH service in mobile cloud computing environment and analyze through at least three main components: bandwidth estimation, bit-rate selection, and chunk scheduling.

References

1. Pande, A., Ahuja, V., Sivaraj, R., et al.: Video delivery challenges and opportunities in 4g networks. IEEE MultiMedia **20**(3), 88–94 (2013)
2. Huang, T.Y., Handigol, N., Heller, B., et al.: Confused, timid, and unstable: picking a video streaming rate is hard. In: Proceedings of the 2012 ACM conference on Internet Measurement Conference, pp. 225–238. ACM (2012)
3. Lai, Y.X.U.N., Wan, J.: Cloud-Assisted Real time Transrating for HTTP Live Streaming. IEEE Wireless Communications 3 (2013)
4. Seferoglu, H., Keller, L., Cici, B., et al.: Cooperative video streaming on smartphones. In: 2011 49th Annual Allerton Conference on Communication, Control, and Computing (Allerton), pp. 220–227. IEEE (2011)
5. Al-Kanj, L., Dawy, Z.: Optimized energy efficient content distribution over wireless networks with mobile-to-mobile cooperation. 2010 IEEE 17th International Conference on Telecommunications (ICT), pp. 471–475. IEEE (2010)
6. Yaacoub, E., Dawy, Z., Abu-Dayya, A.: On real-time video streaming over LTE networks with mobile-to-mobile cooperation. In: 2012 19th International Conference on Telecommunications (ICT), pp. 1–6. IEEE (2012)

7. Abedini, N., Sampath, S., Bhattacharyya, R., et al.: Realtime streaming with guaranteed QoS over wireless D2D networks. In: Proceedings of the fourteenth ACM International Symposium on Mobile ad Hoc Networking and Computing, pp. 197–206. ACM (2013)
8. Sprintson, A., Sadeghi, P., Booker, G., et al.: A randomized algorithm and performance bounds for coded cooperative data exchange. In: 2010 IEEE International Symposium on Information Theory Proceedings (ISIT), pp. 1888–1892. IEEE (2010)
9. ParandehGheibi, A., Médard, M., Ozdaglar, A., et al.: Avoiding interruptions—a qoe reliability function for streaming media applications. IEEE Journal on Selected Areas in Communications 29(5), 1064–1074 (2011)
10. Sodagar, I.: The mpeg-dash standard for multimedia streaming over the internet. IEEE MultiMedia 18(4), 62–67 (2011)
11. Wang, X., Kwon, T.T., Choi, Y., et al.: Cloud-assisted adaptive video streaming and social-aware video prefetching for mobile users. IEEE Wireless Communications 20(3) 2013
12. Li, Z., Huang, Y., Liu, G., et al.: Cloud transcoder: Bridging the format and resolution gap between internet videos and mobile devices. In: Proceedings of the 22nd International Workshop on Network and Operating System Support for Digital Audio and Video, pp. 33–38. ACM (2012)
13. Zhou, C., Lin, C., Zhang, X., et al.: A Control-Theoretic Approach to Rate Adaption for DASH over Multiple Content Distribution Servers (2013)
14. Li, Z., Begen, A.C., Gahm, J. et al.: Streaming video over HTTP with consistent quality. arXiv preprint arXiv:1401.5174 (2014)

Other Topics

Other Topics

Experimental Study on the Performance of Linux Ethernet Bonding

Hoang Tran-Viet[1]([✉]), Toan Nguyen-Duc[1], Kien Nguyen[1,2],
Quang Tran Minh[2], Son Hong Ngo[1], and Shigeki Yamada[2]

[1] Hanoi University of Science and Technology,
1 Dai Co Viet Road, Hanoi, Vietnam
{hoang.tranviet,toan.nguyenduc1}@hust.edu.vn,
sonnh@soict.hust.edu.vn
[2] National Institute of Informatics, 2-1-2 Hitotsubashi,
Chiyoda-ku, Tokyo 101-8430, Japan
{kienng,quangtran,shigeki}@nii.ac.jp

Abstract. Linux bonding is a feature allowing to group multiple physical network interfaces into a logical one on Linux machines. Known as a low-cost method to improve fault tolerance and network throughput, the Linux bonding with seven supported modes is increasingly deployed in various scenarios such as datacenters, home networks, etc. However, the strengths and weaknesses of different modes have not been well investigated. While previous works mostly pay attention on the performance of the popular round-robin mode, this work extensively and additionally evaluates other modes based on three major criteria: throughput improvement, load balancing, and fault tolerance. To the best of our knowledge, this is the first work investigating the capabilities of fault tolerance using Linux bonding. The evaluation results show that the active-backup mode achieves the flow switch-over time, which is the duration of traffic flow discontinuation due to a network failure, as small as 10 milliseconds. Moreover, in the round-robin mode with two bonded network interfaces, Linux machines can achieve the maximum throughput close to double of that in case of non-bonding. However, the out-of-order and switch compatibility issues may limit the utilisation of the round-robin mode in certain scenarios. In the 802.3ad mode, the out-of-order issue can be avoided, although load balancing is not always optimal.

Keywords: Linux bonding · Link aggregation · Fault tolerance · Switch-over · Throughput improvement · Load balancing

1 Introduction

With the continuous development of online applications and services, network operators and service providers have to deal with an ever-increasing bandwidth demand [1]. On the other hand, the customers expect their network services always available, despite the fact that every element in network can fail.

© Institute for Computer Sciences, Social Informatics and Telecommunications Engineering 2014
V.C.M. Leung et al. (Eds.): TridentCom 2014, LNICST 137, pp. 307–317, 2014.
DOI: 10.1007/978-3-319-13326-3_29

A common approach for increasing network resilience and throughput is to combine multiple communication links. In the transport layer, there are many recent works focus on multipath TCP [2,3]. In the network layer, equal cost multipath routing is widely adopted [4]. In the lower layers, the combination is usually done by *interface aggregation*, which means grouping multiple physical network interfaces to form a single logical one. There are several flavours of interface aggregation in networks today. On networking devices, this feature is called EtherChannel [5] by Cisco, or Link Aggregation in 802.3AD standard [6] by IEEE. On servers, this feature is implemented as *Ethernet bonding* [7] in Linux environment, or NIC teaming in Windows environment.

Ethernet bonding feature is currently deployed in various datacenters, server systems, and even in home networks [8]. Additionally, the Ethernet bonding provides a valuable tool for research, for example in building high performance systems [9] or maintaining connectivity during virtual machine migration [10,11]. Despite the popularity of Linux bonding in industrial and research environments, its performance has not been well investigated. For that reason, we extensively measure the performance of different Linux bonding modes. Further, this work is potentially a base for network designers and researchers to choose the right bonding mode for their specific network scenarios and requirements.

Different to previous evaluation works [12,13], we evaluate the performance of Linux bonding based on three major criteria: throughput enhancement, load balancing efficiency, and fault tolerance. To the best of our knowledge, this is the first work evaluating the fault tolerance capability of Linux bonding. Moreover, apart from round-robin mode, several bonding modes are also investigated in our evaluation. The experiment results show that the UDP flow switch-over time is in the range of 5 - 20 milliseconds with active-backup bonding mode. In another experiment, by bonding two physical interfaces in round-robin mode, the transfer duration of a file in FTP is decreased by nearly a half.

To accomplish our evaluations, there are several technical challenges must be overcome. First, measuring the switch-over time of traffic flow is not trivial. In a high-speed network, measurement tools may not work fast enough in recording network events or capturing packets. On the other hand, we need to make sure that our measurements do not impose heavy load on system and affect network performance. Another issue is related to failure detection feature of Network Interface Cards (NICs) hardware. Many NICs do not detect link failures in a timely manner, resulting in a very long flow switch-over time. This requires testing NICs carefully before using them for bonding both in experiment networks and in production networks.

The rest of paper is outlined as follows: after Section 2 mentioning the related work, Section 3 provides a brief overview on Linux bonding feature. In Section 4, after the description of experiment set-up, we present our evaluation results and discussions. Finally, conclusion remark is given in Section 5.

2   Related Work

There are various works related to investigating Linux bonding. The most close ones to our work are [12] and [13], in which the authors evaluated the performance of wired and wireless bonding accordingly. However, the fault tolerance, which is an important aspect of Linux bonding, was not considered in these works. Moreover, the works only examined the round-robin mode although there are seven different modes in Linux bonding. In [8], the authors evaluated Linux bonding in a home network environment. This work analysed the packet loss and throughput improvement of round-robin mode and broadcast mode with varied attenuation level.

3   Overview of Linux Bonding

Linux bonding means aggregating several NICs together into a group on Linux machines. This group of interfaces appears as a single interface to higher network layers. In the Linux bonding, physical interfaces in the group are called *slaves*, while the logical interface is called *master*. When a packet is sent from higher layer to the master interface, the bonding driver will deliver this packet to one (or more) slave interface. Packets can be delivered in several ways, depending on which mode the bonding driver is in. The process of receiving packets is similar to sending process. When a packet comes to a slave from a remote host, the bonding driver will decide to direct this packet to the master or to drop it, depending on the bonding mode.

Linux bonding provides fault tolerance by monitoring link or NIC failure and switching traffic from failed slave to other slaves. Linux bonding uses two methods for link monitoring. The first one is MII monitoring, which relies on NIC driver to maintain its knowledge about local link status. MII monitoring is the default option in Linux bonding and can be used with all modes. The second method is ARP monitoring. With this method, the bonding driver maintains a list of remote peers, periodically sends ARP requests to these peers and monitors whether slave interfaces still send or receive traffic recently. At the time of writing, the latest version of Linux bonding (v3.7.1) supports 7 different bonding modes. Table 1 shows a brief overview [7] of each mode.

Round-Robin Mode. In this mode, each packet is sent to one slave interface in turn. For example, in case of a bonding group with two slave interfaces, the first packet will be sent through slave 1, the second one will be sent through the slave 2, the third one will be sent through slave 1, and so on.

Active-Backup Mode. In this mode, there is one interface is active at a time. Other slaves are in standby state and do not send or receive packets. When the active one is failed, one backup slave will be chosen as the new active one.

Table 1. List of bonding modes

Mode	Fault tolerance	Throughput enhancement
round-robin	Yes	Yes
active-backup	Yes	No
balance-xor	Yes	Yes
broadcast	Yes	No
802.3ad	Yes	Yes
balance-tlb	Yes	Yes
balance-alb	Yes	Yes (for both incoming and outgoing traffic)

Balance-Xor Mode. In this mode, outgoing traffic is balanced per flow of packets. While different flows may be sent over different slaves, all packets belongs to a flow will be sent through the same slave. This ensures all packets of a flow will in order at destination host. Specifically, for each packet coming to bonding group, the bonding driver will decide to send it through which slave by using a XOR hash function on its header information. By default, the outgoing traffic is balanced based on layer 2 information only. Each packet will be sent through the slave with the $SlaveID$ determined by:

$SlaveID = (srcMAC \oplus destMAC) \mod N$

where $srcMAC$ and $destMAC$ are the source MAC address and destination MAC address; N is the number of live slaves in a bonding group. This algorithm let all traffic between two MAC clients go through the same slave. Linux bonding also supports load-balancing based on layer 3 (IP addresses) or layer 4 (TCP or UDP port numbers) information:

$SlaveID = (srcPort \oplus destPort) \oplus (srcIP \oplus destIP) \wedge FFFFh) \mod N.$

Broadcast Mode. Each outgoing packet is copied and broadcast on all bonded interfaces. Currently, this mode is not widely used in real networks.

802.3ad Mode. 802.3ad is an IEEE standard for link aggregation [6], which also includes Link Aggregation Control Protocol (LACP), between two networking devices. In this mode, a Linux host can connect to a LACP-enabled switch through a group of aggregated links. The limitation of this mode is that the 802.3ad requires all links running in full duplex mode at the same speed. Outgoing traffic from Linux host is distributed by the same algorithm as in the balance-xor mode.

Balance-tlb Mode. In this mode, outgoing traffic is balanced per remote host. However, incoming TCP/UDP traffic is always received on one slave.

Balance-alb Mode. This mode is almost similar to the balance-tlb mode, but has a difference in balancing the incoming traffic. By intercepting ARP packets, the bonding driver can decide that traffic from a specific IP address will be received on which slave. However, the interfaces must be able to change their MAC addresses while they are running. The feature that is not supported by commodity NICs is also a big disadvantage of balance-alb mode.

4   Evaluation Method

In this section we present the evaluation of three bonding modes: round-robin mode, active-backup mode, and 802.3ad mode. These modes are chosen because they represent well for three major criteria on which we want to focus: throughput improvement, fault tolerance, and load balancing.

4.1   Experiment Set-Up

Each bonding mode has been evaluated using two network topologies. The first one is host-to-host bonding, as illustrated in Fig. 1a, in which two Linux computers are connected directly through a group of bonded links (i.e., CAT5e Ethernet cables). Each computer (Core i5 Ivy Bridge, 4GB RAM, Ubuntu 13.10 64-bit, kernel version 3.11.0-14, with the latest version of bonding drivers) has several network cards with the same negotiated speed at 100 Mbps. This topology allows us to conveniently monitor how traffic is distributed among bonded links. In real deployments, high performance clustering systems can use this kind of bonding topology. The second topology is shown in Fig. 1b, in which the same Linux computers are used. However, the computers connect to a switch, and the bonding configuration is enabled on one computer (i.e., host 1). In the topology, we use the Pica8 P3295 switch, which has 48 Gigabit Ethernet Ports and supports LACP. The topology allows us to explore how computers with bonding interoperate with networking devices.

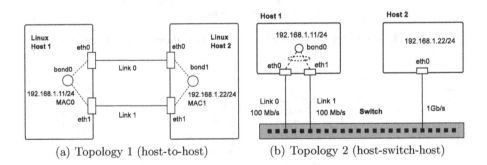

(a) Topology 1 (host-to-host)   (b) Topology 2 (host-switch-host)

Fig. 1. The evaluation topologies

During the bonding initialisation process, it is essential to specify the link monitoring interval; otherwise the mechanism of link failure detection will be disabled. In our evaluations, the monitoring interval is set to 1 ms, which is the minimum value supported on Linux.

4.2 Round-Robin Mode Evaluation

Round-robin is the only mode allowing a TCP/UDP flow to be spread across multiple links. In this evaluation, we use Iperf [14] to generate a UDP flow with 500 Mbps offered rate from host 1 to host 2. Figure 2 shows the total throughput with different UDP datagram sizes in case of topology 2 (Fig. 1b). In case of topology 1 (Fig. 1a), the results are similar. As shown in the figure, when the size of UDP datagram is less than 1472 bytes, the total throughput provided by two NICs or three NICs bonding is nearly double or triple compared to that of non-bonding scenario, respectively. However, the UDP datagrams larger than 1472 bytes are fragmented. With round-robin bonding, different parts of a UDP datagram are sent through different links. Combining with out-of-order issue, these fragments are not re-assembled correctly at the receiver. We also investigate the behavior of round-robin mode in response to link failures. The results for TCP traffic with topology 2 are shown in Fig. 3a. A failure of link 1 (eth1) occurs at $t = 5s$, and then the link is recovered after 5 seconds. We observed

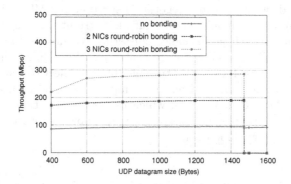

Fig. 2. Round-robin mode, UDP traffic, throughput on Iperf server

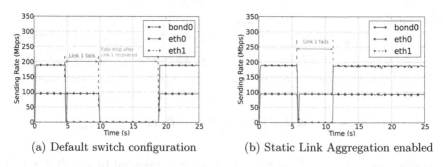

(a) Default switch configuration   (b) Static Link Aggregation enabled

Fig. 3. Round-robin mode, TCP traffic with a link failure on link 1

that even after this link is recovered, from $t = 10s$ to $t = 19s$, the transfer rate is dropped nearly to zero on both slaves. This issue does not happen with topology 1. The root cause of this issue is that the Pica8 switch is not aware that two links are bonded at Linux host, hence the packets go through newly recovered link are dropped at the switch. Although link 0 is still alive, the packet loss on link 1 triggers TCP congestion control to reduce congestion window to 1, hence reducing the sending rate close to zero. To solve this problem, it is necessary to aggregate these switch ports by using Static Link Aggregation (SLA), that is known as 802.3ad without LACP. With SLA enabled, the switch can quickly determine that an aggregated link is recovered, and correctly receive packets from recovered link, as the results of same evaluation in Fig. 3.

Table 2. Round-robin mode, 361 MB file transfer time in FTP (average in 10 runs)

	361 MB file transfer time
no bonding	32.12 seconds
round robin	16.20 seconds

In the case of TCP, significant out-of-order issue will trigger congestion control at the sender to reduce the sending rate. To investigate how this issue affects the throughput performance from application level, we conduct a simple FTP traffic test. We send a 361 MB file in the binary mode of FTP from host 1 to host 2 in topology 2 and measure the file transfer time (FTT). Table 2 shows the FTT value in two cases: host 1 connects to switch by a single link (no bond) or by two bonded links. The results show that FTT has been reduced to nearly a half with round-robin mode, and out-of-order issue only imposes a minor overhead on network performance in this application.

4.3 Active-Backup Mode Evaluation

Active-Backup mode is specifically designed for fault-tolerance, so we focus on evaluating how fast this bonding mode can switch traffic to a backup link when the active link fails. For this purpose, we use flow switch-over time (FST), which is defined as the duration of traffic flow discontinuation due to a network failure, as a criterion to assess fault-tolerance capability. We determine FST as the duration from the time of last data packets on old active slave (that is, just before link failure) to the time of the first data packets on new active slave.

We do the experiments with both topology 1 and 2. While traffic is being sent, failures on the active link happen for every 10 seconds. With the topology 1, we capture all incoming data packets at the receiver (host 2) using Wireshark [15]. Figure 5a shows the FST values of UDP and TCP traffic, each case is measured in 20 times. In the case of UDP, the FST values fall in the range of 5 - 20 ms, however in the case TCP flow, the FST values are divided into two groups:

normal and huge. The huge group contains the values higher than 200 ms. In these cases, the congestion window is reduced to 1, which means that the TCP transmission timeout (RTO) has occurred. This happens if the TCP sender has sent all packets in congestion window, and it has not received acknowledgements during the RTO. It is noted that the minimum value of RTO in Linux TCP is 200 ms by default.

With topology 2, above method cannot be used to measure FST, since all packets are received on a single NIC at the receiver (host 2). In this case, we use another method which based on the port-mirroring feature. Specifically, we mirror the traffic from the port which associated with link 0 to another NIC (eth3) of host 1, as shown in Fig. 4. By using port mirroring, we can determine correctly the FST as the duration from the last packet captured on eth3 and the first packet on eth1. As shown in Fig. 5, the FST results measured with two topologies are similar.

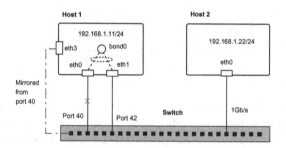

Fig. 4. Measuring FST in topology 2 with port mirroring

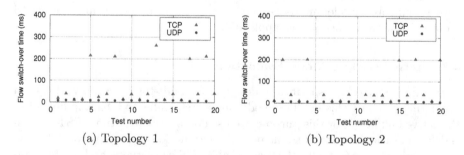

(a) Topology 1   (b) Topology 2

Fig. 5. Flow switch-over time, active-backup mode

4.4 802.3ad Mode Evaluation

This evaluation focuses on load balancing capability supported by hashing algorithms. In the evaluation, we use "layer 3+4" load balancing option, which is based on both IP addresses and layer 4 port numbers. This allows different

TCP/UDP flows between two hosts to be distributed among multiple slaves. The 802.3ad bonding mode works in the two topologies with similar behaviors. The traffic is set up and load-balanced toward the direction from host 1 to host 2. We create four 40 Mbps UDP flows with random UDP port numbers. After that, we measure the receiving rate at both slave interfaces on the host 2, and the results are shown in Fig. 6a. The figure clearly shows the load balancing of the traffic. We repeat same procedure but using the different traffic flows. The link 1 is saturated with one full 100 Mbps flow and three other 40 Mbps flows are on link 0. The results in Fig. 6b show that the load balancing is not optimal. Even though, the link 1 is full, other traffic flows are not switched to the other available link.

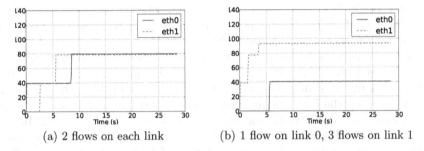

(a) 2 flows on each link   (b) 1 flow on link 0, 3 flows on link 1

Fig. 6. Receiving rate on two links in the Topology1 of 802.3ad evaluation

To further understand the efficiency of the load balancing mechanism, we conduct experiments using two different traffic patterns: pattern 1 with four 10 Mbps flows and pattern 2 with sixteen 2.5 Mbps flows. The direction of flows is from host 1 to host 2. In each case of traffic pattern, we measure the sending and receiving rate in 100 different runs to see how load balancing mechanism allocates flows on each link. Figure 7 shows the number of flows on link 1 with each traffic pattern. For the 4-flow pattern, the worst situation is that all 4 flows run on only one link happened in 10% (10/100 runs). For the other pattern, the situation that all flows run on a single link did not happen in 100 runs. These results indicates the load balancing mechanism of this mode works better in case

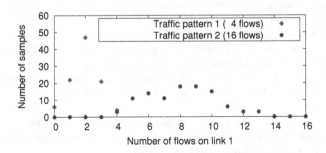

Fig. 7. Distribution of flows on 2 links, 100 runs in 802.3ad mode

of a large number of flows. Furthermore, the evaluation suggests that when the UDP/TCP port numbers are random, the number of flows on a link follows a binominal distribution.

5   Conclusion

In this paper, we have presented the performance evaluation of the three typical Linux bonding modes (i.e., round-robin, active-backup, and 802.3ad modes) on three major criteria: throughput improvement, fault tolerance, and load balancing. With no packet fragmentation, the round-robin mode with two bonded NICs can provide the throughput nearly double of that in the non-bonding case, even for a single flow. However, when the fragmentation happens, the out-of-order issue will affect the throughput performance severely. Moreover, we point out that this mode requires the adjacent peer (i.e., switch) to aggregate ports in order to achieve fault tolerance. In contrast to the round-robin mode, the active-backup mode does not require any special support by the switch and neither suffer from out-of-order issue. The active-backup mode, which is originally designed for the fault tolerance purpose, can provide the FST in the range of 5 - 20 ms with UDP traffic and less than 300 ms with TCP traffic. In the 802.3ad mode, the Linux host can dynamically cooperate with an LACP-enabled switch following in a 803ad standard (or LACP). The hashing algorithms allow the Linux host to load balance outgoing traffic among several physical links; however, the traffic distribution is not optimal.

References

1. Armbrust, M., et al.: A view of cloud computing. ACM Communications **53**(4), 50–58 (2010)
2. Ford, A., Raiciu, C., Handley, M., Bonaventure, O., et al.: TCP Extensions for Multipath Operation with Multiple Addresses. RFC6824 (IETF) (2013)
3. Barré, S., Paasch, C., Bonaventure, O.: MultiPath TCP: From Theory to Practice. In: IFIP Networking, Valencia (May 2011)
4. Augustin, B., Friedman, T., Teixeira, R.: Measuring multipath routing in the Internet. IEEE/ACM Transactions on Networking **19**(3), 830–840 (2011)
5. Cisco EtherChannel - White Paper (accessed January 18, 2014), http://www.cisco.com/en/US/tech/tk389/tk213/tech_white_papers_list.html.
6. IEEE Std 802.3ad-2000 (2000)
7. Davis T., et al.: Linux Ethernet Bonding Driver HOWTO (2011), http://www.kernel.org/doc/Documentation/networking/bonding.txt
8. Yu, Y., Pan, J., Lu, M., Cai, L., Hoffman, D.: Evaluating no-new-wires home networks. In: 33rd IEEE Conference on Local Computer Networks, pp. 869–875. IEEE (2008)
9. Cope, J., Oberg, M., Tufo, H.M., Woitaszek, M.: Shared parallel filesystems in heterogeneous Linux multi-cluster environments. In: Proceedings of the 6th International Conference on Linux Clusters (2005)

10. Dong, Y., Yang, X., Li, J., Liao, G., Tian, K., Guan, H.: High performance network virtualization with SR-IOV. Journal of Parallel and Distributed Computing **72**(11), 1471–1480 (2012)
11. Zhai, E., Cummings, G.D., Dong, Y.: Live migration with pass-through device for Linux VM. In: Proceedings of the 2008 Ottawa Linux Symposium, pp. 261–268 (2008)
12. Aust, S., Kim, J.-O., Davis, P., Yamaguchi, A., Obana, S.: Evaluation of Linux Bonding Features. In: Proceedings of IEEE International Conference on Communication Technology, pp. 1–6 (2006)
13. Jayasuriya, A., Aust, S., Davis, P., Yamaguchi, A., Obana, S.: Aggregation of Wi-Fi links: When does it work? In: Proceedings of IEEE 15th International Conference on Networks, pp. 318–323 (2007)
14. Iperf: The TCP/UDP bandwidth measurement tool (2014)
15. Wireshark - a network protocol analyzer (2014)

Refined Feature Extraction for Chinese Question Classification in CQA

Lei Su[✉], Bin Yang, Xiangxiang Qi, and Yantuan Xian

School of Information Engineering and Automation,
Kunming University of Science and Technology, Kunming 650093, China
s28341@hotmail.com, yangbin0724@126.com, qixiangfighting@163.com,
yantuan.xian@gmail.com

Abstract. Community-based Question Answering (CQA) services, such as Baidu Zhidao, have attracted increasing attention over recent years, where the users can voluntarily post the questions and obtain the answers by the other users from the community. Question classification module of a CQA system plays a very important role in understanding the user intents, which could effectively enhance the CQA systems to identify the similar questions and retrieve the candidate answers. However, the poor semantic information could be obtained from the questions because of the short sentences. This paper proposes a refined feature extraction method for question classification. The method aims to use Wikipedia to expand the semantic knowledge of sentences, and extract the features step by step to overcome the shortness of semantic knowledge. Experimental results on 714,582 Chinese questions crawled from Baidu Knows show that the proposed method could effectively improve the performance of question classification in CQA.

Keywords: Community-based Question Answering · Wikipedia · Question Classification · Semantic Knowledge

1 Introduction

During the last few year, Community-based Question Answering (CQA) websites, such as Baidu Zhidao (zhidao.baidu.com), Sina iAsk (iask.sina.com.cn) and SOSO Ask (wenwen.soso.com), have emerged and become a popular form of online service. In these communities, web users can voluntarily ask and answer questions. Unlike the traditional search engines which retrieve a large number of candidate pages for users, CQA is an interactive platform where the posted questions could get a feedback by other volunteers. CQA provides a similar list of resolved history questions to the post items, where some good quality answers could be obtained by a small number of experts among the large population of users. These communities assure the quality of questions and answers through the mechanisms of voting, badges and reputation [1].

Understanding the user intent behind the questions would help a CQA system to find similar questions, recommend questions and obtain potential answers [2]. The goal of question classification is to accurately label the questions into predefined target categories. Question classification is an essential part of question answering systems, because it can not only impose constrains on the possible answers but also narrow the scope of finding answers. For example, if the question "how much to repair my

© Institute for Computer Sciences, Social Informatics and Telecommunications Engineering 2014
V.C.M. Leung et al. (Eds.): TridentCom 2014, LNICST 137, pp. 318–326, 2014.
DOI: 10.1007/978-3-319-13326-3_30

iphone5?" can be correctly classified into the category of maintenance in Consumer Electronics, the search scope for the answer will be significantly focused on the price instead of each word in the candidate documents.

Various machine learning algorithms have been proposed for question classification, which extract syntactic and semantic features from large quantities of training corpus to build the learning model. D. Zhang and W.S. Lee [3] used a special kernel function called tree kernel to enable the SVM to take advantage of the syntactic structures of questions. A. Moschitti et al. [4] defined tree structures based on shallow semantic encoded in predicate argument structures for question classification. A prominent achievement in Chinese question classification is the modified Bayes model proposed by Y. Zhang [5], where the accuracy rate reaches 72.4% on the 65 Chinese question classes. Compared with normal texts, questions in CQA are usually short and cannot provide sufficient syntactic and semantic features. To tackle the problem of data sparseness, Hotho et al. [6] used the synonym and hypernym included in WordNet to expend the text characteristics. Cai et al. [7] proposed a two-stage approach for question classification in CQA. The large-scale categories are pruned to a small subset, and then the questions are enriched by leveraging Wikipedia semantic knowledge (hypernym, synonym and associative concepts).

Unlike normal texts and documents, questions in CQA are usually short. Therefore, the traditional learning model based on bag-of-word in vector space model extracts a lot of feature value with zero due to the data sparseness. There is another difficulty in question classification in CQA. The traditional methods can classify the questions into several limited categories, while the number of categories in CQA is very large. For example, category level in Baidu Knows is roughly divided into three layers. From the top layer to the bottom layer in the taxonomy, the larger number of categories may cause a significant decline in classification accuracy.

In order to solve the above problems, we propose a refined feature extraction approach for question classification in CQA. First, the Wikipedia semantic library is constructed where the theme relationship can be used to extend the semantic knowledge of questions. Then, the proper nouns table, features extracting from categories and the refined feature extracting method could be employed based on bag-of-word. Experimental results on the 714,582 Chinese questions crawled from Baidu Knows show that the proposed method could significantly improve the classification accuracy in CQA.

The rest of this paper is organized as follows. Section 2 introduces the method of constructing the Wikipedia knowledge library. Section 3 describes the refined feature extraction for question classification. Section 4 reports and analysis the experimental study on the Chinese question classification in CQA. Finally, section 5 summarizes this paper and introduces the future work.

2   Wikipedia Knowledge Library Construction

2.1   Wikipedia Semantic Knowledge

Wikipedia is a free, open-content online collaborative encyclopedia, which provides link designed to guide the user to related pages with additional information. It can be an effective knowledge base resource because of the rich semantic knowledge. In particular, research has been done to exploit Wikipedia for document categorization [8–10] and text cluster [11–13]·

Each article in Wikipedia describes a topic or a concept, and it has a short title, which is a well-formed phrase like a term in a conventional thesaurus. Each article belongs to at least one category, and hyperlinks between articles capture their semantic relations. Specifically, the represented semantic relations are: equivalence (synonymy), hierarchical (hyponymy), and associative [9]. Articles in Wikipedia form a heavily interlinked knowledge base, enriched with a category system emerging from collaborative tagging, which constitutes a thesaurus [14]. Thus, Wikipedia contains a rich body of lexical semantic information, which includes knowledge about named entities, domain specific terms or domain specific word. To use Wikipedia semantic knowledge, we preprocess the Wikipedia articles to construct the topic library and the category library. The topics in Wikipedia are organized as a theme tree, where the topic pages are equivalent to the top nodes and linked to the relational nodes. According to the degree of relationship, each category with the different level can be organized as leaf in the Wiki tree.

Following [5], the semantic relations, such as synonym, polysemy, hypernym and associative relation, can be extracted from the article pages. The synonym relations mainly come from the redirect hyperlinks whose means are usually similar. Wikipedia provides disambiguation for a polysemy concept. Wikipedia categories contain the hypernym relations by hierarchical relations, including relations between categories and links. The associative relation of each hyperlink between Wikipedia articles could be measured by three kinds of method: content-based, out-link category-based and distance-based [10].

(1) Content-based measurement (S_{tfidf}) is based on vector space model. The relatedness of two articles is evaluated by the extent to which they share terms using *tf-idf* scheme.

(2) Out-link category-based measurement (S_{olc}) could be defined as the out-link category similarity. If most of the out-linked categories of two articles focus on several same ones, the concepts described in these two articles are most likely strongly related.

(3) Distance-based method (D_{cat}) measures semantic distance as the number of nodes in the category taxonomy along the shortest path between two conceptual nodes. This measurement is normalized by taking into account the depth of the taxonomy.

The overall relatedness evaluation is defined as:

$$S_{overall}=\lambda_1 S_{tfidf}+\lambda_2 S_{olc}+(1-\lambda_1-\lambda_2)(1-D_{cat}) \tag{1}$$

where λ_1 and λ_2 are the weight parameters.

2.2   Semantic Knowledge Library from Wikipedia

Java-based Wikipedia Library (JWPL) is already freely available for research purpose and is used to construct semantic knowledge library [14]. The category and topic databases from Wikipedia are established respectively.

Categories can reflect semantic relations in Wikipedia, so question expansion could use category information. The category database includes four tables:

(1) Category table: the patent and child categories are stored from Wikipedia, where two fields *CategoryID* (ID of category) and *Name* (name of category) are included.

(2) Category_inlinks table: the relations between the categories and their parent categories are stored, where two fields CategoryID (ID of category) and Inlinks (ID of parent category) are included.

(3) Category_outlinks table: the relations between the categories and their child categories are stored, where two fields CategoryID (ID of category) and Inlinks (ID of child category) are included.

(4) Category_pages table: the relations between the categories and the topic articles which belong to the categories are stored, where two fields CategoryID (ID of category) and Inlinks (ID of topic article) are included. Therefore, the categories and the topics can be connected by this table.

The topic database includes six tables:

(1) Page table: the detailed topics are stored in this table, which is the most important table in the knowledge library. The four fields, *PageID* (ID of page), *Name* (name of page), Text (detailed topics) and *IsDisambiguation* (whether it is a disambiguation page or not), are included in this table.

(2) Page_category table: the relations between the categories and the topic pages are stored, where two fields PageID (ID of page) and CategoryID (ID of category that the page belongs to) are included.

(3) Page_inlinks table: the relations between the pages and the child pages are stored in this table, where two fields PageID (ID of page) and Inlinks (ID of page which links to the page) are included.

(4) Page_outlinks table: the relations between the pages and the parent pages are stored in this table, where two fields PageID (ID of page) and Outlinks (ID of page which the page links to) are included. The associate rules are extracted from this table.

(5) Page_redirects table: the relations between the pages and the disambiguation pages, where two fields PageID (ID of page) and Redirects (ID of page which the page redirects to) are included.

(6) Page_mapline table: the allover information about the redirection pages is stored in this table, where three fields, PageID (ID of page), Name (name of the topic) and Redirects (ID of page which the page redirects to) are included.

The topic pages provide the associative relations through a large number of links. The rich semantic knowledge, such as synonym, polysemy, hypernym and associative relation, could be used to construct the library from the categories in Wikipedia. Therefore, the semantic knowledge library could be applied into question expansion.

3   Refined Feature Extraction

Compared to text documents, questions contain fewer words in each sentence. Therefore, the sparse data is inevitable and maybe degrade the performance of classifier. To tackle this problem of data sparseness for Chinese question classification in CQA, we expand the questions by using Wikipedia semantic knowledge library. The nearest mirror of Wikipedia is used to construct the library, which contains almost 8 hundred thousand topics. The index of topic is constructed to improve the processing speed. Therefore, the corresponding synonyms, hypernym about the topics could be obtained.

3.1   Question Expansion with Wikipedia

ICTCLAS platform (http://ictclas.nlpir.org/) is used to do word segmentation for Chinese questions and stop words are removed. LTP platform [15] is employed to words or phrases disambiguation.

According to Wikipedia knowledge library, the questions could be expanded by using their synonyms. For example, the question "移动定制版三星 Note2 是否可以在美国国际漫游?" is processed into the word list "移动 定 制版 三星 Note2 是否 可以 在 美国 国际漫游 ?" after word segmentation. In this sentence, the term "移动" has three synonym words "中国移动通信",

"运动(物理学)" and "移动电话". Obviously, the first word "中国移动通信" is the most similar to the term and could be added to the sentence according Wikipedia knowledge. The question after expansion is shown in the following figure 1.

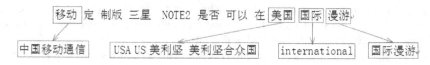

Fig. 1. Question expansion with Wikipedia

After question expansion, the word list has become

"移动 中国移动通信 定 制版 三星 Note2 是否 可以 在 美国 USA US 美利坚 美利坚合众国 国际 international 漫游 国际漫游".

3.2   Refined Feature Extraction Methods

3.2.1   Domain Proper Nouns Table
In Community-based Question Answering system, there are some domain proper nouns which can contribute to category identification. For example, Dungeon-Fighter is a popular game and becomes a hot topic in the game community of Baidu Zhidao. The domain term "地下城" cannot be spitted into "地下 城". Therefore, the domain proper nouns are collected and adopted as a dictionary for word segmentation tools. The dictionary contains 427 domain words and phrases with 13 top categories.

3.2.2   Feature Table upon Category Tree
The categories are organized as a tree from top level to bottom level in CQA. We collect labeled question in CQA belong to the category tree and extract the word feature. On top level, the features with the coarse categories are extracted, and the data sparseness is very obvious because of the huge amount of questions. Therefore, the fine features are extracted according to the bottom level.

We set a predefined dimension D, and extract the high-frequency terms from labeled questions. First, the number of terms belong to the category i with high frequency is $Count_i$, and the number of overall terms is counted as Sum. Then, the proportion of the number of term with high frequency is set to $P_i = Count_i/Sum$. So, the number of features extracted from the labeled questions upon the bottom categories is $N_i = P_i*D$.

3.2.3   Refined Feature Extraction
Considering the poor contributions to the classification by the single words in Chinese questions, these features with single words are removed from the feature table. Then, feature table upon categories tree contains only those features with two words or upon.

Because of the imbalance number of high-frequency words upon each category, the features extracted with types are different. With the increasing of the high-frequency terms on i-th category, the P_i on the feature table is more than others. Because the total number of D is fixed, the number of features extracted upon the other categories is decreased. Therefore, this imbalance maybe affects the classification accuracy. In order to solve this problem, those features where the threshold on frequency is below 10 are removed from the feature table.

4   Experiments

Chinese question data collected from Baidu Zhidao are used as training examples in the experiments. The types in the categories tree can be divided three layers from top to bottom. The top layer contains 13 categories, and the second layer contains 141 categories. In the second layer, there are 41 categories which can be divided into the third layers and then the third layer contains 289 categories.

We collect 714,582 questions from Baidu Zhidao and randomly select 87,149 questions for the training examples because the whole data set is too large. Each question belongs to one category at each category level. Ten times 10-fold cross validation is performed on the experimental data set. In detail, the data set is partitioned into ten subsets with similar sizes and distributions. Each fold is selected once as the test set with 10% examples of the whole set while the remaining nine folds are combined into the training set. The whole above process is repeated for ten times and the results are averaged.

Maxent Entropy Model is a general purpose machine learning framework that has proved to be highly expressive and powerful in NLP community. We employ the Maxent Entropy tool [16] as the classifier for questions classification in CQA.

4.1   Experiments on Top Layer

The top layer contains 13 categories. The high-frequency terms are extracted from the training dataset. According to the different thresholds, the dimensions of features are set to 1,500 and 2,000 respectively. The baseline method is the traditional TF-IDF. The second method uses the domain proper nouns table and the third method imports the feature table upon category tree. Here, the number of iteration in the Maxent Entropy is fixed to 20. The experimental results are as follows in table 1.

Table 1. Experiment Results on Top Layer

The Method of Feature Extraction	Classification Accuracy Rate	
	Dimension	
	1500	2000
TF-IDF	55.98%	59.00%
Domain Proper Nouns Table	60.58%	63.60%
Feature Table upon Category Tree	66.67%	70.79%

From the above experimental results, compared to the TF-IDF method, it can be seen that the accuracy rates could be effectively improved by the method of features extraction after importing both the domain proper nouns table and the feature table upon category tree. For instance, the accuracy rate by feature table upon category tree on 2000 dimension achieved 70.79% and increased clearly compared with TF-IDF.

4.2   Experiments on Middle Layer

Compared to the top layer, the second layer contains more categories. In this experiment on middle layer, the methods importing the domain proper nouns table and the feature table upon category tree are directly used. The dimensions of features are also set to 1,500 and 2,000 respectively. Furthermore, we adopt the refined method to extract features with removing the single words and remove those features whose frequency is bellow 10. Table 2 tabulates the detailed information of the experimental results.

Table 2. Experiment Results on Middle Layer

The Method of Feature Extraction	Classification Accuracy Rate	
	Dimension	
	1500	2000
TF-IDF	50.07%	52.81%
Remove Features with Single Word	57.45%	58.89%
Remove Features Whose Frequency Is Below 10	61.23%	62.23%

From the experiments, it can be observed that the classification accuracy rates are increased with the refined methods. Furthermore, compared to the method of removing single words, the accuracy rates are improved after the low-frequency terms are removed from the feature table. For example, on 1500-dimension, the classification rate by the all above refined method achieved 61.23%.

4.3   Experiments on Bottom Layer

There are 289 categories on the third layer. First, both the domain proper table and the feature table upon categories are used to expand the questions. Then, the refined methods of feature extraction are employed by removing both the single words and the low-frequency words. Figure 3 is the comparison of classification accuracy rates by the different methods.

Table 3. Experiment Results on Bottom Layer

The Method of Feature Extraction	Classification Accuracy Rate	
	Dimension	
	1500	2000
TF-IDF	51.34%	54.61%
Domain Proper Nouns Table and Feature Table upon Category Tree	62.79%	64.18%
Refined Feature Extraction	69.20%	71.21%

From table 3, it can be seen that classification accuracy rates are obviously improved by the proposed refined method of feature extraction. For example, on 2000-dimension, the classification accuracy rate is 71.21% by the refined feature extraction. Note that the accuracy rate obtained on the third layer is even higher than on the second layer. Compared to the second layer, categories on the third layer become more finely. The categories on the third layer may be the most relevant to the features for question classification.

5   Conclusion

Community-based Question Answering has become a hot topic in recent years. Question classification is an important part for CQA systems. In this paper, the Wikipedia knowledge is used to expand the Chinese questions to enrich the features. Then, the refined method of feature extraction is proposed step by step. Experiments show the proposed method could significantly improve the classification accuracy rate in the Chinese question classification. Explore more powerful methods of feature extraction for the Chinese question classification in CQA is an interesting issue for future work.

Acknowledgments. This work was supported by the National Natural Science Foundation of China (No.61365010, 61363044), Yunnan Nature Science Foundation (2011FZ069), Yunnan Province Department of Education Foundation (2011Y387).

References

1. Riahi, F., Zolaktaf, Z., Shafiei, M., Milios, E.: Finding Expert Users in Community Question Answering. In: Proceedings of the 21st International Conference Companion on World Wide Web, 791–798 (2012)
2. Chen, L., Zhang, D., Mark, L.: Understanding User Intent in Community Question Answering. In: Proceedings of the 21st International Conference Companion on World Wide Web, pp. 823–828 (2012)
3. Zhang, D., Lee, W.S.: Question Classification Using Support Vector Machines. In: Proceedings of the 26th Annual International ACM SIGIR Conference on Research and Development in Information Retrieval, Toronto, Canada, pp. 26–32 (2003)
4. Moschitti, A., Quarteroni, S., Basili, R., et. al.: Exploiting syntactic and shallow semantic kernels for question answer classification. In: Proceedings of 45th Annual Meeting of the Association for Computational Linguistics: York, pp. 776–783 (2007)
5. Zhang, Y., Liu, T., Wen, X.: Modified bayesian model based question classification. Journal of Chinese Information Processing **19**(2), 100–105 (2005). (in Chinese)
6. Hotho, A., Staab, S., Stumme, G.: WordNet Improves Text Document Clustering. In: Proceedings of the Semantic Web Workshop of the 26th Annual International ACM SIGIR Conference on Research and Development in Information Retrieval, Toronto Canada, pp. 541–544 (2003)
7. Cai, L., Zhou, G., Liu, K., Zhao, J.: Large-Scale Question Classification in cQA by Leveraging Wikipedia Semantic Knowledge. In: Proceeding of the 20th ACM Conference on Information and Knowledge Management (2011)

8. Gebrilovich, E., Markovitch, S.: Overcoming the brittleness bottleneck using wikipedia: Enhancing text categorication with encyclopedia knowledge. In: IJCAI, pp. 1301–1306 (2006)
9. Wang, P., Domeniconl, C.: Building semantic kernels for text classification using wikipedia. In: KDD (2008)
10. Wang, P., Hu, J., Zeng, H.-J., Chen, L., Chen, Z.: Improving text classification by using encyclopedia knowledge. In: ICDM, pp. 332–341 (2007)
11. Hu, J., Fang, L., Cao, Y., Zeng, H., Li, H., Yang, Q., Chen, Z.: Enhancing text clustering by leveraging Wikipedia semantics. In: SIGIR (2008)
12. Hu, X., Sun, N., Zhang, C., Chua, T.-S.: Exploting internal and external semantics for the clustering of short texts using world knowledge. In: CIKM (2009)
13. Hu, X., Zhang, X., Lu, C., Park, E.K., Zhou, X.: Exploiting wikipedia as external knowledge for document clustering. In: KDD (2009)
14. Zesch, T., Müller, C., Gurevych, I.: Extracting Lexical Semantic Knowledge from Wikipedia and Wiktionary. In: LREC (2008)
15. Che, W., Li, Z., Liu, T.: LTP: A Chinese Language Technology Platform. In: Proceedings of the Coling 2010:Demonstrations, Beijing, China, pp. 13–16 (August 2010)
16. Le, Z.: Maximum Entropy Modeling Toolkit for Python and C++. Software available at. http://homepages.inf.ed.ac.uk/lzhang10/maxent_toolikt.html

Speeding Up Multi-level Route Analysis Through Improved Multi-LCS Algorithm

Pei Tu[1], Xiapu Luo[2,3], Weigang Wu[1]($\boxtimes$), and Yajuan Tang[4]

[1] Department of Computer Science, Sun Yat-Sen University, Guangzhou, China
`tuwantpkyj@hotmail.com, wuweig@mail.sysu.edu.cn`
[2] Department of Computing, The Hong Kong Polytechnic University,
Kowloon, Hong Kong
`csxluo@comp.polyu.edu.hk`
[3] The Hong Kong Polytechnic University Shenzhen Research Institute,
Shenzhen, China
[4] Department of Electronic and Information Engineering,
Shantou University, Shantou, China
`yjtang@stu.edu.cn`

Abstract. Although the multi-level route analysis (e.g., AS, subnet, IP levels) is very useful to many applications (e.g. profiling route changes, designing efficient route-tracing algorithms, etc.), few research investigates how to conduct such analysis efficiently. Regarding routes as sequences, current approaches only handle two routes at a time and they just apply algorithms designed for general sequence comparison. In this paper, we propose and implement a new approach named `Fast-rtd` that contrasts multiple routes simultaneously and exploits the unique features of Internet routes to decrease the computational complexity in terms of time and memory. Our extensive evaluations on real traceroute data demonstrate the efficiency of `Fast-rtd`, such as more than 45% memory reduction, 3% to 15% pruning rate increase, and up to 25% speed improvement.

Keywords: Multi-level route analysis · Multiple LCS · BGP

1 Introduction

Identifying the common and/or the different portions among a set of routes in multiple levels (e.g., AS, subnet, IP levels) is a primitive of route analysis [1]. Such a primitive is very useful to many applications, such as profiling route changes and their impacts [2–6], measuring route asymmetry and diversity [7–10], and designing efficient route-tracing solutions [11], to name a few. Although the primitive's basic idea is straightforward, it is non-trivial to efficiently realize this primitive because of the tremendous volume of data. For example, the Ark project collects 500 million traceroutes in each probing unit and more than 10 billion traceroutes have been recorded. [12]. Moreover, the majority of existing systems process each level independently, thus resulting in redundant processing and high demand of

© Institute for Computer Sciences, Social Informatics and Telecommunications Engineering 2014
V.C.M. Leung et al. (Eds.): TridentCom 2014, LNICST 137, pp. 327–337, 2014.
DOI: 10.1007/978-3-319-13326-3_31

resources [1]. Our previous system, rtd, improves the analysis efficiency by integrating all levels recursively [1].

However, we identify another two deficiencies in existing approaches including rtd. First, existing methods only handle two routes at a time. Applications may need to process multiple routes at the same time, such as locating the invariant portions of the routes collected during a period of time, determining the common IP/Subnet/ASes among a set of routes, etc. Although it is possible to first analyze *each* pair of routes and then synthesize the result, such approach is inefficient because the number of comparisons may increase exponentially. Second, existing approaches usually regard routes as sequences and then apply algorithms designed for general sequences to process routes. In other words, they do not exploit the unique features of Internet routes to optimize the processing. Note that routes are special sequences. For example, each IP address will appear in a correct route once to avoid loop. In this paper, we propose a novel approach named Fast-rtd for multi-level route analysis, which can overcome the above two limitations and achieve higher efficiency. We make three contributions:

1. We identify the limitations of existing multi-level route analysis approaches, including the inefficiency of processing multiple routes and the lack of optimization by exploiting the unique features of Internet routes.
2. We propose a new approach named Fast-rtd that supports contrasting multiple routes at the same time and exploits the unique features of Internet routes to further decrease the computational complexity in terms of time and memory.
3. We implement the new approach in around 800 lines of C++ codes and conduct extensive evaluations on its performance using real traceroute data. The results show that Fast-rtd can achieve more than 45% memory reduction, 3% to 15% pruning rate increase, and up to 25% speed improvement.

The remainder of this paper is organized as follows. Section 2 introduces the multi-level route analysis. We detail the algorithm in Section 3 and evaluate it in Section 4. After introducing related work in Section 5, we conclude the paper in Section 6.

2   Multi-level Route Analysis

Following [1], we define a legitimate route R as an ordered sequence of nodes $r_1 r_2 \ldots r_{|R|}$, where $r_i \neq r_j$ ($i, j \in \{1, 2, \ldots, |R|\}$) to avoid routing loops. Each node r_i, $i \in \{1, 2, \ldots, |R|\}$, is an IP address having n levels of labels, and its t-th level of label is denoted as $L_t(r_i)$. The levels construct an ordered set $\mathcal{L} = \{L_1, ..L_n\}$ with a transitive relation $\succ$ that have the following properties:

1. $L_t \succ L_{t+1} \Rightarrow$ if $L_t(r_i) \neq L_t(r_j)$ then $L_{t+1}(r_i) \neq L_{t+1}(r_j)$.
2. $L_1 \succ L_2 \cdots \succ L_n$.

Note that $L_{t+1}(r_i) \neq L_{t+1}(r_j)$ does not imply $L_t(r_i) \neq L_t(r_j)$, $\forall i, j \in \{1, 2, \ldots, |R|\}$. Following [1–4,7–10], we use $AS(r_i)/SN(r_i)/IP(r_i)$ to denote the AS/subnet/IP-level label of r_i and define $\mathcal{L} = \{\text{AS-level, subnet-level, IP-level}\}$ with

$$AS - level \succ subnet - level \succ IP - level \tag{1}$$

The goal of a multi-level route analysis is two-fold. First, it identifies the common portions among a set of routes R_k ($k = 1, \ldots, M$, $M \geq 2$) on different levels. Then, based on the common portions, it outputs the difference among these routes on different levels. Instead of conducting the comparison on each level independently, our previous work (i.e., rtd) integrates the analysis of all levels recursively [1]. Note that rtd compares two routes at a time using LCS algorithms for general sequence. Although we can use it to analyze each pair of routes and then synthesize the result, it has much larger computation complexity than the algorithms designed for locating LCS of multiple sequences. For example, for a set of M routes, rtd will conduct $\frac{M(M-1)}{2}$ comparisons. In this paper, we propose Fast-rtd to extend rtd's functionality from comparing two routes to multiple routes by using an advanced multi-string LCS algorithm and further improve the performance in terms of time and memory by exploiting Internet routes' features. We will use an example shown in Fig. 1 to introduce the basic idea of multi-level route analysis and then detail Fast-rtd in Section 3.

As shown in Fig. 1, we compare two routes $R_1 = \{$IP1, IP2, IP3, IP4, IP5, IP6, IP7, IP8, IP9, IP10, IP11, IP12, IP13, IP14, IP15$\}$ and $R_2 = \{$IP1, IP2, IP3, IP6, IPa, IPb, IPc, IPd, IPe, IP12, IPf, IP14, IP15$\}$. rtd starts the comparison from the AS level. Since R_1 and R_2 differs in the second AS (i.e., $AS2$ and $AS5$), we know that subnets/IPs belonging to $AS2$ in R_1 and those belonging to $AS5$ in R_2 are different according to Eqn.1. Therefore, rtd will compare subnets in the same ASes (e.g., $AS1$, $AS3$, and $AS4$). Taking $AS1$ as an example, rtd will contrast $AS1$'s subnets in R_1 (i.e., {SN1, SN2, SN3}) and that in R_2 (i.e., {SN1, SN2, SN3}). Since they are the same, rtd will compare the IPs in R_1 (i.e.,{IP1, IP2, IP3, IP4, IP5, IP6}),and those in R_2 (i.e., {IP1, IP2, IP3, IP6}) and identify the common IPs (i.e., {IP1, IP2, IP3, IP6}) and the difference (i.e., {IP4, IP5}). After that, rtd will conduct the same analysis to $AS3$ and $AS4$. As shown in Fig. 1, elements in red box are the differences between R_1 and R_2.

3   Fast-rtd

To extend the comparison from two routes to multiple routes, Fast-rtd adopts the Fast-LCS algorithm [13], which provides a near-linear solution to the problem of finding the longest common subsequence (LCS) among a set of sequences, which is a NP-hard problem [13,14]. Fast-rtd further improves the performance of Fast-LCS in terms of speed and memory usage by exploiting routes' features. Fast-rtd consists of three steps to be elaborated in the following Sections 3.1 - 3.3. The first two steps are the same as those in the Fast-LCS algorithm and our improvements are introduced in the third step.

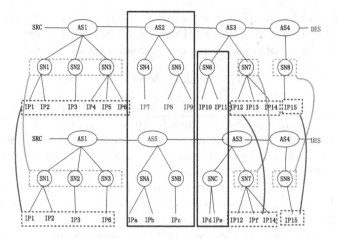

Fig. 1. Example of multi-level route analysis

3.1 Building Successor Tables

Given a set of routes R_k ($k = 1, \ldots, M$, $M \geq 2$), Fast-rtd first constructs a set R_U for containing all unique $r_{k,i}$ ($k = 1, \ldots, M$, $i = 1, \ldots, |R_k|$) and then builds a successor table (denoted as T_k) for each route R_k following [13]. Each element in T_k is defined as follows:

$$T_k(i, j) = \begin{cases} \min\{a | a \in S_k(i, j)\}, & S_k(i, j) \neq \phi \\ -, & otherwise \end{cases} \tag{2}$$

Here, $S_k(i, j) = \{a | R_k(a) = R_U(i), a > j)\}$, it stores the positions of $R_U(i)$ in R_k, where $i = 1, \ldots, |R_U|$ and $j = 0, \ldots, |R_k|$. Since the same r will not appear twice in a route, each row of T_k has only one integer.

	r_1	r_2	r_4	r_3	r_5
r_1	1	-	-	-	-
r_2	2	2	-	-	-
r_3	4	4	4	4	-
r_4	3	3	3	-	-
r_5	5	5	5	5	5

	r_2	r_1	r_4	r_3	r_5
r_1	2	2	-	-	-
r_2	1	-	-	-	-
r_3	4	4	4	4	-
r_4	3	3	3	-	-
r_5	5	5	5	5	5

	r_2	r_1	r_3	r_5
r_1	2	2	-	-
r_2	1	-	-	-
r_3	3	3	3	-
r_4	-	-	-	-
r_5	5	5	5	5

(a) R_1's successor table (T_1).   (b) R_2's successor table (T_2).   (c) R_3's successor table (T_3).

Fig. 2. The successor tables of R_1, R_2 and R_3

We use an example to illustrate how to construct successor tables. Given $R_1 = \{r_1, r_2, r_4, r_3, r_5\}$, $R_2 = \{r_2, r_1, r_4, r_3, r_5\}$, and $R_3 = \{r_2, r_1, r_3, r_5\}$, we build $R_U = \{r_1, r_2, r_3, r_4, r_5\}$ and construct T_1, T_2, and T_3 as shown in Fig. 2.

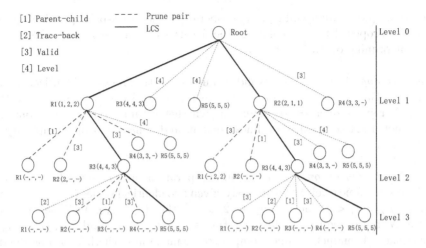

Fig. 3. Example of `Fast-rtd`'s pruning operations

3.2 Constructing LCS Tree

The LCS tree is constructed from the successor tables. We define an identical tuple as $(i_1, \ldots, i_m)$ if $r_{1,i_1} = r_{2,i_2} = \ldots = r_{m,i_m}$. Let $(i_1, \ldots, i_m)$ and $(j_1, \ldots, j_m)$ be two identical tuples. If $i_k < j_k$ for $k = 1, \ldots, m$, $(i_1, \ldots, i_m)$ is a predecessor of $(j_1, \ldots, j_m)$, or $(j_1, \ldots, j_m)$ is a successor of $(i_1, \ldots, i_m)$. For an identical tuple $(i_1, \ldots, i_m)$, its direct successors can be identified through Eqn.3. Starting from the identical tuples on the first level, we can emulate all direct successors and construct a tree.

$$(i_1, \ldots, i_m) \rightarrow (T_1(k, i_1), \ldots, T_m(k, i_m)) \tag{3}$$

From (3) we can see that the operation of producing successor tuples is to couple the elements of the (i_m)th column of T_m.

Following the example in Section 3.1, we enumerate all the first identical tuples: $r_1(1, 2, 2)$, $r_2(2, 1, 1)$, $r_3(4, 4, 3)$, $r_4(3, 3, -)$, $r_5(5, 5, 5)$. The first identical tuples are those whether r_1, r_2, r_3, r_4, r_5 appear firstly in route sequences R_1, R_2 and R_3, individually. Take $r_1(1, 2, 2)$ as an example, we can see $R_1[1] = R_2[2] = R_3[2]$. To generate its direct successors, $r_1(1, 2, 2)$ couples the 1st column of T_1, the 2nd column of T_2, and the 2nd column of T_3 to produce new tuples: $r_1(-, 2, 2)$, $r_2(-, -, -)$, $r_3(4, 4, 3)$, $r_4(3, 3, -)$, and $r_5(5, 5, 5)$. Note that although all tuples can produce its successors, not all its successors are valid. Four pruning operations, to be introduced in the next section, are used to remove the invalid successors.

3.3 Pruning the Tree and Outputting LCSes

Since not all paths in the tree lead to LCSes, we employ four pruning operations to remove tuples that do not belong to LCSes. Two operations (i.e., valid pruning operation and level pruning operation) are from `Fast-LCS` and the other two operations (i.e., parent-child pruning operation and track-back pruning operation) are proposed by us exploiting the features of route sequences. We detail the four pruning operations belows.

Valid Pruning Operation. The valid pruning operation removes identical tuples with $'-'$. Tuples like $(k, -)$ or $(-, k)$ are invalid and can be pruned directly. Given N route sequences, to determine whether a tuple $(i_1, i_2, ..., i_n)$ contains $'-'$ or not, Fast-rtd will do a linear search, and hence the time complexity is $O(N/2)$.

Level Pruning Operation. The level pruning operation removes redundant identical tuples on the same level. More precisely, given two identical tuples $(i_1, \ldots, i_m)$ and $(j_1, \ldots, j_m)$, if $i_1 < j_1$ and $i_k \leq j_k$ (k=2,...,m), then $(j_1, \ldots, j_m)$ will be removed. Given N route sequences, for two tuples $(i_1, i_2, \ldots, i_n)$ and $(j_1, j_2, \ldots, j_n)$, Fast-rtd will conduct N times comparison to make sure whether the one should be pruned or not, thus the time complexity will be $O(N)$.

Parent-Child Pruning Operation. The parent-child pruning operation deletes a child identical tuple if it has the same upper level label as its parent. Given a subsequence $\{r_1, r_2, ...\}$ where $AS(r_1) = AS(r_2) = AS0$ and $AS(r_3) = AS(r_4) = AS1$, in the $AS - level$, the subsequence can be represented as $\{AS0, AS0, AS1, AS1, ...\}$ with redundant $AS0$ and $AS1$. Parent-child pruning operation can help to avoid the redundance during the construction of the LCS tree, because it makes sure that all the tuples have different level label with their parent. As it just processes the level label to decide whether a tuple should be pruned or not, the time complexity of it will be $O(1)$.

Trace-Back Pruning Operation. The trace-back pruning operation deletes tuples whose labels have occurred on the path from itself to the root of the LCS tree. This is motivated by the observation that legitimate route sequences do not contain loops. Given a subsequence $\{r_1, r_2, ...\}$, if $L(r_j)! = L(r_i), (j > i)$, then $L(r_j)! = L(r_k), (0 < k < i)$. Trace-back pruning operation removes all the tuples that may form a loop by tracing back to the root of the LCS tree. The tracing time is $O(D)$, where D is the depth of the tuple in the tree. Since the length of a route is usually short (i.e., less than 30), $O(D)$ can be approximated as $O(1)$.

Example. By applying these four pruning operations during the construction of the LCS tree, Fast-rtd can prune a large amount of tuples during the construction of the LCS tree to improve the efficiency. Fig. 3 demonstrates the LCS tree and how pruning operations remove tuples. The LCS tree begins with the initial tuples $r_1(1, 2, 2)$, $r_2(2, 1, 1)$, $r_3(4, 4, 3)$, $r_4(3, 3, -)$, and $r_5(5, 5, 5)$ on the first level. The valid pruning operation will prune the tuple $r_4(3, 3, -1)$, and then using level pruning operation, we can prune $r_3(4, 4, 3)$ and $r_5(5, 5, 5)$ with $r_1(1, 1, 2)$, $r_2(2, 1, 1)$ left on the first level. Then $r_1(1, 1, 2)$ produces its child tuples $r_1(-, -, -)$, $r_2(2, -, -)$, $r_3(4, 4, 3)$, $r_4(3, 3, -)$, $r_5(5, 5, 5)$ on level 2 and

$r_2(2, 1, 1)$ generates its child pairs $r_1(-, 2, 2)$, $r_2(-, -, -)$, $r_3(4, 4, 3)$, $r_4(3, 3, -)$, $r_5(5, 5, 5)$ on level 2.

On level 2, using the parent-child pruning operation, we prune $r_1(-, -, -)$, $r_2(-, -, -)$. The valid pruning operation removes $r_2(2, -, -)$, $r_1(-, 2, 2)$, $r_4(3, 3, -)$, $r_4(3, 3, -)$ and the level pruning operation removes $r_5(5, 5, 5)$, $r_5(5, 5, 5)$ with the only $r_3(4, 4, 3)$, $r_3(4, 4, 3)$ left on level 2. Then we produce the child tuples of $r_3(4, 4, 3)$, $r_3(4, 4, 3)$, including $r_1(-, -, -)$, $r_2(-, -, -)$, $r_3(-, -, -)$, $r_4(-, -, -)$, $r_5(5, 5, 5)$, $r_1(-, -, -)$, $r_2(-, -, -)$, $r_3(-, -, -)$, $r_4(-, -, -)$, $r_5(5, 5, 5)$ on level 3.

By adopting the parent-child pruning operation, we prune the tuples $r_3(-, -, -)$ and $r_3(-, -, -)$ on level 3. The trace-back pruning operation removes $r_1(-, -, -)$ and $r_2(-, -, -)$, because they have appeared on LCS path to the root. The valid pruning operation eliminates $r_1(-, -, -)$, $r_2(-, -, -)$, $r_4(-, -, -)$, and $r_4(-, -, -)$. Continuing the pruning process, we find that $r_5(5, 5, 5)$ and $r_5(5, 5, 5)$ are the leaf tuples left on the level 3, meaning that the construction of the LCS tree is finished. By tracing back from the two $r_5(5, 5, 5)$ on the level 3 to the root, we will obtain two LCS: $r_1 r_3 r_5$ and $r_2 r_3 r_5$.

3.4   Order of Using the Four Pruning Operations

While there are four pruning operations, we find through extensive experiments against various data sets that they had better be used in the order of parent-child, trace back, valid and finally level pruning. By first using the parent-child pruning operation and the trace-back pruning operation, a large number of tuples on the same level will be pruned. Then the number of tuples to be pruned by the valid pruning operation and/or the level pruning operation will be significantly decreased, thus reducing the computation time.

Analysis. Let N be the number of routes and K denote the number of tuples to be pruned by the valid pruning operation or the level pruning operation in the Fast-LCS algorithm. Since the time complexity of the valid pruning operation and the level pruning operation are $O(N/2)$ and $O(N)$, the time complexity of pruning tuples in the Fast-LCS will be $T_1 = K * O(N)$ if we regard both as $O(N)$. Note that the number of tuples to be pruned by the valid or the level pruning operations is reduced in the Fast-rtd algorithm, because the parent-child and the trace-back pruning operations have pruned a portion of these tuples. Let p be the pruning rate of the parent-child and the trace-back pruning operations. Then the time complexity of using the parent-child or the trace-back pruning operations will be $T_{2_1} = K * p * O(1)$ and that of using the valid or the level pruning operations will be $T_{2_2} = K * (1 - p) * O(N)$. Therefore, the total time complexity in the Fast-rtd algorithm will be $T_2 = T_{2_1} + T_{2_2}$. Compared to the Fast-LCS, we can see that the saved time $T' = T_2 - T_1 = K * p * (O(N) - O(1))$. When N and p increase, Fast-rtd will be more efficient.

Example. Consider the example in Fig. 3 where there are three routes. Tuples $r_3(4, 4, 3)$ on level 2 produces its child tuples $r_3(4, 4, 3)$ and $r_3(4, 4, 3)$, including $r_1(-, -, -)$, $r_2(-, -, -)$, $r_3(-, -, -)$, $r_4(-, -, -)$, $r_5(5, 5, 5)$, $r_1(-, -, -)$,

$r_2(-,-,-)$, $r_3(-,-,-)$, $r_4(-,-,-)$, and $r_5(5,5,5)$ on level 3. In the `Fast-LCS` algorithm, using only the valid pruning operation and the level pruning operation, it will prune the child tuples $r_1(-,-,-)$, $r_2(2,-,-)$, $r_3(-,-,-)$, $r_4(-,-,-)$, $r_1(-,-,-)$, $r_2(2,-,-)$, $r_3(-,-,-)$, and $r_4(-,-,-)$. The time complexity will be $8 * O(N/2)$. However, in the `Fast-rtd`, by using the parent-child operation first, we can prune $r_3(-,-,-)$ and $r_3(-,-,-)$ in 2*O(1), and then prune $r_1(-,-,-)$ and $r_2(-,-,-)$ by using the trace-back pruning operation in 2*O(1). After that, we will prune $r_4(-,-,-)$ and $r_4(-,-,-)$ through the valid pruning operation in time 2*O(N/2). Therefore, the saved time $t = 8 * O(N/2) - 2 * O(N/2) - 4 * O(1) = 6 * O(N/2) - 4 * O(1)$. When N increases, t will increase significantly. Therefore, by first using the parent-child pruning operation and the trace-back pruning operation, the number of tuples on the same level will be largely reduced. Hence, the number of tuples to be pruned by the valid pruning operation or the level pruning operation will decrease, thus reducing computation time.

4   Evaluation

We implement both `Fast-rtd` and `Fast-LCS` for comparisons. They are tested against two sets of real traceroute data. The first one is the iPlane data set [15] from April to July in 2012. The other one contains traceroute data from Planetlab nodes to two subnets in Taiwan, which were collected by ourselves through paris-traceroute [16]. The two data sets have around 100K routes. For each unique IP address in these routes, we get its subnet and AS information through WHOIS database and team cymru's IP to ASN mapping service [17].

Since `Fast-rtd` is designed to handle multiple routes, we evaluate it using three types of routes, which represent different use cases. The first type of data (denoted as S-S) include routes from one IP address to another collected during a period of time. Such kind of data will be examined when a user wants to know the evolving of the routes between two hosts. The second type of data (denoted as M-S) comprises of routes from a set of IPs to one IP, for example, from an AS to one IP. Such type of data is useful for inspecting the multiple routes to a destination. For example, a multi-homing user may have server upstream providers, which provides different paths and even performance for the user to communicate with another IP. The third type of data (denoted as M-M) consists of routes from a set of IPs to another set of IPs, for example, from an AS to another AS. Such type of data may be used by network administrator for investigating the routes between ASes, which are useful to traffic engineering.

`Fast-rtd` improves `Fast-LCS` by taking into account the features of Internet routes. Fig. 4 illustrates the increased pruning rate and decreased memory usages. The X-axis is the number of routes and each point represents an average value from 20 times experiments, where a certain number of routes were randomly selected from our data set. Fig. 4(a) shows that the increased pruning rate is within the range of [3%,15%]. The value increases with the number of routes. The M-M types of routes have much larger pruning rate than the M-S and S-S types of routes. Moreover, the increment of pruning rate is fast for the M-M type

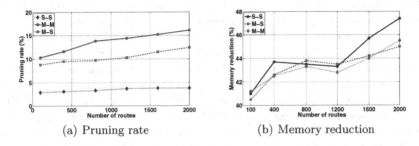

(a) Pruning rate

(b) Memory reduction

Fig. 4. The performance improvement introduced by `Fast-rtd` in different scenarios

of routes when the number of routes increases. The reason may be that the M-M type of routes have much larger number of unique IPs. Fig. 4(a) demonstrates that `Fast-rtd` can lead to more than 40% memory reduction. Moreover, the reduction rate increases along with the number of roues.

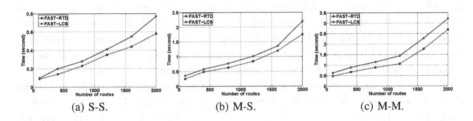

(a) S-S.

(b) M-S.

(c) M-M.

Fig. 5. The speed comparison between `Fast-rtd` and `Fast-LCS` in different scenarios

Fig. 5 compares the time required by `Fast-rtd` and `Fast-LCS` to process different scale of routes in different scenarios. The X-axis is the number of routes and the Y-axis is the computation time. Each point is also an average value from 20 times experiments with randomly selected routes. We can see that `Fast-rtd` uses much less time than `Fast-LCS` and the improvement increases along with the number of routes. For example, when conducting experiments on 2000 routes, we can observe up to 25% speed improvement. When the number of routes is small, the difference is small. The type of data also affects the improvement. For example, as the improvement of pruning rate due to `Fast-rtd` is small for the S-S type of data compared to other type of data as shown in Fig. 4, the time reduction in Fig. 5(a) is less obvious than that in Fig. 5(b) and Fig. 5(c).

5   Related Work

Contrasting routes on different levels is very useful to many applications, such as characterizing route changes [2–6], measuring route asymmetry and diversity

[7–10], and designing efficient route-tracing solutions[11]. Some research uses Jaccard Distance to quantify the changes in routes [4,7,8]. Since this metric does not contain order information, people propose using Edit distance and its variants to profile route changes [2,9,10,18]. However, all these approaches may result in computational redundancy because they process the information on different levels independently [1]. We propose rtd to eliminate redundancy by integrating all levels, thus achieving much better efficiency. However, all these approaches including rtd have two deficiencies. First, they only compare two routes at a time and cannot be easily extended to handling multiple routes. Second, they just apply algorithms designed for processing general sequences to routes without exploiting the unique features in Internet routes. Inheriting the basic idea of integrating all levels, Fast-rtd extends rtd by identifying LCS on multiple routes and improving the performance in terms of time and memory.

6   Conclusion

In this paper, we propose and implement a new approach named Fast-rtd for multi-level route analysis. Different from existing approaches that can only deal with two routes at a time, Fast-rtd can contrasts multiple routes simultaneously. Moreover, instead of directly applying algorithms for processing sequences, Fast-rtd adopts new pruning operation and storage techniques, which are motivated by Internet routes' features, to decrease the computational complexity in terms of time and memory. Our extensive evaluations on real traceroute data demonstrate the efficiency of Fast-rtd, such as more than 45% memory reduction, 3% to 15% pruning rate increase, and up to 25% speed improvement, compared with Fast-LCS, the approach for analysis of general sequences.

Acknowledgments. We thank Ang Chen for his discussion and suggestions. This work is supported in part by the CCF-Tencent Open Research Fund, the Pearl River Nova Program of Guangzhou (No. 2011J2200088), Guangdong Natural Science Foundation (No. S2012010010670), the National Natural Science Foundation of China (No. 60903185), and the Academic Innovation Team Construction Project of Shantou University (No. ITC12001).

References

1. Chen, A., Chan, E., Luo, X., Fok, W., Chang, R.: An efficient approach to multi-level route analytics. In: Proc. IFIP/IEEE IM (2013)
2. Schwartz, Y., Shavitt, Y., Weinsberg, U.: On the diversity, stability and symmetry of end-to-end Internet routes. In: Proc. IEEE GI Symposium (2010)
3. Logg, C., Cottrell, L., Navratil, J.: Experiences in traceroute and available bandwidth change analysis. In: Proc. ACM SIGCOMM Workshop on Network Troubleshooting (2004)
4. Chan, E.W.W., Luo, X., Fok, W.W.T., Li, W., Chang, R.K.C.: Non-cooperative diagnosis of submarine cable faults. In: Spring, N., Riley, G.F. (eds.) PAM 2011. LNCS, vol. 6579, pp. 224–234. Springer, Heidelberg (2011)

5. Fok, W., Luo, X., Mok, R., Li, W., Liu, Y., Chan, E., Chang, R.: Monoscope: Automating network faults diagnosis based on active measurements. In: Proc, IFIP/IEEE IM (2013)
6. Liu, Y., Luo, X., Chang, R., Su, J.: Characterizing inter-domain rerouting by betweenness centrality after disruptive events. IEEE JSAC 31(6) (2013)
7. Pucha, H., Zhang, Y., Mao, Z., Hu, Y.: Understanding network delay changes caused by routing events. In: Proc. ACM SIGMETRICS (2007)
8. Pathak, A., Pucha, H., Zhang, Y., Hu, Y.C., Mao, Z.M.: A measurement study of Internet delay asymmetry. In: Claypool, M., Uhlig, S. (eds.) PAM 2008. LNCS, vol. 4979, pp. 182–191. Springer, Heidelberg (2008)
9. He, Y., Faloutsos, M., Krishnamurthy, S.: Quantifying routing asymmetry in the Internet at the AS level. In: Proc. IEEE GLOBECOM (2004)
10. Han, J., Watson, D., Jahanian, F.: An experimental study of Internet path diversity. IEEE Trans. Dependable and Secure Computing (2006)
11. Beverly, R., Berger, A., Xie, G.: Primitives for active Internet topology mapping: Toward high-frequency characterization. In: Proc, ACM/USENIX IMC (2010)
12. Hyun, Y.: Archipelago measurement infrastructure. http://www.caida.org/projects/ark/
13. Chen, Y., Wan, A., Liu, W.: A fast parallel algorithm for finding the longest common sequence of multiple biosequences. BMC Bioinformatics 7(S4) (2006)
14. Wang, Q., Korkin, D., Shang. Y.: A fast multiple longest common subsequence (MLCS) algorithm. IEEE TKDE 23(3) (2011)
15. Madhyastha, H., Isdal, T., Piatek, M., Dixon, C., Anderson, T.: iPlane: An information plane for distributed services. In: Proc, USENIX OSDI (2006)
16. Augustin, B., Cuvellier, X., Orgogozo, B., Viger, F., Friedman, T., Latapy, M., Magnien, C., Teixeira, R.: Avoiding traceroute anomalies with Paris traceroute. In: Proc. ACM/USENIX IMC (2006)
17. Team Cymru. IP to ASN service. http://www.team-cymru.org/Services/ip-to-asn.html
18. Schwartz, Y., Shavitt, Y., Weinsberg, U.: A measurement study of the origins of end-to-end delay variations. In: Krishnamurthy, A., Plattner, B. (eds.) PAM 2010. LNCS, vol. 6032, pp. 21–30. Springer, Heidelberg (2010)

From Model to Internetware

A Unified Approach to Generate Internetware

Junhui Liu$^{(\boxtimes)}$, Qing Duan, Yun Liao, Lei Su, and Zhenli He

School of Software, Yunnan University, Kunming, Yunnan 650091, China
Key Laboratory for Software Engineering of Yunnan Province, Republic of China
HanksLau@gmail.com,
{qduan,YunLiao,LeiSu,ZhenliHe}@ynu.edu.cn

Abstract. Model driven development has been considered to be the hope of improving software productivity significantly. However, it has not been achieved
even after many years of research and application. Models are only and still
used at the analysis and design stage, furthermore, models gradually deviate
from system implementation. This paper integrates domain-specific modelling
and web service techniques with model driven development and proposes a unified approach, SODSMI (Service Oriented executable Domain-Specific Modelling and Implementation), to build the executable domain-specific model so as
to achieve the target of model driven development. In this work, Domain-
specific modelling is the key to construct xDSM (the eXecutable Domain-
Specific Model). Web services are used as the implementation entities of the
core functions of xDSM with the support of DSMEI (the Domain-Specific
Model Execution Infrastructure). Finally, xDSM is transformed into the form of
internetware to achieve system implementation.

Keywords: Model driven development · Domain-specific modelling · Executable model · Model execution infrastructure · Internetware

1 Introduction

Software is the spirit of a computer system. It has substantial impacts on success in
business today. However, faced with increasing demands and more challenging market pressures, software systems become more and more large and complex. The traditional software development technologies are insufficient for ensuring a successful
outcome that fulfills requirements and quality goals set out [1]. The complexity, variety and changeability make the large software projects have staggering failure rates:
difficult to maintain, low dependability, high cost and the longer time-to-market. The
Standish Report [2] states that nearly a third of projects are cancelled before completion and more than half suffer from serious cost overruns.

Developing and maintaining complex, large-scale, product line of highly customized software systems is difficult and costly. Part of the difficulty is due to the need
to communicate business knowledge between domain experts and application
programmers. Domain specific model driven development (MDD) addresses this

© Institute for Computer Sciences, Social Informatics and Telecommunications Engineering 2014
V.C.M. Leung et al. (Eds.): TridentCom 2014, LNICST 137, pp. 338–347, 2014.
DOI: 10.1007/978-3-319-13326-3_32

difficulty by providing domain experts and developers with domain specific abstractions for communicating designs [3]. Model describes system and its environment from a given view. It is an abstract representation of system and its environment. For a specific aim, model extracts a set of concepts relevant to the subject in order to make developers focusing on the whole system and ignoring irrelevant details [4].

In this paper, we discusses how to build the executable domain-specific model to achieve the target of MDD. This paper proposes an approach to the executable domain-specific modelling based on web services. Domain-specific modelling is the key to construct the eXecutable Domain-Specific Model (xDSM). Web services are used as the implementation entities of the core functions of xDSM with the support of the domain-specific model execution infrastructure which named DSMEI. Finally, xDSM is transformed into the form of internetware to achieve system implementation.

2   Proposed Approach

The role of model for software analysis and design is irreplaceable. Developers establish software analysis and design models in accordance with a variety of software standards, and communicate with each other by models. Model is expected to bring an essential leap of software development, and drive the whole software development process. It means that modelling is not only related to the requirement analysis, software design and software implementation, but also able to support unit testing, system testing, long-term system maintenance and software reuse, etc. The above all require the executability of model. Only executable models can strictly ensure that model validation, system-generation and system maintenance are based on the models.

The key elements of the executability of model lies in whether there are a well-defined models and whether there is a code generator which can automatically and completely generate code. Both of them are mutually constraining and complementary. Code generator can be simple and easy to implement while the model is complete and accurate. On the contrary, code generator must be difficult to achieve with complex structure and required adaptability and flexibility while the model is imprecise. In order to build the executable model, and achieve the automatic transformation from models to system implementation, there are two aspects both need to be concerned. On one hand, models ought to be refined and the degree of abstract ought to be reduced so that models can gradually approach system implementation; on the other hand, code generator ought to have strong adaptability and flexibility to reflect the model description.

This paper is based on domain-specific modelling to construct the executable model. During the process, the key is behaviour modelling. Based on the complete, consistent, detailed and accurate model description by XDML, model parsing and executing mechanism are used to replace code generator, and combine with Domain Framework as the infrastructure of the domain-specific model implementation. Different from other domain specific modelling approach, the abstract level of code implementation is enhanced by the standardised, self-contained, self-describing, modular web services. Encapsulating the details of code implementation, the related domain-specific software functional entities are provided to DSMEI (Domain-Specific Model Execution Infrastructure) by the way of web services cluster. The system running is driven by parsing and executing the behaviour models. The above is the core idea of This paper. The framework of SODSMI (Service Oriented executable Domain-Specific Modelling and Implementation) is shown in Figure 1.

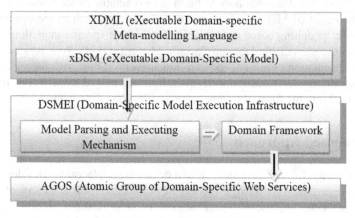

Fig. 1. Framework of SODSMI

SODSMI constructs executable models and their execution infrastructure based on domain-specific modelling through the model refinement and the enhancement of code implement.

From the perspective of functionalities, SODSMI is divided into three levels, corresponding to four core elements:

- xDSM -- Executable Domain-Specific Model
- XDML -- Executable Domain-specific Meta-modelling Language
- DSMEI -- Domain-Specific Model Execution Infrastructure
- AGOS -- Atomic Group of dOmain-specific web Services

XDML is used to describe xDSM. xDSM is parsed and executed in DSMEI. Its execution depends on the corresponding interfaces provided by Domain Framework. Domain Framework provides the core software functional entities through domain-related services of AGOS, and supports the xDSM execution upwards. xDSM, XDML, DSMEI and AGOS constitute the framework of SODSMI together.

3   xDSM – Executable Domain-Specific Model

The primary task of SODSMI is to build executable models, while the executability of model is always an underbelly of MDD for a long time. Software itself is dynamic. Static models can describe some profiles of software, for examples, the subordinate structure and the system hierarchy. But it can describe neither the entire software, nor the running process of software. At the same time, the abstract of models restricts the accuracy of models, which makes models lack of many of the key elements that are used to construct entire software. In MDA system, UML can be used to build models of the system from different perspectives and aspects. Model views represent a part or a profile of the system. However, there are neither positive connections nor constraints among those model views. Model views can be more or less, be concrete or abstract. The process of building a model can be ceased at any phase. It is very difficult for modellers to construct a complete software model unless they understand all the details of code generator. That makes the executable models difficult to achieve in UML system.

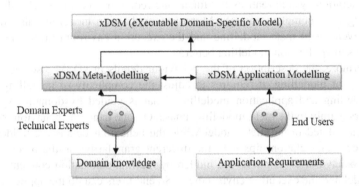

Fig. 2. xDSM Meta-Modelling and Application Modelling

xDSM is constructed based on the domain-specific model, and is technically applied to solve the software development problems existing in a certain application domain. xDSM represents the concepts and rules of the domain. The model is targeted, that narrows the scope of the description effectively and is helpful to define the model accurately. xDSM modelling process is divided into two phases: the xDSM meta-modelling phase and the xDSM application modelling phase. The former is carried out by domain experts and technical experts, and the latter is carried out by end users. The duty and the role of modellers in each modelling phase are different, as shown in Figure 2.

xDSM is required to meet MMLs standards 5 (Modelling Maturity Levels) [5]. It requires the model definition is sufficiently precise. The accuracy here is to describe the details relevant to the modelling objectives accurately rather than to describe all aspects of modelling. The core of xDSM is behaviour modelling. It is required to describe domain concepts and system behaviours unambiguously. In the meta-modelling phase, domain concepts are described unambiguously, including domain objects, relationships, constraints and any operations embodied in the domain concept. In the application modelling phase, the target is to meet all the requirements to software systems. The accurate software behaviour modelling is carried out by using meta-model. The model does not care about the implementation of local software functions, but it does not ignore the necessary details of the behaviour execution yet -- the data flow, the control flow and the related constraints of behaviours must be described in detail.

On one hand, the measurement of the accuracy of models is determined by domain experts and technical experts through xDSM meta-modelling and DSMEI. Namely, if the application model which is built according to the definition of the meta-model can be accurately and completely executed by DSMEI, the models can be regarded accurate enough. On the other hand, the application model which is built in accordance with end users' requirements can ensure the integrity of the model. Namely, if the results of the application model execution meet the system requirements completely, or the generation system realises the functional requirements completely, the models can be regarded complete enough. Moreover, application modelling also facilitates the improvement of meta-modelling and the execution environment, to meet the requirements to application modelling better.

Furthermore, the description of the behaviour details in xDSM also increases the complexity of modelling. It requires to adjust the complexity of modelling through meta-modelling and application modelling. That is guided by domain experts and developers mainly in the meta-modelling phase. On one hand, the behaviour complexity is encapsulated in the meta-model while the behaviour details are hidden in domain objects and relationships with the different granularity; on the other hand, the complex behaviour descriptions are hidden by the implementation convention of the meta-model and the execution environment. So end users can do the application modelling simply and flexibly. So it is easier for end users to build the executable model with high-quality.

4   XDML – Executable Domain-Specific Meta-modelling Language

Following the guide of MMLs5, XDML is defined to describe xDSM meta-model and its application model. XDML extends the semantic basis of XMML language -- a visual meta-modelling language [6], and integrates the well-defined behaviour semantics to support the domain-specific behaviour modelling. XDML defines the concrete syntax of AS&MC which provides accurate definition for dynamic behaviours of models.

XDML improves the description accuracy of the specific domain problem and its solutions, and reduces the complexity of the language itself. XDML is simpler and more accurate in syntax and semantics than the universal modelling languages. That reduces the difficulty of XDML compiler, interpreter and the supporting environment development.

XDML is at a higher abstract level. Generally, the main domain concepts are mapping to the objects in XDML, while other concepts are mapping to the attributes, relationships, sub-model of the object or model links of other languages. Therefore, XDML makes developers use domain concepts directly to construct the domain models. It is able to describe domain concepts, the relationships between domain concepts and domain rules with larger granularity morpheme. Developers can use the domain knowledge elements in XDML directly to develop the application system, rather than develop program code or components that are corresponded to domain concepts from the most basic classes or objects from the scratch. So the system development efficiency is improved effectively.

For enhancing the accuracy of models and the ability of the behaviour modelling in MDA system, OMG issued UML 2.0 which integrates action semantics [7] to improve the ability of the behaviour modelling, and uses OCL to enhance the ability of the accurate model description in MDA system. And ASL (Action Specification Language) is also introduced into xUML to define the system actions in detail. The ultimate goal of above all is to make the behaviour modelling more accurately. UML, OCL and ASL are overlapped in semantics. A part of the abstract syntax of OCL is introduced from the abstract syntax of UML 2.0, especially the introduction of action semantics [8]. ASL is consistent with the action semantics of UML [9]. The coexistence of several sets of abstract syntax of several languages makes it needs a lot of correspondence and references among those languages, and depends on the cohesion of the model reflection interfaces, so as to make the whole syntax architecture huge and complex.

The core of xDSM is the complete and accurate behaviour modelling, with the well-defined behaviour semantics, the accurate model constraints and action specifications as its necessary conditions. XDML is extended based on the semantics of the visual meta-modelling language – XMML. It integrates the well-defined behaviour semantics, supports the domain-specific behaviour modelling adequately, and constructs the concrete syntax of XDML based on XML meta-language. It constructs the textual concrete syntax of AS&MC (Action Specifications and Model Constraints) based on the behaviour semantics of XDML to provide the accurate definition for the dynamic behaviour of models, as shown in Figure 3.

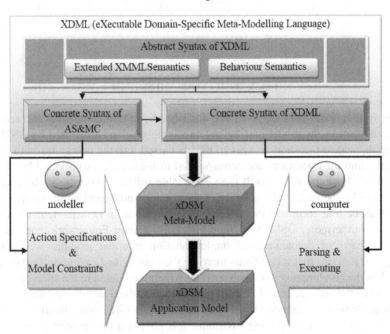

Fig. 3. XDML Architecture and Work Process

5   DSMEI – Domain-Specific Model Execution Infrastructure

Today, the scales of software systems are increasing, and the number of people who are involved in software applications is also increasing, so as to make software architecture more and more complex. The software is no longer limited to a stand-alone desktop system, but gradually evolved into the networked and complex systems which are integrated with each other. In this case, the functionalities of code generator are limited because the generated code may be only a part of the complex software system. Moreover, code generator is also a software product. It is more complex than the generated system, and it is also needed to face the changes of the generated system itself, that requires code generator to be strongly adaptable and flexible [10].

DSMEI is combined with Domain Framework, and employs the model parsing and executing mechanism substituting the code generator to execute xDSM models directly. Domain Framework is used to provide the interface of the underlying platform to the generated code. DSMEI encapsulates the architectures, platforms and concrete implementation of the domain-specific application system into Domain Framework, which reduces the complexity of the generated code significantly, as shown in Figure 4.

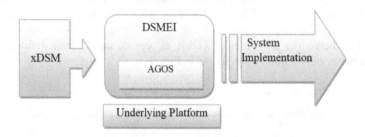

Fig. 4. DSMEI Functional Structure

The system behaviours are able to be described by xDSM completely and accurately. Based on that, the model parsing and executing mechanism is used by DSMEI to replace the code generation process. xDSM is parsed into the operations with precise semantic, and the operations are corresponded to the interfaces provided by Domain Framework. Here the model itself is an executable software product. As the evolution of Domain Framework is independent of the parsing and executing of the model, the model can be transform into the system implementation on DSMEI dynamically and flexibly. Furthermore, DSMEI is combined with Domain Framework, and encapsulates the parts of domain-related implementation into the modular web services through AGOS. So that it can focus more on the parsing and executing of the model, as well as the combination with web services which are related to the specific domain. That makes the architecture of DSMEI general, while the dynamic characteristics and the virtualisation techniques of web services make DSMEI more flexible, so that a common and flexible supporting environment is provided for the model execution by this way.

6   AGOS

To a certain extent, the code is also a model. It is the most refined model, and a language description defined precisely. It can be used to describe a system, but it is also platform-dependent. But such an iterative refinement is not necessary. On one hand, over-refinement makes the scale of model so large that the model loses its abstract nature. On the other hand, to deal with the ever-changing system requirements, even if the advanced language also needs to be added SDK (Software Development Kit) continuously, it must be much harder to the model which only have a weaker descriptive ability. Consequently, a better software functional entity must be found to realise the executable model.

The software functional entity has undergone several evolutions: from functions to objects, from objects to components, then from components to web services. Web services architecture adds and standardises a new layer, named "Service Layer" between the logistic layer and technical implement layer. The standardisation and dynamic characteristics make web services be able to provide the abundant and flexible software functional entities. AGOS adopts web services that is standardised, self-contained, self-described and modulised to enhance the abstract level of the code implementation, encapsulates the details of the code implementation, and provides the related domain-specific software functional entities to DSMEI by the way of web services cluster. Web services are not stand-alone. They depend on the domain-specific application systems and their processes. The development and reuse of web services have already been determined when the xDSM meta-model is constructed. It is a top-down design process. Based on the domain concepts, it describes the domain behaviour process dynamically according to the model, and drives the definition and functionalities of web services according to the realisation requirements of the model. The design principles of web services are as follows: the common parts of the specific domain are encapsulated into web services. The changeable parts are divided into two kinds: one kind that is easy to deal with by xDSM is defined directly by model; the other kind that it is not easy to deal with by xDSM will be transformed into service parameters, and use the parameterised means to handle the change-point. Web services provide the minimal software functional entities in the entire system. It is also the implementation foundation of the entire executable model.

Various web services at the different levels are required to support the problem space involved in the domain-specific modelling. AGOS regards a group related web services of a specific domain as a service cluster. On one hand, it requires a lot of web services entities to provide different functions; on the other hand, there may be several corresponding web services entities to the same functional requirement. So DSMEI is able to not only support the protocol of the service itself, but also deploy web services cluster dynamically in the software life cycle, for examples, querying services, matching services, assembling services, replacement services, load balancing of the service group of the same functional node, and adjustment of the coordinated services, etc. The flexible architecture of DSMEI is the foundation of the above all. It is able to provide Domain Framework dynamically based on web services, and adjusts the existing web service cluster to adapt software changes quickly.

7 Features of SODSMI

SODSMI is aimed at modelling for system implementation, which reduces the model complexity and improves the model accuracy. This method has a holistic and sustainable system to support the transformation from models to system implementation. Compared to other modelling methods, such as MDA system, the proposed approach is more suitable for the establishment and support of executable models, mainly shown as follows:

1. SODSMI is customised for solving software development problems in a certain application areas. It is dedicated and problem-oriented. Although it is at the expense of commonality, it improves the accuracy of the description on domain specific problems and its solutions, and reduces the complexity of modelling.
2. SODSMI improves the abstract level of models, and XDML provides an abstract mechanism to deal with the complexity of specific domains. It provides concepts and rules of the corresponding application domain, rather than those of a certain given programming language. Modellers face the domain concepts with different granularity directly, rather than construct the implementation details in the light of classes and objects, etc.
3. SODSMI pays attention to the integrity of MDD. Its goal is to achieve the system implementation, rather than to simply use models as a means of analysis and design. SODSMI completes the whole process from model establishment to code generation.
4. SODSMI emphasises on the capacity of meta-modelling, and adopts the separation of meta-modelling and domain application modelling to establish models that adapts better to specific domain. At the same time, it is able to separate users' application modelling from domain experts' meta-modelling as well as developers' creating support tools.
5. In SODSMI, the establishment of meta-model and code generator are developed within the organisation. They are mutually complementary: the model establishment is adapted completely to code generator; the generated code is practical, readable, and efficient as same as the code is written by experts who define the code generator. Meanwhile, the establishment of meta-model and code generators implicates a lot of implicit implementation convention that need not be expressed at the model layer, which observably reduces the complexity of models.
6. SODSMI is based on domain engineering, which provides a well support in essence for software reuse; on the contrary, the software reuse techniques also provides a well support for the DSM method.

Acknowledgment. This work is funded by the Open Foundation of Key Laboratory of Software Engineering of Yunnan Province under Grant No. 2011SE13.

References

1. Georgas, J.C., Dashofy, E.M., Taylor, R.N.: Architecture-Centric Development: A Different Approach to Software Engineering. ACM Crossroads **12**(4), 6–23 (2006)
2. Johnson, J.H.: The CHAOS Report. The Standish Group International, Inc. (1994)
3. Hen-Tov, A., Lorenz, D.H., Schachter, L.: ModelTalk: A Framework for Developing Domain-Specific Executable Models. In: Proceedings of the 8th Ann. OOPSLA Workshop Domain-Specific Modeling (DSM 2008), Nashville, TN, USA, pp. 19–20. ACM Press (October 2008)
4. Kuhne, T.: What is Model? Language Engineering for Model Driven Software Development. In: Dagstuhl Seminar Proceedings (2005)
5. Davis, M.D., Sigal, R., Weyuker, E.J.: Computability, Complexity, and Languages. Fundamentals of Theoretical Computer Science. Academic Press, Inc. (2008)
6. Zhou, H., Sun, X.P., Duan, Q., et al.: XMML: A Visual Metamodelling Language for Domain Specific Modelling and its Application in Distributed Systems. In: Proceedings of 12th IEEE International Workshop on Future Trends of Distributed Computing Systems (FTDCS), Kunming, China, pp. 133–139 (October 21-23, 2008)
7. Frankel, D.S.: Model Driven Architecture:Applying MDA to Enterprise Computing. John Wiley & Sons (January 2003)
8. OMG. UML 2.0 OCL Specification. Object Management Group. Framingham, Massachusetts (2003)
9. Mellor, S.J., Balcer, S.J.: Executable UML: A Foundation for Model Driven Architecture. Addison Wesley, Massachusetts (2002)
10. Yang, F., Mei, H., Lu, J., Jin, Z.: Some Discussion on the Development of Software Technology. Acta Electronica Sinica **26**(9), 1104–1115 (2003)

Workshop on Wireless Sensor Network (WSN 2014)

Researches Based on Subject-Oriented Security in the Cyber-Physical System

Caixia Zhang[1(✉)], Hua Li[1], Yuanjia Ma[2], Xiaoyu Wang[3], and Xiangdong Wang[2]

[1] Foshan University, Guangdong 528000, China
zh_caixia@163.com
[2] Guangdong Provincial Key Lab of Petrochemical Equipment Fault Diagnosis,
Guangdong, Maoming 525000, China
[3] The Faculty of Computer, Guangdong University of Technology, Guangzhou 510006, China

Abstract. The security research of Cyber-physical system is a dynamic development process. Because no single technique could ensure the absolute safety of CPS, so its safety problem must be considered from the overall and systematic researches. Based on the structure of CPS, CPS is here divided into some subjects, and various subjects are then discussed in face of security threats in the design of subject oriented CPS security model. This model is supplied with the WPDRRC security system model as a protective layer. With the technology oriented CPS system, subject oriented system security will have superiorities such as initiative, systemic, portability and simplified.

Keywords: Cyber Physical System (CPS) · Security researches · Subject-oriented · The WPDRRC security model

1 Introduction

The technologies in computers, wireless communication, the network control, sensor and embedded technologies are rapidly developed. The physical system emerge. Once the concept was put forward by the literature [1], it is widely intentioned in the domestic and foreign fields in computers, communication, control, health, and so on, because it has wide application prospects and commercial values [2].

In a broad sense, the cyber-physical system is physical network equipment which can be controlled and trusted. At the same time, it can deeply integrate the computation, control and communication. Through the calculation process and physical process of interacting feedback, it can achieve fusion depth and real-time interaction to increase or expand with new functions and CPS monitors, or it can control a physical object entirely in a safe, reliable, efficient and real-time style. The ultimate goal of CPS will surely realize the complete integration of the information and physical worlds, build a controllable, reliable, scalable, secure CPS network, and it will ultimately change the human construction in engineering physics system [3].

Xiangdong Wang: Prioject Supported the National Natural Science Fundation of Guang dong (S2013010014485) and Technology Project of Guangdong Province (2013B020314020).

V.C.M. Leung et al. (Eds.): TridentCom 2014, LNICST 137, pp. 351–359, 2014.
DOI: 10.1007/978-3-319-13326-3_33

At present, the CPS system research is mainly focused on the concept of CPS, CPS architecture, CPS modeling, CPS application and CPS challenges [4–6]. Like all traditional network, security and reliability are very important. For the large information and physical component, interaction has more freedom and equality than the traditional network. Therefore the CPS system will face a series of new security problems. How to construct the CPS security architecture, the completion of the safety communication and security control is an important and challenging problem.

For the security of CPS, scholars at home and abroad have launched a series of discussions from the angle of technology. The security problem about the congestion and tampering with CPS perception data in the CPS system has been discussed [7], which will cause the error of the network state estimation and the error control command. Privacy protection, security controls and security vulnerability assessment technology of CPS have preliminarily been studied. Based on semantic models in CPS, the security analysis of information flow was put forward through information flow tracking and automated analysis process algebra specification [8].Starting from the structure of the CPS, the CPSlayers of security threats and solutions are analyzed in literature [9]. Fine-grained model of CPS was presented [10] in order to ensure the safety of CPS system.

However, the research of CPS security is a dynamic development process. Any single technique is too difficult to guarantee the absolute security, so the safety problem must be considered from the overall and systematic angle. This paper segments subject-oriented and discusses various subjects to solve security threats from the CPS system structure. Based on the theme of the CPS system security, the subject-oriented security model has more advantages than the technology-oriented security model.

2   CPS System Structure

The structure is the most fundamental contents in CPS system, and the scientific and reasonable system structure is the base of the realization of overall safety performance, and it plays an important role in the system safety analysis.

Considering the various definitions of CPS system and the need of completing the various functions, the CPS system is divided into physical layer, network layer and dynamic control execution layer in-depth analysis on the basis of [11–13].

1) Physical Dynamic Layer: The physical dynamic layer refers to the CPS system and the physical environment in close connection with the large number of isomorphic or heterogeneous physical components.

2) The Communication Network Layer: The communication network layer which controls the execution layer provides the real-time and effective multidimensional perceptual information, data and so on..

3) To Control the Execution Layer: The executive control layer in the real-time acquisition is the integrated perception information under premise according to the specific control demands of the semantic rules and the control logic in order to realize the large-scale entity in the real-time control and the global optimization control.

3   CPS System Topic Partition

CPS is a complex dynamic system. From a technical point of view to study the security of the system, and from the technical details of a starting solution which is the emergence of CPS security issues, it will make the CPS system security in a passive position. Facing the new emerging safety concerns, the security must be studied through the analysis to obtain a solution. Then it will enhance the CPS system security research in a chaotic state, and a passive defense situation.

In view of the above analysis, from the angle of technology on CPS system security passive study, the proposed subject oriented CPS system design idea and purpose are the security problems of CPS which is also subject to study, so that CPS system security will break up the whole into parts.

In the depth study of CPS function, on the basis of the system structure and the operation mechanism, the abstract is divided into perceptual systems, storage systems, communications equipment, intelligent network, distributed computing, control system and the implementation of the system. The seven themes are shown in figure 1.

3.1   CPS Theme Connotation and Technical Support

1) CPS system, perception system of dynamic physical layer in various physical components, which track location, condition, environment and other kinds of real time information access, needs a lot of sensing devices. The technical support can be provided by RFID, GPS global positioning technology, sensor technology, image capture apparatus, laser scanning, mobile terminals and other technology development for the perceptual system.

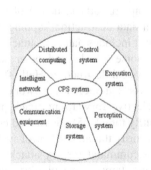

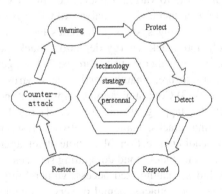

Fig. 1. 7 subjects of CPS   system   **Fig. 2.** The WPDRRC security model

2) Storage system: the perception system generates a large amount of real-time information of data stream, and the control system which produces a large number of parallel control instructions requires powerful storage support. NAS storage technology, cloud storage technology, direct attached storage, network attached storage, storage area network and discs [11] can server storage scheme for CPS system storage system with some technical support;

3) CPS system of communication equipment in dynamic physical layer and application layer is connected to the calculation of a variety of communications equipment for the CPS system in material objects, so people, objects and other information can provide hardware support.

4) CPS intelligent network in real-time communication and the information interaction require a certain transmission pathway of CPS intelligent communication network. CPS intelligent communication network is required in the transmission of information in the course of the digital / analog converter.

5) CPS distributed computing systems require real-time processing massive information system to realize a large number of physical devices with optimal control. The powerful computation and information processing ability are the keys of realizing this goal. Distributed computing, grid computing[14] or cloud computing, distributed computing technology for CPS system are all provided to calculate the theme of technical support.

6) Control system: according to CPS function target and control requirements, the collection and analysis of all kinds of information systems, real-time monitoring and integrated simulation are all generated by applying the control command.

7) Execution system: the implementation system is the control system which generates instruction execution mechanism. CPS system is involved in all walks of life, the performing system also differs in thousands of ways according to different applications.

3.2   CPS System Subject Facing Security Threats

The CPS system is large and complex because it has many hidden security dangers, vulnerable to various attacks, combined with the structure of CPS system, CPS system from themes, and analysis of CPS system potential security threats.

1) Sensing system: it includes hardware, node capture, attack, denial of service, collision attack, energy depletion attack, perception data destruction, tapping, illegal access and other security threats; 2) Storage system: it includes database attack, privacy disclosure, unauthorized access, virus, Trojan horse attacks and other security threats; 3) Communication equipment: it includes physical destruction, Hello flooding attacks, tapping, virtual attacks; 4) Intelligent network: it includes network attack, routing attacks, malicious network, response to selective forwarding attack, tunnel, misleading, direction, black hole attack against security threats; 5) Distributed computing: it includes cloud computing services such as security threat; 6) Control system: it includes unauthorized access, vulnerability, control command forgery attacks, malicious code attacks, denial of service attacks, blocking, tampering with CPS data and other security threats; 7) Execution system: it includes equipment failure, node control, physical destruction, and denial of service attacks, unfair competition and other security threats.

3.3 CPS Security Service Demand

Different from the traditional communication network, computer network, Internet, CPS information in the system and the physical component interaction are more convenient than traditional network. And the frequent, intelligent component can enjoy more freedom and equality. Therefore, the CPS system security problems put forward higher requirements to the social service.

1) Confidentiality: the unauthorized person cannot obtain the content of the message, but CPS system complex network composed of the information is easy to leak, so it must ensure that the system information transmission will not be tapped.

2) Integrity confidentiality guarantees the information safe, but it cannot guarantee that the information is to be modified. CPS system information from emergence to application process is due to transmission network openness, vulnerable to attackers tamper, add, resulting in the loss of information and the data is damaged. The packet message authentication mechanism, data monitoring and other means to identify can ensure data integrity and transfer command.

3) Identity authentication of identity authentication is the most important one of all the security properties; other security services are dependent on the service implementation, the node which can confirm the communication node identity.

4) Access control determines who can access the system, who are able to access the resources system and how to use these resources. The appropriate access control can protect CPS system of massive terminal information from unauthorized physical access.

5) CPS system adaptability to dynamic characteristics of the physical entity must be able to target the change of the external environment, rapid response to the intelligent selection, adaptive adjustment of the balance state, to ensure that the system can adapt the changes in safety.

6) In providing personalized privacy of user experience, CPS can, at the same time, master more user privacy. On the other hand, CPS tasks are normally performed by distrust of the entity in the process of collaboration. The entity output information may cause privacy.

7) Real-time, or timeliness [14]:Once the network delays, the actuator can receive controller command, and the system will not enter into a stable state. The availability of the CPS requirements is more stringent real-time environment than traditional information system.

4 Subject Oriented CPS System Security Model

CPS system security model formulation can be achieved in CPS overall system security protection system, overall, plan and normative, which makes CPS system control flow and data flow information confidentiality. The integrity and availability are comprehensive, reliable protections.

At the beginning of the design, due to the OSI reference model and TCP/IP reference model without consideration of the security problems in network communication, the reference model of any dimension to find security vulnerabilities will be enemy attack. In order to avoid similar situations, the subject oriented CPS system security model design, this paper uses the WPDRRC security system model for the CPS security model of protective layer.

WPDRRC security system model is considering the safety aspects, technology, management, strategy, project the respect such as the process, the design and construction of the security side case strong basis is closely guided here. As is shown in figure 2.

4.1 Subject Oriented CPS System Security Model

In the CPS system security service demand as the basis, the CPS system as the basis, the WPDRRC security system model is introduced into the CPS system security model design, design subject oriented CPS system security model.

1) The Model Center. The model center in perceptual systems, storage systems, communications equipment, intelligent network, distributed computing, control system and the implementation of the system of the seven-theme service requirements of security as the core, in accordance with the overall, systematic thinking, combined with its own characteristics and needs of each subject and theme between interaction design requirements.

2) Model of the System. CPS system architecture consists of physical layer, network layer and dynamic control execution layer, in the design of security model, the three layers require both interrelated and need depend on each other. Therefore, this paper in the CPS system security model design puts forward the interlayer with protective layer of train of thoughts. When a layer of security threats passes through the isolating layer isolation effect, prevents the spread to other levels of security threats. On the other hand, between layers needed to have the cooperation function, as an organic whole, one layer of problems needs the other layer to provide the appropriate security measures, and the CPS system has become an organic whole security defense.

3) Model of the Protective Layer. The security of CPS system needs its own security policy, at the same time, needs protection. Therefore, in the CPS system security model, the WPDRRC security system model is introduced. WPDRRC warning, protection, detection, response, recovery, counter functions of six parts can all complement each other, so that the security of CPS system come into a flow entity.

4) Model, Validation of Safety Standards. Subject oriented CPS system security model in the outer layer is the safety management standard and verification system. The safety standards include CPS security and verification of the lack of universal recognized standards, safety management of security techniques, global trust degree evaluation, collaborative process of privacy protection, system validation considerations from system scheduling capability, system energy consumption, the speed of the system, the system memory usage, deadlock and privacy aspects of the research.

4.2   Oriented CPS Model Comparison

The technology of secure CPS system work flow as is shown in Figure 3.

Along with the rapid development of CPS, new technology also changes rapidly, and a kind of any new technology is not completely safe. Technically oriented research strategy will also need continue to carry out new technology of safety research, to meet a variety of technical and safety requirements.

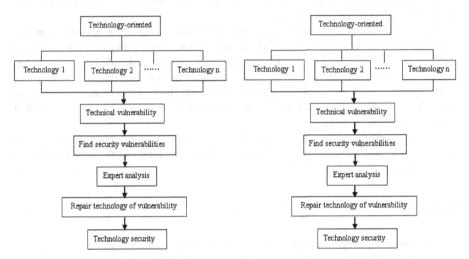

Fig. 3. Subject oriented CPS safety research process

Fig. 4. Technology oriented CPS safety research process

Subject oriented CPS system security research process as is shown in Figure 4.

Researches can be active from each subject's own security needs, forming a closed loop security defense system, and can fundamentally change the CPS system security research in the passive position of state.

Subject-oriented study of safety design strategies leads to themes of safety demand as the research object, and leads to the theme of their own needs as the starting point, so it is relatively stable and oriented with respect to the technical security researches.

Subject-oriented security design research strategy has a better system. Each subject was a safety research. The importance of the theme, the connection and cooperation make it become an organic whole. And in the technical security research, it lacks the whole CPS system security planning, and ignores the CPS system sex.

Subject-oriented study of safety design strategies leads to themes of safety property as the object of study, and it has good portability..

To sum up, subject-oriented CPS system security research is better than the technology research of CPS security initiative, and its changes are numerous for their advantages are brief, systemic, and portable.

5   Summary

In the system, safety is one of development process problems which cannot be ignored. In the Internet design in the initial stage, because of the single attention to the practical application, ignoring the consideration of the system safety, the current Internet has many defects. Internet dependence of TCP/IP protocol has the bigger hidden safety trouble, and it makes Internet security in a passive position. Although active defense has got certain development, Internet security will not be able to reach the ideal state over a period of time.

As a global information technology and information industry's new development trend, the CPS system will be the information world and the physical world, which includes fusion and development of the computer system, embedded systems, industrial control systems, networked control systems, networking, wireless sensor network, hybrid system, permeability and economic life. In all areas of production it can produce far-reaching effect. Therefore, in the initial stage of development, the system security cannot be ignored.

This paper proposes the subject-oriented CPS system security model for CPS security research, and provides a good idea to effectively promote the development of CPS system.

References

1. CPS Steering Group. Cyber-physical systems executive summary (July 2011). http://precise.seas.upenn.edu/events/iccps11/doc/ CPS-Executive-Summary.pdf, Smith, T.F., Waterman, M.S.: Identification of Common Molecular Subsequences. J. Mol. Biol. 147, 195–197 (1981)
2. Wang, Z., Xie, L.: Cyber-physical Systems: A Survey. ACTA AUTOMATICA SINICA 37(10), 1157–1165 (2011)
3. He, J.: Cyber-physical Systems. Communications of China Computer Federation 6(1), 25–29 (2010)
4. Tan, Y., Vuran, M.C., Goddard, S.: Spatio-Temporal Event Model for Cyber-Physical systems. In: Proceedings of the 29th IEEE International Conference on Distributed Computing Systems Work shops, pp. 44–45 (2009)
5. Zhang, F.M., Szwaykowska, K., Wolf, W.: Task. scheduling for control oriented requirements for cyber-physical systems. In: IEEE Proceedings of the Real Time Systems Symposium, Barcelona, Spain, pp. 47–56 (2008)
6. Dillon, T., Potdar, V., Singh, J., Talevski, A.: Cyber-physical systems: Providing Quality of Service (QoS) in a hetero-generous systems-of-systems environment. In: Proceedings of 5th IEEE International Digital Ecosystems and Technologies Conference (DEST), Daejeon, USA, pp. 330–335. IEEE (2011)
7. Cardenas, A.A., Amin, S., Sastry, S.: Secure Control Towards Survivable Cyber-Physical Systems, In: The 28th International Conference on Distributed Computing Systems Workshops, pp. 495–500 (2008)
8. Akella, R., Tang, H., McMillin, B.M.: Analysis of information flow security in cyber–physical systems. International Journal of Critical Infrastructure Protection, 157–173 (2010)

9. Tang, H., Tan, F., Song, B., Li, N.: Cyber-Physical System Security Studies and Research, Multimedia Technology (ICMT), Beijing, 4883–4886 (2011)
10. Codella, C., Hampapur, A., et al.: Continuous Assurance for Cyber Physical System Security (2011).
    http://cimic.rutgers.edu/positionPapers/CPSSW09%20_IBM.pdf
11. Tan, Y., Goddard, P., Rezl, C.: A prototype architecture for cyber-physical systems. SIGBED Review, pp. 51–52 (2008)
12. Kang, W., Son, S.H.: The design of an open data service architecture for cyber-physical systems. ACM SIGBED Review 5(1) (2008)
13. Tan, P., Shu, J., Wu, Z.: An Architecture for Cyber-Physical Systems. Journal of Computer Research and Development, 47 (2010)
14. Wu, M., Ding, C., Yang, L.: Research on Security Architecture and Key Technologies in Cyber-Physical Systems. Journal of Nanjing University of Posts and Telecommunications (natural science) 30(4), 52–56 (2010)

Online Lubricant Monitoring System with WSN Based on the Dielectric Permittivity

YuanJia Ma[1(✉)] and CaiXia Zhang[2]

[1] Guangdong Provincial Key Lab of Petrochemical Equipment Fault Diagnosis,
Guangdong University of Petrochemical Technology, Guangdong, Maoming 525000, China
mayuanjia@foxmail.com
[2] Department of Automation, Foshan University, Guangdong 528000, China
zh_caixia@163.com

Abstract. Through theoretical and experimental methods, the feasibility of the dielectric permittivity as the decay of lubricants evaluation index was verified. To overcome the shortcoming of existing oil monitoring with high costs, complicated operation and poor real-time, it's necessary to develop the wireless online monitoring system. A new type of capacitance sensor for trace moisture measurement was presented. Oil monitoring principle according to the idea of difference was described. Node deploy mode of wireless sensor network is presented in this paper, and asynchronous sleep scheduling algorithm based on the data variation was given. By means of the grey correlation analysis and experiment in allusion to moisture measurement, the results confirm that the accuracy and reliability was improved.

Keywords: Lube · Permittivity · WSN · Grey correlation analysis · Moisture

1   Introduction

The deterioration level of lubricants affects working conditions of the engine directly, and the decay process of the engine lubricating oil is a complicated process. Traditional detecting methods of lubricating oil predominantly use off-line detection, extracting the pre-existing oil sample and bringing it to the special detection mechanism. The off-line detecting method is laborious, time-consuming, costly and requires a long monitoring cycle. Therefore the development of online lubricant monitoring system has very significant theoretical and practical significance.

It shows that moisture in the lubrication system of utility-type unit is one of the important causes leading to the equipment problem, especially in the petrochemical industry. The moisture content in lubricating oil, according to the regulations, should be below 0.03%, and the oil change level is controlled in 0.1%~0.5%. If the standard is not met, lubricating oil will be emulsified, and the lubricating properties of oil will grow poorer, causing parts to rust, axle suspension bush to burn and other machinery accidents. Therefore moisture monitoring in the lubricating oil is particularly important, not only can it monitor the equipment operational condition indirectly, but also provides evidence for the mechanical fault diagnosis.

© Institute for Computer Sciences, Social Informatics and Telecommunications Engineering 2014
V.C.M. Leung et al. (Eds.): TridentCom 2014, LNICST 137, pp. 360–367, 2014.
DOI: 10.1007/978-3-319-13326-3_34

2   Related Work

As the lubricant is oxygenized and polluted, the permittivity becomes increasingly apparent; therefore the permittivity can be seen as the comprehensive evaluation index of the lubricant decay extent. Through the reasonable threshold of the permittivity, the rate of lubricants deterioration can be evaluated comprehensively. Among the lubricant physicochemical index, the change of the metal particles, water, and acid substance are the principal factors which affect the lubricant quality decay. Especially the water, whose permittivity is much larger than the lubricants' and other two factors, plays a key role in the permittivity's change [1].

Currently, the moisture content of lubricating oil online measuring is mainly by the capacitive moisture sensor which based on the variable dielectric permittivity. Authors of literature[2-5] discussed the performance of the capacitance sensor with flat, cylindrical, and probe sensors; experiments were carried out to validate correlation models. The structure of the sensor under the condition of high moisture content performance comparatively ideal, and it is appropriate for detecting water well like crude oil, which moisture content is high. But for lubricating oil, which moisture content is extremely insignificant, the situation is completely different. In the first instance, the sensor's capacitance is too minuscule, usually only a few picofarad. Though some improved sensors[6] with a layer of insulating layer on the plate can increase the capacitance to dozens of picofarad, but the capacitance variation caused by the dielectric permittivity change remains unchanged. This does not increase the sensitivity of the sensor, and it is difficult to distinguish for less than 0.1% moisture. Secondly, we cannot ignore the edge effect, parasitic capacitance, stray capacitance for the sensor's minuscule capacitance, as they impact the mapping relationship between moisture content and capacitance. And lastly, though moisture content has noticeable differences in dielectric permittivity measurement between water and oil, but it is not a single-valued function of the lubricating oil dielectric permittivity; the influence of abrasive particle and temperature on dielectric permittivity cannot be ignored. Therefore, in order to improve the sensitivity and accuracy of trace moisture measurement, it needs to be improved for the sensor and methods of measurement.

3   Design of Lubricant Monitoring System

In this section, the lubricants online monitoring system, which focuses on moisture detecting, is described. Details on hardware and software designing are discussed.

3.1   The Capacitance Sensors

A lot of literature and experiments show that moisture content in lubricating oil has significant influence on the dielectric permittivity; it can go as far as offsetting the effect of other impurities on the oil dielectric permittivity in the interval of high moisture content. However, the absolute variation of the dielectric permittivity of oil, with moisture content less than 1000ppm, is very diminutive; it is difficult to measure with the sensor due to its size and structural limitations. To improve the sensitivity of the sensor, the flat capacitor is reformed, and is designed with a parallel plates capacitance sensor which can be adapted according to the requirements. The structure shown in Figure 1, n is 8, representing the capacitor electrode couple number, including 8 pieces of rotary plate and 8 fixed plate, the radius r=14.4mm, plate thickness is 0.5mm, should be used as far as possible to make the maximum plate opposite area. Due to the ideology of difference, there needs to be two identical sensors. But it is difficult to produce the exact equivalent sensor on both the structures due to limitations of the production process. However, you can move the screw-rotating plate to fine-tune the area by strengthening the nut.

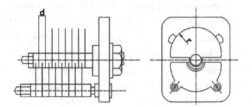

Fig. 1. The structure of sensor

According to research, if consider the influence of edge effect, the plate capacitor expression of limited size is:

$$C = n\varepsilon S\left[1 - \frac{\theta}{\pi}\right]/d + \frac{n\varepsilon S}{\pi}\left[1 + \ln 1 + \frac{2\pi r}{d} + \ln(1 + \frac{2\pi r}{d})\right] \tag{1}$$

According to the theory of dielectric permittivity we know that $\varepsilon = \varepsilon_0 \varepsilon_r$, replacing the ε in formula 1, we get $C = nK\varepsilon_r$.

In the formula:

θ——rotation angle from moving plate to the fixed plate.

n——the couple of the plate.

ε_0 & ε_r——the permittivity of vacuum and relative permittivity of inter-plate oil

K——sensitivity of capacitance on the relative permittivity of one couple plate.

Holding constant the structure and size of the sensor, dielectric permittivity and capacitance value showed a linear relationship in theory. The original capacitance value increases to n times, and reduces the incidence of the parasitic capacitance, which exists in wire and measuring circuit. Furthermore, sensitivity of the sensor enhanced to n times. However, with higher sensitivity, the stability deteriorates. Additionally, the difficulty of the installation and production increases. Therefore, the value of n and s must be considered.

3.2   The Structure of System

From the above formula (1) we can see, the dielectric permittivity and the capacitance are directly linked. Variable permittivity capacitor transforms the permittivity changes of lubricants to the capacitance changes of capacitive sensors in order to achieve the detection purpose. When the permittivity exceeds the threshold of the system, the system alarm will sound. But to date, none of the methods developed is perfect and all are far from ready to be used in practice systems. So it will be followed by a description of how to set up the network of monitoring system, and details on the sensors' structure are discussed in later sections.

The project, which is part of the Maoming Petrochemical rotating machinery fault diagnosis project, provides one-dimensional fault diagnosis evidence for multi-sensor information fusion. The large units of Maoming Petrochemical are equipped with a lubrication system. Lubricating oil filter is an important part of the lubrication system, and its role is to filter and remove impurity and abrasive particle in the lubricant, and to protect life of operation components.

The design is based on the idea of the differential. Sensors with the same structure are mounted in vital parts such as the oil tank, filter, cooler, and dehydrator. By monitoring the permittivity between different nodes, we can calculate the difference to analyze the impact of numerous factors on the oil dielectric permittivity. So the permittivity increment made by moisture, abrasive particle and thermal can be calculated by measuring the difference of capacitance. The structure of the lubricant monitoring system in Maoming Petrochemical is shown in Figure 2.

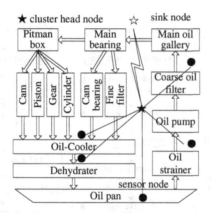

Fig. 2. Diagram of the general design

The monitoring system obtains real-time oil data online generated by sensors mentioned above. Then, it utilizes the Zigbee protocol to communicate between the cluster head node and sensor nodes, by which data is collected. Finally, sink node uses a USB interface and uploads the data to the PC.

The sensor node for each unit is composed of a cluster, using single hop communication between the sensor nodes and the cluster head. The sensor nodes transmit the collected data to the cluster head. Cluster head collects the data from sensor nodes for fusion to remove data redundancy. After that, the cluster head then transfers the data to the sink node. Sensor nodes using regular sleep mechanism wake every ten minutes to collect data from units. And it can also be awakened by the cluster head itself in order to collect data from specific parts of each unit.

When the data is gathered, the sink node uploads the data to the PC by USB interface. Oil expert system can be used for further analysis on the PC, and can also be connected to the larger oil analysis laboratory implementation of remote analysis.

3.3   The Software Design

The diagram of the software is given in figure 3. In order to save the energy of sensor nodes, wireless communication module nodes usually remain dormant and opened only when the value is mutated or when the sink nodes are required to transmit data[7][8]. Considering the energy efficiency and characteristics of oil monitoring, we designed the asynchronous sleep scheduling algorithm based on the data variation as follow. The data are collected by sensor nodes once every ten minutes and compared with preceding data. If changed little, it will be stored in memory and will overwrite the previous data. If the data is mutated, the wireless communication module will power on the wireless communication module for alarm. Sink node will then send the command to WSN to open all nodes when the oil needs to be analyzed, sensor nodes distributed storage data to the cluster-head node, and then send to the sink node by them. Fluids information can be chosen by the sink node at all monitoring points, and can also be separately collected.

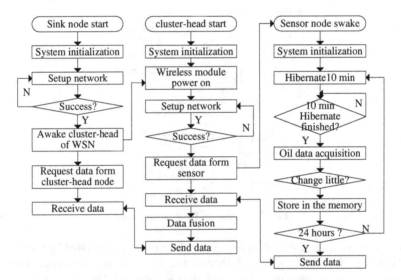

Fig. 3. The flowchart sleep scheduling algorithm

4   Gray Relational Grade Analysis

The dielectric permittivity of the lubricating oil, mainly affected by the moisture, abrasive, temperature and other unknown factors, can give a representative property of physicochemical parameters roundly. It belongs to grey system. The grey system theory put forward the concept of the grey relational grade of various factors, and determines the degree of correlation between factors according to geometry curve similarity of factors. Take water content monitoring for an example, to find out relationship between the sensor output and water content, the bigger correlation degree between factor and moisture content, the more accurate for using it as a monitoring water content index. The major steps are making the original data dimensionless, calculating the correlation coefficient, correlation degree and ranking evaluation index according to the correlation degree.

Set the moisture content as the main sequence $Y=\{Y(k) \mid k = 1, 2, ...,n\}$, and factors as sub sequence $X_i=\{X_i(k) \mid k = 1, 2, ..., n\}$, $i = 1, 2, ..., m$.

The physical meaning of each factor is different, so data dimension is inconsistent. In order to eliminate the influence of dimensional and enhance comparability between different dimensions of factors, we need the grey correlation analysis, and first of all the elements of raw data need to be normalization with non-dimensional treatment, its computation formula is[9]:

$$x_i(k) = \frac{x_i(k)}{x_i(l)}, k = 1,2,\cdots\cdots n; i = 0,1,2\cdots\cdots m \tag{2}$$

According to the definition, the correlation coefficient for main sequence Y(k) and sub sequence Xi(k) is

$$\zeta_i(k) = \frac{\min\limits_i \min\limits_k \Delta_i(k) + \rho \max\limits_i \max\limits_k \Delta_i(k)}{\Delta_i(k) + \rho \max\limits_i \max\limits_k \Delta_i(k)} \tag{3}$$

In the formula the ρ is distinguishing coefficient, the smaller the ρ is, the greater the resolution ratio. The resolution is best, the when the $\rho \leq 0.5463$ or less, usually take $\rho = 0.5$. The correlation degree of sequence of sub factors represents the relationship to the main sequence, the greater the correlation degree of the factors, the influence is more obvious to the main sequence.

5   Experiment

Results of an experiment focus on moisture content we validated are given to illustrate the proposed technique. In the experiment, the actual sample of lubricating oil is measured regularly from a unit in maoming petrochemical company, model for mobil dte25. Take 20 samples of actual oil, and five of them at room temperature, adding suitable amount of water that making lubricating oil moisture volume fraction were 0.01%, 0.1%, 0.3%, 0.5%, 0.3%. And the real moisture content was measured by Karl fischer moisture meter. Stir well for 10 min making water dissolves in lubricating oil. Measuring the capacitance value C_{x1}. Then filter the oil with the precision of 15 microns, measuring the capacitance value C_{x2}. Experimental data measured in temperatures of 26.7℃, 40℃, 55℃, 70℃. The relations between moisture content and capacitance value under different temperature is shown in figure 4 and 5. Obviously, compared with two figures, we know that coincidence degree is higher when using ΔC_w to represent the moisture content than using a single sensor. Therefore, it can reflect real water content more exactly.

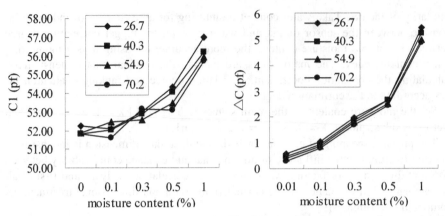

Fig. 4. Relatedness between moisture and C_1 **Fig. 5.** Relatedness between moisture and ΔC_w

Take water content for main sequence, factors correlation calculated according to the equation 4 shown in table 1. It shows that the capacitance sensor using behind filter can improve the correlation about 10% between moisture content and capacitance. And moisture content represented by ΔC_w can lower the cross sensitivity of sensor for temperature. The correlation would be improved by 10% roughly.

Table 1. The correlation coefficient to moisture content

factor	Temperature	Cx0 (pf)	Cx1 (pf)	Cx2 (pf)	ΔCw (pf)
Correlation coefficient (%)	0.2684	0.2960	0.6833	0.7129	0.8186

The data analysis by the method of least squares in experiment shows that the moisture content and ΔC_w fitting relationship is $Y = 0.08473 + 0.208921 * \Delta C_w$. The relative error between actual and predictive value is shown in table 2.

Table 2. The relative error of predicted value

Real (%)	Predicted value（%）	Absolute errors	relative error (%)
0.01	0.0114	-0.001	-13.7 %
0.1	0.1096	-0.010	-9.6 %
0.3	0.3080	-0.008	-2.7 %
0.5	0.4710	0.029	5.8 %
1	1.0100	-0.010	-1.0 %

The result demonstrates that the more moisture content, the higher the testing precision. The deviation is a little larger when moisture content below 0.01% (100 ppm). But if consider the effect of operational error of experiment, compared with the habitual moisture sensor, it has been able to distinguish the trace moisture in the period of low moisture content.

6   Conclusions

1. In this paper, the design of the capacitance sensor with adjustable plates not only has high sensitivity, but also reduces the volume signally than the sensor with the type of cylinder and plate. And it is suitable for the oil online monitoring.
2. Lube oil monitoring for industrial unit needs a large amount of sensor nodes. This requirement has been fulfilled through WSN. According to the characteristics of slowly changing in monitoring data, the design of asynchronous sleep scheduling algorithm based on the data variation can reduce the network energy consumption and prolong the life cycle of the network.
3. A new way to accurately distinguish the ingredient of contaminants in lubricating oil is proposed. Through the idea of difference, reduces the combined impact of multiple factors on oil permittivity. Take measuring trace moisture in oil for example, the method can improve the correlation between moisture and dielectric, by grey relation analysis and experiment validation. It can predict the moisture content in lubricating more accurately. Through the same way can also measure the content of abrasive particle.

Acknowledgments. This work was supported by science and technology plan project of maoming (No.2012B01052), and the open funds of guangdong provincial key lab of petrochemical equipment fault diagnosis (No.512006).

References

1. Wang, H., et al.: Study on Relationship Between Chemical Indicators and Permittivity of Engine Lubricating Oil. J. Journal of Chongqing University of Technology, 13–17 (2010)
2. Tim, C.: An overview of online oil monitoring technologies. In: Fourth Annual Weidmann-ACTI Technical Conference, San Antonio (2005)
3. Hu, L., Toyoda, K., Ihara, I.: Dielectric properties of edible oils and fatty acids as a function of frequency, temperature, moisture and composition. Journal of Food Engineering 88(2), 151–158 (2008)
4. Liu, K.: Oil monitoring method based on the dielectric constant. Lubrication Engineering 1, 030 (2009)
5. Xiao-fei, Z., et al.: Study of Online Oil Monitoring Technology Based on Dielectric Constant Measurement J. Chinese Journal of Sensors and Actuators 12, 026 (2008)
6. Yi-wei, F., Hua-qiang, Li.: Research and Application on Quick Inspecting of Contaminated Lubricating Oil. New Technology & New Process, 22–23 (2005)
7. Emir, H., Narendra, A.: Energy efficient network method using delay tolerant network. In: 2012 International Conference on Green and Ubiquitous Technology (GUT). IEEE (2012)
8. Vimal, U., et al: A Wireless Sensor Network in Vibration Monitoring of Equipments. International Journal, 23–34 (2011)
9. Deng, J.L.: Grey control system: Huzhong Industry College Publishing Company. Wuhan, China (1985)

Workshop on Flexible Architecture of Reconfigurable Infrastructure (FARI 2014)

An Adaptive Fair Sampling Algorithm Based on the Reconfigurable Counter Arrays

Jing Wang[✉], BingQiang Wang, Xiaohui Zhang, and YunZhi Zhu

National Digital Switch System Engineering & Technology Center,
Zhengzhou, 450002, China
Wangjingniu_2003@sina.com,
{wangbingqiang,zhangxiaohui}@ndsc.com.cn, zhuwangzilz@163.com

Abstract. At present, how to trade off the balance between the memory resources and sampling accuracy balance has become one of the most important problems focused on by the network packet sampling algorithms. This paper discusses a novel adaptive fair packet sampling algorithm (AFPS) to solve the above problem by improving the use ratio of memory resources. The key innovation of AFPS is the reconfigurable counter structure composed of two counter arrays, by which the AFPS count the small flow and large flow in a differential way and the size of two arrays can be adjusted adaptively according to the dynamic flow size distribution. The reconfigurable counter structure ensures not only a high memory use ratio value under different network conditions but also accurate estimation of small flows so that the overall sampling accuracy of AFPS is improved. The theoretical analysis and evaluation on real traffic traces show that AFPS can estimate the small flows accurately and the estimation error of the large ones' equals to SGS. Besides AFPS keeps the memory resource use ratio on almost 0.952 under different conditions so that it can use the memory resource efficiently.

Keywords: Network traffic measurement · Packet sampling · Estimation error · Reconfigurable parameter

1 Introduction

Network traffic measurement is essential for network routing, management and security. As the rate of networks links increases rapidly, the confliction between limited measurement resources and measurement accuracy becomes more and more serious. In order to improve the measurement accuracy, packet sampling [1] is usually used. Packet sampling can reduce the number of flow records as well as keep the traffic's primitive characters.

The traditional packet sampling algorithms often keep the flow records in memory resources such as SRAM, DRAM or other fabric structures. The size of memory resources used to store the information of sampled flows affect the accuracy of measurement result directly. Due to the limited memory resources, the information of sampled flows can only be recovered partly. So how to make a trade-off between memory

© Institute for Computer Sciences, Social Informatics and Telecommunications Engineering 2014
V.C.M. Leung et al. (Eds.): TridentCom 2014, LNICST 137, pp. 371–378, 2014.
DOI: 10.1007/978-3-319-13326-3_35

resource and measurement accuracy is the most important problem to be solved. Some algorithms only focus on parts of flows which they are interested in just like SH and MBF [2]. Others adjust sampling rates adaptively according to the flow size or some other conditions [3]. Although these improved sampling algorithms can ensure the accuracy of traffic measurement results partly, they do not use the memory resources efficiently. In the future, the high-speed network bandwidth and the various new network applications will need more and more memory resources to store sampled flows. So a good sampling algorithm in the future network must try to use the memory resources enough as well as ensure a high sampling accuracy.

Recently SDM(software defined measurement) is proposed and discussed [7][8]. In SDM, the tradeoff between resource usage and accuracy is one of the important problems to be solved. Kinds of resources (CPU, memory, network) are be orchestrated by a controller. The memory usage becomes a function of measurement requirement in different spatial and time granularity.

This paper proposes a novel adaptive fair packet sampling algorithm (AFPS). The key innovation of AFPS is the reconfigurable counter structure, which structure is composed of two counter arrays counting packets in a differential way. One counter array named C_m is used to count packets of small flows one by one. The other named C_e is used to count large flows by counting sketch [4]. The two counter arrays share one memory space and the size of each counter array is decided by a reconfigurable parameter TEF (the Threshold to judge Elephant Flow). TEF can be adjusted adaptively according to the dynamic change of the maximal flow size on the link so that the memory resources can be used efficiently under different network conditions. Counting small and large flows in a differential ways ensures that the estimation error of small flows is 0 and the estimation error of large ones' equals to SGS. The dynamic adjustment of TEF makes AFPS estimate more small flow while the maximal flow size becomes small so that AFPS can get small average standard error.

2   Analysis of the Problem

Packet sampling can reduce the number of flow records stored in memory resources. But with the rapid development of network bandwidth and the appearance of some new network applications, existing sampling algorithms can not ensure high sampling accuracy within the constrain of the memory resource.

Especially to the network application such as anomaly detection, collecting as much as traffic information is very important. The information loss on small flows will affect the estimation accuracy of such network application's statistics. Fair sampling is a kind of methodology to settle the above problem. SGS[4] is a classic fair sampling algorithm. It makes the packet sampling probability as a decreasing function of the size of the flow which the packet belongs to. In this way, the packet belongs to the small flows can be sampled with high probability while low sampling probability of the elephant flows will not decrease the estimation accuracy, resulting in much more accurate statistic results.

SGS uses the counting sketch to encode the approximate of all flows. The hash collision in counting sketch might cause more than one flows to be hashed to the same index, resulting in the increasing of estimation error. This inaccuracy has more impactions on small flows than elephant ones.

The existence of hash collision in SGS is due to the limitation of memory resources. Today's memory technique does not support allocate a single counter to each flow. Though the memory resources used as the counters are very limited, SGS wasted lots of memory spaces because of its counting sketch structure. So we try to change the counting structure and improved the use ratio of the limited memory resource.

3   Our Algorithm

To solve the problem that the counting sketch structure used by SGS results in the decreasing of estimation accuracy for flows, the accuracy of the approximation for small flows used to calculate the sampling probability must be improved. This paper proposed an adaptive fair packet sampling algorithm (AFPS) to increase the estimation accuracy of fair sampling algorithm. The key innovation is the reconfigurable counter structure composed of two counter arrays, in which the size of counter arrays can be adjusted according to the changes of dynamic traffic characters on the network. Introducing of this novel counter structure can not only eliminate the hash collision to small flows but also improve the memory use ratio. AFPS can provide better overall accuracy than SGS.

3.1   The Architecture of AFPS

The adaptive fair packet sampling algorithm (AFPS) is mainly composed of three modular: flow counting, packet sampling and adaptive adjusting. The overall architecture of AFPS is shown in figure 1. Once each packet arrives, the AFPS scheme firstly tries to count the size of the flow which the currant packet belongs to by the reconfigurable counter structure. AFPS use the value in counters directly as the unbiased estimation of flow size which is the parameter to calculate the sampling probability. Secondly, the packet sampling modular samples the packet with the probability which is calculated by the decreasing sampling function f of the flow size the packet belongs to. If the packet is sampled, the flow record which the packet belongs to will be update. Finally, at the end of each sampling cycle (a predefined period of time), AFPS adjusts the size of two counter arrays according to the estimation of the maximal flow size during the sampling cycle. The overall architecture is similar to SGS besides the additional adaptive adjusting modular.

The sampling function used by AFPS is :

$$P(i) = 1/(1 + \varepsilon^2 i) \tag{1}$$

Where i is the value of flow size. AFPS simply uses the counter value in the reconfigurable counter structure as the approximation of the concurrent flow size so that AFPS can support full line speed processing. The small flow counter array eliminates the hash collision by counting packet one by one. So AFPS can estimate the small flows accurately. The adaptive adjustment of the counter arrays ensure a high efficiency usage of memory spaces resulting in the increasing of overall estimation accuracy.

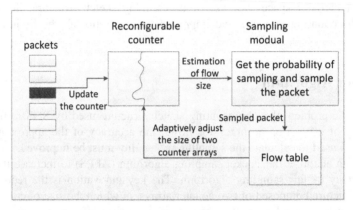

Fig. 1. The overall architecture of AFPS

3.2 The Sturcture of the Reconfigurable Counters

The most important part and the innovation of AFPS is the structure of the reconfigurable counter (RC) which can not only counts packet of small flows one by one but also ensure the high efficiency usage of memory spaces. The structure of RC is shown in figure 2.

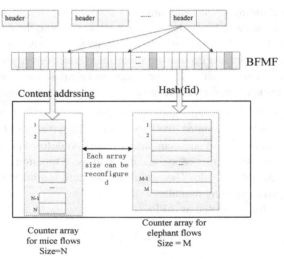

Fig. 2. The structure of RC

AFPS is composed of a Bloom Filter for small flows(BFMF), counter array for small flows C_m, counter array for elephant flows C_e and a reconfigurable parameter: the Threshold to judge Elephant Flow(TEF). The bit length of counters in C_m is smaller than in C_e while the number of counter in C_m is more than in C_e. C_m and C_e share the same memory space. The structure of RC is shown in figure 2.

Upon the arrival of a packet, one counter in RC will be updated. The updating process of RC is described in table1.

Table 1. The updating process of RC

The updating process of RC:
1. Initialize the BFMF, C_m, C_e and TEF;
2. Abstract the flow identification f_{id};
3. Search the BFMF by f_{id}, judge the bit $\phi(h_i(f_{id})), i = 1,...,k$;
4. If $\forall i, i = 1,....,k$ $\phi(h_i(f_{id})) = 1$, then:
5. The packet belongs to a small flow, and then get the counter address of the flow $Addr_m$ in C_m according to the f_{id} by content addressing;
6. If $C_m[Addr_m] < TEF$, then $C_m[Addr_m] = C_m[Addr_m]+1$;
7. Else a new elephant flow appears, then;
8. Get the counter address of the flow $Addr_e$ in C_e according to the f_{id} by $HASH(f_{id})$, update the counter in C_e, $C_e[HASH(f_{id})] \leftarrow C_e[HASH(f_{id})]+C_m[Addr_m]+1$, set the counter in $C_m[Addr_m] = 0$;
9. Remove the current flow record from TEF, Set the bit in TEF to 0;

Based on the above section, we know that the memory resource of AFPS is mainly used by the RC structure. Since the concurrent flow number on the link of back bone is about 0.5 millons or 1 millons[6], the size of each counter arrays in RC is no more than 10^6 bit. So the C_m and C_e can both be implemented on SRAM. Besides the maximal time spent to sample a packet equals $(2k+4)*T$, where k is the number of hash functions in BFMF, T is a memory access time. On the 10Gbps links (OC-192), AFPS can support the line-speed processing.

4   Evaluation and Discussion

4.1   Theoretical Analysis

AFPS aims to improve the accuracy of the estimation of small flows. Since AFPS allocates one counter to each small flow, the hash collision is avoided completely. AFPS can ensure the absolutely accurate flow size estimation for small flows. On the other hand, AFPS use the same counting sketch structure as SGS to count the packet of elephant flows. Thus the estimation error of large flows in AFPS is equal to SGS. Here we define average standard error as the mean of standard error of all flows in one sampling cycle. In table 2, we show the average standard error of AFPS and SGS in different TEF values. In our analysis, we suppose $\varepsilon = 0.1$.

Table 2. Average standard error of the two algorithms under different parameters

	TEF=100	TEF =600	TEF=1000	TEF=1500
AFPS	0.0856	0.0829	0.0734	0.0723
SGS	0.0958	0.0958	0.0958	0.0958

As can be seen from Table 2, the average standard error of AFPS is smaller than SGS. With the increasing of TEF, the average standard error of AFPS becomes smaller and smaller but the average standard error of SGS is a constant. So the sampling accuracy of AFPS is better than SGS.

The use ratio of the memory resources is another important index to measure the performance of sampling algorithms. As discussed in the above sections, the AFPS can keep a high use ratio of memory resources by adjusting the TEF. Here we analyze the use ratio of AFPS theoretically and compare the results to the assumption that the TEF cannot be changed. Figure 3 is the evaluation result where M is the maximal size of flow in the sampling cycles.

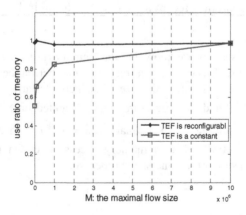

Fig. 3. The use ratio of memory in different schemes

4.2   Evaluation on Real Traffic Trace

The dataset used by the evaluation is from NLARN PMA's 2011[5], which is anonymized to protect the network users' privacy. The dataset file name is COS-1075142054-1.tsh.gz, and the detail information is shown in table 3.

Table 3. Detail information of the dataset

dataset	time	Flow numbers	Packet numbers	Speed of link	File name
NLARN PMA DATA-set	90s	162785	2268944	2.5Gbps	COS-1075142054-1.tsh.gz

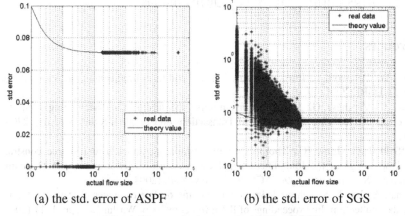

(a) the std. error of ASPF   (b) the std. error of SGS

Fig. 4. The standard error of   ASPF and SGS

As can be seen from Fig. 4, the standard error of small flow size estimated by ASPF is 0 and the one of large flows is very close to the theory value. The flow size estimation of ASPF is more accurate than that of SGS. ASPF is very useful for the network applications which need the traffic information of small flows. The proposed algorithm is an effective way to improve the sampling accuracy with the memory resources constrains.

5   Conclusions and Future Work

In the proposed algorithm, the problem of confliction between memory resources constrain and sampling accuracy is resolved by a novel adaptive fair sampling meth-od. ASPF introduces a reconfigurable counter structure to estimate the small flows and large flows in different way. The reconfiguration of the counter arrays ensures the use ratio of memory almost close to 1 under different network conditions. High use ratio of memory and different counting method for small flows and large flows result in the increasing accuracy of flow size estimation. AFPS is an absolutely effective fair packet sampling algorithm which can estimate small flows with 0 errors as well as do not increase the estimation error of large flows.

In the future, we will do deeper research on the direction of network measurement resource usage. We will study the influence on the measurement accuracy caused by other resource such as CPU or communication bandwidth. Then we want to explore a novel network measurement architecture which can allocate measurement resources between different measurement tasks so that the accuracy can be ensured and the resources can be utilized efficiently.

Acknowledgements. The research work was supported in part by a grant from the National Key Technology Support Program (No. 2012BAH02B01), the National Basic Research Program of China (973 Program)(No. 2012CB315902), the National Natural Science Foundation of China (No.61102074,61170215,61379120), Zhejiang Leading Team of Science and Technology Innovation(No. 2011R50010-03, 2011R50010-12, 2011R50010-19).

References

1. Fang, W., Peterson, L.: Inter-as: Traffic Patterns and their Implications. In: Proceedings of IEEE GLOBECOM (1999)
2. Estan, C., Varghese, G.: New directions in traffic measurement and accounting: focusing on the elephants, ignoring the mice. ACM Transactions on Computer Systems 21(63), 270–313 (2003)
3. Duffield, N.G., Lund, C., Thorup, M.: Flow sampling under hard resource constraints. In: Proceedings of the Joint International Conference on Measurement and Modeling of Computer Systems, pp. 85–96. ACM Press, New York (2004)
4. Kumar, A., Xu, J.: Sketch guided sampling—Using on-line estimates of flow size for adaptive data collection. In: Proceedings of IEEE Infocom 2006, Washington, pp. 1–11 (2006)
5. NLANR. PMA DATA. 2011[OL] (May 2013)
   http://labs.ripe.net/datarepository/data-sets/nlanr-pma-data
6. Tammaro, D., Valenti, S., Rossi, D., Pescap, A.: Exploiting packet-Sampling measurements for traffic characterization and classification. Int. J. Netw. Manag. 22(6), 451–476 (2012)
7. Masoud, M., Minlan, Y., Ramesh, G.: Resource/Accuracy tradeoffs in Software-defined measurement. In: HotSDN 2013, Hong Kong, China (August 16, 2013)
8. Minlan, Y., Jose, L., Rui, M.: Software Defined Traffic Measurement with OpenSketch. In: NSDI (2013)

An Evolving Architecture for Network Virtualization

Shicong Ma(✉), Baosheng Wang, Xiaozhe Zhang, and Tao Li

College of Computer, National University of Defense Technology,
Changsha 410073, Hunan Province, China
{msc91008,wangbaosheng}126.com, {nudtzhangxz,taoli.nudt}@gmail.com

Abstract. Network virtualization realizes new possibilities for the evolution way to future network by allowing multiple virtual networks over a shared physical infrastructure. In this paper, we discuss the shortcoming of current network virtualization and propose our approach, a framework that improves current infrastructure by extending link virtualization with a new component which we call Multi-Hop Virtual Link. At last, we present preliminary design of our proposal.

Keywords: Network Virtualization · Virtual Link · Router Virtualization Architecture

1 Introduction

In a past three decades, Internet has become critical infrastructure for supporting multitude distributed systems, applications, and a widely various networking technology. Just as many successful technologies, Internet has been suffering the adverse effects of inertia [1], and recent efforts show that it is hard to design a one-fit-all network architecture [19]. Network virtualization is considered to be an effective way to fend off this problem [2]. With network virtualization, multiple isolated virtual networks with potentially different routing algorithms, network protocols and data process can share the same physical infrastructure [3].

Network virtualization decouples network functionalities from those physical realization by separating the role of the traditional Internet Service Providers (ISPs) into two parts: infrastructure providers (InPs), who manage the physical network infrastructure, and virtual network operators (VNOs), who create virtual networks by aggregating resources form more than one InP and offer network services based on users needs[5].

In a network virtualization scenario, InPs should maintain a network environment supporting network virtualization which must allow the coexistence of multiple virtual networks with different architectures and protocols over a shared physical infrastructure. Thus, the deployment of network virtualization introduces new requirements in relation to what the architecture of network infrastructure and how virtual network are provisioned, managed and controlled under

© Institute for Computer Sciences, Social Informatics and Telecommunications Engineering 2014
V.C.M. Leung et al. (Eds.): TridentCom 2014, LNICST 137, pp. 379–386, 2014.
DOI: 10.1007/978-3-319-13326-3_36

the condition of virtualization. In conventional network virtualization architecture, the physical network infrastructure is divided into a plurality of slices that are assigned to different users to guarantee resource and support multiple virtual networks [19].

Unfortunately, current networking infrastructure cannot fully meet any of these goals, which causes significant ossification for network operators who want to provide network virtualization services for end-to end users or applications[9]. To fend off this inability, network research communities have made lots of meaningful works to design a framework of infrastructure which can satisfy the needs of network virtualization[4].

In this paper, we begin with revisiting the previous conception of network virtualization and discuss limitations and explain how current works would fall short of our goals. We then explore how we might improve current network virtualization architecture. Roughly, our idea is to be dubbed as two improvements for the existing work, including, i) extend current abstraction mechanism of a network with a more detailed link virtualization abstraction; ii) present a preliminary design of a network virtualization platform, describing how to leverage virtualization primitives in current general-propose hardware. Our modified approaches introduce a new modularity in network infrastructure which we think is necessary to achieve our goals.

We begin this paper at Section 2 by reviewing the basics of current network technologies. We then, in Section 3, introduce our proposal and preliminary design thought. We end with a discussion of the implications of this approach in section 4.

2   Background of Network Virtualization

As shown in Figure 1, previous researches have proposed conventional virtual network architecture running on the sharing infrastructure which must consist of two basic components, virtual node and virtual link [1]. In a networking environment that is capable of supporting network virtualization, each underlying node should be able to contain multiple virtual nodes and bearers more one virtual links[12]. By far, most use cases demand a one-to-one mapping between each virtual node of a virtual network and a physical node. On the other hand, a virtual link is corresponding with a physical path which may consist of more than two physical nodes.

In a common view, virtual node is often considered as virtual router, and data plane virtualization is the basic component of router virtualization[4]. Thus, earlier researches on node virtualization focus on isolation, reconfiguration and partitioning of underlying hardware resources, such as CPU, memory, IO bandwidth, through recent developments in para-virtualization (such as XEN) and operating system virtualization (e.g. OpenVZ). Link virtualization is another central component of network virtualization. Compared with node virtualization, link virtualization is used for forming a virtual network through interconnecting multiple virtual nodes according to the topology of the virtual network. From

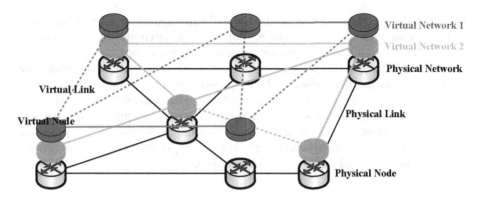

Fig. 1. Basic components of network virtualization

Figure 1, it is easy to see that link virtualization need realize a mapping virtual links between a physical link and guarantee link bandwidth of each virtual link. Particularly, Due to the difference between physical network topology and virtual network topology, there may be some virtual links that traverse more than two physical nodes (in this paper, we call it **multi-hop virtual link**. Due to the existing of multi-hop virtual links, each physical node in a virtual network must play one of two roles, one is one of the two nodes who terminate the virtual link, we call it **Link End Node**; the other is intermediate node which is traversed by the virtual link, we call it **Link Intermediate Node**. At the aspect of implementing link virtualization, some researches argue that time-division multiplexing (TDM) and wavelength division multiplexing (WDM) can be used for isolation and partitioning of link bandwidth and todays common network technology (e.g. MPLS, ATM) can be suitable for building a virtual link.

3   Network Virtualization Extending Design

3.1   Requirements Analysis

While previous works have permitted significant advances in terms of fairness and preference, we consider that there is still room for improvement through recent advances in other domains. In this section we will explore how our proposal in network virtualization framework might be extended to better meet the goals listed in the introduction. There are relevant improvements we consider here:

First, previous studies do not pay enough attention for multi-hop virtual links. Packet processing of multi-hop links on Link Intermediate Node only requires switch hardware to lookups over a small table consisted of multi-hop virtual link tags. Therefore, it unnecessarily couples the whole requirements on Link End Node to packet processing on Link Intermediate Node.

Second, while node virtualization based on operating system virtualization has permitted significant advances in terms of fairness and isolation, but this may introduce additional overhead, especially in support of forwarding plane virtualization with IO-bound feature. Moreover, the environment of forwarding plane virtualization does not require so strict isolation as operating system virtualization. We argue that it is necessary to implement a lightweight forwarding plane virtualization hypervisor without operating system virtualization.

Thus, our proposal is to extend network virtualization architecture in a way that improves some aspects yet still retains current benefits. Then, we will present a preliminary design and prototype implementation of our proposal, describing how to leverage existing virtualization primitives in todays general hardware to achieve ideal network virtualization.

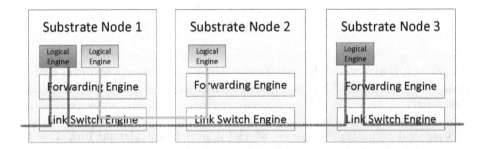

Fig. 2. Proposed Physical Node Model

3.2 Architecture Overview

In this section we explore how the Network Virtualization architectural framework might be extended to better meet the goals listed in the introduction. Our proposal involves two changes for physical nodes in network virtualization environment, which is based on our discussions last section.

Figure 2 shows an example of the proposed architecture. Compared to existing network virtualization, we introduce a new component in physical node supporting network virtualization, which we call Link Switch Engine. Link Switch Engine carries out a simple and fast packet switch process like MPLS, when the physical node acts as a Link Intermediate Node. In this way, we separate packet process of Link End Node and Link Intermediate Node into two separate processes and guarantee individual packet processing ability for multi-hop virtual links. A seemingly natural choice to implement multi-hop virtual link would to refer to simplified hardware, such as OpenFlow or MPLS. For the implementation of Link End Node, there are many solutions based on general-purpose server ,programmable hardware[17], such as FPGA[11][14][16] and additional accelerator, e.g.GPU[15]. Other researchers use IO optimization mechanism[7]

In order to achieve reconfiguration, flexibility and isolation, Link End Nodes should host instances of logical engines which carry out customized forwarding processing of packets that flow through them and require isolation among logical instances. Recent promising technologies proposed by Intel show that software data plane using general-purpose high-preference processors may be a replacement of traditional hardware-based data plane, since it is able to support rates of 10 Gbps[9]. By these results, forwarding hardware could get more improvements in terms of reconfiguration and flexibility. As for isolation, direct mapping each logical instance on an individual core could avoid additional overhead introduced by operating system virtualization [10], which we plan to advance packet processing in Link End Node in future.

3.3 Multi-hop Virtual Link Service Model

Under our modified model, packet processing on a multi-hop virtual link can be represented as a process of packet switch rather than packet forwarding, since it does not need intelligence, just a relatively dumb, but very simple, fast fabric, which we call Link Switch Engine.Even if someone believes that in-network processing will introduce more and more complexity and underlying infrastructure needs to become more flexible, it does not mean that packet processing in a Link Intermediate Node of a multi-hop virtual link and it only need a minimal set of switch primitives without internal forwarding processing. The design of the additional component in network device for Link Switch Engine is a reasonably good analogy for a network virtualization architecture that includes multi-hop virtual links. In a network virtualization environment with multi-hop virtual links, Link End Node will implement network policies and finish encapsulating and decapsulating virtual link tags.

The complexity in the environment lies in mapping the Link End Nodes and Link Intermediate Nodes to physical nodes according requirement of the virtual network for network resources and topology. By the processing of mapping, we embed a virtual network into a given network. There are also four primary mechanisms for this:

Identifying a Multi-hop Virtual Link. As we have described above, packet processing in a Link Intermediate Node differs from in a Link End Node, which is not required to use source or destination addresses for switching. Thus, one option would be to use the identification of the virtual network, since a virtual network only has a multi-hop virtual link instance in a physical node.

Lookup Tables. A Link Intermediate Node will maintain a small table consisted of all multi-hop virtual links through it, and Link Switch Engine delivers a packet to its output interface based on this table. Our proposal is designed around MPLS so we adopt a simple and generalized table structure which can be built around a pipeline of hardware.

Packet Processing in Link Switch Engine. In our proposed architecture, every packet will be identified by virtual network ID. Received packet is firstly checked by Link Switch, judging whether the packet should be processed by it. If not, then, the packet will be delivered to packet forwarding engine. If yes, Link Switch Engine looks up its forwarding table ,make switch decision for the received packet and deliver it to corresponding outport.

Switch Ability Isolation. In a network virtualization environment, isolation of processing resource is a key question for resources guarantee for each virtual network[13]. Therefore, in our proposal, a multi-hop virtual link may be implemented as a tunnel which traverses multi-hop physical nodes. Thus, if a physical node bearer more than one virtual link, Link Switch Engine would be required for strong isolation of switch ability offered to different virtual links.

Beside what we listed above, there are also many practical challenges in implementing such a mechanism we will not cover in this paper. These include control architecture of multi-hop virtual links, the detailed definition of the virtual link tag, and the virtual link tags distributing protocol .etc. We aim to address these challenges in our next phase.

3.4   Feasibility Analysis

There are a multitude of approaches which would be suitable for implementing proposed design presented in the previous section. In what follows, we describe our implementation which we would build as a prototype. While we have proposed the design thought of our implement. Then, we present some of practical issues we have considered in our system.

Multi-hop Virtual Link Switch Engine. In our design, we plan to use a changed MPLS to provide fast switching for multi-hop virtual links, and try to realize it on NetMagic[8], a programmable platform deployed for network innovation. NetMagic can offer multiple simultaneous hardware resources for each multi-hop virtual link and easily reconstructed.

Isolation among Multiple Virtual Links. In order to provide switch ability isolation for multiple virtual links on Link Switch Engine, we prefer to allocate separate hardware to each virtual link, which can facilitate strong isolation among multiple virtual links. For a further work, we are ready to propose a simple but effective scheduling algorithm to enhance isolation among multiple virtual links.

4   Discussion

The approach proposed in this article is conceptually quite simple: rather than requiring forwarding planes to support Link End Node and Link Intermediate Node at the same time, our proposal depends on mapping each of them on an individual element. By separating packet processing element into Packet Forwarding Engine and Link Switch Engine, there will be significant benefits for network infrastructure designed for supporting network virtualization as follow:

Two Free-Running Packet Processing. Independent Link Switch Engines may relieve contradiction between requirements for flexible functions and high preference by mapping the two targets on a flexible packet processing engine and a simple but fast Link Switch Engine. Link Switch Engine only requires the minimal set of packet switch and is suitable for a hardware-based appliance. And flexible packet processing engine could be realized by general-purpose multi-core processors. Based on optimizations on packet I/O and buffers, preference of software packet processing may catch or even exceed hardware-based appliance. Thus, network devices designed based on our proposal will be easy to build, operate and accommodate future innovation.

More Flexible Virtual Network Mapping Model. In traditional network virtualization architecture, the packet processing capacity of a physical node is always described by packet forwarding ability, and in this mapping model, a multi-hop virtual require all Link Intermediate Nodes on its corresponding physical path with forwarding capacity which is equal to its two Link End Nodes. However, in our proposal, by introducing description of Multi-hop Virtual Link and Link Switch Engines, we can get a more flexible virtual network mapping model. Separation of packet processing changes the ability description of physical node into Link Switch capacity and Packet Forwarding capacity. By this approach, our proposal can provide more choices for virtual network mapping.

5   Conclusion

In this paper, we discuss the shortcoming of current network virtualization architecture and give a more detailed description for network virtualization by describing multi-hop virtual link ,a virtual link pass through more than two physical routers. Based on what our description, we propose out extended network virtualization architecture and represent a preliminary design. In order to support multi-hop virtual links, we introduce a new packet component called "Link Switch Engine" used to bear packet switch in a Link Intermediate Node of a multi-hop virtual link. At last, we give our realization idea of our proposal. Although we have discussed a lot of things of our proposal, we clearly know that it is more complex than we consider to give a complete description and realization idea. This approach merits further investigation, as we have only begun to scratch the surface of this idea.

Acknowledgments. Our work is supported by Program for National Basic Research Program of China(973 Program) "TestBed of Flexible Architecture of Reconfigurable Infrastructure", Specialized Research Fund for the Doctoral Program of Higher Education of China(20114307110006)"Research on Technology of Network Quality of Service based on Network Virtualization", and Research on Trustworthy Cross-Domian Information Exchanging Technology Based M-TCM KJ-12-07.

References

1. Carapinha, J., Jimnez, J.: Network virtualization: a view from the bottom. In: Proceedings of the 1st ACM Workshop on Virtualized Infrastructure Systems and Architectures. ACM (2009)
2. Chowdhury, N.M., Boutaba, R.: A survey of network virtualization. Computer Networks 54(5), 862–876 (2010)
3. Anderson, T., et al.: Overcoming the Internet impasse through virtualization. Computer 38(4), 34–41 (2005)
4. Casado, M., Koponen, T., Ramanathan, R., et al.: Virtualizing the network forwarding plane. In: Proceedings of the Workshop on Programmable Routers for Extensible Services of Tomorrow. ACM, p. 8 (2010)
5. Schaffrath, G., Werle, C., Papadimitriou, P., et al.: Network virtualization architecture: proposal and initial prototype. In: Proceedings of the 1st ACM Workshop on Virtualized Infrastructure Systems and Architectures, pp. 63–72. ACM (2009)
6. http://www.edac.org/downloads/resources/profitability/HandelJonesReport.pdf
7. http://www.dpdk.org
8. www.netmagic.org
9. Costa, P., Migliavacca, M., Pietzuch, P., et al.: NaaS: Network-as-a-Service in the Cloud. In: Proceedings of the 2nd USENIX Conference on Hot Topics in Management of Internet. Cloud, and Enterprise Networks and Services, Hot-ICE, vol. 12, p. 1 (2012)
10. Egi, N., Iannaccone, G., Manesh, M., et al.: Improved parallelism and scheduling in multi-core software routers. The Journal of Supercomputing 63(1), 294–322 (2013)
11. Unnikrishnan, D., Vadlamani, R., Liao, Y., et al.: Scalable network virtualization using FPGAs. In: Proceedings of the 18th Annual ACM/SIGDA International Symposium on Field Programmable Gate Arrays, pp. 219–228. ACM (2010)
12. Bhatia, S., Motiwala, M., Muhlbauer, W., et al.: Hosting virtual networks on commodity hardware. Georgia Tech. University., Tech. Rep. GT-CS-07-10 (2008)
13. Wu, Q., Shanbhag, S., Wolf, T.: Fair multithreading on packet processors for scalable network virtualization. In: ACM/IEEE Symposium on Architectures for Networking and Communications Systems (ANCS), pp. 1–11. IEEE (2010)
14. Anwer, M.B., Motiwala, M., Tariq, M., et al.: Switchblade: a platform for rapid deployment of network protocols on programmable hardware. ACM SIGCOMM Computer Communication Review 41(4), 183–194 (2011)
15. Han, S., Jang, K., Park, K.S., et al.: PacketShader: a GPU-accelerated software router. ACM SIGCOMM Computer Communication Review 41(4), 195–206 (2011)
16. Xie, G., He, P., Guan, H., et al.: PEARL: a programmable virtual router platform. IEEE Communications Magazine 49(7), 71–77 (2011)
17. Shimonishi, H., Ishii, S.: Virtualized network infrastructure using OpenFlow. In: 2010 IEEE/IFIP Network Operations and Management Symposium Workshops (NOMS Wksps), pp. 74–79. IEEE (2010)
18. Martins, J., Ahmed, M., Raiciu, C., et al.: Enabling fast, dynamic network processing with clicko. In: Proceedings of the Second ACM SIGCOMM Workshop on Hot Topics in Software Defined Networking. ACM, pp. 67–72 (2013)
19. Turner, J.S., Taylor, D.E.: Diversifying the internet. In: Global Telecommunications Conference, GLOBECOM 2005, vol. 2(6), p. 760. IEEE (2005)

Prologue: Unified Polymorphic Routing Towards Flexible Architecture of Reconfigurable Infrastructure

Kai Pan, Hui Li$^{(\boxtimes)}$, Weiyang Liu, Zhipu Zhu, Fuxing Chen, and Bing Zhu

Shenzhen Engineering Lab of Converged Networks Technology,
Shenzhen Key Lab of Cloud Computing Technology & Application,
Peking University Shenzhen Graduate School, Shenzhen 518055, China
{pankai,wyliu,alexzzp,chenfuxing}@pku.edu.cn,
lih64@pkusz.edu.cn, zhubing@sz.pku.edu.cn

Abstract. Today's Internet architecture was designed and proposed in the 60s and 70s with the intention to interconnect several computing resources across a geographically distributed user group. With the advent of substantially various Internet businesses, traditional Internet is increasingly powerless to satisfy the unprecedented demands. This paper probed the polymorphic routing prototype based on proposed Flexible Architecture of Reconfigurable Infrastructure (FARI) which attempts to emerge as a clean-slate revolution of future Internet and resorts to centralized control manner. Routers in FARI were reconfigurable to adapt to different businesses in terms of identifier type. Moreover, a preliminary framework of FARI is proposed in the end of the article.

Keywords: Polymorphic routing · Prototype · Reconfigurable · Clean-slate

1 Introduction

The over 40-year-old Internet has become an incomparable important component of our daily life in contemporary society and is now facing many unprecedented challenges especially from the market demand. Though its enduring success continues today, the contradiction between single function of Internet and diverse internet business increases day by day. More and more study, work and entertainment rely on the networks which makes the idea of smart terminals and stupid networks unsuitable for the development of Internet. As a result, two opinions represented by clean-slate revolution and incremental evolution have been proposed by the research community to build the future Internet. The former opinion deems that novel network architecture should be built to satisfy the brand-new demands [1], while the latter considers improvement and integration as a better manner for the large scale of current Internet [2].

Actually, Internet experts have been exploring the improvement of Internet including IPv6, firewall, mobile IP, IPsec and so on. Therefore, great development has put on the stage and presented in front of us. However, patchwork is not a thoroughly solution to the defect of Internet, which may even complicate the networks and result in more difficult problems. For example, network address translation

© Institute for Computer Sciences, Social Informatics and Telecommunications Engineering 2014
V.C.M. Leung et al. (Eds.): TridentCom 2014, LNICST 137, pp. 387–394, 2014.
DOI: 10.1007/978-3-319-13326-3_37

(NAT) is introduced to solve the exhaustion of IPv4 address and network security separation, which makes many end-to-end applications disabled and brings in another program called Cross-NAT. Hence, a consciousness to lots of Internet experts is that completely different network architecture must be proposed as quickly as possible.

Future Internet Design (FIND) [3], as a major new long-term initiative research, was announced by National Science Foundation (NSF) several years ago. It was executed by affiliated Computer and Information Science and Engineering (CISE) administrative committee. FIND solicits research across the broad area of network architecture, principles and mechanism design, and helps conceive the future by momentarily letting go of the present - freeing our collective minds from the constraints of the current state of networking. Besides FIND, Future Internet Research and Experimentation (FIRE) [4] from European Union and AKARI [5] from Japan are also clean-slate revolution as FIND.

In this paper, we are going to probe the polymorphic routing prototype in Flexible Architecture of Reconfigurable Infrastructure (FARI) proposed by us as a clean-slate revolution. The rest of the paper is organized as follow. Some useful definitions with proposed FARI are introduced in Section 2. The polymorphic addressing method of FARI is discussed in Section 3. The working mode is given in Section 4. Finally a conclusion together with future work is presented in Section 5.

2   Flexible Architecture of Reconfigurable Infrastructure

The design of novel architecture for future Internet should not only keep open, simple and robust features as traditional one, but also follow some new principles such as interaction, variety and selectiveness. It is interaction rather than a simple expansion of current Internet or extension of telecommunication network. As more and more businesses and demands appear in the Internet, variety and selectiveness are essential to choose the proper service type according to users' demands. In our proposed FARI, the concept of reconfiguration will cover all the features above. As it known to all, demands are multiple and changing, while network service is relatively finite and stable. Thus, the significant discrepancy between them became a bottleneck which has restricted the current network to be a better one. FARI which adopts centralized control can provide flexible, universal, customizable and variant network service.

We introduce definitions that will be useful throughout the paper.

Definition 1 (Atomic Capability, AC): It is the minimum function abstraction of basic transmission capability such as forwarding, fragment, safety etc.

The atomic capability is composed of two parts, the basic and expanded. It is notable that AC cannot be used alone and it only makes sense once combined together according to certain rule. This leads to the following definition.

Definition 2 (Atomic Service, AS): The atomic service consists of several kinds of atomic capabilities according to certain rule and is identified by upper businesses for understanding atomic capability.

In order to realize reconfiguration, polymorphic addressing methods, derived from the ground state addressing method, are essential to adapt to different businesses.

Definition 3 (*Basic Addressing Method, BAM*): It is an AC set of current addressing methods including location, content and the possible future addressing methods.

The BAM is an all-inclusive set which can meanwhile adjust the addressing method corresponding to specific business. It is more like a full described framework or abstraction before specializing to certain addressing method.

Definition 4 (*Polymorphic Addressing Method, PAM*): Polymorphic addressing method is derived from BAM and has different header formats which are used to business distinction during data transmission.

Actually, the mapping between BAM and PAM is a relationship of framework and example, while AC and AS stands for realization and demand.

The BAM in FARI supports four kinds of addressing methods for now which bases on location, identity, service and content as shown in Fig. 1. The specified PAM has a unified format including identifier type prefix and identifier value, and replaces the traditional IP addressing.

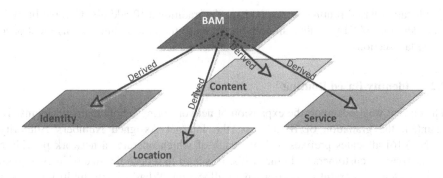

Fig. 1. Four kinds of addressing methods are supported by FARI for now

Definition 5 (*Polymorphic Routing, PR*): The path calculation and updated procedure according to PAM and specific demand is called polymorphic routing.

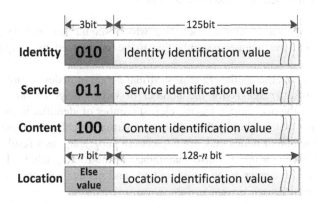

Fig. 2. The source and destination address for PR

In order to achieve PR, a unified Internet protocol we call it Polymorphic Internet Protocol (PIP) is needed to compatible with traditional IP networks. The PIP is based on IPv6 and uses a variant of IPv6 header. Depended on the identifier type prefix in the packet header, the type of addressing method can be ascertained right away. In the 128-bit source and destination address, 3 bits are allocated to the type prefix and the rest bits are used for identifier value such as structural characters for further information as shown in Fig. 2.

3   Polymorphic Routing Methods in FARI

In this section, we are going to discuss the four kinds of PRs mentioned above.

3.1   Location Based Routing

The location based routing corresponds to the traditional IP address. Compatibility is considered in FARI to realize smooth transition to the new architecture as mentioned in the last section.

3.2   Identity Based Routing

The current way to support the expansion of network brings about many problems. To maintain the gradation of IP address, the Internet Assigned Numbers Authority (IANA) [6] allocates prefixes to ISPs, each of which operates a network providing connectivity to customers and other ISPs. It is hard to reduce the size of inter-domain routing table by careful consideration in allocation. What's more, multi-home host and mobility are also difficult problems in current network.

Fortunately, problems mentioned above can be well solved by identity based routing [7]. In the solution, a unique identifier is allocated to each node which can be used to direct routing instead of requiring gradation or address information [8]. A more concrete instruction is described as follow:

(1) Each node has a unique identifier which should not include geographical information, and the uniqueness only has to be guaranteed by assigned numbers authority.

(2) Each node maintains the $r/2$ closest virtual neighbor nodes according to its own value of identifier. r stands for the number of virtual neighbor nodes and virtual neighbor means the node which has the closest number of identifier in the network.

(3) A routing table including the next hop of virtual neighbor is maintained in each node. Virtual neighbor nodes may not adjacent in geography, as a result the next hop of the virtual neighbor node is also maintained in the routing table. Moreover, each node may have the chance to be a middle node and maintain routing information for the other nodes.

3.3   Service Based Routing

Service means the solution of some demand proposed by individual or group. It needs some price to achieve and sometimes with certain restrictions. Moreover, service can be regarded as a logical cell which has the following properties:

(1) Functionality: service has a specify function.

(2) Combination: service can be combined with each other what means different services can be requested at the same time.

(3) Descriptiveness: the function of service can be defined clearly.

(4) Visibility: services are visible to the requesters.

Due to the limited function of single service, demands may be difficult to be satisfied with. As a result, service combination is an important technical approach in the future service oriented network. Service combination refers to combine the services which are independently developed to obtain stronger new service. Service combination is also an important thought in the service oriented architecture (SOA) [9]. Network can provide customized service by defining and constraining the interaction between different services. For example, if a packet header is constructed through service combination, any running node in the network can add control module to the header according to the demand of specific network function. Actually, similar idea as service combination is adopted in Just-In-Time protocol by communicating with Silos instead of TCP/IP [10].

3.4   Content Based Routing

As an important branch of PR, content based routing is also a major research topic in Content Centric Network (CCN) [11].

There are three kinds of information tables in CCN's router: forwarding information base (FIB), content store (CS) and pending interest table (PIT). FIB stores the next port of getting to the CS. CS preserves the buffer content and PIT records the Interest packet that hasn't been responded and the face it arrived on in order to send a Data packet back (a face in CCN is corresponding to a port in router).

The procedure of forwarding model in CCN is as following:

When a node receives an Interest packet, if there is already a Data packet in the CS that matches, it will be sent out the face the Interest arrived on and the Interest will be discarded. Otherwise, if the Interest is not in the PIT, it will be added in and then forwarded according to the FIB.

Content based routing mainly cares about two problems:

(1) How to represent infinite name space with finite state routing.

(2) Multi-path forwarding strategy.

As the widely used routing protocol in the Internet, Open Shortest Path First (OSPF) [12] has high-quality open-source implementations. However, OSPF only finds out one shortest path in the network which may not suitable for content centric network. As a result, multi-path forwarding is needed to choose the suboptimal path when necessary.

4   Working Mode for Polymorphic Routing

Due to centralized control of FARI, A three-plane model including manage plane, control plane and data plane, which interacts with each other for common goal, is used to describe the functional structure of polymorphic routing.

The manage plane is realized by intra-domain server and is responsible for perceiving and maintaining the network. It allocates the PR identifier and differentiates the type of communication subject. Moreover, as the management center of the structure, it is also in charge of the realization of PR and provides basis to the control level for business cognition.

The control plane sustains responsibility of establishing PR path, collecting and monitoring routing resources which is realized in the routers. On one hand, it provides guidance of transmission path for data through current routing table entry updated in terms of network state information. On the other hand, it judges from the communication subject result provided by the manage plane and identifier type by executing PIP to achieve PR scheme. Actually, the control plane exists as an executer in the structure.

Data plane, the lowest plane in the structure, plays a simple but important part in the routing realization. It is mainly responsible for data forwarding. When data is transmitted in the network, the data plane will respond respectively base on different identifier.

There are four kinds of routing tables corresponding to four PRs maintained by each router. After a host joined in a network, it immediately informed its node property and identifier type to the intra-domain server on manage plane, and then a unique identifier was allocated to it by some manager instantiated by the server.

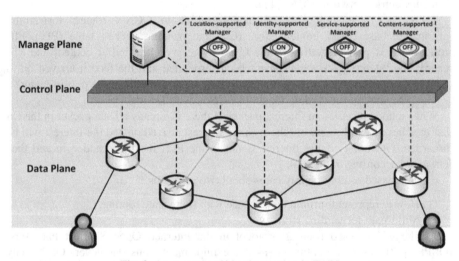

Fig. 3. An example of identity routing in FARI

Here is an example shown in Fig. 3 of identity routing in FARI. Assuming a host (on the left side) wants to communicate with another host (on the right side), it first connects to the nearest router and sends a packet with identity identifier to it. Due to unconsciousness of the next hop, the router will hand the packet to identity-supported manager (which is labeled ON in Fig. 3). Then the identity-supported manager will help calculate the shortest path to the destination according to specific business (identity based in this example) by providing the basis of updating the routing table to the control plane. Once routing table is finished updating communication can be carried on along the path (as shown by yellow in Fig. 3).

Actually, different managers can be instantiated to support diverse business simultaneously with FARI. The working mode mentioned above only happens in one domain. It is more complicated when communication takes place between different domains and it will be the future work.

5   Conclusion and Future Work

In this paper, we probed the polymorphic routing based on proposed FARI which attempts to emerge as a clean-slate revolution of future Internet and resort to centralized control manner. Once instantiating different managers, it is convenient for network to choose a proper routing manner in terms of specific demand. Depending on the identifier type prefix in the packet header, routers can ascertain the next hop by looking up corresponding routing table. The routing tables in each router are updated based on the current network state information provided by the control plane.

However, it is a preliminary framework of FARI and communication only in the same domain is considered in the paper. There is still a huge development space for FARI. In the future, we will continue to research the polymorphic routing method and take inter-domain communication into consideration. Moreover, emulation system of FARI will be built up to test the novel architecture.

Acknowledgment. This work is supported in part by the National Basic Research Program of China (973 Program) under Grant 2012CB315904, the National Natural Science Foundation of China under Grant NSFC61179028, the Natural Science Foundation of Guangdong Province under Grant NSFGD S2013020012822, the Basic Research of Shenzhen under Grant SZ JCYJ20130331144502026.

References

1. Feldmann, A.: Internet Clean-Slate Design: What and Why? ACM SIGCOMM Comp. Comm. Review **37**(3), 59–64 (2007)
2. Rexford, J., Dovrolis, C.: Future Internet Architecture: Clean-Slate versus Evolutionary Research. Comm. of the ACM **53**(9), 36–40 (2010)
3. NSF NeTS FIND Initiative. http://www.nets-find.net
4. European Future Internet Portal. http://www.future-internet.eu/activities/fp7-projects

5. AKARI Architecture Design Project for New Generation Network. http://akari-project.nict.go.jp
6. Internet Assigned Numbers Authority (IANA) Home Page. http://www.iana.org
7. Caesar, M.C.: Identity Based Routing. Ph.D Thesis, University of California, Berkeley (September 2007)
8. Caesar, M.C., Condie, T., Kannan, J.: ROFL: Routing on Flat Labels. In: ACM SIGCOMM (September 2006)
9. Papazoglou, M.P., Georgakopoulos, D.: Introduction to a special issue on Service-Oriented Computing. Communications of the ACM **46**, 24–28 (2003)
10. Wei, J.Y., McFarland, R.I.: 'Just-in-time signaling for WDM optical burst switching networks. Journal of Lightwave Technology **18**, 2019–2037 (2000)
11. Content Centric Networking. http://www.parc.com/work/focus-area/content-centric-networking
12. Moy, J.: OSPF version 2. RFC 2328 (April 1998)

A Network Controller Supported
Open Reconfigurable Technology

Siyun Yan[✉], Chuanhuang Li, Ming Gao, Weiming Wang,
Ligang Dong, and Bin Zhuge

Zhejiang Gongshang Universit, Hangzhou, 310018, China
1161864548@qq.com, chuanhuang_li@mail.zjgsu.edu.cn,
{gaoming,wmwang,zhugebin}@zjsu.edu.cn,
donglg@zjgsu.edu.cn

Abstract. In open reconfigurable architecture, the network devices realize the separation of the control plane and data plane. This paper study the control center of entire open reconfigurable network device: control element. It provides independent exclusive platform for control plane resources, which can enhance its scalability, control ability and efficiency significantly. The hierarchical structure of reconfigurable network and architecture of control element software are discussed. Then, core components of control element, which include protocol middleware and the development of user operating management system are introduced in details. Experiments of middleware software are illustrated for running routing protocols, network management, interface test etc. The experiment results show the feasibility of the control element design.

Keywords: Control element · Open reconfigurable technology

1   Introduction

In open reconfigurable network, a NE (e.g., a router/switch) is systematically separated into a control plane and a forwarding plane, disperse the control and forwarding / switching functions into different processors in the physical network devices. With the expansion of the network, data plane can reach a large capacity through a multistage (whether Clos or Benes cascade), as control plane have independent exclusive platform , it is possible to enhance its expansion significantly, control ability and efficiency by independent upgrade, to solve the capacity contention issues for control plane and data plane in a single network device.

In term of the Network Service Provider, the central control unit can assemble those contained units in data plane which is departed in physical space, loosely-coupled into a logical entirety which can provide IP network service to the customers. At the same time, it can avoid various IP network service from scrambling the IP infrastructure resources as they are all coordinated by the central control unit.

Xbind [1] has studied a set a set of the distributed software components which is used to create, deployment and management of multimedia services on the ATM

© Institute for Computer Sciences, Social Informatics and Telecommunications Engineering 2014
V.C.M. Leung et al. (Eds.): TridentCom 2014, LNICST 137, pp. 395–405, 2014.
DOI: 10.1007/978-3-319-13326-3_38

network early. Click software router project [2] [3]in MIT provides a modular and scalable network device structure. W.Louati [4] used the / proc file system in Linux as a communication mode between kernel and user to achieve dynamic configuration function in Click. I.Houidi[5] used the CORBA component model to realize Click. There are two open source programmable networking platform: Open Contrail[6], Open Daylight[7].ForTER[8] ,analyze and implement an open programmable router based on forwarding and control elements separation. Section 2 described the architecture of open reconfigurable network and CE . Section 3 presented the implementation details of key elements in CE. Section 4 introduced some experiments and tests result

2   Architecture

2.1   Hierarchical Structure of Reconfigurable Network

In reconfigurable network, management node and open reconfigurable router are important parts of it, its specific structure is showed in Figure 1, which has developed a set of software architecture specification for open reconfigurable router. Management node can be divided into the business layer and the service layer , open reconfigurable router can be divided into logical functional layer and the service layer . According to ForCES structure, open reconfigurable router can also be divided into a control element (referred to as CE) and forwarding element (referred to as FE). Service layer is consist of the service access unit, service management unit and other modules. Service access unit is mainly to complete the communication between the open reconfigurable router and management nodes, and service management unit is primarily responsible for the management of services, deployment of services (on the managed node) or configuration (on the open reconfigurable router) of LFC .The logical functional layer of open reconfigurable router mainly to complete the main resource management of LFC and support services can be reconstructed.

2.2   Software Architecture of the Control Element

In the CE software architecture which is based on ForCES middleware, the core is ForCES middleware and various third-party software. According to achieve different specific application services (such as: path discovery service, user management services, etc.),R & D personnel select the corresponding third-party software and design different application software abstract adaptation (eg: routing information management adaptation, user management adaptation)for each third-party software , the operating of application services via abstract adaptation unified transformation into standardized operating which is provided by reconfigurable component model. And multiple applications can use same abstract adaptation, such as OSPF, RIP, network management and other applications services can use interface management adaptation in the meantime. Figure 2 is the schematic of control element software architecture based on ForCES middleware.

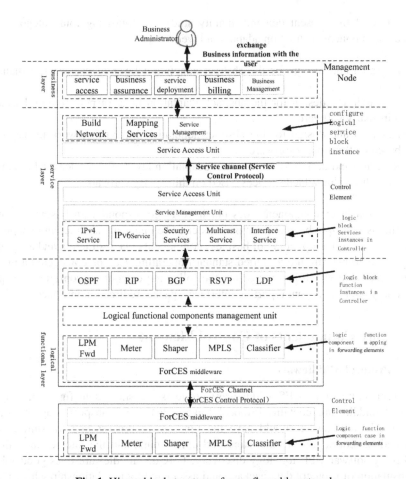

Fig. 1. Hierarchical structure of reconfigurable network

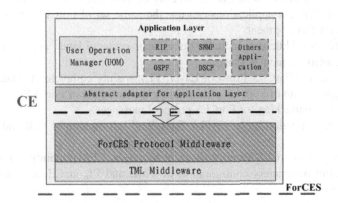

Fig. 2. Software architecture of reconfigurable control element based on ForCES middleware

In view of the present demand, mainly study the following four categories for business component abstraction adaptation layer :

❖   Research and design for the abstract adaptation layer of user central management.
❖   Research and design for the abstract adaptation layer of path finding based on third-party software
❖   Research and design for the abstract adaptation layer of network management based on third-party software
❖   Research and design for the abstract adaptation layer of   service quality control and other value-added services based on third-party software

Adaptation layer component does not have to correspond with business component, that is: multiple business components can use one same abstract and adaptation layer component, the operating of business components via abstraction and adaptation components transform into a unified standard operating. Can be considered a unified abstract interface which is divided into the following categories: configure the interface, query interface, event reporting interfaces, packet redirection interface.

3   Core Components of Control Element

3.1   Protocol Middleware

The architecture of ForCES middleware products are showed in figure 3, ForCES protocol middleware contains Protocol Layer (PL) and Transport Mapping Layer (TML). All middleware should have the function of process and transmit control information, redirection of data, store and access data, and the interaction with the third-party software, FE topology discovery. ForCES middleware does good job on encapsulation of protocol data package and associated logic relationship which ForCES protocol need to complete, and lay a good foundation for the development of all types of network device which based on ForCES protocol. ForCES structure network products for different applications can use the same set of ForCES middleware, can avoid iterative development.

The ForCES middleware includes three parts: protocol layer, application function layer and control element manager.

Protocol layer (ForCES Protocol Layer, PL): mainly complete the functions such as building the chain of ForCES , maintaining the link state of ForCES, the operations of packing and unpacking for ForCES protocol messages.

Application Function Layer (,AFL): Saving all information of LFB and attribution in FE.

CE managers (ForCES Control Element Manager, CEM): mainly to complete the related startup parameters configuration of TML and PL in CE, such as: all FEID controlled by CE.

Concrete block diagram of ForCES architecture which based on middleware is showed in Figure 2

3.2   Develop User Operating Management System in Control Element

User operating management system (UOM) is an important part of supporting open reconfigurable generic network equipment control element , which is essentially a special third-party software application. Its main purpose is to provide users with a common graphical operating management, so as to bring convenience for the user in the management of open reconfigurable device.

The main functions of UOM

1) Verification for login of user, and supports the three levels management authority of user.
2) Use tree as resource overview map in the network device which allow users to deployment management property of nodes in a tree .
3) Topology management is not only convenient for the user to view the distribution of resources in the FE, but also supports online reconstructed network resources , and thus meet the rapid escalation of network resources and deployment needs.
4) Supports view, add , delete routing table, and deployment management RIP, OSPF and other routing protocols.
5) Filter provide deployment management of security policies and security associations for the application layer.
6) Open third-party software management interface, support integration of routing software (Zebra, Xorp etc.) and SNMP network management software.

3.2.1   Internal Structure of UOM

As shown in Figure 3, UOM adopt B / S mode, the overall is divided into server and client : the former relying on Tomcat , the latter is runned by downloading in the IE browser , can be flexibly deployed on Linux and Window platforms . In UOM, the data layer reflect on the underlying layer of ForCES middleware , UOM is divided into four layers , graphical user interface (GUI) layer, message management layer, and background processing layer and plug-in layer, each function is as follows:

1. Graphical user interface (GUI) layer , provides a graphical user operating interface .
2. Message management layer , in the B / S mode, the message communication layer between client and server, now encrypt http object flow data interaction form is used to guarantee the security of the system.
3. Background processing layer, according to message information, control the movements of background data , and its business operating.
4. Plug-in layer , set up a bridge between the UOM and ForCES middleware, to achieve seamless between the two.

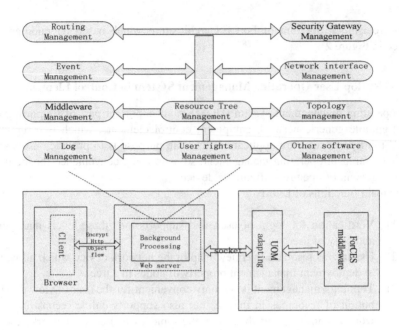

Fig. 3. Internal structure of UOM

3.2.2   UOM Interface Design

UOM main interface include eight major areas ,in particular: 1.the main menu area ; 2.tree operating area ; 3 .node property configuration and topology display area ; 4.tab page; 5.event notification area ; 6.the operating results prompt area ; 7 .login display ; 8.the progress bar. UOM main interface is shown in Figure 4.

➢   Main menu area

In the main menu area users can complete all operating except for the tree operating. Specifically includes : System Login / Logout , deployment management of PL and TML , subscribe / cancel / view for LFC events , LFC topology management , third-party software management (support routing software (Zebra and Xorp) and multiple SNMP agent) , the routing table management, network interfaces management, security gateway management, log management , user privilege management.

➢   Node property configuration and topology display area

When the user double-click a node on the tree operating area, it will show attribute information of node in detail in this area , then you can modify attribute according to the actual situation and click "Apply" button to take effect. In addition, this area also displays LFC topology .Shown in Figure 5.

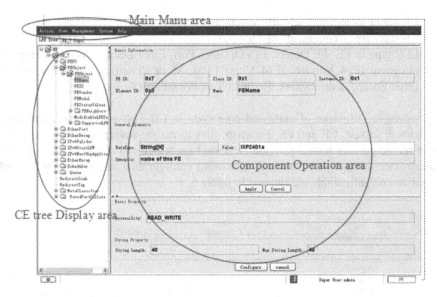

Fig. 4. Software interface of user management platform

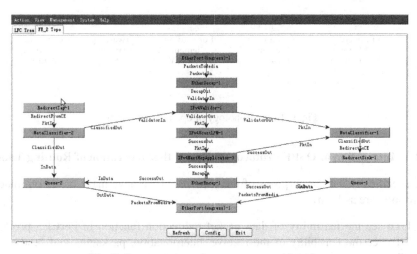

Fig. 5. Component topology management interface

4   Experiment

4.1   Test Environment

Support the open reconfigurable control element software apply to open reconfigurable router system, open reconfigurable router connected directly by a single control element (CE) and more than one forwarding elements (FE) through the switch, while running middleware software in CE and FE .its test environment as follows:

> CE hardware environment: PC machine;
> CE software environment: Red hat 9.0
> LFC type in FE: FE Object, FEPO, Ether Port, Ether Decap,IPv4 Next Hop Application, IPv4 Validor, IPv4 Ucast LPM, Meta Classifier, Scheduler, Queue, Ether Encap, Redirect Sink, Redirect Tap, Forwd Port Collate;

Executable filename of compiled core code in CE : ce; executable filename of FE named: fe_test, CE and FE use script files to realize startup. Control element of open reconfigurable routers provide web services, which can access open reconfigurable router through web terminal. Hardware configuration of open reconfigurable router and reconfigurable are showed in figure 6.

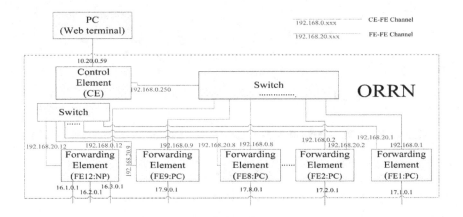

Fig. 6. Router topology of open reconfigurable

4.2   Interaction of OSPF Protocol Stack and the Generation of Routing Table

We specifically list the purposes of the experiment we have made based on middleware software as follows:

(1)To see the feasibility of data packet redirection function in ForCES protocol,
(2)To see the feasibility of the receive, interpretation, packaging and sending for redirect message

Its test ID is 1.4, and the test configuration description is showed in figure 7.

Test process(operation / signal flow):

(1)Connect a port (FE12 here in Port 2)of open reconfigurable router with the port 2 (SMB1-2)of SmartBits network tester's LAN-3321A module gigabit mouth;
(2)According to the testing requirements configure corresponding IP address for test equipment, use Tera Routing Tester test simulated network topology (IP address starts with 200 for each IP network segment), start SmartBits internal OSPF protocol;

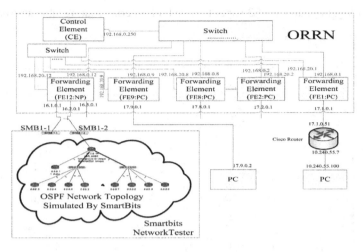

Fig. 7. Description of the test configuration

(3) Run OSPF on a port of FE12 (IP address: 16.2.0.1)in CE, starts OSPF protocol in the CE;

(4)Wait for internal interaction of Smartbits network with open reconfigurable
routers through by OSPF ;

(5)Based on web terminal interface in 2.2 section, click on View / Routing table to
open the route lookup dialog box to view the dynamic routing tables generated by the
CE;

(6)Log in a FE HyperTerminal, enter "route-n" command to view if the dynamic
routing being added correctly.

1) View the dynamic routing table which generated by CE on routing query dialog
   box:

From the results, after the interaction, CE has been properly learned Smartbits dynamic routing table.

2) After logging into the FE3 super terminal, FE3 kernel routing table shows:

```
[root@f3 root]# route -n
Kernel IP routing table
Destination     Gateway         Genmask         Flags Metric Ref    Use Iface
200.0.12.0      192.168.20.12   255.255.255.0   UG    0      0        0 eth1
200.0.13.0      192.168.20.12   255.255.255.0   UG    0      0        0 eth1
200.0.14.0      192.168.20.12   255.255.255.0   UG    0      0        0 eth1
200.0.15.0      192.168.20.12   255.255.255.0   UG    0      0        0 eth1
192.168.20.0    0.0.0.0         255.255.255.0   U     0      0        0 eth1
200.0.8.0       192.168.20.12   255.255.255.0   UG    0      0        0 eth1
200.0.9.0       192.168.20.12   255.255.255.0   UG    0      0        0 eth1
200.0.10.0      192.168.20.12   255.255.255.0   UG    0      0        0 eth1
192.168.0.0     0.0.0.0         255.255.255.0   U     0      0        0 eth2
200.0.11.0      192.168.20.12   255.255.255.0   UG    0      0        0 eth1
200.0.4.0       192.168.20.12   255.255.255.0   UG    0      0        0 eth1
200.0.5.0       192.168.20.12   255.255.255.0   UG    0      0        0 eth1
200.0.6.0       192.168.20.12   255.255.255.0   UG    0      0        0 eth1
200.0.7.0       192.168.20.12   255.255.255.0   UG    0      0        0 eth1
200.0.16.0      192.168.20.12   255.255.255.0   UG    0      0        0 eth1
200.0.1.0       192.168.20.12   255.255.255.0   UG    0      0        0 eth1
200.0.17.0      192.168.20.12   255.255.255.0   UG    0      0        0 eth1
200.0.2.0       192.168.20.12   255.255.255.0   UG    0      0        0 eth1
200.0.18.0      192.168.20.12   255.255.255.0   UG    0      0        0 eth1
200.0.3.0       192.168.20.12   255.255.255.0   UG    0      0        0 eth1
```

From the chart, CE in open reconfigurable router learned new routing table through OSPF, and issued to the FE3, realize dynamic update of routing tables.

Results 1 and 2 shows data packet redirection between CE and FE correctly, containing receiving, interpretation, packaging and sending of reception message.

4.3   Support Management Functions for Open Reconfigurable Control Element Software and Interface Test

To see the feasibility of providing all the trees in FE and all interface to query information of LFC. Its test id is 2.1, and test configuration description is OSPF test configuration diagram remove configuration in the dashed box in the lower left.

Testing process (operation / signal flow): view the Web terminal in LFC Tree Domain . Test results:

1) Report LFC ability and display information: figure 4 show user management platform software interface

Tree structure shows the LFC in FE and details of each LFC.

(2)Topology information of LFC in FE: figure 5 component topology management interface

This topology shows the connection relationship between FE7 of each LFC.

From the above results, support ForCES protocol connection negotiation process which is realized by open reconfigurable network generic equipment control element software , and in the link stage, the connection messages are received ,interpreted, sending and package correctly.

5   Conclusion

In this paper, we introduced the hierarchical structure of reconfigurable network and architecture of control element software. Then, core components of control element, which include   protocols middleware and the development of user operating management system are introduced in details.

Experiments of middleware software are illustrated for running routing protocols, network management, interface test etc. More importantly, the experiments have, as a result, actually illustrated the feasibility of control element.

Generic network devices which support open reconfigurable in this paper has been used in the development of open reconfigurable routing products, established two application demonstration in Shanghai Broadband Technology Center and the IETF ForCES working group during the project period, and the system has been deployed and tested in the application demonstration.

Acknowledgement. This work was supported in part by a grant from the National Basic Research Program of China (973 Program) (No. 2012CB315902), the National Natural Science Foundation of China (No.61102074, 61170215, 61379120), Zhejiang Leading Team of Science and Technology Innovation (No. 2011R50010-03, 2011R50010-12, 2011R50010-19).

References

1. The Xbind Research Project. http://comet.columbia.edu/xbind/
2. The Click Modular Router Project. http://www.pdos.lcs.mit.edu/click/
3. Kohler, E., et al.: The click modular router. In: ACM Transactions on Computer Systems, **18** (3) 2000
4. Louati, W., Jouaber, B., Zeghlache, D.: Configurable Software-based Edge Router Architecture. In: 4th IEEE Workshop on Applications and Services in Wireless Networks, 2004. (Also appear in Elsevier Computer Communications, Vol.28(14) (2005)
5. Houidi, I., Louati, W., Zeghlache, D.: An extensible software router data-path for dynamic low-level service deployment. IEEE Workshop on High Performance Switching and Routing 2006, Poland, pp. 161–166 (June 2006)
6. Open Contrail. http://opencontrail.org/
7. Open Daylight. http://www.opendaylight.org/
8. Wei-Ming, W., Li-Gang, D., Bin, Z.: Analysis and Implementation of an Open Programmable Router Based on Forwarding and Control Elements Separation, journal of computer science and technology, **23**(5) (2008)

AdaFlow: Adaptive Control to Improve Availability of OpenFlow Forwarding for Burst Quantity of Flows

Boyang Zhou[1], Wen Gao[1], Chunming Wu[1(✉)], Bin Wang[1],
Ming Jiang[2], and Yansong Wang[3]

[1] College of Computer Science, Zhejiang University, Hangzhou 310027, China
{zby,gavingao,wuchunming,bin_wang}zju.edu.cn
[2] Hangzhou Dianzi University, Hangzhou 310018, China
jmzju@163.com
[3] ZTE Corporation, Nanjing 210012, China
wang.yansong@zte.com.cn

Abstract. The Software-Defined Networking (SDN) separates the control plane from the data plane to increase the flexibility. In the data plane, the unavailability of data forwarding is a common problem preventing a switch from configuring a new arrival flow into its flow table. When the burst flows arrived at the switch, the flow table can be consumed, causing the unavailability occurred. However, the problem is more complicated than in Internet due to the limited channel bandwidth for detecting the table usage. Hence, we propose a transparent core layer in the controller. The mechanism of the layer improves the availability in such way, configuring switches adapting to arrival patterns of flows to prevent the resource of switch exceeding its limit. This paper introduces the design and mechanisms of the layer as well as their algorithms. We further use a real flow trace from a Internet core router to evaluate the performance of layer. By emulating on on miniNet-HiFi, the results demonstrate that the layer can smooth the burst flows without making the flow table exceeding its size, without the layer, the switch lost 8% ingress flows. Meanwhile, the control throughput is lowered by 25.8% than before.

Keywords: Software-Defined Networks · Network management

1 Introduction

The Software-Defined Networking (SDN) separates the data plane from the control plane to improve the control flexibility [1,2]. The control plane is consisted of multiple controllers. In the data plane, each controller configures its switches via the control channel that supports the OpenFlow (OF) protocol [1]. Each switch has a flow table to define the forwarding rules. By matching against the rules, the ingress flows are forwarded by a switch to output ports of the switch.

Generally, a flow is mismatched due to either new flow arrivals or expiration of the rule. At that time, the switch first queries its controller to retrieve the new rules for the flow and then programs the rules into the flow table. Such process

© Institute for Computer Sciences, Social Informatics and Telecommunications Engineering 2014
V.C.M. Leung et al. (Eds.): TridentCom 2014, LNICST 137, pp. 406–415, 2014.
DOI: 10.1007/978-3-319-13326-3_39

generates the control traffic in the channel between controller and switch. However, such process has a problem: new ingress flows can be lost by the switch if the flow table is full or the control channel is congested, thus negatively impacting on the availability of switch forwarding for the ingress flows.

When applying SDN to the wide-area networks (WANs), the problem is more challenging than the current applications of SDNs, since the flows are large-scale, burst, transient and intermittent. These features impact the flow table and the channel on their performance along with variation of new flow arrivals. Hence, by exploiting these resources, the performance of data forwarding can be further exploited, yielding a new adaptive control policy to optimize switch's flows.

Realizing such policy is complicated by the separated architecture in SDNs. It is because the policy should be made based on the statistics of switch resources, however, the channel only has the limited bandwidth. The current work on SDN architecture have not improved the availability.

In this paper, we propose a novel transparent core layer (named as the AdaFlow layer) to adaptively control the active count of flow table entries according to the flow arrival patterns, so as to improve the forwarding availability. The mechanism of the layer is consisted of three workflows: (i) The optimization workflow predicts the expiration of an new flow entry according to a estimated flow throughput, smoothing the active count for the burst flows; (ii) The resource workflow predicts the active count by history; and (iii) The estimation workflow estimate the throughput of a flow according to the flow arrival pattern. The workflows (ii) and (iii) provides the estimation inputs to the workflow (i).

We evaluate the performance of the layer by using miniNet-HiFi. The results demonstrate that the layer can smooth a burst quantity of ingress flows without making the switch exceeding the size of flow table. In comparison, without the layer, the switch lost 8% ingress flows. In addition, the control throughput is lowered by 25.8% than before.

The rest of the paper is organized as follows. Section 2 analyzes and states the problem in depth. Section 3 proposes the design and mechanism of AdaFlow layer. Section 4 evaluate the performance of the layer. Section 5 and 6 discuss the related work and conclude the paper.

2   Problem Statement

In this section, we first give the system model of the SDN control on switch and then formulize the problem of availability of switch as a time series problem.

2.1   System Analysis

In SDN, a controller, denoted as c, configures the forwarding table of the i-th switch, denoted as s_i, via the i-th channel, denoted as h_i. All the switches of c are denoted as $S_c = \{s_1, s_2, ..., s_i, ..., s_m\}$, where m is the number of the switches. Fig. 1 gives such an example which shows a common scenario for the OF forwarding. The controller c and its OF switches s_a, s_b and s_i. The bandwidth of h_i

competes with other switches belonging to the controller within a limited physical bandwidth. In the switch s_i, the flow table is consisted of multiple flow table

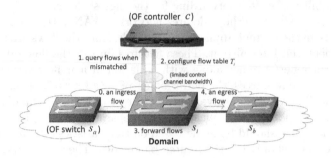

Fig. 1. OpenFlow forwarding example

entries, and each entry is consisted of forwarding rules, actions, hard timeout of flow and idle timeout of flow. The switch executes the actions by matching headers of ingress packets of a flow with the corresponding rules. Formally, we denote the flow table of i-th switch as $T_i = \{f_1, f_2, ..., f_j, ..., f_Q\}$, where f_j is the j-th table entry and Q is the number of the active table entries (thus termed as the active count). The physical size of the table is denoted as L_i. In addition, the idle timeout of the j-th flow entry for the i-th switch is denoted as $k_{i,j}$. It is note that the hard timeout will not be considered in our work as settings of values of the timeouts are different from service to service.

Wherein, the flow table of each switch is initially set to be null. When an ingress flow from s_a is mismatched at s_i, s_i queries new configuration to c via the channel h_i, and then forwards the flow to its output port, e.g., s_b. When the hard timeout of the entry is exceeded or no packet is arrived within the idle timeout, the entry is expired from the table.

For each switch in S_c, the total throughput of the control channel, denoted as λ_{all}, equals to the sum of two types of control traffics for all the switches, namely, configuring the flow tables, and making controllers connections. The latter one is a constant for the number of switches. Formally, the total throughput is specified as Eq. 1, where $C(L)$ is a constant value of L, α_i^t is the hit ratio of the flow table at the time tick t and $\tilde{\theta}_i^t$ is the expiration rate of the flow table of the i-th switch at t. We denote the upper limit of channel bandwidth as Z.

$$\lambda_{all} = \sum_{s_i \in S_c} (1 - E(\tilde{\theta}_i^t \times (1 - \alpha_i^t)) + C(L) \tag{1}$$

Based on the model, we denote the availability ratio of s_i at the time tick t as β_i^t. β_i^t is the probability that the configurations of the flow table entries of s_i, when its ingress flows are arrived in the recent unit time, can be correctly programmed into s_i.

2.2   Problem Statement

The problem is to find the configurations of idle timeouts for all the table flow entries of a switch to minimize the control throughput of the switch restricted by the lower limit of the availability of the switch, given by a continuous time series of ingress flow headers of the switch. We formulize such problem as below.

For a switch s_i at t, we denote the time series of ingress flow arrivals as $G_t = (g_0, g_1, g_2, g_2, g_3, ..., g_b, ..., g_t)$, where b is the time tick of arriving of an ingress flow ranging from 0 to t and g_b is a valuable identifies the arrival flow by uniquely hashing the header of the flow. The controller c controls the s_i, and c defines the lower limit of the availability ratio of switch as β_i for all the time ticks. The idle timeouts of T_i are $K = \{k_{i,1}, k_{i,2}, ..., k_{i,Q_t}\}$, where N_t is the size of flow table at t. The problem is specified as Eq. 2, where $\tilde{v}$ is estimated value of v, and H^t is estimated throughputs of part flows in G_t held in the controller.

$$\underset{K \in N^{Q_t}}{\text{argmin}} \, (\tilde{S_c}^{t+1}) \text{ , subject to:}$$
$$\tilde{\beta}_i^{t+1} \geq \beta_i \text{ and } \lambda_{all}^{t+1} \leq Z \qquad (2)$$
$$\text{Given by } G_t \text{ and } H = \{\tilde{\lambda}^t(g_b) : g_b \in F_t \text{ and } 0 \leq t \leq t\}$$

Such minimization problem is challenging as it requires the controller to predict β and λ_{all} with the limited knowledge of H^t. In next, we discuss an heuristic solution.

3   Design and Mechanism of Adaptive Flow Control

In this section, we propose an adaptive control mechanism to address problem of the availability of switch forwarding when there is a burst quantity of ingress flows arrived at the switch. We also introduce its algorithms.

3.1   Overall Design

In general, the proposed adaptive control mechanism ensures the availability of data plane by predicting the flow arrival patterns and by efficiently measuring the resource usage of the flow table. The mechanism is implemented as a transparent AdaFlow layer in Beacon controller [2]. The layer locates between the network services and the OpenFlow protocol stack. The layer optimizes the service performance by changing the idle timeout in the FLOW_MOD message to make it subject to Eq. 2 and then performing the configuration by sending the message to the switch via the OF stack.

Fig. 2 shows the internal design of the layer. It has three concurrent workflows. The optimization workflow decides the idle timeouts of new arrival flows by receiving the two inputs: (i) the flow table usage that is produced by the resource workflow, and (ii) the input of estimated throughput of the ingress flows that is produced by the estimation workflow.

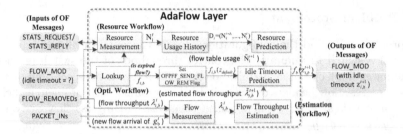

Fig. 2. Internal Design of the AdaFlow Layer

Wherein, the estimation workflow is the simplest. It predicts the throughput of the flow by averaging on all the thoughputs sent by the FLOW_REMOVED messages [3]. The workflow outputs $\lambda_{i,b}^{t+1}$ to the prediction workflow.

We detail the rest of two workflows as follows.

3.2   Optimization Workflow

The optimization workflow decides the optimal value of idle timeout for flow configurations sent from the service. In the workflow, only are the flows with the duration time of larger than γ considered, because that most of survival times of flows live for a very short term even in a core router of a WAN, e.g. 2 seconds (see Subsection 4.1). In next, we give the algorithm of the workflow in the Alg. 1. It has the three steps as following.

First, the lookup step first receives FLOW_MOD message, denoted as f_b. Then, the lookup step lookups f_b to decide it is an expired flow. If not, the idle timeout is set to be a default value, in our prototype, 2 seconds (see lines 5-8 in the Alg. 1). Otherwise, the workflow decides the optimal value for the idle timeout in the next last step.

Second, when received the FLOW_MOD message, the set flag step tag OFPFF_SEND_FLOW_REM to the message to measure its throughput (see the line 10 in the Alg. 1).

Last, the idle timeout prediction step first decides an optimal idle timeout for the flow, denoted as $f_b(Z^{i,b})$, and then send $f_b(Z^{i,b})$ to the OF stack. When the flow table reaches to full with the probability of the availability ratio of switch β_i, the step sets the idle timeout to 1 to ensure the availability (see the line 12 in the Alg. 1). Otherwise, the step uses Eq. 3 to compute the timeout with the availability ratio. The mathematical deduction of Eq. 3 is given by Th. 1.

Such workflow provides an adaptive approach to provide a heuristic solution to the problem that is presented in Eq. 2.

Theorem 1 (Idle Timeout). *Given a flow entry f_b, the estimated throughput of the flow $\lambda_{i,b}^{t+1}$, and a timeout probability $1 - \beta$, the idle timeout should be set to Eq. 3, considering the ingress flow is in a Poisson distribution.*

$$k_{i,b}^{t+1} = 1 + \frac{1}{1 - \beta_i} + \frac{1}{\lambda_{i,b}^{t+1}} \tag{3}$$

Algorithm 1. Optimization Workflow

Require:
  FLOW_MOD message: f_b
  Flow throughput estimation: $\lambda_{i,b}^{t+1}$
  Active count estimation: $\tilde{N}_i^{t+1}$
  Availability ratio of switch: β_i
Ensure: f_b with idle timeout: $f_b(k_{i,b}^{t+1})$
  1: $FLOWS = \{\}$
  2: **repeat**
  3:    wait for receiving a FLOW_MOD message f_b
  4:    **if** $f_b \in FLOWS$ **then**
  5:       $FLOWS = FLOWS \cap \{f_b\}$
  6:       $k_{i,b}^{t+1} = \gamma$
  7:       send $f_b(k_{i,b}^{t+1})$ to s_i via the OF stack
  8:       continue
  9:    **end if**
  10:   tag OFPFF_SEND_FLOW_REM to f_b
  11:   **if** $\tilde{N}_i^{t+1} > L_i$ **then**
  12:      $k_{i,b}^{t+1} = 1$
  13:   **else**
  14:      $k_{i,b}^{t+1} = 1 + 1/(1 - \beta_i) + 1/\lambda_{i,b}^{t+1}$
  15:   **end if**
  16:   send $f_b(k_{i,b}^{t+1})$ to s_i via the OF stack
  17: **until** true

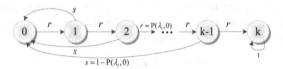

Fig. 3. Transition for timer state of idle timeout

Proof. The state of the timeout value can be modelled by using the Markov chain as follows. Fig. 3 depicts behaviors of the state transition of the timer, where k is the idle timeout, $r = P(\lambda_i, 0)$ is an event when no packet of the flow arrives in a unit time tick, and $s = 1 - P(\lambda_i, 0)$ is the opposite event of r. Each circle represents a state and each arrow is a transition between the states. The state $0 \leq w \leq k - 1$ reaches to $w + 1 \leq k$ with r, and the state k only can reach to itself. We denoted such transition as a matrix M, where $M(w, v)$ is the probability of transiting from the state w to v. In addition, we denoted a vector, $x = [x_0, x_1, .., x_k]$, as the probabilities at each state, where x_q is the probability of timer at q-th state.

$$\tilde{x} = \frac{r^k}{r^k \times k - r^k + 1} \times [1, \frac{1}{r}, \frac{1}{r^2} - \frac{1}{r} + 1, \frac{1}{r^3} - \frac{1}{r^2} + 1, ..., \frac{1}{r^k} - \frac{1}{r^{k-1}} + 1] \quad (4)$$

$$1 - \beta = P_\theta(f_i, t) = \frac{r^k}{r^k \times k - r^k + 1} \times (\frac{1}{r^k} - \frac{1}{r^{k-1}} + 1) \tag{5}$$

The stationary states of M is when $xM = x$, denoted as $\tilde{x}$. By solving the linear equations, $\tilde{x}$ is computed as Eq. 4. Thus, the probability of state at the timeout is denoted as $1 - \beta = P_\theta(f_i, t)$ as Eq. 5. Last, we solve k in Eq. 5 by differentiating on k to get Eq. 3. Proof is done.

3.3   Resource Workflow

The resource workflow predicts the active count of flow table entries, named as the active count, by periodically querying the switch. It has the three steps as following (see the three white rectangles in the top of Fig. 2). First, it measures the active count of flow table entries of the i-th switch at the time tick t, denoted as N_i^t. Then, it saves N_i^t into the memory of controller to form the time series history, denoted as $D = (N_i^{t-\delta}, N_i^{t-\delta+1}, ..., N_i^t)$. The layer only maintains the δ size of the history. Last, it predicts $\tilde{N}_i^{t+1}$ based on the history.

   In detail, the algorithm of the prediction is given in the Alg. 2 as below. The algorithm gives the upper limit of active count in the next tick given by the availability ratio of switch β_i. In the lines 4-12, the controller c measures the performance statistics of all the OF switch in S_c for the recent δ seconds in a periodical mode. The statistics cover on all the statistics fields defined the OF specification 1.0 [3], e.g., the active count of flow table entries. In addition, we add two extra statistics, namely, the count of flows removed and the rate of flow modifications (see lines 6-7 in Alg. 2). Based on those statistics, the workflow predicts the active count by Eq. 6 (see lines 13-16 in Alg. 2). In line 13, we use the fast Poisson algorithm to compute the confidence value range for the β_i.

   The algorithm output of $\tilde{N}_i^{t+1}$ is utilized by the prediction workflow to compute the optimal idle timeout of the flow (see Subsection 3.1).

$$\tilde{N}_i^{t+1} = \tilde{\lambda}_i^{t+1} + N_i^{t+1} - \theta_i^{t+1} \tag{6}$$

The correctness of the algorithm holds since Eq. 6 exploits the Markov property of state of the active count of flow table entries. Because the state of N_i^{t+1} only depends on the state of N_i^t. Thus, the state can be predicted by its state in the current time tick and patterns of ingress flows, as Eq. 7 shows, where E is the variable expectation, $\tilde{\theta}_i^t$ is the expiration rate of the flow table of the i-th switch at t. Eq. 7 indicates that variation states of N_i^t depends on ingress flows. Hence, Alg. 6 is correct.

$$E(N_i^{t+1}) - E(N_i^t) \approx E(\tilde{\lambda}_i^t) \times (1 - \alpha_i^t) - E(\tilde{\theta}_i^t) \tag{7}$$

4   Evaluation

4.1   Performance Preliminaries

The AdaFlow layer is implemented on the Beacon controller 1.0.3 [2] with support of OF 1.0.3 protocol [3]. The layer registers the listeners for all the OF

Algorithm 2. Resource Workflow

Require:
    OF messages: STATS_REQUEST, FLOW_MOD and FLOW_REMOVED
    The availability of switch: β_i
Ensure: Flow table usage: $\tilde{N}_i^{t+1}$
  1: $D_{1 \leq i \leq |S_c|} = ()$
  2: **repeat**
  3:    wait for a new second t
  4:    **for** $s_i \in S_c$ **do**
  5:      $features = send(s_i, \text{STATS\_REQUEST})$
  6:      $features.add(\# \text{ of modFlows for } s_i)$
  7:      $features.add(\text{rate of flowRemoved for } s_i$
  8:      **if** $|D_i| > \delta$ **then**
  9:        $D_i.dequeue()$
10:      **end if**
11:      $D_i.enqueue(features)$
12:    **end for**
13:    $\tilde{\lambda}_i^{t+1} = PoissonPdf(mean(D_i.modFlows), \beta_i)$
14:    $N_i^{t+1} = mean(D_i.activeCount)$
15:    $\theta_j^{t+1} = mean(D_i.flowRemoved)$
16:    $\tilde{N}_i^{t+1} = \tilde{\lambda}_i^{t+1} + N_i^{t+1} - \theta_i^{t+1}$
17: **until** true

---

messages required. We test the performance of AdaFlow layer by using the routing service provided by the Beacon itself.

We setup a basic topology as the Fig. 1 shows, to simplify the problem. We emulate the topology by using the miniNet-HiFi [4]. It provides the traffic shaping for links and the cgroup based isolation of resources. We limit the bandwidth of all the links to 1000Mbps. In detail, s_a is emulated as a packet generator by using the TcpReplay tool. The traffic is generated at maximum speed of link. s_b is emulated as a flow receiver that is replaced by the tcpdump tool. And s_i is an OpenvSwitch [5] with supporting of the OF 1.0.3 protocol [3]. We limit the table size of s_i to 25000 in the controller which is slightly larger than the average rate of new flow arrival rate, so that we can emulating the burst events of the flows.

Wherein, the generator replays a real packet trace of a core Internet router amount of 544040 flows[1]. We replay the trace in the speed of 99 seconds, since OS is hard to emulate the trace in its real speed. We count the cumulative distribution function (CDF) of the living time of all the flows in the trace. In the trace, we find the 79.55% of flows only live for less than 2s. Thus, in the Alg. 1, γ is set to 2 seconds. In the Alg. 2, δ is set to 60 seconds. In addition, the availability ratio β_i is set to 0.95 (see Subsection 2.2).

---

[1] The trace file can be downloaded from the following URL:
http://data.caida.org/datasets/passive-2013/equinix-chicago/20130529-130000.
UTC/equinix-chicago.dirA.20130529-130100.UTC.anon.pcap

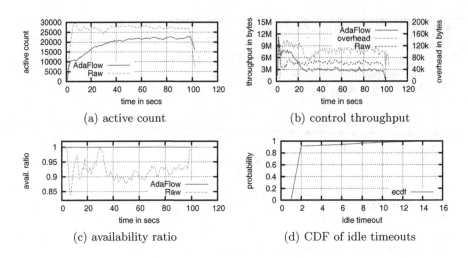

Fig. 4. Performance of AdaFlow Layer

4.2   Performance Results

The availability ratio of switch forwarding for s_i is denoted as β_i (see Subsection 2.2). In practical, $\beta_i^t = \#$ of mod flows$/\tilde{\lambda}_i^t$. In the following, we compare performance of the AdaFlow version of the Beacon controller with its raw implementation version by using the same trace previously discussed.

The evaluation results are given in Fig. 4. Fig. 4(a) shows the active count of flow table for the AdaFlow version is decreased by 26.4% than the raw on the average. The means of the active counts for them are 19073 and 25917 (see Fig. 4(a)). In addition, in Fig. 4(b), the control throughput of the AdaFlow version is decreased by 25.8% than the raw on the average. The means of the throughputs for both of them are 3.504MBps and 4.724MBps. For the AdaFlow, the FLOW_REMOVED messages only consume throughput of 100.582KBps. When a burst amount of flows arrived, the availability of switch forwarding can be much improved by such a sharply decreasing. Fig. 4(c) shows the availability ratio of the AdaFlow version is increased by 8% comparing to the raw. The means of the ratios for them are 1 and 0.9261. Fig. 4(d) shows the CDF of the idle timeouts for the AdaFlow version.

5   Related Work

The recent work on the efficiency of control protocol in SDN focus on strengthening the controller architectures in these three ways: (i) The architecture enables the features of multi-threading, multi-core and I/O batching when the controller processes OF messages [6,7], e.g. OpenDayLight [8], Beacon [2] and Maestro [9].

(ii) The architecture clusters several controllers in the same domain to load balance the arrival of OF messages from the switches, e.g. OpenDayLight uses the shared pool to distribute the messages among the controllers [8].

And (iii) The architecture moves part of controller functions to the switch side to improve the performance of switch, e.g. DevoFlow [10] and NOSIX [11].

Hence, none of these researches considers optimizing the OpenFlow protocol itself by controlling the flows according their arrival patterns. In addition, our approach improves performance of these architecture and does not conflict with these ways. Our work is innovative in dealing with the patterns.

6 Conclusion

We propose a novel adaptive control mechanism for SDN by exploiting the arrival patterns of flows and detecting the active count of flow table. The mechanism can smooth a burst quantity of ingress flows to ensure their availability being processed by the switch, meanwhile, lowering the control throughput. We demonstrate these benefits by using a real flow trace from an Internet core router. Our solution provides an easy way to improve performance of SDN services.

Acknowledgments. This work is supported by the National Basic Research Program of China (973 Program) (2012CB315903), the Key Science and Technology Innovation Team Project of Zhejiang Province (2011R50010-05) and the National Natural Science Foundation of China (61379118 and 61103200). This work is sponsored by the Research Fund of ZTE Corporation.

References

1. McKeown, N., Anderson, T., Balakrishnan, H., et al.: Openflow: enabling innovation in campus networks. In: ACM SIGCOMM (2008)
2. Erickson, D.: The beacon openflow controller. In: ACM SIGCOMM Workshop on HotSDN (2013)
3. Openflow switch specification, version 1.0.0, Open Networking Foundation (2009)
4. Handigol, N., Heller, B., Jeyakumar, V., et al.: Reproducible network experiments using container-based emulation. In: ACM International Conference on Emerging Networking Experiments and Technologies (2012)
5. Pfaff, B., Pettit, J., Amidon, K., et al.: Extending networking into the virtualization layer. In: Hotnets (2009)
6. Tootoonchian, A., Gorbunov, S., Ganjali, Y., et al.: On controller performance in software-defined networks. In: USENIX Hot-ICE (2012)
7. Yeganeh, S.H., Tootoonchian, A., Ganjali, Y.: On scalability of software-defined networking. IEEE Communications Magazine **51**(2), 136–141 (2013)
8. Ortiz Jr., S.: Software-defined networking: On the verge of a breakthrough? IEEE Computer **46**(7), 10–12 (2013)
9. Ng, E.: Maestro: A system for scalable openflow control, Technical Report of Rice University (2011)
10. Curtis, A.R., Mogul, J.C., Tourrilhes, J., et al.: Devoflow: scaling flow management for high-performance networks. In: ACM SIGCOMM (2011)
11. Yu, M., Wundsam, A., Raju, M.: Nosix: A lightweight portability layer for the sdn operating system. ACM Computer Communication Review (2014)

Optimization-Based Atomic Capability Routing Model for Flexible Architecture of Reconfigurable Infrastructure

Weiyang Liu[✉], Hui Li, Fuxing Chen, and Kai Pan

Shenzhen Engineering Lab of Converged Networks Technology,
Shenzhen Key Lab of Cloud Computing Technology & Application,
Peking University Shenzhen Graduate School, Shenzhen 518055, China
{wyliu,chenfuxing,pankai}@pku.edu.cn, lih64@pkusz.edu.cn

Abstract. There are more and more emerging problems in today's Internet, indicating today's Internet architecture can not meet the quality requirement of various applications and service. With conventional Internet under mounting pressure, a new future Internet architecture named as Flexible Architecture of Reconfigurable Infrastructure (FARI) has been developed and implemented in China. Aiming at designing a routing mechanism which is one of the most essential issue in any Internet architecture, this paper explores to establish an optimization-based atomic capability routing model that is able to optimally select or generate a routing protocol based on the current network quality of service (QoS) requirement. In experiments, the feasibility of this routing model is verified and results of complexity analysis are satisfying.

Keywords: Combinatorial Optimization · FARI · Atomic Capability · Routing Protocol

1 Introduction

The transmission capacity becomes increasingly crucial under the rapid development of today's Internet. Specifically, the transmission capability usually does not match the certain service requirement, which leads to terrible user experience. Moreover, the IP/TCP based Internet can not give sufficient support to mobility, security, quality of service (QoS), network convergence etc, indicating that conventional Internet is no longer suitable for our various service nowadays.

Dedicated to solving the existing various problems and improving QoS, Flexible Architecture of Reconfigurable Infrastructure (FARI) has benn proposed by the 973 program [1,2]. To be simple, FARI is no longer a static Internet architecture but a dynamic self-adaptive one. The novelty of this brand new Internet architecture lies in its reconfigurable and extensible transmission ability that can automatically match the service requirement. That is to say, there is nearly no transmission capability that is wasted by unreasonable resource allocation.

© Institute for Computer Sciences, Social Informatics and Telecommunications Engineering 2014
V.C.M. Leung et al. (Eds.): TridentCom 2014, LNICST 137, pp. 416–424, 2014.
DOI: 10.1007/978-3-319-13326-3_40

There two importance concepts in the routing model of FARI that need to be explained in detail. One is the basic routing state and the other is the polymorphic routing state. To be specific, the basic routing state refers to the protocol library which contains all the existing routing protocols and its extension. It is like a combination of all existing routing mechanism. The polymorphic routing state is a specific routing protocol or routing mechanism generated from the basic state, namely the protocol library. Both the basic routing state and the polymorphic routing state constitute the two aspects of the routing model of FARI.

One of the most essential part of FARI is the routing architecture, or routing mechanism. In the light of optimization theory and atomic capability theory, we proposed the optimization-based routing model for FARI in this paper. The outline of this paper is as follows. Section 2 comprehensively introduces the atomic capability theory. Section 3 presents the optimization-based atomic capability routing model for FARI. Experiments is discussed in Section 4, followed by concluding remarks given in Section 5.

2 Atomic Capability

2.1 Introduction of Atomic Capability

Atomic capabilities, which are defined as the smallest and undecomposable functionality in a routing protocol, are essential for the optimization-based routing model. For now, we have already defined the basic state as a set of every routing protocol and routing forwarding mechanism and the polymorphic state as many possible subsets containing one specific routing protocol. This definition is far away from satisfying for us because it is hard to be described in mathematical form and therefore difficult to be applied to build a routing model. So we need to give mathematical expression for atomic capabilities and also describe the way atomic capabilities are generated.

Similar to the relation between atoms and material, atomic capabilities are the smallest functional components for any routing protocols. That is to say, if the decomposition of the atomic capability is proceeded anyway, we will not obtain any component with a complete function. As a result, it is why we call them the smallest functional components. Atomic capabilities consists of the basic atomic capabilities and the extra atomic capabilities. Simply speaking, the basic atomic capabilities are the necessary and indispensable functions which are shared by all routing protocols, and the extra atomic capabilities are the special and optional functions that just a few routing protocols have.

2.2 Generation of Atomic Capability

The atomic capability is abstracted from similarities that are shared by existing routing protocols such as RIP [4], OSPF [5] etc. Existing routing protocols constitute a library-like basic routing state. Atomic capabilities stand for the smallest

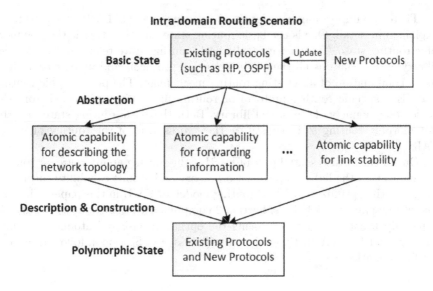

Fig. 1. Generation of Atomic Capability

functionality of the routing protocol and are abstracted and generated from the existing routing protocols. As mentioned above, the atomic capability contains the basic atomic capability and the extended atomic capability. The basic atomic capabilities are the necessary components of a routing protocol and represent the similarities among routing protocols while the extended atomic capabilities are the extra functionalities of a routing protocol and stand for the difference among routing protocols. The brief generation process of the atomic capabilities is shown in Fig.1.

2.3   Mathematical Expression of Atomic Capability

We divide the atomic capabilities into two general categories. One is the basic atomic capabilities and the other is the extended atomic capabilities. The basic atomic capabilities derive from the similarities among all the routing protocols while the extended atomic capabilities come from the difference and particular characteristics among all the routing protocols. In conclusion, basic atomic capabilities are essential to a routing protocol while extended atomic capabilities are selectable.

We depute the set of all basic atomic capabilities as the matrix S_{BAC} and the set of all extended atomic capabilities as the matrix S_{EAC}.

$$S_{BAC} = (S_1, S_2, \cdots, S_n) \tag{1}$$

where $S_i, 1 \leq i \leq n$ stands for the ith basic atomic capability. Similarly, the extended atomic capability is defined as follows.

$$S_{EAC} = (S_{E1}, S_{E2}, \cdots, S_{Ep}) \tag{2}$$

where $S_{Ei}, 1 \leq i \leq p$ represents the ith extended atomic capability.

As for the specific atomic capability, we define it as a vector containing its feasible multiple schemes. Taking the basic atomic capability S_i as an example, we show the constitution of the vector S_i.

$$S_i = (s_{i1}, s_{i2}, \cdots, s_{im})^T \tag{3}$$

And the extended atomic capability shown as follows is similar to S_i.

$$S_{Ei} = (s_{Ei1}, s_{Ei2}, \cdots, s_{Eim})^T \tag{4}$$

To show the optionality of the extended atomic capability, we should modify S_{Ei} by assigning $s_{Ei1} \equiv 0$, which will turn (4) into the following equation.

$$S_{Ei} = (0, s_{Ei2}, \cdots, s_{Eim})^T \tag{5}$$

There is another important issue that has been brought up above. It is the determination of the value of m. In order to take all the schemes in every atomic capability into account, we should let m exceed the maximum of the number of schemes in the atomic capabilities. So we assign m as follows.

$$m = \max_{1 \leq i \leq n, 1 \leq r \leq p} \{row(S_i), row(S_{Er})\} \tag{6}$$

where $row(.)$ is the row of this matrix. Therefore, after defining all the atomic capabilities, we can obtain three large matrixes, namely the basic atomic capability matrix, the extended atomic capability matrix and the general atomic capability matrix

$$
\begin{aligned}
S_{GAC} &= (S_{BAC} \mid S_{EAC}) \\
&= (S_1, S_2, \cdots, S_n \mid S_{E1}, S_{E2}, \cdots, S_{Ep}) \\
&= \begin{pmatrix} s_{11} & \cdots & s_{n1} & s_{E11} & \cdots & s_{Ep1} \\ \vdots & \ddots & \vdots & \vdots & \ddots & \vdots \\ s_{1m} & \cdots & s_{nm} & s_{E1m} & \cdots & s_{Epm} \end{pmatrix}
\end{aligned} \tag{7}
$$

2.4 Mathematical Expression of Protocol Based on Atomic Capability

In the light of atomic capability theory, we know that all the routing protocols are turned into the combination of several atomic capabilities and some constraint conditions among these atomic capabilities just like Fig.2.

Assume X be the scheme selection matrix which stands for the chosen protocol. X is the following form:

$$X = [\delta(x_1), \cdots, \delta(x_n) \mid \delta(x_{n+1}), \cdots, \delta(x_{n+p})] \tag{8}$$

where $\delta(x)$ is a m dimensions row vector with xth element equal to 1 and others equal to 0. In particular, $\delta(x)$ is a zero row vector when $x = 0$.

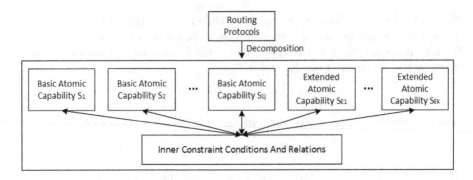

Fig. 2. Decomposition of a Routing Protocol

We have given a mathematical expression for protocol which is

$$pr = diag\left(S_{GAC}^{T} \cdot X\right) \tag{9}$$

Protocols can also be represented by the following form.

$$pr = [pr_1, \cdots, pr_n \mid pr_{n+1}, \cdots, pr_{n+p}] \tag{10}$$

3   Routing Model

3.1   General Framework

The fundamental idea of this framework is to regard the process of the construction from the basic state to the derived state as an optimization process. The abstract form of the routing architecture selection model is shown as follows.

$$\min \quad res\,(protocol)$$

$$\text{subj. to} \begin{cases} TimeDelay > a_1 \\ BandWidth > a_2 \\ \quad \vdots \\ Reliability > a_n \end{cases} \tag{11}$$

where, $res(\cdot)$ stands for the hardware resource that the generated protocol will consume and the constraint conditions in (11) represent the quantitative description of the communication service that users need. This optimization target can be replaced by the other feasible target such as the $TimeDelay$ ($TimeDelay$ denotes -1 times the allowable time delay) and so on. The constraint conditions may be much more than we have listed and the evaluation index may also be different. However, it will not affect how our model works. For illustrative purposes, we can summarize all the constraint conditions shown in (11) as the service requirements.

The optimization model can be written in a more specific form. Before further explaining this part, we first introduce the atomic capabilities partition model.

3.2 Mathematical Form of the Optimization-Based Model

We can turn the minimum consumed hardware resource into the following optimization target by adding the inner requirements and relation conditions to the constraint conditions in the optimization expression.

$$\min_X \quad C \cdot X$$

$$\text{subj. to} \begin{cases} diag(S_{GAC}{}^T \cdot X) \in P \\ constraint\,(S_{GAC}) \\ SR - A > 0 \end{cases} \tag{12}$$

$$\text{where, } SR = \begin{bmatrix} TimeDelay \\ BandWidth \\ \vdots \\ Reliability \end{bmatrix}, \, A = [a_1, a_2, \cdots, a_2]^T \tag{13}$$

and C represents a cost vector, denoting the resource cost of the system and P is the universal set of all possible protocols. $constraint(\cdot)$ denotes the inner constraint of atomic capabilities in a routing protocol. To sum up, the purpose of this model is to select a optimal routing protocol for the different QoS requirements, which can be also summarized as "service-adaptive".

4 Experiments and Results

This section is to simulate the optimization-based routing model. There are 2 experiments containing the scenario simulation and the complexity experiment.

4.1 Specific Optimization Model in Experiments

The specific optimization model shown as follows has been simplified from the previous one.

$$\min_X \quad C \cdot X$$

$$\text{subj. to} \begin{cases} diag(S_{GAC}{}^T \cdot X) \in P \\ SR - A > 0 \end{cases} \tag{14}$$

$$\text{where, } SR = \begin{bmatrix} TimeDelay \\ BandWidth \end{bmatrix}, \, A = [a_1, a_2, \cdots, a_2]^T \tag{15}$$

4.2   Scenario Simulation

Considering there are three available routing protocols: RIP, OSPF and IS-IS
[6], we only take Interior Gateway Protocol (IGP) into consideration. The basic
idea is to determine which protocol is optimal under different QoS requirements.
All links in this topology have 20ms delay.

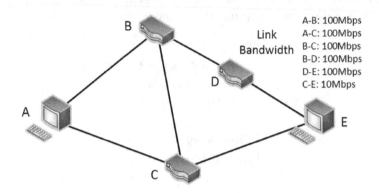

Fig. 3. Process of Atomic Capability Abstraction from Existing Protocols

We apply the optimization-based atomic capability routing model to find
the optimal routing protocol under different QoS guarantee. First we let the
bandwidth guarantee be the independent variable and find the proper routing
protocol to meet the bandwidth requirement. Results are shown in Fig.4, in
which the blue bar represents this protocol is available under the bandwidth
requirement. Then we change the bandwidth guarantee to the time delay guarantee and proceed the similar experiment whose results are shown in Fig.5.

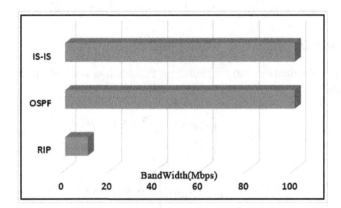

Fig. 4. Available Routing Protocols under Bandwidth Guarantee

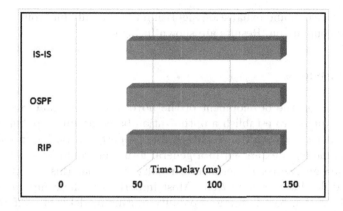

Fig. 5. Available Routing Protocols under Time Delay Guarantee

From Fig.4 and Fig.5, we can see that this model can effectively select a proper routing protocol to meet the current network QoS requirement.

4.3 Complexity Analysis

In the complexity experiment, we assume there are total 50 available routing protocols and the number of atomic capabilities is set as 10. For simplification, we regard all the atomic capabilities as the basic ones. Binary search and exhaustion are both adopted to solve the atomic capability routing model, and we also

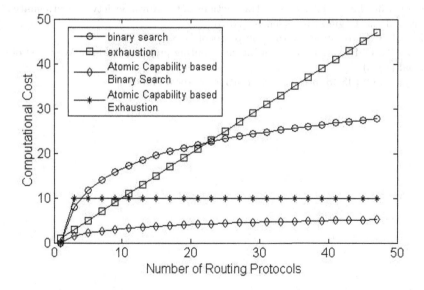

Fig. 6. Comparison of Computational Cost

apply binary search and exhaustion algorithm to optimally find routing protocol directly for comparison. Results are shown in Fig.6.

5   Conclusions

Concentrating on the development of the novel routing mechanism for FARI, this paper explores to establish a optimization-based atomic capability routing model in order to achieve the reconfigurable property in routing mechanism of FARI. This model is expressed in a general form and could be specified under different QoS guarantee. Experimental results show that this routing model is feasible and flexible to some extent. Most importantly, the computational cost of the optimization-based atomic capability routing model is also affordable.

Acknowledgments. Our work is supported in part by the National Basic Research Program of China (973 Program) under Grant 2012CB315904, the National Natural Science Foundation of China under Grant NSFC61179028, the Natural Science Foundation of Guangdong Province under Grant NSFGD S2013020012822, the Basic Research of Shenzhen under Grant SZ JCYJ20130331144502026.

References

1. Lan, J.L., Xing, C.Q., Hu, Y.X., Cheng, D.N.: Reconfiguration Technology and Future Network Architecture. Telecommunications Science **8**, 16–23 (2013)
2. Lan, J.L., Xing, C.Q., Hu, Y.X., Cheng, D.N.: Initial Analysis on Intelligence Mechanisms of Reconfigurable Network. Telecommunications Science **8**, 105–112 (2012)
3. Liu, Y., Wu, J., Wu, Q., et al.: Recent progress in the study of the next generation Internet in China. Philosophical Transactions of the Royal Society A, Mathematical, Physical and Engineering Sciences (2013)
4. Hedrick, C.L.: Routing information protocol (1988)
5. Moy J.T.: OSPF: anatomy of an Internet routing protocol. Addison-Wesley Professional (1998)
6. Oran, D.: OSI IS-IS intra-domain routing protocol (1990)

An Early Traffic Sampling Algorithm

Hou Ying[(⊠)], Huang Hai, Chen Dan, Wang ShengNan, and Li Peng

National Digital Switching System Engineering & Techological R&D center,
ZhengZhou, 450002, China
ndschy@139.com, hh@mail.ndsc.com.cn, cd@mail.ndsc.com.cn

Abstract. The first several packets of a flow play key role in the on-line traffic managements. Early traffic sampling, extracting the first several packets of every flow, is raised. This paper proposes a structure named CTBF, combination of counting Bloom Filter and time Bloom Filter. Based on it, the algorithm is designed to realize automatically removing the space occupied by the timeout flow. The analyses and experiments demonstrate that the sampling accuracy of CTBF is better than that of LRU and Fixed-T algorithm in the same space.

Keywords: Traffic classification · Bloom Filter · Early Traffic Sampling

1 Introduction

The first several packets of a flow play key role in early traffic classification, traffic monitor and early warning etc. Early traffic classification has become an essential means for network security. Researchers collect and analyze the first several packets of the flow to identify the application of the traffic [1][2]. In [3], Zhang.H.L has proved that it can get relatively high accuracy of traffic classification through the statistical features of the first four packets. With the increasing of network bandwidth, the costs of storage and calculation increase sharply. Thus, the early traffic sampling, how to collect the early packets in establishment stage of a flow, is proposed, especially in high-speed network.

The early traffic sampling is different with the classical uniform random sampling and fixed periodic sampling. It can be defined as follows:

Let F denote the sequence of packets $\{f_1, f_2, \ldots f_N, f_{N+1}, \ldots f_M\}$, N is the number of packets to be sampled. The sample probability of the ith packets is p_i, and

$$p_i = \left\{ \begin{array}{l} 1, \text{ when i} \leq \text{N} \\ 0, \text{ when i>N)} \end{array} \right\} \tag{1}$$

As data preprocessing, the accuracy of the early traffic sampling directly determines the accuracy of the subsequent traffic identification. The core of the early

This research was supported by a research grant from the National Natural Science Foundation of Chinese government [61309019].

V.C.M. Leung et al. (Eds.): TridentCom 2014, LNICST 137, pp. 425–433, 2014.
DOI: 10.1007/978-3-319-13326-3_41

traffic sampling in high speed network is how to quickly and correctly locate and record the information of each flow. The early traffic sampling has remained elusive.

The contributions of this paper are: First, We raise the meaning and give the definition of early traffic sampling. Second, we propose a CTBF (Counter and Timer Bloom Filter) structure suitable of early traffic sampling. At last, the accuracy, space complexity and time complexity of CTBF are analyzed.

This paper is organized as follows. In section 2, we review the previous work in traffic sampling algorithm. Section 3 presents the structure CTBF and describes the principle. Section 4 focuses on the theoretical analysis. Section 5 gives the experimental results of evaluation in accuracy, space and time complexity. Section 6 is the summary of this paper.

2   Related Works

For early traffic sampling, the common approach is to maintain per-flow state table and record the number of the sampled packets. When receiving a packet, locate the position of the corresponding flow in the table by hash functions, query the number of the sampled packets and compare the number with N to judge whether to sample. Drawback of this method is that hash collisions will lead to leakage and the cost is too high to resolve the conflicts with linked list. So it is not suitable for high-speed network.

CBF, Count Bloom Filter [4], usually used in long flows identification, can also be used for early traffic sampling. CBF can improve packet processing speed and reduce the computational complexity. Drawback of this method is: as the IP flow length in the internet obeys heavy-tailed distribution, where a few flows with large bytes occupy most of the network traffic, and in the life cycle of long flow, the counter of bloom filter must remain valid. So as the time goes by, more and more counters become nonzero, resulting in the increasing of leakage sample probability. For normal TCP flow, we can judge the end to clear the counter by FIN/RST. But in the real network, there are more and more UDP and abnormal TCP flows. Usually they rely on the timeout mechanism to judge the end. In the field of network measurement, many researchers have focused on how to set up a reasonable timeout mechanism for these flows. If the timeout is set longer, the end flows occupy memory and increase the processing load of the system. And the shorter timeout may lead to a single flow be mistaken for multi flows.

In [5], Claffy judged the end of flow by the fixed-T mechanism. The timeout is set to be 64s. The experiments verified that this method has a good effect in most cases. But when the short flow peak appears (DDoS attack or worm outbreak), short flows cannot be timely released. That will increase the consumption of system resource. Some researchers designed adaptive timeout mechanism to judge the end of flow [6][7].In [6], Ryu B proposed MBET algorithm, according to the number and the interval of packets to dynamically adjust the timeout of a flow. That algorithm judges the end of flows and releases the resource as soon as possible. But adaptive timeout mechanisms require history information to calculate the flow characteristics, thereby adjusting the timeout. That is too complicated and cannot be applied to high speed networks.

LRU (least recently used) algorithm was proposed in [8] to detect the long flows. That can be used in the early traffic sampling. The core of the algorithm is that the least recently used flow is replaced when a new flow arrives. This algorithm only maintains the current active link and need not periodically scan the table to release the flow. That reduces the cost of system. But this algorithm needs hash function to locate the flow table. The complexities of time and space to solve the hash conflict are large. And when a large number of sudden small flows arrive, the active flows may be replaced.

In addition, the time Bloom filter flow sampling algorithm [9] extracts the first packet of per flow. That cannot meet the needs of early flow sampling.

3   Description of CTBF

CTBF structure consists of k independent hash function $h_1, h_2, ..., h_k$ and two vectors, V_1 and V_2. The numerical value of each hash function are independent and the range is $\{1, 2, ... , m\}$. Each dimension of the vector V_1 is set to be a counter, denoted as $C(i)$. Each dimension of the vector V_2 is set to be a timer, denoted as $t(i)$. Both of the initial values are set to zero.

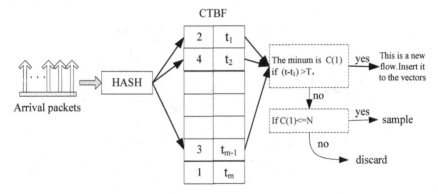

Fig. 1. CTBF structure

Figure 1 is the schematic diagram of the CTBF structure and the sampling algorithm. Assuming that N is the sampling number of per flow and T is a preset timeout of flow interval. The main process of the CTBF algorithm is:

1) When a packet arrives at time t, extract flow identification (five-tuple: source IP address, source port number, destination IP address, destination port number , protocol type) as the input of hash function and get k hash results $h_j(s)(1 \leq j \leq k)$.

2) Calculate $\Delta t_j = t - t(h_j(s))$, $1 \leq j \leq k$.

3)   update the timer in V_2: $t(h_j(s)) = t$.

4)   When one $\Delta t_j \geq T$, the packet is the first of a new flow. Sample this packet and update the counter in V_1: $c(h_i(s)) = 1$, where i satisfy $\Delta t_i \geq T$ and $1 \leq i \leq k$.

5)   If for any j ($1 \leq j \leq k$), $\Delta t_j \leq T$, then the flow has begun sampling. Judge the sampling number by $c\_min = \min(c(h_j(s)))$. If $c\_min < N$, sample and update the counters in V_1: $c(h_j(s)) = c(h_j(s))+1$, $1 \leq j \leq k$. Otherwise discard this packet.

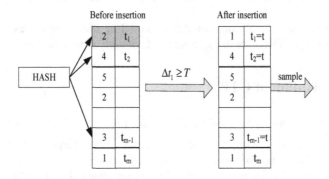

Fig. 2. When first packet of a new flow arrives at t moment

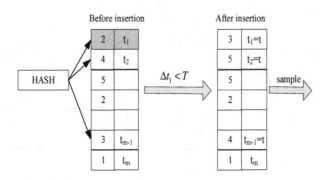

Fig. 3. When a packet of an existing flow arrives at t moment

Figure 2 and figure 3 show the vector's modification when a new flow arrives and when a packet of an existing flow arrives at t moment.

4   Algorithm Analyses

Early traffic sampling algorithm is evaluated from space complexity, accuracy and computational complexity. This several aspects restrict each other. The general goal is reducing computation complexity and space complexity in the range of accepted false probability.

4.1   False Positive Probability of CTBF

The false positive probability of early traffic sampling algorithm is defined as: when the i-th packet, i<N, arrives, the packet doesn't be sampled. As a concise synopsis data structure, there is false positives probability in Bloom filter. According to the principle of the CTBF algorithm, the algorithm makes mistakes in the following circumstances: when first packet of a new flow arrives, for any j （$1 \leq j \leq k$）, $\Delta t_j \leq T$. The following is the theoretical analysis of false positive probability of the CTBF algorithm.

Suppose there are n concurrent flows and m is the length of vector V_1. Since the threshold N is very small, to simplify the analysis, assume the hash functions' result is completely random, and the concurrent flows number don't change before a new flow been sampled. So the probability that the counter in the vector equals zero is $p = (1-\dfrac{1}{m})^{nk}$. The probability has nothing to do with sampling threshold. A new flow is false judged when all $\Delta t_j \leq T$ （$1 \leq j \leq k$）. Then the new flow will not be sampled because it is judged as an existing flow. Therefore, the false positive probability of a new flow is:

$$p_{ctbf} = \left(1-p\right)^k = \left(1-(1-\frac{1}{m})^{kn}\right)^k \approx \left(1-e^{-kn/m}\right)^k$$

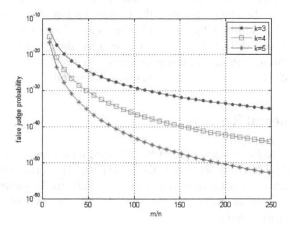

Fig. 4. False positive probability with diffident m/n, in different k

Figure 4 shows the change of p_{CTBF} with the ratio of m/n, when k is 3,4 and 5. It can be seen that p_{CTBF} monotonically decreases with m/n increasing. And the larger k makes the smaller p_{CTBF}.

The figure also shows that the false positive probability is associated with n, the number of concurrent flows. So it is associated with timeout threshold T. Therefore the choice of timeout threshold T influences the false positive probability.

4.2   Time Complexity

The algorithm can be divided into the following sections:

T_h: Time of calculating the k hash functions.
T_q: Time of determining whether $\Delta t_j \leq T$ $(1 \leq j \leq k)$.
T_i: Time of verifying the vectors.

For a packet, CTBF algorithm needs computing the k hash functions, judging whether it is a new flow according to Δt_j and modifying V_2, and then deciding whether sampling by V_1 and modifying V_1. So the average handling time of every packet in CTBF algorithm is:

$$T_{ctbf} = T_h + 2 \times (T_q + T_i)$$

Considering $T_q + T_i$ is far less than T_h, so time of CTBF algorithm is almost the time of calculating the k hash functions

4.3   Space Complexity

The space complexity of Bloom filter is measured by the total bits occupied by the vector. When the vector length m is fixed, the algorithm storage space positively correlated with a single counter-digit. However, if the counter-digit is too small, it will lead the counter to be overflow and impact false positives. According to the [4], the width of V_1 is set to be 16bits, assuring the counter cannot overflow in acceptable false probability. The width of V_2 is set to be 32bits and the unit is set to be 100ms. Then the time vector overflow time is 4971 days after algorithm running. That can satisfy the conventional measurement requirements.

So the space of CTBF algorithm is: 16×m+32×m=48×mbit.

5   Experimental Results

Our experiments are based on the passively collected data opened by "National Laboratory for Applied Network Research" (NLANR)[10]. The form of the file is ERF. We use the real trace collected from campus net of Waikato. To protect the privacy, there are only the head of packets in the data file. The duration of the trace is 24 hours. See Table 1 for details.

Table 1. Information of the experimental trace

Data set	File name	duration	Number of flows	Number of Packets
Waikato network	20110407-000000-0	24 hours	31169027	331999280

Set k=4, sampling number N=4. The vectors' length was set to 1000000 and occupied space was 6M bytes. We calculated the accuracy of CTBF when T is from 8 seconds to 96 seconds. The sampling experimental results are shown in Figure 5.

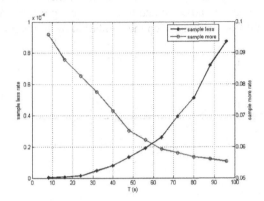

Fig. 5. Sampling results of CTBF with different T

From figure 5 we can see that with T increasing, the less sampling probability increases. That is because the longer the timeout, the more the number of concurrent flow. It is equivalent to m/n decrease, resulting in less sampling. On the other hand, with the decrease of T, some flow may be sampled several times. The reason is that one flow may be truncated into several short flows, resulting in over sampling. We can see that when T=64, the result is more balanced.

The next experiment is compare the sampling result of CTBF, LRU, and Fixed-T with the same space and T=64s. The results are shown in Table 2. The experimental results show that, under the same conditions, the CTBF algorithm over sampling rate is about 4 times less than other algorithms. This is because the other two algorithms need to store five-tuple and linked list pointer, limited by the space. When in the same space, the flow table records are small, resulting in active flow be swapped out. That leads to over sampling. On the other hand, the less sampling rate of CTBF algorithm is between that of LRU and Fixed_T. The reason is in LRU, even though the active flows have been swapped out, the subsequent packets of the flow produce a new flow record and sample again. So LRU algorithm can only produce over sampling but cannot produce less sampling. But in Fixed-T algorithm, when the space is not enough, the packet is discarded. That easily leads to less sampling. So the comprehensive accuracy of CTBF is better than that of the other two algorithms.

Table 2. Information of the experimental trace

	CTBF	LRU	Fixed_T
Over sample（10e-2）	1.72	4.11	3.96
Less sample（10e-2）	0.0026	0	4.93

We evaluated the time complexity of the CTBF, LRU and Fixed-T, base on the Waikato campus dataset. The experiments are conducted on a laptop with Intel i5 CPU, 2.50GHz frequency and 4Gbytes RAM.

To avoid the affect of the disc IO on the conduct time, we read the first hour data of the set to the memory in advance and test with the algorithms. We got PPS (Packets Per Second) of the algorithms when the number of hash functions is 1-7.

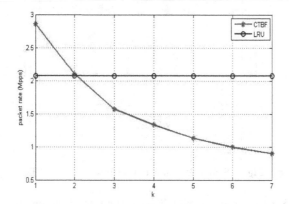

Fig. 6. The rate of CTBF and LRU in different hash functions

The results are shown in figure 6. The latter two algorithms' conduct rates are almost equal. With the increasing of hash functions, the handle rate of CTBF decreases rapidly. Serially handling with hash functions occupies the most time in the emulation and consumes lots of the resource of CPU. When designing an actual system, we can design parallel processing in hardware to raise the rate.

6   Conclusions

The contribution of the paper is the proposed of early traffic sampling. And this paper presents a structure and algorithm suitable for early traffic sampling. The structure consists of two vectors, counting Bloom Filter and timer Bloom Filter. The two vectors cooperate to realize early traffic sampling. The counting Bloom Filter for high rate sampling counting saves storage space. The timer Bloom filter automatic releases the space when timeout, avoiding scanning the flow table regularly. The accuracy, space complexity and time complexity are analyzed and experiments are conducted on the real trace from internet. The experimental results show that when in the same space, CTBF gets better comprehensive accuracy than LRU and Fixed_T algorithm.

References

1. Bernaille, L., Teixeira, R., Akodkenou, I.: Traffic classification on the fly. ACM SIGCOMM Computer Communication Review **36**(2), 23–26 (2006)
2. Li, W., Canini, M., Moore, A.W., Bolla, R.: Efficient application identification and the temporal and spatial stability of classification schema. Computer Networks **53**(6), 790–809 (2009)

3. ZHANG, H.-L., LU G.: Machine Learning Algorithms for Classifying the Imbalanced Pro-
    tocol Flows: Evaluation and Comparison.Journal of Software, 23(6):1500–1516 (2012)
4. Fan, L., Cao, P., Almeida, J., Broder, A.Z.: Summary Cache: A Scalable Wide-area Web
    Cache Sharing Protocol. IEEE/ACM Transactions on Networking 8(3), 281–293 (2000)
5. Claffy, K.C., Braun, H.W., Polyzos, G.C.: A parameterizable methodology for Internet
    traffic flow profiling. IEEE Journal on Selected Areas In Communications 12(8), 1481–
    1494 (1995)
6. Ryu, B., Cheney, D., Braun, H.W.: Internet flow characterization: adaptive timeout strate-
    gy and statistical modeling. In Proc, Passive and Active Measurement workshop (2001)
7. Cai, J., Zhang, Z., Zhang, P., et al.: An adaptive timeout strategy for profiling UDP flows.
    Networking and Computing (ICNC), 2010 First International Conference on. 44–48, IEEE
    (2010)
8. Smitha, InkooKim, NarasimhaReddy, A.L.: Identifying Long-term High-bandwidth Flows
    at a Router. In: Proceedings of the 8thInternational Conference on High Performance
    Computing. Hyderabad, India, 361–371(2001)
9. Kong, S., He, T., Shao, X., An, C., Li, X.: Time-Out Bloom Filter: A New Sampling
    Method for Recording More Flows. In: Chong, I., Kawahara, K. (eds.) ICOIN 2006.
    LNCS, vol. 3961, pp. 590–599. Springer, Heidelberg (2006)
10. NLANR. National Laboratory for Applied Network Research [EB/OL]. http://
    pma.nlanr.net/

On the Routing of Wide-Sense Circuit

Based on Algebraic Switching Fabric

Qian Zhan, Hui Li[✉], Li Ma, and Shijie Lv

Shenzhen Eng. Lab of Converged Networks Technology,
Shenzhen Key Lab of Cloud Computing Tech. & App, Shenzhen Graduate School,
Peking University, Shen Zhen, China
Zhanqian0218@gmail.com, lih64@pkusz.edu.cn,
mali5057@163.com, iamlvshijie@qq.com

Abstract. In order to ensure high quality of service for Next Generation Network, we focus our study on the Wide-Sense Circuit proposed in Flexible Architecture of Reconfigurable Infrastructure. First we construct the functional structure of Wide-Sense Circuit and then explore the switching mechanism and module for it, which is called the Multipath Self-routing Switching Mechanism. Its detailed working process includes traffic classification, establishment and adjustment of Wide-Sense Circuit and data forwarding three parts. For underlying data forwarding, we introduce an innovative Load-Balanced Multipath Self-routing Switching Architecture and start on the implementation on an Altera StratixIV FPGA. The inspiring test results prove that our theory and practiceguarantee the high communication transmission quality for Wide-Sense Circuit.

Keywords: Wide-Sense Circuit · Multipath Self-routing Switching Mechanism · Load-Balanced Multipath Self-routing Switching Architecture

1   Introduction

The present network's architecture is designed for data switching, and TCP/IP, as its fundamental mechanisms, suffers from single function and services as a barely satisfactory schema.That reveals the bottleneck of the general function innetworks, and also contributes the weak adaptability of the capability and structure of networks in different need, which could be seen as the incapability in current network to satisfy more advanced need, like ubiquitous, interconnection, quality, integration, isomerism, credibility, manageability, expandability.

In recent years, efforts have been made by many countries on new types of network architecture, reconfigurable technologies and, routing and switching architectures, such as FIND program in United States, AUTOI program from Challenge One Project in European Unionand AKIRA program in Japan.In China, Information Engineering University proposed the complete system of theories and application test platform of flexible architecture of reconfigurable infrastructure (FARI) [1], including network Atomic Capability (AC), Polymorphic Addressing, Routing and reconfigurable network. Among all, AC theory takes the enhancement of network

© Institute for Computer Sciences, Social Informatics and Telecommunications Engineering 2014
V.C.M. Leung et al. (Eds.): TridentCom 2014, LNICST 137, pp. 434–443, 2014.
DOI: 10.1007/978-3-319-13326-3_42

fundamental capacities directly as an entry point, rather than amending or expanding the original networks, which has drawn our academic attention.

AC theory holds that features and requirements of network businessesjobs are diverse and versatile variant with inspect to the finity and certainty. A feasible approach to mitigate this difference, as the core of network AC theory,is to abstract the features and requirements of network jobs as well as network service into a specific, top-down schema of business, Atomic Service(AS) and Atomic Capability.

According to the definition of AS, the network switching mechanism capable of this service is part of AC and satisfies new AS requirements through dynamical adjustment. Wide-Sense Circuit (WSC) [2], as a new basic data transfer mode, is introduced. WSC is an adaptive circuitry built dynamically for network business flow with identical transfer path, aiming to enhance basic data transfer mode in terms of performance, security, multicasting, mobility and extensionality.

Most of the large-scale switching architecture at present relies on principles of IO Queue and Slot scheduling, whose bottleneck is central scheduling and waiting delay induced from queuing. Additionally, the support of multicasting is realized by dividing into several multiple unicasts, so hardware logic fanout cannot be achieved. As a result, WSC cannot be implemented on current switching architecture. In this article, we propose a solution–a novel two-stage, load-balanced, multipath, self-routing switching architecture. The first stage has a load-balanced function and the second one is designed for self-routing. The self-routing module is based on concentrator which can absorb traffic bursts of network, and Algebraic Switching Fabric (ASF), is characterized by fully distributed self-routing, no scheduling of port matching, no delay and jitter of buffer, group building positionally and recursive extension. This solution is implemented on Stratix IV FPGA platform from Altera Inc. and results of tests show that this architecture can achieve 100% payload, low delay, and no jitter. So this proposal supports WSC in theory.

The content followed includes the structure and function of WSC(part II), setting up switching mechanisms corresponsive to WSC(part III), building switching models supporting WSC based on switching mechanisms(part IV), and the summary.

2   The Functional Structure of Wide-Sense Circuit

WSC is builtdynamically for network business stream with identical transfer path to support Quality of Service (Qos) of data transfer. To achieve this, the structure is designed as a 'management-control-data' model. The management layer is responsible for the deployment of WSC, the control layer is responsible for execution of management part, and the data layer is responsible for WSC data transmitting. These three layers exchange information to realize the function of WSC as shown in Fig. 1.

2.1   The Management Plane

The management plane's functionality, realized by domain's server, consists of acquitting current network status, computing WSC's location, and transmitting orders, such as setting up, adjusting and removing WSC. This layer serves as the core layer and management center of WSC.

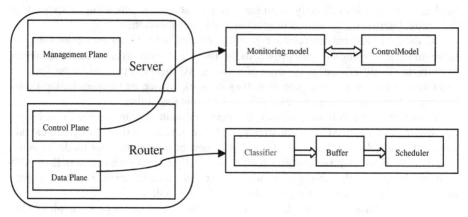

Fig. 1. The relationship of three planes of WSC

2.2   The Control Plane

This plane, realized in router, takes orders from the management layer and takes charge of execution, such as setting up, adjusting, and removing WSC according to WSC protocol. In this layer, monitoring module and control module are designed: the monitoring module collects information of flow and resource and reports it to the status acquisition module in the management layer; the control module executes orders from the management layer and communicates with other network WSC's control layer.

2.3   The Data Plane

Definition 1. Along the WSC, network set up a virtual circuit, which is called Wide-Sense Circuit Passway (WSCP).

This plane, realized in router, sets up WSCP and routes packets. When data is transmitted in WSC, WSCP is set up and corresponding labels are inserted into label switching table at entry point of WSCP. Afterwards, this layer will route packets and certify the QoS of different data flow simultaneously. This layer is the concrete key of realization of the functionality of WSC—for network nodes with built WSC, packets classifier, buffer and scheduler will react to the specific data flow accordingly to meet the requirements of data flow transmitting.

3   Switching Mechanism and Module for Wide-Sense Circuit

3.1   The Overall Structure of Reconfigurable Router

WSCis a new kind of data transmission mechanism, which guarantees the QoSaccording to the category of the traffic. Its working process includes traffic classification, establishment and adjustment of WSC and data forwarding three parts, which all happen in Reconfigurable Router. The overall architecture of Reconfigurable

Router is shown in Fig. 2. The flows are classified based on three key QoS indicators: delay, jitter and loss. The classification is mainly conducted by the classifier within Data Plane. The establishment and adjustment of WSC is under the decision of the server within Management Plane. And after making a decision, the work is completed by Control Plane in which the monitoring module is responsible for monitoring the bandwidth occupancy of various flows and the control module carries out the commands in detail. In Data Plane, if a WSC has been set up, there will be a private channel for it, calledWSCP, the place data switching proceeds. In addition, we need an advanced switching mechanism to ensure all types of QoS requirements. Next, we will carry on the detailed introduction of the three parts above-mentioned.

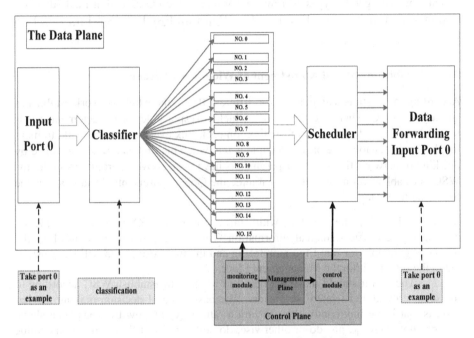

Fig. 2. The overall architecture of Reconfigurable Router

3.2   Traffic Classification

WSC sorts kinds of network flows in accordance with their different data transmission requirements, which consist of a series of QoS parameters. Here, to simplify our modeling, we just focus on delay, jitter and loss three indicators as the classification basis, and assume that boundary nodes have got all the relevant information.

Definition 2. The QoS requirements of data flow F is <delay, jitter, loss >.

Among them, delay indicates the time delay requirement, namely the time should be no more than delay (ms) when a packet is transferred from the source to its destination. Jitter defines the time jitter requirement, that is to say, the time jitter for a full packet must not exceed the maximum value: jitter (ms). Loss means the packet loss requirement, which limits the largest proportion of the discarded packets.

Next, we divide delay into [0, 100], (100, 400], (400, 1000] and (1000, ∞) four intervals. Jitter is divided into [0, 50] and (50, ∞) two intervals, and for loss: [0, 0.1%] and (0.1%, 1). In this way, we can use X, Y, and Z to represent the three QoS categories, and determine its specific number for each interval under a certain kind of category. The definite means are as follows:

1) If 0ms < delay ≤100ms, X = 1. If 100ms < delay ≤400ms, X=2. For 400ms < delay ≤1000ms, X=3. And if delay > 1000ms, X=4.

2) If 0ms < jitter ≤50ms, Y=1. If jitter > 50ms, Y=2.

3) For 0 ≤ loss ≤ 0.1%, Z = 1. And for loss > 0.1%, Z = 2.

Thus, we can get 16 types of flows according to the classification method: F_{XYZ}. And they are F_{111} F_{112}, F_{121}, F_{211}, F_{122}, F_{212}, F_{221}, F_{311}, F_{222}, F_{312}, F_{321}, F_{411}, F_{322}, F_{412}, F_{421} and F_{422}.

3.3   Establishment and Adjustment of Wide-Sense Circuit

According to the statistical analysis for different flows, the whole network establishes and adjusts WSC. Therefore the server, which is responsible for management, needs to collect each kind of traffic information on each link every once in a while to making the final decision. The basic principle is that when the link bandwidth occupied by one kind of network flow or other parameters have been above a certain threshold, the WSC is established on the link to guarantee the QoS requirements. Details are as the following three steps.

1) Calculating the link bandwidth utilization ratio UXYZ of flow FXYZ according to the traffic statistical information. This work is under the control by the monitoring module for real-time monitoring and the monitoring data will be transmitted to the server within the Management Plane.

2) The server should make the decision whether to establish WSC according to the setup criteria and related parameters. The basic idea of decision-making mechanism is that if the link bandwidth utilization ratio U_{XYZ} of flow F_{XYZ} has been above the threshold $U_{XYZ, th}$, just do it, otherwise, do nothing. For different flows, the value of $U_{XYZ, th}$ is not necessarily the same. Usually, for the business which requires high quality of service or high service priority, its $U_{XYZ, th}$ should be low, otherwise set high threshold, to achieve the purpose of distinguishing different service. To take an extreme example, setting $U_{111,th}=U_{112,th}=U_{211,th}=U_{212,th}=0$ and $U_{421,th}=U_{422,th}=1$, that is to say, we must establish WSC for flows F_{111}, F_{112}, F_{211}, F_{212} but not for flows F_{421}, F_{422}.Detailed scheme is in Table 1.

Table 1. Different values of $U_{XYZ, th}$ for different flows

NO.	0	1, 2, 3	4, 5, 6, 7	8, 9, 10, 11	12, 13, 14	15
flow	F_{111}	F_{112},F_{121},F_{211}	$F_{122},F_{212},F_{221},F_{311}$	$F_{222},F_{312},F_{321},F_{411}$	F_{322},F_{412},F_{421}	F_{422}
threshold	3.4%	4.6%	5.7%	6.8%	7.9%	9.1%

We can see that threshold priority is divided into 3.4%, 4.6%, 5.7%, 6.8%, 7.9% and 9.1% six levels and the same threshold value can be used by some different types of flows, in which the smaller the label NO., the higher the internal priority. Firstly, we decide to set up WSC or not for a certain kind of network flow by comparing its link bandwidth utilization ratio with its threshold. After completing the establishment of all the qualified WSC, if the bandwidth resources are still remaining, we could use the rest flows to fill the bandwidth in the order of label numbers.

3)   The control module within control plane performs the decisions such as establish or dismantle WSC, which is responsible for establishing WSCP, etc. When WSC deployment is completed, this WSC can provide sufficient bandwidth for the corresponding traffic. And to ensure kinds of QoS requirements, matched scheduling algorithm and discard algorithm are also be used for distinguishing or configuring.

3.4   Data Forwarding

WSC realizes virtual circuit connection with the method of label switching and packets are forwarded within WSCP. WSC supports Multiple Input Multiple Output (MIMO), therefore, packets can enter into WSC as long as there is a node within the coverage area of the WSC. Similarly, packets can leave in any node.

In WSC ingress node,when a network flow arrives, the node will retrieve the label switching table according to the category information and destination address of packets. In WSCintermediate node, the node will retrieve the label switching table again, but according to the message header of WSC this time, and then forwards the matched packets.In WSC exit node, the node will drop the message header and forward the data as common packets.

4   Switching Mechanism and Module for Data Forwarding

4.1   2×2 Basic Sorting Unit

The 2×2basic sorting unit is a sequential logiccircuit, with two inputs and two outputs (respectively called 0/1 port).According to the theory of algebraic distributive lattices [3], we define the two inputs as Ω_0 and Ω_1, each of which has three kinds of data: the one going to output0, the one going to output1 and the invalid data. As is shown in Fig. 3(a) and (b), the sorting unit has two essential states: Cross and Bar. That means the inputs go to the different outputs: input0/input1 to output1/output0 and input0/input1 to output0/output1, corresponding to Cross and Bar,respectively.If the inputs compete for the same one output, the state will be Conflict and the final choice of BAR or CROSS will depend on their priority, shown in Fig. 3(c).

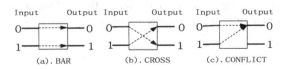

Fig. 3. 2×2 basic sorting unit and its states

4.2   Multipath Self-routing Switching Structure

An N×N ($N=2^n$) routing network is a Multistage Interconnection Network (MIN) built by 2×2 basic sorting units. By using first stage permutation σ_0, inter-stage permutation $\sigma_1, \sigma_2...\sigma_{(n-1)}$ and last stage permutation σ_n, the network can be represented as $[\sigma_0: \sigma_1: \sigma_2:...: \sigma_{(n-1)}:\sigma_n]$. Each colon symbolizes a stage of 2x2 units. We can define a Trace sequence and a Guide sequence[4] as follows:

$$T_k=(\sigma_0\sigma_1...\sigma_{K-1})^{(-1)}(n) \quad 1\leq k\leq n. \tag{1}$$

$$G_k=(\sigma_0\sigma_1...\sigma_{K-1})(n) \quad 1\leq k\leq n. \tag{2}$$

Route is specified by Trace or Guide. As Fig. 2 shows, for the network [: (43): (42)(31): (43):], data from the origination address $I_1I_2I_3I_4$ finally gets to the destination $O_1O_2O_3O_4$ with the decision at each stage by the Trace (4, 3, 2, 1) or Guide (1, 2, 3, 4).

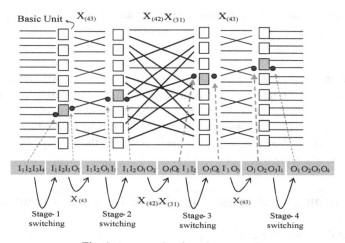

Fig. 4. An example of routing network

Multipath Self-routing Switching Structure (MSSS)[5] is an innovative structure, which combines MIN with concentrators.

To construct MSSS, we substitute each basic for 2G-to-G concentrator sorting unit and replace the single cable with a bundle of G cables. For the multipath structure (N=128 M=16 and G=8) which is based on a 16×16 routing network, G shows the size of group, M is the number of group and N=M×G indicates the whole number of input/output ports ($G=2^g$, $M=2^m$, $N=2^n$, n=m+g, n, m, g are positive integers). Acting as an indispensable part of MSSS, the 2G-to-G concentrator [6] separates the larger G signals of the whole 2G inputs from the other G signals, finally forming two output groups. And the output order within each group is arbitrary.

4.3   Load-Balanced Self-routing Switching System

As shown in Fig. 5,two MSSSs are used in series to compose the Load-BalancedMultipath Self-routing Switching Structure (Load-Balanced MSSS), with the VOGQs (Virtual Output Group Queues)[7]ahead of the firstfabric and the assemblages at the end of the second fabric.   Actually, by using simple algorithms and small buffers,the first stage fabric serves as a balancer, which spreadsthe incoming traffic to all the ingress ports of the second stage fabric. Then the second stage fabric forwards the data in a self-routing manner to their final destinations. Every G inputs/outputs are bundled into an input/output group, thus N input lines form M groups on the input side(N=M×G), so is the output side. To ease presentation, IG/OG denotes input/output group, and MGrepresents a line group between the two stages.In the project, there are 4 IGs, 4 MGs and 4 OGs. Each group has 8 lines. .

VOGQs are responsible for storing packets and making data ready for IGs. We use VOGQ(i,j) to denote the VOGQ whose packets are destined forOGj from IGi.

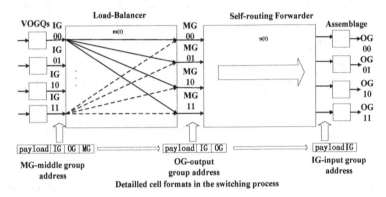

Fig. 5. Load-Balanced MSSS

Generally, for the structure we proposed, the processing of arriving packets in each time slot is composed by severalsequential phases which are shown as follows. In addition, to achieve maximum processing speed, we should use pipeline structure as far as possible.

1. *Preparatoryphase*: With checking and judging, the arriving packet which is destined forOGj from IGi is stored into VOGQ (i,j).
2. *Splitting phase*: Packets in VOGQs are split into cells. And each cell will be added with some certain packet headers.
3. *Balancing phase*: With the help of MG tags, cells will be routed to every middle group simultaneously and uniformly. When the cells reach the middle groups, MG tags will be dropped.
4. *Routing phase*: Cells are further to their final destinations directed by OG tags. When they get through the second stage fabric, OG tags will be discarded.
5. *Assembling phase*: Cells are to be assembled to originalpackets.When completed, packets will be output from the OGs.

4.4   System Test with Real Network Traffic

IXIA400T network tester is our leading network test instrument. We use four test modules of all the interfaces on the test board, which can generate or capture standard Ethernet frames transmitted at the rate of 10/100/1000 Mb/s. It is so powerful that we can set, if we want to, every Byte of a frame to be sent and get detailed and comprehensive information about the frames captured. The tester also provides remote management capabilities. And coupled with the automated platformset up by Tclscripting language, we can implement remote automated testing.

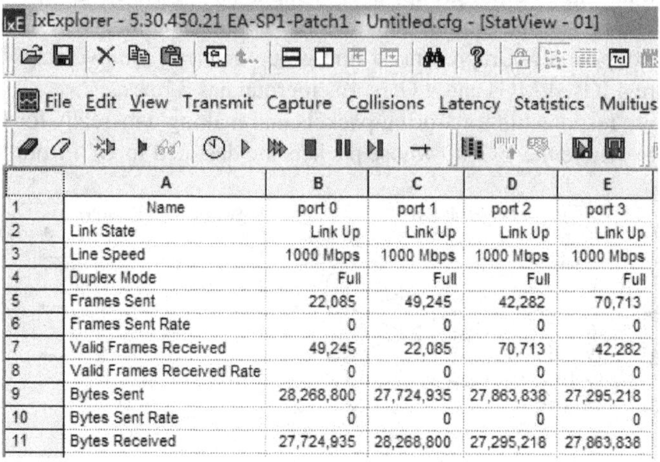

IxExplorer - 5.30.450.21 EA-SP1-Patch1 - Untitled.cfg - [StatView - 01]

File Edit View Transmit Capture Collisions Latency Statistics Multius

	A	B	C	D	E
1	Name	port 0	port 1	port 2	port 3
2	Link State	Link Up	Link Up	Link Up	Link Up
3	Line Speed	1000 Mbps	1000 Mbps	1000 Mbps	1000 Mbps
4	Duplex Mode	Full	Full	Full	Full
5	Frames Sent	22,085	49,245	42,282	70,713
6	Frames Sent Rate	0	0	0	0
7	Valid Frames Received	49,245	22,085	70,713	42,282
8	Valid Frames Received Rate	0	0	0	0
9	Bytes Sent	28,268,800	27,724,935	27,863,838	27,295,218
10	Bytes Sent Rate	0	0	0	0
11	Bytes Received	27,724,935	28,268,800	27,295,218	27,863,838

Fig. 6. Statistic views of IXIA

Fig. 6 shows us the finalstatistical result of a test for four ports. According to our configuration, port 0 prepares to receive the output data sent form all the four ports (including itself). And port2, port3 and port4 follow the same way. We can see that there is no one Byte data dropped at each port in the case of a large number of input data.

5   Conclusions

Multipath Self-routing Switching Mechanism (MSSM) belongs to the physical vision of packet transmission in AC, which is also the foundation of WSC. It is a high quality basic network structure inherited from the existing network system, directly providing the network survivability and robustness. Above all it provides the material foundation for the construction of WSC and the reconfiguration. Based on the powerful transmittability of MSSM, WSC can also possess the new information foundation of the communication network and the new connotation of network interconnection transmission capacity. These enhanced foundational capabilities, especially for data transfer mode, ensure the lower delay of packet transmission, wire-speed forwarding, efficient multicast and security. MSSM gives effective technical support to build a new type of WSC, so as to make WSC be the supporting factor of reconfigurable ability, together with the packet transmission.

The research in this direction goes well: we have accomplished the single-stage switching system which supports unicast and multicast and the two-stage load balancing switching system which supports unicast only.Good results have been achieved in a series of tests. So far, our system is based on the MSSS (M=4, G=8). And next step, we plan to increase it to M=8, G=16. Meanwhile, the design of large-scale wire-speed multicast base on Load-Balanced MSSS we constructed will be the focus, which needs more excellent design and more thorough support system.

Acknowledgment. Our work is supported in part by the National Basic Research Program of China (973 Program) under Grant 2012CB315904, the National Natural Science Foundation of Chinaunder Grant61179028, the Natural Science Foundation of Guangdong Provinceunder Grant201101000923 and 2013020012822, the Basic Research of Shenzhenunder Grant201104210120A and 20130331144502026.We also acknowledge the valuable feedback from Le Yang and Qing Ma (Depaul University, Chicago, USA) for helping me improve my Englishduring the preparation of this paper.

References

1. Lan, J., Xinget, C., et al.: Reconfiguration Technology and Future Network Architecture. Telecommunications Science, 10.3969/j.issn.1000-0801.2013.08.003
2. The 2013 Annual Report of NationalBasic Research Program of China (973 Program, No. 2012CB315904), Zhenzhou
3. Nojima, S., et al.: Integrated services packet network using bus matrix switch. IEEE J. of Select Areas Commun. 5, 1284–1292 (1987)
4. Li, S.Y.R.: Algebraic switching theory and broadband applications. Academic Press (2001)
5. Li, H., He, W., Chen, X., Yi, P., Wang, B.: Multi-path Self-routing Switching Structure by Interconnection of Multistage Sorting Concentrators. In: IEEE CHINACOM 2007, Shanghai (August 2007)
6. Li, S.Y.R.: Algebraic Switching Theory and Broadband Applications. Academic Press (2001)
7. He, W., Li, H., Wang, B., et al.: A Load-Balanced Multipath Self-routing Switching Structure by Concentrators. In: IEEE ICC (2008)

Semi-Centralized Name Routing Mechanism for Reconfigurable Network

Fuxing Chen[✉], Weiyang Liu, Hui Li, and Zhipu Zhu

Shenzhen Engineering Lab of Converged Networks Technology,
Shenzhen Key Lab of Cloud Computing Technology & Application,
Peking University Shenzhen Graduate School, Shenzhen 518055, China
{chenfuxing,wyliu,zhuzhipu}@pku.edu.cn, lih64@pkusz.edu.cn

Abstract. Dedicated to overcoming weakness of current Internet architecture, some novel internet architectures have been proposed recently. Examples of these architectures contain Information Centric Networking (ICN), Name Data Networking (NDN), reconfigurable networking etc. As far as we know, the most efficient name based routing mechanism which suites the new architectures has not been found yet. This paper proposed a Semi-Centralized Name Routing (SCNR) protocol for reconfigurable network to enhance the routing efficiency. Results of this paper show that SCNR has good performance in ICN, which can be regarded as one of the many sub-networks in reconfigurable network.

Keywords: Name based Routing · Reconfigurable Network · OpenFlow · FARI

1 Introduction

The networking paradigm is shifting from communication between hosts to communication for data. The information-centric networking is one of the significant results of different international Future Internet research activities, which has been explored by a number of research projects, such as CCN [1], DONA [2] and NDN [3].

Flexible Architecture of Reconfigurable Infrastructure (FARI) is proposed and funded by one of National Basic Research Programs of China. FARI not only keep open, simple and robust features as tradition, but also follow some new principles such as interaction, variety and selectiveness. It is more than a simple expansion of current network or extension of telecommunication network, and it can also provide flexible, universal, customizable and variant network service. In other words, the target of FARI is to construct some sub-networks, e.g. Content-Centric Network (CCN), Name Data Network (NDN), Information Centric Network (ICN), Service Centric Network (SCN), traditional IP-centric network, and any networks which would be proposed in the future, in a single physical network by isolating infrastructure resource. For convenience, we propose an efficient routing algorithm over ICN, a sub-network of Reconfigurable network.

© Institute for Computer Sciences, Social Informatics and Telecommunications Engineering 2014
V.C.M. Leung et al. (Eds.): TridentCom 2014, LNICST 137, pp. 444–452, 2014.
DOI: 10.1007/978-3-319-13326-3_43

In this paper we discuss a Name data Routing based on Link State algorithm which is called Semi-Centralized Name Routing (SCNR) in sub-network ICN for FARI. We will refer the lookup-and-cache routing mechanism of Content Network (CONET) [4] architecture to design the SCNR algorithm, and deploy it in OpenFlow [5]. In Section 2, we describe the Lookup-and-Cache Architecture. Section 3 gives the design of the name link state routing. Section 4 gives the simulation results. Section 5 contains the conclusion.

2   The Lookup-and-Cache Routing Mechanism

The concept of lookup-and-cache is first proposed in [4], which is used to update CONET name-based routing tables. Because of the inefficient aggregation of names, the prefix-dissemination could produce big name-based routing tables. In order to support the above case, the lookup-and-cache is proposed, since it is not feasible to include all possible names in the routing table. In this method, a CONET node uses a fixed number of rows of its name-based *routing table* as route cache. When a node lacks of the routing info, it requires an interest packet to looks up its routing entry in a *name-routing-system* and inserts this entry in the route cache.

In this paper, we refer to the lookup-and-cache mechanism in SCNR algorithm to cope with the capacity issue of the FIB and with the cost issue of the RIB. We plan to use the FIB of a Reconfigurable node's Forwarding Engine as *route cache*, and to deploy a centralized routing system that serves all the nodes of an Autonomous System (AS). Fig. 1 gives an example of Lookup-and-Cache operations. Node *N1* receives an interest message for "icn.com/video/chunk1". When the FIB lacks the related route, firstly, the node temporarily queues the interest message, secondly, the node lookups the route in a remote RIB, and then gets the routing information and stores it in the FIB. In the following, we give the brief rationale underlying the Lookup-and-Cache architecture.

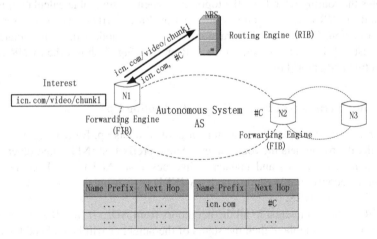

Fig. 1. Lookup-and-Cache concept

FIB as route cache, As we all know, the number of flows of Interest message is very large. However, the Reconfigurable ICN node concurrently route-by-name is even much smaller than ICN routes. Thence, the FIB is proposed as route cache, and contains the entire set of active-routes. When the FIB is short of a route, the node lookups the route in a remote RIB and then stores the route in its FIB.

Centralized routing engine, All routes are contained in the RIB of a routing engine in the NRS, which serves all the nodes of AS and runs on a logical centralized serve, named Name Routing System (NRS) node. Therefore, a single network device can replace all the network nodes, and this approach reduces the cost greatly for network operator.

[6] has described the "data-plane" of Lookup-and-Cache architecture. However, the Lookup-and-Cache architecture needs "routing-plane" procedures that runs on NRS nodes and whose goal is to setup the RIBs. This paper proposes SCNR and gives the collaborative design of SCNR algorithm in local reconfigurable ICN node and NRS.

3   Name Based Centralized Routing for Reconfigurable Network

The Name routing is deployed both in NRS Controller and reconfigurable ICN routers. [1] proposed Link-state Intra-domain Routing technique and also discussed about both IS-IS and OSPF for nodes to discover and describe their local connectivity and to establish adjacencies. This paper adapts the idea of IP OSPF protocol and develops SCNR over ICN.

The ICN nodes will advertise their adjacency and name prefix of the content in the network. Neighbors receive this advertisement and build Link State Data Base (LSDB) from the adjacency advertisement and forward it to NRS, and then the NRS calculates the routing table from the topology. When routing table calculation is complete, and the NRS has the Routing Information Base (RIB) of name prefixes. From this information, Forwarding Information Base of ICN node will be formulated, and the interest will be routed based on the FIB entries. Fig. 2 shows the SCNR internal constructing and algorithm.

3.1   The Operations of Router Booting/Rebooting Up

Router read configuration file as soon as it boots/reboots up. By reading the configuration file, the router sets the router-name, Name prefix List (NPL), and other configuration parameter, builds and updates Adjacency List (ADL). SCNR connects to a Daemon of reconfigurable routing node (SCNRD) synchronizing the Link State Data Base (LSDB) with NRS.

SCNR sends info interest to all the neighbors from ADL. If SCNR receives a reply for the info from neighbors then the status of the neighbor will be updated to "active" from "down" state. For any neighbor, if info interest is timed out in appointed times, then status remains unchanged for that neighbor. Neighbor's SCNR hear "info" interest replies with content containing information of its LSDB version and info version.

3.2   LSDB Synchronization

Two kinds of LSA are carried out by router, Name LSA origination and Adjacency LSA origination. Router reads the name prefixes from list, builds Name LSA and installs it to its own LSDB. Adjacency LSA is built by including the active neighbors from the neighbors list by checking the status of the neighbors. If there is any change in neighbor list status then router will build Adjacency LSA by including all the active neighbors and install the LSA in own LSDB. The LSDB synchronization is done in five steps as follows.

A.   Sending LSDB interest

In the first step of LSDB synchronization, SCNR sends interest "lsdb", received from neighbors in exclusion filter, on name prefix for all the active neighbors in ADL including the last version of LSDB. In reply it hears from neighbors then performs the work described in subsection 3). But if SCNR does not hear any reply from any neighbors, it will try sending "lsdb" interest promissory times. If interest for any neighbor is timed out for promissory times, then that neighbor will be considered down, and SCNR will update its ADL accordingly and will also schedule building of Adjacency LSA.

B.   Sending LSDB Summary by Neighbors

Neighbor's SCNR hearing interest for "lsdb" will check the version number. If the version number in exclusion filter is older than the version number of LSDB, the SCNR will prepare "LSDB Summary Content" with all the header information of all LSA and reply back to neighbors. On the other hand, if the version in exclusion filter is not older than the version number of LSDB, then SCNR will reply with NACK content.

C.   Sending LSA interest

In this step, if SCNR gets NACK reply content from neighbors, and then does nothing as it is already synchronized with that neighbor. But if SCNR gets "LSDB Summary Content" from neighbors, then for every LSA header in LSDB Summary Content, first it will check its own LSDB for existence. Secondly if the LSA does not exist in LSDB then sends "lsa" interest to neighbors.

D.   Sending LSA by neighbors

Neighbor's SCNR hearing interest for "lsa", will check its LSDB with header information provided in interest name, prepare content with LSA information and reply back with the content.

E.   LSA installation

SCNR receiving LSA content from neighbor will install it into LSDB. Installation process checks whether LSA is new/newer or not. If LSA is new then it will be added into LSDB. If LSA is newer than delete old LSA and add the new one. However, if LSA is newer and is checked valid, then delete old LSA and install new one. If LSA is not valid, then delete the old LSA and discard new LSA.

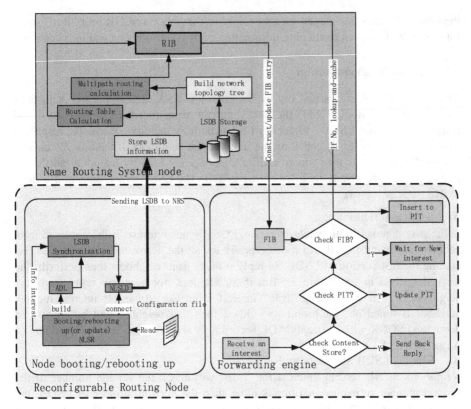

Fig. 2. SCNR algorithm

4   Performance Analysis of SCNR

The matrices used for comparing performance of SCNR are: success rate, routing overhead and end-to-end delay [7]. If a query acquires the requested content, that is called successful. The ratio of total number of successful queries to the total number of queries is defined as success rate. The higher success rate value means better result. The success rate (*Sr*) is written as:

$$Sr = \sum_{1}^{N} SucPkts \bigg/ \sum_{1}^{n} ReqPkts \qquad (1)$$

The average time interval between the generation of request packet at a source node and the successful reception at the data source node is called end-to-end delay. It includes all possible delays, which may be caused by propagation, queuing and processing. The lower end-to-end delay value means the better result. The end-to-end delay (*De2e*) is given like follow formula:

$$De2e = \sum_{1}^{N} (SedTi - RecTi) \Big/ \sum_{1}^{n} RecPkts \qquad (2)$$

The ratio of statistical number of routing packets generated in the network to the statistical number of request packets generated by all the simulated networks is defined as routing overhead. It reveals the utilization of the network bandwidth. The higher value of routing overhead means poorer throughput and longer delay. The lower routing overhead indicates a better result. The routing overhead (*Or*) is written as:

$$Or = \sum_{1}^{N} RouPktsN \Big/ \sum_{1}^{n} ReqPktsS \qquad (3)$$

4.1 Simulated Network Assumptions

The simulated network comprises sixty routers, thirty HTTP traffic sources and ten data sources. All content stores were initially empty, and they got filled in with data as simulation continued. In this simulated network, this paper made following assumptions corresponding with [7] in order to facilitate comparison with SCNR.

1) The topology of the network is generated by manipulator software based on Power Law (Rank Exponent) distribution with r=3[8][9].
2) Traffic generation is an important part of the simulation. In this experiment, the appropriate traffic load is generated by simultaneously starting forty distinct content request flows.
3) The results of Sandvine's fall 2011 "Global internet Phenomena Spotlight" Survey showed that Hypertext Transfer Protocol HTTP traffic dominates Internet traffic [10]. Therefore, the HTTP over this simulated network will be taken.
4) The data networks traffic is characterized by extreme variability. In this experiment, the different heavy-tailedness of inter-arrival interval times is experimented by utilizing different values for alpha parameter of Pareto distribution for example 0.5, 1.0, 1.5 and 2.0.

4.2 Simulation Architecture and Results

As shown in Fig. 3, there are two planes in architecture of ICN network based on OpenFlow:

1) A data plane with the Serving Nodes (content producers), the End-Nodes (content requesters/consumers) and the Reconfigurable ICN nodes.
2) A control plane with the Name Routing System (composed by NRS Nodes). The two planes communicate with an extended OpenFlow interface, by using the NRS nodes to control one or more Reconfigurable ICN nodes. In this architecture, the NRS is responsible for name-based routing by implying ICN functionality as a set of OpenFlow controllers.

Table 1. Comparison of lookup-and-cache, flooding, expanding ring, random walk, alpha=1

	Success Rate (Sr)	Routing Overhead (Or)	Average End-to-End Delay (De2e)
Lookup-and-Cache	99.9	50	0.48
Flooding	99.9	268	1.10
Expanding Ring	99.6	231	1.09
Random Walk	99.9	141	0.79

Table 2. Comparison of Lookup-and-Cache, Flooding, Expanding Ring, Random Walk, Alpha=1.5

	Success Rate (Sr)	Routing Overhead (Or)	Average End-to-End Delay (De2e)
Lookup-and-Cache	99.9	32	0.29
Flooding	99.9	102	0.73
Expanding Ring	99.7	99	0.93
Random Walk	99.9	50	0.60

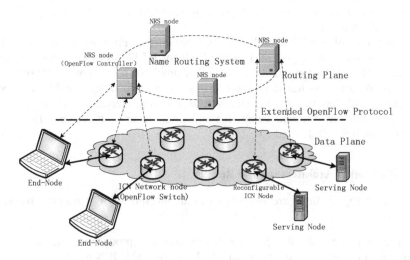

Fig. 3. ICN network based on OpenFlow

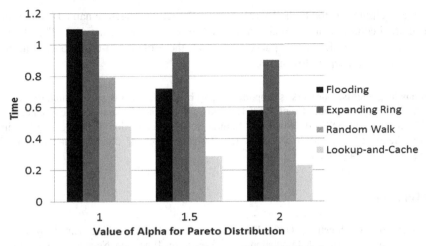

Fig. 4. Comparison of Averaged End-to-End Delay

The work of realizing ICN on OpenFlow, and its architectural in [6] can be referenced by us. Hence we focus on comparison of evaluation performance between Lookup-and-cache in SCNR and flooding, random walk, expanding ring presented in [7]. The averaged end-to-end delay behaviors of Lookup-and-cache, flooding, random walk, and expanding ring over two hours duration are shown in Fig. 4. We should note that the reconfigurable ICN nodes and NRS system needs a little time to initialize and configure. The RIB calculation in NRS will finish as soon as the nodes boot up, and subsequently the FIB stored in router's forwarding module will be constructed completely. Therefore the queries are satisfied from router's cache thereby reducing end-to-end delay greatly.

Tables 1, 2 give the comparison of success rate, packet overhead and end-to-end delay for lookup-and-cache, flooding, random walk and expanding ring for value of alpha equal to 1.0 and 1.5 respectively.

The simulation results show that the Lookup-and-Cache has the minimal routing overhead per request packet. The success rate of lookup-and-cache, flooding and random walk are comparable. The success rate of expanding ring is less than others, because the requested content cannot be accessed with initial TTL value with high probability. However, lookup-and-cache offers the smallest end-to-end delay followed by others.

5   Conclusion

In this paper, we implemented SCNR algorithms over OpenFlow and carried out a comparison with the similar transfer scenario of [7]. The SCNR algorithm separates the FIB from the RIB which is generated by calculating routing tables. This scenario can overcome two severe problems. First, the current FIB technology is impractical to contain all name-based routes. Second, the cost of implementing a large RIB in routing equipment is too high. Therefore the RIB-FIB architecture named lookup-and-cache architecture is an efficient solution to the reconfigurable network. The elementary simulation results of this paper show that, the lookup-and-cache offers the best performance over OpenFlow network.

Acknowledgements. Our work is supported in part by the National Basic Research Program of China (973 Program) under Grant 2012CB315904, the National Natural Science Foundation of China under Grant NSFC61179028, the Natural Science Foundation of Guangdong Province under Grant NSFGD S2013020012822, the Basic Research of Shenzhen under Grant SZ JCYJ20130331144502026.

References

1. Jacobson, V., Smetters, D.K., Thornton, J.D., et al.: Networking named content. In: Proceedings of the 5th International Conference on Emerging Networking Experiments and Technologies, pp. 1–12. ACM (2009)
2. Koponen, T., Chawla, M., Chun, B.G., et al.: A data-oriented (and beyond) network architecture. ACM SIGCOMM Computer Communication Review **37**(4): 181–192 (2007)
3. Named Data Networking (NDN). http://www.named-data.net/
4. Detti, A., Blefari, M.N., Salsano, S., et al.: CONET: a content centric inter-networking architecture. In: Proceedings of the ACM SIGCOMM Workshop on Information-Centric Networking, pp. 50–55. ACM (2011)
5. McKeown, N., Anderson, T., Balakrishnan, H., et al.: OpenFlow: enabling innovation in campus networks. ACM SIGCOMM Computer Communication Review **38**(2), 69–74 (2008)
6. Detti, A., Salsano, S., Blefari-Melazzi, N.: IPv4 and IPv6 Options to support Information Centric Networking. Internet Draft, draft-detti-conet-ip-option-02, Work in progress (2011)
7. Ul Haque, M., Pawlikowski, K, Willig, A., et al.: Performance analysis of blind routing algorithms over content centric networking architecture. In: 2012 International Conference on Computer and Communication Engineering (ICCCE), pp. 922–927. IEEE (2012)
8. Faloutsos, M., Faloutsos, P., Faloutsos, C.: On power-law relationships of the internet topology. ACM SIGCOMM Computer Communication Review **29**(4), 251–262 (1999)
9. Magoni, D.: nem: A software for network topology analysis and modeling. In: Proceedings of the 10th IEEE International Symposium on Modeling, Analysis and Simulation of Computer and Telecommunications Systems, 2002, MASCOTS 2002, pp. 364–371. IEEE (2002)
10. Sandvine, Global Internet Phenomena Spotlight Europe, Fixed Access, Fall 2011, (accessed On: April 14, 2012).
    http://www.sandvine.com/news/globalbroadbandtrens.asp

Workshop on Mobile Cloud Computing (MCC 2014)

Research on Cloud Computing in the Application of the Quality Course Construction

HuiKui Zhou and MuDan Gu[⌂]

Nanchang Institute of Science & Technology, Jiangxi, China
583517476@qq.com

Abstract. In order to solve the Four Problems in present quality course establishing and the redundancy in Cloud Service, this paper studies the effective ways of improving the Cloud Service, and also introduces the Chord algorithm into Cloud Computation. A multiple Chord loop model is constructed based on a master-slave structure system, and after analyzing the routing list of the nodes in the loops a new calculation formula of the routing list is put forward. As the study shows, the improved calculation decreases obviously in the average routing hops and average network delay, thus the effectiveness of resource searching is improved.

Keywords: Cloud computation · Course establishing · Chord algorithm

1   Introduction

With the popularity of Internet, network teaching is more and more enjoyed by the learners. Through the excellent courses construction, promote discipline construction and teaching reform in colleges and universities. Course of information construction has obtained certain achievements, but the four problems existing in the course construction: access, compatible, update, interactive, hindered the further development of exquisite course construction. How to make use of cloud computing technology to promote the development of the fine course construction, which is an important research significance. This paper mainly studies how to use cloud computing to solve the four problems and study the effective ways to improve the cloud service.

2   High-Quality Course Construction Problem

Since starting construction project, the major national fine course construction is developing, but there are still many problems in the curriculum resources application, outstanding performance at the four problems [1].

(1) Hardly access

The current number of fine courses online sharing is very handsome, but due to the different colleges and universities in the process of making excellent courses hard software and the use of the network language is not the same, especially dependent plug-ins. There is much broadband audio video content in the course, it is difficult for

This work was supported by jiangxi subject project: JXJG-13-27-8.

© Institute for Computer Sciences, Social Informatics and Telecommunications Engineering 2014
V.C.M. Leung et al. (Eds.): TridentCom 2014, LNICST 137, pp. 455–462, 2014.
DOI: 10.1007/978-3-319-13326-3_44

the visitors to the curriculum for curriculum resources effectively. The bandwidth of the part of the course website is limited, prone to access congestion and can't open the website. So the curriculum resource access difficultly is become a bottleneck problem of exquisite course application sharing [2].

(2) Difficultly update

According to the requirements of the department in charge of education, fine courses should be updated regularly, but only 20% of survey data show that the recent one year or so. Because of the course update control platform design is not convenient, the school's network management is responsible for the curriculum information update slowly. [3]

(3) Difficultly Compatible

Due to the lack of mandatory for material requirements of technical standard, the ministry of education of different colleges and universities in the process of making excellent courses hard software and the diversity of network language influence the universality and compatibility of courseware resources sharing, this is especially an obvious on the video file sharing. [4]Video file format is the lack of diversity, speed slowly, factors such as lack of restricted access to users in the course, ultimately affect the use effect of the curriculum resources.

(4) Difficultly interactive

Most of the courses are not possible to exchange the discussion for the users and lack of interaction, school-teachers are difficult to accurately grasp the students' feedback information, etc. Colleagues, download courses are mainly composed of self-study students, teachers and students lack of interactive learning atmosphere [5].

3   Cloud Computing in the Application of the Quality Course Construction

In order to solve the four problems in the construction of excellent courses, the application of cloud computing in the construction of excellent courses. Make full use of the advantages of cloud computing, can better play in the exemplary role of excellent courses, promote the co-construction and sharing of subject construction. The current cloud computing with powerful computing and storage capacity, the cloud chart as shown in figure 1. Based on the data storage center, the data information can be strictly and effective management and control, and has a very high safety and reliability connection properties [6].

3.1   Building Exquisite Course of Cloud Platform

Application of cloud computing in the construction of excellent courses does not need to data information platform to make many changes, which realize the integration of education resources to the greatest extent. The main role of cloud computing in the high-quality goods curriculum construction as shown in figure 2, high share technical advantages of cloud computing to the existing high-quality goods curriculum resources into a super resources "cloud" as a whole, make the high quality curriculum resources can be developed with equal sharing among colleges and universities in underdeveloped areas.

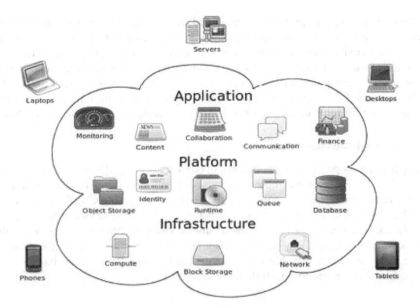

Fig. 1. Cloud computing

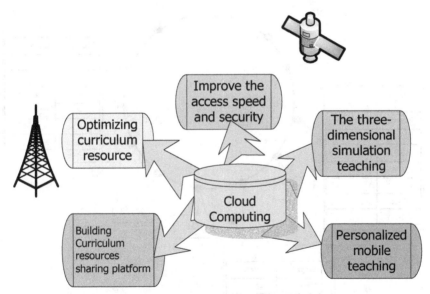

Fig. 2. Cloud computing application in curriculum construction

Appear easily in the construction process of different colleges and universities to build a course at the same time, the mutual relationship between their respective problems will lead to the same high quality courses construction, the use of cloud computing for excellent courses can give full play to the cloud computing sharing and optimization of the technological advantage, this can solve the problem of data redundancy and waste of resources [7].

Cloud computing can provide an integrated computing environment, all data are stored in the cloud, the user with access to the use of cloud computing can achieve the same working environment, user can choose according to their requirements in terms of curriculum resources. Cloud computing to build learning school teaching groups, users need to update a computer hardware and software upgrades, and only need to install a web browser on the computer, it is not affected by time and space limit to carry out teaching activities, implementation of personalized mobile excellent courses teaching.

3.2   Study Chord Algorithm

The application scope of excellent courses in order to meet the demands of the masses of users in a timely manner, improving the speed and security of the curriculum re-source access is more and more important. The cloud computing Chord algorithm [8] can solve the problem of difficult access, but there is also some disadvantages, For example, the heterogeneity of nodes and redundant routing table is too large, when the network scale, these problems will seriously restrict the performance of the network resources in the search. So this article study Chord algorithm, on the basis of the original Chord algorithm to do a little improvement.

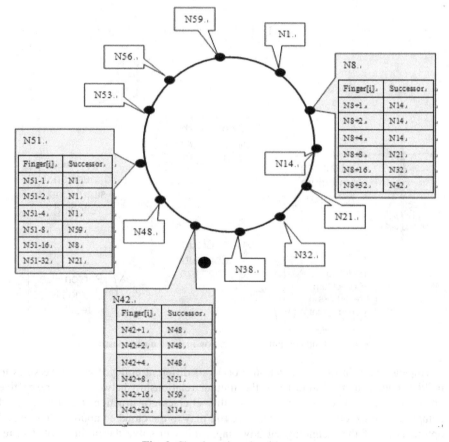

Fig. 3. Chord routing algorithms

From a macro perspective to look at the cloud computing network, because of the cloud computing network is composed of a number of cloud server together, we make a cloud server in the network, a node called cloud, as constitute the basic elements of network topology, and Chord link points. Basic structure of Chord routing algorithms such as figure 3, cloud node in the ability of processing data, storage, online there are differences in time and bandwidth.

Specific idea is: first of all, every cloud nodes in the network IP address, the same cloud nodes in the network number as a group, a Chord from the ring. And then in each group, a node evaluate the performance of the comparison of cloud, according to the result of the comparative evaluation, choose the best performance for super cloud node, and in the other group super cloud node according to the Chord algorithm of Chord main ring; Select performance after super node as a backup cloud node, in this super cloud node failure or leave the network, to take his work as new super cloud node. in order to facilitate description, we established in this definition the model for MC - Chord, concrete model structure as shown in figure 4.

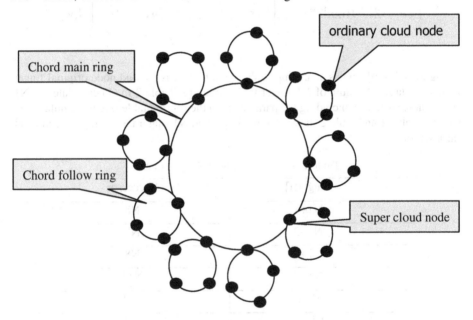

Fig. 4. MC-Chord

3.3 The Design of the Routing Table

In this model, the first super cloud node is the subordinate to the Chord from one member of the ring, so I need a table from the ring finger to show in each cloud node from the ring, the relationship between the super node is part of the Chord ring Lord of cloud, so you also need a main ring finger table to represent the main ring on the rela-tionship between the various super cloud node. For ordinary cloud nodes, only need one from the ring finger to indicate where the relationship between the each cloud node from the ring. Considering the particularity of back-up cloud node, in addition to said there is a node of the relationship between the ring clouds from the ring finger table, must also have a completely different and this group of super cloud nodes of the main ring finger table.

For each finger table above, in order to improve the routing efficiency, in this paper, on the basis of MC - Chord, finger table of node calculation formula is modified, the modified model is called the MFC - Chord. First of all, I consider it step by step, and the formula of introducing a parameter d, d said the distance between the current and subsequent cloud node. Due to the consistent hash function can make all the physical node roughly uniform distribution on the Chord ring, so any cloud node and its successor cloud node distance are roughly equal. The improved calculation formula is as follows:

$$
\text{Finger}[j] = \begin{cases} (n+d)\bmod 2^m \cdots\cdots 1 \leqslant i \leqslant \left\lfloor \log_2^d + 1 \right\rfloor, j = 1 \\ (n+2^{i-1})\bmod 2^m \cdots\cdots \left\lfloor \log_2^d + 1 \right\rfloor < i \leqslant m, j = i - \left\lfloor \log_2^d \right\rfloor \end{cases}
$$

(1)

Figure 4 Chord ring as an example, shown in table 1 is a cloud node original finger table calculation formula of N1 finger table structure. Table 2 in (1) calculate the N1 finger table structure, including the parameters in the routing table finger formula d = 6. Contrast table 1 and table 2 shows that the improved N1 finger table without redundant information.

Table 1. The original Chord N1 finger table

Finger[i]	Successor
N1+1	N8
N1+2	N8
N1+4	N8
N1+8	N14
N1+16	N21
N1+32	N38

Table 2. Conclusion by type (1) N1 finger table

Finger[i]	Successor
N1+6	N8
N1+8	N14
N1+16	N21
N1+32	N38

Resources localization process

From the ring to find in the first place, if you can find the required resources, looking for an end to; Otherwise, and then to find between ring, until find relevant resources, the main steps are as follows:

(a)   Cloud node query, first of all nodes in the cloud resource list query, if found direct return; Otherwise, turn to (b).

(b)   In this cloud nodes belonging to a Chord from the ring shall be carried out in accordance with the routing policy lookup, if we can find the resources needed to deposit target cloud node, it returns the query results, or into (c).

(c)   Whether the cloud node from the ring to belong to super node of cloud, if yes, are converted to (e); Otherwise to (d).

(d)   This cloud node will request from the ring to belong to super cloud node.

(e)   Super cloud nodes on the Chord ring Lord carried out in accordance with the routing lookup strategy to find the target from the ring's super cloud node, if successful, turn to the next step; Otherwise the query fails.

(f)   Goals from the ring's super cloud node according to the routing lookup strategy in the node from the ring to find target cloud, if we can find, the query is successful, returns the query result; Otherwise, the query fails.

4   Conclusion

Based on the introduction of cloud computing in the construction of excellent courses, building the cloud service platform and optimizing the Chord algorithm in cloud computing, MC - Chord model was established. On the one hand, This model build a super node of cloud, solve the Chord system without considering the heterogeneity of the nodes, on the other hand the Chord routing table algorithm is improved, and reduce the redundant information routing table, expanded the coverage of the routing table. Experiment proves that the construction of excellent courses of cloud service platform can effectively solve the four problems in the construction of excellent courses. But a perfect quality courses cloud service platform structures requires more information resource and high configuration of the server hardware, need much money and skilled technical support. It is difficult to achieve a school. We need the government department report, enterprises and schools of cooperation to do together.

References

1. Shi, S.: Research on cloud computing and services framework of marine environmental information management. Acta Oceanologica Sinica **10**, 57–66 (2013)
2. Kim, W., Diko, M., Rawson, K.: Network Motif Detection: Algorithms. Parallel and Cloud Computing, and Related Tools, Tsinghua Science and Technology. **5**, 469–489 (2013)
3. Saripalli, P., Walters, B.A.: Quantitative Impact and Risk Assess-ment Framework for Cloud Security. In: Proceedings of IEEE 3rd International Conference on Cloud Computing, pp. 280–288 (2010)
4. Tian, W.: CRESS: A Platform of Infrastructure Resource Sharing for Educational Cloud Computing. China Communications. **9**, 43–52 (2013)

5. Wu, H.: A benefit-aware on-demand provisioning approach for multi-tier applications in cloud computing. Frontiers of Computer Science in China. **4**, 459–474 (2013)
6. Guo, L.-Z.: Particle Swarm Optimization Embedded in Variable Neighborhood Search for Task Scheduling in Cloud Computing. Journal of Donghua University. **30**(2), 145–152 (2013)
7. Mei, J.-Q., Ji, H., Li, T.: Cross-layer optimized Chord protocol for separated ring convergence in MANET. The Journal of China Universities of Posts and Telecommunications. **4**, 84–90 (2009)
8. Burresi, S., Canali, C., Renda, M.E., et al.: MeshChord: a location-aware, cross-layer specialization of Chord for wireless Mesh networks (concise contribution). In: Proceedings of the 6th Annual IEEE International Conference on Pervasive Computing and Communications (PerCom 2008), Hong Kong, China, March 17–21, 9.06–212. IEEE, Piseataway (2008)
9. Wei, D., Iyengar, S.S.: Bootstrapping Chord over MANETs: all roads lead to rome. In: Proceeding of the IEEE Wireless Communications and Networking Conference (WCNC 2007), Hung Kong, China, March 11–15, pp. 3501–3506. IEEE, New York (2007)

The Study on the Network Security Simulation for HITLS Technology

MuDan Gu[1(✉)], HuiKui Zhou[1], YingHan Hong[2], and Li Zhang[1]

[1] Nanchang Institute of Science & Technology, Jiangxi, China
583517476@qq.com
[2] Hanshan Normal University, Guangdong, China

Abstract. Network security simulation model for HITLS technology is established, which aims to solve the problems in present network security simulation, that is, the network vulnerability and lack of network attack responses. This paper studies the implement methods of this model from the angle of basic structure, network security simulation frame and simulation controlling. The simulation environment based on network security simulation model for HITLS technology can provide fast and safe prototyping, demonstration, testing, and analysis, which evaluates the safety and performance of the equipment. By comparing the numbers of success for network communication before and after signaling and link attacking, the effectiveness of this method is verified. The model has broad application prospects.

Keywords: HITLS technology · Network security simulation · Attack effect simulation

1 Introduction

HITLS refers to the loop simulation, under the premises of meeting the conditions, which puts the object into the simulation system as much as possible and replaces the corresponding mathematical model. So simulation system is closer to the actual situation, and the credibility of the simulation can be drawn. There are some key technologies which needed to be solved in network security simulation, such as difficulties in network security model, lack of responses to the network attack in application and there is no uniform standard to evaluate the effect of such attacks on network security. Loop simulation system can have the actual hardware and software modules, so the loop simulation network simulation is not only more accurate than a simple inspection of protocols and algorithms, but also requires fewer hardware and software resources than the actual number of experiments with more good experimental manipulation, which can achieve a repeatable experiment, and can achieve a larger-scale network security simulation [1].

2 Network Security Model

2.1 Formal Description of Network Security Modeling Environment

Firstly, abstracted from the static model of computer network [2], namely supposes R is first in the network router set, H is the main engine set, L is the point-to-point link

---

This work was supported by jiangxi subject project: JXJG-13-27-8.

V.C.M. Leung et al. (Eds.): TridentCom 2014, LNICST 137, pp. 463–471, 2014.
DOI: 10.1007/978-3-319-13326-3_45

set, C is the sharing link set, then the whole network of routing topology is $T = (R, L, \varphi)$, and the mapping $\varphi : L \rightarrow R \times R$ said adjacency relations. If H and C is not empty then there is a division of $\{H_1, H_2, \cdots, H_n\}$ and $\{C_1, C_2, \cdots, C_n\}$, so $\forall i \in [1, n], \exists r \in R$ and $N_i = (\{r\} \cup H_i, C_i, \varphi_i)$ constitutes a fully connected graph, including n for LAN quantity.

On the other hand, Data packet transmission based on the discrete dynamics of computer networks and discrete event systems (DEVS) match[3]. Thus, according to automata theory and discrete event systems, Network Modeling presented a general formal description of the environment. Modeling environment automaton M, namely a 7-tuple $(Q, V, \Sigma, \Gamma, Y, q_0, F)$, where :

① Q representative state sets;

② V representative Area. in set;

③ Σ Representative external events set;

④ Γ Representative internal affair sets;

⑤ Y Representative transfer function sets, and: $Y = \begin{cases} \{\delta_{ext}, \delta_{int1}\} & \Sigma \neq \Phi \\ \{\delta_{int2}\} & \Sigma = \Phi \end{cases}$

$$\begin{pmatrix} \delta_{ext} : Q \times \sum \times V \times N \xrightarrow{c_1} Q \times \Gamma \\ \delta_{int1} : Q \times \Gamma \times N \xrightarrow{c_1, c_2} Q \times \Psi(\Gamma) \times \Psi(\sum) \\ \delta_{int2} : Q \times \Gamma \longrightarrow Q \times \Psi(\Gamma) \times N \end{pmatrix}$$

And in the formula, N expresses the real clock, Ψ expressed that (event) the output function, c_1 and c_2 are the real-time constraints.

⑥ $q_0 \in Q$ for initial state;

⑦ $F \in Q$ for termination state sets;

Here, V of the element indicates the reception and processing of those events, so $V \subseteq R \cup H \cup L \cup C$, Σ is M and external interaction packets sets. A list used to manage internal event to be processed, the table element $(\lambda, v, t) \in \Gamma$ value that is characterized by λ inside the event, will always be received and processed by v at t time. M, able to generate a variety of network models rely mainly on the rich behavior of the transfer function, where:

$\delta_{ext}(q_1, p, v, t) = (q_2, e)$, in state q_1 that receives the external event p (Area. in v, Time t) will cause the state transition to q_2, and produce internal affair e.

$\delta_{int1}(q_1,e_1,t)=(q_2,E,P)$, in state q_1 that receives the internal affair e (Time t) will cause the state transition to q_2, produce internal affair E and external events subset P.

$\delta_{int2}(q_1,e_1)=(q_2,E,t_1)$, in state q_1 that receives the internal affair e_1 will cause the state transition to q_2, Time advance to t and a subset of internal events generated E.

c_1 : $rt(\delta)<t_\delta$, Which $rt(\delta)$ return after the execution time value δ for the execution of $(\lambda_\delta,v_\delta,t_\delta)$ after δ list of minimum value of t event.

c_2 : $\delta_{int1}(q_1,(\lambda_1,v_1,t_1),t)=(q_2,E,P)$ established, if and only if $0\le t-t_1\le\varepsilon$, where t is the current time, and ε for the regulator.

2.2   Network Security Model of Virtual Degrees Are Classified

According to the description of modeling environment formalization , definition of models of virtual degrees division was further got. $M=(Q,V,\Sigma,\Gamma,Y,q_0,F)$ [4] :

① When $V=R\cup L$ and $\Sigma\ne\Phi$, the resulting network model is semi-virtual. Model only subnet for virtual communication, the host is located external to interact with the data model.

② When $V=R\cup H\cup L\cup C$ and $\Sigma\ne\Phi$, the resulting network model is quasi-virtual. Events within the model were extended to receive and process all network elements can be abstract, so the model must complete the network virtualization layers.

③ When $V\subseteq R\cup H\cup L\cup C$ and $\Sigma=\Phi$, the resulting network model is all virtual.

2.3   The Network Security Model and Scale Fidelity

Modeling environment using the network model has generated the fidelity problem, that is, accuracy in expressing the real system model. Fidelity is a major measure for modeling, but because of the complexity and diversity of the real system, it is difficult to obtain the fidelity of the quantitative indicators, therefore it has to be measured from the model range, the details of the number, effectiveness and other a qualitative measure of respect. [5]

3   Based on HITLS Network Security Simulation Model

The simulation model of network security based on HITLS mainly includes the following several systems: HITLS technology network security test simulation

subsystem, credibility validation subsystem, subsystems of safety evaluation simulation. The subsystems based on high level architecture[6], (HLA) were integrated together, convenient for users to use simulation control platform and the demo surveillance system simulation real-time monitoring and results check.

3.1   HITLS Network Security Simulation Model of Basic Structure

Network security simulation [7] can be divided into the following steps: preparation, execution and analysis. In the implementation process, monitor the whole process of simulation when making use of simulation and control platform, to ensure HITLS network simulation loop network data conversion completed in real time and interactive, while the simulation process can be collected in the corresponding statistical data. In addition, in order to improve simulation credibility, a subsystem for verifying the credibility of a simulation should be established to inspect and verify the whole process of simulation. Diagram of network security simulation model based on HITLS as shown in Fig. 1.

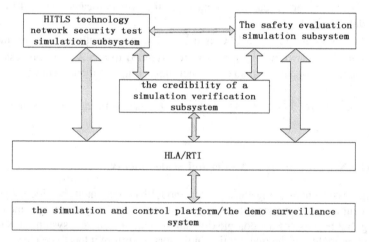

Fig. 1. HITLS diagram of network security model simulation

Network security simulation model based on simulation HITLS node will directly use the real network protocol stack TCP/IP protocol stack for the communication, the construction of the virtual node with a virtual network card, making the virtual node close to the real web presence. The virtual node network API calls directly through real TCP/IP network protocol stack to communicate with other nodes. The simulation environment management node is responsible only for construction of the link between the analog channels. And because of the direct use of real network protocol stack, the simulation results are reliable and accurate. Network simulation model is shown in Fig.2.

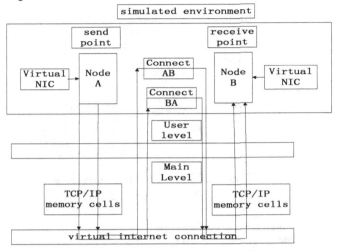

Fig. 2. Simulation model based on network security diagram HITLS

3.2   HITLS Based Simulation Framework for Network Security

Based on the above model of new network simulation, we join simulation of the network environment and the real network environment due to the need for loop network simulation, Then we also need to provide a network emulation package intercepted, the implementation framework is shown in Fig.3 based on the design goals of general-purpose database. Intermediate driver: operate in the system kernel, and provide the underlying system functions and the hardware abstraction layer functions for the network interface user-level programs, to achieve hardware independence.

User-level library: operate in the user level, provide the main program with further abstract unified interface of the application program, call the intermediate driver to the next interface. Main documents: the application through the library calls interface applications that operate in the project that simulation platform.

3.3   Based on Network Security Simulation Control of HITLS Technology

Simulation control is in the process of simulation, and operation of various simulation resources coordination and scheduling in general, including initialization, start, pause, resume, synchronization, stop, cancel, monitoring. In the OPNET simulation primarily through external control technology to achieve an external program of ESA OPNET simulation process control, ESA API is a set of OPNET provides external program interface functions, including simulation of process control, interface to access, input and output, blending the four function sets. Among them, the simulation process control functions are used to set an OPNET simulation and control events to advance and keep OPNET simulation clock. The interfaces to the main function is to provide external nodes and internal between the nodes for communication interface. Input/Output function will be responsible for the OPNET simulation data read or write. ODB provides the use of mixed-function to debug and observe the distribution of memory cells in memory and interaction.

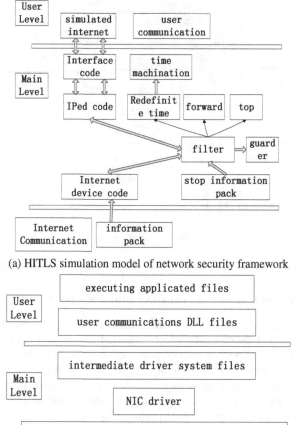

(a) HITLS simulation model of network security framework

(b) File system simulation model of network security map

Fig. 3. Simulation Model Based on HITLS network security implementation framework

4   Based on Applications of HITLS Network Security Simulation Model

4.1   Simulation of Network Security Equipment

Simulation environment is established according to the network simulation model based on HITLS, provides fast prototyping, demonstration, testing and analysis. Specifically, establish the safety model and environment model under the premise of studying the basic functions and implementation principles of the safety equipment, according to the design methodology and technical documents, and then design a variety of simulation experiments on the important security features and performance indicator simulation, and thus evaluate the safety and performance of the equipment.

4.2 Simulation of Network Attacks

Network attack simulation needs to establish the corresponding mathematical model or simulator using real network attacks, as many of the integration of existing instances of attacks and attack, for example, DOS attacks, worm propagation, DDOS [8] attacks, spoofing attacks, and then use these attacks against the system model or a variety of simulation experiments to study and verify the network parameters, the attacker when the attack effect parameters changes.

4.3 Simulation of Attack Effects

Target network and its traffic model for voice transmission to a public telephone network and its traffic model, attack models, including model and link signaling device attacks against equipment model, simulate, respectively, blocking malicious interference call and two e-attacks. Attack and attack the signaling link to the target network device model, the simulation run the entire network.

The simulation network operations, network operations in the process of collecting data such as throughput, delay and connection rate and so on. The connection rate, for example, attacks by adding, respectively, before and after the completion rate is shown in Fig.4 and Fig.5, by comparison, to analyze the attack effect. From the simulation results we have the following conclusions:

(1) Through the link to block interference, it can affect the data transmission route, add a link load, and interfere with the normal user's connection rate.

(2) By signaling attacks, for example, prevalent malicious network call information can be gathered to increase the network load, the user's information through the interference with the normal rate, in turn, can interfere with the normal operation of communication networks.

(3) Link blocking attack is to block a link, so that communication data transmitted by other routes, increasing the burden on other links. Signaling is active against a large amount of malicious traffic information transmitted through the network, increasing the burden of communication networks.

(4) Evaluation by means of attack, attack on the network effect was measured, and the link attacks and the effect of signaling the value of attack, the results are shown in Tab.1, table m that network communication distance.The average effect of two attacks were 3.27 and 1.68. Evaluation criteria for the attacker are able to give the following conclusions: the attack of two attack effect "significant"; signaling attack effect is slightly better than the link attack effect.

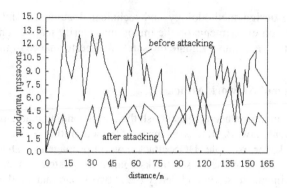

Fig. 4. Signaling attacks before and after the success of the number of network communication

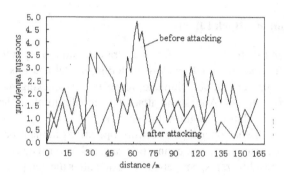

Fig. 5. Link attack before and after the success number of network communication

Table 1. Two attacking effect values

	Effect Value (link attack)	Effect Value (signaling attack)
m=0	3.0	3.0
m=15	2.0	3.7
m=30	4.3	2.3
m=45	3.2	1.2
m=60	4.0	2.4
m=75	2.0	1.5
m=90	6.3	1.2

5   Conclusions

Loop simulation is introduced into the network security simulation model, which establishes the simulation model of network security based on HITLS, including the formalized description, classification methods of virtual degrees and fidelity modeling of the network security modeling.

The simulation model of network security based on HITLS is established, which expounds on the system structure, the basic framework and the control of the network security simulation model.

The application of simulation model for network security based on HITLS is discussed, which studies the numbers of success of network traffic before and after signaling and link, and verifies the validity of the method. The model has broad application prospects.

References

1. Chen, Z.: TIFAflow: Enhancing Traffic Archiving System with Flow Granularity for Forensic Analysis in Network Security. Tsinghua Science and Technology **4**, 406–417 (2013)
2. Arun, M., Krishnan, A.: Functional Verification of Signature Detection Architectures for High Speed Network Applications. International Journal of Automation and Computing **4**, 395–402 (2012)
3. Saripalli, P., Walters, B.A.: Quantitative Impact and Risk Assess-ment Framework for Cloud Security Proceedings of IEEE 3rd International Conference on Cloud Computing, pp. 280–288 (2010)
4. Sjodin, M.: A study of Modeling and Simulation for computer and network security. University of Stockholm/Royal Institute of Technology (2005)
5. Tian, G.: A New Network Simulation Model Based on half Material Object-in-the-loop Simulation. Computer Engineering and Applications (2006)
6. Wang, S.Y., Kung, H.T.: A New Methodology for Easily Constructing Extensible and High-Fidelity TCP/IP Network Simulators. Computer Networks **40**(2), 257–278 (2002)
7. Yang, Xuelin: High-speed optical binary data pattern recognition for network security applications. Frontiers of Optoelectronics **5–3**, 271–278 (2012)
8. Webb, R.P., Yang, X.L., Manning, R.J., Maxwell, G.D., Poustie, A.J., Lardenois, S., Cotter, D.: All-optical binary pattern recognition at 42 Gb/s. Journal of Lightwave Technology **27**(13), 2240–2245 (2009)
9. Webb, R.P., Dailey, J.M., Manning, R.J., Maxwell, G.D., Poustie, A.J., Lardenois, S., Harmon, R., Harrison, J., Kopidakis, G., Athanasopoulos, E., Krithinakis, A., Doukhan, F., Omar, M., Vaillant, D., Di, N.F., Koyabe, M., Di Cairano-Gilfedder, C.: All-optical header processing in a 42.6 Gb/s optoelectronic firewall. IEEE Journal of Selected Topics in Quantum Electronics 18(2), 757–764 (2012)
10. Ren, W., Jiang, X H., Sun, T.F.: RBFNN-based prediction of networks security situation. Computer Engineering and Applications 42(31), 136–139 (2006)

An Improved Access Control Model for the CSCD Environment

Ai Fei[✉] and Zhang Ping

School of Computer Science & Engineering, South China University of Technology,
Guangzhou, China
{aifei,pzhang}@scut.edu.cn

Abstract. For the Computer Supported Collaborative Design (CSCD) environment's groups, dynamics and distribution characteristics, the paper proposes a Task & Role-Based access control model (T & RBAC) and makes the informal definition of the model. The T & RBAC model is based on the T-RBAC model, and extends the definition of the Users, Roles, Tasks, Permissions and the other factors. In the T&RBAC model, Roles are classified into two classes: job position and business role. As a passive role, permissions are preasigned to the job function Role. By the other way, the business role is assigned to the task in the business process, and the permissions are actived by the context of the task's excuted status, so that the paper realizes the active and passive access control. Finally, we applied the T&RBAC model in the CSCD system and validated the model.

Keywords: CSCD · Access control · T-RBAC · Task · Role

1 Introduction

The Computer Supported Collaborative Design (CSCD) is based on the computer technology, multimedia technology and network communication technology, it supports the members of team to work together in order to accomplish a mutual design project in a shared environment by the interactive consultations, division of the works and the mutual collaboration [1] [2]. In the collaborative environment, the members of the team share the design resources through internal and external networks, but the shared resources are all the business securities of the enterprise. How to ensure these resources' availability, accuracy, and how to avoid hacking have been the critical problems in collaborative work environment [3] [4].

From the system's point of view, the CSCD system is passive and provides the functional HCI. But by the perspective of the collaboration work, the collaborative design is the business process and is active. The collaborative environment changes in the context of the design tasks' executed. The purpose of this paper is to propose a proper model of the access control for the CSCD's environment. The improved access control model named the Task and Role-based access control model (T & RBAC) is founded on the two core concepts of the Task and the Role, which reflect the characteristics of CSCD environment.

© Institute for Computer Sciences, Social Informatics and Telecommunications Engineering 2014
V.C.M. Leung et al. (Eds.): TridentCom 2014, LNICST 137, pp. 472–479, 2014.
DOI: 10.1007/978-3-319-13326-3_46

The remainder of this paper is organized as follows: Section 2 reviews the previous research related to the access control, including the weaknesses of their applications in the CSCD environment. Section 3 describes the work modes in the CSCD environment, and those modes induce the different access modes of the information objects for the user. Section 4 proposes the T&RBAC model and makes formal definitions of the model. Section 5 depicts the T & RBAC model's implement in a CSCD system which supports the collaborative industrial design work among the team members who distribute in the different regions. Section 6 presents the conclusion of this paper.

2   Related Work

International Organization for Standardization (ISO) divided the security service into five levels: authentication, access control, data security, data integrity, and denying. The access control is one of the important security parts. Access control [5] is the means to make a proper access to the protected resources, it's final objective is to ensure the authenticated users to access the authorized resources availably, in order to avoid damaging fault to make the resources to be outflowed.

So far, many traditional access control models have been developed. The main ones include the Discretionary access control (DAC), Mandatory Access Control (MAC), Role-Based Access Control (RBAC), and Task-Role-based access control (T-RBAC). DAC [6,7] depends on the object's owner, who can not only access the own object but also pass the access rights of the object to the others. DAC is very flexible to the owner, but it is too weak in the access control area, for it cannot guarantee the "need-to-do" and separation of duty(SOD) principles. On the contrary, MAC [8] is too strong. It sets the security levels on the objects and users mandatorily. Only those users whose security level is higher than the object's can access the object.

In the early 1990s, National Institute of Standards and Technology(NIST)[9] proposed a role-based access control model (RBAC). The core concept of the RBAC [10] is Role. From an enterprise perspective, the notion of the role is a job position or an organization, the role collects the access privileges. As shown in fig. 1, the users get the object's access rights through the role.

Fig. 1. RBAC Approach. This shows the approach how the user to get the permissions of the object in the RBAC model.

Although RBAC is policy neutral and can perfectly reflect organization of the enterprise environment, but the access control strategy is based on passive access control and cannot fit the active access control. T-RBAC [11] is based on the RBAC. It not only contains the concepts of the RBAC, but also imports an other core concept of the Task. Task is the foundational unit of the business work, the model classifies the task into four classes and deals with each task differently according to it's class. The users obtain the permissions through the role assigned to the task. As shown in fig. 2, the permissions are granted to the task, and the task is some like the sub-role of the role.

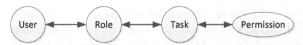

Fig. 2. T-RBAC Approach. This shows the approach how the user to get the permissions of the object in the T-RBAC model.

In conclusion, DAC is very flexible for the object owner, but it is too weak in access control. By the way, it is based on the control list . As the amount of the objects and users increases, the control list size will become larger and be more complicated to be managed; DAC is more used in the Operation System. MAC is too strong. It is based on the security levels attached to the users and objects, and guarantees the confidentiality and integrity of the information. However, it is difficult for "information shared" in the enterprise environment and inconvenient to the business process; RBAC is based on the organizational structure or group of users. The relationships between the role and permission are predefined, and the administrator only allocates the user to the role. RBAC decreases the complexity of the permission management, but it is not suitable for the workflow environment. Le Yang, Xiao Daoju, LI Cheng-kai, [12] [13] [14] have done a lots of works in the RBAC. They applied the RBAC in the CSCW environment by extending the RBAC model. T-RBAC is based on the role and the task. In the session, the user activates the access privileges by his business work. Currently, most of the collaborative work environments adopt T-RBAC model as their access control policy [15][16][17][18].

3   Requirements of Access Control in CSCD Environments

CSCD is one of the concurrent engineering[19] methodology ,it's objectives are better product quality, shorter lead-time, more competitive cost and higher customer satisfaction [20]. With the advancement of the computer and information technology, CSCD has been wildly applied in the product design field. CSCD not only supports the multidisciplinary design teams, but also crosses the boundaries of the area and time zones.

As an engineering process, CSCD is mainly based on the project. As shown in fig. 3, CSCD is structured on the organizations and projects. The users access the information by their business actives and job functions. The one type of the tasks are related to the job position in the organization. In general, such tasks are management actives which are assigned to the users according to their job positions, and they are passive; the others are related to the business role in the project. These tasks compose the business process, and on the IT's view, they are actives of the workflow. In the project, the users are allocated to the tasks by their business role, and such tasks own the special properties, such as task status, start time, end time, mutual relationship (serial, parallel, and feedback), input and output data. As a logical unit of the workflow, the active task can be completed by a person or by more people. Additionally, the task of the workflow is not insulated to each other, but depends on the other task. For example: task B is activated only after the Task A has been finished ; the output data of the task A is the Task B's input data; while the failure of the Task B occurs , the workflow would   return back to the task A, etc.

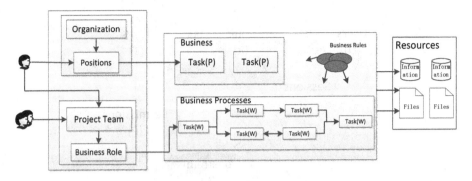

Fig. 3. CSCD's Features. This shows the features that the user gets the resources in the enterprise.

4   T & RBAC Access Control Model

As shown above, the previous works on access control do not fully meet the requirements in the CSCD environment. We presented a proved access control model T&RBAC based on the T-RBAC. T&RBAC contains the concepts of the T-RBAC, but it considers the factors in the CSCD environment more. In T-RBAC, the access rights only are assigned to the task. However in the T&RBAC, the users get the access right through the roles and the assigned tasks. The role is mapped to the job position in the organization, and the task is the active of the product design workflow. Table 1 shows Relationship between factors of CSCD and components of T&RBAC.

Table 1. Relationship between factors of CSCD and components of T&RBAC

The factors in the CSCD environment	The base components in T&RBAC
Information	Object
User, Agent	User
job position, business role	Role
Task	Task
Business process	Workflow

4.1   Formal Description of T & RBAC

Fig. 4 shows the brief overviews of T&RBAC. In the T&RBAC model, the permissions are assigned to the job position roles and the tasks. During a session, the user accesses the HCI of the CSCD system by the role according to his job position. What informations can user access by the HCI is bounded to the task that is allocated to the role of the user.

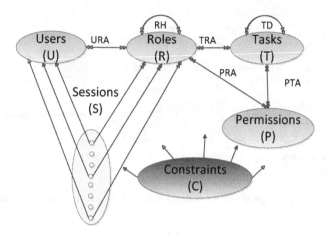

Fig. 4. T & RBAC Model. This shows the components in the T&RBAC model.

The base components in the T&RBAC are defined as follows:

Users (U): Users is a set of users and agents in the CSCD environment.

Roles (R): Roles contain two aspects. One is the position in the organization, and the other one is the business role in the business process.

Tasks (T):Task is an active of the co-design business process , it is atomic and finishes a unit of job.

Sessions (S): A session is the life time while the user is bounded to the active roles and the tasks in the workflow. When the tasks are finished or suspended, or when the user logouts from the CSCD system, the session will end.

Permissions (P): Permissions is an access policy that the authorized subject can interact on the object, including the set of the access objects and the set of operations which affect on the objects;

Constraints (C): Constraints is the abstraction of the business rules in collaborative design process, including role inheritance constraints, permissions conflict constraints, the task dependency constraints, the access scope of the Object, permissions' being activated constraints, etc.

Properties 1 (role inheritance RH). $RH \subseteq 2^R$, means that there is a hierarchy in the roles. We take senior role as the ancestor role and the junior role as the descendant role. Such hierarchy relationship can also be described as a partial order relation ($\geq$).

1) While the ancestor role is active in a session, the permissions assigned to the descendant role are inherited to the ancestor role;

$$P_i, P_j \in P, P_i \in PRA(R_i), P_j \in PRA(R_j), R_i \geq R_j \Rightarrow \{P_i, P_j\} \subseteq PRA(R_i)$$

2) While the ancestor role's permissions exclude from the permissions of the descendant role, the resolution is remaining the prior permissions. For instance, descendant role R_i is not permitted to read the object Ob_j , while the ancestor role R_j can write object Ob_j , then the ancestor role remains the write operation to the Ob_j;

$$P_i, P_j \in P, P_i \in PRA(R_i), P_j \in PRA(R_j), R_i \leq R_j, P_i \leq P_j \Rightarrow \{P_j\} \subseteq PRA(R_j)$$

Properties 3 (Users-Roles assign URA). $URA \subseteq R \times U$, a many-many relationship between the Users and Roles.

1) While a ancestor role and its descendant role are assigned to a user together, the user activates the permissions assigned to the ancestor role in a session.

$$R_i, R_j \in URA(U), R_i \leq R_j \Rightarrow Activated(R_j)$$

Properties 4 (Tasks-Roles assign TRA). TRA $\subseteq$ R $\times$ T, a many-many relationship between the Tasks and Roles.

1) If R_i excludes from R_j, the two roles could not be assigned to the tasks together. For example, the designer role and the auditor role cannot be assigned to a task .

$$R_i, R_j \in TRA(T) \Rightarrow R_i \notin Excluding(R_j)$$

Properties 5 (Tasks-Tasks dependence TD). T$\times$T $\subseteq 2^{TD}$, TD = { serial, parallel, feedback }.

Properties 6 (Roles-Permissions assign PRA). PRA $\subseteq$ P$\times$R, a role has a set of Permissions to execute the job. The mutual-exclusive Permissions cannot be assigned to one role.

Properties 7 (Tasks-Permissions assign PTA). PTA $\subseteq$ P$\times$T, a task has a set of permissions, and the permissions' being activated bases on the task status(TS).

Properties 8(Task Status TS). The task in the business process has executing status, including static, active, executive, suspending, and end status. When the status is static, suspending, or end state, task-related privileges will be revoked. While the task status is active or executive state, the task will activate all permissions assigned to itself till the status changes into other state.

4.2   Access Control Policy

In the section 3, we have described the features of the CSCD environment and the requirements of the access control. From the perspective of the CSCD environment, T & RBAC model supports the active and passive access control policy. Fig. 5 shows the approach of the T&RBAC model, the user accesses the CSCD system to complete the management jobs assigned to his job position in the organization. The permissions are pre-assigned to the role which reflects the structure of the organization, such role is a passive access control policy. On the collaborative design process, the project team members are the executor of the tasks. The task's status decides the user's permissions.

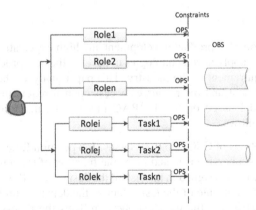

Fig. 5. T & RBAC Approach. This shows the approach that user accesses the object in the T & RBAC model.

5   T & RBAC Model's Implement in CSCD System

In this paper, we applied the T&RBAC model in the industrial product collaborative design platform. The platform supports the collaborative design between the multi-users who come from different departments, companies, or regions. These users compose of the project team. The market department submits the requirements of the new product to the product design department. The product manager makes a development plan of the new product according to the demand. The top leader of the enterprise audits the plan and decides to whether to start the product develop plan or not. Then the product design department appoints a project leader and allocates the mission book to the project leader. the project leader will establish a project team, and the members of the team come from multi-department or even multi-company . Then the leader decomposes the tasks, allocates the resources to the tasks. A new product development project management processes are shown in figure 6.

Industry Product Design Project Management Workflow

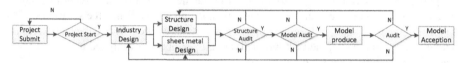

Fig. 6. Industry product design workflow

In the collaborative design process, according to the different types of the tasks, we defined the following roles in our collaborative design platform, such as shown in Table 2. Based on the management jobs in the organization and the tasks in the design process, the roles in the CSCD environment are granted the appropriate permissions to access the resources flexibly and safely.

Table 2. List of roles

Roles	Technical director, design manager, project leader, designer, reviewer, marketer, customer

6   Conclusion

The increasingly complex product development and high expectation of the customers drive the industry to apply new technologies to develop the new products. The CSCD is emerged in the requirement of the industry. This paper analyzes the characteristics of the CSCD environment and the resources access control requirements, and proposes the T&RBAC model based on the T-RBAC model. The main contributions of the T&RBAC are as follows:

1) Classify the Roles of CSCD in two classes: Job position Role and Business Role. Job position Role is a passive role and maps the function of the position in the organization; Business Role is assigned in the task of the design workflow, it is an active role.

2) Define the new attribute of the task which is the dependent relationship between the tasks. By this attribute, the model properly reflects the access control of the information in the business process.

3) Supports the active and passive access control. According to the management job in the organization structure, the permissions are pre-assigned to the roles. In the business process, the permissions can also be assigned to the tasks and be activated by the task status.

Lastly, we developed an industrial product collaborative design platform, and applied the T&RBAC to the platform to effectively control the access of the shared information between the multi-users.

References

1. Haibin, Y., Yun, Z.: Collaborative manufacturing. Tsinghua University Press, Beijing (2004)
2. Shen, W., Hao, Q., Li, W.: Computer Supported Collaborative Design: Retrospective and perspective. Computers in Industry 59(9), 855–862 (2008)
3. Patel, A.: Security management for OSI networks. Computer Communications 17(7), 544–553 (1994)
4. Stergiou, T., Leeson, M.S., Green, R.J.: An alternative architectural framework to the OSI security model. Computers and Security 23(23), 137–153 (2004)
5. Defense, AD0.TnlstedComPuterSystemEvaluationCriteria (August 15, 1983)
6. Pfleger, C.P.: Security in Computing, 2nd edn. Prentice-Hall International Inc., Englewood Cliffs (1997)
7. Joshi, J., Aref, W., Ghafoor, A., Spafford, E.: Security model for web-based applications. Communications ACM 44 (2) (2001)
8. Amoroso, E.G.: Fundamental of Computer Security Technology. PTR, Prentice-Hall, Englewoods Cliffs (1994)
9. Ferraiolo, D.F., Gilbert, D.M., Lynch, N.: An Examination of Federal and Commercial Access Control Policy Needs. In: Proc. NIST-NCSC National Computer Security Conf., Nat'l Inst. Standards and Technology, Gaithersburg, Md., pp. 107–116 (1993)
10. Sandhu, R.S., Coyne, E.J., Feinstein, H.L., Youman, C.E.: Role-based access control models. Computer (1996)
11. Sejong, O.: Seog Park. Task-role-based access control model, Information Systems 28, 533–562 (2003)
12. Yang, L., Choi, Y., Choi, M., Zhao, X.: FWAM: A Flexible Workflow Authorization Model using Extended RBAC
13. Daoju, X., Chao, L., Xiaosu, C.: The Security model of CSCW system based on RBAC. J. Huazhong Univ. of Sci. & Tech. (Nature Science Edition) 32(5) (May 2004)
14. Cheng-kai, L.I., Yong-zhao, Z.H.A.N., Bing, M.A.O., Li, X.I.E.: A Role-Based Access Control Model for CSCW Systems. Journal of Software 11(7), 931–937 (2000)
15. Jun, Z., Yong, T.: Study of the Role and Task-based Access Control Technology for CSCW System. Computer Science 37(7) (2010)
16. Ji-Bo, D., Fan, H.: Task-Based Access Control Model. Journal of Software 14(1) (2003)
17. Fan, H., Xiaofei, Z.: Task-based access control model and its implemention, Huazhong. J. Univ. of Sci. & Tech. (Nature Science Edition) 30(1) (January 2002)
18. Quan-bing, C., Hui-jin, W.: An improved access control model based on Task-Role. Journal of Jinan University (Natural Science) 31(1) (2010)
19. Hartley, J.: Concurrent Engineering, Cambridge. Productivity Press, Mass. (1992)
20. Zongkai, L.: Collaborative design will design and CAD technology-induced changes. Journal of Software, Supplement 9, 126–130 (1998)
21. Myers, B.A.: A brief history of human-computer interaction technology interactions. 5(2), 44–54 (1998)

Designation of Green Computer Terminal Supported by Cloud Computing

Guohua Xiong[(✉)]

GuangDong Construction Vocational Technology Institute, Baiyun District,
Guangzhou, Guangdong, China
xiongguohua2005@126.com

Abstract. Due to the rapid development of cloud computing and information technologies, traditional computer is replaced by novel terminal gradually. This paper conducts a full research on the design of computer terminal equipment accessing the cloud server. On the basis of the analysis of a large number of existing terminal equipment performance and presenting an effective solution, we design the device by hardware and software integration method, by selecting the appropriate hardware to optimize the communication protocol. The test results of our scheme is a feasible method to solve some problems of traditional solution, which is a kind of green energy-saving product with stable performance and cheap price.

Keywords: Cloud computing · Energy-saving · Green computer · Cloud terminal

1   Introduction

Cloud computing is a method to provide the shared software and hardware resource information to computers and other equipment for computation as needed via internet [1-3]. Users can acquire the service provided by "Cloud" simply via internet with no need to know details of cloud computing environment. "Cloud" here is a graphic metaphor, actually, it is to provide service for users with many distributed interconnected computers to form cloud service platform through unified resource management and scheduling and then by virtue of the internet[4-5]. Users use it on demand just as water, electricity and other public services and it is charged based on the amount of usage. Cloud computing provides virtualization services mainly at three levels [6], namely: (Infrastructure as a Service, IaaS), services such as storage, hardware, server, network components, etc. are available for users via internet. Service providers possess these hardware resources and distribute them according to the demands of different users, and users pay for each application. Main products include Amazon EC2 and Sun Grid. (Platform as a Service, PaaS), at the same time service providers will provide a basic computation platform for users instead a specific application. Users can construct their own application through this computation platform, besides, cooperation among many users is also allowed in this platform, such as Google App Engine. (Software as a Service, SaaS), it is a new delivery software mode. Software service providers deploy application software uniformly to their own servers, and provide paid online

© Institute for Computer Sciences, Social Informatics and Telecommunications Engineering 2014
V.C.M. Leung et al. (Eds.): TridentCom 2014, LNICST 137, pp. 480–488, 2014.
DOI: 10.1007/978-3-319-13326-3_47

application service via internet to customers. Only by logging in the website of SaaS service providers, customers can place and order for even use the needed application software service according to their own actual needs. Such as mail server which is a natural SaaS-mode system. Cloud computing is mainly fulfilled by relaying on virtualization technology [7-8].

Cloud server virtualization mainly refers to the optimization of "Computation" while desktop virtualization is the combination of "Computation" optimization and "Communication" optimization, which shows the essence of "Centralization" computing mode to a greater extent. Generally speaking: foreground virtualization and background centralization are to place the foreground terminal operation system and the applied physical computation into background data center so as to achieve the centralization of actual computation and relevant data at the background; the foreground is only used for displaying and user's operation interface, and all data, applications, etc. are presented in virtual forms before end-users. With such foreground and background relationship, communication technology between foreground and background is necessarily needed to offer support so as to form complete technology system. Cloud computing represents a kind of new computing and service providing method, and only a simple terminal device is needed for future users to enable "Cloud" to fulfill any needed service. Cloud computing integrates computing resources and storage resources to provide huge computing and storage capabilities for end users; according to the philosophy of cloud computing, as long as there is network, high-quality services will be available for users. As for how to utilize network band width effectively, compressing communication data is a relatively effective method. Terminal equipment with rapid compression and decompression technologies is in critical shortage in current market, therefore, it is extremely urgent to launch computer terminal equipment with extraordinary performance and green energy-saving features [9-11].

2   Key Technologies

To meet the above customer demands, surveys are made on three global cloud computing service providers; there are two ways to access cloud server: one is to access through practical network application program of browser, such as Google Apps, and the other is to access through remote desktop protocol, thereby customers can use the cloud server just as local computer. With user demand and actual situation of cloud computing server, the system shall be up to the three points: to realize green energy saving and cheap price, it is a must to abandon traditional PC mode and adopt the current system-on-chip with low power consumption. PC mode needs to be installed with operation system and other software; software licensing fee is required; PC is relatively not green and will consume a large amount of electricity, which go against low-carbon requirement; besides, the utilization rate of PC is less than 20% and they are left to be used at most of time according to the statistics of the concerned authority. While SOC adopts embedded Linux operation system which saves the software licensing fee and consumes low power; generally, the power consumption of the entire machine is less than 20W, which saves a large amount of electricity and protects the environment. Second, according to the analysis and test on current remote desktop protocol, accessing cloud server with the improved remote desktop access technology can hardly meet the current user demands; while the remote desktop protocol with image compression technology can reduce the network data transmission amount, improve transmission efficiency, and avoid time delay, as if the computing was made locally. At the same time, with Web2.0 technology browser, users can use and give full play to the performance of cloud server; in addition, it keeps traditional entertainment functions, such as movie playing, etc. With the above discussion combined, the integrated design of hardware and software is performed [12].

A. Hardware Design

In this solution, S5PV210 chip of ARM CortexTM-A8 core is used as   main control chip and also   ARM V7 instruction set is adopted, frequency is 1GHZ, 64/32-bit internal bus structure, 32/32KB data/instruction first-level cache, 512KB second-level cache, and 2000DMIPS (operating 0.2 billion instruction sets per second) high-performance computing capability. With low power consumption, it supports Linux and android operation systems, and it has built-in MFC (Multi Format Codec) , supports the encoding and decoding of videos with MPEG-1/2/4, H.263, H.264 and other formats, and supports simulated/digital TV output. With JPEG hardware encoding and decoding, the supported resolution ratio can be up to 8000x8000; it is inbuilt with high-performance PowerVR SGX540 3Dgraphics engine and 2D graphics engine, supports 2D/3D graphics acceleration, and is the fifth generation of PowerVR product. Its polygon formation rate is 28 million polygons/s, pixel fill rate can be up to 0.25 billion/s, and it supports PC level display technologies such as DX9, SM3.0, OpenGL2.0, etc..   It is the equipment with IVA3 hardware accelerator, with excellent graphics decoding performance, supports full-definition and multi-standard video encoding, can play , record smoothly video documents of 1920×1080 pixel (1080p) at 30 frame/s, and encode high-quality graphics and videos more rapidly. At the same time, it is inbuilt with HDMIv1.3 so that high-definition videos can be transmitted to external display. It has great multi-media performance capability, supports hard decoding of many graphic formats such as JPEG; video encoding supports MPEG1, MPEG2, MPEG4, H.264, VC-1 and RV, and audio encoding supports MP3, WMA, EAAC+ and AC3; with the cooperative work of software and hardware, FULL HD (1080P) high-definition video movies are clearly and vividly brought to people's daily entertainment through the HDMI output of digital TV to meet the entertainment function of users, apart from which,   S5PV210 also provides 3D accelerator which can enrich the design of the next generation of GUI or other graphic application. Hardware system provides various video input, HDMI and LVDS interfaces, and even the function enabling users to get "cloud computing" service by directly connecting traditional TVs. To meet the storage need of users, the system provides USB2.0/SD/CF interface, to which, users can connect various portable storage devices; it also supports SATA hard disk interface and has infinite storage expansion capability. Overall hardware design frame is shown in Figure 1:

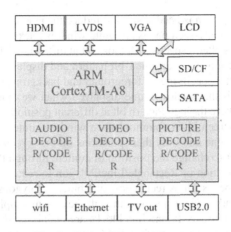

Fig. 1. Hardware System Frame

B. Software Design

Traditional remote desktop transmission protocols are diversified, such as VNC and RDP. In VNC system, it is divided into Client and Server. The design of VNC Viewer is very simple, i.e. it is purely responsible for receiving the keyboard or mouse signal input by users, then pack it into TCP packet, and transmit to far-end server through network; the communication protocol used between VNC Server and Client is named as Remote Frame Buffer Protocol (RFB Protocol) which regards Server as a virtual display card at far end; the produced screen images (FrameBuffer) can not only be displayed on native computer but also can be transmitted to far-end Client. This transmission protocol is pretty perfect in theory, however, in actual use, the transmission speed is relatively low and it falls behind RDP to some extent.

RDP transmission protocol is relatively sophisticated among remote desktop transmission protocols and its performance is more excellent. The purpose of RDP is to transmit the display and other data information on the Windows terminal server to clients smoothly. The client here can be PC or Non-PC equipment with different systems and in different structures, such as computers operating various different OS platforms such as UNIX and Linux and so on. Through RDP protocol, the computer at client can interact with the operating service program in remote server to acquire corresponding service.

Except connection and synchronization functions of RDP, the most important is the updating of the displayed images. Compared with other systems in which screen images are all transmitted in graphics, RDP uses rectangle, polygon and texts to strengthen display effect, therefore, it is also faster than other transmission protocols. With Cache technology, most of the used texts and graphics of RDP will remain in the Cache of the internal memory for within a period of time for future re-use, in this way, there is no need for Server to transmit the same materials to client the next time and will reduce transmission amount. The following technologies are also used in RDP to improve transmission performance.

Memory blt is to display the cache graphics stored in internal memory onto the designated position of the screen. The same graphic can be displayed at different positions but only one-time transmission is needed so as to reduce the amount of data. In general Windows, the most commonly-seen one is all-white window background, and it is to display white 64*64 graphics after respective Memory blt at different positions of the image.

Pattern blt instruction is to transmit 1 bit pattern and display it at the designated position on the screen after specifying its foreground and background colors. The most commonly-seen pattern is the window frame displayed when we drag the window, and it is formed by single pattern through Pattern blt at different positions.

The method of Screen blt is common when window content is dragged. As images are completely the same and only their positions on the screen are changed, it is only needed for the Sever to change the position of content through this instruction.

The maximum function of Rectangle/Line/Polygon to reduce data amount in RDP is to display basic shapes, such as rectangles, line blocks, polygons, etc. which can form various different window elements even though they seem simple. Rectangles are often used to compose window itself, and line blocks are mainly used to add bottom lines for word serials, while polygons can be found in Cache patterns added into Powerpoint.

Text: texts are ubiquitous in windows, covering function table, title list, webpage content, Command Line, etc.; in other previous systems, all texts are transformed into graphics for representation; as most texts are tall and thin and classified as high-frequency area in graphics, therefore, if distortion compression is used together, the texts will become illegible. So RDP Server allows texts with pure background to be shown in the form of dot matrix font while texts with complicated environment remain to be shown in the form of graphics. As for the word serial shown in the form of dot matrix graphic words, RDP Server will designate the font, id and index of word serial word Cache, its displaying position on the screen, etc..

The above transmission mechanisms make advantages for RDP among numerous remote desktop transmission protocols but the current demand can not be satisfied, mainly reflected in two aspects: 1. The playing of movies is awfully unsatisfactory, and the refreshing speed is very low when the window is in full screen; 2. Serious motion trailing occurs when browsing more than one pictures. According to the display of network monitoring results, there is huge amount of data transmitted in network under the above two situations. Based on the analysis of the data, there are the following reasons:

When movies are played in RDP, RDP Server has no idea about whether users are playing movies but only those frames are changing, therefore, all of them are transmitted to the connected Client end, which greatly increases the transmission amount for several times.

Movie playing or multi-picture previewing generally includes many graphics of various colors and with complicated structures, therefore, non-distortion compression inbuilt in RDP can not reduce effectively data amount, instead, it can increase it. Sometimes, RDP Server can even determine the uncompressed graphics directly transmitted, as low compression rate of graphics will produce additional burden to network.

To solve the above problems, the solution proposed the improvement method, which makes full use of original advantages of RDP and reduces data transmission amount by improving RDP image compression rate. There are many compression technologies; the hardware system of the solution is installed with JPEG hard decoding chip, therefore, images processed by JPEG compression at RDP Server end can be decoded easily without adding burden to embedded CPU so as to reduce data transmission amount without adding time delay caused by image decoding. The processing method is: RDP Server end adopts JPEG encoding when transmitting images, and sends the compressed images to Client after encoding; then the Client end adopts JPEG Decoder hard decoding chip to decode and display them on the screen. Therefore, the key of this system is to transform the originally transmitted documents in BMP format at the RDP Sever end into JPEG format through encoding, as shown in Figure 2.

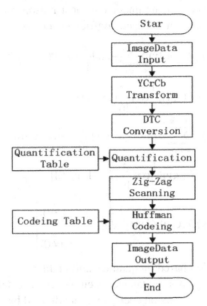

Fig. 2. JPEG Encoding Processing Procedure

3   Key Algorithms

A. Color Space Conversion
It is regulated in JPEG standard that information source image can be colored or black and white; if it is colored image, it is usually composed of luminance component Y and chrominance component Cr and Cb; it is shown in research results that the visual system of human beings has strongest resolution capability in the luminance of light, and the resolution rate of chrominance is approximately 1/4 of that of the luminance; then RDP signals are encoded after transforming luminance and color difference signal relying on the perception of human visual system on colors. The conversion formula is as Formula (1).

$$Y = 0.299R + 0.587G + 0.144B - 128$$
$$Cr = 0.500 - 0.4187G - 0.0813B \tag{1}$$
$$Cb = -0.1687R - 0.3133G + 0.500B$$

B. 2D forward discrete cosine transform
With 2D forward discrete cosine transform, the input images are first decomposed into 8*8 blocks, and then transform each block for 2D DCT; the transformation formula is shown as Formula (2); then the coefficient of DCT transform is encoded and

transmited; perform 2D DCT inverse transformation for each 8*8 image block when decoding, finally, the inverse transform of data blocks are combined into a pair of images. For common images, the values of most DCT coefficients are close to zero. If these DCT coefficient values close to zero are discarded, the image quality will not decline significantly when image is reconstructed. Therefore, compressing and coding images with DCT will save large storage space. The compression should be done with minimum quantity of coefficients under the most reasonable situation similar to the original image. The number of the used coefficients determines the compression rate.

$$G(u,v) = C(u)C(v)\sum_{y=1}^{8}\sum_{x=1}^{8}\{\frac{1}{2}\cos[\frac{\pi}{16}(u-1)(2x-1)]\}$$

$$F(x,y)\{\frac{1}{2}\cos[\frac{\pi}{16}(2y-1)(v-1)]\}$$

$$F(x,y) = \sum_{u=1}^{8}\sum_{v=1}^{8}C(u)C(v)\{\frac{1}{2}\cos[\frac{\pi}{16}(u-1)(2x-1)]\}$$ (2)

$$G(u,v)\{\frac{1}{2}\cos[\frac{\pi}{16}(2y-1)(v-1)]\}$$

$$while, C(u),C(v) = \begin{cases} \frac{1}{\sqrt{2}} ....if(u,v=0) \\ 1........if(u,v\neq0) \end{cases}$$

C. Uniform quantification based on quantification table:

In JPEG standard, linear uniform quantizer is employed. The definition of uniform quantification is that 64 DCT conversion coefficients are divided by corresponding quantification step to take the round number by rounding off, as is shown in Formula (3).

$$Q(u,v) = IntegerRound(Y(u,v)/S(u,v))$$ (3)

S(u, v) in the formula refers to quantification step pitch. Quantification is to quantify DCT coefficients through quantification table, i.e. to perform mod operation for 8*8 blocks of DCT coefficients with 8*8 quantification tables as templates in turn, and the result will be the quantified coefficient.

Good quantification table can improve compression rate and reduce image distortion. Quantizer step is the key of quantification while the best value of quantification step is determined by the characteristics of input image and image display equipment, for which, quantification table provides quantification steps. It makes use of the feature so that it is difficult for human vision to sense high space frequency distortion and the quantification step increases with the improvement of space frequency. As human eyes are sensitive to luminance but not to color difference, different quantification steps are used for luminance and color difference. The quantification step of luminance is divided more specifically while that of chrominance is more generally; the step of the low-frequency part at the upper left corner of quantification table is slightly small while that of the high-frequency part at the lower right corner is much larger. As the energy of most images is gathered at the upper left corner after DCT conversion, their quantification step is also small. High-frequency part will show some 0 after 8*8 DCT coefficients are quantified, which fulfills compression, and distortion also mainly occurs at this moment. As human eyes are not sensitive to high-frequency component, the distortion at high-frequency can not be easily found by human eyes. JPEG compression of images is mainly finished at the quantification part. For image compression, such spatial filtering with the lower right corner eliminated and the upper left corner remained is equivalent to a low-pass filter of space. The result after quantification is still 64 coefficients of 8*8 Q(u, v); the quantification does not change the nature of coefficients, and similarly, Q(0,0) is DC coefficient and other 63 coefficients Q(u, v) are AC coefficients.

D. Huffman Coding [13,14]

The code length of Huffman coding is changing. For information with high-frequency occurrence, the length of coding is short; while for information with low-frequency occurrence, the coding length is long. Thus, the overall code length to process all information is surely less than the symbol length of actual information. Compared with general coding method, Huffman coding seems a little complicated, mainly including Huffman coding part and preorder traversal Huffman tree function. Main procedures of Huffman coding mainly include initialization of original data, making statistics for the probability of message occurrence, sequencing message according to the occurrence probability, and finally combining two messages with the lowest occurrence probability into one, to construct the leaf nodes of Huffman tree; then, repeat the above processes till all coding work is finished, i.e. Huffman tree is completely built. Traversal of Huffman tree function is mainly used to fulfill Huffman compression coding. The processing flow chart is shown in Figure 3.

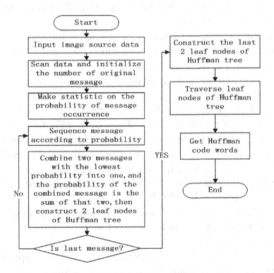

Fig. 3. Huffman Coding Processing Procedure

4   Conclusion

The solution is realized through embedded technology, and it has the following specific advantages: 1. Low power consumption, low heat productivity, simple maintenance, low maintenance cost; 2. Adopt the browser with Webkit core and it is flexible to use network application programs, such as Google Apps; 3. Support 1080p high-definition playing, and meet the multi--media entertainment function for users; 4. The remote desktop protocol is improved; the network transmitted data amount and time delay is decreased greatly; and end users are more significantly satisfied. But there are also still many aspects needing improvement, such as 3D application, about which, it does not support 3D desktop effect and large network game which are yet to be improved in the future.

References

1. Mell, P., Grance, T.: The NIST definition of cloud computing. National Institute of Standards and Technology (2009)
2. Liu, J., Peng, H.: Designation and application of Cloud computing terminal equipment. The 2nd International Conference on E-Business and E-Government ShangHai China, pp. 4988–4991 (May 2011) (EI: 20112914161296)
3. Marinos, Alexandros, Briscoe, Gerard: Community Cloud Computing. In: Jaatun, Martin Gilje, Zhao, Gansen, Rong, Chunming (eds.) Cloud Computing. LNCS, vol. 5931, pp. 472–484. Springer, Heidelberg (2009)
4. Liu, J., Wang, Q., Wan, J., Xiong, J., Zeng, B.: Towards key issues of disaster aid based on wireless body area networks. KSII Transactions on Internet and Information Systems 7(5), 1014–1035 (2013) (SCI:WOS:000320007300005)
5. Hewitt, C.: ORGs for Scalable, Robust Privacy-Friendly Client Cloud Computing. IEEE Internet Computing, 96–99 (2008)
6. Buxmann, P., et al.: Software as a Service. Wirtschaftsinformatik 50, 500–503 (2008)
7. Liu, J., Zhou, H., Chen, C.: A Novel Interpolation Fingerprint Localization Supported by Back Propagation Neural Network. Sensors & Transducers 158(11) (November 2013)
8. Hazari, S., Schnorr, D.: Leveraging student feedback to improve teaching in web-based courses. The Journal 26, 30–38 (1999)
9. Liu, J., Wang, Q., Chen, X., Zeng, B.: A Trilaminar Data Fusion Localization Algorithm Supported by Sensor Network. Sensors & Transducers 157(10) (October 2013)
10. Velte, A., Velte, T.: Microsoft virtualization with Hyper-V. McGraw-Hill, Inc. (2009)
11. Turner, M., et al.: Turning software into a service. Computer 36, 38–44 (2003)
12. Liu, J., Yan, H., Zou, C., Suo, H.: Architecture of Desktop as a Service Supported by Cloud Computing. Advanced Technologies. In: Embedded and Multimedia for Human-centric Computing, pp.355–361 (2014)
13. Gonciari, P.T., Al-Hashimi, B.M., Nicolici, N.: Variable-length input Huffman coding for system-on-a-chip test. IEEE Transactions on Computer-Aided Design of Integrated Circuits and Systems 22(6) 783–796 (2003)
14. Hashemian, Reza: Condensed table of Huffman coding, a new approach to efficient decoding. IEEE transactions on communications 52(1), 6–8 (2004)

A Novel Concept Lattice Merging Algorithm Based on Collision Detection

Caifeng Zou[1], Jiafu Wan[2(✉)], and Hu Cai[3]

[1] College of Information Engineering, Guangdong Mechanical & Electrical College,
Guangzhou, China
caifengzou@gmail.com
[2] School of Mechanical and Automotive Engineering,
South China University of Technology, Guangzhou, China
jiafuwan_76@163.com
[3] College of Electrical Engineering and Automation,
Jiangxi University of Science and Technology, Ganzhou, China
396210149@qq.com

Abstract. Concept lattice has been widely used in machine learning, pattern recognition, expert systems, computer networks, data analysis, decision analysis, data mining and other fields. The algorithms of constructing concept lattices are introduced. This work proposes a novel concept lattice merging algorithm based on collision detection, which can remove the redundant information in distributed construction of concept lattice. Further research to distributed concept lattice construction algorithm is needed.

Keywords: Concept lattice · Distributed construction · Merging algorithm · Collision detection

1 Introduction

The concept is the basic unit of human cognition and an important research object of artificial intelligence disciplines. German mathematician Wille proposed Formal Concept Analysis(FCA) in 1982 [1]. He systematically studied the hierarchies of concepts, properties of lattice algebra, and the isomorphic nature of concept lattice and formal context, which established foundations for the field of Formal Concept Analysis (FCA).

FCA is a powerful tool for data analysis and rule extraction from the formal context. FCA expresses concepts, attributes, and relationships of the ontology with formal context. According to the context, concept lattice is constructed to show the structure of the ontology clearly, and describe the generalization and specialization of the concept. Concept Lattice, also known as Galois Lattice, is the core data structure of FCA. In concept lattice, each node is a formal concept. Formal concept consists of extension part and intension part [2]. Extension of the concept is considered as the set of all objects belonging to this concept, and intension is considered as the set of the common characteristics or attributes of all these objects [3]. Concept lattice essentially describes the affiliation between objects and features, and shows the relationships

© Institute for Computer Sciences, Social Informatics and Telecommunications Engineering 2014
V.C.M. Leung et al. (Eds.): TridentCom 2014, LNICST 137, pp. 489–495, 2014.
DOI: 10.1007/978-3-319-13326-3_48

of generalization and specialization between the concepts. The corresponding Hasse diagram contributes to data visualization.

The basic concepts of FCA include formal context, concept lattice, Hasse diagram, senior concept and parental concept, sympatric formal context and sympatric concept lattice, independent context and independent concept lattice, and so on [4].

(1) Formal context

Formal context is defined as a triple K (U, A, I), where U is a set of objects, A is a set of attributes, and I is a binary relation between object U and attribute A, ie. $I \subseteq U \times A$. If there is $(x, a) \in I$, then xIa shows that object x has attribute a. The form of two-dimensional data table is also a type of formal context. The tuple represents object or instance, and the column represents attribute.

When there is
$$X^* = \{a \mid a \in A, \forall x \in X, xIa\}, X \subseteq U$$
$$B^* = \{x \mid x \in U, \forall a \in B, xIa\}, B \subseteq A$$

if $\exists X^* = B$ and $B^* = X$, then (X, B) is called a formal concept or simply a concept. X is defined as the extension of concept (X, B). B is defined as the intension of concept (X, B). Extension of the concept indicates the set of all objects belonging to this concept, and intension of the concept indicates the set of the common attributes of all these objects. For example, $C((1,5), \{b, c, e\})$ indicates that concept C covers two objects 1 and 5. The common attribute of these two objects is $\{b, c, e\}$.

(2) Concept lattice

Concept lattice is used to indicate the relationship between attributes and objects. There is a kind of partially ordered relationship between the nodes of concept lattice. Given $C_1(X_1, B_1), C_2(X_2, B_2)$, then $C_1 < C_2 \Leftrightarrow B_1 < B_2$.

This partially ordered relationship means that $C_1(X_1, B_1)$ is a senior concept of $C_2(X_2, B_2)$, or $C_1(X_1, B_1)$ is a generalization of $C_2(X_2, B_2)$.

For formal context (U, A, I), there is a unique partially ordered set in relationship I. This partially ordered set produces a lattice structure. Lattice L generated from the context (U, A, I), is called the concept lattice. The concept lattice of a formal context is unique.

2   Main Construction Algorithms of Concept Lattice

Algorithm for constructing concept lattice is the basis for the concept lattice research. Concept lattice construction is a concept clustering process. The completeness of the concept lattice means the concept lattice generated from the same data is unique. The current concept lattice construction algorithms can be divided into three categories: batch processing algorithm, incremental algorithm and distributed algorithm. The first two algorithms are stand-alone construction algorithms, in which the incremental algorithm is considered to be more promising. With the rapid growth of data-scale, distributed algorithm for constructing concept lattice has also become an important research content.

2.1   Batch Processing Construction Algorithm

Batch algorithm generates all nodes at a time, then generates edges according to the relationship of direct predecessor and direct successor of nodes, and establishes the whole concept lattice ultimately. There are many batch processing algorithms of constructing the concept lattice, in which only a few algorithms can generate Hasse diagram.

The main idea of Bordat algorithm [5] is top-down construction of the lattice starting from supremum. Firstly the topmost node is established, then all the child nodes of the topmost node are generated, and the child nodes are added to the lattice and connected to the parent node. Then the processes are executed iteratively for each child node. The defect of Bordat algorithm is: the number of repeated emergence of each child node (concept) is equal to the number of its parent nodes in the final concept lattice. This method is not suited to the concept lattice construction of large-scale formal context. Bordat algorithm can generate the concept lattice and Hasse diagram.

Ganter algorithm [6] uses feature vectors to enumerate the attribute sets of the lattice. The length of each vector is the cardinality of the attribute set. If the value of an attribute appears in the vector, then the corresponding bit is set to 1, otherwise it is set to 0. This algorithm does not generate Hasse diagram.

Chein algorithm [7] is a bottom-up lattice construction algorithm. The algorithm starts from the first layer l_1, which consists of the set of all of the pairs $(\{x\}, f(\{x\}))$ of X. Then it uses an iterative approach to construct the concept lattice from down to up layer by layer. It merges two pairs in layer l_k to create a new pair in layer l_{k+1}. The merging process is to find the intersection of all pairs in layer l_k, and test whether the intersection has appeared before. If the intersection has appeared in the upper layer, then the intersection in the upper layer is not complete pair, and should be marked for remove at the end of this layer. Chein algorithm does not generate Hasse diagram.

2.2   Incremental Construction Algorithm

The idea of the incrementally constructing concept lattice is: firstly the concept lattice is initialized to be the whole concept and the empty concept, and then the concept lattice is incrementally constructed using different operations according to the difference of the intersection of inserted object's attributes and the intension of the concept lattice nodes. When the context changes, such as adding an instance, the incremental construction method can maximize the use of existing concept lattice to avoid constructing the lattice from the beginning each time.

Godin algorithm [8] is a typical incremental concept lattice construction algorithm. This algorithm starts from a single object, and the new object is added into the lattice one by one, with only the necessary structural updates each time. This method can produce not only complete pair of the concept lattice, but also Hasse diagram.

Kuznetsov [9] pointed out that Godin algorithm is more suitable for sparse formal context. When the formal context becomes dense, the performance of Godin algorithm declines sharply.

Z. Xie [10] proposed an incremental algorithm for constructing concept lattice which organized the concept lattice nodes by tree structure. Y. Jiang [11] proposed an incremental concept lattice construction algorithm based on the list structure, which use list structure to organize the lattice nodes, and use the index table to achieve a quick update on concept lattice. H. Mao [12] presented a concept lattice incremental construction algorithm based on the binary tree structure according to the features of a certain kind of concept lattice.

2.3   Distributed Construction Algorithm

With the development of distributed systems and database technology, distributed computing, parallel computing and cloud computing has become the mainstream technologies [13, 14]. In practical applications, mass data distributed storage technology has been used very widely. For large databases, batch processing and incremental construction method of concept lattice still need to cost a lot of time. It has become a hot topic to get the global concept lattice from distributed database and establish the whole structure of the concept lattice.

P. Valtchev [15] proposed a divide and conquer method to construct concept lattice. It forms distributed multiple sub-contexts through the split of the formal context, then constructs the corresponding sub-lattices, and combines the sub-lattices to obtain a complete concept lattice. Y. Li [16], L. Zhang [17], and W. Wang [18] also studied the distributed algorithm for constructing concept lattice.

3   Concept Lattice Merging and Distributed Construction

With the development of cloud computing and big data processing technology, distributed storage and parallel data processing has become an inevitable trend. For concept lattice construction of big data, it is necessary to break the formal context up into several sub-sets, and then construct and merge them.

When a formal context splits into multiple sub-contexts, the corresponding concept lattice is called the sub-concept lattice. Concept lattice corresponding to formal context can be obtained by merging the sub-context concept lattices. This construction method of concept lattice uses the divide and conquer strategy, namely the distributed construction model of concept lattice. Concept lattice distributed construction is based on the form context merging. For example, when the company establishes workers file (formal context), each employee will fill in some fixed contents (properties) and hand to the department manager, then the department manager organizes the sector information (sub formal context) and turn them over to the company personnel department.

For the formal context merging, Wille proposed overlay and juxtaposition [2]. Overlay is vertical merging of the formal contexts, which possess the same attribute items and the different object domains. Juxtaposition is horizontal merging of the formal contexts, which have the different attribute items and the same objects domains. In distributed construction of concept lattice, the formal context is split to construct the corresponding sub-lattices, then the generated sub-lattices are merged to obtain the complete concept lattice. Overlay and juxtaposition of formal context is based on the consistency of extension or intension, and the consistent formal contexts need some processing before merging. Maedche proposed the similarity method in 2002 [19].

Distributed construction of concept lattice requires a lot of comparisons in the merging of sub-lattices. Some useless comparisons are redundant information, and can not affect the structure of concept lattice. The redundant comparisons will reduce the performance of the algorithm. The larger scale data will result in the more lattice nodes, and the more redundant information. Elimination of redundant information can significantly improve the distributed construction efficiency of concept lattice.

4 Concept Lattice Merging Algorithm Based on Collision Detection

Because of completeness of concept lattice, the distributed concept lattice construction algorithm often need to search for a large number of irrelevant concepts, which will increase the number of comparisons in the construction process, and reduce construction efficiency, but will not affect the structure of concept lattice. These irrelevant concepts are called redundant information. The formal context of distributed concept lattice is usually constructed by the massive high-dimensional data, which will generate a lot of redundant information. It is necessary to improve the distributed construction algorithm of concept lattice to remove redundant information and improve construction efficiency. This paper presents the method of removing redundant information in distributed merging of concept lattice. The collision detection technology is used to eliminate redundant information generated in the sub-lattice merging, and reduce the duplicate comparison of concept intension, in order to improve the construction efficiency of concept lattice.

The basic unit of the collision is concept C1, C2, ..., Cn. If there is an association between the two concepts, such as a common property, then a collision will occur. For example, if two concepts $Ci = (Ui, Ai)$ and $Ci' = (Ui', Ai')$ comprise at least one common attribute, then the collision between Ci and Ci' will occur.

In the merging of concept lattice, the detection sub-process is executed step by step, and the time interval between adjacent detection steps is a constant which is set as t. Meanwhile, the collision weight from concept Ci to Ci' is denoted by w(Ci, Ci', t) in step t, and the merging probability of concept Ci and Ci' is denoted by P(Ci, t) and P (Ci ', t). In step t, the change rate of P(Ci, t) is the accumulation result of collision between concept Ci and other related concepts as shown in Figure 1.

As Figure 1 shown, the collision effect of the concept Ci' to Ci is defined as the product of collision weight of the concept Ci' to Ci and the merging probability of the concept Ci', i.e., $w(Ci', Ci, t)p(Ci', t)$. For concept Ci, the collision effect of the concept

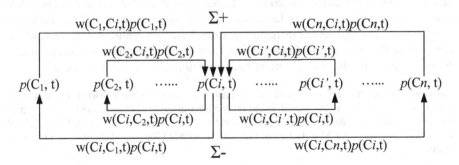

Fig. 1. Collision between concept Ci and other association concepts

Ci' to Ci is positive, which can enhance the merging probability of concept Ci, while the collision effect of the concept Ci to Ci' is negative, which can reduce the merging probability of concept Ci. The difference of positive effect and negative effect is the integrated effect. For the concept Ci, the integrated collision effect between concept Ci' and Ci is w(Ci' , Ci, t) p(Ci' , t)- w(Ci , Ci', t) p(Ci , t). The change rate of p(Ci, t) is the accumulation result of collision effect between concept Ci and other related concepts. If the collision directions between concepts are not considered, then the collision reaction equation of concept Ci is defined as follows:

$$\frac{\partial p(c_i,t)}{\partial t} = \sum_{i'=1}^{n} [w(c_{i'},c_i,t)p(c_{i'},t) - w(c_i,c_{i'},t)p(c_i,t)] \qquad (1)$$

$\partial p(c_i,t)/\partial t$ is the change rate of $p(c_i,t)$. According to Euler equation, the merging collision reaction equation of concept lattice can be expressed as follows:

$$p(c_i,t+1) = p(c_i,t) + h\sum_{i'=1}^{n} [w(c_{i'},c_i,t)p(c_{i'},t) - w(c_i,c_{i'},t)p(c_i,t)] \qquad (2)$$

According to equation (2), $p(c_i,t+1)$ can be calculated by iteration pattern:

$$p(c_i,t+1) = p(c_i,t) + h \cdot p_t^{'}(c_i,t) \qquad (3)$$

$p_t^{'}(c_i,t) = \partial p(c_i,t)/\partial t$, wherein, h is the iteration step length and is set to be 1.

The target of collision reaction is expanding the difference between the merging probabilities of the concepts. When the change of the merging probability of the concept is small, the collision reaction ends and the final result of the collision reaction is obtained. Based on the collision reaction result, the concept lattice can be effectively merged.

5   Conclusions

Concept lattice is gaining more and more attention of the researchers because of its unique advantages. It has been widely used in machine learning, pattern recognition, expert systems, computer networks, data analysis, decision analysis, data mining and other fields. However, it is still a young and rapidly developing field. There are many problems on concept lattice needed to study deeply, such as distributed concept lattice construction algorithm, concept lattice merging algorithm, and so on. This work proposes a novel concept lattice merging algorithm based on collision detection, which can remove the redundant information in distributed construction of concept lattice. Further research to distributed concept lattice construction algorithm is needed.

Acknowledgment. The authors would like to thank the National Natural Science Foundation of China (No. 61262013), the High-level Talent Project for Universities, Guangdong Province, China (No. 431, YueCaiJiao 2011), and the Open Fund of Guangdong Province Key Laboratory of Precision Equipment and Manufacturing Technology (PEMT1303) for their support in this research.

References

1. Wille, R.: Restructuring lattice theory: an approach based on hierarchies of concept, ordered sets. In: Rival, I. (ed.), pp. 445–470 (1982)
2. Ganter, B., Wille, R.: Formal concept analysis: mathematical foundations. Springer, Berlin (1999)
3. Yang, Q., Zhao, M.: Progress in concept lattice research. Computer Engineering and Design 29(20), 5293–5296 (2008)
4. Cai, Y., Cercone, N., Han, J.: An attribute-oriented approach for learning classification rules from relational databases. In: Proceedings of Sixth International Conference on Data Engineering, pp. 281–288 (1990)
5. Bordat, J.P.: Practical Calculation of Lattice Galois correspondence. Mathematiques et Sciences Humaines 96, 31–47 (1986)
6. Ganter, B.: Two Basic Algorithms in Concept Analysis. In: Kwuida, L., Sertkaya, B. (eds.) ICFCA 2010. LNCS, vol. 5986, pp. 312–340. Springer, Heidelberg (2010)
7. Chein, M.: Algorithme de recherche des sous-matrices premieres d'une matrice. Bull. Math. Soc. Sci. Math. Roumanie, R.S. 13, 1–25 (1969)
8. Godin, R., Missaoui, R., Alaoui, H.: Incremental concept formation algorithms based on Galois (concept) lattices. Computational Intelligence 11(2), 246–267 (1995)
9. Kuznetsov, S.O., Obiedkov, S.A.: Comparing performance of algorithms for generating concept lattices. Journal of Experimental & Theoretical Artificial Intelligence 14(2–3), 189–216 (2002)
10. Xie, Z., Liu, Z.: A Fast Incremental Algorithm for Building Concept Lattice. Chinese Journal of Computers 25(5), 490–496 (2002)
11. Jiang, Y., Zhang, J., Zhang, S.: Incremental construction of concept lattice based on linked list structure. Computer Engineering and Applications 43(11), 178–180 (2007)
12. Mao, H., Xhang, Z.: Algorithm of generating concept lattice based on binary tree. Computer Engineering and Applications 45(33), 35–37 (2009)
13. Wan, J., Zou, C., Ullah, S., Lai, C.F., Zhou, M., Wang, X.: Cloud-enabled wireless body area networks for pervasive healthcare. IEEE Network 27(5), 56–61 (2013)
14. Zou, C., Deng, H., Qiu, Q.: Design and Implementation of Hybrid Cloud Computing Architecture Based on Cloud Bus. In: 2013 IEEE Ninth International Conference on Mobile Ad-hoc and Sensor Networks (MSN), Dalian, China, pp. 289–293 (2013)
15. Valtchev, P., Missaoui, R., Lebrun, P.: A partition-based approach towards constructing Galois (concept) lattices. Discrete Mathematics 256(3), 801–829 (2002)
16. Li, Y., Liu, Z., Chen, L., Xu, X., Cheng, W.: Horizontal Union Algorithm of Multiple Concept Lattices. ACTA Electronica Sinica 32(11), 1849–1854 (2004)
17. Zhang, L., Shen, X.-J., Han, D.-J., An, G.-W.: Vertical union algorithm of concept lattices based on synonymous concept. Computer Engineering and Applications 43(2), 95–98 (2007)
18. Wang, W., Wu, Y.: Research on a Divide-and-conquer Algorithm for Constructing Concept Lattice. International Journal of Advancements in Computing Technology 4(11), 96–105 (2012)
19. Maedche, A., Zacharias, V.: Clustering Ontology-Based Metadata in the Semantic Web. In: Elomaa, T., Mannila, H., Toivonen, H. (eds.) PKDD 2002. LNCS (LNAI), vol. 2431, p. 348. Springer, Heidelberg (2002)

Sleep Scheduling Method Based on Half-Sleep State in the Distributed Sensor Network

Pan Deng[1], Jianwei Zhang[2], Feng Chen[1], Jiafu Wan[3(✉)],
Biying Yan[1], and Long Zhao[2]

[1] Lab. of Parallel Software and Computational Science,
Institute of Software Chinese Academy of Sciences, Beijing, China
{dengpan,chenfeng,biying}@iscas.ac.cn
[2] State Key Laboratory of Software Development Environment,
Beihang University, Beijing, China
hitzjw@163.com, zhaolong@nslde.buaa.edu.cn
[3] College of Electrical Engineering & Automation,
Jiangxi University of Science and Technology, Ganzhou, China
jiafuwan_76@163.com

Abstract. In order to extend the sensor's lifetime, this paper researched deeply into the sleep scheduling mechanism in the distributed sensor network. Now, the commonly used sleep scheduling methods based on the coverage have the problem of response delay, so we proposed a sleep scheduling method based on the half-sleep state to overcome this shortcoming. Under the control of regional agent node, this method adopts a minimum coverage algorithm based on the approximate solution to select the minimum coverage node set. Experimental results show that the proposed scheduling method can both reduce power consumption of the whole network effectively and extend the lifetime of the sensor noticeably.

Keywords: Sensor Network · Sleep Scheduling · Half-sleep

1   Introduction

In recent years, sensor networks and related techniques such internet of things and cyber-physical systems are developing very rapidly [1-3]. To save energy and make the lifetime of sensor longer, most of sensor network usually put part of sensor nodes in sleep state during the operation, whereas other sensor nodes which can cover the monitoring area keep in work [4-7]. The above mechanism is so-called sleep scheduling mechanism.

In order to realize the above sleep scheduling mechanism, it is necessary to decide which nodes should go to sleep and which should keep work. Now two kinds of methods usually are used to realize the scheduling. The first one is each sensor node go to sleep with probability p and keep work with probability 1-p. The strategy based on the probability is divide again into two kinds, which includes static probability and alterable probability. Static probability method means that each sensor node goes to

© Institute for Computer Sciences, Social Informatics and Telecommunications Engineering 2014
V.C.M. Leung et al. (Eds.): TridentCom 2014, LNICST 137, pp. 496–505, 2014.
DOI: 10.1007/978-3-319-13326-3_49

sleep with a predefined probability [4]. Alterable probability method can compute the probability of becoming a redundant node according to the perception of the nodes within its radius. This method can adjust dynamically the probability of becoming redundant, which has a lot of flexibility [8]. Beside the method based on the probability, another widely used method is to select some nodes which can cover the monitoring region, and at the same time close all the other nodes. Now, many sleep scheduling mechanism are based on this idea, for example the scheduling mechanism based on DELLC protocol [9], the two-phase sleep scheduling mechanism, and the dynamic sleep scheduling mechanism based on the pre-wakeup idea [6], and so on.

The above probability method will achieve the coverage region at a certain probability, so it is not used when the users need to realize the full coverage. The other method can achieve the full coverage, but after selecting the monitoring node, it will put all the other node go to sleep, and then these sleeping nodes will wakeup periodically to determine whether it will go to work. When an event occurs, the above mechanism will has some response delay, so we proposed a half-sleep scheduling mechanism to expend the lifetime of the sensor, and at the same time, to avoid the problem of the delay. Half-sleep state is a kind of sensor state, which refers to that the sensor under this state will close the data collection module, and only keep its communication module.

2   Related Definitions

Suppose all the sensors are placed in R which is a two-dimensional rectangle, and the coverage region of each sensor s is a circular (recorded as $C(s)$) with the center at s and the radius equal to r. If S is the sensor node set, the coverage region of S (recorded as $C(S)$) is the union of the coverage regions of all the sensors, i.e. $C(S) = \bigcup_{s \in S} C(s)$.

Definition 1: Suppose R is a region and S is a node set. If the coverage region of S can cover R, i.e. $R \subseteq C(S)$, the node set S is called the coverage set of region R.

Definition 2: For a given region R and a node set S, and S' is the subset of S. If S' is also a coverage set of R, and any proper subset of S' is not the coverage set of the region R, we then call S' as the least coverage set. And the least coverage set with the smallest node is called the minimum coverage.

Let's take Fig. 1 as an example. There are eleven sensors in that rectangle, and the monitoring area of each sensor is a circle with the radius equal to r. It is easy to see that in order to monitor the whole area, the three black sensors nodes are enough.

Definition 3: We call the node under the monitoring state as the monitoring node, and call the node which closes the monitoring module, under the half-sleep state as the half-sleep node. The half-sleep nodes keep half-sleep state for all the most time, and they will become into the monitoring node when they receive the wakeup message from the monitoring node and then open the monitoring module.

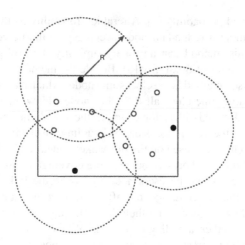

Fig. 1. Minimum coverage

3   Half-Sleep Scheduling Mechanism

This paper used the approximate solution to realize the half-sleep schedule which has the following goodness: on the one hand using the approximate solution can control the time complexity under the polynomial magnitude; on the other hand, the number of the solution of the least coverage set is larger than that of the minimum coverage set, the difference between the number can make the half-sleep schedule more fairly.

3.1   Basic Ideas

Region agent node will periodically send wakeup or sleep message to the ordinary node in the network to decide the state of the ordinary node. Once the ordinary node receives the message, it will determine whether it needs to open its data collection module. If the node will go to sleep according to the message, it should send the collective data to the certain nodes before it go to sleep.

The whole process of the sleep scheduling mechanism includes the following four steps:

Step1: set the random factor (the setting method of which will be introduced in the following section), the aim of which is to make all the nodes go to sleep relatively fairly.

Step2: according to the above random factor, using the minimum coverage algorithm to get an approximate solution to create the monitoring nodes set;

Step3: traverses each node in the coverage set, and sends the wakeup message to each node until receiving all the answers from each node.

Step4: send sleep message to all the nodes which are not selected as the new monitoring node. The process of this sleep scheduling mechanism is over.

During the process, if it can't receive the answer from any of the nodes in Step3, this process will be pronounced a failure, and then begin a new scheduling process after deleting the node which don't send back the answer.

3.2   Minimum Coverage Algorithm Based on MRC

In order to find out the least coverage set of the monitoring nodes, we divide the wakeup process to the following three steps:

(1) According to the random factor φ ($\dfrac{\sqrt{2}}{2} \leq \varphi < 1$) , the process firstly divides the whole network into several rectangles, the width of which is φR .

(2) Secondly, find the least coverage set for every rectangle.

(3) Finally, merge all the least coverage sets of each rectangle to achieve the coverage set of the whole network.

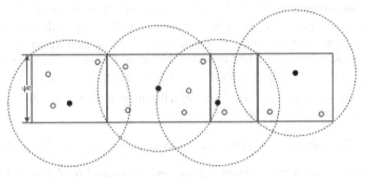

●   candidate detection node

○   candidate sleep node

Fig. 2. Rectangle division

Fig. 2 gives an instance of the rectangle division based on the random factor, where the black node represent the candidate nodes under the monitoring state. The algorithm to find a least coverage set for the rectangle is as follows:

(1) Suppose the node set in the rectangle is $BS = \{bs1, bs_2, ... bs_m\}$, and all the monitoring radii of each node are R;

(2) For the circle arc the node bs_i coverage, its right half part will intersect the rectangle at two pointes (proved by the following **Theorem 1**), and record the smaller X-coordinate value of the one of the two point as $x_{right}(bs_i)$;

(3) Begin from x_{left} which lies in the leftmost of the rectangle to find two nodes which can cover the left part of the rectangle, and record the node with the largest $x_{right}(bs_i)$ as bs_i;

(4) Set x_{left} to $x_{right}(bs_i)$, and put bs_i into the least coverage set; continue the process until $x_{left} \geq x_{right}$;

(5) Return the node set, and the algorithm is end.

The above algorithm cannot always get the optimum solution, but there isn't the big difference between the achieved solutions and the optimum solution because the value of random factor φ is limited to $\dfrac{\sqrt{2}}{2}$ to 1. This conclusion can be proved by Theorem 2.

Theorem 1: When the value of the random factor φ is smaller than 1, the right part of the cover circle of each node within the rectangle will intersect with the rectangle at two points.

Theorem Proving: The prerequisite of a circle and a line not intersecting is the distance from the circle center to the line is smaller than the radius of the circle. The width of the rectangle is $b = \varphi R$, so for every node in the rectangle, the distances from the node to the upper side of the rectangle or to the bottom side of the rectangle will satisfy with the relation: $d \leq b$; Circle center is also a node within the rectangle, so the distances from the circle center to the upper side or to the bottom size are $d_c \leq b$. So it can be deduced that $d_c \leq b = \varphi R < R$. So the coverage circle of the node in the rectangle is sure to intersect with the upper side and the bottom size at the same time. The proving is over.

Theorem 2: When the value of the random factor φ ranges from $\dfrac{\sqrt{2}}{2}$ to 1, the ratio between the appropriate resolutions set size and the optimal resolutions set size will not more than 2.

Theorem Proving: Suppose the achieved coverage network under the optimal resolutions is $\{g1, g_2,... g_m\}$, the set size achieved under the appropriate resolutions is $|MRC|$, and the set size achieved under the optimal resolutions is $|OPT|$. Now we use the induction to prove the theorem, which as follows: when $m = 1$, the optimal resolutions use one node (g_1) to cover the monitoring region. In the worst case, if the nodes selected under the appropriate resolutions locate in the edge of the network, it will need two nodes at most, so $|MRC_1| \leq 2 = 2|OPT_1|$. Now, we begin to induce, suppose we will have $|MRC_k| \leq 2|OPT_k|$ when $m = k$. When $m = k + 1$, g_{k+1} will need at most two nodes to cover, so we will have $|MRC_{k+1}| \leq |MRC_k| + 2 \leq 2|OPT_k| + 2 \leq 2|OPT_{k+1}|$, i.e. $|MRC_{k+1}| \leq 2|OPT_{k+1}|$. So the ratio between the appropriate resolutions set size and the optimal resolutions set size will not more than 2. The proving is over.

4   Experimental Results and Analysis

4.1   Analysis of Scheduling Results

Fig. 3 is a 10×10 region, and within which there are 200 randomly-generated nodes, and each node is supposed to represent a sensor with the monitoring radius is 2. Now, we adopt the minimum coverage algorithm to select a minimum coverage set.

The algorithm finally selected 20 nodes from the 200 nodes, and the coverage is 100% based on the Monte Carlo method, which can satisfy the monitor need.

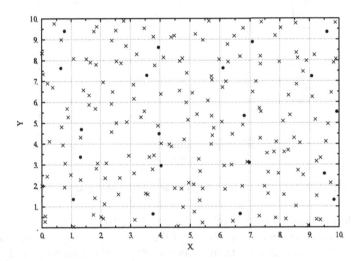

Fig. 3. Diagram of scheduling results of half-sleep scheduling

4.2   Analysis of System Power Consumption

The power consumption of the sensor consists of two parts, which are message handling consumption m and data collection consumption d. In order to test the saving of the system power consumption under the half-sleep scheduling mechanism, we adopt the energy-saving coefficient r, which is the ratio between the energy-saving under the sleep state with the total consumption when all the sensors are wakeup. The bigger the coefficient r, the lower the system power consumes. The coefficient r is computed as follows:

$$r = \frac{(N-n)*d}{N*(m+d)} = (1-\frac{n}{N})*\frac{d}{m+d} \tag{1}$$

where N is the total number of the sensors, n is the monitoring nodes the above minimum coverage algorithm select to keep work, and all the other node beyond the n nodes are all go to sleep. $d/(m+d)$ is a constant predefined according to the specific monitoring equipment, so the finally value of the coefficient r is determined by the number of nodes in the half-sleep state, i.e. $r' = 1 - n/N$.

Suppose we need to monitor a 100×100 region, the following tests analyze the system power consumption from two aspects, which are the monitoring radius R of each sensor and the total number SN of the sensors.

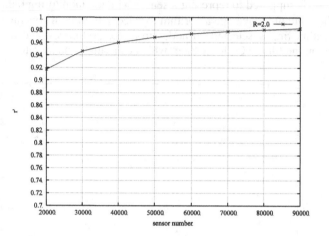

Fig. 4. Relations between energy saving coefficient and sensors number

(1) The affect of the total number of the sensors ($R = 2.0$)
The curve in Fig. 4 represents the change of the coefficient along with the increase of the total number of the sensors (from 20000 to 90000), where the monitoring radius is 2.0. From the curve we can see that the system achieves good energy saving effect along with the increase of the total number. In a certain static region, when the monitoring radius is set down, the number of the sensors need to monitor this region is also in a relatively fixed range. So, with the increase of the total number, the system energy saving coefficient will increase at a speed of 1 - 1/x.

(2) The affect of the monitoring radius ($SN = 20000$)
The curve in Fig. 5 represents the change of the coefficient along with the increase of the monitoring radius (from 2 to 9), where the total number of sensors is set to 20000. Similar with the curves in Fig. 4, the system achieves good energy saving effect along with the increase of monitoring radius. The curve in Fig. 5 is steeper than that in the Fig. 4, which is because that the relation between the monitoring area and the radius is a kind of square relation.

In the main, we can increase the energy-saving coefficient through either increasing the total number of the sensors or increasing the monitoring radius. But increasing the total number of the sensor will increase the total power consumption, so in the actual environment, we should make an effort to increase the monitoring area of each sensor to decrease the system power consumption.

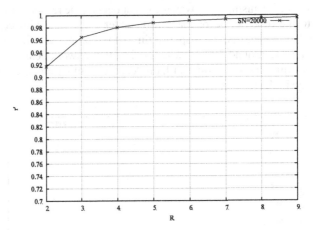

Fig. 5. Relations between energy saving coefficient and monitoring radius

4.3   Analysis of Response Time of the Half-Sleep Scheduling

Compared to the traditional sleep scheduling mechanism, the half-sleep scheduling mechanism has an advantage in response time. In order to verify this, we now give the simulate tests about the response time, where include 1,000 nodes. Fig. 6 gives the result of the traditional sleep scheduling mechanism. In the simulate tests, each node works for 10 seconds, and then go to sleep for *stime* second. The curve in Fig. 6 is got with the value of *stime* range from 1000 to 9000. At the same time, we do another nine tests about the time need to wake up a sensor when it is under the half-sleep state, and the result is shown in Fig. 7. From the above figures we can see that in the traditional

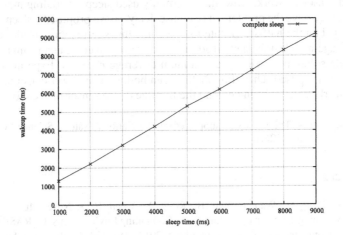

Fig. 6. Wakeup response time of traditional sleep mode

sleep scheduling mechanism, when wakeup event occurs, the response time is basically proportional to the time period of the sensor under sleep state plus certain network delay. But, in these nine tests, the response time of the proposed half-sleep scheduling mechanism is always around 300ms, which is just the network delay. From this comparison, we can find that the proposed half-sleep scheduling mechanism has the absolute advantage in the response time.

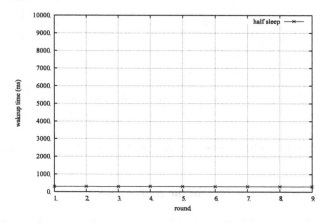

Fig. 7. Wakeup response time of half-sleep mode

5   Conclusions

Most of the sensor networks usually adopt sleep scheduling mechanism, but traditional method has the shortcoming of response time delay. In order to extend the sensor's lifetime, this paper researched deeply into the sleep scheduling mechanism in the distributed sensor network. Now, the commonly used sleep scheduling methods based on the coverage have the problem of response delay, so we proposed a sleep scheduling method based on the half-sleep state to overcome this shortcoming. Under the control of regional agent node, this method adopts a minimum coverage algorithm based on the approximate solution to select the minimum coverage node set. Experimental results show that the proposed scheduling method can both reduce power consumption of the whole network effectively and extend the lifetime of the sensor noticeably.

Acknowledgements. The work was supported by the National Natural Science Foundation of China (No. 61100066, 61262013).

References

1. Zhang, J., Deng, P., Wan, J., Yan, B., Rong, X., Chen, F.: A Novel Multimedia Device Ability Matching Technique for Ubiquitous Computing Environments. EURASIP Journal on Wireless Communications and Networking 2013, 181 (2013), doi: 10.1186/1687-1499-2013-181

2. Wan, J., Chen, M., Xia, F., Li, D., Zhou, K.: From Machine-to-Machine Communications towards Cyber-Physical Systems. Computer Science and Information Systems **10**(3), 1105–1128 (2013)
3. Wan, J., Zhang, D., Sun, Y., Lin, K., Zou, C., Cai, H.: VCMIA: A Novel Architecture for Integrating Vehicular Cyber-Physical Systems and Mobile Cloud Computing. ACM/Springer Mobile Networks and Applications **19**(2), 153–160 (2014)
4. Ren, Q., Li, J., Gao, H., Cheng, S.: A Two-Phase Sleep Scheduling Based Protocol for Target Tracking in Sensor Networks. Chinese Journal of Computers **32**(10), 1971–1979 (2009)
5. Shi, G., Liao, M.: Stochastic Sleeping for Energy-Conserving in Large Wireless Sensor Networks. Journal of Computer Research and Development **43**(4), 579–585 (2006)
6. Liu, Y., Wu, J., Chen, Z., Xiong, Z.: A Dynamic Sleep Scheduling Mechanism for Localization in Mobile Sensor Networks. Journal of Computer Research and Development **45**(8), 1330–1337 (2008)
7. Zhu, J., Li, J., Liu, Y., Gao, H.: Data-Driven Sleeping Scheduling Mechanism in Sensor Networks. Journal of Computer Research and Development **45**(1), 172–179 (2008)
8. Liu, M., Cao, J., Zheng, Y., Chen, L., Xie, L.: Analysis for Multi-Coverage Problem in Wireless Sensor Networks. Journal of Software **18**(1), 127–136 (2007)
9. Mao, Y., Liu, M., Chen, L., Chen, D., Xie, L.: A Distributed Energy-Efficient Location-Independent Coverage Protocol in Wireless Sensor Networks. Journal of Computer Research and Development **43**(2), 187–195 (2006)

Author Index

Wojciech Cellary · Mohamed F. Mokbel
Jianmin Wang · Hua Wang
Rui Zhou · Yanchun Zhang (Eds.)

Web Information Systems Engineering – WISE 2016

17th International Conference
Shanghai, China, November 8–10, 2016
Proceedings, Part II

 Springer

Editors

Wojciech Cellary
Poznań University of Economics
Poznan
Poland

Mohamed F. Mokbel
University of Minnesota
Minneapolis, MN
USA

Jianmin Wang
Tsinghua University
Beijing
China

Hua Wang
Victoria University
Melbourne, VIC
Australia

Rui Zhou
Victoria University
Melbourne, VIC
Australia

Yanchun Zhang
Victoria University
Melbourne, VIC
Australia

ISSN 0302-9743   ISSN 1611-3349   (electronic)
Lecture Notes in Computer Science
ISBN 978-3-319-48742-7   ISBN 978-3-319-48743-4   (eBook)
DOI 10.1007/978-3-319-48743-4

Library of Congress Control Number: 2016955509

LNCS Sublibrary: SL3 – Information Systems and Applications, incl. Internet/Web, and HCI

Preface

Welcome to the proceedings of the 17th International Conference on Web Information Systems Engineering (WISE 2016), held in Shanghai, China, during November 8–10, 2016. The series of WISE conferences aims to provide an international forum for researchers, professionals, and industrial practitioners to share their knowledge in the rapidly growing area of Web technologies, methodologies, and applications. The first WISE event took place in Hong Kong, China (2000). Then the trip continued to Kyoto, Japan (2001); Singapore (2002); Rome, Italy (2003); Brisbane, Australia (2004); New York, USA (2005); Wuhan, China (2006); Nancy, France (2007); Auckland, New Zealand (2008); Poznan, Poland (2009); Hong Kong, China (2010); Sydney, Australia (2011); Paphos, Cyprus (2012); Nanjing, China (2013); Thessaloniki, Greece (2014); Miami, USA (2015); and this year, WISE 2016 was held in Shanghai, China, supported by Fudan University, China.

A total of 233 research papers were submitted to the conference for consideration, and each paper was reviewed by at least three reviewers. Finally, 39 submissions were selected as full papers (with an acceptance rate of 16.7 % approximately), plus 31 as short papers. The research papers cover the areas of social network data analysis, recommender systems, topic modeling, data diversity, data similarity, context-aware recommendation, prediction, big data processing, cloud computing, event detection, data mining, sentiment analysis, ranking in social networks, microblog data analysis, query processing, spatial and temporal data, graph theory and non traditional environments.

In addition to regular and short papers, the WISE 2016 program also featured a special session on Data Quality and Trust in Big Data (QUAT-16) and a medical big data forum.

QUAT is a forum for presenting and discussing novel ideas and solutions related to the problems of exploring, assessing, monitoring, improving, and maintaining the quality of data and trust for big data. It aims to provide researchers in the areas of web technology, e-services, social networking, big data, data processing, trust, and information systems and GIS with a forum for discussing and exchanging their recent research findings and achievements. This year, the QUAT 2016 program featured eight accepted papers on data cleansing, data quality analytics, reliability assessment, and quality of service for domain applications. As the organizers of QUAT 2016, Prof. Deren Chen, Prof. William Song, Dr. Xiaolin Zheng, Dr. Johan Håansson, and Prof. Shaozhong Zhang, we would like to thank all the authors for their enthusiastic high-quality submissions, the reviewers (Program Committee members) for their careful and timely reviews, and the Organizing Committee, Dr. Roger Nyberg, Dr. Zukun Yu, Dr. Xiaofeng Du, and Dr. Xiaoyun Zhao, for their excellent publicity.

The medical big data forum aims to promote the analysis and application of big data in healthcare. Experts and companies related to the domain of big data in healthcare were invited to present their reports in this forum. Many hot research points of big data in healthcare were discussed, including analysis and mining, application and value exploration, interoperability standards, security and privacy protection. The objective of this forum is to provide forward-looking ideas and views for research and application of big data in healthcare, which will promote the development of big data in healthcare, accelerate practical research, and facilitate the innovation and industrial development of mobile healthcare. The forum was organized by Prof. Yan Jia, Prof. Weihong Han, and Prof. Hua Wang.

We also wish to take this opportunity to thank the honorary conference chair, Prof. Maria Orlowska; the general co-chairs, Prof. Hong Mei, Prof. Marek Rusinkiewicz, and Prof. Yanchun Zhang; the program co-chairs, Prof. Wojciech Cellary, Prof. Mohamed F. Mokbel, and Prof. Jianmin Wang; the special area chairs, Prof. Xueqi Cheng, Prof. Yan Jia, and Prof. Jianhua Ma; the workshop co-chairs, Prof. Zhiguo Gong and Prof. Yong Tang; the tutorial and panel chair, Prof. Xuemin Lin; the publication co-chairs, Prof. Hua Wang and Dr. Rui Zhou; the publicity co-chairs, Dr. Jing Yang and Dr. Quan Bai; the website chair, Dr. Rui Zhou; the local arrangements chair, Prof. Shangfei Zhu; the finance co-chairs, Ms. Lanying Zhang and Ms. Irena Dzuteska; the sponsor chair, Dr. Tao Li; and the WISE society representative, Prof. Xiaofang Zhou. The editors and chairs are grateful to Ms. Sudha Subramani and Mr. Sarathkumar Rangarajan for their help in preparing the proceedings and updating the conference website.

We would like to sincerely thank our keynote and invited speakers:

- Professor Maria Orlowska, Fellow of the Australian Academy of Sciences, Vice-President of the Polish-Japanese Institute of Information Technology, former Secretary of State in the Ministry of Science and Higher Education, Poland
- Professor Binxing Fang, academician of CAE (Chinese Academy of Engineering) and the former president of BUPT (Beijing University of Posts and Telecommunications), China
- Dr. Phil Neches, Advisor, Member of National Academy of Engineering, Chairman of Foundation Ventures LLC, founder of Teradata Corporation, USA
- Professor Ramamohanarao (Rao) Kotagiri, Fellow of the Institute of Engineers Australia, Fellow of the Australian Academy Technological Sciences and Engineering, and Fellow of Australian Academy of Science, The University of Melbourne, Australia.

In addition, special thanks are due to the members of the international Program Committee and the external reviewers for the rigorous and robust reviewing process. We are also grateful to Fudan University, China, Victoria University, Australia, and the International WISE Society for supporting this conference. The WISE Organizing Committee is also grateful to the QUAT special session organizers and medical big data forum organizers for their great efforts to help promote web information system research to broader domains.

We expect that the ideas that emerged at WISE 2016 will result in the development of further innovations for the benefit of scientific, industrial, and social communities.

November 2016

Wojciech Cellary
Mohamed F. Mokbel
Jianmin Wang
Hua Wang
Rui Zhou
Yanchun Zhang

Organization

Honorary Conference Chair

Maria Orlowska   Polish-Japanese Institute of Information Technology, Poland

General Co-chairs

Hong Mei   Shanghai Jiao Tong University, China
Marek Rusinkiewicz   New Jersey Institute of Technology, USA
Yanchun Zhang   Victoria University, Australia and Fudan University, China

Program Co-chairs

Wojciech Cellary   Poznań University of Economics, Poland
Mohamed F. Mokbel   University of Minnesota, USA
Jianmin Wang   Tsinghua University, China

Special Area Chairs

Big Data Area Chair

Xueqi Cheng   Chinese Academy of Sciences, China

Medical Big Data Analysis Area Chair

Yan Jia   National University of Defense Technology, China

Transparent Computing and Service Area Chair

Jianhua Ma   Hosei University, Japan

Tutorial and Panel Chair

Xuemin Lin   The University of New South Wales, Australia and East China Normal University, China

Workshop Co-chairs

Zhiguo Gong   University of Macau, Macau, China
Yong Tang   South China Normal University, China

Publication Co-chairs

Hua Wang   Victoria University, Australia
Rui Zhou   Victoria University, Australia

Publicity Co-chairs

Jing Yang   Chinese Academy of Sciences, China
Quan Bai   Auckland University of Technology, New Zealand

Conference Website Chair

Rui Zhou   Victoria University, Australia

Conference Finance Co-chairs

Lanying Zhang   Fudan University, China
Irena Dzuteska   Victoria University, Australia

Local Arrangements Chair

Shangfeng Zhu   Fudan University, China

Sponsorship Chair

Tao Li   Florida International University, USA

Wise Society Representative

Xiaofang Zhou   The University of Queensland, Australia
                  and Soochow University, China

Program Committee

Karl Aberer   EPFL, Switzerland
Imad Afyouni   GIS Technology Innovation Center, Saudi Arabia
Marco Aiello   University of Groningen, The Netherlands
Mohammed Eunus Ali   Bangladesh University of Engineering and Technology,
                         Bangladesh
Toshiyuki Amagasa   University of Tsukuba, Japan
Farnoush   University of Colorado Denver, USA
   Banaei-Kashani
Jie Bao   Microsoft Research Asia, China
Denilson Barbosa   University of Alberta, Canada
Boualem Benatallah   University of New South Wales, Australia
Azer Bestavros   Boston University, USA

Antonis Bikakis   University College London, UK
Bin Cao   Zhejiang University of Technology, China
Barbara Catania   University of Genoa, Italy
Richard Chbeir   LIUPPA Laboratory, France
Cindy Chen   University of Massachusetts Lowell, USA
Jinchuan Chen   Renmin University of China, China
Jacek Chmielewski   Poznań University of Economics, Poland
Alex Delis   University of Athens, Greece
Schahram Dustar   Vienna University of Technology, Austria
Islam Elgedawy   Middle East Technical University, Turkey
Hicham Elmongui   Alexandria University, Egypt
Marie-Christine Fauvet   Université Grenoble Alpes, France
Yunjun Gao   Zhejiang University, China
Thanaa Ghanem   Metropolitan State University, USA
Claude Godart   Université de Lorraine, France
Daniela Grigori   Laboratoire LAMSADE, Université Paris Dauphine,
                           France
Venkata Gunturi   IIIT-Delhi, India
Hakim Hacid   Bell Labs, USA
Armin Haller   Australian National University, Australia
Mohammad Hammoud   CMU Qatar, Qatar
Tanzima Hashem   Bangladesh University of Engineering and Technology,
                           Bangladesh
Rafiul Hassan   King Fahd University of Petroleum and Minerals,
                           Saudi Arabia
Xiaofeng He   East China Normal University, China
Yuh-Jong Hu   National Chengchi University, Taiwan
Peizhao Hu   Rochester Institute of Technology, USA
Jianbin Huang   Xidian University, China
Marta Indulska   University of Queensland, Australia
Yoshiharu Ishikawa   Nagoya University, Japan
Adam Jatowt   Kyoto University, Japan
Yan Jia   National University of Defense Technology, China
Lili Jiang   Max Planck Institute for Informatics, Germany
Wei Jiang   Missouri University of Science and Technology, USA
Peiquan Jin   University of Science and Technology of China, China
Byeong Ho Kang   University of Tasmania, Australia
Raymond Lau   City University of Hong Kong, Hong Kong, SAR China
Dan Lin   Missouri University of Science and Technology, USA
Shuai Ma   Beihang University, China
Murali Mani   University of Michigan-Flint, USA
Natwar Modani   Adobe Research, India
Mikolaj Morzy   Poznań University of Technology, Poland
Wilfred Ng   Hong Kong University of Science and Technology,
                           Hong Kong, SAR China

Kjetil Nørvåg	Norwegian University of Science and Technology, Norway
Mitsunori Ogihara	University of Miami, USA
George Pallis	University of Cyprus, Cyprus
Wen-Chih Peng	National Chiao Tung University, Taiwan
Olivier Pivert	ENSSAT, France
Tieyun Qian	Wuhan University, China
Jarogniew Rykowski	Poznań University of Economics, Poland
Yucel Saygin	Sabanci University, Turkey
Wei Shen	Nankai University, China
John Shepherd	University of New South Wales, Australia
Lawrence Si	University of Macau, Macau, SAR China
Dandan Song	Beijing Institute of Technology, China
Shaoxu Song	Tsinghua University, China
Reima Suomi	University of Turku, Finland
Stefan Tai	Karlsruhe Institute of Technology, Germany
Dimitri Theodoratos	New Jersey Institute of Technology, USA
Yicheng Tu	University of South Florida, USA
Xiaojun Wan	Peking University, China
Hua Wang	Victoria University, Australia
Junhu Wang	Griffith University, Australia
De Wang	Google, USA
Ingmar Weber	Qatar Computing Research Institute, Qatar
Adam Wojtowicz	Poznań University of Economics, Poland
Jei-Zheng Wu	Soochow University, Taiwan
Takehiro Yamamoto	Kyoto University, Japan
Hayato Yamana	Waseda University, Japan
Yanfang Ye	West Virginia University, USA
Hongzhi Yin	The University of Queensland, Australia
Tetsuya Yoshida	Nara Women's University, Japan
Ge Yu	Northeastern University, China
Jeffrey Xu Yu	Chinese University of Hong Kong, Hong Kong, SAR China
Qi Zhang	Fudan University, China
Xiangmin Zhou	RMIT University, Australia
Xingquan Zhu	Florida Atlantic University, USA

QUAT General Co-chairs

| Deren Chen | Zhejiang University, China |
| William Song | Dalarna University, Sweden |

QUAT Program Committee Co-chairs

Xiaolin Zheng   Zhejiang University, China
Johan Håkansson   Dalarna University, Sweden
Shaozhong Zhang   Zhejiang Wanli University, China

QUAT Organizing Committee Co-chairs

Roger G. Nyberg   Dalarna University, Sweden
Zukun Yu   Britich Telecom, UK
Xiaofeng Du   British Telecom, UK
Xiaoyun Zhao   Dalarna University, Sweden

QUAT Program Committee

Adriana Marotta   Universidad de la República, Uruguay
Anders Avdic   Dalarna University, Sweden
Fei Chiang   McMaster University, Canada
Hasan Fleyeh   Dalarna University, Sweden
Jacky Keung   City University of Hong Kong, Hong Kong, SAR China
Jun Hu   Nanchang University, China
Preben Hansen   Stockholm University, Sweden
Rajeev Agrawal   North Carolina A&T State University, USA
Sheng Zhang   Nanchang Hangkong University, China
Yuansheng Zhong   Jiangxi University of Finance and Economics, China
Yuhao Wang   Nanchang University, China

QUAT Sponsors

Complex Systems & Microdata Analysis, Dalarna University, Sweden
E-Service Research Center, Zhejiang University, China

Contents – Part II

Non-traditional Environments

Special Session on Data Quality and Trust in Big Data

Contents – Part I

Prediction

Big Data Processing

Cloud Computing

Event Detection

Data Mining

Sentiment Analysis

Dynamic Topic-Based Sentiment Analysis
of Large-Scale Online News

Peng Liu[(✉)], Jon Atle Gulla, and Lemei Zhang

Department of Computer and Information Science, NTNU, Trondheim, Norway
{peng.liu,jon.atle.gulla,lemei.zhang}@idi.ntnu.no

Abstract. Many of today's online news websites and aggregator apps
have enabled users to publish their opinions without respect to time
and place. Existing works on topic-based sentiment analysis of product
reviews cannot be applied to online news directly because of the following two reasons: (1) The dynamic nature of news streams require
the topic and sentiment analysis model also to be dynamically updated.
(2) The user interactions among news comments can easily lead to inaccurate topic and sentiment extraction. In this paper, we propose a novel
probabilistic generative model (DTSA) to extract topics and the specified sentiments from news streams and analyze their evolution over time
simultaneously. DTSA incorporates a multiple timescale model into a
generative topic model. Additionally, we further consider the links among
news comments to avoid the error caused by user interactions. Finally, we
derive distributed online inference procedures to update the model with
newly arrived data and show the effectiveness of our proposed model on
real-world data sets.

Keywords: Topic-based sentiment analysis · Topic model · User
interaction · Online inference

1 Introduction

With the growing popularity of both the social media and mobile news apps, an
increasingly amount of significant information concerning user opinions and sentiments is being stored online. As important platforms used to describe events
happening around the world, online news and comments are the efficient means
of conveying positive or negative emotions underlying an opinion and also communicating an affective state, such as happiness, fearfulness, or surprise. It is
valuable to extract topics as well as sentimental information from these texts.
The governments can detect public sentiments toward policies and emergencies
and give feedback in time. The marketers are able to acquire knowledge about
the public sentiment environment which supports further analysis and decisions.
However, the analysis is impossible to complete manually due to the huge amount
of data, and the unstructured data increases the difficulty of machine analysis.

Most earlier studies [1–3] embrace topics or domains into sentiment analysis
model, to improve the accuracy of sentiment classification. To a large extent,

© Springer International Publishing AG 2016
W. Cellary et al. (Eds.): WISE 2016, Part II, LNCS 10042, pp. 3–18, 2016.
DOI: 10.1007/978-3-319-48743-4_1

it is due to the tightly reliance on domains or topics of sentiment description. The same word in different topics may convey various sentiment polarities. For instance, the word "offensive" is used as positive orientation in the phrase "offensive player" when discussing sports news, whereas it also has negative orientation when used in the phrase "offensive behaviour" referring to political news comments. Thus, sentiment analysis based on topic or domain has far-reaching significance.

In recent years, among the many researches on the approaches to extract topic-based sentiments, most works have focused on analyzing product comments, which are very different from the comments on news and events [4]. More specifically, current studies assume that words in documents have static co-occurrence patterns, which may not be suitable for the task of capturing topic and sentiment shifts in a time-variant data corpus. What is more, the most popular topic models for sentiment analysis rely on batch mode learning which assumes that the training data are all available prior to model learning. When fitting large-scale news streams, the time and memory costs of such approaches will scale linearly with the number of documents analyzed. In addition, many algorithms regard comments as independent individuals, ignoring their connections. In fact, the socialized characteristic of the media platform makes it easier for users to interact with each other, which will result in more connections.

To have a better understanding of user interaction, we list some real comments with interactions of the WALB News website and their corresponding polarities and types in Fig. 1. The first comment shows a negative sentiment towards the shooting news. The second comment agrees with the first comment's opinion using positive expressions whereas the third person has a little disagreement with the first one. The last comment is based on the previous critiques. In such a situation, we find some drawbacks in the existing methods. First, for example, in the comment "Well said", the existing methods cannot extract the corresponding topics unless considering the interaction with the original news comment. Second, the normal sentiment polarities of positive and negative cannot precisely describe the sentiment polarities of news comments between

News Comments	Type (comment/response)	Polarity of News (positive/negative)	Polarity of Existing Methods (positive/negative)
That's so stupid. She can drive a fucking lambo or a shitty honda, she can drive whatever the fuck she wants. In no way does that justify this crazy white bitch's actions.	comment	negative	negative
Well said.	response	negative	positive
True but it's more likely shit will go down if you're showing off. Just saying.	response	negative	negative
Women who dress provocatively are asking to be raped, too.	response	negative	negative

Fig. 1. News comments and the interactions between them.

interactions, so the sentiment classification results will be inaccurate using existing methods. Therefore, user interaction affects both the extraction of topics and sentiments, which renders existing methods less useful.

In this paper, we propose a dynamic topic-based sentiment analysis model (DTSA) which is capable of extracting topics and topic-specific sentiments from the online news comment and tracking their evolution over time simultaneously. The DTSA model incorporates the links among new comments to avoid the error caused by user interactions. To efficiently handle streaming data, we derive online inference procedures based on a stochastic Expectation Maximization (EM) algorithm, in which the model is sequentially updated using newly arrived data and the parameters of the previously estimated model. We applied our model to several real data sets and the experimental results demonstrate promising and reasonable performance of our approach.

This paper makes the following contributions:

- It proposes a DTSA model where the generation of current sentiment-topic-word distributions are influenced by the multiple timescale word distributions at the previous epoch. Considering both the long-timescale dependency and the short-timescale dependency improves the robustness of the model.
- Two special sentiments which represent the transformation of user sentiments–approval and disapproval are introduced to model the links among news comments, which could improve the accuracy of topic-based sentiment classification.
- The proposed DTSA approach adopts a distributed online inference procedure to update the model with newly arrived data, which can be generalized to perform dynamic topic-based sentiment analysis on other large-scale social media streams.

The remainder of the paper is organized as follows. Section 2 introduces the related work. In Sect. 3, we present our new model. We describe the data sets, experiment settings and the prior information we use in Sect. 4. Section 5 shows our experiment results. Finally, we present the conclusions and future work in Sect. 6.

2   Related Work

Although much work has been done in detecting topics [5–7], these works mainly focused on discovering and analyzing topics of documents alone, without any analysis of sentiments in the text, which limit the usefulness of the mining results. Other works [8,9] addressed the problem of sentiment detection at various levels (i.e. from word/phrase level, to sentence and document level). However, none of them can model the mixture of topics and sentiment classification, which again makes the results less informative to users.

Some of the recent works [1–3] have been aware of this limitation and tried to capture sentiments and the mixture of topics simultaneously. Lin and He [1] introduced sentiment polarities into topic modeling and presented a model called

JST which can extract the mixture of aspects and different sentiment polarities for products and services. Aspect-and-Sentiment Unification Model (ASUM) [2] and Sentiment-Topic model with Decomposed Prior (STDP) [3] are all based on LDA, which extract sentiments about topics in a static way without consideration of the dynamic nature of documents. Besides, these methods do not take into account the sentiment polarity transformation caused by user interactions.

In recent years, there has been a surge of interest in developing topic models to explore topic evolutions over time. The continuous time dynamic topic model (cDTM) [10] used Brownian motion to model the latent topics through a sequential collection of documents. [12] proposed online multiscale dynamic topic models (OMDT) which could trace the topic evolution with multiple timescales. It was on the basis of the Dirichlet-multinomial framework by assuming that current topic-specific distributions over words were generated based on the multiscale word distributions of the previous epoch. Wang et al. [13] proposed a Temporal-LDA or TMLDA method to mine streams of social text such as the Twitter stream for an author, by modeling the topics and topic transitions that naturally arised in such data. Different from the work of [10], it focused more on learning the relationship among topics.

None of the aforementioned models take into account time-aware topic–sentiment analysis. Mohamed et al. [14] proposed an LDA based topic model for analyzing topic-sentiment evolution over time by modeling time jointly with topic and sentiments, and derived inference algorithm based on Gibbs Sampling process. However, this time-aware topic-sentiment (TTS) model could not consider adjusting model parameters in realtime and process online news streams. [15] presented probabilistic model called topic sentiment trend model (TSTM), based on probabilistic latent semantic analysis (PLSA) model. Thus it exists the problems of inferencing on new documents and overfitting the data.

Our model DTSA is partly inspired by the previously proposed multiscale topic models [12] and explores the generation process of online comments, considering the co-effects caused by user interactions and the time factor for the first time. The results show that the DTSA model makes a significant improvement on both topics and topic-specific sentiments extraction.

3   The DTSA Model

In this section, we propose a novel dynamic topic-based sentiment analysis model (DTSA) for large-scale online news. Firstly, the problem is defined, including the relevant general terms and notations. Then a multiple timescale model and a graphical model are presented in detail. Finally, we describe the estimation and prediction of parameters.

3.1   Problem Definition

For convenience of describing the graphical model, we here define the following terms and notations:

In a time-stamped news comments collection, we assume comments are sorted in the ascending order of their time stamps. At each epoch t where the time period for an epoch can be set arbitrarily at an hour, a day, or a year. A stream of comments $C^t = \{c_1^t, c_2^t, c_3^t, ..., c_D^t\}$ are received with their order of publication time stamps preserved.

In C^t, D is the number of comments, K is the number of topics, S_1 is the number of normal sentiments (positive and negative), S_2 is the number of special sentiments (approval and disapproval), and $M = S_1 + S_2$ is the total number of sentiments. n_d^s is the number of sentiment words in comment d and n_d^o is the number of topic words in comment d. There are K topic models $\varphi_{z=1...K}^o$ which denotes the multinomial distribution of words specific to topic z. For each topic z, there are S_1 topic-specific normal sentiment models $\varphi_{l=1...S_1,z}^n$, which denotes the multinomial distribution of words specific to normal sentiment label l and topic z. There are S_2 special sentiment models $\varphi_{m=1...S_2}^s$, which is the multinomial distribution of words specific to special sentiment label m. The variable θ denotes the distribution of topics in comment d, the variable π denotes the distribution of sentiments in comment d. Let d' be the comment that d interacts with, then the variables θ' and π' denote the distribution of topics and sentiments in comment d'.

In particular, we define an evolutionary matrix of topic z and sentiment label l, $E_{l,z}^t$, where each column is the word distribution of topic z and sentiment label l, $\sigma_{l,z,s}^t$, generated for comments received within the time slice specified by s. We then attach a vector of weights $\mu_{l,z}^t = \{\mu_{l,z,0}^t, \mu_{l,z,0}^t, \mu_{l,z,0}^t, ..., \mu_{l,z,s}^t\}$, each of which determines the contribution of time slice s in computing the priors of $\beta_{l,z}^t$.

The Key Task of Dynamic Topic-based Sentiment Analysis (DTSA) is to estimate the model parameters σ^t, μ^t, θ^t, π, φ^o, φ^n and φ^s using a stochastic EM algorithm, then to extract topics and topic-specific sentiments of the online news and analyze their evolution over time simultaneously. Table 1 summarizes the notations of frequently used variables.

3.2   Multiple Timescale Model

Following the previous work [12], we could account for the influence of the past at different timescales to the current epoch. For example, we set time slice s equivalent to 2^{S-1} epochs. Hence, if S = 3, we would consider three previous sentiment-topic-word distributions where the first distribution is between epoch $t - 4$ and $t - 1$, the second distribution is between epoch $t - 2$ and $t - 1$, and the third one is at epoch $t - 1$. This would allow taking into consideration of previous long and short timescale distributions. However, this model would take more time and memory spaces and effective algorithm needs to be performed in order to reduce time/memory complexity.

Figure 2 illustrates the relationship among μ, E and β when the number of historical time slices accounted for is set to 3. Here, $\sigma_{l,z,s}^t$, $s \in 1...3$ is the historical word distribution of topic z and sentiment label l within the time slice specified by s. As a form of smoothing to avoid the zero probability problem for unseen words, we set $\sigma_{l,z,0}^t$ for the current epoch as the uniform

Table 1. Notations used in the paper.

Symbol	Description
t	The index of timestamp
K	Number of topics
D	Number of comments
S_1	Number of normal sentiments (positive and negative)
S_2	Number of special sentiments (approval and disapproval)
M	The total number of sentiments
N_d^s	Number of sentiment words in comment d
N_d^t	Number of topic words in comment d
γ	Symmetric prior for sentiment labels
α	The prior for the topic distribution
β	The prior for the word distribution conditioned on sentiment labels and topics
φ_z^o	The multinomial distribution of words specific to topic z
$\varphi_{l,z}^n$	The multinomial distribution of words specific to normal sentiment label l and topic z
φ_m^s	The multinomial distribution of words specific to special sentiment label m
λ	The word prior for sentiment polarity information
θ	The distribution of topics in comment d
π	The distribution of sentiments in comment d
θ'	The distribution of topics in the comment that d interacts with
π'	The distribution of sentiments in the comment that d interacts with
$E_{l,z}^t$	Evolutionary matrix of sentiment label l and topic z at epoch t
$\mu_{l,z}^t$	Weight vector which determines the contribution of time slice s in computing the priors of $\beta_{l,z}^t$
$\sigma_{l,z,s}^t$	The multinomial word distribution of sentiment label l and topic z with time slice s at epoch t

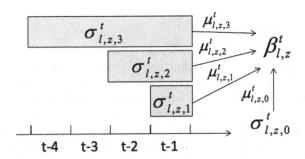

Fig. 2. The relationship among μ, E and β.

distribution where each element takes the value of 1/(vocabulary size). The evolutionary matrix $E_{l,z}^t = \{\sigma_{l,z,0}^t, \sigma_{l,z,1}^t, \sigma_{l,z,2}^t, \sigma_{l,z,3}^t\}$, and the weight matrix $\mu_{l,z}^t = \{\mu_{l,z,0}^t, \mu_{l,z,1}^t, \mu_{l,z,2}^t, \mu_{l,z,3}^t\}^T$. The Dirichlet prior for sentiment-topic-word distributions at epoch t is $\beta_{l,z}^t = \mu_{l,z}^t E_{l,z}^t$.

3.3 Graphical Model

According to the real-world observation, we give two assumptions on sentiments as follow: (1) The sentiments of a comment do not exist independently, but depend on the comment it replies to and their relationship. (2) News comments can be divided into the reply comments and the original comments. The reply often omits the topic information, because it has the same topic with the original. We call this characteristic of user interaction "Topic Consistency".

The graphical representation of DTSA is shown in Fig. 3. The parameter definitions are shown in Table 1.

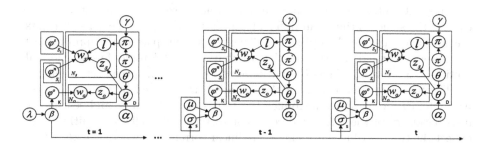

Fig. 3. DTSA model.

Assuming we have already calculated the evolutionary parameters $\{E_{l,z}^t, \mu_{l,z}^t\}$ for the current epoch t, the formal generative process of DTSA model as shown in Fig. 3 at epoch t is given as follows:

1. For each normal sentiment $l \in \{1, ..., S_1\}$:
   i. For each topic $z \in \{1, ..., K\}$:
      Compute $\beta_{l,z}^t = \mu_{l,z}^t E_{l,z}^t$
2. For each topic $z \in \{1, ..., K\}$:
   i. Choose a distribution $\varphi_z^o \sim Dir(\beta_z^o)$
   ii. For each normal sentiment $l \in \{1, ..., S_1\}$
      Choose a distribution $\varphi_{l,z}^n \sim Dir(\beta_{l,z}^n)$
3. For each special sentiment $m \in \{1, ..., S_2\}$:
   Choose a distribution $\varphi_m^s \sim Dir(\beta_m^s)$
4. For each comment $d \in \{1, ..., D\}$:
   i. Choose a distribution $\theta_{temp} \sim Dir(\alpha)$:
      Create a new distribution θ_d by combining θ_{temp} and $\theta_{d'}'$
   ii. Choose a distribution $\pi_{temp} \sim Dir(\gamma)$:
      Create a new distribution π_d by combining π_{temp} and $\pi_{d'}'$
   iii. For each topic word $w_{d,i}^o$ where $i \in \{1, ..., n_d^o\}$:
      (a) Choose a topic $z_i^o \sim Mult(\theta_d)$
      (b) Choose a word $w_{d,i}^o$ from the distribution φ^o over words defined by the topic z_i^o.

iv. For each sentiment word $w_{d,j}^s$ where $j \in \{1, ..., n_d^s\}$:
  (a) Choose a topic $z_j^s \sim Mult(\theta_d)$
  (b) Choose a sentiment label $l_j \sim Mult(\pi_d)$
  (c) If l_j is a normal sentiment, choose a sentiment word $w_{d,j}^s$ from the distribution φ^n over words defined by the topic z_j^s and sentiment l_j. Otherwise, choose a special sentiment word $w_{d,j}^s$ from the distribution φ^s over words defined by the sentiment m_j.

In the proposed model, we divide the words into topic words and sentiment words. A sentiment lexicon and POS tagging are used to identify the sentiment words. There are two kinds of sentiments in the model-normal and special ones. The normal sentiments are topic-sensitive, where users use different words to express the same sentiment in different topics. However, the special sentiments are not topic-sensitive. According to [16], there are some patterns in approval and disapproval. Therefore, we choose the distributions of all k topics for each normal sentiment S^n, but only one distribution is chosen for each special sentiment S^s.

The topics and sentiments of the comment are affected by the comment a user interacts with, so we introduce the topics distribution θ' and sentiments distribution π' of the interacted comment to reflect this effect. Intuitively, we expect the two distributions θ and θ' are linear correlation, where $\theta = p\theta' + (1-p)\theta_{temp}$. The greater p value means a better topic consistency, which depends on the data set. We also expect $\pi = q\pi' + (1-q)\pi_{temp}$. Approximately, a larger q represents more weight on user interactions. The setting for p and q was determined empirically.

3.4   Online Inference

We use a stochastic EM algorithm to sequentially update the model parameters at each epoch using the newly arrived data and the parameters of the previously estimated model. At each EM iteration, we infer latent sentiment labels and topics using the collapsed Gibbs sampling and estimate the hyperparameters using maximum likelihood [17]. Due to the space limit, we leave out the derivation details and only show the sampling formulas.

Model Parameters Estimation. The sampling formulas of model parameters $\theta^t, \pi^t, \varphi_t^o, \varphi_t^n$ and φ_t^s at epoch t given the evolutionary parameters E^t, μ^t are follow:

$$\theta_{d,k}^t = \frac{N_{d,k,t}^o + N_{d,k,t}^s + \alpha_k^t}{\sum_{k=1}^{K}(N_{d,k,t}^o + N_{d,k,t}^s + \alpha_k^t)} \tag{1}$$

$$\pi_{d,m}^t = \frac{N_{d,m,t}^s + \gamma_m^t}{\sum_{m=1}^{M}(N_{d,m,t}^s + \gamma_m^t)} \tag{2}$$

$$\varphi_{k,v,t}^o = \frac{N_{k,v,t}^o + \sum_S \mu_{k,s,v}^t \sigma_{k,s,v}^t}{\sum_{v=1}^{V}(N_{k,v,t}^o + \sum_S \mu_{k,s,v}^t \sigma_{k,s,v}^t)} \tag{3}$$

$$\varphi^n_{k,m,v,t} = \frac{N^n_{k,m,v,t} + \sum_S \mu^t_{k,m,s,v}\sigma^t_{k,m,s,v}}{\sum_{v=1}^{V}(N^n_{k,m,v,t} + \sum_S \mu^t_{k,m,s,v}\sigma^t_{k,m,s,v})} \tag{4}$$

$$\varphi^s_{m,v,t} = \frac{N^s_{m,v,t} + \sum_S \mu^t_{m,s,v}\sigma^t_{m,s,v}}{\sum_{v=1}^{V}(N^s_{m,v,t} + \sum_S \mu^t_{m,s,v}\sigma^t_{m,s,v})} \tag{5}$$

where $N^o_{d,k,t}$ is the number of topic words assigned to topic k in document d at epoch t. $N^s_{d,k,t}$ is the number of sentiment words assigned to topic k in document d at epoch t. $N^s_{d,m,t}$ is the number of sentiment words assigned to sentiment m in document d at epoch t. Other variables containing N are defined similarly.

Evolutionary Parameters Estimation. There are two sets of evolutionary parameters to be estimated, the weight parameters μ and the evolutionary matrix E. The update formulas are:

$$(\mu^t_{k,m,s})^{new} \leftarrow \frac{\mu^t_{k,m,s}\sum_v \sigma^t_{k,m,s,v}A}{B} \tag{6}$$

where $A = \psi(N^t_{k,m,v} + \sum_{s'} \mu^t_{k,m,s'}\sigma^t_{k,m,s',v}) - \psi(\sum_{s'} \mu^t_{k,m,s'}\sigma^t_{k,m,s',v})$ and $B = \psi(N^t_{k,m} + \sum_{s'} \mu^t_{k,m,s'}) - \psi(\sum_{s'} \mu^t_{k,m,s'})$, $N^t_{k,m,v}$ is the number of times word v assigned to sentiment label m and topic k at epoch t, $N^t_{k,m} = \sum_v N^t_{k,m,v}$.

The evolutionary matrix E^t accounts for the historical word distributions at different time slices. The derivation of E^t therefore requires the estimation of each of its elements, $\sigma^t_{k,m,s,v}$, the word distribution in topic k and sentiment label m at time slice s, which can be calculated as follows:

$$\sigma^t_{k,m,s,v} = \frac{C^t_{k,m,s,v}}{\sum_v C^t_{k,m,s,v}} \tag{7}$$

where $C^t_{k,m,s,v}$ is the expected number of times word v is assigned to sentiment label m and topic k at time slice s. For the Multi-scale model, a time slice s might consist of several epochs. Therefore, $C^t_{k,m,s,v}$ is calculated by accumulating the count $N^{t'}_{k,m,v}$ over several epochs. The formula for computing $C^t_{k,m,s,v}$ is $C^t_{k,m,s,v} = \sum_{t'=t-2^{s-1}}^{t-1} N^{t'}_{k,m,v}$.

Distributed Model Training. To handle large scale data sets, we design a parallel training program for DTSA model on Hadoop, which is a Java-based open source distributed computing framework. Hadoop implemented the MapReduce framework proposed by Jeffrey et al. [18], and it can effectively handle a large amount of data. In Hadoop, all data are stored as key-value pairs. For our proposed model training program, the key is document id, and the value is the words and sentiments in the comment with their corresponding latent topics. The global model parameters include the Dirichlet prior α^t, γ^t, the weight parameter μ^t and the element of evolutionary matrix σ^t. Initially, a comment set is randomly split into N equal parts for N parallel executing processes. In the Map stage, every process loads the global model parameters from the last iteration, and uses them to sample the comments in its own part. The posterior distribution of hidden variables θ^t, π^t, φ_t^o, φ_t^n and φ_t^s are computed. In the Reduce stage, the posterior distribution θ^t, π^t, φ_t^o, φ_t^n and φ_t^s from all processes are aggregated to generate a new version of global model parameters.

4   Experimental Setup

We evaluate our proposed model on two kinds of datasets: news and twitter. For news datasets, we crawl the comments of four hot news events occurred from February 2014 to April 2014 using the Guardian Open Platform API[1]. (1) MH370 event: Malaysia airlines MH370 B777-200ER loses contact with air traffic control. (2) Crimea event: Russia dispatches troops to Crimea. (3) Sochi event: Sochi 2014 Winter Olympics are held successfully. (4) India event: India holds the largest president election ever. In order to evaluate our model's generality, we also crawl the tweets of Facebook events occurred on February 2014 from Twitter Search API[2]. Facebook event: Facebook buys WhatsApp for 19 Billion US Dollars. Each dataset contains the comments interacted with other comments by reply. Detail statistics of the datasets and sentiment distribution are shown in Table 2.

Table 2. Some statistics of the datasets and sentiment distribution.

Dataset	MH370	Crimea	Sochi	India	Facebook
Documents	351041	46722	405000	289900	101900
Tokens	2565490	382419	3518923	2359761	1026950
# of positive/negative documents	7/12	3/8	7/2	5/4	4/7

DTSA is an unsupervised model. As preprocessing, we first perform stemming and remove stopwords. Then we use Stanford POS Tagger[3] to tag the comments. In prior information, we use the sentiment lexicon SentiWordNet[4], containing 2290 positive and 4800 negative words with score over 0.6, as normal sentiment. Words contained in the sentiment lexicon are automatically labeled as sentiment words. For special sentiment, we use some seed words as prior information for approval, such as "praise", "agree", "support", and we use the discourse markers and swear words as prior information for disapproval, such as "what?", "nonsense" [16]. Other words, which are not labeled as normal/special sentiment words, are regarded as topic words. To quantitatively evaluate our model,

---

[1] http://open-platform.theguardian.com/.
[2] http://apiwiki.twitter.com/.
[3] http://nlp.stanford.edu/software/tagger.shtml.
[4] http://sentiwordnet.isti.cnr.it/.

we randomly select 500 comments from five datasets separately, and manually label each word as topic, normal and special sentiment word.

In our experiments, the unit epoch is set to daily. The number of topics K is set to be 20, the number of normal sentiments S_1 is set to be 2, the number of special sentiments S_2 is set to be 2. We set the Gibbs sampling iterations to be 5000. Following [6], we fix $\alpha = 50/K$, $\gamma = 50/(S_1 + S_2)$.

5 Experiments

In this section, we evaluate the performances of our proposed models with three experiments. In the first experiment, we show the topics and topic-specific sentiments extracted by DTSA with some qualitative analysis. The second experiment evaluates the computational time of our models. In the third experiment, we apply a document-level sentiment classification task to compare our models with several baselines.

5.1 Qualitative Results

In Table 3 we show the evolution of topics and topic-specific sentiments identified by the DTSA model with the number of time slices set to 4. Due to space limit, we only take an example of news comments on the MH370 event. For each topic, we list the top 5 topic words and the related sentiment words.

We can see that DTSA can extract topics and topic-based sentiments well. For example, the topic words are "MH370" and "disappeared" while the specific negative sentiment words are "painful" and "cruel". We also notice that the evolution of topics is well consistent with the actual news stories in real world. In addition, one improvement of the proposed model is that DTSA could automatically adjust the polarity of sentiment words. For example, in Epoch 9, the word

Table 3. News MH370 lose contact.

Time	Epoch 5	Epoch 6	Epoch 7	Epoch 8	Epoch 9	Epoch 10
Topic	MH370	MH370	officials	MH370	Boeing	MH370
	Malaysia	disappeared	MH370	military	fuel	aircraft
	flight	passenger	search	sea	MH370	underwater
	missing	plane	scientists	evidence	died	Sumatra
	search	terrorism	Australian	found	people	search
Senti_Positive	hopeful	optimistic	advanced	support	hopeful	prospective
	prospective	hopeful	optimistic	hopeful	promising	optimistic
	extreme	cheerful	sophisticated	sustained	likely	strong
	promising	confident	powerful	sufficient	confident	huge
	optimistic	huge	support	powerful	high	advanced
Senti_Negative	sad	cruel	miserable	tragic	hopeless	hopeless
	bad	sorrily	painful	unwilling	sad	ruefully
	dangerous	ruefully	tearing	hate	despairing	painful
	unbelievable	painful	sorrily	cruel	suffering	sad
	tragic	tearing	fierce	sorrowful	believe	misery

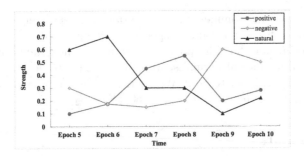

Fig. 4. Sentiment dynamics of MH370 event.

"believe" becomes negative while it is positive in lexicon. In the comment "So what? We just believe they are alive!", "believe" should have labeled this comment positive, but the prior information "what?" makes this comment labeled as disapproval. And because this comment is a reply to a comment which approves of the news topic, we change the sentiment distribution of this comments to disapprove of the topic, which makes "believe" becomes negative words.

In Fig. 4, we plot and compare the topic life cycle and its sentiment dynamics on MH370 event, where the strength distribution of a sentiment l in document d associated with the topic z, over the comment set C^t in each epoch t is calculated as:

$$P(z, l) = \frac{1}{|C^t|} \sum_{d \in C^t} P(z|l, d)P(l|d) \tag{8}$$

From Fig. 4, we can see that in the first 2 days, the neutral sentiment dominates the opinions, for everyone talks about the facts during that time. However, the positive sentiment rises obviously over the next 2 days, reaching the peak at day 4, since the search and rescue operations. After that, the negative sentiment shoots up for 24 h, peaking at day 5. This is mainly because the Boeing 777 has run out of fuel and passengers have little chance of survival. All these results show that DTSA is effective to extract topics and topic-specific sentiments.

5.2 Evaluation of Computational Time

In order to evaluate the effectiveness of DTSA in modelling dynamics, we compare the computational time of the DTSA model with the non-dynamic version of LDA [5] and JST [17], namely, LDA-one, JST-one, and JST-all. LDA-one and JST-one only use the training data in the current epoch whereas JST-all uses all the past data for model learning.

According to the previous work [10,11], we also compare our proposed model with the other two different ways of setting the history influence on the generation of documents at current epoch: sliding-DTSA and skip-DTSA.

– **sliding-DTSA**: the current sentiment-topic-word distributions are dependent on the previous sentiment-topic specific word distributions in the last S epochs.

– **skip-DTSA**: we take history sentiment-topic-word distributions into account
  by skipping some epochs in between. For example, if S = 3, we only consider
  previous sentiment-topic-word distributions at epoch $t - 2^2$, $t - 2^1$ and $t - 2^0$.

Figure 5 shows the average training time per epoch with the increasing number of time slices. sliding-DTSA, skip-DTSA and DTSA have similar average
training time across the number of time slices. JST-one has less training time
than the DTSA models. LDA-one uses least training time since it only models
3 sentiment topics while others all model a total of 20 sentiment topics. JST-
all takes much more time than all the other models as it needs to use all the
previous data for training.

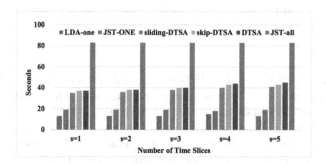

Fig. 5. Computational time per epoch with different number of time slices.

5.3 Sentiment Classification

In this section, we present the results of sentiment classification with the number
of time slices fixed at S = 4. We use the above mentioned datasets (see Table 2)
to do the experiment. DTSA is a probabilistic model, we run 10 times for each
experiment, and list the average F1-score in Table 4.

We compare the performance of our model with JST-one and JST-all [17].
In order to prove the importance of user interactions, we introduce two special
sentiments to JST-one and JST-all, making the new model called JST-one+
and JST-all+ which could identify approval and disapproval. For evaluating the
advantage of using multiple timescale model, we also compare the DTSA model
with sliding-DTSA and skip-DTSA.

As can be seen from Table 4, the performance of DTSA, sliding-DTSA and
skip-DTSA are better than JST-one and JST-one+ method on all data sets.
This is because JST-one and JST-one+ only use the data in the previous epoch
for training and do not model dynamics. While our models take into account the
influence of history sentiment-topic-word distributions, which can improve the
sentiment classification metrics. Compared to sliding-DTSA and skip-DTSA, our
model DTSA achieve the highest F1-score, which proves the effective of multiple
timescale model.

Table 4. The F1-score of sentiment classification results.

Dataset	DTSA	sliding-DTSA	skip-DTSA	JST-one	JST-one+	JST-all	JST-all+
MH370/Topic	**0.865**	0.811	0.859	0.674	0.683	0.786	0.790
MH370/Senti	**0.831**	0.792	0.803	0.613	0.679	0.715	0.767
Crimea/Topic	**0.837**	0.793	0.828	0.607	0.615	0.776	0.782
Crimea/Senti	**0.812**	0.733	0.769	0.579	0.631	0.727	0.731
Sochi/Topic	**0.896**	0.795	0.869	0.683	0.690	0.765	0.765
Sochi/Senti	**0.853**	0.763	0.783	0.602	0.668	0.734	0.760
India/Topic	**0.879**	0.815	0.853	0.657	0.662	0.790	0.803
India/Senti	**0.848**	0.778	0.793	0.613	0.659	0.716	0.765
Facebook/Topic	**0.857**	0.806	0.848	0.637	0.637	0.753	0.762
Facebook/Senti	**0.828**	0.749	0.776	0.591	0.629	0.687	0.733

In addition, we can see that JST-one+ and JST-all+ significantly improve the accuracy of sentiment classification on all data sets. This suggests that the special sentiments have a significant impact to the sentiment classification result. Furthermore, the DTSA outperforms the JST-all and JST-all+ methods on all data sets. JST-all+ could detect the user interactions, but does not use the user interactions to adjust the topic and sentiment distribution of comments, making them can not avoid the error caused by user interaction on both topic and sentiment.

We also analyze the influence of the topic number settings on the DTSA model performance. With the number of time slices fixed at $S = 4$, we vary the topic number $T \in \{1, 5, 10, 15, 20, 25\}$. Figure 6 shows the average sentiment classification accuracy over epochs with different number of topics. As can be seen from Fig. 6, increasing the number of topics leads to a slight drop in accuracy. This trend is more evident on the twitter data set.

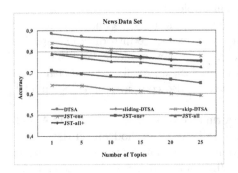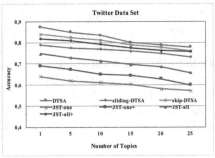

Fig. 6. Sentiment classification accuracy with different number of topics.

6   Conclusion

In this paper, a novel dynamic topic-based sentiment analysis model (DTSA) is proposed to extract topics and topic-specific sentiments from online news stories and comments. It could be used to decrease the error caused by user interactions, handle long-term and short-term dependency and automatically adjust model parameters in real time to improve the accuracy of classification based on sentiment recognition. The model is deployed on distributed online systems thus making improvements of efficiency of data process. The model has been tested on two kinds of data sets and displays promising results.

In the future, more semantic information such as relationships between terms and more features like sarcasm could be used into this model to further improve the accuracy of sentiment analysis. Besides, we should study the performance of the various evaluation methods in topic words extraction tasks.

References

1. Lin, C., He, Y.: Joint sentiment/topic model for sentiment analysis. In: Proceedings of the 18th ACM Conference on Information and Knowledge Management, pp. 375–384. ACM (2009)
2. Jo, Y., Oh, A.H.: Aspect and sentiment unification model for online review analysis. In: Proceedings of the Fourth ACM International Conference on Web Search and Data Mining, pp. 815–824. ACM (2011)
3. Li, C., Zhang, J., Sun, J.T., et al.: Sentiment topic model with decomposed prior. In: SIAM International Conference on Data Mining (SDM 2013). Society for Industrial and Applied Mathematics (2013)
4. Balahur, A., Steinberger, R., Kabadjov, M., et al.: Sentiment analysis in the news (2013). arXiv preprint: arXiv:1309.6202
5. Blei, D.M., Ng, A.Y., Jordan, M.I.: Latent Dirichlet allocation. J. Mach. Learn. Res. **3**, 993–1022 (2003)
6. Blei, D.M.: Probabilistic topic models. Commun. ACM **55**(4), 77–84 (2012)
7. Titov, I., McDonald, R.: Modeling online reviews with multi-grain topic models. In: Proceedings of the 17th International Conference on World Wide Web, pp. 111–120. ACM (2008)
8. Kim, S., Zhang, J., Chen, Z., et al.: A hierarchical aspect-sentiment model for online reviews. In: AAAI (2013)
9. Zhao, Y., Dong, S., Li, L.: Sentiment analysis on news comments based on supervised learning method. Int. J. Multimed. Ubiquit. Eng. **9**, 333–346 (2014)
10. Wang, C., Blei, D., Heckerman, D.: Continuous time dynamic topic models (2012). arXiv preprint: arXiv:1206.3298
11. Wang, X., McCallum, A.: Topics over time: a non-Markov continuous-time model of topical trends. In: Proceedings of the 12th ACM SIGKDD International Conference on Knowledge Discovery and Data Mining, pp. 424–433. ACM (2006)
12. Iwata, T., Yamada, T., Sakurai, Y., et al.: Online multiscale dynamic topic models. In: Proceedings of the 16th ACM SIGKDD International Conference on Knowledge Discovery and Data Mining, pp. 663–672. ACM (2010)

13. Wang, Y., Agichtein, E., Benzi, M.: TM-LDA: efficient online modeling of latent topic transitions in social media. In: Proceedings of the 18th ACM SIGKDD International Conference on Knowledge Discovery and Data Mining, pp. 123–131. ACM (2012)
14. Dermouche, M., Velcin, J., Khouas, L., et al.: A joint model for topic-sentiment evolution over time. In: 2014 IEEE International Conference on Data Mining (ICDM), pp. 773–778. IEEE (2014)
15. Zheng, M., Wu, C., Liu, Y., et al.: Topic sentiment trend model: modeling facets and sentiment dynamics. In: 2012 IEEE International Conference on Computer Science and Automation Engineering (CSAE), pp. 651–657. IEEE (2012)
16. Wang, L., Cardie, C.: Improving agreement and disagreement identification in online discussions with a socially-tuned sentiment lexicon. In: ACL 2014, p. 97 (2014)
17. Lin, C., He, Y., Everson, R., et al.: Weakly supervised joint sentiment-topic detection from text. IEEE Trans. Knowl. Data Eng. **24**(6), 1134–1145 (2012)
18. Dean, J., Ghemawat, S.: MapReduce: simplified data processing on large clusters. Commun. ACM **51**(1), 107–113 (2008)

Improving Object and Event Monitoring on Twitter Through Lexical Analysis and User Profiling

Yihong Zhang$^{(\boxtimes)}$, Claudia Szabo, and Quan Z. Sheng

School of Computer Science, The University of Adelaide, Adelaide, SA 5005, Australia
{yihong.zhang,claudia.szabo,michael.sheng}@adelaide.edu.au

Abstract. Personal users on Twitter frequently post observations about their immediate environment as part of the 500 million tweets posted everyday. These observations and their implicitly associated time and location data are a valuable source of information for monitoring objects and events, such as earthquake, hailstorm, and shooting incidents. However, given the informal and uncertain expressions used in personal Twitter messages, and the various type of accounts existing on Twitter, capturing personal observations of objects and events is challenging. In contrast to the existing supervised approaches, which require significant efforts for annotating examples, in this paper, we propose an unsupervised approach for filtering personal observations. Our approach employs lexical analysis, user profiling and classification components to significantly improve filtering precision. To identify personal accounts, we define and compute a mean user profile for a dataset and employ distance metrics to evaluate the similarity of the user profiles under analysis to the mean. Our extensive experiments with real Twitter data show that our approach consistently improves filtering precision of personal observations by around 22 %.

Keywords: Twitter · Microblog content classification · User profiling

1 Introduction

Micro-blogging services such as Twitter have become widely used in recent years. Twitter allows its users to create and publish short messages of maximum 140 characters, called *tweets*. Currently, around 284 million active Twitter users generate 500 million tweets every day[1], and around 80 % of Twitter users use their mobile phones to create tweets[1]. The use of mobile platforms for tweeting implies that users can report observed events and objects in their physical vicinity. For example, personal tweets have been used for tracking the movements of earthquakes and typhoons in Japan [12]; tweets about flood, hurricane, and riots have also been used for crime and disaster location [7]. In a previous work, we

---

[1] https://about.twitter.com/company.

© Springer International Publishing AG 2016
W. Cellary et al. (Eds.): WISE 2016, Part II, LNCS 10042, pp. 19–34, 2016.
DOI: 10.1007/978-3-319-48743-4_2

showed that news generated based on personal observation messages on Twitter can often be hours earlier than the first news appearing in traditional media, even for the most newsworthy events such as shooting incidents [19].

Current work on microblog and short text analysis mostly relies on supervised machine learning methods [2,12], which require the manual preparation of training samples. This has several drawbacks, such as the need for significant manual effort for annotating examples, and a lack of quality guarantees of the classification solutions, when the classifier is applied to a wider pool of tweets beyond its training data. *Unsupervised methods* have the potential to address these issues. In the domain of microblogs and short texts, however, due to the complexity and uncertainty of human user data, works on unsupervised methods are still at an early stage [1,17]. The informal and unstructured text messages used on microblogs creates uncertainty for any kind of classification models, and solutions and models effective in one application often will not be as effective in another application. For example, the work in [8] has shown that the effect of user roles in Twitter rumor classification varies significantly for different rumor instances. Thus a challenge for a specific application using unsupervised methods is to find a particular model that is effective for that application and domain.

In this paper, we focus on filtering personal observations of objects and events on Twitter using an unsupervised method. To address the challenges discussed above and provide high classification accuracy, we advance a novel approach that employs lexical analysis and user profiling. The lexical analysis module filters *observation messages* based on two attributes, part-of-speech (POS) tag and message objectivity. The user profiling module separates *personal accounts* from other types of accounts based on four analyzed attributes, namely, *objectivity, interactivity, originality*, and *topic focus*. We conduct extensive experiments using real Twitter data collected for a variety of events, with significantly improved results over the existing works. Our main contributions are:

- We propose a novel unsupervised method for filtering personal observations on Twitter. Our method utilizes various natural language processing techniques in lexical analysis and user profiling.
- We propose a novel model for profiling Twitter users based on four dimensions, including *objectivity, interactivity, originality*, and *topic focus*. We also propose algorithms that can effectively distinguish personal accounts from specific-purpose accounts.
- We test our method extensively with real Twitter datasets. For controlled datasets, our method consistently improves the precision by around 22 %. We obtain even higher improvement for crowd-sourced datasets. Our method also out-performs some of the most effective supervised techniques.

2   Related Work

Twitter as a public media and news source has been studied in several works. Wu et al. [18] investigated the demographics of influential Twitter users, whom they grouped into media, organization, celebrity, and blogger. Their study concludes that bloggers are popular personal accounts that produce the most influential tweets. Kwon et al. [5] investigated supervised methods for identifying rumors on Twitter using a number of prominent features, including propagation peaks, friendship network graph, and linguistic properties based on LIWC (Linguistic Inquiry and Word Count). They found that selecting the right features is critical to classifier accuracy. Sriram et al. [14] similarly studied supervised tweet classification for five types of tweets: news, opinions, deals, events, and private messages. Although various machine learning techniques are compared, they also found selecting the right features is the key factor for classification accuracy.

Despite the fact that messages on Twitter are very often informal and incomplete [3], researches have used Twitter information for disaster location [6], object tracking [12], and event detection [16]. For example, Lingad et al. [7] studied locations mentioned in disaster-related messages in order to identify the position of natural disasters and affected areas. However, accurately classifying object or event-related messages is a challenging task. Sakaki et al. [12] developed a system that tracks the movement of earthquakes and typhoons based on personal reports detected on Twitter. They compared a number of features for building the event-related message classifier, with the best-performing feature set achieving a precision of 63.64 %. Li et al. [6] studied the use of tweets for detecting crime and disaster events (CDE) as they were reported on Twitter. They trained a classifier based on the words present in identified CDE tweets, and achieved a precision of 30 % and a recall of 85 %.

Due to the amount of effort required for manually annotating a large number of messages, a supervised method, however, is in many cases impractical. Unsupervised methods have the advantage of needing less manual effort. Current unsupervised methods for microblog analysis are still at an early stage of research. Carroll et al. [1] developed an unsupervised method for determining the objectivity of in Chinese microblog texts. They defined objectivity as sentiment neutrality, but the application is limited to brand and company reputation analysis. Unankard et al. [16] developed a framework for predicting election results using Twitter messages, in which message and user sentiments are calculated based on positive and negative word counts. Since observation messages are not strongly related to message sentiments, filtering personal observations, however, requires technique beyond sentiment analysis.

3   Filtering Methodology

Our method filters observations of objects and events from personal accounts, by performing the following steps. First, we identify observations from collected tweets for a specific keyword. Second, using also the collected tweets, we distinguish personal accounts from other types of accounts. A personal account is a Twitter account employed for personal use, and is assumed to be free from business or propaganda interests. Our insight is that tweets from personal accounts often contain realtime and localized observations of objects and events. Finally, from the observation tweets identified in the first step, we retain only those made from personal accounts. These personal observations of objects and events have proved useful in previous works for scenarios such as disaster location and rumor detection [5,12].

An overview of our method is shown in Fig. 1. To identify observation tweets, we run lexical analysis on tweet texts based on the par-of-speech (POS) tagging, objectivity analysis, and originality test. To identify personal accounts, we first analyze four attributes for each user, namely, *objectivity*, *interactivity*, *originality*, and *topic focus*. Then we use a clustering algorithm for classifying personal accounts based on the attribute values. We describe our method below.

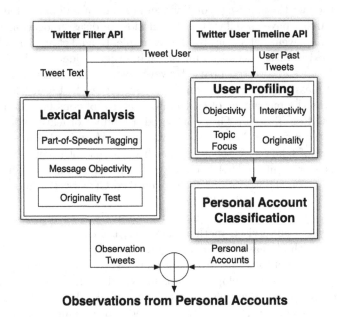

Fig. 1. Method overview

3.1   Observation Filtering

After using the Twitter Filter API[2] to obtain tweets that contain the object or event keyword such as "rainbow" or "car accident", our lexical analysis method focuses on extracting observation tweets. Not all tweets containing the keywords are observations of objects and events, since in some cases the keywords can have another semantic, context-based meaning, and the objects and events can be mentioned in general comments instead of specific observations, e.g., "I dislike car accidents". We address this by utilizing three techniques, namely, *par-of-speech* (POS) tagging, *objectivity analysis*, and *originality test*. POS tagging allows filtering of messages in which the object or event keyword is not used as a subject of observation. Objectivity analysis allows filtering of uncertain messages, such as questions and general comments. Originality test removes messages that are not originally created by the user, such as retweets or quotations.

---

[2] https://dev.twitter.com/streaming/public.

Filtering Based on Part-of-Speech Tagging. Our insight is that the objects and events mentioned in an observation are most likely to be nouns and gerunds, such as in "I just saw a rainbow", or "A shooting outside my home". On the other hand, keywords not used as nouns and gerunds often indicate that the tweet is not a specific observation. Some examples of non-observation tweets are shown in Table 1, with the role of the keyword determined by POS tagging.

Table 1. Non-observation tweets filtered by POS tagging, for monitoring flight delay, shooting incidents, and rainbows

Tweet text	POS
Keep praying for the typhoon to magically **delay** my flight a day	VB
Can we pretend that airplanes, in the night sky, are like **shooting** stars?	JJ
This guy got on a **rainbow** colored LV belt	JJ

VB = base form verb, JJ = adjective.

POS tagging is a technique that matches words in a text with their part-of-speech categories, such as modal, noun, verb, and adverb [13]. We use a filtering rule on top of POS tagging to effectively remove a portion of tweets that are clearly not observations. After performing POS tagging for a tweet, we accept it if the POS tag for the keyword is **NN** (Noun, singular or mass), **NNP** (proper noun, singular), and **VBG** (verb, gerund or present particle). The tweet is rejected if the keyword has other POS tags.

Filtering Based on Objectivity Analysis. Our insight is that a specific observation of an object or event usually is written in a more objective tone than a general tweet. Generally, the objectivity of a message is affected by sentimental words and uncertain words, such as "great", "bad", "maybe", "anyone". Sentimentality and uncertainty as factors for determining message objectivity has already been proposed in existing works [1,10]. We calculate tweet objectivity based on both sentimentality and uncertainty, using the following formula:

$$objectivity(t) = 1 - [senti_p(t) + 0.5 \times senti_n(t)]$$
$$\times (1 - \sqrt{uncertainty(t)})$$

where $senti_p$ is the positive sentiment and $senti_n$ is the negative sentiment. In our previous works, we have found that negative sentiments have a large presence in observation messages [20]. We follow this insight here and we weight down the effect of negative sentiments on reducing the objectivity in the formula. Furthermore, since uncertainty plays an important role in determining the objectivity of a message, as discovered in [10], we increase the effect of uncertainty by scaling it to a larger value.

For sentiment analysis, we employ previously proven effective methods, which employ a positive/negative words dictionary and the slang sentiment dictionary [16]. The positive and negative sentiments of a tweet text t are measured as:

$$senti_p(t) = \frac{count_p(t)}{count_w(t)}$$

$$senti_n(t) = \frac{count_n(t)}{count_w(t)}$$

where $count_p(t)$ and $count_n(t)$ are the word count for positive and negative words in t, and $count_w(t)$ is the word count of t.

For uncertainty analysis, we use a dictionary of uncertain words based on the LIWC category of hesitation words [15]. To measure the uncertainty of tweet t, we consider the number of uncertain words in the text, and whether it is a question.

$$uncertainty(t) = \begin{cases} 0.5, \text{ if } t \text{ ends with a question mark} \\ \frac{count_u(t)}{count_w(t)}, \text{ otherwise} \end{cases}$$

where $count_w(t)$ is the word count for uncertain words in t.

Originality Test. Our analysis of various datasets show that sometimes personal users may repeat some messages created by other users, which do not count as their own observations. The repeated messages not only produce redundancy, but also generate noises for analysis. Thus it is crucial to determine message originality. We proposed a set of rules to determine non-original messages based on message content, as shown in Table 2. A message satisfies any of the rules in the table is considered non-original, and will be filtered out.

Table 2. Originality test rules

Rule	Explanation
Retweet	Contains the word RT
Quotation	Contains quotation marks
Speech	Mention or capitalized word before colon
News title	All words capitalized before link
Repeat	Contains "says", "claims", "via", or "according to"
News mention	Mention contains "news", "radio", or "breaking"
News agent	Mention contains news agent name such as "ABC" or "CNN"

Some repeated messages are easy to identify, such as retweets, which have "RT" at the beginning of the messages. Other forms of repeated messages can be more difficult to spot, such as indirect quotes, which often but not necessarily contain the word "says" or "claims". Given the various ways a message may be repeated, the rules listed in Table 2 do not cover all non-original messages. Nevertheless, we found these rules to filter out most of the repeated messages.

Algorithm 1. Lexical Analysis on Single Tweets

INPUT: keyword w, tweet set T, objectivity threshold θ
OUTPUT: obervation labels O
1: set all $o \in O$ as *false*
2: **for** each $t \in T$ **do**
3:     run POS tagging for t
4:     **if** POS tag for $w \in \{\mathbf{NN, NNP, VBG}\}$ **then**
5:         $pp \leftarrow true$
6:     **end if**
7:     **if** $objectivity(t) > \theta$ **then**
8:         $po \leftarrow true$
9:     **end if**
10:     **if** t fails all rules in Table 2 **then**
11:         $pt \leftarrow true$
12:     **end if**
13:     $o_t \leftarrow pp \wedge po \wedge pt$
14: **end for**

Lexical Analysis Algorithm. Algorithm 1 describes our lexical analysis method. The input is a keyword w, and a set T of tweet texts containing the keyword. The output is a set of predictions of whether each tweet text $t \in T$ is an observation, O. In line 7, we use a parameter θ to control the level of objectivity a tweet requires to meet to be considered an observation. The default value for θ is the first quartile of overall objectivity in the tweet set.

3.2   User Profiling for Personal Account Classification

Previous works have shown that news generated from personal observations on Twitter can be much faster than traditional media, and the implicitly-associated location data can be used for localizing the object or the event [12, 19]. However, there are many Twitter accounts that are not for personal use, and do not have the same time and location association for their observation messages, and while they add noises to the data collected, it is usually difficult to distinguish them from personal accounts. The main issue is that all accounts on Twitter uses the same format to store data, and usually there is no effective way to judge the type of account other than looking at the content of the account posts directly. These accounts include news, business, activist and advertisement accounts. We call these latter types of accounts *specific-purpose accounts*, and show some well-known examples in Table 3.

Table 3. Examples of specific-purpose accounts

News	@cnnbrk @wsj @foxnews @huffingtonpost @bbcworld @politico
Business	@AdamDenison @GMblogs @MarriottIntl @chicagobulls @Marvel
Activist	@Greenpeace @femmajority @OU_Unheard @freedomtomarry

Our study of personal and specific-purpose accounts leads to the following observations:

– News accounts tweet about various topics in a strictly objective tone. Their tweets usually contain links to Web articles. Depending on the specialty, a media account can cover a wide range of topics.
– Business accounts contain conversations, observations, and product promotions, but the range of topic is limited to the specific business.
– Activist and advertisement accounts rarely use objective tone, and their range of topics is also limited.

A personal account, however, does not have such clear-cut characteristics as specific-purpose accounts, and usually contains a mix of information sharing, conversation with other users, and original content that covers various topics. We propose that:

Conjecture 1. A personal account has moderate levels in objectivity, interactivity, originality, and topic focus.

We use various statistics generated from Twitter data to calculate the levels of *objectivity, interactivity, originality,* and *topic focus* for Twitter users. Here we assume these user qualities are consistent over time and do not easily change. There are rare cases that the profile of a user changes drastically, for example, caused by a job change, but currently we do not consider such cases. To profile a user, first we collect a set of past tweets made by the user, H. Then we select the original tweets in H based on the rules described in Table 2, as $OH = \{oh_1, oh_2, ..., oh_l\}$, where $|OH| = l$.

The objectivity of a user is calculated based on the objectivity of each tweet in OH:

$$u_{objectivity} = \frac{\sum_{i=1}^{l} objectivity(oh_i)}{l}$$

The interactivity of a user is calculated based on the number of tweets containing mention mark "@" in H:

$$u_{interactivity} = \frac{count_@(H)}{|H|}$$

The originality of a user is calculated based on the fraction of original tweets in H.

$$u_{originality} = \frac{l}{|H|}$$

To calculate a user's topic focus, we count the frequency of each topic word for all topic words appearing in OH. For simplicity, we consider a topic word as a word that starts with a capital letter. The first word in a sentence is ignored. Once we have a descendingly-sorted list of topic word occurrences $\{nt_1, nt_2, ..., nt_k\}$, the topic focus of a user is calculated based on the fraction of the first quarter of the most frequent topic words:

$$u_{focus} = \frac{\sum_{i=1}^{n/4} nt_i}{\sum_{j=1}^{n} nt_j}$$

A user is thus profiled by the quadruple:

$$u = \{u_{objectivity}, u_{interactivity}, u_{originality}, u_{focus}\}$$

3.3   Personal Account Classification with Profiles

We propose an algorithm for automatically identifying personal accounts based on the user profile. First we define the difference between two user profiles u_1 and u_2 as the Euclidian distance between two profiles:

$$d(u_1, u_2) = \sqrt{\sum (u_1 - u_2)^2}$$

where

$$\sum (u_1 - u_2)^2 = (u_{objectivity1} - u_{objectivity2})^2$$
$$+ (u_{interactivity1} - u_{interactivity2})^2$$
$$+ (u_{originality1} - u_{originality2})^2$$
$$+ (u_{focus1} - u_{focus2})^2$$

Following Conjecture 1, we see that the attributes of a personal account are usually closer to a set of mean values while a specific-purpose account usually holds more extreme values. Therefore we propose that:

Conjecture 2. Given a set of user profiles U, which contains personal account profiles P and specific-purpose account profiles S, there exists a mean profile $\bar{u}$, such that $\sum_{p \in P} d(p, \bar{u}) < \sum_{s \in S} d(s, \bar{u})$.

While it is difficult to prove Conjecture 2, we find it generally true in our analysis, as we will show with our experiments. Given a set of user profiles U, and a mean profile $\bar{u}$, we can separate from U a subset C that is more likely to contain personal accounts, by selecting profiles that have shorter distance to $\bar{u}$.

We devise an iterative algorithm for finding the mean profile $\bar{u}$. Intuitively, we can use the mean attribute values of all profiles in U. However, the extreme attribute values of the specific-purpose account profiles can bias the mean significantly, making it inaccurate for deciding personal accounts. In Algorithm 2, we use an iterative approach and a cluster size threshold δ for selecting a cluster of $|U| \times \delta$ profiles that are close to an unbiased $\bar{u}$. Starting from an initial mean profile $\bar{u}_0$, the algorithm alters between cluster updating (line 2, 6) and mean updating (line 4 and 5). In the cluster updating step, a number of profiles close to the mean are selected. In the mean updating step, a new mean is calculated based on the selected profiles. If there are extreme values that cause a bias in the cluster, the mean will move away from the bias, and replace the extreme value profiles with more average profiles in the cluster. The output of the algorithm, F, is a set of personal account predictions.

Algorithm 2. Predicting Personal Accounts

INPUT: user profiles U, mean profile $\bar{u}_0$, selected cluster size δ
OUTPUT: F
1: set all $f \in F$ as *false*
2: $C \leftarrow |U| \times \delta$ profiles closest to $\bar{u}_0$
3: **while** $C \neq C'$ **do**
4:    $C' \leftarrow C$
5:    $\bar{u} \leftarrow$ mean attribute values of profiles in C
6:    $C \leftarrow |U| \times \delta$ profiles closest to $\bar{u}$
7: **end while**
8: **for** each $u \in U$ **do**
9:    **if** $u \in C$ **then**
10:       $f_u \leftarrow true$
11:    **end if**
12: **end for**

While Algorithm 2 generally finds a good mean profile that separates personal accounts and specific-purpose accounts. However, depending on the choice of the initial mean $\bar{u}_0$, the algorithm sometimes produces undesirable results. To address this issue, we derive a particle swarm optimization (PSO) algorithm for finding the optimal $\bar{u}_0$.

PSO is an optimization technique that takes a population of solutions, and iteratively improves the quality of the solutions by moving them toward the best solution in each iteration [4]. A solution in our PSO algorithm is an initial mean $\bar{u}_0$ to be given to Algorithm 2. A PSO algorithm requires the definition of the quality measure and the solution movement. To define the quality of a solution, we rely on our initial observation that personal accounts exhibit higher variance than any types of specific-purpose accounts. Therefore we propose that:

Conjecture 3. Given two user profile clusters C_1 and C_2, if the profiles in C_1 are more diverse than C_2, than C_1 is more likely to contain personal accounts.

We use pairwise profile differences to calculate the diversity of profiles in a cluster, $C = \{c_1, c_2, ..., c_k\}$,

$$div(C) = \frac{2 \times \sum_{i=1}^{k-1} \sum_{j=i+1}^{k} d(c_i, c_j)}{k \cdot (k-1)}$$

For the solution movement in PSO, we set a moving speed v so in each iteration, a solution p moves towards the best solution p_b as:

$$p \leftarrow p + (p_b - p) \cdot v \tag{1}$$

Our PSO algorithm is shown as Algorithm 3. It starts with a number of random solutions (line 1) and for each solution, a profile cluster is generated using Algorithm 2 (line 2 to 4). Then iteratively, the PSO algorithm moves the best solution towards an optimal solution by comparing the cluster diversity with each solution (line 5 to 13).

Algorithm 3. PSO for Finding Optimal $\bar{u}_0$

INPUT: user profiles U, selected cluster size δ, number of particles n, speed v
OUTPUT: p_b
1: randomly choose n solutions P in the solution space
2: **for** each $p \in P$ **do**
3:      generate a cluster C_p using Algorithm 2
4: **end for**
5: $p_b \leftarrow p$ with highest $div(C_p)$
6: **while** $p_b \neq p'_b$ **do**
7:      $p'_b \leftarrow p_b$
8:      **for** each $p \in P$ **do**
9:          $p \leftarrow p + (p_b - p) \cdot v$
10:         generate a cluster C_p using Algorithm 2
11:     **end for**
12:     $p_b \leftarrow p$ with highest $div(C_p)$
13: **end while**

The optimal initial mean produced by Algorithm 3 can then be used in Algorithm 2 for selecting the cluster of personal account profiles. Although Algorithm 3 requires two more parameters, during our experiments we find the effect of changing n and v negligible for any $n > 1,000$ and $v < 0.2$, as the solution already reaches optimal values. Therefore we can confidently set n and v to fixed values. The only parameter that still affects the classification result is the cluster size parameter δ, which controls the portion of profiles in the data to be selected as personal account profiles.

Algorithm 4. Filter Observations from Personal Accounts

INPUT: keyword w, messages M, objectivity threshold θ, selected cluster size δ
OUTPUT: R
1: set all $r \in R$ as *false*
2: $T \leftarrow$ tweet text from M
3: $U \leftarrow$ user profiles from M
4: $O \leftarrow$ run Algorithm 1 with w, T, θ
5: $p_b \leftarrow$ run Algorithm 3 with U, δ
6: $F \leftarrow$ run Algorithm 2 with U, p_b, δ
7: **for** each $m \in M$ that has text t and user profile u **do**
8:      **if** $o_t \wedge f_u$ **then**
9:          $r_m \leftarrow true$
10:     **end if**
11: **end for**

3.4   Overall Algorithm

Algorithm 4 identifies observations from personal accounts. Given the input of a keyword w and a set of tweets M, and the control parameter θ and δ, the output is a set of predictions, R, of whether each respective tweet is an observation of the object or event of interest from personal accounts.

4   Experimental Analysis

We tested the effectiveness of our method for filtering personal observations on Twitter with two real Twitter datasets, comprising of a controlled dataset and a crowd-sourced dataset. In this section, we present the setup, measurement, baseline methods, and results of our experiments in detail.

4.1   Experiment Setup

We implemented the algorithms presented in the previous section in Java. The experiments were run on a MacBook Pro laptop computer, with 2.3 GHz Intel Core i7 CPU and 8 GB 1600 MHz DDR3 memory. We deployed an existing implementation for POS tagging. After comparing several existing POS tagging implementations including OpenNLP and LingPipe, we chose StanfordNLP POS module to run our POS tagging because it is relatively fast and provides a high tagging accuracy of around 95 % [9].

For parameter θ in Algorithm 1, we chose the first quartile of overall objectivity in the dataset for all experiments, which generally provides good results. For parameter δ, we compared three different values, including 0.7, 0.8, and 0.9. To ensure the consistency of the experiments, instead of randomly choosing initial values for the particles in Algorithm 3, we chose combinations of evenly distributed values for the four attributes as the initial values, i.e., 0.2, 0.4, 0.6, 0.8, and 1. Our analysis shows that randomly initialized particles provide similar results. For user profiling, up to 1,000 recent tweets were collected for each user using Twitter Timeline API.

4.2   Baseline Methods and Comparison Metrics

We compared our approach with three baseline filtering strategies, namely, *Accept All, Sakaki* filter, and *Sriram*. Accept All takes all tweets in the dataset as the positive for personal observations. Sakaki classifier, proposed by Sakaki et al. in [12], is a supervised method that deploys a Support Vector Machine (SVM) classifier with linear kernel built on manually annotated training data. Among the three feature sets proposed in [12], we implemented the reportedly most effective set, Feature Set A, which is based on word counts and keyword positions. We deployed an existing SVM implementation in an R language package called e1071[3]. We used a weighting function according to class imbalance to ensure optimal performance of the classifier. The performance of the Sakaki classifier was measured using the three-fold cross validation. One drawback of the

---

[3] https://cran.r-project.org/package=e1071.

Sakaki classifier is that it requires the presence of a keyword. The user profiling in our approach, though, does not have this requirement.

The Sriram classifier, proposed by Sriram et al. in [14], is also a supervised method that is based on eight features and the Naive Bayes model. The eight features include author name, use of slang, time phrase, opinionated words, and word emphasis, presences of currency signs, percentage signs, mention sign at the beginning and the middle of the message. The evaluation is based on the five-fold cross validation. The Sriram classifier is shown to be effective in classifying tweets into categories such as news, opinions, deals and events, but has not been tested in other applications.

All datasets for evaluation were manually annotated according to whether each tweet is a personal observation of an object or event of interest, which were considered ground truth in our experiments. The output of the filtering methods were compared with the manual annotations. If a filtering output is positive in manual annotations, it is considered a *true positive*. We use *precision, recall* and *f − value* as the measurements of filtering accuracy, where given the set of positive filtering results P and the set of true positives in the dataset TP, The $precision = \frac{|P \bigcap TP|}{|P|}$, $recall = \frac{|P \bigcap TP|}{|TP|}$, and f-value $= 2 \cdot \frac{precision \cdot recall}{precision + recall}$.

4.3   Effectiveness on Controlled Datasets

We first tested our method on two controlled datasets. We collected a dataset of around 5,000 tweets containing the keyword *hailstorm* during August, 2015, and a dataset of around 5,000 tweets containing the keyword *car accident* during September, 2015. After removing retweets and tweets containing links, we manually labelled the remaining tweets as positive or negative examples, according to whether the message is about a direct observation of a hailstorm or a car accident. The resulted *hailstorm* dataset contains 675 tweets, with 251 positive examples and 424 negative examples. The labelled *accident* dataset contains 954 tweets, with 347 positive examples and 607 negative examples.

We tested the filtering methods on the two datasets. Accuracy results for the baseline methods, lexical analysis-only filtering (LX), and lexical analysis combined with personal account filtering using three δ values, PA($\delta = 0.9$), PA($\delta = 0.8$), and PA($\delta = 0.5$), are presented in Table 4.

As shown in the table, the Accept All strategy captured all the positives in the annotations and had the maximum recall of 1. All other methods improved the precision by sacrificing the recall to some degree. Personal account filtering with δ set to 0.9 achieved the highest overall performance, indicated by the highest f-value. Using lexical analysis only and PA with $\delta = 0.9$ and $delta = 0.8$ all performed better than the Sakaki classifier and the Sriram classifier, the latter of which provided almost no filtering effect in the hailstorm dataset. Setting δ to a lower value improved the precision but also lowered the recall. When setting δ to 0.5, PA achieved the highest precision, while still held a relatively high f-value. The performance of all methods were consistent across two datasets, with LX improving precision from the Accept All strategy by around 15 % and PA($\delta = 0.9$) further improved it by 5 %–7 %.

Table 4. Filtering accuracy for hailstorm and car accident datasets

	Accept all	Sakaki	Sriram	LX	PA($\delta = 0.9$)	PA($\delta = 0.8$)	PA($\delta = 0.5$)
Hailstorm dataset							
Precision	0.37	0.43	0.37	0.53	0.62	0.64	**0.70**
Recall	1	0.70	0.98	0.80	0.76	0.71	0.46
f-value	0.54	0.53	0.54	0.63	**0.68**	0.67	0.56
Car accident dataset							
Precision	0.38	0.50	0.44	0.53	0.58	0.59	**0.60**
Recall	1	0.73	0.84	0.76	0.74	0.69	0.43
f-value	0.55	0.60	0.57	0.63	**0.65**	0.64	0.50

4.4   Effectiveness on Crowd-Sourced Dataset

We tested our approach on a publicly available dataset produced by Castillo et al. [11], and is available online[4]. The dataset contains around 20,000 tweets related to crisis events, such as the Colorado wildfires and the Pablo typhoon in 2012, and the Australia bushfire and New York train crash in 2013. These crisis tweets were manually annotated by hired workers on Crowdflower, a crowd-sourcing platform[5]. The tweets were labelled according to their relevance to the crisis event, and the type of information they provide into four categories, namely, *related and informative, related but not informative, not related*, and *not applicable*. The seven information types include Eyewitness, Government, NGOs, Business, Media, Outsiders, and Not applicable.

We consider that the Eyewitness-type tweets in the dataset are personal observations, while other types of tweets are not. Hence we expect our approach to filter Eyewitness tweets from other tweets. With this goal, we re-organized the dataset. First we selected two categories of related tweets from the dataset. Then we selected five information types of tweets: Eyewitness, Government, NGOs, Business and Media. We then produced a list of labels, with Eyewitness tweets as positives, and other types of tweets negatives. We also removed retweets from the data. Our labelled dataset had 3,646 tweets with 528 positives.

Since the tweets do not contain a specific keyword, we did not run POS and objectivity analysis. The Sakaki classifier is not applicable without a keyword. As such we ran the originality test in the lexical analysis and the personal account classification, and compared only to the Sriram classifier (Table 5).

The results are similar to previous experiments, where PA($\delta = 0.9$) achieved the highest f-value and PA($\delta = 0.5$) achieved the highest precision. The lexical analysis was particularly effective for this dataset, improving the precision by around 38 %, mainly because the dataset includes a large portion of news messages, which failed the originality test. After the lexical analysis, PA($\delta = 0.9$) further improved the precision by 12 %. Both LX and PA($\delta = 0.9$) significantly outperformed the Sriram classifier.

---

[4] http://crisislex.org/.
[5] http://www.crowdflower.com/.

Table 5. Filtering accuracy for the crisis dataset

	Accept all	Sriram	LX	PA($\delta = 0.9$)	PA($\delta = 0.8$)	PA($\delta = 0.5$)
Precision	0.14	0.32	0.52	0.64	0.64	**0.65**
Recall	1	0.52	0.47	0.50	0.48	0.27
f-value	0.24	0.40	0.47	**0.56**	0.55	0.38

5 Conclusion

Personal observations of objects and events published on micro-blogging platforms such as Twitter are an invaluable information source, and can be utilized in applications such as natural disaster tracking and crime monitoring. However, given the various ways users post messages and the large variety of account types, information about a particular object or event is usually noisy and misleading. Thus it is critical to develop a novel approach that filters out noises before the information can be further utilized. Current filtering approaches based on supervised machine learning techniques require large manual efforts and thus are impractical in many scenarios.

In this paper, we propose an unsupervised message filtering approach that consists of a lexical analysis module, which examines the message, and a personal account classification module, which examines the message history of the user and determines if the user account is a personal account. We tested our approach extensively on real Twitter datasets. For the controlled dataset, our method consistently improves the precision by around 22 %, with the lexical analysis module improves it by 15 %, and personal account classification further improves it by 7 %. We see even higher improvement in a crowd-sourced dataset, increasing the precision from 14 % to 65 %. Compared with the Sakaki classifier and the Sriram classifier, our approach was able to achieve more than 10 % higher accuracy. In the future, we will continue to investigate unsupervised methods for further filtering accuracy improvement by incorporating location and name-entity analysis.

References

1. Carroll, T.Z.J.: Unsupervised classification of sentiment and objectivity in Chinese text. In: Third International Joint Conference on Natural Language Processing, p. 304 (2008)
2. Castillo, C., Mendoza, M., Poblete, B.: Information credibility on Twitter. In: Proceedings of the 20th International World Wide Web Conference, pp. 675–684 (2011)
3. Chung, D.S., Nah, S.: Media credibility and journalistic role conceptions: views on citizen and professional journalists among citizen contributors. J. Mass Media Ethics **28**(4), 271–288 (2013)
4. Kennedy, J.: Particle swarm optimization. In: Sammut, C., Webb, G.I. (eds.) Encyclopedia of Machine Learning, pp. 760–766. Springer, Heidelberg (2010)

5. Kwon, S., Cha, M., Jung, K., Chen, W., Wang, Y.: Prominent features of rumor propagation in online social media. In: Proceedings of 13th International Conference on Data Mining, pp. 1103–1108 (2013)
6. Li, R., Lei, K.H., Khadiwala, R., Chang, K.-C.: TEDAS: a Twitter-based event detection and analysis system. In: Proceedings of 28th International Conference on Data Engineering, pp. 1273–1276 (2012)
7. Lingad, J., Karimi, S., Yin, J.: Location extraction from disaster-related microblogs. In: Proceedings of the 22nd International World Wide Web Conference Companion, pp. 1017–1020 (2013)
8. Maddock, J., Starbird, K., Al-Hassani, H., Sandoval, D.E., Orand, M., Mason, R.M.: Characterizing online rumoring behavior using multi-dimensional signatures. In: Proceedings of the 18th ACM Conference on Computer Supported Cooperative Work and Social Computing, pp. 228–241 (2015)
9. Manning, C.D., Surdeanu, M., Bauer, J., Finkel, J., Bethard, S.J., McClosky, D.: The stanford CoreNLP natural language processing toolkit. In: Proceedings of 52nd Annual Meeting of the Association for Computational Linguistics: System Demonstrations, pp. 55–60 (2014)
10. Mukherjee, S., Weikum, G., Danescu-Niculescu-Mizil, C.: People on drugs: credibility of user statements in health communities. In: Proceedings of the 20th ACM International Conference on Knowledge Discovery and Data Mining, pp. 65–74 (2014)
11. Olteanu, A., Castillo, C., Diaz, F., Vieweg, S.: CrisisLex: a lexicon for collecting and filtering microblogged communications in crises. In: Proceedings of the 8th International AAAI Conference on Weblogs and Social Media, pp. 376–385 (2014)
12. Sakaki, T., Okazaki, M., Matsuo, Y.: Tweet analysis for real-time event detection and earthquake reporting system development. IEEE Trans. Knowl. Data Eng. **25**(4), 919–931 (2013)
13. Santorini, B.: Part-of-speech tagging guidelines for the penn treebank project (3rd revision). Technical report MS-CIS-90-47, University of Pennsylvania Department of Computer and Information Science Technical (1990)
14. Sriram, B., Fuhry, D., Demir, E., Ferhatosmanoglu, H., Demirbas, M.: Short text classification in Twitter to improve information filtering. In: Proceedings of the 33rd International ACM SIGIR Conference on Research and Development in Information Retrieval, pp. 841–842 (2010)
15. Tausczik, Y.R., Pennebaker, J.W.: The psychological meaning of words: LIWC and computerized text analysis methods. J. Lang. Soc. Psychol. **29**(1), 24–54 (2010)
16. Unankard, S., Li, X., Sharaf, M., Zhong, J., Li, X.: Predicting elections from social networks based on sub-event detection and sentiment analysis. In: Benatallah, B., Bestavros, A., Manolopoulos, Y., Vakali, A., Zhang, Y. (eds.) WISE 2014. LNCS, vol. 8787, pp. 1–16. Springer, Heidelberg (2014). doi:10.1007/978-3-319-11746-1_1
17. Unankard, S., Li, X., Sharaf, M.A.: Emerging event detection in social networks with location sensitivity. World Wide Web Journal (2015, in press)
18. Wu, S., Hofman, J.M., Mason, W.A., Watts, D.J.: Who says what to whom on Twitter. In: Proceedings of the 20th International World Wide Web Conference, pp. 705–714 (2011)
19. Zhang, Y., Szabo, C., Sheng, Q.Z.: Sense and focus: towards effective location inference and event detection on Twitter. In: The Proceedings of the 16th International Conference on Web Information Systems Engineering (2015)
20. Zhang, Y., Szabo, C., Sheng, Q.Z., Fang, X.S.: Classifying perspectives on Twitter: immediate observation, affection, and speculation. In: The Proceedings of the 16th International Conference on Web Information Systems Engineering (2015)

Aspect-Based Sentiment Analysis Using Lexico-Semantic Patterns

Kim Schouten[✉], Frederique Baas, Olivier Bus, Alexander Osinga,
Nikki van de Ven, Steffie van Loenhout, Lisanne Vrolijk, and Flavius Frasincar

Erasmus University Rotterdam, PO Box 1738, 3000 DR Rotterdam, The Netherlands
{414224fb,419325ob,427832ao,356202nv,431068sl,413096lv}@student.eur.nl,
{schouten,frasincar}@ese.eur.nl

Abstract. With its ever growing amount of user-generated content, the Web has become a trove of consumer information. The free text format in which most of this content is written, however, prevents straightforward analysis. Instead, natural language processing techniques are required to quantify the textual information embedded within text. This research focuses on extracting the sentiment that can be found in consumer reviews. In particular, we focus on finding the sentiment associated with the various aspects of the product or service a consumer writes about. Using a standard Support Vector Machine for classification, we propose six different types of patterns: lexical, syntactical, synset, sentiment, hybrid, surface. We demonstrate that several of these lexico-syntactic patterns can be used to improve sentiment classification for aspects.

Keywords: Lexico-semantic patterns · Support Vector Machines · Aspect-based sentiment analysis

1 Introduction

With its ever growing amount of user-generated content, the Web has become a trove of consumer information. Consumers everywhere are invited to share their experiences with products or services they bought and these experiences are in turn shared with prospective buyers to inform their decision making. In this, the Web has transformed the marketplace, putting the electronic word-of-mouth at the core of the decision making process. While reviews are marketed as being useful for prospective consumers, companies are even more interested in all of the expressed opinions toward their products and services. That information enables them to improve their products and optimize marketing strategies.

Unfortunately, the free text format of reviews prevents direct analysis of sentiment. Hence, data mining and natural language processing techniques are used to extract the highly valuable sentiment information. Before sentiment can be extracted, however, the sentiment scope has to be determined, since sentiment can be extracted for complete documents, sentences, or aspects. The advantages

© Springer International Publishing AG 2016
W. Cellary et al. (Eds.): WISE 2016, Part II, LNCS 10042, pp. 35–42, 2016.
DOI: 10.1007/978-3-319-48743-4_3

of the first two options are that they are easier to do. The disadvantage is that they can not cope with situations where within the unit of analysis (i.e., the document or the sentence), two or more things are discussed that have conflicting sentiment values. To deal with this, sentiment analysis has moved to the aspect level, where sentiment is associated with actual characteristics of the product or service under review. This naturally solves the problem of conflicting sentiment, but the process becomes more complex since the aspects themselves have to be found first. In our research, we focus on the sentiment analysis only, using the aspects that are already provided in the labeled data.

More specifically, we want to investigate the use of lexico-semantic patterns for sentiment analysis, based on the hypothesis that people tend to use similar linguistic structures to express sentiment. For this, we look at lexical patterns, Part-of-Speech (i.e., word types like nouns, verbs, etc.) patterns, and synset (i.e., a set of synonyms that have a single meaning) patterns, and, in addition, at combinations of these. For example, a pattern like 'low' followed by 'quality' denotes a different sentiment than 'low' followed by 'price'. This shows the difficulty of sentiment analysis and it forms the basis why we want to consider various combinations of attributes. We pose that an extended analysis of patterns will contribute to the existing sentiment analysis literature.

The paper is structured as follows. We start by discussing some of the related work in Sect. 2, followed by the description of the types of features we want to investigate in Sect. 3. We then describe our methodology and its evaluation in Sect. 4. We give our conclusions and possible directions for future work in Sect. 5.

2   Related Work

This work is a continuation of [7], which argues that patterns, either over adjacent words or over the grammatical structure of a text, can be employed together with a classifier to perform sentiment analysis. The scope in that work is still the sentence level, with all the advantages and disadvantages as discussed in the previous section. The features used are synset-based features, lexical features, and features that use the grammatical structure instead of word adjacency. We extend this research by first moving to the aspect level. Furthermore, we investigate n-grams up to $n = 4$, including some hybrid patterns like a synset followed by a Part-of-Speech tag. However, we only use word adjacency for our patterns, so grammatical relations are not employed to create patterns of non-adjacent words.

Using n-grams instead of just unigrams has been shown to increase performance and it is straightforward to implement [2,4]. For example, [4] uses both unigrams and bigrams to estimate aspect sentiment. However, the unigram feature still proved to be the most important in the ablation experiment, where this feature was left out to measure the drop in performance compared to including it in the feature set.

Part-of-Speech information, or grammatical word categories, has been used in text classification for a long time. In [3], for example, Part-of-Speech is used to filter out certain words, as this research focuses on the sentiment orientation of adjectives. One of the main conclusions from this research is that adjectives that are linked to each other with a conjunction like 'and' often have the same or at least a similar sentiment value. The opposite is true when adjectives are linked with 'but'. Furthermore, Part-of-Speech can to some extent be used to detect negated information. Negations are crucial for proper sentiment analysis. People are more likely to use negations with negative sentiment than with positive sentiment, so positive words are negated to become negative, but negative words are usually not negated to get positive words [5].

In [5], the authors investigated Part-of-Speech patterns for sentiment analysis on Twitter data. For example, sequences such as "I just", "I seriously", "I never", etc., are all patterns of the form 'Personal Pronoun followed by Adverb'. In their research, this pattern proved to be associated with negative sentiment. The top 100 best patterns, ranked by their Information Gain score, is included as features, which significantly improves the performance compared to only using unigram features.

3   Lexico-Semantic Patterns

The various features we investigate in this research can be placed in six categories: synset, lexical, syntactical, sentiment, hybrid, and surface features. Synsets are a part of semantics, and are sets of synonyms that have a single meaning. Hence, synsets are more specific than the original words, since any ambiguity is eliminated. Both unigrams and bigrams are used here, with the caveat that for synset bigrams we ignore the order of the adjacent synsets. We believe this will make the features more robust, at only a small cost to accuracy. Hence, seeing synsets A and B is the same as seeing synsets B and A.

The lexical category consists of word patterns, where we use the lemma, or dictionary form, of each word in the patterns. We investigate unigrams through quadgrams, since n-grams with n larger than four are too sparse to be of practical use. The syntactical patterns are all sequences of Part-of-Speech (POS) labels. These labels match with any word in that particular word group (i.e., the 'Noun' label will match any noun). As such these patterns are more generic than lexical patterns, making them more robust, but less descriptive. We investigate POS patterns ranging from bigrams to quadgrams.

Furthermore, we look at negator-POS bigrams, which are in fact hybrids between syntactical and lexical features. The bigram consists of a negator, from a list of negator words like 'not' and 'never', followed by a Part-of-Speech label. It effectively splits the Part-of-Speech bigrams that start with an adverb into negating and non-negating bigrams, since words like 'not', 'very', and 'highly' all have the same Part-of-Speech label. We also look at hybrid patterns that combine a Part-of-Speech label and a synset in one bigram.

Since the task is sentiment classification, it makes sense to include sentiment related features as well. For that we use the SentiWordNet dictionary [1], where synsets are given a positive, negativity, and objectivity score that always sum up to one. We compute a sentiment score from those by subtracting the negativity score from the positivity score. This is denoted as a sentisynset. We also look at negator-sentisynset bigrams where a negator is followed by a sentisynset, since this will invert the influence it has on the sentiment classification.

The surface feature is actually not related to patterns, but instead it determines how much of the surrounding context in a sentence is taken into account when creating features for a given aspect. Whenever the exact location of an aspect within a sentence is provided in the annotated data, we use that to create a window of words around that aspect. The words within that window are the only source of information from which to create features for that specific aspect. This allows us to predict different sentiment classes for aspects that are in the same sentence. Unfortunately, for some aspects, the exact location within a sentence is not provided, in which case we cannot specify a specific window and are limited to use the whole sentence as a source for features. The window is defined as k words before the aspect and j words after the aspect, but bound to be within the same sentence.

4   Methodology

For the experiments, we use a linear multi-class Support Vector Machine (SVM). We perform a 10-fold cross-validation to ensure stable results, and from the 90 % training data, we designate 20 % as validation data. The latter is used to perform feature selection. The rest is used to train the SVM model itself. The final results, as reported in Table 5, are obtained by training on 80 % of the training data, using 20 % of the training data as a validation set, and evaluating on the official SemEval2015 test data for both data sets.

To determine which types of features perform the best, a forward feature selection is performed. In each round the effect of adding just an isolated feature type is measured. The feature type that gives the highest increase in performance is added to the selected set of features. Again, all remaining types of features are tested, until no increase in performance is measured. The baseline score is simply the majority class. For our data, the 'positive' sentiment class is the most prevalent, as can be seen in Table 1.

The two datasets that are used in our experiments are the English restaurant review data set and the English laptop review data set from SemEval 2015 [6].

The first part of the evaluation is dedicated to the feature selection, showing the effect of each type of feature on performance. First, starting with no features at all, the baseline always predicts positive (the majority class). Every type of

Table 1. Sentiment value distributions for the two used data sets.

	Positive	Neutral	Negative	Total
Restaurants	1198	53	403	1654
Laptops	1103	106	765	1974

Table 2. The effect of using an additional particular feature type versus the majority baseline for both data sets.

	Laptops	Restaurants
Baseline	0.497	0.637
+ *word unigram*	**0.754**	0.694
+ *word bigram*	0.738	**0.713**
+ *word trigram*	0.572	0.637
+ *word quadgram*	0.500	0.637
+ *POS bigram*	0.599	0.634
+ *POS trigram*	0.602	0.640
+ *POS quadgram*	0.525	0.637
+ *synset unigram*	0.696	0.669
+ *synset bigram*	0.597	0.672
+ *synset-POS bigram*	0.663	0.675
+ *negator-POS bigram*	0.555	0.637
+ *sentisynset unigram*	0.580	0.637
+ *negator-sentisynset bigram*	0.497	0.637

feature is added in isolation and the performance is measured. This is the first step in the forward feature selection and the results of this step are presented in Table 2. As expected, word unigrams and word bigrams are the two strongest types of features in this setup. Interestingly, the various feature types perform differently on the two data sets. Features that are useful for the laptop data are not beneficial for the restaurant data and the other way around. This shows how domain dependent sentiment analysis is.

Carrying out the forward feature selection procedure results in an optimal set of *word unigram, synset bigram, sentisynset unigram,* and *synset unigram* for the laptop domain and an optimal set of *word unigram, synset bigram, sentisynset unigram, POS bigram,* and *negator-POS bigram* for the restaurant domain.

Table 3. Results of the ablation experiments for both data sets. The '-' in the first column denotes set difference.

	Laptops accuracy	Restaurants accuracy
Using optimal feature set	76.80 %	73.18 %
- *word unigram*	−9.95 %	−0.99 %
- *synset bigram*	−2.49 %	−2.20 %
- *sentisynset unigram*	−1.94 %	−1.58 %
- *synset unigram*	−0.29 %	Not selected
- *POS-bigram*	Not selected	−2.21 %
- *negator bigram*	Not selected	−0.95 %

Reversing the above process is known as an ablation experiment. Here we start with the optimal set of features, and record the effect of removing one of the feature types. These results are shown in Table 3. Of interest is that while the word unigram features are very important for laptops, this is less true for restaurants, where synset bigrams and POS bigrams are the most important. In contrast, the sentisynset unigram feature is about as equally important for both domains.

Subsequently, the optimal window size is computed that limits the words from which features are extracted for a given aspect. This is only of interest for the restaurant data, since only there exact aspect locations are provided for many of the aspects. We find that the optimal window size is 8 words before and 8 words after the aspect (but always limited by sentence bounds). However, with $k = j = 7$ and $k = j = 9$, roughly the same performance is achieved, losing only 1.27 % in accuracy.

To go one level deeper, we looked at the weight of individual features as assigned in the trained SVM model. To make interpretation of these weights easier, we removed the 'neutral' class, resulting in a binary classifier (i.e. positive and negative only). Note that some words only appear with or even have just a single meaning. In that case, the (senti)synset feature has the same weight as the lexical feature of the same word (e.g., 'amazing' in the first column). Of interest are the domain specific words that appear with high weights, such as 'soggy' which is obviously negative for the restaurant domain, but is not used in the laptops domain, and 'Dell' which for this data set is an indicator of negative sentiment for laptops, but of course irrelevant for restaurants (Table 4).

The scores of the best performing feature sets for each data set are reported in Table 5. These use the optimal window size as discussed above. Overall, we obtain an F_1-score of 69 % for restaurant reviews and 73.1 % for laptops reviews. Looking at the precision and recall values for the different sentiment values, we can see that on the restaurant data, the SVM tends to classify too many aspects as positive, since both the precision for positive and the recall for negative is relatively low. This seems less the case for the laptops data, resulting in a higher overall score.

Table 4. The most influential features, according to the weight (positive or negative) assigned by the SVM. The feature types are denoted as folows: W is word unigram, SS is synset unigram, and SSS is sentisynset unigram. The SVM is run using the optimal set of feature types.

Restaurants				Laptops			
Positive		Negative		Positive		Negative	
Best (SSS)	0.348	Be (SSS)	−0.639	Be (SS)	0.893	Not (W)	−0.621
Be (SSS)	0.317	Not (SSS)	−0.562	Love (W)	0.696	Be (SS)	−0.593
Amazing (W)	0.31	Soggy (W)	−0.473	Amazing (W)	0.564	Worst (W)	−0.503
Amazing (SSS)	0.31	Worst (W)	−0.408	Great (W)	0.516	Worst (SS)	−0.503
Love (W)	0.304	Worst (SSS)	−0.408	Love (SS)	0.508	Dell (W)	−0.458

Table 5. Overview of classifications on the SemEval 2015 restaurants and laptops test data using the optimal features.

	Restaurants			Laptops		
	Precision	Recall	F_1-score	Precision	Recall	F_1-score
Positive	68.1 %	87.4 %	76.6 %	76.5 %	86.7 %	81.3 %
Neutral	33.3 %	4.4 %	7.8 %	22.2 %	10.1 %	13.9 %
Negative	72.7 %	53.2 %	61.4 %	72.6 %	66.0 %	69.1 %
All	69.0 %	69.0 %	69.0 %	73.1 %	73.1 %	73.1 %

5   Conclusion

In this work we employ and investigate lexico-semantic patterns for aspect-based sentiment analysis. We show that some of the investigated patterns improve the sentiment classification. For laptops the combination of word unigrams, synset unigram, synset bigrams, and sentisynset unigrams prove to be the best performing from amongst the feature types included in our experiments. It is interesting to see that semantical features such as synsets are preferred over other types of features such as the more syntactical Part-of-Speech (POS) bigrams. For restaurants, the best performing combination of feature types is word unigrams, synset bigrams, sentisynset unigram, POS-bigram, and negator-POS bigram. Again, the synset bigram is included, but additionally, the POS bigram and negator-POS bigram are included as well. Evidently, in the restaurant reviews, sentiment is expressed using more consistent syntactical patterns. This points to a difference in language use for reviews about laptops compared to reviews about restaurants. Exactly what these differences entail and why this phenomenon occurs is an interesting avenue for future research.

Another option for future work is to include even more feature types, as there are types of features that, as of yet, were not included in our experiments. Examples of these include additional lexicons and features based on grammatical relations. In conclusion, lexico-semantic patterns prove to be powerful predictors for sentiment analysis, as shown by the 69.0 % and 73.1 % F_1-score for restaurant and laptop reviews, respectively, but more research is needed to provide definitive answers.

Acknowledgments. The authors are partially supported by the Dutch national program COMMIT.

References

1. Baccianella, S., Esuli, A., Sebastiani, F.: SentiWordNet 3.0: an enhanced lexical resource for sentiment analysis and opinion mining. In: Proceedings of the Seventh International Conference on Language Resources and Evaluation (LREC 2010), vol. 10, pp. 2200–2204 (2010)

2. Brychcín, T., Konkol, M., Steinberger, J.: UWB: machine learning approach to aspect-based sentiment analysis. In: Proceedings of the 8th International Workshop on Semantic Evaluation (SemEval 2014), pp. 817–822. Association for Computational Linguistics and Dublin City University (2014)
3. Hatzivassiloglou, V., McKeown, K.R.: Predicting the semantic orientation of adjectives. In: Proceedings of the 35th Annual Meeting of the Association for Computational Linguistics and 8th Conference of the European Chapter of the Association for Computational Linguistics (ACL 1997), pp. 174–181. Morgan Kaufman Publishers and Association for Computational Linguistics (1997)
4. Kiritchenko, S., Zhu, X., Cherry, C., Mohammad, S.: NRC-Canada-2014: detecting aspects and sentiment in customer reviews. In: Proceedings of the 8th International Workshop on Semantic Evaluation (SemEval 2014), pp. 437–442. Association for Computational Linguistics and Dublin City University (2014)
5. Koto, F., Adriani, M.: The use of POS sequence for analyzing sentence pattern in Twitter sentiment analysis. In: Proceedings of the 29th IEEE International Conference on Advanced Information Networking and Applications Workshops (WAINA 2015), pp. 547–551. IEEE (2015)
6. Pontiki, M., Galanis, D., Papageorgiou, H., Manandhar, S., Androutsopoulos, I.: SemEval-2015 Task 12: aspect based sentiment analysis. In: Proceedings of the 9th International Workshop on Semantic Evaluation (SemEval 2015), pp. 486–495. Association for Computational Linguistics (2015)
7. Schouten, K., Frasincar, F.: The benefit of concept-based features for sentiment analysis. In: Gandon, F., Cabrio, E., Stankovic, M., Zimmermann, A. (eds.) ESWC 2015. CCIS, vol. 548, pp. 223–233. Springer, Heidelberg (2015)

Multilevel Browsing of Folksonomy-Based Digital Collections

Joaquín Gayoso-Cabada, Daniel Rodríguez-Cerezo,
and José-Luis Sierra(⊠)

Fac. Informática, Universidad Complutense de Madrid,
C/Prof. José García Santesmases 9, 28040 Madrid, Spain
{jgayoso,drcerezo,jlsierra}@fdi.ucm.es

Abstract. This paper describes how to extend the usual one-level tag selection navigation paradigm in folksonomy-based digital collections to a *multilevel browsing* one, according to which it is possible to incrementally narrow down the set of selected objects in a collection by sequentially adding more and more filtering tags. For this purpose, we present a browsing strategy based on finite automata. As well, we provide some experimental results concerning the application of the approach in *Clavy*, a system for managing digital collections with reconfigurable structures in digital humanities and educational settings.

Keywords: Multilevel browsing · Folksonomy · Indexing · Navigation automata

1 Introduction

Folksonomies are cataloguing schemes defined and applied collaboratively by communities of users. In this way, users not only apply folksonomies to organize digital resources, but also actively contribute to their creation and maintenance [12]. In this context, accommodating any but the simplest interaction models can become a substantial technical challenge.

An example of a particularly difficult-to-achieve interaction model is general, unconstrained, *multi-level browsing* [5]. In this setting, users sequentially select tags, and, in each stage, the set of objects tagged by all the selected tags is filtered. Even for collections of moderate size, computing these sets of objects can in some cases be too costly to be achieved within acceptable response times. By establishing predefined orders in which tags can be selected and by using these orders to create and maintain navigation trees, response times can be dramatically enhanced, but this rigid and aprioristic organization is contrary to the dynamic and agile nature of folksonomies, where tag sets are continuously changing. In this paper we address this interaction style in its most unconstrained and general form.

The rest of the paper is organized as follows. Section 2 introduces the basis of folksonomy-like organizations of digital collections. Section 3 introduces the multilevel browsing paradigm for this kind of collections and describes how to enable such a browsing style efficiently. Section 4 presents some related work. Finally, Sect. 5 outlines the final conclusions and some lines of future work.

© Springer International Publishing AG 2016
W. Cellary et al. (Eds.): WISE 2016, Part II, LNCS 10042, pp. 43–51, 2016.
DOI: 10.1007/978-3-319-48743-4_4

2 Folksonomy-Based Digital Collections

Collections organized with folksonomies typically comprise the following parts (see Fig. 1 for an example):

- On one hand, there are the *resources* in the collection. For instance, the small collection depicted in Fig. 1 includes six image archives as resources, corresponding to photographs of artistic objects from the Prehistoric and Protohistoric artistic periods in Spain (Fig. 1 actually shows thumbnails of these images).
- On the other hand, there is the *annotation* of the resources. This annotation consists of associating descriptive *tags* with resources. These tags are useful when cataloguing resources and, therefore, they enable future uses of the collection (navigation, search, etc.). For instance, in Fig. 1, resource number 1 has the tags *Cave-Painting*, *Cantabrian* and *Prehistoric* associated.
- Finally, there is a *tag cloud* that groups all the tags that can be used to annotate the resources. Thus, the tag cloud shown in Fig. 1 groups all the tags that annotate resources in the collection. As usual, the size of tags in this cloud represents the presence (number of tagged resources) of the tag in the collection.

Consequently, the internal organization of this kind of collection is very similar in appearance to classic keyword-based systems [15]. However, what distinguishes these collections from classic keyword-based systems is the social and inductive nature in the creation of the cataloguing schemata (i.e., the tag clouds). Indeed, folksonomy-based systems actively involve user communities that add, modify, delete and tag resources, using existing tags or creating new ones as needed. In this way, tag clouds are not explicitly defined nor explicitly maintained, but emerge from the collaborative behavior of communities of practice [12]. While this somewhat uncontrolled and anarchic approach to tagging digital resources can additionally bring up some relevant concerns and critiques from a cataloguing point of view (e.g., existence of synonymous, irrelevant or very generic tags, etc.) [14], the fact is that these systems are extensively used in many scenarios (and especially in computer-mediated social ones) [3]. Therefore, in this paper we will not focus on the critiques and potential shortcomings of the approach, but on efficient ways of enabling sophisticated interaction strategies (multi-level browsing, in particular).

Folksonomy-like systems support a simple one-level browsing strategy in a straightforward way. According to this strategy, it is possible to select one tag in the tag cloud and recover all the resources tagged with said tag. Figure 2(a) illustrates this approach with the small collection from Fig. 1.

One-level browsing can be accomplished efficiently in a straightforward way by using and maintaining an *inverted index* [19], i.e., a data structure that provides a reference to the set of resources tagged by each tag and therefore directly links to the results for each selection. This simple and efficient implementation explains why most folksonomy-based systems include this interaction style as a primary browsing strategy. However, this style prevents more sophisticated exploratory behaviors involving two or more tags simultaneously. In the rest of the paper we will examine how to deal with more than one browsing level.

Tag cloud	Tartesian Megalithic Plateau **Levant** **Prehistoric** Punic **Protohistoric** Cave-Painting **Cantabrian** Phoenician Penibaetic

Annotation				
	Resource 1	Cave-Painting, Cantabrian, Prehistoric	**Resource 4**	Tartesian, Plateau, Protohistoric
	Resource 2	Cave-Painting, Levant, Prehistoric	**Resource 5**	Phoenician, Penibaetic, Protohistoric
	Resource 3	Megalithic, Cantabrian, Prehistoric	**Resource 6**	Punic, Levant, Protohistoric

Resources				
	Resource 1	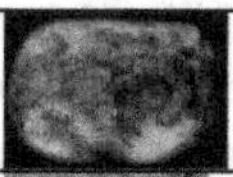	**Resource 4**	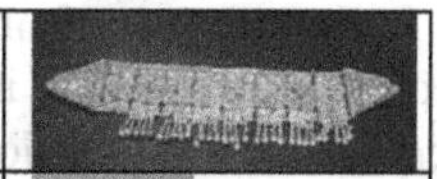
	Resource 2		**Resource 5**	
	Resource 3		**Resource 6**	

Fig. 1. A small digital collection

3   Multilevel Browsing in Folksonomy-Based Systems

This section addresses the multi-level browsing style in folksonomy-based systems. Subsect. 3.1 introduces the basic interaction behavior. Subsect. 3.2 characterizes this behavior as a finite state machine. Finally, Subsect. 3.3 gives some experimental results.

3.1   The Browsing Model

Conceptually, the extension from one-level to multi-level browsing in folksonomy-like systems is simple. Basically, when a tag is selected, not only is the set of resources narrowed down but also the tag cloud: the resulting tag cloud will be the one *induced* by the set of filtered resources **R**. Such a tag will contain all the tags annotating some resource in **R** with the exception of those tags annotating *all* the resources in **R** (since, in this case, the selection would not refine the set of resources). This makes it possible

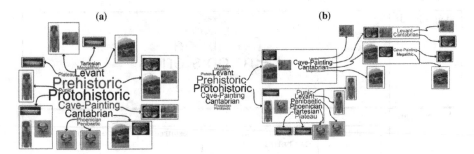

Fig. 2. Examples of (a) one-level browsing; (b) multi-level browsing

to carry out new selections successively on the narrowed tag clouds until a state containing an empty tag cloud is reached. The expected behavior is partially illustrated in Fig. 2(b), which shows the set of resources and the associated tag clouds after some browsing actions on the collection in Fig. 1.

As in the case of one-level browsing, multi-level browsing behavior can also be accomplished by using inverted indexes. However, now an evaluation of a conjunctive query in each interaction state is needed in order to determine the resources to be filtered. Although extensive research has been carried out on how to speed up these operations [2], in some cases the time inverted can negatively impact the user's interactive experience.

3.2   Navigation Automata

In order to accelerate multi-level browsing, it is necessary to have a suitable index structure. Ideally this structure should link to the set of resources selected by each meaningful set of tags $t_1, ..., t_n$, in the same way, an inverted index directly provides the set of resources selected by a tag in the one-level approach. A way of providing such a structure is by using a finite state machine characterizing all the possible interactions and interaction states. This state machine will be called a *navigation automaton*. This automaton will consist of *states* labelled by sets of resources, and *transitions* labelled by tags (as an example, Fig. 3a shows the navigation automaton for the collection of Fig. 1). More precisely:

- There will be an initial state labelled by all the resources in the collection.
- Given a state **S** labelled by a set of resources **R**, for each tag **t** in the tag cloud induced by **R** there will be a state **S'** labelled by all the resources in **R** annotated by **t**, as well as a transition from **S** to **S'** labelled by **t**.

Since the navigation automaton contains all the possible ways of multi-level navigation, it can support multi-level browsing in a straightforward way. Unfortunately, in some cases the number of states in this automaton can grow very quickly (in the worst case, exponentially with respect to the number of resources). The most extreme case, in which the number of states is 2^n-1 (with n the number of resources), arises, for instance, by distinguishing each pair of resource annotations in a single tag. In order to

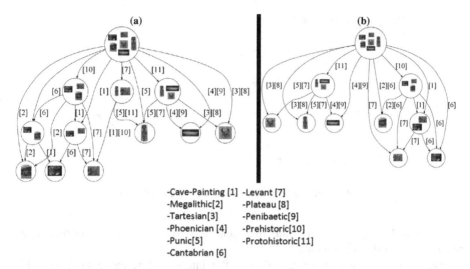

-Cave-Painting [1] -Levant [7]
-Megalithic[2]   -Plateau [8]
-Tartesian[3]   -Penibaetic[9]
-Phoenician [4]   -Prehistoric[10]
-Punic[5]   -Protohistoric[11]
-Cantabrian [6]

Fig. 3. (a) Navigation automaton for the collection in Fig. 1; (b) A non-deterministic version of the automaton in (a)

avoid this potential exponential factor in the explicit construction of navigation automata, it is possible to maintain non-deterministic versions of these automata, in such a way that only states representing disjoint partitions of their parent states are maintained. Figure 3b shows a feasible non-deterministic automaton equivalent to the one shown in Fig. 3a (it is worthwhile to point out that this solution may not be unique).

3.3   Experimental Evaluation

In order to evaluate our multilevel browsing approach, we have implemented it in *Clavy*, an experimental system for managing digital collections that lets users define organization schemata in a collaborative way.[1] In order to provide some structure to facilitate navigation, *Clavy* makes it possible to group tags in categories that are organized hierarchically. Nevertheless, this hierarchy is not pre-established, but can be edited by *Clavy* users at any time (see Fig. 4). Therefore, backstage, multi-level browsing support in *Clavy* must resort to the basic model described in Sect. 3, since the hierarchy is also subjected to continuous change and evolution. In addition to the automata-based browsing framework described in this paper, we have also implemented an inverted index-based solution in *Clavy*, using Lucene [13], a robust and highly optimized framework for implementing information retrieval applications.

In this context, we set up an experiment consisting of adding the resources in *Chasqui* [17],[2] a digital collection of 6283 digital resources on Pre-Columbian

---

[1] http://clavy.fdi.ucm.es/Clavy/.

[2] http://oda-fec.org/ucm-chasqui.

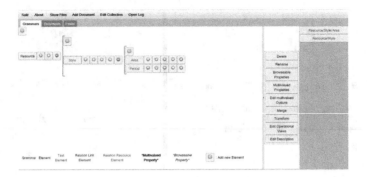

Fig. 4. Editing a hierarchy of tag categories with *Clavy*.

American archeology, to *Clavy* and simulating runs concerning hierarchy reconfiguration and browsing operations.

Each run was customized as follows. We interleaved resource insertion with hierarchy reconfiguration/browsing rounds. Each insertion round consisted of 100 resource insertions (with the exception of the last one, in which all the remaining resources where inserted). In turn, each browsing/reconfiguration round consisted of executing $0.1n$ browsing operations randomly interleaved with $0.01n$ reconfigurations (n being the number of resources inserted so far). Each browsing operation in turn consisted of selecting a feasible tag and computing the next set of active objects, or of establishing the initial state as the active one in case of unavailability of feasible tags; once the next interaction state was determined, all the filtered resources were visited. In both the cases of inverted indexes and automata, in-memory indexes were used in order to avoid the side effects of persistence that might disturb the experiment.

Figure 5 shows the results obtained from the two runs. The experiment was run on a PC with Windows 10, with a 3.4 GHz Intel microprocessor, and with 8 Gb of DDR3 RAM. The horizontal axis corresponds to the number of operations carried out so far. The vertical axis corresponds to cumulative time (in seconds). As is made apparent, the automata-based approach clearly outperforms inverted indexes (regardless of the fact that we are using a highly optimized framework, like Lucene, for inverted indexing vs. our own in-house experimental implementation for navigation automata).

4   Related Work

There are several systems that, like our proposal, implement several sorts of multi-level browsing onto folksonomy-based systems. Systems like the one described in [7, 9] are supported by inverted index approaches. Other systems, like that described in [11], are supported by extensible data adapters that interface between synchronized tag clouds and underlying database management systems. Instead of relying on inverted indexes and/or conventional database layers, our approach starts by characterizing the intrinsic behavior of multi-level browsing onto a folksonomy-like system in terms of navigation

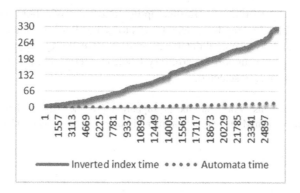

Fig. 5. Cumulative time of inverted indexes vs. automata

automata, and then tries to approximate this model with a non-deterministic version that provides reasonable time and space tradeoffs. In [4] we propose a representation of these non-deterministic automata inspired by *dendrograms* such as those used in hierarchical clustering settings [8].

Our navigation automata model is actually similar to lattice-based proposals to browse information spaces, as described in the seminal work of [5]. This organization is actually the main subject of the fertile theory of *formal concept analysis* [16]. Similarly, there are several proposals on using lattices as the underlying indexing structures for enabling multi-level browsing [6, 18]. However, all these approaches are limited by the intrinsic complexity of formal concept analysis [10]. This is why we have proposed a simpler but still practical approximation based on non-deterministic versions of navigation automata.

5   Conclusions and Future Work

Folksonomy-based digital collections are living entities in which not only digital resources, but also organization schemata, are subject to continuous change and evolution. This changing and evolving nature makes the accomplishment of sophisticated interaction paradigms particularly challenging. In this paper we have addressed the efficient inclusion of multilevel browsing strategies in these settings, in which sets of selected resources can be successively refined through the selection of sequences of tags. For this purpose we have modeled this behavior as a finite state machine, the *navigation automaton*, taking into account all the possible ways of navigating the collection by using tags. Unfortunately, we have also showed how, in some cases, the number of states in this automaton can increase exponentially with respect to the collection's size. In order to address this potential exponential factor we have proposed using non-deterministic versions of these automata. Some experiments with a real collection gave us evidence on how the automata-based technique can outperform more conventional and widely used ones, like those based on inverted indexes.

We are currently working on further optimizing our navigation automata representation. We are also looking for efficient ways to make all this information persistent, either by using standard relational databases or alternative NoSQL approaches. Finally, we also hope to include support for arbitrary Boolean queries and for alternative ways of exploring the resources selected.

Acknowledgements. This work has been supported by the BBVA Foundation (grant HUM14_251) and Spanish Ministry of Economy and Competitiveness (grant TIN2014-52010-R)

References

1. Chodorow, K.: MongoDB: The Definitive Guide. O'Reilly, Sebastopol (2013)
2. Culpepper, J-S., Moffat, A.: Efficient set intersection for inverted indexing. ACM Trans. Inf. Syst. **29**(1) (2010)
3. du Preez, M.: Taxonomies, folksonomies, ontologies: what are they and how do they support information retrieval? Indexer **33**(1), 29–37 (2015)
4. Gayoso-Cabada, J., Rodríguez-Cerezo, D., Sierra, J-L.: Browsing digital collections with reconfigurable faceted thesauri. In: 25th International Conference on Information Systems Development (ISD), Katowize, Poland (2016)
5. Godin, R., Saunders, G.: Lattice model of browsable data space. Inf. Sci. **40**(2), 89–116 (1986)
6. Greene, G-J.: A generic framework for concept-based exploration of semi-structured software engineering data. In: Proceedings of the 30th IEEE/ACM International Conference on Automated Software Engineering, pp. 894–897 (2015)
7. Hernandez, M-E., Falconer, S-M., Storey, M-A., Carini, S., Sim, I.: Synchronized tag clouds for exploring semi-structured clinical trial data. In: Proceedings of the 2008 Conference of the Center for Advanced Studies on Collaborative Research: Meeting of Minds (CASCON), article 4 (2008)
8. Jain, A.-K., Murty, M.-N., Flynn, P.-J.: Data clustering: a review. ACM Comput. Surv. **31**(3), 264–323 (1999)
9. Koutrika, G., Zadeh, Z-M., Garcia-Molina, H.: CourseCloud: summarizing and refining keyword searches over structured data. In: Proceedings of the 12th International Conference on Extending Database Technology (EDBT), pp. 1132–1135 (2009)
10. Kuznetsov, S.: On computing the size of a lattice and related decision problems. Order **18**(4), 313–321 (2001)
11. Leone, S., Geel, M., Müller, C., Norrie, M.C.: Exploiting tag clouds for database browsing and querying. In: Proper, E., Soffer, P. (eds.) CAiSE Forum 2010. LNBIP, vol. 72, pp. 15–28. Springer, Heidelberg (2011)
12. Mathes, A.: Folksonomies – cooperative classification and communication through shared metadata. Comput. Mediat. Commun. – LIS590CMC **47**(10), 1–13 (2004)
13. McCandless, M., Hatcher, E., Gospodnetic, O.: Lucene in Action, 2nd edn. Manning Publications, Greenwich (2010)
14. Peterson, E.: Beneath the metadata: some philosophical problems with folksonomy. D-Lib Mag. **12**(11) (2006)
15. Salton, G., McGill, M.J.: Introduction to Modern Information Retrieval. McGraw-Hill, Maidenherd (1986)

16. Sarmah, A.-K., Hazarika, S.-M., Sinha, S.-K.: Formal concept analysis: current trends and directions. Artif. Intell. Rev. **44**(1), 47–86 (2015)
17. Sierra, J.-L., Fernández-Valmayor, A., Guinea, M., Hernanz, H.: From research resources to learning objects: process model and virtualization experiences. Educ. Technol. Soc. **9**(3), 56–68 (2006)
18. Way, T., Eklund, P.: Social tagging for digital libraries using formal concept analysis. In: Proceedings of the 17th International Conference on Concept Lattices and their Applications (CLA) (2010)
19. Zobel, J., Moffat, A.: Inverted files for text search engines. ACM Comput. Surv. **33**(2) (2006). Article 6

Ranking in Social Networks

Faderank: An Incremental Algorithm for Ranking Twitter Users

Massimo Bartoletti[1]([✉]), Stefano Lande[1], and Alessandro Massa[1,2]

[1] Università degli Studi di Cagliari, Cagliari, Italy
bart@unica.it
[2] Xorovo.com, Cagliari, Italy

Abstract. User reputation is a crucial indicator in social networks, where it is exploited to promote authoritative content and to marginalize spammers. To be accurate, reputation must be updated periodically, taking into account the whole historical data of user activity. In big social networks like Twitter and Facebook, these updates would require to process a huge amount of historical data, and therefore pose serious performance issues. We address these issues in the context of Twitter, by studying a technique which can update user reputation in constant time. This is obtained by using an arbitrary ranking algorithm to compute user reputation in the most recent time window, and by combining it with a summary of historical data. Experimental evaluation on large datasets show that our technique improves the performance of existing ranking algorithms, at the cost of a negligible degradation of their precision.

Keywords: Reputation · Social networks · Performance

1 Introduction

The global growth of electronic communication facilities like peer-to-peer and social networks brought out two major problems: how to filter out low quality information, and how to enforce safe interactions. In many contexts, these issues are not completely disjoint: e.g., interacting safely in peer-to-peer networks may correspond to only download trusted contents or files. A possible way to address these issues is to associate each object (peer, user or resource) with an index, usually called *reputation*, which reflects the opinion the network has towards such object. The underlying assumption is that, by analysing the past interaction history of an object, one can predict the quality of its future interactions [10, 22].

In the specific context of social networks, like e.g. Twitter and Facebook, reputation has several applications: for instance, it has been exploited to rank users [1,21], to marginalize spammers [26] and dishonest services [5], to distributed moderation among users [13,14], to maximize information spread in viral marketing strategies [11], and to refine search results [18].

Designing effective reputation systems for social networks is not an easy task, for two main reasons. First, they have to deal with the impressive amount of data generated by social networks: for instance, Twitter counts ∼10 M daily active

© Springer International Publishing AG 2016
W. Cellary et al. (Eds.): WISE 2016, Part II, LNCS 10042, pp. 55–69, 2016.
DOI: 10.1007/978-3-319-48743-4_5

users and ∼500 M tweets per day [2], while Facebook counts ∼900 M daily active users, ∼44 M comments and ∼4.5 B likes per day [3]. Second, reputation system must protect themselves from misbehaving users who try to undermine the ranking mechanism in order to obtain unwarranted service or to prevent honest participants from obtaining legitimate service [8]. Although some defence techniques against these attacks have been proposed over the years [6,17,23,29,30], currently there is no reputation system which is (either provably or empirically) resilient to all kinds of attacks.

To make the situation even more complex, the problem of efficiency and that of security are strictly related. On the one hand, if a system tries to improve efficiency by reducing the frequency of reputation updates, an adversary could easily build a positive reputation in a first period of time, and then exploit it to carry on attacks in the time window where reputation is not updated. On the other hand, frequently recomputing reputation gives rise to a performance problem: ideally, for each update we have to process all the historical data, besides the new data. A possible approach to mitigate this issue is to truncate data older than a certain time: for instance, Klout—a popular reputation aggregator—only considers the last 90 days of user interaction [21]. However, this mechanism can be subject to *whitewashing attacks* where an adversary abuses the system for a while, and then simply waits some time before rebuilding a fresh reputation.

Contributions. In this paper we propose and evaluate a technique to reduce the overhead of keeping updated the reputation of Twitter users. Instead of naïvely truncating historical data, our technique aggregates it in constant time and space, by adapting the *fading memories* technique of [23]. The actual reputation of a user is computed by taking into account its recent (raw) behaviour, its behaviour in the aggregated history, and the gradient of behaviour change. In this way, we reach two goals. First, since the amount of data to be processed at each update is (on average) constant, the average execution time of an update is constant as well. Second, since the past interaction history is taken into account (although in aggregated form), we mitigate *whitewashing attacks* like the ones outlined above. A further feature of our technique is that it is parametric with respect to the reputation algorithm used to process raw data. Overall, one can choose the algorithm which offers the required defences on raw reputation, and calibrate the weights of the raw/aggregated/gradient components to obtain similar properties on the optimized algorithm.

We validate our technique, called *Faderank*, using two raw reputation algorithms: TURank [28], and a variant of PageRank [20] suited to rank Twitter users. In our experiments we use three real datasets, obtained by crawling Twitter for several weeks. Our datasets contain tweets, retweets, and follow relations of ∼10 K users, spanning over a period of eleven months. Assuming a monthly reputation update, we compare the completion time of FadeRank, TURank and PageRank, showing that Faderank is a constant-time algorithm, while the computation time of the raw algorithms grows linearly on the size of the input. To evaluate the precision of Faderank we use the *Kendall τ rank distance* [12]. More precisely, for each dataset, for each iteration, and for each raw algorithm (TURank and PageRank), we measure two distances: the distance between the ranking obtained by Faderank and the raw algorithm, and the distance between the latter and its *forgetful* version, where the history is truncated every month. Our experiments show that, in all datasets, there is a little degradation of the precision of Faderank w.r.t. the raw algorithms, but Faderank is still more precise than their forgetful versions. Further, we show that, compared with the forgetful algorithms, Faderank is more resilient to whitewashing attacks.

The sources of our FadeRank tool, as well as the experimental data used for its validation, are available online at tcs.unica.it/software/faderank.

2   Related Work

In this section we briefly survey the literature on reputation systems, with special emphasis on those used for ranking users of social networks.

Pagerank. Many reputation systems are based on PageRank [20], an algorithm originally introduced by Google to rank web pages. PageRank models the web as a directed graph (V, E), where V is the set of web pages, and E is the set of hyperlinks (i.e., references) from a page to another. The reputation of a web page is proportional to the reputation of the web pages that reference it. Being based on a single object-object relation, the PageRank model does not precisely capture the rich topology of social networks. In Twitter, for instance, users can follow other users, and send "tweets" which can be "retwitted" by other users. Designing a reputation system which flattens this structure to a single user-user relation may affect the precision of the results; hence, subsequent works have refined the PageRank model to take into account more complex structures.

ObjectRank. ObjectRank [4] generalises the PageRank model by considering different kinds of edges and nodes. Each node gives a part of its reputation to the nodes linked to it. The exact amount of this reputation is determined by (i) the weight on the edge which links the two nodes, and (ii) the reputation of the source node. To account for the fact that different kind of relations may affect the reputation in different ways, ObjectRank allows to associate a different weight to each kind of edge.

To apply ObjectRank to a new domain, one has to instantiate an *authority transfer schema graph* (V_S, E_S, w_S), where V_S is the set of *node kinds*, E_S is the set of *edge kinds*, and $w_S : E_S \to \mathbb{R}$ associates weights to edge kinds. From this schema graph and the dataset, ObjectRank constructs an *authority transfer graph* (V, E, w, k), which is used to compute the reputation. The component V is the set of nodes (the actual objects in the dataset), while E is the set of edges (associated to an edge kind by $k : E \to E_S$). The component $w : E \to \mathbb{R}$ associates a weight to each edge as follows:

$$w(e) = \frac{w_S(k(e))}{OutDeg_{k(e)}(u)} \tag{1}$$

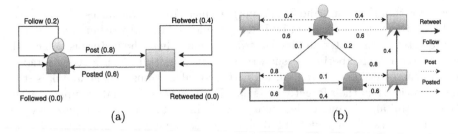

Fig. 1. In 1a, the user-tweet schema graph; in 1b, a user-tweet graph.

where $OutDeg_{e_S}(u) = \#\{e \in E \mid fst(e) = u \text{ and } k(e) = e_S\}$ is the number of edges of type e_S originating from the node u.

Similarly to PageRank, the reputation is a vector $\boldsymbol{r} \in \mathbb{R}^{|V|}$, defined as the fixed point of the following equation:

$$\boldsymbol{r} = d \, \boldsymbol{A} \, \boldsymbol{r} + \frac{(1-d)}{|V|}[1,\ldots,1]^T \tag{2}$$

where d is a real constant (called *damping factor*), and $\boldsymbol{A} = (a_{uv})$ is the *transition matrix* where each element a_{uv} is given by

$$a_{uv} = \begin{cases} w((u,v)) & \text{if } (u,v) \in E \\ 0 & \text{otherwise} \end{cases} \tag{3}$$

ObjectRank computes $\boldsymbol{r}$ through an iterative algorithm, which converges whenever the transition matrix $\boldsymbol{A}$ is irreducible and aperiodic [19]. The first condition is guaranteed by a suitable choice of the damping factor d, while the second one happens to be true for real-world datasets.

TURank. The reputation system proposed in [28], called TURank, instantiates the authority transfer schema graph of ObjectRank into a *user-tweet schema graph* $UTG_S = (V_S, E_S)$, displayed in Fig. 1a. The set of nodes V_S comprises just two elements (*user* and *tweet*). The set of edges E_S renders the fact that Twitter users can: (i) dispatch *tweets*, (ii) *follow* users (i.e., when a user A follows B, she will receive all tweets posted by B), and (iii) *retweet* the messages they receive (i.e., if B retweets a message of A, this message will be received by all the followers of B). The weights associated to edges reflect the following assumptions: (i) authoritative users tend to follow other authoritative users; (ii) tweets retweeted by many authoritative users are likely to be interesting; (iii) users who post many interesting tweets are likely to be authoritative.

The authority transfer graph instantiated from the schema and the dataset is called *user-tweet graph*, a minimalistic example of which is displayed in Fig. 1b. TURank analyses this graph, using Eq. (2) to compute the reputation of Twitter users. Note that, as anticipated in Sect. 1, to update the reputation one must considering both historical data and new data to reconstruct the user-tweet graph and analyse it. We discuss in Sect. 3 how our proposal reduces the computational overhead of this operation.

Other Adapations of Pagerank. Several other papers propose reputation systems for social networks by taking inspiration from PageRank and ObjectRank. Weng *et al.* [27] propose an algorithm also takes into account the topic similarity between the users (i.e., two users are similar to the extent they tweet on similar topics). More precisely, the algorithm in [27] can associate to each user many reputation values, i.e. one for each topic. To this aim, the PageRank model is modified in [27] so to have a different transition probability between each node (i.e. the values of the transition matrix), depending on the topic similarity between them. Haveliwala [7] propose a similar algorithm to improve PageRank using topics, but they use a different "teleportation" vector (the $[1, \ldots, 1]^T$ vector in Eq. (2)) for each topic, instead of changing the transition matrix.

Time-Sensitive Algorithms. Mariani *et al.* [16] investigate the problem of how temporal aspects affect reputation systems based on PageRank, reaching the conclusion that not considering these aspects undermines their accuracy. Hu *et al.* [9] address this issue in the field of social networks, by adapting PageRank to take into account three time factors: the age of an edge, the frequency with which edges are created, and the topic similarity of the nodes linked by new edges in a certain amount of time, under the assumption that trustworthy users focus their activity in a certain topic for a period of time.

Algorithms Based on Other Techniques. Many works propose reputation systems for social networks which do *not* employ the link-structure analysis with the PageRank model, and exploit instead machine learning techniques. Uysal and Croft [24] compute a reputation for the incoming tweets of a user. The reputation of a tweet is proportional to the probability that the recipient will retweet it, and it is computed using a decision tree. To do that, they propose several features, like e.g. the number of followers of the author, the number of retweets, and the contents of the tweet itself. Wang [26] proposes a similar approach, using a Bayesian classifier to detect spam tweets. Differently from [24], the algorithm in [26] uses features obtained from a graph similar to the user-tweet graph of TURank. Vosecky *et al.* [25] propose a filter model that uses a SVM classifier to discard low quality tweets, and a rank model that uses Rank SVM to order tweet by reputation. They use two sets of features: content-based (like e.g. punctuation, spelling, grammatical indicators), and link-based, that utilizes the implicit relations between tweets, hyper-links, and users. Ma *et al.* [15] associates a reputation to tweets, rather than users. The reputation of a tweet is a measure of its popularity, and it is computed using a *sigmoid function*, taking into account the number of retweets, the number of possible views (i.e., number of user that can see the tweet because they follow the author or other users that retweeted it), and a model of the temporal dynamics of a tweet.

3   FadeRank

In this section we illustrate our technique, which is obtained by suitably combining three basic ingredients:

- an *arbitrary ranking algorithm*, used to compute the *raw reputation* from the data collected in a time interval;
- the *dependable trust model*, used to compute the *aggregated reputation* from the raw reputation and the historical data;
- the *fading memories* technique, used to aggregate the historical data in constant time and space.

Overall, we call FadeRank the combination of these three ingredients. Before introducing in Sect. 3.3 our algorithm, we present in Sects. 3.1 and 3.2 the dependable trust model and the fading memories technique.

3.1   Dependable Trust Model

We exploit the dependable trust model of [23] to compute the *aggregated reputation* of users, taking as input the raw reputation obtained by an arbitrary ranking algorithm. The aggregated reputation of a given user at time interval $i \geq 0$, denoted by $AR[i]$, is the weighted sum of three components:

$$AR[i] \;=\; \alpha \cdot R[i] \;+\; \beta \cdot H[i] \;+\; \gamma(i) \cdot D[i] \qquad (4)$$

where:

- $R[i]$ is the raw reputation of the user at time interval i;
- $H[i]$, defined by Eq. (5) below, aggregates in a single value the *history* of the user reputation over the time intervals $0, \ldots, i - 1$;
- $D[i]$, defined by Eq. (6) below, represents the change of reputation of the user in the last time interval.

More precisely, the value $H[i]$ is computed as follows:

$$H[i] \;=\; \sum_{k=1}^{n} R[i-k] \cdot \frac{w_k}{\sum_{j=1}^{n} w_j} \qquad \text{where } n = \begin{cases} maxH & \text{if } i \geqslant maxH \\ i & \text{otherwise} \end{cases} \qquad (5)$$

and where $maxH$ is the number of past raw reputation values stored by the system, and w_k is a weight. Some possible choices for w_k (taken from [23]) and their effects are displayed in Fig. 2.

The value $D[i]$ is computed as the difference between the aggregated history and the current raw reputation as follows:

$$D[i] = R[i] - H[i] \qquad (6)$$

The weights α, β, and γ in Eq. (4) can be tuned to change the response of the reputation system to attacks. A larger value of α gives more weight to the

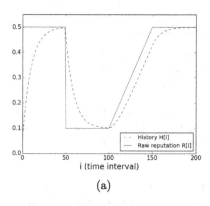

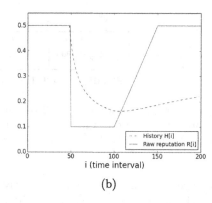

Fig. 2. The figures show a simulation of a whitewashing attack. We compare the trend of the history values $H[i]$ (solid lines) to the raw reputation values $R[i]$ (dashed lines), i.e. the behaviour of the attacker, for two different choices of w_k. Figure 2a shows an *optimistic* choice, i.e. $w_k = \rho^{k-1}$ (with $\rho < 1$), for which Eq. (5) becomes an exponentially weighted sum. Instead, Fig. 2b shows a *pessimistic* choice, i.e. $w_k = \frac{1}{R[i-k]}$, which yields a harmonic mean.

recent behaviour, while a larger value of β gives more weight to the past history (to address e.g., whitewashing attacks [10]).

The weight $\gamma(i)$ at time interval i is given by:

$$\gamma(i) = \begin{cases} \gamma_1 & \text{if } D[i] \geqslant 0 \\ \gamma_2 & \text{otherwise} \end{cases} \tag{7}$$

where γ_1 and γ_2 are two constants. A possible choice of these constants, as suggested by [23], could be $\gamma_1 < \beta < \gamma_2$. In the first case ($D[i] \geq 0$) we reward by a factor γ_1 an amelioration of the user behaviour, while in the second one ($D[i] < 0$) we penalise by a factor γ_2 its deterioration.

3.2   Fading Memories

When computing the history value $H[i]$ in Eq. (5), we assume that the system stores the raw reputation values for a user for the past $maxH$ intervals. If, to account for the distant past, we were storing a large number $maxH$ of values, we would cause a large memory footprint, as well as an increase of the time needed to compute $H[i]$ upon each update. On the other hand, a small value of $maxH$ would make the malicious behaviour of a user forgotten after $maxH$ intervals, so paving the way to whitewashing attacks.

To cope with this issue, we exploit the *fading memories* technique of [23], which allows to compute a bounded digest of the *whole* past history, and so to compute the value $H[i]$ in constant time and space. To do that, we store only the most recent raw reputation values exactly, while we aggregate (*fade*) the older values, with an accuracy that decreases proportionally to their age.

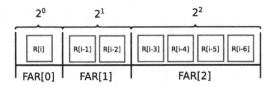

Fig. 3. Fading memories with $b = 2$ and $m = 3$, which aggregate $b^m - 1 = 7$ past raw reputation values into m values. The faded values $FAR[i]$ (for $i \in 0 \ldots 2$) are obtained by aggregating $b^0 = 1$, $b^1 = 2$, and $b^2 = 4$ past raw reputation values.

More precisely, fixed two strictly positive integer constants b and m, the fading memories aggregate into m values the past reputation values: the i-th value is the digest of b^i reputation values. The 0-th fading memory is a digest of the b^0 most recent reputation value (i.e., just $R[i]$), the 1-th is a digest of b^1 values (i.e., $R[i-1], \ldots, R[i-b]$), and so on. Since $\sum_{i=0}^{m-1} b^i = b^m - 1$, the m fading memories actually represent a digest of the last $b^m - 1$ reputation values. Figure 3 shows an example of fading memories with $b = 2$ and $m = 3$. The memories for the recent past aggregates a smaller number of raw reputations than the one for the old past, thus making the former more precise.

To update the fading memories at the stroke of a new time interval we use Eq. (8) below, where we denote with $FAR^t[i]$ (for $0 \le i \le m - 1$) the i-th faded past reputation value at interval t of a given user:

$$FAR^{t+1}[i] \;=\; \frac{FAR^t[i] \cdot (b^i - 1) \;+\; FAR^t[i - 1]}{b^i} \tag{8}$$

3.3   The FadeRank Algorithm

Our FadeRank algorithm is illustrated in Algorithm 1. The main routine is FADERANK (lines 1–7), which takes as input *newData*, the user-tweet graph corresponding to the interactions in the most recent time interval. This graph is then passed to a ranking algorithm (line 2), which computes the raw reputations on *newData* (i.e., the ranking algorithm considers *newData* as the whole history of interactions). The call to COMPUTEREPUTATION (line 4) updates the reputation of a user, exploiting the dependable trust model described in Sect. 3.1.

The function COMPUTEREPUTATION takes as input the current fading memories vector *far*, and the *score* for the interval computed before. At line 9 we aggregate the *far* values into a single value to compute *history*, according to Eq. (5). The *score* and *history* values are then used to compute the change of reputation *diff* (line 10) according to Eq. (6). At line 11 we compute the weight γ as in Eq. (7), and then at line 12 we compute the new reputation of the user, exploiting Eq. (4). The last step is the update of *far* (line 5), performed by the function UPDATEFAR, that employs Eq. (8) (line 16).

Algorithm 1. FadeRank

1: **procedure** FADERANK($newData$)
2:     $rawScores \leftarrow$ REPUTATIONALGORITHM($newData$)
3:     **for** $i{=}1$ to $|users|$ **do**
4:         $users_i.score \leftarrow$ COMPUTEREPUTATION($users_i.far, rawScores_i$)
5:         $users_i.far \leftarrow$ UPDATEFAR($users_i.far, rawScores_i$)
6:     **end for**
7: **end procedure**

8: **function** COMPUTEREPUTATION($far, score$)
9:     $history \leftarrow \sum\limits_{i=1}^{|far|} far_i \cdot \dfrac{w_i}{\sum\limits_{k=1}^{|far|} w_k}$
10:     $diff \leftarrow score - history$
11:     $\gamma \leftarrow$ **if** $diff \geqslant 0$ **then** γ_1 **else** γ_2
12:     **return** $\alpha \cdot score + \beta \cdot history + \gamma \cdot diff$
13: **end function**

14: **function** UPDATEFAR($far, score$)
15:     **for** $i{=}1$ to m **do**
16:         $newFAR_i \leftarrow \dfrac{far_i \cdot (b^i - 1) + far_{i-1}}{b^i}$
17:     **end for**
18:     **return** $newFAR$
19: **end function**

4 Validation

In this section we validate FadeRank in terms of its performance and precision with respect to two raw ranking algorithms, i.e. TURank [28] and a variant of PageRank [20] tailored to Twitter[1]. Additionally, we compare the precision of both instances of FadeRank with the *forgetful* versions of the raw ranking algorithms, which truncate the history every month.

Hereafter, we shall denote with:

– FadeRank$_T$: the instance of FadeRank which uses TURank as source of raw reputation;
– FadeRank$_P$: the instance of FadeRank which uses our variant of PageRank;
– Forget$_T$: the forgetful version of TURank;
– Forget$_P$: the forgetful version of PageRank.

Datasets. To the purpose of validation we have constructed three datasets, obtained by a custom crawler which downloads data (i.e., the tweet, retweet

---

[1] Note that we cannot use PageRank *as is* because of limitations of Twitter APIs, which do not allow to obtain temporal information about the "follow" relation. To circumvent this limitation, our variant of PageRank operates on the "tweet" and "retweet" relations, by assigning to each user the sum of the score of its tweets.

and follow relations) exploiting the Twitter APIs. Table 1 shows the details of the datasets; all of them cover a time-span of 11 months. The datasets D1 and D3 contain data of Italian users (the former has a relevant portion of influential users; the latter contains mostly normal users), while the dataset D2 contains data of American users.

In the rest of this section we present the validation results only for dataset D1; the analysis of the other datasets leads to very similar results, so to save space we make it available online at tcs.unica.it/software/faderank.

Table 1. Datasets details.

Dataset	#Users	#Tweet	#Follow	#Retweet
D1	∼11 K	∼14 M	∼15 M	∼5 M
D2	∼12 K	∼12 M	∼15 M	∼4 M
D3	∼12 K	∼11 M	∼11 M	∼3 M

Partitioning the Datasets in Time Intervals. We are interested in evaluating and relating the performance and the precision of *incremental* algorithms (i.e. FadeRank$_\mathbf{T}$, FadeRank$_\mathbf{P}$, Forget$_\mathbf{T}$, and Forget$_\mathbf{P}$) with respect to *non-incremental* ones (i.e., TURank and PageRank). To this purpose, we partition each dataset in 11 time intervals, each one comprising data spanning over 30 days. Then, we execute the algorithms to update user reputation, with the following criteria:

- incremental algorithms: for each time interval, process only the data contained in such interval;
- non-incremental algorithms: for each time interval i, process the data from the first to the i-th time interval.

Choice of the Parameters. For the purpose of the validation, we have to fix actual values for several parameters:

- the weights α, β, γ_1, γ_2 of the function AR in Eqs. (4) and (7);
- the weight function w_k in Eq. (5);
- the values for the parameters b and m of the fading memories (Eq. (8)).

The choice of the parameters for the dependable trust model aims at equalizing the scale and behaviour of FadeRank and of the raw reputation algorithm (TURank and PageRank). To this purpose, we choose $w_k = \rho^{k-1}$ as in Fig. 2a (with $\rho = 0.9$), and we compute the weights α, β, γ_1, γ_2 as follows:

1. we start by executing FadeRank$_\mathbf{T}$ (resp. FadeRank$_\mathbf{P}$) on dataset D1, simulating an update of the user reputation in 30-days intervals;
2. for each update, we save the raw reputation (denoting with R_t^n the raw reputation of user n at interval t) and the *history values* (denoting with H_t^n the history value of user n at interval t);

3. we execute TURank (resp. PageRank) with the data from interval 0 to t, so to compute the reputation of each user (denoting with T_t^n the reputation of user n at the interval t);
4. we solve the over-determined linear system obtained with the equations in the form $\alpha \cdot R_t^n + \beta \cdot H_t^n = T_t^n$, using the minimum least squares method;
5. finally, we use the solution of the linear system as initial values of α and β, which we fine-tune to mimic the behaviour of TURank (resp. PageRank); using the same criteria we choose the parameters γ_1 and γ_2[2].

For the fading memories parameters we choose $b = 2$ and $m = 3$, so to have a small number (i.e., $2^3 - 1 = 7$) of values to store. Note that, by increasing the number of fading memories (i.e., choosing bigger values for b and m), the FadeRank algorithm would take account for the past more precisely. Table 2 summarizes the choice of parameters used in the validation.

Table 2. Choice of the parameters of FadeRank$_T$ and FadeRank$_P$.

Algorithm	α	β	γ_1	γ_2	w_k	ρ	b	m
FadeRank$_T$	0.3	0.9	0.1	0.1	ρ^{k-1}	0.9	2	3
FadeRank$_P$	0.3	1.2	0.1	0.1	ρ^{k-1}	0.9	2	3

Performance Analysis. Figure 4 shows the execution time of FadeRank$_T$ vs. TURank (Fig. 4a), and of FadeRank$_P$ vs. PageRank (Fig. 4b). As expected, the experimental results show that the execution time of the non-incremental algorithms grows linearly with time (because the amount of data to be analysed grows at each update), while the execution time of FadeRank remains more or less constant. Note that the execution time of FadeRank cannot be exactly constant, because the size of the partition of the dataset is not constant (e.g., the monthly number of tweets may vary). The execution time of the forgetful versions of the algorithms (not shown in the figure) are very close to that of FadeRank.

Precision Analysis. To evaluate the precision of FadeRank, we consider *rankings*, i.e. list of Twitter users sorted by their reputation (computed each month). More precisely, we compare the ranking of FadeRank$_T$ (resp. FadeRank$_P$) with the ones obtained by TURank and Forget$_T$ (resp. PageRank and Forget$_P$). To compare two rankings we use the Kendall's τ [12], similarly to [27]. The Kendall's τ is a value in the range $[-1; +1]$ which measures the correlation between two rankings: in particular, $\tau = +1$ indicates that the two rankings perfectly agree (i.e. they are the same), while $\tau = -1$ indicates perfect disagreement (i.e., a ranking is the inverse of the other), and $\tau = 0$ denotes no correlation.

---

[2] Note that we cannot compute the γ-weights by solving the linear system, because the value D_t^n is a linear combination of the other two (i.e., $D_t^n = R_t^n - H_t^n$).

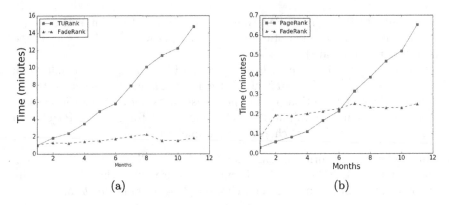

Fig. 4. In 4a, the execution time of FadeRank$_T$ (dashed line) and TURank (solid line) for dataset D1. In 4b, the same for FadeRank$_P$ and PageRank.

Figure 5 shows the results of our experiments on dataset D1. We see that, despite its constant-time execution, FadeRank$_T$ loses a small amount of precision with respect to TURank, but it is still more precise than Forget$_T$ on the long term. The comparison of FadeRank$_P$ and PageRank shows similar results: in this case, the gain of precision of FadeRank with respect to the forgetful algorithm is evident from the starting time intervals.

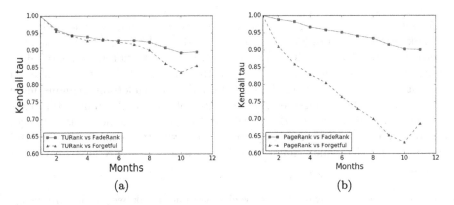

Fig. 5. In 5, the Kendall's τ correlation between the rankings of FadeRank$_T$ *vs.* TURank (solid line), and Forget$_T$ *vs.* TURank, on dataset D1. In 5b, the same for FadeRank$_P$, Forget$_P$ and Pagerank.

To further compare the precision of FadeRank with that of the forgetful algorithms, we have experimented on an artificial dataset which represents a whitewashing attack scenario. The dataset, containing 500 users and 400 K tweets spanning over 11 months, contains 30 % of spammers, who—after being ranked low in the past—begin to share high-quality content in the attempt to whitewash their reputation. Since TURank and FadeRank process the whole past behaviour of users, they can address this attacks, by letting the reputation of spammers increase slowly. Conversely, the forgetful algorithms discard the past history every month, hence they are susceptible to such whitewashing attacks.

The results of our experiments, reported in Fig. 6, show that the hybrid approach adopted by FadeRank, which only records a bounded digest of the past history (namely, $b^m - 1 = 7$ fading memories), is enough to address the whitewashing attack. More precisely, the diagram in Fig. 6a shows the expected drop of precision for Forget$_T$ with respect to TURank starting at the seventh month, while the precision of FadeRank remains within $\tau > 0.9$.

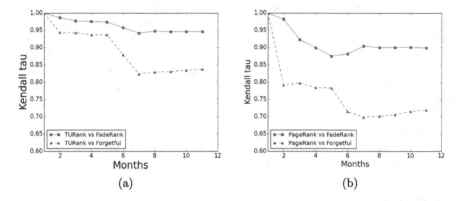

(a)   (b)

Fig. 6. In 6a, the precision of FadeRank$_T$ and Forget$_T$ for the whitewashing dataset. In 6b, the same for FadeRank$_P$ and Forget$_P$.

5   Conclusions

We have proposed an incremental reputation algorithm for Twitter, which updates the user reputation in (roughly) constant time. In this way we address a performance issue of reputation algorithms, which typically either consider the whole historical data at every update (so suffering from a huge computational overhead), or just discard the past (so being subject to whitewashing attacks).

Our algorithm, named FadeRank, exploits the technique introduced in [23] to summarize the past history in a bounded number of values—the *fading memories*. FadeRank combines the fading memories with the raw reputation computed in the most recent time interval, obtained (in constant time) by an arbitrary reputation algorithm. The actual behaviour of FadeRank depends on the weights associated to these components. A dominant weight on the raw component makes the reputation adapt very quickly to the most recent behaviour: a consequence of this choice is that spammers, i.e. malicious users that frequently tweet uninteresting or misleading content, could adopt a *strategic oscillation behaviour*, leading to a whitewashing attack [10]. A user who adopts this behaviour oscillates between building reputation, behaving non-maliciously, and then "milking" reputation, behaving maliciously. Instead, a dominant weight on the historical component makes the reputation adapt more slowly to the recent behaviour, so offering a defence against the above-mentioned attack.

We have validated FadeRank by comparing its performance and precision with those of two standard ranking algorithms, i.e. TURank [28] and a variant of PageRank [20] tailored to rank Twitter users. To perform the validation we have developed a crawler, through which we have downloaded from Twitter three large datasets of tweet/retweet/follow data, spanning over a period of 11 months. Our experiments show that, although the execution time of FadeRank is nearly constant at each reputation update (while, as expected, the execution time of TURank and PageRank grows linearly at each update), the loss in precision with respect to the raw algorithms is very limited. Further, FadeRank outperforms in precision the *forgetful* versions of the raw reputation algorithms, which naïvely truncate the past history. In particular, our experiments show that these algorithms suffer from a huge loss of precision in the presence of whitewashing attacks, while the ranking obtained by FadeRank is still quite close to that of the raw algorithms.

Acknowledgments. This work has been partially supported by Aut. Reg. of Sardinia P.I.A. 2013 "NOMAD", and by EU COST Action IC1201 "Behavioural Types for Reliable Large-Scale Software Systems" (BETTY).

References

1. Lithium Technologies Acquires Klout. http://www.lithium.com/company/news-room/press-releases/2014/lithium-technologies-acquires-klout. Accessed 09 April 2016
2. Twitter Usage Statistics. Internetlivestats.com http://www.internetlivestats.com/twitter-statistics. Accessed 09 April 2016
3. The top 20 valuable Facebook statistics, December 2015. Zephoria.com https://zephoria.com/top-15-valuable-facebook-statistics. Accessed 09 April 2016
4. Balmin, A., Hristidis, V., Papakonstantinou, Y.: Objectrank: authority-based keyword search in databases. In: VLDB, vol. 30, pp. 564–575 (2004)
5. Bartoletti, M., Cimoli, T., Murgia, M., Podda, A.S., Pompianu, L.: A contract-oriented middleware. In: Braga, C., Ölveczky, P.C. (eds.) FACS 2015. LNCS, vol. 9539, pp. 86–104. Springer, Heidelberg (2016). doi:10.1007/978-3-319-28934-2_5
6. Dimitriou, T., Karame, G., Christou, I.T.: SuperTrust: a secure and efficient framework for handling trust in super-peer networks. In: ACM PODC, pp. 374–375 (2007). http://doi.acm.org/10.1145/1281100.1281180
7. Haveliwala, T.H.: Topic-sensitive pagerank. In: WWW, pp. 517–526. ACM (2002)
8. Hoffman, K.J., Zage, D., Nita-Rotaru, C.: A survey of attack and defense techniques for reputation systems. ACM Comput. Surv. **42**(1), 1 (2009)
9. Hu, W., Zou, H., Gong, Z.: Temporal pagerank on social networks. In: Wang, J., Cellary, W., Wang, D., Wang, H., Chen, S.-C., Li, T., Zhang, Y. (eds.) WISE 2015. LNCS, vol. 9418, pp. 262–276. Springer, Heidelberg (2015). doi:10.1007/978-3-319-26190-4_18
10. Jøsang, A., Ismail, R., Boyd, C.: A survey of trust and reputation systems for online service provision. Decis. Support Syst. **43**(2), 618–644 (2007)

11. Kempe, D., Kleinberg, J., Tardos, É.: Maximizing the spread of influence through a social network. In: ACM SIGKDD, pp. 137–146. ACM (2003)
12. Kendall, M.G.: A new measure of rank correlation. Biometrika **30**(1/2), 81–93 (1938)
13. Lampe, C., Johnston, E.W., Resnick, P.: Follow the reader: filtering comments on slashdot. In: CHI, pp. 1253–1262 (2007)
14. Lampe, C., Resnick, P.: Slash(dot) and burn: distributed moderation in a large online conversation space. In: CHI, pp. 543–550 (2004)
15. Ma, H., Qian, W., Xia, F., He, X., Xu, J., Zhou, A.: Towards modeling popularity of microblogs. Front. Comput. Sci. **7**(2), 171–184 (2013)
16. Mariani, M.S., Medo, M., Zhang, Y.C.: Ranking nodes in growing networks: when pagerank fails. Scientific reports 5 (2015)
17. Michiardi, P., Molva, R.: Core: a collaborative reputation mechanism to enforce node cooperation in mobile ad hoc networks. In: Communications and Multimedia Security, IFIP Conference Proceedings, vol. 228, pp. 107–121. Kluwer (2002)
18. Mislove, A., Gummadi, K.P., Druschel, P.: Exploiting social networks for internet search. In: HotNets, p. 79 (2006)
19. Motwani, R., Raghavan, P.: Randomized Algorithms. Chapman & Hall/CRC, London (2010)
20. Page, L., Brin, S., Motwani, R., Winograd, T.: The pagerank citation ranking: bringing order to the web. Technical report 1999-66, Stanford InfoLab (1999)
21. Rao, A., Spasojevic, N., Li, Z., DSouza, T.: Klout score: measuring influence across multiple social networks. In: Big Data, pp. 2282–2289. IEEE (2015)
22. Resnick, P., Kuwabara, K., Zeckhauser, R., Friedman, E.: Reputation systems. Commun. ACM **43**(12), 45–48 (2000)
23. Srivatsa, M., Xiong, L., Liu, L.: TrustGuard: countering vulnerabilities in reputation management for decentralized overlay networks. In: WWW, pp. 422–431. ACM (2005)
24. Uysal, I., Croft, W.B.: User oriented tweet ranking: a filtering approach to microblogs. In: ACM CIKM, pp. 2261–2264. ACM (2011)
25. Vosecky, J., Leung, K.W.-T., Ng, W.: Searching for quality microblog posts: filtering and ranking based on content analysis and implicit links. In: Lee, S., Peng, Z., Zhou, X., Moon, Y.-S., Unland, R., Yoo, J. (eds.) DASFAA 2012, Part I. LNCS, vol. 7238, pp. 397–413. Springer, Heidelberg (2012)
26. Wang, A.H.: Don't follow me: spam detection in Twitter. In: SECRYPT, pp. 1–10. IEEE (2010)
27. Weng, J., Lim, E.P., Jiang, J., He, Q.: TwitterRank: finding topic-sensitive influential twitterers. In: ACM WSDM, pp. 261–270. ACM (2010)
28. Yamaguchi, Y., Takahashi, T., Amagasa, T., Kitagawa, H.: TURank: Twitter user ranking based on user-tweet graph analysis. In: Chen, L., Triantafillou, P., Suel, T. (eds.) WISE 2010. LNCS, vol. 6488, pp. 240–253. Springer, Heidelberg (2010)
29. Yu, H., Gibbons, P.B., Kaminsky, M., Xiao, F.: SybilLimit: a near-optimal social network defense against sybil attacks. In: IEEE S&P, pp. 3–17 (2008)
30. Yu, H., Kaminsky, M., Gibbons, P.B., Flaxman, A.D.: SybilGuard: defending against sybil attacks via social networks. IEEE/ACM Trans. Netw. **16**(3), 576–589 (2008)

Personalized Re-ranking of Tweets

Yukun Zhao[1], Shangsong Liang[2], and Jun Ma[1(✉)]

[1] Shandong University, Jinan, China
`yukunzhao.sdu@gmail.com`, `majun@sdu.edu.cn`
[2] University College London, London, UK
`shangsong.liang@ucl.ac.uk`

Abstract. In microblogs, the problem of information overload has troubled many users especially those with numerous followees. Users receive hundreds of tweets in chronological order and have to scan through pages of tweets to find useful information. In this paper, we propose a personalized tweet re-ranking framework for re-ranking the tweets received by a user based on his preference such that interesting tweets are ranked higher for the user. With the personalized re-ranked tweets, the user can find his interesting tweets conveniently. Modeling users' preference in the context of tweet streams is more challenging than modeling that in the context of long documents as it is difficult to capture users' interests with sparse short text documents like tweets. To address this challenge, we propose a media awareness tweet re-ranking model, MATR for short, to incorporate WeMedia accounts (WeMedia is a type of accounts in microblogs that only has media attributes publishing original and valuable messages), and explicitly calculate the influence of the publishers of these tweets. Experimental results demonstrate the effectiveness of our method compared to state-of-the-art baselines.

Keywords: Personalized tweet re-ranking · Topic modeling · Microblog

1 Introduction

With the rising of social media, microblogs such as Twitter[1] and Sina Weibo[2] have become increasingly popular for their important roles in information sharing and interpersonal communication. When a user logs in with his own account, there would be a large amount of tweets shown to the user especially when he has many followees. Almost half of the tweets pushed to him are pointless babble while the rest of them are news, conversations, self-promotions and trashes [8,9,13,16,18]. Some important and useful tweets would be flooded by other tweets that the users do not care. This problem of information overload problem troubles the users, since all tweets are posted to them in chronological order and considered equally important regardless of the users' personalized interests.

---

[1] http://twitter.com.
[2] http://weibo.com.

© Springer International Publishing AG 2016
W. Cellary et al. (Eds.): WISE 2016, Part II, LNCS 10042, pp. 70–84, 2016.
DOI: 10.1007/978-3-319-48743-4_6

One effective solution to assist a user to access the tweets he is interested in is to re-rank the tweets posted to him based on his personal interests. Users' interests modeling has been widely studied including [4,7,15,19,22,24,26,28], who model users' interests in terms of topics. Tweet ranking and recommendation [2,5,11,25,30], integrate tweet contents and other features including tweet history and social relations to infer users' preferences. All of these methods do not consider media attributes of microblogs and big data behind the users' followees.

To effectively retrieve interesting tweets for a specific user, we propose a personalized media awareness tweet re-ranking model, abbreviated as MATR. We estimate a user's personalized preference based on the tweets he posted and the WeMedia accounts he is following. Our approach builds on the previous work [7,17,26–28,30], but we explicitly consider the big data behind the users' followed WeMedia accounts and the influence of tweet publishers. We briefly describe our model in the following two paragraphs.

Users' media attributes have been discussed in [8,10,12,14,20,29]. WeMedia [20,29] is a type of accounts which focuses on vertical specialization areas such as technology, finance, automobile etc. These WeMedia accounts do publish lots of original and valuable contents [20]. In general, WeMedia accounts publish a large amount of tweets and the texts obey common text rules with more meaningful nouns, phrases and universal grammars. Intuitively speaking, the reason why a user follows a WeMedia accounts is that there are some topics the user concerns in the contents he published. We then incorporate the tweets' texts published by the WeMedia accounts the user is following and the user's published tweets to infer a global topic mode (GTM), via which we can infer the user's topic distribution.

Words can have different meanings in different contexts. For example, if a user often tweets about IT, iphone, coding, android, we need the word "apple" to indicate a product of Apple Inc. instead of fruit when he says "Apple is amazing". In order to solve this problem of word ambiguity, for each document (tweet), we use all the tweets published by the WeMedia account who is the original publisher of the tweet, to build a local topic model (LTM). We use two hierarchical topic models (GTM and LTM) to infer the topic distributions of each tweet and the user's interests. We calculate the user's preference score on a tweet based on the topical similarity between the user and the tweet. And, we calculate the influence of the tweet publisher, including the authority of the publisher, the quality of tweets and social interactions between the user and the publisher. Experimental results show that our approach captures each user's interests more accurately and recalls more useful tweets.

The main contributions of this paper are as follows:

(1) We propose a personalized media awareness tweet re-ranking model (MATR) to re-rank the tweets posted to a user based on the his preference for these tweets.
(2) We alleviate sparsity of data, topic coarse in modeling users' interests by incorporating those large amount of WeMedia accounts the user is following.

(3) We propose to use the local topic models for the tweets to alleviate word ambiguity and understand what the tweets talk about better.

(4) We compute the influence of the publishers of tweets on the user's preference for these tweets explicitly.

The rest of this paper is organized as follows. We review related work in Sect. 2. We give our proposed framework in Sect. 3. Section 4 shows experiments and evaluation. We give conclusions in Sect. 5.

2   Related Work

Our approach builds on the earlier work in automatic WeMedia accounts detection, topic modeling, tweet ranking and tweet recommendation.

2.1   WeMedia

Kwak et al. [8] and Shayne and Willis [29] prove that the microblog service is not only a social network but also a news media platform, while some accounts exist as media accounts and publish many valuable tweets. These accounts who publish vast original and useful messages, are regarded as WeMedia accounts [20]. Liu and Zhang [20] study WeMedia accounts from posting behaviors and posting contents and then propose a method to detect WeMedia accounts automatically, while the method of WeMedia accounts detection is used in our work.

2.2   Topic Modeling

Topic models [1,6] are widely used to project high-dimensional words into low-dimensional latent topics, where each document and each word are viewed as multinomial distributions over a set of topics. The latent topics extracted from users' documents and words are used to infer users' interests [15,19,24,28,35]. When dealing with short texts, Wan and Xiao [31,32] add extra neighbor documents for topic decomposition. But the finding of neighbor documents are usually arbitrary. These methods introduce too much noise and result in topic drift when the document and its so-called neighbor documents do not talk about the same topics. Liu et al. [21] and Matthew and Macskassy [23] aim to find the topics to represent interests for users in Twitter by identifying the entities they mentioned in the tweets. Zhao et al. [4] extract representative key words from tweets with considering the setting of Twitter and classify latent topics into "back-ground" topics and "personal" topics. Inspired by these methods, we represent a user's interests and a tweet in both topic level and word level.

2.3   Tweet Ranking and Recommendation

Weng et al. [33] propose a graph-based ranking strategy to rank tweets posted to each user based on the relevance between users' interests and tweet contents.

Duan et al. [3] use a learning-to-rank approach for general tweet ranking. Feng and Wang [5] incorporates all sources of information like users' profile, tweet quality, interaction history to rank the tweets for each users. Vosecky et al. [30] utilizes topic models and language models to represent words in both topic level and word level, which gives an efficient method to calculate topic affinity between users and tweets. Chen et al. [2] propose to recommend tweets based on collaborative ranking strategy and other useful contextual information. Similarly, recommending "novel" tweets to users are studied in [25]. These methods consider many information including social relations and other explicit features to represent the user's preference for each tweet, but when to infer each user's interests they still decompose the user's tweet contents into topic level using traditional topic models simply without solving the coarse topics and the problem of word ambiguity.

Our work is different from the above related works in the following important ways: (1) We incorporate long tweets published by WeMedia accounts which have meaningful nouns, meaningful phrases and universal grammars to alleviate data sparsity when infer users' interests in the setting of microblogs and (2) we then explicitly calculate the influence of the tweet publisher on the users' preference for a tweet.

3 Media Awareness Tweet Re-ranking

3.1 Overview

We aim to re-rank the tweets that are posted to each user during a certain time period for each user. That is: our task is to estimate each user's preference on each tweet. We use u to represent a user and i to indicate an item (a tweet posted to the user u). A user u's interests are represented as a multinomial distribution of topics M_u, and an item i is represented as a multinomial distribution Q_i. The score $\widehat{r_{u,i}}$ of user u's preference on tweet i is obtained as follows:

Table 1. Main notations used in this paper

Notation	Gloss
K	Number of topics
V	The vocabulary size
u	A user
i	A new posted tweet (item, document)
d	A tweet or retweet
w	A word presenting in a tweet, $w \in d$
M_u	Multinomial distribution of user u
Q_i	Multinomial distribution of item i
b_i	Influence of publisher of tweet i
$\widehat{r_{u,i}}$	Estimation of u's preference on item i
N_u	The WeMedia accounts user u followed
θ_d	Multinomial distribution of tweet d
ϕ_k	Multinomial distribution of topic k
z_w, z_d	Topic assignment on word w and tweet d
α, β	Hyper parameters in our topic model
μ, λ, η	Hyper parameters in MATR

$$\widehat{r_{u,i}} = b_i + sim(M_u, Q_i), \quad (1)$$

where $sim(M_u, Q_i)$ represents the similarity between a user's topic distribution and the distribution of item i. b_i is the influence of the publisher of tweet i. The main notations we use in this paper is summarized in the Table 1.

We show the method to calculate topical similarity between a user and an item in Subsect. 3.2. Then we detail the influence of the publisher of tweet i on the user u's preference for tweet i in Sect. 3.3.

3.2   Topical Similarity Between a User and an Item

We split the user u's set of published tweets into two subsets. The first subset D_u contains all the user's original tweets, while the second subset R_u contains tweets that are retweeted from other users. In order to represent the user's interests M_u, we need to infer topic distribution M_{D_u} and topic distribution M_{R_u}. They relationship of these three multinomial distributions is the following:

$$M_u = \lambda M_{D_u} + (1 - \lambda) M_{R_u}, \tag{2}$$

where λ is free parameter that measures the importance of original tweets in inferring user u's interests. We use Jelinek Mercer smoothing method [34] to incorporate topic distributions of original tweets and retweets.

Topic Distribution of Original Tweets M_{D_u}: We use LDA [1] to infer a topic distribution of each document, in our case, tweet, and then average all distributions to infer M_{D_u}. We use a tweet set D_u published by the user's followees and himself to build a global topic model abbreviated as GTM. We use GTM to infer the topic distribution on tweet d as θ_d, $\theta_{d,k}$ representing the k-th dimension of θ_{t_j}, $d \in D_u, k \in [1, K]$. w is a word in tweet d. ϕ_k^{GTM} is a topic-word distribution being the probability of a set of words generated under topic k. $P(w|\phi_k^{GTM})$ indicates the probability of word w being generated under topic k. $\theta_{d,k}^{GTM}$ represents the probability of a document d being assigned to topic k in GTM. The user's original tweets topic distribution M_{u,D_u} on topic k can be formulated:

$$M_{D_u,k} = \frac{1}{|D_u|} \sum_{j=1}^{|D_u|} \theta_{d_j,k}^{GTM}. \tag{3}$$

Then we introduce how to incorporate the WeMedia accounts the user is following to infer topic distributions of retweets.

Topic Distribution of Retweets M_{R_u}: For each user u, we identify the WeMedia accounts user u followed as N_u using the method [20]. Inspired by [30], we use both words and topics to represent the user's interests. For each tweet $d \in R_u$, there is a publisher $N_{u_d} \in N_u, N_{u_d} \neq u$. We use the tweets published by the WeMedia account N_{u_d} to train a local topic model LTM^d. Then we get document-topic distribution $\theta_d^{LTM^d}$ for document d and topic-word distribution $\phi_k^{LTM^d}$ for each topic k.

We assign the document d a single topic by choosing the topic that maximizes the probability of $\theta_{d,k}$. Then the topic assignment on tweet d is z_d:

$$z_d = \arg\max_k \theta_{d,k}^{LTM^d} = \arg\max_k \prod_{w \in d} P(w|\phi_k^{LTM^d}). \tag{4}$$

Similarly, one single topic assignment z_w on word $w \in d$ is obtained by choosing the topic that maximizes the probability of $\phi_{k,w}^{\mathrm{LTM}^d}$:

$$z_w^{\mathrm{LTM}^d} = \arg\max_k P(w|\phi_k^{\mathrm{LTM}^d}). \tag{5}$$

For each word $w \in d$, select top-N words in the topics whose topic is $z = z_w^{\mathrm{LTM}^d}$ and add these words into document d, leading the document d has more precise and sufficient words to express its topics. Then we get document d expanded to d', and the retweet set R_u expanded to R'_u. At the same time, users have similar interests with the publisher as mentioned below. After incorporate the WeMedia contents, we formulate the topic distributions of retweet set R_d on topic k as follows:

$$M_{R_u,k} = \frac{1}{|R'_u|} \sum_{d'=1}^{|R'_u|} \theta_{d',k}^{\mathrm{GTM}}. \tag{6}$$

After the two steps inferring M_{D_u} and M_{R_u}, we infer the user u's interests M_u by combining topic distributions of his original tweets M_{D_u} and topic distributions of all retweets M_{R_u}. The k-th dimension of M_u is formulated as:

$$M_{u,k} = \lambda M_{D_u,k} + (1-\lambda)M_{R_u,k}$$

$$= \lambda \frac{1}{|D_u|} \sum_{d=1}^{|D_u|} \theta_{d,k}^{\mathrm{GTM}} + (1-\lambda)\frac{1}{|R'_u|} \sum_{d'=1}^{|R'_u|} \theta_{d',k}^{\mathrm{GTM}}. \tag{7}$$

Topical Representation of an Item Q_i: If the publisher of tweet(item) i is an ordinary user, we use GTM to obtain its topic distribution Q_i. The k-th dimension of Q_i is obtained as follows:

$$Q_{i,k} = \frac{\prod_{w \in i} P(w|\phi_k^{\mathrm{GTM}})}{\prod_{w \in i} \sum_z P(w|\phi_z^{\mathrm{GTM}})}. \tag{8}$$

If the publisher of tweet i is a WeMedia account, we get the tweet i expanded to i'. We add similaring words under the identical topics in LTM^i as metioned before. Then, we get the topic distribution on tweet i Q_i, while the dimension k of Q_i is obtained as follows:

$$Q_{i,k} = \frac{\prod_{w \in i'} P(w|\phi_k^{\mathrm{GTM}})}{\prod_{w \in i'} \sum_z P(w|\phi_z^{\mathrm{GTM}})}. \tag{9}$$

As we represent each user and each item via a multinomial topic distribution, we calculate the cosine similarity between each user and each item. Then the remaining problem is to calculate the influence of the publisher, which is shown in the next Subsect. 3.3.

3.3   Calculation of Publisher Influence

We formulate the publisher's influence on the user u's preference on item i as b_i. The publisher's explicit features are deduced in the following three primary parts:

Interest Affinity Weight $w_I(\boldsymbol{N}_{u_i}, \boldsymbol{u})$: We use N_{u_i} to indicate the publisher of tweet i, and $w_I(N_{u_i}, u)$ to indicate the affinity of interests between the user u and the user N_{u_i}. Generally, the user tend to retweet a tweet when the tweet publisher has similar interests with him. We measure the similarity of interests between the user u and the publisher N_{u_i} via their latent topic profiles using inverse KL-divergence:

$$w_I(N_{u_i}, u) = 1/KL(M_u, M_{N_{u_i}}). \tag{10}$$

Publisher Authority Weight $w_A(\boldsymbol{N}_{u_i}, \boldsymbol{u})$: The authority of a publisher is indicated by the number of followers, the number of tweets and the number of mentioned times. We use c_{follow} to indicate the number of followers of user N_{u_i}, and use $c_{followAvg}$, $c_{followMax}$ indicate the average number of followers a user is following and the maximal number of followers a user is following respectively. The number of tweets infer the user's activeness in microblogs. c_{tweet} is number of tweets published by user N_{u_i}, $c_{tweetAvg}$, $c_{tweetMax}$ are the average number of tweets a user published and the maximum number of tweets a user published respectively. Mentioned counts are the times the publisher has been mentioned in other tweets, the frequency indicating the popularity of the publisher. c_{ment}, $c_{mentAvg}$ and $c_{mentMax}$ represent the number of times user N_{u_i} being mentioned in other tweets, the average number of times a user being mentioned and the maximum number of times a user being mentioned. The authority weight is normalized as follows:

$$w_A(N_{u_i}, u) = \eta_1 \frac{c_{follow} - c_{followAvg}}{c_{followMax}} + \eta_2 \frac{c_{tweet} - c_{tweetAvg}}{c_{tweetMax}} + \eta_3 \frac{c_{ment} - c_{mentAvg}}{c_{mentMax}}. \tag{11}$$

Content Quality Weight $w_C(\boldsymbol{N}_{u_i}, \boldsymbol{u})$: The quality of a tweet is estimated by the length of the tweet, retweeted times of the tweet, the number of comments in the tweet. Tweets which are long and retweeted or commented many times could be awarded as high quality tweets. We use $c(awardedTweet)$ to indicate the number of high quality tweets and use $(c(tweet)$ to indicate the number of tweets the user N_{u_i} published. The weight of the quality of publisher's contents is estimated by $w_C(N_{u_i}, u)$:

$$w_C(N_{u_i}, u) = \frac{\log(c(awardedTweet))}{\log(c(tweet))}. \tag{12}$$

The overall weight of the influence of publisher N_{u_i} on user u is formulated as:

$$b_i = \mu_1 w_I(N_{u_i}, u) + \mu_2 w_A(N_{u_i}, u) + \mu_3 w_C(N_{u_i}, u), \qquad (13)$$

where $\mu_1, \mu_2, \mu_3 \in [0, 1]$ indicates the weight of different factors, $\sum_j \mu_j = 1$.

Using Eqs. 3, 7, 8, 9 and 13, the user $u's$ preference score $\widehat{r_{u,i}}$ on item i is formulated as follows:

$$\widehat{r_{u,i}} = \cos(M_u, Q_i) + \mu_1 w_I(N_{u_i}, u) + \mu_2 w_A(N_{u_i}, u) + \mu_3 w_C(N_{u_i}, u). \qquad (14)$$

4 Experiments

4.1 Experimental Setup

In this paper, we use Sina Weibo as our default setting of microblog service. We work with a dataset crawled from Sina Weibo. The dataset contains 896 users including all their published tweets from the date of their registration up to May 1, 2015 and their social relations. For each user, we crawl all the followees he followed including the tweets and user-information. Finally, we get 21058 users in total. The average number of tweets an ordinary user published is 1,137, including 156 original tweets and 981 retweets. In these 981 retweets, 563 of them are published from WeMedia accounts while the rest of them are published from ordinary users. An ordinary user follows 133 users averagely, and 64 of them are WeMedia accounts. Table 2 shows the statistics of the dataset.

Table 3 shows the difference between ordinary users and WeMedia accounts. We get 4864 WeMedia accounts and 16194 ordinary users in this dataset. Averagely, a WeMedia account has 12798 followers while an ordinary user only has 433 followers. The average number of tweets and average retweeted times per tweet published by a WeMedia account are 9799 and 97 respectively, while the values are 1137 and 0.86 respectively published by an ordinary user. The average length of a original tweet published by a WeMedia account is 76 while the value is

Table 2. For each user, #tweets to be trained, #followees, #WeMedia accounts he followed, #tweets, #retweets

Training tweets	Followees	WeMedia accounts	Original tweets	Retweets
2.3M	133	64	156	981

Table 3. Comparison between WeMedia accounts and ordinary users, #, #followers, #tweets(including original tweets and retweets), retweeted times per tweet, average length of each tweet

Account type	#	#followers	#tweets	Retweeted times	Tweet length
WeMedia accounts	4864	12798	9799	97	76
Ordinary users	16194	433	1137	0.86	23

only 23 when published by a ordinary user. The numbers of key words of a tweet published by ordinary users and WeMedia accounts are shown in Subsect. 4.5.

In this dataset, the retweeted tweets are regarded as positive samples and the others are negative samples. For each user, we depart the tweets in two parts based on their chronological order, and the first three fourths of the tweets are used for training while the rest of them are used for validation.

4.2 Effectiveness of MATR

We use precision to indicate the ratio of tweets in the ranked list that are retweeted finally, and use recall to indicate how many tweets the user has retweeted can be found by our method. We use Mean-F1 measure to evaluate our method. Mean-F1 is obtained by averaging F1 values of the all 896 users.

Now we show the performance of our method compared to other four methods. The detailed implementations are listed below:

Chronological: The tweets are regarded as equally important and posted in chronological order. This strategy indicates the default user experience in microblogs.

Retweeted Times: We re-rank the tweets based on its retweeted times, for the retweeted times is an objective estimation of the popularity of a tweet. This method ignores personalized users' interests and regards all users' interests are the same as the public.

LDA: In LDA [1], user interests are represented from the majority of tweets he published. Known the distribution of user u and tweet d, we calculate the preference score as below:

$$y_{u,d} = \sum_{d_0 \in Tweets(u)} D_{KL}(d_0||d) + b_d \qquad (15)$$

Here $D_{KL}(d_0||d)$ express the KL-divergence between the topic distribution of two tweets, b_d express tweet bias.

CTR: Collaborative tweet recommendation [2], a representative method in the state-of-art, which incorporates users' contents and social relations. On the one hand, CTR decompose users' tweet contents into topic level using traditional latent topic models to capture user personal interests. On the other hand, CTR take social relation factors and explicit features into account to represent each users' preference to each particular tweet.

Figure 1 shows the performance of five compared methods. In general, the re-ranked tweet lists should be compact, then the length of re-ranked tweet lists are 10, 30, 50 and 100 in our experiments.

In Fig. 1, we see that chronological strategy shows poor results with Mean-F1 value 0.095 when the length of a list is only ten, which indicates users can almost retweet no more than one status in the ranking list. When the length of ranking list increase to 30, 50 and 100, its Mean-F1 value is 0.1, 0.1 and 0.12. It is obvious that users scan the tweets but do not retweet frequently. This method in our experiments is regarded as a random order to present statuses to a personalized user and the performance is depended on the ratio of positive samples.

The performance based on retweeted times obtains a slight improvement compared with chronological order, whose Mean-F1 values range from 0.19 to 0.23. It is still a poor result for there are many positive samples in test dataset indicating that even if we rank the tweets randomly we can obtain a comparable performance with retweeted times strategy. The result verify the necessity of personalized tweet re-ranking while personalized users' interests are not very similar to the popular interests.

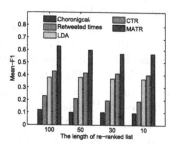

Fig. 1. Mean-F1 of five compared methods in different length of tweet lists.

LDA outperforms the two mentioned methods because it use users' tweets to infer their interests, and the Mean-F1 values are 0.367 to 0.38. When the length of tweet list varies from 10 to 30, the Mean-F1 values vary from 0.367 to 0.37. The Mean-F1 value slightly improves to 0.38 with the length of re-ranked item list increased to 50 and 100.

Then we come to CTR, the collaborative tweet ranking method obtain a large improvement compared with three previous methods, whose Mean-F1 values are 0.40, 0.41, 0.416 and 0.43 and the corresponding length the lists are 10, 30, 50 and 100. Our method MATR is built on the basis of CTR, whose Mean-F1 value is improved to 0.63 when the list length is 100, which means we can capture users' preference on the tweets more accurately and precisely with just recommending the top 100 tweets. We see Mean-F1 value will be 0.60, 0.57 and 0.57 when the item list length decreases to 50, 30 and 10.

In the setting of Sina Weibo, a page is composed of three subpages within 45 tweets but mostly users only scan the previous 2 subpages meaning that they only scan top 30 tweets. We select top 30 items from the ranked item list and show the Mean-F1 value and recall value in Table 4. Mean-F1 values of chronological order method, retweeted times, LDA, CTR and MATR are 0.1, 0.195, 0.37, 0.41 and 0.57 respectively as we analyzed before. Recall values of compared four methods are 0.12, 0.26, 0.42, 0.60 and 0.78 respectively. Users scan pages to pages of tweets in microblogs and they concern more about how many tweets they likes can be recalled, thus the big improvement to recall useful tweets demonstrate the efficiency and practicability of our method.

Table 4. When the length of ranked item list is 30, Mean-F1 and recall of chronological, retweeted times, LDA, CTR and MATR

	Chronological	Retweeted times	LDA	CTR	MATR
Mean-F1	0.1	0.195	0.37	0.41	0.57
Recall	0.12	0.26	0.42	0.60	0.78

4.3   Effectiveness of Components

In the previous subsection, we have validated the effectiveness of our proposed method MATR. The Fig. 2 shows the influence of each component, i.e., publisher influence and WeMedia.

The implementation of LDA for personalized tweet ranking has been discussed above. "MATR - WeMedia" represents we exclude WeMedia accounts to the inference of users' interests but consider the tweet publisher's influence. "MATR - Publisher Influence" represents that we incorporate his followed WeMedia accounts to inter the user's interests, without considering publisher influence. MATR is the complete model we have proposed in this paper.

In this Fig. 2, the x-axis is the length of item list 10, 30, 50 and 100 while the y-axis is recall value. Performance of LDA is shown for comparison. The result shows when integrate publisher influence, the values of recall are 0.625, 0.56, 0.56, 0.55 better than LDA whose values of recall are 0.41, 0.424, 0.42, 0.42. Considering the publisher influence means a tweet would be ranked front if its publisher is a popular person or a friend. When incorporate WeMedia accounts, we see recall is improved to 0.75 compared with LDA in 100 ranked items. This big improvement testify the effectiveness of incorporating WeMedia accounts for personalized tweet ranking. The better ranking performance is due to integrating the vast compact tweet contents, which are published by WeMedia accounts, to infer user interests more accurately. "MTAR - Publisher Influence" outperforms "MTAR - WeMedia", which means WeMedia accounts have bigger contribution on personalized tweet re-ranking than publisher influence. We conclude that both publisher influence and WeMedia are helpful in personalized tweet re-ranking.

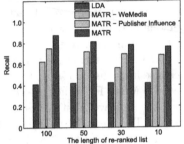

Fig. 2. Comparison of components with different item list length.

4.4   Analysis of Parameters

We trained our model and other baseline topic models using 500 iterations and set $\alpha = 0.5, \beta = 0.1, K = 50$. When we train each LTM, the size of topics is also $K = 50$. Other parameters, i.e., the publisher influence on tweet b_i is calculated explicitly as we mentioned before, and the weights of different factors in publisher influence σ_i are all set 0.33. Figure 3 shows the influence of parameter λ.

λ describes the weight of a user's original published tweets in modeling the user's interests. In the Fig. 3, we see when λ is around 0.3 the recall reaches top. When λ exceeds 0.3, λ increases but recall decreases. This phenomenon shows that larger weight of user's original tweets lead to less ideal ranking results. When λ reaches to 0.9 or more, recall stay close to 0.4 which is close to the performance of LDA method. We conclude that model with smaller λ value means bigger influence from WeMedia accounts leading to a better ranking performance. This result validates the necessity and effectiveness to incorporate WeMedia accounts for personalized tweet re-ranking.

4.5   Quality in Modeling User Interests

We use terminology "user original tweet" to denote the tweets originally published by ordinary users (not retweets), "WeMedia account tweet" to denote the tweets originally published by some WeMedia accounts. Figure 4 show average tweet length and average number of key words in a tweet published by ordinary users and WeMedia accounts repectively. As can be seen in Fig. 4(a), the ratio of tweets of which the length is less than 50 words is about 36.5 % from ordinary users, while that is 29.0 % from WeMedia accounts, which indicates that the ratio of tweet length

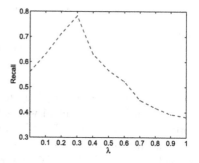

Fig. 3. Influence of λ on recall, with the length of item list being 30.

exceeds 50 words is about 71 % published by WeMedia accounts while this ratio is only 63.5 % published by ordinary users. From Fig. 4(b) we see that the number of key words per tweets published by WeMedia tend to be larger than those published by common users. The ratio of number of key words less than 20 is 50.6 % published by ordinary users while the ratio is only 25.5 % published by WeMedia accounts. This phenomenon testify our intuition that tweets published by common users are always short and noisy but tweets published by WeMedia tend to have more compact and expressive words.

Then we shows some words in a tweet represented by topics produced by LTM+GTM and LDA. The tweets are written in chinese originally. For understanding, we translate it into english as follows, 1st tweet: "No matter you are single or married now, please believe that your life will never be lonely when you

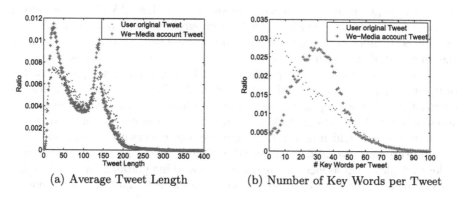

(a) Average Tweet Length   (b) Number of Key Words per Tweet

Fig. 4. The ratio of average tweet length and the number of key words per tweet, published by the ordinary users and the WeMedia accounts respectively.

Table 5. The expanded words of original tweets extracted by our method LTM+GTM and LDA, respectively. Words marked blue represent the most coherent words; Words marked green represent less coherent words and others represent irrelevant words.

	Single, married, life									
LTM + GTM	Love	Dream	My dear	Life	Youth	Beijing	Time	Women	Movie	Story
LDA	Dream	Youth	Child	Today	Drama	Friend	Bullshit	Time	Dress up	Brain
	God, good luck									
LTM + GTM	God	Bad luck	Future	Creature	Safeness	Constellation	Legend	Smile	Life	Pisces
LDA	Year	Wine	Child	Variation	Bad luck	God	Creature	Senior	Work	House

get old." After do POS tagging and key phrase extraction we get words "single, married, life" as the central words for this tweet. Then we use LTM to get the words "single", "married", "life" expanded. The top-10 words in the correlate topics is shown in Table 5. The 2nd tweet: "The most cute God, retweet it and you will get good luck." We get the words "God", "good luck" to be trained in our topic model. Each word is assigned a topic and get expanded. We extract top ten words with maximum likelihood in the topics to represent the original tweet in Table 5.

From Table 5, we see that LTM+GTM methods discovers more meaningful and related words for the tweet. And the words in the topic are more coherent. The results demonstrate that we can alleviate word ambiguity and understand what the tweets talk about better. We use consistent topics to get words expanded enhancing their expressibility. In fact, we incorporate long tweets(documents) published by WeMedia accounts instead of directly applying LDA, to alleviate data sparsity, topic coarse in modeling users' interests.

5   Conclusion

In this paper, we propose a novel and efficient framework, MATR, to re-rank the tweets posted to a specific user based on the his preference for the tweets he receives. First, we propose to incorporate each user's followed WeMedia accounts, whose published tweets are always with meaningful nouns, phrases and universal grammars, to infer each user's personal interests. Then, we explicitly calculate the influence of the publishers of tweets including social interactions, the quality of tweet contents and the publishers' authority. Finally, we provide a list of tweets having been re-ranked to the personalized user. Experimental results demonstrate that we capture a user's interests more precisely by better understanding what the tweets are talking about, and our approach recall more useful tweets to the user which is helpful to improve user experience in microblogs.

As future work, we need to improve the efficiency of our proposed algorithm in order to deploy such service on a real social networking platform. Another future work is to focus on the topic extraction on short texts and find the semantic relations in different environments not limited to microblogs.

Acknowledgements. This work is supported by the Natural Science Foundation of China (61672322, 61672324, 61272240, 71402083), the Natural Science foundation of Shandong province (ZR2012FM037), the Excellent Middle-Aged and Youth Scientists of Shandong Province (BS2012DX017) and the Fundamental Research Funds of Shandong University.

References

1. Blei, D.M., Ng, A.Y., Jordan, M.I.: Latent Dirichlet allocation. J. Mach. Learn. Res. **3**, 993–1022 (2003)
2. Chen, K., Chen, T., Zheng, G., Jin, O., Yao, E., Yu, Y.: Collaborative personalized tweet recommendation. In: SIGIR, pp. 661–670 (2012)
3. Duan, Y., Jiang, L., Qin, T., Zhou, M., Shum, H.-Y.: An empirical study on learning to rank of tweets. In: COLING, pp. 261–270 (2010)
4. Zhao, W.X., et al.: Topical keyphrase extraction from twitter. In: ACL (2011)
5. Feng, W., Wang, J.: Retweet or not? Personalized tweet re-ranking. In: WSDM (2013)
6. Hofmann, T.: Probabilistic latent semantic indexing. In: SIGIR, pp. 50–57 (1999)
7. Krieger, M., Ahn, D.: TweetMotif: exploratory search and topic summarization for twitter. In: ICWSM (2010)
8. Kwak, H., Lee, C., Park, H., Moon, S.: What is twitter, a social network or a news media? In: WWW (2010)
9. Liang, S.: Fusion and diversification in information retrieval. Ph.D. thesis, University of Amsterdam (2014)
10. Liang, S., de Rijke, M.: Finding knowledgeable groups in enterprise corpora. In: SIGIR 2013 (2013)
11. Liang, S., de Rijke, M.: Burst-aware data fusion for microblog search. Inf. Process. Manag. **51**(2), 89–113 (2015)
12. Liang, S., de Rijke, M.: Formal language models for finding groups of experts. Inf. Process. Manag. **52**(4), 529–549 (2016)
13. Liang, S., Rijke, M., Tsagkias, M.: Late data fusion for microblog search. In: Serdyukov, P., Braslavski, P., Kuznetsov, S.O., Kamps, J., Rüger, S., Agichtein, E., Segalovich, I., Yilmaz, E. (eds.) ECIR 2013. LNCS, vol. 7814, pp. 743–746. Springer, Heidelberg (2013). doi:10.1007/978-3-642-36973-5_74
14. Liang, S., Ren, Z., de Rijke, M.: Fusion helps diversification. In: SIGIR, pp. 303–312 (2014)
15. Liang, S., Ren, Z., de Rijke, M.: Personalized search result diversification via structured learning. In: KDD, pp. 751–760 (2014)
16. Liang, S., Ren, Z., Rijke, M.: The impact of semantic document expansion on cluster-based fusion for microblog search. In: Rijke, M., Kenter, T., Vries, A.P., Zhai, C.X., Jong, F., Radinsky, K., Hofmann, K. (eds.) ECIR 2014. LNCS, vol. 8416, pp. 493–499. Springer, Heidelberg (2014). doi:10.1007/978-3-319-06028-6_47
17. Liang, S., Ren, Z., Weerkamp, W., Meij, E., de Rijke, M.: Time-aware rank aggregation for microblog search. In: CIKM, p. 10 (2014)
18. Liang, S., Yilmaz, E., Kanoulas, E.: Dynamic clustering of streaming short documents. In: KDD. ACM (2016)
19. Liang, S., Cai, F., Ren, Z., de Rijke, M.: Efficient structured learning for personalized diversification. IEEE Trans. Knowl. Data Eng. (to appear)
20. Liu, J., Zhang, M.: A study on we media account detection in Sina Weibo. In: CCIR (2014)

21. Liu, X., Zhang, S., Wei, F., Zhou, M.: Recognizing named entities in tweets. In: ACL (2011)
22. Liu, Z., Chen, X., Zheng, Y., Sun, M.: Automatic keyphrase extraction by bridging vocabulary gap. In: CoNLL, pp. 135–144 (2011)
23. Matthew, M., Macskassy, S.A.: Discovering users' topics of interest on twitter: a first look. In: Proceedings of the Fourth Workshop on Analytics for Noisy Unstructured Text Data, pp. 73–80 (2010)
24. O'Connor, B., Krieger, M., Ahn, D.: TweetMotif: exploratory search and topic summarization for twitter. In: ICWSM (2010)
25. Pennacchiotti, M., Silvestri, F., Vahabi, H., Venturini, R.: Making your interests follow you on twitter. In: CIKM (2012)
26. Ren, Z., Liang, S., Meij, E., de Rijke, M.: Personalized time-aware tweets summarization. In: SIGIR (2013)
27. Ren, Z., Peetz, M.-H., Liang, S., van Dolen, W., de Rijke, M.: Hierarchical multi-label classification of social text streams. In: SIGIR, pp. 213–222 (2014)
28. Rosen-Zvi, M., Griffiths, T., Steyvers, M., Smyth, P.: The author-topic model for authors and documents. In: UAI, pp. 487–494 (2004)
29. Shayne, B., Willis, C.: We Media: How Audiences are Shaping the Future of News and Information. Media Center at The American Press Institute, Reston (2003)
30. Vosecky, J., Leung, K.W.-T., Ng, W.: Collaborative personalized twitter search with topic-language models. In: SIGIR (2014)
31. Wan, X., Xiao, J.: Collabrank: towards a collaborative approach to single-document keyphrase extraction. In: COLING, pp. 969–976 (2008)
32. Wan, X., Xiao, J.: Single document keyphrase extraction using neighborhood knowledge. In: AAAI (2008)
33. Weng, J., Lim, E.-P., Jiang, J., He, Q.: Twitterrank: finding topic-sensitive influential twitterers. In: WSDM (2010)
34. Zhai, C.X.: Statistical Language Models for Information Retrieval. Synthesis Lectures on Human Language Technologies. Morgan & Claypool, San Rafael (2008)
35. Zhao, Y., Liang, S., Ren, Z., Ma, J., Yilmaz, E., de Rijke, M.: Explainable user clustering in short text streams. In: SIGIR, pp. 155–164 (2016)

Ranking Microblog Users via URL Biased Posts

Yongjun Ye[1,2], Peng Li[1,2(✉)], Rui Li[1,2], Meilin Zhou[1,2], Yifang Wan[1,2], and Bin Wang[1,2]

[1] Institute of Information Engineering, Chinese Academy of Sciences, Beijing, China
{yeyongjun,lipeng,lirui,zhoumeilin,wanyifang,wangbin}@iie.ac.cn
[2] University of Chinese Academy of Sciences, Beijing, China

Abstract. Finding high-quality users to follow is essential for acquiring information in microblogging systems. Measuring user's quality according to its published posts is effective but also needs a large computation considering the volume and the diversity of the posts. In this paper, we explore using only the posts with URLs, i.e., a subset ($\sim$20%) of the whole posts, for ranking microblog users and propose an iterative graph based ranking algorithm called UBRank to simultaneously rank users and URLs with the assumption that the importance of users and URLs can be mutually boosted. Experiments based on a Chinese microblog corpus demonstrate the effectiveness of the proposed approach.

Keywords: User quality measure · User behavior model · Graph based ranking

1 Introduction

Nowadays, microblogging service has become one of the most important information portals for the Web. It is estimated that 500 million messages[1] are published every day in Twitter.

According to the current system, people have to follow other users (called followees) to keep track of the recent information. The posts of the followees will completely determine the information presented. Identifying high quality users would not only help people to choose followees meeting their interests, but also benefit many applications such as recommendation and information filtering.

Existing works have studied the problem as identifying authority users [1]. However authority does not necessarily means "good" for information seekers. Authority users do provide high quality and credible information, but they may update information very rarely. Those high quality users should also act as information hubs, i.e., people can obtain various and relevant information by following them. The most natural way to measure user quality is to evaluate their posts directly, i.e., representing users by their posts. Previous work [2] has explored to use User-Tweet graph for user ranking, where all of the posts are considered as input. However, from the computation perspective, it may not be that efficient since many posts do not contain valuable information.

---

[1] http://www.internetlivestats.com/twitter-statistics/.

© Springer International Publishing AG 2016
W. Cellary et al. (Eds.): WISE 2016, Part II, LNCS 10042, pp. 85–93, 2016.
DOI: 10.1007/978-3-319-48743-4_7

In this paper, we explore using only posts with URLs (or posted URLs equally) for measuring user quality. Specifically, our contributions are as follows:

(1) We find that user's posts with URLs are good enough indicators for representing user quality.
(2) We propose to use posted URLs and the related user publish and retweet behaviors for computing user quality. On extracting these behavior data, we only use the posts with URLs as our input instead of all the posts.
(3) We propose a graph based ranking algorithm called UBRank which combines the authority factor and the hub factor together to measure user quality.

The rest of the paper is organized as follows: Sect. 2 introduces related works. Section 3 studies the quality of the posts with URLs and its advantage for representing user quality. Section 4 presents our proposed ranking algorithm. Experiments and evaluation results are provided in Sect. 5. We conclude our paper and discuss possible future work in Sect. 6.

2   Related Work

The most related works are about identifying influential users through using different kinds of information available in Twitter. Measuring user's influence is a well studied problem since the born of microblog [3–6]. Recent works attempt to make a detailed distinction, i.e., identifying topic specific influential users or topical experts [7–9]. In the above studies, influential uses are defined as people with certain authority within its social network [8]. However, none of the above works considered measuring user's importance as an information hub. One notable work is [2]. Specially, [2] construct a user-tweet graph which takes all the tweets into accounts. The number of user's tweets will affect user's quality score. Similar to [2], we evaluate user's quality by considering authority and hub factors simultaneously. The advantage of our work is that we build a more concise graph using only posted URLs, which can significantly accelerate the user evaluation process.

From the perspective of information types, the following relationship [1,2,7, 8], publish behavior [2], retweet behavior [1,2,5] and text contents of posts [1,5,8] have all been explored. The above studies all take the user following relationship into consideration for user ranking. Besides, Twitter Lists, which are contributed by micro-blog users, were also explored for finding topical authority [11] and it was found that they can yield more accurate prediction than the systems based on user's bio or tweet content, but the Lists information may not be that common.

From the perspective of methodology, existing studies on ranking users are mostly based on graph ranking algorithms such as PageRank (Page et al. [12]) and HITS (Klienberg et al. [13]). Different structure and iterative algorithm are proposed for different purposes [2,8,10]. Other methodology for finding topical users are based on prediction algorithm, which used many attributes for ranking user quality [1].

3   Analyzing Posts with URLs

3.1   Dataset Construction

We select Sina Weibo as our data source[2] and selected the top 10 seed users with the most followers and who tagged itself with Natural Language Processing (NLP) or Machine Learning (ML). Then expanded the seed users by their following relationship and filtered users by their tags. After filtering, we have got 3,122 users for statistical analysis. In this section, we try to keep as many users for statistical analysis while actually the most related tags are the top 10 tags, which corresponds to 1,073 users. For each user, we crawled the recent 6,000 posts at most. The final dataset contains 5,503,824 posts, for which the publish date range from 2009-08-14 to 2016-01-08.

3.2   Quality Study

The quality of a post is judged on a scale of 0–2 with 0 meaning irrelevant, 1 meaning relevant and 2 meaning "more relevant and interesting" (the criteria is similar to the criteria of NDCG in Information Retrieval Evaluation). The relevance is judged based on the post's topic to the publisher's tags. To label the quality, we sampled users and posts considering the huge volume.

Let Θ_{URL} be the mean average quality score across users for the posts with URLs; $\Theta_{\overline{URL}}$ be the corresponding mean average quality score for the posts without URLs. The null hypothesis is $H_0 : \Theta_{URL} = \Theta_{\overline{URL}}$ and the alternative hypothesis is $H_1 : \Theta_{URL} > \Theta_{\overline{URL}}$. Through manual labeling, we observed that $\Theta_{URL} = 0.93$ while $\Theta_{\overline{URL}} = 0.29$. We conducted the student's t-test and the Wilcoxon signed-rank test (the non-parametric form). Both results show that the null hypothesis is rejected, where $p = 1.6e^{-15}$ and $p = 4.1e^{-11}$ separately. This indicates that posts with URLs have higher quality than posts without URLs.

We further analyzed the average quality score against the number of followers. Figure 1 presents the scatter plot of average post score of each user.

Besides, we made a statistical description on the whole post set. The posts with URLs accounts for 20.8 % of the whole. Figure 2 presents the scatter plot of average retweet count for each user. Obviously, the posts with URLs have a larger retweet counts than the posts without URLs. This means it is easier to evaluate the quality of the posts with URLs than to evaluate the posts without URLs since they have more information available. Another interesting point in Fig. 2 is that the user who has got the largest average retweet count is not the user with the most followers. This shows that the number of user followers cannot fully determine the user's influence, which has been confirmed in [8].

---

[2] Sina Weibo is one of the most popular microblogging service in China.

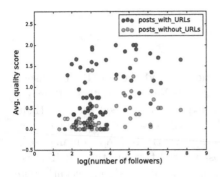

Fig. 1. Avg. quality score for the posts with (without) URLs vs. the number of followers

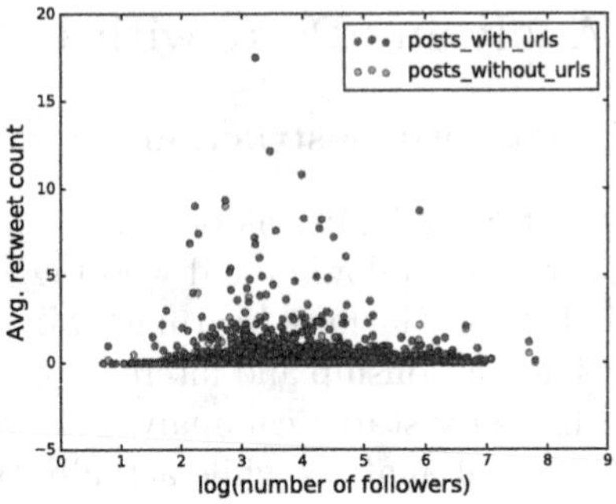

Fig. 2. Avg. retweet counts for the posts with (without) URLs vs. the number of followers

4   URL Biased User Rank (UBRank)

In this section, we describe our approach to calculate user quality score based on the publish behavior and retweet behavior.

4.1   Graph Construction

User-User Graph. Given the user collection $S = \{S_i \mid 1 \leq i \leq m\}$, the User-User graph is a directed graph where each user is considered as a node and a directed edge between two users is formed if one user retweet any post of another user. Specifically, if S_i retweets a post from $S_j(i \neq j)$, then we construct a directed edge from S_i to S_j, donated by $S_i \rightarrow S_j$. The weight from S_i to $S_j(i \neq j)$ is set to the number of total retweet counts from S_i to S_j, donated by $\sum S_i \rightarrow S_j$. For better formalization, we use an adjacency matrix U to represent weights between user pairs. $U = [U_{ij}]_{m \times m}$ is defined as follows:

$$U_{ij} = \begin{cases} \sum S_i \rightarrow S_j, & \text{if } i \neq j \\ 0, & \text{otherwise} \end{cases} \quad (1)$$

U can be normalized to $\widetilde{U}$ to make the sum of each row equal to 1:

$$\widetilde{U}_{ij} = \begin{cases} \sum S_i \rightarrow S_j \big/ outdegree(S_i), & \text{if } outdegree(S_i) \neq 0 \\ 0, & \text{otherwise} \end{cases} \quad (2)$$

User-URL Graph. Given the URL collection $T = \{T_i \mid 1 \leq i \leq n\}$ which are extracted from posts, the User-URL graph is an undirected graph where each URL and user is considered as a node. If user S_i posts or retweets a post with URL T_j, donated by $S_i \leftrightarrow T_j$, then we construct an undirected edge from S_i

to T_j. The weight for each edge is set to 1. We use an adjacency matrix V to represent weights for each edge. $V = [V_{ij}]_{m \times n}$ is defined as follows:

$$V_{ij} = \begin{cases} 1, & \text{if } S_i \leftrightarrow T_j \text{ exists} \\ 0, & \text{otherwise} \end{cases} \tag{3}$$

The weight from user to URL V is normalized to $\widetilde{V}$. The weight from URL to user, donated by V^T, can be normalized to $\widehat{V}$ in the same way.

4.2 Iterative Algorithm

Given the user quality score $v = [v(s_i)]_{m \times 1}$ and the URL quality score $\nu = [\nu(t_j)]_{n \times 1}$. The score of user is determined by the scores of its neighbor users and its posts. The corresponding matrix form is:

$$v = \alpha \widetilde{U}^T v + \beta \widehat{V}^T \nu, \quad \nu = \widetilde{V}^T v \tag{4}$$

where α and β determine the importance of quality scores contributed from the homogeneous nodes and the heterogeneous nodes respectively. $\alpha + \beta = 1$.

On constructing graph, the main differences between our work and TuRank [2] are as follows: (1) We model retweet action as user relation instead of post relation and we consider the join effect accumulated from each retweet instead of using retweet to measure each post quality. (2) We do not take user following relationship into the graph though they can be easily incorporated.

5 Experimental Evaluation

5.1 Methods for Comparison

To validate the effects of our proposed approach, we implemented the following methods for user ranking:

UBRank: As described in Sect. 4, UBRank focuses on the posts with URLs and is based on the User-User Graph and the User-URL Graph. The parameter α and β are both set to 0.5, as obtained by training.

RTRankU: This method constructs the User-User graph based on the retweet information of the posts with URLs and ignores the User-URL Graph.

RTRankA: This method constructs the User-User graph based on the retweet information of all the posts including the posts without URLs and ignores the User-URL Graph.

TuRank: TuRank takes following behavior, publish behavior and retweet behavior into consideration. Especially, the constructed graph contains all the post nodes and the reweet action is expressed as the relationship between posts. The edge weights for different relations are set to the values in [2].

TwitterRank: This model is a simplified version of work [8]. We skip the process of calculating user topics from posts, since our users are already picked up within a certain topic. This method constructs a User-User graph based on the following relationship.

Besides, we also implemented some heuristic methods for comparison.

Follower_Count: The users are ranked based on the number of followers.
URL_Count: The Users are ranked based on the number of its posted URLs.
URL_RT_Count: The users are ranked based on the number of total retweet counts of all the user's posts with URLs.
ALL_RT_Count: The users are ranked based on the number of total retweet counts of all the user's posts whether the post has URLs or not.

5.2 Evaluation Results

In this paper we take a similar paradigm for evaluation: we only consider the top ranked users of each method and manually label their quality. Specifically, top 10 users were selected for pooling as [1]. After the pooling, we have 46 unique users for labeling. To be fair for the compared methods, we use all the posts with or without URLs to evaluate user's quality.

Considering the large amount, we use stratified sampling to sample posts and then label their quality. This sampling paradigm is similar to statMAP procedure for IR evaluation. To measure the performance of each method, we use Kendall's τ as our evaluation metric as [8]. A large τ value means the rank is closer to the human judgment.

Effects of UBRank: The evaluation results are given in Table 1. Obviously, the proposed UBRank outperforms other baselines over all seven metrics. The advantage of using URL biased posts can also be seen by comparing RTRankU and RTRankA. Specifically, RTRankU only considers the posts with URLs while RTRankA considers all the posts on the graph construction. The rest of the process is the same for the two methods. The performance of RTRankU is better than RTRankA. The result is consistent with our finding that the posts with URLs have higher quality than the posts without URLs, for which the "vote" from the retweet of the posts without URLs is not that accurate for measuring user authority.

From Table 1, we can also find that the performance of RTRankA is comparable to the performance of TwitterRank, which indicates that the following relationship has almost the same effect for measuring user quality. The performance of TuRank is better than RTRankA and TwitterRank shows that by combining the following information and retweet information improvement can be achieved. The most effective information for evaluating user quality is the reweet action of the posts with URLs: RTRankU outperforms RTRankA, TwitterRank at the same time. This indicates that the retweet information based on the posts with URLs (URL biased) is the most effective beating the following

Table 1. Performances based on Top 10 users

Model	Kendall's τ
UBRank	**0.9449**
RTRankU	**0.8436**
RTRankA	0.8167
TuRank	**0.8680**
TwitterRank	0.8103
Follower_Count	0.6077
URL_Count	0.6474
URL_RT_Count	0.6436
ALL_RT_Count	0.618

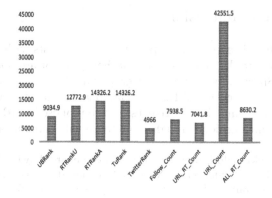

Fig. 3. Average post number

information and retweet information of all the posts on measuring user quality. Also, considering the quantity scale, the posts with URLs is a promising resource.

Table 2. List of top 10 users (with quality score)

UBRank(score)	RTRankA(score)	TuRank(score)	TwitterRank(score)
爱可可-爱生活(11,849)	爱可可-爱生活(11,849)	百度(455)	王斌_IIEIR(3,161)
好东西传送门(6,300)	百度(455)	爱可可-爱生活(11,849)	李航博士(1,172)
丕子(3,493)	199IT-互联网数据中心(465)	199IT-互联网数据中心(465)	唐杰THU(507)
1000sprites(3,919)	互联网分析沙龙(1,057)	互联网分析沙龙(1,057)	余凯_西二旗民工(810)
LR机器学习计算机视觉(2,308)	刘江总编(882)	刘江总编(882)	刘挺(583)
gootobe(2,880)	梁斌penny(1,389)	梁斌penny(1,389)	刘知远THU(3,058)
duin_shawe(3,018)	开源中国(4,206)	开源中国(4,206)	孙茂松(308)
数据娃掘-刘壮(1,709)	EMC中国研究院(1,886)	EMC中国研究院(1,886)	梁斌penny(1,389)
小诺_Noah(1,462)	CSDN云计算(871)	张栋_机器学习(2,024)	刘康_自动化所(1,512)
IBM_Huiwen_Watson(2,197)	张栋_机器学习(2,024)	CSDN云计算(871)	好东西传送门(6,300)

Table 2 present the top 10 users generated by different methods. The score here is the standard user quality score based on the human judgments. Specifically, UBRank can find users who may not be very famous but they do update high quality contents; RTRankU and RTRankA have similar results but different preferences for users; As we expected, TwitterRank can find authority users who are quite famous in the studied domain. The advantage of our UBRank is that it can find the users who may not be very famous offline but they accumulate many high quality contents (URLs) which are well accepted in the studied domain. An example is the user "1000sprites", who only appears in our top 10 results. He has only 119 followers, but the sum of its post quality is up to 3,919.

We also present the average number of the posts for the top 10 users (Fig. 3) generated by different methods. Obviously, our method UBRank is not aggressive to pick up the users with the most posts but with the posts at a moderate scale due to the consideration of post quality.

6   Conclusion

In this paper, we propose to use only posts with URLs to compute user quality, where the hub factor and authority factor are both important for measurement. Specifically, we propose a graph based iterative algorithm called UBRank to rank microblog users. Experiments demonstrate the advantage of using URL biased posts and the effectiveness of the proposed UBRank for measuring user quality, which achieves a high consistence with human judgments.

Acknowledgments. This work is supported by the National Natural Science Foundation of China (grant No. 61402466 and 61572494) and the Strategic Priority Research Program of the Chinese Academy of Sciences (grant No. XDA06030200).

References

1. Pal, A., Counts, S.: Identifying topical authorities in microblogs. In: Proceedings of the Fourth ACM International Conference on Web Search and Data Mining, pp. 45–54. ACM (2011)
2. Yamaguchi, Y., Takahashi, T., Amagasa, T., Kitagawa, H.: TURank: Twitter user ranking based on user-tweet graph analysis. In: Triantafillou, P., Suel, T., Chen, L. (eds.) WISE 2010. LNCS, vol. 6488, pp. 240–253. Springer, Heidelberg (2010)
3. Bakshy, E., Hofman, J.M., Mason, W.A., et al.: Everyone's an influencer: quantifying influence on Twitter. In: Proceedings of the Fourth ACM International Conference on Web Search and Data Mining, pp. 65–74. ACM (2011)
4. Lee, C., Kwak, H., Park, H., et al.: Finding influentials based on the temporal order of information adoption in Twitter. In: Proceedings of the 19th International Conferenceon World Wide Web, pp. 1137–1138. ACM (2010)
5. Romero, D.M., Galuba, W., Asur, S., Huberman, B.A.: Influence and passivity in social media. In: Gunopulos, D., Hofmann, T., Malerba, D., Vazirgiannis, M. (eds.) ECML PKDD 2011, Part III. LNCS, vol. 6913, pp. 18–33. Springer, Heidelberg (2011)
6. Cha, M., Haddadi, H., Benevenuto, F., et al.: Measuring user influence in Twitter: the million follower fallacy. ICWSM **10**(10–17), 30 (2010)
7. Tunkelang D.: A Twitter analog to pagerank. The Noisy Channel (2009)
8. Weng, J., Lim, E.P., Jiang, J., et al.: TwitterRank: finding topic-sensitive influential twitterers. In: Proceedings of the Third ACM International Conference on Web Search and Data Mining, pp. 261–270. ACM (2010)
9. Kong, S., Feng, L.: A tweet-centric approach for topic-specific author ranking in micro-blog. In: Tang, J., King, I., Chen, L., Wang, J. (eds.) ADMA 2011, Part I. LNCS, vol. 7120, pp. 138–151. Springer, Heidelberg (2011)
10. Gupta, P., Goel, A., Lin, J., et al.: WTF: the who to follow service at Twitter. In: International World Wide Web Conferences Steering Committee on Proceedings of the 22nd International Conference on World Wide Web, pp. 505–514 (2013)
11. Ghosh, S., Sharma, N., Benevenuto, F., et al.: Cognos: crowdsourcing search for topic experts in microblogs. In: Proceedings of the 35th International ACM SIGIR Conference on Research and Development in Information Retrieval, pp. 575–590. ACM (2012)

12. Suh, B., Hong, L., Pirolli, P., et al.: Want to be retweeted? Large scale analytics on factors impacting retweet in Twitter network. In: 2010 IEEE Second International Conference on Social Computing (SOCIALCOM), pp. 177–184. IEEE (2010)
13. Antoniades, D., Polakis, I., Kontaxis, G., et al.: we.b: The web of short URLs. In: Proceedings of the 20th International Conference on World Wide Web, pp. 715–724. ACM (2011)

Identifying Implicit Enterprise Users from the Imbalanced Social Data

Zhenni You, Tieyun Qian[(✉)], Baochao Zhang, and Shi Ying

State Key Laboratory of Software Engineering, Wuhan University, Wuhan, China
{znyou,qty,bczhang,yingshi}@whu.edu.cn

Abstract. Identifying the implicit enterprise users in social media enables the improvement of data quality for many applications like user profiling and targeted advertisement, as they register as ordinary users but act like enterprise ones and hence become the noises in the data. The recognition of implicit enterprise users confronts two challenges: (1) it needs to be handled quickly with little cost due to the very nature of preprocessing, and (2) it is necessary to deal with the highly skewed distribution of implicit enterprise users and ordinary users, which is about 1:10 in a social media site Sina Weibo in China. To the best of our knowledge, this problem is so far unexplored.

In this paper, we present an efficient class-imbalance learning framework which involves several types of new features from the users' profile. Specifically, a cost sensitive learning strategy is designed to overcome the problem arising from the skewed data, and a set of novel features are extracted from the profile rather than the main contents to greatly reduce the overhead of crawling and processing the microblogs. We conduct extensive experiments on a real data set consisting of 2200 users (2000 ordinary users and 200 implicit enterprise users, respectively) in Sina Weibo. The results demonstrate that our method significantly outperforms the baselines by a large margin.

Keywords: User classification · Implicit enterprise users · Feature extraction · Imbalanced data

1 Introduction

There are a special group of enterprise users in social media like Sina Weibo in China, who register as *ordinary users* (OUs) but act like enterprise ones. In other words, the account is mainly used for brand or product promotion rather than the personal interaction with other people. We call this kind of users as *implicit enterprise users* (IEUs). Although Sina Weibo defines a special user type, known as Blue V, which we call them *explicit enterprise users* (EEUs), many small enterprises do not choose to be verified as the Blue V users due to the strict or long verification procedure. They still register as ordinary users and become implicit enterprise users. The account of an implicit enterpriser user can stand for an object like a shop, a company, or a society rather than a human

© Springer International Publishing AG 2016
W. Cellary et al. (Eds.): WISE 2016, Part II, LNCS 10042, pp. 94–101, 2016.
DOI: 10.1007/978-3-319-48743-4_8

being. It will be harmful if we include implicit enterpriser users into the corpus when doing user profiling or demographic analysis [3,5,6,11]. Thus it is necessary to eliminate the implicit enterprise users before starting such tasks. In this paper, we treat it as a two-class classification problem, one for implicit enterprise users and the other for ordinary users.

Due to the similarity to the EEUs (Blue V), the IEUs can be recognized by simply using a set of high-frequency words like "company", "center", and "community". However, our preliminary investigation finds that many IEUs do not follow this rule. For example, a user with the name of 'the alliance of dream chasing" is a ordinary user while another username "Feeling the beauty of painting" looks like a nickname of a sentimental person, but it actually belongs to an implicit enterprise user. We will show in the experiment part that the performance of such a straight-forward approach is quite poor. Moreover, by analyzing the application scenario of the task of implicit enterprise user, we find that (1) this task is usually regarded as a preprocessing component and needs to be handled quickly with little cost, and (2) the ratio of IEUs to OUs is highly skewed, i.e., about 1/10 in a sample we investigate.

Based on the above observations, we present an efficient class-imbalance learning framework which involves several types of new features extracted from the users' profile. In particular, a cost sensitive learning strategy is designed to overcome the problem incurred by the skewed data, and the profile features rather than the content features are used to greatly save the time overhead of crawling and processing the microblogs.

The contributions of this paper are as follows:

1. We present a first-of-a-kind problem for detecting implicit enterprise users who are a special type of noises in social media.
2. We extract a set of new features from the user profile which capture the intrinsic properties of the implicit enterprise users.
3. We design an efficient class-imbalance learning framework for accurately recognizing the implicit enterprise users.

2   Related Work

Real word data are usually imbalanced, i.e. some classes have much more samples than others. The imbalanced learning problem has drawn a great amount of studies [4,12]. The most commonly used approach is the sampling method which alters the sizes of training sets. More sophisticated sampling like SMOTE [1] carefully create artificial data considering the relationship between examples. The cost-sensitive learning considers the costs associated with misclassifying examples [8,9]. It uses different weights to represent the costs for misclassifying any samples in the data. Overall, the cost-sensitive learning is more efficient and is often superior to sampling methods in terms of classification performance. Hence we adopt it to solve our problem.

Spammer detection is another related field to our study. Finding good features is a main focus in this area. Most of existing studies used the content features including duplicate reviews [2,10], the urls [15], the posting relations [13], profile features such as the ratio of sent/acceptance invitation [14]. In general, the features useful for spammer detection may be ineffective in recognizing enterprise user. In this paper, we present a number of new features for effectively recognizing implicit enterprise users.

3   Overall Framework for Identifying Implicit Enterprise Users in Imbalanced Data

3.1   Novel Profile Features

Sina Weibo allows users to register their basic information in the profile and post microblogs in his/her homepage. Developers are provided with APIs to access the profile and microblogs. Normally, the profile information is easier to get than the microblogs since it costs much more requests to access the microblogs. If we can remove most of the implicit enterprise users merely using the profile information, the resources will be greatly saved for later processing. For the fast identification of implicit enterprise users, we use features from the profile instead of using features from microblogs.

We extract six types of features from users' profiles. The privacy features reflect whether the user would disclose his/her personal information such as blood type and profession to the public. The contact features measure the degree to which the user would connect to the others. The personalized features describe users' tags and description. The status features are assigned by Sina, which record how frequently a user logs into the system. Both the friend constitution and character n-gram features are proposed to analyze how the user's screenname and interests are related to different types of users.

3.2   Class-Imbalance Learning Approach

After extracting the profile features, each user can be represented as a vector in the designated feature space. We then follow a class-imbalance learning framework for detecting the implicit enterprise users in the imbalanced social data.

The objective of class-imbalance learning is to improve the identification performance on the minor (positive) class. By associating the positive samples with a higher value, the cost sensitive learning denotes a higher importance of correctly identifying these samples. Since the cost sensitive learning only changes the weight for each sample in the data set, it can be combined with any supervised learning algorithms such as support vector machine (SVM) or logistic regression (LR). SVM needs a careful tuning to reach high performance. In contrast, LR is less sensitive to the parameters and is more efficient than SVM in most of the cases. Hence we use LR as our classifier.

We briefly describe the basic concepts in two-class LR classification. Let $L = \{(x_i, y_i)\}$ (i = 1..N) be a set of training samples, where each $x_i \in R^n$ is the feature vector of user u_i; y_i is a class label in Y = {0,1}. The logistic regression assumes the following probability model: $P(y|x, w, b) = \frac{1}{1+e^{-y(w^T x+b)}}$, where $w \in R^n$ and $b \in R$ are the parameters of the model. For a simpler derivation, we omit the bias term b and represent $[w^T; b]$ as $[w^T]$, and then the model is defined as:

$$P(y|x, w) = \frac{1}{1 + e^{-y(w^T x)}} \tag{1}$$

To solve the problem is to find parameters fitting well for the training data. Usually the parameters are estimated using the likelihood function $\prod_{i=1}^{N} P(y_i|x_i, w)$. It can be transformed to maximize the log-likelihood function, which is defined as:

$$\max_{w} L(w) = -\sum_{i=1}^{N} log(1 + e^{-y_i * (w^T x_i)}) \tag{2}$$

It can be further transformed into the dual problem to minimize the negative log-likelihood:

$$\min_{w} f(w) = \sum_{i=1}^{N} log(1 + e^{-y_i(w^T x_i)}) \tag{3}$$

In order to enhance the generalization ability, we add a L_2 regularization factor on $f(w)$. The objective for LR on balanced data is defined as:

$$\min_{w} f_b(w) = (\frac{1}{2}w^T w + \lambda \sum_{i=1}^{N} log(1 + e^{-y_i(w^T x_i)})) \tag{4}$$

where λ is a parameter to balance the two terms in Eq. 4.

Suppose that we have $L^+ = \{(x_i, y_i)\}$ (i = 1..N^+) and $L^- = \{(x_j, y_j)\}$ (j = 1..N^-) minor and major samples, respectively. For a class-imbalance problem where $N^+ \ll N^-$, we need differentiate the samples in the minor and major class. Hence we associate a weight of cost item $c_i \in [0, r]$ for each training example in L^+ and L^-. For simplicity, we assign the same costs to all the minor (major) samples. The objective for LR on imbalanced data is then defined as:

$$\min_{w,b} f_i(w) = (\frac{1}{2}w^T w + \alpha \sum_{i=1}^{N^+} log(1 + e^{-y_i(w^T x_i)}) + \beta \sum_{j=1}^{N^-} log(1 + e^{-y_j(w^T x_j)})) \tag{5}$$

where α and β is the cost for minor and major samples, respectively.

Both Eqs. 4 and 5 are the optimization problem and can be solved by a number of approaches like gradient descent or Newton method. In this paper, we adopt the Newton method. The detailed steps for the overall framework for class-imbalance learning are given in Algorithm 1.

In Algorithm 1, line 1 initializes the variables. Lines 2 to 8 are used to update the parameters in an iterative way. Line 9 assigns the parameters using the values returned from the last round. Line 10 computes the probability of y_i for t_i. Lines 11 to 15 finish the class label assignments for test samples.

Algorithm 1. $IEUFinder^{imb}$

Require: the minor and major training data set $L+$ and $L-$, a test data set $T = \{t_1, t_2, ...t_n\}$, the objective function $f_i(w)$, the gradient $g(w) = \triangledown f_i(w)$, the Hessian matrix $H(w)$ of $f_i(w)$, the termination criterion ε.
Ensure: the class label assignment for each t_i in T.
 1: Initialize w^0, $g_0 = g(w^0)$, set $k = 0$
 2: **while** $||g_k|| >= \varepsilon$ **do**
 3:    Compute $g_k = g(w^k)$
 4:    Compute $H_k = H(w^k)$
 5:    Compute $s_k = -H_k{}^{-1}g_k$
 6:    $w^{k+1} = w^k + s_k$
 7:    $k = k + 1$
 8: **end while**
 9: $w = w^k$
10: Compute the probability for t_i using equation Eq. 1.
11: **if** $P(y = 0|t_i, w) > P(y = 1|t_i, w)$ **then**
12:    $y(t_i) = 0$
13: **else**
14:    $y(t_i) = 1$
15: **end if**

---

4 Experimental Evaluation

4.1 Experiment Setup

We conducted experiments on a real data set from Sina Weibo. It contains 200 IEUs and 2000 OUs, respectively. We conduct 5 fold cross-validation. The results are averaged over five folds. We report the F1 score for the minor class as the evaluation metric. Since no existing works are tailed for our task, we propose the following six baselines for comparison.

(1) *MatchBV*: We sort the character n-grams (n = 2, 3) of the screennames of Blue V users in descending order, and then choose a certain percent of character n-grams to match the screenname in the test set. If matched, then we label the test data as an implicit enterprise user.

(2) *MatchOU*: We sort the character n-grams (n = 2, 3) of the screennames of ordinary users in descending order, and then choose a certain percent of character n-grams to match the screenname in the test set. If matched, then we label the test data as an ordinary user.

(3) *NaiveBayes(NB)*: We first calculate the probability of each character n-gram (n = 2,3) in Blue V and ordinary users. Then we sum the probability values of all the character n-grams in one user's screenname. The user is assigned a label with a larger value.

(4) $IEUFinder^{bal}$: We use the same profile features as those used in $IEUFinder^{imb}$. The model is also the logistic regression with L2 regularization. The only difference is that $IEUFinder^{bal}$ does not distinguish the costs for samples in minor and major classes, i.e., $\alpha = \beta = 1$.

(5) *SplitData*: We apply the under-sampling strategy on the data, i.e., the samples in the major class are randomly split into n parts. Then a LR with L2 regularization classifier is applied to each partition. Finally the results from the n classifiers are further ensembled to get better performance [7].

(6) *SplitFeature*: We apply under-sampling strategy on the features. All the other settings are similar with *SplitData*.

Please note that the first four baselines are classic learning methods and the last two baselines are class-imbalance learning.

4.2 Effects of Cost Items

We then evaluate the performance of $IEUFinder^{imb}$ by varying the ratio of cost item α (for minor class) to β (for major class). The results are shown in Fig. 1. The left and right sub-figures show the effects of cost items for $\alpha > \beta$ and $\alpha < \beta$, respectively.

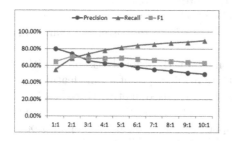 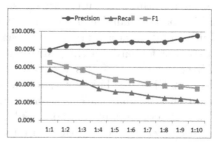

Fig. 1. Effects of cost items α and β

It is clear that setting high cost weight on major class (the right sub-figure) severely damages the performance. The F1 curve is very steep, its value decreasing from 64.88 % to 36.77 %. In contrast, the F1 curve in the left sub-figure is steady. Overall, with the increase ratio of α:β ($\alpha > \beta$), the recall continuously ascends and the precision descends. This is intuitive as more users are recognized as IEUs with larger weight on minor class. The best F1 value (70.71 %) is got when α:β is set to 2:1, showing a 5.83 % improvement over the start point. In the following, we will use α:$\beta = 2$:1 as our default setting.

4.3 Comparison with Baselines

We now compare our proposed algorithm $IEUFinder^{imb}$ with the six baselines. The results are presented in Table 1. For *MatchBV* and *MatchOU*, we select the top 0.001, 0.005, 0.01, 0.05, 1, 5, and 10 percent of high frequency words from the EEUs and the OUs, respectively, for matching the test cases, and then select the best results for comparison. For *SplitData* and *SplitFeature*, we also vary n from 1 to 10 and present their best results.

Table 1. Comparison with baselines

Approaches	Precision	Recall	F1
MatchBV	22.57	66.50	33.68
MatchOU	10.97	96.00	19.68
NB	24.17	81.00	37.16
IEUFinder^{bal}	80.21	55.50	64.88
SplitData	45.46	87.50	59.24
SplitFeature	45.00	88.50	59.13
IEUFinder^{imb}	**74.28**	**69.00**	**70.71**

We have the following important notes.

- The F1 score for *MatchOU* is only 19.68 %, the worst among all methods. This is because many of the character n-grams in the ordinary users are widely used. They can be easily matched by both implicit enterprise users and ordinary users, resulting in all users are classified as ordinary ones.
- *NB* is better than *MatchBV* and *MatchOU*. This infers that using the distribution of character n-grams in the screenname is more reasonable than using a straight-forward matching strategy.
- *IEUFinder*^{bal} performs the best among four traditional baselines with a 64.88 % F1 score. This suggests that the multiple types of profile features are more effective than the character n-gram features used in other three baselines.
- Two under-sampling methods *SplitData* and *SplitFeature* are worse than *IEUFinder*^{bal}, showing that an improper class-imbalance learning approach may hurt the performance. Another finding is that while their F1 scores are worse than that of *IEUFinder*^{imb}, their recall values are much higher. This is intuitive because when the data or features are split, the gap between the size of the minor and major class is reduced. Hence samples in minor class are easier to be found.
- *IEUFinder*^{imb} is the best. It is much better than all four classic learning approaches, and it also significantly outperforms two under-sampling methods, showing a huge increase on F1. This clearly demonstrates that our cost sensitive learning approach is very effective in dealing with the introduced imbalanced learning problem.

5   Conclusion

We introduce a new research problem of identifying implicit enterprise users in social media. This problem is expected to be solved efficiently in a skewed data distribution. To this end, we present a class imbalance learning framework which involves several types of new features extracted from users' profile. The cost-sensitive classification is effective in handling imbalanced data. By using the profile features rather than the content ones, we greatly save the costs in crawling and processing the microblogs. We conduct extensive experiments on a real data set. Results demonstrate that our proposed method is very effective in recognizing implicit enterprise users. It also significantly outperforms all the baselines with a large margin.

We wish this study will initiate the research of the noise removal in the area of social media processing. In the future, we plan to explore more features to further improve the performance and compare our problem with the task of spammer detection to see if they can be put into a unified framework.

Acknowledgements. The work described in this paper has been supported in part by the NSFC projects (61572376, 61272275, 61373038), and the 111 project (B07037).

References

1. Chawla, N., Bowyer, K., Hall, L., Kegelmeyer, W.: Smote: synthetic minority over-sampling technique. J. Artif. Intell. Res. **16**, 321–357 (2002)
2. Chen, C., Wu, K., Srinivasan, V., Zhang, X.: Battling the internet water army: detection of hidden paid posters. In: Proceedings of ASONAM, pp. 116–120 (2013)
3. Filippova, K.: User demographics and language in an implicit social network. In: Proceedings of EMNLP, pp. 1478–1488 (2012)
4. He, H., Garcia, E.A.: Learning from imbalanced data. TKDE **21**(9), 1263–1284 (2009)
5. Kosinski, M., Stillwell, D., Graepel, T.: Private traits and attributes are predictable from digital records of human behavior. PNAS **110**, 5802–5805 (2013)
6. Li, J., Ritter, A., Hovy, E.: Weakly supervised user profile extraction from Twitter. In: Proceedings of ACL, pp. 165–174 (2014)
7. Liu, X.Y., Wu, J., Zhou, Z.H.: Exploratory under-sampling for class-imbalance learning. In: Proceedings of ICDM, pp. 965–969 (2006)
8. Liu, X.Y., Zhou, Z.H.: Training cost-sensitive neural networks with methods addressing the class imbalance problem. TKDE **18**, 63–77 (2006)
9. McCarthy, K., Zabar, B., Weiss, G.: Does cost-sensitive learning beat sampling for classifying rare classes? In: Proceedings of International Workshop Utility-Based Data Mining, pp. 69–77 (2005)
10. Mukherjee, A., Kumar, A., Liu, B., Wang, J., Hsu, M., Castellanos, M., Ghosh, R.: Spotting opinion spammers using behavioral footprints. In: Proceedings of KDD, pp. 632–640 (2013)
11. Nguyen, D., Trieschnigg, D., Doğruöz,, A.S., Grave, R., Theune, M., Meder, T., de Jong, F.: Why gender and age prediction from tweets is hard: lessons from a crowdsourcing experiment. In: Proceedings of COLING, pp. 1950–1961 (2014)
12. Sun, Y., Kamel, M.S., Wong, A.K., Wang, Y.: Cost-sensitive boosting for classification of imbalanced data. Pattern Recogn. **40**, 3358–3378 (2007)
13. Wu, F., Shu, J., Huang, Y., Yuan, Z.: Social spammer and spam message co-detection in microblogging with social context regularization. In: Proceedings of the 24th ACM International on Conference on Information and Knowledge Management, pp. 1601–1610 (2015)
14. Yang, Z., Wilson, C., Wang, X., Gao, T., Zhao, B.Y., Dai, Y.: Uncovering social network sybils in the wild. ACM Trans. Knowl. Discov. Data **8**, 2 (2014)
15. Zhang, X., Li, Z., Zhu, S., Liang, W.: Detecting spam and promoting campaigns in Twitter. ACM Trans. Web **10**(1), 4:1–4:28 (2016)

Microblog Data Analysis

Understanding Factors That Affect Web Traffic via Twitter

Chunjing Xiao[1,2,3](✉), Zhiguang Qin[2], Xucheng Luo[2],
and Aleksandar Kuzmanovic[3]

[1] School of Computer and Information Engineering,
Henan University, Kaifeng, China
chunjingxiao@gmail.com
[2] School of Information and Software Engineering, UESTC, Chengdu, China
{qinzg,xucheng}@uestc.edu.cn
[3] Department of EECS, Northwestern University, Evanston, USA
akuzma@cs.northwestern.edu

Abstract. Currently, millions of companies, organizations and individuals take advantage of the social media function of Twitter to promote themselves. One of the most important goals is to attract web traffic. In this paper, we study the problem of obtaining web traffic via Twitter. We approach this problem in two stages. First, we analyze the correlation between important factors and the click number of URLs in tweets. Through measurements, we find that the commonly accepted method, increasing followers by reciprocal exchanges of links, has limited effects on improving the number of clicks. And characteristics of tweets (such as the presence of hashtags and tweet length) exert different impacts on users with different influence levels for obtaining the click number. In our second stage, based on the analyses, we introduce the Multi-Task Learning (MTL) to build a model for predicting the number of clicks. This model takes into account the specific characters of users with different influence levels to improve the predictive accuracy. The experiments, based on Twitter data, show the predictive performance is significantly higher than the baseline.

Keywords: Popularity · Prediction · Web traffic · Twitter

1 Introduction

Web traffic is one of the key indicators of a website's success, and most of individuals and companies rank websites mainly on the basis of their web traffic, such as the well-known Alexa[1]. Thus, website owners constantly strive to increase their web traffic by implementing various strategies, such as advertisements or audience analyses. The popularity of Twitter provides a new mean of promoting websites. In fact, Twitter has become new influential media for information sharing [18]. Thus, millions of organizations, companies, and individuals register

---

[1] http://www.alexa.com/.

© Springer International Publishing AG 2016
W. Cellary et al. (Eds.): WISE 2016, Part II, LNCS 10042, pp. 105–120, 2016.
DOI: 10.1007/978-3-319-48743-4_9

accounts on that and publish their URLs to attract web traffic, and Twitter has been a beneficial platform for a number of the websites [3, 21].

Although the capability of Twitter to generate web traffic is widely accepted, little work focuses on examining the factors that affect obtaining web traffic via Twitter, and a serial of questions in this field keep unknown. For example, the previous work shows that the number of followers does not necessarily reflect their influence in terms of retweets or mentions [8], however, the reason is still unknown. To increase the follower number, users may randomly follow others in the hope that they follow back [23], and this phenomenon is called reciprocal links by Ghosh et al. [12]. Whereas it is not clear whether these types of followers can enhance content diffusion. In addition, there is a need to understand how hashtags and mentions in tweets impact the click number of URLs and whether these factors have the predictive power of the click number.

Our approach to answering these questions begins with an extensive characterization of important affecting factors, such as the follower number, presences of hashtags and mentions, as well as tweet length. To understand the impact of followers, we analyze the correlation between the numbers of clicks and followers, and find their correlation is not as strong as expected, which is consistent with the finding in [8]. However, the difference in the numbers of followers and reciprocal links has an obviously higher coefficient of correlation with the number of clicks. Therefore, reciprocal links are a key reason why the number of user followers does not necessarily reflect their influence in terms of the click number. And our further analyses also show reciprocal links have limited effects on content diffusion, although it is widely used to increase the number of followers.

Besides, we exploit the effect of tweet characteristics on the click number, such as the presences of hashtags and mentions and tweet length. And we find that the correlation between the number of clicks and these characteristics exhibits different trends for users with different influence levels (Here the influence level is measured by the difference between the numbers of followers and reciprocal links). Specifically, in terms of hashtags, URLs in tweets with hashtags obtain more clicks for users with low influence, but less for users with high influence. And for tweet length, when tweets have 50 and 120 characters, their URLs attract a similar maximum number of clicks for users with low influence. However, it is hardly affected by tweet length for users with high influence.

The second part of work for answering these questions is to conduct prediction about the number of clicks. Because the above analyses show that hashtags, mentions and tweet length exert different effects on users with different influence levels for obtaining the number of clicks, the model should take into account these different effects to improve predictive performance. To this end, we cast the predictive problem as a Multi-Task Learning (MTL) problem.

Specifically, we build a SVM+MTL model to predict the number of clicks. In this model, users are placed into different groups based on their influence levels, and each group is treated as a task. The model considers both the common properties of all the users and specific characters of users with different influence levels to improve predictive performance. Based on the Twitter data, the experiment results show the accuracy of our model is significantly higher than the baseline.

2   Related Work

There is little work focusing on the number of clicks on Twitter, however, the number of clicks, to some extent, can be a measure of popularity. Therefore, our work is related to the fields of popularity, which mainly consist of two threads of work: analyzing factors that affect popularity and predicting popularity in social media.

For the analyses of affecting factors, Suh *et al.* [24] examine a number of features that might affect the retweets. They find that URLs, hashtags and the numbers of followers and friends affect the retweets. Comarela *et al.* [10] identify factors that influence user response or retweet probability. They find that some basic textual characteristics, such as message size and the presence of hashtags, mentions and URLs, affect the replies or retweets. Liu *et al.* [20] evaluates eleven extrinsic factors that may influence the response rate in social question and answering from Sina Weibo. They show that the features, such as the number of followers, frequency of posting, hashtags and emotion, can be used to predict the number of responses. Apart from microblogs, Khosla *et al.* [16] and Bakhshi *et al.* [4] study the important factors that impact the popularity of images and quality of reviews respectively. Compared with these studies, we, beyond analyzing basic factors, explore the reason of existed phenomenons, and study whether tweet characteristics (such as hashtags, mentions and tweet length) exert different impacts on URLs in tweets of users with different influence.

For the popularity prediction, the studies fall into two main genres: conducting prediction before and after content publication. For the former, because the distribution of cascade sizes is very skewed, predicting the exact number of cascade sizes remain relatively unreliable [5]. Hence, rather than predicting exact integer values, most of the researchers define several categories to represent the popularity levels and predict which categories contents will belong to. For example, Hong *et al.* [13] define several categories to represent popularity of tweets and use logistic regression to predict the categories of tweets. Jenders *et al.* [15] predict whether a given tweet will be more frequently retweeted than a certain threshold. They firstly analyze the correlation between the retweet frequency and user features, and then they use the probabilistic models to conduct prediction. Vasconcelos *et al.* [27] categorize reviews into various popularity levels and predict the levels using multivariate linear regression and SVM models.

To achieve higher accuracy of prediction, many studies predict popularity after content publication. In this case, the early number of retweets or views within a short period after content publication can be used for prediction. Some work uses the early information to predict the exact integer values. For example, Szabo *et al.* [25] find the early number of retweets or views is strongly correlated with the later number on Digg and YouTube, and predict the popularity of content based on this finding. Kupavskii *et al.* [17] and Bao *et al.* [7] improve the performance of popularity prediction by exploiting the features of the cascade flow and structural characteristics respectively And Zhao *et al.* [28] develop a self-exciting Point Process Model to predict tweet popularity.

Other work still uses the early information to predict the categories which represent the popularity levels. For example, Gao *et al.* [11] predict whether a tweet will be popular based on temporal features of first 10 retweets using the bagged decision trees model. Given a cascade that currently has size k, Cheng *et al.* [9] predict whether it grow beyond the median size 2k by using the temporal and structural features. They use a variety of learning methods, including logistic regression classifier, naive Bayes and SVM for the prediction.

The method of popularity prediction after content publication generally achieves better performance than that of before content publication, but it is still crucial for the prediction before content publication. Because (*i*) publishers always want to know popularity of their contents before publication, (*ii*) and this method can clearly measure the importance of static factors in affecting popularity. Therefore, we conduct prediction before content publication. And our MTL-based predictive model is built based on our findings. To the best of our knowledge, we are the first to predict popularity using MTL.

3   Data Description

3.1   Background of URL Clicks

In this section, we present information about clicks of short URLs. Due to the limitation of tweet length, users tend to publish shortened URLs on Twitter. Therefore, the service of shortening long URLs is provided by many companies, and Bitly is among the most popular ones. Furthermore, Bitly APIs[1] provide the information about the click number of URLs in tweets. These number can be classified into two types: the *exact click number* referring to the number of clicks from a given tweet of the user; the *global click number* referring to the number of clicks from all the domains and platforms, including Twitter, Facebook and so on. For these two kinds of numbers, the exact click number can be considered as the ability of the tweet to attract web traffic. Therefore, the exact click number are used as the standard for analyzing factors that affect web traffic via Twitter. And the global click number can be used to reflect the popularity of the tweet content, and will be used as one of the features to predict the exact click number. Below the click number will refer to the exact click number for simplicity.

3.2   Twitter Data

As our goal is to analyze users who are aiming to attract web traffic via Twitter, we need to select users who tend to publish tweets with short URLs. In our study, we only select short URLs hosted by Bitly, because their exact click number can be obtained, and they are the most popular ones, taking about 50 % of all the URLs in Twitter [3].

---

[1] http://dev.bitly.com/api.html.

To select targeted users, we firstly extract domains hosted by Bitly based on a random sample of public tweets (around 790 million) collected by Twitter streaming APIs. And we obtain 6,524 domains hosted by Bitly, including many well-known companies and organizations, such as nyti.ms (New York Times), wapo.st (Washington Post) and es.pn (ESPN). Secondly, from these 790 m tweets, we extract the users whose language is English and whose tweets include at least one short URL hosted by Bitly. Base on this, we further select users who tend to publish Bitly URLs and tend to increase their websites via Twitter. According to these rules, we select users whose ratios of Bitly URLs are more than 50 %, and whose domain focuses are more than 50 %. Here the domain focus is defined as the degree of short URLs redirecting to the same domain, and can be calculated as follows: $D_i = \frac{1}{V_i} \max_k v_{ik}$, where V_i refers to the summary of URLs of user i, and v_{ik} refers to the number of URLs with the domain k of user i. If all the URLs published by a user redirect to one domain, its domain focus will be 1. Finally, 214,293 users are selected as our targeted users.

For these selected users, by Twitter APIs, we download their profiles, followers, and friends, as well as their tweets during June 2014, as shown in Table 1. And by Bitly APIs, we collect the click information of short URLs extracted from these tweets.

Table 1. Summary of Twitter data

Number of users	214,293
Number of follower links	1,261,721,039
Number of friend links	180,803,547
Number of tweets	46,286,824
Number of short URLs	34,338,613

4   Analyses of Affecting Factors

We firstly describe the effect of user followers and tweet characteristics on the click number. The results in the section are the foundation for the predictive method, which is presented later.

4.1   The Role of User Followers

The number of followers is frequently used to gauge influence or reputation of users [14,23], and compare to other criterions, such as the number of retweets and mentions [8,18]. Therefore, we first analyze how the number of followers is correlated with the number of clicks received by URLs in tweets.

Figure 1(a) shows the correlation between the numbers of followers and URL clicks. The X-axis is the number of user followers, and the Y-axis is the sum of

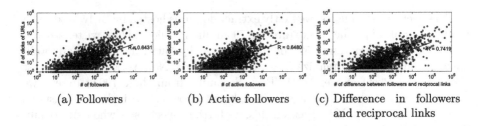

(a) Followers   (b) Active followers   (c) Difference in followers
                                                               and reciprocal links

Fig. 1. The correlation between the numbers of followers and clicks

the number of clicks. This figure shows that the coefficient of linear correlation, 0.64, is not as high as expected. This finding is consistent with the previous work, which shows that popular users with a high number of followers do not necessarily have high influence in terms of retweets or mentions [8] and the global click number of short URLs [22].

This observation raises the question why the number of followers is not very strongly correlated with the number of clicks. To address this question, we conduct analyses from two perspectives. (*i*) How do inactive followers affect the relationship between the numbers of followers and clicks? Thomas *et al.* [26] show that numerous accounts on Twitter have been suspended because of spamming issues or similar reasons. Moreover, some users tend to register multiple accounts but use only a part of them or stop using Twitter. We, therefore, attempt to evaluate the correlation between the numbers of active followers and clicks to analyze the effect of inactive followers. (*ii*) How do reciprocal links affect the relationship of the number of followers and clicks? On Twitter, a part of users randomly follow other users in the hope that they will follow back, whereas, some users join groups in which each member agrees to follow all of the other members in that group [23]. This phenomenon, which is called the reciprocal links by Ghosh *et al.* [12], is a way to increase one's number of followers, and users are recommended to increase their followers through this way to gain more web traffic [1]. However, whether these reciprocal links increase the diffusion effect of content remains unclear. Therefore, we attempt to explore the correlation between the numbers of reciprocal links and clicks to answer these questions.

To analyze the effect of inactive followers, we first identify whether a user is active. In general, Twitter regard users who log in at least once a month as active ones [2]. However, considering that we cannot obtain information about logging in activities, we regard users who publish at least one tweet, including any kind of tweets such as retweets and replies, within the last two months as active ones. After collecting the recent tweets by Twitter APIs, we can compute the active followers for each user. Further, the correlation between the numbers of active followers and clicks is plotted in Fig. 1(b). The coefficient of correlation, 0.6480, is nearly the same as that of the numbers of followers and clicks. We also analyze the correlation between numbers of active followers and all followers, and find that a strong linear relationship exists between them. These results suggest that inactive followers are not the main reason behind the moderate relationship between the number of followers and clicks.

For reciprocal links, we first collect the follower and friend list of each user, and then compute the intersection between the follower set and the friend set. This intersection is regarded as the reciprocal links. Based on this data, the correlation between the number of clicks and the difference in followers and reciprocal links is calculated, as shown in Fig. 1(c). Compared with Fig. 1(a) and 1(b), the points in Fig. 1(c) are centered around the straight line and a stronger correlation exists between the number of clicks and the difference in followers and reciprocal links. The coefficient, 0.7419, is approximately 10 % higher than that of followers and clicks. These results indicate that reciprocal links considerably affect the correlation between numbers of followers and clicks. And when reciprocal links are removed, the number of followers becomes more strongly correlated with the number of clicks.

To further evaluate the effect of reciprocal links in improving the number of clicks, we analyze the correlation between reciprocal links and clicks, as well as the correlation between reciprocal links and friends. the coefficient of the former, 0.1632, indicates that reciprocal links are not significantly correlated with clicks. The coefficient of the later is 0.9125, suggesting that most of the friends originate from reciprocal links.

Therefore, based on these analyses, we conclude that although reciprocal links are widespread to be used to increase the number of followers, they have limited effects on improving the number of clicks. And the difference of followers and reciprocal links can be a better measure of user influence. Hence, below this difference is regarded as the measure of user influence (levels), and user followers refer to this difference except Sect. 5.2.

4.2 The Role of Tweet Characteristics

In this section, we analyze the impact of two kinds of tweet characteristics on the click number of URLs: tweet types (i.e., the presences of hashtags and mentions in tweets) and tweet length.

Tweet Types. On Twitter, tweets contain two widely used objects: hashtags and mentions. The former is used to mark keywords or topics in a tweet and to categorize messages, whereas the latter is a form of conversation on Twitter. Users are often encouraged to include hashtags to increase the click number of URLs on some web pages, such as [1]. Therefore, we explore how tweets that contain hashtags or mentions affect the number of clicks.

For this purpose, we group the tweets into four types: *hashtag tweets*, which are tweets that include at least one hashtag; *mention tweets*, which are tweets that include at least one mention; *hashtagMention tweets*, which are tweets that include both hashtags and mentions; and *normal tweets*, which are tweets without hashtags and mentions. To avoid any preference for users who tend (not) to publish more hashtag or mention tweets, we also analyze users with at least one hashtag, mention, or hashtagMention tweet.

Figure 2 shows the number of clicks per URL in different tweet types for different user sets. The Y-axis presents the average number of clicks for a given

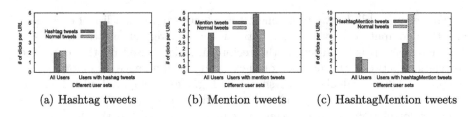

Fig. 2. Tweet type vs. number of clicks

user set. For hashtag tweets, shown in Fig. 2(a), the average number of clicks of hashtag tweets is lower than that of normal tweets for all users; however, the values are reversed for users with at least one hashtag tweet. Therefore, we cannot fully ascertain how tweets that contain hashtags correlate the number of clicks. For mention tweets, depicted in Fig. 2(b), the average number of clicks of mention tweets is always higher than that of normal tweets for both user sets. This result suggests that a positive correlation exists between tweets containing mentions and the number of clicks. For hashtagMention tweets, presented in Fig. 2(c), the trends are also inconsistent for different users.

Considering the unclear results about the effect of hashtags, we further explore whether hashtags and mentions exert the different effect on the number of clicks for users with different influence levels. For this purpose, we place users into buckets according to an interval of 200 followers. We use numbers to denote the buckets, i.e., the bucket 1 represents users with 0–200 followers, bucket 2 represents users with 200–400 followers, and so on. For each bucket, we group the tweets into four types: *hashtag tweets*, *mention tweets*, *hashtagMention tweets*, and *normal tweets*, and compute the average number of clicks for each type.

We compare the click number of the first three types of tweets with that of normal tweets, and the results are shown in Fig. 3. The figures do not show all of the buckets because of space constraints. The X-axis shows the bucket number. The Y-axis denotes the average number of clicks per URL for the particular bucket.

The results of the hashtag tweets are shown in Fig. 3(a). For the bucket 7 and 8 (referring to users with 1200–1400 and 1400–1600 followers respectively), the click numbers of the hashtag and normal tweets are very close. While, for the bucket 1 to 6, the hashtag tweets obtain a higher number of clicks than the normal tweets. However, the reverse is true for bucket 9 and beyond. These

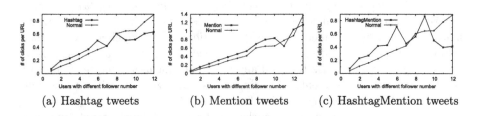

Fig. 3. Tweet type vs. number of clicks for users with different influence levels

results indicate that tweets with hashtags do not always achieve additional clicks, i.e., they can obtain more clicks for users with lower influence but not for that with higher influence.

For the mention tweets, presented in Fig. 3(b), from the bucket 1 to 10, the mention tweets generate a higher number of clicks than the normal tweets. While, for other buckets, the click numbers of both are interlaced with each other. That is, when users have less than roughly 1,800 followers, their tweets with mentions can attract additional clicks; however, when users have a higher number of followers, mentions do not contribute to improving the number of clicks. Affected by both hashtags and mentions, the hashtagMention tweets, presented in Fig. 3(c), exhibit a similar trend to hashtag tweets. The average number of clicks shows a small fluctuation because of their small number.

These results indicate that contrary to what people commonly assume, tweets with hashtags cannot always obtain more clicks. In fact, the hashtags and Mentions exhibit a different effect on users with different influence levels for obtaining the number of clicks.

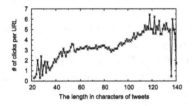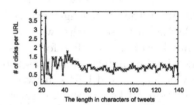

Fig. 4. All the users   **Fig. 5.** Users with 2000–2200 followers

Tweet Length. Here, we explore the correlation between the tweet length and number of clicks. We first analyze this correlation for all users, and the results are shown in Fig. 4. The X-axis denotes the length of the tweets. The minimum length is 20 because the tweet contain the short URL with no less than 20 characters. The Y-axis refers to the average number of clicks with a particular length. From the figure, we can see that the number of clicks generally increases with the tweet length. And short URLs in tweets with approximately 120 characters tend to attract more clicks.

We further explore how the effect of tweet length differs for users with different influence levels. As in the previous section, we place the users into buckets according to an interval of 200 followers. For each bucket, we plot the correlations between the tweet length and number of clicks. By observing the trend of each figure, we find that these figures can be divided into two categories: users with 0–2,000 followers and users with more than 2,000 followers. For the former, all of the buckets exhibit a similar trend. In view of space constraints, we present the figures of three buckets: users with 1–200 followers, users with 600–800 followers and users with 1600–1,800 followers, as shown in Fig. 6. This category has the similar trend that the number of clicks exhibits a double hump phenomenon,

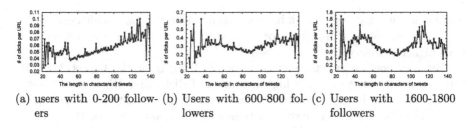

(a) users with 0-200 follow- (b) Users with 600-800 fol- (c) Users with 1600-1800
ers   lowers   followers

Fig. 6. Tweet length vs. number of clicks for users with 0 to 2000 followers

and this trend becomes even more significant with the rise in the number of followers. For example, when the number of followers reaches 1,600–1,800, this trend becomes the most significant, and the two peaks of the click number are twice the minimum number of clicks. For users with more than 2,000 followers, we present the figures of users with 2,000–2,200 followers in Fig. 5, and all of the other buckets exhibit a similar trend. The number of clicks fluctuates because of the small amount of tweets when the tweet length is near 40, but it remains stable when the tweet length exceeds 50.

Basing on these results, we can conclude that the effect of tweet length on the number of clicks differs for users with different influence levels. Specifically, users with low influence, such as those with 0–2,000 followers, can be affected by tweet length, and URLs in tweets with around 50 to 120 characters tend to obtain more clicks. However, users with high influence, such as those with more than 2,000 followers, can hardly be affected by tweet length.

5   Methodology

5.1   Method of Prediction

The above analyses indicate that hashtags, mentions and tweet length place the different impact on users with different influence levels for obtaining the number of clicks. Therefore, the predictive model should take into account this different impact to achieve higher accuracy. However, a global model, such as logistic regression and SVM, will ignore this different impact. One way to address this challenge is to create and apply numerous models to the user sets with different influence levels. However, the data of some user sets, especially for user set with high influence levels, is very sparse and cannot build model accurately. Hence, to overcome this problem, we introduce the Multi-Task Learning (MTL) to predict the click number of URLs. MTL seeks to simultaneously learn the commonality as well as the differences between the multiple tasks. Therefore, we divide users into different groups based on their influence levels and treat prediction of each group as a task. And the MTL model is used to improve the performance by considering both the common properties of all users and specific characters of users with different influence levels. Here, we introduce an extension of SVM+ approach to multi task learning called SVM+MTL [19] to build the model.

In SVM+MTL, the training set T is the union of task specific sets $T_r = \{x_{ir}, y_{ir}\}_{i=1}^{l_r}$. For each task the learned weights vector is decomposed as $w + w_r, r \in (1, 2, ..., t)$ where w and w_r respectively model the commonality between tasks and task specific components. The optimization problem of SVM+MTL is formulated as follows:

$$\min_{w,b} \frac{1}{2}(w, w) + \frac{\beta}{2} \sum_{r=1}^{t}(w_r, w_r) + C \sum_{r=1}^{t} \sum_{i=1}^{l_r} \xi_{ir} \tag{1}$$

$$st : y_{ir}((w, \phi(x_{ir})) + b + (w_r, \phi_r(x_{ir})) + d_r) \geq 1 - \xi_{ir} \tag{2}$$

$$\xi_{ir} \geq 0, i = 1, ..., l_r, r = 1, ..., t \tag{3}$$

Here, all w_r's and the common w are learned simultaneously. β regularizes the relative weights of w and w_r's. ξ_{ir}'s are slack variables measuring the errors w_r's make on the t data groups. y_{ir}'s denote training labels while C regulates the complexity and proportion of nonseparable samples.

The goal of SVM+MTL is to find t decision functions $f_r(x) = (w, \phi(x)) + b + (w_r, \phi_r(x)) + d_r, r = 1, ..., t$. Each decision function f_r comprises two parts: the common weights vector w with bias term b, and the group-specific correction function w_r with bias term d_r.

5.2 Feature Spaces

In this section, we introduce the features which are used in the predictive model, including the attributes of user influence, publishing behavior, and short URLs.

Features of user influence describe the characteristics of the social topology of users. Based on the user profiles we can download by Twitter APIs, we use the metadata relative to user influence as the features, such as the number of followers, friends, lists and son on. Further, based on our analyses, we exploit the features related to influence: the active followers and differences between followers and reciprocal links, which can more accurately reflect user influence. The features are detailed in Table 2.

Features of publishing behavior are composed of the items which users can control when publishing tweets. The tweet characteristics, such as the presences of hashtags and mentions as well as tweet length, are also placed into this set, because users can determine whether their tweets include hashtags or mentions and how long their tweets are.

Features of short URLs describe the information collected by Bitly APIs. Among these features, the global click number of URLs can reflect the popularity of the tweet content, because the global click number is the sum of clicks from all the domains and platforms, and URLs in tweets are generally the key points of the tweets. The referrer number can also be a measure of popularity for URLs, because it means the sum of resources where clicks originated, i.e., the higher referrer number is, the more popular the URL is. Therefore, in the experiments later, we can evaluate whether the popularity of content has the predictive power of the exact click number by using the features about the global click number and referrer number.

Table 2. Summary of features

Feature sets	Name	Description
User influence	Followers	The number of followers
	Friends	The number of friends
	Lists	The number of lists including this user
	Active-followers	The number of active followers
	Diff-followers	Difference between followers and reciprocal links
Publishing behavior	Hashtags	The presence of hashtags in tweets
	Mentions	The presence of mentions in tweets
	Tweet length	The length of tweets
	Published time	The published time of tweets
	Average tweets	Average number of Tweets per day in our dataset
	Ratio of URLs	Ratio of numbers of tweets with URLs and all tweets
Short URLs	Global number	The global click number from all the domains and platforms
	Created time	Difference of tweet published time and URL created time
	Referrer number	The number of resources where clicks originated
	Domain ranking	Ranking in Alexa.com of the domain of expanded URLs

6 Prediction Results

Based on the method and features, we predict the click number of URLs in tweets. We describe the experiment setup and compare the results of SVM+MTL with the original SVM.

6.1 Experiment Setup

We conduct prediction before tweets publication, because compared with prediction after tweets publication, this kind of prediction can more clearly measure the factors that affect the number of clicks. As in [6,13,27], we define several categories to represent the levels of the click number and predict which categories the URL will belong to, instead of predicting the exact number. Because the latter is harder, particularly given the skewed distribution of popularity [5], and the former should be good enough for most purposes. Specifically, we divide URLs into five categories depending on the click number. That is we put URLs with 0, 1~10, 11~100, 101~1,000, and more than 1,000 clicks into the category 1, 2, 3, 4 and 5 respectively. We select the same number of URLs for each category randomly, because the URLs in category 1 are dominant, accounting for around 70 % of all the URLs. When considering all the URLs for the experiments, the accuracy of prediction will reach 70 % even if we label all URLs as category 1.

The SVM+MTL takes into account both the common properties and specific characters of users with different influence levels. Hence, we place users into buckets according to an interval of 200 followers, and treat prediction of each bucket as a task. And the SVM is used as the baseline.

We use the classification accuracy and F-score to measure the performance. And the accuracy is defined as the proportion of true results in the population, and the F-score combines recall and precision with an equal weight. And to evaluate the predictive performance, we randomly divide the URLs of each user into two sets: 50 % for training and 50 % for testing.

6.2 Results and Discussion

The accuracy and F-score of the SVM and SVM+MTL predictors are presented in Table 3 for the combination of the different feature sets. The best results (biggest accuracy) for each model are emphasized in boldfaced numbers. The first observation is that although the SVM model can perform reasonably well with around 69 % accuracy using all features, the performance of SVM+MTL, 81.77 %, is significantly higher than that of SVM. Besides, no matter which feature sets are used for prediction, the accuracies of SVM+MTL are always approximately 10 % higher than that of SVM. This indicates that grouping users based on user influence levels is appropriate for SVM+MTL, and by considering both the common properties of all users and specific characters of users with different influence levels, SVM+MTL can achieve expected predictive results.

In addition, we proceed to the feature set level to determine the importance of features in predicting the click number. Unsurprisingly, for the SVM+MTL model, the accuracies of using the influence feature set and behavior feature set arrive at 74.35 % and 72.46 % respectively, which suggest that both feature sets play an important role in predicting the levels. Interestingly, the features of short URLs cannot perform as better as that of user influence and behavior. Among the short URL features, both the global click number and referrer number can, to some extent, reflect the popularity of the URL content. But they fail to have a predictive power of the exact click number. This indicates that not every user can achieve more clicks by publishing popular URLs. We also compute the coefficient of correlation between the global click number and exact click number. The lower coefficient, about 0.38, also provides support for this point.

Table 3. The predictive results

Feature sets	SVM		SVM MTL	
	Accuracy (%)	F-score (%)	Accuracy (%)	F-score (%)
Influence	65.11	64.32	74.35	73.41
Behavior	62.33	61.48	72.46	72.14
URLs	57.68	58.13	68.74	69.85
Influence + behavior	66.04	66.84	75.26	74.11
Influence + URLs	65.3	65.91	76.18	77.14
Behavior + URLs	60.27	61.05	71.49	70.28
All features	**69.49**	69.74	**81.77**	81.37

7   Conclusions

In this paper, we conducted analyses and predictions about the click number of URLs in tweets. Through the analyses, we showed that the correlation of the click numbers and followers is not as strong as expected. This is due to reciprocal links, not inactive followers. And our further analysis suggested reciprocal links have limited effects on content diffusion, although it is widely used to increase the number of followers. We also found that hashtags and tweet length place different impacts on users with different influence levels for obtaining the number of clicks. Specifically, in terms of hashtags, URLs in tweets with hashtags achieve more clicks for users with low influence, but less for users with high influence. And for tweet length, URLs in tweets with 50 and 120 characters attract a similar maximum number of clicks. However, users with higher influence are hardly affected by tweet length. Based on these analyses, we built a SVM+MTL model to predict the click number. In this model, users with different influence levels are treated as different predictive tasks, and the commonality of all users and differences of users with different influence levels are learned simultaneously. The experiments, based on Twitter data, showed our predictive performance is significantly higher than the baselines.

Acknowledgment. This work is supported by the National Natural Science Foundation of China (No. 61402151 and 61272527), Science and Technology Foundation of Henan Province of China (No. 162102410010), and Open Research Fund of Network and Data Security Key Laboratory of Sichuan Province of China (No. NDS2015-02).

References

1. How to use twitter to increase web traffic. http://www.wikihow.com/Use-Twitter-to-Increase-Web-Traffic
2. Twitter announces 100 million active users. http://mashable.com/2011/09/08/twitter-has-100-million-active-users
3. Antoniades, D., Polakis, I., Kontaxis, G., Athanasopoulos, E., Ioannidis, S., Markatos, E.P., Karagiannis, T.: we.b: the web of short URLs. In: Proceedings of the 20th international conference on World Wide Web, pp. 715–724 (2011)
4. Bakhshi, S., Kanuparthy, P., Shamma, D.A.: Understanding online reviews: funny, cool or useful? In: Proceedings of the 18th ACM Conference on Computer Supported Cooperative Work, pp. 1270–1276 (2015)
5. Bakshy, E., Hofman, J.M., Mason, W.A., Watts, D.J.: Everyone's an influencer: quantifying influence on Twitter. In: Proceedings of the Fourth ACM International Conference on Web Search and Data Mining, pp. 65–74 (2011)
6. Bandari, R., Asur, S., Huberman, B.A.: The pulse of news in social media: forecasting popularity. In: The Sixth International AAAI Conference on Weblogs and Social Media, pp. 26–33 (2012)
7. Bao, P., Shen, H.W., Huang, J., Cheng, X.Q.: Popularity prediction in microblogging network: a case study on Sina Weibo. In: Proceedings of the 22nd International Conference on World Wide Web, pp. 177–178 (2013)

8. Cha, M., Haddadi, H., Benevenuto, F., Gummadi, K.P.: Measuring user influence in twitter: the million follower fallacy. In: Proceedings of International AAAI Conference on Weblogs and Social Media (2010)

9. Cheng, J., Adamic, L., Dow, P.A., Kleinberg, J.M., Leskovec, J.: Can cascades be predicted? In: Proceedings of the 23rd International Conference on World wide web, pp. 925–936 (2014)

10. Comarela, G., Crovella, M., Almeida, V., Benevenuto, F.: Understanding factors that affect response rates in Twitter. In: Proceedings of the 23rd ACM Conference on Hypertext and Social Media, pp. 123–132 (2012)

11. Gao, S., Ma, J., Chen, Z.: Effective and effortless features for popularity prediction in microblogging network. In: Proceedings of the 23rd International Conference on World Wide Web, pp. 269–270 (2014)

12. Ghosh, S., Viswanath, B., Kooti, F., Sharma, N.K., Korlam, G., Benevenuto, F., Ganguly, N., Gummadi, K.P.: Understanding and combating link farming in the Twitter social network. In: Proceedings of the 21st International Conference on World Wide Web, pp. 61–70 (2012)

13. Hong, L., Dan, O., Davison, B.D.: Predicting popular messages in Twitter. In: Proceedings of the 20th International Conference Companion on World wide Web, pp. 57–58 (2011)

14. Hutto, C., Yardi, S., Gilbert, E.: A longitudinal study of follow predictors on Twitter. In: Proceedings of the SIGCHI Conference on Human Factors in Computing Systems, pp. 821–830 (2013)

15. Jenders, M., Kasneci, G., Naumann, F.: Analyzing and predicting viral tweets. In: Proceedings of the 22nd International Conference on World Wide Web, pp. 657–664 (2013)

16. Khosla, A., Das Sarma, A., Hamid, R.: What makes an image popular? In: Proceedings of the 23rd International Conference on World Wide Web, pp. 867–876 (2014)

17. Kupavskii, A., Ostroumova, L., Umnov, A., Usachev, S., Serdyukov, P., Gusev, G., Kustarev, A.: Prediction of retweet cascade size over time. In: Proceedings of the 21st ACM International Conference on Information and Knowledge Management, pp. 2335–2338 (2012)

18. Kwak, H., Lee, C., Park, H., Moon, S.: What is Twitter, a social network or a news media? In: Proceedings of the 19th International Conference on World Wide Web, pp. 591–600 (2010)

19. Lichen, L., Cherkassky, V.: Connection between SVM+ and multi-task learning. In: Proceedings of the International Joint Conference on Neural Networks, pp. 2048–2054 (2008)

20. Liu, Z., Jansen, B.J.: Factors influencing the response rate in social question and answering behavior. In: Proceedings of the 2013 Conference on Computer Supported Cooperative Work, pp. 1263–1274 (2013)

21. Rodrigues, T., Benevenuto, F., Cha, M., Gummadi, K., Almeida, V.: On word-of-mouth based discovery of the web. In: Proceedings of the 2011 ACM SIGCOMM Conference on Internet Measurement Conference, pp. 381–396 (2011)

22. Romero, D.M., Galuba, W., Asur, S., Huberman, B.A.: Influence and passivity in social media. In: Proceedings of the 2011 European Conference on Machine Learning and Knowledge Discovery in Databases, pp. 18–33 (2011)

23. Stringhini, G., Wang, G., Egele, M., Kruegel, C., Vigna, G., Zheng, H., Zhao, B.Y.: Follow the green: growth and dynamics in Twitter follower markets. In: Proceedings of the 2013 Conference on Internet Measurement Conference, pp. 163–176 (2013)

24. Suh, B., Hong, L., Pirolli, P., Chi, E.H.: Want to be retweeted? Large scale analytics on factors impacting retweet in Twitter network. In: Proceedings of the 2010 IEEE Second International Conference on Social Computing, pp. 177–184 (2010)
25. Szabo, G., Huberman, B.A.: Predicting the popularity of online content. Commun. ACM **53**, 80–88 (2010)
26. Thomas, K., Grier, C., Song, D., Paxson, V.: Suspended accounts in retrospect: an analysis of Twitter spam. In: Proceedings of the 2011 ACM SIGCOMM Conference on Internet Measurement Conference, pp. 243–258 (2011)
27. Vasconcelos, M., Almeida, J.M., Goncalves, M.A.: Predicting the popularity of micro-reviews: a foursquare case study. Inf. Sci. **325**, 355–374 (2015)
28. Zhao, Q., Erdogdu, M.A., He, H.Y., Rajaraman, A., Leskovec, J.: SEISMIC: a self-exciting point process model for predicting tweet popularity. In: Proceedings of the 21th ACM SIGKDD International Conference on Knowledge Discovery and Data Mining, pp. 1513–1522 (2015)

Analysis of Teens' Chronic Stress on Micro-blog

Yuanyuan Xue[1,2(✉)], Qi Li[1], Liang Zhao[1], Jia Jia[1], Ling Feng[1], Feng Yu[3], and David A. Clifton[4]

[1] Department of Computer Science and Technology,
Tsinghua University, Beijing, China
{xue-yy12,liqi13,jing-zhao11}@mails.tsinghua.edu.cn,
{jiajia,fengling}@mail.tsinghua.edu.cn
[2] Department of Computer Technology and Application,
Qinghai University, Xining, China
[3] Department of Psychology, Tsinghua University, Beijing, China
yufeng10@sem.tsinghua.edu.cn
[4] Institute of Biomedical Engineering, University of Oxford, Oxford, UK
davidc@robots.ox.ac.uk

Abstract. Statistics show that more and more teenagers today are under the stress in all areas of their lives from school to friend, work, and family, and they are not always able to use healthy methods to cope with. Long-term stress without proper guidance will lead to a series of potential problems including physical and mental disorders, and even suicide due to teens' shortage of psychological endurance and controllability. Therefore, it is necessary and important to sense teens' long-term stress and help them release the stress properly before the stress starts to cause illness. In this paper, we present a micro-blog based method to recognize teens' chronic stress by aggregating stress detected from micro-blog. In particular, we analyze the characteristics of teens' chronic stress, and identify five types of chronic stress level change patterns. We evaluate the framework through a user study at a high school where the 48 participants are aged 16–17. The result provides the evidence that sensing teens' chronic stress is feasible through the open micro-blog, and the identified stress level change patterns allow us to find useful regulations of teens' stress transition and to give sensible interpretations.

Keywords: Teens · Chronic pressure · Stress transition · Micro-blog

1 Introduction

1.1 Motivation

No one lives a stress-free life. Anything that poses a challenge or a threat to our well-being is a stress. The American Heritage Medical Dictionary defines *stress* as a physical or psychological stimulus that can produce mental or physiological reactions which may lead to illness [1]. Stress can be divided into *acute stress* or *chronic stress.* Acute stress is usually short-lived and can be beneficial, as it can

© Springer International Publishing AG 2016
W. Cellary et al. (Eds.): WISE 2016, Part II, LNCS 10042, pp. 121–136, 2016.
DOI: 10.1007/978-3-319-48743-4_10

enhance alertness and improve productivity [2]. In contrast, chronic stress is long-lived. It is the response to emotional pressure suffered for a prolonged period over which an individual perceives s/he has no control. While the immediate effects of stress hormones are beneficial in a particular situation, long-term exposure to stress creates a high level of these hormones that remains constant. This may lead to high blood pressure and subsequently heart disease, damage to muscle tissue, inhibition of growth, suppression of the immune system, and damage to mental health [3]. In view of the severe consequence of chronic stress, it is quite important to catch it in time.

With the rapid economic development, chronic stress has become an epidemic in our modern society, and people almost accept it as a way of life. Particularly for teenagers, they have to face heightened stress due to the many changes experienced concomitantly. When teens are overloaded with long-term chronic stress, inadequately managed stress can lead to anxiety, withdrawal, aggression, physical illness, or poor coping skills such as drug/alcohol use. It could also trigger or worsen depression [4], social isolation, and aggressive miss-behaviors [5]. To the extreme, injury to either teenagers themselves or others will happen. The campus gunman, Elliot Rodger, posted a video of himself on YouTube, saying he had been suffering long-lasting stress of loneliness before the campus killing in Santa Barbara in USA [6].

Hence, being aware of the existence of chronic stress and helping stressful teenagers control and manage chronic stress before it becomes severe enough to cause illness are particularly important.

1.2   Existing Solutions

Traditional stress analysis and detection techniques use subjective questionnaires or various objective sensors to monitor the changes and predict the trends of *physiological signals* and/or *physical signals* for people under stress [7–9]. *Smart phones* as a kind of speech sensor were also exploited in [10,11], focusing on cognitive stress and stressor frequency estimation rather than the type and severity of stress. The limitations of these methods are the invasion or inconvenience caused by the body contact and the deviation induced by physical excise. Recently, micro-blog offers another low-cost sensing channel to obtain people's self-expressed contents and behaviors, from which some emotional signals could be captured and analyzed. [12–16] evaluated whether people are in the risk of depression by analyzing their twitting behaviors. Oriented at the youth group, [17–19] investigated a number of teens' typical tweeting behaviors that may reveal adolescent stress, and built a micro-blog based platform to sense and help ease teenagers' mental stress. But, aforementioned analysis stopped at detecting adolescent stress category and stress level from teenagers' tweets. None investigates further to design an approach to differentiate whether a teen suffers chronic stress upon the aggregation of stress of tweets within time periods on micro-blog.

1.3 Our Work

The aim of this study is to analyze and distinguish teenagers' acute and chronic stress through the social media micro-blog. Chronic stress could appear continuously or discontinuously and its level may vary over time during the stress period. Understanding teens' chronic stress level change patterns and features could help us track and predict teens' stress trend, then further provide proper intervention to avoid possible severe consequences.

Here, we turn to micro-blog for teens' chronic stress detection for the following reasons. Firstly, micro-blog keeps track of teens' long-term tweeting contents and behaviors, and it is possible to detect and associate stress within different time scopes, which is difficult for wearing body-contact sensors and taking the measurements. Secondly, teenagers tend to record details of their daily life and feelings on micro-blog, making the acquisition of teens' emotional states possible. Furthermore, based on the sensing results, effective and prompt intervention and interaction with teens under stress can be easily implemented through the lively micro-blog channel.

The contributions of this paper can be summarized as follows.

- By aggregating teens' stress levels from individual tweets, we design a method to differentiate teen's chronic stress over a time period.
- We analyze the characteristics of teens' chronic stress, and identify five types of chronic stress change patterns.
- We conduct a user study testing the accuracy of the proposed method with teenagers recruited from a local school, and experimentally analyze the reasons for different chronic stress level change patterns.

To our knowledge, this is the first attempt in the literature to analyze and identify teenagers' chronic stress, as well as different chronic stress level change patterns, on micro-blog social media.

2 Related Work

2.1 Stress Detection by Subjective Questionnaires and Psychologists

The first method uses subjective questionnaires or individual/group meetings with psychologists to analyze users' stress situations. This method needs high cooperation of users and relies on people's ability to recall their experiences.

2.2 Stress Detection from Physiological Signals

Because stress will induce the variation of physiological and physical signals of the body, there is a rich body of work using objective physiological and physical signals to detect stress. Typical physiological measures include galvanic skin response (GSR), heat rate variability (HRV), electroencephalogram

(EEG), electrocardiogram (ECG), blood pressure, electromyogram, and respiration. [20] found skin conductivity and heart rate metrics have close correlations with driver's stress level, and used electrocardiogram, electromyogram, skin conductance, and respiration for driver's stress detection [21]. [22] applied the non-linear system identification technique to HRV for continuous mental stress monitoring. The above experimental results came from the laboratories where subjects were under a stationary state. For people on the move, [23] combined ECG, GSR, and accelerometer gathered from 20 participants across three activities (sitting, standing, and walking) to differentiate physiological signals generated between physical activity and mental stress. [24] investigated the differences of EEG characteristics (overall complexity and spectrum power of EEG bands) collected from two groups of people - high stress versus moderate stress. The results showed that those with chronic stress have higher left prefrontal power.

2.3   Stress Detection from Physical Signals

Although physiological measures can achieve good accuracy in mental stress detection, it may make people discomfort, slightly conflicting air, or even more stressful increase due to its invasiveness. Some physical measures (e.g., voice, gesture and interaction, facial expressions, eye gaze, pupil dilation and blink rates) are thus taken for stress detection as non-invasive measures, since they do not need to put the contact sensors on human bodies. Voice-based stress detection has received much attention in recent years due to its observable variability when response to stressors. [25] presented a stress detection method by computing prosodic, voice quality, and spectral features on variable window sizes. Smart phones were also used as a kind of sensor to detect people's mental stress by analyzing their voice variation in diverse conversational situations [10,11]. Besides voice, [26] analyzed people's mouse movements and found that people click mouse button harder as their stress decrease. [27] proposed a stress recognition method based on pupil videos obtained from video camera. Considering the contact sensors need specialists to install and monitor, which causes inconvenience to people's daily life, [28] used a low-cost webcam that recovered the instantaneous heart rate signal from video frames of human faces for mental stress detection. [29] further used features extracted from GSR and/or speech signals to train four types of classifiers, and the result showed that SVM classifiers can reach better accuracy than other classifiers for stress detection.

2.4   Stress and Depression Detection from Micro-blog

The popularity of micro-blog offers another medium for sensing people's mood. [13,14] built a statistical classifier to estimate whether people are in the risk of depression by analyzing their twitting behaviors before being diagnosed. The experimental results demonstrated that social media contained useful cues in predicting individual's depression tendency. Recently, [17] investigated a number of teens' typical tweeting behaviors that may reveal adolescent stress, and applied five classifiers to teens' stress detection. [18] trained a deep sparse neural network to detect psychological stress from cross-media micro-blog. So far, teen's stress detection is conducted on the basis of individual tweets. Aggregation of stress levels revealed from tweets over a time period to identify teen's chronic stress and different chronic stress change patterns, have not been investigated yet. In this paper, a user study recruits 48 teenagers from a local high school and estimates the accuracy of the proposed method. Besides, some interesting findings are also found through the user study.

3   Problem Statement

Considering the characteristics of teenagers' micro-blog behaviors, [17,18] developed techniques to sense teenagers' stress level from each individual tweet of the four major categories: study, self-cognition, inter-personal, and affection. Six ranks: *none, very light, light, moderate, strong, very strong* are adopted to measure stress levels, where *none* indicates no stress. For computation purpose, we use integer set $S = \{0, 1, 2, 3, 4, 5\}$ to represent the above labels. Let (t, w) be a tweet w posted at time t. Function $Stress(t, w) = s$ returns a detected stress level $s \in S$ from tweet w.

To further sense chronic stress, we investigate a sequence of teen's tweets during a time period and aggregate the detected stress level of each single tweets.

Definition 1. *Let $I = [I.s, I.e]$ be a time period I starting time $I.s$ and ending time $I.e$. The temporal length of I is $|I| = I.e - I.s$, which can be a day, a week, a month, etc. Let $W(I) = \langle (t_1, w_1), (t_2, w_2) \cdots, (t_m, w_m) \rangle$ (for $I.s \le t_1 \le \cdots \le t_m \le I.e$) denote a **tweet sequence within time period I**, where tweets $w_1, w_2, \cdots, w_m$ were posted by a teenager chronologically on micro-blog at time $t_1, \cdots, t_m$, respectively.*

Definition 2. *Applying the stress detection function $Stress(t, w)$ upon each tweet in $W(I)$, we can obtain a corresponding **stress level sequence in time period I**, denoted as $S(W(I)) = \langle Stress(t_1, w_1), Stress(t_2, w_2), \cdots, Stress(t_m, w_m) \rangle = \langle s_1, s_2, \cdots, s_m \rangle$, where for $\forall i$ $(1 \le i \le m)$ $(s_i \in S)$. I is called a **stress existing time period**, if and only if $\exists i (1 \le i \le m)$ $(s_i > 0)$.*

As chronic stress is only meaningful for a relatively long time interval, and should exist frequently across the whole period, we give the following definition for chronic stress.

Definition 3. *Let $\mathcal{I} = [I_1, I_2, \cdots, I_n]$ be a time interval, which is divided into n successive time periods of equal temporal length, where for $\forall i$ $(1 \le i \le n-1)$ $(I_i.e = I_{i+1}.s) \wedge (|I_1| = |I_2| = \cdots = |I_n|)$. For a list of tweet sequences posted within $\mathcal{I}$, $\mathcal{W} = [W(I_1), W(I_2), \cdots, W(I_n)]$, and a list of stress level sequences within $\mathcal{I}$, $\mathcal{S}(\mathcal{W}) = [S(W(I_1)), S(W(I_2)), \cdots, S(W(I_n))]$, the **stress coverage ratio within $\mathcal{L}$** is computed as the number of stress-existing time periods in $\mathcal{I}$ versus the total time periods number n.*

Assume $\mathcal{I}$ is a stress existing time period. $\mathcal{I}$ is called a **chronic stress existing time period**, *if and only if (1) the temporal length of $\mathcal{L}$ is greater than threshold τ_t, and (2) the stress coverage ratio within $\mathcal{L}$ is greater than a threshold τ_c. Based on teenagers' regular schedule, $\tau_t = 1$ month, and $\tau_c = 100\%$ for simplification of basic model in this study.*

4 Method

4.1 Gaussian Process for Single Tweet Stress Detection

We extract 9 features from teens' micro-blogs to characterize the postings related to stress. The features can be categorized into two types: content-centric (i.e., linguistic content, number of negative emotion words, shared music/picture genres, number of positive and negative emoticons, number of exclamations and question marks, emotional degree lexicons) and context-centric (abnormal tweeting time and frequency). From each teen's tweeting/retweeting behavior, we extract and analyze these features, and then employ a Gaussian Process classifier to perform single-tweet based stress detection. Several of these features are motivated from [17], where greater details can be accessed by the readers.

Based on the content and context features extracted from teens' tweets, we employ the Gaussian Process (GP) framework to learn the stress level (categorized into 6 levels: "No Stress", "Very Light", "Light", "Moderate", "Strong", "Very Strong") for each tweet, which offers a principled means of performing inference over noisy data. The significant reasons we adopt Gaussian Process are the notion of GP as a distribution over functions and its best performance for stress detection on micro-blog [17], thus it is suitable to analyze teens' tweets. Here, we still use 6 stress levels defined in previous work to measure individual's stress extent in single tweet. Detailed derivations can be found in [17].

4.2 Stress Aggregation on Single Tweets

Considering teens' routines of study and rest vary weekly, we set the granularity of time interval as "week", namely for the successive time interval $\mathcal{I} = [I_1, I_2, \cdots, I_n, I_m]$, the length $|I_i| (1 \leq i \leq m)$ is a week. Thus, for each teen, we first aggregate stress of single tweets weekly, using three typical functions Avg, Max, Sum to calculate the average, minimal, and maximal stress levels in a week. The aggregated stress value indicates the stress state of each week (whether the teen endures stress in this week or not).

Let $W(I) = \langle (t_1, w_1), (t_2, w_2) \cdots, (t_m, w_m) \rangle$ be a tweet sequence in time period I, and let $S(W(I)) = \langle Stress(t_1, s_1), Stress(t_2, s_2), \cdots, Stress(t_m, s_m) \rangle = \langle (t_1, s_1), (t_2, s_2), \cdots, (t_m, s_m) \rangle$ be a list of stress level sequences detected from $W(I)$ (*Definition 1 and 2*). We have $Avg(S(W(I))) = \frac{\sum_{i=1}^{m} s_i}{m}$, $Max(S(W(I))) = arg_{1 \leq i \leq m} \ max(s_i)$, and $Sum(S(W(I))) = arg_{1 \leq i \leq m} \ min(s_i)$.

We label the aggregation stress result (by $Avg/Max/Sum$ functions) in $|I_i| (1 \leq i \leq m)$ as $\mathcal{S}(W(I_i))$. Thus for a stress level sequence $S(\mathcal{W})$ in time interval $\mathcal{I}$, the aggregation result is $\mathcal{S}(\mathcal{W})$. In our later results presentation, we proved that teens' stress (aggregated weekly) has consistent changing trends under three aggregation methods.

4.3 Detecting Chronic Stress Level Change Patterns

Teen's stress state usually changes over time influenced by environment and personality during the chronic stress interval (for example, stress level rises fast or drops slowly). The changing of teens' stress reflects in the variation between low level and high level stress. Thus, in this paper, we define two stress states: *lower stress* and *higher stress*, and focus on their mutual transition.

Within the continuous chronic stress interval $\mathcal{I} = [I_1, I_2, \cdots, I_m]$ (where the length of $|I_i| (1 \leq i \leq m)$ is one week, $S(W(I_i)) > 0$), a teen has two different stress states *lower stress* and *higher stress*, measured by the stress value threshold τ. For the aggregated stress value $\mathcal{S}(W(I_i))$ of each time period $I_i (1 \leq i \leq m)$, if $\mathcal{S}(W(I_i)) \leq \tau$, I_i is in *lower stress* state; or else I_i is in *higher stress* state. The setting of τ is subject to teen's personality and daily behaviors (here we set τ to be 5 based on the fact of 5 working days in a week).

We define *lower stress* interval as $\mathcal{I}_l = [I_p, I_{p+1}, \cdots, I_k]$, and the adjacent *higher stress* interval as $\mathcal{I}_h = [I_{k+1}, I_{k+2}, \cdots, I_q]$ in time interval $\mathcal{I}$ ($1 \leq p \leq k \leq q \leq m$), satisfying the following two conditions:

Condition 1: For $\forall i$ ($p \leq i \leq k$), $\mathcal{S}(W(I_i)) \leq \tau$;

Condition 2: For $\forall i$ ($k+1 \leq i \leq q$), $\mathcal{S}(W(I_i)) > \tau$.

Teen's chronic stress state changes from $\mathcal{I}_l$ to $\mathcal{I}_h$ when stress starts worsening. Similarly, transition from *lower stress* to *higher stress* happens when time interval $\mathcal{I}_h$ is in front of $\mathcal{I}_l$ in time line.

Within the *higher stress* time interval $\mathcal{I}_h$, we find the maximal stress level $S_{peak}(I_h) = S(W(I_{peak}))$, where $S(W(I_{peak})) = arg_{p \leq i \leq k} Max(S(W(I_i)))$ ($p \leq i \leq k$). I_{peak} (the time interval with peak stress value), together with I_p (the start time of $\mathcal{I}_l$) and I_q (the end time of $\mathcal{I}_h$), and divide the stress state transaction from *lower stress* to *higher stress* into three phases in the time line:

Phase 1. Early-Starting Phases stress level increases from *lowerstress* state to *higherstress* state, from I_p to I_k, in time span $T_1 = k - p$ (indicated in Fig. 1 with $p1$).

Phase 2. Middle-Rising Phases stress level increases from $S(W(I_k))$ to peak value $S_{peak}(\mathcal{I}_h)$, from I_{k+1} to I_{peak}, in time $T_2 = peak - (k + 1)$ (indicated in Fig. 1 with $p2$).

Phase 3. Late-Decreasing Phases stress level decreases from peak value $S_{peak}(\mathcal{I}_h)$ to *lower stress* state, from I_{peak} to I_q, in time $T_3 = q - peak$ (indicated in Fig. 1 with $p3$).

Note that the transition between *lower stress* and *higher stress* may occur repeatedly and alternately within a continuous chronic stress interval in reality. We measure the stress level changing speed (in *Phase2*) with the slope from I_k

	Pattern ID	Pattern Description	Sub-pattern		
			early (p1)	middle (p2)	late (p3)
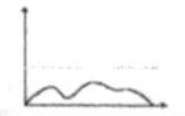	Pattern 1	stable chronic stress	-	-	-
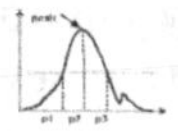	Pattern 2	stable chronic stress →intensive stress →stable chronic	Fast	Slow	Slow
			Fast	Slow	Fast
			Fast	Fast	Slow
			Fast	Fast	Fast
			Slow	Slow	Slow
			Slow	Slow	Fast
			Slow	Fast	Slow
			Slow	Fast	Fast
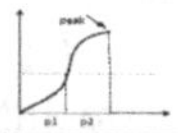	Pattern3	Stable chronic →intensive stress	Fast	Slow	-
			Fast	Fast	-
			Slow	Slow	-
			Slow	Fast	-
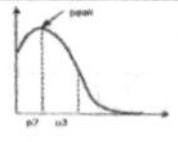	Pattern4	Intensive stress →stable chronic	-	Fast	Fast
			-	Fast	Slow
			-	Slow	Fast
			-	Slow	Slow
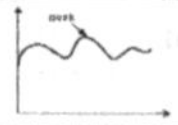	Pattern 5	Last intensive stress	-	-	-

Fig. 1. Five chronic stress level change patterns.

to I_{peak}, denoted as $Speed_{up} = (\mathcal{S}(W(I_{peak})) - \mathcal{S}(W(I_k)))/T_2$. We measure the speed of *Phase1* and *Phase2* by using the time span T_1 and T_2. In our case study, we found 287 stress level transaction cases from 48 teens' tweets, and further calculated the average changing speed of three phases respectively from the 287 transactions, thus obtaining three thresholds for measuring the changing speed of each phase, which are denoted as $\lambda_1, \lambda_2, \lambda_3$.

Further, we present five stress level change patterns based on the transaction between *lower stress* and *higher stress* states, within the chronic stress interval $\mathcal{I} = [I_1, I_2, \cdots, I_m]$. For each pattern, sub-patterns are defined according to the changing speed (*fast* or *slow*) of three phases, as shown in Fig. 1.

- Pattern 1: within the chronic stress interval $\mathcal{I}$, if for $\forall i \ (1 \leq i \leq m)$, $\mathcal{S}(W(I_i)) \leq \tau$, we call $\mathcal{I}$ a *smooth stress pattern*, indicating that no *higher stress* state appears in this chronic stress interval.
- Pattern 2: within the chronic stress interval $\mathcal{I}$, if there exists three conjoint sub time intervals, $\mathcal{I}_l, \mathcal{I}_h, \mathcal{I}_l$ in time line, namely stress state changes from *lower stress* to *higher stress* state, then back to *lower stress* state, we call it a *burst stress pattern*.
- Pattern 3: within the chronic stress interval $\mathcal{I}$, if there exists two conjoint sub time intervals, $\mathcal{I}_l$ and $\mathcal{I}_h$ in time line, namely stress state changes from *lower stress* to *higher stress* state and lasts to the end of $\mathcal{I}$, we call it a *gradually intensified and long-lasting pattern*.
- Pattern 4: within the chronic stress interval $\mathcal{I}$, if there exists two conjoint sub time intervals, $\mathcal{I}_h$ and $\mathcal{I}_l$ in time line, indicating that stress changes from

higher stress (at the beginning of $\mathcal{I}$) to *lower stress* state, we call it a *downward stress pattern*.

- Pattern 5: within the chronic stress interval $\mathcal{I}$, if $\forall i$ ($1 \leq i \leq m$), $\mathcal{S}(W(I_i))$ $\geq \tau$, we call $\mathcal{I}$ *intensive stress pattern*, showing that the teen keeps in *higher stress* state.

5   User Study

5.1   PSS-14 Questionnaires

Cohen's Perceived Stress Scale (PSS-14) [30] is commonly used to measure human's stress level worldwide in psychology. We take the PSS-14 score value (from 0 to 75, corresponding to none, light, moderate, and strong stress level respectively) as the ground-truth of our general stress detection results.

We invited 48 students (26 girls and 22 boys, aged 16–17) with micro-blog accounts from Xining No. 4 High School to participate in our case study. Getting their consents, we guided the students to fill in the Chinese PSS questionnaire [31] based on their emotional feelings in the last month (from Nov.26,2014 to Dec.26,2014).

Besides, we also add two questions to ask participants to label their characters and micro-blog usage: (1) *"Do you think you are introvert or extrovert?"* and (2) *"Do you prone to express emotions through tweets?"*

5.2   Teens' Tweets from Tencent Micro-blog Platform

We collected 30,041 tweets before 26 December, 2014 of the above 48 students from Tencent Micro-blog Platform, which is similar to Twitter in China. For each teen, the number of tweets ranges from 28 to 3,288, and the time span ranges from 25 weeks to 261 weeks. These tweets provide us with abundant information to detect chronic and acute stress of the participants, and to further analyze their chronic stress level change patterns.

To verify our detection results for chronic stress according to our ground-truth (based on PSS-14 questionnaires), we collected tweets of the 48 teens in the corresponding month (from November 26, 2014 to December 26, 2014). For each teen, the number of tweets ranges from 1 to 94, and the time span ranges from 1 week to 5 weeks.

6   Results

To match the four stress levels of PSS-14, we merged our detected *"very light"* and *"light"* stress levels into *"light"* stress level, and *"very strong"* and *"strong"* stress levels into *"strong"* stress level.

6.1   Experiment 1: Teens' General Stress Detection

In this experiment, we used the subset of collected tweets (posted from November 26, 2014 to December 26, 2014), to guarantee the timeliness of our ground-truth (based on PSS-14 questionare). For each student, we detected the stress level of every single tweet, and further computed his/her average stress level in this month. By comparing the stress levels reflected by PSS-14 questionnaire and detected by our approach of each 48 students, the average detection accuracy of our approach is 77.1 %. 25 out of 29 students, who are identified as suffering strong stress by PSS-14, are detected correctly by our approach.

Effect of "Introvert" or "Extrovert" Character on Detection Performance. Figure 2(a) and (b) show the ranking results of PSS-14 and our approach based on the stress levels of 26 introvert students, and 22 extrovert students respectively. We draw the fitting straight line and use R^2 (ranging from 0 to 1) to show the linear correlation degree of data in each sub-figure. The R^2 of 22 extrovert students in Fig. 2(b) shows a higher value of 0.64 than that of 26 introvert students in Fig. 2(a). The difference of R^2 indicates that the ranking result of extrovert teens has a higher linear correlation degree than that of introvert teens.

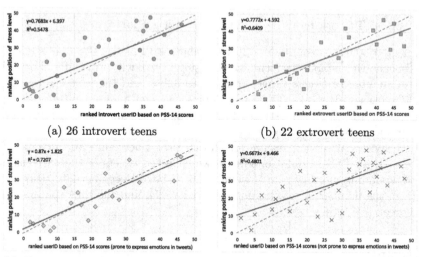

(a) 26 introvert teens   (b) 22 extrovert teens

(c) 19 teens prone to express emotions   (d) 29 teens not prone to express emotions

Fig. 2. Ranking results comparison based on stress levels detected by our approach and PSS-14. We rank the PSS-14 scores among 48 teens, and also rank the average stress level of them detected by our approach. We compare the two rank results, using the data fitting method, where the result R^2 ranging from 0 to 1. The greater value of R^2 indicates higher fitting degree of the two ranks.

Students Who Likely Express Emotions on Micro-blog Get Higher Performance. Figure 2(c) and (d) show the ranking results of PSS-14 and our approach based on the stress levels of 19 teens who are prone to expressing emotions in tweets and 29 teens who are not prone to expressing emotions in tweets. The fitting straight line in Fig. 2(c) is nearer to the $y = x$ line and obtains a very high value of $R^2 = 0.72$, which is much higher than $R^2 = 0.48$ in Fig. 2(d), and also higher than the results in Fig. 2(a) and (b).

6.2 Experiment 2: Chronic Stress Detection

In this part, we used whole set of teens' tweets to detect teens' chronic stress and to analyze its change patterns during entire posting time. Given the above definition, in this research, we focused on stress level rather than stress type while detecting chronic stress.

Aggregation Performance. For each teen, we aggregated stress level of single tweets weekly by using three methods: (1) the maximal stress level in a week, (2) the average stress level in a week, (3) the accumulated stress level in a week.

Sensibility of Chronic Stress Intervals. According to the psychological theory, time span of chronic stress could be recognized as "months to years" [32]. Combined with the application scenarios (per semester lasting for 4 months in Chinese high school), the length threshold for chronic stress interval (in Definition 3) is set to 1, 2, 3 and 4 months respectively to explore teens' chronic stress reactions with different baseline time.

Result in Fig. 3 shows that the number of teens suffering from chronic stress gradually decrease as baseline time extended. Combing detection results and teens' tweets, we have observed that nearly half of teens release the stress when semester ends or vacation starts. The rest of teens endure stress coming from families, peers, or bad self-regulation capabilities, which are less affected by outside

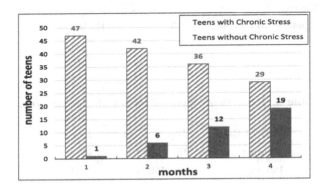

Fig. 3. Number of students with chronic stress, under different settings

world. When time span is set to 1 month, we find that most teens are suffering chronic stress with different periods. So we suggest that coaching or intervention once per month for teenagers be planned, to avoid potential consequences caused by chronic stress.

Performance of Chronic Stress Detection. To evaluate chronic stress detection performance, all participants were asked a question ("In the last year, do you feel nervous and stressed?" 1. Never 2. Seldom 3. Sometimes 4. Often 5. Always), which is regarded as ground-truth for detection result of each teen. To match question answers into the aggregation results (here we choose the average aggregation method, and the other two methods performing the similar trends can also be adopted), we set the rule: answer 1. Never mapping to "None", "2. Seldom" and "3. Sometimes" mapping to "Occasional", and "4. Often" and "5. Always" mapping to "Frequent". Here, we considered the label of "None" as no stress, "Occasional" as temporary stress, and "Frequent" as the chronic stress. Then we chose the minimal size of "1 month" as the threshold of chronic stress interval. The accuracy of detection result is presented in Table 1. Besides, the precision and recall of chronic stress detection can reach to 80.00 % and 66.67 % respectively. Causing relative low recall may be because some participants only posted few tweets during the posting period.

From another perspective, we compared our detection results with the rank of teens' PSS-14 scores (in descending order). Consequently, it reveals that most teens with chronic stress rank high in the list of PSS-14 results. As Table 2 shows, 10 teens with chronic stress are in the top 15, 13 teens are in the top 20, and 15 teens are in the top 25.

Table 1. Confusion matrix of stress detection

PSS-14	Detect		
	None	Occasional	Frequent (chronic)
None	1 (50 %)	1	0
Occasional	1	24 (77.42 %)	6
Frequent (chronic)	0	3	12 (80 %)

Table 2. Top n(15–25) ranks of teens with chronic stress

PSS-14 Rank	Top 15	Top 20	Top 25
Number of teens	10	13	15
Percent	66.67 %	86.66 %	100 %

6.3   Experiment 3: Chronic Stress Change Patterns

According to Definition 5, we explored all the varying patterns existing in the continuous chronic stress intervals of 48 teens. What we concerned more were the duration of low-level stress before its worsening, and the speed of worsening and alleviating. Five patterns were subclassified further in this trial. To describe the properties mentioned above, three parameters were used, including the lasting time of lower stress state $Lastingtime_{low}$, the transition speed from lower state to higher state $Speed_{up}$, and the transition speed from higher state to lower state $Speed_{down}$. We marked $Lastingtime_{low}$ as *slow* when it was greater than average value of lasting time of 48 teens, and marked $Speed_{up}$ and $Speed_{down}$ as *slow* when they were less than average value, the other way round. In such cases, stress level change patterns were classified into 18 sub-patterns (in Definition 4).

Table 3 shows the comparison of occurrence proportion of 5 patterns when the baseline time is set to 1, 2, 3 and 4 months. In general, the overall proportion do not markedly change with baseline time variation. Among these patterns, pattern 1 is the dominant one and then is pattern 2, which means teens usually are under the lower stress while suffering from chronic stress. But when their stress intensifies, it usually turns into a way of increasing first and then decreasing. The small change of percentage of pattern 1 and pattern 2 indicate that the ratio of stress worsening will rise with baseline time increasing.

Table 3. Distribution of 5 chronic stress change patterns in different baseline time

	Pattern 1	Pattern 2	Pattern 3	Pattern 4	Pattern 5
1 month	75.04 %	15.91 %	3.47 %	4.86 %	0.69 %
2 month	74.32 %	17.96 %	3.50 %	3.85 %	0.35 %
3 month	72.06 %	20.37 %	3.39 %	4.01 %	0.15 %
4 month	67.15 %	25.24 %	3.18 %	4.16 %	0.24 %

The proportion of sub-patterns in pattern 2 in 1 month baseline time is shown in Fig. 4 (only one pattern is reported here due to the space restriction). It shows that an overwhelming majority of teens (87.37 %) turns to the stage of intensive stress only after a short period of lower stress, which might be because teens easily feel anxious when facing stress due to their immaturity. Besides, the most prominent sub-pattern is sub-pattern 4, in which the speed of both stress ascent and decline are "fast", which seems like "easy come easy go" when teens' stress get worse. But an important thing to know is there are still 45.6 % teens keep "slow" speed at stress alleviating stage. For these teens, intervention or psychology guidance should be imported early to help them release stress.

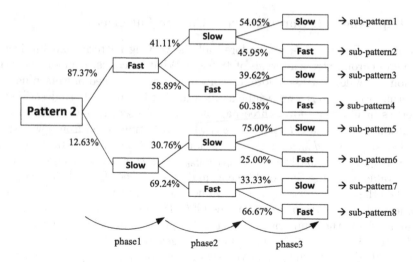

Fig. 4. Detected proportions of 8 sub-patterns in pattern 2

7 Conclusion

Chronic stress can lead to a series of physical and mental health problems. Especially for adolescents, it may result in more serious consequences such as suicide, due to their shortage of psychological endurance and controllability. Therefore, it is particularly necessary to timely detect adolescents' chronic stress and guide them to cope with it. In this study, we propose a framework for chronic stress detection by aggregating individual tweet's stress detection results. We identify five chronic stress change patterns, and give explanations and some advices based on the findings from a user study with 48 students of age 16–17 recruited from a high school. In the future, we plan to implant a personalization model upon the framework to automatically or semi-automatically adapt to different teens' stress detection.

Acknowledgments. The work is supported by National Natural Science Foundation of China (61373022 and 61370023).

References

1. The American Heritage Medical Dictionary. Houghton Mifflin Company (2008)
2. Benson, H., Allen, R.: How much stress is too much? Harvard Bus. Rev. **58**(5), 86–92 (1980)
3. Stress. http://psychology.wikia.com/wiki/Stress
4. Stress contributes to range of chronic diseases, review shows (2007). http://www.sciencedaily.com/releases/2007/10/071009164122.htm
5. Mineur, Y., Prasol, D., Belzung, C.: Agonistic behavior and unpredictable chronic mild stress in mice. Behav. Genet. **33**(5), 513–519 (2003)

6. Psychology today (2014). http://www.psychologytoday.com/blog/web-loneliness/201405/the-loneliness-elliot-rodger
7. Shi, Y., Ruiz, N., Taib, R., Choi, E., Chen, F.: Galvanic skin response (GSR) as an index of cognitive load. In: Proceedings of CHI, pp. 2651–2656 (2007)
8. Hamid, N., Sulaiman, N., Aris, S., Murat, Z., Taib, M.: Evaluation of human stress using EEG power spectrum. In: Proceedings of CSPA, pp. 1–4 (2010)
9. Hosseini, S., Khalilzadeh, M.: Emotional stress recognition system using EEG and psychophysiological signals: using new labelling process of EEG signals in emotional stress state. In: Proceedings of ICBECS, pp. 1–6 (2010)
10. Lu, H., Rabbi, M., Chittaranjan, G., Frauendorfer, D., et al.: Stresssense: detecting stress in unconstrained acoustic environments using smartphones. In: Proceedings of Ubicomp, pp. 351–360 (2012)
11. Bauer, G., Lukowicz, P.: Can smartphones detect stress-related changes in the behaviour of individuals? In: Proceedings of PERCOM Workshop, pp. 423–426 (2012)
12. Park, M., McDonald, D., Cha, M.: Perception differences between the depressed and non-depressed users in Twitter. In: Proceedings of ICWSM, pp. 476–485 (2013)
13. Choudhury, M., Gamon, M., Counts, S., Horvitz, E.: Prediction depression via social media. In: Proceedings of ICWSM, pp. 128–137 (2013)
14. Choudhury, M., Counts, S., Horvitz, E.: Social media as a measurement tool of depression in populations. In: Proceedings of ACM Web Science, pp. 47–56 (2013)
15. Shen, Y.-C., Kuo, T.-T., Yeh, I.-N., Chen, T.-T., Lin, S.-D.: Exploiting temporal information in a two-stage classification framework for content-based depression detection. In: Pei, J., Tseng, V.S., Cao, L., Motoda, H., Xu, G. (eds.) PAKDD 2013. LNCS (LNAI), vol. 7818, pp. 276–288. Springer, Heidelberg (2013). doi:10.1007/978-3-642-37453-1_23
16. Wang, X., Zhang, C., Ji, Y., Sun, L., Wu, L., Bao, Z.: A depression detection model based on sentiment analysis in micro-blog social network. In: Li, J., Cao, L., Wang, C., Tan, K.C., Liu, B., Pei, J., Tseng, V.S. (eds.) PAKDD 2013. LNCS (LNAI), vol. 7867, pp. 201–213. Springer, Heidelberg (2013). doi:10.1007/978-3-642-40319-4_18
17. Xue, Y., Li, Q., Jin, L., Feng, L., Clifton, D.A., Clifford, G.D.: Detecting adolescent psychological pressures from micro-blog. In: Zhang, Y., Yao, G., He, J., Wang, L., Smalheiser, N.R., Yin, X. (eds.) HIS 2014. LNCS, vol. 8423, pp. 83–94. Springer, Heidelberg (2014). doi:10.1007/978-3-319-06269-3_10
18. Lin, H., Jia, J., Guo, Q., Xue, Y., Li, Q., Huang, J., Cai, L., Feng, L.: User-level psychological stress detection from social media using deep neural network. In: Proceedings of MM (2014)
19. Li, Q., Xue, Y., Jia, J., Feng, L.: Helping teenagers relieve psychological pressures: a micro-blog based system. In: Proceedings of EDBT Demo (2014)
20. Healey, J., Picard, R.: Detecting stress during real-world driving tasks using physiological sensors. IEEE Trans. Intell. Trans. Syst. 6(2), 156–166 (2005)
21. Rigas, G., Goletsis, Y., Fotiadis, D.: Real-time driver's stress event detection. IEEE Trans. Intell. Trans. Syst. 13(1), 221–234 (2012)
22. Choi, J., Gutierrez-Osuna, R.: Using heart rate monitors to detect mental stress. In: Wearable and Implantable Body Sensor Networks, pp. 219–223 (2009)
23. Sun, F., Kuo, C., Cheng, H., Buthpitiya, S., Collins, P., Griss, M.: Activity-aware mental stress detection using physiological sensors. In: Proceedings of Social Informatics and Telecommunications Engineering, pp. 211–230 (2012)

24. Peng, H., Hu, B., Zheng, F., Fan, D., Zhao, W., Chen, X., Yang, Y., Cai, Q.: A method of identifying chronic stress by EEG. Pers. Ubiquit. Comput. **17**(7), 1341–1347 (2013)
25. Soury, M., Devillers, L.: Stress detection from audio on multiple window analysis size in a public speaking task. In: Proceedings of Affective Computing and Intelligent Interaction, pp. 529–533 (2013)
26. Liao, W., Zhang, W., Zhu, Z., Ji, Q.: A real-time human stress monitoring system using dynamic Bayesian network. In: Proceedings of CVPR (2005)
27. Mokhayeri, F., Akbarzadeh-T, M.-R.: Mentail stress detection based on soft computing techniques. In: Bioinformatics and Biomedicine, pp. 430–433 (2011)
28. Bousefsaf, F., Maaoui, C., Pruski, A.: Remote assessment of the heart rate variability to detect mental stress. In: Proceedings of Pervasive Computing Technologies for Healthcare Workshops, pp. 348–351 (2013)
29. Kurniawan, H., Maslov, A., Pechenizkiy, M.: Stress detection from speech and galvanic skin response signals. In: Proceedings of CBMS, pp. 209–214 (2013)
30. Cohen, S., Kamarck, T., Mermelstein, R.: A global measure of perceived stress. J. Health Soc. Behav., 385–396 (1983)
31. Cheng, T., Wu, J., Chong, M., Williams, P.: Internal consistency and factor structure of the Chinese health questionnaire. Acta Psychiatr. Scand. **82**(4), 304–308 (1990)
32. Contrada, R.J.: The Handbook of Stress Science. Springer Publishing Company. LLC, New York (2011)

Large-Scale Stylistic Analysis of Formality in Academia and Social Media

Thin Nguyen[✉], Svetha Venkatesh, and Dinh Phung

Deakin University, Burwood, Australia
{thin.nguyen,svetha.venkatesh,dinh.phung}@deakin.edu.au

Abstract. The dictum 'publish or perish' has influenced the way scientists present research results as to get published, including exaggeration and overstatement of research findings. This behavior emerges patterns of using language in academia. For example, recently it has been found that the proportion of positive words has risen in the content of scientific articles over the last 40 years, which probably shows the tendency in scientists to exaggerate and overstate their research results. The practice may deviate from impersonal and formal style of academic writing. In this study the degree of formality in scientific articles is investigated through a corpus of 14 million PubMed abstracts. Three aspects of stylistic features are explored: expressing emotional information, using first person pronouns to refer to the authors, and mixing English varieties. Trends of these stylistic features in scientific publications for the last four decades were discovered. A comparison on the emotional information with other online user-generated media, including online encyclopedias, web-logs, forums, and micro-blogs, was conducted. Advances in cluster computing are employed to process large scale data, with 5.8 terabytes and 3.6 billions of data points from all the media. The results suggest the potential of pattern recognition in data at scale.

Keywords: Big data · Apache Spark · Stylistic features · Academia · Social media

1 Introduction

Publication pressure has influenced the way researchers present study results, emerging patterns of presentations in scientific publications. Recently a pattern in expressing emotional information in academic papers has been found: the proportion of positive words has risen in the content of academic articles for the last 40 years [2,13], linking with the possibility of exaggeration or distortion of study findings [7,13], in order to give the papers more chance to be accepted. As emotional expression is said to be avoided in academic writing [1] or to associate with informal writing [11], the writing mode may not follow a formal style.

Other informal elements include using first person pronouns to refer to the authors [4,5]. Academic writers are advised that *'leave their personalities at the door'* [6] and *'traditional formal writing does not use I or we in the body of the paper'* [12].

© Springer International Publishing AG 2016
W. Cellary et al. (Eds.): WISE 2016, Part II, LNCS 10042, pp. 137–145, 2016.
DOI: 10.1007/978-3-319-48743-4_11

Another requirement for scientific publications is the consistency in the use of English. In the guide to authors by several journals, such as *Journal of Phonetics*[1] or *Information Sciences*,[2] it is written '*Please write your text in good English (American or British usage is accepted, but not a mixture of these)*'.

This work adapts a data-driven and lexicon-based approach to capture the language style conveyed in PubMed articles. Not only two linguistic categories – positives and negatives, but other stylistic features expressed in the content of PubMed abstracts will also be extracted. They include the proportion of sentiment-bearing words in the content and their affective scores, the extent of using first person pronouns to refer to the authors, and the degree of mixing English spelling in academic writing. Trends of these stylistic features in scientific publications for the last four decades will be investigated. The emotional information will be compared with that of other media, consisting of online encyclopedia (Wikipedia), online diaries (web-logs, e.g., Live Journal), online forums (Reddit), and micro-blogs (Twitter). Advanced framework in cluster computing will be employed to process approximately six terabytes of data containing billions of data points from all the media.

A key contribution of this work is to provide a set of stylistic features for scientific articles as well as trends of these features for the last 40 years. This would probably help to understand the evolution of scientific writing, as well as anomalies along the development. The trends may also imply changes in the extent of acceptability of certain stylistic features over the course of the period.

The paper is organized as follows. Section 2 outlines the proposed methods, data collections, and experimental setup. Section 3 presents the results. Section 4 concludes the paper and proposes possible future work.

2   Method

2.1   Datasets

Data from PubMed, Wikipedia, Live Journal, Reddit, and Twitter were crawled or downloaded. The time range, number of instances, and the volume for these corpora is shown in Table 1.

For PubMed, on 20 January 2016, through http://www.ncbi.nlm.nih.gov/pubmed/, English articles having abstracts were queried. The site returned 14,334,783 records of articles, in XML format. For each record, the content of certain tags, such as article title, article abstract, and publication date, was extracted.

For Wikipedia, the 05 March 2016 dump of English Wikipedia was downloaded.[3] This contains 8,374,298 articles. However, many of them do not have

---

[1] https://www.elsevier.com/journals/journal-of-phonetics/0095-4470/guide-for-authors, 2016.

[2] https://www.elsevier.com/journals/information-sciences/0020-0255/guide-for-authors, 2016.

[3] https://dumps.wikimedia.org/enwiki/20160305, downloaded on 31 March 2016.

Table 1. Corpora used in the experiments.

Dataset	Time range	#Instance	Volume
PubMed	01/12/1948 – 20/01/2016	14,334,783	150 GB
Wikipedia	05/11/2002 – 05/03/2016	5,760,798	52 GB
Live journal	14/05/1999 – 23/04/2005	33,152,794	64 GB
Reddit posts	24/01/2006 – 31/08/2015	196,531,736	251 GB
Reddit comments	15/10/2007 – 31/05/2015	1,659,361,605	908 GB
Twitter	07/06/2013 – 14/03/2016	1,673,497,746	4,542 GB

the content. They are referrals of other articles and were removed, resulting in 5,760,798 articles.

For Live Journal, a corpus of RSS (Rich Site Summary) feeds provided by the authors of [8] was used. This dataset contains more than 33 million blog posts written in English. More than half of the posts are tagged with moods, probably suggesting a sentiment-bearing and less formal data source.

For Reddit, both corpora of posts and comments were downloaded, including approximately 200 million posts and 1.6 billion comments.[4]

For Twitter, we introduce a new dataset of tweets written in English, geo-tagged with a US location, and time-stamped from 07 June 2013 to 14 March 2016.

2.2 Features

To characterize PubMed articles, three types of features were extracted: (1) affective information conveyed in the content, (2) informal elements, and (3) the mixing of American and British English. For other media, the affective information was extracted.

Affective Information. To compute the proportion of affective words in a document, *positive emotions* and *negative emotions* lexicons from LIWC [10] were employed. To estimate the sentiment score of sentiment-bearing words, ANEW ratings [3], employed to infer mood patterns in [9], was used. Words in this lexicon are rated in term of valence (*very unpleasant* to *very pleasant*), arousal (*least active* to *most active*), and dominance (*submissive* to *dominant*).

Using First Person Pronouns. In this work, using first person pronouns to refer to the authors was used as an example of informal elements. In particular, the proportion of abstracts containing *We* and *I* was calculated.

Generally, *We* is used more in co-authored papers than in sole-authored ones, and the other way around for *I*. So, in addition to the proportion calculated for all papers, those computed with respect to sole- and co-authored papers are included.

---

[4] Posts: http://bit.ly/1MvQobz, comments: http://bit.ly/1RmhQdJ, retrieved October 2015.

Mixing of American (AmE) and British English (BrE) Spelling. This work examined differences between AmE and BrE in term of spelling. From http://www.studyenglishtoday.net/british-american-spelling.html,[5] all words with different spelling between AmE and BrE were selected as the initial set. Then those words highlighted as misspelling by Notepad++ version 6.7.5 and their British counterparts were chosen, resulting in a list of 60 American and British word couples.[6]

This list was employed as the vocabulary to determine if a mixture of American and British spelling was used in a document of the media. For example, if both 'behavior' and 'colour' were found in a document, the document would be considered to have a mixture of English varieties in the content.

2.3   Trends in Academic Writing

To examine trends of stylistic features in scientific articles, annual values of each feature were examined. Correlation of the values with time would roughly show how the features have been changed over time. In this work, Pearson correlation between the annual value of the features and the time was used to detect the evolution of academic writing in PubMed articles for the last four decades, from 1975 to 2015. A positive correlation possibly means that the feature has increased over the time, and vice versa.

2.4   Computing Environment

All the processing of the big corpora in this work was conducted using Apache Spark, an emerging cluster computing platform [14]. A Spark cluster of eight worker nodes was employed. Each node features a dual eight-core Intel® Xeon® E5-2670@2.60 GHz processors, 128 GB of main memory, and CentOS 7.2 operating system.

3   Results

3.1   Affective Information

Proportion of Positive and Negative Words in the Content. Figure 1 shows the use of positive and negative words in PubMed abstracts for the last four decades. The use of positive words has increased for the period, with the correlation with time of 0.79, partly confirming recent findings that the proportion of positive words has risen in the content of scientific articles [2,13,15]. On the other hand, virtually no trend is observed for the use of negative words over the time.

---

[5] Retrieved February 2016, cached: http://bit.ly/1UNOeWa.
[6] The list could be accessed at http://bit.ly/1Sb1E9Z.

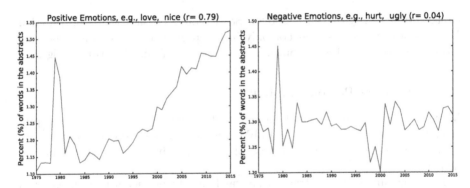

Fig. 1. The use of positive and negative words in PubMed abstracts for the last 40 years.

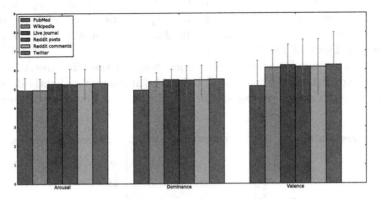

(a) Mean of the affective scores across the media.

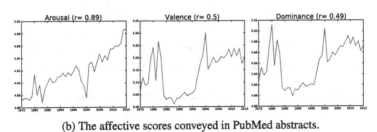

(b) The affective scores conveyed in PubMed abstracts.

Fig. 2. The affective scores for all the media and the affective scores for PubMed articles for the last 40 years.

Affective Score of Subjective Words. Figure 2a shows the mean of three affective scores for the content of all the media. The value for PubMed abstracts is lowest in all the affective scores.

However, all the scores for PubMed abstracts have increased for the last 40 years, as shown in Fig. 2b. Especially, the trend is clear for *arousal* score, with strong correlation with time, at 0.89. So, it could be said that, for PubMed abstracts, an increase is seen not only in the proportion of sentiment-bearing words in the content (Fig. 1), but also in the scores of affective words (Fig. 2b).

3.2   Using First Person Pronouns

Figure 3 shows the use of one of the informal elements – using first person pronouns to refer to the authors – in PubMed publications for the last 40 years. In general, an increase is seen in the use of *We* and *I* in PubMed abstracts over the period.

In particular, for all abstracts, *We* was found to be increasingly used, from less than 10 % of papers in 1975 to almost 50 % in 2015, a five times higher, shown in the left figure of Fig. 3a. A similar trend is observed for the proportion of *We* papers (papers with *We* in the abstracts) in co-authored papers, shown in the right figure of Fig. 3a. An increase in the proportion of co-authored papers is also seen, from less than 82 % in 1975 to almost 96 % in 40 years later, shown in the middle figure of Fig. 3a.

On the other hand, for all abstracts, as shown in the left figure of Fig. 3b, the percentage of *I* papers (papers with *I* in the abstracts) is slightly decreased over the time. However, the reason for this decrease is due to the sharp drop

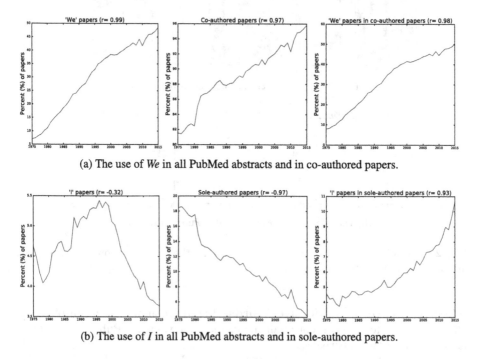

(a) The use of *We* in all PubMed abstracts and in co-authored papers.

(b) The use of *I* in all PubMed abstracts and in sole-authored papers.

Fig. 3. The use of first person pronouns in all PubMed abstracts, as well as with respect to co-authored or sole-authored papers, for the last 40 years.

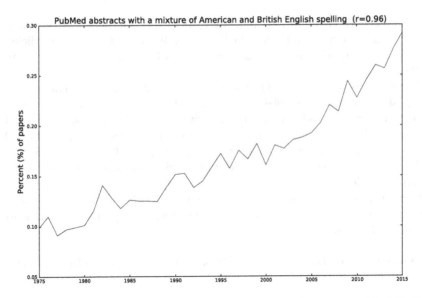

Fig. 4. Proportion of PubMed abstracts with a mixture of American and British English spelling over the last 40 years.

in the proportion of sole-authored papers, from more than 18 % in 1975 to 4 % in 2015, shown in the center figure of 3b. Indeed, the percentage of I papers in sole-authored papers has increased for the last 40 years, from 4.5 % to more than 10 %, a more than two times higher, shown in the right figure of Fig. 3b.

The increases in the proportions of *We* and I papers in co-authored and sole-authors, respectively, probably imply a rise in the degree of acceptability of the informal element in academic writing.

3.3   Mixing of American and British English Spelling

As shown in Fig. 4, the rate of PubMed articles containing a mixture of English spelling has increased for the last 40 years. In 1975, only 0.1 % of PubMed abstracts had a mixture of American and British English spelling. In 2015, this number is almost 0.3 %, a three times higher in 40 years.

4   Conclusion and Future Work

The work investigated stylistic features expressed in PubMed papers published for the last 40 years, with a comparison on the affective information with a variety of media, consisting of online encyclopedia, online diaries, online forums, and micro blogs. Advances in cluster computing framework were utilized to process almost 6 terabytes of data. Emerging trends in academic writing have been discovered. Among others, there exists the tendency of using first person pronouns to refer to the authors and mixing English spelling in the abstracts for the last four decades. Results also indicated differences in the affective information between academia and other media. The work demonstrated the efficiency of advanced computing framework in dealing with big data, providing prompt results.

The result is limited to publications in bio-medical and life sciences. Future studies should consider scientific articles in other fields to further validate the findings. Future research would also benefit from conducting sub-analyses for scientific publications, such as broken by journal impact factors and author affiliations (or English as the first or the second language for the authors). This would help to gain deeper insight into stylistic differences among sub-cohorts of academic articles.

Furthermore, other informal elements as well as other differences among the English varieties should be included in future work to capture a comprehensive view of academic writing.

Acknowledgment. This work is partially supported by the Telstra-Deakin Centre of Excellence in Big Data and Machine Learning.

References

1. Ahmad, J.: Stylistic features of scientific English: a study of scientific research articles. English Lang. Lit. Stud. **2**(1), 47 (2012)
2. Ball, P.: 'Novel, amazing, innovative': positive words on the rise in science papers. Nature (2015)
3. Bradley, M.M., Lang, P.J.: Affective norms for English words (ANEW): instruction manual and affective ratings (1999)
4. Burrough-Boenisch, J.: Negotiable acceptability: reflections on the interactions between language professionals in Europe and NNS 1 scientists wishing to publish in English. Curr. Issues Lan. Plan. **7**(1), 31–43 (2006)
5. Chang, Y.Y., Swales, J.: Informal elements in English academic writing: threats or opportunities for advanced non-native speakers. In: Writing: Texts, Processes and Practices, pp. 145–167. Longman (1999)
6. Hyland, K.: Options of identity in academic writing. ELT J. **56**(4), 351–358 (2002)
7. Lazarus, C., Haneef, R., Ravaud, P., Boutron, I.: Classification and prevalence of spin in abstracts of non-randomized studies evaluating an intervention. BMC Med. Res. Methodol. **15**(1), 1 (2015)
8. Leshed, G., Kaye, J.J.: Understanding how bloggers feel: recognizing affect in blog posts. In: Proceedings of Conference on Human Factors in Computing Systems, pp. 1019–1024 (2006)
9. Nguyen, T.: Mood patterns and affective lexicon access in weblogs. In: Proceedings of ACL Student Research Workshop, pp. 43–48 (2010)
10. Pennebaker, J.W., Boyd, R.L., Jordan, K., Blackburn, K.: The development and psychometric properties of LIWC2015. Technical report, University of Texas at Austin (2015)
11. Rosen, L.D., Chang, J., Erwin, L., Carrier, L.M., Cheever, N.A.: The relationship between 'textisms' and formal and informal writing among young adults. Commun. Res. **37**(3), 420–440 (2010)

12. Spencer, C.M., Arbon, B.: Foundations of Writing: Developing Research and Academic Writing Skills. National Textbook Company, Lincolnwood (1996)
13. Vinkers, C.H., Tijdink, J.K., Otte, W.M.: Use of positive and negative words in scientific PubMed abstracts between 1974 and 2014: retrospective analysis. BMJ **351**, h6467 (2015)
14. Zaharia, M., Chowdhury, M., Franklin, M.J., Shenker, S., Stoica, I.: Spark: cluster computing with working sets. In: Proceedings of 2nd USENIX Conference on Hot Topics in Cloud Computing, p. 10 (2010)
15. Zimmer, C.: Staying afloat in the rising tide of science. Cell **164**(6), 1094–1096 (2016)

Discriminative Cues for Different Stages of Smoking Cessation in Online Community

Thin Nguyen[1]($\boxtimes$), Ron Borland[2], John Yearwood[1], Hua-Hie Yong[2],
Svetha Venkatesh[1], and Dinh Phung[1]

[1] Deakin University, Geelong, Australia
{thin.nguyen,john.yearwood,svetha.venkatesh,dinh.phung}@deakin.edu.au
[2] Cancer Council Victoria, Melbourne, Australia
{ron.borland,hua.yong}@cancervic.org.au

Abstract. Smoking is one of the leading causes of preventable death, being responsible for about six million deaths annually worldwide. Most smokers want to quit, but many find quitting difficult. The Internet enables people interested in quitting smoking to connect with others via online communities; however, the characteristics of these discussions are not well understood. This work aims to explore the textual cues of an online community interested in quitting smoking: www.reddit.com/r/stopsmoking – *"a place for redditors to motivate each other to quit smoking"*. A total of approximately 5,000 posts were randomly selected from the community. Four subgroups of posts based on the cessation days of abstainers were defined: S0: within the first week, S1: within the first month (excluding cohort S0), S2: from second month to one year, and S3: beyond one year. Psycho-linguistic features and content topics were extracted from the posts and analysed. Machine learning techniques were used to discriminate the online conversations in the first week S0 from the other subgroups. Topics and psycho-linguistic features were found to be highly valid predictors of the subgroups, possibly providing an important step in understanding social media and its use in studies of smoking and other addictions in online settings.

Keywords: Feature extraction · Textual cues · Web community · Smoking cessation

1 Introduction

Internet is increasingly being used for the exchange of information, support, and advice on a range of health concerns, including dealing with certain addictions, such as, smoking, drinking, and drug abuse. Reddit is one such avenue for people who share a common interest to connect and form communities with a specific interest. Such communities are known as subreddits and their members are called redditors. Online users can contribute to these subreddits by making posts and getting them discussed and commented on. For dealing with addiction, people may join subreddits of their interest, e.g., "r/stopsmoking", "r/stopdrinking",

© Springer International Publishing AG 2016
W. Cellary et al. (Eds.): WISE 2016, Part II, LNCS 10042, pp. 146–153, 2016.
DOI: 10.1007/978-3-319-48743-4_12

or "r/stopgaming". In these communities abstainers could exchange their own health story, encourage others, or record their journey of self-treatment, such as getting rid of smoking, drinking, or gaming. However, to date, little is known about the topics discussed within these communities or the language features that characterize these discussions.

This study aims to examine the topics and linguistic features in an online community interested in smoking cessation www.reddit.com/r/stopsmoking – "*a place for redditors to motivate each other to quit smoking.*" A large corpus of data was crawled including thousands of posts made by thousands of users within the community. We present an analysis focusing on the topics and psycholinguistic processes expressed in the content of users' posts, to identify predictive feature sets.

A key contribution of this work is to provide a comprehensive view based on topics of interest and language styles of members of an addiction community who self-identified as smokers who have quit smoking. Another contribution is to provide a set of predictors to differentiate users in different stages of smoking cessation. This work helps to improve our understanding of online addiction communities and illustrates the potential of machine learning for improving health care research and practice.

The current paper is organized as follows. Section 2 presents related work. Section 3 outlines the proposed methods and experimental setup. Section 4 presents the performance of topics and language styles in classifying posts into different stages of quitting. Section 5 concludes the paper and notes the prospect for future research.

2   Related Work

Several studies have considered Reddit as a new venue for exploration. For example, subreddits "r/stopsmoking" and "r/stopdrinking" were investigated to gain insight into smoking and drinking cessation [8]; "r/suicidewatch" was explored to discover changes in its content following celebrity suicides [4]; "r/stopsmoking", "r/hookah", and "r/electronic_cigarette" were examined to investigate into people's experiences with different tobacco products [2].

To conceptualize the content, two feature sets have been widely used: (1) topics: *what* people are writing about and (2) language styles: *the way* they express the story. To extract topics, latent Dirichlet allocation (LDA) [1] – a Bayesian probabilistic topic modeling – is often employed. To capture language styles conveyed in the content, packages proposed in psychology, such as LIWC [7], is widely used. For example, both topics and language styles were used as the base to detect community [5]. These two representations also potentially provide insights into mental health status of individuals. Indeed, these features have been found to be strong predictors of autism, and differentiate mental health communities from other online communities [6].

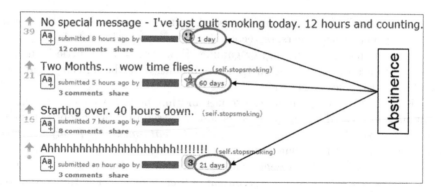

Fig. 1. Examples of posts made in www.reddit.com/r/stopsmoking.

3   Method

3.1   Data

In this paper Reddit data were chosen since they allow people to create or join communities with a common interest. In particular, data from the largest Reddit community interested in stop smoking – www.reddit.com/r/stopsmoking – were crawled.

The community was founded on 6 November 2009 and as of October 2015, 17,030 users (redditors) have made 33,278 posts in the forum. Figure 1 shows examples of posts made in the community. As seen from the figure, some authors are tagged with their cessation time. There were 8,828 authors who had declared their cessation time. Based on the cessation badge of authors, the cessation days for posts were calculated, which refer to the number of days the authors were abstinent from smoking when making the posts. In this work, we are interested in the posts made from day 1 of current cessation and exclude those made before that day, resulting in 13,566 posts. We categorized these posts into four mutually exclusive subgroups as below to learn how the textual features of the authors change as smoking cessation progresses:

- S0: Within the first week.
- S1: Within the first month (excluding cohort S0).
- S2: From second month to one year.
- S3: Beyond 1 year.

To create a balanced dataset, which is convenient for the evaluation of the classification afterwards, the same number of posts (based on the smallest number of posts, 1,220, which appeared in S3 cohort) for each of the four cohorts was randomly selected into the study, resulting in a corpus of 4,880 posts. This corpus was used in the experiments.

3.2 Feature Sets

In this work, topics, extracted using LDA [1], and language styles, extracted using LIWC package [7], were used to characterize posts made in different stages of quitting smoking. For language styles, LIWC package returns 68 psycho-linguistic categories, such as linguistic, social, affective, cognitive, perceptual, biological, relativity, personal concerns and spoken.

Table 1. The accuracy in the two-class classifications of posts into S0 versus later stages by different classifiers with different features. Best results for each feature set are shown in bold.

LIWC	S1	S2	S3	Topic	S1	S2	S3	Joint LIWC & Topic	S1	S2	S3
Lasso	**54.5**	**62.1**	**71.1**	Lasso	60.2	64.3	61.3	Lasso	60	64.3	75.4
LR	51	59.4	68.6	LR	60.2	64.8	63.7	LR	57.4	61.9	69.9
NB	50.2	59.2	59	NB	59.4	60.9	60.7	NB	61.9	63.5	60.7
SVM	49.8	54.7	55.5	SVM	49.2	49.6	49.4	SVM	48.8	54.3	54.9

3.3 Classifiers

Our experimental design examines the effect of topics and language styles in classifying a post into one of four different stages of quitting smoking. We are interested in not only which sets of features perform well in the classification but also which features in the sets are strongly predictive of the cessation stages. For this purpose, the least absolute shrinkage and selection operator (Lasso) [3], a regularized regression model, is chosen. Lasso does logistic regression and selects features simultaneously, enabling an evaluation on both the classification performance and the importance of each feature in the classification. Particularly, in prediction of S0 versus S1, S2, and S3 stages for a post, Lasso assigns positive weights to features more likely to be used in S0 and negative weights to those less to be used in S0. To the features irrelevant to the prediction, Lasso assigns zero weight. Thus, by examining its weights, we can learn the importance of each feature in the prediction.

For comparison with the classification performed by Lasso, classifiers from other paradigms were also included: Naive Bayes (NB), Support vector machines (SVM), and Logistic regression (LR). These classifiers will perform the binary classifications of posts into either S0 or S1/S2/S3 stages, using LIWC, topics, and a combination of them as the feature sets. The accuracy is used to compare with that of Lasso on the same classification.

4 Classification

4.1 Performance

The Lasso model [3] is used for the classification. Using the coefficients derived from the Lasso method, we implemented three pair-wise classifiers classifying

Table 2. Lasso model with language styles as the features to discriminate S0 versus later stages. Features with same coefficient signs across the three binary classifiers were colored. Reds are the positive predictors of S0 and blues are the positive predictors of S1, S2, and S3.

Feature	Example	S1	S2	S3	Feature	Example	S1	S2	S3
(Intercept)		-0.59	-0.45	-0.75	Anger	Hate, kill	0.21		
Word count		0.67	0.31		Sadness	Crying, grief	-0.96		
Words per sentence		-1.92	0.14	6.94	Cognitive	Cause, know	0.14		
Dictionary words		0.95			Insight	Think, know	-0.73		
Words > 6 letters		0.66			Causation	Because, effect	-0.78		
Total function words		-0.64			Discrepancy	Should, would	-0.04		
1st pers singular	I, me	1.83	1.45	1.45	Tentative	Maybe, perhaps	0.38	0.63	
1st pers plural	We, us	-0.24	-0.12		Certainty	Always, never	-1.35	-2.3	
2nd person	You, your	-0.57	-2.11	-3.93	Inhibition	Block, constrain	0.28		
3rd pers singular	She, her	-0.99			Inclusive	And, with	0.55		
3rd pers plural	They, their	-0.24			Exclusive	But, without	-0.31		
Articles	A, an	-0.09			Perceptual	Observing, heard	-1.2		
Auxiliary verbs	Am, will		0.14	0.37	See	Appearance, look	-0.52	-1.26	-0.24
Past tense	Went, ran	-0.61	-0.5		Hear	Listen, hearing	0.63	0.71	
Present tense	Is, does	-0.37			Feel	Feels, touch	1.88	1.12	1.16
Future tense	Will, gonna	1.1			Biological	Eat, blood	-0.91		
Adverbs	Very, really	-1	-0.2		Body	Cheek, hands		0.14	0.82
Prepositions	To, with	0.57	0.13		Health	Clinic, flu	-0.36		
Conjunctions	And, but	0.08	0.57	0.51	Sexual	Horny, love	-0.99		
Negations	No, not	-0.08			Time	End, until	0.53		
Quantifiers	Few, many	-0.06	0.48		Work	Job, majors	1.38	0.5	
Swear words	Damn, piss	3.74	0.24		Achievement	Earn, hero	0.16	0.82	
Social	Mate, talk		-0.07	-0.07	Leisure	Cook, chat	-1.63	-0.06	
Humans	Adult, baby	0.12	-0.06		Home	Apartment, kitchen	0.03		
Positive emotion	Love, nice	-0.56	-0.46		Money	Audit, cash		-1.73	-1.29
Negative emotion	Hurt, ugly	0.46	0.26	1.04	Religion	Altar, church	1.25		
Anxiety	Worried, fearful	-0.61			Assent	Agree, OK	-2.87	-0.53	

input posts into *S0* versus *S1*, *S2*, or *S3* stages, using three feature sets: LIWC, topics, and a combination of them. The accuracy of this classifier in different feature sets is shown in Table 1, accompanied by that of SVM, NB, and LR. Lasso outperformed other classifiers when LIWC and a combination of LIWC and topics were used as the features, and was second to LR when topics were the features. However, Lasso used a smaller number of features than did the best, LR. So, for the sake of brevity, only results by Lasso are reported hereafter.

In general, the result of the classification by Lasso is better when the gap of the stages is wider. In other words, the performance of S0 versus S3 classification is the best, that of S0 versus S2 is in between, and that of S0 versus S1 is the worst. A possible reason is that as cessation progresses the topics and language styles of people in later stages are markedly different from those expressed during the first stage. An exception is the drop in performance on using topics as features to classify posts into S0 versus S3 stages, implying a similarity in the topics discussed by both junior and senior abstainers. It could be because the seniors may talk about their early days of the journey or advise novices on what they may face in the battle, making the use of topics in stage S0 and S3 indistinguishable.

Topics outperformed language styles as the features in S0 versus S1 and S2 classifications. However topics fell behind language styles in the roles of features in S0 versus S3 classification, possibly due to a bigger gap in the use of certain language processes than in the use of topics between the two categories.

Observably, a fusion of the features gained the best performance in S0 versus S3 classification. This shows the potential of using multi-cues for making prediction of people in different stages of quitting an addiction.

4.2   Linguistic Features as the Predictors

Table 2 shows the Lasso model using language style cues as features to predict S0 versus S1, S2, and S3 posts. Obviously, *negative* emotion is a positive predictor of posts made in the first week of smoking abstinence. Likewise, it is also observed that *first personal singular pronouns* is another positive predictor of first-week posts while, *second personal pronouns* is an indicator of posts made in later stages.

An interesting observation is that *feel(ing)* is a positive predictor of S0, while *see(ing)* (e.g., *appearance, look, weight*) is a negative predictor of this early stage. This is understandable given that those in the initial stage of quitting tend to experience the feeling of craving, whereas for the seniors they tend to look back and talk about *before and after*, for example, commenting on their appearances, such as *"Skin looks better - Before I'd look pale, dry, wrinkly, like a dying man. Now I feel I have lesser wrinkles. Skin looks more alive. Must also be due to the fact that I'm much better hydrated now..."* or *"You'll only gain weight if you let yourself. If you don't eat junk food as a replacement, you won't gain weight. It's really that simple..."*.

4.3   Topics as the Predictors

Table 3 shows the classification model inferred by Lasso [3] to predict S0 versus S1, S2, and S3 posts using topics as features.[1]

Table 4 shows the word cloud of topics with the same sign of coefficients for all classifications. Strong positive predictors of S0 abstainers include topic numbered 18 about the theme of determination of quitting ("quit", "decided"), topic 23 (the failure in past attempts – "failed", "past", "previous", "attempts"), and topic 47 (methods of quitting smoking – "gum", "vaping"). Other strong predictors of S0 include topic 15, which is on looking for generic advice in Reddit, such as on posts, comments, or edit. This could be because the abstainers in the first week are novices to Reddit.

On the other hand, strong positive predictors of posts made by abstainers in later stages are feeling proud after succeeding months of smoking abstinence (topic 10 – "month", "proud", "passed", "hit", "mark"), being happy about winning the challenge (topic 20 – "smoke-free", "cigarette-free", "nicotine-free", "challenge", "glad"), or struggling to deal with the temptation and staying strong (topic 26 – "stay-strong", "struggle", "temptation").

---

[1] The list of all topics can be accessed via http://bit.ly/21Z0o4r.

Table 3. Lasso model with topics as the features to discriminate posts made in S0 versus those made in later stages of quitting smoking. Features with the same coefficient signs across the three classifiers were colored. Those in red are the positive predictors of S0 and those in blue are the positive predictors of S1, S2, and S3.

Feature	S1	S2	S3	Feature	S1	S2	S3	Feature	S1	S2	S3
(Intercept)	0.36	−0.13	−0.24	T18	0.39	1.38	1.14	T35		0.14	
T1			−1.34	T19	−0.14	−0.66	−0.51	T36		−0.05	−0.53
T2		0.01	−0.27	T20	−0.04	−0.74	−0.95	T37	1.26	−2.12	−0.47
T3			−1.15	T21		−0.89	−0.94	T38		0.37	2.01
T5		1.37	0.36	T22		−0.05		T39	−0.41		−0.44
T6			0.21	T23	0.37	2.49	2.72	T40			−0.85
T8			−0.79	T24	0.75	0.82	0.75	T41			0.38
T9		−0.33	−0.44	T25	−3.55	−1.03		T42			−1.59
T10	−0.09	−2.26	−1.19	T26	−0.52	−0.85	−2.17	T43		0.74	1.14
T11		0.46		T28		0.71	3.31	T44	−0.43		0.13
T12		−0.11	−1.84	T29		0.35		T45		−0.1	
T13		0.44	0.41	T30	0.16	1.25	0.43	T46			−0.69
T14		0.8	2.83	T31		0.5	1.3	T47	0.48	1.18	1.53
T15	0.06	0.75	0.76	T32		−1.13	−2.26	T48	−0.37		−1.1
T16		0.4	1.57	T33		−0.45	−1.16	T49		−0.43	−0.06
T17			0.99	T34		0.16	1.01	T50			2.8

Table 4. Topics selected into the prediction models with the same coefficient signs in the three classifiers. Red indicate positive predictors of S0 and blue indicates its negative predictors.

Topic	Word cloud	Topic	Word cloud
T15	reddit advice post comments edit — tips group update reddit-comments ...	T47	nicotine gum — using vape vaping addiction ...
T18	quit decided turkey — quit-turkey decided-quit ...	T10	month proud mark — hit passed star milestone ...
T23	cig tried cigs quit tried-quit ...	T19	smoked dream dreams woke — smoking realized woke remember ...
T24	pack buy half smoked bought — ...	T20	free smoke smoke-free ...
T30	started smoking — quit started-smoking ...	T26	strong stay stay-strong — quitters fellow proud ...

5   Conclusion

This study investigated the topics and linguistic features of the discussions among members in an online community interested in quitting smoking. Machine learning techniques were used to discriminate the textual features among posts made in early and late stages of quitting smoking. It was found that distinct topics and linguistic styles differentiate abstainers in the first week from those in later stages, probably providing textual factors for both failure and success in smoking cessation. The results of this study suggest that data mining of low-cost social media has the potential to detect meaningful patterns of addiction problems confronted by society, likely offering an effective tool for policy makers. The findings also highlight the potential applicability of machine learning to health care practice and research.

This work has explored the markers of different stages in the current cessation attempt. Since Reddit does not record the cessation badge for previous attempts, manual annotations could be conducted to collect all the attempts. When this information is available, future work could investigate into the causes of relapsing among abstainers.

Acknowledgment. This work is partially supported by the Telstra-Deakin Centre of Excellence in Big Data and Machine Learning.

References

1. Blei, D.M., Ng, A.Y., Jordan, M.I.: Latent Dirichlet allocation. J. Mach. Learn. Res. **3**, 993–1022 (2003)
2. Chen, A.T., Zhu, S.-H., Conway, M.: What online communities can tell us about electronic cigarettes and hookah use: a study using text mining and visualization techniques. J. Med. Internet Res. **17**(9), e220 (2015)
3. Friedman, J., Hastie, T., Tibshirani, R.: Regularization paths for generalized linear models via coordinate descent. J. Stat. Softw. **33**(1), 1 (2010)
4. Kumar, M., Dredze, M., Coppersmith, G., De Choudhury, M.: Detecting changes in suicide content manifested in social media following celebrity suicides. In: Proceedings of the ACM Conference on Hypertext & Social Media, pp. 85–94 (2015)
5. Nguyen, T., Phung, D., Adams, B., Venkatesh, S.: A sentiment-aware approach to community formation in social media. In: Proceedings of the International AAAI Conference on Weblogs and Social Media, pp. 527–530 (2012)
6. Nguyen, T., Phung, D., Venkatesh, S.: Analysis of psycholinguistic processes and topics in online autism communities. In: Proceedings of the IEEE International Conference on Multimedia and Expo, pp. 1–6 (2013)
7. Pennebaker, J.W., Francis, M.E., Booth, R.J.: Linguistic Inquiry and Word Count (LIWC) [Computer software]. LIWC Inc. (2007)
8. Tamersoy, A., De Choudhury, M., Chau, D.H.: Characterizing smoking and drinking abstinence from social media. In: Proceedings of the ACM Conference on Hypertext & Social Media, pp. 139–148 (2015)

Query Processing

POL: A Pattern Oriented Load-Shedding for Semantic Data Stream Processing

Fethi Belghaouti[1], Amel Bouzeghoub[1(✉)], Zakia Kazi-Aoul[2], and Raja Chiky[2]

[1] SAMOVAR, Telecom SudParis, CNRS, Universite Paris-Saclay,
9 rue Charles Fourier, 91011 Evry Cedex, France
{fethi.belghaouti,amel.bouzeghoub}@telecom-sudparis.eu
[2] Institut Superieur d'Electronique de Paris,
28 rue Notre-Dame des Champs, 75006 Paris, France
{zakia.kazi-aoul,raja.chiky}@isep.fr
http://www.telecom-sudparis.eu, www.isep.fr

Abstract. Nowadays, high volumes of data are generated and published at a very high velocity, producing heterogeneous data streams. This has led researchers to propose new systems named RDF Stream Processors (RSP), to deal with this new kind of streams. Unfortunately, these systems are fallible when their maximum supported speed is reached especially in a limited system resources environment. To overcome these problems, recent efforts have been made in the field. Some of them decrease the volume of RDF data streams using compression or load-shedding techniques, mostly according to a probabilistic approach. In this paper we propose POL: a Pattern Oriented approach to Load-shed data from RDF streams based on a deterministic approach. As a pre-processing task through a unique pass, the approach extracts the exact needed semantic data from the stream. The conducted experiments on public available datasets have demonstrated the effectiveness of our approach.

Keywords: BigData · Semantic data stream · Graph patterns detection · Load-shedding

1 Introduction

In the very near past, queries were volatile when data was persistent. Today, we are witnessing the inversion of roles. Thus, data is becoming extremely dynamic when the queries are persistent. Indeed, data is generated continuously as a stream by different sources such as sensors, social networks, GPS, e-commerce and weather stations to cite only few and is heterogeneous (various formats such as JSON, XML, RSS, CSV, etc.). This fact leads to an interoperability problem.

Today, in order to provide useful information, such as contextual data, for target applications and increase interoperability, initiatives such as the Semantic Sensor Web (SSW)[1] have semanticized their descriptions and their observation data using semantic web technologies [6][2], giving rise to semantic data streams.

---

[1] http://en.wikipedia.org/wiki/Semantic_Sensor_Web.
[2] http://www.w3.org/standards/semanticweb/.

© Springer International Publishing AG 2016
W. Cellary et al. (Eds.): WISE 2016, Part II, LNCS 10042, pp. 157–171, 2016.
DOI: 10.1007/978-3-319-48743-4_13

However, given the specificity of this type of streams, neither Data Stream Management Systems (DSMS) [1,3] nor standard semantic web technologies were adapted to process this new type of data flows. This has favored the emergence of a new research axis from the semantic web community and led researchers to propose RDF Stream Processing systems (*RSP*) as a solution to deal with this new kind of streams. We cite C-SPARQL [5], CQELS [15], SPARQL Stream [8], Sparkwave [12], EP-SPARQL [2] and Streaming SPARQL [7]. This community has created recently the W3C RSP Group[3] in order to define "a common model for producing, transmitting and continuously querying RDF Streams" (see footnote 3).

Dealing with huge volumes of dynamic data could overload the system, which causes a significant increase in response time and an inevitable degradation of response quality and sometimes even to its unavailability. In addition, none of the proposed RSPs includes yet a quality of service policy (QoS) [13], which makes them fallible when their maximum supported speed is reached or the resources of the system hosting them are saturated. To overcome such situations, in contrast to the existing probabilistic solutions, inspired by the DSMS domain techniques ([17,21,27]), we propose a deterministic approach named POL: a Pattern Oriented approach for Load-shedding semantic data streams. Our approach proposes to use basic boolean operations as a "low cost" pre-processing. After constructing the binary pattern of the continuous query, for each received RDF graph, a conjunction operator (AND) is applied between its online binary detected pattern and the binary representation of the query. This determines, very quickly, the relevant part of the data to send to the RSP engine and the irrelevant ones to load-shed according to the particular query. To implement our solution, we consider the existing RSP systems as black boxes. The objective of our solution is to reduce the volume of the input stream and to optimize the memory and CPU usage increasing thus the system processing capacity and ensuring its availability while guaranteeing its recall at 100 %.

The remainder of the paper is organized as follows: Sect. 2 presents the related work, giving a critical overview of existing approaches for decreasing the load on RDF Stream Processors. We present the Pattern Oriented Load-shedding approach in Sect. 3. Section 4 reports the empirical evaluation. Finally, we conclude and give some research perspectives in Sect. 5.

2   Related Work

Obviously, processing and storing the entire data of a stream, which is an infinite set of tuples is impossible, in particular, if the system has a restricted set of processing and storage resources. To deal with those constraints, two types of approaches have been adopted by researchers.

The first type, which has a financial impact, considers the elasticity of the system, using Cloud Computing technologies to allocate as many resources as necessary. As far as we know, there are two works dealing with elasticity.

---

[3] http://www.w3.org/community/rsp/.

In [18], Hoeksema and Kotoulas implement partial RDFS reasoning as part of the C-SPARQL query language on the S4 streaming platform[4], which enables to split the processing load over multiple machines to increase the overall system throughput. In [19], Le Phuoc et al. propose CQELS Cloud which allows nodes to join or leave, and re-assigns operators to nodes accordingly.

The second type of existing approaches has no financial impact and considers the inflexible and rigid aspects of the system, where the only resources to allocate are the ones that are physically available. Consequently, when the data stream volume and/or rate reach some maximum threshold, the system could be saturated causing a significant degradation in response's quality and time and probably makes the system itself unavailable. To overcome such situations, this type of approaches uses techniques from DSMS domain [4,10,17,21] which consist of reducing the input load by shedding a part of its data to avoid the system resources saturation.

In their work, Jain et al. in [20] have extended CQELS by adding new operators and implementing three sampling algorithms: Uniform Random Sampling, Reservoir Sampling and Chain Sampling. Depending on the algorithm and the sampling rate passed as parameters to the query, this approach consists in ignoring the RDF triple or passing it to the target system.

In [14], Nguyen et al. propose eviction strategies for semantic flow processing by dropping variable bindings instead of data, unlike what is done in load shedding approaches. This probabilistic eviction is based on the fact that a query is represented by a tree of algebra expressions. The variable bindings are propagated from the leaves to the root, representing the result. Each algebra expression has a cache where the variable bindings are stored. Thus, based on the probability that its result set is not empty, the algorithm decides to evict a binding. Nevertheless, these probabilities are computed offline, which means that they must be calculated beforehand. Moreover, this strategy does not take into account the structure of the graph.

In [11], authors propose CLOCK, a data-aware eviction strategy that extends Last Recently Used (LRU) algorithm. Indeed, it considers not only the last time the variable binding has been used, but also the importance of past usefulness in order to estimate the likelihood of a future one and evict bindings from the cache based on this estimation. In this approach, every binding is associated with a score. The scores are stored in a circular buffer, and a pointer points at the position p. If the cache is full, then the score at position p is depreciated and if it is lower than a chosen threshold, the corresponding element is evicted. If not, the pointer moves to the next element and so on until an element gets evicted. If a binding contributes to a join, its score is increased. This strategy is more efficient than LRU, but it needs an extra-buffer.

These techniques are recently used in RSP community (see footnote 3). Even if they avoid systems overload and/or crash, they however decrease the quality of their responses trying to maximize their recall. In addition, they are all based on a probabilistic data-oriented approach and some of them need off-line computations.

---

[4] http://incubator.apache.org/s4/.

To overcome these disadvantages, we proposed in a previous work [24], a graph-oriented approach for load-shedding semantic data streams. The main idea of this work is to prove that semantic data streams should be processed as a stream of sub-graphs instead of triples. We have shown that the graph-oriented approach preserves the links between data which leads to a higher semantic level and best performances comparing to the triple-based approach which destroys the links between nodes during the load-shedding and thus decreases the semantic level of the RDF stream. Table 1 summarizes and compares the existing works in the literature according to some criteria such as the handled data vs graph structure, processing type (online vs offline) and whether the method is probabilistic or deterministic.

Table 1. Comparative study of existing works.

Approaches	Data vs structure	Offline vs online	Probabilistic vs deterministic
Jain et al. [20]	Data	Online	Probabilistic
Gao et al. [11]	Data	Online	Probabilistic
Nguyen et al. [14]	Data	Offline	Probabilistic
Belghaouti et al. [24]	Graph	Online	Probabilistic
POL	Graph	Online	Deterministic

In this paper, we propose POL: a Pattern Oriented approach for Load-shedding semantic data streams. This new approach, that guarantees a 100 % of the system recall, is based on an exact matching between the continuous query pattern and the input stream one using Boolean operations. We detail this algorithm in the next section.

3 Pattern Oriented Load-Shedding: POL

Our approach performs the load-shedding through three steps:

- (1) The online predicates pattern detection and their hash table (*PHT*) construction detailed in Sect. 3.2,
- (2) The RDF graph and continuous query bit vectors construction presented in Sect. 3.3, and
- (3) The load-shedding mechanism described in Sect. 3.4.

Before detailing these steps, we first give some necessary definitions that will be used in the following subsections.

3.1 Definitions

Let $\mathcal{S} = \{G_1, .., G_n\}$ be an RDF stream where each graph G_i is a finite set of RDF triples:

$$G_i = \{(s_{i1}, p_{i1}, o_{i1}), (s_{i2}, p_{i2}, o_{i2}), ..., (s_{im}, p_{im}, o_{im})\}$$

We assume that every complex tree-based RDF graph can be divided into a set of star graphs with a unique subject [25].

The graph is thus reduced to a set of triples having the same subject:

$$G_i = \{(s_i, p_{i1}, o_{i1}), (s_i, p_{i2}, o_{i2}), ..., (s_i, p_{im}, o_{im})\}$$

Hence, we can formalize our understanding of a graph in an RDF stream and the notions of graph and query patterns as follows:

Property 1. Each graph in an RDF Stream can be represented as a directed star-graph $G_i(V, E)$, where $V = \{v_0, v_1, v_2, ..., v_m\}$ is the set of vertices with v_0 the central vertex and vi the leaf vertices for $i = 1..m$ and $E = \{(v_0, v_1), (v_0, v_2), ..., (v_0, v_m)\}$ is the set of edges labeled with the predicates.

Definition 1 (Graph Pattern). *Let $P = \{p_1, ..., p_n\}$ be the set of predicates in the graph stream $\mathcal{S}$, $GP_i = \{p_k \in P \mid k \leq n\}$ a subset of P and $G_i \in \mathcal{S}$ a graph in the stream.*

$$GP_i \text{ is a graph pattern of } G_i \text{ iff}$$

$$\forall p_k \ (p_k \in GP_i \rightarrow p_k \in G_i)$$

Definition 2 (Query Pattern). *Let $P = \{p_1, ..., p_n\}$ be the set of predicates in the graph stream $\mathcal{S}$, $QP_j = \{p_l \in P \mid l \leq n\}$ a subset of P and Q_j a continuous query.*

$$QP_j \text{ is a query pattern of } Q_j \text{ iff}$$

$$\forall p_l \ (p_l \in QP_j \rightarrow p_l \in Q_j)$$

3.2 Frequent Predicates Detection and PHT Construction

The pseudo Algorithm 1 explains how we construct the Predicate Hash Table (*PHT*) by analyzing the predicates of the RDF stream. This table contains all the detected predicates in RDF graphs of an input stream. *PHT* is an indexed table where each new detected predicate is inserted. When the PHT is empty at the beginning of the stream (Algorithm 1, line 2), each time an RDF graph is received (Algorithm 1, line 4), for all its predicates, if the predicate is not present in the *PHT*, it is inserted with a new index (Algorithm 1, lines 5 to 14). Note that those indexes will serve later to point the bits in the *GraphBV* and the *QueryBV*.

Algorithm 1. Frequent RDF Predicates Detection

Data: RDF Stream
Result: Predicates Hash Table (PHT)
```
 1  begin
 2  │   HashTable PHT<predicate, index>
 3  │   int i ← 0                                    /* Index initialization */
 4  │   foreach graph ∈ RDF Stream do
 5  │   foreach predicate ∈ graph do
 6  │   begin
 7  │   │   if predicate ∈ PHT then
 8  │   │   │   NOP                                  /* already existing predicate */
 9  │   │   else
10  │   │   │   ind ← i
11  │   │   │   PHT.put(predicate, ind)             /* Insert the new predicate */
12  │   │   │   i ← i+1                             /* Update the bit index */
13  │   │   end
14  │   end
15
16
17  │   return PHT
18  end
```

3.3   Query and Graph Bit Vectors Construction

As stated in Sect. 3.1, since each RDF graph can be considered as a set of RDF star graphs, each graph can be represented as a bit vector that we call *GraphBV*. Each bit at index i of this vector is set to 1 or 0 according to the presence or not of the corresponding predicate in the graph. Figure 1 illustrates how the two bit vectors are constructed. In this example, the graph contains the predicates a, b, c, d; and the query contains the predicates a and c.

We consider in this section two bit vectors: *GraphBV* with size m associated to each graph pattern GP and *QueryBV* with size k associated to each graph query GQ. p_i and p_j are predicates belonging to *PHT*.

$$\forall\, i \in [0, m-1],\ GraphBV[i] = \begin{cases} 1 \text{ if } p_{i+1} \in GP \\ 0 \text{ else.} \end{cases}$$

And

$$\forall\, j \in [0, k-1],\ QueryBV[j] = \begin{cases} 1 \text{ if } p_{j+1} \in GQ \\ 0 \text{ else.} \end{cases}$$

When a query is received by the RSP, the *QueryBV* is initially set to zero (Algorithm 2, line 2). Then, for each predicate of the query, the corresponding bit is set to 1 (according to the *PHT*). If the predicate does not exist in the *PHT*, it is inserted as new predicate pattern and its corresponding bit is set to "1" (Algorithm 2, lines 3 to 12). The bit vector *GraphBV*, associated to the RDF

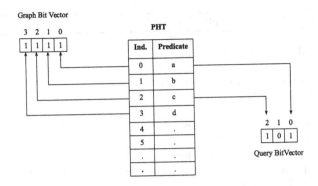

Fig. 1. Construction of the query and graph BitVectors (patterns).

Algorithm 2. Query Pattern Detection

Data: RSP Continuous Query, Predicate Hash Table (PHT)
Result: Query Bit Vector (QueryBV)

```
1  begin
2  |    BitVector QueryBV ← 0                          /* Query bitvector initialization */
3  |    foreach predicate ∈ Query do
4  |    begin
5  |    |    if predicate ∈ PHT then
6  |    |    |    ind ← PHT.get(predicate)             /* Get the predicates bit index */
7  |    |    |    QueryBV[ind] ← 1                      /* Set the relevant bit to 1 */
8  |    |    else
9  |    |    |    Insert(predicate) into PHT           /* Insert the new predicate */
10 |    |    |    Update(ind)
11 |    |    |    QueryBV[ind] ← 1                      /* and set the relevant bit to 1 */
12 |    |    end
13 |    end
14 |
15 |    return QueryBV                                 /* Return the Query Pattern */
16 end
```

---

graph received from the stream, is constructed in the same way (the algorithm is not presented to avoid redundancy).

3.4 The Load-Shedding

Our Pattern oriented Load-Shedding approach consists in a continuous process that filters the incoming RDF stream, thus keeping only the requested ones for the RSP engine. Based on using bitwise operations like the conjunction *(binary AND)* and hash table accesses, our approach avoids the RSP system doing complex operations on RDF graphs that are usually very "costly".

Pseudo Algorithm 3 explains how, for each graph in the RDF stream (line 3), we drop all the triples that contain predicates which are not requested by the query. The only ones that are transmitted (not dropped) to the RSP engine are those having their index-bits set to 1 in both *GraphBV* and *QueryBV* (lines 7,10).

Algorithm 3. Pattern Oriented Load-Shedding

Data: RDF Stream, QueryBV, PHT
Result: Load-Shedded RDF Stream

```
 1 begin
 2 │   Query Pattern Detection(QueryBV)
 3 │   foreach graph ∈ RDF Stream do
 4 │   begin
 5 │   │   foreach triple t ∈ graph do
 6 │   │   begin
 7 │   │   │   if t.predicate ∈ PHT then
 8 │   │   │   │   ind ← PHT.get(t.predicate)  /* Get the existing predicates
 │   │   │   │   bit index */
 9 │   │   │   │   if QueryBV[ind] = 1 then
10 │   │   │   │   │   NOP                           /* Keep the triple */
11 │   │   │   │   else
12 │   │   │   │   │   drop(t)   /* The irrelevant triple is Load-Shedded */
13 │   │   │   │   end
14 │   │   │   else
15 │   │   │   │   drop(t)       /* The irrelevant triple is Load-Shedded */
16 │   │   │   end
17 │   │   end
18 │
19 │   │   return graph              /* return the lightweighted graph   */
20 │   end
21 │
22 end
```

3.5 Proof of Concept: Load-Shedding Semantic Data Streams Using the Graph (data) and Query Patterns

Let suppose that we have a continuous query q as in listing 1.1.

```
SELECT ?x ?y ?z
FROM STREAM <http://MyStream> [NOW 10s SLIDE 10s]
WHERE {?x a ?y ;
          c ?z .
      }
```

Listing 1.1. Continuous query example

Figure 2 illustrates the content of the current window that contains the data received from the stream during the last ten seconds, as mentioned in the query q (Listing 1.1). Our approach consists of constructing the patterns of the query and its bit vector (once). Then, every time an RDF graph is received, the Load-Shedding algorithm computes a Boolean operation AND between those two bit vectors $GraphBV$ and $QueryBV$ dealing to update the $GraphBV$ value ($GraphBV'$ in Fig. 2). According to the result, we keep only triples of the

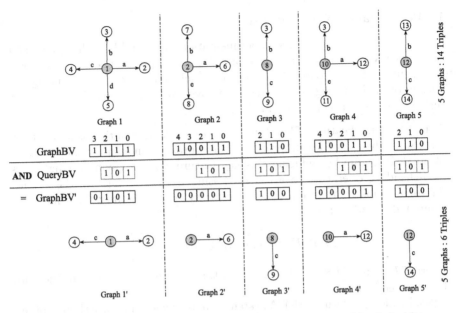

Fig. 2. RDF data stream example: applying pattern oriented load-shedding.

incoming RDF graph that contain the predicates of the query. This operation reduces the memory consumption, enhances the system workload and of course guarantees its good quality of response.

Thus, Fig. 2 shows that with a $QueryBV{=}101$, the algorithm reduces the volume of data in the current window from 5 graphs containing 14 triples to 5 graphs containing only 6 triples. For example, Graph1 is reduced from $\{(1, a, 2), (1, b, 3), (1, c, 4), (1, d, 5)\}$ to $\{(1, a, 2), (1, c, 4)\}$ and graph2 is reduced from $\{(2, a, 6), (2, b, 7), (2, e, 8)\}$ to $\{(2, a, 6)\}$ and so on.

4   Evaluation and Discussion

POL algorithm has been implemented using Java language on the top of Ubuntu-64 14.04 LTS OS and a personal laptop (Intel core i7-4500 4X1,8 GHz with 6 GB of RAM). For the experimentation purpose, we choose C-SPARQL as an RSP engine. However, as explained previously, any other RSP engine could be used. In order to assess the effectiveness of our approach, we launch C-SPARQL queries twice (1st time with POL and the 2nd time without POL).

In this section we present the Key Performance Features that we aim to achieve, the 5 public datasets used in the conducted experimentations, and a case study to illustrate the proposal on a real extracted semantic data stream. Finally we will explain the evaluation results and give a final discussion.

4.1   Performance Key Features

Before presenting the conducted experimentation, we detail here the three main Performance Key features that our approach must improve. These keys are useful to highlight the contribution of our approach that is to say, enhancing the efficiency of an RSP engine in a restricted system resources environment. We describe these performance keys in the following:

- Time Efficiency Feature (TE). A system is more efficient in time than another, if it can do the same task in less time. Our approach can enhance the efficiency of an RSP engine by reducing this key feature when applying a single pass load-shedding operation to avoid processing irrelevant data by the engine, improving thus its time efficiency and the system scalability. This metric is computed as follows:

$$Time\ Efficiency\ in\%\ (TE) = \frac{ET}{ETLS}$$

where ET and $ETLS$ are the execution time of the engine without and with POL respectively.

- Space Efficiency Feature (SE). A system is more efficient in space than another, if it can do the same task using less memory space. Our approach decreases the memory space system usage by load-shedding an extract of input data stream (irrelevant data). It enhances the space efficiency, and thus the system scalability. This feature is the ratio between the number of the triples processed by the engine without and with Load-Shedding (POL). It is computed as follows:

$$Space\ Efficiency\ in\%\ (SE) = \frac{NTriples}{NTriples - NLSTriples}$$

where $NTriples$ and $NLSTriples$ are respectively the total Number of Triples in the stream and the Number of Load-Shedded Triples using POL.

- Recall Feature (SRecall). The system Recall is usually defined as the number of correct returned results divided by the number of all the relevant results. When applying a probabilistic load-shedding algorithm to a data stream, the recall of the target system is necessarily reduced. Our approach can ensure a 100 % recall, even if -depending of the query- more than half of the volume of the input data is shedded. We define SRecall (Stream Recall) as a specific recall where its value is the result of the division of the number of the tuples returned by the engine when using POL by the one without using it. This key shows how POL can preserve the quality of response of the system.

$$SRecall = \frac{NRLS}{NR} \times 100\%$$

4.2   Datasets Description

AEMET-1 and AEMET-2 are two datasets provided by the Spanish Meteorological Office (AEMET). They represent meteorological information, taken from weather stations in Spain [9] according to different schemas. The Petrol dataset provides metadata about credit cards transactions in petrol station, furnished by a Spanish start-up (Localidata[5]). Charley and Katrina are two datasets within others delivered by Linked Observation Data (LOD)[6]. They represent sensor observations of different weather parameters. Those observations represent meteorological phenomena like humidity, temperature, pressure, visibility, precipitation, etc.

4.3 Case Study

Figure 3 presents an example of a C-sparql query and illustrates the resulted Query Bit Vector ($QueryBV$) based on the PHT. As explained in Sect. 3.3, Algorithm 2 constructs it by checking the presence of the query predicates one by one (I) and setting to 1 each corresponding bit (here indexes 1, 2, 3 and 5). The returned value is thus 101110 (46) (II).

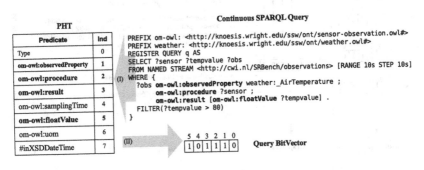

Fig. 3. Example of query bit vector construction using the PHT table.

Figure 4 shows an extract of an RDF stream on which we apply our approach. At the right side the evolution of the RDF stream over the time is depicted. At the left side, we can see the constructed $GraphBV$ corresponding to each graph pattern and the new graph bit vector corresponding to the results of the AND operation between $GraphBV$ and $QueryBV$ for each graph of the stream ($GraphBV$ AND $QueryBV$). All data in red will be dropped. The RSP engine will receive only the relevant data (in black), which will contribute significantly to save space and time.

4.4 Evaluation Results

Table 2 lists the experimental datasets, reporting: number of triples (# RDF Triples), number of RDF graphs (# RDF Graphs), the space efficiency key (SE), the time efficiency key feature (TE) and finally the SRecall.

---

[5] http://www.localidata.com/.
[6] http://wiki.knoesis.org/index.php/LinkedSensorData#Linked_Observation_Data.

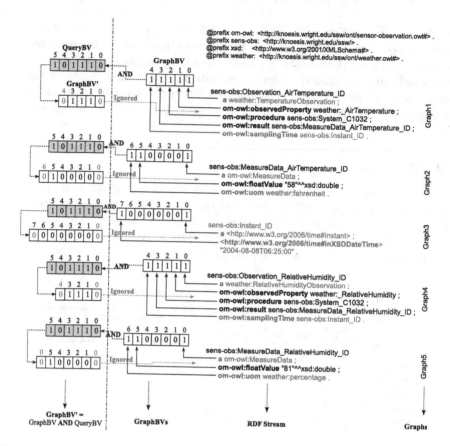

Fig. 4. Pattern oriented load-shedding on LOD data stream extract.(Black: kept data, Red: Shedded data). (Color figure online)

We can clearly notice how POL contributes on scaling up an RSP by decreasing its memory consumption more than 11 times (aemet-1 dataset for example) and similarly multiplying its execution speed by approximatively the same rate.

Table 2. Pattern oriented load-shedding approach applied on different datasets.

DataSet	# RDF triples	# RDF graphs	SE	TE	SRecall
aemet-1	1 018 815	33 095	**11,10**	**11,73**	101 %
aemet-2	2 788 429	398 347	**3,50**	**3,50**	101 %
Petrol	3 356 616	419 577	**4,00**	**4,03**	98 %
Charley	108 644 569	25 303 346	**2,34**	**2,32**	110 %
Katrina	179 128 408 (*944 510)	41 600 926	**1,30**	**1,31**	103 %

Depending on the size of RDF graphs in the stream and the graph of the continous query, the ratio of the data to ignore could be different. The load-shedding is inversely proportional to the query graph size and directely proportional to the RDF graphs size. For example in the aemet-1 dataset, we obtain the higher value of Space and Time efficiencies since the query asks only three predicates while RDF graphs may contain 59 predicates. This explains the high value of the ratio of ignored data. In contrast, in the Charley dataset, the size of RDF graphs is most time less than five predicates, while the query graph size is four predicates. In this case most of the data are passed to the RSP engine.

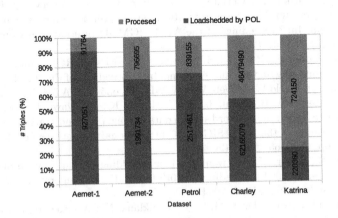

Fig. 5. Space efficiency results.

Figure 5 highlights space efficiency results and illustrates the processed triples vs. the unprocessed ones (dropped by POL). As we can see, the system supported by POL may process only relevant data (in red). This result directly affects in a positive way time efficiency of the system. The other interesting result is that the SRecall is between 98 % and 110 %. This is explained by the fact that (i) the stream processor may give different valid results (unlike a DBMS) and (ii) our approach for load-shedding reduces the probability to lose data during the windowing process.

5 Conclusion

We present in this paper a new deterministic approach for load-shedding RDF data streams named POL. Our Pattern Oriented Load-shedding approach is able to increase the scalability of any RSP system at least 1.3 times to more than 11 times the space and time efficiency without any degradation on the quality of responses. Moreover, it increases the number of the engine answers, thus, its quality of services. All those contributions are based on very "low cost" operations as a boolean operation and a hash table access. In our future works, we will explore the scalability of RSPs in an unlimited system resources environment. We plan to use Cloud Computing technologies to offer them horizontal scalability.

Acknowledgments. This work is partially funded by the French National Research Agency (ANR) project CAIR (ANR-14-CE23-0006).

References

1. Abadi, D., Carney, D., Cetintemel, U., Cherniack, M., Convey, C., Erwin, C., Galvez, E., Hatoun, M., Maskey, A., Rasin, et al.: Aurora: a data stream management system. In: Proceedings of the ACM SIGMOD International Conference on Management of Data (2003)
2. Anicic, D., Fodor, P., Rudolph, S., Stojanovic, N.: EP-SPARQL: a unified language for event processing and stream reasoning. In: Proceedings of the 20th International Conference on World Wide Web, WWW 2011, pp. 635–644. ACM, New York (2011)
3. Arasu, A., Babcock, B., Babu, S., Datar, M., Ito, K., Nishizawa, I., Rosenstein, J., Widom, J.: Stream: the stanford stream data manager (demonstration description). In: Proceedings of the ACM SIGMOD International Conference on Management of Data, pp. 665–665. ACM (2003)
4. Babcock, B., Datar, M., Motwani, R.: Load shedding for aggregation queries over data streams. In: 2004 Proceedings of 20th International Conference on Data Engineering, pp. 350–361, March 2004
5. Barbieri, D.F., Braga, D., Ceri, S., Grossniklaus, M.: An execution environment for c-SPARQL queries. In: Proceedings of the 13th International Conference on Extending Database Technology, EDBT 2010, pp. 441–452. ACM, New York (2010)
6. Berners-Lee, T., Hendler, J., Lassila, O., et al.: The semantic web. Sci. Am. **284**(5), 28–37 (2001)
7. Bolles, A., Grawunder, M., Jacobi, J.: Streaming SPARQL - extending SPARQL to process data streams. In: Bechhofer, S., Hauswirth, M., Hoffmann, J., Koubarakis, M. (eds.) ESWC 2008. LNCS, vol. 5021, pp. 448–462. Springer, Heidelberg (2008). doi:10.1007/978-3-540-68234-9_34
8. Calbimonte, J.-P., Corcho, O., Gray, A.J.G.: Enabling ontology-based access to streaming data sources. In: Patel-Schneider, P.F., Pan, Y., Hitzler, P., Mika, P., Zhang, L., Pan, J.Z., Horrocks, I., Glimm, B. (eds.) ISWC 2010, Part I. LNCS, vol. 6496, pp. 96–111. Springer, Heidelberg (2010)
9. Corcho, Ó., Garijo Verdejo, D., Mora, J., Poveda Villalon, M., Vila Suero, D., Villazón-Terrazas, B., Rozas, P., Atemezing, G.A.: Transforming meteorological data into linked data. Semantic Web (2012)
10. Das, A., Gehrke, J., Riedewald, M.: Approximate join processing over data streams. In: Proceedings of the ACM SIGMOD International Conference on Management of Data, pp. 40–51. ACM (2003)
11. Gao, S., Scharrenbach, T., Bernstein, A.: The clock data-aware eviction approach: towards processing linked data streams with limited resources. In: Presutti, V., d'Amato, C., Gandon, F., d'Aquin, M., Staab, S., Tordai, A. (eds.) ESWC 2014. LNCS, vol. 8465, pp. 6–20. Springer, Heidelberg (2014)
12. Komazec, S., Cerri, D., Fensel, D.: Sparkwave: continuous schema-enhanced pattern matching over RDF data streams. In: DEBS, pp. 58–68. ACM (2012)

13. Margara, A., Urbani, J., van Harmelen, F., Bal, H.: Streaming the web: reasoning over dynamic data. Web Semant.: Sci. Serv. Agents World Wide Web **25**, 24–44 (2014)
14. Nguyen, M.K., Scharrenbach, T., Bernstein, A.: Eviction strategies for semantic flow processing. In: SSWS@ ISWC, pp. 66–80 (2013)
15. Phuoc, D.L.: A native and adaptive approach for linked stream data processing. Ph.D. thesis, Digital Enterprise Research Institute, National University of Ireland, Galwa (2013)
16. Prudhommeau, E., Carothers, G., Machina, L.: Rdf 1.1 turtle terse RDF triple language. W3C Recommendation, 25 February 2014
17. Tatbul, N., Çetintemel, U., Zdonik, S.B., Cherniack, M., Stonebraker, M.: Load shedding in a data stream manager. In: VLDB, pp. 309–320 (2003)
18. Jesper, H., Spyros, K.: High-performance distributed stream reasoning using S4. In: Ordering Workshop at ISWC (2011)
19. Le-Phuoc, D., Nguyen Mau Quoc, H., Le Van, C., Hauswirth, M.: Elastic and scalable processing of linked stream data in the cloud. In: Alani, H., Kagal, L., Fokoue, A., Groth, P., Biemann, C., Parreira, J.X., Aroyo, L., Noy, N., Welty, C., Janowicz, K. (eds.) ISWC 2013, Part I. LNCS, vol. 8218, pp. 280–297. Springer, Heidelberg (2013)
20. Jain, N., Pozo, M., Chiky, R., Kazi-Aoul, Z.: Sampling semantic data stream: resolving overload and limited storage issues. In: Herawan, T., Deris, M.M., Abawajy, J. (eds.) Proceedings of the First International Conference on Advanced Data and Information Engineering (DaEng-2013). LNEE, vol. 285, pp. 41–48. Springer, Heidelberg (2014). doi:10.1007/978-981-4585-18-7_5
21. Brian, B., Mayur, D., Rajeev, M.: Load shedding in data stream systems. In: Aggarwal, C.C. (ed.) Data Streams. ADS, pp. 127–147. Springer, Heidelberg (2007). http://www-cs-students.stanford.edu/datar/papers/mpds03.pdf
22. Agrawal, R., Imieliski, T., Swami, A.: Mining association rules between sets of items in large databases. ACM SIGMOD Rec. **22**(2), 207–216 (1993)
23. Hoan, Q., Mau, N., Le Phuoc, D.: An elastic and scalable spatiotemporal query processing for linked sensor data. In: Proceedings of the 11th International Conference on Semantic Systems. ACM (2015)
24. Belghaouti, F., Bouzeghoub, A., Kazi-Aoul, Z., Chiky, R.: Graph-oriented load-shedding for semantic data stream processing. In: 2015 International Workshop on Computational Intelligence for Multimedia Understanding (IWCIM). IEEE, October 2015
25. Belghaouti, F., Bouzeghoub, A., Kazi-Aoul, Z., Chiky, R.: FreGraPaD: frequent graph patterns detection for semantic data streams. In: Tenth IEEE International Conference on Research Challenges in Information Science - RCIS (2016)
26. Dell'Aglio, D., Calbimonte, J.-P., Balduini, M., Corcho, O., Della Valle, E.: On correctness in RDF stream processor benchmarking. In: Alani, H., Kagal, L., Fokoue, A., Groth, P., Biemann, C., Parreira, J.X., Aroyo, L., Noy, N., Welty, C., Janowicz, K. (eds.) ISWC 2013, Part II. LNCS, vol. 8219, pp. 326–342. Springer, Heidelberg (2013)
27. Tu, Y.-C., Liu, S., Prabhakar, S., Yao, B.: Load shedding in stream databases: a control-based approach. In: Proceedings of the 32nd International Conference on Very-Large Data Bases, pp. 787–798. VLDB Endowment (2006)

Unsupervised Blocking of Imbalanced Datasets for Record Matching

Chenxiao Dou[1,2(✉)], Daniel Sun[1,2], and Raymond K. Wong[1,2]

[1] School of Computer Science and Engineering,
University of New South Wales, Sydney, Australia
`chenxiaod@cse.unsw.edu.au`
[2] Data61, Commonwealth Scientific and Industrial Research Organisation (CSIRO),
ACT, Sydney, Australia

Abstract. Record matching in data engineering refers to searching for data records originating from same entities across different data sources. The solutions for record matching usually employ learning algorithms to train a classifier that labels record pairs as either matches or non-matches. In practice, the amount of non-matches typically far exceeds the amount of matches. This problem is so-called imbalance problem, which notoriously increases the difficulty of acquiring a representative dataset for classifier training. Various blocking techniques have been proposed to alleviate this problem, but most of them rely heavily on the effort of human experts. In this paper, we propose an unsupervised blocking method, which aims at automatic blocking. To demonstrate the effectiveness, we evaluated our method using real-world datasets. The results show that our method significantly outperforms other competitors.

Keywords: Record matching · Blocking · Imbalance · Heuristics

1 Introduction

A crucial step in integrating data from multiple sources is detecting and eliminating duplicate records [9]. This process is called Entity Matching, Record linkage, or Record Matching, which is a well known problem that arises in many applications such as address matching and citation de-duplication [3,5,6,16]. The goal of record matching is to identify records that represent the same real-world entities from a variety of data sources.

Machine learning has been playing an increasingly important role in the Record Matching problem. Some classical algorithms such as Support Vector Machine (SVM) and Decision Tree are adopted to predict whether a record pair is matched or not, based on the similarities between the entries [5,16]. However, selecting a training dataset is one of the most significant steps before learning process. To achieve a good classifier in terms of accuracy and recall, people have to label as many samples as possible, and consequently hiring human experts to hand-label the instances is too expensive in general.

© Springer International Publishing AG 2016
W. Cellary et al. (Eds.): WISE 2016, Part II, LNCS 10042, pp. 172–186, 2016.
DOI: 10.1007/978-3-319-48743-4_14

In a real-world record matching task on a dataset with n records, it is obvious that the number of truly matched pairs is not larger than n. However, the total number of candidate pairs including matched pairs and non-matched pairs can reach $\theta(n^2)$. To reduce the number of candidate pairs, blocking techniques have been proposed to filter out the pairs that are unlikely matched [8,15].

The general idea is to divide the records into several blocks and only the records in the same blocks need to be compared. For the records in different blocks, it assumes that the pairs are unlikely to match. Take a dataset of academic publications for example. When detecting the duplicates, we may partition the dataset into small groups according to conference names. Papers published in different conferences cannot refer to the same real-world entities. To increase comparison opportunities for truly matched records, users may employ several blocking criteria to ensure that every duplicated pair is assigned into at least one block [18]. However, most of blocking criteria are designed manually and decided based on human experience.

In this paper, we propose a new blocking method that can automatically filter record pairs. For many imbalanced datasets, most candidate record pairs have low similarity. As a result, in a similarity space, areas resided by non-matched pairs have higher density than those with matched pairs. Therefore, unlike most blocking methods that take similarity thresholds as input parameters, our method uses density as the measure and requires two thresholds (to be discussed in detail later) of density provided by users. We target at matched and non-matched pairs that are entangled in a similarity space. Furthermore, to improve the efficiency of our method, we admit the monotonicity assumption on detecting the target region. Through our empirical studies, it is explicit that the property of monotonicity generally holds in real-world datasets. Our results demonstrate that the proposed method can significantly block non-matched pairs. In summary, the contributions of this paper are summarized as follows:

- Compared to manually blocking methods, our method is able to determine complex blocking criteria automatically.
- The performance of the proposed density based approach will not be affected as much by the selection of similarity functions.
- The monotonicity of datasets is examined and used to improve the efficiency of the proposed method.

The remainder of this paper is structured as follows. We discuss related work in Sect. 2. In Sect. 3, we present the background of this paper including the problem, the assumptions, and the definitions. Our proposed method is then presented in Sect. 4. After that, the proposed method is evaluated in Sect. 5. Finally, we conclude this paper in Sect. 6.

2   Related Work

Entity matching is a well-studied problem of determining whether two records refer to the same entity or not. To measure the similarity between records, a variety of similarity functions have been proposed. EditDistance, Jaccard similarity, Cosine similarity are three widely used measures for this problem [7]. These different similarity measures are the key criteria to identify truly matched records.

Many researchers have explored machine learning techniques [5,16] to solve the entity matching problem. Each similarity is regarded as a data feature, whose importance weight is automatically decided by a learning algorithm. But, there exists an imbalance issue that greatly affects the learning, that is, no learning algorithm can achieve an outstanding performance with an extremely imbalanced training set.

In order to reduce non-matched pairs, various blocking techniques are used to filter out the pairs that are unlikely matched. The traditional blocking criteria are manually designed according to the attributes of datasets [14]. Some learning algorithms are adopted to produce the blocking criteria automatically in [4,13]. Canopy Clustering [12] fast groups record pairs into overlapping sets with a loose threshold and then filters the non-matches with a tight threshold. An inappropriate blocking criterion may separate the truly matched records into different clusters. Most of the existing work use several blocking criteria to increase the chance of assigning the matched records to the same clusters. Whang et al. [18] proposed an iterative blocking framework, which enables record matching across different clusters. After that, they discussed how to update the existing blocking rules when new records are added in [17].

Most of the previous methods [3,4,6,12,13] use textual similarity as the main measure to filter pairs. In our work, we employ the density of pairs on a similarity space as the measure to find the non-matches. We also adopt the monotonicity assumption to improve the efficiency of our proposed density based method. The monotonicity assumption has also been introduced in [3,6] but they focused on the precision during learning, while in our approach, we focus on the property of monotonicity on the density during blocking.

3   Background

3.1   Problem Definition

In Table 1, the upper table contains three citation records from DBLP dataset, and the other has two records from ACM dataset. As shown in the tables, only the last records in the two tables are matched and the other three are non-matched. Thus, out of all 6 possible pairs between the two tables, there is only one matched pair, and this results in the imbalance problem. Given the entire datasets, the matched and the non-matched will be extremely unbalanced, and consequently from such datasets, it is difficult to sample a balanced training set, whose quality is important for the following learning process.

We denote the set of all record pairs as $\mathbb{C}$, the set of all matched pairs as $\mathbb{C}_{match}$, and the set of all non-matched pairs as $\mathbb{C}_{non}$. Our goal is to design a blocking method that could prune pairs in $\mathbb{C}_{non}$ and preserve pairs in $\mathbb{C}_{match}$ as many as possible in order to achieve a balanced data pool (the ideal imbalance

Table 1. Citation dataset

Title	Authors	Venue	Year
Safe query languages for constraint databases	Peter Z. Revesz	TODS	1998
Efficient filtering of XML documents for selective dissemination of information	Mehmet Altinel, Michael J. Franklin	Very large data bases	2000
Standards for databases on the grid	Susan Malaika, Andrew Eisenberg, Jim Melton	ACM SIGMOD record	2003
Title	Authors	Conf.	Year
Database techniques for the World-Wide Web: a survey	D. Florescu, A. Levy, A. Mendelzon	SIGMOD	1998
Standards for databases on the grid	S. Malaika, A. Eisenberg, J.	SIGMOD	2003

ratio is 1 : 1). The set of all blocked pairs is denoted as $\mathbb{B}$. Since it is difficult to prune the instances perfectly, the aim of our work is to make the output closely approximate the ideal result. It is measured based on three metrics: *Recall*, *Reduction Ratio* and *Imbalance Ratio*. We do not use *Precision* as a metric, because the aim of blocking is to balance the dataset other than classify the instances, and the high imbalance ratio will prevent any algorithm from directly finding the true matches.

$$Recall = 1 - \frac{\sum_{x \in \mathbb{C}_{match}} 1[x \in \mathbb{B}]}{|\mathbb{C}_{match}|} \tag{1}$$

$$Reduction\ Ratio = \frac{\sum_{x \in \mathbb{C}_{non}} 1[x \in \mathbb{B}]}{|\mathbb{C}_{non}|} \tag{2}$$

$$Imbalance\ Ratio = \frac{\sum_{x \in \mathbb{C}_{non}} 1[x \notin \mathbb{B}]}{\sum_{x \in \mathbb{C}_{match}} 1[x \notin \mathbb{B}]} \tag{3}$$

3.2 Similarity Space

Textual similarity is one of the main measures to decide whether two records are matched or not. Given a record pair $(r, s) \in R \times S$, we can use a variety of similarity functions to measure the similarity between attributes of R and attributes of S. Without loss of generality, we assume the returned scores from all the similarity functions are in $[0, 1]$. Given d different similarity measures, we can map a pair $(r, s) \in R \times S$ into a point $(s_1, \ldots, s_d) \in [0, 1]^d$ where s_i is the similarity score returned by the i-th similarity measure. We call $[0, 1]^d$ *similarity space.* Each dimension represents one similarity measure to evaluate a similarity between r and s.

In this paper, for the convenience of discussion, a similarity space is partitioned into regular cells. A *region* refers to a sub-space consisting of several consecutive cells and an *area* refers to an arbitrary sub-space in the similarity space.

3.3   Monotonicity

Monotonicity has been assumed for entity matching in [3,6]. For example, Arvind et al. [3] have studied the monotonicity of precision on improving the efficiency of their algorithm. In practice, the monotonicity assumption generally holds in many datasets. Table 1 is example records in two citation tables. Jaccard similarity on *Name* and EditDistance on *Title* are two frequently used similarity in Citation datasets. When we map the record pairs onto a 2D similarity panel shown in Fig. 1, we can observe that the dark area of lower similarity has much more points than the area of high similarity. Generally, in the similarity space $[0,1]^d$, the area of lower similarities may contain more points. We call this phenomenon as *Monotonicity of Density*. Intuitively, a pair of records with a lower textual similarity would have less possibilities to be matched. Thus, in this paper, we focus on how to use the monotonicity assumption to block record pairs.

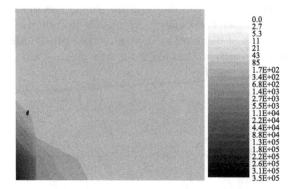

Fig. 1. Contour of citation pairs. The data are the publication records from DBLP and Google Scholar [1]. The panel on the left is the similarity space of two similarities. The right are the contour levels, which represent the numbers of points per unit area.

Prior to formally introducing *Monotonicity of Density*, we first give a formal definition of density. Due to the imbalance issue, the number of matched points is much smaller than that of non-matched ones after record pairs are mapped into $[0,1]^d$. So the density of non-matches around a given point is roughly defined as follows:

Definition 1. *Given a threshold r and a point f, the density of point f, denoted as $\rho(f)$, is defined as the number of points within a certain distance r to f.*

And then, we define the density of region as follow:

Definition 2. *In a similarity space $[0,1]^d$, the density of a region is represented by the density of point f that has the lowest $\rho(f)$ among all points in the same region.*

We also define a partial ordering $\preceq$ on the points in a similarity space.

Definition 3. *Given two points $f = (f_1, \ldots, f_d)$ and $f' = (f'_1, \ldots, f'_d)$, if $f_i \leq f'_i$ for all $1 \leq i \leq d$, we say that f' dominates f, denoted as $f \preceq f'$; if $f \preceq f'$ and $f_i \neq f'_i$ for some $1 \leq i \leq d$, it is denoted as $f \prec f'$.*

Then, we formalize *Monotonicity of Density* as follows (Table 2):

Definition 4. *In a similarity space, for any two points f and f' such that $f \preceq f'$, if $\rho(f) \geq \rho(f')$, we say that the density is monotonic w.r.t. $\preceq$.*

Table 2. Notation table

Notation	Description
$\mathbb{C}$	The set of all pairs
$\mathbb{C}_{match}$	The set of matched pairs
$\mathbb{C}_{non}$	The set of non-matched pairs
$\mathbb{B}$	The set of blocked pairs
$\preceq, \prec$	The partial ordering (*dominate*) defined in Sect. 3
$\rho(f)$	The density of point f
d	The number of dimensions of similarity space
r	The distance threshold for computing density
T_1	The tight threshold
T_2	The loose threshold
k	The granularity parameter
p, f	The points
R, S	The datasets
$\mathbb{V}$	The set of granulated points
$\mathbb{M}$	The set of *MaxBound* points
$\mathbb{U}$	The set of *MinUnknown* points
$\mathbb{Z}$	The set of enumerated points with density no less than T_2

4   Proposed Method

4.1   Overview of Method

Motivated by the observation that non-matched pairs crowd greatly in the area of low similarity, we propose a heuristic method that can automatically block the non-matches. Our method consists of three main steps:

- **Preprocessing.** After mapping entity pairs into the similarity space, the number of points is rather huge. Due to the huge number, it is too expensive to compute the density of every points for finding the region of high density. To improve the efficiency, we split the similarity space into finite cells and only consider the corners of each cell as the candidate boundary points of high density region.
- **Search for the region with density no less than T_1.** The property of monotonicity notably holds in the region of rather low similarity. So in the second step, we use a *Binary Search* algorithm to find all sub-regions with density at least equal to T_1. The union of every sub-region is the target region where the density is at least equal to T_1. An example is shown in Fig. 2.
- **Search for the points with density no less than T_2.** In some region, the monotonicity may not hold strictly as well as in the region of density T_1, but there still exist many non-matches. Thus, in the rest of space, we run a recursive algorithm to enumerate the points of density no less than T_2, as shown in Fig. 2.

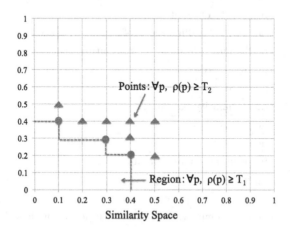

Fig. 2. Overview of the proposed method. The region with the density no less than T_1 will be blocked in the second step. The points with the density no less than T_2 will be blocked in the third step.

4.2   Preprocessing

In our method, the most expensive operation is to compute the defined density $\rho(f)$ of time complexity $\mathcal{O}(|\mathbb{C}|)$. As $\rho(f)$ is called frequently in the algorithms, we use an *R-tree* index[1] to mark the points and lower the complexity to $\mathcal{O}(\log(|\mathbb{C}|))$.

When searching the boundary points of high density region, it is infeasible to compute the density of every points in the similarity space. To improve the efficiency, we use an approximation technique that split the similarity space into finite cells and only check the points at the corners of each cell (Table 3).

Table 3. Search the region with the density no less than T_1.

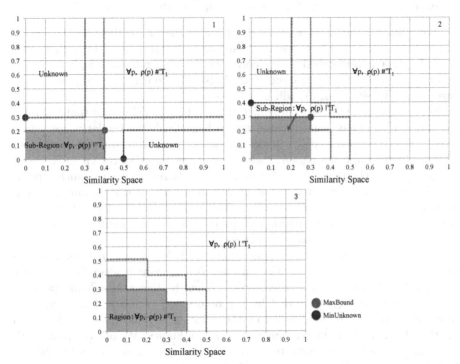

In order to split the space, we fix an integer value k, called *granularity para-meter*. Then we define a set $\mathbb{V}$ of points, any of which is in the form $(v_1, \ldots, v_d)$ where $v_i = j/k, j \in 0, 1, \ldots, k$. The set $\mathbb{V}$ partitions the similarity space into $(1+k)^d$ *cells*. And a *region* is an area formed by several consecutive cells. When considering the density of region, we only need to check the $(1 + k)^d$ points in $\mathbb{V}$. The points are at the grid line crosses in Fig. 2.

---

[1] *R-tree* is a kind of tree data structures for indexing multi-dimensional information [10].

4.3   Search for the Region with Density No Less Than T_1

Now we show our solution of exploiting the monotonicity of density. Given two points $p \preceq p'$, if the monotonicity holds, $\rho(p) \geq \rho(p')$. From the practical experience in Fig. 1, this monotonicity generally applies in the region when the similarities are rather low. Considering the monotonicity of density, if we can find a point f with $\rho(f) \geq T_1$ and $\forall f' \succ f, \rho(f') < T_1$, this implies that the points f'' with $f'' \preceq f$ are all in the regions with the density no less than T_1. Formally, we define such point f as following:

Definition 5. *Given a threshold T_1 and Monotonicity of Density, we say a point $p \in [0,1]^d$ is maximally dense if $\rho(p) \geq T_1$ and $\forall p' \succ p, \rho(p') < T_1$. Such a point is called* MaxBound *point. And the set of such points is denoted as* $\mathbb{M}$.

According to the monotonicity, the point p that have the property $\exists p' \in \mathbb{M}, p \preceq p'$ should be in the region of density at least equal to T_1. In order to find the redundant non-matched points correctly, we set a relatively high threshold T_1 for enumerating the *MaxBound* points in $\mathbb{M}$. The detected record pairs, which have higher density than T_1, will be blocked out.

Next we propose our searching algorithm. The general idea is that when we locate one *MaxBound* point, it could always help divide the similarity space into three parts: unknown density, density at least equal to T_1 and density lower than T_1. In the unknown region, every point p has the property $\forall p' \in \mathbb{M}, p \not\prec p'$ and $p \not\succ p'$. For the point $f \preceq \forall f'$ in one unknown region, we call such a point f as *MinUnknown* point, which has minimum density in this unknown region. And the set of all *MinUnknown* points is denoted as $\mathbb{U}$. To detect the density of unknown regions, our algorithm repeats the process of finding the *MaxBound* points on the remaining unknown regions.

Our algorithm starts at the point $(1/k, \ldots, 1/k)$ because it should be the first *MinUnknown* point in $\mathbb{U}$. Then we use *Binary Search* algorithm on every dimension to locate the *MaxBound* point. When finding a *MaxBound* point f, we know that the region resided by the points $p \preceq f$ has a density at least equal to T_1 and the region resided by the points $p \succ f$ has a density less than T_1. But the density of the remaining region is unknown. We put the point with minimum density of unknown region into $\mathbb{U}$ and start a new round of *Binary Search* on next *MinUnknown* point in $\mathbb{U}$. Repeat the same process until no region is unknown in $[0,1]^d$. We give a simple example on the 2-D similarity space in Fig. 2. In the first round, our algorithm starts at $(0.1, 0.1)$. After the process of *Binary Searching*, the first found *MaxBound* point, $(0.4, 0.2)$, divides the space into four regions. The one resided by the *MaxBound* point is one sub-region of the target region of density T_1. The two unknown ones are the regions which need to be detected in next iteration. And the left one is the region with density less than T_1. In the second round, we start the searching algorithm from the two *MinUnknown* points founded in the last round, $(0, 0.3)$ and $(0.5, 0)$. After this round, the area of unknown regions is reduced and a new sub-region of density T_1 is formed as shown in the second step of Fig. 2. Then, we repeatedly detect the remaining unknown regions until the similarity space has been entirely explored.

The union region of all founded sub-regions is the target region with density no less than T_1.

As *MaxBound* points in $\mathbb{M}$ are on the boundary of region with density at least equal to T_1, we then enumerate each point $f \in \mathbb{M}$ and block all the points $p \preceq f$. According to *Monotonicity of Density*, the blocked points must have a density no less than T_1. For the second step, since we use *Binary Search* to locate the *MaxBound* points, the total number of points enumerated is $\mathcal{O}(\log k \cdot d \cdot |\mathbb{M}|)$.

```
1  Procedure EnumerateAllMaxBound(T₁)
2  |   U = {(1/k,...,1/k)}
3  |   foreach point p ∈ U do
4  |   |   if ρ(p) ≥ T₁ then
5  |   |   |   p_max ← FindMaxBound( p, T₁ )
6  |   |   |   M ← M ∪ p_max            /* p_max is a MaxBound Point        */
7  |   |   |   U ← UpdateMinUnknown( U, p_max )
8  |   |   end
9  |   end
10 Procedure UpdateMinUnknown(U, p_max)
11 |   U_new ← ∅
12 |   foreach point p ∈ U do
13 |   |   if p ≺ p_max then
14 |   |   |   for i ← 1, d do
15 |   |   |   |   p' ← p                 /* p' is a MinUnknown point         */
16 |   |   |   |   p'[i] ← p_max[i] + 1/k  /* p'[i] is the i-th dimension of p' */
17 |   |   |   |   U_new ← U_new ∪ p'
18 |   |   |   end
19 |   |   end
20 |   end
21 Procedure FindMaxBound( p, T₁)
22 |   for i ← 1, d do
23 |   |   hi = 1
24 |   |   lo = p_i while hi − lo ≥ 2 do
25 |   |   |   p[i] ← (hi + lo)/2
26 |   |   |   if ρ(p) ≥ T₁ then
27 |   |   |   |   lo = p[i]
28 |   |   |   else
29 |   |   |   |   hi = p[i]
30 |   |   |   end
31 |   |   end
32 |   end
33 |   return p
```

Algorithm 1. Enumerate all *MaxBound* points

```
 1  Z ← M
 2  foreach point p ∈ Z do
 3      for i ← 1, d do
 4          for j ∈ {−1, 1} do
 5              p′ ← p               /* p′ is a neighbour point of p        */
 6              p′[i] ← p′[i] + j/k   /* p′[i] is the i-th dimension of p′   */
 7              if  p′ ∉ Z and ρ(p′) ≥ T₂ then
 8                  |  Z ← Z ∪ {p′}
 9              end
10          end
11      end
12  end
```

Algorithm 2. Enumerate points with density no less than T_2

4.4 Search for the Points with Density No Less Than T_2

As mentioned above, the monotonicity property can coarsely distinguish points, but in some region distinguish-ability is not so strong. For a finer grain solution, the points in non-distinguishable region but with a high density should also be blocked out. In this section, we present a recursive algorithm to find the points.

In this step, we set another threshold $T_2 < T_1$ and search for the points of density no less than T_2. Our algorithm starts at some point p in the $\mathbb{M}$. If the neighbour point p' of p has $T_2 \leq \rho(p') < T_1$, we put it into an enumeration set $\mathbb{Z}$, which is equal to $\mathbb{M}$ at the very beginning. Then, we repeat this enumeration process at points in $\mathbb{Z}$, until no more eligible points are found and added into $\mathbb{Z}$. With assuming that the points close to a point $f \in \mathbb{Z}$ would also have a density at least equal to T_2, our blocking strategy is to remove all points within r to any one point in $\mathbb{Z}$.

The time consumption of this step is determined by T_2. The case that takes the longest time is when the density of each point in $\mathbb{V}$ on the rest space is just equal to T_2. When computing the density of point $p \in \mathbb{V}$, we need to count the number of points that are within a distance r to p. With some value of r, the density of p may count some points that are also counted by other $2d$ neighbour points of p in $\mathbb{V}$. To make the density identical, the number of shared points counted by two adjacent points in $\mathbb{V}$ should be same and equal to $T_2/2d$. After the last blocking step, the number of remaining points in $\mathbb{C}$, denoted as N_C, and the number of remaining points in $\mathbb{V}$, denoted as N_V, are known to users. There should exist $\frac{N_C}{T_2/2d}$ groups of points counted by two adjacent points in $\mathbb{V}$. And for each point, its density would be counted on $2d$ groups of shared points. Thus, if the maximal number of iterations does not exceed N_V, it can be represented as $\frac{N_C}{T_2/2d} \times \frac{2}{2d}$ equal to $\frac{2N_C}{T_2}$. The result shows the number of iterations does not matter with d. Even though the time complexity is $\mathcal{O}(\frac{N_C}{T_2})$, it should be noticed that N_C is much smaller than $|\mathbb{C}|$. The reason is that most of the non-matches are located in the region of high density and have been blocked in the last step.

5 Experiments

Our experiment were conducted on three datasets: *Restaurant, Goods* and *Citation. Restaurant* [1] is a collection of addresses of real-world restaurants. *Citation* [2] dataset contains a variety of publication records from DBLP and Google Scholar. *Goods* [2] is a dataset recording the product information on the websites of Google and Amazon. All of the datasets have two tables for record matching. The statistics of records in the datasets are shown in Table 4.

Table 4. Statistics of records

Datasets	Table A	Table B	Matched pairs
Restaurant	533	331	112
Citation	2294	2616	2224
Goods	1363	3266	1300

5.1 Method Comparison

In this section, we compare our method with *Standard Blocking* (SB) method [11] and *Canopies* (CANOPY) [12]. The two methods exploit different metrics for blocking. *Standard Blocking* clusters the records that share the same blocking keys into one block. In this experiment, we take the attributes of a dataset as the blocking keys. After having tried a variety of attribute combinations, we pick the one with good performance in terms of *Reduction Ratio* and *Recall* for comparison.

Canopies is an unsupervised clustering algorithm, which requires one loose similarity threshold θ_1 and one tight similarity threshold θ_2. It clusters the records that are textually similar to one block. From the similarity thresholds in the range $[0.3, 0.9]$, we choose the setting that achieves higher scores of *Reduction Ratio* and *Recall* for comparison.

Our method is a density-based clustering algorithm, which requires a loose threshold and a tight threshold of density. It blocks the records that are in high-density areas in the similarity space. We have four parameters all related to density computation. To simplify the process of tuning, we fixed $k = 20$ $r = 0.15$ and vary T_1, T_2 in $[100, 10000]$. In the following, the results are shown in Tables 5, 6, 7.

From the results, we can observe that the three methods all work well on *Citation* and *Restaurant*. The reason why there is no significant difference is that the two datasets have been cleaned, that is, they do not contain much noisy information. In such a scenario, similarity functions are highly credible, grading non-matched pairs a low score and fully duplicated pairs a high score. But for *Goods*, a dataset with noise, the two competitors do not work well. As the noise generally exists in the attributes of the dataset, the similarity scores

Table 5. Restaurant

	SB	CANOPY	OURS
Reduction ratio	0.847	0.924	0.992
Recall	1.000	1.000	0.982
Imbalance ratio	376	253	24

Table 6. Citation

	SB	CANOPY	OURS
Reduction ratio	0.824	0.944	0.986
Recall	1.000	0.999	0.994
Imbalance ratio	393	151	38

Table 7. Goods

	SB	CANOPY	OURS
Reduction ratio	0.831	0.997	0.996
Recall	0.274	0.377	0.885
Imbalance ratio	180	25	15

of truly matched data pairs may decrease to the level of non-matches'. Thus, a method targeting at the pairs with high similarity scores may not work anymore. As shown in Table 7, *Canopy* only captures 37.7 % matched pairs that reside in the area of high similarity.

Our method achieves an outstanding result when noise exists. As the algorithms are to search for the area of non-matches, the noise does not make an influence. For *Goods* dataset, the noise makes matched points enter into the low-similarity area, but also makes non-matched points move to the area with further low similarity. It is still possible to locate the area of non-matches, with using the property of density. Though some matches of low similarity cannot be found, our density-based method still achieves a high recall 0.885 on *Goods* dataset.

5.2 Evaluation on Density

As the density is defined as the number of instances in the area centered with r, the value of r plays an important role in the algorithms. A small r would make density more local and a big r is closer to the global density. In this section, we focus on studying the value of r.

Table 8. Restaurant

r	0.05	0.1	0.125	0.15	0.2
Reduction ratio	0.074	0.074	0.731	0.971	0.992
Recall	1.000	1.000	1.000	1.000	0.982
Imbalance ratio	3081	3081	895	96	24

Table 9. Citation

r	0.05	0.1	0.125	0.15	0.2
Reduction ratio	0.388	0.388	0.902	0.934	0.986
Recall	1.000	1.000	1.000	0.996	0.994
Imbalance ratio	1666	1666	266	178	38

Table 10. Goods

r	0.05	0.1	0.125	0.15	0.2
Reduction ratio	0.429	0.996	0.996	0.996	0.997
Recall	0.987	0.889	0.881	0.881	0.877
Imbalance ratio	1895	15	15	15	11

To study the effect of r, we fixed $k = 20, T_1 = 1000, T_2 = 200$ and vary the value of r in $\{0.05, 0.1, 0.125, 0.15, 0.20\}$. The experiment is conducted on three datasets as shown in Tables 8, 9, 10.

From the results, we can make two conclusions: First, with the increase of value of r, *Reduction Ratio* tends to be greater, while *Recall* and *Imbalance Ratio* tend to be smaller; Second, with a smaller r, our method does not have a good performance.

For the first conclusion, when r becomes greater, according to the definition of density, the thresholds T_1 and T_2 become relatively looser. For a point p with $\rho(p) \leq T_2$, after the increase of r, the area centered at p would become larger and include more points, making the new value returned by $\rho(p)$ possibly larger than T_2. Thus, with a loose threshold, there should be more pairs being blocked by the algorithm, and this leads to a higher *Reduction Ratio* and a lower *Recall*. The second conclusion is due to the noise. When enumerating the points with density no less than T_2, if the algorithm finds a point p with $\rho(p) < T_2$, the neighbour point $p' \succeq p, \rho(p') \geq T_2$ will have no chance to be enumerated. p is the noise point that may make our algorithm early stop, and is the reason why the results of $r = 0.05$ in all tables are bad. With a smaller r, the density has more chance to be affected by some noise points. But with a greater r, the effect of the noise would be balanced off, as shown in the experiment that the results of $r = 0.15, 0.2$ are all good.

6   Conclusion

In this paper, we studied the problem of blocking records for entity matching. Unlike the methods using similarity to filter entities, we used density as main measure for blocking. Our proposed method also exploits the monotonicity of density on improving the algorithm efficiency. Finally, we compared our density based approach with one similarity based approach and one index based approach. We evaluated our method on real datasets and demonstrate the superiority of our approach in terms of *Reduction Ratio* and *Recall*.

References

1. http://archive.ics.uci.edu/ml/
2. http://dbs.uni-leipzig.de/en/research/projects/object_matching
3. Arasu, A., Götz, M., Kaushik, R.: On active learning of record matching packages. In: Proceedings of ACM SIGMOD International Conference on Management of data, pp. 783–794. ACM (2010)
4. Bilenko, M., Kamath, B., Mooney, R.J.: Adaptive blocking: learning to scale up record linkage. In: 6th International Conference on Data Mining, ICDM 2006, pp. 87–96. IEEE (2006)
5. Bilenko, M., Mooney, R.J.: Adaptive duplicate detection using learnable string similarity measures. In: KDD, pp. 39–48 (2003)
6. Chaudhuri, S., Chen, B.-C., Ganti, V., Kaushik, R.: Example-driven design of efficient record matching queries. In: Proceedings of 33rd International Conference on Very Large Data Bases, pp. 327–338. VLDB Endowment (2007)
7. Cohen, W.W.: Data integration using similarity joins and a word-based information representation language. ACM Trans. Inf. Syst. (TOIS) 18(3), 288–321 (2000)
8. Dalvi, N.N., Rastogi, V., Dasgupta, A., Sarma, A.D., Sarlós, T.: Optimal hashing schemes for entity matching. In: WWW, pp. 295–306 (2013)
9. Elmagarmid, A.K., Ipeirotis, P.G., Verykios, V.S.: Duplicate record detection: a survey. IEEE Trans. Knowl. Data Eng. 19(1), 1–16 (2007)
10. Guttman, A.: R-trees: a dynamic index structure for spatial searching. ACM SIGMOD Rec. 14, 47–57 (1984). ACM
11. Jaro, M.A.: Advances in record-linkage methodology as applied to matching the 1985 census of Tampa, Florida. J. Am. Stat. Assoc. 84(406), 414–420 (1989)
12. McCallum, A., Nigam, K., Ungar, L.H.: Efficient clustering of high-dimensional data sets with application to reference matching. In: Proceedings of 6th ACM SIGKDD International Conference on Knowledge Discovery and Data Mining, pp. 169–178. ACM (2000)
13. Michelson, M., Knoblock, C.A.: Learning blocking schemes for record linkage. In: Proceedings of National Conference on Artificial Intelligence, vol. 21, p. 440. AAAI Press, MIT Press, Menlo Park, London (2006) (1999)
14. Newcombe, H.B.: Handbook of Record Linkage: Methods for Health and Statistical Studies, Administration, and Business. Oxford University Press Inc., Oxford (1988)
15. Shu, L., Chen, A., Xiong, M., Meng, W.: Efficient spectral neighborhood blocking for entity resolution. In: IEEE 27th International Conference on Data Engineering (ICDE), pp. 1067–1078. IEEE (2011)
16. Tejada, S., Knoblock, C.A., Minton, S.: Learning domain-independent string transformation weights for high accuracy object identification. In: Proceedings of 8th ACM SIGKDD International Conference on Knowledge Discovery and Data Mining, pp. 350–359. ACM (2002)
17. Whang, S.E., Garcia-Molina, H.: Incremental entity resolution on rules and data. VLDB J. 23(1), 77–102 (2014)
18. Whang, S.E., Menestrina, D., Koutrika, G., Theobald, M., Garcia-Molina, H.: Entity resolution with iterative blocking. In: SIGMOD Conference, pp. 219–232 (2009)

Partially Decompressing Binary Interpolative Coding for Fast Query Processing

Xi Fu[1,2], Peng Li[1(✉)], Rui Li[1], and Bin Wang[1,2]

[1] Institute of Information Engineering,
Chinese Academy of Sciences, Beijing, China
{fuxi,lipeng,lirui,wangbin}@iie.ac.cn
[2] University of Chinese Academy of Sciences, Beijing, China

Abstract. Inverted index is the core data structure in large scale information retrieval systems such as Web search engine. Index compression techniques are usually used to reduce the storage and transmission time from disk to memory. Many index compression schemes have been proposed and among them Binary Interpolative Coding (IPC) is one of the most widely used schemes due to its superior compression ratio (CR). However, the decompression speed of IPC is relatively slow, thus fully decompressing (FD) IPC will slow down the whole process of online query processing. In this paper, we first point out that it is unnecessary to fully decompress all the IPC nodes in query processing and then propose a partial decompression (PD) algorithm for IPC. Experimental results on two publicly available standard corpora show that compared with normal IPC our algorithm performs 40 % faster for Boolean conjunctive queries and 20 % faster for Rank queries without additional storage consumption.

Keywords: Index compression · Binary interpolative coding · Inverted file

1 Introduction

Information retrieval systems have been widely used in many online applications including search engine, library system and e-commerce system etc. To speed up the retrieving process an important data structure named inverted index file (IF) has been proposed. In general, IF needs to be read from disk into memory during online processing, however, the uncompressed inverted index is almost as large as original collection [1]. Therefore, lots of compression schemes have been proposed [2–8]. In general, schemes aiming at high compression ratio (CR) usually have a slower decompressing speed, so most methods try to make a tradeoff between memory occupation and decompression speed. Binary interpolative coding (IPC) [8] is one of those schemes with high CR while its decompressing speed is relatively slower.

Because of its high CR, IPC can be used in those extremely high CR required situation. For example, when compressed *IF* is larger than the internal memory space, high CR schemes help to maintain more cache in internal memory and also reduce the amount of data read from external memory. For instance in [13] IPC is used to compress the huge versioned document collections. However, the relatively heavy time consummation during online query processing limits its further use. Any improvement

© Springer International Publishing AG 2016
W. Cellary et al. (Eds.): WISE 2016, Part II, LNCS 10042, pp. 187–195, 2016.
DOI: 10.1007/978-3-319-48743-4_15

of its processing speed is not trivial. Many researchers have realized acceleration of online processing is meaningful and proposed some improvements [9, 10]. Most of these improvements use extra space to exchange with time which weakens the advantage of high CR. Our work aims at exploring the acceleration potential of query processing when *IF* is compressed in IPC form while without additional space consummation.

We analyze its decompressing procedure in detail and find that not every node needs to be decompressed during query processing. Therefore, we propose a PD algorithm. We will describe our algorithm in detail and finally validate its efficiency.

Our contributions are double fold. First, we propose a partial decompression (PD) algorithm to process Boolean conjunctive query and Rank query when *IF* is compressed in IPC form. Second, we experimentally validate its efficiency on two publicly available corpora.

This paper is organized as follows. We briefly introduce the IPC and background in Sect. 2. In Sect. 3 we will explain our algorithm. We will check its efficiency by experiment in Sect. 4. Finally, we give our conclusion.

2   Background and Related Work

2.1   Background

An inverted index file (*IF*) consists of a term dictionary and an inverted list (also called posting list) for each term; we mainly focus on the decompression of inverted lists in this paper.

A term t and its inverted list can be described as $\{f_t : d_{t,1}, d_{t,2}, d_{t,3} \ldots d_{t,f_t}\}$, where f_t is the total number of documents containing the term t and $d_{t,1}, d_{t,2}, d_{t,3} \ldots d_{t,f_t}$ are IDs of them which are usually sorted in increasing order.

IF is a convenient tool to process queries, however, *IF* is almost as large as original document file so storing them simply will need too much space. Therefore, it needs compression before being read into memory. Until now many compression methods are proposed. Some methods are designed for delta values [3–5]. Among them OPTPFD [7] is competitive both in time and space so widely used in SE system. We use OPTPFD as one of the baseline methods.

Methods designed for delta values utilize the distribution of deviation; its efficiency relies on some assumption of distribution. Another type of methods [2, 6, 7] designed for the original value utilizes the property of monotonously increasing list. Among them EF [6] is another competitive method and will be used as another baseline method in this paper. Partitioned-EF [7] is the improvement of EF and can be regard as one of the state-of-the-art methods.

Although many coding have been proposed, IPC is still competitive for its incomparable CR. We will check its detail in next section.

2.2   Binary Interpolative Coding and Its Improvements

Binary Interpolative Coding (IPC) [8] is a useful coding for its high CR. IPC is designed for original values which numbers are listed in strictly increasing order. Its idea is limiting each number by its order and interval to minimize its entropy. Use the classic example on [8], the inverted list is <7:3, 8, 9, 11, 12, 13, 17> with a range of [1, 20]. Firstly we encode the middle number 11, which have 3 numbers on either side. Its range is [1 + 3, 20 − 3] with a length of 17 − 4 + 1 = 14, so it needs 4 bits and is encoded to 11 − 4 = 7, 0111. The next number is the middle number in the left part, which is 8 with one number on either side. Its range is [1 + 1, 10 − 1] with a length of 9 − 2 + 1 = 8, so it needs 3 bits and is encoded to 8 − 2 = 6, 110, etc. It is a recursive procedure as a binary tree which is called IPC tree. See Fig. 1. Finally we record it in pre-order traversal order (also called PLR order: parents, leftchild, rightchild). The above list is recorded as: 0111, 110, 010, 0, 000, 011. Note the commas do not need to be stored, because length of each node is already determined by its parent nodes.

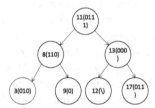

Fig. 1. The encoding process tree of IPC

Decompressing process will reverse the process. To restore the list we need computations about many messages of each node, which are expensive and will slow down the query processing. Researchers have realized to accelerate processing time is helpful and proposed some improvements. To our best knowledge the following two papers are found. In 2004 Cheng proposed a unique-order IPC [9]. They cut *IF* into fixed length of pieces and claimed at least two advantages would be taken. With fixed length g of IPC pieces the decoding process can be accelerated by pre-computer order, another advantage is that skipping is feasible during intersection. However, parameter g is difficult to determine because the length of list varies from few to million. In 2010 Teuhola proposed a log-time IPC [10]. Their idea is to compute the longest possible length of an interval with a particular number of elements, then encoding that part of list with its longest possible length. By this it is easy to locate a particular element for skipping and random access. However it requires additional space and its space occupation might be larger than OPTPFD from the report. These two improvements try to accelerate decompressing of IPC by using additional space so that the advantage of high CR has been weakened. Our work aims at developing the acceleration potential without reducing its CR (do not change its structure).

3   PD and FD in Query Processing

3.1   Analyze of FD Process in Conjunctive Boolean Query Processing

Firstly we introduce the algorithm of FD. We need to rebuild the binary tree in Fig. 1 during FD. Because data in IPC is arranged in PLR order, the rebuilding procedure also proceeds in PLR order. For each node we need to compute the information of its *left* (number of nodes on the left sub-tree), *right*, *max*, *min* and *len* (length of bits read from *IF*) by parents' values, next we read *len* bits from *IF* to get the *tmpvalue*, then we can restore this node and its children. Here we proposed an algorithm using stack to decompress IPC tree. We need a stack *S* of structure contains the necessary message of each node including the fields mentioned above. We unitize the algorithm of in-order traversing of binary tree with stack and restore each value recursively. Each value can be computed by its parents' nodes. A global point *CurPointer* is initialized as the start address of the according list in *IF*. Finally we put original values into a list in order, which is just the inverted list. Next work is intersecting all those restored lists. We start at the shortest one so the intersection list is always short. However in experiment we find the processing of FD occupies at least 90 % of the total processing time which means decompression needs acceleration.

Note the structure of IPC coding is a binary sort tree which might apply skipping operations in conjunctive Boolean query. Refer to [12] we get following two conclusions: First, skip list can accelerate conjunctive query processing. Second, most of the Boolean queries involve only conjunction operations. So we also want to apply skipping to implement partial decompression in IPC tree which however cannot be used as skip list directly. That is because in a skip list a skipped node should have an additional pointer point to the next skipped node. Besides, values in IPC tree are not stored in order. However we have Observation 3.1 which makes skipping possible.

Definition 3.1: For any sub-tree in IPC tree with a root of *R*, there is a path from root to leaf generated by each time travels the left branch. Then we reverse the path, nodes on the reversed path can be regarded as a list and defined as **left list**.

Observation 3.1: Values of nodes on *left list* in any sub-tree are sorted in increasing order. For each node on *left list*, all the values of nodes on its right sub-tree are between the value of current node and next node on *left list* (or the overall maximal).

Observation 3.1 can be easily explained by the property of binary sort tree. By Observation 3.1 IPC tree can be regarded as recursive levels of skip list. Consider the same example in Sect. 2.2, its IPC tree is showed in Fig. 1. We could also change it into a multilayer skip list by rotating the tree clockwise till its *left list* to be horizontal. We could find that the nodes 3, 8, 11 could be viewed as skipped nodes in skip list. Skipped nodes and nodes in its right sub-tree could be viewed as an inner block. But not like skip list IPC coding use pre-order to store data. For a tree in IPC it is stored by two parts including nodes on *left list* which will be stored by the reversed *left list* order and right sub-tree of each node on *left list* which will be stored by *left list* order. For example in Fig. 1 the storing order is {11, 8, 3, {9}, {13, 12, 17}}.

Consider the compression order we know after having accessed the root node we could easily decompress the entire *left list* without decompressing other nodes.

However to locate the start point of a right sub-tree of a particular node *N* we have to compute the stored length of right sub-tree of all nodes which are before *N* in the *left list*. For instance if we have a list of {1, 13} to intersect with IPC tree in Fig. 1, after we restored the *left list* and finish comparison we decide to skip the right sub-tree of node 3 and 8, we need to know the length of sub-tree {9} then we can locate the second sub-tree on *IF*. It seems computation on sub-tree is inevitable. However we find the computation of the length of a sub-tree is faster than restoring the total tree.

Definition 3.2: During query processing a tree compressed in IPC, if we do not restore all the values of nodes on the tree, instead we just compute its length in *IF*, we call this operation as **skipping the tree**. Nodes on that tree are called **skipped nodes**.

Observation 3.2: Skipping a tree is faster than restoring (or decompressing).

The reasons are as follows. First, to skip a node we just need to know its *left, right, len* and *tmpvalue*. Next, computations of *max, min* and original value usually involve with operation of big integers. Last, skipping operation in leaf nodes, which have a large amount in a tree, is so fast that do not even need to allocate an addition node. By experiment we find skipping a large tree costs almost 3/4 time of restoring.

Another noticeable advantage of PD is sometimes we can terminate the traversal of tree earlier. For example we have a list of {1, 2} and intersect it with the tree in Fig. 1, after we restore the *left list* of root node we can safely ignore remain ones.

In conclusion, the normal processing of IPC in conjunctive query is fully decompressing the inverted list and then doing intersection while our idea is doing decompressing with intersection simultaneously. We decompress only the nodes which are possible to be a result and skip (or ignore) the others.

3.2   PD Process in Conjunctive Boolean Query and Rank Query Processing

We check Boolean query first. Firstly we describe our skipping function to skip a sub-tree with a particular root. Skipping function is similar with restoring function and shares the stack. We need only the message of *left, right, length* and *tmpvalue*, which consist a structure of skipped node. When the skipped node is a leaf, we just need to move the pointer on *IF* while without restoring the node. Next we check the timing for executing skipping. We denote the restored list as L and list compressed in IPC as T. For a node in the *left* list of a particular node in T, we denote the maximal of range of its right sub-tree as m ($m = max + right$). When the current value in L is larger than m, the total right sub-tree can be skipped. See Fig. 2 for example.

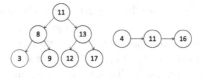

Fig. 2. An example of skipping

The left tree is compressed in IPC while the right one is totally restored. First we decompress the *left list* of root node in the IPC tree, which is {3, 8, 11}. Next we process the intersection of *left list* and the restored list. When we process at the node 8 on IPC, the current pointer on the restored list stays at the node 11. We find value m of node 8 is 10 and less than 11, so we could skipped the right sub-tree (*right skip*) of node 8. When we process at node 13, the current pointer on the restored list stays at the node 16. We can safely skip the left sub-tree (left *skip*) of node 13. In algorithm for each outer loop left skip may occur only when start the outer loop and before restoring the left edge. Here is the algorithm. Let L be the list totally restored, T be the *IF* and Q be the intersection result array. *Lcur* and *Qcur* are current pointers on L and Q separately and initialized as 0.

```
Restore root node of T and push into stack S
1.while(Tcur=S[top]!=null)
2.   if(L[Lcur]>=root->orgvalue)
3.      Skip left child of root //execute the left skip
4.   else
5.      Restore left list of sub-tree with the root Tcur
from T and push them by decompression order into S
6.      while(true)   //loop for array L
7.         if(L[Lcur]<=Tcur->orgvalue)
8.            if (L[Lcur]==Tcur->orgvalue)
9.               Q[Qcur++]=L[Lcur]   //copy the node into result
list
10.        else if(Lcur<maxlength) //maxlength of array L
11.           Lcur++
12.           continue
13.           else
14.           return //array L have reached the end and ignore
the remain nodes in T
15.        else
16.           pop S
17.           if((L[Lcur]<(Tcur->rightvalue+Tcur->maxvalue))&&
Tcur->right>0) //need to check its right child
18.              restore right child of temp and push it into S
19.              break //break into the outer loop

20.           skip   right   child   of   temp
              //execute the right skip
```

Next work is simple. We choose the shortest inverted list and totally decompress it. Then use it as L to intersect with following list to get the result list of query.

Rank queries are similar. Although rank queries are more like disjunctive Boolean query we can use the *continue* strategy in [12] to execute skipping when processing the ID list. After having processed the ID list we will record the position of the result of intersection into a list. We can utilize this list to access the according values on frequency IPC tree and skip the unnecessary nodes.

4 Experiments

We process experiments on the following corpus. PPD (PeopleDaily91–93) is a collection of short news reported by Chinese official news agency: NCNA (New China News Agency). It contains 135,193 documents and 3,171,009 terms. Gov2 is the TREC 2004 Terabyte Track test collection which includes millions of documents crawled from.gov website. Gov2 are mainly in English and with 9,122,147 documents and 164,443,902 terms. For data in Chinese we use *ansj* (http://www.ansj.org/) for Chinese word segmentation, we do not need stemming technology and remove stop word. For data in English we use Porter2 stemmer and have removed stop word. The experiment machine has a CPU of Inter Core i5-2400, main memory of 4G and WIN7 32 OS. All online processing programs are coding in C++ and we use g++ 4.3 for complier. Queries are randomly chosen from segments of some documents.

Next we will check the efficiency of PD during query processing. Our space consummation remains the same with PD and we focus on its time consummation.

Above Tables show the result of PD compared with FD, PFD and Elias-Fano coding. Actually in practical PD will perform better than above because our programs are all running in inner memory and the advantage of less amount of data transmission between inner and external storage have not been showed.

From Table 1 we find in Boolean conjunctive query PD is comparable with that of Elias-Fano. From Table 2 we know PD in Rank query do not performed as well as Boolean conjunctive query. We find in large corpus PD will take more advantage, but even in Gov2 PD is about a quarter slower compared with the popular coding OPTPFD. That partly because more lists needs to be totally restored in Rank query.

Table 1. Average running time of Boolean conjunctive query

Length of query	FD per query ave time ($\bar{t}$) (ms)		PD ($\bar{t}$) (ms)		OPTPFD [7] ($\bar{t}$) (ms)		Elias-Fano [8] ($\bar{t}$) (ms)	
	PPD	Gov2	PPD	Gov2	PPD	Gov2	PPD	Gov2
2	0.244	1.502	0.196	1.161	0.164	1.064	0.172	1.069
4	0.475	2.997	0.330	2.047	0.290	1.858	0.325	1.954
6	0.663	4.288	0.448	2.453	0.379	2.504	0.431	2.667
8	0.875	5.474	0.596	3.399	0.498	3.186	0.569	3.372
10	1.079	6.561	0.728	4.160	0.619	3.812	0.699	4.015

Table 2. Average running time of Rank query (Acu = 1000 on PPD and 5000 on Gov2)

Length of query	FD Per query ave time ($\bar{t}$) (ms)		PD ($\bar{t}$) (ms)		OPTPFD [7] ($\bar{t}$) (ms)		Elias-Fano [8] ($\bar{t}$) (ms)	
	PPD	Gov2	PPD	Gov2	PPD	Gov2	PPD	Gov2
2	0.6551	6.7909	0.6568	6.7990	0.4092	4.5840	0.5267	5.6436
4	1.0104	11.6633	0.9539	11.100	6.5575	8.494	7.633	9.307
6	1.6994	19.4289	1.5144	17.117	1.0978	15.1139	1.2439	15.183
8	2.4501	28.1508	2.1775	23.957	1.513	18.917	1.7984	21.957
10	3.1960	38.9273	2.8412	32.459	2.472	26.120	2.612	31.268

5 Conclusion

IPC is an effective coding in CR with a relatively slower processing speed, any improvement on its processing speed is not trivial. We proposed a partially decompression algorithm which can accelerate query processing speed. We try to reduce the time consummation by saving any computation unnecessary and we prove our method is useful. Our algorithm is about 40 % faster for Boolean conjunctive query and 20 % faster for Rank query without additional storage consumption compared with FD.

Acknowledgments. We would like to thank the anonymous reviewers for their valuable comments and suggestions. This work is supported by the National Natural Science Foundation of China (grant No. 61402466, 61572494), the Strategic Priority Research Program of the Chinese Academy of Sciences (grant No. XDA06030200), and the National Key Technology R&D Program (grant No. 2012BAH46B03).

References

1. Zobel, J., Moffat, A.: Adding compression to a full-text retrieval system. Softw. Pract. Exp. **25**(8), 891–903 (1995)
2. Golomb, S.W.: Run-length encodings. IEEE Trans. Inf. Theor. **12**(3), 399–401 (1966)
3. Williams, H.E., Zobel, J.: Compressing integers for fast file access. Comput. J. **42**(3), 193–201 (1999)
4. Zukowski, M., Heman, S., Nes, N., Boncz, P.: Superscalar RAM-CPU cache compression. In: Proceedings of the 22nd International Conference on Data Engineering (ICDE), no. 59, pp. 1–12. IEEE (2006)
5. Yan, H., Ding, S., Suel, T.: Inverted index compression and query processing with optimized document ordering. In: Proceedings of the 18th International Conference on World Wide Web (WWW), pp. 401–410. ACM (2009)
6. Vigna, S.: Quasi-succinct indices. In: Proceedings of the 6th International Conference on Web Search and Data Mining (WSDM), pp. 83–92. ACM (2013)
7. Ottaviano, G., Venturini, R.: Partitioned Elias-Fano indexes. In: Sigir (2014)
8. Moffat, A., Stuiver, L.: Binary interpolative coding for effective index compression. Inf. Retrieval **3**(1), 25–47 (2000)

9. Cheng, C.S., Shann, J.J.J., Chung, C.P.: Unique-order interpolative coding for fast querying and space-efficient indexing in information retrieval systems. Inf. Process. Manag. **42**(2), 407–428 (2006)
10. Teuhola, J.: Interpolative coding of integer sequences supporting log-time random access. Inf. Process. Manag. **47**, 742–761 (2011)
11. Anh, V.N., Moffat, A.: Pruned query evaluation using pre-computed impacts. In: SIGIR, pp. 372–379. ACM, New York (2006)
12. Moffat, A., Zobel, J.: Self-indexing inverted files for fast text retrieval. Systems **14**(4), 349–379 (1996)
13. He, J., Yan, H., Suel, T.: Compact full-text indexing of versioned document collections. In: Proceedings of the 18th ACM Conference on Information and Knowledge Management, 02–06 November, Hong Kong, China (2009)

Using Changesets for Incremental Maintenance of Linkset Views

Vânia M.P. Vidal[1]([⊠]), Marco A. Casanova[2], Elisa S. Menendez[2],
Narciso Arruda[1], Valeria M. Pequeno[3], and Luiz A. Paes Leme[4]

[1] Federal University of Ceará, Fortaleza, CE, Brazil
{vvidal,narciso}@lia.ufc.br
[2] Department of Informatics, Pontifical Catholic University of Rio de Janeiro,
Rio de Janeiro, RJ, Brazil
casanova@inf.puc-rio.br, elisasmenendez@gmail.com
[3] INESC-ID, Porto Salvo, Portugal
vmp@inesc-id.pt
[4] Fluminense Federal University, Niteroi, RJ, Brazil
lapaesleme@ic.uff.br

Abstract. In the Linked Data field, data publishers frequently materialize linksets between two datasets using link discovery tools. However, when the datasets are continually updated, a materialized linkset must also be updated since the links may no longer meet the linkage rules. To help solve this problem, this paper presents an approach for maintaining linksets, which treats linksets as materialized views, is based on changesets and adopts an incremental strategy. The paper formalizes the materialized linkset maintenance problem based on changesets and indicates that our approach correctly maintains materialized linksets views. Finally, it suggests an architecture and describes an implementation and experiments to validate the proposed approach.

Keywords: RDF dataset interlinking · Linked data · View maintenance

1 Introduction

The Linked Data initiative [1] defines best practices for publishing and interlinking data on the Web using RDF triples to represent the data. Briefly, a *dataset* is simply a set of RDF triples. A *link* is an RDF triple of the form (s, p, o), where s and o are resources defined in two distinct datasets. A *linkset* is a set of links.

Link discovery tools help create and materialize linksets. These tools are typically semi-automatic in the sense that users have to define a set of *linkage rules* that specify conditions that resources must fulfill to be interlinked. However, when datasets are continually updated, the maintenance of a materialized linkset requires attention since the links may no longer meet the linkage rules that originated the linkset. To inform consumers about changes, an RDF dataset should publish *changesets* [3] to indicate the difference between two states of the dataset.

In this paper, we present an approach for maintaining materialized linksets. The approach we propose: (1) treats linksets as materialized views, called *linkset views*;

© Springer International Publishing AG 2016
W. Cellary et al. (Eds.): WISE 2016, Part II, LNCS 10042, pp. 196–204, 2016.
DOI: 10.1007/978-3-319-48743-4_16

(2) accounts for the facts that a linkset is computed by (complex) linkage rules and that the linkset does not contain the property values used by the linkage rules; (3) uses the changesets published by the source datasets to compute the changes that must be applied to a materialized linkset to keep it consistent with the new states of the source datasets; (4) adopts an incremental strategy. The proposed approach has two main steps. The first step uses the changesets, published by the source datasets, to compute the set of updated resources that are relevant to the materialized linkset. The second step updates the links for the relevant resources.

The contributions of the paper are: (i) we formalize the materialized linkset maintenance problem based on changesets; (ii) we define an approach that uses changesets to incrementally maintain materialized linksets and informally illustrate how it works; (iii) we provide two theorems that indicate that the proposed algorithms correctly maintains materialized linksets views; (iv) we describe an implementation and experiments to validate the approach.

Several tools were designed to create linksets [4, 5, 9]. The introduction of views, as suggested in [2], would simplify the configuration of the tools designed to create links. In another direction, tools, such as DSNotify [6], were designed to inform database administrators about dataset changes and to allow them to preserve link integrity. The proposed approach is based on, but not reducible to such incremental view maintenance strategies. Indeed, a linkset is not a regular view computed by querying two datasets, but it is created using linkage rules that frequently involve computing entity similarity. Furthermore, a linkset does not contain the property values that the linkage rules use. Endris et al. [3] presented a framework for interest-based RDF update propagation that can consistently maintain a full or partial replication of large LOD datasets. This framework is also based on changesets, but the solution can only be applied when the view mappings are direct mappings. The approach proposed in this paper goes further and considers linkset views defined by expressive mappings.

The paper is organized as follows. Section 2 introduces basic definitions and a running example. Section 3 presents our approach for maintaining linksets views. Section 4 describes an implementation and experiments to validate the proposed approach. Finally, Sect. 5 contains the conclusions.

2 Linkset Views

2.1 Linkset View Definition

To make the paper self-contained, we introduce an abstract notation to define *catalogue views* and *linkset views* with the help of mapping rules [7]. In the rest of this paper, $\sigma_S(t)$ denotes the state of S in time t, where S can be a source dataset or a view, and M [$\sigma_S(t)$] denotes the set of triples defined by a set M of mapping rules against $\sigma_S(t)$.

A *catalogue view definition* is a triple $\mathbf{V} = (V_V, S_V, M_V)$, where

- V_V is the vocabulary of $\mathbf{V}$, also called the *view vocabulary*, and consists of a single class and a set of datatype properties
- S_V is the source dataset which exports the view $\mathbf{V}$, described by a vocabulary V_S

- M_V is a set of mapping rules that map concepts of V_S to concepts of V_V, called the *view mapping*.

A *materialization* of view **V** at time t is obtained by computing $M_V[\sigma_{S_V}(t)]$ and storing it as part of a dataset.

A *linkset view definition* is a quintuple **L** = (P, V_L, **F**, **G**, μ), where

- P is an object property
- V_L is the *match vocabulary* of L and consists of a single class and a set of datatype properties
- **F**= (V_F, S_F, M_F) and **G**= (V_G, S_G, M_G) are catalogue view definitions where
- $V_F = V_G = V_L$. Thus, V_L is the common vocabulary for exported views **F** and **G**
- μ is a *2n*-relation, called the *match predicate* of **L**.

Let V_L ={C, $P_1,...,P_n$} be the match vocabulary of **L**. Let $\sigma_F(t)$ and $\sigma_G(t)$ be states respectively of **F** and **G** in time t. The *state* of **L** in time t is the set $\sigma_L(t)$ defined as: *(s, p,o)* $\in \sigma_L(t)$ iff there are triples *(s, rdf:type, C)*, *(s, P_1, s_1)*, ..., *(s, P_n, s_n)* $\in \sigma_F(t)$ and *(o, rdf:type, C)*, *(o, P_1, o_1)*, ..., *(o, P_n, o_n)* $\in \sigma_G(t)$ such that *($s_1,...,$ s_n, $o_1,...,$ o_n)* $\in \mu$

2.2   Running Example

In this section, we illustrate how to define a linkset view. Consider the *MusicBrainz* (http://musicbrainz.org/doc/about) dataset, which uses the Music ontology. Figure 1 shows a fragment of the Music ontology, which reuses terms from three well-known vocabularies: *FOAF* (Friend of a Friend), *MO* (Music Ontology) and *DC* (Dublin Core). Consider the DBpedia (http://wiki.dbpedia.org/about) dataset, which uses the *DBpedia* Ontology *(dbo)*. Figure 2 shows a fragment of *DBpedia* ontology.

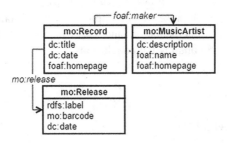

Fig. 1. A fragment of the *Music Ontology*

Fig. 2. A fragment of the *DBpedia Ontology*

Suppose that a user wants to create *sameAs links* between instances of the class *Record* in the *MusicBrainz* dataset and instances of the class *Album* in the *DBpedia* dataset. For this purpose, the user creates the linkset view definition $\mathbf{L} = (owl{:}sameAs,$ $V_{\mathbf{L}}, \mathbf{F}, \mathbf{G}, \mu)$, where: $V_{\mathbf{L}}=\{mo{:}Record, dc{:}title, mvl{:}artistName, dbo{:}releaseDate\}$; the vocabulary $V_{\mathbf{L}}$ reuses terms from *DBpedia and Music Ontologies* and defines a new term *mvl:artistName*; $\mathbf{F}$ and $\mathbf{G}$ are catalogues views exported by *DBpedia* and *MusicBrainz*, respectively, with mapping rules $M_{\mathbf{F}}$ and $M_{\mathbf{G}}$ from *DBpedia and Music Ontology* to common vocabulary $V_{\mathbf{L}}$, respectively:

$M_{\mathbf{F}}$: *mo:Record(x)* ← *dbo:Album(x)*
dc:title(x, y) ← *dbo:Album(x); foaf:name(x, y)*
mvl:artistName(x, y) ← *dbo:Album(x); dbo:artist(x, z); foaf:name(z, y)*
dbo:releaseDate(x, y) ← *dbo:Album(x); dbo:releaseDate(x, y)*
$M_{\mathbf{G}}$: is omitted here due to space limitation

and μ is the match predicate defined as

$$(s_1, s_2, s_3, o_1, o_2, o_3) \in \mu \text{ iff } \sigma(s_k, o_k) \geq a, \text{ for each } k = 1, 2, 3$$

where σ is the 3-gram distance and $\alpha = 0.5$. The match predicate compares the *title*, *artistName* and *releaseDate* of instances of *Record* from both views $\mathbf{F}$ and $\mathbf{G}$.

3   Linkset Incremental Maintenance Based on Changesets

In this section, we present our approach to correctly compute the changeset for a linkset view $\mathbf{L}$, based on the changesets published by $S_{\mathbf{F}}$ and $S_{\mathbf{G}}$. A *changeset* of an RDF dataset S from the state $\sigma_S(t_0)$ in time t_0 to the state $\sigma_S(t_1)$ in time t_1 is a pair $<\Delta_S^-(t_0, t_1), \Delta_S^+(t_0, t_1)>$, where $\Delta^-{}_S(t_0, t_1)$ is the set of triples removed from $\sigma_S(t_0)$ and $\Delta_S^+(t_0, t_1)$ is the set of triples added $\sigma_S(t_0)$ to create $\sigma_S(t_1)$ (for a formal definition see [8]). The approach we suggest to compute $\Delta_{\mathbf{L}}(t_0,t_1)$ follows two main steps: (1) Compute $R_{\mathbf{F}}(t_0,t_1)$, the set of resources that are affected by $\Delta_{S\mathbf{F}}(t_0,t_1)$ w.r.t $\mathbf{F}$, and $R_{\mathbf{G}}(t_0,t_1)$, the set of resources that are affected by $\Delta_{S\mathbf{G}}(t_0,t_1)$ w.r.t $\mathbf{G}$; (2) Compute $\Delta_{\mathbf{L}}(t_0,t_1)$ using the resources in $R_{\mathbf{F}}(t_0, t_1)$ and $R_{\mathbf{G}}(t_0, t_1)$.

3.1   Computing the Affected Resources

In this section we present an algorithm to compute $R_{\mathbf{F}}(t_0,t_1)$, the set of resources that are affected by $\Delta_{S\mathbf{F}}(t_0,t_1)$ w.r.t $\mathbf{F}$. We say that a resource s is *affected* by $\Delta_{S\mathbf{F}}(t_0,t_1)$ iff the state of s in $\sigma_{\mathbf{F}}(t_o)$ is different from the state of s in $\sigma_{\mathbf{F}}(t_1)$. More formally, a resource s *is affected by* $\Delta_{S\mathbf{F}}(t_0,t_1)$ w.r.t $\mathbf{F}$ iff $s[\sigma_{\mathbf{F}}(t_o)] \neq s[\sigma_{\mathbf{F}}(t_1)]$. To compute $R_{\mathbf{F}}(t_0,t_1)$, we have to consider two situations:

(i)   If all mappings in $M_{\mathbf{F}}$ are simple mappings, $R_{\mathbf{F}}(t_0,t_1)$ can be directly computed from $\Delta_{S\mathbf{F}}(t_0,t_1)$ [8].

(ii)   Otherwise, the computation of $R_{\mathbf{F}}(t_0,t_1)$ requires, besides $\Delta_{S\mathbf{F}}(t_0,t_1)$, the old state $\sigma_{S\mathbf{F}}(t_0)$ of $S_{\mathbf{F}}$. But, $\sigma_{S\mathbf{F}}(t_0)$ is no longer available when the changeset is published.

To account for the second case, we introduce the notion of *auxiliary view* A_F for F, defined as a triple $A_F = (V_{AF}, S_{AF}, M_{AF})$, where:

- V_{AF} consists of all classes and properties in V_F that are relevant to S_F
- $S_{AF} = S_F$
- M_{AF} is a set of direct mappings from the vocabulary of S_F to V_{AF}.

In the suggested architecture (see [8]), the auxiliary view A_F is materialized, while the view F is virtual. Algorithm 1, shown in Table 1, computes $R_F(t_0, t_1)$ when an auxiliary view is required. Theorem 1 in [8] shows that Algorithm 1 correctly computes the set of affected resources.

Table 1. Algorithm 1

Input: $\sigma_{AF}(t_0)$, $\Delta_{SF}(t_0, t_1)$

Step 1.1: Compute $\Delta^-_{AF}(t_0, t_1) = M_{AF}[\Delta^-_{SF}(t_0, t_1)]$ and $\Delta^+_{AF}(t_0, t_1) = M_{AF}[\Delta^+_{SF}(t_0, t_1)]$;

Step 1.2: Compute $R^-(t_0, t_1) = \{s \mid s$ is the subject of a triple t in $\sigma_F(t_0)$ and t is affected by a triple in $\Delta^-_{AF}(t_0, t_1) \}$;

Step 1.3: Compute $\sigma_{AF}(t_1) = (\sigma_{AF}(t_0) - \Delta^-_{AF}(t_0, t_1)) \cup \Delta^+_{AF}(t_0, t_1)$;

Step 1.4: Compute $R^+(t_0, t_1) = \{s \mid s$ is the subject of a triple t in $\sigma_F(t_1)$ and t is affected by a triple in $\Delta^+_{AF}(t_0, t_1) \}$;

Step 1.5: Return $R_F(t_0, t_1) = R^-(t_0, t_1) \cup R^+(t_0, t_1)$.

To illustrate the computation of $R_F(t_0, t_1)$ by Algorithm 1, consider the linkset view L over the catalogue views F and G exported from *DBpedia* and *MusicBrainz*, defined in Sect. 2.2. The auxiliary view for F is $A_F = (V_{AF}, S_{AF}, M_{AF})$, where: $V_{AF} = \{dbo:$ *Album, foaf:name, dbo:artist, dbo:releaseDate* $\}$; S_{AF}: http://host/dbpedia; M_{AF} is a set of direct mappings from *DBpedia's* vocabulary to V_{AF}. The auxiliary view for G is $A_G = (V_{AG}, S_{AG}, M_{AG})$, where: $V_{AG} = \{mo:Record, dc:title, foaf:maker, foaf:name, mo:$ *realese, dc:date*$\}$; S_{AF}: http://host/MusicBrainz; M_{AG} is a set of direct mappings from *MusicBrainz's* vocabulary to V_{AG}. Assume that:

- Table 2 shows the states of the catalogue views F and G, the auxiliary view A_F and linkset view L, on Sep 10, 2015 at 10:00 AM (t_0) and the triples published by the DBpedia Live extractor for the changes made on Sep 10, 2015 between 10:00 AM (t_0) and 11:02 PM (t_1).
- *MusicBrainz* did not release new changeset on Sep 10, 2015 between 10:00 AM (t_0) and 11:02 PM (t_1).

Algorithm 1 computes the set $R_F(t_0, t_1)$ in 5 steps:

Step 1.1: Compute $\Delta^-_{AF}(t_0, t_1)$ and $\Delta^+_{AF}(t_0, t_1)$. From Algorithm 1, we have:
$\Delta^-_{AF}(t_0, t_1) = \{$(dbr:b1 *foaf:name* "Jackson Michael")$\}$.
$\Delta^+_{AF}(t_0, t_1) = \{$(dbr:a1 *dbo:releaseDate* "1982-11-29"), (dbr:a1 *foaf:name* "Thriller"), (dbr:b1 *foaf:name* "Michael Joseph Jackson")$\}$.

Table 2. $\sigma_F(t_0)$, $\sigma_G(t_0)$, $\sigma_{AF}(t_0)$, $\sigma_{AF}(t_1)$, $\sigma_L(t_0)$, $\Delta^-_{DBpedia}(t_0, t_1)$ and $\Delta^+_{DBpedia}(t_0, t_1)$

$\sigma_F(t_0)$ = {	(dbr:a2 *dbo:artist* dbr:b1),
(dbr:a1 rdf:type *mo:Record*);	(dbr:b1 *foaf:name* "Michael Joseph
(dbr:a1 *mvl:artistName* "Jackson Michael");	Jackson")}
(dbr:a2 rdf:type *mo:Record*);	$\sigma_G(t_0)$ = {
(dbr:a2 *dc:title* "Thriller 25");	(mbr:r1 rdf:type *mo:Record*);
(dbr:a2 *mvl:artistName* "Jackson Michael");	(mbr:r1 *dc:title* "Thriller");
(dbr:a2 *dbo:releaseDate* "2008-02-08")}	(mbr:r1 *mvl:artistName* "Michael Joseph
$\sigma_{AF}(t_0)$ = {	Jackson");
(dbr:a1 rdf:type *dbo:Album*);	(mbr:r1 *dc:releaseDate* "1982-11-29");
(dbr:a1 *dbo:artist* dbr:b1);	(mbr:r2 rdf:type *mo:Record*);
(dbr:a2 rdf:type *dbo:Album*);	(mbr:r2 *dc:title* "Thriller 25");
(dbr:a2 *foaf:name* "Thriller 25");	(mbr:r2 *mvl:artistName* "Michael Joseph
(dbr:a2 *dbo:releaseDate* "2008-02-08");	Jackson");
(dbr:a2 *dbo:artist* dbr:b1);	(mbr:r2 *dc:releaseDate* "2008-02-08")}
(dbr:b1 *foaf:name* "Jackson Michael")}	$\sigma_L(t_0)$ = {(dbr:a2 *owl:sameAs* mbr:r2)}
$\sigma_{AF}(t_1)$ = {	$\Delta^-_{DBpedia}(t_0, t_1)$ = {
(dbr:a1 rdf:type *dbo:Album*),	(dbr:b1 *foaf:name* "Jackson Michael")}
(dbr:a1 *foaf:name* "Thriller"),	$\Delta^+_{DBpedia}(t_0, t_1)$ = {
(dbr:a1 *dbo:releaseDate* "1982-11-29"),	(dbr:a1 *dbo:releaseDate* "1982-11-29");
(dbr:a2 rdf:type *dbo:Album*),	(dbr:a1 *foaf:name* "Thriller");
(dbr:a2 *foaf:name* "Thriller 25"),	(dbr:b1 *foaf:name* "Michael Joseph
(dbr:a2 *dbo:releaseDate* "2008-02-08"),	Jackson")}
(dbr:a1 *dbo:artist* dbr:b1),	

Step 1.2: Compute $R^-(t_0, t_1)$. First we have to compute which triples in $\sigma_F(t_0)$ are affected by triples in $\Delta^-_{AF}(t_0, t_1)$. For example, consider the triple $\mathbf{y}$ = (dbr:b1 *foaf:name* "Jackson Michael") in $\Delta^-_{AF}(t_0, t_1)$. The triples (dbr:a1 *mvl:artistName* "Jackson Michael") and (dbr:a2 *mvl:artistName* "Jackson Michael") in $\sigma_F(t_0)$ are affected by $\mathbf{y}$ because those triples are generated by substituting *foaf:name(z, y)* by $\mathbf{y}$ in the mapping rule "*mvl:artistName(x, y)* ← *dbo:Album(x); dbo:artist(x, z); foaf:name(z, y)*". Therefore, $R^-(t_0, t_1)$ = {dbr:a1, dbr:a2}.

Step 1.3: Compute $\sigma_{AF}(t_1)$ = $(s_{AF}(t_0) - \Delta^-_{AF}(t_0, t_1))$ ∪ $\Delta^+_{AF}(t_0, t_1)$ (See Table 2).

Step 1.4: Compute $R^+(t_0, t_1)$. First we have to compute the triples in $\sigma_F(t_1)$ that are affected by triples in $\Delta^+_{AF}(t_0, t_1)$. The triples (dbr:a1 *dbo:releaseDate* "1982-11-29"), (dbr:a1 *dc:title* "Thriller"), and (dbr:a1 *mvl:artistName* "Jackson Joseph Michael") in $\sigma_F(t_1)$ are affected by triples in $\Delta^+_{AF}(t_0, t_1)$. Therefore, $R^-(t_0, t_1)$ = {dbr:a1, dbr:a2}.

Step 1.5: Compute $R_F(t_0, t_1)$ = $R^-(t_0, t_1) \cup R^+(t_0, t_1)$
$R_F(t_0, t_1)$ = {dbr:a1, dbr:a2}.

3.2   Computing the Changeset for L

Algorithm 2 in Table 3 returns $\Delta_L(t_0, t_1)$, a changeset for **L**. Theorem 2 in [8] shows that the changeset $\Delta_L(t_0, t_1)$ returned by Algorithm 2 correctly maintains **L**. To illustrate

Table 3. Algorithm 2

Input: $\sigma_L(t_0)$, $\sigma_{AF}(t_1)$, $\sigma_{AG}(t_1)$, $R_F(t_0,t_1)$, $R_G(t_0,t_1)$

Step 2.1: Compute

$\quad D_F = \{ (s, p, o) \,/\, (s, p, o) \in \sigma_L(t_0)$ and $s \in R_F(t_0,t_1)\}$

$\quad I_F = \{ (s, p, o) \,/\, s \in R_F(t_0,t_1), o \in M_F[\sigma_{AF}(t_1)]\};$

Step 2.2: Compute

$\quad D_G = \{ (s, p, o) \,/\, (s, p, o) \in \sigma_L(t_0)$ and $s \in R_G(t_0,t_1)\}$

$\quad I_G = \{ (s, p, o) \,/\, s \in R_G(t_0,t_1), o \in M_G[\sigma_{AG}(t_1)]\};$

Step 2.3: Compute $\Delta^-_L(t_0,t_1) = D_F \cup D_G$;

Step 2.4: Compute $\Delta^+_L(t_0,t_1) = I_F \cup I_G$;

Step 2.5: Return $\Delta_L(t_0, t_1) = < \Delta^-_L(t_0,t_1), \Delta^+_L(t_0,t_1) >$.

---

the computation of $\Delta_L(t_0,t_1)$ by Algorithm 2, consider the set $R_F(t_0,t_1)$ computed in Sect. 3.1. Since we assume that *MusicBrainz* did not release new changesets in the time interval considered, $R_G(t_0,t_1) = \varnothing$. Algorithm 2 computes $\Delta_L(t_0,t_1)$ in 5 steps.

Step 2.1: Compute D_F and I_F. From Algorithm 2, we have:

$D_F = \{(dbr:a2\ owl:sameAs\ mbr:r2)\};$

$I_F = \{(dbr:a1\ owl:sameAs\ mbr:r1), (dbr:a2\ owl:sameAs\ mbr:r2)\}.$

Step 2.2: Compute D_G and I_G. From Algorithm 2, we have:

$D_G = \varnothing; I_G = \varnothing.$

Step 2.3: Compute $\Delta^-_L(t_0,t_1)$. From Algorithm 2, we have:

$\Delta^-_L(t_0,t_1) = \{(dbr:a2\ owl:sameAs\ mbr:r2)\}.$

Step 2.4: Compute $\Delta^+_L(t_0,t_1)$. From Algorithm 2, we have:

$\Delta^+_L(t_0,t_1) = \{(dbr:a1\ owl:sameAs\ mbr:r1), (dbr:a2\ owl:sameAs\ mbr:r2)\}.$

Step 2.5: Return $\Delta_L(t_0, t_1) = < \Delta^-_L(t_0,t_1), \Delta^+_L(t_0,t_1) >$

The new state of **L** is computed by $\sigma_L(t_1) = (\sigma_L(t_0) - \Delta^-_L(t_0,t_1)) \cup \Delta^+_L(t_0,t_1)$. Therefore, $\sigma_L(t_1) = \{(dbr:a1\ owl:sameAs\ mbr:r1), (dbr:a2\ owl:sameAs\ mbr:r2)\}.$

4   Implementation and Experiments

The *Linkset Maintainer* tool was developed using Java, JBoss 7, Open Link Virtuoso as the triple store, and Silk as the link discovery tool. In order to evaluate the performance of the incremental strategy, we selected two datasets: a *Music Brainz* dump, and the *DBpedia* endpoint. Additionally, *DBpedia* daily provides sets of changed triples extracted from Wikipedia, called *DBpedia* Changesets (available at http://live.dbpedia. org/changesets/), which are organized by year, month, day, and hour; and also separated by the type of update (added, removed, reinserted, and clear).

We defined views about music records released after 2010 for each dataset. The "MusicBrainz_Records" view had 311,374 resources and the "DBpedia_Records" view had 35,651resources. Then, we materialized an *owl:sameAs* linkset of records, using these views, by comparing their titles, artist names and release dates. The linkset had 14,716 links and the runtime to compute it using Silk was around 4 h. To test the performance of the incremental strategy, we processed and analyzed one entire day (October 3th, 2015) of DBpedia changesets. We computed the total number of inserted and deleted resources, the sets $\Delta_{\mathbf{AF}}^{-}(t_0, t_1)$, $\Delta_{\mathbf{AF}}^{+}(t_0, t_1)$, R^{-} and R^{+}, and the runtime to maintain the linkset. Table 4 summarizes the results for the whole day.

Table 4. Analysis of DBpedia Changesets.

	Total	Sets	Avg	Max
Deleted resources	144385	720	200,5	1230
Auxiliary view deleted resources $\left(\Delta_{\mathbf{AF}}^{-}(t_0, t_1)\right)$	7453	720	10,35	85
View deleted resources (R^{-})	318	720	0,4	16
Inserted resources	134887	720	187,3	1072
Auxiliary view inserted resources $\left(\Delta_{\mathbf{AF}}^{+}(t_0, t_1)\right)$	7614	720	10,58	85
View inserted resources (R^{+})	372	720	0,5	16
Runtime	12 h	720	1 min	5 min

Note that, on the average, there are 200,5 deleted resources per changeset, of which only an average of 0,4 resources affected the view. Also note that the max number of R^{-} and R^{+} was only 85. We highlight that the max runtime to process a changeset was 5 min, which included the time to download and decompress the changeset file, compute R^{-} and R^{+}, and update the linkset. Recall that the runtime to materialize the linkset was 4 h, which is much higher than the max runtime to incrementally maintain the linkset using a changeset. Therefore, in these experiments, we showed that the incremental strategy, by far, outperformed the re-materialization strategy.

5   Conclusions

Data publishers frequently materialize linkset views between two source datasets using link discovery tools. However, when the source datasets are updated, the materialized linkset views must also be updated. To help solve this problem, we presented a formal framework for maintaining linkset views that adopts changesets and an incremental strategy. The changesets, published by the source datasets, are used to compute the set of updated resources that are relevant to a linkset view; the incremental strategy updates the links only for the relevant resources. We provided a formalization of our approach and indicated that the framework correctly maintains the linkset views. We also described experiments to validate the proposed framework.

Acknowledgments. This work was partly funded by CNPq under grants 153908/ 2015-7, 557128/2009-9, 444976/2014-0, 303332/2013-1, 442338/2014-7 and 248743/ 2013-9, by FAPERJ under grants e E-26-170028/2008 and E-26/201.337/2014 and by FCT – Fundação para a Ciência e Tecnologia, under grant SFRH/BPD/76024/2011.

References

1. Berners-Lee, T.: (2006). http://www.w3.org/ DesignIssues/LinkedData.html
2. Casanova, M.A., Vidal, V.M.P., Lopes, G.R., Leme, L.A.P.P., Ruback, L.: On materialized sameAs linksets. In: 25th International Conference on Database and Expert Systems Applications, pp. 377–384 (2014)
3. Endris, M.K., Faial, S., Orlandi, F., Auer, S., Scerri, S.: Interest-based RDF update propagation. In: 14th International Semantic Web Conference, pp. 650–665 (2015)
4. Isele, R., Jentzsch, A., Bizer, C.: efficient multidimensional blocking for link discovery without losing recall. In: 14th International Workshop on the Web and Databases (2011)
5. Ngomo, A.C.N., Auer, S.: Limes: a time-efficient approach for large-scale link discovery on the web of data. In: 22nd International Joint Conference on Artificial Intelligence, pp. 2312–2317 (2011)
6. Popitsch, N., Haslhofer, B.: DSNotify – a solution for event detection and link maintenance in dynamic triplesets. J. Web Semant. **9**(3), 266–283 (2011)
7. Vidal, V.M.P., et al.: Specification and incremental maintenance of linked data mashup views. In: 27th International Conference on Advanced Information Systems Engineering, pp. 214–229 (2015)
8. Vidal, V.M.P., Casanova, M.A., Menendez, E.S., Arruda, N.: A formal approach based on changesets for the incremental maintenance of linkset views. Technical report 015, Department of Informatics, PUC-Rio, Brazil (2015)
9. Volz, J., Bizer, C., Gaedke, M., Kobilarov, G.: Discovering and maintaining links on the web of data. In: 8th International Semantic Web Conference, pp. 650–665 (2009)

Spatial and Temporal Data

Graph-Based Metric Embedding for Next POI Recommendation

Min Xie[1], Hongzhi Yin[2(✉)], Fanjiang Xu[1], Hao Wang[1], and Xiaofang Zhou[2]

[1] Science and Technology on Integrated Information System Laboratory,
Institute of Software, Chinese Academy of Sciences, Beijing 100190, China
{xiemin2014,fanjiang,wanghao}@iscas.ac.cn
[2] School of Information Technology and Electrical Engineering,
The University of Queensland, Brisbane, QLD 4072, Australia
db.hongzhi@gmail.com, zxf@itee.uq.edu.au

Abstract. With the rapid prevalence of smart mobile devices and the dramatic proliferation of location-based social networks (LBSNs), point of interest (POI) recommendation has become an important means to help people discover attractive and interesting places. In this paper, we investigate the problem of next POI recommendation by considering the sequential influences of POIs, as a natural extension of the general POI recommendation, but it is more challenging than the general POI recommendation, due to that (1) users' preferences are dynamic, and the next POI recommendation requires tracking the change of user preferences in a real-time manner; and (2) the prediction space is extremely large, with millions of distinct POIs as the next prediction target, which impedes the application of classical Markov chain models. In light of the above challenges, we propose a graph-based metric embedding model which converts POIs in a low dimensional metric and tracks the dynamics of user preferences in an efficient way. Besides, the knowledge of sequential patterns of users' check-in behaviors can be exploited and encoded in the POI embedding, which avoid the time-consuming computation of the POI-POI transition matrix or even cube as the Markov chain-based recommender models have done. In other words, our proposed method effectively unifies dynamic user preferences and sequential influence via the POI embedding. Experiments on two real large-scale datasets demonstrate a significant improvement of our proposed models in terms of recommendation accuracy, compared with the state-of-the-art methods.

Keywords: Next POI recommendation · Metric embedding · Sequential influence · Dynamic user preferences

1 Introduction

With the rapid development of Web 2.0, location acquisition and wireless communication technologies, a sufficient number of location-based social networks (LBSNs) have emerged in recent years, such as Foursquare, Facebook Places,

© Springer International Publishing AG 2016
W. Cellary et al. (Eds.): WISE 2016, Part II, LNCS 10042, pp. 207–222, 2016.
DOI: 10.1007/978-3-319-48743-4_17

Gowalla and Loopt, where users can check in at point-of-interests (POIs), e.g., stores, restaurants, sightseeing sites, and share their life experiences in the physical world via mobile devices. To help users navigate a huge number of POIs and suggest the most suitable POIs to meet their personal preferences, POI recommendation has become an important means and played a critical role in LBSN services. POI recommendation aims at learning users' preferences based on their check-in records and then predicting users' preferred POIs for recommendation. Recently, many various recommender models have been proposed for POI recommendation by exploiting and integrating geographical influence [18], social influence [5], temporal cyclic effect [6,26], word-of-mouth effect [9,25], content effect [15,24] and their joint effect [9,22,25].

Next POI recommendation [2], as a natural extension of general POI recommendation, is recently proposed. There are relatively few studies on this new problem and it is very challenging. Different from general POI recommendation that focuses on estimating users' static preferences on POIs, next POI recommendation requires provides satisfactory recommendations promptly based on users' latest preferences and their most recent checked-in POIs, which requires producing recommendation results in a real-time manner. However, most of existing general POI recommender models is incapable of supporting real-time recommendation, and they would suffer from the following two drawbacks: (1) Delay on model updates caused by the expensive time cost of re-running the recommender model; and (2) Disability to track changing user preferences due to the fact that latest check-in records used for updating recommendation models are often overwhelmed by the large data of the past. Accurately capturing the change of user preferences in a real-time manner is very helpful for next POI recommendation. Since each check-in provides valuable information about the user's preferences, recommender model must respond immediately to new check-in information.

On the other hand, several Markov chain-based recommender models [2,28,29] have been recently developed to capture the sequential patterns of POIs. But, they encounter from the huge parameter prediction space. Suppose there are a collection of V POIs and the next POI depends on the previous n ones. These recommendation methods then need to estimate $|V|^{n+1}$ free parameters in the nth order Markov chain model, which is extremely computational-expensive. To reduce the size of the prediction space, most related studies [2,29] exploit sequential influence using a first-order Markov chain, which considers only the last one in a sequence of locations visited by a user to recommend a new location for her. Although the parameter space can be decreased to $|V|^2$, it may still be huge considering that V is usually a large number in LBSNs. Hence, we aim to develop a new method with a small number parameters to incorporate the influence from all recently visited locations, rather than just the last one.

More recently, methods of embedding items in a low-dimension Euclidean space have been widely adopted in a variety of fields, including natural language processing, text mining and music information retrieval. Tang et al. [13] predicted text embeddings based on heterogeneous text networks which showed great potential in document classification. Chen et al. [1] proposed a Logistic

Markov embedding (LME) to map each song to one point (or multiple points) in a latent Euclidean space for playlists generating, which also verifies the effectiveness of embedding methods.

In this paper, we stand on the recent advances in embedding learning techniques and propose a graph-based metric embedding method called GME to effectively learn the embeddings of POIs in a low-dimension Euclidean space. Then, we track the dynamic user preferences and provide recommendations based on the embeddings of the user's check-in POIs and their timestamps. Specifically, we adopt a time-decay manner to compute the user's dynamic preferences from his/her checked-in POIs, i.e., if a POI is visited by the user more recently, it will be more important and assigned with a higher weight. Just like the classic item-based collaborative filtering method [8], our proposed recommendation method has the nice properties of making fast response to new check-in information, producing dynamic recommendations in realtime and scaling to massive data sets, and our GME model only needs to be trained once to obtain the embeddings of POIs. Note that the computation of POI-POI correlation (or similarity) in our method is based on the learnt POI embeddings, which effectively overcomes the issue of data sparsity encountered by the item-based CF. To further improve the effectiveness of our method in next POI recommendation, we extend the GME model to GME-S by exploiting the sequential patterns of POIs. Since the knowledge of sequential patterns is encoded in the POI embeddings, we do not need to integrate the sequential influence to next POI recommendation in an explicit way as the Markov chain-based recommendation method do. In our GME-S model, the parameter space is $|V| \times d$ where d is the dimension of POI embedding that tends to be smaller than 100. Thus, the parameter space in our model is much smaller than $|V| \times |V|$.

To summarize, we make the following contributions:

– We develop a graph-based metric embedding (GME) model to learn the representation of POIs in a low-dimension latent space. Then, we propose a time-decay method to track and represent the dynamic user preferences based on the learnt POI embeddings.
– To model the sequential influence of POIs, we further extend our GME to GME-S model by exploiting and integrating the sequential patterns in the learning process of POI embeddings. To the best of our knowledge, this is the first work that uses the metric embedding method to unify dynamic user preferences and the sequential influence in a principled manner.
– We conduct comprehensive experiments to evaluate the performance of our proposed methods on two large scale real datasets. The results show the superiority of our proposals in recommending next POIs for users by comparing with the state-of-the-art techniques.

The remainder of the paper is organized as follows. Section 2 details our proposed recommendation approach. We report the experimental results in Sect. 3. Section 4 reviews the related work and we conclude the paper in Sect. 5.

2   Graph-Based Metric Embedding

In this section, we first formulate the problem definitions, and then present our proposed Graph-based Metric Embedding (GME) model, as well as its extension GME-S which incorporate the sequential influence.

2.1   Problem Definitions

For ease of presentation, we define the key data structures and notations used in this paper. Table 1 also lists them.

Table 1. Notations used in this paper.

Variable	Interpretation
U, V	The set of users and POIs
D_u	The profile of user u
$\mathbb{R}^d$	d dimensional metric
$\boldsymbol{p}_{u,t}, \boldsymbol{q}_v$	Time-aware user embedding and POI embedding
S_u	The sequence of user u
$\triangle T$	The time period threshold

Definition 1 *(POI)*. *A POI is defined as a uniquely identified specific site (e.g., a restaurant or a cinema). We use v to represent a POI.*

Definition 2 *(Check-in Activity)*. *A user check-in activity is represented by a triple (u, v, t) that means user u visits POI v at time t.*

Definition 3 *(User Profile)*. *For each user u, we create a user profile D_u, which is a set of check-in activities associated with u. The dataset D used in our model includes all user profiles, i.e., $D = \{D_u : u \in U\}$.*

Since we use graph-based method to embed POIs, now let us begin with formally defining of the POI-POI graph, POI embedding and user embedding. The toy example of generating the POI-POI graph is show in Fig. 1.

Definition 4 *(POI-POI Graph)*. *A POI-POI co-occurrence graph, denoted as $G = (V, E)$, captures the POI co-occurrence information in a user profile D_u. V is a set of POIs and E is the set of edges between POIs. In general, if a user u has checked in two POIs v_i and v_j, there will be an edge e_{ij} between v_i and v_j. The weight w_{ij} of edge e_{ij} is defined as the number of times that the two POIs co-occured in the whole dataset D.*

Definition 5 *(POI Embedding)*. *Each POI v in the dataset D will be represented by a POI embedding $\boldsymbol{q}_v$ in the $\mathbb{R}^d$ metric.*

(a) user check-in data   **(b) POI-POI graph**

Fig. 1. A toy example of generating POI-POI graph from user profile D_u.

Definition 6 *(User Embedding).* *For each user u in the dataset D, his/her dynamic preferences will be represent as a time-aware user embedding $\boldsymbol{p}_{u,t}$ in the $\mathbb{R}^d$ metric.*

The POI-POI graph captures the POI co-occurrences which is resemble to the item-based collaborative filtering that mines the item similarity. Our goal is to project POIs in a low dimensional metric $\mathbb{R}^d$ through the graph information, thus we can get the POI embedding $\boldsymbol{q}$, then we calculate the cosine similarity between POIs. Intuitively, if two POIs are often checked in together, their cosine similarity will be larger in $\mathbb{R}^d$: if a user has visited one of them, he is probably to check in the other one.

Given a dataset D as the union of a collection of user profiles, we are aim to provide next POI recommendations for querying users and time, stated as follows.

Problem 1 (**Next POI Recommendation**). Given a user activity dataset D and a querying user u at time t (i.e., the query is $q = (u,t)$), our goal is to recommend a list of POIs that u would be interested in next.

2.2   Model Description and Inference

In this section, we first propose a graph-based embedding model (GME) to learn POI representation in the latent space, and then present how to track and represent the dynamic user preferences.

Predictive POI Embedding. Given the POI-POI graph $G = (V, E)$, where V is the set of POIs and E is the set of edges between them. For each edge e_{ij} whose source node is v_i, target node is v_j in the graph, we first define the conditional probability of vertex v_j generated vertex v_i as:

$$p(v_j|v_i) = \frac{\exp(\boldsymbol{q}_j^{\mathrm{T}} \cdot \boldsymbol{q}_i)}{\sum_{k=1}^{|V|} \exp(\boldsymbol{q}_k^{\mathrm{T}} \cdot \boldsymbol{q}_i)} \tag{1}$$

where q_i is the embedding vector of vertex v_i, and q_j is the embedding vector of vertex v_j, Eq. 1 defines a conditional distribution $p(\cdot|v_i)$ over all the vertices. To preserve the weight w_{ij} on edge e_{ij}, we can make the conditional distribution $p(\cdot|v_i)$ be close to its empirical distribution $\hat{p}(\cdot|v_i)$, which can be defined as $\hat{p}(v_j|v_i) = \frac{w_{ij}}{deg_i}$. Then minimize the following objective function:

$$O = \sum_{i \in V} \lambda_i d(\hat{p}(\cdot|v_i), p(\cdot|v_i)) \tag{2}$$

where $d(\cdot, \cdot)$ is the KL-divergence between two distributions, λ_i is the importance of vertex v_i in the network, which can be set as the degree $deg_i = \sum_j w_{ij}$. Omitting some constants, the objective function Eq. 2 can be calculated as:

$$O = - \sum_{(i,j) \in E} w_{ij} \log p(v_j|v_i) \tag{3}$$

By learning $\{q_i\}_{i=1...|V|}$ that minimize Eq. 3, we are able to represent every POI v_i with a d dimensional embedding q_i in metric $\mathbb{R}^d$.

Model Inference. Optimizing objective function Eq. 3 is computationally expensive, as calculating the conditional probability $p(\cdot|v_i)$ need to sum over the entire set of vertices. To address this problem, we sample multiple negative edges according to some noisy distribution for each edge e_{ij} following the negative sampling approach proposed in [10]. For each edge e_{ij}, it specifies the following objective function:

$$\log \sigma(q_j^T \cdot q_i) + \sum_{n=1}^{K} E_{v_n \sim P_n(v)}[\log \sigma(-q_n^T \cdot q_i)] \tag{4}$$

where $\sigma(x) = 1/(1 + exp(-x))$ is the sigmoid function, K is the number of negative edges. We set $K = 5$, $P_n(v) \propto d_v^{3/4}$ from the empirical setting of [10], d_v is the out-degree of vertex v. Then we adopt the asynchronous stochastic gradient algorithm (ASGD) [11] for Eq. 4. If an edge e_{ij} is sampled, the gradient w.r.t. the embedding vector q_i of vertex v_i will be calculated as:

$$\frac{\partial O}{\partial q_i} = w_{ij} \cdot \frac{\partial \log p(v_j|v_i)}{\partial q_i} \tag{5}$$

However, when the weights of edges have a high variance there will be a problem, because it is very hard to find a good learning rate. If we select a large learning rate according to the edges with small weights, the gradients on edges with large weights will explode, while the gradients will become too small if we select the learning rate according to the edges with large weights. To overcome this dilemma, we follow the edge sampling approach using in [14]. Let $W = (w_1, w_2, ..., w_{|E|})$ denote the ranking sequence of edge weights. First, we calculate the sum of the weights $w_{sum} = \sum_{i=1}^{|E|} w_i$. Then, sample a value within $[0, w_{sum}]$ to see which interval $[\sum_{j=0}^{i-1} w_j, \sum_{j=0}^{i} w_j)$ the random value falls into.

In the latter procedure, we use alias table method [7] to draw a sample, thus reduce the sampling complexity to $O(1)$. Moreover, optimization with negative sampling takes $O(\eta \times (K + 1))$ time cost, where K is the number of negative samples and η is the time taking for one sampling. Thus, the entire step takes $O(\eta \times K)$ time. In fact, the number of steps used for optimization is usually proportional to the number of edges $|E|$. Therefore, the overall time complexity of optimization is $O(\eta \times K \times |E|)$, while η, K are all constants. The proposed edge sampling method is very efficient since it is linear to the number of edges $|E|$, and does not depend on the number of vertices $|V|$.

Predictive Dynamic User Embedding. General recommender models (e.g. latent factor models) achieves the dynamic update of user preferences via retraining the model or applying the online learning techniques, which is very time-consuming. We aim to propose an efficient approach that tracks the dynamic of user preferences in a linear time complexity. To achieve this, we map dynamic user preferences to the same dimensional metric $\mathbb{R}^d$ as POIs, and utilize the learnt POI embeddings to represent the dynamic user preference embedding. More precisely, we assume that an individual's preferences at time t are affected by the whole set of POIs he has visited in the user profile D_u before time t. Note that, the check-ins in D_u are ranked according to their check-in timestamps in an increasing order. Therefore, we can learn the embedding $\boldsymbol{p}_{u,t}$ of u's preferences at time t by utilizing the vectors of POIs he has visited before t in the form of exponential decay. That is, if a user u has checked in a set of POIs before time t, his/her preferences at time t can be computed as:

$$\boldsymbol{p}_{u,t} = \sum_{(v_i,t_i)\in D_u \cap (t_i < t)} exp^{-(t-t_i)} \cdot \boldsymbol{q}_i \tag{6}$$

where $\boldsymbol{q}_i$ is the embedding of POI v_i, (v_i, t_i) is u's check-in record in D_u before time t; the later the POI is visited, the bigger the exponential is. In this way, we can dynamically track the user's preferences in a linear time.

2.3   Incorporating Sequential Influence

Since it has been shown in multiple studies that human movement in LBSNs clearly demonstrates sequential patterns [27,28], we further extend our GME model by incorporating sequential influence and propose GME-S model, which unifies the sequential influence and dynamic user preferences in a principled way. Intuitively, if two POIs have been checked in by a user together with a big time interval, they may not have a strong link. To describe our GEM-S model clearly, we first define the notations behind, and it is also listed in Table 1.

Definition 7 (Sequence). *A sequence of user u, consists of an ordered list of elements, denoted by $S_u = \{(v_1, t_1), (v_2, t_2), ..., (v_n, t_n)\}$, where each element (v_i, t_i) indicates that user u visited POI v_i at time t_i ($1 \leq i \leq n$ and $t_1 \leq t_2 \leq ... \leq t_n$).*

In the GME-S model, there is also a kind of POI-POI graph, but it is different from that in the GME model as it incorporates the sequential patterns of POIs. To distinguish the two graphs, we call it sequential POI-POI graph which is defined as follow.

Definition 8 *(Sequential POI-POI Graph). A sequential POI-POI co-occurrence Graph, denoted as $G = (V, E)$, captures the check-in sequence of POIs in a user profile D_u. V is a set of POIs and E is the set of edges between POIs.* ***Given a time period threshold $\triangle T$, for each check-in pair*** *$\{(v_i, t_i), (v_j, t_j)\}$* ***in user's sequence S_u,*** *if $0 < t_i - t_j \leq \triangle T$,* ***there will be an edge e_{ij} between v_i and v_j.*** *The weight w_{ij} of edge e_{ij} is defined as the number of times that the two POIs sequentially co-occur in the whole dataset D.*

The learning algorithm for POI embeddings on the sequential POI-POI graph is the same as that of GME model, and we will study the impact of $\triangle T$ on the quality of next POI recommendation in Sect. 3.3. Thus, the sequential information is encoded in the POI embeddings.

2.4   Next POI Recommendation

Our proposed GME and GME-S models are employed to make next POI recommendation as follows. Given a user u at time t (that is, the query is $q = (u, t)$), our task is to recommend top-k POIs that u wishes to visit from the POIs that the user has not visited before. More precisely, given the user u and time t, for each POI v which has not been visited by u, we compute its ranking score as in Eq. 7, and then select the k ones with the highest ranking scores as recommendations.

$$S(u, v, t) = \boldsymbol{p}_{u,t}^{\mathrm{T}} \cdot \boldsymbol{q}_v \tag{7}$$

where $\boldsymbol{p}_{u,t}$ is the representation of u's preferences at time t, which can be computed in Eq. 6, and $\boldsymbol{q}_v$ is the embedding of POI v. From the above Equation, we can see that we do not explicitly integrate the sequential influence, as the sequential information has been captured by the POI embeddings. Thus, we avoid computing the huge POI-POI transition matrix or even cube as other Markov chain-based recommender model have done.

3   Experiments

In this section, we move forward to evaluate the effectiveness of the proposed GME and GME-S model for next POI recommendation. The experiments are set up as the following.

3.1   Experimental Settings

Datasets. Our experiments are performed on two real large-scale LBSNs datasets: Foursquare and Twitter. The basic statistics of them are shown in Table 2. The two real datasets are publicly available[1].

---

[1] https://sites.google.com/site/dbhongzhi/.

Table 2. Basic statistics of datasets

	Foursquare	Twitter
# of users	4,163	114,508
# of POIs	121,142	62,462
# of check-ins	483,813	1,434,668

Foursquare. This dataset contains 483,813 check-in histories of 4,163 users who live in the California, USA. The whole dataset covers 121,142 POIs around the world.

Twitter. This dataset is based on the publicly available Twitter dataset in [3]. The dataset contains 1,434,668 check-in histories of 114,508 users over 62,462 POIs.

Comparative Approaches. We compare our GME and GME-S with the following three methods representing the state-of-the-art next POI recommendation techniques.

BPR. BPR [12] is a generic Bayesian method for learning models for personalized ranking from implicit feedback which absolutely meet the top-k recommend requirements according to user check-in data compared to matrix factorization based methods. However, BPR does not contain sequential influence, thus we use it to compare with our proposed GME model.

SPORE. SPORE [16] is a sequential personalized POI recommendation framework, which introduces a novel latent variable topic-region to model and fuse sequential influences and personal interests in a latent and exponential space, which considers the user preferences and sequential influence simultaneously as the GME-S do.

PRME. PRME [4] is a personalized ranking metric embedding algorithm that jointly models the sequential transition of POIs and user preferences. It also exploits the metric embedding method for the next POI recommendation, but utilize two latent spaces: one is the sequential transition space and the other is the user preferences space.

Evaluation Methods. Given a user profile D_u in terms of a collection of user activities, we first extracted the activity sequence of each user S_u, then divide the user's activities into a train set and a test set, and make sure the timestamp of check-ins in the test set happened behind that in the train set. Besides this constraint, we randomly select 20 % of the activity records as test set and the rest the train set. Therefore, we split the user activity dataset D into the train set D_{train} and the test set D_{test}. To evaluate the recommendation methods, we adopt the evaluation methodology and measurement Accuracy@k proposed in

[5,19,21,24,25]. Specifically, for each activity record (u, v, t) in D_{test} as well as its associated query q we make the following procedure:

- First, to track user's current interests, we compute $\boldsymbol{p}_{u,t}$ which means the querying user u's preferences at time t on basis of Eq. 6.
- Second, we calculate the ranking score for POI v and all other POIs which are unvisited previously by u through Eq. 7.
- Third, according to the ranking scores of all these POIs, we form a ranked list ordered by the scores. Let p denote the position of v within this list. Obviously, we expect POI v precedes all the other unvisited POIs, which means $p = 1$.
- Fourth, we formed a top-k recommendation list by picking the k top ranked POIs from the list. If $p \leq k$ (i.e., the ground truth POI v appears in the top-k recommendation list), we have a hit. Otherwise, we have a miss.

We define hit@k for a single test case as either the value 1, if the ground truth POI v appears in the top-k results, or the value 0, if otherwise. The overall Accuracy@k is defined by averaging over all test cases which proceeds as Eq. 8 shows:

$$Accuracy@k = \frac{\#hit@k}{|D_{test}|} \tag{8}$$

where $\#hit@k$ denotes the number of hits in the whole test set, and $|D_{test}|$ is the number of test cases.

3.2   Recommendation Effectiveness

In this part, we present the effectiveness of all the recommendation methods with well-tuned parameters. Figure 2 reports the performance of the recommendation methods on Foursquare and Twitter datasets respectively. Note that, we only show the performance when $k = \{1, 5, 10, 15, 20\}$, since a greater value of k is usually ignored for the top-k recommendation task.

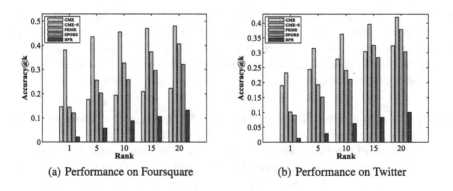

(a) Performance on Foursquare   (b) Performance on Twitter

Fig. 2. Recommendation effectiveness

In our proposed methods, we set $d = 60$, $\triangle T = 5$ days on Foursquare dataset, while $d = 70$, $\triangle T = 20$ on Twitter dataset, the selection of these two parameters will be shown in Sect. 3.3. It is obvious that our proposed GME-S model outperforms other competitor models significantly, and GME also show a fairish result compared to the model without considering sequential influence. Several observations made from the results are presented following:

(1) GME and GME-S have a Higher Ability to Place Ground Truth in Top-1 Position. It is apparent that the competitor recommendation methods have significant performance disparity in terms of the top-k accuracy, while GME and GME-S will get a relatively high accuracy no matter how small the k is. Top-1 result takes up 65.8 % of top-20 result in GME and 79.4 % of top-20 result in GME-S on Foursquare (35.6 % in PRME, 37.7 % in SPORE and 15.9 % in BPR respectively). The result on Twitter dataset also verifies this phenomenon, top-1 result occupies 58.6 % of top-20 result in GME and 55.5 % of top-20 result in GME-S (26.9 % in PRME, 30.0 % in SPORE and 12.9 % in BPR).

(2) Sequential Influence Plays an Important role in next POI Recommendation. GME-S model is more efficient than GME model on both datasets which demonstrate the beneficial brought by incorporating sequential influence. The accuracy gap between GME and GME-S is bigger on Foursquare dataset than that on Twitter dataset is mainly because that the users in Foursquare dataset visited more POIs per capita than that in Twitter dataset, which may bring more noise edges in POI-POI graph in GME model. Moreover, PRME and SPORE outperform BPR and GME on Foursqaure dataset also shows the importance of sequential influence as these methods also considered the sequential factor.

(3) Metric Embedding Methods Outperform Other Competitors. GME, GME-S and PRME are all metric embedding based methods, they get a better efficiency than other competitors (GME-S and PRME outperform SPORE and GME outperforms BPR) which may imply consistent interpretation is important in top-k recommendation. Moreover, GME-S does better than PRME which may be because GME-S embeds all information into one latent space while PRME uses two latent spaces to embed user preferences and sequential patterns, respectively.

(4) Observations About the Datasets. GME performs better on the Twitter dataset than the Foursquare dataset, it is because the data covers 4 years on Foursquare dataset while half year on Twitter dataset, which brings in too many noise edges in POI-POI graph as we generate edges only consider POI co-occurrences in GME. However, the GME-S method can overcome this deficiency easily and get a high effectiveness. Meanwhile, the high user check-in density makes accuracy on Foursquare dataset is better than that on Twitter dataset in all other methods.

3.3   Impact of Model Parameters

Tuning model parameters is critical to the performance of the proposed models. There is the metric dimension d to be studied in GME and the metric dimension d and time period threshold $\triangle T$ to be tested in GME-S since we consider sequential influence in GME-S. The impact of d in GME is similarly to that in GME-S, we therefore show the impact of d and $\triangle T$ in GME-S in this subsection.

Impact of Metric Dimension d. Table 3 depicts the impact of the metric dimension d. From the results, we observe that the recommendation accuracy of GME-S first increased with the increasing number of dimension d, and then it does not change significantly when the number of dimension is larger than 60 on Foursquare dataset and 70 on Twitter dataset. The reason is that high dimensions can better embody the latent metric relationships, but when d exceeds a threshold (e.g., $d = 60$ on Foursquare dataset and $d = 70$ on Twitter dataset), the dimension is enough to embed the relationships. At this point, it is less helpful to improve the model performance by increasing d. Empirically, we set $d = 60$ on Foursquare dataset and $d = 70$ on Twitter dataset in our experiments, which achieves a satisfying trade off between recommendation accuracy and efficiency.

Table 3. Impact of metric dimension d

(a) Impact of d on Foursquare

d	Accuracy@k				
	$k = 1$	$k = 5$	$k = 10$	$k = 15$	$k = 20$
30	0.160	0.221	0.249	0.267	0.281
40	0.263	0.317	0.340	0.354	0.366
50	0.363	0.417	0.428	0.450	0.461
60	**0.381**	**0.436**	**0.456**	**0.470**	**0.480**
70	0.382	0.436	0.456	0.471	0.480
80	0.383	0.436	0.456	0.471	0.481

(b) Impact of d on Twitter

d	Accuracy@k				
	$k = 1$	$k = 5$	$k = 10$	$k = 15$	$k = 20$
40	0.193	0.282	0.333	0.365	0.388
50	0.213	0.295	0.341	0.372	0.395
60	0.223	0.310	0.359	0.390	0.418
70	**0.233**	**0.315**	**0.363**	**0.396**	**0.420**
80	0.233	0.316	0.363	0.396	0.420
90	0.234	0.316	0.363	0.397	0.421

Impact of Time Period Threshold $\triangle T$. Table 4 investigates the impact of time period threshold $\triangle T$ in GME-S. From the experimental results, we observe

Table 4. Impact of time period threshold $\triangle T$

(a) Impact of $\triangle T$ on Foursquare

$\triangle T$	Accuracy@k				
	$k = 1$	$k = 5$	$k = 10$	$k = 15$	$k = 20$
1	0.233	0.267	0.284	0.297	0.307
3	0.246	0.299	0.327	0.342	0.351
5	**0.381**	**0.436**	**0.456**	**0.470**	**0.480**
7	0.304	0.361	0.385	0.402	0.414
9	0.165	0.226	0.255	0.276	0.289
∞	0.146	0.176	0.194	0.209	0.222

(b) Impact of $\triangle T$ on Twitter

$\triangle T$	Accuracy@k				
	$k = 1$	$k = 5$	$k = 10$	$k = 15$	$k = 20$
10	0.216	0.278	0.315	0.339	0.359
15	0.226	0.302	0.345	0.373	0.395
20	**0.233**	**0.315**	**0.363**	**0.396**	**0.420**
25	0.230	0.311	0.356	0.386	0.408
30	0.212	0.295	0.322	0.361	0.388
∞	0.190	0.244	0.279	0.304	0.324

that the performance first improves quickly with the increase of $\triangle T$ and then drop down rapidly. Note that, when $\triangle T = \infty$, GME-S reduces to GME model. The reason of accuracy disparity is that, when $\triangle T$ is small, GME-S may prune too many POI co-occurrence edges which makes the train set too small to completely training, while $\triangle T$ is large, GME-S may incorporate too many noise edges, which may lead to lower accuracy in test set. Thus, we choose $\triangle T = 5$ days on Foursquare dataset and $\triangle T = 20$ days on Twitter dataset to get the best result. Moreover, due to the denser check-in data on Foursquare dataset compared to that on Twitter dataset, the $\triangle T$ is smaller on Foursquare dataset than that on Twitter dataset.

4 Related Work

In this section, we discuss existing research related to our work, including next POI recommendation and metric embedding.

Importance of POI recommendation has attracted a significant amount of research interest on developing recommendation techniques [12,18,20,23,24,26], while the next POI recommendation which requires providing satisfactory recommendations promptly based on users' latest preferences and their most recent checked-in POIs has received relatively little research attention. Most of the studies developed the Markov chain-based methods to capture the sequential patterns of POIs and predict the next check-ins. To reduce the size of the prediction space, Cheng et al. [2] exploited sequential influence using the first-order Markov chain which only considers the latest location in a user's visiting sequence to recommend a new location for the user. Zhang et al. [28] predicted the next location probability through an additive Markov chain, and assumed recent check-in locations usually have stronger influence than those locations checked-in long time ago. Although the parameter space in these approaches can be decreased to $|V| \times |V|$, it may still be huge considering that V is usually a large number in LBSNs. To reduce the prediction space, Wang et al. [16] modeled the sequential effect at the topic-region level. However, its accuracy fell behind us. In our proposed GME-S model, the parameter space is only $|V| \times d$, where d is the dimension of POI embedding that tends to be smaller than 100, thus the parameter space is much smaller than $|V| \times |V|$.

Embedding methods have been long studied and proved to be effective in capturing latent semantics of how items (e.g. words in sentences) interact with each other. For example, Tang et al. [14] learned words embedding to make document classification, and verified its effectiveness. There are also a line of music recommendation research using metric embedding based methods. Chen et al. [1] adopted metric embedding in the music playlist prediction and proposed a Logistic Markov embedding (LME) for generating the playlists. The research [17] proposed by Wu et al. embeds users and songs into a common latent space to represent the personalized Markov chain. The POI recommendation using metric embedding methods is relatively less. PRME proposed by Feng et al. [4] and BPR developed by Rendle et al. [12] are the typical ones which exploits pair-wise ranking scheme. However, our work is a graph-based method, which can embed large-scale information efficiently into a graph and represent POIs and users in a unified metric while PRME embeds user preference and sequential patterns in two different metric respectively. Moreover, we track and represent the dynamic user preferences in the form of time-decay which can make recommendation in a real-time manner based on users' latest preferences.

Our work in this paper distinguishes itself from previous researches in several aspects. Firstly, to the best of our knowledge, it is the first effort that uses the metric embedding method to unify dynamic user preferences and the sequential influence in a principled way. Secondly, although research [4] exploited the metric embedding for next POI recommendation, it embedded user preferences and sequential transition into two different spaces which may lose some potential relationship between users and POIs. In contrast, our proposed methods embed all the information into a unified space via graph based method and make next POI recommendation by tracking the change of user preferences in a real-time manner. Thirdly, we proposed a novel effective and efficient method to exploit and encode the knowledge of sequential patterns of users' check-in behaviors in the POI embedding and track the dynamics of user preferences in an efficient way.

5   Conclusions

In this paper, we proposed a novel graph-based metric embedding (GME) model for next POI recommendation which can learn the representation of POIs in a low-dimension latent space and track the dynamic user preferences in the form of time-decay based on the learnt POI embeddings. To model the sequential influence, we further extend our GME to GME-S model by exploiting and integrating the sequential patterns in the learning process of POI embeddings. To the best of our knowledge, this is the first work that uses the metric embedding method to unify dynamic user preferences and the sequential influence in a principled manner. Extensive experiments were conducted to evaluate the performance of GME and GME-S on two real datasets. The results showed superiority of our proposals over other competitor methods. Besides, we studied the impact of time interval of sequential patterns and verified the importance of sequential influence in next POI recommendation. According to the experimental results, our approach significantly outperforms existing recommendation methods in effectiveness and efficiency.

Acknowledgments. This work was supported by National Basic Research Program of China (2013CB329305), ARC Discovery Early Career Researcher Award (DE160100308) and ARC Discovery Project (DP140103171). It was also partially supported by National Natural Science Foundation of China (61572335, 61303164, 61402447 and 61502466), Development Plan of Outstanding Young Talent from Institute of Software, Chinese Academy of Sciences (ISCAS2014-JQ02) and Jiangsu Natural Science Foundation of China (BK20151223).

References

1. Chen, S., Moore, J.L., Turnbull, D., Joachims, T.: Playlist prediction via metric embedding. In: KDD, pp. 714–722 (2012)
2. Cheng, C., Yang, H., Lyu, M.R., King, I.: Where you like to go next: successive point-of-interest recommendation. In: IJCAI, pp. 2605–2611 (2013)
3. Cheng, Z., Caverlee, J., Lee, K., Sui, D.Z.: Exploring millions of footprints in location sharing services. In: ICWSM (2011)
4. Feng, S., Li, X., Zeng, Y., Cong, G., Chee, Y.M., Yuan, Q.: Personalized ranking metric embedding for next new poi recommendation. In: AAAI, pp. 2069–2075 (2015)
5. Ference, G., Ye, M., Lee, W.-C.: Location recommendation for out-of-town users in location-based social networks. In: CIKM, pp. 721–726 (2013)
6. Gao, H., Tang, J., Hu, X., Liu, H.: Exploring temporal effects for location recommendation on location-based social networks. In: RecSys, pp. 93–100 (2013)
7. Li, A.Q., Ahmed, A., Ravi, S., Smola, A.J.: Reducing the sampling complexity of topic models. In: KDD, pp. 891–900 (2014)
8. Linden, G., Smith, B., York, J.: Amazon.com recommendations: item-to-item collaborative filtering. IEEE Internet Comput. **7**(1), 76–80 (2003)
9. Liu, B., Fu, Y., Yao, Z., Xiong, H.: Learning geographical preferences for point-of-interest recommendation. In: KDD, pp. 1043–1051 (2013)
10. Mikolov, T., Sutskever, I., Chen, K., Corrado, G.S., Dean, J.: Distributed representations of words and phrases and their compositionality. In: Advances in NeuralInformation Processing Systems, pp. 3111–3119 (2013)
11. Recht, B., Re, C., Wright, S., Niu, F.: HOGWILD: a lock-free approach to parallelizing stochastic gradient descent. In: Advances in Neural Information Processing Systems, pp. 693–701 (2011)

12. Rendle, S., Freudenthaler, C., Gantner, Z., Schmidt-Thieme, L.: BPR: Bayesian personalized ranking from implicit feedback. In: UAI, pp. 452–461 (2012)
13. Tang, J., Meng, Q., Mei, Q.: PTE: predictive text embedding through large-scale heterogeneous text networks. In: KDD, pp. 1165–1174 (2015)
14. Tang, J., Meng, Q., Wang, M., Zhang, M., Yan, J., Mei, Q.: LINE: large-scale information network embedding. In: WWW, pp. 1067–1077 (2015)
15. Wang, W., Yin, H., Chen, L., Sun, Y., Sadiq, S., Zhou, X.: Geo-SAGE: a geographical sparse additive generative model for spatial item recommendation. In: KDD, pp. 1255–1264 (2015)
16. Wang, W., Yin, H., Sadiq, S., Chen, L., Xie, M., Zhou, X.: SPORE: a sequential personalized spatial item recommender system. In: ICDE (2016)
17. Wu, X., Liu, Q., Chen, E., He, L., Lv, J., Cao, C., Hu, G.: Personalized next-song recommendation in online karaokes. In: RecSys, pp. 137–140 (2013)
18. Ye, M., Yin, P., Lee, W.-C., Lee, D.-L.: Exploiting geographical influence for collaborative point-of-interest recommendation. In: SIGIR, pp. 325–334 (2011)
19. Yin, H., Zhou, X., Cui, B., Wang, H., Zheng, K., Nguyen, Q.V.H.: Adapting to user interest drift for poi recommendation. IEEE Trans. Knowl. Data Eng. **PP**(99), 1–14 (2016)
20. Yin, H., Cui, B.: Spatio-Temporal Recommendation in Social Media, 1st edn. Springer Publishing Company, Heidelberg (2016)
21. Yin, H., Cui, B., Chen, L., Zhiting, H., Zhang, C.: Modeling location-based user rating profiles for personalized recommendation. TKDD **9**(3), 19:1–19:41 (2015)
22. Yin, H., Cui, B., Huang, Z., Wang, W., Wu, X., Zhou, X.: Joint modeling of users' interests and mobility patterns for point-of-interest recommendation. In: ACM Multimedia, pp. 819–822 (2015)
23. Yin, H., Cui, B., Sun, Y., Zhiting, H., Chen, L.: LCARS: a spatial item recommender system. ACM Trans. Inf. Syst. **32**(3), 11:1–11:37 (2014)
24. Yin, H., Sun, Y., Cui, B., Zhiting, H., Chen, L.: LCARS: a location-content-aware recommender system. In: KDD, pp. 221–229 (2013)
25. Yin, H., Zhou, X., Shao, Y., Wang, H., Sadiq, S.: Joint modeling of user check-in behaviors for point-of-interest recommendation. In: CIKM, pp. 1631–1640 (2015)
26. Yuan, Q., Cong, G., Ma, Z., Sun, A., Thalmann, N.M.: Time-aware point-of-interest recommendation. In: SIGIR, pp. 363–372 (2013)
27. Zhang, J.-D., Chow, C.-Y.: Spatiotemporal sequential influence modeling for location recommendations: a gravity-based approach. TIST **7**(1), 11:1–11:25 (2015)
28. Zhang, J.-D., Chow, C.-Y., Li, Y.: LORE: exploiting sequential influence for location recommendations. In: SIGSPATIAL, pp. 103–112 (2014)
29. Zheng, Y.-T., Zha, Z.-J., Chua, T.-S.: Mining travel patterns from geotagged photos. TIST **3**(3), 56:1–56:18 (2012)

Temporal Pattern Based QoS Prediction

Liang Chen[1(✉)], Haochao Ying[2], Qibo Qiu[2], Jian Wu[2], Hai Dong[1],
and Athman Bouguettaya[1]

[1] School of Computer Science and Information Technology,
RMIT, Melbourne, Australia
jasonclx@gmail.com, {hai.dong,athman.bouguettaya}@rmit.edu.au
[2] College of Computer Science and Technology, Zhejiang University,
Hangzhou, China
{haochaoying,vincent2014,wujian2000}@zju.edu.cn

Abstract. Quality-of-Service (QoS) is critical for selecting the optimal
Web service from a set of functionally equivalent service candidates. Since
QoS performance of Web services are unfixed and highly related to the
service status and network environments which are variable against time,
it is critical to obtain the missing QoS values of candidate services at
given time intervals. In this paper, we propose a temporal pattern based
QoS prediction approach to address this challenge. Clustering approach
is utilized to find the temporal patterns based on services QoS curves
over time series, and polynomial fitting function is employed to predict the missing QoS values at given time intervals. Furthermore, a data
smoothing process is employed to improve prediction accuracy. Comprehensive experiments based on a real world QoS dataset demonstrate the
effectiveness of the proposed prediction approach.

Keywords: Service Computing · QoS prediction · Temporal pattern

1 Introduction

A Service-Oriented Computing (SOC) paradigm and its realization through standardized Web service technologies provide a promising solution to the seamless
integration of single-function applications to create new large-grained and value-
added services. Web services are software systems designed to support interoperable machine-to-machine interaction over a network. Typically, a service-oriented
application consists of multiple Web services interacting with each other in several tiers.

Quality of Service (QoS) has been widely employed for evaluating the
non-functional characteristics of Web services [16]. With the explosive growth
of functionality-equal services, non-functional characteristic of Web service is
becoming a popular research concern and kinds of QoS-based approaches were
proposed in various of Service Computing areas, such as service composition [1,2], fault-tolerant web services [5], and service selection [4,18].

© Springer International Publishing AG 2016
W. Cellary et al. (Eds.): WISE 2016, Part II, LNCS 10042, pp. 223–237, 2016.
DOI: 10.1007/978-3-319-48743-4_18

A common premise of previous research is that the values of QoS properties are already known and fixed. However, user-dependent QoS values always
vary over time in the real-world scenario. Figure 1(a)[1] shows the variation curve
of one service's response time (response time is one important QoS property)
when continually invoked by the same user along 64 time intervals. It could be
found that the response time varies largely from 1 s to 20 s. Actually, the QoS
performance of Web services observed from the users perspective is usually quite
different from that declared by the service providers in Service Level Agreement
(SLA), due to the following reasons [17]:

- QoS performance of Web services is highly related to invocation time, since
  the service status (e.g., workload, number of clients, etc.) and the network
  environment (e.g., congestion, etc.) change over time.
- Service users are typically distributed in different geographical locations. The
  user-observed QoS performance of Web services is greatly influenced by the
  Internet connections between users and Web services. Different users may
  observe quite different QoS performance when invoking the same Web service.

Based on above reasons, it is becoming essential to collect time-aware QoS
information of Web services for QoS-based Service Computing research issues.
However, in reality, a service user usually only invokes a limited number of Web
services, thus the QoS values of the other Web services are missing (unknown)
for the target user. Without sufficient time-aware QoS information, the accuracy
of QoS-based research work, i.e., QoS-based service selection, QoS-base service
composition, could not be guaranteed. Therefore, it is becoming urgent to build
a time-aware QoS prediction approach for efficiently estimating missing QoS
values of Web services for target users.

In this paper, we propose to address the problem of time-aware QoS prediction by exploring the advantages of temporal patterns. Temporal patterns and
related techniques have been used and demonstrated in social media area to
solve the problems such as video popularity prediction in Youtube [12], retweet
number prediction in Twitter [15], etc. An intuitive idea is that the influences
of factors (i.e., network environment, location, etc.) behind the QoS temporal
variation could be reflected in the uncovered patterns, and the missing values
in each QoS carve could be predicted by using the most similar temporal pat-
ter to fit for. Particularly, a curve clustering approach is proposed to uncover
QoS temporal patterns, and polynomial fitting function is employed to predict
the missing QoS values. Moreover, A curve smoothing approach is employed to
improve prediction accuracy, due to the noises in QoS curves. Experiments based
on 20+ million service invocation records demonstrate the effectiveness of the
proposed prediction approach.

In summary, this paper makes the following contributions:

1. We formally identify the critical problem of time-aware Web service QoS prediction and propose the concept of temporal pattern in this research area. Particularly, temporal patterns are extracted from QoS curves over time series.

---

[1] Due to the space limitation, Fig. 1 is placed in Page 5.

2. We propose a novel Temporal Pattern based QoS Prediction approach TPP, which utilizes temporal patterns to predict the missing QoS values via polynomial fitting. Moreover, a data smoothing process is employed to improve the prediction accuracy. We consider TPP as the first temporal pattern based QoS prediction approach.

3. Comprehensive experiments based on a real world Web service QoS dataset are implemented to evaluate the performances of TPP and other state-of-the-art approaches. Compared with other approaches, TPP achieves 35.8 %~52.0 % improvement in terms of MRE metric.

The rest of this paper is organized as follows. Section 2 highlights the related work of QoS prediction. Section 3 formally define the problem and introduces the details of data smoothing, pattern clustering, and the prediction algorithm. Experimental results and analysis are presented in Sect. 4, whereas Sect. 5 concludes this paper.

2   Related Work

Quality of Service (QoS) has been widely employed for evaluating the non-functional characteristics of Web services [16]. Among QoS properties, values of server-side QoS (e.g., price, popularity) are identical for different users while others (e.g., response time, throughput) observed from the user-side may change over time due to the unpredictable network conditions and heterogeneous user environments [8]. With the explosive growth of functionality-equal services, non-functional characteristic of Web service is becoming a popular research topic and kinds of QoS-based approaches are proposed in various of Service Computing areas, such as service composition service composition [1] fault-tolerant web services [5] and service selection [4].

A common premise of previous research is that the values of user-dependent QoS properties are already known. However, in reality a user typically has engaged a limited number of Web services in the past and cannot exhaustively invoke all the available candidate services. Thus, it is fundamental to predict the missing QoS values for any QoS-based Service Computing research.

In web service QoS prediction, Collaborative filtering approaches have been widely adopted. Generally, traditional recommendation approaches could be classified into two categories: memory-based [13,19] and model-based [3]. Memory-based approaches, also known as neighborhood-based approaches, are one of the most popular prediction methods in collaborative filtering systems. Shao et al. [11] first use collaborative filtering approach to predict QoS values from similar users. Zheng et al. [20] propose a hybrid user-based and item-based approach to predict QoS values for the current user by employing historical web service QoS data from other similar users and similar web services. Although memory-based algorithms implement easily, high computation complexity makes it difficult to deal with a large and sparse time-aware dataset. Model-based algorithms employ statistical and machine learning techniques to learn a sophisticated model based on history QoS invocation records, including clustering models [14], latent semantic models [6], latent factor models [9], etc. Zheng et al. use PMF algorithm to predict missing failure probability values in user-service matrix [19], and propose NIMF to improve prediction accuracy by balancing the global information and local information [21]. Compared with memory-based approaches, model-based QoS prediction approaches usually have better performance but lack of interpretation.

Time is an important context factor which affects QoS prediction accuracy, since service status (e.g. number of clients and workload) and network environments (e.g. congestion) change over time. QoS values will fluctuate when the same user invoke the same service at different time interval. Limited QoS prediction works consider the influence of time to QoS values. Hu et al. propose a time-aware similarity model which considers two aspects: (1) More temporally close QoS experience from two users on a same service contributes more to the user similarity measurement; (2) More recent QoS experience from two users on a same service contributes more to the user similarity measurement [7]. Zhang et al. construct a three dimensional matrix by adding time factor, and then employ tensor factorization to extract user-specific, service-specific, and time-specific latent features from historical QoS values for prediction [17]. In this paper, we take advantage of model-based concept and propose a temporal pattern based approach with better interpretability. In this paper, we analyze a set of 430,000 response-time curves, each curve means one user invokes one service at 64 continuous time intervals. The surprising thing is that temporal patterns of QoS values could be accurately represented by using limited number of curves. Moreover, a data smoothing process is employed to improve the performance of QoS prediction.

3   QoS Prediction Based on Temporal Patterns

In this section, we first formally define the problem and analyze the research challenges in Sect. 3.1, and then introduce the details of corresponding solutions in Sects. 3.2 and 3.3, respectively. Finally, QoS prediction algorithm is presented in Sect. 3.4.

3.1   Problem Definition and Research Challenges

In previous works, most of QoS prediction approaches origin from recommender system. Concretely, they predict the missing QoS values in the user-service or user-service-time QoS matrix, which is generated from historical service invocation by users [11,17,22]. Unlike above works, we propose a novel method to predict QoS value based on temporal patterns in this paper.

Let U be the set of m users, S be the set of n Web services, and T be the set of c time intervals. From the collection of QoS attribute from user-side, the observed QoS value of user i invoking service j at time interval t_k can be formally represented by q_{ijk}, where $i \in 1, ..., m$, $j \in 1, ..., n$, $k \in 1, ..., c$ and q_{ijk} is one of QoS attributes (e.g., response time or throughput). For convenience, the length of time internals is fixed. For example, the real-world dataset employed in this paper is over 64 consecutive time slices at 15 min interval. Intuitively, the shape of q_{ij} measures how user i invokes service j changed over time. In practice, each user typically uses a few of services so that we can get the set H of complete curves which we know all QoS values of user invoked service at each time interval. However, component service can be replaced automatically in service-oriented architecture (SOA). Therefore, the records of user invoked service at some intervals may be missed, which formally represented by the set Δ. Our goal is to use the complete curves in H to predict the missing value in Δ.

In the scenario of QoS prediction, there are two challenges to efficiently predict the missing value. First, due to the influence of dynamic network conditions and varying server loads, the QoS value at each interval fluctuates quickly and may exist noise. If we directly use the original data, the performance of prediction may reduce. Secondly, To predict the missing value, the naive method is to compare the curve with missing value with each complete curve and then use the most similar curve to predict the missing value. However, although each user invokes a few services, millions of complete curves may be collected if we have large number of users and services. Therefore, this approach is time-consuming and not efficiently.

3.2   Data Smoothing

To deal with the first challenge, we design a data transformation method for QoS data to reduce noises. Figure 1 presents an example of a complete QoS (i.e., response time) curve of one user invoked a service. It is obvious that the curve is too diverse to directly compare with others by using distance measure. Fortunately, We can also observe that the QoS value at time t is close to the value at the previous $(t-1)$ and forward $(t+1)$ time slice. It is intuitive that

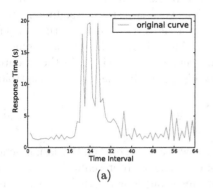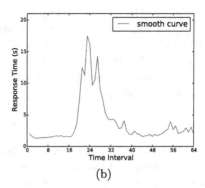

Fig. 1. An example of curves smooth in response time. (a) is the original curve and QoS values fluctuate sharply. (b) is the smoothed curve. To some extent this curve reduces noise and keep overall changing shape of QoS values.

the value in continue intervals should be similar. Based on this observation, the data transformation is defined as follows:

$$q_{ijk} = \begin{cases} \dfrac{2q_{ijk} + q_{ijk+1}}{3} & k = 1 \\[2mm] \dfrac{2q_{ijk} + q_{ijk-1}}{3} & k = c \\[2mm] \dfrac{q_{ijk-1} + 2q_{ijk} + q_{ijk+1}}{4} & \text{otherwise} \end{cases} \qquad (1)$$

Our data smoothing method takes more weights to current observed QoS values and simultaneously consider QoS values in adjacent time. From Fig. 1(b), we can find that the smoothed curve retains the changing shape of QoS values and reduces noise to some extent.

3.3 Temporal Pattern Generation

To deal with the second challenge, we employ K-Means clustering algorithm to find the clusters of QoS curves that share distinct temporal pattern. The reason that we choose K-Means algorithm is its simpleness and efficiency.

Given the set H of complete QoS curves and the number of clusters K, our goal is to find an assignment set C_k of curves for each cluster, and the centroid u^k of each cluster minimizes the following function:

$$F = \sum_{k=1}^{K} \sum_{q_{ij} \in C_k} d(q_{ij}, u^k) \qquad (2)$$

where $d(q_{ij}, u^k) = \sum_{t=1}^{c} (q_{ijt}, u_t^k)^2$ is the square of Euclidean distance. We start the K-Means algorithm with random initial K centroids. As an iterative refinement algorithm, K-Means proceeds by alternating between two steps: assignment step and update step. In the assignment step, we assigns each curve to the cluster with the closest centroid based on $d(q_{ij}, u^k)$. After finding the new assignment set C_k for each curve, we calculate the new centroid for each C_k in the update step, according the average of all curves in C_k. Formally, the updated centroid should be as follows:

$$u^k = \frac{1}{|C_k|} \sum_{q_{ij} \in C_k} q_{ij} \qquad (3)$$

After updating many times, the algorithm will converge when the assignment no longer changes. Finally, the centroid of each cluster represents the temporal pattern. Figure 2 presents an example for clustering four original curves. It is obvious that the two temporal patterns catch the most important characters in each cluster. In the next section, we will use these temporal patterns to predict the missing QoS values.

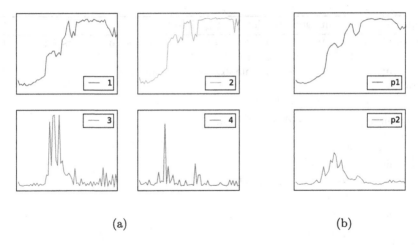

(a)   (b)

Fig. 2. An example of curves clustering. (a) is the four original curves of response time. After smoothing and clustering, (b) shows the centroids of two clusters.

3.4 QoS Prediction

After smoothing and clustering, we get K temporal patterns. Suppose that we have a curve q_{ij} with some QoS values at the corresponding time intervals missing. For simplify, q_{ij} misses the value in interval t. Now, the question is how to use these pattern to predict the missing QoS value q_{ijt}.

First, we compute the distance between the observed values of q_{ij} and each pattern in corresponding time interval under different metric. In the experiments, we compare three distance approaches (i.e., cosine, euclidean, and cityblock) and choose the best metric to measure the distance. After this step, the most similar pattern p can be obtained based on the distance. An intuitive way is to directly use the value of p in interval t to predict the q_{ijt}. However, it is unwise because the pattern p can not match q_{ij} completely and we can not eliminate the fixed distance in interval t. In this paper, we use a function to map the pattern p to the curve q_{ij}. In general, the map function is polynomial fitting function as follows:

$$\hat{q}_{ij} = map(p) = w_0 + w_1 p + w_2 p^2 + \cdots + w_d p^d \qquad (4)$$

where w is the weights and d is the order.

After finding the order and weights of polynomial based on sum of least square between q_{ij} and $\hat{q}_{ij}$ in the observed values, the predicted value q_{ijt} could be obtained through $map(p_t)$. Note that we just compare the linear and square fitting in the experiments to avoid overfitting. The pseudo code of our algorithm for QoS prediction is provided in Algorithm 1.

4   Experiments

In this section, comprehensive experiments are implemented to evaluate the proposed approach based on a real-world dataset. Experimental evaluation will

---

Algorithm 1. Our QoS Prediction Algorithm.

Input : The set H of complete QoS curves; The number of clusters K; The set Δ of incomplete QoS curves

Output: The QoS prediction of unobserved value in Δ

1 **for** $q \in$ H **do**
2 　　smooth q by Equation 1;

3 random initial K centroids $u^1, u^2, ..., u^K$;
4 **repeat**
5 　　set each cluster $C_1, .., C_K$ to null;
6 　　**for** $j = 1$ *to* $|H|$ **do**
7 　　　　$k \longleftarrow argmin_{k=1,..,K} d(p_j, u^k)$;
8 　　　　$C_k \longleftarrow C_k \cup j$;

9 　　**for** $i = 1$ *to* K **do**
10 　　　　$u_i \longleftarrow \frac{1}{|C_k|} \sum\limits_{q_{ij} \in C_k} q_{ij}$;

11 **until** *centroids converge*;
12 **for** $q \in \Delta$ **do**
13 　　find the most similar pattern p based on observed value in q;
14 　　polynomial fit $q \longleftarrow map(p)$;
15 　　predict unobserved value of q in each interval t by $map(p_t)$;

---

answer the following questions: (1) What are the evaluation metrics? (2) How does our approach compare with other state-of-the-art ones? (3) What is the impact of data smoothing, similarity approach, and the order of polynomial fit?

4.1 Data Preprocessing

In the experiments, we mainly focus on $\underline{R}$esponse $\underline{T}$ime (RT), one of the most important QoS properties, to evaluate QoS prediction methods. Response time (RT) is the length of time between the end of an inquiry on a computer system and the beginning of a response. All experiments are implemented in a machine with a 2.2 GHz Intel CPU and 16 GB RAM, running OS X Yosemite.

For the sake of application in practice, all experiments are implemented based on a public real-world Web service QoS dataset which is collected by 142 users invoking 4532 web services in 16 hours with a time interval of 15 min [17]. In particular, the users are 142 computers of PlanetLab[2] located in 22 countries, and the services are 4532 public available real world web services distributed in 57 countries. Through the observation, we find quite a lot of noises exist in the dataset. For example, the response time value will be set to -1, if the response time is over 20 s in this invocation. Furthermore, some Web services have not been invoked by any user. Thus, we do some data cleaning work on this dataset, and macroscopic statistics & data distribution of the generated dataset

---

[2] PlanetLab is a global research network that supports the development of new network services. Details could be found in https://www.planet-lab.org/.

are presented in Figs. 3 and 4, respectively. It could be found the experimental evaluation utilizes more than 20 million records, which partly demonstrate reliability and scalability of the experiments. It should be noted that the proposed approach could be utilized for the prediction of any other QoS property (e.g., throughput), even though only response time is studied in this paper.

Statistics	Values
#Users	135
#Services	3952
#Time slices	64
#Time interval	15min
#Records	20,138,880
RT scale	$(0, 20)$
RT mean	0.8442

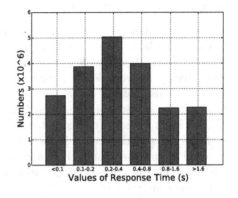

Fig. 3. Statistics of QoS dataset   **Fig. 4.** RT value distribution

4.2 Evaluation Metric

We evaluate the prediction accuracy of our proposed approach in comparison with other existing methods by using the following metrics.

- **MAE** (Mean Absolute Error). MAE is average prediction accuracy between prediction results and corresponding observations, which is defined as follows:

$$MAE = \frac{\sum_{i,j} \left| \hat{R}_{ij} - R_{ij} \right|}{N} \qquad (5)$$

where R_{ij} denotes the real QoS value of service j observed by user i, $\hat{R}_{ij}$ is the predicted QoS value by a method, and N is the total number of predicted values.

- **NMAE** (Normalized Mean Absolute Error). NMAE normalizes the differences range of MAE by computing:

$$NMAE = \frac{MAE}{\sum_{ij} R_{ij}/N} \qquad (6)$$

- **MRE** (Median Relative Error). MRE measures the median value of relative errors between observed value and predicted value:

$$MRE = median \left| \hat{R}_{ij} - R_{ij} \right| / R_{ij} \qquad (7)$$

Due to the large variance of QoS values, we focus more on relative error metric, i.e., MRE, which is more appropriate for QoS prediction evaluation. Since many papers use MAE and NMAE, they are also included for comparison purpose.

4.3   Performance Comparisons

In order to show the effectiveness of our proposed QoS prediction approach, we compare the prediction accuracy of the following methods:

- **UPCC**: This method employs the information of similar users (measured by Pearson Correlation Coefficient) to predict the QoS values [3].
- **IPCC**: This method is widely-used in recommendation system, which employs the similarity between services for QoS prediction [10].
- **UIPCC**: This method combines UPCC and IPCC model, which fully uses the similarity of users and services [20].
- **PMF**: This is a classic matrix factorization method, which has been employed in [19]. User-service matrix is factorized into two matrices under low-rank assumption and then using the matrices predict QoS values.
- **WSPred**: This is a tensor factorization-based prediction method with average QoS value constraint [17].

In the experiments, user-service records are randomly divided into two parts: 80 % records as the training data and the rest 20 % as the testing data. In order to evaluate the performance of different approaches in reality, we randomly choose $\frac{m}{16}$ ($m = 1$, 2, 3, 4, 5, 6, 7, 8) of the training data for pattern clustering, and the others (i.e., $\frac{16-m}{16}$ of the training data) for cross validation. Equation (1) is employed for data smoothing, and Eqs. (2) and (3) are employed for the pattern clustering. Through the observation of experimental results, we find that the proposed approach could get similar temporal patterns in any density setup. That is, the proposed pattern clustering approach is quite stable and even $\frac{1}{16}$ of training data is enough to get appropriate patterns. Polynomial fit is employed for QoS prediction, once temporal patters are generated. Since a user usually only invokes a small number of services, the testing matrix density is randomly thinned to the same $\frac{m}{16}$. The prediction accuracy is evaluated by comparing the original value and the predicted value of each removed entry in testing matrix. Without lost of generality, the number of patterns is set as 4 in this paper. Detailed impact of data smoothing, similarity approach, and polynomial order is studied in Sects. 4.4, 4.5, and 4.6, respectively.

The QoS value prediction accuracies evaluated by MAE, NAME, and MRE are shows in Table 1. For each row in the table, we highlight the best performer among all methods. As we can observe, our approach significantly outperforms the other ones over MRE, while still achieving best results on MAE and NMAE. Concretely, our approach achieves 35.8 %~52.0 % improvement on MRE, 1.8 %~2.7 % improvement on MAE, and 2.0 %~3.0 % improvement on NMAE at different matrix densities. Note that all improvements are computed as the percentage of how much our approach outperforms the other most competitive approach.

Table 1. Comparison of performance (a smaller value means a better performance)

Method	Density = 2/16			Density = 3/16			Density = 4/16		
	MAE	NMAE	MRE	MAE	NMAE	MRE	MAE	NMAE	MRE
UPCC	0.5226	0.6211	0.5334	0.492	0.5845	0.477	0.4745	0.5637	0.4497
IPCC	0.5946	0.7066	0.6671	0.5675	0.6741	0.6395	0.5376	0.6386	0.5992
UIPCC	0.5215	0.6197	0.5225	0.4912	0.5835	0.473	0.4719	0.5606	0.4467
PMF	0.5219	0.6208	0.4764	0.4925	0.5855	0.4496	0.4765	0.5659	0.4327
WSPred	0.4583	0.5445	0.4519	0.4358	0.5168	0.4293	0.4253	0.504	0.4112
TPP	**0.4501**	**0.532**	**0.2167**	**0.4253**	**0.5025**	**0.2249**	**0.4138**	**0.4888**	**0.2308**
Improve. (%)	1.8 %	2.3 %	52.0 %	2.4 %	2.8 %	47.6 %	2.7 %	3.0 %	43.9 %
Method	Density = 5/16			Density = 6/16			Density = 7/16		
	MAE	NMAE	MRE	MAE	NMAE	MRE	MAE	NMAE	MRE
UPCC	0.462	0.549	0.4323	0.4517	0.5368	0.4185	0.4435	0.5272	0.4069
IPCC	0.5204	0.6184	0.5776	0.5071	0.6029	0.5606	0.4954	0.5891	0.5453
UIPCC	0.4588	0.5452	0.4307	0.4482	0.5327	0.4182	0.4394	0.5223	0.4072
PMF	0.4633	0.55	0.4262	0.4536	0.5386	0.4231	0.4444	0.5277	0.408
WSPred	0.4148	0.4913	0.3895	0.4125	0.4884	0.3894	0.4084	0.4834	0.3814
TPP	**0.4075**	**0.4817**	**0.2375**	**0.4026**	**0.4756**	**0.2419**	**0.3985**	**0.4709**	**0.2448**
Improve. (%)	1.8 %	2.0 %	39.0 %	2.4 %	2.6 %	37.9 %	2.4 %	2.6 %	35.8 %

We also find that although UIPCC achieves higher accuracy than UPCC and IPCC over MAE and NMAE, and WSPred achieves better performance compared with the first three Collaborative Filtering based approaches (i.e., UPCC, IPCC, and UIPCC) and PMF, all these approaches have large errors over MRE. Thus, only focusing on minimizing the absolute error may lead to large relative error, which is not suitable for QoS prediction problem.

4.4   Impact of Data Smoothing

Data smoothing process is employed to reduce noises in QoS curves for the purpose of improving prediction accuracy, and is one of main contributions in this paper. In order to study its impact, we implement two versions of our proposed approach: one with the proposed data smooth process, i.e., Eq. (1), and the other without it. Figure 5 shows the prediction accuracy comparison between the above two versions. From Fig. 5, We can observe that the version with data smoothing largely outperforms the other version in terms of MAE, NMAE, and MRE. This is because the remove of noise points in QoS curves facilitates the generation of temporal patterns. In short, The process smooths out data fluctuations and improves QoS prediction accuracy.

4.5   Impact of Similarity Approach

In the process of the proposed TPP approach, we have to choose the most similar pattern for the target QoS curve for predicting the missing values in

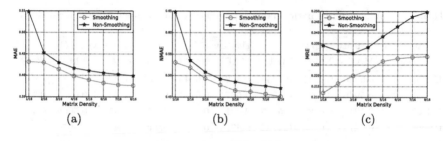

Fig. 5. Impact of data smoothing

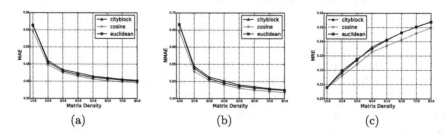

Fig. 6. Impact of similariy approach

the curve. Thus, the choice of similarity measure approach is very important for the final prediction accuracy. In the experiments, we employ three widely accepted approaches to compute the similarity between pattern and the choose data points in testing data. Specifically, the three similarity measure approaches are cosine, euclidean, and cityblock.

To present a comprehensive evaluation of these approaches, we vary the matrix density from 1/16 to 8/16. Other parameter settings are #pattern = 4, order of polynomial = 1. Figure 6 shows the performance comparison of different similarity approaches in terms of MAE, NAME, and MRE. From Fig. 6, we can find cosine similarity method always outperforms the other methods over three metrics when the data density varies from 1/16 to 8/16. This observation demonstrates that cosin similarity measurement is more suitable for computing similarity between curves. Furthermore, we can also observe that as the density increases, every similarity approach can achieve better prediction results in terms of absolute error metrics, i.e., MAE and NMAE. This is because more data points provided in testing data, more information could be gained for prediction. However, it is not suitable for the trend of relative error, i.e., MRE.

4.6   Impact of Order of Polynomial Fit

Once the optimal pattern is selected, polynomial fitting function is employed to predict the missing QoS values in testing data. In this section, we evaluate the impact of different polynomial fitting functions, that is, order of polynomial fit. For simplicity, we only compare the performance of QoS prediction when order

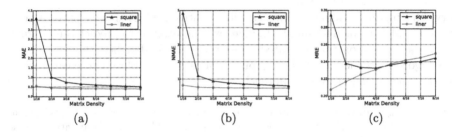

Fig. 7. Impact of order of polynomial fit

is 1 (liner) and 2 (square), since the trend could be easily illustrated by this comparison. Other parameter settings are #pattern = 4, similarity = cosine.

Figure 7 shows the prediction accuracy comparison of linear and square polynomial fit with the increase of density. For Fig. 7, we observe that the linear polynomial fit outperforms the square in most cases. As the increase of density, the prediction accuracy of square polynomial fit improves (the MAE and NMAE decreases) due to more information provided. However, compared with square one, it could be observed that linear polynomial fit is quite stable with the increase of density. That means, linear polynomial fit approach is very suitable for the case of cold-start and data sparsity, that is, online QoS prediction.

Further, we can find the prediction accuracy of square polynomial fit is quite bad when the density is 1/16, which means this sparsity condition causes an overfitting problem. From another perspective, the performance gap of linear and square polynomial fit decreases with the increase of matrix density. That means the overfitting phenomenon alleviates with more provided information. In all, linear polynomial fit is quite suitable for our problem.

5   Conclusion

With the explosive growth of functionality-equal services, non-functional characteristic of Web service is becoming a popular research concern and kinds of QoS-based approaches were proposed in various of Service Computing research areas. Since QoS performance of Web services are unfixed and highly related to the service status and network environments which are variable against time, it is critical to obtain the missing QoS values of candidate services at given time intervals. In this paper, we propose a temporal pattern based QoS prediction approach to address this challenge. Clustering approach is utilized to find the temporal patterns based on services QoS curves over time series, and polynomial fitting function is employed to predict the missing QoS values at given time intervals. Furthermore, a data smoothing process is employed to improve prediction accuracy. Comprehensive experiments based on a real world QoS dataset demonstrate the effectiveness of the proposed prediction approach.

For future work, we will investigate more techniques to improve the performance of temporal pattern generation and QoS prediction. Particularly, QoS curve shifting and scaling techniques will be introduced for better pattern generation, and machine learning techniques will be utilized to predict the missing QoS values based on the generated temporal patterns. Further, the datasets of other QoS properties (e.g., throughput) will also be employed to evaluate the performance of the proposed approach.

Acknowledgement. This research was made possible by NPRP 9-224-1-049 grant from the Qatar National Research Fund (a member of The Qatar Foundation). The statements made herein are solely the responsibility of the authors. This research was partially supported by the Natural Science Foundation of China under grant of No. 61379119, Science and Technology Program of Zhejiang Province under grant of No. 2013C01073, the Open Project of Qihoo360 under grant of No. 15-124002-002.

References

1. Alrifai, M., Risse, T.: Combining global optimization with local selection for efficient QoS-aware service composition. In: Proceedings of the 18th International Conference on World Wide Web, pp. 881–890. ACM (2009)
2. Alrifai, M., Risse, T., Nejdl, W.: A hybrid approach for efficient web service composition with end-to-end QoS constraints. ACM Trans. Web (TWEB) **6**(2), 7 (2012)
3. Breese, J.S., Heckerman, D., Kadie, C.: Empirical analysis of predictive algorithms for collaborative filtering. In: Proceedings of the Fourteenth conference on Uncertainty in artificial intelligence, pp. 43–52. Morgan Kaufmann Publishers Inc. (1998)
4. Chen, L., Kuang, L., Wu, J.: Mapreduce based skyline services selection for QoS-aware composition. In: 2012 IEEE 26th International Parallel and Distributed Processing Symposium Workshops & PhD Forum (IPDPSW), pp. 2035–2042. IEEE (2012)
5. Fang, C.L., Liang, D., Lin, F., Lin, C.C.: Fault tolerant web services. J. Syst. Archit. **53**(1), 21–38 (2007)
6. Hofmann, T.: Latent semantic models for collaborative filtering. ACM Trans. Inf. Syst. (TOIS) **22**(1), 89–115 (2004)
7. Hu, Y., Peng, Q., Hu, X.: A time-aware and data sparsity tolerant approach for web service recommendation. In: 2014 IEEE 21th International Conference on Web Services (ICWS), pp. 33–40. IEEE (2014)
8. Menasce, D.: QoS issues in web services. IEEE Internet Comput. **6**(6), 72–75 (2002)
9. Mnih, A., Salakhutdinov, R.: Probabilistic matrix factorization. In: Advances in Neural Information Processing Systems, pp. 1257–1264 (2007)
10. Resnick, P., Iacovou, N., Suchak, M., Bergstrom, P., Riedl, J.: GroupLens: an open architecture for collaborative filtering of netnews. In: Proceedings of the 1994 ACM Conference on Computer Supported Cooperative Work, pp. 175–186. ACM (1994)
11. Shao, L., Zhang, J., Wei, Y., Zhao, J., Xie, B., Mei, H.: Personalized QoS prediction for web services via collaborative filtering. In: IEEE International Conference on Web Services, ICWS 2007, pp. 439–446. IEEE (2007)
12. Szabo, G., Huberman, B.A.: Predicting the popularity of online content. Commun. ACM **53**(8), 80–88 (2010)
13. Wu, J., Chen, L., Feng, Y., Zheng, Z., Zhou, M.C., Wu, Z.: Predicting quality of service for selection by neighborhood-based collaborative filtering. IEEE Trans. Syst. Man Cybern.: Syst. **43**(2), 428–439 (2013)

14. Xue, G.R., Lin, C., Yang, Q., Xi, W., Zeng, H.J., Yu, Y., Chen, Z.: Scalable collaborative filtering using cluster-based smoothing. In: Proceedings of the 28th Annual International ACM SIGIR Conference on Research and Development in Information Retrieval, pp. 114–121. ACM (2005)

15. Yang, J., Leskovec, J.: Patterns of temporal variation in online media. In: Proceedings of the Fourth ACM International Conference on Web Search and Data Mining, pp. 177–186. ACM (2011)

16. Zeng, L., Benatallah, B., Ngu, A.H., Dumas, M., Kalagnanam, J., Chang, H.: QoS-aware middleware for web services composition. IEEE Trans. Softw. Eng. 30(5), 311–327 (2004)

17. Zhang, Y., Zheng, Z., Lyu, M.R.: WSPred: a time-aware personalized QoS prediction framework for web services. In: 2011 IEEE 22nd International Symposium on Software Reliability Engineering (ISSRE), pp. 210–219. IEEE (2011)

18. Zhao, L., Ren, Y., Li, M., Sakurai, K.: Flexible service selection with user-specific QoS support in service-oriented architecture. J. Netw. Comput. Appl. 35(3), 962–973 (2012)

19. Zheng, Z., Lyu, M.R.: Personalized reliability prediction of web services. ACM Trans. Softw. Eng. Methodol. (TOSEM) 22(2), 12 (2013)

20. Zheng, Z., Ma, H., Lyu, M.R., King, I.: QoS-aware web service recommendation by collaborative filtering. IEEE Trans. Serv. Comput. 4(2), 140–152 (2011)

21. Zheng, Z., Ma, H., Lyu, M.R., King, I.: Collaborative web service QoS prediction via neighborhood integrated matrix factorization. IEEE Trans. Serv. Comput. 6(3), 289–299 (2013)

22. Zhu, J., He, P., Zheng, Z., Lyu, M.R.: Towards online, accurate, and scalable QoS prediction for runtime service adaptation. In: 2014 IEEE 34th International Conference on Distributed Computing Systems (ICDCS), pp. 318–327. IEEE (2014)

Searching for Data Sources for the Semantic Enrichment of Trajectories

Luiz André P. Paes Leme[1](✉), Chiara Renso[2], Bernardo P. Nunes[3,4],
Giseli Rabello Lopes[5], Marco A. Casanova[3], and Vânia P. Vidal[6]

[1] Fluminense University, Niterói, RJ, Brazil
`lapaesleme@ic.uff.br`
[2] ISTI-CNR, Pisa, PI, Italy
`chiara.renso@isti.cnr.it`
[3] PUC-Rio, Rio de Janeiro, RJ, Brazil
`{bnunes,casanova}@inf.puc-rio.br`
[4] Federal University of the State of Rio de Janeiro, Rio de Janeiro, RJ, Brazil
`bernardo.nunes@uniriotec.br`
[5] Federal University of Rio de Janeiro, Rio de Janeiro, RJ, Brazil
`giseli@dcc.ufrj.br`
[6] Federal University of Ceará, Fortaleza, CE, Brazil
`vvidal@lia.ufc.br`

Abstract. The fast growing number of datasets available on the Web inspired researchers to propose innovative techniques to combine spatio-temporal data with contextual data. However, as the number of datasets has increased relatively fast, finding the most appropriate datasets for enrichment also became extremely difficult. This paper proposes an innovative approach to rank a set of datasets according to the likelihood that they contain relevant enrichments. The approach is based on the intuition that the sequence of places visited during a trajectory can induce the best datasets to enrich the trajectory. It relies on a supervised approach to learn rules of association between visited places and meaningful datasets.

Keywords: Trajectories · Semantic enrichment · Movement data

1 Introduction

The personal position-enabled mobile devices are becoming our companions in everyday life, leaving tracks of our movements during our daily routine. The tracks collected by mobile devices describe the so-called *raw trajectories* that represent the geometric facets of movement data. Social media have also been proposed as complementary sources of mobility data. Georeferenced social media can be used as sparse and freely annotated movement traces [2,12] or, possibly, can be used to enrich raw GPS data thus getting semantically richer data with high positional accuracy [5].

© Springer International Publishing AG 2016
W. Cellary et al. (Eds.): WISE 2016, Part II, LNCS 10042, pp. 238–246, 2016.
DOI: 10.1007/978-3-319-48743-4_19

The approach presented in this paper tackles the problem of searching the most appropriate datasets to enrich mobility data. It is based on the intuition that the sequence of places visited during a movement, i.e., the sequence of stops, can induce the purpose of the movement and hence suggest the set of datasets for enrichment. For example, assume that a traveler visits the sequence of places [hotel, stadium, restaurant, hotel] in Rio de Janeiro. Also assume that the dataset of tourist attractions available in the Open Data Portal of the government of the city of Rio de Janeiro contains data about the Maracanã stadium. The sequence of places suggests that the person can be a tourist because tourists frequently stay in hotels and visit the Maracanã Stadium in Rio de Janeiro. Therefore, one could attempt to match the place labeled as stadium with the entry *Maracanã stadium* in the dataset. It is important to notice that this is not a deterministic problem that could be solved with an a priori rule such as if a person visited a stadium then search for enrichments in the dataset of attractions since there is no obvious evidence, for someone who doesn't know the content of the dataset, that the dataset of attractions would contain an entry that could be matched with the place stadium. However, this can be learned from previous trajectory enrichments: if most trajectories similar to this one, in terms of the places visited, are enriched with the dataset of attractions then one can select that dataset as a potential source of enrichment for the new trajectory.

In this paper we take advantage of social media traces of movement and their user annotations to propose a technique for searching potentially useful datasets for the enrichment of trajectories. As for related work, the process of semantic enrichment of spatial and spatiotemporal data can be automatic [2,5,10] or semi-automatic [8]. Automatic approaches can use machine learning techniques such as Hidden Markov Models [10,12], probabilistic models [7], similarity measures [2] or simple proximity heuristics [2] to attach annotations. Recent techniques have also stressed the relevant role of the emerging and fast growing Web of Data [3] in the enrichment process. All existing works have used predefined sets of sources. Developers have favored popular sources such as DBpedia, Open Street Map, Open Weather Map, etc. and neglected less popular ones such as government open data and domain specific datasets. The fundamental reason for that is the lack of techniques to crawl and search for potentially useful datasets for enrichment.

The rest of this paper is organized as follows. Section 2 introduces the basic concepts used throughout the paper and describes the proposed ranking technique. Section 3 addresses the preparation of the test dataset. Section 4 presents the experiments for assessing the technique and Sect. 5 contains the conclusions.

2   The Problem of Searching for Sources of Enrichments

A *raw trajectory* of a moving object o is a sequence $\rho_o = (p_1, p_2, ..., p_n)$ of spatio-temporal points such that the timestamp of p_i is earlier than the timestamp of p_{i+1}. A *segment* g of a raw trajectory ρ_o is a continuous subsequence of ρ_o.

A *segmented trajectory* of a raw trajectory ρ_o is a sequence $\sigma_o = (g_1, g_2, ..., g_n)$ of segments of ρ_o such that $s = g_1 \| ... \| g_n$, that is, s is the concatenation of $g_1, ..., g_n$. A segment of a raw trajectory is a fragment of the whole raw trajectory where a given property holds.

The notion of semantic trajectory goes further and enriches a segmented trajectory with contextual information retrieved from external datasets. A *contextual resource* r of a dataset d is a pair (r, d) with $r \in d$. We use the notion r^d rather than (r, d). A *contextual information* of a segment g of a segmented trajectory σ_o, denoted by c, is a set, of contextual resources $c = \{r_1^{d_1}, ..., r_n^{d_n}\}$. In this way, we say that c *enriches* g. Intuitively, a contextual information is a set of resources that can be used to describe a trajectory. A *semantic trajectory* for a segmented trajectory σ_o is a sequence $\tau_o = (< g_1, c_1 >, ..., < g_n, c_n >)$, such that $< g_i, c_i >$ is a pair indicating that g_i is enriched with contextual information c_i.

We also define a particular kind of enriched trajectory, called *labeled trajectories*. Labeled trajectories arise from mobility data captured from social media. We define labeled trajectories as follows. A *labeled trajectory* for a segmented trajectory σ_o is a sequence $\lambda_o = (< g_1, l_1 >, ..., < g_n, l_n >)$, such that $< g_i, l_i >$ is a pair indicating that segment g_i is enriched with a set l_i of labels.

Given a labeled trajectory $\lambda_o \in \Lambda$ of a segmented trajectory σ_o and a set D of available datasets, generate a list $R = [d_1, ..., d_n]$ of datasets such that $d_i \in D$ and d_i likely contains the resources for the semantic enrichment of σ_o. The list should be ranked according to the likelihood that a dataset contains semantic enrichments for σ_o. More formally, let

   i. Σ be a set of segmented trajectories
   ii. Λ be a set of labeled trajectories of the trajectories in Σ
   iii. T be a set of semantic trajectories of the trajectories in Σ
   iv. Δ be the set of datasets of the contextual resources of the trajectories in T
   v. P be an assessment function that estimates the likelihood that a dataset d_i contains enrichments for $\sigma_o \in \Sigma$ with respect to $\lambda_o \in \Lambda$.

One wants to find a ranking function $rank : \Lambda \mapsto \bigcup_{n=1}^{\infty} \Delta^n$ such that if $rank(\lambda_o) = [d_1, ..., d_n]$ then $P(\lambda_o, d_i) > P(\lambda_o, d_{i+1})$, for $i = 1, ..., n - 1$. We segment trajectories with the stop-and-move strategy [11] and label each segment with taxonomic classifications of the place visited at the end of the segment. We cast the problem as a supervised multi-class classification problem. If one takes the set of available datasets as classes of trajectories, one can induce a ranking function as follows. A *classification model* is a function $C : \Lambda \mapsto \bigcup_{n=1}^{\infty} (\Delta \times \Re)^n$ that assigns each labeled trajectory λ_o to a list with n pairs (d, s), where $d \in \Delta$ is a dataset and s is the *assessment score* of d, represented by a Real number. Let C be the set of all classification models. Let $2^{\Lambda \times T}$ be the set of sets of pairs (λ_o, σ_o). Intuitively, $\Theta \in 2^{\Lambda \times T}$ is a set of pairs (λ_o, σ_o), where λ_o is a labeled trajectory and σ_o is a semantic trajectory, such that the pairs in Θ will be used for training a classification model. Then, we introduce the function $Modeling : 2^{\Lambda \times T} \mapsto C$ to represent a machine-learning-based process that takes as input sets of pairs of labeled trajectories and that corresponding semantic trajectories, called a *training set*, and outputs a classification model.

Finally, the *ranking function induced by a classification model C* is defined as $rank(\lambda_o) = sortDescending(C(\lambda_o))$, where *sortDescending* sorts pairs by the second coordinate in descending order.

As for the features of trajectories, we tested four types of sets: the set of labels of the places visited in a trajectory (W_{λ_o}), e.g. {Residence, Law School, Pizza Place}, boolean model of the set of labels (X_{λ_o}), as used by Information Retrieval (IR) techniques, the set of all valid sequences of labels visited by a trajectory (Y_{λ_o}), e.g. {(Residence, Law School, Pizza Place), (Residence, Pizza Place), (Residence, Law School), ...}, and the boolean model of the sequences of labels (Z_{λ_o}), also as in IR.

3   Dataset Preparation

This section describes the preparation of the dataset used as training data to validate the proposed technique, i.e., the set of labeled and semantic enriched trajectories. We used a set of 9,594,421 geolocated tweets, between June and July 2014 generated in the city of Rio de Janeiro, as trails of movement of people during the FIFA World Cup 2014. A trajectory is defined as the movement of one person between 4:00 AM and 4:00 AM of the next day. There were 912,643 trajectories with 11 samples (tweets) on the average. Each trajectory was segmented using a stop/move heuristic, labeled with place check-ins and semantically enriched with entities from a set of datasets available on the Web.

Labeled Trajectories - Highly dense sampled trajectories are usually segmented using the *speed* and *minimal stop time* criteria. However, low density trajectories, like social media tracks, are not suitable for this kind of segmentation due to the impossibility of correctly computing the speed. We adopted a simpler heuristic for segmenting low density trajectories, yet following the stop-and-move strategy.

The segmentation is based on the intuition that if the time interval between two consecutive tweets is above a given threshold, the user might have moved from one position to another and, therefore, there would be a move segment from the position of the first tweet to the position of the second tweet. On the other hand, if the time interval is short, the user might be stopped or on the move. This last condition is justified because some mobile applications checks-in users automatically. In some cases, it was observed a series of consecutive tweets with short intervals of time and space, giving the idea that the user was on the move. All consecutive tweets considered to be part of the same move segment can be merged into a single segment, while the tweets in the same static position can be merged with the previously identified segment.

Recall from Sect. 2 that the modeling process receives as input a set of labeled trajectories. The trajectories were labeled with the categories of the places visited by users and enriched with the entities from the datasets of Table 1. The places visited by users were captured from Foursquare check-ins made available through tweets. Each Foursquare check-in contains metadata about the place which includes its classification according to the Foursquare taxonomy. This taxonomy is a three-level hierarchy that has, at the highest level, general categories, such as Food and Event. On the other hand, the lowest level is a very specific classification that contain, for example, the categories Preschool and Private School. Both levels, however, would lead to a poor discrimination regarding to the class association. The classification model would either over-associate trajectories with classes or discard some associations. Therefore, the trajectories were enriched with the intermediary level of classification, such as Breakfast Spot, Coffee Shop and Beach. The labeling procedure labels segments with information about the place at the end of the segment.

It is important to remark that only trajectories that visited three or more places were selected. It seems not make sense to classify trajectories with small sets of visited places since the induced purpose of the trajectories might be hidden. Therefore, we empirically considered trajectories with three or more places. So, the total number of trajectories was reduced from 912,643 to 8,730.

Semantic Trajectories - Regarding semantic enrichment, we used datasets (Table 1) made available through the open data portals http://dados.gov.br (Portal Brasileiro de Dados Abertos - ODBr) and http://data.rio.rj.gov.br (Portal de Dados abertos da Prefeitura do Rio - ODRio). The enrichment process was semi-automatic and matched the metadata of the places visited by the users (captured from the Foursquare check-ins) with the metadata of entities contained in each dataset.

Table 1. Datasets used for semantic enrichments of the trajectories.

Dataset URI	Source	Alias
http://dados.gov.br/dataset/instituicoes-de-ensino-basico	ODBr	schools
http://dados.gov.br/dataset/instituicoes-de-ensino-superior	ODBr	universities
http://data.rio.rj.gov.br/dataset/pontos-turisticos-e-culturais	ODRio	attractions
http://data.rio.rj.gov.br/dataset/hoteis	ODRio	hotels
http://data.rio.rj.gov.br/dataset/museus	ODRio	museums
http://data.rio.rj.gov.br/dataset/teatros	ODRio	theaters
http://data.rio.rj.gov.br/dataset/estabelecimentos-de-saude	ODRio	hospitals
http://data.rio.rj.gov.br/dataset/unidades-administrativas	ODRio	offices

The matching process consisted in computing a similarity measure between places p and entities e and manually deciding the matchings. The similarity function used is defined as follows.

$$sim_N(p, e) = 1 - \frac{levenshteinDistance(p[name], e[name])}{p[name].length + e[name].length} \tag{1}$$

$$sim_G(p, e) = \frac{1}{(0.19 \cdot geoDistance(p[position], e[position]) + 1)} \tag{2}$$

$$sim(p, e) = harmonicMean(sim_N(p, e), sim_G(p, e)) \qquad (3)$$

The sim_G is defined such that $sim_G = 1$ for $distance = 0$, $sim_G = 0$ for $distance \to \infty$ and $sim_G = 0.05$ for $distance = 100$ m. A place and an entity are matching candidates iff $sim(p, e)$ is greater than 0.95. The matching task only aimed at providing a Gold Standard.

4 Experiments

The main goal of the experiments was to assess the performance of the ranking function. As for the performance measure, the experiments computed the Mean Average Precision (MAP) of the ranking. The next subsections describe the creation of the classification model, the ranking function and the ranking assessment.

Classification Model - We investigated different classification algorithms and concluded that the best classification function is a combination of binary classifiers using the JRip algorithm [1]. Table 2.a compares the F-Measure of different classification algorithms, JRip, J48 [6], OneR [4], ConjunctiveRule [9] and DecisionStump [9], with respect to a positive classification for the classes offices, theaters, hotels, hospitals, museums, attractions, ies, schools. This experiment used the set of valid sequences of places (Z_{λ_o}) for the features of trajectories. As we show, none of the algorithms statistically improves the performance of the reference algorithm (JRip). The statistic significance was determined by the paired T-Test method using a set of 10 randomly partitions of the test dataset of the type 2/3 *for training set* + 1/3 *for test set.*

Table 2. F-measure of classification algorithms.

a) Using binary vector of sequences of places.

Dataset	(1)	(2)	(3)	(4)	(5)
offices	0.66	0.10	0.00 ●	0.00 ●	0.00 ●
theaters	0.82	0.63	0.66	0.66	0.66
hotels	0.14	0.03 ●	0.03 ●	0.00	0.00
hospitals	0.53	0.32	0.26 ●	0.00 ●	0.00 ●
museums	0.58	0.28 ●	0.16	0.00 ●	0.00 ●
attractions	0.69	0.69	0.53 ●	0.62	0.53 ●
universities	0.82	0.81	0.78	0.73	0.78
schools	0.72	0.71	0.71	0.68	0.71
Average	0.62	0.45	0.39	0.34	0.34

b) Multi-class version of JRip binary vector of sequences of places

Class	F-Measure
offices	0.31
theaters	0.67
hotels	0.06
hospitals	0.33
museums	0.63
attractions	0.65
universities	0.79
schools	0.69
None	0.90
Average	0.56

o, ● statistically significant improvement or degradation

(1) rules.JRip '-F 3 -N 2.0 -O 6 -S 1'
(2) trees.J48 '-C 0.25 -M 2'
(3) rules.OneR '-B 6'
(4) rules.ConjunctiveRule '-N 3 -M 2.0 -P -1 -S 1'
(5) trees.DecisionStump "

The low performance of the classification with respect to the dataset `hotels` can be explained by its generality. That is, a `hotel` can be a stop in several different sequences of places, which makes it more difficult to find a pattern of correlation between trajectories and datasets. The average performance of JRip was 62%. Table 2.b shows the performance of the multi-class version of JRip, which has an average performance of 56%. The binary classifiers, therefore, proved to be more efficient. Tables 3.a and b show the performance measures using the set of features in Definitions W_{λ_o} and X_{λ_o}. The best performance was achieved with the JRip algorithm using the categories of the places visited by a trajectory (Definition X_{λ_o}), which was 61%. These results corroborate the intuition that using sequences of places is more discriminating. For example, a sequence of places (Definition Z_{λ_o}) such as [Residence, School, Residence] could indicate that the person is a Student, while a sequence [Residence, School, School, School, Residence], if the schools are different, could indicate that the person is, for example, a professional delivery boy. Both cases, however, have the same set of features. In the first example, the enrichment with a dataset of schools would make sense, while in the last one it seems not to be the case.

Table 3. F-measure of classification algorithms.

a) Using sets of categories as features.

Dataset	(1)	(2)	(3)	(4)
offices	0.17	0.07	0.07	0.00
theaters	0.62	0.53	0.53	0.00 ●
hotels	0.00	0.10	0.10	0.00
hospitals	0.27	0.08 ●	0.08 ●	0.00 ●
museums	0.44	0.27	0.27	0.00 ●
attractions	0.61	0.66	0.66	0.00 ●
universities	0.77	0.62 ●	0.62 ●	0.00 ●
schools	0.71	0.58	0.58	0.00 ●
Average	0.45	0.36	0.36	0

b) Using binary vector of categories as features.

Dataset	(1)	(2)	(3)	(4)
offices	0.00	0.00	0.53 ○	0.57 ○
theaters	0.67	0.67	0.86	0.86
hotels	0.26	0.26	0.12	0.14
hospitals	0.28	0.28	0.52 ○	0.45 ○
museums	0.24	0.24	0.72 ○	0.64 ○
attractions	0.68	0.68	0.69	0.74 ○
universities	0.69	0.69	0.83 ○	0.83
schools	0.68	0.63	0.69 ○	0.69
Average	0.43	0.43	0.62	0.62

○, ● statistically significant improvement or degradation

(1) bayes.NaiveBayesUpdateable "
(2) bayes.NaiveBayes "
(3) rules.JRip '-F 9 -N 2.0 -O 6 -S 1'
(4) trees.J48 '-C 0.25 -M 2'

Ranking Assessment - Rankings were generated, as before, using a set of 10 randomly partitions of the enriched dataset such that 2/3 were used for training set and 1/3 for test set. We used sets of binary classifiers, one for each dataset, based on JRip algorithm which is a rule-based classifier that, while trained, generates classification rules such as

Rule: if the a person visited a place of type States & Municipalities and did not visit a Residence and moved from a place of type States & Municipalities to a place of type Food then classify trajectory as attraction

The training step computes, for each rule, its precision, recall and F-measure. We used the F-measure as an estimate of the confidence of the rule, since intuitively the higher the precision and recall are, the higher the confidence on the classification will be. The confidence, therefore, was used as the *assessment score* (Sect. 2) output by the *classification model*.

To assess the ranking function we computed the Mean Average Precision (MAP) of the rankings of a set of trajectories. We assessed the ranking function on 2,508 trajectories out of the 8,730 trajectories available in the dataset. These trajectories had 1.5 relevant datasets on the average and the computed MAP was 66%, which means that one would need, on the average, just the three top most entries of the rank to find two datasets for enrichments.

5   Conclusions

This work proposes a novel approach for finding datasets for semantic enrichment based on the types of places visited. The technique takes advantage of place check-ins available on social networks to identify the sequences of places. It is a supervised approach that uses a set of semi-automatically enriched trajectories to learn correlations between the places visited and the datasets available for enrichment. We investigated different classification algorithms and different sets of features for the trajectories. The best performance was obtained with the JRip algorithm and sets of features that contain all possible sequences of places for a trajectory. The resulting ranks obtained, on the average, a MAP of 66% in the experiments.

Acknowledgements. This work has been funded by CNPq/BR and FAPERJ under grants E-26-170.028/2008, 557128/2009-9, 248743/2013-9, 248987/2013-5, 303332/2013-9, 442338/2014-7, 444976/2014-0 and E-26-201.337/2014.

References

1. Cohen, W.W.: Fast effective rule induction. In: the 12th International Conference on Machine Learning, pp. 115–123. Morgan Kaufmann (1995)
2. Fileto, R., Krüger, M., Pelekis, N., Theodoridis, Y., Renso, C.: Baquara: a holistic ontological framework for movement analysis using linked data. In: Ng, W., Storey, V.C., Trujillo, J.C. (eds.) ER 2013. LNCS, vol. 8217, pp. 342–355. Springer, Heidelberg (2013)
3. Heath, T., Bizer, C.: Linked Data: Evolving the Web into a Global Data Space, vol. 1. Morgan & Claypool, San Rafael (2011)
4. Holte, R.C.: Very simple classification rules perform well on most commonly used datasets. Mach. Learn. **11**(1), 63–91 (1993)
5. Nabo, R.G.B., Fileto, R., Nanni, M., Renso, C.: Annotating trajectories by fusing them with social media users posts. In: the XI Brazilian Symposium on GeoInformatics, pp. 25–36 (2014)
6. Quinlan, J.R.: C4.5: Programs for Machine Learning. Morgan Kaufmann, Burlington (1993)

7. Spinsanti, L., Celli, F., Renso, C.: Where you stop is who you are: understanding peoples activities. In: the 5th Workshop on Behaviour Monitoring and Interpretation–User Modelling (2010)

8. Uzun, A.: Linked crowdsourced data - enabling location analytics in the linking open data cloud. In: 2015 IEEE International Conference on Semantic Computing, pp. 40–48. IEEE (2015)

9. Witten, I.H., Frank, E., Hall, M.A.: Data Mining: Practical Machine Learning Tools and Techniques. Morgan Kaufmann, Burlington (2011)

10. Yan, Z., Chakraborty, D., Parent, C., Spaccapietra, S., Aberer, K.: SeMiTri: a framework for semantic annotation of heterogeneous trajectories. In: The 14th International Conference on Extending Database Technology, pp. 259–270 (2011)

11. Yan, Z., Chakraborty, D., Parent, C., Spaccapietra, S., Aberer, K.: Semantic trajectories: mobility data computation and annotation. Trans. Intell. Syst. Technol. 4(3), 49 (2013)

12. Yuan, J., Liu, X., Zhang, R., Sun, H., Guo, X., Wang, Y.: Discovering semantic mobility pattern from check-in data. In: Benatallah, B., Bestavros, A., Manolopoulos, Y., Vakali, A., Zhang, Y. (eds.) WISE 2014. LNCS, vol. 8786, pp. 464–479. Springer, Heidelberg (2014). doi:10.1007/978-3-319-11749-2_35

On Impact of Weather on Human Mobility in Cities

Jun Pang[✉], Polina Zablotskaia, and Yang Zhang

Computer Science and Communications, University of Luxembourg,
Luxembourg, Luxembourg
jun.pang@uni.lu

Abstract. Although researchers have demonstrated that human mobility is constrained by space, time and social relations, one important factor, namely weather, has been often ignored in the literature. Not only influences what people wear everyday, weather also has a major impact on their mobility. In this paper, we conduct the first large-scale analysis of weather's impact on human mobility in cities. Focusing on a number of major cities, we construct a human mobility dataset from the social network Instagram. We discover that in general nice weather (e.g., moderate temperature and high pressure) has a positive impact on human mobility. Through analyzing mobility at locations of different categories, we further discover that human mobility is less influenced by weather at certain categories such as residences than others including stores and entertainment places.

1 Introduction

Urbanization is a massive process happening in this century. Every year, more and more people are moving to cities. According to a UN report[1], by 2050 more than 6 billion people will live in cities. Although living in cities brings a lot of convenience to people, it also causes major problems, such as air pollution and traffic congestion. While much effort has been taken to tackle these problems, one fundamental challenge is to fully understand how people move, i.e., human mobility in cities.

Human mobility has attracted the research community a considerable amount of interest during the past decade. Researchers have demonstrated that human mobility is constrained by space, time [1] and social networks [2]. On the other hand, another important factor, i.e., weather, receives much less attention and is often ignored. Weather as a natural phenomenon influences our mobility in many ways. When people check weather reports, they not only decide what to wear, but also where to visit. For instance, few people are willing to walk in a park on a cloudy winter afternoon.

Understanding the relationship between mobility and weather can result in positive benefits for multiple stakeholders: for example, city governors can design

---

[1] http://bit.ly/1N3gAH6.

© Springer International Publishing AG 2016
W. Cellary et al. (Eds.): WISE 2016, Part II, LNCS 10042, pp. 247–256, 2016.
DOI: 10.1007/978-3-319-48743-4_20

Table 1. Dataset summary.

City	#Check-ins	#Users	#Locations	City	#Check-ins	#Users	#Locations
New York	2,728,705	788,980	30,644	Washington DC	542,822	185,687	10,601
Los Angeles	2,011,106	607,380	27,716	San Francisco	635,842	225,438	9,620
Tokyo	891,029	300,111	26,586	Chicago	725,223	233,844	12,407
London	1,441,658	516,640	15,571	Rome	232,305	102,022	6,267
Paris	633,868	253,516	11,112	Milan	296,353	122,481	5,917
Boston	465,615	165,166	7,619	Barcelona	245,298	113,997	5,457
Hongkong	191,899	87,413	4,203				

specific plans for different weather conditions to control traffic flow; shop owners can provide suitable benefits to attract customers; city residents can choose to visit less crowded places on weekends. In the current work, we conduct the first large-scale analysis of weather's impact on human mobility in cities. Our contributions can be summarized as follows:

- We construct a mobility dataset under different weather parameters for 13 major cities across the world (Sect. 2). We gather more than 10 millions of users' location records, namely check-ins, from Instagram and weather data from Forecast.io.
- We analyze the relationship between users' general mobility behaviors and different weather parameters such as temperature and humidity (Sect. 3). We quantify users' mobility through average check-in volumes, average movement volumes and average movement distances. Our discoveries, for example, include both low and high temperature have negative effects on mobility; high pressure on the other hand positively affects mobility. Interestingly, we also discover that humidity affects mobility negatively in coastal cities while positively in inland cities.
- We take one step further to analyze users' mobility at different location categories under different weather parameters (Sect. 4). We discover that users' average check-in volumes at locations of certain categories, such as store, entertainment and professional places, are more correlated with weather than others such as residence places. Moreover, people' movement patterns among location categories are less diverse under a uncomfortable weather condition than a comfortable one.

2   Dataset Construction

Check-in Data. We collect the geo-tagged photos, i.e., check-ins, in 13 major cities worldwide from Instagram by using its public API from August 1st, 2015 until December 15th, 2015. We first resort to Foursquare to extract all location ids within each city we are interested in, meanwhile collect each location's category information. Then for each Foursquare's location id, we query Instagram's API to get its corresponding location id in Instagram. After obtaining

Instagram's location ids, we query each location's recent check-ins several times a day. In the end, more than 10M check-ins have been collected. Table 1 summarizes the dataset. As Foursquare organizes location categories into a tree structure, we take its first level categories including *entertainment, food, bar, outdoor, professional, residence, store* and *transportation* to label each location.

Weather. We exploit Forecast.io's API to extract weather data. Forecast.io is a weather application started in 2013, it gathers the data from multiple sources such as NOAA and Met Office, and provides users with the aggregated results. Forecast.io's API provides daily weather data covering temperature (°C), humidity (relative humidity), wind speed (miles per hour), pressure (millibar). In addition, as people normally do not feel the difference when the temperature varies one or two degrees, we bucket temperature into bins of 3° starting from 0°C (−2°C–0°C) to 30°C (28°C–30°C).

3 Weather and Mobility

For weather, four parameters are considered including temperature, pressure, wind speed and humidity. For mobility, we focus on two aspects. The first one is the average number of check-ins, namely *average check-in volumes*, under each value of each weather parameter. The second one is related to users' movements, including the average number of movements, namely *average movement volumes* and *average movement distances* (km). Here, we consider a user checking in at two locations within a certain time threshold τ as one movement. In this paper, we choose τ to be 3 hours which we believe is a reasonable transition time for a user. The same formulation has been used in [3] as well. Note that our mobility quantification is at a general level instead for each individual user, i.e., we calculate the mean of users' total number of check-ins, number of movements and movement distances under each value of each weather parameter.

Temperature. Figure 1 depicts the average check-in volumes under different temperature (bucketed by 3°C) in Paris and Boston. We observe that people check in more often under a moderate temperature than low (≤6 °C) and high (≥24 °C) temperature in both cities. We further fit the data into a Gaussian

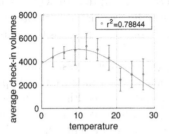
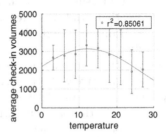

Fig. 1. Temperature vs. average check-in volumes in Paris (left) and Boston (right).

Table 2. r^2 Between temperature and average check-in volumes.

City	r^2	b	c	City	r^2	b	c
New York	0.90	12.76	25.72	Washington DC	0.84	14.45	19.21
Los Angeles	0.36	17.97	17.78	San Francisco	0.86	12.52	17.21
Tokyo	0.67	13.77	22.92	Chicago	0.45	13.64	23.62
London	0.24	10.97	18.92	Rome	0.85	14.71	15.78
Paris	0.78	9.83	14.39	Milan	0.91	10.52	15.36
Boston	0.85	12.10	20.37	Barcelona	0.64	16.82	21.11
Hongkong	0.77	22.22	21.14				

Table 3. r between pressure and mobility ($r1$: average check-in volumes, $r2$: average movement volumes, $r3$: average movement distances).

City	$r1$	$r2$	$r3$	City	$r1$	$r2$	$r3$
New York	0.23	0.60	0.68	Washington DC	0.74	0.69	0.66
Los Angeles	0.16	0.21	0.12	San Francisco	0.31	-0.20	-0.22
Tokyo	0.81	0.64	0.55	Chicago	0.30	0.35	0.39
London	0.63	0.60	0.63	Rome	0.57	0.09	0.05
Paris	0.54	0.48	0.47	Milan	0.48	0.18	0.18
Boston	-0.05	0.56	0.59	Barcelona	-0.17	-0.43	-0.53
Hongkong	0.25	0.18	0.18				

function defined as $avg\_ci(t) = a \cdot \exp(-(\frac{t-b}{c})^2)$. In the formula, $avg\_ci(t)$ is the average check-in volume at temperature t (bucketed by 3°C), a, b and c are the parameters of the function: a represents the height of the curve peak, b marks the center of the curve and c controls the width. As shown in Fig. 1, a high coefficient of determination, i.e., r^2, is obtained for the fitting, meaning that a Gaussian curve captures the relation between temperature and average check-in volumes. Table 2 lists r^2 together with parameters b and c for all the cities. We make two interesting observations. First, data for most cities fit the Gaussian function well, except for Los Angeles and London with relatively weak results. This indicates that there exists a universal pattern of temperature's impact on human mobility. Second, the central point of the Gaussian function, i.e., b, varies across the cities. Cities located in hot regions such as Hongkong and Los Angeles have higher values for b, as people living there are used to hot weather, compared to cities located in cold regions, e.g., London.

For the second aspect of mobility, i.e., average movement volumes and average movement distances, as an example we plot the average movement volumes in Rome and the average movement distances in Washington DC as a function of temperature in Fig. 2, respectively. Consistently, we see – similar to average check-in volumes – both average movement volumes and distances fit Gaussian functions well.

From the above analysis, we first conclude that human mobility is more adapted to moderate temperature than both low and high temperature.

Pressure. High pressure is a whirling mass of cool and dry air which generally brings good weather, while low pressure is normally associated with bad weather such as cloud, rain and wind. We expect that pressure has positive effects on users' mobility.

Table 3 lists three correlation coefficients (r) between pressure and mobility, pressure indeed positively affects users' mobility in most of the cities. Especially for Tokyo and London, we observe strong correlations (see Fig. 3). On the other hand, Barcelona is the only city with three negative correlation coefficients, indicating that pressure has negative effects on human mobility in Barcelona. In addition, most of the cities show consistency between average check-in volumes ($r1$) and movements ($r2$, $r3$), except for San Francisco and Boston. People in San

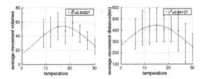 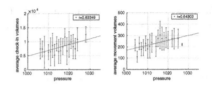

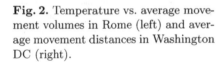

Fig. 2. Temperature vs. average movement volumes in Rome (left) and average movement distances in Washington DC (right).

Fig. 3. Pressure vs. check-in volumes in London (left) and movement volumes in Tokyo (right).

Francisco have more check-ins but less and shorter movements on high pressure days. In Boston, high pressure does not affect average check-in volumes much, instead it leads to more and longer movements.

Wind Speed. Wind speed is an important aspect of weather. Through analysis, we discover that average check-in volumes in most cities receives negative wind speed effects (Table 4). Figure 4 (left) presents the result in Barcelona as an example.

The relation between wind speed and movements, on the other hand, is more complicated. For some cities including Los Angeles (see Fig. 4 (right)), Tokyo, Paris, Washington DC and Hongkong, wind speed has similar effects on movements as on check-in volumes. On the other hand, in New York, Boston, San Francisco and Barcelona, the (negative) effects of wind on movements become weaker. Moreover, in Chicago, Rome and Milan, there exist positive effects of wind speed on movements. One explanation could be wind negatively affects cycling and walking which results in more car and public transportation usage in these cities. In turn, this leads to the increases in movement volumes and distances. In the end, we observe that in London wind speed has weak effects on average check-in volumes but strong (negative) effects on movements.

Humidity. People normally feel uncomfortable when humidity is low (≤ 0.3) or high (≥ 0.8). Therefore, similar to the case of temperature, we expect the relation between mobility and humidity to follow a Gaussian curve as well. However, analysis results show that humidity (mostly between 0.3 and 0.8) and mobility are linearly correlated in most of the cities. More interestingly, we observe contradictory linear correlations in different cities. As shown in Fig. 5, humidity has positive effects on mobility in Rome while negative effects in Hongkong. Table 5 lists correlation coefficients for both kinds of cities (the results for movements are quite similar and omitted).

Fully understanding the correlation between humidity and mobility involves multiple factors, such as city location, temperature or even culture background, which is out of the scope of the current work. On the other hand, by only studying the dataset, we observe that most of the cities with positive humidity effects are inland cities except for Barcelona and Boston. On the other hand, cities with negative effects are all coastal cities where humidity is normally high.

Table 4. r between wind and mobility ($r1$: average check-in volumes, $r2$: average movement volumes, $r3$: average movement distances).

Table 5. r between humidity and average check-in volumes.

City	$r1$	$r2$	$r3$	City	$r1$	$r2$	$r3$
New York	−0.47	−0.05	−0.07	Washington DC	−0.29	−0.25	−0.24
Los Angeles	−0.60	−0.60	−0.55	San Francisco	−0.50	−0.16	−0.16
Tokyo	−0.37	−0.40	−0.31	Chicago	−0.26	0.26	0.30
London	0.02	−0.57	−0.56	Rome	−0.05	0.33	0.45
Paris	−0.16	−0.28	−0.36	Milan	−0.31	0.24	0.21
Boston	−0.40	−0.03	−0.01	Barcelona	−0.56	−0.18	-0.07
Hongkong	0.07	0.12	0.02				

City	r	City	r
Hongkong	−0.70	Rome	0.68
Los Angeles	−0.54	Paris	0.61
New York	−0.28	London	0.59
Tokyo	−0.19	Milan	0.56
San Francisco	−0.14	Barcelona	0.50
		Boston	0.33
		Chicago	0.16
		Washington DC	0.12

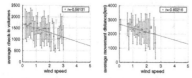

Fig. 4. Wind vs. average check-in volumes in Barcelona (left) and average movement distances in Los Angeles (right).

Fig. 5. Humidity vs. average check-in volumes in Hongkong (left) and Rome (right).

We conjecture that humidity negatively affects human mobility in coastal cities while positively in inland cities.

4   Weather and Location Category

In this section we take one step further to analyze weather's influences on mobility at different location categories. We start by analyzing average check-in volumes at each category, then discuss movement patterns among categories.

4.1   Average Check-In Volumes

Temperature. We exploit Gaussian function to model the relation between temperature and average check-in volumes at each location category, assuming that users are more adapted to moderate temperature than both low and high temperature (Sect. 3). Through analysis, we obtain high correlation of determination (r^2) for Gaussian function fitting at entertainment, professional, outdoor and store places. On the other hand, residence is the category with the lowest r^2 values, followed by food and bar. Figure 6 (left) further plots the results in Los Angeles, London and Chicago.

Since Gaussian function cannot capture the correlation between temperature and average check-in volumes at residence, food and bar places, we further examine the data of these categories. Figure 7 depicts the average check-in volumes at

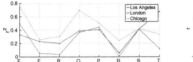
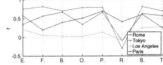
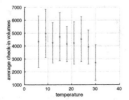
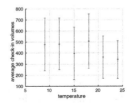

Fig. 6. r^2 of fitting between average check-in volumes and temperature at location categories (left), r between average check-in volumes and pressure at different location categories (right) (each category is denoted by its first letter).

Fig. 7. Average check-in volumes at food places in New York (left) and bar places in San Francisco (right) under different temperature.

food places in New York and bar places in San Francisco as a function of temperature; no clear correlation can be observed. This means whether people going to a bar (a restaurant or a residence) is not strongly dependent on temperature. One reason could be that places of these categories are mostly indoor places, thus not weather-exposed. We conclude that human mobility is more affected by temperature at entertainment, professional, outdoor and store places while it is less affected by temperature at food, bar and residence places.

Pressure. Section 3 states that pressure positively affects users' mobility, this result holds for most of the location categories as well. In addition, in most cities, users' mobility at entertainment, professional and store places receives more positive pressure effects than mobility at other categories. On the other hand, the correlation at residence places is rather weak. For instance, in Fig. 6 (right), correlation coefficients (r) at residence places in Tokyo, Rome, Los Angeles and Paris drop quickly when compared to other categories. Meanwhile, there also exist subtle differences among the cities. For instance, users' average check-in volumes at food places have the highest pressure effects in Tokyo while food places have the lowest pressure effects for Paris.

Wind Speed. Previously, we have shown that even though wind speed has different effects on movements (average movement volumes and distances) in different cities (Table 4), it still negatively affects average check-in volumes in most cities. However, when conducting analysis at the location category level, similar pattern between wind speed and average check-in volumes cannot be observed. To give an example, we discover that the impact of wind speed at residence places decreases (similar to the cases of temperature and pressure) in some cities, while in other cities the wind's negative impact even gets stronger.

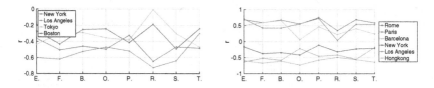

Fig. 8. r between average check-in volumes and wind speed (left) humidity (right) at different location categories.

Fig. 9. Movements among categories in London at $12\,°C$ (left) and $24\,°C$ (right).

Fig. 10. Movements among categories in Los Angeles at humidity 0.56 (left) and 0.8 (right).

From Fig. 8 (left), we see that Tokyo and Boston belong to the former case while New York and Los Angeles represent the latter one.

Humidity. Effects of humidity on users' mobility are positive in some cities while negative in others. For most cities with positive humidity effects, residence is again the category with the lowest correlation coefficients (r) while entertainment, professional and store places have the highest (similar to the results of pressure). For cities with negative humidity effects, we cannot observe a clear pattern. Figure 8 (right) plots the results of a few cites: Rome, Paris and Barcelona for the first case, New York, Los Angles and Hongkong for the second.

4.2   Movements Among Location Categories

Since each location is associated with a location category, we further study the weather's impact on movements among different categories. In the current work, we focus on the direct movements between two categories, e.g., from professional places to food places.

Temperature. Among all the 13 cities, we discover that users' movements among location categories under a moderate temperature are more diverse than those under low and high ones. Figure 9 plots two chord diagrams in London under a moderate temperature ($12\,°C$) and a high temperature ($24\,°C$). Each location category is represented by its first letter (capitalized) on the circle, links having the same color as a category are movements starting from that category. Width of each link is proportional to the number of movements. In Fig. 9, there exist more links among categories when temperature is $12\,°C$ than $24\,°C$. For example, there are many links from entertainment to outdoor and transportation places in the left part of Fig. 9, while the number of links decreases on the right part of Fig. 9; the most likely destinations for people after checking in at transportation places are bar places when temperature is 12 °C, while they are professional places when temperature is 24 °C.

Humidity. Similar to the case of temperature, users' movements among location categories are more diverse under a comfortable humidity condition than a uncomfortable one. Figure 10 plots the chord diagrams in Los Angeles under two humidity conditions, i.e., 0.56 and 0.8. There are more links in Fig. 10 with humidity condition 0.56 than with 0.8, e.g., many more movements end at outdoor places in the left chord diagram than in the right one. Similar results are obtained for pressure as well.

5 Related Work

To the best of our knowledge, the current work is the first large-scale study on weather and human mobility. One close line of work is the study on weather and transportation carried out by the transportation community [4].

Comparing to these studies, our work has the following advantages. (1) Most of the studies conducted by the transportation community focus on weather's impact on people's transportation modes such as public transportation, bicycle or walk. Especially, bicycle usage attracts a lot of attentions (e.g., see [5,6]). On the other hand, we focus on users' mobility without any constrains, this makes our analysis more general than theirs. (2) Our dataset is at the global level, i.e., we focus on the mobility of users among 13 cities located in Asia, Europe and North America, while most of the datasets used by the transportation community concentrate on a single city or country. Besides, since our mobility data is from Instagram, the user sample is much bigger than those works whose data is normally collected by conducting surveys.

6 Conclusion

We have conducted the first large-scale analysis on the relationship between weather and human mobility in cities. Our discoveries include (1) nice weather, characterized by moderate temperature, high pressure, slow wind speed and suitable humidity, has positive effects on users' mobility; (2) users' mobility at certain location categories, e.g., residence places, is less influenced by weather than mobility at other categories including entertainment, professional and store places.

References

1. Gonzalez, M., Hidalgo, C., Barabasi, A.L.: Understanding individual human mobility patterns. Nature **453**, 779–782 (2008)
2. Cho, E., Myers, S.A., Leskovec, J.: Friendship and mobility: user movement in location-based social networks. In: Proceedings of 17th ACM Conference on Knowledge Discovery and Data Mining (KDD), pp. 1082–1090. ACM (2011)

3. Noulas, A., Shaw, B., Lambiotte, R., Mascolo, C.: Topological properties and temporal dynamics of place networks in urban environments. In: Proceedings of 24th International Conference on World Wide Web (WWW Companion), pp. 431–441. ACM (2015)
4. Böcker, L., Dijst, M., Prillwitz, J.: Impact of everyday weather on individual daily travel behaviours in perspective: a literature review. Transp. Rev. **33**(1), 71–91 (2013)
5. Hanson, S., Hanson, P.: Evaluating the impact of weather on bicycle use. Transp. Res. Rec. **629**, 43–48 (1977)
6. Nankervis, M.: The effect of weather and climate on bicycle commuting. Transp. Res. Part A: Policy Pract. **33**(6), 417–431 (1999)

Graph Theory

Minimum Spanning Tree on Uncertain Graphs

Anzhen Zhang$^{(\boxtimes)}$, Zhaonian Zou, Jianzhong Li, and Hong Gao

Harbin Institute of Technology, Harbin 150001, China
azzhang@hit.edu.cn

Abstract. In recent years, lots of data in various domain can be represented and described by uncertain graph model, such as protein interaction networks, social networks, wireless sensor networks, etc. This paper investigates the most reliable minimum spanning tree problem, which aims to find the minimum spanning tree (MST) with largest probability among all possible MSTs on uncertain graphs. In fact, the most reliable MST is an optimal choice between stability and cost. Therefore it has wide applications in practice, for example, it can serve as the basic constructs in a telecommunication network, the link of which can be unreliable and may fail with certain probability. A brute-force method needs to enumerate all possible MSTs and the time consumption grows exponentially with edge size. Hence we put forward an approximate algorithm in $O(d^2|V|^2)$, where d is the largest vertex degree and $|V|$ is vertex size. We point out that the algorithm can achieve exact solution with expected probability at least $(1-(\frac{1}{2})^{(d+1)/2})^{|V|-1}$ and the expected approximation ratio is at least $(\frac{1}{2})^{d|V|}$ when edge probability is uniformly distributed. Our extensive experimental results show that our proposed algorithm is both efficient and effective.

1 Introduction

Recently, lots of data in various domain can be represented by graph model, such as the web, social networks, and cellular systems. Such networks are often subject to uncertainties caused by noise, incompleteness and inaccuracy in practice [1]. Incorporating uncertainty to graphs leads to uncertain graphs, each edge of which is associated with an edge existence probability to quantify the likelihood that this edge exists in the graph. For example, in a telecommunication network, a link can be unreliable and may fail with certain probability [14]; in a social network, the probability of an edge may represent the uncertainty of a *link prediction* [6]; in a wireless sensor network, communication links between sensor nodes often suffer from inevitable physical interference [15]. The uncertain graph, also referred as probabilistic graph, addresses such scenarios conveniently in a unified way.

There has been extensive research on the minimum spanning tree on exact graphs which are precise and complete. Given a connected exact graph $G = (V, E)$, each edge has a non-negative weight, a spanning tree T of G is a tree whose edges connect all the nodes in G, the sum weight of all edges in T is the cost

© Springer International Publishing AG 2016
W. Cellary et al. (Eds.): WISE 2016, Part II, LNCS 10042, pp. 259–274, 2016.
DOI: 10.1007/978-3-319-48743-4_21

of T. Among all spanning trees the one with minimum cost is minimum spanning tree, which is short for MST. A number of algorithms have been proposed to compute MST for exact graph, among which Prim and Kruskal gave two classical algorithms in polynomial time [2,3].

The problem of computing MST is fundamental for uncertain graphs, just as they are for exact graphs. Obviously we can still obtain the MST with minimum cost in uncertain graph by neglecting the possibility of edges and treat the uncertain graph as exact graph. We call the obtained MST *minimum cost MST*, however, it suffers from low reliability and may fail to exist since we leave the possibility of edges out of consideration. Actually we can obtain the MST with largest probability by setting the weight of edge e to be $-log(p(e))$ and executing MST algorithm for exact graphs. The MST obtained this way has the largest existing probability but has no guarantee for the cost, we call it *maximum probability MST* for simplicity. To make a balance between those two types of MST, we propose *the most reliable MST* which has largest probability among all possible MSTs and it can be found in a wide range of network applications.

In a telecommunication network, the most reliable MST can serve as the basic constructs to help connect all nodes in the network at least cost while the stability of network can still be guaranteed [16]. In the scenario of advertisement promotion in social network with edge uncertainty measures the intimacy between two friends and edge weight quantifies the cost of spreading, the most reliable MST can help discover a most effective propagation path with minimum advertisement cost. Another practical application is data aggregation tree in wireless sensor network [15]. Most reliable MST can serve as an optimal initial data aggregation tree with sink node to be the root and source nodes to be leafs since it takes transmission energy cost and link failure probability into consideration, which contributes to the construction of data aggregation tree that maximizes the network lifetime.

In uncertain graph, possible instantiations of the graph are commonly referred to as worlds or implicated graph, the probability of a world is calculated based on the probability of its edges, as will shown in later section. There exists at least one MST in each connective implicated graph, all MSTs of the connective implicated graphs form the MST set of the uncertain graph and the most frequent MST in the set is the most reliable one, denoted by MST_{max}.

A brute-force method is to enumerate all connected implicated graphs and compute MST for each of them, however, enumerating all implicated graph needs $O(2^{|E|})$ time, where $|E|$ is the edge size. The exact algorithm is not feasible since the scale of graph is large in practical applications. Hence we present an approximate algorithm in $O(d^2|V|^2)$, where d is the maximum degree of vertexes and $|V|$ is vertex size. Our theoretical analysis shows that it has pretty good performance in aspects of accuracy and approximate ratio. Extensive experiment results on synthetic sets show that our approximate algorithm outperforms the other three algorithms in terms of stability and cost.

The rest of the paper is organized as follows. We define the most reliable MST problem in Sect. 2. An approximate algorithm and its performance analysis is presented in Sect. 3. We show experimental studies in Sect. 4 and present related work in Sect. 5. Finally, we conclude this paper in Sect. 6.

2 Problem Formulation

In this section, we formally present the uncertain graph model and introduce the problem of most reliable MST in an uncertain graph.

2.1 Model of Uncertain Graphs

Let $\mathcal{G} = (V, E, P, W)$ be an uncertain graph, where V and E denote the set of vertexes and edges respectively. $P : E \rightarrow (0, 1]$ is a function assigning existence possibility values to edges. W is weight function, and $w(e)$ is the weight of edge $e \in E$.

An uncertain graph has many existence forms due to the uncertainty of edges, each deterministic form $g = (V, E_g)$ is called *implicated graph* and is denoted by $\mathcal{G} \Rightarrow g$. Each edge $e \in E_{\mathcal{G}}$ is selected to be an edge of g with probability $P(e)$. The total number of implicated graphs is $2^{|E|}$ since each edge has two cases as to whether or not that edge is present in the graph. We assume that all existence possibilities of edges are independent, the probability of an uncertain graph $\mathcal{G}$ implicating an exact graph g is

$$P(\mathcal{G} \Rightarrow g) = \prod_{e \in E(g)} P(e) \prod_{e' \in E(G) \setminus E(g)} (1 - P(e')) \tag{1}$$

where $P(e)$ is the existence possibility of edge e. To gain more intuition on the uncertain graph model and the implicated graph, We present a simple example in the following.

Example 1. Consider the uncertain graph $\mathcal{G}$ in Fig. 1(a). There are $2^3 = 8$ implicated graphs, and the probability of each graph is calculated based on Eq. (1), as shown in Fig. 1(b). Take $g2$ for example, $P(\mathcal{G} \Rightarrow g2) = 0.4 \times (1 - 0.9) \times (1 - 0.7) = 0.012$. The probability of the other implicated graphs are calculated in the same way.

2.2 Most Reliable MST

There exists at least one MST in each connective implicated graph of uncertain graph $\mathcal{G}$ with probability same as the implicated graph containing it, all possible MSTs form MST set $\{MST_1, MST_2, \cdots\}$, and MST_i denotes the edge set of the ith MST.

Obviously a MST for an implicated graph may be MST for another implicated graph, hence each MST in MST set is accompanied with certain frequency and the one with maximum frequency is most reliable, that is MST_{max}. The existing probability $P(MST_i)$ of MST_i is determined by the implicated graph it belongs

(a) Uncertain graph G

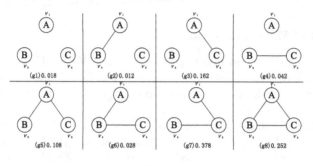

(b) Imp(G)

Fig. 1. A simple example

to. As we mentioned above, MST_i could be MST of several implicated graphs, so $P(MST_i)$ is the sum probability of all implicated graphs whose MST is MST_i and can be mathematically quantified as follows.

$$P(MST_i) = \sum_{g \in Imp(G)} P(G \Rightarrow g) \cdot I_1(g) \cdot I_2(g) \tag{2}$$

where $I_1(g)$ and $I_2(g)$ are indicator functions.

$$I_1(g) = \begin{cases} 1 & \text{if } g \text{ is connected} \\ 0 & \text{otherwise} \end{cases}$$

$$I_2(g) = \begin{cases} 1 & \text{if } MST_i \text{ is MST of } g \\ 0 & \text{otherwise} \end{cases}$$

Now we give the formal definition of MST_{max}, that is the MST with maximum probability.

$$MST_{max} = argmax\{P(MST_i)\} \tag{3}$$

In the following example, we show how to exactly compute MST_{max} of uncertain graph G in Fig. 1(a).

Example 2. There are 8 implicated graphs of G as shown in Fig. 1(b), only 4 of them are connected, namely, $g5$, $g6$, $g7$ and $g8$. After computing the MST of

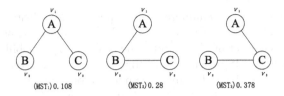

Fig. 2. MST set of graph G

the four subgraphs respectively, we get three different MSTs, MST_1, MST_2 and MST_3 as shown in Fig. 2. The MSTs of $g6$ and $g8$ are actually same to each other, that is MST_2. We can compute the existing probability of MST_i using Eq. (3), $i \in 1, 2, 3$.

$$P(MST_1) = P(\mathcal{G} \Rightarrow g5) = 0.108$$
$$P(MST_2) = P(\mathcal{G} \Rightarrow g6) + P(\mathcal{G} \Rightarrow g8) = 0.028 + 0.252 = 0.28$$
$$P(MST_3) = P(\mathcal{G} \Rightarrow g7) = 0.378.$$

According to Eq. (3), MST_{max} is the MST with largest probability in MST set, which refers to MST_3 in our example, thus we obtain the most reliable MST $MST_{max} = \{AC, BC\}$, and $P(MST_{max}) = P(MST_3) = 0.378$. We denote the cost of MST as $|MST|$, then $|MST_{max}| = |MST_3| = 5 + 2 = 7$.

An intuitive way to compute MST_{max} is to enumerate all implicated subgraphs and compute corresponding MSTs of the connected subgraphs, each MST is with a corresponding existing probability and the one with largest probability is the MST_{max}. Detailed algorithm is shown in Algorithm 1.

Algorithm 1. Naive Algorithm

Input: Uncertain graph $\mathcal{G} = (V, E, P, W)$
Output: The edge set A of MST_{max}

1: $MST\_Edge = \varnothing; MST\_P = 0; MST\_W = 0; Imp = \varnothing;$
2: $map < Edge, (P, W) > MST\_SET$
3: **for** $i \leftarrow 2^{|V|-1} - 1$ to $2^{|E|} - 1$ **do**
4:    Transform i to its binary form, denoted by i_binary // i.e.100111
5:    **if** The number of 1's in i_binary is not smaller than $|V| - 1$ **then**
6:        Add all edges whose index corresponds to 1 in i_binary in Imp
7:        $MST\_P = \prod_{e \in Imp} P(e) \prod_{e' \in E \setminus Imp} (1 - P(e'))$
8:        $MST\_Edge, Imp\_W = Prim(Imp)$
9:        **if** MST_Edge is not in MST_SET **then**
10:            Add $(MST\_Edge, (MST\_P, MST\_W))$ in MST_SET
11:        **else if** MST_Edge is in MST_SET **then**
12:            Modify $P = MST\_P \cdot P$ in original $< Edge, (P, W) >$ pair whose $Edge = MST\_Edge$
13: return $Edge$ with maximum probability in MST_SET

In Naive Algorithm, we enumerate all implicated algorithms and compute MST using Prim algorithm. To find the MST with largest frequency, we use a map whose key is edge set of MST, and value is a pair of probability and weight, the map can hash all MSTs with same edge set together. After computing all MSTs of connected implicated graphs, we find the one with largest probability, that is MST_{max}. There are total $2^{|E|}$ implicated graph of $\mathcal{G}$, the efficiency of the brute-force algorithm is unsatisfactory when applied to large-scale graphs due to its exponential growing rate.

2.3   Edge Induced Combinational Method

According to the definition of most reliable MST in Sect. 2.2, it is not easy to find the most reliable MST in polynomial time. However, we find out another way to compute the probability of MST in a combinational way. Without lose of generality, we suppose that the edge weight is different from the others. For MST_i in MST set, the set of all edges not in MST_i is denoted by R_i, $R_i = E - MST_i$ by definition. For an edge e_i in R_i, adding e_i in MST_i will form a circle due to the connectivity of MST_i. Next we give the definition of safe edge and dangerous edge in R_i.

Definition 1. *Safe edge. For an edge e_i in R_i, it is a safe edge to MST_i if it has largest weight in the circle when adding e_i in MST_i.*

Definition 2. *Dangerous edge. For an edge e_i in R_i, it is a dangerous edge to MST_i if it does not has largest weight in the circle when adding e_i in MST_i, in other words, there exists an edge whose weight is larger than $e_i's$.*

Based on the above definition, we divide the remaining edge set R_i into two separate sets, namely, RS_i and RD_i. All safe edges in R_i are placed in RS_i, and all dangerous edges are in RD_i. Now we move on to give a combinational way to compute the probability of MST_i and we prove that the probability computed in this way is same as that given by Eq. 2.

$$P(MST_i) = \prod_{e_i \in MST_i} p(e_i) \cdot \prod_{e_j \in RD_i} (1 - P(e_j)) \tag{4}$$

Theorem 1. *The probability calculated by Eq. 4 is equal to that obtained by Eq. 2.*

Proof. We only give a sketch of the proof, the detailed proof is omitted due to page limit. Apparently, the MST_i itself is a implicated graph whose MST is MST_i, based on this we can further add any safe edge to MST_i and they will not affect the MST of newly constructed implicated graphs, that is MST_i. This is because safe edge has largest weight in the circle and will be discarded. Further more, we can prove that any dangerous edge added to MST_i will affect the original structure, therefore all edges in RD_i can not exist, which is shown in Eq. 4.

Example 3. BC is a dangerous edge to MST_1, according to Eq. 4, we have $P(MST_1) = P(AB) \cdot P(AC) \cdot (1 - P(BC)) = 0.4 \times 0.9 \times (1 - 0.7) = 0.108$, which is same as the result in Example 2. $P(MST_2)$ and $P(MST_3)$ can be computed in a similar way.

3 Greedy Algorithm

In this section, we present an approximate algorithm of the most reliable MST. The detailed algorithm description is shown in Sect. 3.1 and we analyse the performance of our approximate algorithm in Sect. 3.2. The complexity analysis is in Sect. 3.3.

3.1 Algorithm Description

The greedy algorithm on uncertain graph is similar to Prim algorithm on exact graph. Specifically, given connective uncertain graph $\mathcal{G} = (V, E, P, W)$, we maintain a tree A, which starts from a random root r and spans an edge at each step until A covers all nodes in V. At each step, a *light edge with largest probability* connecting A and an isolated node in $\mathcal{G}_A = (V, A)$ will be added in A, $\mathcal{G}_A = (V, A)$ is a forest whose node set is same to $\mathcal{G}$, but edge set is A. Initially $\mathcal{G}_A = (V, A)$ is a forest with $|V|$ isolated nodes, with the spanning of A, $\mathcal{G}_A$ adds edges in A increasingly. Intuitively A spans an edge whose one endpoint is in A but the other one is not. *light edge* refers to edge with minimum weight in E, the *light edge with largest probability* is defined as follows.

Definition 3. *Light edge with largest probability(LELP). Add all edges connecting A and isolated node in forest $\mathcal{G}_A = (V, A)$ into queue S, sort S by edge weight in ascending order, for the ith edge in S, say e_i, the probability of adding e_i to A is calculated by Eq. 5, denoted by $\widehat{P}(e_i)$, which is called join probability, the edge with largest join probability in S is LELP.*

$$\widehat{P}(e_i) = (\prod_{j=1}^{i-n_i-1} (1 - P(e_j))) \cdot P(e_i) \tag{5}$$

where $1 \leq i \leq |S|$. n_i is the number of edges whose weight is same to the ith edge but position is ahead of it.

The complete algorithm is outlined in Algorithm 2. The input is an uncertain graph $\mathcal{G}$ and the edge set A of MST_{max} is the output. The probability of A is given in Eq. 6, which is the product of the join probability of all edges in A. To gain a better understanding of Algorithm 2, we compute MST_{max} of a simple uncertain graph step by step in the following example.

$$\hat{P}(A) = \prod_{e_i \in A} \hat{P}(e_i) \tag{6}$$

Algorithm 2. Greedy Algorithm

Input: Uncertain graph $\mathcal{G} = (V, E, P, W)$
Output: The edge set A of approximate MST_{max}

1: $MST\_V = \varnothing; A = \varnothing; S = \varnothing; \hat{P}(A) = 1$
2: Randomly select a root node , say r, add it in MST_V
3: Add all edges connected with r in queue S
4: **while** $|MST\_V| < |V|$ **do**
5:     Sort S by weight in ascending order
6:     Calculate the probabality of each edge joinning in A by Eq. 5;
7:     Get the edge with maximum probabiity by max heap, say (u, v)
8:     Add (u, v) in A, suppose u is already in MST_V, v is not,then add v in MST_V
9:     Update $\hat{P}(A) = \hat{P}(A) \cdot \hat{P}(u, v)$
10:     Delete all edges connecting v in S
11:     Add edges whose one endpoint is v but the other endpoint is not in MST_V in S
12: return A

Example 4. The input uncertain graph $\mathcal{G}'$ is in Fig. 3 with four vertexes and four edges, the weight and existence probability are labeled as binary group on edges.

Initially, we select a node randomly, say a, add a in MST_V and add edges connecting a in S, that is (a, b) and (a, h). sort S in ascending order of weight. We calculate the probability for each edge adding in A using Eq. 4. $\hat{P}(a, b) = P(a, b) = 0.8$, $\hat{P}(a, h) = (1 - P(a, b)) \cdot P(a, h) = 0.12$. We maintain a max heap H to obtain the edge with maximum probability, (a, b) in this case. Add (a, b) in A and the new node b in MST_V.

Next adjust S, delete edges which contains vertex b in S, that is (a, b), then add all edges whose one endpoint is b but the other one is not in MST_V, that is (b, h) and (b, c). Sort S again according to edge weight. Compute the probability of edges in S, $\hat{P}(a, h) = P(a, h) = 0.6$, $\hat{P}(b, c) = P(b, c) = 0.2$, $\hat{P}(b, h) = (1 - P(a, h)) \cdot (1 - P(b, c)) \cdot P(a, b) = 0.224$. The edge with largest probability is (a, h), add it to A and vertex h in MST_V and delete (a, h) and (b, h) in S. Only (b, c) is in S, so we add it in A directly and insert vertex c into MST_V, the MST_{max} edge set $A = (a, b)(a, h)(b, c)$, $\hat{P}(MST_{max}) = \hat{P}(a, b) \cdot \hat{P}(a, h) \cdot \hat{P}(b, c) = 0.096$.

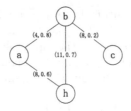

Fig. 3. Uncertain graph G'

3.2 Greedy Selectivity

In this section, we will evaluate the performance of the greedy algorithm we proposed from two aspects, namely, accuracy rate and approximate ratio. To begin with, we analyse the greedy selectivity of our problem.

Suppose we have already known the structure of MST_{max}, that is edges in MST_{max} are given, we can redefine the join probability $\widehat{P}(e_i)$ as Eq. 7. For the ith edge e_i in queue S, we put all edges whose weight is lighter than ei in a set SA_i, $SA_i = \{e_1, e_2 \ldots e_{i-n_i-1}\}$.

$$\widehat{P}'(e_i) = P(e_i) \cdot \Big(\prod_{j=1}^{i-n_i-1} (1 - P(e_j)) + \sum_{k=1}^{|SA_i|} \sum_{e_{z1} \ldots e_{zk} \in SA_i}$$
$$\{ \prod_{x=1}^{x=k} P(e_{zx}) \cdot \prod_{\substack{e_m \neq e_{zj} \\ j \in [1,k] \\ e_m \in SA_i}} (1 - P(e_m)) \cdot I_3(e_{z1} \ldots e_{zk}) \} \Big)$$

(7)

where $I_3(e_{z1} \ldots e_{zk})$ is a indicator, which indicates whether there exists a path from e_{zx} to e_i in MST_{max} so that $w(e_i)$ is smaller than some edge on that path, $x \in [1, k]$. If no such edge exists, another case in which $I_3(e_{z1} \ldots e_{zk}) = 1$ is that there is no path from e_{zx} to e_i for all $x \in [1, k]$.

$$I_3(e_{z1} \ldots e_{zk}) = \begin{cases} 1 & \exists x \in [1, k], w(e_i) \text{ is smaller than} \\ & \text{some edge on the path from } e_{zx} \\ & \text{to } e_i \text{ or } \forall x \in [1, k] \text{ there has no} \\ & \text{path from } e_{zx} \text{ to } e_i \text{ in } MST_{max} \\ 0 & \text{otherwise} \end{cases}$$

We modify line 6 of Algorithm 2 by using Eq. 7 instead of Eq. 5, the other lines remain unchanged. The MST obtained this way is denoted by MST_{new} and the MST obtained by original algorithm is named MST_{old}. The probability of MST_{new} is $P(MST_{new}) = \prod_{e_i \in MST_{new}} \widehat{P}'(e_i)$ and we can prove the following theorem is true. We omit the proof due to the page limit.

Theorem 2. *For 2-connected uncertain graph* $\mathcal{G} = (V, E, P, W)$, MST_{new} *obtained from modified Algorithm 2 is same as* MST_{max} *in Algorithm 1, that is they have the same edge set and their probability and weight are equal. Formally,* $MST_{new} = MST_{max}$, $P(MST_{new}) = P(MST_{max})$ *and* $W(MST_{new}) = W(MST_{max})$

Next we will analyse the performance of the approximate algorithm we proposed in Sect. 3.1. Suppose the queue S contains $\{e_1, e_2, e_3 \cdots \}$ in ascending order of their weight currently, then we have the following lemma.

Lemma 1. *If the existence probability of edge obeys uniform distribution in (0,1), then the probability of* $\widehat{P}'(e_1) > \widehat{P}'(e_k)$ *is at least* $\frac{1}{2}$ *for* $k > 1$.

Proof. $E[P(e_i)] = \frac{1}{2}$, $P(P(e_i) \geq \frac{1}{2}) = \frac{1}{2}$, $P(P(e_i) < \frac{1}{2}) = \frac{1}{2}$, $\widehat{P}'(e_1) = P(e_1)$ and $\widehat{P}'(e_2) = P(e_2)[(1 - P(e_1)) + P(e_1)I_3(e_1)]$, suppose $P(I_3(e_1) = 0) = p_0$.

The first case is that $P(e_1) \geq \frac{1}{2}$ and $P(e_2) \geq \frac{1}{2}$. If $I_3(e_1) = 0$, $\widehat{P}'(e_2) = P(e_2) \cdot (1 - P(e_1)) < \frac{1}{2}P(e_2) < \frac{1}{2} < P(e_1) = \widehat{P}'(e_1)$. However, if $I_3(e_1) = 1$, $\widehat{P}'(e_2) = P(e_2) > \frac{1}{2}$, then $\widehat{P}'(e_1)$ has $\frac{1}{2}$ probability larger than $\widehat{P}'(e_2)$. Thus the probability in this case is $\frac{1}{2} \cdot \frac{1}{2} \cdot [p_0 + (1 - p_0) \cdot \frac{1}{2}]$. The probability in the other three cases can be computed in a similar way. The total probability of $\widehat{P}'(e_1) > \widehat{P}'(e_2)$ is $\frac{1}{2} + \frac{7p_0}{48}$. Besides, the probability of $\widehat{P}'(e_1) > \widehat{P}'(e_k)$ is obviously larger than $\frac{1}{2}$ for $k > 2$.

Theorem 3. *For 2-connected uncertain graphs $\mathcal{G} = (V, E, P, W)$, if the edge probability is independent and identically distributed in $(0, 1)$ uniformly, the greedy algorithm can obtain the accurate MST_{max} with expected probability at least $(1 - (\frac{1}{2})^{d/2})^{|V|-1}$.*

Proof. In our former analysis, we should select an edge e_i with largest $\widehat{P}'(e_i)$ at each step, so that we can obtain the accurate MST_{max}. However, we apply $\hat{P}(e_i)$ in our approximate algorithm, there are two cases that e_i can still be selected in MST_{max}. The first case is that e_i with largest $\widehat{P}'(e_i)$ also has largest $\hat{P}(e_i)$ among all candidate edges in queue S. The second case is that all indicate function $I_3(e_k) = 0$ for $k \in [1, i - 1]$. The expected correct probability for e_i is at least $(\frac{1}{2} + \frac{1}{2} \cdot (1 - (\frac{1}{2})^{(d-1)/2}))$. The detailed proof is omitted due to the page limit.

Theorem 4. *The expected approximate ratio is at least $(\frac{1}{2})^{d|V|}$.*

Proof. We consider the worst case in which $\widehat{P}'(e_i) = P(e_i)$ but $\hat{P}(e_i) = P(e_i) \cdot \prod_{k=1}^{k=i-1}(1 - P(e_k))$, the approximation ratio is $r = \prod_{k=1}^{k=i-1}(1 - P(e_k))$. Due to $P(e_i)$ is independent random variable, we have $E[\prod P(e_i)] = \prod E[P(e_i)]$, hence $E[r] = E[\prod_{k=1}^{k=i-1}(1 - P(e_k))] = \prod_{k=1}^{k=i-1} E[(1 - P(e_k))] = (\frac{1}{2})^{i-1}$, for $|V| - 1$ edges, the ratio is $r^{|V|-1} > (\frac{1}{2})^{d|V|}$

3.3   Complexity Analysis

In this section, we analyse running time in the worst case. We denote the maximum vertex degree as d, it is obvious to see $1 \leq d \leq |V - 1|$, the length of S in ith iteration is denoted as $|S_i|$, then we have the following relations:

$$\begin{cases} |S_1| \leq d \\ |S_{i+1}| \leq (|S_i - 1|) + (d - 1) \end{cases} \tag{8}$$

The general term formula of arithmetic progression is $|S_i| \leq (d - 2) \cdot i + 2 = O(di)$. The total run time is $T(n) = \sum_{i=1}^{|V|}(O(d^2 i) + O(lgdi) + O(1) + O(di) + O(d)) = O(d^2|V|^2)$.

4   Experiments

In this section, we present experimental results studying the effectiveness and efficiency of greedy algorithm.

4.1   Environment and Datasets

Our algorithms were implemented using C++ and the Standard Template Library(STL), and were conducted on a 2.4 GHz Dual Core Intel(R) core(TM) CPU with 2.0 GB RAM running Ubuntu 12.04.

We conduct our experiments on two kinds of synthetic datasets, one of which is generated from real datasets and the other is generated randomly. The first dataset is obtained by assigning a random weight to each edge of real uncertain graphs, the weight is a integer among $[0, 100]$, The real datasets in our experiments are Nature and Flickr, Nature is a protein-protein interaction(PPI) uncertain graph and Flickr is a social network, the scale and connectivity of these two graphs is shown in Table 1, where $N(MST)$ is the number of connected components in graph.

Table 1. Synthetic datasets

Uncertain graph	Graph scale(V,E)	Connectivity	N(MST)
Nature	(2708,7123)	No	63
Flickr	(21594,1008258)	No	1732

The second datasets is generated randomly, to be specific, the edges between vertexes and the edge weight and probability are generated randomly after fixing vertex size, edge weight is a integer among $[0, 100]$ and the probability is among $(0, 0.99]$. We generated three random datasets, the first one is characterized by its average vertex degree, which is 1.23, but the size of vertexes grows from 1k to 10k, we denote this dataset as *man-made1*. The second dataset contains 10 graphs whose vertex sizes are fixed to be 1k, but average vertex degree grows from 3 to 7.5. The third dataset is a set of small uncertain graphs whose vertex size is between 4 to 50 and average degree is 3, we denote it as *man-made3*.

4.2   Analysis of Greedy Algorithm

If the uncertain graph is not connective, we calculate the most reliable forest MSF_{max}. Specifically, when greedy algorithm terminates with a spanning tree A, the vertex size of A is smaller than that of G, we add A in MSF_{max} and randomly select a new root node not in A at the same time, repeat this process until all vertexes in G are covered by MSF_{max}. Next, we analyse the effect of vertex size $|V|$ and average vertex degree $\bar{d}$, as they are two main factor affect the runtime of greedy algorithm.

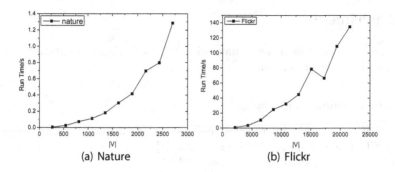

Fig. 4. Execution time with different $|V|$

Effect of $|V|$. In this experiment, we tested the runtime under different graph scales. We extracted subgraphs from 10 % to 100 % of Nature and Flickr and executed greedy algorithm on subgraphs separately. the results are shown in Fig. 4.

Through the curve in Fig. 4, we can see runtime exhibited parabolically trend increase with the $|V|$, which agrees with our theoretical analysis in Sect. 3.3. However, when we look into Fig. 4(b) carefully we find that the runtime at graph scale (17273,102356) is less than that at (15113,97743) , this is because the average vertex degree $\overline{d}$ of graph (17273,102356) is smaller than that of graph (15113,97743). Therefore we tested the effect of $\overline{d}$ on running time in following experiments.

Effects of $\overline{d}$. We ran greedy algorithm on man-made1 dataset, since the average degree on man-made1 is set to be 1.23, we can examine the single effect of $|V|$ on runtime, as shown in Fig. 5(a). The result shows that runtime grows more smoothly when $\overline{d}$ is fixed and no outliers occur. Next we fix $|V|$ and test the effect of $\overline{d}$ on runtime, we apply greedy algorithm on man-made2 dataset whose vertex size is fixed to be 1k and the edge size grows from 3k to7.5k, which means

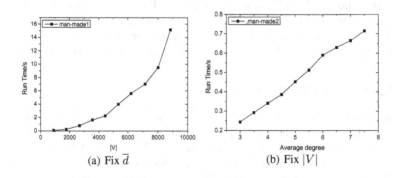

Fig. 5. Execution time with different $\overline{d}$

$\bar{d}$ is in $[3, 7.5]$, the result of this experiment is shown in Fig. 5(b). We can see that runtime grows linearly as $\bar{d}$ increases when $|V|$ is fixed.

Accuracy. To quantify the accuracy of greedy algorithm, we compare probability and weight of resulting MST with the other three algorithms. We conduct our experiment on man-made3 dataset since the time complexity of exact algorithm is in $O(2^{|E|})$. Furthermore, the probability of MST is very small for graphs whose edge existing probability is relatively small, with the increasing of edges in MST, the probability decreases sharply and it is not convenient for us to record and analyse. Hence we amplify the probability of each edge by computing its log value since log function increases monotonically. Here we have the equation $log \prod_i P_i = \sum_i log P_i$.

We design two contrast experiments to see the effectiveness of our proposed greedy algorithm. The first one is adapted Prim algorithm, which obtains the MST with minimum cost by neglecting the probability on each edge. The other one is a random algorithm, we randomly select one edge and add it in MST.

We compare the probability and weight of MSTs obtained from four algorithms, namely, exact algorithm, greedy algorithm, Prim algorithm and Random algorithm, as shown in Fig. 6(a) and (b). From the figures we can see that the probability and weight of MST obtained by greedy algorithm is same as exact algorithm in most cases. Furthermore, greedy algorithm provides a better approximation to exact solution on probability compared with the other two algorithms.

Next we extend our experiment on larger scale graphs without exact algorithm as shown in Fig. 7(a) and (b). We can see greedy algorithm can achieve better probability all the time with a little loss of weight.

Through the experiments conducted above, we come to the following conclusions. First, there are mainly two factors that effect runtime of greedy algorithm, vertex size and vertex degree, furthermore, the grow trend of runtime roughly agrees with our theoretical analysis. Second, our greedy algorithm provides a good approximation to exact algorithm not only on probability but also on weight.

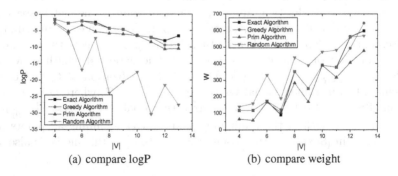

(a) compare logP   (b) compare weight

Fig. 6. Compare exact algorithm and greedy algorithm

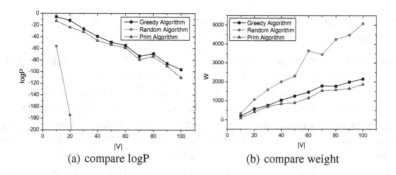

Fig. 7. Compare greedy algorithm and the other two algorithm

5 Related Work

The minimum spanning tree problem have been studied extensively in the literature under the term stochastic geometry. The main work focus on computing the
expected lengths of the MST in stochastic graphs, to the best of our knowledge,
there has no previous work on most reliable MST in uncertain graph. To begin
with, we survey the work about MST in stochastic graph model, specifically, it
mainly includes existential uncertainty model, locational uncertain model and
randomly weighted graph model.

Existential Uncertain Model. Given a complete, weighted undirected graph $G = (V, E)$, on n node and m edges, called the master graph, where each node v_i
is active(or present) with independent probability p_i. When a node is inactive,
all of its incident edges are also absent. We compute the expected minimum
spanning tree cost for G, namely, $\sum p(H)MST(H)$, where the sum is over all
node-induced subgraphs H of G, $p(H)$ is the probability with which H appears,
and $MST(H)$ is the cost of its minimum spanning tree. This problem has been
proven to be #P-hard by Kamousi and Suri in [7].

Locational Uncertainty Model. Given a metric space P. The location of each
node $v \in V$ in the stochastic graph G is a random point in the metric space and
the probability distribution is given as the input. We assume the distributions
are discrete and independent of each other. We use p_{vs} to denote the probability
that the location of node v is point $s \in P$. The expected length of MST is
$E[MST] = \sum_{\mathbf{r} \in R} Pr[\mathbf{r}] \cdot MST(\mathbf{r})$, where $\mathbf{r}$ is a realization of G and can be
represented by an n-dimensional vector $(r_1, \ldots, r_n) \in P^n$, where point r_i is the
location of node v_i for $1 \leq i \leq n$, $\mathbf{r}$ occurs with probability $Pr[\mathbf{r}] = \prod_{i \in [n]} p_{v_i r_i}$,
$MST(\mathbf{r})$ is the length of the minimum spanning tree spanning all points in $\mathbf{r}$.
Huang and Li in [8] showed that computing $E[MST]$ in this model is also #P-
hard.

Randomly Weighted Graph Model . In this model edge weights are independent nonnegative variables, Frieze and Steele in [9,10] showed that the expected

value of the minimum spanning tree on such a graph with identically and independently distributed edges is $\varsigma(3)/D$ where $\varsigma(3) = \sum_{j=1}^{\infty} 1/j^3$ and D is the derivative of the distribution at 0.

Another line is network reliability problem, which computes a measure of network reliability given failure probabilities for the arcs in a stochastic network where each arc can be in either of two states: operative or failed. The state of an arc is a random event that is statistically independent of the state of any other arc. J.Scott has proven that the functional reliability analysis of all-terminal problem is #P-complete in [5].

So far we have quickly reviewed minimum spanning tree problem on stochastic graphs, next we briefly survey problems under the semantic of uncertain. Researchers have studied many kinds of queries on uncertain database, such as Top-k query [12], k-nearest neighbors querey [1], Probabilistic skylines [13]. In addition, lots of work have been done on uncertain graph, including discovering highly reliable subgraphs [14], discovering frequent subgraphs [4] and so on. However, to the best of our knowledge, there is no literature to date on discovering most reliable minimum spanning tree on uncertain graphs. This paper is the first one to investigate this problem.

6   Conclusion

This paper investigates the problem of the most reliable minimum spanning tree on uncertain graph data. The most reliable MST is an optimal choice between stability and cost, which has wide applications in practical. Since accurate algorithms take exponential time to enumerate all possible worlds, an approximate algorithm in polynomial time was proposed to discover an approximate MST and we analysis the accuracy and approximation rate of the approximate algorithm theoretically. The experimental results show that our greedy algorithm has high efficiency and approximation quality.

References

1. Potamias, M., Bonchi, F., Gionis, A., et al.: K-nearest neighbors in uncertain graphs. In: VLDB (2010)
2. Prim, R.C.: Shortest connection networks and some generalizations. Bell Syst. Tech. J. **36**(6), 1389–1401 (1957)
3. Kruskal, J.B.: On the shortest spanning subtree of a graph and the traveling salesman problem. Proc. Am. Math. Soc. **7**(1), 48–50 (1956)
4. Zou, Z., Gao, H., Li, J.: Discovering frequent subgraphs over uncertain graph databases under probabilistic semantics. In: SIGKDD (2010)
5. Provan, J.S., Ball, M.O.: The complexity of counting cuts and of computing the probability that a graph is connected. SIAM J. Comput. **12**(4), 777–788 (1983)
6. Sevon, P., Eronen, L., Hintsanen, P., Kulovesi, K., Toivonen, H.: Link discovery in graphs derived from biological databases. In: Leser, U., Naumann, F., Eckman, B. (eds.) DILS 2006. LNCS, vol. 4075, pp. 35–49. Springer, Heidelberg (2006). doi:10.1007/11799511_5

7. Kamousi, P., Suri, S.: Stochastic minimum spanning trees and related problems. In: ANALCO (2011)
8. Huang, L., Li, J.: Minimum spanning trees, perfect matchings and cycle covers over stochastic points in metric spaces. In: arXiv preprint arXiv (2012)
9. Frieze, A.M.: On the value of a random minimum spanning tree problem. Discret. Appl. Math. **10**(1), 47–56 (1985)
10. Steele, J.M.: On Frieze's (3) limit for lengths of minimal spanning trees. Discret. Appl. Math. **18**(1), 99–103 (1987)
11. Ball, M.O.: Computational complexity of network reliability analysis: an overview. IEEE Trans. Reliab. **35**(3), 230–239 (1986)
12. Soliman, M.A., Ilyas, I.F., Chang, K.C.-C.: Top-k query processing in uncertain databases. In: ICDE (2007)
13. Pei, J., Jiang, B., Lin, X., et al.: Probabilistic skylines on uncertain data. In: VLDB (2007)
14. Jin, R., Liu, L., Aggarwal, C.C.: Discovering highly reliable subgraphs in uncertain graphs. In: SIGKDD (2011)
15. Wu, Y., Fahmy, S., Shroff, N.B.: On the construction of a maximum-lifetime data gathering tree in sensor networks: NP-completeness and approximation algorithm. In: INFOCOM (2008)
16. Manfredi, V., Hancock, R., Kurose, J.: Robust routing in dynamic manets. In: Annual Conference of the International Technology Alliance (2008)

A Block-Based Edge Partitioning for Random Walks Algorithms over Large Social Graphs

Yifan Li[1,2], Camelia Constantin[1], and Cedric du Mouza[2(✉)]

[1] LIP6, University Pierre et Marie Curie, Paris, France
{yifan.li,camelia.constantin}@lip6.fr
[2] CEDRIC Lab., CNAM, Paris, France
dumouza@cnam.fr

Abstract. Recent results [5,9,23] prove that *edge partitioning* approaches (also known as *vertex-cut*) outperform *vertex partitioning* (*edge-cut*) approaches for computations on large and skewed graphs like *social networks*. These vertex-cut approaches generally avoid unbalanced computation due to the *power-law degree distribution* problem. However, these methods, like *evenly random assigning* [23] or *greedy assignment strategy* [9], are generic and do not consider any computation pattern for specific graph algorithm. We propose in this paper a vertex-cut partitioning dedicated to random walks algorithms which takes advantage of graph topological properties. It relies on a blocks approach which captures *local communities*. Our split and merge algorithms allow to achieve load balancing of the workers and to maintain it dynamically. Our experiments illustrate the benefit of our partitioning since it significantly reduce the *communication cost* when performing *random walks*-based algorithms compared with existing approaches.

1 Introduction

Random walks-based algorithms, such as personalized PageRank (PPR) [10] and personalized SALSA [4] have proven to be effective in personalized recommender systems due to their scalability. Some recent proposals rely on multiple random walks started from *each vertex* on graph, *e.g.* Fully personalized PageRanks computation using Monte Carlo approximation [3]. We call this intensive computation Fully Multiple Random Walks (FMRWs).

Graph partitioning is a key area of distributed graph processing research, and plays an increasingly important role in both vertex-centric computation, like in *Pregel* model, and query evaluation. Recent results exhibit that *edge partition (vertex-cut)* turned out to be more efficient [5,9] than traditional vertex partitioning (edge-cut) for computation on real-world graphs like social networks. As a consequence, several popular graph computation systems based on this approach have emerged, such as PowerGraph (GraphLab2) [9] and GraphX [23]. However their graph partitioning strategies are generic and do not depend on the algorithms performing the different computations. So they distribute edges evenly over partitions either randomly, *i.e.* a hash function of vertex ids in Giraph [2]

© Springer International Publishing AG 2016
W. Cellary et al. (Eds.): WISE 2016, Part II, LNCS 10042, pp. 275–289, 2016.
DOI: 10.1007/978-3-319-48743-4_22

and GraphX, or using a greedy or dynamic algorithm like in PowerGraph and GPS [19]. Due to the power-law nature of the Web and social network graphs, this edge allocation may lead to an important workload imbalance between the resources. Besides, in contrast with *light-weight* algorithms like PageRank whose messages transmitted between vertices are only rank values, the simulation of *heavy-communication* algorithms, such as *fully (multiple) random walks* in this paper, have a more important communication cost since (*i*) some extra path-related information of walks must also be delivered, and (*ii*) more than one message (walk) start from each vertex at one time. In this case, reducing communication cost is crucial for computation performance guarantee.

We propose in this paper a novel block-based, workload-aware graph(-edge) partitioning strategy which provides a balance edge distribution and reduce the communication costs for random walks-based computations. To the best of our knowledge, this is the first time a partitioning strategy dedicated to fully multiple random walks algorithms is proposed in Pregel model. Finally, the experiments show that our partitioning made significant improvements on both communication cost and time overhead.

Contributions. In summary, our contributions are:

1. a *block-based* partitioning strategy which considers graph algorithms specificities and the topological properties of real-world large graphs along with a seeds selection algorithm for building the blocks;
2. algorithms for merging and splitting blocks to achieve a dynamical load-balancing of the partitions;
3. an experimental comparison of our partitioning approach with several existing random methods over large real social graphs.

After the related work introduced in Sect. 2, Sect. 3 presents our block building strategy while Sect. 4 describes our blocks merge and refinement algorithms. Section 5 presents our experimental results and Sect. 6 concludes and introduces perspectives.

2 Related Work

Pregel [16] has become a popular distributed graph processing framework due to the facilities it offers to the developers for large-graph computations, especially compared with other data-parallel computation systems, *e.g.* Hadoop. Pregel is inspired by *Bulk Synchronous Parallel* [21] computation model where computations on a graph consists of several iterations, also called *super-steps*. During a super-step, each vertex first receives all the messages which were addressed to it by other vertices in the previous super-step. Each vertex performs the actions defined by user-specific function, namely *vertex.compute()* [19] or *vertex.program()* [9], in parallel, using the updated values received in the messages. Then each vertex may decide to halt computing or to pass to other vertices the messages to be used in next super-step. When there is no message transmitted over graph during a super-step (*i.e.* every vertex has decided to halt) the computation stops. Due to *Pregel* success, several optimizations have been recently proposed in literature like the function *Master.compute()* [19] to incorporate global computations or *Mirror Vertices* [14] to reduce communication.

Traditional methods from 2-way cut by local search to multi-level approaches, like Kernighan-Lin [12], PageRank Vectors [1] and METIS-based [11] algorithms, follow a vertex-partitioning (edge-cut) strategy. They propose partitionings which assign (almost) evenly vertices between partitions while minimizing the number of edges cut (edges between two partitions). These algorithms are efficient for small graphs, using in-memory computation. However for real world graphs the large size and the power-law distribution lead to an unbalanced load over edge-cut partitions. More recent partitioning proposals in Pregel-like systems, such as Giraph, GPS, Gelly and Chaos [18] shard the graph using an *edge-cut* strategy which also generates unbalancing for power-law graphs, as introduced in [9].

While there exists a large literature and several implementations for vertex-partitioning, few recent works propose edge-partitioning. The two principal ones are GraphX [23] and PowerGraph [9]. However GraphX only offers random/hash partitioning where edges are evenly allocated over partitions with some constraints of communication between nodes. The underlying graph property, like *local communities in social networks*, is not properly explored. Unlike the hash-like partitioning, PowerGraph uses a heuristic partitioning method, *Greedy Vertex-Cuts*, which has shown significant better performance than random placement in any cases [9]. However, it also ignores the graph topological property and only focus on how to minimize the future communication on previous partitioning situation during edges distribution among partitions. Additionally, unlike our proposal, GraphX and PowerGraph partitionings can not be updated dynamically with graph evolution.

Our approach also takes advantage from the existence of communities. In [8] authors state that, due to the heavy-tailed degree distributions and large clustering coefficients properties in social networks, considering only the direct neighbors of a vertex allows to construct good clusters (communities) with low conductance. In [22] authors improve this method to detect communities over graph, but neither edge partitioning nor workload balancing problem is studied. Moreover, the overlapping communities approach for graph partitioning are not suitable to Pregel-like systems.

3   Block-Based Graph Partitioning

3.1   Principle

Most existing edge partitioning methods, like random [23] or greedy [9] approaches achieve a balanced workload, which means each partition has the same number of edges. Our objective is to go beyond workload balancing and to lower graph processing time by reducing the communication between partitions during graph computation. In *edge-partitioning* approach, a vertex is possibly allocated to multiple partitions and communications between partitions occur when updating the different replicas (mirror vertices) at each Pregel super-step. Consequently, Vertex Replication Factor (VRF) firstly defined in [9] is often used as a communication measurement. So, given an edge partitioning, the communication cost is generally estimated in Pregel, as

$$cost_{Comm} = O(L \times (VRF \times |V|)) \tag{1}$$

where L is the number of supersteps (iterations) during graph computation.

However, in most real graphs, like social networks, there exist many clusters (communities). Our objective is to take advantage of this topological characteristic in our block construction. *Local Access Pattern (LAP)* is described in [24] for first time as one of three kinds of query workload in graphs. We propose to rely on its principles and analysis when proposing our edge-partitioning strategy for random walks-based algorithms considering graph communities to reduce communication costs.

As a consequence we consider that, while VRF is a good estimator of communication cost for some graph algorithms, it is not suitable for the random walks-based algorithms which follow a LAP, since the number of visits of each vertex is different for these algorithms. In other words, communications are conducted unevenly on graph. So our objective is to design a new edge partitioning strategy dedicated to random walks-based algorithms which takes into consideration both the power-law topology of the graph and the LAP characterizing these algorithms.

Our Approach. A block corresponds to a tightly knit cluster in graph, *e.g.* a community in social network. In the *Pregel* approach, we consider the block as a set of edges which are "close" one to another, and these blocks become the component units of each partition in computation, but also the allocation units for workload over machines. Similar to the methodology adopted in vertex partitioning [8,22], we propose to compute a set of K blocks by exploring the graph. An edge is allocated to a block based on its connectivity score from this block. We start a breadth-first search exploration (BFS) from a pre-defined set of K seeds. For each edge encountered we update its connectivity score with respect to all blocks. When the exploration step ended, we allocate the edges to the closest block.

3.2   Connectivity Score of an Edge

In graph computation, how to measure the closeness between a pair of nodes is a fundamental question and it has been studied in many existing works. One interest of these connectivity score measures is to detect cluster in graph (see Sect. 3.3). But based on the observation that for several graph algorithms like random walk, nearest neighbors, breadth-first search, etc., the communications during computations mainly occur between vertices belonging to the same cluster, several approaches extended this cluster detection to perform graph partitioning. For instance [1] proposed a PageRank vector method to find a "good" partition w.r.t. an initial vertex and several pre-set configurations. Besides, there are some proposals like [20] which describes how to obtain these partitions by conducting random walks.

For our edge-partitioning approach, we propose here to estimate the *connectivity score* between an edge and a *query* vertex, e.g. the seed in our paper. We adapt the inverse P-distance [10] used for connectivity score computation between two vertices.

Vertex to Vertex Connectivity Score. Inverse P-distance captures the connectivity: the more numerous and short paths between two vertices, the closer they are in graph topology.

So, the connectivity score $conn_v(i,j)$ from vertex i to vertex j in a directed graph G can be calculated by the paths between them, as follows:

$$conn_v(i,j) = \sum_{p \in P_{ij}} S(p) \tag{2}$$

where the P_{ij} denotes the set of paths from i to j. $S(p)$ is the inverse distance score value of path p defines below.

According to the idea of inverse P-distance score, we introduce the concept of "reachability" into connectivity score computation between vertices. The reachability means the probability for a random walk starting from i to arrive at j. So, for path p: $v_0, v_1, ..., v_{(k-1)}$ with length k, $S(p)$ can be defined by:

$$S(p) = (1-\alpha)^k \cdot \prod_{i=0}^{k-1} \frac{1}{outDeg(v_i)} \tag{3}$$

where $\alpha \in (0,1)$ is the teleporting probability, *i.e.*, the probability to return to the original vertex, and $outDeg(v_i)$ is the out-degree of vertex v_i.

Vertex to Edge Connectivity Score. Based on the vertex to vertex connectivity score introduced above, we define a vertex to edge connectivity score. We adopt the following definition:

Definition 1 (Edge connectivity score). *The connectivity score $conn_e(a,b)$ from a vertex a to an edge $b = (i,j)$ is:*

$$conn_e(a,b) = \theta(conn_v(a,i), conn_v(a,j))$$

where θ is an aggregation function.

In our experiment we choose the average function for θ but other functions like *min* or *max* may also be considered.

3.3   Edges Allocation Algorithm

Based on our edge connectivity score we can now design an edge allocation algorithm. Our algorithm can be decomposed into three steps:

  (i) selection of a subset of vertices, namely *seeds*
  (ii) connectivity score computation from each edge to all the seeds
  (iii) edges allocation to the different blocks

Seeds Selection. We consider for our block-partitioning a seed-expansion strategy: we select a vertex as seed for each block and add each edge to one of the existing blocks. Obviously the result of the partitioning, in term of size-balancing or communication during the computation, is highly dependent on the choice of the seeds. This problem has been studied in literature for instance in [22] to detect communities on graph or in [7] where authors propose and experiment for the pre-computation step of their recommendation algorithm several landmark selection strategies.

Here we adopt the simple but efficient seeds selection procedure, based on *Spread Hubs* method (see [22]), which can be easily deployed on existing graph processing systems. There are two main measurements we used in seeds selection: (1) vertex degree, and (2) connectivity score to other existing seeds. Our seeds selection algorithm is:

1. first we sort the vertices in ascending order, according to their global (in + out) degrees;
2. then we scan the sorted list of vertices, and check if the current one is not *too close* to any existing seed, otherwise we discard it.

The rationale for this algorithm is that a vertex with a large global degree is a vertex with a centrality property and its connected vertices are likely to join its block. Moreover observing a minimum connectivity score between seeds allows a better distribution of the seeds within the graph. Since BFS is efficiently implemented in Pregel, we use it to measure the *distance* between seeds. So we start a BFS from the seed candidate and report the number of hops required to reach the first existing seed. We observe experimentally that we achieve a good partitioning with this algorithm even when the depth of each seed's BFS is set to 1 (so a new seed is not allowed to be the direct neighbor of an existing seed).

Number of Seeds. In our approach, each seed will determine a block which implies to have at least as many seeds as the number of final partitions. However we argue that we can achieve a better partitioning when setting this number to a larger value because:

- the *expansion* of each block can be processed independently, thus can be deployed easily on Pregel-like architecture;
- the combination of small blocks needs *much less* overhead cost than splitting (*i.e.*, refinement) of large blocks when trying to minimize the VRF;
- the more blocks we pre-computed, the higher the level of reusability our partitioning will be.

Connectivity Score Computation. For the second step of our algorithm, we compute first the distance scores of each vertex to all seeds. To perform this connectivity score computation efficiently in our Pregel-like architecture, we proceed to a parallel BFS exploration starting from each seed. Consider a set of seeds $S = (s_1, s_2, \ldots, s_N)$. We maintain for each vertex ν a connectivity score vector $conn(\nu) = (d_1, d_2, \ldots, d_N)$ where $d_i = conn_\nu(s_i, \nu)$ is connectivity score to the seed s_i. This vector is updated for each vertex encountered during the BFS exploration.

Since the BFS exploration in large graphs is very costly, we propose to limit the depth of BFS. Indeed we observe in most of the large graphs (like social graphs) a community phenomenon which we capture by selecting the seeds among the vertices with the largest degrees, representing the center of these communities. Intuitively, the distance from the community center is short to other vertices inside the community. Actually, from our experiment results and "Six Degrees of Separation" theory [17], we observe that the *radius of block*, *i.e.*, the connectivity score from seed to potential community members is small and consequently the BFS depth can be set to a small value.

For instance, during the experiment on Livejournal [13] social network, we found the vertex/edge coverages of 200 seeds can reach around 88 % and 96 % by limiting the BFS only to 3 and 4 hops respectively.

Finally we compute a connectivity score vector for each edge in the graph. Consider an edge $e(\nu, \nu')$ and the connectivity score vectors for its vertices $conn(\nu) = (d_1, d_2, \ldots, d_N)$ and $conn(\nu') = (d'_1, d'_2, \ldots, d'_N)$. Based on Definition 1 we compute the edge connectivity score vector $conn(\varepsilon) = (D_1, D_2, \ldots, D_N)$ as:

$$\forall i \in [1..N], \ D_i = conn_e(s_i, \varepsilon)$$

Edges Allocation. Finally we can allocate the different edges to the blocks according to their edge connectivity score vector. We decide that an edge belongs to the block whose seed is the *closest* to this edge. For edges without any connectivity score value (which means its end vertices have not be reached by any seed during the BFS step), we allocate them in an extra-block.

Example 1. We illustrate the *edge allocation* process with the example in Fig. 1. We assume we have already computed the vertex connectivity score vectors for vertices i and j, considering three seeds s1, s2 and s3. Notice that the '*' value means that the current vertex can not be reached by the seed s_3 in our BFS exploration step. We sum (or make the average) the two vectors to determine the edge connectivity score vector for $e(i, j)$: $conn(i, j) = (0.64 + 0.53, 0.61 + 0.88, 0.62 + 0.0) = (1.17, 1.49, 0.62)$. Here we can clearly point out that the edge e should be allocated to s2 since it has maximum closeness value to this seed.

Observe that some optimizations are possible for storing the vertex connectivity score vectors and for the edge connectivity score vector computation. For instance we can avoid keeping all connectivity score values to every seed, since

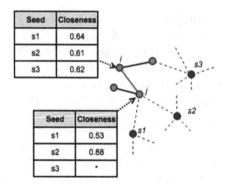

Seed	Closeness
s1	0.64
s2	0.61
s3	0.62

Seed	Closeness
s1	0.53
s2	0.88
s3	•

Fig. 1. Example of edge allocation

in this *edge allocation* step, only the maximum value is used to allocate an edge to a block. So we could keep only a *top-k* values for each vertex, with $k \leq |\mathcal{S}|$. Of course the larger k is, the more precise our final result is.

4   Blocks Merge and Refinement Algorithms

Our block partitioning respects the topological properties of the (social) graph, *e.g.* local communities and power-law degree distribution to significantly reduce the communication costs compare to a random allocation strategy.

Given a number of servers P, we must determine how to allocate the different blocks to these servers considering two criteria:

– minimizing the global communication cost;
– balancing the storage and computation workload between servers.

These conditions can be captured by Definition 2.
The first part of the definition allows to control the size of a partition to fit the server capacity and to have an almost balanced edges distribution. The second part of the definition means the partitioning $\mathcal{A}$ is the one which minimizes the *Vertex Replication Factor* (VRF). The VRF measure adopted for instance in [9] means the less partitions the vertex span on average, the less communication across partitions the system initiates for vertices synchronization before running into the next superstep. With respect to Definition 2 we can proceed to the final partitioning based on the different blocks we built.

Definition 2 (Balanced edge partitioning). *Consider a graph $G(V,E)$ where V is the set of vertices and E the set of edges, a set of blocks $\mathcal{B}$ and a number of servers P. The balanced edge partitioning $\mathcal{A}(\mathcal{B}, P)$ is defined as:*

$$\mathcal{A}(\mathcal{B}, P) \in 2^{\mathcal{B}}, \ such \ that \begin{cases} \forall i \in [1..P], \eta\frac{|E|}{P} \leq |Edge(p_i)| \leq \lambda\frac{|E|}{P} \\ \\ \forall \mathcal{A}' \in 2^{\mathcal{B}} \ satisfying \ above, \\ \frac{1}{|V|}\sum_{v\in V}|alloc(v, \mathcal{A})| \leq \frac{1}{|V|}\sum_{v\in V}|alloc(v, \mathcal{A}')|, \\ otherwise, \ relax \ \eta \ and(or) \ \lambda \ to \ find \ the \ \mathcal{A}. \end{cases}$$

where p_i is a partition (server) and $Edge(p_i)$ the edges it contains, $alloc(e, \mathcal{A})$ is the set of partitions to which edge e is assigned with the partitioning $\mathcal{A}$ (more than one if the vertex is replicated) and $(0 \leq \eta \leq 1 \leq \lambda)$ are small factors to control the storage in each partition.

Block Split. Since the edges allocation to blocks is only based on a connectivity score criterium some blocks may not fit the maximum size allowed for a partition (second part of Definition 2). Consequently we propose a simple split strategy. Assume that the size of a partition p_i is $(\beta - 1)\lambda\frac{|E|}{P} \leq |Edge(p_i)| < \beta\lambda\frac{|E|}{P}$. We then apply our block building algorithm to the partition p_i with β seeds to split it into β sub-blocks. We potentially iterate the process for any of the sub-blocks which exceeds the partition size.

Blocks Merge. Our block building may also result in producing some blocks whose size is lower than the minimal size (*i.e.* $\eta\frac{|E|}{P}$, see Definition 2). For such a block we re-allocate its edges without considering its seed anymore. Observe that this may lead in turn to some block splits.

Block Allocation. We assume that, possibly after some required splits, the size of all blocks respect the partition size limit. To allocate the blocks to the different partitions, two strategies may be considered: based only on the balancing of the partition sizes, or on minimizing the replication factor between partitions.

Considering this latter approach, we exhibit the following drawbacks: (1) there is an exponential complexity for finding the best blocks allocation considering this criterion, (2) the final size of each partition may highly differ one from another, (3) reducing the global replication factor will not reduce that much the cost of the random-walks algorithms since a path starting in one block and finishing in another is unlikely (according to our blocks building) and finally (4) this partitioning could not evolve dynamically and the partitioning must be re-built when many edges are added or removed.

Consequently we decide to adopt a blocks allocation considering only the size criterion, to achieve a balanced partitioning. We propose a simple but efficient *greedy* algorithm. We allocate the largest block to the partition with the smallest size, and we iterate this strategy until all blocks are allocated. Consequently this allocation is in $O(|\mathcal{B}|)$ where $\mathcal{B}$ represents the set of blocks.

The whole algorithm is presented in Algorithm 1 where *split* refers to a function which proceeds to the block split introduced above, *sortSize* is a function which sorts a set of blocks according to their size, from the largest to the smallest one, and *first* returns the first element from an ordered set.

Managing Graph Dynamicity. Large graphs, especially for social network applications, are often characterized by a high dynamicity. One important aspect of our partitioning algorithm is its ability to manage this dynamicity. Indeed when adding a new edge (for instance when adding a friend on Facebook or an

---

Algorithm 1. Block allocation algorithm

---

    input : a set $\mathcal{B} = \{b_1, \ldots, b_n\}$ of blocks, a set $\mathcal{P} = \{p_1, \ldots, p_m\}$ of partitions
    output: each block is allocated to a $p_j \in \mathcal{P}$

1 // Initialization to avoid large blocks
2 $\mathcal{B}' = \emptyset$
3 **foreach** b_i *in the* $\mathcal{B}$ **do**
4   **if** $b_i.size > \lambda \frac{|E|}{n}$ **then**
5 | $\mathcal{B}' = \mathcal{B}' \cup split(b_i)$
6   **end**
7     $\mathcal{B}' = \mathcal{B}' \cup b_i$
8 **end**
9 // Sort the set of blocks in descending size order
10 $\mathcal{B}' = sortSize(\mathcal{B}')$
11 $b = first(\mathcal{B}')$; **while** $\mathcal{B}' \neq \emptyset$ **do**
12     $p_i = smallest(\mathcal{P})$;
13     $p_i = merge(p_i, b)$; //merge b with the smallest partition
14     $\mathcal{B}' = \mathcal{B}' - \{b\}$;
15     $b = first(\mathcal{B}')$;
16 **end**
17 Return $\mathcal{P}$;

---

url on a Website) we simply have to aggregate the two vertex connectivity score vectors of the two vertices of the edge if both vertices were already present in the graph to compute its edge connectivity score vector. Then we allocate the edge to the block, and consequently to the partition, with the highest connectivity score score. If one of the vertices is new, we have first to perform the BFS exploration from that vertex and compute its vertex connectivity score vector. Potentially this edge allocation may lead to a block split which can be handled with our split algorithm. Oppositely when removing an edge, the size of a block may become too small and we proceed to our block merge algorithm.

5   Experiments

This section presents experiments on our block-based partitioning strategy. We compare it with existing edge partitioning methods: the hash-based approaches [23] and greedy algorithm [9].

5.1 Setting

Computation are performed using GraphX [23] APIs in Spark [25] (version 1.3.1), on a 16 nodes cluster. Each machine has 22 cores with 60 GB RAM running Linux OS. For our experiments we set teleporting probability α to a classical value 0.15. The depth of the BFS exploration (*i.e.*, the maximum length considered for paths from seed to other vertices).

Data Sets . We validate our approach on two datasets: LiveJournal [6] with 4.8M vertices and 68.9M edges, and Pokec [15] with 1.6M vertices and 30.6M edges. These datasets can be downloaded from *SNAP* [1].

Competitors . *Hash Partitioning*. There are four wide used random(hash)-like partitioning methods[2], introduced in GraphX:

– RandomVertexCut: allocates edges to partitions by hashing the source and destination vertex IDs.
– CanonicalRandomVertexCut: allocates edges to partitions by hashing the source and destination vertex IDs in a canonical direction.
– EdgePartition1D: allocates edges to partitions using only the source vertex ID, co-locating edges with the same source.
– EdgePartition2D: allocates edges to partitions using a 2D partitioning of the sparse edge adjacency matrix.

Greedy Vertex-Cuts. PowerGraph proposes a greedy heuristic for edge placement process which relies on the previous allocation of vertices to determine the partition next edge should be assigned.

5.2   Communication

Our approach aims at reducing the runtime graph processing thanks to a significant reduction of the communication costs.

Vertex Replica Factor (VRF). VRF is the traditional way to compare two partitionings regarding the communication costs, independently of the algorithm executed. We compare the VRF of our *Block-based* partitioning with the one of the competitors for different numbers of partitions. Results are depicted on Fig. 2. We observe that, as observed in [9], partitioning strategies based on topology outperform as expected hash-based methods: VRF decreased by 30–60 % (resp. 60–80 %) for Powergraph (resp. our block strategy) compare to the strategies used in GraphX. This experiment also illustrates the benefit of our global approach for edge allocation compare to a greedy approach with on average a 40 %-lower VRF.

Number of Messages. VRF is a general criterion to compare two partitioning strategy independently from the algorithms, but we expect our partitioning to exhibit even better results for random walks-based algorithms. Consequently to estimate the benefit of our approach we simulate fully multiple random walks (FMRW) and we measure the number of messages exchanged between partitions. From each vertex we perform 2 random walks of length 4 and we report

---

[1] https://snap.stanford.edu/data/index.html.
[2] See details and implementations at http://spark.apache.org/docs/latest/api/scala/index.html.

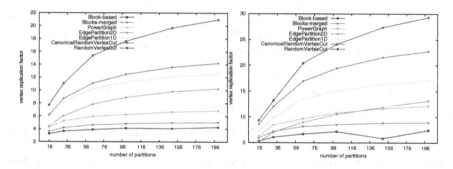

Fig. 2. VRF w.r.t. edge partitioning methods on LiveJournal (left) and Pokec (right)

experimental results in Table 1. We observe that our method reduces significantly the number of messages exchanged between partitions. For instance with 100 partitions, 61.8 million messages are necessary for processing the FMRW with our method while 381.9 million are transmitted with Random-Vertex-Cut method, so a drop of 84 %. This result was expected since the VRF is 3–4 times lower with our method than with Random-Vertex-Cut. But we notice that if the reduction of the number of messages and of the VRF were proportional, the system should exchange 89.4 million message. This 30 % gain in the number of messages transmitted validates our intuition that random walks intend to stay in the local cluster (community). So low-replicated vertices (close to the seed in block) are accessed more times, and oppositely few random walks reach the farthest, high-replicated, vertices. Similar results are obtained from experiments on Pokec.

Table 1. Messages transmitted in FMRW (LiveJournal)

#Partitions	Random-vertex-cut [23]		Block-based partitioning			
	VRF	Real mess	VRF	Real mess	Expected mess	Ratio
64	15.38	303.5 m	3.90	55.3 m	76.9 m	0.72
100	17.61	381.9 m	4.13	61.8 m	89.4 m	0.69
150	19.68	464.8 m	4.07	70.6 m	96.1 m	0.73
200	21.12	525.6 m	4.26	76.0 m	106.0 m	0.72

5.3   Runtimes

We propose to evaluate how the runtime of different graph processing algorithms benefits our partitioning, compared to other methods. First, we launch FMRW, a heavy-communication algorithm, on LiveJournal and Pokec datasets respectively, with 3 random walks of length 4 started from each vertex. From the results

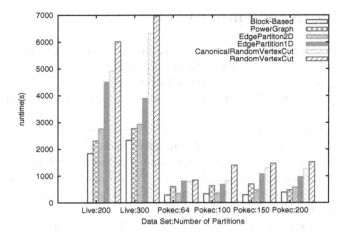

Fig. 3. Runtimes for FMRW with different partitionings for LiverJournal and Pokec

in Fig. 3, we see that our partitioning can save up between from 20 to 65 % of runtime, compared with other partitionings, for both datasets.

We also test our method with traditional PageRank algorithm. We consider the static (fixed number of iterations) and dynamical (with convergence and a threshold value) approaches. We consider there are 200 partitions and we proceed to resp. 30, 50 and 100 iterations for static PageRank and to dynamical PageRank with resp. 0.005 and 0.001 convergence factor. Figure 4 depicts results and confirms that our partitioning method outperforms other ones. While we observe a small 5–20 % gain for the static implementation of PageRank, we reach a 20–55 % gain for the dynamical implementation.

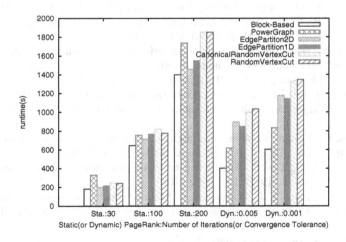

Fig. 4. Runtimes for static and dynamic PageRank for LiverJournal

6   Conclusion and Future Work

We present in this article a vertex-cut partitioning for random-walks-based algorithms relying on the topology to build blocks which respect local communities. We propose *split* and *merge* algorithms to get and to maintain the final partitioning. We experimentally demonstrate that our proposal outperforms existing solutions.

As future work we plan to investigate different seeds selection algorithms. While this problem has been studied in different contexts (see [7,22]) we believe that the nature of the graph algorithms, here random walks-based algorithms, must be considered when selecting the seeds. We also intend to study the 5–10 % of vertices which are not reached by the BFS exploration issued at seeds. They are located on the periphery of social graph and are poorly connected. While we currently place them to an extra-block, we will design a strategy to allocate them to existing blocks.

References

1. Andersen, R., Chung, F., Lang, K.: Local graph partitioning using PageRank vectors. In: FOCS, pp. 475–486 (2006)
2. Apache. Giraph. http://giraph.apache.org
3. Bahmani, B., Chakrabarti, K., Xin, D.: Fast personalized PageRank on MapReduce. In: SIGMOD, pp. 973–984 (2011)
4. Bahmani, B., Chowdhury, A., Goel, A.: Fast incremental and personalized PageRank. Proc. VLDB Endow. **4**(3), 173–184 (2010)
5. Bourse, F., Lelarge, M., Vojnovic, M.: Balanced graph edge partition. In: SIGKDD, pp. 1456–1465 (2014)
6. Chierichetti, F., Kumar, R., Lattanzi, S., Mitzenmacher, M., Panconesi, A., Raghavan, P.: On compressing social networks. In: SIGKDD, pp. 219–228 (2009)
7. Dahimene, R., Constantin, C., du Mouza, C.: RecLand: a recommender system for social networks. In: CIKM, pp. 2063–2065 (2014)
8. Gleich, D.F., Seshadhri, C.: Vertex neighborhoods, low conductance cuts, and good seeds for local community methods. In: SIGKDD, pp. 597–605 (2012)
9. Gonzalez, J.E., Low, Y., Gu, H., Bickson, D., Guestrin, C.: PowerGraph: distributed graph-parallel computation on natural graphs. In: OSDI, pp. 17–30 (2012)
10. Jeh, G., Widom, J.: Scaling personalized web search. In: WWW, pp. 271–279 (2003)
11. Karypis, G., Kumar, V.: A fast and high quality multilevel scheme for partitioning irregular graphs. SIAM J. Sci. Comput. **20**(1), 359–392 (1998)
12. Kernighan, B.W., Lin, S.: An efficient heuristic procedure for partitioning graphs. Bell Syst. Techn. J. **49**(2), 291–307 (1970)
13. Leskovec, J., Lang, K.J., Dasgupta, A., Mahoney, M.W.: Community structure in large networks: natural cluster sizes and the absence of large well-defined clusters. Internet Math. **6**, 29–123 (2008)
14. Low, Y., Bickson, D., Gonzalez, J., Guestrin, C., Kyrola, A., Hellerstein, J.M.: Distributed GraphLab: a framework for machine learning and data mining in the cloud. VLDB Endow. **5**(8), 716–727 (2012)

15. Lubos Takac, M.Z.: Data analysis in public social networks. In: Present Day Trends of Innovations, pp. 1–6 (2012)
16. Malewicz, G., Austern, M.H., Bik, A.J.C., Dehnert, J.C., Horn, I., Leiser, N., Czajkowski, G.: Pregel: a system for large-scale graph processing. In: SIGMOD, pp. 135–146 (2010)
17. Newman, M., Barabasi, A.-L., Watts, D.J., Structure, T.: Dynamics of Networks: (Princeton Studies in Complexity). Princeton University Press, Princeton (2006)
18. Roy, A., Bindschaedler, L., Malicevic, J., Zwaenepoel, W.: Chaos: scale-out graph processing from secondary storage. In: SOSP, pp. 410–424 (2015)
19. Salihoglu, S., Widom, J.: GPS: a graph processing system. In: SSDBM, pp. 22:1–22:12 (2013)
20. Sarkar, P., Moore, A.W.: Fast nearest-neighbor search in disk-resident graphs. In: SIGKDD, pp. 513–522 (2010)
21. Valiant, L.G.: A bridging model for multi-core computing. J. Comput. Syst. Sci. **77**(1), 154–166 (2011)
22. Whang, J.J., Gleich, D.F., Dhillon, I.S.: Overlapping community detection using seed set expansion. In: CIKM, pp. 2099–2108 (2013)
23. Xin, R.S., Gonzalez, J.E., Franklin, M.J., Stoica, I.: GraphX: a resilient distributed graph system on spark. In: GRADES, pp. 1–6 (2013)
24. Yang, S., Yan, X., Zong, B., Khan, A.: Towards effective partition management for large graphs. In: SIGMOD, pp. 517–528 (2012)
25. Zaharia, M., Chowdhury, M., Das, T., Dave, A., Ma, J., McCauley, M., Franklin, M.J., Shenker, S., Stoica, I.: Resilient distributed datasets: a fault-tolerant abstraction for in-memory cluster computing. In: NSDI, p. 2 (2012)

Differentially Private Network Data Release via Stochastic Kronecker Graph

Dai Li[1], Wei Zhang[1,2]($\boxtimes$), and Yunfang Chen[1]

[1] College of Computer, Nanjing University of Posts and Telecommunications,
Nanjing, China
zhangw@njupt.edu.cn

[2] Jiangsu High Technology Research Key Laboratory for Wireless Sensor Networks,
Nanjing 210003, Jiangsu, China

Abstract. Excessive sensitivity problem due to complication of data has been a non-negligible challenge to data privacy protection under differential privacy recently. We design a private data release framework called DPDR-SKG (Differentially Private Data Release via Stochastic Kronecker Graph), which focuses on releasing social network data under differential privacy and uses a two-phase privacy budget allocation. Firstly, we cluster the similar communities of network according to Stochastic Kronecker graph parameter. Secondly, we implement optimized privacy budget allocation in terms of cluster distribution. Experimental results show that the DPDR-SKG outperforms in preserving the privacy of network structure and effectively retaining the data utility.

Keywords: Social network graph · Differential privacy · Privacy budget · Network model · Community structure

1 Introduction

Social network data contain lots of valuable and sensitive information. Since Samarti and Sweeney obtained the governor's health information in 1998 by connecting Massachusetts health information table with the voter registration form, personal privacy protection has become the social focal topic [2]. For traditional structural data, the privacy protection models often appear very weak in the face of attacks based on background knowledge. Differential privacy was firstly proposed by Dwork [1] in 2006. It is a new kind of definition for statistical database privacy disclosure issues that whether a single record exists in the data set or not, has almost negligible impact on the calculation results. So, the privacy risks are controlled within the tiny and acceptable scope. The algorithm utilizes parameter ε to denote privacy budget or privacy protection level. The mechanism of differential privacy protection is adding an appropriate amount of interference noise to the query function return value. Existing privacy budget

W. Zhang—Project supported by the National Natural Science Foundation of China under grants 61272422, 61202353.

W. Cellary et al. (Eds.): WISE 2016, Part II, LNCS 10042, pp. 290–297, 2016.
DOI: 10.1007/978-3-319-48743-4_23

allocation methods often can't reflect social network properties and structure. DPDR-SKG is inspired by community features of the social network, then optimizes privacy budget allocation methods, eventually releases network data which satisfies differential privacy.

2   Related Work

Faced with various attacks and analysis methods, some privacy protection methods were proposed, such as K-anonymity [2], but the defects of these protection models gradually revealed because They overly depend on the assumptions of the background knowledge and cannot provide quantitative analysis. In order to solve above problems, Dwork in 2006, brought up the strict concept of differential privacy, privacy risks are controlled within tiny and quantifiable scope, so differential privacy has become a prime choice in data privacy research. Since rigorous concept does not apply to complex data in reality, Dwork et al. [3] presented the extensive optimization concept of global sensitivity: smooth sensitivity for practical application. Zhu [4] defined a new form of sensitivity, the correlated sensitivity.

Social network data release under differential privacy is divided into interactive and non-interactive release. The current data research focuses on the non-interactive release. Meanwhile Karwa and Slavković [5] also studied the network degree sequence differential privacy. So as to better protect the structure of network properties, Sala et al. [6] developed a differentially private graph model called Pygmalion, which can extract graphs structure into degree correlation statistics DK series. DK series maintains as much structural similarity to G as possible, while supporting abundant sub-graph counting queries. Xiao et al. [7] claimed that social network data can be converted to Hierarchical Random Graph (HRG) model, which mixes network structure and statistical inference. Lus work [8] suggests that social network graph can be converted to several parameters of Exponential Random Graph Model (ERGM). Generally protecting network parameters from identification can help protect the privacy of the entire network. Mir and Wright [9] introduced maximum likelihood estimation algorithm to SKG graph model. Our paper also uses SKG model to analyse community structure instead of whole network.

3   Preliminaries

3.1   Definition of Differential Privacy

Definition 1 (Differential Privacy): A randomized algorithm M with domain $N^{|\chi|}$, is (ε, δ)-differentially private for all $S \subseteq Range(M)$ and for all $x, y \in N^{|\chi|}$, the randomized mechanism satisfies:

$$\Pr[M(x) \in S] \leq \exp(\varepsilon) \Pr[M(y) \in S] + \delta \qquad (1)$$

The sensitivity of a function Δf is defined as the maximum difference in function output when one single domain is modified.

Definition 2 (Neighboring Dataset): Given two dataset D and D', they share the same structure and property, $|D\Delta D'|$ indicates the number of records they differ, once $|D\Delta D'| = 1$, we call D and D' neighboring datasets.

Definition 3 (Global Sensitivity): For $f : D \rightarrow R^d$, the global sensitivity of f is defined as

$$GS_f = \max_{D,D'} \|f(D) - f(D')\|_1 \tag{2}$$

3.2 SKG Model

Parametric network model assumes that the observed data is generated by a series of probability estimation, $P = \{f(x, \theta) : \theta \in \Theta\}$, in which θ represents the unknown parameters or vectors from the value space Θ. In this way, the structure and features of network need to be protected by defending the parameters. In the paper, we select SKG (Stochastic Kronecker Graph) model. The graph model effectively captures some key patterns of real-world graphs and can deal with very large and complex networks due to the fast and scalable MLE algorithm.

Definition 4 (Stochastic Kronecker Graph): Given an $N \times N$ matrix: Θ, $\theta_{i,j} \in \Theta$ represents the probability that edge (i, j) exists in the graph, $\theta_{i,j} \in (0, 1)$. Then the k-th Kronecker power $P = \Theta^{[k]}$, is a stochastic matrix where each value $p_{u,v} \in P$ encodes the probability of edge (u, v) appearing. A stochastic graph is generated from the stochastic Kronecker matrix. The calculation of $p_{u,v}$ is as follows:

$$p_{uv} = \prod_{i=0}^{k-1} \Theta \left[\left\lfloor \frac{u-1}{N^i} \right\rfloor (\mathrm{mod}\, N) + 1, \left\lfloor \frac{v-1}{N^i} \right\rfloor (\mathrm{mod}\, N) + 1 \right] \tag{3}$$

Gleich and Owen [10] propose the so-called moment-based estimation of the model parameter, we refer model parameters of the original graph from the observed statistics. Four statistics for matching are considered: number of edges (E), number of triangles (Δ), number of 2-stars (H) and number of 3-stars (T). They consider graphs with a $2*2$ initiator matrix of the form $\hat{\Theta} = \begin{pmatrix} a & b \\ b & c \end{pmatrix}$

Definition 5 (SKG Function): Given an undirected graph G, according to the SKG model, we get the definition of SKG function:

$$SKG(G) : G \rightarrow \hat{\Theta} = \begin{pmatrix} a & b \\ b & c \end{pmatrix} \tag{4}$$

4 Differentially Private Data Release via SKG

Since one social network has been divided into some communities, we convert each community to a single SKG parameter. And then we cluster the communities with the similar SKG parameters into the same group. Afterward, we allocate the privacy budget in the groups according to the number of communities in each group.

4.1   Clustering Communities

We replace a SKG parameter vector of the whole network with a set of SKG parameters vector of the communities, whose advantages are listed below (1) Network structure is better preserved because community structure is simpler and more distinctive than whole network structure; (2) Community treatment ignores the influence of the bridge edges between the communities, and the independence of the sensitivity calculation will be proved in the following section; (3) DPDR-SKG decomposed the parameters model privacy protection into division, each local divisions satisfies differential privacy, so does the whole network.

It is obvious that similar parameters infer the similar network structures, meanwhile SKG parameters are determined by initial matrix. As a consequence, similar initial matrix denotes analogical network structure. The proposed clustering process puts the similar communities indicated by the similar $\hat{\Theta}$, in one group, and the similarity is decided by the Euclidean distance of $\hat{\Theta}$.

Definition 6 ($\hat{\Theta}$ Euclidean Distance): Given a SKG matrix of sizes $N \times N$,

$$\Theta = \begin{pmatrix} a_{11} & \cdots & a_{1n} \\ \vdots & \ddots & \vdots \\ a_{m1} & \cdots & a_{mn} \end{pmatrix}, \Theta_x, \Theta_y \text{ have the same size, the Euclidean Distance is}$$

defined below:

$$d_{x,y} = \sqrt{\sum_{j=1}^{n} \sum_{i=1}^{n} (a_{i,j} - a'_{i,j})^2} \tag{5}$$

We adopt a threshold clustering approach that calculates the Euclidean distance between all parameters and form a distance matrix. After the approach, we can get

$$\{\hat{\Theta}_1, \hat{\Theta}_2, \ldots, \hat{\Theta}_n\} \rightarrow \{\Gamma_1, \Gamma_2 \ldots \Gamma_k\}, k <= n \tag{6}$$

so n communities are clustered into k groups and the distance of any pair communities in one group is less than the threshold.

4.2   Allocating Privacy Budget

The core of the two phase budget allocation is the more communities the group has, the less privacy budget the group needs. In the first phase, privacy budget allocation is mainly based on the number of communities in each group. According to the parallel composition, we assume the whole privacy budget is ε. In the worst situation, we assign the budget to the group who has the least number of communities to make sure that the whole network data are protected under differential privacy. Afterwards, we allocate privacy budget to other groups due to the numbers of communities inside. According to our method, we have the following equations, n_{min} denotes the minimum number of communities in single group:

$$\varepsilon_{\Gamma_i} = \varepsilon \cdot \frac{n_{min}}{n_{\Gamma_i}} \tag{7}$$

Table 1 shows the example of privacy budget allocation. The whole network is divided into 4 groups, consisting of 1, 4, 7, 8 communities. Group A has only 1 community, least number among other groups. According to our method, the budget of Group B is computed, $\varepsilon_B = \varepsilon \cdot \frac{n_{min}}{n_{r_i}} = \frac{\varepsilon}{4}$, group C and group D get privacy budget $\frac{\varepsilon}{7}$ and $\frac{\varepsilon}{8}$.

In the second phase, the privacy budgets are divided based on the community unit. The sensitivity calculation of each community is independent ,the proof is introduced in Sect. 4. We just need to inject some noise to the key statistics to preserve parameter privacy.we give considerations to the structure and numbers of communities inside the group. Each community receives the same privacy budget on account of the similar parameters.

Table 1. Example of privacy budget allocation

Groups	Group A	Group B	Group C	Group D
Community numbers	1	4	7	8
Group budget	ε	0.25ε	0.143ε	0.125ε
Community budget	ε	0.25ε	0.143ε	0.125ε

4.3   Differentially Private Algorithm

We compute a differentially private estimator based on the above theories. Whole privacy budget is divided into 2 parts for private approximation to parameters. One is for injecting noise to E, H, and T by computing approximation to the degree sequence vector of G and the other is for adding noise to the number of triangles in G respectively. Finally, we generate the synthetic graphs using the output estimator and release the data to the public for research purposes.

Lemma 1. *DPDR-SKG meets the definition of edge differential privacy*

Proof. Two situations are discussed below: (1) Edge privacy within communities; (2) Edge privacy between communities. According to [10], the SKG parameters are decided by 2 statistics, which are degree sequence and the numbers of triangle. We need to discuss edge privacy analysis on degree sequence and triangle numbers. The method to inject noise to degree sequence was proposed in [11]. Given an undirected graph community G_C, let d be the degrees sequence of G_C, Hay proposed a method of computing a differentially private approximation d^* of the sorted degree vector d_S by adding a vector of appropriate Laplace noise. Therefore, we compute $(\epsilon, 0)$ -differentially private approximations of E', H', T'. Injecting noise to the numbers of triangle adopts the methods mentioned in [3]. The smooth sensitivity can be used to compute a (ε, δ)-differentially private approximation of Δ. In conclusion, we prove that the computation of (E', H', T', Δ') meets $(2\varepsilon, \delta)$ differentially private within the community.

Assuming that d_{Ci} represents the degree sequence of i-th community, d_{Cj} denotes the j-th community. The proof proceeds by the following the hypothesis: The sensitivity of d_{Ci} is influenced by the changes of d_{Cj}. The augment or removal of single edge only affects the degrees of 2 corresponding nodes. Assuming node m, which has x edges, is in community C_i, node n, which has y edges, is in community C_j, if we add one edge between node m and node n, the degree of m and n becomes $x+1$, $y+1$, the sensitivity of degree sequence of community C_i changes to 1, so does community C_j. The above results are opposite to the hypothesis. Therefore we prove that sensitivity calculation of degree sequence is independent. Triangle consists of three vertices and corresponding 3 edges between vertices. If we remove or add an edge across 2 communities, it has no effect for internal triangle numbers of two communities respectively.

So we conclude that sensitivity calculation of triangle number is also independent. Through the above analysis, our two-phase method definitely meets the definition of differential privacy.   □

5 Experiment Evaluation

In this session, we mainly introduce the performance of proposed methods applied in real datasets. We select 3 real-world data sets, which are WBLOGS, NetScience [12] and BIO [13]. WBLOGS represents the social network graph data. NetScience and Bio-celegans contain a co-authorship network. All data are pre-processed into undirected graph whose edges are un-weighted without self-loops.

In the experiment, we compare DPDR-SKG with other data release approaches, such as HRG and DK-2 models, as well as the original graph data. Due to the randomness, we examine the variances of its performance by running the algorithm ten times on each network and compute various expected statistics. In the following figures, Original refers to the original graph, HRG and DK-2 represents the data release method proposed by [6, 7] respectively. We summarize 3 statistics briefly, Degree distribution, Clustering coefficient and Eccentricity distribution.

Figure 1 shows the degree distributions of the released data under privacy budget $\varepsilon = 1$. It can be seen that, DPDR-SKG protects the properties of both

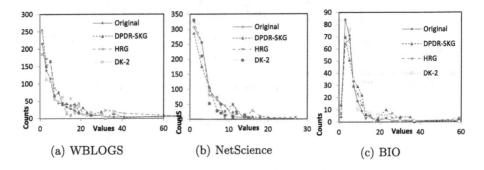

(a) WBLOGS   (b) NetScience   (c) BIO

Fig. 1. Degree distribution, $\varepsilon = 1$

high-degree nodes and low-degree nodes better, comparing with other cases. From the above figures, we observe that released data by 3 methods all perform well and match the original graph.

Figure 2 compares the eccentricity centrality for each graph data. We observe that our method efficiently captures the important nodes locating in the center of the network. By observing our method, we can also see the decrease of long path length. We believe that is due to the influence of edges changed between the communities, but this does not have a big influence on the structure of network.

Figure 3 indicates the average clustering coefficient of released data for each network. We only focus on our method and want to find out how our method responds to different privacy budgets. To be fair, we also plot the graph data without injecting noise, and change $\varepsilon = 0.5\ 1\ 5\ 10\ 100$. It can be observed that the average clustering coefficient of released data matches closely with original graph with small privacy budget. When we increase the privacy budget, the accuracy varies greatly and the statistics arent stable and robust, which destroys the utilization of released data. For privacy concerns, it is better to limit privacy budget to small scale, our method performs well with robustness.

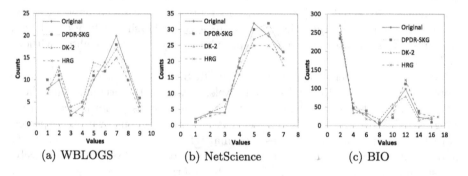

(a) WBLOGS   (b) NetScience   (c) BIO

Fig. 2. Eccentricity distribution

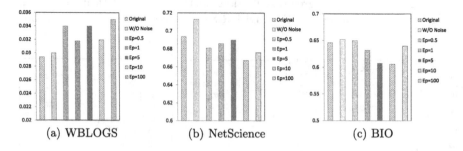

(a) WBLOGS   (b) NetScience   (c) BIO

Fig. 3. Average clustering coefficient

6 Conclusions

We propose a graph mechanism to release graph data while protecting individual privacy. The results of experiments show that our method not only effectively protect the original structure of the network graph, but also guarantee the utilization of released data. There are several research directions for future work. For example, we intend to find more suitable graph models, such as ERGM. Furthermore, the privacy allocation strategy can still be optimized to achieve higher accuracy.

References

1. Dwork, C.: Differential privacy. In: Bugliesi, M., Preneel, B., Sassone, V., Wegener, I. (eds.) ICALP 2006. LNCS, vol. 4052, pp. 1–12. Springer, Heidelberg (2006)
2. Sweeney, L.: Achieving k-anonymity privacy protection using generalization and suppression. Int. J. Uncertain. Fuzziness Knowl.-Based Syst. **10**(05), 571–588 (2002)
3. Dwork, C., McSherry, F., Nissim, K., Smith, A.: Calibrating noise to sensitivity in private data analysis. In: Halevi, S., Rabin, T. (eds.) TCC 2006. LNCS, vol. 3876, pp. 265–284. Springer, Heidelberg (2006)
4. Zhu, T., Xiong, P., Li, G., Zhou, W.: Correlated differential privacy: hiding information in non-IID data set. IEEE Trans. Inf. Forensics Secur. **10**(2), 229–242 (2015)
5. Karwa, V., Slavković, A.B.: Differentially private graphical degree sequences and synthetic graphs. In: Domingo-Ferrer, J., Tinnirello, I. (eds.) PSD 2012. LNCS, vol. 7556, pp. 273–285. Springer, Heidelberg (2012)
6. Sala, A., Zhao, X., Wilson, C., Zheng, H., Zhao, B.Y.: Sharing graphs using differentially private graph models. In: Proceedings of 2011 ACM SIGCOMM Conference on Internet Measurement Conference, pp. 81–98. ACM (2011)
7. Xiao, Q., Chen, R., Tan, K.L.: Differentially private network data release via structural inference. In: Proceedings of 20th ACM SIGKDD International Conference on Knowledge Discovery and Data Mining, pp. 911–920. ACM (2014)
8. Lu, W., Miklau, G.: Exponential random graph estimation under differential privacy. In: Proceedings of 20th ACM SIGKDD International Conference on Knowledge Discovery and Data Mining, pp. 921–930. ACM (2014)
9. Mir, D.J., Wright, R.N.: A differentially private graph estimator. In: IEEE International Conference on Data Mining Workshops, ICDMW 2009, pp. 122–129. IEEE (2009)
10. Gleich, D.F., Owen, A.B.: Moment-based estimation of stochastic Kronecker graph parameters. Internet Math. **8**(3), 232–256 (2012)
11. Hay, M., Li, C., Miklau, G., Jensen, D.: Accurate estimation of the degree distribution of private networks. In: 9th IEEE International Conference on Data Mining, ICDM 2009, pp. 169–178. IEEE (2009)
12. Rossi, N.A.R.: Network repository (2012–2016). http://networkrepository.com/index.php
13. DuBois, C.L.: UCI network data repository (2008)

An Executable Specification for SPARQL

Mihaela Bornea[1], Julian Dolby[1]([✉]), Achille Fokoue[1],
Anastasios Kementsietsidis[2], Kavitha Srinivas[1], and Mandana Vaziri[1]

[1] IBM Thomas J. Watson Research Center, Yorktown Heights, NY, USA
{mbornea,dolby,achille,ksrinivs,mvaziri}@us.ibm.com
[2] Google Research, Mountain View, CA, USA
anastasios@alumni.utoronto.ca

Abstract. Linked Data on the web consists of over 1000 datasets from a variety of domains. They are queried with the SPARQL query language. There exist many implementations of SPARQL, and this rich ecosystem has demanded a precise specification and compliance tests. However, the SPARQL specification has grown in complexity, and it is increasingly difficult for developers to validate their implementations. In this paper, we present a declarative specification for SPARQL, based on relational logic. It describes SPARQL with just a few operators, and is executable: queries written in it can be directly executed against real datasets.

Linked Data on the web consists of over 1000 datasets from a variety of domains: curated medical literature [14], geographical data [6], financial data [13], crowd-sourced general knowledge [4], government data [3] and many more. Across many domains, programming against datasets increasingly involves querying with the SPARQL query language [10,12].

However, the SPARQL specification is *operational*, i.e., given by translating the language to an algebra, and is non-trivial for complex queries. We present an alternative, declarative specification for SPARQL based on *relational logic*, where relations are first-class entities and can be composed via relational and logical operators to form *constraints*. A *solution* to a relational constraint is an assignment of data to the relations that satisfies the constraint. The graph-based nature of RDF is a natural fit for relational logic: subject-predicate-object expressions are represented as relations and the meaning of queries is given in terms of relational operators. Our specification is *declarative*, i.e., the structure of SPARQL queries is mapped directly to relational constraints whose solutions represent answers to the query.

We have validated our specification by applying the compliance tests provided by SPARQL. This was done by writing our relational-loic semantics in Kodkod and running it on compliance tests.

1 Semantics

In this section, we give meaning for the SPARQL core. We cover the graph patterns as defined in the specification (see [10], Sects. 5–10 and 19.8, grammar rules 53–68): basic graph pattern (BGP), union, optional, filter, minus, bind and values.

© Springer International Publishing AG 2016
W. Cellary et al. (Eds.): WISE 2016, Part II, LNCS 10042, pp. 298–305, 2016.
DOI: 10.1007/978-3-319-48743-4_24

The meaning of a query Q for a dataset D is the set of bindings of the variables of Q such that the denoted subgraph appears in D. $\mathfrak{T}(Q, D)$ denotes the formula in the free variables of Q that satisfies Q in D; $\mathfrak{T}$ is defined in Fig. 3. The semantics of graph patterns makes use of expressions in some cases, which is defined in Fig. 4.

1.1 Graph Patterns

We introduce and motivate $\mathfrak{T}$ with a series of examples that cover the core.

Basic Graph Patterns. An example dataset is shown in Fig. 1(a), along with a simple SPARQL query in Fig. 1(b). This is a basic pattern specifying two variables ?a and ?b, and matches pairs of triples where a binding for ?a has :p edges to ?b and to :n. Given the dataset on the left, the query in the middle evaluates to the answer on the right, Fig. 1(c), since :x has a :p relation to :n, which can satisfy the second triple pattern (T2). Both :n and :y can satisfy the first triple pattern (T1). Our basic approach is to express the query as a logical formula. For a triple $\langle a, b, c \rangle$, we simply require the triple be in the dataset: $\mathfrak{T}(\langle a, b, c \rangle) \equiv \langle a, b, c \rangle \in G$. For the join between the two triples, we use logical and: $\mathfrak{T}(T_1.T_2) \equiv \mathfrak{T}(T_1) \wedge \mathfrak{T}(T_2)$. Applying $\mathfrak{T}$ in this case, we get the following formula

$$\langle a, :\mathrm{p}, b \rangle \in G \wedge \langle a, :\mathrm{p}, :\mathrm{n} \rangle \in G$$

To obtain the answer, i.e. all pairs a, b, we define a set comprehension of the formula over all its free variables

$$\{\langle a, b \rangle \,|\, \langle a, :\mathrm{p}, b \rangle \in G \wedge \langle a, :\mathrm{p}, :\mathrm{n} \rangle \in G\}$$

Filter. The same approach can be elaborated to cover the core of the SPARQL pattern matching language. The first elaboration is that not all variables are free. Consider the slightly more complicated query in Fig. 2a that adds a filter that makes sure that an additional triple ?c :q ?b exists in the dataset. In SPARQL 1.1, filters are expressions, and their definitions are in Fig. 4.

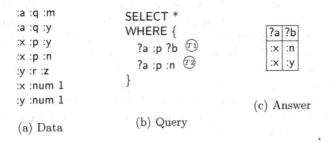

(a) Data

(b) Query

(c) Answer

Fig. 1. BGP example

SELECT * WHERE { T_1	SELECT * WHERE { T_1	SELECT * WHERE { T_1
?a :p ?b	?a :p ?b	?a :p ?b
?a :p :n	?a :p :n	?a :p :n
FILTER EXISTS { T_2	UNION { T_2	OPTIONAL { T_2
?c :q ?b	?c :q ?b	?c :q ?b
}}	}}	}}
(a) FILTER EXISTS	(b) UNION	(c) OPTIONAL example

Fig. 2. Examples

The variable ?c is not mentioned in the main pattern, so the formulation is a little different; there must be some value for c for any pair a, b in the solution. Specifically, in our example, because ?c does not even appear in the main pattern, the set of variables in the filter T_2 that are unbound in the main pattern T_1 is statically known, and consists only of the variable c. Hence, for simple cases where the set $\{v_1 \ldots v_k\}$ of variables in the filter expression T_2 that are unbound in the main pattern T_1 is statically known, we define $\mathfrak{T}(T_1 \exists\, T_2) \equiv \mathfrak{T}(T_1) \wedge \exists v_1 \ldots v_k \mathfrak{T}(T_2)$. However, we shall see later in this section that it gets more complex (due to the fact that variables in T_1 can be dynamically bound in general). For now, we get the following formula once we wrap it in a set comprehension over the free variables

$$\{\langle a, b\rangle \,|\, \langle a, :\mathrm{p}, b\rangle \in G \wedge \langle a, :\mathrm{p}, :\mathrm{n}\rangle \in G \wedge \exists\, c\, \langle c, :\mathrm{q}, b\rangle \in G\}$$

The FILTER NOT EXISTS construct is the same except the existential is negated.

So far, the queries have all had the same set of bound variables for all answers, but there are two SPARQL constructs that do not have this property: UNION and OPTIONAL.

Union. UNION has the expected meaning of combining two child patterns and hence denotes a logical or in our formalism; $\mathfrak{T}(T_1 \cup T_2) \equiv \mathfrak{T}(T_1) \vee \mathfrak{T}(T_2)$. However, UNION also illustrates one of the more thorny parts of SPARQL, which is that variables get bound dynamically. Specifically, in our example in Fig. 2b, if the left branch of the UNION produces mappings, then only ?a and ?b are bound, but ?c is not (similarly, the right branch binds only ?b and ?c). If both branches produce mappings, then a specific solution mapping μ can have either ?a and ?b bound, or ?b and ?c bound. Simply expressing union as an $\vee$ does not capture this; that formula would be $u = \{\langle a, b, c\rangle \,|\, ((\langle a, :\mathrm{p}, b\rangle \in G \wedge \langle a, :\mathrm{p}, :\mathrm{n}\rangle \in G) \vee \langle c, :\mathrm{q}, b\rangle \in G)\}$. Some solutions for Fig. 2b bind only ?a and ?b; this corresponds to the left branch of the *or* in the set comprehension u; in that case there is no constraint on ?c and so every value for ?c would be a valid answer.

We need to capture in our formula that the left branch of the union binds only ?a and ?b; we introduce $dom(T)$ to denote variables bound in a solution. Thus, $dom(T1) = \{?\mathrm{a}, ?\mathrm{b}\}$ and $dom(T2) = \{?\mathrm{b}, ?\mathrm{c}\}$. Combining these for $dom(T)$ is slightly tricky: which other variable is bound depends on which side of the union was taken; we need to ensure that $dom(T)$ is either $dom(T_1)$ or $dom(T_2)$. A simple union will not suffice for this, so we use an auxiliary variable τ_i to denote the chosen branch:

$$dom(T) \equiv \exists \tau_i \begin{cases} dom(T1) \; \tau_i \\ dom(T2) \; \neg\tau_i \end{cases}$$

We also introduce a helper function $valid(x) \equiv \text{`x'} \in dom(T) \vee x = \emptyset$ to mean that a variable is either bound or is null; i.e. $valid$ ensures that variables unbound in the pattern must be null rather than ranging over all possible values. We use `x' to denote the name of a variable, and we will use $valid(x_1, \ldots, v_n)$ to mean element-wise application of $valid$.

The formal definition of $dom(T)$ is given in Fig. 3. Given $dom(T)$, we get the following formula for this example. Hereinafter, we will implicitly add to every top level comprehension the constraint that all free variables are valid

$$\left\{ \langle a, b, c \rangle \; \middle| \; \left(\left(\begin{matrix} \langle a, \texttt{:p}, b \rangle \in G \wedge \\ \langle a, \texttt{:p}, \texttt{:n} \rangle \in G \end{matrix} \right) \vee \langle c, \texttt{:q}, b \rangle \in G \right) \wedge valid(a, b, c) \right\}$$

Optional. OPTIONAL patterns are optional in the sense that, if the pattern matches in the dataset, any additional variables bound in the optional pattern are bound in the overall pattern; if the optional pattern fails to match, those variables are left unbound. As shown in Fig. 2c, OPTIONAL patterns are also a complex kind of pattern since they generate two kinds of results: the first is when both the left and right hand sides are true, and the second is when the left hand side is true and the right hand side cannot be matched given the bound variables in the left hand side, which is essentially a filter not exists pattern

$$\mathfrak{T}(T_1 \text{ optional } T_2) \equiv (\mathfrak{T}(T_1) \wedge \mathfrak{T}(T_2)) \vee \mathfrak{T}(T_1 \# T_2)$$

and

$$dom(T_1 \text{ optional } T_2) \equiv \begin{cases} dom(T_1) \cup dom(T_2) \; \mathfrak{T}(T_2) \\ dom(T_1) \qquad\qquad\quad otherwise \end{cases}$$

The complication with OPTIONAL is that to define the notion of the right hand side T_2 that cannot be matched given the bound variables in the left hand side T_1, we need to handle the dynamism of mappings of T_1, so for OPTION-ALs, dom directly impacts the variables used in the existential quantification of subformulae. Hence, we define a helper logical operator for quantification, $\exists^T$. Intuitively, if a free variable v of $\mathfrak{T}(T_2)$ is bound in T_1, then $\exists^{T_1} v \, \mathfrak{T}(T_2)$ is simply $\mathfrak{T}(T_2)[v^{T_1}/v]$, the formula obtained after replacing all occurrences of v in $\mathfrak{T}(T_2)$ by v^{T_1} (where v^{T_1} refers to the constant to which v is bound in pattern T_1); otherwise, $\exists^{T_1} v \, \mathfrak{T}(T_2)$ corresponds to the normal existential quantification $\exists v \, \mathfrak{T}(T_2)$. This is precisely the behavior we want to account for the dynamism of mappings. We now formally define $\exists^T$ as follows: for a logical formula Q and a non-empty subset $\{v_1, \ldots, v_n\}$ of free variables of Q, $\exists^T v_1, \ldots, v_n Q$ means

$$\exists v_1, \ldots, v_n (\text{`v}_1\text{'} \in dom(T) \to v_1 = v_1^T) \wedge \ldots \wedge (\text{`v}_n\text{'} \in dom(T) \to v_n = v_n^T) \wedge Q$$

where v_i^T refers to the constant to which v_i is bound in pattern T. With a slight abuse of notation, when the set of variables is empty, we define, for a given formula Q, $\exists^T Q$ as $\exists^T Q \equiv Q$.

Going back to the FILTER EXISTS example in Fig. 2a, with the definition of $\exists^T$, the proper meaning of the FILTER EXISTS construct that accounts for

---

$FVars(\mathfrak{I}(T)) \equiv$ set of free variables of $\mathfrak{I}(T)$

$\quad\quad v^T \equiv$ the constant to which the variable v is bound in pattern T

$\exists^T v_1 \ldots v_k Q \equiv \exists v_1 \ldots v_k \left(`\mathbf{v_1}` \in dom(T) \to v_1 = v_1^T \right) \wedge \ldots \wedge \left(`\mathbf{v_k}` \in dom(T) \to v_k = v_k^T \right) \wedge Q$

$\quad\quad \exists^T Q \equiv Q$

$\nexists^T v_1 \ldots v_k Q \equiv \neg(\exists^T v_1 \ldots v_k Q)$

$$\mathfrak{I}(T,G) \equiv \begin{cases} \langle a,b,c \rangle & \equiv \langle \mathfrak{G}, a, b, c \rangle \in G \\ \text{VALUES } v_1 \ldots \{\{c_{1,1} \ldots\} \ldots\} & \equiv (v_1 = c_{1,1} \wedge \ldots) \vee \ldots \\ \text{BIND } v \text{ AS } E_1 & \equiv V(E_1, T) \wedge v = \mathfrak{E}(T, E_1) \\ s \text{ path } o & \equiv \langle s, o \rangle \in \mathfrak{P}(path) \\ \text{GRAPH } g \ \{T_1\} & \equiv \text{let } \mathfrak{G} = g \text{ in } \mathfrak{I}(T_1) \\ T_1 . T_2 & \equiv \mathfrak{I}(T_1) \wedge \mathfrak{I}(T_2) \\ T_1 \text{ FILTER } E_1 & \equiv \mathfrak{I}(T_1) \wedge V(E_1, T) \wedge \mathfrak{E}(T, E_1) \\ T_1 - T_2 & \equiv \begin{cases} \mathfrak{I}(T_1 \nexists T_2) & (dom(T_1) \cap dom(T_2)) \neq \emptyset \\ \mathfrak{I}(T_1) & otherwise \end{cases} \\ T_1 \cup T_2 & \equiv \mathfrak{I}(T_1) \vee \mathfrak{I}(T_2) \\ T_1 \text{ optional } T_2 & \equiv (\mathfrak{I}(T_1) \wedge \mathfrak{I}(T_2)) \vee \mathfrak{I}(T_1 \nexists T_2) \end{cases}$$

$$dom(T) \equiv \begin{cases} \langle a,b,c \rangle & \equiv \text{names of all variables in the triple} \\ \text{VALUES } v_1 \ldots \{\{c_{1,1} \ldots\} \ldots\} & \equiv \{`v_1` \ldots\} \\ \text{BIND } v \text{ AS } e & \equiv \{`v`\} \\ \text{GRAPH } g \ \{T_1\} & \equiv \begin{cases} \{`g`\} \cup dom(T_1) & g \text{ is a variable} \\ dom(T_1) & otherwise \end{cases} \\ T_1 . T_2 & \equiv dom(T_1) \cup dom(T_2) \\ T_1 \text{ FILTER } E_1 & \equiv dom(T_1) \\ T_1 - T_2 & \equiv dom(T_1) \\ T_1 \cup T_2 & \equiv \begin{cases} dom(T_1) & \mathfrak{I}(T_1) \wedge \neg\mathfrak{I}(T_2) \\ dom(T_2) & \mathfrak{I}(T_2) \wedge \neg\mathfrak{I}(T_1) \\ \exists \tau_i \in \{true, false\} \text{ such that} \\ \text{if } \tau_i \text{ } dom(T_1) \text{ else } dom(T_2) & \mathfrak{I}(T_1) \wedge \mathfrak{I}(T_2) \end{cases} \\ T_1 \text{ optional } T_2 & \equiv \begin{cases} dom(T_1) \cup dom(T_2) & \mathfrak{I}(T_2) \\ dom(T_1) & \neg\mathfrak{I}(T_2) \end{cases} \end{cases}$$

$$\mathfrak{P}(p) \equiv \begin{cases} \mathfrak{P}(link : p) \equiv \{<x,y> | \langle \mathfrak{G}, x, : p, y \rangle \in G\} \\ \mathfrak{P}(inv : p) \equiv \{<x,y> | \langle \mathfrak{G}, y, : p, x \rangle \in G\} \\ \mathfrak{P}(NPS(p_1 \ldots p_n)) \equiv \{<x,y> | \exists q \ q \notin p_1 \ldots p_n \wedge \langle \mathfrak{G}, x, q, y \rangle \in G\} \\ \mathfrak{P}(seq(p_1, p_2)) \equiv (\mathfrak{P}(p_1).\mathfrak{P}(p_2)) \\ \mathfrak{P}(alt(p_1, p_2)) \equiv (\mathfrak{P}(p_1) \cup \mathfrak{P}(p_2)) \\ \mathfrak{P}(OneOrMorePath(p_1)) \equiv \hat{}\mathfrak{P}(p_1) \\ \mathfrak{P}(ZeroOrOnePath(p_1)) \equiv \mathfrak{P}(p_1) \cup \{\langle x,x \rangle | \exists y, z \ \langle \mathfrak{G}, x, y, z \rangle \in G \vee \langle \mathfrak{G}, y, z, x \rangle \in G\} \\ \mathfrak{P}(ZeroOrMorePath(p_1)) \equiv \mathfrak{P}(alt(OneOrMorePath(p_1), ZeroOrOnePath(p_1))) \end{cases}$$

Fig. 3. Pattern semantics. (We use $T_1 \nexists T_2$ to mean T_1 FILTER NOT EXISTS T_2). Note that this handles *named graphs*, which essentially generalize triples to quads. For ease of explanation, our examples just use triples.

the dynamism of mappings is as follows: $\mathfrak{T}(T_1 \exists T_2) \equiv \mathfrak{T}(T_1) \wedge \exists^{T_1} v_1 \ldots v_k \mathfrak{T}(T_2)$ where $\{v_1 \ldots v_k\}$ is the set of free variables of $\mathfrak{T}(T_2)$.

Now, we can define $\not\exists^T$ as follows: for a logical formula Q and a subset $S = \{v_1, \ldots, v_n\}$ of free variables of Q (S may be empty), $\not\exists^T v_1, \ldots, v_n Q \equiv \neg(\exists^T v_1, \ldots, v_n Q)$. Finally, we can formally define the FILTER NOT EXISTS construct: $\mathfrak{T}(T_1 \not\exists T_2) \equiv \mathfrak{T}(T_1) \wedge \not\exists^{T_1} v_1 \ldots v_k \mathfrak{T}(T_2)$ where $\{v_1 \ldots v_k\}$ is the set of free variables of $\mathfrak{T}(T_2)$.

Minus. MINUS is essentially the same as filter not exists, but it adds the constraint that the left and right hand sides must have at least one variable in common in order for subtraction to occur. That is captured by adding a *dom* constraint to filter not exists:

$$\mathfrak{T}(T_1 - T_2) \equiv \begin{cases} \mathfrak{T}(T_1 \not\exists T_2) & (dom(T_1) \cap dom(T_2)) \neq \emptyset \\ \mathfrak{T}(T_1) & otherwise \end{cases}$$

Property Paths. A significant new feature in SPARQL 1.1 is property paths, which essentially allow specification of a regular expression over predicates to connect a given subject and object. Relational logic is natural to define such predicates as relations. We define property paths as $\mathfrak{P}$ in Fig. 3.

Aggregation. Aggregation is specified over a set comprehension, as defined in Fig. 4; We illustrate with the query select ?a (max(?n) as ?m) where ?a :q ?b . ?b :num ?n GROUP BY ?a. The group is specified in this case as those answers sharing the same value of ?a given a formula P:

$$G(P) = (\text{let } a_g = a \text{ in } \{\langle a, b, n \rangle \,|\, \mathfrak{T}(P) \wedge a = a_g \})$$

Then the aggregation function is applied; first the expression being aggregated is evaluated for each group member,

$$E(G) = \{n \,|\, \langle a, b, n \rangle \in G\}$$

and then the aggregate function itself is computed:

$$max(E) \in E \wedge \not\exists max' \in E \wedge max' > max(E)$$

1.2 Expressions

Expressions appear in filter and bind patterns, and represent values computed from other variables and constants. Expression semantics $\mathfrak{E}$ is presented in Fig. 4. An example using bind is Figure ??. This expression appears normal, as it simply adds two variables together.

Validity means that evaluation is allowed only when every portion of the expression is valid, i.e. applicable to its arguments, if any. It is analogous to type correctness in dynamic languages, but tests simply fail when they are invalid rather than aborting the computation with a type error. Note that && and || operations swallow errors when possible. && returns false if either argument is valid and returns false, regardless of whether the other argument is valid. || is analogous.

$$\mathfrak{E}(E,T) \equiv \begin{cases} E_1 == E_2 \equiv \begin{matrix} \text{let } v_1 \leftarrow \mathfrak{E}(E_1,T), v_2 \leftarrow \mathfrak{E}(E_2,T) \text{ in} \\ v_1 == v_2 \qquad\qquad\qquad\qquad B(T(v_1)) \wedge B(T(v_2)) \\ S(v_1) == S(v_2) \wedge T(v_1) == T(v_2) \; \textit{otherwise} \end{matrix} \\ E_1 \neq E_2 \equiv \begin{matrix} \text{let } v_1 \leftarrow \mathfrak{E}(E_1,T), v_2 \leftarrow \mathfrak{E}(E_2,T) \text{ in} \\ v_1 \neq v_2 \; B(T(v_1)) \wedge B(T(v_2)) _2 \\ \textit{false} \quad \textit{otherwise} \end{matrix} \\ \neg E_1 \equiv \neg\mathfrak{E}(E_1,T) \\ E_1 \;\&\&\; E_2 \equiv \mathfrak{E}(E_1,T) \wedge \mathfrak{E}(E_2,T) \\ E_1 \;\|\; E_2 \equiv \mathfrak{E}(E_1,T) \vee \mathfrak{E}(E_2,T) \\ bound(v) \equiv 'v' \in dom(T) \\ \text{EXISTS } T_1 \equiv \exists^T v_1...v_k \; \mathfrak{T}(T_1) \;\text{ with } v_i \in FVars(\mathfrak{T}(T_1)) \\ \text{NOT EXISTS } T_1 \equiv \nexists^T v_1...v_k \; \mathfrak{T}(T_1) \;\text{ with } v_i \in FVars(\mathfrak{T}(T_1)) \end{cases}$$

$$V(E,T) \equiv \begin{cases} E_1 == E_2 \equiv V(E_1,T) \wedge V(E_2,T) \\ E_1 \neq E_2 \equiv V(E_1,T) \wedge V(E_2,T) \\ \neg E_1 \equiv V(E_1,T) \\ E_1 \;\&\&\; E_2 \equiv (V(E_1,T) \wedge V(E_2,T)) \vee (V(E_1,T) \implies \neg\mathfrak{E}(E_1,T)) \vee (V(E_2,T) \implies \neg\mathfrak{E}(E_2,T)) \\ E_1 \;\|\; E_2 \equiv (V(E_1,T) \wedge V(E_2,T)) \vee (V(E_1,T) \implies \mathfrak{E}(E_1,T)) \vee (V(E_2,T) \implies \mathfrak{E}(E_2,T)) \\ \textit{otherwise} \quad \textit{true} \end{cases}$$

$$\mathfrak{G}(T, e_{1...n}) \equiv \text{let } e_1' = e_1, \ldots e_n' = e_n \text{in} \left\{ FVars(\mathfrak{T}(T)) \Big| \mathfrak{T}(T) \wedge e_1' = e_1 \wedge \ldots e_n' = e_n \right\}$$

$$\mathfrak{A}(T, a_{1...m}, e_{1...n}) \equiv \mathfrak{T}(T) \wedge var(a_1) = agg(a_1) \left(\{exp(a_1)(t) \,|\, t \in \mathfrak{G}(T, e_{1...n})\}\right) \wedge \ldots$$

$T(v) \equiv$ RDF type of value v

$S(v) \equiv$ literal string of value v

$B(t) \equiv$ true if type t is built in

Fig. 4. Expression semantics

1.3   Blank Node Equivalence

Entailment regimes [5] define how SPARQL query answers change for RDF graphs under a range of OWL [7,8] semantics. We cover RDF entailment, under which two RDF graphs G_1 and G_2 are equivalent if they differ only in the labels of their blank nodes, denoted $G_1 =_{RDF} G_2$.

2   Conclusion

To our knowledge, we present the most complete semantics for SPARQL that is not based on translation or has actually been run. Previous work based on directly assigning meaning to SPARQL constructs [1] focuses on a limited subset of SPARQL. Other formalisms for SPARQL have been defined based on translations to Answer Set Programming (ASP) [9], Datalog [11] and relational algebra [2]. None of these have been subject to automated verification.

We presented a formal definition of the core of SPARQL 1.1 that parsimoniously distills the language down to a few constructs, succinctly capturing subtle issues like the meanings of negation. This semantics is expressed in relational logic, and has been mechanically checked by implementing it.

References

1. Arenas, M., Pérez, J.: Querying semantic web data with SPARQL. In: Lenzerini, M., Schwentick, T. (eds.) Proceedings of 30th ACM SIGMOD-SIGACT-SIGART Symposium on Principles of Database Systems, PODS 2011, Athens, Greece, 12–16 June 2011, pp. 305–316. ACM (2011). http://doi.acm.org/10.1145/1989284.1989312

2. Cyganiak, R.: A relational algebra for SPARQL. Technica report, Digital Media Systems Laboratory, HP Laboratories Bristol (2005)

3. data.gov. http://data.gov/

4. DBPedia SPARQL Endpoint. http://dbpedia.org/sparql

5. Sprql 1.1 entailment regimes. http://www.w3.org/TR/sparql11-entailment/

6. GeoNames Semantic Web. http://datahub.io/dataset/geonames-semantic-web

7. Owl 2 web ontology language document overview. http://www.w3.org/TR/owl2-overview/

8. Owl 2 web ontology language mapping to RDF graphs. www.w3.org/TR/owl2-mapping-to-rdf/

9. Polleres, A., Wallner, J.P.: On the relation between SPARQL 1.1 and answer set programming. J. Appl. Non-Class. Log. **23**(1–2), 159–212 (2013)

10. Prud'hommeaux, E., Seaborne, A.: SPARQL query language for RDF, January 2008. http://www.w3.org/TR/2008/REC-rdf-sparql-query-20080115/

11. Schenk, S.: A SPARQL semantics based on datalog. In: Hertzberg, J., Beetz, M., Englert, R. (eds.) KI 2007. LNCS (LNAI), vol. 4667, pp. 160–174. Springer, Heidelberg (2007)

12. Semantic web use cases. http://www.w3.org/2001/sw/sweo/public/UseCases/

13. Semantic XBRL. http://datahub.io/package/semantic-xbrl

14. UniProt SPARQL Endpoint. http://beta.sparql.uniprot.org

Non-traditional Environments

Towards a Scalable Framework for Artifact-Centric Business Process Management Systems

Jiankun Lei, Rufan Bai, Lipeng Guo, and Liang Zhang$^{(\boxtimes)}$

School of Computer Science, Shanghai Key Laboratory of Data Science,
Fudan University, Shanghai, China
{jklei,rfbai,lpguo,lzhang}@fudan.edu.cn

Abstract. Over the last decade, we have witnessed the success of artifact-centric approach in business process management (BPM). However, the scalability issue was neglected by almost all its implementation frameworks. A non-scalable framework will severely hamper applicability of corresponding artifact-centric BPM systems in large-scale applications. Considering distinct characteristics of the Representational State Transfer (REST) architectural style, we propose a distributed artifact-centric BPM framework based on REST principles. A prototype is developed using Docker-based micro services for continuously delivering of process engine instances. Through extensive experiments against a typical process-aware application, we confirm that the proposed framework is promising to support scalable artifact-centric BPM systems.

Keywords: Artifact-centric business process · REST · Scalable framework

1 Introduction

Over the last decade, the artifact-centric approach [4,13] has emerged as a popular perspective in business process management (BPM). Comparing to traditional activity-centric BPM, the artifact-centric BPM approach focuses on data with lifecycle, known as *artifacts*, in business processes and provides a better balance between process-centric and data-centric modeling [20]. As it rapidly develops, more and more artifact-centric BPM systems are deployed to support enterprises' operational tasks, the systems inevitably have to handle a large number of users and business process instances in some process-aware applications. This tendency requires corresponding infrastructures, e.g. the frameworks and implemented process engines, to be scalable enough to meet the challenge.

Unfortunately, due to its infancy, almost all the implementation frameworks of the artifact-centric BPM, ranging from ArtiFlow [10] (and its successor EZ-Flow [3]), to ACP [12], and Barcelona [7], have not yet addressed the scalability issue properly. Taking the ACP framework [12] as an example, the process engine exploits a centralized rule evaluation facility (i.e. Drools) to actuate services which have artifacts transferred along their lifecycles. The centralized nature of the rule engine prevents ACP from being heavily-distributed deployed,

© Springer International Publishing AG 2016
W. Cellary et al. (Eds.): WISE 2016, Part II, LNCS 10042, pp. 309–323, 2016.
DOI: 10.1007/978-3-319-48743-4_25

which severely hurts the scalability. Our previous studies focus on the realization of artifact-centric workflows [10] or a workflow engine [3], had no concerns about scalability, too. From our experiments, we can find that Barcelona behaves poorly in terms of scalability as well.

Speaking of scalability, it is widely acknowledged that the World Wide Web (WWW) is a successful, distributed, and scalable platform [6]. The success is built so much on the underlying Representational State Transfer (REST) architectural style. REST provides principles behind the WWW, which is responsible for many desirable properties, such as scalability, modifiability, and interoperability [5,18]. We believe that it would be promising to introduce the REST style to artifact-centric BPM systems for the purpose of scalability.

In fact, there are some studies in the area of the RESTful business process modeling. Kumaran *et al.* [9] has proposed a RESTful architecture for business processes based on business entities modeled as Mealy machines. Other researches [14,21] take the resource-oriented approach of REST for activity-centric business processes to improve the simplicity of interfaces and interoperability of services. However, on one hand, approaches like [14,21], cannot take advantage of the artifact-centric approach, and on the other hand, the three studies all lack implementation or experiments. As a result, we cannot confirm the scalability of these approaches.

To bridge the gap between the study of artifact-centric BPM and scalable BPM framework, we propose a distributed artifact-centric BPM framework, named ArtiREST, based on REST principles. We also develop a prototype by using Docker-based micro services for continuously delivering of process engine instances. Extensive experiments towards the scalability demonstrate the superiority of the framework over other available ones.

The technical contribution of this paper can be summarized as:

- Identifying the scalability issue in artifact-centric BPM;
- Proposing a distributed artifact-centric BPM framework leveraged by the REST style and developing a prototype to prove the feasibility of the framework, and
- Confirming the applicability of REST style in artifact-centric BPM in pursuit of better scalability.

The remainder of this paper is organized as follows. Section 2 presents a running example to illustrate the proposed framework in subsequent sections. Section 3 specifies the scalability from many dimensions. Section 4 presents the ArtiREST in detail, and Sect. 5 evaluates framework in terms of scalability by experiments. Section 6 compares our approach with some related work. Finally, we give the conclusion and our future work.

2   A Running Example

Artifacts are business-relevant entities that are created and evolved through business processes. An artifact class (hereafter artifact) defines an information model and its lifecycle [4]. Consider a traditional loan approval process [16] (the middle part), and its artifact-centric representation (the upper part) in Fig. 1. The later defines an artifact *Loan*, which consists of an information model (right part) and a lifecycle (upper left). There are six states in the lifecycle (e.g. *Pending*) and five external services in the process (e.g. *Create* on the bottom). A client can instantiate the process by creating a loan artifact instance, and follows the process to choose a loan type to apply. A manager can approve or cancel the loan application. If it is approved and confirmed by the bank business services, current loan rate will be assigned to the *rate* attribute of the *Loan* artifact instance. Business rules (shaded diamonds) and services (rounded rectangles) work together to update attributes in the information model and have the artifact instance traveled from one state to another along its lifecycle.

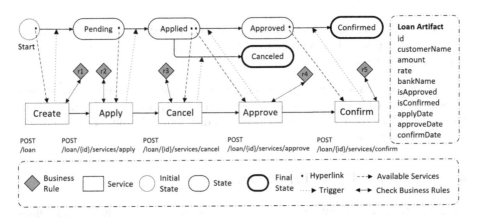

Fig. 1. An artifact-based view of a loan approval process

One of the significant innovations of artifact-centric BPM is that it focuses on what can be done (goals and progresses) instead of what should be done (tasks or corresponding services) [1]. Nevertheless, the advantages of artifact-centric BPM rely on the scalability of the underlying framework. Before discussing our framework, it is the time to elaborate on the scalability first.

3 Scalability

Scalability is a desirable property of a system, especially in the case as its load increases. Usually, scalability refers to the capability of a system, network, or process to handle a growing amount of work, or its potential to be enlarged in order to accommodate the growth [2]. In our context, we define scalability as,

Definition 1 (Scalability). A system is scalable if it can provide services and varies the quality of services (QoS) gracefully under light, moderate, to heavy loads.

The QoS can be measured from different angles. In this study, we are interested in performance. Hence, we choose the transaction per second (TPS) and the average response time (ART) as two indictors of QoS. As we know, investing more resources in a system can improve its QoS to some extent. Methods of adding more resources to a system fall into two broad categories: horizontal and vertical scaling.

Definition 2 (Horizontal Scalability). A system is horizontally scalable (or scale out/in) if it is scalable as adding more nodes to (or removing nodes from) the system.

Since Barcelona [7] and ACP [12] frameworks are implemented on a single server rather than a distributed platform, we need to consider vertical scalability as well.

Definition 3 (Vertical Scalability). A system is vertically scalable (or scale up/down) if it is scalable as adding resources to (or removing resources from) a single node in the system.

Technically, scalability improvement strategies include changing scheduling rules over shared resources, avoiding centralized control, or leveraging parallelism. We adopt these strategies to develop a distributed framework for artifact-centric BPM systems.

4   ArtiREST BPM Framework

In this section, we present the artifact-centric business process model, and elaborate its RESTful representation, which results in the ArtiREST, a distributed framework for artifact-centric BPM systems.

4.1   Artifact-Centric Business Process Modeling

There are plethoric studies to specify artifact-centric business process models, formally or informally. But they reach a consensus that such a business process is dominated by business artifacts.

In this study, we adopt the ACP model [12] with some modifications. Specifically, an artifact class is a tuple (A, Q, s, F), where A is a finite set of attributes, Q is a finite set of states, $s \in Q$ denotes the pseudo initial state and $F \subseteq Q$ is a set of final states. Let Z be a schema of artifacts, which is a finite set of artifact classes. A business rule r is a triple (λ, β, v) where λ is pre-condition and β is post-condition. Table 1 shows a business rule of our running example.

An artifact instance is actuated along its lifecycle by services constrained by business rules. Without loss of generality, we define services as RESTful web services [15].

Table 1. An example of business rule in the loan approval process

Post-condition	$instate(L, Pending)$
r2: Apply for loan L	
Pre-condition	$instate(L, Pending) \wedge defined(L, amount) \wedge defined(L, bankName)$ $\wedge\, amount > 10000$
Service	$apply(L)$
Post-condition	$instate(L, Applied)$

Definition 4 (Service). A service over a schema Z is a tuple (n, u, m, V_r, V_w), where n is a unique service name, u the URI and m a REST method (e.g. GET, PUT, POST, DELETE, etc. in the context of HTTP). V_r and V_w are finite sets of variables of artifact classes in Z.

As illustrated in Fig. 1, each state contains links (dots) to available services that might make state transitions. In this sense, the model conforms to the famous HATEOAS principle of REST [6]. It is worth emphasizing the importance of HATEOAS in our framework. Relying on the principle, we reverse the relation of business rules and services in traditional ACP model, which relieves us from the centralized control. A process engine needs only to evaluate those business rules (shaded diamonds) bound to a service (rounded rectangle) locally, instead of all rules globally when receiving an event like ACP. For example, if it is going to invoke service *apply*, the engine now only evaluates business rule *r2*. This modification to ACP can improve scalability drastically. In our modified ACP model, business rules are guards to guarantee the correct invocation of services and the proper transition among states. A service invocation is correct only if its pre-conditions hold before invoking the service and the post-conditions hold after the service has been invoked. A proper transition between two states happens only if the post-condition of the business rule stands.

```
{ "name": "Loan",                          {"name":"rule4_approved",
  "status" : "DEPLOYED",                     "preConditions":[
  "information_model": [                        {"artifact":"Loan","state":"applied","type":"INSTATE"},
    {"name": "customerName","type": "String"},  {"artifact":"Loan","attribute":"approveStatus",
    , ... ],                                      "operator":"EQUAL","type":"SCALAR ",
  "lifecycle": [                                 "value":"approved" }, ... ],
    {"name": "applied", "type": "NORMAL",     "postConditions":[ ... ],
     "nextStates": ["canceled","approved"]}   "action":{"service":"approve", "transitions":[
    , ... ],                                     {"artifact":"Loan", "fromState":"applied",
  "instances": [ ... ]                            "toState":"canceled"}, ...]}}
}                                          }
```

Fig. 2. A JSON representation of artifact classes *Loan* in resource /{process}/{process_id}/artifacts/{artifact} (left); A JSON representation of business rules *r4* in resource /{process}/{process_id}/rules/{rule}

4.2   RESTful Business Processes

The core abstraction of information in RESTful systems is a resource with a
URI [6]. In ArtiREST, we use templates in Table 2 to represent resources related
to an artifact-centric business process at the different levels of granularity. In
addition to them, we can zoom in on the lifecycle of an artifact as Fig. 2 (left)
or on the business rules affiliated to it as Fig. 2 (right).

Both of business information model and its lifecycle of an artifact
can be easily organized as web resources. RESTful services and business
rules can be also represented as resources. Back to our running example,
`/loan/1/services/apply` represents the URI of the service *apply* in Fig. 1,

Table 2. Uniform interface semantics for process-related resources

Method	Description
Process:/{process}	
GET	Retrieve a representation of the process, with links to its instances
PUT	Deploy or update the process
DELETE	Undeploy the process
POST	Create a new process instance, which may instantiate some artifact intances
Process instance:/{process}/{process_id}	
GET	Retrieve a representation of the process instance. With links to its artifact instances
DELETE	Delete the process instance
Artifact:/{process}/{process_id}/artifacts/{artifact}	
GET	Retrieve a representation of an artifact, with links to its instances
POST	Instantiate a new artifact instance
Artifact instance:/{process}/{process_id}/artifacts/{artifact}/{instance}	
GET	Retrieve the information of the artifact instance, including current state, attributes, state transitions and logs
PUT	Update the attributes of the instance
DELETE	Delete the artifact instance
Service:/{process}/{process_id}/services/{service}	
GET	Retrieve a representation of the service
PUT	Bind or update the service
DELETE	Unbind or delete the service
POST	Invoke the service initiatively
Business rule:/{process}/{process_id}/rules/{rule}	
GET	Retrieve a representation of the business rule, with its pre-condition, post-condition, corresponding service and etc.
PUT	Update the business rule
DELETE	Delete the business rule

where 1 is the process instance id and *apply* is the service name. To invoke a service, we apply standard HTTP verbs on its URI. For example, a client can simply invoke the interface `POST /loan/1/services/apply` with proper parameters to apply for a new loan.

4.3 Design Issues

REST is an architectural style for building Internet-scale distributed hypermedia systems [6]. Its scalability comes from its style principles, such as global addressability, client-server, stateless interaction, uniform interface, and layered system. ArtiREST inherits REST's desirable architecture properties, e.g. performance, scalability, simplicity, modifiability, and interoperability by enforcing these principle constraints in both the framework and its system architecture. A system architecture conforms to ArtiREST framework is shown in Fig. 3.

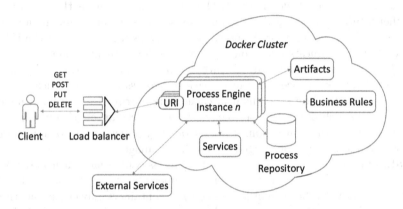

Fig. 3. A distributed architecture for ArtiREST system

- **Layered System.** The architecture is organized as multiple layers, including proxy, backend servers, cache, and database. The proxy layer provides load balancing of services across multiple networks and backend servers.
- **Stateless.** Each request from a client contains all information necessary for the server to understand and no client context is stored on the server between requests [6].
- **Uniform Interface.** A client can only make requests through HTTP verbs, i.e. GET, PUT, POST, DELETE, etc.
- **Cacheable.** The architecture employs multiple layers of cache, such as proxy cache and database cache.

We implement a light-weight and web-based BPM prototype, also named ArtiREST. Comparing with the existing artifact-centric BPM systems, we have made few decisions on some design issues.

- **Distributed Process Engines.** Like ACP [12], ArtiREST supports automated realization of artifact-centric models under one prerequisite: all services have been implemented, registered, and deployed. It is practical because the service-oriented approach promotes services registration. Unlike ACP and other centralized control implementations, ArtiREST advocates distributed evaluation by incorporating REST's HATEOAS and micro services. Each process engine is capable of evaluating those rules related to particular service independently. New engine instance can be instantiated on demand.
- **Cluster.** We deploy our prototype in a Docker Swarm Cluster, which enables booting a large number of containers in a very short time. Each container is built with all system services and is capable of serving all requests from clients. As the number of request increases, we can quickly scale up the container or scale out containers to improve the QoS of the system.
- **Sessions.** Session management in a distributed system is tough because of synchronization across servers. However, there should be no session according to the stateless principle of REST. One trick we are using is the token-based authentication [17], instead of keeping user sessions. After logging in, a unique token will be generated for the user. This mechanism requires that the HTTP header of any requests must contain the token for authentication.
- **Instance synchronization.** To further improve performance and scalability, we don't save process instances back to process repository once they are updated. Instead, we keep them in cache temporarily. Two mechanisms can be used to synchronize data between cache and backend repository: scheduled or fixed-point synchronization. It is controlled by policies that are application-sensitive and could be leveraged by a policy manager.
- **Data consistency.** The data in the database is consistent, but it may not be true in caches. Inconsistency frequently happens since the number of containers may vary with the current loads and some containers may crush sometimes. Many cache algorithms are proposed to ensure data consistency in the industry so we can use them directly.

4.4   Improving Scalability

Considering our model and system framework design, we address the following essential points for improving scalability specifically.

- **Decentralized business rules evaluation.** As mentioned in Sect. 4.1, we have well-defined REST services bound with related business rules. According to HATEOAS principle, a process instance regardless of any state only has limited available services. A user must explicitly invoke a specific service with self-describing messages, so the business engine only needs to evaluate the bound business rules.
- **RESTful architecture.** According to REST principles [6], *layered system, stateless, cacheable* mainly contributes to the system scalability. Load balancing can be performed among process engine instances in a distributed Docker

Swarm cluster. No centralized session (*stateless*) also improves scalability. Caches of business process models and instances on the server side further improve scalability.

4.5   BPM with ArtiREST

The concepts and technologies relevant to BPM can be outlined as a business process lifecycle: *design & analysis, configuration, enactment*, and *evaluation*, in a cyclical structure with logical dependencies [19]. In this section, we discuss how to support BPM with the ArtiREST prototype.

– **Design & Analysis.** We implemented a web-based graphic tool to support business process modeling. The tool is used to define artifacts, business rules, and service interfaces. Since the design model is serialized and saved in a standard format (XML/JSON), model validation can be done through the validation checking of XML or JSON. Verification of instances is supported as the execution model reflects the conceptual model according to ACP claims [12]. So far simulation is not automated, human participation must be involved to write or execute simulation cases.
– **Configuration.** Configuration becomes easier since we ship our services into Docker containers, which facilitates the system configuration and startup.
– **Enactment.** Process instantiation, service invocation and instance monitoring are involved in the enactment phase. According to the artifact-centric approach, the instantiation of artifact classes represents the process instantiation. Artifact instances can be serialized for persistence and transmission. Similarly, processes instance monitoring can be made via monitoring the artifact instances. The creation, update, or state transitions of an artifact will be logged, which provides information for monitoring. So far artifacts monitoring and logging have been implemented in our prototype while performance monitoring is absent. Process execution is accomplished by request resources and invoking RESTful web services.

Taking the loan approval process in Fig. 1 as an example, the execution procedure is shown in Fig. 4. A client applies for a loan by invoking a service named *Apply*. The POST request is submitted to invoke the service, and the server will get the corresponding business rule *r2* and check whether the state and attributes of the artifact *Loan* satisfy the pre-conditions. If it is satisfied, the Process Engine will invoke the service and then check if the new state of the

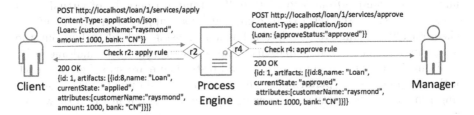

Fig. 4. The enactment of a process of loan approval in ArtiREST

artifact satisfied the post-condition. If everything is successful, the server will response to the client with the applied *Loan* artifact. Otherwise, an alarm is pending. Similarly, a manager can approve the loan application via a POST request to invoke service *Approve*.

– **Evaluation.** Evaluation involves improvement on process models and implementations by some techniques, such as monitoring and process mining on instance logs. Thanks to the artifact-centric approach, it is easier to monitor artifacts than tracking a traditional activity-centric process instance.

5 Evaluation

The technical evaluation towards the artifact-centric business process modeling and realization were given in ACP framework [12]. We dont repeat the evaluation here but focus ourselves on scalability. We are going to test if ArtiREST can provide services and varies QoS gracefully under light, moderate, to heavy loads. We also compare the scalability of our prototype with the two famous implementations of artifact-centric BPM tools Barcelona [7] and ACP [12]. All experiments are conducted with the loan approval process as shown in Fig. 1.

5.1 Load Testing

Load testing makes it practical to measure a systems QoS by simulating user behavior [11]. There are two primary QoS factors we are interested: availability and response time. In the following experiments, we ensure services to be always available and focus on the response time and transactions per second.

The systems to be tested are deployed in a Docker Swarm cluster with ten physical nodes, including seven process engine nodes, one load balancer, one cache node, and one database node. Each physical node has 32 GB RAM and four cores with hyper-threading. So we treat each node as a computer with 8 (logical) CPUs in following experiments.

We are interested if we can use low-cost (limited resources) process engines to handle heavy loads. As the QoS drops, we will supply more engines to the system. In other words, we care about the horizontal scalability. To do so, we ship an engine into a Docker container with only 1 GB RAM and 1 CPU.

We use Apache JMeter[1] to simulate virtual users and monitor performance. Apache JMeter is convenient to generate heavy load with many server protocol types, such as HTTP, REST, SOAP, etc. We use it to simulate that a growing number, for example from 0 to 2000 in 45 s (ramp-up period), of virtual users invoke 5 RESTful web services to complete a loan approval process in Fig. 1. Theoretically, we want to simulate a linear increasing of load to find out the maximum number of users (capability) that a system can serve simultaneously.

Figure 5 shows the result of partial load tests. There are six subgraphs, each of them represents the performance curves with a certain number (1–6) of running process engine instances. For example, the first graph in Fig. 5 shows the

---

[1] Apache JMeter: http://jmeter.apache.org.

performance delivered by one process engine. The TPS reaches to a maximum value (about 40) before the response time begins to increase sharply. We call it a saturation point, usually happens when resources are exhausted in a system.

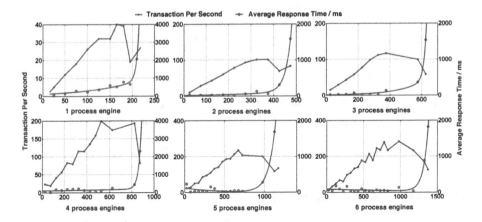

Fig. 5. Performance versus number of users. Here we observe two key performance metrics, i.e. the ART (average response time) on the left vertical axis, and TPS (transactions per second) on the right vertical axis. The annotation "3 process engine" indicates there are 3 active process engine instances.

5.2   Horizontal Scalability Evaluation

Usually, horizontal scalability can be measured by increasing loads steadily until the SLA (Service-Level Agreement) is achieved or the target resource utilization is reached. Resource utilization of distributed containers is difficult to measure, so we calculate the maximum TPS before saturation point as the SLA indicator.

Figure 5 shows that ArtiREST behaves well regarding horizontal scalability. As the increase of the number of process engine instances, the TPS rises steadily, from 40 up to 250, and supports more active users, from 150 up to 1000. Before saturation points, the response time is usually lower than 1 s.

Figure 6(a) shows the average number of maximum TPS before the saturation points vary with the number of process engines. In the linear fit, the equation is $y = 33.378x + 60.152, R^2 = 0.96415$, where y is an average number of the maximum TPS and x is the number of containers in the cluster. In the polynomial fit, the equation is $y = -1.238x^2 + 58.704x - 21.686, R^2 = 0.99683$. We can see that after the number of process engine instances exceeds 15, the TPS increases slowly. It is a normal phenomenon since we have only 10 physical nodes in the cluster, including process engines, cache, database, and load balancer. After the number of process engines exceeds a certain number, the cluster begins to saturate because of the limited resources for networks, database, cache, etc. We believe that the TPS can increase much faster and higher by adding more machines in the cluster and not restricting the RAM volume of each engine.

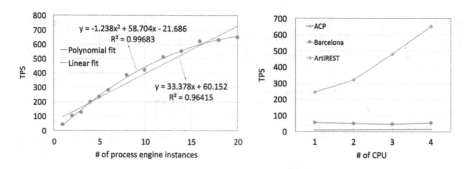

(a) Horizontal scalability: maximum TPS   (b) Vertical scalability: maximum
versus the number of process engines   TPS versus the number CPU

Fig. 6. Result of horizontal scalability and vertical scalability

5.3 Vertical Scalability Evaluation

The two mainstream implementations of artifact-centric BPM frameworks, Barcelona [7] and ACP [12], cannot scale out. Hence, we compare them with ArtiREST to investigate the vertical scalability by increasing the number of CPU in a single machine. To do it, we designed models for the loan process in accordance with ACP and Barcelona languages, respectively.

Figure 6(b) reveals the fact that ArtiREST scales vertically much better than the two competitors. By analysis, we know the huge difference results from many factors. On one hand, traditional frameworks focus on the realization of artifact-centric models but neglect the scalability. On the other hand, there are some flaws in design and implementation. For example, from the point view of design, ACP heavily relies on the business rule engine, in exchange for the flexibility processes modeling, it has to pay for the cost of centralized control. Consider the implementation techniques, there only exists a single thread in ACP framework as the centralized rule engine, and each business process instance is also realized as a single thread. Both the poor design and implementation flaws seriously harm its performance.

It should be noted that the maximum TPS with one business engine of ArtiREST reaches as high as 220 in Fig. 6(b), much higher than the previous experiments in Fig. 5 (about 40 there). This is because in this experiment, we just consider the number of CPU in a single machine but let the RAM free (32 GB) when performing the vertical scalability evaluation.

5.4 Dynamic Scalability

In the previous discussions, we start a certain number of process engine instances simultaneously and test the maximum TPS as its capability. In the real world, one interesting problem is the ability to dynamically adjust the engine instances according to the current system loads. Dynamically scaling is attractive because it adapts to the growing of loads without restarting the system. Figure 7 shows the result of a simple dynamic scalability experiment. It depicts the behaviors of TPS and ART against the number of users as process engine instances steadily increased. From the three subgraphs, we can see that when the number of users reaches 173, 390, and 510 respectively, the system begins to saturate. However, new engines start and join the cluster so that it breaks all saturation point by lowering response time and increasing TPS. Of course, the result is not perfect yet. First, the latency of starting an engine is too high (more than 10 s). Second, we dont know the perfect timing to start new engines. However, it does provide some findings that the ArtiREST is dynamically scalable. This indicates that the framework is much promising in pursuit of better scalability. Scaling dynamically is difficult, which involves loads monitoring, loads prediction, and scaling without interrupting and latency. We will study these issues in future work.

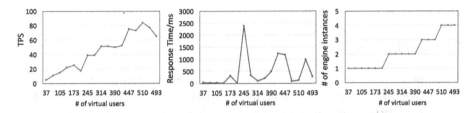

Fig. 7. Dynamically scaling the process engine instances according to the loads

6   Related Work

The study in this paper is about the scalability of artifact-centric BPM frameworks. We could classify related work into three categories, i.e. artifact-centric BPM implementation frameworks, BPM based on RESTful style, and a combination of artifact-centric approach that following RESTful style.

Since the birth of the artifact-centric approach [13], a number of implementation frameworks have emerged. Barcelona [7] and ACP framework [12] are arguably the most important frameworks among them. Barcelona [7] is a homegrown environment from IBM research, the inventor of the artifact-centric approach. The formal model GSM [8] and its open-sourced implementation BizArtifact[2] could be considered as the benchmark in the area of artifact-centric BPM. In the open-source world, there is another implementation ACP [12]. Besides its public accessibility, we prefer ACP because it reflects the original idea [13] of artifact-centric approach faithfully. Hence, in this study, we adopt the ACP model and adapt it to RESTful style. When evaluating the scalability, we choose them as our references. As indicated in Fig. 6(b) we found that both of them are underperforming in vertical scalability, aside from inability

---

[2] BizArtifact: https://sourceforge.net/projects/bizartifact.

in horizontal scalability. Similarly, our previous frameworks, ArtiFlow [10] and EZ-Flow [3] have no concerns about scalability.

Parallel with artifact-centric BPM researches, there exist some explorations of application of REST architectural styles on activity-centric BPM [16,21]. Besides the perspective difference, most works in this direction focus on design principles or guidelines, instead of the concrete framework implementation.

The work of Kumaran *et al.* [9] is closest to the our work. They propose a RESTful architecture for service-oriented business process execution in which business entities are modeled as Mealy machines, and the framework uses resource brokers to handle service requests and manage business entities. Contrasting to their indirect approach subject to the REST constraints, ArtiREST gives a straight answer. Moreover, they focus on the discussion of desirable properties, such as flexibility, interoperability, and scalability, but leave the implementation aside. As result, they provide neither experiments nor evidence to prove their claims in scalability.

7   Conclusion

In this paper, we studied the scalability issue in artifact-centric BPM systems, which was neglected by other researches on artifact-centric approaches. We then proposed a distributed framework ArtiREST based on the REST architectural style. Extensive experiments demonstrate the advantage of ArtiREST in both horizontal and vertical scalabilities over mainstream implementations of artifact-centric BPM. It can serve as a convincing evidence that the RESTful framework is effective and promising to reach a scalable artifact-centric BPM system.

In future work, we are going to improve the framework to support more management aspects of BPM such as performance monitoring and transaction support. It is also interesting to study how to scale out/in and up/down dynamically of the number of process engine instances according to current loads and loads prediction.

Acknowledgments. The work is supported by National NSFC (No. 60873115), Shanghai Science and Technology Development Funds (No. 13dz2260200 & No. 13511504300), and National Hi-Tech. Project (2012AA02A602).

References

1. Bhattacharya, K., Gerede, C.E., Hull, R., Liu, R., Su, J.: Towards formal analysis of artifact-centric business process models. In: Alonso, G., Dadam, P., Rosemann, M. (eds.) BPM 2007. LNCS, vol. 4714, pp. 288–304. Springer, Heidelberg (2007). doi:10.1007/978-3-540-75183-0_21
2. Bondi, A.B.: Characteristics of scalability and their impact on performance. In: Proceedings of the 2nd International Workshop on Software and Performance, pp. 195–203. ACM (2000)
3. Chen, Y., Xu, W., Zhang, L., Su, J.: EZMS: a workflow management system for EZ-Flow (in Chinese). Comput. Technol. Dev. **22**(12), 1–6 (2012)

4. Cohn, D., Hull, R.: Business artifacts: a data-centric approach to modeling business operations and processes. Bull. IEEE Comput. Soc. Tech. Committee Data Eng. **32**(3), 3–9 (2009)
5. Fielding, R.T., Taylor, R.N.: Principled design of the modern web architecture. ACM Trans. Internet Technol. (TOIT) **2**(2), 115–150 (2002)
6. Fielding, R.T.: Architectural styles and the design of network-based software architectures. Ph.D. thesis, University of California, Irvine (2000)
7. Heath III, F.T., Boaz, D., Gupta, M., Vaculín, R., Sun, Y., Hull, R., Limonad, L.: Barcelona: a design and runtime environment for declarative artifact-centric BPM. In: Basu, S., Pautasso, C., Zhang, L., Fu, X. (eds.) ICSOC 2013. LNCS, vol. 8274, pp. 705–709. Springer, Heidelberg (2013). doi:10.1007/978-3-642-45005-1_65
8. Hull, R., Damaggio, E., De Masellis, R., Fournier, F., Gupta, M., Heath III., F.T., Hobson, S., Linehan, M., Maradugu, S., Nigam, A., et al.: Business artifacts with guard-stage-milestone lifecycles: managing artifact interactions with conditions and events. In: Proceedings of the 5th ACM International Conference on Distributed Event-Based System, pp. 51–62. ACM (2011)
9. Kumaran, S., Liu, R., Dhoolia, P., Heath, T., Nandi, P., Pinel, F.: A RESTful architecture for service-oriented business process execution. In: Proceedings of IEEE International Conference on e-Business Engineering, pp. 197–204 (2008)
10. Liu, G., Liu, X., Qin, H., Su, J., Yan, Z., Zhang, L.: Automated realization of business workflow specification. In: Dan, A., Gittler, F., Toumani, F. (eds.) ICSOC/ServiceWave 2009. LNCS, vol. 6275, pp. 96–108. Springer, Heidelberg (2010). doi:10.1007/978-3-642-16132-2_9
11. Menascé, D.A.: Load testing of web sites. IEEE Internet Comput. **6**(4), 70–74 (2002)
12. Ngamakeur, K., Yongchareon, S., Liu, C.: A framework for realizing artifact-centric business processes in service-oriented architecture. In: Lee, S., Peng, Z., Zhou, X., Moon, Y.-S., Unland, R., Yoo, J. (eds.) DASFAA 2012. LNCS, vol. 7238, pp. 63–78. Springer, Heidelberg (2012). doi:10.1007/978-3-642-29038-1_7
13. Nigam, A., Caswell, N.S.: Business artifacts: an approach to operational specification. IBM Syst. J. **42**(3), 428–445 (2003)
14. Pautasso, C.: BPMN for REST. In: Dijkman, R., Hofstetter, J., Koehler, J. (eds.) BPMN 2011. LNBIP, vol. 95, pp. 74–87. Springer, Heidelberg (2011). doi:10.1007/978-3-642-25160-3_6
15. Pautasso, C.: RESTful web services: principles, patterns, emerging technologies. In: Bouguettaya, A., Sheng, Q.Z., Daniel, F. (eds.) Web Services Foundations, pp. 31–51. Springer, New York (2014)
16. Pautasso, C., Wilde, E.: Push-enabling RESTful business processes. In: Kappel, G., Maamar, Z., Motahari-Nezhad, H.R. (eds.) ICSOC 2011. LNCS, vol. 7084, pp. 32–46. Springer, Heidelberg (2011). doi:10.1007/978-3-642-25535-9_3
17. Tan, W., Hsu, J., Pinn, F.: Method and system for token-based authentication (Feb 23 2001), US Patent App. 09/792,785
18. Webber, J., Parastatidis, S., Robinson, I.: REST in Practice: Hypermedia and Systems Architecture. O'Reilly Media, Inc., Sebastopol (2010)
19. Weske, M.: Business Process Management. Concepts, Languages, Architectures. Springer, Heidelberg (2012)
20. van der Aalst, W.M.P.: Business process management: a comprehensive survey. ISRN Softw. Eng. **2013**, 1–37 (2013). doi:10.1155/2013/507984
21. Xu, X., Zhu, L., Kannengiesser, U., Liu, Y.: An architectural style for process-intensive web information systems. In: Chen, L., Triantafillou, P., Suel, T. (eds.) WISE 2010. LNCS, vol. 6488, pp. 534–547. Springer, Heidelberg (2010)

Bridging Semantic Gap Between App Names: Collective Matrix Factorization for Similar Mobile App Recommendation

Ning Bu$^{(\boxtimes)}$, Shuzi Niu, Lei Yu, Wenjing Ma, and Guoping Long

Institute of Software, Chinese Academy of Sciences,
4# South Fourth Street, Zhong Guan Cun, Beijing, China
{buning13,shuzi,yulei,wenjing,guoping}@iscas.ac.cn

Abstract. With the increase of mobile apps, i.e. applications, it is more and more difficult for users to discover their desired apps. Similar app recommendation, which plays a critical role in the app discovering process, is of our main concern in this paper. Intuitively, name is an important feature to distinguish apps. So app names are often used to learn the app similarity. However, existing studies do not perform well because names are usually very short. In this paper, we explore the phenomenon of the ill performance, and dive into the underlying reason, which motivates us to leverage additional corpus to bridge the gap between similar words. Specifically, we learn app representation from names and other related corpus, and formalize it as a collective matrix factorization problem. Moreover, we propose to utilize alternating direction method of multipliers to solve this collective matrix factorization problem. Experimental results on real-world data sets indicate that our proposed approach outperforms state-of-the-art methods on similar app recommendation.

Keywords: Mobile application · Similar app recommendation · Collective matrix factorization · Alternating direction method of multipliers

1 Introduction

Mobile apps, i.e. applications, are ubiquitous along with the smart phones, and play a more and more important role in our daily life. However, it is a daunting task to discover the desired apps for users from the vast number of apps. Similar app recommendation is such a useful way to enhance user experience. For instance, a list of similar apps is presented for each app in Google Play, users can obtain other similar or related apps with minimal effort when browsing a certain app. Thus we focus on how to obtain such a list for similar app recommendation.

Two apps are supposed to be similar if their meta information is semantically related. This is called High Level Software Similarity in previous work [3]. Here app meta information means the name, description, rating, reviews, screen shots and all other information describing the app itself. Among all kinds of app meta information, name is often used as the meaningful identifier to distinguish

© Springer International Publishing AG 2016
W. Cellary et al. (Eds.): WISE 2016, Part II, LNCS 10042, pp. 324–339, 2016.
DOI: 10.1007/978-3-319-48743-4_26

different apps. App developers use name to summarize one app as two or three discriminative, impressive words. App users use names to search a particular app. According to a survey [27], 88 % query terms are from app names. Generally, name functions as keywords of all the meta information for each app.

As important feature, name arouses much research interest, but few of them make full use of names in app representation learning. Because the app name usually contains a small number of words, two or three for example, the word independence assumption in traditional vector space model is supposed to be false for short texts. Existing studies on the similarity between short texts usually leverage additional information to help model the word dependency, but such additional information is often obtained with great effort, especially for those private information such as query log. Besides, these methods usually relies on the particular kind of information. Thus how to learn app representation from names systematically is a challenge in the similar app recommendation task.

We first explore the reason of introducing additional corpus to model word dependency. Then, we propose a systemic method to utilize this additional corpus to help learn representation from names. The word dependency is modeled as the word co-occurrence in the additional corpus. We jointly utilize the vector space model and word dependency to derive the app representation by formalizing it as a collective matrix factorization problem [20]. In this paper, we take description for example because it can be as easily obtained from app stores as app names. Finally, we propose a new optimization algorithm to solve this collective matrix factorization problem. In contrast to the optimization algorithm proposed in [20], the alternating direction method of multiplier avoids the computation of Hessian matrix and converges faster without loss of performance. We investigate our proposed approach on real-world data sets crawled from Google Play. Experimental results show that our proposed approach outperforms state-of-the-art methods in the similar app recommendation task.

Our method will help app developers promote their new apps, help app stores attract more app users, and help app users find their desired apps. In all, the major contributions of this paper lie in the following three aspects:

- the exploration of the necessity of introducing additional corpus to help representation learning from names.
- the formalization of the app representation learning with the help of additional corpus as the collective matrix factorization problem.
- the proposal to adopt alternating direction method of multiplier to solve the problem above.

The rest of the paper is organized as follows: Sect. 2 discuss related work; Sect. 3 describe our motivation for introducing additional corpus for names; Sects. 4 and 5 present the problem formulation and the optimization algorithm respectively; Sect. 6 show the empirical results; Sect. 7 concludes the paper.

2 Related Work

In this paper, we investigate the role that app name plays in the app representation for similar app recommendation task. As a typical kind of short text, app name can be treated as document, sentence, words or phrase, but not exactly the same. Statistical patterns of human word usage can be used to figure our what people mean. In other words, if units of text have similar vectors in a text frequency matrix, then they tend to have similar meanings. This is statistical semantics hypothesis [15]. According to different kinds of statistical semantics hypothesis, we review the related work in terms of document similarity based on bag of words hypothesis and word similarity based on distributional hypothesis.

Document Similarity. Treating the document similarity as its content similarity, there are a bundle of classical methods to model the document content, like TF-IDF [17], LSI [19], LDA [2]. LSI [19] employs matrix factorization methods of the document-term matrix, such as singular value decomposition (SVD), to generate the low-dimensional document representations. LDA [2], short for Latent Dirichlet Allocation, is a three-level hierarchical Bayesian model of text corpora, in which each document in the collection is modeled as a finite mixture over an underlying topics, and each topic is modeled as an infinite mixture over words of topic probabilities. All the three methods are mainly based on vector space model [6], which is supposed to be the first practical, useful algorithm for exacting semantic information from word usage [15]. Bag of words hypothesis says that If documents have similar column vectors in a document-term matrix, then they tend to have similar meanings. To enrich the short texts, various related studies [10,12,18,23] propose to leverage external resources, such as web search results, to improve the semantical similarity between text segments.

Phrase/Word Similarity. Words that occur in similar contexts tend to have similar meanings [7,19]. Distributional hypothesis states that if words have similar row vectors in a word-context matrix, then they tend to have similar meanings. A lot of recent studies are based on this hypothesis, such as [9,16,21]. word2vec [21] learns word vectors from word-context matrix through neural network model, then it is extended to sentence and paragraph [16], namely Doc2vec in this paper. The focus shift from document to word provides more possibilities, for instance the context may be words, phrases, sentences, paragraphs, chapters, documents, sequences of characters and so on.

App Similarity. Existing studies [3,4,14,25] focus on the app representation learning from meta information in different tasks. For **app classification**, Zhu et al. [25] enrich the app representation by exploiting the additional Web knowledge from the Web search engine. For **app search**, AppLDA [14] is proposed to introduce user reviews to bridge the vocabulary gap between app developers and users to learn app representation by extending LDA. MobileWalla [1], a mobile application search engine, computes the semantic similarity between app based on the WordNet [5]. Panorama [4], a semantic-aware application search framework, propose the App Topic Model that integrates the text, link and category information in order to discover the latent semantics from apps. For **similar app recommendation**, SimApp [3] is the state-of-the-art framework to employ multiple heterogeneous kinds of app information to detect similar apps.

Different from the related studies on document and phrase or word similarity, our method takes the word dependency into consideration for the short app name the and leverages external source without too much effort. Distinguished from existing studies on app similarity, we put emphasis on the importance of names in learning app representation. SimApp [3] considers the app name as a short string of characters and utilizes the well-known string kernel [8], referred to as SSK (subsequence kernel) to model the similarity between apps as string matching without considering their semantics.

3   Motivation

App name is such an important feature that cannot be ignored in the app presentation learning. First, app names are usually originated from the summarization of the description, so words in app names are representative and less noisy. Second, though not unique, app names are often used as the identifier where one app is different from the others, so words in app names are discriminative. Finally, users identify similar apps usually by names intuitively. However, experimental results in existing studies [3,4,14,25] show app names do not play the most significant role in similar app recommendation. This phenomenon arouses our curiosity to study this problem.

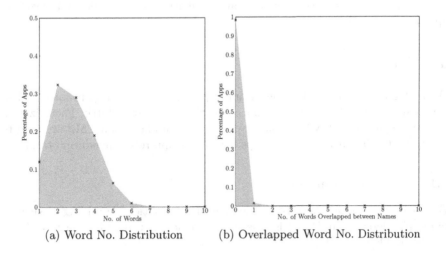

(a) Word No. Distribution   (b) Overlapped Word No. Distribution

Fig. 1. Word statistics in crawled app names

Words in app names are usually representative. Here we mean words in app names can be treated as the keywords of app description texts. We simply use the TF-IDF to predict the keywords in app description texts, and top k words are selected. Therefore the accuracy of this simple keyword extraction method can be coarsely estimated as the representativeness of words in app names, such as Precision@1 and Precision@2. Statistical results on our crawled more than 20 thousand apps show that Precision@1 and Precision@2 are 5 %, 4 % respectively.

Words in app names are often discriminative. Simply we use the literal difference between two app names to measure the discrimination of words, the word overlap between any two app names. On average, the number of words overlapped between any two app names is nearly 0.02. Among 200 million app pairs, 98 % pairs with no word in common. These results suggest app developers tend to use different words from existing app names even when two apps are semantically related. This characteristic of word usage will lead to the failure of word independence assumption in measuring the similarity between app names.

However, the number of words in app names are always smaller than ever. For instance, a common short text is microblog with the averaged number of words 5 or so. Statistical results on our crawled apps show that the averaged number of words is 2.8 for each app name in Fig. 1. In Fig. 1, more than 90 % apps have no more than 4 words in their names, and almost all the apps have no more than 6 words in their names. The small number of words in app names will cause the sparsity of models based on word independence assumption directly.

Generally, both the discriminative words and the smaller number of words in app names make it more difficult to learn a better semantic space for apps from names. Therefore we cannot connect "Uber" and "Yandex.Taxi" by looking at words alone. With the help of auxiliary text documents where these words co-occur frequently, we may establish a strong semantic similarity between words. As a result, it is necessary to incorporate auxiliary word dependency in learning app representation from names.

4   Methods

We first give a formal definition of app representation learning problem. Then we show this problem can be reduced to the Collective Matrix Factorization problem, denoted as CMF. Finally, app vectors obtained from CMF are used to compute the similarity between apps for similar app recommendation task.

4.1   Problem Definition

For each app $a \in \mathcal{A}$, there is a collection of information describing a, such as name E_a, description D_a. $\mathcal{A}$ is a set of n mobile apps. In this paper, we focus on the problem as follows.

Definition 1 (App Representation Learning). *Let E describe app names and L describe the semantic relation between two words for all apps in $\mathcal{A}$, our app representation learning problem aims at learning a latent semantic space for each app from both E and L.*

Given the name-word matrix E for all the apps in $\mathcal{A}$ and their associated auxiliary document-word matrix L, we hope to bridge the gap between word that are potentially semantically related. Here we use the app description as the auxiliary documents for example. As illustrated in Fig. 2, we construct a two-layer bipartite graph among app names, words and app descriptions.

Specifically, the left layer of bipartite graph is used to represent the relationship between names and words. Each app name can be represented as a vector of word occurrences and some app names share one or multiple word. If names of two apps have one or more words in common, they are supposed to be semantically related. Similarly, if two words co-occur in the same auxiliary document, they will be semantically related. This relationship between words and auxiliary documents is represented in the right layer of bipartite graph.

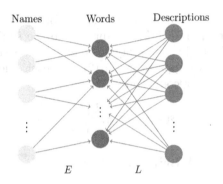

Fig. 2. Two-layer bipartite graph: name-word bipartite graph E and description-word bipartite graph L

4.2   Collective Matrix Factorization

We use the typical vector space model to obtain the name-word matrix $E \in \mathbb{R}^{n \times l}$, where n is the number of apps, and l is the size of app name dictionary. $E = (e_{ij})_{n \times l}$ where e_{ij} means TFIDF of word j in the name of app i, $E_{i\cdot}$ is the representation of app i in the original space. We derive the latent semantic space $U \in \mathbb{R}^{n \times k}$ by LSI [19] as $E = UV_1^T$, where $U_{i\cdot}$ is the latent semantic representation of app i, and k is the dimension of this latent semantic space.

$L \in \mathbb{R}^{n \times l}$ is a document-word matrix, where $L = (l_{ij})_{n \times l}$, l_{ij} means the count of word j in the description of app i, such as TF-IDF, TF and binary value. Here we use the TF value for example. $L_{i\cdot}$ is the representation of the description of app i. Using Latent Semantic Indexing [19], we obtain the latent semantic representation by $L = WV_2^T$.

In order to bridge the gap between words that are likely to be semantically related, we propose to learn the latent semantic representation U by decomposing E and L jointly with the constraint $V_1 = V_2$. This is called collective matrix factorization, denoted as CMF, which was proposed by Singh and Gordon [20].

Our **App** representation **L**earning problem can be reduce the following CMF problem in Eq. (1), denoted as AppLe-CMF[1].

$$\begin{aligned} \min \quad & \lambda_E\|E - UV_1^T\|_F^2 + \lambda_L\|L - WV_2^T\|_F^2 + \Omega(U, V_1, V_2, W) \\ s.t. \quad & V_1 = V_2 \end{aligned} \tag{1}$$

In the optimization objective function of AppLe-CMF as Eq. (1), λ_E and $\lambda_L(0 \le \lambda_E, \lambda_L \le 1, \lambda_E + \lambda_L = 1)$ are trade-off parameters between the factorization error of E and L. $\|M\|_F$ is the Frobenius Norm of M. $\Omega(U, V_1, V_2, W)$ is the regularized term to control the complexity of U, V_1, V_2 and W. In this paper, we defined this term as $\gamma_1\|U\|_F^2 + \gamma_2\|V_1\|_F^2 + \gamma_3\|V_2\|_F^2 + \gamma_4\|W\|_F^2$.

4.3   App Similarity

We obtain the latent semantic representation U for all apps by optimizing the objective function of AppLe-CMF. To apply it to the similar app recommendation, we employ the cosine similarity to compute the semantically similarity $s(a_i, a_j)$ between any two apps as in Eq. (2). For each query app, top d apps with higher similarity are recommended.

$$s(a_i, a_j) = \frac{U_{i.} U_{j.}}{\|U_{i.}\|\|U_{j.}\|} \tag{2}$$

5   Optimization Algorithm

The remaining question is how to optimize the objective function of AppLe-CMF in Eq. (1). First, we introduce the augmented Lagrangian function for better convergence. Second, we apply the alternating direction method of multiplier to solve the collective matrix factorization problem. Finally, we analyze the time complexity of our optimization method.

5.1   Augmented Lagrangian Function

We transform the constrained optimization problem AppLe-CMF into the unconstrained optimization problem by introducing the Lagrangian function

$$\lambda_E\|E - UV_1^T\|_F^2 + \lambda_L\|L - WV_2^T\|_F^2 + \Omega(U, V_1, V_2, W) + \Lambda \bullet (V_1 - V_2),$$

where Λ is the Lagrangian multiplier. The scalar product $\bullet$ is the sum of all element-wise products of two matrices A and B of the same size, i.e., $A \bullet B = \sum_{i,j} a_{ij}b_{ij}$. Although this Lagrangian function is non-convex with all the four matrices U, V_1, V_2 and W, it is convex with respect to any one matrix while fixing the other three.

Existing alternating methods [22] optimize one matrix by fixing the others iteratively until the results converges. The only difference among different

---

[1] Core code is available at https://github.com/bnn2010/iscas2016_AppSimilarity.

alternating methods lies in the update step. Some methods utilize the conjugate gradient descent step [26], other methods employ the Newton-Raphson step [20].

Compared with the classical alternating methods [20,22,26], the ADMM algorithm converge much faster due to the addition of the quadratic term $\|V_1 - V_2\|_F^2$, which can be interpreted as quadratic Tikhonov regularization [13]. This damping term encourages $V_1^{(t)}$ not to be very far from $V_2^{(t)}$ after t iterations. As the ADMM algorithm converges, $V_1^{(t)}$ gets close to $V_2^{(t)}$, so the effect of the quadratic regularization goes to zero. In other words, the quadratic regularization contributes a term to the gradient that decreases to zero as the algorithm proceeds. Therefore, the augmented Lagrangian function of the original problem AppLe-CMF in Eq. (1) is

$$
\begin{aligned}
\mathcal{L}(U, V_1, V_2, W, \Lambda) = &\lambda_E \|E - U V_1^T\|_F^2 + \lambda_L \|L - W V_2^T\|_F^2 + \Omega(U, V_1, V_2, W) \\
&+ \Lambda \bullet (V_1 - V_2) + \alpha \|V_1 - V_2\|_F^2,
\end{aligned}
\tag{3}
$$

where Λ is a lagrangian multiplier and $\alpha > 0$ is a penalty parameter. The Lagrangian multiplier Λ is a dual variable associated with the consensus constraint $V_1 = V_2$, which means the violation degree of the constraint.

5.2   Alternating Direction Method of Multipliers for Collective Matrix Factorization

The alternating direction method of multipliers for the augmented Lagrangian function in Eq. (3) is derived by successively minimizing $\mathcal{L}$ with respect to U, V_1, V_2, W, one at a time while fixing others at their most recent values, then updating the multiplier Λ. For each iteration $t+1$, the update includes two parts:

1. update U, V_1, V_2 and W

$$
\begin{aligned}
U^{(t+1)} &= \arg\min \mathcal{L}(U, V_1^{(t)}, V_2^{(t)}, W^{(t)}, \Lambda^{(t)}) \\
V_1^{(t+1)} &= \arg\min \mathcal{L}(U^{(t+1)}, V_1, V_2^{(t)}, W^{(t)}, \Lambda^{(t)}) \\
V_2^{(t+1)} &= \arg\min \mathcal{L}(U^{(t+1)}, V_1^{(t+1)}, V_2, W^{(t)}, \Lambda^{(t)}) \\
W^{(t+1)} &= \arg\min \mathcal{L}(U^{(t+1)}, V_1^{(t+1)}, V_2^{(t+1)}, W, \Lambda^{(t)})
\end{aligned}
\tag{4}
$$

2. update the dual variable Λ

$$
\Lambda^{(t+1)} = \Lambda^{(t)} + 2\eta\alpha(V_1^{(t+1)} - V_2^{(t+1)})
\tag{5}
$$

where η is a step length.

Considering the convexity of each primal variable to $\mathcal{L}$, the minimization in each step is achieved by the local minimum using the most recent values of the other primal variables and the dual variables. Thus we obtain the closed form of the minimization problem in each step as Eq. (6).

$$U^{(t+1)} = \arg\min\{\lambda_E \|E - UV_1^{(t)T}\|_F^2 + \gamma_1 \|U\|_F^2\}$$
$$= \lambda_E E V_1^{(t)} (\lambda_E V_1^{(t)T} V_1^{(t)} + \gamma_1 I_{k \times k})^{-1}$$
$$V_1^{(t+1)} = \arg\min\{\lambda_E \|E - U^{(t+1)} V_1^T\|_F^2 + \gamma_2 \|V_1\|_F^2 + \Lambda^{(t)} \bullet V_1 + \alpha \|V_1 - V_2^{(t)}\|_F^2\}$$
$$= (2\lambda_E E^T U^{(t+1)} + 2\alpha V_2^{(t)} - \Lambda^{(t)})(2\lambda_E U^{(t+1)T} U^{(t+1)} + (2\gamma_2 + 2\alpha) I_{k \times k})^{-1}$$
$$V_2^{(t+1)} = \arg\min\{\lambda_L \|L - W^{(t)} V_2^T\|_F^2 + \gamma_3 \|V_2\|_F^2 - \Lambda^{(t)} \bullet V_2 + \alpha \|V_1^{(t+1)} - V_2\|_F^2\}$$
$$= (2\lambda_L L^T W^{(t)} + 2\alpha V_1^{(t+1)} + \Lambda^{(t)})(2\lambda_L W^{(t+1)T} W^{(t+1)} + (2\gamma_3 + 2\alpha) I_{k \times k})^{-1}$$
$$W^{(t+1)} = \arg\min\{\lambda_L \|L - W V_2^{(t+1)T}\|_F^2 + \gamma_1 \|W\|_F^2\}$$
$$= \lambda_L L V_2^{(t+1)} (\lambda_L V_2^{(t+1)T} V_2^{(t+1)} + \gamma_4 I_{k \times k})^{-1}$$

$$(6)$$

Algorithm 1. Alternating Direction Method of Multipliers for Collective Matrix Factorization

---
1: **Input:**
2:    the matrix $E, L \in \mathbb{R}^{n \times l}$;
3: **Output:** the latent semantic space $U \in \mathbb{R}^{n \times k}$.
4: **begin**
5: set V_1, V_2 as a random matrix
6: set $\alpha, \eta > 0$,
7: set U, W and Λ as zero matrix of appropriate sizes
8: **while** $\Delta \mathcal{L}(U, V_1, V_2, W, \Lambda) \geq \epsilon$ **do**
9:    update (U, V_1, V_2, W) as Eq. (6);
10:    update Λ as Eq. (5);
11: **end while**
12: return U
13: **end**

As shown in Algorithm 1, the stopping criterion is met when the following condition is satisfied: $\frac{|\mathcal{L}_{t+1} - \mathcal{L}_t|}{\mathcal{L}_0} \leq \epsilon$. $\mathcal{L}_{t+1}$ and $\mathcal{L}_t$ are objective values in the iteration $t+1$ and t respectively. ϵ is usually a small value.

5.3   Time Complexity

Each iteration in the Algorithm 1 consists of updating the five matrices U, V_1, V_2, W and Λ. Then we analyze the time complexity for each iteration.

The most time-consuming computation in updating U lies in the multiple matrices multiplication and the matrix inversion in Eq. (6). Time complexity for obtaining the matrix to be inverse and computing the inversion of a matrix with size $k \times k$ is about $\mathcal{O}(lk^2)$ and $\mathcal{O}(k^3)$ respectively. Computing the multiplication of three matrices with size $n \times l$, $l \times k$ and $k \times k$ separately cost about $\mathcal{O}(nlk + \max\{n, l\}k^2)$. Therefore the overall complexity is $\mathcal{O}(k^3 + lk^2 + \max\{n, l\}k^2 + nlk)$.

Similarly, the time complexity for updating V_1, V_2, W and Λ is $\mathcal{O}(k^3 + lk^2 + nk^2 + nlk)$, $\mathcal{O}(k^3 + lk^2 + nk^2 + nlk)$, $\mathcal{O}(k^3 + lk^2 + \max\{n, l\}k^2 + nlk)$

and $\mathcal{O}(lk)$ separately. For each iteration in Algorithm 1, the time complexity is $\mathcal{O}(k^3+lk^2+\max\{n,l\}k^2+nlk)$. Its leading complexity $\mathcal{O}(nlk)$ is the same as that in gradient descent method. In this sense, the ADMM is nearly as efficient as the gradient descent method. Suppose the algorithm converges after T iterations, the overall complexity is $\mathcal{O}(nlkT)$, which is comparable to those of baseline methods, such as LDA [2], LSI [19] and Doc2vec [16].

6 Experiments

First we present our crawled apps from Google Play, which are used as our datasets, and other experimental settings. Then we conduct comprehensive experiments on our datasets in terms of accuracy analysis and parameter sensitivity analysis in similar app recommendation task. To make a further step towards the performance improvement, we analyze an illustrative example in detail and compare the word vector for better understanding.

6.1 Experimental Setting

Datasets. We establish our original data set in two steps. First, we use the app meta-information provided in [3] and obtain 15,282 apps which belong to 42 categories, after removing some noisy apps. For each app, name and description are preprocessed by removing the punctuation, stop words and low-frequency words, stemming. Thus there are 3,835 distinct words in names and 41,773 words in descriptions. Then, we crawl similar app lists presented in Google Play Store because the test collection is not provided in [3]. The ground truth for app similarity is generated from our crawled tens of thousands of similar app lists. Like [3], two apps are considered to be similar if they co-occur in the same similar app list more than once.

Baselines. In this section, we explain the process of our empirical study and briefly review several state-of-art algorithms we compared to as baselines. We compared our proposed AppLe-CMF with three kinds of typical baseline methods: (1) Document Similarity Models: TF-IDF [17], LSI [19], LDA [2]; (2) Word Similarity Models: Doc2vec [16]; (3) String Similarity Models: the string kernel [8] used in SimApp [3] denoted as SimApp_S. For those latent space models like LSI, LDA, Doc2vec and AppLe-CMF, we choose the dimension of latent space from 10 to 100 with step 10 and from 200 to 1000 with step 100. Additionally, our proposed method AppLe-CMF need to adjust a trade-off parameter from 0.1 to 0.9 with step 0.1. All these performances shown in the following sections are in the best configuration. We set α as $1.91\times10^{-4}\frac{\max\{\|E\|_F,\|L\|_F\}\max\{n,l\}}{k}$ like [24]. ϵ in the stopping criterion is 10^{-6} and η is 1.618 as [24] in our experiments.

Evaluation. For rank-based evaluation, we set each app as query app, and its similar apps can be obtained from the similar app lists. After removing those query apps with the number of similar apps less than 5, we obtain $4,457$

query apps. Based on the unreliable assumption that apps out of app a's similar app list are dissimilar to a, we choose dissimilar apps for each query app as in SimApp [3]. To avoid the bias of the unreliable assumption, we randomly select different numbers of dissimilar apps, such as 50, 100, 200. Therefore we obtain three test data sets with each query app corresponding to a list of more than 5 similar apps (labeled with 1) and a number of dissimilar apps (labeled with 0), denoted as AppSet50, AppSet100, AppSet200. We evaluate the performance of various methods for similar app recommendation with rank-based measures [11], i.e. Precision@k(denoted as P@k) and NDCG@k.

6.2   Ranking Accuracy Analysis

With P@5 and NDCG@5 as evaluation measures, the best averaged performance over all the query apps is shown in Table 1. For all the three data sets, the optimal parameter setting of k is 900, 200, 300, 1000 for LSI, LDA, Doc2vec and AppLe-CMF separately and the optimal λ_L is 0.9 for AppLe-CMF. Statistical significance tests are also done for performance comparisons.

Table 1. Performance comparison between AppLe-CMF and baseline methods

Approach	AppSet50		AppSet100		AppSet200	
	P@5	NDCG@5	P@5	NDCG@5	P@5	NDCG@5
Doc2vec	0.232847	0.232050	0.140273	0.141457	0.079649	0.079178
TFIDF	0.669598	0.702618	0.624680	0.658857	0.583980	0.616297
LSI	0.698093	0.726622	0.653130	0.680771	0.607494	0.633038
LDA	0.641239	0.666057	0.576576	0.598272	0.496433	0.513752
SimApp_S	0.702580	0.733794	0.652188	0.683939	0.597846	0.628773
AppLe-CMF	0.714158[a]	0.738584[a]	0.669778[a]	0.692549[a]	0.613058[a]	0.634468[a]

[a]Performance differences between AppLe-CMF and any baseline are statistically significant with p-value < 0.01 for paired t-tests.

As shown in Table 1, our proposed method AppLe-CMF achieves the best performance on all the three data sets among all the methods. For example, P@5 of AppLe-CMF on AppSet100 is 6.7%, 2.3%, 11.4%, 1.6%, 377.48% higher than TF-IDF, LSI, LDA, SimApp_S and Doc2vec separately. Obviously, both typical document similarity models (i.e., TF-IDF, LSI, LDA) and word similarity model (i.e. Doc2vec) perform not so well as string similarity model (i.e. SimApp_S) mainly because the string kernel used in SimApp makes full use of the limited words of names in terms of characters. Generally, the introduction of word dependency brings about the performance improvement of AppLe-CMF.

With the increase of the dissimilar app number from each dataset in Table 1, the performance of each method decreases. Taking SimApp_S for example, NDCG@5 on AppSet100 and AppSet200 is 6.8% and 14.3% less than that on

AppSet50 respectively. This performance deduction can be explained by two reasons. One is that the similar app recommendation task becomes more difficult as the dataset size increases. The other is the unreliable assumption that there is some similar apps labeled with 0 as mentioned before. In that case, these noisy labels have no effect on our performance comparison results.

Table 2. Similar apps for "Uber" from AppLe-CMF and baselines

	LDA	LSI	AppLe-CMF	SimApp_S	TFIDF	Doc2vec
1	Duel Quiz	CNHandwriting for GO Keyboard	Taxibeat Free taxi app	Battery Widget Lightsaber	Alaska Airlines Travel App	GalaxSim Unlock
2	SugarSync	GalaxSim Unlock	inTaxi: order taxi in Russia	Het Weer in Nederland	The Economic Times	Easy Taxi, Cab App for Drivers
3	Lyft	inTaxi: order taxi in Russia	Yandex.Taxi	Water Drop Live Wallpaper	Het Weer in Nederland	Hill Climb Racing
4	BiTaksi	Pinball Pro	Tappsi Taxista	Meru Cabs	Essential Memo	TapTaxi
5	PipeRoll	Duel Quiz	EST: Call Taxi?	Calorie Counter	Yandex.Taxi	BusyBox X

Specifically for the query app "Uber", which is a well-known taxi booking app, we list top 5 apps names for each method in Table 2. One app is similar (not similar) to the query app if its name is in black (red) color. Note that in Table 2, "Taxibeat Free taxi app", "BiTaksi", "Yandex.Taxi", "Lyft" etc. are all taxi booking apps. This qualitative example illustrates the better performance of AppLe-CMF. TF-IDF and SimApp_S cannot capture the latent semantic relation between "Uber" and "taxi", which are well related in AppLe-CMF. The semantic similarity between word vectors may explain the better performance of AppLe-CMF, which inspires us to explore the underlying reason further.

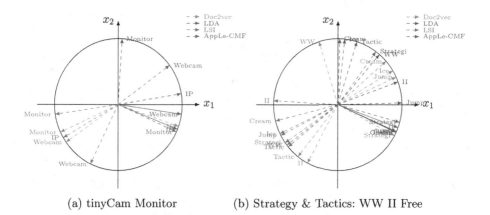

(a) tinyCam Monitor   (b) Strategy & Tactics: WW II Free

Fig. 3. Word vectors in latent space

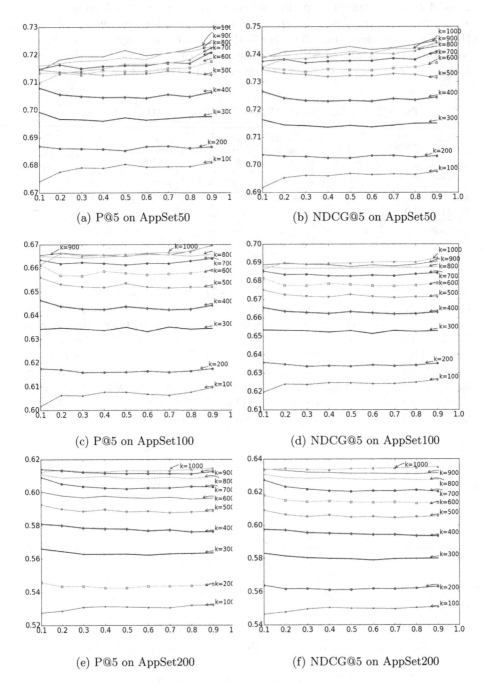

Fig. 4. Performance variation with k and λ_L

6.3 Word Vector

To illustrate the learned word vector, we present the latent space with 2-dimension in Fig. 3. Due to the cosine similarity adopted in all the methods, we focus on the angle between two word vectors. Thus all the word vectors are mapped to the unit circle for better comparison. We select two similar app pairs ("tinyCam Monitor FREE", "IP Webcam") and ("Strategy & Tactics: WW II FREE", "Ice Cream Jump"), where the former means the query app and the latter means the app to be ranked. After preprocessing, there remains three words ("Monitor", "IP", "Webcam") in the first example, and seven words except "FREE" in the second example.

Both examples in Fig. 3 are similar pairs, so they are supposed to have a small angle between words from different apps. For the first example in Fig. 3a, the query app is for remote surveillance or control your private or public network/IP cameras, video encoders, DVRs and Webcams. For our understanding, both angles between vectors "monitor" and "Webcam", vectors "monitor" and "IP" are small. AppLe-CMF reflects our understanding well while baselines do not. This seems to reveal the underlying reason for the improvement of AppLe-CMF.

6.4 Parameter Sensitivity

There are two parameters in our proposed AppLe-CMF. k is the dimension of the latent space, and λ_L is the trade-off parameter, where $\lambda_E = 1 - \lambda_L$. Here we investigate its sensitivity to different parameter settings. Experimental results are shown in Fig. 4, k ranges from 100 to 1000 with step 100 and λ_L ranges from 0.1 to 0.9 with step 0.1.

In Fig. 4, the relative performance changes with λ_L is stable. For example, on AppSet50, NDCG@5 increases by 1.22 % and P@5 increases by 1.80 % from 0.1 to 0.9 when $k = 1000$. However, the performance increases fast with k from 100 to 1000. For $\lambda_L = 0.9$ on AppSet100, P@5 and NDCG@5 improvement is 9.87 % and 10.59 % respectively. Thus the setting of k has more effect on the performance of our proposed method.

7 Conclusions and Future Work

We mainly focus on learning app representation from app names for similar app recommendation. First, we explore the characteristics of names and find the reason why additional information is needed lies in the discriminative and fewer words in app names. Then we incorporate the word dependency from auxiliary documents, such as app descriptions, into name-word matrix and formulate this app representation learning as the collective matrix factorization problem, referred to as AppLe-CMF. Finally, for better convergence, Alternating direction method of multipliers is employed novelly for AppLe-CMF. Experimental results show that our proposed method outperforms state-of-the-art baselines.

In the future work, we will extend our AppLe-CMF to all the heterogeneous data in apps, such as links, images and other texts, to obtain a comprehensive app representation. Moreover, our AppLe-CMF will be applied to the app search task and how to model query will become of our main concern. Finally, AppLe-CMF in the supervised scenario will be attractive.

Acknowledgments. This paper is supported in part by the National High-tech R&D Program of China (No. 2012AA010902), and NSFC (No. 61303059).

References

1. Kajanan, S., Pervin, N., Datta, A., Dutta, K.: Mobilewalla: a mobile application search engine. IEEE Trans. Mob. Comput. (2011)
2. Blei, D.M., Ng, A.Y., Jordan, M.I.: Latent dirichlet allocation. JMLR **3**, 993–1022 (2003)
3. Chen, N., Hoi, S.C., Li, S., Xiao, X.: Simapp: a framework for detecting similar mobile applications by online kernel learning. In: WSDM 2015, pp. 305–314 (2015)
4. Leung, K.W.T., Ng, W., Di Jiang, K., Vosecky, J.: Panorama: a semantic-aware application search framework. In: Extending Database Technology (2013)
5. Fellbaum, C.: WordNet: An Electronic Lexical Database. MIT Press, Cambridge (1998)
6. Yang, C.S., Salton, G., Wong, A.: A vector space model for automatic indexing. Commun. ACM **18**(11), 613–620 (1975)
7. Harris, Z.: Distributional structure. Word **10**(23), 146–162 (1954)
8. Shawe-Taylor, J., Cristianini, N., Watkins, C., Lodhi, H., Saunders, C.: Text classification using string kernels. JMLR **2**, 419–444 (2002)
9. Manning, C.D., Pennington, J., Socher, R.: Glove: Global vectors for word representation (2014)
10. Jones, R., Rey, B., Madani, O., Greiner, W.: Generating query substitutions. In: WWW 2006, pp. 387–396 (2006)
11. Manning, C.D., Raghavan, P., Schütze, H.: Introduction to Information Retrieval. Cambridge University Press, Cambridge (2008)
12. Metzler, D., Dumais, S.T., Meek, C.: Similarity measures for short segments of text. In: Amati, G., Carpineto, C., Romano, G. (eds.) ECiR 2007. LNCS, vol. 4425, pp. 16–27. Springer, Heidelberg (2007)
13. Parikh, N., Boyd, S.: Proximal algorithms. Found. Trends Optim. **1**(3), 127–239 (2014)
14. Park, D.H., Liu, M., Zhai, C., Wang, H.: Leveraging user reviews to improve accuracy for mobile app retrieval. In: SIGIR 2015, pp. 533–542 (2015)
15. Peter, P.P., Turney, D.: From frequency to meaning: vector space models of semantics. J. Artif. Intell. Res. **37**(1), 141–188 (2010)
16. Mikolov, T., Le, Q.: Distributed representations of sentences and documents (2014)
17. Rajaraman, A., Ullman, J.D., Leskovec, J.: Mining of Massive Datasets, vol. 1. Cambridge University Press, Cambridge (2012)
18. Sahami, M., Heilman, T.D.: A web-based kernel function for measuring the similarity of short text snippets. In: WWW 2006, pp. 377–386 (2006)
19. Furnas, G.W., Landauer, T.K., Harshman, R., Scott, D., Dumais, S.T.: Indexing by latent semantic analysis. J. Am. Soc. Inf. Sci. **41**(6), 391–407 (1990)
20. Singh, A.P., Gordon, G.J.: Relational learning via collective matrix factorization. In: KDD 2008, pp. 650–658 (2008)

21. Chen, K., Corrado, G.S., Dean, J., Mikolov, T., Sutskever, I.: Distributed representations of words and phrases and their compositionality. In: NIPS (2013)
22. Von Neumann, J.: Functional Operators: The Geometry of Orthogonal Spaces. Princeton University Press, Princeton (1950)
23. Yih, W.-T., Meek, C.: Improving similarity measures for short segments of text. In: AAAI, vol. 7, pp. 1489–1494 (2007)
24. Zhang, Y.: An alternating direction algorithm for nonnegative matrix factorization (2010, preprint)
25. Zhu, H., Chen, E., Xiong, H., Cao, H., Tian, J.: Mobile app classification with enriched contextual information. IEEE Trans. Mob. Comput. 13(7), 1550–1563 (2014)
26. Zhu, Y., Chen, Y., Lu, Z., Pan, S.J., Xue, G.R., Yu, Y., Yang, Q.: Heterogeneous transfer learning for image classification. In: AAAI (2011)
27. Zhuo, J., Huang, Z., Liu, Y., Kang, Z., Cao, X., Li, M., Jin, L.: Semantic matchingin app search. In: WSDM 2015, pp. 209–210 (2015)

Summarizing Multimedia Content

Natwar Modani[1]([⊠]), Pranav Maneriker[1], Gaurush Hiranandani[1],
Atanu R. Sinha[1], Utpal[1], Vaishnavi Subramanian[1], and Shivani Gupta[2]

[1] BigData Experience Lab, Adobe Research, Bangalore, India
{nmodani,pmanerik,ghiranan,atr,utp,vasubram}@adobe.com
[2] Adobe India, Noida, India
shivanig@adobe.com

Abstract. Today multimedia content comprising both text and images
is growing at a rapid pace. There has been a body of work to summarize
text content, but to the best of our knowledge, no method has been developed to summarize multimedia content. We propose two methods for
summarizing multimedia content. Our novel approach explicitly recog-
nizes two desirable, normative characteristics of a summary - good coverage and diversity of the respective text and images, and that text and
images should be coherent with each other. Two methods are examined -
graph based and a modification to the submodular approach. Moreover,
we propose a metric to measure the quality of a multimedia summary
which captures coverage and diversity of text and images as well as coherence between the text and images in the summary. We experimentally
demonstrate that the proposed methods achieve good quality multimedia
summaries.

Keywords: Summarization · Text and images · Multimedia content ·
Algorithms

1 Introduction

Today multimedia content is growing at a rapid pace on the web. To cater to
readers, publishers such as The New York Times and The Wall Street Journal
offer briefings of content with text and images. The growing shift to mobile
devices calls for summarizing multimedia content. Text summarization has been
addressed. Our research fills a void by examining summarization of multimedia
content - text and images.

The first of two formulations we propose is graph based, inspired by [13]. Each
fragment of either content type is a node, the edge weight within a content type is
the similarity between two fragments, and the edge weight between fragments of
two different types is the coherence between them. The node weight signifies the
amount of information in the fragment. The objective function includes all three
properties. The second approach uses sub-modular functions, inspired by [9]. The
objective function models coverage and diversity of both content types in the summary, but introduces an additional term for the coherence between these types.

© Springer International Publishing AG 2016
W. Cellary et al. (Eds.): WISE 2016, Part II, LNCS 10042, pp. 340–348, 2016.
DOI: 10.1007/978-3-319-48743-4_27

In the absense of ground truth, information coverage and diversity of a summary are used to measure its quality. We extend this notion to images, while also incorporating the coherence of the images and text to define quality for the new concept of multimedia summary. A quality metric, labeled MuSQ (Multimedia Summary Quality) is introduced. With a small manually annotated data set, we demonstrate that the proposed metric shows better agreement with human judgement when compared to traditional metrics such as retention/compression rate and KL divergence. We then evaluate the proposed algorithms using this metric, and the experimental results show that our proposed algorithms perform better compared to the baseline methods.

2   Related Work

While text summarization has been an active area of research for several years, summarizing multimedia content is relatively unexplored. Recent work has presented a multimedia summarizer system for retrieving relevant information from web repositories based on the extraction of semantic descriptors of documents [1]. In this approach, images are not treated as primary objects, but are chosen secondarily based on the selected text summary. Notably, the content of the images is not leveraged, instead only its metadata is used, making the summary potentially less accurate.

The literature on summarization of multimedia data [3] focuses largely on video summarization. Other works [2], based on video/audio features, exploit natural language engines to create textual summaries.

For text summarization, the two broad approaches are: abstractive and extractive. In this research paper, we will be focusing on extractive summarization only.

Starting with Luhn [10] automated (text-only) extractive document summarization has been examined by researchers in Information Retrieval and Computational Linguistics [14]. Algorithms such as support vector machine (SVM) and regression models have been used. However, Wu et al. [17] found that certain graph-based algorithms (for example, TextRank [11]) perform better than SVM and regression methods.

Solving the summarization problem for product reviews, [13] proposed a graph based formulation which uses a fast and scalable greedy algorithm. They considered the informativeness and diversity of the sentences to select the summary of the reviews.

The papers mentioned above follow the bag of words approach, which rely on frequency of words in documents. In a different approach, [5] used continuous vector representations for semantically aware representations of sentences as a basis for measuring similarity. Our technology extends the approach presented in [5,13] to incorporate images in the summary.

With our goal of multimedia summary it is necessary to associate segments of text with segments of images. Approaches that describe contents of images are formulated either by mapping images to a fixed set of human-constructed sentences [4,15], or by automatically generating novel captions [8,12]. Other approaches use Kernel Canonical Correlation Analysis [16] to align images and sentences; however their reliance on computing kernels, quadratic in number of images and sentences, make them not easily scalable. We use the framework developed by [6] to map the text and images onto a common vector space in our work.

3   Problem Definition

First, we present five desirable qualities of multimedia summary qualitatively, by extending well-established concepts in text summarization.

- The text (image) part of the summary should provide good coverage of the text (image) part of the document.
- The text (image) part of the summary should be diverse.
- The text and image part of the summary should be coherent.

We start by defining the content fragment which is either a text unit (typically, a sentence), or an image segment. The desired size of the summary images is a configuration parameter of our system. The image segments are generated as follows. First, we apply an image segmentation algorithm [7] to identify informative objects in an image. Then, each image segment is bounded by a box. This is achieved by finding the smallest rectangle parallel to boundaries that completely encloses the informative object as identified above. If the rectangle is smaller than desired size, it is merged with other image segments that overlap with it. Eventually, when the bounding rectangle is at least of the desired size, we re-size it (by zoom out) to fit the desired size. Now, each such rectangle is an image segment.

The similarity between a pair of text units (sentences) is determined by first applying a recursive auto-encoder based vector representation to both the text units and then taking the cosine similarity between the two vectors. For finding the similarity between a pair of image segments, we apply the deep learning based CNN (convolutional neural network) technique [6] to transform images into a vector of size 4096, and then assess the cosine similarity between these two vectors. To find the similarity between a text unit and an image segment, we apply the transformation to project them into a common vector space [6] and then we compute the cosine similarity between the vectors representing the image and the text.

3.1   Graph Based Approach

In this approach, (inspired by [13]), we construct a graph to represent the document. Each node represents a content fragment. We draw an edge between two nodes, representing two content fragments, with the edge weight as their similarity. We also assign a reward to each content fragment. A text unit is assigned the reward score as the number of nouns, adverbs, adjectives, verbs and half of the number of pronouns. An image fragment is assigned the reward score based on the information content. We take the image segment reward as the average level of similarity with all other image segments.

We attach a cost to each content fragment. The cost of a text fragment is taken in units of sentences, word or characters, and the cost of an image segment is taken as one unit, as all image segments are resized to the desired level. The user also specifies the upper limit on the size of summary for the text and image parts separately, called as budget for the text and image parts, respectively, and represented as b_T and b_I.

We follow an iterative greedy strategy [13] to select the content fragments to include in the summary. In particular, we find the gain G_i of including an available content fragments i in the summary, given by:

$$G_i = \sum_{j=1}^{n} w_{ij} * R_j + \sum_{k=1}^{m} \hat{w}_{ik} * \hat{R}_k \tag{1}$$

Here, w_{ij} is the edge weight between the ith content fragment and j^{th} text unit, and $\hat{w}_{ik}$ is the edge weight between the ith content fragment and k^{th} image segment. Further, R_j is the reward of the jth text unit, and $\hat{R}_k$ is the reward for the kth image segment.

Then we find the content fragment, with the maximum gain to cost ratio, and include it in the summary. Note that we do not impose any order while choosing the text and image fragments for the summary, although the number of text units and image segments selected are controlled by the individual budgets for those two parts of the summary. When a content fragment is included in the summary, the rewards for all other content fragments are updated, per following rules. If a content fragment is the same type as the selected content fragment, its rewards is multiplied by $(1 - w_{ij})$, and if the content fragment in question is of a different type compared to the selected content fragment, its reward is multiplied by $(1 + w_{ij})$. This ensures diversity because the value of including another content fragment that is similar and of the same type as the summary is reduced. At the same time, coherence is achieved since the value of including a content fragment that is similar but of a different type is increased.

3.2   Coverage-Diversity Based Approach

In this approach, inspired by the sub-modular approach to text summarization [5], we have a five part objective function. We have a text coverage term, and a text diversity reward term. Along similar lines, we define the image coverage term, and an image diversity reward term. Finally, we define a coherence term which captures the similarity between text and image(s) selected in the summary. For document D, we denote the summary of the text T as S and of the images V as I. The objective function is defined as

$$F(S, I) = \alpha_1 * C_T(S) + \alpha_2 * R_T(S) + \alpha_3 * C_V(I) + \alpha_4 * R_V(I) + \alpha_5 * H(S, I) \tag{2}$$

Here, α's represent the weights which can be tuned by the user.

The term $C_T(S)$ represents the coverage of the text T of the document by the summary text S, defined in the same way as [5]

$$C_T(S) = \sum_{i \in T} min\{\sum_{j \in S} w_{ij}, \; \alpha \sum_{j \in T} \{w_{ij}\}\} \tag{3}$$

The term $R_T(S)$ is the reward for diversity of the text summary S with respect to the text of the document, defined in the same way as [9]

$$R_T(S) = \sum_{i \in S} \sqrt{\sum_{j \in P_i \cap S} r_j} \; \text{ where } \; r_j = \frac{1}{n} \sum_{i \in T} w_{ij} \tag{4}$$

where P_i is a partition of the ground set T into separate clusters and r_j is the singleton reward of including sentence j in the empty summary. The clustering is done using CLUTO with the 4096 sized vector representation of the sentences derived from [5] with number of clusters as 0.2 times the number of sentences (so, on average, each cluster would have 5 sentences), a direct K-mean clustering algorithm is used following the same choice as made in [9]. The term r_j is defined again in the same manner as [9] where n is the number of sentences in T and w_{ij} is the similarity between sentences i and j. By replacing T with V and S with I, we can define the corresponding terms for images and their summary.

The term $H(S,I)$ represents the coherence between the summary text and summary images. It is defined as the sum of all pairs of text units and image fragments, i.e.,

$$H(S,I) = \sum_{i \in S} \sum_{j \in I} \hat{w}_{ij}$$

here, $\hat{w}_{ij}$ represents the similarity between the text fragment i in the text part of the summary and image fragment j in the image part of the summary.

4   Multimedia Summary Quality

Measuring quality of a summary relative to its original source is important. Since the problem of multimedia summarization has not been addressed, no quality metrics have been proposed. We propose *MuSQ*, or *Multimedia Summary Quality*, which includes the desirable characteristics stated in Sect. 3. This metric does not require ground truth.

Let the similarity between a content fragment (text or image) u and another content fragment v be given by $Sim(u,v)$. Consider a text sentence v present in the document text T and a sentence u in the summary text S.

Now consider a metric μ_T defined as

$$\mu_T = \sum_{v \in T} R_v * \max_{u \in S} \{Sim(u,v)\} \tag{5}$$

The term $\max_{u \in S} Sim(u,v)$ represents the maximum level of similarity between a sentence v in the document text and any sentence in the summary S.

Recall that the term R_v is the reward value of the sentence v, and contribution of the sentence v towards the quality of the summary is accordingly $R_v * \max_{u \in S} Sim(u, v)$. Note that due to the *max* function, if there are two sentences which are similar to the given sentence v, it will not lead to enhanced contribution of the sentence to the quality of the summary. On the other hand, if the summary is having a sentence similar to a sentence in the document, it leads to increase in the metric value for the summary quality. In this way, the function μ_T is able to simultaneously capture the diversity and the information content of the summary with respect to the text of the original document T.

We define the overall quality metric *MuSQ* as:

$$\mu_M = \mu_T + \mu_I + \sigma_{T,I} \tag{6}$$

$$\mu_I = \sum_{w \in V} \hat{R}_w * \max_{x \in I} \{Sim(w, x)\} \tag{7}$$

$$\sigma_{T,I} = \sum_{v \in S} \sum_{w \in I} \{Sim(v, w) * R_v * \hat{R}_w\} \tag{8}$$

The terms μ_T and μ_I are diversity aware information coverage measure for the text part and the image part of the summary, respectively. The third term $\sigma_{T,I}$ measures the degree of cohesion between the text and the image part of the summary, as the sum of similarities between the sentences and the images in the summary, across all pairs.

5   Experimental Results

Now, we describe experimental results to validate our algorithms, as well as the proposed quality metric. First, on a small dataset we check whether the quality metric *MuSQ* correlates well with human judgment about the quality of multimedia summary, since obtaining human input for a large dataset is very expensive. Once *MuSQ* is validated, it is used to evaluate the proposed summarization algorithms on a larger dataset.

The small dataset comprised ten articles from the *New York Times* for each of which we created two summaries. In a survey, participants were shown the original article, the two summaries and were asked which one of the two summaries was better, or whether they were almost of similar quality. To control the order effect, the summaries were randomly placed first or second (without regard to their *MuSQ* scores), and the participants were not given any information about how the summaries were generated.

We define agreement level in three different ways. The first definition treats the 'Equal' option as half agreement and half disagreement, i.e., $AL1 = 100 * (A+0.5E)/(A+E+D)$, where $AL1$ is the agreement level according to definition 1, A is number of agreements (i.e., the human judge preferred the summary which had higher *MuSQ* score), E is number of times both summaries were deemed to be of same quality by the human judge, and D is the number of disagreements (i.e., the human judge preferred the summary which had lower *MuSQ* score).

Second definition treats the 'Equal' option as disagreement, i.e., $AL2 = 100 * A/(A + E + D)$. Third definition ignores the 'Equal' option completely, i.e., $AL3 = 100 * A/(A + D)$.

In total, 22 human judges provided 128 responses. Out of these, 87 responses favoured summaries with higher $MuSQ$ scores, whereas 14 responses found the summaries to be almost equal in quality. The remaining 27 responses disagreed with the ranking based on the $MuSQ$ scores. This translates to 68 % agreement for the $MuSQ$ scores (where, as a conservative approach 'equal' is classified as a disagreement), and 76 % agreement ignoring the votes for 'equal'. The Pearson correlation coefficient between the agreement levels (AL1, AL2 and AL3) and the fractional difference in the $MuSQ$ scores is approximately 0.51 for all the three definitions of agreement levels, which shows that our proposed quality metric correlates well with human judgment.

Now, we describe the experiments performed on a larger dataset, considering $MuSQ$ as the quality metric. We collected 1,000 articles from *New York Times*, which typically have text and images, both. We kept only those articles which had at least 20 and at most 100 sentences, and at least 1 image. This resulted in selecting 703 articles for the experiment. Further, the size of the summary was specified as 3 sentences and 1 image of size $200 * 200$ pixels.

The image segmentation algorithm takes the number of objects to be identified as input. We choose to identify 20 objects, with a further constraint that each class of objects does not occur more than 10 times. This ensures that the objects from a general class, such as background, do not end up as the only objects in the segments. Also, we used [9] to compute the similarity between two sentences. The similarity between two images, as well as, between a text sentence and an image was computed in the same way as [6].

We evaluated the two approaches proposed in this paper using the $MuSQ$ score. As a baseline, we used the text only version of these two algorithms for finding the three summary sentences, and augmented this summary with the first (whole) image from the article (hitherto only known method). The graph based approach we propose achieves the highest score 539 times, and the coverage-diversity based approach achieves the highest score 90 times. Only 103 times out of 703 articles, one of the two baseline approaches outperform our proposed approaches, and 587 times our proposed approaches outperform the baseline approaches. This means that our proposed approaches are better 83.5 % of the times and equally good another 1.5 % of the times. As the $MuSQ$ scores are dependent on the size of the original document, it is not appropriate to compare them across articles.

We also report the traditional text only performance metric for the summary quality for the four algorithms in Table 1, as well as the newly proposed metric $MuSQ$. As expected, the $MuSQ$ score is higher for the enhanced versions compared to the baseline methods. One finds that both for retention rate and KL-Divergence, the baseline approaches perform better than the enhanced approaches, which are to be expected. However, note that the performance degradation is fairly small and less severe for the graph based approach. Hence, the algorithms proposed by us provide significant value for summarizing multimedia content.

Table 1. Quality metric for the four approaches (retention rate and KL-Divergence are measured only for the text part of the summary)

Metric	Enhanced approaches		Baseline approaches	
	Submodular	Graph based	Submodular	Graph based
MuSQ	1528.37	1592.18	1519.95	1564.78
Retention rate	0.3704	0.4608	0.3896	0.4652
KL-Divergence	1.2052	0.8980	1.0822	0.8725

6 Conclusion

Today multimedia content in the form of text and images are commonplace across publishing sites and devices. The need for the summarization of such content to comprise both text and images is stronger than ever before. The results provide strong evidence in support of our proposed methods and validate the new quality metric. These summaries are better than the summaries generated only using text part and then adding the first image, which is the only known multimedia summary method. We hope that future work will advance our understanding and knowledge in multimedia summarization to parallel that of text summarization.

References

1. dAcierno, A., Gargiulo, F., Moscato, V., Penta, A., Persia, F., Picariello, A., Sansone, C., Sperl, G.: A multimedia summarizer integrating text and images. In: Intelligent Interactive Multimedia Systems and Services, pp. 21–33. Smart Innovation, Systems and Technologies (2014)
2. Ding, D., Metze, F., Rawat, S., Schulam, P.F., Burger, S.: Generating natural language summaries for multimedia. In: Proceedings of the Seventh International Natural Language Generation Conference, pp. 128–130. Association for Computational Linguistics (2012)
3. Ding, D., Metze, F., Rawat, S., Schulam, P.F., Burger, S., Younessian, E., Bao, L., Christel, M.G., Hauptmann, A.: Beyond audio and video retrieval: towards multimedia summarization. In: Proceedings of the 2nd ACM International Conference on Multimedia Retrieval, p. 2. ACM (2012)
4. Farhadi, A., Hejrati, M., Sadeghi, M.A., Young, P., Rashtchian, C., Hockenmaier, J., Forsyth, D.: Every picture tells a story: generating sentences from images. In: Daniilidis, K., Maragos, P., Paragios, N. (eds.) ECCV 2010, Part IV. LNCS, vol. 6314, pp. 15–29. Springer, Heidelberg (2010). doi:10.1007/978-3-642-15561-1_2
5. Kageback, M., Mogren, O., Tahmasebi, N., Dubhashi, D.: Extractive summarization using continuous vector space models. In: Proceedings of the 2nd Workshop on Continuous Vector Space Models and their Compositionality (CVSC), pp. 31–39. EACL (2014)
6. Karpathy, A., Joulin, A., Fei-Fei, L.: Deep fragment embeddings for bidirectional image sentence mapping. Archive, Cornell University Library (2014). http://arXiv.org/abs/1406.5679

7. Krähenbühl, P., Koltun, V.: Geodesic object proposals. In: Fleet, D., Pajdla, T., Schiele, B., Tuytelaars, T. (eds.) ECCV 2014, Part V. LNCS, vol. 8693, pp. 725–739. Springer, Heidelberg (2014). doi:10.1007/978-3-319-10602-1_47

8. Kulkarni, G., Premraj, V., Dhar, S., Li, S., Choi, Y., Berg, A.C., Berg, T.L.: Baby talk: understanding and generating simple image descriptions. In: CVPR (2011)

9. Lin, H., Bilmes, J.: A class of submodular functions for document summarization. In: Proceedings of the 49th Annual Meeting of the Association for Computational Linguistics: Human Language Technologies, HLT 2011, Stroudsburg, PA, USA, vol. 1, pp. 510–520 (2011)

10. Luhn, H.: The automatic creation of literature abstracts. IBM J. Res. Dev. **2**(2), 159–165 (1958)

11. Mihalcea, R.: Language independent extractive summarization. In: ACLdemo, pp. 49–52 (2005)

12. Mitchell, M., Han, X., Dodge, J., Mensch, A., Goyal, A., Berg, A., Yamaguchi, K., Berg, T., Stratos, K., Hal Daum, I.: Midge: generating image descriptions from computer vision detections. In: EACL (2012)

13. Modani, N., Khabiri, E., Srinivasan, H., Caverlee, J.: Graph based modeling for product review summarization. In: WISE (2015)

14. Nenkova, A., McKeown, K.: A survey of text summarization techniques. In: Aggarwal, C.C., Zhai, C.X. (eds.) Mining Text Data, pp. 43–76. Springer, New York (2012)

15. Ordonez, V., Kulkarni, G., Berg, T.L.: Im2text: describing images using 1 million captioned photographs. In: NIPS (2011)

16. Socher, R., Fei-Fei, L.: Connecting modalities: semi-supervised segmentation and annotation of images using unaligned text corpora. In: CVPR (2010)

17. Wu, J., Xu, B., Li, S.: An unsupervised approach to rank product reviews. In: FSKD, pp. 1769–1772 (2011)

Bridging Enterprise and Software Engineering Through an User-Centered Design Perspective

Pedro Valente[1,2]([⊠]), Thiago Silva[1], Marco Winckler[1],
and Nuno Nunes[2]

[1] Institut de Recherche en Informatique de Toulouse (IRIT),
Université Paul Sabatier, Route de Narbonne, 118, 31400 Toulouse, France
pvalente@uma.pt, {rocha,winckler}@irit.fr
[2] Madeira Interactive Technologies Institute (MITI), University of Madeira,
Caminho da Penteada, 9020-105 Funchal, Portugal
njn@uma.pt

Abstract. The development of Web-based Information Systems is crucial in the quest to maintain and develop the enterprise competiveness. However, capturing requirements from Business Processes (BP) is still an issue, as existing methods mostly focus, or on human aspects and the user interface, or on business concerns as rules and workflow coordination, and therefore do not specify all the Software Architectural components which are relevant for software development. We present the Goals Approach, which analyzes BPs and User Tasks and details them in the process of methodically designing and structuring the User Interface, the Business Logic and the Database of the Information System given a Model-View-Controller (MVC) architectural pattern. In this paper we focus on how to obtain the Goals business model of requirements based on the DEMO method. The approach can be used for in-house software development, and the method is straightforward fitting Small and Medium Enterprises agility needs.

Keywords: Web-based applications · Enterprise engineering · Software engineering · User-Centered Design · Software architecture

1 Introduction

Software development within enterprises still lacks effectiveness as project full-success rates are still as low as about 30 % [1, 2]. Despite this fact, efforts in SE have at least taken us from a chaotic state of the practice [3], to a more inspiring situation where expertized executive management support, user involvement in the development process and agile techniques are appointed as factors of project success [4, 5].

In our quest to integrate the enterprise and the software engineering perspectives as a solution to align business and Information Technology (IT) and create the conditions to increase software success rates, we bridge both domains by means of a User-Centered Design perspective that allows the modeling of Web-based applications. We presents the Goals Approach, which models the business and uses it as the back-bone of the software architecture. This paper focuses on the business model elaboration from DEMO [6], as a way to enhance business analysis performance and explain our method.

W. Cellary et al. (Eds.): WISE 2016, Part II, LNCS 10042, pp. 349–357, 2016.
DOI: 10.1007/978-3-319-48743-4_28

1.1   Foundations and Software Development Process

The Goals Approach is founded on five methods: Wisdom [8], which is a software engineering and architectural method; Goals [9], which establishes a relation between business and software architectures; DEMO [6], that models the enterprise by means of an ontology; Activity Modeling (AM) [10], which models human activity and designs the user interface, and BDD [11], which models user interface and system behavior.

The Software Development Process defines a method that integrates the Enterprise Engineering and Software Engineering perspectives, concerning a given Business Process Improvement (BPI) [12], in two phases. The Analysis Phase identifies Business Processes (Step 1), User Tasks (Step 2), Interaction Spaces (Step 3), Business Rules (Step 4) and Data Entities (Step 5), composing an Enterprise Structure of business requirements, which components are presented in Table 1.

Table 1. Enterprise structure's component's definition, origin and symbol.

Component	Brief Definition	Origin	Symbol
Business Process (BP)	*A Network of UTs that lead to a Goal*	DEMO	
User Task (UT)	*A Complete Task within a BP*	AM	
Interaction Space (IS)	*The Space that supports a UT with the same BRs and DEs.*	Wisdom	
Business Rule (BR)	*A Restriction on the DE's Structural Relations*	DEMO	
Data Entity (DE)	*Persistent Information about a Business Concept*	Wisdom	

The Design Phase applies a User-Centered Design perspective to the Enterprise Structure in order to specify User Tasks (Step 6), design the User Interface (Step 7), structure the Business Logic (Step 8) and the Database (Step 9), finishing (Step 10) by elaborating the Software Architecture based on a MVC architectural pattern [13] in order to support for any possible combination of BPs that may structure the enterprise service.

Table 2. Software Architecture components definition, origin and symbol.

Component	Definition	Origin	Symbol
Aggregation Space	*A User Interface*	Hydra	
Interaction Component	*Tool of a User Interface*	Goals	
Interaction Object	*A User Interface Object that triggers SRs*	Goals	
User Interface SR	*A SR that provides support for User Interface presentation*	Goals	
Database SR	*A SR that manages Data Entities*	Goals	

Each Software Architecture component is presented in Table 2, where SR stands for System Responsibility. The Software Architecture is elaborated by means of composing one Aggregation Spaces [14] per each User Task (UT), which architecturally uses the ISs which are associated to the UT, ensuring the application of BRs over identified DEs and ensuring traceability between business and software implementation.

Goals establishes a relation with DEMO by means of the concepts of BP, UT, BR and DE which are compatible with the DEMO concepts of Transaction, Coordination Act, Action Rule and Object Class, respectively. Goals adds the Interaction Space (IS) which as the key to build-up the Enterprise Structure. We define three patterns of derivation (A, B and C) which are used to identify Goals component from DEMO models. The patterns are introduced in Fig. 1, and Steps 1 to 5 which explain the derivation of components in a top-down process are presented in Sects. 2.1, 2.2, 2.3, 2.4 and 2.5.

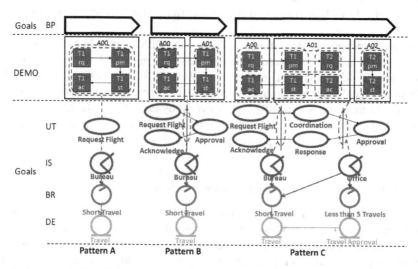

Fig. 1. Patterns A, B and C of component (BP, UT, IS, BR and DE) derivation from DEMO.

2 Analysis Phase

The elaboration of the Enterprise Structure is presented in Steps 1 to 5.

2.1 Step 1 – Business Process (BP) Identification

Goals definition of BP is compliant with the notion of Business Process provided by DEMO as a "set of interrelated or enclosed Transactions". One Transaction is a sequence of Coordination Acts {namely: request (rq), promise (pm), state (st) and accept (ac)} performed by two actors, or by a single actor directly in the system.

Figure 1 presents the BP derivation patterns based on the DEMO Process Structure Diagram (PSD). Pattern A includes a single Transaction (T1) performed by Actor A00, pattern B includes a single Transaction (T1) performed by two Actors (A00 and A01), and pattern C has two Transactions (T1 and T2) performed by three Actors (A00, A01 and A02). In all cases the relation between Goals and DEMO BPs is of one-to-one.

2.2   Step 2 – User Task (UT) Identification

Contrarily to DEMO, Goals considers that an Actor always carries on a only single task (a UT) and never two consecutive tasks or Coordination Acts (C-Acts). This aims Business Process clarification, user performance and software conception efficiency in order to deploy the necessary tools for the execution of the task by reducing articulatory distance and therefore, the user effort [15]. Hence, Goals considers any consecutive DEMO C-Acts {request (rq), promise (pm), state (st) and accept (ac)] as a single UT.

Figure 1 presents the derivation of UTs from the DEMO PSD. In pattern A a single UT is considered for the four consecutive C-Acts {rq, pm, st and ac}. In pattern B the consecutive C-Acts {pm and st} performed by Actor A01 are considered as a single UT ("Request Flight"), and in pattern C, Actor A01 is responsible for transposing the BP execution from Actor A00 to A02 and viceversa by carrying on the UTs "Coordination" and "Response", which are merged from consecutive C-Acts, namely {T1 pm - T2 rq} and {T2 ac - T1 st} respectively.

2.3   Step 3 – Interaction Space (IS) Identification

One IS supports the interaction between two users in person or remotely while each one carries on his own UT. Even if many UTs are carried by many Actors, the UTs will still be different, and if two Actos carry on the same UT of the BP remotely, then they are performing cooperative work [16]. The derivation of ISs does not depend on DEMO models as this method does not consider the space where human activity occurs.

Figure 1 illustrates the derivation of the IS from the relation of UTs, as each IS (e.g. "Bureau" in Pattern B) supports the communication between any two or more Actors, the line that divides the swim-lanes of each Actor represents an IS. Given that DEMO only predicts the interaction between two Actors, when applied to DEMO models, this pattern of derivation will always result in a direct relation between one IS (e.g. ISs "Bureau" and "Office" for Transactions T1 and T2 in Pattern C) per Transaction.

2.4   Step 4 – Business Rule (BR) Identification

BRs represent regulations or requirements that should be elicited during the Analysis Phase in order to facilitate the understanding of the restrictions which the user is subject to when carrying on a User Task within a certain Interaction Space, and represent restrictions which are applied to existing Data Entities. BRs are the grounding foundation of the Business Logic (given an MVC pattern), as they are the more specific programmed system responsibility regarding the structuring of this layer, the middleware of the system.

Figure 1 illustrates a situation in which both T1 and T2 define a BR each ("Short Travel" and "Less than 5 Travels"), which are also used by the Interaction Spaces of Transactions T1 and T2. BRs are constantly executed in order to ensure that a given restriction is ensured regarding the transfer of information between Interaction Spaces and Data Entities. BR should also be used by Interaction Spaces in order to restrict the introduction of invalid information by the user, therefore preventing usage mistakes.

2.5   Step 5 – Data Entity (DE) Identification

DEs are business concepts which are recognized within the enterprise domain by those who have knowledge about it (the enteprise). DEs are compliant with the concept of Class and relation of Classes used in UML [17]. And this definition is compatible with DEMO Object Classes (OC) which structures facts and Transactions. Goals derivation of DEs is carried out using the Object Fact Diagram (OFD) by establishing a direct relation between one DE per OC.

Figure 2 which presents the relation between OCs and Transactions in the OFD horizontal swim-lane. Transactions 1 and 2 use each a single DE, and these are related in a multiplicity of 1 to many (from "Travel" to "Travel Approval"). The resulting Enterprise Structure is presented above the DEs representation, and is composed by every identified component until this moment with no changes and is representative of the social interaction in terms of stable and essential norms, which is known as the organizational kernel [18].

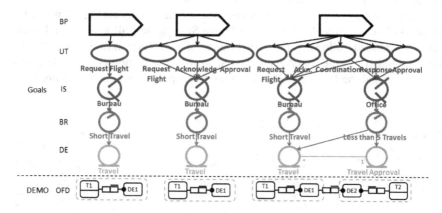

Fig. 2. Enterprise structure and derivation of DEs from OFD diagram.

3 Analysis Phase

The Design Phase elaborates the Software Architecture which is conceived in a top-down process that detailing the User Interaction (Step 6), the User Interface (Step 7), the Business Logic (Step 8) and the Database layer (Step 9), finishes with the composition of the Software Architecture (Step 10).

3.1 Step 6 – Task Model

The Task Model details User Tasks (UTs) in order to obtain information in order to carry on the User Interface design, which happens in Step 7. The Task Model follows the technique applied in the Wisdom methodology in order to specify the UT in terms of User Intentions (steps that the user takes to complete the task) and System Responsibilities (that provide the necessary information), following a traditional decomposition of an Essential Use Case (EUC) by means of the application of the Concur Task Trees (CTT) technique [19].

3.2 Step 7 – Interaction Modeling

The User Interface Design is carried out by means of the application of the Behavior Driven Development (BDD) method [11]. BDD is an agile software development method that produces pseudo-code as User Stories in order to specify a system feature (a UT) which is used within a certain scenario (an Aggregation Space).

User Stories specify a flow of user interactions that matches the User Intentions of the Task Model, specifying one Interaction Components per User Intention, and one Interaction Object per User Interaction, and related system behavior in terms of User Interface and Database System Responsibilities (SRs).

Figure 3 presents a User Story example for User Task "Request Flight" where three Interaction Components (A, B and C) and three SRs (the last SR is always a Database SR) are identified following the specification of four User Interactions. The User Interface Design specifies the Aggregation Space which is composed by the Interaction Components and the Interaction Objects (one to support each User Interaction).

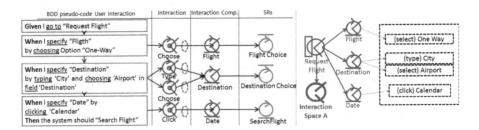

Fig. 3. Interaction model and user interface example.

3.3   Step 8 – Business Logic Structuring

The Business Logic Structuring is carried out by defining the relations that each System Responsibility (SR) to the existing to Data Entities (DE) based on the semantics and current state about identified business concepts. Given the current example and given Pattern A of derivation, we assume that DEs "Travel" and "Approval" are inherited from the Enterprise Structure. "Flight Choice" has been mapped to "Travel", and it is assumed that the "Airport" Fields belongs to a new DE "Airport". By means of the analysis of "SearchFlight", we assume that it uses a new DE "Flight".

3.4   Step 9 – Database Structuring

The Database Structuring is possible once all new DEs and Fields are already identified. The structuring od carried out according to the principles of elaboration of a Domain Model [17], in terms of Classes and Attributes which suffer simple transformation in order to structure the final Database [20]. According to our example, two new DEs have been identified ("Flight" and "Airport"), and for purposes of exemplification, we assume that DE "Travel" can only be related to a single record of those new DEs, and that DE "Flight" can is related to more than one "Airport" (usually two).

3.5   Step 10 – Software Architecture Composition

The composition of the Software Architecture is carried out by relating in a single diagram the every identified component by means of the execution of Steps 1 to 9. Figure 12 presents the Software Architecture, which relates all the identified components in a single Software Architecture, including the User Interface components associated to UT "Request Flight", the elaborated Business Logic and Database components, including the components which are architectural inherited from the Enterprise Structure.

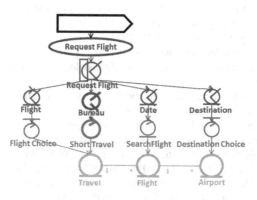

Fig. 3. Software Architecture example.

4 Related Work

Our approach can be compared to ArchiMate [21] and BPMN [22] in the perspective that it provides an Enterprise and Software Structuring language. It is different in the perspective that it applies a methodology to derive software implementation specifications. Regarding the specific User-Centered Design perspective, the closest solutions are methods settle for user interface conception based on user task and domain models, such as Sukaviriya's [23] and Sousa's [24]. Our approach is different as it complementarily conceives the Business Logic layer based on enterprise business rules and coordination structures that operate the user interface and domain processing execution. Considering the enterprise-driven development, it is different from the DEMO-based GSDP [25] as it specifies a structured user interface.

5 Conclusions

Our approach inherently aims at facilitating requirements elicitation, focuses on user needs, and simplifies traceability between business requirements and software implementation, witch match project management needs and user involvement in the SDP. The Goals Approach strategy, which is based on BPI, fits most successfully sized projects. Based on Standish Group statistical reports, projects under 1 M$ (one million dollars) cost are believed to be up to 10 times more successful than 10 M$ projects [4]. It suits Small and Medium Enterprises (SME) in-house development needs of agility concerning the achievement of tangible results in limited amounts of time [7].

References

1. The Standish Group: Chaos Report 2014 (2014)
2. Valente, P., Aveiro, D., Nunes, N.: Improving software design decisions towards enhanced return of investment. In: Proceedings ICEIS 2015, pp. 388–394 (2015)
3. Morgenshtern, O., Raz, T., Dvir, D.: Factors affecting duration and effort estimation errors in software development projects. IST **49**, 827–837 (2007)
4. The Standish Group: Chaos Report 2013 (2013)
5. Version One. The 10th Annual State of Agile Report (2016)
6. Dietz, J.: Enterprise Ontology - Theory and Methodology. Springer, Berlin (2006). ISBN 978-3540331490
7. Gerogiannis, V., Kakarontzas, G., Anthopoulos, L., Bibi, S., Stamelos, I.: The SPRINT-SMEs. In: Proceedings of ARCHIMEDES III (2013)
8. Nunes, N.: Object modeling for user-centered development and user interface design: the wisdom approach. Ph.D. thesis, Universidade da Madeira (2001)
9. Valente, P.: Goals Software Construction Process: Goal-Oriented Software Development. VDM Verlag Dr. Müller, Germany (2009). ISBN 978-3639212426
10. Constantine, L.: Human Activity Modeling - Toward a Pragmatic Integration of Activity Theory and Usage-Centered Design. Springer, Berlin (2009)

11. Chelimsky, D., Astels, D., Helmkamp, B., North, D., Dennis, Z., Hellesoy, A.: The Rspec Book (2010). ISBN: 1934356379
12. Lodhi, A., Köppen, V., Saake, G.: Business process improvement framework and representational support. In: Proceedings of the 3rd International Conference on Intelligent IHCI (2011)
13. Zukowski, J.: The model-view-controller architecture. In: John Zukowski's Definitive Guide to Swing for Java 2 (1999). ISBN: 978-1430252511
14. Costa, D., Nóbrega, L., Jardim Nunes, N.: An MDA approach for generating web interfaces with UML ConcurTaskTrees and canonical abstract prototypes. In: Coninx, K., Luyten, K., Schneider, K.A. (eds.) TAMODIA 2006. LNCS, vol. 4385, pp. 137–152. Springer, Heidelberg (2007)
15. Winckler, M., Cava, R., Barboni, E., Palanque, P., Freitas, C.: Usability aspects of the inside-in approach for ancillary search tasks on the web. In: Abascal, J., Barbosa, S., Fetter, M., Gross, T., Palanque, P., Winckler, M. (eds.) INTERACT 2015. LNCS, vol. 9299, pp. 211–230. Springer, Heidelberg (2015). doi:10.1007/978-3-319-22668-2_18
16. Grudin, J.: Computer-supported cooperative work: history and focus. Computer 27, 19–26 (1994)
17. Booch, G., Jacobson, I., Rumbaugh, J.: The Unified Modeling Language Users Guide. Addison-Wesley, Wokingham (1998)
18. Stamper, R.: On developing organisational semiotics as an empirical science: the need for scientific method and rigorous debate. In: Proceedings of 14th ICISO, pp. 1–13 (2013)
19. Paternò, F.: Model-Based Design and Evaluation of Interactive Applications. Springer, London (1999)
20. Awang, M., Labadu, N.: Transforming object oriented data model to relational data model. New Comput. Archit. Appl. 2(3), 402–409 (2012)
21. Archimate Foundation: Archimate Made Practical (2008)
22. Völzer, H.: An overview of BPMN 2.0 and its potential use. In: Mendling, J., Weidlich, M., Weske, M. (eds.) BPMN 2010. LNBIP, vol. 67, pp. 14–15. Springer, Heidelberg (2010). doi:10.1007/978-3-642-16298-5_3
23. Sukaviriya, N., Sinha, V., Ramachandra, T., Mani, S., Stolze, M.: User-centered design and business process modeling: cross road in rapid prototyping tools. In: Baranauskas, C., Abascal, J., Barbosa, S.D.J. (eds.) INTERACT 2007. LNCS, vol. 4662, pp. 165–178. Springer, Heidelberg (2007)
24. Sousa, K., Mendonça, H., Vanderdonckt, J., Rogier, E., Vandermeulen, J.: User interface derivation from business processes: a model-driven approach for organizational engineering. In: Proceedings of 2008 ACM SAC, pp. 553–560 (2008)
25. Kervel, S., Dietz, J, Hintzen, J., Meeuwen, T., Zijlstra, B.: Enterprise ontology driven software engineering. In: Proceedings of ICsoft 2012 (2012)

Special Session on Data Quality and Trust in Big Data

Region Profile Based Geo-Spatial Analytic Search

Xiaofeng Du$^{(\boxtimes)}$ and Zhan Cui

British Telecom, London, UK
xiaofeng.du@bt.com

Abstract. In geo-spatial related data analysis, an important task of geo-data analysts is to quickly find the things that they are interested from their data, such as spatial-temporal patterns, spatial clusters, co-location patterns, and spatial hotspots etc. Currently, most of the geo data analytic tools are exploratory based and lack of facilities that can help analysts to define what they are looking for and quickly find them from data. In this paper, we proposed a region profile based geo-spatial data analytic solution that tackles exactly the issue. The proposed solution captures analysts' interests in so called region profiles and then uses those region profiles to quickly locate the data that satisfy those interests either manually or automatically. Through the proposed solution, analysts can easily find what they are looking for in their data. They also can validate their results in a collaborative analytic environment and share and reproduce analytic results across a group of analysts.

Keywords: GIS · Geo-spatial data analytics · Spatial analysis · Point pattern analysis · Spatial statistics

1 Introduction

As the generation of information proliferates, vast quantities of data are created by systems, software, devices, sensors and all manner of other entities. Some data is intended for human review, problem identification or diagnosis, scanning, parsing or mining. As data sets are generated and stored in greater quantities, at greater rates, and with potentially greater levels of complexity and detail, the "big data" problem of storing, handling, processing or using the data arises.

Data from sensors, recorded events, astronomical, medical, computer network and other data can have associated spatial attributes such as geo-spatial coordinates or other relative or absolute spatial location information. For example, traffic, crime, health and social data can be associated with spatial locations in a map. Network data can be associated with real or virtual spatial locations in a network arrangement or topology. Furthermore, data can be associated with temporal attributes such as a measure of an absolute or relative time of occurrence at a relevant degree of granularity and precision. Spatial and spatiotemporal data analysis techniques are known in the art for the analysis of data sets by identifying co-occurrences of data events, similarity of data events and rules or models of data events [6]. For example, in genetics, spatiotemporal gene expression is employed to identify patterns of gene expression [9]. On another scale,

© Springer International Publishing AG 2016
W. Cellary et al. (Eds.): WISE 2016, Part II, LNCS 10042, pp. 361–370, 2016.
DOI: 10.1007/978-3-319-48743-4_29

epidemiological data can be analysed using similar techniques to observe rules relating data events, such as socio-economic events or factors and their association with health conditions [3]. In crime recording, spatiotemporal analysis techniques can identify relationships between criminal occurrences and proximity of certain resources, facilities and times of day, season etc. A variety of analytic techniques and functions can be employed, e.g. spatial or spatiotemporal clustering; co-location pattern analysis; spatiotemporal pattern analysis.

While a variety of analytic techniques and functions exist, their application to potentially large data sets across multi-dimensional spaces such as two-dimensional geographic areas involves considerable analytical effort. Typically, the process of data analytics involves gathering data, loading data into analytic tools, and applying exploratory based statistical models or data mining methods. Through this process, something potentially useful could be discovered, such as clusters, rules, and patterns. However, such an approach is slow and resource intensive and prone to fail to identify analytical results that the analysts are most interested in, especially in the Big Data era with large amount of data coming in at high velocity and rapid changing of analysts' interests. To mitigate these challenges, a system with better utilities that can help geo-data analysts to easily identify interesting information from their data is needed.

We believe that exploratory based data analytic [1, 4, 6–8] only works most effectively at the very beginning stage of the data analytic process, i.e. when an analyst receives a new set of data and needs to be familiar with it. At the later stages, usually the analysts will know what they are looking for in the data, but do not have effective ways of describing and searching for it. At this stage, very often the questions they ask are "the crime pattern I discovered in this city, does it happen in other cities as well?" or "in this area, my products have good sales in the places where there is a retirement home nearby, is this true in other areas too or just a coincident?". For these questions, the analysts need quick answers rather than go through another complex analytic process. In this paper, we propose a system that employs a flexible region profile based geo-spatial analytic search method that can not only discover something interesting from data, but also help analysts to encapsulate the similar questions mentioned above as region profiles and find the data that produce their desired analytic results. The key contributions of our work is summarised as follows:

- **Developing the concept of region profile**. A region profile is a capsule that encapsulates desired analytic results that analysts are looking for and how the results are produced. A region profile is a template spatial region having a shape and dimensions, an identification of a plurality of analytic functions, a specification of one or more parameters for each identified function, and a result set including output of each of the functions applied to events associated with a spatial region of the space in accordance with the template and based on the parameters. More details of profile will be discussed in later sections.
- **Developing an interactive visual analytics environment for users to create/modify region profiles**. Under this environment, users can highlight their interested geo-regions on map, perform statistical and spatial-data mining analytics to get insights into their data in the highlighted regions, and save their desired

results as region profiles for further analysis later. The region profile can be easily shared with other analysts.

- **Developing an interactive search facility for users to quickly locate subsets of data that match pre-defined region profiles.** The search facility can search for subsets of data that match to the profile either automatically or manually controlled by users.

This paper is structured as follows. Section 2 reviews related work. After give the details of what a region profile is in Sect. 3, we will discuss how region profiles can be used in geo-data analytics in Sect. 4. Finally, we discuss the limitations and future work in Sect. 5.

2 Related Work

In this section, we review some of the geospatial data analytic tools that are most related to our work. We will also discuss why our solution is different.

ArcGIS [1] is one of the most comprehensive GIS tool. It provides the system for editing, storing, visualizing and analysing geographic data. Spatial data analysis is one of its strength. It supports extendable analytic capabilities through extensions. However, it is an exploratory based data analytic tool and does not have any functionality that supports users to capture what they are looking for and search through data based on it. Chen et al. [8] developed a system that focuses specifically on discovering people movement pattern through social media data. It allows users to filter and select reliable data from each derived movement category, based on the guidance of uncertainty model and interactive selection tools. By iteratively analysing filtered movements, users can explore the semantics of movements, including the transportation methods, frequent visiting sequences and keyword descriptions. It does mention pattern which has some similarity to region profile, but it is limited to movement analysis only. GeoVISTA Studio [4] is an open source Java-based visual programming environment and is commonly used for developing geo-visualization applications. Another general system is QGIS [7]. It is an open-source desktop GIS application, which supports exploratory data analysis and data editing.

3 Region Profile

As discussed previously, when data analytics progress to certain stages, the analysts should approximately know what they are looking for in their data. The rest of the analytic tasks should be focusing on looking for which part of the data contains their desired interests. This is especially true in geo-spatial data analytics due to spatial data's spatial dependence [5] and spatial heterogeneity [10] characteristics. Once analysts discover some interesting result, they need to validate whether the result holds true in other geographical locations or just a local phenomenon. Traditionally, to validate the result, the analyst can simply load data from other geo regions into the model he/she built to see if they generate the same results because all the data are local and the analyst does not work collaboratively. However, this solution has some major drawbacks, especially in the Big Data era with a group of analyst performing data analytics simultaneously:

- **Low efficiency**. The model needs to go through the whole data set in order to find interests in other areas. As there is no clearly defined "local area", the model also needs to figure out where to start and when to stop the analysis to find interests in other areas and at the same time does not lose data locality.
- **Insufficient privileges to access required data**. In the modern data analytics, especially with the emerging of Big Data, data set are getting extremely large and distributed. More often than not, an analyst does not have access to all the data that he/she needs to validate the results.
- **High complexity and error prone to reproduce results**. It takes considerable amount of efforts and analytical knowledge to share a pre-designed model among analysts and produce the same results. It is even more difficult to share the model with people who have no analytical knowledge.

To overcome the above issues, we propose the concept of region profile. A region profile is a capsule that encapsulates desired analytic results that analysts are looking for and how the results are produced. There are few key elements that are essential in a region profile, such as a clear defined region, a time window, and the analytic functions that are used etc. formally a region profile is defined as follows:

Definition 3.1. A region profile RP is a tuple, $RP = (S, T, D, F, P, R)$, where:

- $S = ((x_1, y_1), (x_2, y_2), ..., (x_n, y_n))$ is a sequence of coordinates of a polygon that defines a local region on map. It can be a predefined region, such as a shape of a city boundary, or a hand drawn shape, such as a circle.
- $T = [t_1, t_2]$ is a time interval between t_1 and t_2.
- $D = \{d_1, d_2, ..., d_n\}$ is a set of data that used to produce the results.
- $F = \{f_1, f_2, ..., f_n\}$ is a set of analytic functions.
- $P = \{p_1, p_2, ..., p_n\}$ is a set of analytic processes. $p \in P$ is a tuple $(F_p, \textbf{Trans})$, where $F_p \in F$ is a set of analytic functions and **Trans** is a set of transition relations between element of F_p.
- $R = \{r_1, r_2, ..., r_n\}$ is a set of results. Each result r is define as a tuple (i, o, f, p), where i is a set of inputs, o is a set of outputs, $f \in F$ is a analytic function produces the result, which can be **null** if the result is produced by a analytic process, and $p \in P$ is a analytic process produces the result, which can be **null** if the result is produced by a analytic function.

From above definition we can see that a region profile contains all the information that an analyst needs to reproduce an analytic results. It provides a generic description, which is not platform dependent, data dependent, and scenario dependent. Therefore, the analytic results can be easily shared between analysts to reproduce or validate.

The region profile is described in extensible markup Language (XML). Any analytic system that has parser to parse the XML description and have access to the analytic functions will be able to reproduce the results. A typical region profile's structure is listed as follows:

```
<Profile>
    <Name></Name>
    <StartTime></StartTime>
    <EndTime></EndTime>
    <Data>
        <Type></Type>
        <Source></Source>
        <Filter></Filer>
        <Aggregation></Aggregation>
    </Data>
    <Polygons>
        <Polygon>
            <Coordinates></<Coordinates>
        </Polygon>
        ...
    </Polygons>
    <Functions>
        <Function>/<Function>
        ...
    </Functions>
    <Processes>
        <Process>/<Process>
        ...
    </Processes>
    <Results>
        <Result></ Result >
        ...
    </Results>
</Profile>
```

In the following section, we will discuss how a region profile is constructed and how it can enhance geo-spatial data analytics through our analytic search system.

4 Region Profile Analytic Search

The region profile analytic search is carried out through two processes in our system: the region profile construction process and the region profile based search process, see Fig. 1. Each process involves several components to help analysts to construct region profiles to capture their interests and use these profiles to find data that match their interest.

4.1 Region Profile Construction Process

The aim of this process is to create a region profile to capture the analysts' interests. This is achieved through few steps:

1. **Highlight a geographical region on map**. At this step, users need to highlight a region on map that is in their interests. This can be done by either loading a predefined shape on map or manually drawing a shape.
2. **Select data to plot in the highlighted region**. At this step, users need to load their data into this region. The data can be from different sources, such as database,

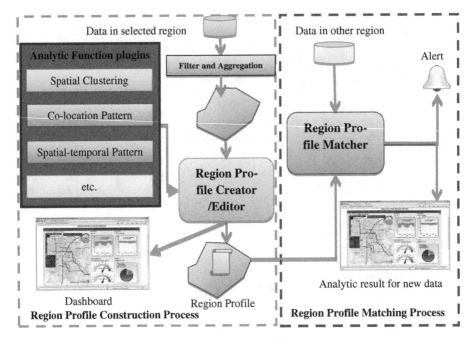

Fig. 1. System structure

Big Data, and spreadsheet etc. The key challenge here is how to bring all the data together and handle them in a uniformed way. In our system, this is done through data pre-processing and integration. Data pre-processing is to make sure that data from different sources are pre-processed into the same format before plotting on map and passing to analytic functions. Data integration is to bring non-geographical data onto the map by linking them with data that have geo-location information. To support the analysis of large amounts of data, users can apply multiple filters on their data and aggregate data in different aspects, including locations, periodicity, and attributes.

3. **Exploratory geo-data analyses with analytic functions and processes**. Once data are loaded into the selected region, users can start to analyses them and decide what should be included in their region profile. The data analysis can start with exploratory analysis if users do not know what the data can tell them. However, the exploratory analysis here is only performed on the subset of user's data within the selected region, not the whole data set. If users know what exactly they are looking for, they can directly select the analytic functions to produce the results. The system provides a selection of analytic functions, such as spatial clustering, Co-location pattern analysis, spatial-temporal pattern analysis etc. External analytic functions are supported through plug-ins. Data can also be analysed by a sequence of analytic functions in order to produce desired results, i.e. analytic processes. The system provides users with a dashboard facility to visualise the analytic results if it is possible, see Fig. 2. (For data protection purpose, the quality of the image is reduced.)

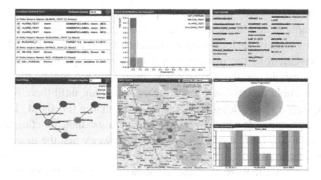

Fig. 2. Dashboard view of analytic results

4. **Save desired analytic results as region profile**. Once users decide which analytic functions and processes with their result should be included in a region profile, generate the region profile and save it is very straight forward. The analytic search system will automatically parse the information related to the region profile, e.g. data, analytic functions, processes, related parameters, and their results etc., and generate an XML description. The description can be either saved as a file or stored in a database.

4.2   Region Profile Matching Process

The aim of this process is to help users to find the data that can produce similar results as defined in region profiles. The process itself is very straight forward. Users open a predefined region profile and decide whether let the system automatically find the data that match the profile for them or manually find the data themselves. If the manual option is chosen, users need to drag the shape defined in the profile to other regions of the map and see how the data in those regions match to the region profile. However, there are few challenges in this process need to be discussed.

The first challenge is, in the automatic mode, how the system can efficiently and effectively go through the map space and find the data that satisfy users' region profiles. The simplest way for a system to go through a map space is by dividing the map into portions the same size of the minimum bounding box of the shape in a region profile, see Fig. 3, and going through them one by one. The major problems of this solution are, firstly, an interesting data cluster may be divided into several boxes and therefore lost their analytical features; secondly, this solution is not efficient. As we mentioned before, due to spatial heterogeneity, data are not evenly distributed over a map space. It is totally wasting time and computational power when the system goes through the areas like oceans, desert, and rural areas, which do not contain data at all. To solve this problem, we propose a solution called density based traversal. The algorithm starts with a density analysis in order to know how the data are distributed over a map space and where are the densest points. It will then pick few points with the highest density to start with. At each high density point, the algorithm will move the minimum bounding box of the shape step by step in a hub and spoke style from high density area towards the low density area in all directions that have data, see Fig. 4. At each step, the system will examine how closely the local data are matched to the criteria defined in the region profile. The movement of the minimum bounding box stops when the density level drops below a threshold and the data that have been analysed will be removed from the map space. The whole process will repeat again and again until there is no more data left in the map space or the density of data is lower than a threshold. The distance of each step is configurable. It can be a fixed value or a gradient function that generates values according to the current density, e.g. move slower when the density is high and faster when the density is low. The advantage of this algorithm is that it only analyses the areas in a map space that are relevant and always starts with the most relevant areas. The density based traversal algorithm is performed behind the scenes. Although we talked about map space, there is no need for a map to be present physically. All calculations are done virtually.

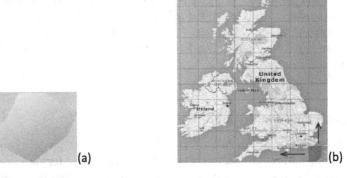

Fig. 3. (a) The Minimum bounding box for a shape (the pink rectangle); (b) Dividing map into minimum bounding boxes (Color figure online)

The second challenge is, how to compare the results generated by a sub-set of data to the region profile in order to know whether they are similar or not. As we discussed previously, a region profile can contain analytic results from a list of analytic functions and processes. If we consider each analytic function or analytic process as an attribute of the region profile, then we can consider a region profile as a complex object with many attributes, where the values of attribute are the results of analytic functions or processes. To compare the similarity between complex objects, we adopted the Term Weighted Cosine Coefficient [2] from the vector based similarity measurement methods to calculate the similarity. Suppose we have two objects O_1 and O_2 and their property vectors $V_1 = (t_1, t_2, ..., t_j)$ and $V_2 = (t_1, t_2, ..., t_j)$ then we can apply the following formula:

$$Cos\theta_{V_1,V_2} = \frac{\sum_{k=1}^{j} w_{1k} \bullet w_{2k}}{\sqrt{\sum_{k=1}^{j} w_{1k}^2} \bullet \sqrt{\sum_{k=1}^{j} w_{2k}^2}} \tag{1}$$

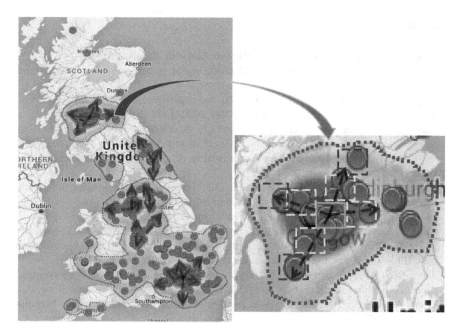

Fig. 4. An illustration of density based traversal

Where, the variable w_{ik} represents the vector V_i's *k-th* term's weighted value. It is normally calculated based on the importance of the properties of an object. Here we assume that although all the results in a region profile are in the analysts' interest, some of the result might have higher impact than others, hence we use weighted value rather than the original value.

At the end of the process, any sub-sets of data that closely matched to the region profile will be reported back to users.

5 Conclusion

As we discussed previously, most of the geo-data analytic tools are exploratory based and lack of facilities that can help analysts to define what they are looking for and quickly find them in their data. In this paper, we introduced the concept of region profile and how it can be used to help geo-data analysts to capture their analytic interests and efficiently find or validate those interests in other data sets.

The system proposed in this paper has a good user base in our organisation. Several patents have been filed around the ideas in this work. In the future work, we will make the system more efficient and scalable by utilising the technologies from the Big Data technology stack, such as Apache Spark.

References

1. ArcGIS. http://www.esriuk.com/software/arcgis. Accessed 20 July 2016
2. Berry, M.W., Drmac, Z., Jessup, E.R.: Matrices, vector spaces, and information retrieval. SIAM Rev. **41**(2), 335–362 (1999)
3. Jacquez, G.M., Greiling, D., Kaufmann, A.: Spatial pattern recognition in the environmental and health sciences: a perspective. IJERPH **7**(4), 1302–1329 (2010)
4. Geovista studio. http://www.geovistastudio.psu.edu. Accessed 20 July 2016
5. Knegt, De, Coughenour, M.B., Skidmore, A.K., Heitkönig, I.M.A., Knox, N.M., Slotow, R., Prins, H.H.T.: Spatial autocorrelation and the scaling of species–environment relationships. Ecology **91**, 2455–2465 (2010)
6. Longley, P.A., Goodchild, M.F., Maguire, D.J., Rhind, D.W.: Geographic Information Science and Systems, 4th edn. Wiley, London (2015). ISBN EHEP003247
7. QGIS. http://www.qgis.org/en/site. Accessed 20 July 2016
8. Chen, S., Yuan, X., Wang, Z., Guo, C., Liang, J., Wang, Z., Zhang, X., Zhang, J.: Interactive visual discovering of movement patterns from sparsely sampled geo-tagged social media data. IEEE Trans. Vis. Comput. Graph. **22**(1), 270–279 (2016)
9. Shestopalov, I.A., Chen, J.K.: Spatiotemporal control of embryonic gene expression using caged morpholinos. Methods Cell Biol. **104**, 151–172 (2011)
10. Wang, J.F., Zhang, T.L., Fu, B.J.: A measure of spatial stratified heterogeneity. Ecol. Ind. **67**, 250–256 (2016)

Segmentation and Enhancement of Low Quality Fingerprint Images

Hasan Fleyeh[(⊠)]

Computer Engineering Department, School of Technology and Business Studies,
Dalarna University, Falun, Sweden
hfl@du.se

Abstract. This paper presents a new approach to segment low quality fingerprint images which are collected by low quality fingerprint scanners. Images collected using such readers are easy to collect but difficult to segment. The proposed approach focuses on automatically segment and enhance these fingerprint images to reduce the detection of false minutiae and hence improve the recognition rate.

There are four major contributions of this paper. Firstly, segmentation of fingerprint images is achieved via morphological filters to find the largest object in the image which is the foreground of the fingerprint. Secondly, specially designed adaptive thresholding algorithm to deal with fingerprint images. The algorithm tries to fit a curve between the gray levels of the pixels of each row or column in the fingerprint image. The curve represents the binarization threshold of each pixel in the corresponding row or column. Thirdly, noise reduction and ridge enhancement is achieved by invoking a rotational invariant anisotropic diffusion filter. Finally, an adaptive thinning algorithm which is immune against spurs is invoked to generate the recognition ready fingerprint image.

Segmentation of 100 images from databases FVC2002 and FVC2004 was performed and the experiments showed that 96 % of images under test are correctly segmented.

1 Introduction

Fingerprint recognition becomes more popular to identify and verify people. There are many commercial applications which require the fingerprint of a person to be read by a sensor in order to be recognized by this application. Recognition of fingerprints often takes place by finding a number of minutiae on the fingerprint image, then the recognition algorithm matches these minutiae with those in application database. Segmentation is the step prior to minute extraction in which a fingerprint image is usually divided into non-overlapping regions; the *foreground* and the *background*. The *foreground* is the area of scanner surface which is in contact with the finger surface and includes the necessary information needed for fingerprint recognition. While the *background* is the noisy area which should be removed by the segmentation process. Therefore, the result of fingerprint segmentation is a fingerprint image in which the background is removed (Akram et al. 2008; Maio et al. 2009). Incorrect segmentation can lead to serious consequences on the recognition as the foreground can be labelled

© Springer International Publishing AG 2016
W. Cellary et al. (Eds.): WISE 2016, Part II, LNCS 10042, pp. 371–384, 2016.
DOI: 10.1007/978-3-319-48743-4_30

as background and vice versa. Furthermore, false minutiae can be generated which gives negative impact on the recognition rate.

When dealing with segmentation fingerprint images, there are two issues to think about. The first one is that the number of images the segmentation algorithm to deal with is huge. A robust segmentation algorithm should be able to deal with all kind of fingerprint images. The second one is that each fingerprint image represents unstructured data which requires specific algorithms to find patterns in the image. Furthermore, dealing with low quality fingerprint images makes extracting these patterns even more difficult.

Most of the segmentation algorithms aim to use one level of features to achieve segmentation (Akram et al. 2008; Bazen and Gerez 2001; Feng et al. 2009; Helfroush and Mohammadpour 2008; Weixin et al. 2009; Yu et al. 2008). In general, there are two approaches for fingerprint segmentation: block-wise based or pixel-wise based (Ren et al. 2008). In the block-wise approach, the fingerprint image is divided into blocks and each block is classified into foreground or background based on features calculated for the block. While in the pixel-wise method, segmentation is achieved on the pixel level.

This paper proposes a new technique to segment fingerprint images. Segmentation is achieved by morphological filters to find the largest object in the fingerprint image. An adaptive threshold algorithm specially designed for fingerprint images is also proposed. This algorithm considers the gray levels of each row or column in the fingerprint image as 2D function and fits a curve among the highest and lowest values. The fitted curve represents the adaptive threshold values for each pixel in this row or column. The thresholded fingerprint image is enhanced by removing noise and reconnecting separated ridges by rotational invariant anisotropic diffusion filter. Finally an adaptive thinning algorithm which is able to remove all spurs is invoked to generate the final fingerprint image.

The rest of the paper is organized as follows. In the next section state of the art of fingerprint segmentation is presented. In Sect. 3 the proposed method is illustrated. The experimental results based on the proposed method are given in Sect. 4, and in Sect. 5 the conclusion is presented.

2   Literature Review

In recent years, biometric authentication became a big field of research because of its importance to identify and verify people. Automated Fingerprint Identification System (AFIS) is one among many other fields which was developed rapidly. In this section, the recent state of the art is presented.

Sankaran et al. ((2017) proposed a method to automatically segment latent fingerprints in order to distinguish between ridge and non-ridge patterns. The authors invoked machine learning algorithms to achieve the latent segmentation. The fingerprint image was divided into non-overlapping blocks and for each block a number of features were computed and fused to construct a feature vector. Features include Saliency, Intensity, Gradient Ridge, and quality features were fused to create the feature vector. A random forest classifier was employed to segment the image into foreground and background blocks. Results showed high segmentation accuracy of about 96 % on inked fingerprint datasets.

Thai et al. (2016) proposed a novel factorized directional bandpass (FDB) segmentation method for texture extraction based on the directional Hilbert transform of a Butterworth bandpass Directional Hilbert Butterworth

Bandpass filter (DHBB) filter interwoven with soft-thresholding. The original image was transformed into the Fourier domain and filtered first by the DHBB factor obtaining 16 directional sub-bands. Next, soft-thresholding was applied to remove spurious patterns. The feature image was reconstructed from these sub-bands using a second DHBB factor. Finally, the feature image was binarized and the ROI is obtained by morphological operations.

Thai and Gottschlich (2016) developed a segmentation method by global three-part decomposition (G3PD). Based on global variational analysis, the G3PD method decomposed the fingerprint image into cartoon, texture and noise parts. After decomposition, the foreground region was obtained from the non-zero coefficients. The proposed method was evaluated by the segmentation of 10560 images.

Ezeobiejesi and Bhanu (2016) proposed an algorithm to segment latent fingerprint which was based on fractal dimension features and weighted extreme learning machine. The feature vectors, which were built from the local fractal dimension features, were invoked as input to a weighted extreme learning machine ensemble classifier. The result of classification was two classes; fingerprint and non-fingerprint classes. The proposed segmentation algorithm was evaluated by achieving better results than the state of the art regarding the false detection rate (FDR) and overall segmentation accuracy compared to the existing approaches.

Nimkar and Mishra (2015) developed an algorithm for fingerprint segmentation. The proposed algorithm was named as Adaptive (scale) and Orientation (vector). The basic idea of the proposed algorithm was originated from the total variation models, along with two features of fingerprints; namely, scale and vector. The result of the algorithm was to decompose the fingerprint image into two regions; noisy and texture. The algorithm was tested on two different fingerprint datasets and PNSR was invoked to check the efficiency of the algorithm.

Carneiro et al. (2014) achieved a comparative study to analysis four thresholding techniques (Niblack, Bernsen, Fisher, Fuzzy), two thinning techniques (Stentiford and Holt) and a feature extraction (Cross Number) technique for fingerprint applications. The authors tested and analyzed the algorithms on a set of 160 fingerprint images. The results pointed out the positive and negative sides of the different algorithms.

3 The Proposed Approach

The proposed approach for fingerprint segmentation and enhancement is depicted in Fig. 1. It consists of five stages:

1. Pre-processing
Fingerprint images with low contrast, false traces ridges or noisy complex background cannot be segmented correctly. Therefore, such images should be enhanced. The pre-processing applied in this paper is mean and variance normalization. A fingerprint

image $\mathbf{I}[x, y]$ is normalized by specifying its desired mean and variance values denoted m_0 and v_0 as shown in Eq. 1.

$$\mathbf{I}'[x, y] = \begin{cases} m_0 + \sqrt{(\mathbf{I}[x, y] - m)^2 . v_0/v} & \textit{if } \mathbf{I}[x, y] > m \\ m_0 - \sqrt{(\mathbf{I}[x, y] - m)^2 . v_0/v} & \textit{otherwise} \end{cases} \qquad (1)$$

This process produces a fingerprint image $\mathbf{I}'[x, y]$ according to m_0 and v_0. In this equation, m and v are the mean and variance of the fingerprint image $\mathbf{I}[x, y]$.

2. Segmentation

The proposed segmentation approach segments the fingerprint image in two non-overlapping regions; the foreground and the background according to the following relationship:

$$\mathbf{I} = \cup (Fo, Ba) \qquad (2)$$

where $\mathbf{I}$ is the fingerprint image, Fo is the foreground region and Ba is the background region.

Since the fingerprint foreground represents the object with the largest area in the image, locating this object in the image means locating its foreground. Figure 2 depicts the steps followed to isolate this object from the rest of the image. The process starts by binarizing the fingerprint image using the Otsu thresholding method (Otsu 1979). To isolate the foreground from the rest of the image, dilation is applied to force the detached ridges to attach to each other. A square structuring element whose size is related to that of the image under consideration is created. The fingerprint foreground becomes a large single object dominating the image. By applying a modified version of connected component labelling algorithm (Suzuki et al. 2003) and targeting the largest object, the foreground of the fingerprint is located and extracted. Extraction of this object takes place by a simple IF THEN rule which checks the presence of a white pixel in the image contacting the largest foreground object. Figure 4C depicts the largest object in the fingerprint image while Fig. 4D presents the results of this segmentation.

3. Adaptive Thresholding

Due to the fact that gray levels of pixels representing fingerprint's ridges varies widely from an image to another and from one position in a certain image to another one, traditional thresholding algorithms may not produce robust results. Therefore, the need for an adaptive algorithm which eliminates such problems is essential. In this paper, a special thresholding algorithm for fingerprints analysis is proposed. Consider a strip of one pixel width taken laterally or longitudinally anywhere in a fingerprint image where ridges and valleys exist. Plotting this strip gives a wave similar to that shown in Fig. 3. In this plot, the x-axis represents the location of the pixels in the strip, while the y-axis is the gray level of each pixel. The highest amplitude point of each cycle of the wave represents a ridge while the lowest amplitude point corresponds to a valley.

The main idea of the proposed adaptive thresholding algorithm is find a curve which fits the ridge-valley wave and separates it into two parts; an upper part

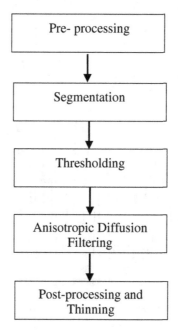

Fig. 1. The proposed Approach for fingerprint segmentation and enhancement.

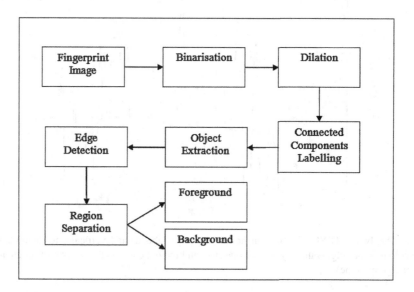

Fig. 2. Segmentation of fingerprint images.

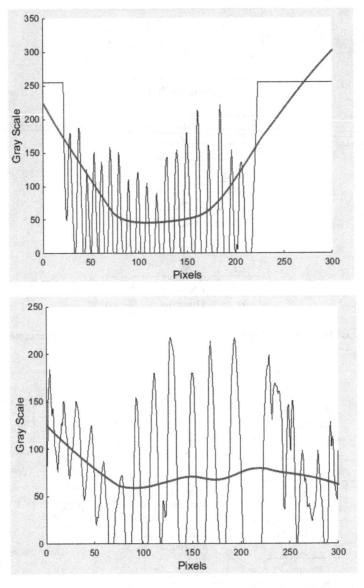

Fig. 3. Applying LOWESS fitting on horizontal strips (above) and vertical one (below). The blue colour is the ridge-valley system of one strip and the red curve is the resultant fitting curve. (Color figure online)

represents the ridges and the lower one represents the valleys. The fitting algorithm which can achieve this job is called Locally Weighted Scatter-plot Smoothing (LOWESS) (Cleveland 1979; Cleveland and Devlin 1988). This is a method to fit a smooth curve between two variables where one variable is the ridge and the other one is the valley. The method is nonparametric because the linearity assumptions of

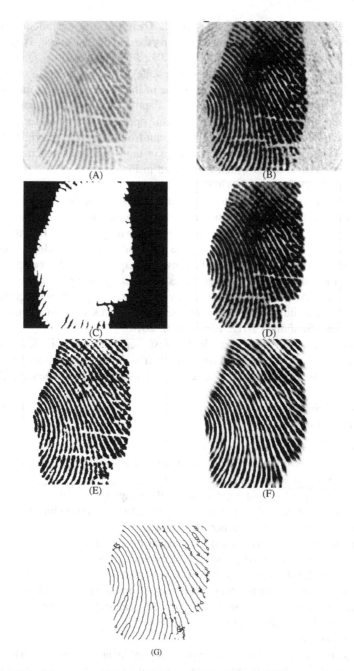

Fig. 4. Details of the proposed approach. (A): Original Image. (B): Fingerprint image after Pre-processing. (C): Image of the largest object. (D): Extracted foreground. (E): Thresholding a fingerprint strip by LOWESS. (F): Rotational Invariant Anisotropic Diffusion Filter. (G): Thinning and Post-processing

conventional regression methods are relaxed. Therefore, the overall uncertainty is measured as how well the estimated curve fits the population curve. Applying this method upon the ridge-valley curve depicted in Fig. 5 generates a curve (the red curve) which fits between the ridges and the valleys. The intersection of this curve with the ridge–valley system is a unique value of threshold calculated for each cycle of the wave (a ridge and a valley). Once these adaptive threshold values are computed, the strip is converted into black and white. This operation is applied for each image row from the top to the bottom and each column from the left to the right. The final binary image is generated by an OR operation of the two images generated from the horizontal and vertical strips which is depicted in Fig. 4E.

4. Anisotropic Diffusion Filtering

Many fingerprint matching systems employ minutiae for matching. With the presence of noise in the image, many true minutiae can be missed and false minutiae can be detected instead. Therefore, the recognition process will be affected. In order to avoid these errors, it is essential to improve the fingerprint image quality. Anisotropic Diffusion filter is designed to reduce the noise in images while preserving the region edges, and to smooth along the image edges removing gaps due to noise.

The basis of the method was introduced by Weickert (Weickert and Scharr 2002). Modifications and improvements were presented by (Kroon and Slump 2009) (Gottschlich and Schönlieb 2012; Kroon et al. 2010).

The method consists of two steps. In the first step, the image is described by a structure tensor called the second-moment matrix. While in the second step, the structure tensor is transformed into a diffusion tensor for edge enhancing diffusion filtering.

The details of this approach is given in (Kroon and Slump 2009) which can be summarized as follows:

1. Smooth the image by a Gaussian filter.
2. Calculate Hessian from every pixel of the Gaussian smoothed image.
3. Gaussian Smooth the Hessian.
4. Calculate eigenvectors and eigenvalues of the image from step 3. Note that image edges give large eigenvalues, and the eigenvectors corresponding to those large eigenvalues describe the direction of the edge.
5. The eigenvectors are used as diffusion tensor directions.
6. The diffusion is performed by a finite difference scheme.
7. Back to step 2, till a certain diffusion time is reached.

Applying this approach on the fingerprint images produced by the former step will improve image quality by removing the noise and enhancing and preserving ridge's edges. Results of this enhancement is depicted in Fig. 4F.

5. Post-processing

In this stage, the skeleton of the enhanced fingerprint image is generated. The skeleton algorithm invoked in this stage was designed to handle situations where spurs are to be minimized which fits the requirements of fingerprint recognition applications. It is assumed that skeleton points are those which sit at the center of a circle that touches the edge of the shape to be skeletonized at multiple points. The gray-level of each pixel on the skeleton depends upon the shortest distance to travel around the perimeter of the shape to be skeletonized to connect the most distant two points. Thus spurs in the skeleton due to small edge perturbations will have low intensity even if they are very long which fits the requirements of fingerprint applications. Finally a threshold should be selected depending on the expected size of any noisy protrusions in the silhouette (Howe 2016). An example of an image which is treated with post-processing is depicted in Fig. 4G.

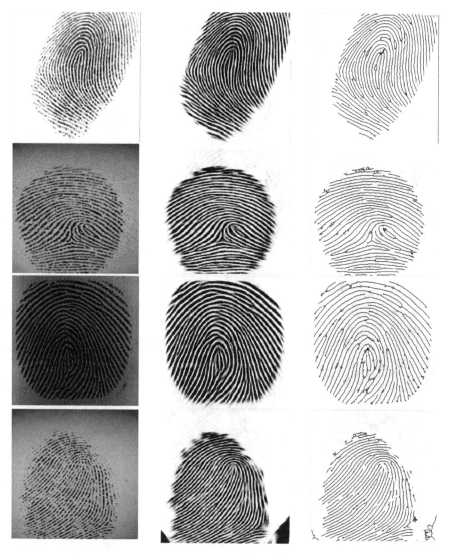

Fig. 5. Segmentation and enhancement results from FVC2002. Left column: Original image. Middle column: Results of rotational invariant anisotropic diffusion filter. Right column: Thinning and post processing. Row 1: FVC2002-DB1-A-9_3. Row 2: FVC2002-DB2-A-2_7. Row 3: FVC2002-DB3-A-4_3. Row 4: FVC2002-DB4-A-17_1

4 Experiments and Results

To test the proposed algorithm, two different datasets are employed. The first one is the second fingerprint verification competition FVC2002 (2002) which consists of 4 datasets (3 real and 1 synthetic). There are 31 participants who voluntarily submit their fingerprints. The second dataset is FVC2004 (2004) which has fingerprints of 43

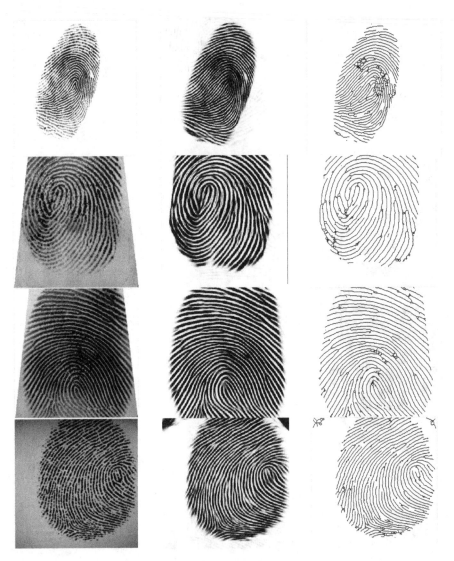

Fig. 6. Segmentation and enhancement results from FVC2004. Left column: Original image. Middle column: Results of rotational invariant anisotropic diffusion filter. Right column: Thinning and post processing. Row 1: FVC2004-DB1-B-107_6. Row 2: FVC2004-DB2-B-103_1. Row 3: FVC2004-DB2-B-109_4. Row 4: FVC2004-DB2-B-105_4

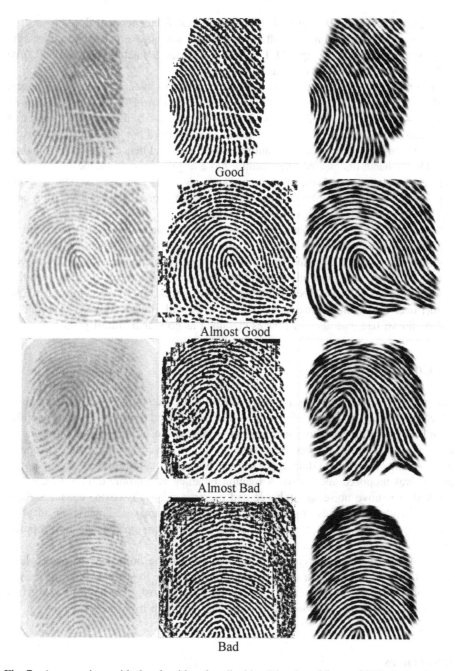

Good

Almost Good

Almost Bad

Bad

Fig. 7. A comparison with the algorithm described by (Fleyeh and Jomaa 2010). Left column: Original images. Middle column: segmentation from (Fleyeh and Jomaa 2010). Right column: results from current approach.

participants including 29 industrial, 6 academics and 8 independent developers. It is very important to mention that different scanning sensors were used to collect the fingerprint images and dealing with FVC2004 databases is much harder than 2002 due to the perturbations deliberately introduced.

The proposed approach was tested by 100 fingerprint images which were selected randomly and without repetition from the FVC2002 database DB1-A, DB2-A, DB3-A, and DB4-A, and from FVC2004 DB1-B, DB2-B and DB4-B. These images represent unstructured data which should be cleaned and prepared for classification. Wrong segmentation may increase false minutiae in the image and hence reduce classification rate. On the hand, undetected true minutiae has a negative impact on the classification rate. The validation test showed that the proposed algorithm could segment 96 % of the images under test. Samples of segmented images from datasets FVC2002 and FVC2004 are depicted in Figs. 5 and 6, respectively.

A comparison with the method proposed by Fleyeh and Jomaa (2010) to segment images from FVC2000 shows that the current approach performs much better than the other one. The results depicted in Fig. 7 show that segmentation is good even with images which are previously classified as bad by the other approach. It can be seen that great improvements have been achieved by the current approach compared to the former one. These improvements are not only clear with images formerly classified as bad or almost bad, but also for images classified as good and almost good.

5 Conclusion

The problem of fingerprint segmentation is one of the pattern classification paradigms which are not fully solved yet. Fingerprint images collected as forensic evidences suffer from background noise. This paper proposes a new approach to segment and enhance low quality fingerprint images. Segmentation was achieved by morphological opera-tions. An adaptive thresholding approach which was specially designed for fingerprint images was proposed and tested. A rotation invariant anisotropic diffusion filter was invoked to remove noise and enhance and preserve ridges. This step enhances ridge structure and reduces false minutiae in the segmented images. Finally, an adaptive thinning algorithm which was able to remove spurs was included in the proposed approach.

A set of experiments were performed to evaluate the proposed approach which showed high robustness. The proposed approach was able to segment 96 % of images used for testing. All images which were segmented as almost good, almost bad and bad can now be segmented as good, which indicates that high robustness is achieved.

References

Akram, M.U., Nasir, S., Tariq, A., Zafar, I., Khan, W.S.: Improved fingerprint image segmentation using new modified gradient based technique. Paper presented at the 2008 Canadian Conference on Electrical and Computer Engineering, Niagara Falls, Canada, 4–7 May 2008

Bazen, A.M., Gerez, S.H.: Segmentation of fingerprint images. Paper presented at the ProRISC 2001 Workshop on Circuits, Systems and Signal Processing, Veldhoven, The Netherlands, November 2001

Carneiro, R., Bessa, J., Moraes, J.D., Neto, E., Alexandria, A.D.: Techniques of binarization, thinning and feature extraction applied to a fingerprint system. Int. J. Comput. Appl. **103**(10), 1–8 (2014)

Cleveland, W.: Robust locally weighted regression and smoothing scatterplots. J. Am. Stat. Assoc. **74**, 829–836 (1979)

Cleveland, W., Devlin, S.: Locally weighted regression: an approach to regression analysis by local fitting. J. Am. Stat. Assoc. **83**, 596–610 (1988)

Ezeobiejesi, J., Bhanu, B.: Latent fingerprint image segmentation using fractal dimension features and weighted extreme learning machine ensemble. Paper presented at the IEEE Conference on Computer Vision and Pattern Recognition Workshops (2016)

Feng, W., Xiuyou, W., Lin, X.: An improved fingerprint segmentation algorithm based on mean and variance. Paper presented at the 2009 International Workshop on Intelligent Systems and Applications, Wuhan, China, 23–24 May 2009

Fleyeh, H., Jomaa, D.: Segmentation of Low Quality Fingerprint Images. Paper presented at the IEEE International Conference on Multimedia Computing and Information Technology (MCIT-2010), Sharja, UAE, 2–4 March 2010

FVC2002 (2002). http://bias.csr.unibo.it/fvc2002/

FVC2004 (2004). http://bias.csr.unibo.it/fvc2004/

Gottschlich, C., Schönlieb, C.: Oriented diffusion filtering for enhancing low-quality fingerprint images. IET Biom. **1**, 105–113 (2012)

Helfroush, M., Mohammadpour, M.: Fingerprint segmentation. Paper presented at the 3rd International Conference on Information and Communication Technologies: From Theory to Applications, Damascus, Syria (2008)

Howe, N.: Implementation of Contour-Pruned Skeletonization (2016). http://cs.smith.edu/~nhowe/research/code/index.html#binarize

Kroon, D., Slump, C.: Coherence filtering to enhance the mandibular canal in cone-beam CT data. Paper presented at the IEEE-EMBS Benelux Chapter Symposium (2009)

Kroon, D., Slump, C., Maal, T.: Optimized anisotropic rotational invariant diffusion scheme on cone-beam CT. Paper presented at the International Conference on Medical Image Computing and Computer-Assisted Intervention (2010)

Maio, D., Maltoni, D., Jain, A., Prabhakar, S.: Handbook of Fingerprint Recognition, 2nd edn. Springer, London (2009)

Nimkar, R., Mishra, A.: Fingerprint segmentation using scale vector algorithm. Paper presented at the IEEE 2015 5th International Conference on Communication Systems and Network Technologies (CSNT) (2015)

Otsu, N.: A threshold selection method from gray level histogram. IEEE Trans. Syst. Man Cybern. SMC **9**(1), 62–66 (1979)

Ren, C., Yin, Y., Ma, J., Yang, G.: A linear hybrid classifier for fingerprint segmentation. Paper presented at the IEEE 4th International Conference on Natural Computation, Jinan, China (2008)

Sankaran, A., Jain, A., Vashist, T., Vatsa, M., Singh, R.: Adaptive latent fingerprint segmentation using feature selection and random decision forest classification. Inf. Fusion **34**, 1–15 (2017)

Suzuki, K., Horiba, I., Sugie, N.: Linear-time connected component labelling based on sequential local operations. Comput. Vis. Image Underst. **89**, 1–23 (2003)

Thai, D., Gottschlich, C.: Global variational method for fingerprint segmentation by three-part decomposition. IET Biom. **5**(2), 120–130 (2016)

Thai, D., Huckemann, S., Gottschlich, C.: Filter design and performance evaluation for fingerprint image segmentation. PLoS ONE **11**(5), 154–160 (2016)

Weickert, J., Scharr, H.: A scheme for coherence-enhancing diffusion filtering with optimized rotation invariance. J. Vis. Commun. Image Represent. **13**, 103–118 (2002)

Weixin, B., Deqin, X., Yi-Wei, Z.: Fingerprint segmentation based on improved active contour. Paper presented at the IEEE Computer Society International Conference on Networking and Digital Society (2009)

Yu, C., Xie, M., Qi, J.: An effective algorithm for low quality fingerprint segmentation. Paper presented at the IEEE 3rd International Conference on Intelligent System and Knowledge Engineering, Chengdu, China (2008)

Feature Selection and Bleach Time Modelling of Paper Pulp Using Tree Based Learners

Karl Hansson, Hasan Fleyeh$^{(\boxtimes)}$, and Siril Yella

Computer Science Department, Dalarna University, 791 31 Falun, Sweden
{khs,hfl,sye}@du.se
http://www.du.se

Abstract. Paper manufacturing is energy demanding and improved modelling of the pulp bleach process is the main non-invasive means of reducing energy costs. In this paper, time it takes to bleach paper pulp to desired brightness is examined. The model currently used is analysed and benchmarked against two machine learning models (Random Forest and TreeBoost). Results suggests that the current model can be superseded by the machine learning models and it does not use the optimal compact subset of features. Despite the differences between the machine learning models, a feature ranking correlation has been observed for the new models. One novel, yet unused, feature that both machine learning models found to be important is the concentration of bleach agent.

Keywords: Feature selection · Machine learning · CFS · Random forest · TreeBoost · XGBoost · Paper manufacturing

1 Introduction

Paper manufacturing is intrinsically energy demanding. According to the Confederation of European Paper Industries, its members consumed about 101 TWh in 2013 [1]. To put this in perspective, the EU-28 countries consumed a total of 3262 TWh electricity in the same year, roughly a third were consumed by industries [2]. The paper manufacturing in Europe thus accounted for roughly 8.5 % of the total usage of electrical energy in the industrial sector. The collaborative partner in this work is one of the largest paper mills in Sweden. Even relatively small improvements in terms of energy efficiency leads to substantial energy savings and competitive advantages in terms of cost effectiveness. The time when paper production goes from producing paper of one quality to another is called a changeover. During changeovers, produced paper cannot be sold since the quality of the product is not in any marketable state. Since the production is continuous, the manufacturing plant still consumes the same amount of energy as in a non-changeover state. Paper produced during a changeover must be recycled and there is, therefore, a two folded energy waste. Reducing changeover time is among the most effective mean a paper manufacturer can do to reduce costs. A success factor for reducing the changeover time is to better understand

© Springer International Publishing AG 2016
W. Cellary et al. (Eds.): WISE 2016, Part II, LNCS 10042, pp. 385–396, 2016.
DOI: 10.1007/978-3-319-48743-4_31

and model the bleaching process, a process that is hard to observe directly as it possesses long lead times. If brightness of the paper is to be changed, a bleaching process must be initiated hours in advance. Better prediction of bleach time would improve planing and preparations for coming changeovers. Currently the company models the bleach process by looking at mass transport of paper pulp within the paper production plant.

The main objective of this article is to investigate and ensure whether if all the necessary features are incorporated in the current model for predicting the bleach time. The proposed method is based on a pre-study, that outlines ideas of feature selection and modelling of high dimensional manufacturing systems [3]. The investigation is done by first using Hall's filter technique Correlation-based Feature Selection [4], and append this new feature set to the existing feature set used by the pre-existing model. Collected data from the paper plant was then invoked to benchmark the current model and also to train two strong models based on Brieman's Random Forest [5] and Friedman's TreeBoost algorithm [6]. The models are then benchmarked against each other to examine if the extended feature set offered means of more precise predictions of the bleach time using novel data. The machine learning models are compelling as both offer functionality for assessing feature importance. This article presents and analyse feature rankings suggested by the new models.

This article is organized as follows. In Sect. 2, available data is discussed. Section 3 discusses the models employed in this work. Section 3 presents measuring of variable importance and in Sect. 4 experimental results are shown. Results are discussed in Sect. 5 and the article is concluded in Sect. 6.

2   Data

It is essential to monitor manufacturing plants. Sensors are placed throughout the entire process, with the primary function of letting operators and control loops observe the current state of production. Such sensor readings are stored in a data warehouse to let the manufacturer evaluate past performance of the production. In this case, thousands of different variables have been stored in a data warehouse. In this article, only data stored between the bleach tower and the point where the brightness of the paper pulp is measured are used.

The manufacturer continuously stores a product code describing the type of paper that is currently produced. The product code contains information regarding several properties of the paper, one among them is brightness. By looking at the recorded product codes in the period March 2013 to October 2015, it could be determined at what timestamps the plant started to produce a new product with a different brightness. Furthermore, given these timestamps it was possible to match if changes in the concentration of bleaching agent in the bleach tower had preceded the change in brightness. A total of 231 observations of changes in bleach agent within 12 hours of a brightness change was identified. The time difference between change in bleach agent level and brightness change in the final product was used as the target feature to evaluate model performance. If several

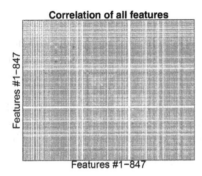

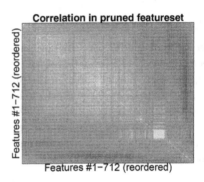

Fig. 1. Correlation between the 847 variables. Lighter greys indicates higher correlation, completely white lines are features with zero variance.

Fig. 2. Correlation between the 712 features after removal of zero variance features. Reordered rows and columns to visualize closely correlated features.

changes in the bleach agent occurs within a time frame, the one closest to the brightness change was the one considered. One problem with the target value worth commenting on is that it included both the time it takes for the bleaching as well as the time of the actual changeover. There are 847 different candidate features extracted from the companies data warehouse to create a dataset which were used to predict bleach time. These features represents set points and sensor readings from the pulp manufacturing part of the plant and the paper machine itself. The vast majority of the features are numerical, but some of them can be treated as categorical as they only take binary values. In industrial environments, missing values are common and often carries information regarding the status of the machinery. It was neither suitable to omit nor impute them. However, 135 of the features never change in any of the observations. Figure 1 depicts all features and their corresponding correlations, lighter greys signifies a higher correlation and the white lines are features with zero variance (never changing). The features with zero variance are removed since they cannot add any information to the data driven models. Removing the non-changing ones reduces the number of features to 712, where 80 of them are binary. Furthermore, a number of features are fully correlated to each other, because of the nature of the production process. This is not directly apparent in Fig. 1 but if the rows and columns of the correlation matrix are reordered the correlation becomes clear as shown in Fig. 2.

3   Models

In this section, three different types of models are described. First, the current model of the bleach time in the paper plant is presented. It is then followed by presenting the two machine learning algorithms that are proposed to be used to identify additional features.

3.1   The Current Model

The current model used by the paper manufacturer to predict bleach time has been constructed from a set of differential equations that describes flow of paper pulp between storage tanks in the paper manufacturing plant. In total 7 features, $\{x_1, x_2, \ldots, x_7\}$, and 3 numerical constants, $\{\alpha_1, \alpha_2, \alpha_3\}$, are used to predict the bleach time given the current state of the production plant. These features and numerical constants have been selected by domain experts. Feature and constant names have been replaced by dummy names due to confidentiality reasons. The model itself is shown in Eq. 1.

$$\hat{y} = \frac{\alpha_1 x_1 x_2}{(\alpha_2 - x_3)(x_4(\alpha_2 - x_6) - \alpha_2 x_5)(\alpha_2 - x_7)} + \alpha_3 \qquad (1)$$

3.2   Machine Learning Models

Tree based ensemble learners have in the past few years emerged as the top performing algorithms for modelling complex systems based on structured data [7–10]. The strength of ensembles has been analytically confirmed by Tumer and Ghosh [11]. The authors proved that an ensemble of weak learners, which are not strongly correlated to each other, improves the combined generalization ability. Ensemble techniques are especially useful when the training data is in limited supply. Single decision trees are sensitive to the training data in the sense that minor changes in the training data can produce widely different trees [12,13] which also motivates the use of ensemble techniques. Both machine learning models used in this article are based on the CART tree, introduced by Breiman et al. [12], which has been widely employed due to its simplicity and predictive capabilities. The CART tree is a binary tree that splits the feature space in two parts at each node, leafs in the tree describes the final regression/classification. A CART tree, $h(\mathbf{x})$, partitions the input space into J disjunct regions, $R_1, \ldots, R_J$. A value is associated with each of the regions, b_j, it is this value that constitutes the prediction of individual trees. The individual tree model is expressed in Eq. 2, where $1(\mathbf{x} \in R_{jm})$, is the binary indicator function.

$$h(\mathbf{x}) = \sum_{j=1}^{J} b_j 1(\mathbf{x} \in R_j) \qquad (2)$$

3.3   Random Forest

The Random Forest, RF, is a modelling technique that employs bagging [14], which reduces variance and overfitting of a classifier. Bagging means that given a training set $\mathcal{D}$ with size n, re-sample $\mathcal{D}$ uniformly with replacements into m new datasets $\mathcal{D}_i$ each with size n'. Usually $n' = n$ is chosen, then $1 - 1/e$ of the samples are expected to be unique within each of the produced subsets [15]. After re-sampling, a model of choice is fitted for each $\mathcal{D}_i$. The final prediction is made by having a majority vote from the weak learners, each being equally weighted. RF was introduced by Breiman [5], RF extends the idea of bagging by not only sub-sample datasets but also by random sampling of which features each tree in the forest uses. Predictions using an RF model is done via a majority vote as shown in Eq. 3.

$$\hat{y}(\mathbf{x}) = \frac{1}{K} \sum_{k=1}^{K} h_k(\mathbf{x}) \tag{3}$$

Measuring variable importance in an RF works by randomly permuting individual feature to measure how much the sum of squares errors (SSE) increases when a feature becomes noisy. The rationale behind this argument is that when an important feature randomly changes the prediction error increases. Given feature data $\mathcal{D} = \{\mathbf{x_1}, \mathbf{x_2}, \ldots, \mathbf{x_m}\}$, corresponding targets $\mathbf{Y}$ and an RF model, $H(\mathbf{x})$, variable importance is then calculated as follows.

1. Calculate the unaltered SSE, $e_0 = \sum (Y - H(\mathcal{D}))^2$.
2. Permute each feature, $i \in \{1, \ldots, m\}$ while keeping the rest fixed. The dataset $\mathcal{D}_i$ denotes a permuted i:th feature.
3. Recalculate SSE, $e_i = \sum (Y - H(\mathcal{D}_i))^2$ for each $\mathcal{D}_i$.
4. For each i calculate the variable importance ratio, $I_i = e_i/e_0$

3.4 TreeBoost

In 2001 Friedman [6] proposed a gradient boosting machine extending on Schapire's work with boosting [16]. The algorithm is generic with regards to predictor, but can easily be optimized for CART trees, this variant is called TreeBoost. In this article an R implementation of Friedman's TreeBoost has been used, called XGBoost. The fundamental idea of TreeBoost is to create an ensemble via boosting of decision trees of a fixed size. A TreeBoost model is built iteratively, adding one tree at the time beginning with constant prediction at round zero. The ensemble can be viewed in Eq. 4. Selecting which tree to add is done via gradient decent of an objective function, which consists of a loss part (squared loss) and a regularization part. Details of XGBoost can be found in [17].

$$H(\mathbf{x})_i^{(t)} = \sum_{k=1}^{t} h_k(\mathbf{x}_i) = H(\mathbf{x})_i^{(t-1)} + h_t(\mathbf{x}_i) \tag{4}$$

To asses feature importance of boosted trees, it is essential to understand how individual trees in the ensemble measure feature importance. Variable importance of an individual tree, $h()$, the estimated importance squared of a feature, j, in a CART tree is expressed in Eq. 5. Where $J-1$ is the number of non-terminal nodes. $1()$ is a binary indicator function which indicates if a non-terminal node splits on feature j and $\hat{i}_t^2$ is the empirical improvement in squared error of the split. Friedman generalized this idea to measure feature importance over the whole ensemble, of M tree, by arguing that feature importance for the ensemble could be estimated as the mean of the features importance of the individual trees, as shown in Eq. 6.

$$\hat{I}_j^2(h) = \sum_{t=1}^{J-1} \hat{i}_t^2 1(v_t = j) \tag{5}$$

$$\hat{I}_j^2 = \frac{1}{M} \sum_{m=1}^{M} \hat{I}_j^2(h_m) \tag{6}$$

4   Results

In this section, data pre-processing and feature set are described along with performance of the current model, the machine learning models and their respective variable importance indications. The section is finalized by comparing the feature importance found by the two models to each other.

4.1   Data Processing and Feature Selection

Beside reducing number of features from 847 to 712, additional reduction was performed by using Correlation-based Feature Selection (CFS) [4], which reduced the number of features to 23. The intersection of the feature set selected by CFS and the one selected by domain experts showed that two features were shared among both sets. The union of the two sets generated a feature set with 28 different features (23 from CFS, 7 from experts, but 2 features are common in both sets). The union set was employed by the learning algorithms. The features correlations are displayed in Fig. 3, where $\{x_1, x_2, \ldots, x_7\}$ are the features selected by domain experts and the rest are features selected by the CFS.

To evaluate the performance of the current model, all 231 samples (28 features) are used. While for the machine learning models a 50-50 split is used to create a training and testing set, respectively.

4.2   Performance of the Current Model

Figure 4 is produced by applying the current model to all available samples and subtracting the actual time taken before the brightness changes in the final paper. The figure shows the error of the current model in terms of frequency. A mixture of two normal distributions was used to produce the density function which approximates the histogram. A standard EM algorithm was used to estimate the distribution [18]. The fitted density function is described in Eq. 7.

$$f_{mix}(\mathbf{x}) = \frac{\lambda_1}{\sigma_1, \sqrt{2\pi}} e^{-\frac{(\mathbf{x}-\mu_1)^2}{2\sigma_1^2}} + \frac{\lambda_2}{\sigma_2, \sqrt{2\pi}} e^{-\frac{(\mathbf{x}-\mu_2)^2}{2\sigma_2^2}} \tag{7}$$

It is worth noting that the mode of the distribution is shifted to the right. The empirical bias of the distribution described in Eq. 7 can be calculated by

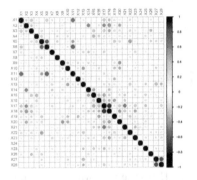
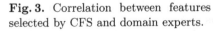

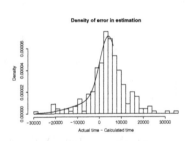

Fig. 3. Correlation between features selected by CFS and domain experts.

Fig. 4. Histogram showing error of current model, solid line is an estimated density function via a mixture of two normal distributions.

employing Eq. 8 to the estimated μ:s and λ:s. In the case of the current model, evaluated on the entire dataset, the value of μ_{mix} was 4130.

$$\mu_{mix} = \lambda_1\mu_1 + \lambda_2\mu_2 \tag{8}$$

The empirical variance of the current model was computed by Eq. 9. The standard deviation was $\sigma_{mix} = 8942$ s.

$$\sigma_{mix}^2 = \lambda_1\sigma_1^2 + \lambda_2\sigma_2^2 + \left[\lambda_1\mu_1^2 + \lambda_2\mu_2^2 - (\lambda_1\mu_1 + \lambda_1\mu_1)^2\right] \tag{9}$$

rMSE is used to compare the current model with the machine learning models, as they are trained with rMSE as evaluation criteria. rMSE is given in Eq. 10, where n is the number of samples, y is the target value and $\hat{y}$ is the target estimated by the model. The rMSE of the current model is 9568.

$$rMSE = \sqrt{\sum_{i=1}^{n} (\hat{y}_i - y_i)^2} \tag{10}$$

4.3 Random Forest Results

To find optimal settings for an RF model leave-one-out cross validation was used in the parameter grid search. It was found that that parameter settings $p = 25$ and $K = 1000$ yielded the best performance. Figure 5 depicts one profile from the tuning of the parameter p, using fixed $K = 1000$. This figure suggests that $p \approx 25$ gives good generalization.

The RF model's performance was then measured against testing dataset. Figure 6 shows the error distribution as a histogram together with the estimated mixed model of normal distributions.

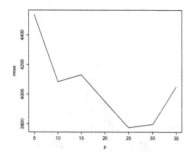

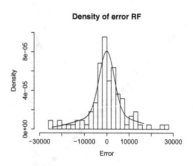

Fig. 5. Figure showing the RMSE for different values of p when training and evaluating the RF model using leave-one-out cross-validation, and $K = 1000$

Fig. 6. Histogram showing the empirical error for the RF model on previously unseen data. A mixture of normal distributions was used to estimate the error frequency.

Using the methodology described earlier, the mean of the estimated mixed distribution was $\mu_{mix} = -45$ s, the empirical standard deviation was $\sigma_{mix} = 8533$ s and the $rMSE$ was 8147. It is evident that the RF model performs much better than the current model. It is interesting to investigate if RF utilizes other variables compared to the current model. However, due to random sampling of the subsets, different variable importance in terms of increased MSE, could differ between runs. To minimize such effect, 100 different RF models were created and evaluated in order to find the average variable importance. The results are shown in Fig. 9.

4.4 TreeBoost Results

The parameters of TreeBoost model was tuned in a similar manner to RF. TreeBoost requires two parameters to be tuned, the learning rate η, and the maximum depth of the trees D_{max}. The results from the grid search is visualized in Fig. 7. The performance of TreeBoost was noisy regarding its parameter settings, although a general trend is observed such that a low value of η yields a lower RMSE. The best setting was found at Depth $= 7$ and $\eta = 0.2$. When evaluating this model on the test set, an rMSE of 8176 is achieved. Similarly, a mixture of normal distributions was fitted to the errors depicted in the histogram of Fig. 8. The fitted distribution has $\mu_{mix} = 320$ s and $\sigma^2_{mix} = 8170$ s. The TreeBoost model, thus, has a slightly larger bias but lower variance compared to the RF model.

Results from the tuned TreeBoost model is shown in Fig. 10. Again, 100 models were trained and evaluated with regards to variable importance to negate effects of random sampling.

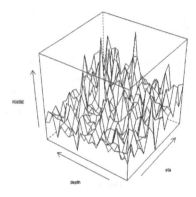

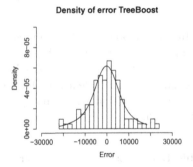

Fig. 7. Training error for different settings of TreeBoost, using leave-one-out cross validation.

Fig. 8. A histogram showing the error distribution as well as a fitted mixture of normal distributions to describe the error.

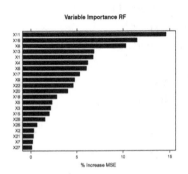

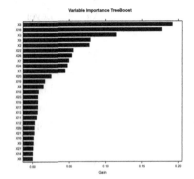

Fig. 9. Average variable importance for 100 different RF models. All using $p = 25$ and 1000 trees.

Fig. 10. Average variable importance for 100 different TreeBoost models. All using $\eta = 0.2$ and Depth $= 7$.

4.5   Comparing Variable Importance

From Figs. 9 and 10, it is clear that the different algorithms did not rank the feature identically. This is due to two facts. The algorithms do not measure feature importance in the same way and the algorithms uses two different methods to perform the ensemble. However, it is interesting to investigate if there is a correlation in the feature ranking. To measure this, Spearman's Rank Correlation was used. Given two rank vectors x and y, the rank correlation can be calculated by using Eq. 11. Where x describes the ranking of feature importance from RF and y describes the feature rankings from the TreeBoost model. Where n is the total number of features. The resulting Spearman's Rank Correlation are $\rho = 0.3218$, and $p = 0.0952$. These values suggest that the hypothesis that there is a weak correlation between the ranking of the two models is not rejected with an alpha-level of 0.1.

$$\rho = 1 - \frac{6\sum(x-y)^2}{n^3 - n} \tag{11}$$

In Table 1 presents the top most important features as selected by the learning models together with those selected by the experts. Features selected by the models are those which gives 50 % increase/gain compared that given of the maximum important feature. Due to confidential reasons on behalf of the paper plant, numerical values are not provided but instead their physical interpretations are given.

Table 1. Top most important features found by both machine learning models, as well as the features selected by domain experts.

Feature	Type	Unit	Origin
X_1	Flow	m^3/h	Expert, RF
X_2	Level	%	Expert, TB
X_3	Level	%	Expert, TB
X_4	Flow	m^3/h	Expert
X_5	Flow	m^3/h	Expert, TB
X_6	Flow	m^3/h	Expert
X_7	Level	%	Expert
X_8	Concentration	%	RF, TB
X_{11}	Volume	m^3	RF
X_{13}	Level	%	RF
X_{16}	Voltage	kV	RF, TB

5   Discussion

It is interesting that the set of features found by CFS had an overlap with those selected by domain experts. This is promising since CFS could select any among the 712 features. Since the final pruned dataset (28 features) were created by taking the union between the current dataset and the one selected by CFS, it was expected that some of the variables would have high correlation between each other.

When comparing the feature importance rankings from the two machine learning models, indications of correlations are evident. It was found that X_{11} had high correlation with both X_1 and X_6. This is an interesting outcome as X_{11} were selected as the most important feature by the RF model, which in line with what the domain experts had deemed important for the system. On the other hand, TreeBoost did not select X_{11} as an important predictor and selected X_1 instead. Suggesting that both machine learning algorithms have an implicit agreement regarding the importance of these features. Since features are correlated, ranking them directly is hard. It was, therefore, encouraging to observe that the two different methods had an agreement in the ordering of the feature importance.

Despite the fact that only half of the samples were used for training, the machine learning models were able to outperform the current model for unseen data, with regards to bias, variance as well as rMSE. It has been seen that the machine learning models were able to drastically reduce the bias compared to the current model. This is expected since the current model does not try to actively predict the time of a changeover, but only the time it takes for bleaching to take effect. Unfortunately, it has not been possible to segregate the two time parts out of the target variable. However, given the assumption that changeovers are relatively constant in time, it is clear that the machine learning models were able to produce a significantly lower variance compared to the current model. This showed that, with the help of the extended feature set, it is possible to increase the performance when estimating the bleach time compared to the current model.

A feature that seems promising for future investigation is the feature X_8. What this feature describes is the new concentration of bleaching agent after the bleaching process is initiated. It is reasonable that such information could have predictive capabilities in how long the actual bleaching will take. X_8, as a reminder, was classified as the topmost important feature by the TreeBoost model and third most important by the Random Forest model. As this features is not used by the current model, it seems feasible to extend it by utilizing X_8 in order to increase its predictive capability. This is something that for practical reasons is good, as the two machine learning models are rather large and not practical to implement in the current control system used by the paper manufacturer. Results from this work indicate that improvements in bleach time production is possible.

6   Conclusion

In this work, an exploratory analysis of feature importance for predicting bleach time in a large paper manufacturing plant has been conducted. Different machine learning techniques, RF and TreeBoost, have been used to model bleach time. It has been shown that machine learning algorithms were able to reduce the prediction's bias, variance as well as rMSE. Further, by using Spearman's Rank Correlation, it is suggested that the feature importance ranking from the different machine learning algorithms were correlated. The big take-away from this article a new feature, X_8, were identified as important factor in estimating bleach time. This feature describes the concentration of bleach agent after the bleach process had been initiated. Future work will aim to incorporating X_8 into the pre-existing model such that it achieves improved predictive performance while still being in a format which is suitable for the current infrastructure used at the paper plant.

References

1. Key statistics, European pulp and paper industry (2014). http://www.cepi.org/system/files/public/documents/publications/statistics/2015/Key%20Statistics%202014%20FINAL.pdf. Accessed 11 Apr 2016
2. Electricity and heat statistics, eurostat. http://ec.europa.eu/eurostat/statistics-explained/index.php/Electricity_and_heat_statistics. Accessed 11 Apr 2016
3. Karl, H., Yella, S., Dougherty, M., Fleyeh, H.: Machine learning algorithms in heavy process manufacturing. Am. J. Intell. Syst. **6**, 1–13 (2016)
4. Hall, M.A.: Correlation-based feature selection for discrete and numeric class machine learning, pp. 359–366. Morgan Kaufmann (2000)
5. Breiman, L.: Random forests. Mach. Learn. **45**, 5–32 (2001)
6. Friedman, J.H.: Greedy function approximation: a gradient boosting machine. Ann. Stat. **29**, 1189–1232 (2001)
7. Caruana, R., Niculescu-Mizil, A.: An empirical comparison of supervised learning algorithms. In: Proceedings of the 23rd International Conference on Machine Learning, ICML 2006, pp. 161–168. ACM, New York (2006)
8. Laha, D., Ren, Y., Suganthan, P.N.: Modeling of steelmaking process with effective machine learning techniques. Expert Syst. Appl. **42**(10), 4687–4696 (2015)
9. Halawani, S.M.: A study of decision tree ensembles and feature selection for steel plates faults detection. Int. J. Tech. Res. Appl. **2**(4), 127–131 (2014)
10. Deng, H., Runger, G.C.: Feature selection via regularized trees (2012). CoRR, vol. abs/1201.1587
11. Tumer, K., Ghosh, J.: Error correlation and error reduction in ensemble classifiers. Connect. Sci. **8**(34), 385–404 (1996)
12. Breiman, L., Friedman, J., Olshen, R., Stone, C.: Classification and Regression Trees. Wadsworth and Brooks, Monterey (1984)
13. Quinlan, J.R.: C4.5: Programs for Machine Learning. Morgan Kaufmann Publishers Inc., San Francisco (1993)
14. Breiman, L.: Bagging predictors. Mach. Learn. **24**, 123–140 (1996)
15. Aslam, J.A., Popa, R.A., Rivest, R.L.: On estimating the size and confidence of a statistical audit. In: Proceedings of the USENIX Workshop on Accurate Electronic Voting Technology, EVT 2007, p. 8. USENIX Association, Berkeley (2007)
16. Schapire, R.E.: The strength of weak learnability. Mach. Learn. **5**, 197–227 (1990)
17. Introduction to boosted trees. http://xgboost.readthedocs.org/en/latest/model.html. Accessed 11 Mar 2016
18. Van Dyk, D.A., Meng, X.L., Rubin, D.B.: Maximum likelihood estimation via the ECM algorithm: computing the asymptotic variance. Technical report (1994)

Trust Model of Wireless Sensor Networks Based on Shannon Entropy

Jun Hu[1(⊠)] and Chun Guan[2]

[1] School of Software, Nanchang University, Nanchang,
Jiangxi, China
hujun@ncu.edu.cn
[2] School of Information Engineering, Nanchang University,
Nanchang, Jiangxi, China
guanchun@yeah.net

Abstract. Trust between nodes is the foundation of communication security in wireless sensor network. A new entire trust model of wireless sensor network is constructed in terms of comprehensive trust value of nodes. The direct trust value is deduced on basis of node trusted elements system, according to the Shannon entropy theory. Experiments show that trust model of wireless sensor network based on Shannon entropy can improve the stability, speed and security of networks efficiently.

Keywords: Shannon entropy · Wireless sensor networks · Trust model

1 Introduction

Sensor nodes of Wireless Sensor Networks (WSN) are always deployed in hostile region or severe environment which is difficult to maintenance safely via manual method, and gain, collect, process and transfer information of local area or research objects [1–5]. There are many uncontrollable and variable factors in the environment of nodes, such as temperature, moisture, wind force, and pressure etc. Due to existence of those factors, nodes of sensors are ease to be attacked and malfunctioned, and it can make whole networks to be anomaly, even to be broken down. For example, when sensor nodes are deployed into hostile military area and are caught by enemy, the data from our networks would be leaked and modified maliciously, even camouflage node would be connected into our networks. In another scenario, if sensor nodes are deployed into severe outside natural area, internal modules of nodes are easily malfunction and cause network to break down, owning to influence of severe environment. Besides the influence of environment, sensor nodes are possible to behave selfishly, cause error or date lose, and break the function or lifetime of networks, in consideration of its limitation of communication, memory, power, computation, and unbalanced distribution. All external factors and internal limitation to damage WSNs are named as attack of WSNs.

Generally, the source of WSNs' attack can be classified into external attack and internal attack [6]. External attack includes information interception, information listening, camouflage node, fake route distribution, fake information transfer, service rejection etc. Internal attack includes package discarding, information resend,

© Springer International Publishing AG 2016
W. Cellary et al. (Eds.): WISE 2016, Part II, LNCS 10042, pp. 397–403, 2016.
DOI: 10.1007/978-3-319-48743-4_32

information steal, fake data distribution and data modification etc. About external attack, there are many effective approaches against it, including general access control, intrusion detection, data authorization, digital watermarking, key security system etc. However, internal attack is difficult to defend effectively in that its indiscoverable and undetectable features, which don't exist in external attack, invalidate most general key security techniques. Thus, information security and efficiency of networks are threatened seriously in terms of general key security systems are entirely malfunctioned under internal attack. In this scenario, as the complement of general key security systems, trust model and trust management technique of WSNs, which depend on nodes' trust relationship and trust degree to judge anomaly behavior, are critical research fields of WSNs' security. Therefore, establishment of nodes' trust relation is essential condition to evaluate networks' functionality, since operation and maintenance of WSNs do generally rely on the trust between sensor batch nodes.

2 Related Work

Nowadays, domestic and international scholars, who research WSNs trust [7–12], generally focus on basic principle, behavior of nodes, trust degree of nodes, confidential degree of nodes, structure of networks, and coordination of nodes etc. Fuzzy theory, Subject Logical theory, Bayesian theory and Uncertainty deduction etc. are leveraged to construct trust model. Moreover, trust issues of WSNs are integrated into other theories, such as Cloud theory, Rasch theory, Social Networks theory, Analytic Hierarchy Process, and Grey theory etc., and correlate trust models are constructed on the basis of those theories [13–20].

However, there are still various defects in those theories and models, including:

1. Complicate computation and evaluation of trust value. Massive and delicate parameters for computation need more memory and CPU of nodes, which burden nodes' loads and energy consumption heavily.
2. Historical Storage of computing parameters. There are enormous parameters in the communication between nodes, history information of which need to store in the nodes' memory for a long time.
3. Simplification and deletion of parts of parameters. There are some unnecessary parameters that need to be simplified or deleted in terms of loose couple for actual application or weak effect for trust results.
4. Inaccuracy of trust results. In consideration of effect of only one or few elements in trust values, it will separate the relation among elements of trust system. Moreover, manual configuration or prior configuration for element weights will cause inaccuracy of trust values' evaluation.

3 Trust Model Based on Shannon Entropy

In landmark paper published in 1948, entitled "A Mathematical Theory of Communication", C. E. Shannon addressed conception of entropy, which analyzes and evaluates quantity of information in message.

Generally, signals from information source are uncertain, so that uncertainty can be evaluated by probability of occurrence. Probability of occurrence is more, uncertainty is less; on the other side, probability of is less, uncertainty is more.

Function of uncertainty F is monotonic decreasing function of Probability P, and the uncertainty function of two independent signals occurred in same time equals to the sum of uncertainty function of each signal, $F(p_1, p_2) = F(p_1) + F(p_2)$, named Additivity. The function F, which can satisfy Additive property and Monotonic decreasing property, shall be logarithmic function, $F(p) = \log \frac{1}{p} = -\log p$.

During analysis of quantity in information, it is not just consideration of uncertainty of one signal's occurrence, but average uncertainty of all signal's occurrence from source. If there are n values in signals from source: $U_1 \cdots U_i \cdots U_n$, the probability of occurrence is $P_1 \cdots P_i \cdots P_n$, and occurrence of each signal is independent, the average uncertain degree of source is statistic mean E of each signal's uncertainty $F(p_i)$, named Entropy, is defined as $H(U) = E(F(P_i)) = -\sum_{i=1}^{n} P_i \log p_i$, where base of logarithm is 2, and unit is bit, U represent collection of all signals may occurrence.

In consideration of massive and complicate information from sensor nodes in WSNs, this paper combines Shannon entropy, fuzzy trust model and trust model of Social Networks to deduce trust value of nodes precisely.

3.1 Direct Trust Elements System of Nodes

Direct trust of nodes is influenced by various trust elements, so that direct trust elements system of nodes is the foundation and prerequisite of computation of direct trust. The choice of trust elements shall conform to the features of WSNs and Wireless Sensor. Therefore, trust elements are classified into trust elements of nodes communication, trust elements of node structure, and other elements.

(1) Trust elements of nodes communication, include speed of data process, indicator of data process, transmit power of node signal.

Speed of processing data is data which are processed for same task in unit time by nodes, is defined:
Speed of processing data = Amount of processing data/processing time.
Indicator of processing data is rate of transfer data to receive data for same task during a time cycle by nodes, is that:
Indicator of processing data = Amount of transferring data/Amount of receiving data.
Transmit power of node signal is transmit power of sensor node during data transmission.

(2) Trust elements of node structure, include variation of memory capacity and consumption of power.

Variation of memory capacity is variation of memory capacity from beginning to end of data transfer by node for same task, is that variation of memory capacity = memory capacity at end of data transfer – memory capacity at beginning of data transfer.

Consumption of power means the power consumption of node for same task in unit time, is that:

Consumption rate of power = power consumption of node/Processing time.

(3) Other elements, include success rate of mission accomplished, distance between nodes, amount of neighbor nodes, distortion rate of data, and count of node communication.

Success rate of mission accomplished is that:

Success rate of mission accomplished = amount of mission accomplished/amount of mission.

Distortion rate of data is discrepancy rate of receive data of present node to receive data of prior node. It is that:

Distortion rate of data = amount of discarding data in a node/amount of receiving data in prior node.

Count of node communication is that user can deliver command of append node to all nodes in networks, when a new node appears and is added by user. Otherwise, if the node appears suddenly, its trust will be evaluated by count of node communication.

3.2   Weight Computation of Trust Elements Based on Shannon Entropy

Evaluating Node collects related data of trust elements from evaluated node. Suppose there are m evaluated nodes, n trust elements, value matrix of trust elements is that:

$$
X = \begin{bmatrix}
x_{11} & x_{12} & \cdots & x_{1n} \\
x_{21} & x_{22} & \cdots & x_{2n} \\
\vdots & \vdots & \vdots & \vdots \\
x_{m1} & x_{m2} & \cdots & x_{mn}
\end{bmatrix},
$$

where $x = (x_{ij})_{mn}$. In the case of a trust element, large fluctuation of evaluated node x_{ij} means that this node is anomaly, need to be marked as anomaly node and deleted from networks in order to less effect for evaluation matrix.

Steps of weight computation of trust elements based on entropy, is described as following:

(1) Normalize of matrix:

$$
x'_{ij} = \frac{x_{ij} - \min\{x_j\}}{\max\{x_j\} - \min\{x_j\}}
$$

(2) Computing weight of trust element j for node i, is $p(x_{ij})$.

$$p(x_{ij}) = \frac{x_{ij}}{\sum\limits_{i=1}^{m} x_{ij}}$$

(3) Computing entropy of trust element j:

$$e_j = -k \sum\limits_{i=1}^{m} p(x_{ij}) \ln p(x_{ij})$$

(4) Computing discrepancy factor of trust element j, $d_j = 1 - e_j$. If discrepancy factor is less, the influence to trust element j is less. If discrepancy factor is bigger, the influence to trust is more, and element is more important and will set more weight during the computation of direct trust.
(5) Computing weight of element j:

$$w_j = \frac{d_j}{\sum\limits_{j=1}^{n} d_j}$$

(6) Evaluating trust value of elements:

$$s_{ij} = w_j \times x'_{ij}$$

4 Validation from Simulation Experiment

This paper compares suggested novel trust model and trust propagation algorithm with general trust model and algorithm via MATLAB simulation software, and analyzes con and pro of these models and algorithms. Configurations of experiment environment are as following:

(1) Deploy 200 node from Uniform distribution in area 100*100.
(2) Element attributes of nodes includes speed of data process, indicator of data process, transmit power of node signal, variation of memory, consumption of power, success rate of mission accomplished, distortion rate of data, and count of node communication, distance with other node, and count of neighbor nodes.
(3) All nodes are kept in initial state at beginning of experiment. After running of simulation, element attributes of nodes start to be variable.
(4) All nodes are kept in trust state at beginning of experiment. After running of simulation, untrusted nodes will be generated.
(5) Via 100 iteration of simulation, variation in practical scenario of WSNs will be simulated.

Critical subject of trust model is to simplify and speed computation of trust value, in order to reduce consumption of resource, such as power, memory capacity and bandwidth etc. Moreover, precision of trust value can be increased, and stability, speed, security of networks can be fortified.

From Fig. 1, trust values of nodes in suggested trust model increase rapidly at beginning of experiment 1. After that, the trust values of nodes in suggested trust model tend to be stable gradually, which means the networks are more stable. On the contrary, trust value of nodes in general trust model increase slowly. After that, more fluctuation and low level of trust value in general trust model happened during the procedure of simulation. Therefore, suggested trust model of WSNs based on entropy can improve the stability, speed and security of networks efficiently.

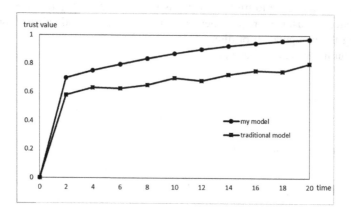

Fig. 1. Variation of trust value in trusted nodes

5 Conclusion

Information security and efficiency of WSNs are threatened seriously in terms of general key security systems are entirely malfunctioned under internal attack. In this scenario, as the complement of general key security systems, trust model and trust management technique of WSNs, which depend on nodes' trust relationship and trust degree to judge anomaly behavior, are critical research fields of WSNs' security. In this paper, a new entire trust model of wireless sensor network is constructed in terms of comprehensive trust value of nodes, which synthesize direct trust value and recommended trust value. The direct trust value is deduced on basis of node trusted elements system, according to the entropy of information theory. Simulation experiments show that the trust mode based on entropy can improve the stability, speed and security of networks efficiently. The following work will study how to compute recommend trust value according to the theory of social relational networks.

Acknowledgment. This work is supported by the Special Visiting Scholar Foundation for the Young Teacher Development Plan in Ordinary Universities of Jiangxi Province.

References

1. Han, G., Jiang, J., Shu, L., et al.: Management and applications of trust in wireless sensor networks: a survey. J. Comput. Syst. Sci. **80**(3), 602–617 (2014)
2. Aftab, M.U., Ashraf, O., Irfan, M., et al.: A review study of wireless sensor networks and its security. Commun. Netw. **7**(4), 172–179 (2015)
3. Ishmanov, F., Kim, S.W., Nam, S.Y.: A secure trust establishment scheme for wireless sensor networks. Sensors **14**(1), 1877–1897 (2014)
4. Alzaid, H., Alfaraj, M., Ries, S., Jøsang, A., Albabtain, M., Abuhaimed, A.: Reputation-based trust systems for wireless sensor networks: a comprehensive review. In: Fernández-Gago, C., Martinelli, F., Pearson, S., Agudo, I. (eds.) IFIPTM 2013. IAICT, vol. 401, pp. 66–82. Springer, Heidelberg (2013). doi:10.1007/978-3-642-38323-6_5
5. Misra, S., Vaish, A.: Reputation-based role assignment for role-based access control in wireless sensor networks. Comput. Commun. **34**(3), 281–294 (2011)
6. He, D., Chen, C., Chan, S., et al.: Retrust: attack-resistant and lightweight trust management for medical sensor networks. IEEE Trans. Inf. Technol. Biomed. Publ. IEEE Eng. Med. Biol. Soc. **16**(4), 623–632 (2012)
7. Zhou, P., Jiang, S., Irissappane, A.A., et al.: Towards energy-efficient trust system through watchdog optimization for WSNs. IEEE Trans. Inf. Forensics Secur. (tifs) **10**(3), 613–625 (2015)
8. Feng, R., Che, S., Wang, X., et al.: Trust management scheme based on D-s evidence theory for wireless sensor networks. Int. J. Distrib. Sens. Netw. **2013**(1), 130–142 (2013)
9. Renjian, F., Xiaofeng, X., Xiang, Z., et al.: A trust evaluation algorithm for wireless sensor networks based on node behaviors and D-s evidence theory. Sensors **11**(2), 1345–1360 (2011)
10. Mármol, F.G., Pérez, G.M.: Providing trust in wireless sensor networks using a bio-inspired technique. Telecommun. Syst. **46**(2), 163–180 (2011)
11. Mármol, F.G., Pérez, G.M.: Trust and reputation models comparison. Internet Res. **21**(2), 138–153 (2011)
12. Shen, S., Huang, L., Fan, E., et al.: Trust dynamics in WSNs: an evolutionary game-theoretic approach. J. Sens. **2016**, 1–10 (2016)
13. Liu, A., Liu, X., Long, J.: A trust-based adaptive probability marking and storage traceback scheme for WSNs. Sensors (basel, Switzerland) **16**(4), 451 (2016)
14. Liu, L., Li, C., Jia, H.: Social Milieu oriented routing: a new dimension to enhance network security in WSNs. Sensors **16**(2), 247 (2016)
15. Vamsi, P.R., Kant, K.: Trust and location-aware routing protocol for wireless sensor networks. IETE J. Res., 1–11 (2016)
16. Dogan, G., Avincan, K.: MultiProTru: a Kalman filtering based trust architecture for two-hop wireless sensor networks. Peer-to-peer Netw. Appl., 1–14 (2016)
17. Ahmed, A., Bakar, K.A., Channa, M.I., et al.: A secure routing protocol with trust and energy awareness for wireless sensor network. Mob. Netw. Appl. **21**, 1–14 (2016)
18. Das, A.K.: A secure and robust temporal credential-based three-factor user authentication scheme for wireless sensor networks. Peer-to-peer Netw. Appl. **9**(1), 223–244 (2016)
19. Kaur, J., Gill, S.S., Dhaliwal, B.S.: Secure trust based key management routing framework for wireless sensor networks. J. Eng. **2016**(3), 1–9 (2016)
20. Dogan, G, Avincan, K, Brown, T.: DynamicMultiProTru: an adaptive trust model for wireless sensor networks. In: 2016 4th International Symposium on Digital Forensic and Security (ISDFS), pp. 49–52 (2016)

Assessing the Quality and Reliability of Visual Estimates in Determining Plant Cover on Railway Embankments

Siril Yella[✉] and Roger G. Nyberg

Department of Computer Engineering and Informatics,
Dalarna University, 78170 Borlänge, Sweden
{sye, rny}@du.se

Abstract. This study has investigated the quality and reliability of manual assessments on railway embankments within the domain of railway maintenance. Manually inspecting vegetation on railway embankments is slow and time consuming. Maintenance personnel also require extensive knowledge of the plant species, ecology and bio-diversity to be able to recommend appropriate maintenance action. The overall objective of the study is to investigate the reliable nature of manual inspection routines in favour an automatic approach. Visual estimates of plant cover reported by domain experts' have been studied on two separate railway sections in Sweden. The first study investigated visual estimates using aerial foliar cover (AFC) and sub-plot frequency (SF) methods to assess the plant cover on a railway section in Oxberg, Alvdalsbanan, Sweden. The second study investigated visual estimates using aerial canopy cover method on a railway section outside Vetlanda, Sweden. Visual estimates of the domain experts were recorded and analysis-of-variance (ANOVA) tests on the mean estimates were investigated to see whether if there were disagreements between the raters'. ICC(2, 1) was used to study the differences between the estimates. Results achieved in this work indicate statistically significant differences in the mean estimates of cover ($p < 0.05$) reported by the domain experts on both the occasions.

1 Introduction

Presence of vegetation on and alongside railway tracks is a serious problem. Vegetation on the tracks reduces the elasticity of the ballast and increase water retention eventually contributing to the deterioration of wooden sleepers. Vegetation alongside railway tracks (especially in curves and level crossings) severely challenges visibility, as a result of which, trains have to be slowed down. Proper control and maintenance is therefore necessary to ensure smooth operational routines. Inspections aimed at measuring vegetation on and alongside railway tracks and embankments in Sweden (and elsewhere in the world) are currently performed manually by a human operator. Such inspections are, to a large extent are carried either by visually inspecting the track on-site, or by manually looking at video clips collected by maintenance trains. A decision concerning the condition is given by the inspector and is normally only explicit in cases of poor condition, for which the inspector recommends further maintenance action. Manually

© Springer International Publishing AG 2016
W. Cellary et al. (Eds.): WISE 2016, Part II, LNCS 10042, pp. 404–410, 2016.
DOI: 10.1007/978-3-319-48743-4_33

inspecting vegetation is slow and time consuming. Such inspection routines require that the maintenance personnel have extensive knowledge of the plant species to be able to recommend appropriate maintenance action. Further, preservation of the ecology and maintaining its diversity are yet other important issues [1–5]. The aim of this study is to investigate and assess the quality and reliability of such manual assessments; more specifically to compare the visual estimates (VE) of plant cover reported by the domain experts to be able to evaluate disagreements (if any).

Previous investigations on the problem reported significant difference between the raters' [6, 7]. Such work has mainly investigated the observers' ability to assess plant cover from images acquired on railway tracks to verify proof of concept. Results achieved from the above work indicate that seven out of the nine ANOVA tests conducted in this study have demonstrated significant difference in the mean estimates of cover (p < 0.05). The current article aims to extend the aforementioned work by carrying out cross investigations between domain experts on site as opposed to assessing vegetation from photographs. Work reported in this article is part of a major research project aimed at automating the process of detecting vegetation on railway embankments. A good description of the research project aimed at automatic vegetation detection on railway embankments is out of the scope of this article but could be found elsewhere [5, 8, 9]. Study of the prevalent differences between domain experts (if any) is therefore necessary to be able to advocate automatic procedures in favour of slow and time consuming manual routines.

The rest of the paper is organised as follows. Section 2 presents methodology; a brief introduction to the methods is also provided for the benefit of the readers unfamiliar with the methods. Section 3 presents results of the visual estimates reported by the different raters'. The paper finally presents concluding remarks.

2 Data Acquisition and Methodology

Studies aimed at investigating the VE of plant cover on railway embankments were carried out on two separate sites as follows.

2.1 On-Site Visual Estimates from Alvdalsbanan, Oxberg, Sweden

The first set of estimates was collected along the Alvdalsbanan railway track in Oxberg, Sweden. Two domain experts visually estimated the total plant cover of woody plants, herbs and grass separately (in %) using aerial foliar cover (AFC) and sub-plot frequency (SF) methods. In the context of assessing vegetation AFC is the area of ground covered by the vertical projection of the aerial portions of the plants. Small openings in the canopy and intra-specific overlap are excluded. In contrast, SF is a measure of the number of sub-plots that contain the target species. A good discussion concerning the methods could be found elsewhere [10]. At this stage it is worth mentioning that the raters' had long standing experience in estimating plant cover within the railway domain. Note that VE of mainly woody plants were reported along the Alvdalsbanan due to their dominant presence along the track. All the estimates were made by within a sample area of 1×1 m with the assistance of a boundary of a square meter (a.k.a. grid). The grid consisted of a sub-plot frame quadrat where each sub-plot measured 10*10 cm (see Fig. 1).

Fig. 1. Square meter grid with sub-plots

Different VE per plot were reported from a total of five plots in Oxberg as follows:

1. VE of the total cover using the AFC (no grid)
2. VE of the total cover using AFC and the square meter grid
3. VE of the woody plants using AFC and the square meter grid
4. VE of total cover using SF and the square meter grid
5. VE of woody plants cover using SF and the square meter grid

2.2   On-Site Visual Estimates from Vetlanda, Sweden

The second set of VE was collected from a section outside Vetlanda, Sweden. Three domain experts provided estimates on-site in 12 out of a total 179 sample areas. Twelve sample areas were selected by a systematic sampling method in which the starting position (of the first sample area) was chosen at random, and every eighth sampling area was assessed accordingly. Each sample area was represented by a rectangular area comprising of five ballast areas in between six sleepers on a railway track. VE in this particular case were reported using only the aerial canopy cover (ACC) method. ACC is the area of ground covered by the vertical projection of the outermost perimeter of the natural spread of foliage of plants, also known as the convex hull. Small openings within the canopy were included and in situations when it was practically impossible to identify individual plants, raters' agreed (in prior) to report such plant clusters as one plant.

At this stage it is worth mentioning that the railway section in this particular case was investigated twice in June and August 2013; to study the effect of a vegetation management routine that was carried out in between the sessions (see Table 2). The plant cover reported before and after the vegetation management routine (mainly herbicide treatment), expressed in percentage is presented in Table 2.

Note that no time limits were applied for gathering VE and the raters' reported their estimates independently on both sessions. All the observations were recorded and their mean estimates were computed for further analysis (see Table 1). Before proceeding any further it is worth mentioning that all the data was log10 transformed for all further parametric analysis. This is because a preliminary visual analysis of the raters' mean and median histogram plots has indicated an irregular, positively skewed distribution. The fact that log10-transformation makes a positively skewed data distribution less skewed justifies our choice [9].

Table 1. On-site visual estimates of plant cover (in %) at Oxberg, Alvdalsbanan, Sweden

Method	Rater	Plot 1	Plot 2	Plot 3	Plot 4	Plot 5	Mean diff. between the raters'
VE of total cover using AFC without a grid	Rater A	50	55	40	25	15	16
	Rater B	45	20	15	15	10	
	Relative difference between the raters	5	35	25	10	5	
VE of total cover using AFC and a grid	Rater A	62	37	16	15	13	5.6
	Rater B	52	28	20	18	15	
	Relative difference between the raters	10	9	4	3	2	
VE of woody plants cover using AFC and a grid	Rater A	30	21	15	14	9	2.2
	Rater B	25	22	13	13	7	
	Relative difference between the raters	5	1	2	1	2	
VE of total cover using SF and a grid aid	Rater A	86	59	46	61	47	17.8
	Rater B	94	81	68	73	72	
	Relative difference between the raters	8	22	22	12	25	
VE of woody plants cover using SF and a grid aid	Rater A	64	49	43	51	39	8.4
	Rater B	34	52	49	50	41	
	Relative difference between the raters	30	3	6	1	2	

Table 2. On-site visual estimates of plant cover at Vetlanda, Sweden

	(%) cover in June	(%) cover in August
Mean	12.89	2.6
Std. deviation	1.55	1.8
Max.	29	7
Min.	4	0

Analysis-of-variance (ANOVA) tests were tried and tested to investigate whether if there were differences between the estimates i.e. test the null hypothesis (H0) to check whether if the means of estimates are equal between the raters'. Density plots of the residuals obtained from the log10 transformed data were approximately normally distributed again justifying our choice of the ANOVA test. Intra-correlation coefficient (ICC) was used to be able to assess inter-rater reliability. Inter-rater reliability is the degree of agreement (a.k.a. ratings) between the raters' by comparing the variability of different ratings of the same subject with the total variation across all ratings and all subjects. The ICC coefficient can theoretically vary between 0 and 1.0, where an ICC value of 0 indicates no agreement whereas an ICC value of 1.0 indicates perfect agreement/reliability. A complete discussion of the classes is out of the scope of this article but could be found elsewhere [11]. In this particular article, ICC (2, 1) class was chosen (Eq. 1.).

$$ICC(2,1) = \frac{var(\beta)}{var(\alpha) + var(\beta) + var(\varepsilon)} \tag{1}$$

In addition to the ICC (2,1) method the Krippendorff's α was calculated using Eq. 2; where D_0 is the observed disagreement and D_e is the expected random disagreement.

$$\alpha_{Kripp} = 1 - \frac{D_0}{D_e} \tag{2}$$

3   Results and Discussion

Differences in the VE between the raters' were computed using ANOVA test and their reliability was assessed using the ICC (2,1) and the Krippendorff's α coefficient. Results achieved from the investigation at Oxberg, and Vetlanda have been tabulated in Tables 3 and 4 for the sake of simplicity.

Table 3. Inter-rater reliability between the visual estimates reported by the two raters' in Oxberg, Alvdalsbanan, Sweden

Method	Reliability ICC(2,1)	ICC(2,1) p-value	Krippendorrf's α
VE of total cover using AFC (no grid)	0.42	0.094	0.291
VE of total cover using AFC (grid aid)	0.94	0.0037	0.93
VE of woody plants cover using AFC (grid aid)	0.94	0.0012	0.935
VE of total cover using SF (grid aid)	0.46	0.016	0.283
VE of woody plants cover using SF (grid aid)	−0.58	0.83	−0.354

Table 4. Inter-rater reliability between the visual estimates reported by the three raters' in Vetlanda, Sweden

Method	Reliability ICC(2,1)	ICC(2,1) p-value	Krippendorrf's α
VE of total cover using ACC in June	0.53	$3.9 * 10^{-7}$	0.05
VE of total cover using ACC in August	0.51	$3.15 * 10^{-6}$	0.05

VE from Oxberg, Alvdalsbanan, Sweden indicate that better estimates were observed when the raters' had used the grid while estimating vegetation cover. Reliability coefficients while assessing the total cover and woody plants cover using AFC method assisted by a grid were relatively better. Reliability coefficients while assessing the woody plants cover using SF method assisted by a grid was in between moderate to poor and can be attributed to the high mean difference (17.8 %) in the VE for that trial. See Table 1. The reliability coefficient values of the VE while assessing the woody plants cover using SF method assisted by a grid were all negative. This indicates that the raters' estimates were worse than random. In particular remarkable differences have been observed when the raters' assessed the first plot. Post VE interviews revealed that individual interpretations as of how to assess bigger woody plants using SF methods led to the huge differences [9].

VE from Vetlanda, Sweden obtained in June and August 2013 were investigated using two one way ANOVA tests. Results achieved in both the cases showed a statistically significant difference between the three domain experts estimates ($p < 0.05$); indicating that the raters' disagreed on both the occasions. It was not in the interest of this investigation to identify which raters' differed from the others. Reliability of the raters' was assessed using ICC (2,1); see Table 4. ICC2 coefficient values in the current case could be considered as showing moderate reliability for a single rater i.e., how accurate a single rater would be if they made the estimates on their own [9].

4 Conclusions

Current day vegetation assessments within railway maintenance are (to a large extent) carried out manually; either through visual inspection onsite or by looking at video clips collected by maintenance trains. The overall objective of the study is to expose the unreliable nature of the (slow and time consuming) manual vegetation inspection regime in favour an automatic approach. The quality and reliability of such manual assessments have been investigated for the purpose by studying the visual estimates (VE) of plant cover reported by domain experts' on-site on two separate railway sections in Sweden. The first study investigated VE of domain experts using aerial foliage cover (AFC) and sub-plot frequency (SF) to assess the plant cover on a railway section in Oxberg, Alvdalsbanan, Sweden. A second study investigated VE of domain experts on a railway section outside Vetlanda, Sweden. VEfrom two separate occasions (in June and August 2013) were recorded using the aerial canopy cover method (ACC) on the same track with maintenance routine carried out in between the assessments.

VE of raters' were recorded and analysis-of-variance (ANOVA) tests on the mean estimates were investigated to see whether if there were disagreements between the raters'. ICC(2, 1) was used to study the differences between the estimates. Results achieved through ANOVA and ICC(2,1) tests clearly indicate that VE of plant cover are quite unreliable thereby suggesting the need for an automatic approach. Results achieved also highlight the importance of a well-defined protocol be presented to the personnel (in prior) to reduce systematic errors as a result of misinterpretation while assessing vegetation cover. There are other areas within the domain of railway maintenance that are (to this day) heavily reliant on manual inspections to ensure smooth operations. It would be interesting to extend the work further by investigating other immediately relevant areas and report if similar differences persist.

References

1. Hulin, B., Schussler, S.: Measuring vegetation along railway tracks. In: Proceedings of the IEEE Intelligent Transportation Systems Conference, pp. 561–565 (2005)
2. Banverket: Vegetation Maintenance Manual, Bvh 827.1, Original title in Swedish: Handbok om vegetation (2000)
3. Banverket: Vegetation Maintenance Requirements, Bvh 827.2, Original title in Swedish: behovsanalys infor vegetationsreglering (2001)
4. Banverket: Safety Inspections Manual, Bvf 807.2, Original title in Swedish: sakerhetsbesiktning av fasta anlaggningar (2005)
5. Yella, S., Nyberg, R.G., Payvar, B., Dougherty, M., Gupta, N.: Machine vision approach for automating vegetation detection on railway tracks. J. Intell. Syst. **22**(2), 179–196 (2013). ISSN: 2191–026X
6. Yella, S., Nyberg, Roger, G., Gupta, Narendra, K., Dougherty, M.: Reliability of manual assessments in determining the types of vegetation on railway tracks. In: Wang, J., Cellary, W., Wang, D., Wang, H., Chen, S.-C., Li, T., Zhang, Y. (eds.) WISE 2015. LNCS, vol. 9419, pp. 391–399. Springer, Heidelberg (2015). doi:10.1007/978-3-319-26187-4_37
7. Nyberg, R.G., Yella, S., Gupta, N., Dougherty, M.: Inter-rater reliability in determining types of vegetation on railway track beds, accepted for publication. In: The 3rd International Workshop on Data Quality and Trust in Big Data in Conjunction with the 16th International Conference on Web Information Systems Engineering (WISE), Miami, USA (2015)
8. Nyberg, R.G., Gupta, N.K., Yella, S., Dougherty, M.: Machine vision for condition monitoring vegetation on railway embankments. In: Proceedings of the 6th IET Conference on Railway Condition Monitoring (RCM 2014), Birmingham, UK (2014)
9. Nyberg, R.G.: Automated condition monitoring of vegetation on railway track beds and embankments, Ph.D. thesis, Edinburgh Napier University, UK (2015)
10. Coulloudon, B., Eshelman, K., Gianola, J., Nea, H.: Sampling vegetation attributes. Interagency Technical Reference BLM/RS/ST- 96/002+1730, Bureau of Land Management's National Applied Resource Sciences Center, Bureau of Land management. National Business Center. BC-650B. P.O. Box 25047. Denver, Colorado 80225–0047 (1999)
11. Shrout, P., Fleiss, J.: Intraclass correlations: uses in assessing rater reliability. Psychol. Bull. **86**, 420–428 (1979)

Community-Based Message Transmission with Energy Efficient in Opportunistic Networks

Sheng Zhang[1(✉)], Xin Wang[1], Minghui Yao[1],
and William Wei Song[2]

[1] School of Information Engineering, Nanchang Hangkong University,
Nanchang, China
{zwxzsl68,wxl991210}@126.com, hiyaominghui@163.com
[2] Business Intelligence and Informatics, Dalarna University, Borlänge, Sweden
wso@du.se

Abstract. An Opportunistic Networks is a wireless self-organized network, in which there is no need to build a fixed connectivity between source node and destination node, and the communication depends on the opportunity of node meeting. There are some classical message transmission algorithms, such as PRoPHET, MaxProp, and so on. In the Opportunity Networks with community characteristic, the different message transmission strategies can be sued in inter-community and intra-community. It improves the message successful delivery ratio significantly. The classical algorithms are CMTS and CMOT. We propose an energy efficient message forwarding algorithm (EEMF) for community-based Opportunistic Networks in this paper. When a message is transmitted, we consider not only the community characteristic, but also the residual energy of each node. The simulation results show that the EEMF algorithm can improve the message successful delivery ratio and reduce the network overhead obviously, in comparison with classical routing algorithms, such as PRoPHET, MaxProp, CMTS and CMOT. Meanwhile the EEMF algorithm can reduce the node's energy consumption and prolong the lifetime of network.

Keywords: Opportunistic networks · Message transmission · Community characteristic · Energy efficient

1 Introduction

An Opportunistic Networks (ON) is a network of wireless connected nodes. Nodes may be either mobile or fixed. The network topology may change due to node mobility or node activation and node deactivation. There is no a fixed connectivity between source node and destination node, and the communication depends on the opportunity of node meeting [1]. Due to the short-distance wireless mobile devices (such as smart phones, smart bracelets, Apple Watches, iPads, etc.) are widely used, the direct communication and data sharing for each other are becoming more and more convenient [2]. The typical applications of Opportunistic Networks are booming, such as the pocket

© Springer International Publishing AG 2016
W. Cellary et al. (Eds.): WISE 2016, Part II, LNCS 10042, pp. 411–423, 2016.
DOI: 10.1007/978-3-319-48743-4_34

switched networks (PSN) [3], the mobile vehicular networks (VN) [4], and the wireless sensor networks (WSN) [5].

In Opportunistic Networks, the communication among nodes shows intermittent connectivity due to the node's moving. Therefore the Opportunistic Networks only depends on the encounter opportunity among nodes to forward messages. Consequently, the "Storage-Carry-Forward" strategy is usually used to deliver messages in Opportunistic Networks. In addition, the nodes generally tend to congregate together according to social relations in Opportunistic Networks, show community characteristic. The node is much active in itself community, while it hardly move to other communities. There are just a few nodes which can visit other communities according to their interests, they are likely to set up the ties between different communities.

Another feather of Opportunistic Networks is that most of nodes supply with batteries. The power of a battery is usually limited, and charging is not convenient in some case. So it is very important to save energy. In this case, how to forward efficiently messages from source node to destination node in the community-based opportunistic networks is a huge challenge.

The remainder of this paper is organized as follows. Section 2 describes the exiting message transmission mechanism and energy efficient solutions. Section 3 introduces the community division and message buffer for saving energy. Section 4 shows the energy efficient message forwarding algorithm (EEMF) for community-based Opportunistic Networks that we propose in this paper. In Sect. 5, we set the simulation scenario and analyze the experiment results. And Sect. 6 concludes overall paper and lists future work.

2 Related Work

Many researches have done the considerable works on message forwarding in Opportunistic Networks. Due to the intermittent connectivity of nodes, the message forwarding or not is mainly based on the encounter probability between the nodes. The typical message forwarding algorithms based on probability are PRoPHET [6], and MaxProp [7]. These algorithms rely on the meeting opportunity between nodes to achieve the goal node of forward, so as to improve the delivery successful ratio. But these algorithms do not consider the community characteristic of Opportunistic Networks. Some research scholars considered the community characteristic and proposed corresponding algorithms, such as CMTS [8], CMOT [9], OSNLMTS [10], etc. But these algorithms mainly considered to improve the message delivery successful ratio and reduce the network latency, did not take into account the energy consumption of networks.

At present, the research on the node energy consumption in Opportunistic Networks had made some progress. The research is mainly two directions.

Firstly, it is mainly considered in the hardware layer. Let the node sleep according to a certain way, or lower the power of node's scan and receive to get the goal of energy conservation based on the environment.

The literature [11] takes sleep mode. It saves energy according to sleep mode. And designed a framework makes nodes in sacrificing a small amount of communication opportunity can save energy, on the basis of the framework effectively balance the energy saving and node connectivity problems.

The literatures [12, 13] design an energy-saving MAC scheme. They propose as a kind of MAC layer routing protocol for WSN, named S-MAC. In order to reduce energy consumption when the S-MAC listen the idle channel, node periodically sleeps. It forms a virtual cluster with neighbor nodes at the same time. In the node dormancy, neighbor nodes automatically in sync.

The literatures [14, 15] design moving plan of node to reduce energy consumption. In the range of communication, MULEs collects data from the sensors, stores and transmit messages to the nodes which close the MULEs by wireless.

Secondly, energy consumption is considered in software layer. It uses suitable routing algorithm to reduce the amount of data packet transmission, achieves the goal of energy saving.

The literature [16] propose IC-Routing algorithm. In the environment of natural disaster, node's mobility and encounter show the characteristics of periodic. We choose a more worthy trust path by evaluating routing delay and the transmission probability, and control the message copies to reduce the network overload.

In this paper, we build a community-based network model and propose an energy efficient message forwarding algorithm (EEMF) for community-based Opportunistic Networks. We assume that there are n nodes in Opportunistic Networks. And we set a threshold value δ, if the encounter probability of node i and node j is bigger than δ, node i and j are belong to the same community. After the network runs for a period of time, the n nodes are assigned into different communities according to the encounter probability each other. The EEMF includes two parts: intra-community forwarding and inter-community transmission. The former adopts multi-copy forwarding strategy according to the node residual energy and the counter probability between nodes within a community, while the latter selects optimal path between the connected communities according to nodes' transmission probability. As this scheme considers both the local community characteristic and the connectivity among communities in global network, meanwhile adopts energy efficient strategy, it would be feasible to achieve the optimal performance.

3 Community Division and Message Buffer

3.1 Community Division

The node moves in Opportunistic Networks and shows community characteristic. The nodes have a high encounter probability in the same community, while there is a low encounter probability in different community. When the encounter probability is greater than the threshold δ, the two nodes will be divided into the same community. It can effectively reduce the weak connection problem by setting the threshold.

The process of community division is described as following.

Firstly, we initialize the local community of node i as $C_i = \{i\}$.

Secondly, when node i and j meet together, we update the encounter probability as $P_{(i,j)}$.

Thirdly, if $p_{(i,j)}$ is bigger than the threshold δ, then put the node j into the community of node i.

Newman and Girvan [17] proposed modularity to measure the performance of community division. The modularity function Q is used to measure the quality of community division. The Q would be bigger, when the nodes in the same community have a strong relation and the nodes in different communities have a weak relation. The bigger of Q value, the better of the community division quality. Because of different value of threshold δ would have different number of community, so there is different community division result with different threshold value δ. We can select different threshold δ, compare the modularity function Q, would get the best threshold δ.

By experiment verification, the best threshold δ is 0.25 in this paper.

The above-mentioned method can get the best community division result. We don't need to know the number of community in the network in advance. And the location and size of community are changed with the node moving. It's more flexible, suitable to the real situation.

3.2 Message Buffer

If the copies of message are too many in the network, it will waste the network resource. We introduce ACK mechanism to eliminate redundant message copies. When a message gets to the destination node, the destination node immediately broadcasts a respond message of ACK into the network. When a node gets the respond message, compares the message ID with messages in message buffer, and deletes the message with the same ID. When the message's time to live (TTL) is over the threshold, delete it.

4   Message Transmission Strategies of EEMF

4.1   Intra-community Forwarding Strategy

The PRoPHET is a classical probability-based transmission algorithm, defines the delivery predictability to measure delivery probability metric between nodes. If the delivery predictability of node j is larger than that of node i which carries with messages, the node j can gain a copy of the messages from node i. Since nodes move in a community frequently, the encounter probability between nodes is high, there are large number of message copies in network. In this case, a great deal of unnecessary messages are forwarded, they waste a lot of network resources. Therefore we propose an improved PRoPHET algorithm for intra-community message transmission in this paper. We select one-hop nodes for destination node as relay nodes and consider the residual energy of node. This way ensures high delivery ratio and reduce redundant message copies with energy efficiency.

Encounter Probability Between Nodes. Each node holds an encounter probability vector to store encounter probability between nodes. Whenever node i encounters node j, the encounter probability should be updated according to the formula (1), where

$p_{init} \in [0, 1]$ is an initialization constant. This formula ensures that nodes have high delivery predictability when they are often encountered.

$$P_{(i,j)} = P_{(i,j)_{old}} + (1 - P_{(i,j)_{old}}) \times p_{init} \tag{1}$$

If node i does not encounter node j during a time interval, they are less likely to become good forwarders of messages to each other. As a consequence, the delivery predictability must age. The aging equation is shown in formula (2), where $\gamma \in [0, 1]$ is the aging constant, and k is the number of time units. The time unit can be different, and should be defined based on the average interval of nodes encounter within the community.

$$P_{(i,j)} = P_{(i,j)_{old}} \times \gamma^k \tag{2}$$

The simulation results shown in Sect. 5 reveal that $p_{init} = 0.75$ and $\gamma = 0.98$ are the most appropriate values.

The residual energy factor σ of node can be gotten by the following formula (3), where σ_j is the residual energy factor of node j, E_j^c is the current residual energy of node j, and E_j^i is the initial energy of node j.

$$\sigma_j = \frac{E_j^c}{E_j^i} \tag{3}$$

We define the forwarding probability for considering the residual energy of encounter probability. So, the forwarding probability from node i to node j is shown in formula (4), where λ is weighting factor.

$$p'_{(i,j)} = \lambda p_{(i,j)} + (1 - \lambda)\sigma_j \tag{4}$$

Message Forwarding Process in a Community. Intra-community message forwarding depends on the forwarding probability of node. When two nodes encounter, the EEMF compares the forwarding probability, and the messages always forward to the node whose forwarding probability is larger. If a node forwards a message to another node, it does not delete the message. If a node relays a message, it stores and manages the message in accordance with the "first-in first-out" principle, until the TTL (the time to live) value expires or the message is transferred to the destination node.

Meanwhile, If the messages are forwarded to the destination node, an ACK packet that carries the ID of the received message is sent to the network. When a node receives the ACK packet, it will eliminate the redundant message copies based on the ACK information.

From the perspective of energy saving, this message forwarding method selects the node with the highest forwarding probability as a relaying node to ensure the reliability of delivery. And it selects only one-hop node as the relaying node to reduce the number of redundant copies in the network.

4.2   Inter-community Transmission Strategy

The core of inter-community message transmission is to find the optimal path from the source node community to the destination node community.

Community Transmission Probability. We reference the concept of community transmission probability in literature [9]. Each node holds a community transmission probability table which stores the transmission probability from the node to each community. The community transmission probability is divided into two categories: the accessible community transmission probability and the inaccessible community transmission probability. For the local community, the value of community transmission probability is 1. For the accessible community and the inaccessible community, the values of community transmission probability are calculated as following.

The accessible community transmission probability of a node is the probability that the node visits the accessible community, is calculated by formula (5). Where p_{ic_j} is the community transmission probability of node i visiting community c_j, C_a is the accessible community set of the node i, N_{ic_j} is the number which node i visits community c_j.

$$p_{ic_j} = \frac{N_{ic_j}}{\sum_{c_k \in C_a} N_{ic_k}} \tag{5}$$

The inaccessible community transmission probability can be calculated by the accessible community transmission probability and the encounter probability. We assume that there are three communities: c_x, c_y, and c_z. c_x is the local community of node i, c_y is the local community of node j and the accessible community of node i, and c_z is the accessible community of node j and the inaccessible community of node i. The scenario is shown in Fig. 1.

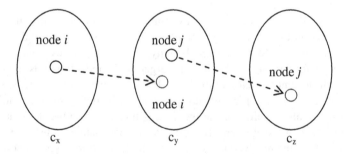

Fig. 1. The community path ($c_x \rightarrow c_y \rightarrow c_z$) is built by the node i and j

If the node i and j encounter each other, they exchange the community transmission probability table. A communication path from community c_x to community c_z (i.e. $c_x \rightarrow c_y \rightarrow c_z$) is established when the node i encounter the node j. The node i has an opportunity to transfer messages from c_x to c_z through c_y.

Equation (6) shows the inaccessible community transmission probability of the node i to the inaccessible community c_z.

$$p_{ic_z} = p_{ic_y} \times p_{(i,j)} \times p_{jc_z} \tag{6}$$

Where p_{ic_y} indicates the accessible community transmission probability of the node i to the community c_y, and builds the community path $c_x \rightarrow c_y$. Likewise, p_{jc_z} indicates the accessible community transmission probability of the node j to the community c_z, and builds the community path $c_y \rightarrow c_z$. $p_{(i,j)}$ indicates the encounter probability of node i and node j and provides the opportunity that the messages can transmit from the community c_x to the community c_z.

When we consider the energy efficient, we need replace the $p_{(i,j)}$ with the $p'_{(i,j)}$, then, the formula (6) change to formula (7).

$$p_{ic_z} = p_{ic_y} \times p'_{(i,j)} \times p_{jc_z} \tag{7}$$

Inter-community Message Forward Process. When messages are forwarded between communities, the community transmission probability of a node to the target communities is used to choose the best community communication path. Thus the node with the highest community transmission probability is often chosen as a relay node between communities, until the message is delivered to the target communities.

5   Simulations Scenario and Results Analysis

5.1   Simulation Scenario

In this paper, we use the ONE (Opportunistic Network Environment) to simulate, and compare with typical algorithms such as PRoPHET, CMTS, MaxProp and CMOT. The Fig. 2 shows the interface of the ONE simulation software.

Before the simulation begins, the pretreatment process of 10000 s completes the community division. The specific simulation parameters are set in Table 1.

5.2   Experimental Results and Analysis

Based on the above scenario, we compare the performance of five algorithms with different nodes average speed and messages TTL. The metrics include the successful delivery ratio, the average overhead and the residual energy. We still discuss the effects on energy consumption by selecting different λ value.

The effects of energy consumption by changing λ value To get the best energy saving, we need to seek the suitable value of λ. The simulation results are shown in Fig. 3, when λ is 0.7, 0.75, .80.8, 0.85, 0.9. When we set $\lambda = 0.85$, then network owns the best energy saving state. So we select $\lambda = 0.85$ in following experiments.

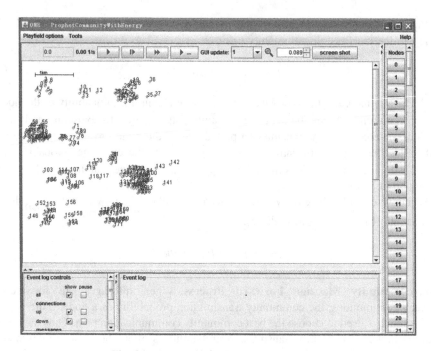

Fig. 2. The simulation interface of the ONE

Table 1. The parameters of simulation scenario

Category	Parameter (unit)	Values
Scenario features	Simulation time (s)	43200
	Threshold δ	0.25
	Simulation region (m^2)	8500 m × 8500 m
Community and node characteristics	Movement model	Community movement
	Initial energy (mA.H)	1000 k
	Energy in scan consumption (mA.H)	60
	Energy in transmit consumption (mA.H)	300
	Movement speed (m/s)	1~7
	Transmission rate (KB/s)	250
	The maximum transmission range (m)	30
	Cache size (MB)	10
	Wait time (s)	5~10
Data packet characteristics	Event generator	Message event generator
	Data packet size (MB)	0.5~1.5
	TTL (s)	1000/2000/4000/6000/8000/10000/12000
	The total number of data packets	1000

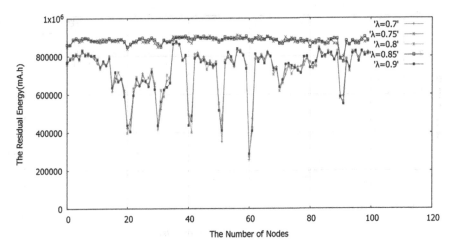

Fig. 3. The nodes energy consumption for different λ value

The effects in Different Average Speed of Nodes. We set the message TTL is 6000 s. As shown in Fig. 4, when the average speed increases, the successful delivery ratio improves for all algorithms. The EEMF and CMOT have the highest successful delivery ratio. When the average speed is less than 5 m/s, the successful delivery ratio increases linearly. Figure 5 shows the change of network average overhead, when the average speed increases. The EEMF and CMOT is lower network overhead than PRoPHET, CMTS, and MaxProp. Except for the MaxProp, other algorithms are not sensitive to the change of the average speed. When the average speed is greater than 5 m/s, the average overhead almost remain the same.

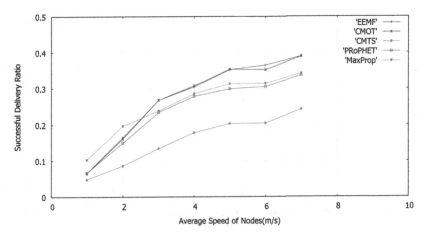

Fig. 4. Comparison of delivery ratio in different average speed of nodes

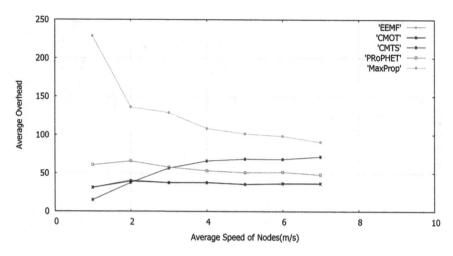

Fig. 5. Comparison of average overhead in different t average speed of nodes

The Effects in Different Messages TTL. We set the average speed of nodes is 5 m/s. Figure 6 shows that the successful delivery ratios of all algorithms are low when the message TTL is small. When the message TTL increases, the successful delivery ratio improves for all algorithms. When the message TTL is greater than 6000 s, all algorithm have slow increase of successful delivery ratio, except for CMTS. Meanwhile the CMTS is lower successful delivery ratio than that of other algorithms. Figure 7 shows that the EEMF and CMOT have lower overhead ratio than other algorithms. With the message TTL increasing, the average overhead of CMTS increase, while the average overhead of other algorithms decrease.

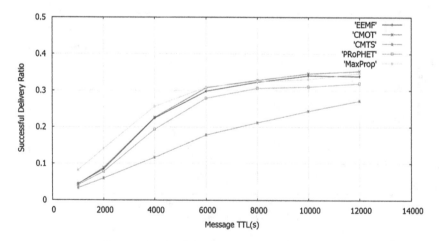

Fig. 6. Comparison of successful delivery ratio in different message TTL

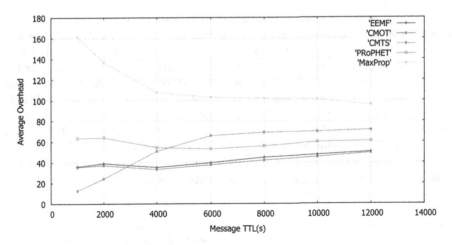

Fig. 7. Comparison of average overhead in different message TTL

The Comparison of Nodes' Residual Energy. We set the average speed of nodes is 5 m/s, and the message TTL is 6000 s. After the network runs in above different algorithms, the residual energy of all nodes are shown in Fig. 8. We can see that the EEMF and CMTS have the best energy saving effect.

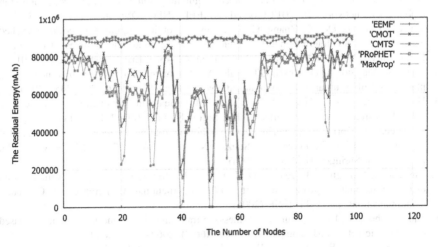

Fig. 8. The nodes residual energy after running different algorithm

6   Conclusion and Future Work

According to the community characteristic of nodes in Opportunistic Networks, We still consider the limited power supply by battery, propose an energy efficient message forwarding algorithm (EEMF) for community-based Opportunistic Networks.

The EEMF algorithm can reduce the node's energy consumption and prolong the life of network. Our major contributions are summarized as following. Firstly, we propose a new community division method, which is more suitable the community-based opportunistic networks. Secondly, on the basis of CMOT algorithm, we consider the energy saving strategy which can prolong the lifetime of network. The simulation results show that the EEMF and CMOT algorithm are better than the PRoPHET, MaxProp and CMTS algorithm in the successful delivery ratio and network overload. At the same time, the EEMF and CMTS algorithm are better than the CMOT, MaxProp and PRoPHET algorithm in energy saving effect. In short, the EEMF algorithm combines the advantages of other algorithms, improves the successful delivery ratio, reduces the network overload and energy consumption of nodes at the same time, so as to prolong the network lifetime.

Acknowledgment. This work is partially supported by the National Natural Science Foundation of China (61162002, 61661037), and the Jiangxi province National Natural Science Foundation of China (20151BAB207038).

References

1. Xiong, Y.P., Sun, L.M., Niu, J.W., Liu, Y.: Opportunistic networks. J. Softw. **20**(1), 124–137 (2009)
2. Wu, J., Xiao, M., Huang, L.: Homing spread: community home-based multi-copy routing in mobile social networks. In: 2013 Proceedings IEEE, INFOCOM, pp. 2319–2327 (2013)
3. Ma, C., Yang, J., Du, Z., Zhang, C.: Overview of routing algorithm in pocket switched networks. In: 9th International Conference on Broadband and Wireless Computing, Communication and Applications (BWCCA), pp. 42–46. IEEE Computer Society (2014)
4. Gaito, S., Maggiorini, D., Rossi, G.P., Sala, A.: Bus switched networks: an ad hoc mobile platform enabling urban-wide communications. Ad Hoc Netw. **10**(6), 931–945 (2012)
5. Hu, S.C., Wang, Y.C., Huang, C.Y., Tseng, Y.C.: Measuring air quality in city areas by vehicular wireless sensor networks. J. Syst. Softw. **84**(11), 2005–2012 (2011)
6. Lindgren, A., Doria, A., Schelén, O.: Probabilistic routing in intermittently connected networks. In: Dini, P., Lorenz, P., Souza, JNd (eds.) SAPIR 2004. LNCS, vol. 3126, pp. 239–254. Springer, Heidelberg (2004)
7. Burgess, J., Gallagher, B., Jensen, D., Levine, B.N.: MaxProp: routing for vehicle-based disruption-tolerant networks. In: 25th IEEE International Conference on Computer Communications, pp. 1–11. IEEE (2006)
8. Niu, J., Zhou, X., Liu, Y., Sun, L.: A message transmission scheme for community-based opportunistic network. J. Comput. Res. Dev. **46**(12), 2068–2075 (2009)
9. Zhang, S., Tan, P., Bao, X., Song, W.W., Liu, X.: Community-based message opportunistic transmission. In: Vogel, D., Guo, X., Linger, H., Barry, C., Lang, M., Schneider, C. (eds.) Transforming Healthcare Through Information Systems. LNISO, vol. 17, pp. 79–93. Springer, Heidelberg (2016)
10. Liu, Y., Gao, Y., Qiao, J., Tan, C.: Community-based message transmission scheme in opportunistic social networks. J. Comput. Appl. **33**(5), 1212–1216 (2013)

11. Feeney, L.M., Nilsson, M.: Investigating the energy consumption of a wireless network interface in an ad hoc networking environment. In: Proceedings - IEEE INFOCOM, vol. 3, pp. 1548–1557 (2001)
12. Singh, S., Raghavendra, C.S.: PAMAS – power aware multi-access protocol with signalling for ad hoc networks. ACM SIGCOMM Comput. Commun. Rev. **28**(3), 5–26 (1998)
13. Ye, W., Heidemann, J., Estrin, D.: An energy-efficient MAC protocol for wireless sensor networks. In: Global Telecommunications Conference, GLOBECOM 2005, vol. 3, pp. 1567–1576. IEEE (2008)
14. Ramiro, S., Stolwijk, C., Dougados, M., van Tubergen, A.: Data mules: modeling and analysis of a three-tier architecture for sparse sensor networks. Ad Hoc Netw. **1**(2–3), 215–233 (2003)
15. Juang, P., Oki, H., Wang, Y., Martonosi, M., Peh, L.S., Rubenstein, D.: Energy-efficient computing for wildlife tracking: design tradeoffs and early experiences with ZebraNet. In: International Conference on Architectural Support for Programming Languages and Operating Systems, vol. 37, pp. 96–107 (2002)
16. Uddin, M.Y.S., Ahmadi, H., Abdelzaher, T., Kravets, R.: A low-energy, multi-copy inter-contact routing protocol for disaster response networks. In: IEEE Communications Society Conference on Sensor, Mesh and Ad Hoc Communications and Networks, SECON 2009, pp. 637–645. IEEE (2009)
17. Newman, M.E.J., Girvan, M.: Finding and evaluating community structure in networks. Phys. Rev. E Stat. Nonlinear Soft Matter Phys. **69**(2 Pt 2), 026113 (2004)

A Multi-Semantic Classification Model of Reviews Based on Directed Weighted Graph

Shaozhong Zhang[1(✉)], William Wei Song[2], Minjie Ding[1], and Ping Hu[1]

[1] School of Electronic and Computer Science, Zhejiang Wanli University, Ningbo 315100, Zhejiang, China
dlut_z88@163.com
[2] Information Systems and Business Intelligence, Dalarna University, 79188 Borlänge, Sweden
wso@du.se

Abstract. Semantic and sentimental analysis plays an important role in natural language processing, especially in textual analysis, and has a wide range of applications in web information processing and management. This paper intends to present a sentimental analysis framework based on the directed weighted graph method, which is used for semantic classification of the textual comments, i.e. user reviews, collected from the e-commerce websites. The directed weighted graph defines a formal semantics lexical as a semantic body, denoted to be a node in the graph. The directed links in the graph, representing the relationships between the nodes, are used to connect nodes to each other with their weights. Then a directed weighted graph is constructed with semantic nodes and their interrelationships relations. The experimental results show that the method proposed in the paper can classify the semantics into different classification based on the computation of the path lengths with a threshold.

Keywords: Directed weighted graph · Reviews · Semantic classification

1 Introduction

Semantic analysis is a branch of natural language processing. It studies the meanings and characteristics of a given text through analyzing its vocabulary. In recent years, with the development of social network systems and increasing interactive activities performed by users, reviewing the web services and products has been considered and required over all aspects of various networks, including social, economic, political, and commercial networks. Particularly, as e-commerce products and websites have rapidly booming, users, including buyers, sellers, and go-betweens are increasingly required to provide their comments (i.e. reviews) on merchandises, products, services, and even business activities and behaviors. Undoubtedly, reviews have become an important factor in improving the quality of businesses, products, services, and even ways of doing businesses. However, although there are many researches on investigation of using user reviews to support businesses, to dig into the semantics (semantic and sentimental analysis) of the user reviews remains less touched. Therefore, it is significant to carry out the study of reviews semantic analysis of e-commerce and social networks.

W. Cellary et al. (Eds.): WISE 2016, Part II, LNCS 10042, pp. 424–435, 2016.
DOI: 10.1007/978-3-319-48743-4_35

Generally, given an entity, its semantics consists of five components, a semantics target, properties of the semantic target, meaning, semantic holders, and a time when the entity pertains the semantic. In previous studies, generally, researchers considered to use entity to represent semantic targets (objects) [1]. An entity can be a product, a service, a topic, a person, an organization, or an event. Usually, an entity has a hierarchical structure and is described as a set of properties. Each property of an entity at different levels has its own value [2]. Sentimental values usually represent some semantics of the entity, expressing the sentiment of an entity as a positive, negative, or neutral style. Of course, a higher intensity of the sentiments at different levels can also be defined to describe opinions at great details [3–5].

A general task of a sentiment analysis is, for a given review text, to mine and extract its entity semantics and characteristics. A key task of sentimental analysis is achieved through its name (or naming) entity [6–8]. With the entity naming recognition, we try to classify entities into different categories, to which similar entities belong [9, 10]. The characteristics and classifications of entities form attributes of the entities used to represent the sentiments of the entities and the research of semantic-sentimental classification analysis is the key issue to the obtainment of an overall sentiment of a given review text (or a review document). Conventional machine learning methods used for semantic categorization of entity sentiments include support vector machines (SVM), maximum entropy, and naive Bayesian classifier. [11–13]. These methods are mainly used for topic-based semantic classification. However, with the quick increase and great diversity of item reviews provided by various types of users, many problems occur when processing the sentiments of the user reviews, including (1) uncertainty – a review being less relevant to a given text; (2) short texts – being hard to determine the exact meaning without context; (3) randomness – review target may change; and (4) being not strictly comply with the integrity of information. Furthermore, a target entity included in a review text is not just one; there may be more than one target entity. The semantics of the given review text may differ from one entity to another. That is, in one same review, it may exhibit one sentiment to an entity while to another entity it may present another sentiment. Hence, it is the most important issue of how to distinguish different semantic classification of different entities in the same review. That is a so called multi-classification problem of semantic-sentimental analysis study.

2 Related Work

In recent years, extensive researches have been carried out in the field of semantic analysis and opinion mining to analyze the review textual contents from the social networks and the web information systems. The purpose of semantic analysis and opinion mining is to find out what a user's views, such as attitudes and emotions, are on a particular entity. The entities represent an individual, an event, or a theme. Currently, most of the methods, dealing with users' opinions and emotions, focus on the research of classification and similarity of text data [14]. The existing semantic classification methods are divided into supervised and unsupervised ones. In their report [9], the authors presented a machine learning algorithm based on distance monitoring, which divides the Twitter information into two types, positive and negative, and uses distant supervision to classify the sentiment of Twitter messages. In their paper [15], Li and Liu proposed a TF-IDF weighting method and apply it to the voting mechanism and importing term scores, which provide an acceptable and stable clustering result. This approach displays an investigation direction of positive and negative polarity classification. A rule-based sentiment polarity calculation method is applied for extracting sentiment features from Chinese reviews [16], based on a sentiment word dictionary to calculate the basic polarity of the sentiment features. The method also considers to judge the dynamic sentiment word's polarity and to adjust the polarity according to the context information. Pak and Paroubek proposed an automatic method to collect a corpus of positive and negative sentiments without human interference and a corpus of objective texts [17]. The size of the collected corpora can be arbitrarily large. The method performs a statistical linguistic analysis on the collected corpus to generate a sentiment classification. In their paper [18] the authors developed a sentiment analysis system for reviews with Chinese sentimental orientation. The system analyzes the problems of tendency of semantic content of the reviews based certain characteristics and following a particular categorization. They propose the concept of dependencies to identify reviews' sentimental orientation.

3 Sentiment Analysis Framework

3.1 Semantic and Objects

Definition (Semantics): A semantic is a quadruple, (g, s, h, t), where g is the semantic target, also called object, s is the semantic about the object, h is the semantic holder, and t is the time when the semantic was expressed. In practice, the object can often be decomposed and described in a structured manner with multiple levels, which greatly facilitate both mining of semantic s and later use of the mined semantic results [1].

Definition (Object Structure): An object o is a product, service, topic, issue, person, organization, or event. It is described with a pair, o: (T, W), where T is a hierarchy of parts, sub-parts, and so on, and W is a set of attributes of o. Each part or sub-part also has its own set of attributes [1].

The relationship between semantic and object is shown in Fig. 1.

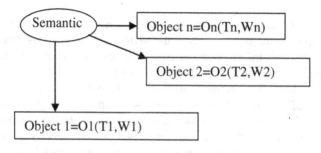

Fig. 1. Construction of semantic and objects

Look at Example 1. There is a review on a hotel on booking.com. "Loved the decor of the hotel and the location was perfect for shopping (1) and very close to the train station (2). Friendly and professional front desk staff (3). But it was very hot in our rooms because of the weather (4). I feel that this hotel needed air conditioning because my husband and I didn't sleep any of the nights because of being so uncomfortable (5). Would visit this hotel again only in the cooler months (6). Also the breakfast wasn't satisfactory (7). They kept running out of fruit and fruit salad - and for someone with allergies to other things, you rely on fruit (8)."

The semantic of the above can be decomposed into eight objects and corresponding attributes of the object and represented as pairs. This definition essentially describes a hierarchical decomposition of an object based on the part of relation. The root node is the name of the object, e.g., Review on Hotel. All the other nodes are parts and sub-parts, etc. A semantic can be expressed on any node and any attribute of the node.

Considering Example 2, in our example review above, the sentences (1), (2), (3) and (6) express positive opinions about the hotel. The sentences (4), (5), (7) and (8) express negative comments on the hotel. Clearly, one can also express semantics about parts or components of the hotel.

This object as a hierarchy of any number of levels needs a nested relation to represent it, which is often too complex for applications. The main reason is that since NLP is a very difficult task, recognizing parts and attributes of an object at different levels of details is extremely hard [1]. We use a directed graph to denote object and path for relation.

3.2   Directed Weighted Graph

In order to describe and extract semantic, emotional tendencies, we use a directed weighted graph to represent the structure of reviews text. We consider that the theory and method of graph structure is suitable for textual semantic analysis. Formally, a directed weighted graph is a set of triples. A triple is a collection of nodes, a set of links, and a collection of weights.

Definition (Directed Weighted Graph): A directed weighted graph is G defined as $G = <V, E, K>$, where V represents a set of nodes, E a set of edges, K a set of weights.

In the directed weighted graph, we consider to use the *markedness* and *orderliness* to describe the tags of semantic and emotion vocabulary appearing in a review text. For a given node v in the graph G, based on the order of the review text, we consider a (time) sequential relationship among other nodes connected to v by using the directed weighted graph. In the directed weighted graph G are there three types of nodes, i.e., text data nodes V^T, semantic and emotion tags nodes V^S, and sematic classification nodes V^C. So $V = \{V^T, V^S, V^C\}$. A text data node represents a text in the reviews. A semantic and emotion tag node corresponds to a particular emotion or specific semantic tags.

Definition (Links): In the space of nodes V of G, there are n nodes, $V_1, ..., V_n$. For any two nodes V_i and V_j, a directed link E_{ij} goes from V_i to V_j if $i < j$ (V_j appears after V_i), denoted to be $E_{ij} = V_i \rightarrow V_j$.

The value (weight) of a directed link between two nodes represents the strength of semantics and tendentious. The value can be calculated with the weights of a link. Directed links connect text nodes with tags nodes, tags nodes with others tags nodes, and tags nodes with semantic nodes. The strength of a connection is represented by a weight function of links.

Definition (Weighted Function): A weight function K_{ij} of links is used to compute the directed link weights of E_{ij} connecting any two nodes V_i and V_j, $i,j = 1, ..., n$.

With this method the semantics of a text can be represented by a path consisting of a set of weights and a series of tags and the strength of the semantics can be calculated by the weights in the path.

3.3   Semantic Classification Model

Basically, the idea of a semantic classification model is based on the directed weighted graph, i.e. $G = <\{V^T, V^S, V^C\}, E, K>$. The essential factors are described as follows. Firstly, given a review text data node, V^T, its properties are expressed as $V^T = <ReviewerID, Data>$. Secondly, considering V^S as the semantic keywords, tags and other feature nodes extracted from a review text, we have $V^S \in <SignTagSet>$. Here *SignTagSet* is a known semantic lexicon library and contains two parts (signs), a positive part and a negative part. Thirdly, all the vocabularies are signs with certain scores. V^C denotes a set of semantic classification nodes. It represents different semantics and tendentiousness.

Definition (Semantic Classification): A semantic classification is defined as V^C, and the ith element V_i^C in VC is defined to be:

$$V_i^C = (V_i^T, V_j^S, V_k^S, E_{ij}, E_{jk} | E_{ij}, E_{jk} \in E,)$$

Here V_i^C, a node set, is the *ith* classification; V_i^T is the node of the *ith* review text; V_j^S is the set of the *jth* semantic keywords in semantic lexicon; V_k^S is the kth tags node set of the meaning objects; E_{ij} connects the node V_i^T to the node set V_j^S, and E_{jk} connects the node set V_j^S to the node set V_k^S.

4   Weights and Semantic Classification Algorithm

4.1   Weights of K_{ij} Between Nodes in G

A weight on a link represents a frequency of some tags nodes in text, the tightness between tags nodes, and the similarity relationship between tags node and a particular semantic content node. The K_{ij} represents the weight of a directed link which is from a node V_i to another node V_j. We define a function $N(V_{ij})$ to be the number of the directed links from V_i to V_j. A junction-weight K_{ij} between two nodes and a sum of the junction-weights can be defined as:

$$K_{ij} = \sum_{V_j \in (N(V_i) \cap N(V_j))} N(V_{ij}) \text{ and } \sum_{ij} K_{ij} \leftarrow |V(V^T, V^S, V^C)|$$

Algorithm (To compute the weights of K)

Input: the node set V_i^T of a review text and the set of semantic nodes extracted from the reviews V_j^S;

Output: All values of K that between the nodes;

Step 1: Initialization: $i = 1, j = 1, k = 1$;

Step 2: For each text node in V_i^T, calculate its frequency that its feature values appeared in the other tags node set, i.e. $N(V_{ij})$.

Step 3: Move to next tag node in V_j^S and $j = j + 1$;

Step 4: Return to Step 2, until searching all the tag nodes in V_j^S. For each tag node Calculate its number of frequencies of the junction from V_i^T;

Step 5: For a tag node in V_k^S calculate the frequency of characteristic value from V_k^S to another tag node marker, i.e. $N(V_{kj})$;

Step 6: Next tag node in V_k^S, $k = k+1$, return to Step 5 for all the nodes in V_k^S;

Step 7: For a text node of V_i^T, $i = i+1$, return to Step 2, for all the nodes in V_i^T;

Step 8: Compute the following formula $K_{ij} = \sum_{V_j \in (N(V_i) \cap N(V_j))} N(V_{ij})$ and $K_{kj} = $

$\sum_{V_j \in (N(V_k) \cap N(V_j))} N(V_{kj})$

With the above algorithm we calculate the semantic closeness from the review text nodes to all the tag nodes, as well as all the other tag nodes. By setting different thresholds, we connect two nodes with a link with the values of path weights reaching a certain range, i.e. a directed link E_{ij} between V_i and V_j. Hence we construct a directed weighted graph with reviews text nodes and some semantic tag nodes.

4.2   Algorithm of Semantic Classification

The basic idea of semantic classification is to estimate the value of each path from a review text node to a tag node. Every weight on the path will calculate cumulatively. The objective is to identify a set of paths having their path length being not greater than a certain threshold. Each set of nodes on a path represents one kind of meaning or opinion of a review text, which can be as a classification of the reviews. In the actual calculation, using the path length to calculate the path weight is more convenient. The reciprocal of a path length is considered to be the weight of the path. The larger the value of weight is, the shorter the path length. Now our task is to find a list of different kinds of paths, with their sum of the path length being within a certain threshold. The nodes on one path give one similar semantic and can be classified in one category. By setting different thresholds, we obtain different paths lengths, thus generate a semantic classification of the reviews (i.e. different semantics or opinions).

We define the reciprocal of a weight as the length of a path from a node V_i to another node V_j, denoted $S_{ij} = S(V_i, V_j) = 1/K_{ij}$. Obviously, when a weight of a link is zero, i.e. $K_{ij} = 0$, the path length of the link $S(V_i, V_j) = \infty$. When the path length of a link (from one node to another) is shorter, the tightness between the nodes is higher. When searching the nodes that form all the paths, we can identify similar semantic content of some nodes linked together through a path. In this way, we can produce a series of paths whose nodes have different semantic similarities (i.e. classification of opinion semantics) by setting a range of thresholds for the path lengths. Of all these semantic classifications, the semantic class with the shortest path contains the review texts having closest semantics (the same or similar meaning). Semantic classification may vary when the range of path lengths is adjusted through the thresholds. This forms different types of semantic classification, termed Multi-Semantic Classification. The algorithm of Multi-Semantic Classification is given below.

Algorithm (To compute Multi-Semantic Classification)

Input: review text nodes V_i^T and tag nodes V_j^S; the weight value between nodes K_{ij} and K_{kj}.

Output: A collection of semantic classification: $V^C|Max(W_i|W_i = \sum E_{ij})$.

Step 1: Initialize the paths, $s \leftarrow V_i^T$, $R = \{s : V_i^T\}$, set the path length threshold.

Step 2: Select a tag node from V_j^S, and decide: If $S_{ij} = S(s, V_j) = 1/K_{ij} > \varepsilon$ (indicating that the tightness is smaller than the expectation), discard the node. Otherwise, if $S_{ij} <= \varepsilon$, add the node and continue.

Step 3: If the node V_j^S is already in the set R of path nodes the process has completed, go on to Step 2; if not, add V_j^S to R. Set the node V_j^S as the source node s, represented as $Q_{V_j^S}$, i.e. $R = R \cup \{V_j^S\}$, $Q_{V_j^S} \leftarrow s$.

Step 4: For each node V_k^S on the path from s to V_j^S, judge:

(1) If the distance of $s \rightarrow V_k^S$ is the shortest then add the path to s;
(2) If the V_k^S is an intermediate node of the path and the node is on the path from s to the node V_j^S, then delete V_k^S, and connect s to V_j^S;
(3) If the path from $V_k^S \rightarrow V_j^S$ is on the way of the path from s to V_j^S, i.e. $V_k^S \rightarrow V_j^S$ is a subset of $s \rightarrow V_j^S$, then add the nodes in the path to V_j^S until no such nodes exist as $V_k^S \rightarrow V_j^S$ on the path $s \rightarrow V_j^S$. If there is a subset of nodes on a path, which is a node set on another path, delete the path and then fusion junction as one node, that means the path already exist and not need give a new one.
(4) Calculate the shortest path to V_j^S on the global path:

$$\bar{S}(s, V_j^S) = \min(\sum_{k=1, j=1} (S(s, V_j^S)|Q(V_k^S, V_j^S)))$$

Step 5: Select next node of review text V_j^S and go to Step 1 until all review text nodes to be addressed.

Step 6: Select and set the tightness classification threshold function $f(\varepsilon)$, and proceed as follows:

For all nodes V_j^S, do while not end of j:if there is $\bar{S}(s, V_k^S) \le f(\varepsilon)$ then all the nodes on the path form a valid path, and correspond a semantic classification, denoted as V_i^C;

Step 7: Output V_i^C and all the nodes on the corresponding path.

We obtain different semantics and its orientations about the reflection of review texts using the Algorithms 1 and 2. The semantics obtained is the meaning mined from one review text or a number of review texts. By analyzing the semantics, we can understand the review texts and grasp the dynamics of people public opinions.

5 Experiment and Discussion

5.1 Dataset

Obviously a collection of internationally recognized data is more supportive to be used to test the effect of our proposed approach. The dataset we use is from Amazon.com collected by Stanford University [19, 20], whose characteristics are shown in Table 1.

Table 1. Review dataset of Amazon

Category	Reviews	Items
Books	22.5M	2.37M
Electronics	7.82M	498K
Sports and outdoors	1.32M	532K
Video games	3.26M	51K
Baby	915K	71.3K

The data set contains 24 categories, about 83.06 million reviews and 9.4 million Items. Each review is composed of *reviewerID* representing the ID of the reviewer, *reviewerName* representing the name of the reviewer, *helpful* representing helpfulness rating of the review, *reviewText* representing the text of the review, *overall* representing the rating of the product, *summary* representing the summary of the review, and the *time* of the review. Each Item is composed of ID of the product, *title* representing the name of the product, *price* representing the price in US dollars (at the time of crawl), *imUrl* representing the url of the product image, as well as *related* representing the related products (i.e. *also bought, also viewed, bought together, buy after viewing*).

In order to facilitate the experiment, we did some preliminary processing for raw data. In this experimental, the data set is divided into two parts: training data and test data. We use the Reviews data as the training set and as a test set the Item with corresponding ID of the product to the reviews. We also randomly select 100K Review data as the test data. Another test set is the 1M samples data obtained from the Review data collection covering the following five datasets, Books, Electronics, Sports and Outdoors, Video Games, Baby. Each corresponding data are also extracted from the Item data set according to the ID of the product in the Review data set. The *related* content of *also bought, bought together, buy after viewing* of related products indicates that a user purchases another commodity when he have bought or viewed some kind of similar goods. This user behavior reflects that these users have a similar tendency. From the views of semantic analysis, the user who has bought the same goods tends to share similar semantic in their comments. Therefore, it is feasible to maintain the accuracy of user's semantic classification of reviews by considering whether the users have purchased the same items.

5.2   Experimental Results and Analysis

Experiment 1 is to analyze the number of semantic classification under different path lengths. Path length is controlled by the threshold function $f(\varepsilon)$, see the Algorithm 2. The higher the value of ε is, the longer the path and there are more nodes contained in the same type of classification. This is reflected that the number of semantic classifications is small in the overall number. Conversely, if the value ε is smaller one the semantic relationship between the nodes is closer and there may be less number of nodes to be included in a semantic classification. The number of total classification of semantic is increased. The comparison of the five semantic classifications is shown in Fig. 1.

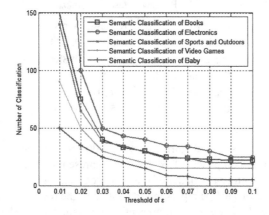

Fig. 2. Comparisons of five semantic classifications under different thresholds

As shown in Fig. 1, it can be observed that when the value of ε is small, the number of semantic classification is larger. The number of classification will increase rapidly when the threshold is less than 0.01. The number of semantic classification will close to a certain value when the threshold value is a larger one. Theoretically, when ε is close to zero, the number of semantic classification is close to the number of reviews of all the users. When it is close to 1, the number of semantic classification will be close to 1. Under the same situation of ε, the number of semantic classification of electronics is large indicates that there are more divergent of user reviews of this kind of commodities. The semantic classifications of the books and sports classes have close numbers whereas the type of baby has smaller number of semantic classifications. It indicates that these users of the baby type have a consensus in opinion.

Experiment 2 is a comparison of the number of semantic classification under different training samples. As we can see from Fig. 3, the number of training samples has a greater impact on the number of semantic classification. When there is a small sample size, the number of semantic classification is lower. When the sample size is increased, the number of semantic categories also increased. The Increasing of the number of semantic classification of will be flattening gently when the number of samples reaches a certain level. Wherein there is a more of electronics semantic types and the types of books and sports are in the intermediate level, there is less semantic type in baby type.

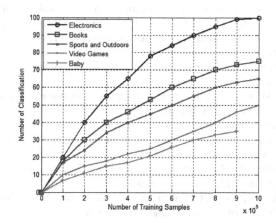

Fig. 3. Comparison of the number of semantic classification under a different number of training samples

The accuracy of the model using for semantic classification is analyzed by the test sample data set. The analysis method uses the proportion of users who buy the same number of items which is belong to the same semantic classification of users, and the proportion of users who purchased the same goods but not in the same semantic classification of users to verify the accuracy. The proportion of user who bought the same product at the same time in the same classification represents an accurate ratio. The proportion of users who buy the same product but not in the same semantic types of users represents the error rate. The comparison of the experimental results is shown in Fig. 2.

Acknowledgments. This paper is a part of research work in the Dalarna University in Sweden. This work was supported by the Natural Science Foundation of Zhejiang (LY16G020012), Major Research Projects of Humanities and Social Sciences in Colleges and Universities of Zhejiang (2014GH015), Science and Technology Innovation Team of Ningbo (2013B82009), Social Development Projects of Ningbo (2012C50045), Research Project of Humanities and Social Sciences of The Ministry of Education (14YJC630210), Public Technology Research and Application Project of Zhejiang (No. 2015C33065).

References

1. Liu, B.: Web Data Mining: Exploring Hyperlinks, Contents, and Usage Data. Springer, Berlin (2008)
2. Liu, B.: Sentiment analysis and subjectivity. In: Indurkhya, N., Damerau, F.J. (eds.) Handbook of Natural Language Processing, 2nd edn. Chapman & Hall, London (2010)
3. Cambria, E., Grassi, M., Hussain, A., Havasi, C.: Sentic computing for social media marketing. Multimedia Tools Appl. **59**(2), 557–577 (2012)
4. Liu, B.: Sentiment analysis and opinion mining. Synth. Lect. Hum. Lang. Technol. **5**(1), 1–167 (2012). doi:10.2200/S00416ED1V01Y201204HLT016
5. Wilson, T., Wiebe, J., Hoffmann, P.: Recognizing contextual polarity in phrase-level sentiment analysis. In: HLT 2005 Proceedings of Conference on Human Language Technology and Empirical Methods in Natural Language Processing, Vancouver, pp. 347–354, October 2005
6. Hobbs, J.R., Riloff, E.: Information extraction. In: Handbook of Natural Language Processing, pp. 1–31 (2010)
7. Bunescu, R.C., Mooney, R.J.: Subsequence kernels for relation extraction. In: Advances in Neural Information Processing Systems, pp. 171–178 (2005)
8. Sarawagi, S.: Information extraction. Found. Trends Databases **1**(3), 261–377 (2008)
9. Go, A., Bhayani, R., Huang, L.: Twitter sentiment classification using distant supervision. CS224N Project report, Stanford (2009)
10. Kennedy, A., Inkpen, D.: Sentiment classification of movie reviews using contextual valence shifters. Comput. Intell. **22**(2), 110–125 (2006)
11. Hu, M., Liu, B.: Mining and summarizing customer reviews. In: Proceedings of 10th ACM SIGKDD International Conference on Knowledge Discovery and Data Mining, pp. 168–177. ACM Press, New York (2004)
12. Pang, B., Lee, L.: Opinion mining and sentiment analysis. Found. Trends Inf. Retr. **2**(1–2), 1–135 (2008)
13. Turney, P.D.: Thumbs up or thumbs down? Semantic orientation applied to unsupervised classification of reviews. In: Proceedings of ACL-2002, 40th Annual Meeting of Association for Computational Linguistics, USA, pp. 417–424 (2002)
14. Venugopalan, M., Gupta, D.: Exploring sentiment analysis on twitter data. In: 2015 Eighth International Conference on Contemporary Computing (IC3), Noida, pp. 241–247, 20–22 August 2015
15. Li, G., Liu, F.: A clustering-based approach on sentiment analysis. In: 2010 International Conference on Intelligent Systems and Knowledge Engineering (ISKE), Hangzhou, pp. 331–337, 15–16 November 2010
16. Liu, R., Xiong, R., Song, L.: A sentiment classification method for Chinese document. In: 2010 5th International Conference on Computer Science and Education (ICCSE), Hefei, 24–27 August 2010, pp. 918–922 (2010)
17. Pak, A., Paroubek, P.: Twitter as a corpus for sentiment analysis and opinion mining. In: Proceedings of 7th Conference on International Language Resources and Evaluation (LREC 2010), pp. 1320–1326, May 2010
18. Kao, H.Y., Lin, Z.Y.: A categorized sentiment analysis of chinese reviews by mining dependency in product features and opinions from blogs. In: 2010 IEEE/WIC/ACM International Conference on Web Intelligence and Intelligent Agent Technology (WI-IAT), Toronto, ON, vol. 1, 456–459, 31 August – 3 September 2010

19. McAuley, J., Targett, C., Shi, J., van den Hengel, A.: Image-based recommendations on styles and substitutes. In: SIGIR 2015 Proceedings of 38th International ACM SIGIR Conference on Research and Development in Information Retrieval, pp. 43–52. ACM, New York (2015)
20. McAuley, J., Pandey, R., Leskovec, J.: Inferring networks of substitutable and complementary products. In: KDD 2015 Proceedings of 21th ACM SIGKDD International Conference on Knowledge Discovery and Data Mining, pp. 785–794. ACM. New York (2015)

Data Warehouse Quality Assessment Using Contexts

Flavia Serra[✉] and Adriana Marotta

Facultad de Ingeniería, Universidad de la República, Montevideo, Uruguay
{fserra, amarotta}@fing.edu.uy

Abstract. Data Warehousing Systems (DWS) are of great relevance for supporting decision making and data analysis. This has been proven over time, through the generalization of its development and use in all kind of organizations. Many researchers have presented the need to incorporate and maintain Data Quality (DQ) in DWS. However, there is no consensus in the research community on how or whether it is possible to define a set of quality dimensions for DWS, since such set may depend on the purpose for which the data are used. Moreover, quality requirements may vary among different domains and among different users. The contribution of this paper is twofold: a study of existing proposals that relate DQ with DWS and with contexts, and a proposal of a framework for assessing DQ in DWS. This proposal is the starting point of a broader and deeper investigation that will allow quality management in DWS.

Keywords: Data quality · Data warehousing system · Data warehouse · Context

1 Introduction

Data Quality (DQ) evaluation in Data Warehouse Systems (DWS) is a very important issue, considering that the main goal of these systems is to give support to decision making. However, despite the existing efforts towards its solution, there are still many open aspects [1–3]. We believe that when considering DQ at least two objectives should be achieved by the system: providing to the final user DQ information about the data he obtains, and controlling and improving DQ throughout its data transformation and loading process.

DWS typically have various components with different goals and characteristics: data sources, ETL (Extraction, Transformation and Load) components, Data Warehouse (DW), data marts (DM), front-end components. Data in each of these components are in different states, regarding granularity, quality, structure, etc. We think that in order to effectively manage DQ in DWS, we must address the problem differently in each DWS component, taking into account the particularities of data and related processes in each one.

The importance and influence of data context in DQ has been stated many years ago [4], and is widely accepted. Also the *fitness for use* approach [5], where it is considered that DQ completely depends on the fitness of the data to the use they will have, is adopted by most of DQ researchers.

© Springer International Publishing AG 2016
W. Cellary et al. (Eds.): WISE 2016, Part II, LNCS 10042, pp. 436–448, 2016.
DOI: 10.1007/978-3-319-48743-4_36

The approach of this work is to assess DQ in DWS by means of considering each system component and the corresponding data context in each one. For example, the context of data in the DW component may be given by associated data from inside and outside the DW, while the context of data in the front-end component may be given by the profile of its user.

In this paper we propose a framework for assessing DQ in DWS using contexts, which is implemented through Datalog rules, and we present an example of its application. Our proposal is based on a thorough study of the existing literature relating DQ, DW and Contexts. Some of the results of this study are also presented in this paper. The contribution of this paper is twofold: (i) a study of existing proposals that relate DQ, DWS and contexts, and (ii) a proposal of a framework for assessing DQ in DWS.

The rest of the document is organized as follows: in Sect. 2 we present some preliminary concepts regarding DQ, DW and Contexts, in Sect. 3 we present the existing work that relate these areas, in Sect. 4 we present our proposal for assessing DQ in DWS, in Sect. 5 we present an example using the proposal framework and finally, in Sect. 6 we present some conclusions and future work.

2 Preliminaries

For the research community DQ is a multi-faceted concept, which is represented by DQ dimensions that address different aspects of data. At the same time, the approach of DQ as *fitness for use* has been widely adopted by this community. A huge set of DQ dimensions have been defined in the literature in the last 20 years, existing a subset that is used by most of the authors, with similar notions and/or definitions. Some works that gather definitions of DQ and DQ dimensions [6, 7], show that there is not an standard or agreement about the set of dimensions that characterize DQ. Recently, in [3] a new effort for organizing DQ dimensions was presented, where six clusters are proposed, which intend to cover the main dimensions: *accuracy, completeness, redundancy, readability, accessibility, consistency, usefulness* and *trust*.

In this work we consider a DQ metamodel for managing DQ, which consists of: *DQ dimensions*, which represent general quality aspects, *DQ factors*, which are more specific quality characteristics that are grouped in each dimension, and *DQ metrics*, which define the way the DQ factors are measured. This way, a DQ dimension may have many corresponding DQ factors and a DQ factor may have many corresponding DQ metrics. For example, for the DQ dimension *accuracy* we can consider the DQ factors *syntactic accuracy* and *semantic accuracy*. Meanwhile, for the DQ factor *syntactic accuracy*, we can consider a DQ metric that calculate it by searching the data value in a dictionary, and another one that applies a rule that determines if the data value has a valid format.

A DW is a database whose data are the result of the extraction, integration, cleaning and diverse transformations of heterogeneous source data, with the goal of giving support to decision-oriented analysis. The most commonly used model for this kind of data is the Multidimensional Model [8], whose intention is to give the analyst a natural way for manipulating the subjects and indicators of the analysis. Data in this model are presented in a n-dimensional space, called *data cube*, where the axis are the *dimensions* of analysis and the points in the space contains the indicators, called *measures*. Each coordinate of the cube is called a *fact*. The dimensions are structured in *hierarchies* that give the criteria for data aggregation, which is an essential operation in multidimensional analysis. Besides, the hierarchies are composed by *levels*, and the instances of a level are called *members*. For example, in the dimension *Time* there may be a hierarchy composed by levels *date, month, quarter, year*. "Q1", "Q2", "Q3", "Q4" are members of the level *quarter*. Figure 1 shows an example of a data cube [8].

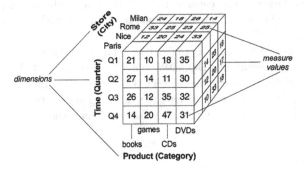

Fig. 1. A three-dimensional cube for sales data having dimensions store, time and product, and a measure amount.

A DWS is an information system whose main component is a DW, and whose general architecture is composed by different components that make possible the whole process from the data sources towards the end-user. In [9] different architectures are presented, but the two-tired architecture, shown in Fig. 2, is stated as the most referenced one. It remarks the separation between the sources and the DW, although it represents the four main stages in the data flow: source layer, data staging, DW layer, and analysis. Moreover, the metadata repository is used in all DWS lifecycle; there

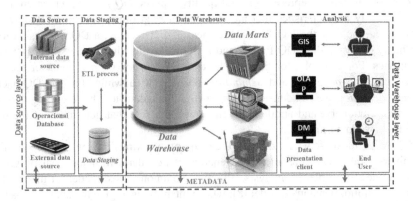

Fig. 2. Two-tier architecture in data warehouse.

exists information about the sources, DM schemes, results of the data quality assessment, users data, etc.

As said before, the importance of considering the context in DQ management is widely recognized. However, it is not possible to find in the literature a concise and globally accepted definition for the concept of context. In fact, there are a lot of conceptualizations and definitions for it, whose approaches depend on the research domain where it is applied. For example, in [10], the context is defined as the possibility of selecting data according to the user environment, while in [11] the authors consider that the context is a set of variables of interest that influence the actions of an agent. In [12] a set of definitions extracted from the Web are analyzed. The authors consider that is difficult to find a relevant definition that satisfies all disciplines and they mention that there are still few ideas about the relevant properties that should be considered when modeling context.

In this work we are interested in *data context*, and the notion of context we use, which is based on the literature, can be synthesized as: the relevant information that influences data content, its interpretation, and the actions over it.

3   Existing Work

In this Section we comment the most important conclusions obtained from a literature review of the existing work that relates the three research topics Contexts, DQ and DW. Afterwards, we present an analysis of these works, putting the focus on DQ tasks and DQ dimensions.

3.1   Connecting Three Research Areas: Context, DQ and DW

The used approach for analysing the research advances in *the use of Contexts in DQ evaluation in DWS* was to also study the proposals that address the combinations of two of the involved topics. Therefore, we present an analysis of the works that focus on DQ-DW, Context-DW and Context-DQ, and then an analysis of the works that address the three topics (Context-DQ-DW).

Data Quality and Data Warehouse (DQ-DW). In spite of the existing consensus on the importance of incorporating and maintaining DQ in DWS, there is not an agreement in the literature on how to do it. Neither is identified the best moment or component in the construction of the DWS, for performing DQ management. Most of the works focus on data cleaning during ETL process, such as the ones presented in [13, 14], and on solving DQ problems in the sources selection stage [15]. The task of evaluating DQ throughout the whole DWS lifecycle is in general ignored or only mentioned but not addressed. In [1] the authors consider that DQ problems in multidimensional repositories still need to be correctly ordered.

In [16] the authors emphasize on the subjectivity of DQ in DWS, considering two aspects: (i) DQ problems may be relevant or not, depending on the decisions to be made, and (ii) data analysts may have different notions and expectations about DQ.

Finally, although many works associate DQ dimensions to DWS [2], an adequate set of DQ dimensions for these systems has not yet been identified and agreed. This fact leads us to question if it is possible or not to define a unique set of DQ dimensions for DWS.

Contexts and Data Warehouse (Context-DW). Some authors consider that the context in a DW is defined by its dimensions, since they are the ones that gives meaning and allow the analysis of the DW measures [17, 18]. Other authors consider that the context is defined by documents content [19, 20], being very frequent that non-structured data obtained from sources as the enterprise intranet, the web or emails, have a relationship with the entities and relationships stored in the DW. They consider that in the data analysis stage the context of the DW facts is also described in documents [20]. On the other hand, they mention that the OLAP (On-line Analytical Processing) performed by the user determines the context of the decision making. The authors claim that although contextual information should be consider when exploiting a DW, there has been very little research in the integration of context in DWS.

Contexts and Data Quality (Context-DQ). Many authors consider that the concept *fitness for use* means that DQ depends on the context where data are used [2, 13, 17, 21–23]. In [23, 24] they consider the context as the data users and their tasks at hand. Besides, in [24] the authors propose to manage DQ considering the construction of information as a process, so DQ is a dynamic measure. In this case, during the information construction, from data to knowledge, DQ would go through different contexts. Additionally, in [23] DQ and information quality are considered different. In particular, for the authors, information quality metrics are necessarily context-dependent while DQ metrics may be absolute.

Many works found in the literature are based on the DQ dimensions classification given in [4], where DQ dimensions are classified in intrinsic, contextual, representational and accessibility, for example [22]. In this work the authors claim that due to the dependence of DQ on the context, despite the wide discussions about DQ dimensions existing in the literature, it does not exist a unified set of DQ dimensions. In [21] the authors remark that most of existing DQ approaches are context-dependent, however the contextual dimension is in general not represented.

Contexts, Data Quality and Data Warehouse (Context-DQ-DW). Few works relating the three research areas are found in the literature. The proposal presented in [2] integrates DQ during the whole DW development process, in particular in the requirements analysis phase. The authors mention that some DQ dimensions are objective and others are subjective, and the subjectivity is given by the users by their DQ requirements.

Meanwhile, in [17] contexts are represented through dimensions that include hierarchies. According to the authors, DQ cannot be evaluated without a contextual knowledge about the production and use of data.

Finally, in [25] the authors remark that DQ is context-sensitive by nature, and therefore it must be evaluated in the context of the business where data will be used.

They also state that research in DQ evaluation has only focused on the identification of DQ dimensions and factors, and in particular for decision support systems relevant DQ factors has not been identified and context has not been considered.

3.2   Analysis from DQ Perspective

In this Section, the reviewed works are analyzed with respect to two aspects: first, the DQ tasks presented and the consideration of the context for the proposal, and second, the DQ dimensions used or defined in the proposal.

DQ Tasks. Different DQ tasks are addressed in the considered literature: data profiling, data cleaning and data evaluation, and only some of the works propose the use of context when performing the task. Table 1 shows the references of the works that address each task and if they consider or not the context for their proposal.

Table 1. Data quality tasks

Task	Takes into account the context	
	Yes	No
Analysis	[23, 26]	[15, 21, 22, 24, 25, 27, 28]
Data cleaning	[29]	[13, 14, 17, 26, 27, 30]
Measurement	[23, 25, 26, 29, 31]	[15, 21, 22, 24, 27, 28]

As can be observed, DQ Measurement tasks are the ones that most use context in the analyzed proposals. The authors of these works remark the importance of context consideration in the DQ metrics definitions, and show how context elements such as the user task, can modify the DQ measurement results.

Quality Dimensions. Another important result obtained from the literature review, is the identification of the DQ dimensions proposed in the different works. We group the papers according to their topics, in Context-DQ and DQ-DW, and for each group we present the proposed DQ dimensions. Table 2 show the most relevant DQ dimensions (for space reasons, 13 from 54) proposed in Context-DQ papers, while Table 3 shows the most relevant DQ dimensions (for space reasons 10 from 21) presented in DQ-DW papers.

It is worth noting the variety of terminology and concepts for DQ dimensions that can be found in the bibliography, for example *accuracy* and *correctness*, which refer to the same concepts. This confirms the lack of standardization of the concepts in DQ research area. As can be seen, much more DQ dimensions have been found in the works of DQ and context than in the ones of DQ and DW. In both cases the dimensions *accuracy*, *completeness* and *timeliness* are the most referred.

Table 2. Quality dimensions in articles focused on DQ and CTX.

Dimension	Article
Accessibility	[22]
Accuracy	[22, 28, 31]
Completeness	[21, 22, 28, 31]
Consistency	[21, 28]
Correctness	[24]
Freshness	[31]
Granularity	[25]
Precision	[31]
Relevancy	[22, 25]
Security	[22, 31]
Timeliness	[21–23, 28]
Traceability	[22]
Usefulness	[24]

Table 3. Quality dimensions in articles focused on DQ and DW.

Dimension	Article
Accuracy	[1, 27, 30]
Completeness	[1, 27, 30, 32]
Consistency	[1, 27, 32]
Correctness	[32]
Reasonableness	[15]
Temporality	[15]
Timeliness	[1, 15, 30]
Transparency	[32]
Trust-worthiness	[15, 32]
Uniqueness	[1]

4   Framework for DQ Assessment in DWS

According to the articles analyzed before, we develop a proposal whose purpose is to define a framework that gives support to DQ assessment in DWS. For this, we consider the different components that make up the SDW (see Fig. 2) and the different contexts that have influence on such components. One purpose of this work is to define contexts, which may influence DQ assessment, along the entire lifecycle of the DWS, considering the different contexts that data go across from the DW until they are used by the end-users [24]. Our proposal does not focus on data sources and ETL layers quality issues, since many researches have already addressed them (especially data cleaning inclusion in ETL).

4.1   Context in Each DW Component

In this section we present and define contexts for the components in the DW layer. Each component with its context is presented in Fig. 3. In the following we describe the elements that determine each context.

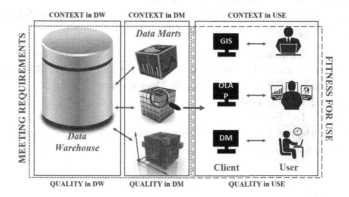

Fig. 3. Two quality approaches in a DWS to evaluate data quality according to the context.

Context in the Data Warehouse (DWC): It is defined by data in the DW, documents, e-mails and other data external to the DW. All these elements are related to data stored in the DW.

Context in the Data Mart (DMC): A Data Mart contains a subset of the data stored in the DW, which had been transformed, and is directed to a specific analysis domain (e.g. a section in the organization). Hence, for us, the DMC is determined by a set of rules that describe properties, constraints and quality requirements specific to the corresponding analysis domain.

Context in Use (CiU): The CiU is the context in the data presentation layer, and is determined by data that describe the end-user. These data can be geographical location, language, role, requirements (of data or quality), etc. The context could be one of them or a combination of them. For example, the DQ requirements could be a minimum level of data accuracy or data completeness.

4.2   Data Quality According to the Context

For the quality assessment in the DW components, taking into account the contexts introduced before, this work is supported by two quality approaches: *Crosby's Meeting Requirements* (compliance with the requirements) [33] and *Juran's Fitness for Use* (meeting the needs of the user) [5]. The former is applied for DQ assessment in two components, DW and DM, while the latter is applied for DQ assessment in the data presentation layer (shown in Fig. 3). Based on these quality approaches DQ is defined according to the context in each DW component:

Quality in the Data Warehouse (DWQ) depends on the DWC, therefore the DQ metrics for the DW are defined using this context.

Quality in the Data Mart (DMQ) depends on the DMC, therefore the DQ metrics for the DM are defined using this context.

Quality in Use (QiU) depends on the CiU, therefore the DQ metrics for the presentation layer are defined using this context.

The concepts we have just defined constitute the base to apply the following steps for defining the DQ metrics for assessing DQ in DWS:

1 – Select the **component** to be assessed: DW, DM or Presentation
2 – If the component is DM then specify **Domain** and **Domain Rule(s)** Else
If the component is Presentation, specify **User data**
3 – Determine **DQ dimension**
4 – Determine **DQ factor**
5 – Define **DQ metric**: Name, contextualizing object, contextualized object, granularity, description and result type.

4.3   Implementation Using Datalog

We implement the context-based DQ metrics using Datalog, since it allows us to represent the DWS data, the defined contexts and the metrics as a set of logical rules, which can also be executed performing the DQ measurements. Our model is based on the model of [34], and the example used for applying it, is a supermarket chain called "BigSales" that maintains information about its sales in a DWS. Figure 4 shows the conceptual multidimensional model (following MultiDim model [8]), where the DW dimensions (Products, Time and Store) with their hierarchies and levels, and the DW dimensional relationship (Sales) with its measure (amount-of-sales), are shown.

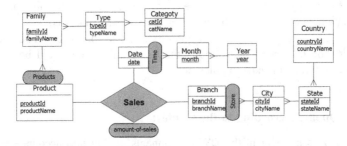

Fig. 4. Hierarchies for each dimension in the DW and the dimensional relationship "Sales".

According to the model of [34], facts are represented through abstract entities, e.g. *AFactQty*(Sales, s1,50), where s1 is a fact identifier and 50 is its measure value. The *aggr* predicate associates an abstract fact with a level member, e.g. *aggr*(X, Store, branchId, 31) means that the dimension is Store, the level is branch and the member has branchId 31, for the abstract fact X. The rules represent the rollup operations between level members and for our example they are of the form:

aggr(X, Products, familyId, chocolate) :- aggr(X, Product, productID, chocolate bars)

The rollup operations between the level members productId and familyId

aggr(X, Store, cityId, MVD) :- aggr(X, Store, branchId, 30)

The rollup operations between the level members branchId and cityId

aggr(X, Time, month, 5 − 2013) :- aggr(X, Time, date, 30−5−2013)

The rollup operations between the level members date and month

idToName(MVD, Montevideo). Given an id returns the corresponding name

AFactQty(Sales, s1, 50). s1 is a fact identifier and 50 is its measure value

5 Using the Framework

Due to lack of space, we only present one case, out of six developed, that illustrates how the proposed framework is used.

Metric Definition

Component: DM   **Domain:** Sales

Domain Rule (R_{Sales}): "The branch's name structure must be p_1-p_2-p_3, where p_1 is the supermarket's name, p_2 is the city's name to which it belongs (cityName in the city level) and p_3 is the branch's identifier (branchId in the branch level)"

Quality dimension: Accuracy   **Quality factor:** Syntactic accuracy

Quality metric: *dmq_Example*   **Contextualizing object:** R_{Sales}

Contextualized object: branch level members of Store dimension

Granularity: Attribute

Description: For each level member (with branchName b) of the branch level, the metric verifies that b has the structure p_1-p_2-p_3 where p_1 must be "BigSales" (Supermarket's name), p_2 must be the value in cityName and p_3 the value in brancheId.

Result: 1 (if the attribute value verifies R_{Sales}), 0 otherwise.

Metric Implementation

The *Contextualizing object* is the domain rule R_{Sales}, and the rules *aggr*(X, Store, branchId, B), *aggr*(X, Store, cityId, A) and *idToName*(A, C) are used to represent it. The *dmq_Example* DQ metric uses this context and other rules.

context(**X,B,C**):-aggr(X,Store,branchId,B),aggr(X,Store,cityId,A),idToName(A, C).

Where *A* is the id of a city, *B* is the id of a branch and *C* is the city's name for *A*. For each abstract fact X, the *context* predicate returns the id of the branch and the city's name for this branch.

dmq_Example(X, N):- context(X,B,C), aggr(X,store,branchId,S), idToName(S,N), branchStructName1(S,Y), branchStructName2(S,Z), branchStructName3(S,W), 'BigSales' = Y, B = Z, C = W.

Where S is the branchId, N is the branchName in the DW for the brancheId, Y is the real value of p_1 in the branchName's structure (p_1-p_2-p_3), Z is the real value of p_2, W is the real value of p_3. For each abstract fact X, the *dmq_Example* DQ metric returns the names of all branches that meet the rule R_{Sales} (which correspond to the result = 1 specified in the metric definition)

6   Conclusion and Future Work

In this work we presented a literature review that showed the importance of considering the context when assessing DQ, in particular in DWS. Based on the performed literature analysis and some obtained results, a framework for DQ assessment in DWS was presented. This framework allows and leads the user to the consideration of the contextual nature of data quality, which was widely analyzed in the literature, however, we have not yet found a research solving this issue in DWS.

The proposed framework is based on the definition of contexts for the different DWS components, and DQ metrics that use these contexts. It contains a set of steps that must be applied for defining the context-based DQ metrics. The main advantage of this framework is that it helps the DQ expert to identify the context that influences DQ in each DWS component, and to define appropriate context-based DQ metrics.

An implementation using Datalog is presented too, which allows the representation of the metrics and their execution. Finally, an example is shown as a proof of concept.

As ongoing work we are implementing a case study with real data, where the framework is applied, and as future work we are planning to formalize the proposed models and develop a complete framework that allows DWS DQ assessment.

References

1. Gongora de Almeida, W., de Sousa, R.T., de Deus, F.E., Amvame Nze, G.D., Lopes de Mendonca, F.L.: Taxonomy of data quality problems in multidimensional data warehouse models. In: 8th Iberian Conference on Information Systems and Technologies (CISTI), pp. 1–7 (2013)
2. Munawar, M., Salim, N., Ibrahim, R.: Towards data quality into the data warehouse development. In: IEEE Ninth International Conference on DASC, pp. 1199–1206 (2011)
3. Batini, C., Scannapieco, M.: Data and Information Quality – Dimensions, Principles and Techniques. Data-Centric Systems and Applications. Data-Centric Systems and Applications. Springer, Heidelberg (2016). ISBN 978-3-319-24104-3
4. Strong, D.M., Lee, Y.W., Wang, R.Y.: Data quality in context. Commun. ACM **40**(5), 103–110 (1997)
5. Juran, J., Godfrey, A.B.: Quality Handbook. Republished McGraw-Hill, New York (1999)
6. Batini, C., Scannapieco, M.: Data Quality: Concepts Methodologies and Techniques. Springer, Heidelberg (2006)
7. Scannapieco, M., Catarci, T.: Data quality under a computer science perspective. Arch. Comput. **2**, 1–15 (2002)

8. Malinowski, E., Zimányi, E.: Advanced Data Warehouse Design: From Conventional to Spatial and Temporal Applications. Data-Centric Systems and Applications. Springer, Heidelberg (2008)
9. Golfarelli, M., Rizzi, S.: Data Warehouse Design: Modern Principles and Methodologies. McGraw-Hill Inc., New York (2009)
10. Ciaccia, P., Torlone, R.: Modeling the propagation of user preferences. In: Jeusfeld, M., Delcambre, L., Ling, T.-W. (eds.) ER 2011. LNCS, vol. 6998, pp. 304–317. Springer, Heidelberg (2011). doi:10.1007/978-3-642-24606-7_23
11. Bolchini, C., Curino, C.A., Orsi, G., Quintarelli, E., Rossato, R., Schreiber, F.A., Tanca, L.: And what can context do for data? Commun. ACM 52(11), 136–140 (2009)
12. Bazire, M., Brézillon, P.: Understanding context before using it. In: Dey, A., Kokinov, B., Leake, D., Turner, R. (eds.) CONTEXT 2005. LNCS, vol. 3554, pp. 29–40. Springer, Heidelberg (2005)
13. Ali, K., Warraich, M.A.: A framework to implement data cleaning in enterprise data warehouse for robust data quality. In: ICIET International Conference, pp. 1–6 (2010)
14. Santos, V., Belo, O.: Modeling ETL data quality enforcement tasks using relational algebra operators. Procedia Technol. 9, 442–450 (2013). CENTERIS 2013
15. Prat, N., Madnick, S.: Measuring data believability: a provenance approach. In: Proceedings of the 41st Annual Hawaii International Conference on System Sciences, pp. 393–393 (2008)
16. Daniel, F., Casati, F., Palpanas, T., Chayka, O.: Managing data quality in business intelligence applications. In: QDB/MUD, pp. 133–143 (2008)
17. Hamad, M.M., Jihad, A.A.: An enhanced technique to clean data in the data warehouse. In: Developments in E-systems Engineering (DeSE), pp. 306–311 (2011)
18. Silva Souza, V.E., Mazón, J.N., Garrigós, I., Trujillo, J., Mylopoulos, J.: Monitoring strategic goals in DW with awareness requirements. In: SAC 2012, pp. 1075–1082. ACM, New York (2012)
19. Thollot, R., Brauer, F., Barczynski, W.M., Aufaure, M.A.: Text-to-query: dynamically building structured analytics to illustrate textual content. In: EDBT 2010, pp. 14:1–14:8. ACM (2010)
20. Perez, J.M., Berlanga, R., Aramburu, M.J., Pedersen, T.B.: Towards a data warehouse contextualized with web opinions. In: IEEE International Conference on ICEBE 2008, pp. 697–702 (2008)
21. Helfert, M., Foley, O.: A context aware information quality framework. In: Fourth International Conference on COINFO 2009, pp. 187–193 (2009)
22. Moges, H.T., Dejaeger, K., Lemahieu, W., Baesens, B.: A multidimensional analysis of data quality for credit risk management: new insights and challenges. Inf. Man 50(1), 43–58 (2013)
23. Alberts, D.S., Vassiliou, M., Agre, J.: C2 information quality: an enterprise systems perspective. In: MILCOM 2012, pp. 1–7 (2012)
24. McNab, A.L., Ladd, D.A.: Information quality: the importance of context and trade-offs. In: 47th Hawaii International Conference on HICSS, pp. 3525–3532 (2014)
25. Sundararaman, A.: A framework for linking data quality to business objectives in decision support systems. In: 3rd International Conference on TISC 2011, pp. 177–181 (2011)
26. Milani, M., Bertossi, L., Ariyan, S.: Extending contexts with ontologies for multidimensional data quality assessment. In: IEEE 30th International Conference on ICDEW 2014, pp. 242–247 (2014)
27. Sidi, F., Ramli, A., Jabar, M.A., Affendey, L.S., Mustapha, A., Ibrahim, H.: Data quality comparative model for data warehouse. In: International Conference on CAMP 2012, pp. 268–272 (2012)

28. Hazen, B.T., Boone, C.A., Ezell, J.D., Jones-Farmer, L.A.: Data quality for data science, predictive analytics, and big data in supply chain management: an introduction to the problem and suggestions for research and applications. Int. J. Prod. Econ. **154**, 72–80 (2014)
29. Dasu, T., Loh, J.M., Srivastava, D.: Empirical glitch explanations. In: KDD 2014, pp. 572–581. ACM, New York (2014)
30. Huang, Z., Peng, H.: Improving uncertain data-quality through effective use of knowledge base. In: 4th International Conference on WiCOM 2008. pp. 1–4 (2008)
31. Zheng, D., Wang, J., Kerong, B.: Evaluation of quality measure factors for the middleware based context-aware applications. In: 11th IEEE/ACIS, ICIS 2012, pp. 403–408 (2012)
32. Wieder, B., Ossimitz, M.L.: The impact of business intelligence on the quality of decision making a mediation model. Procedia Comput. Sci. **64**, 1163–1171 (2015)
33. Crosby, P.B.: Quality Is Free: The Art of Making Quality Certain. McGraw-Hill, New York (1979)
34. Marotta, A., Vaisman, A.: Rule-based multidimensional data quality assessment using contexts. In: Madria, S., Hara, T. (eds.) DaWaK 2016. LNCS, vol. 9829, pp. 299–313. Springer, Heidelberg (2016). doi:10.1007/978-3-319-43946-4_20

Author Index